OUTDOORS

P9-CCL-585

CALIFORNIA CAMPING

TOM STIENSTRA

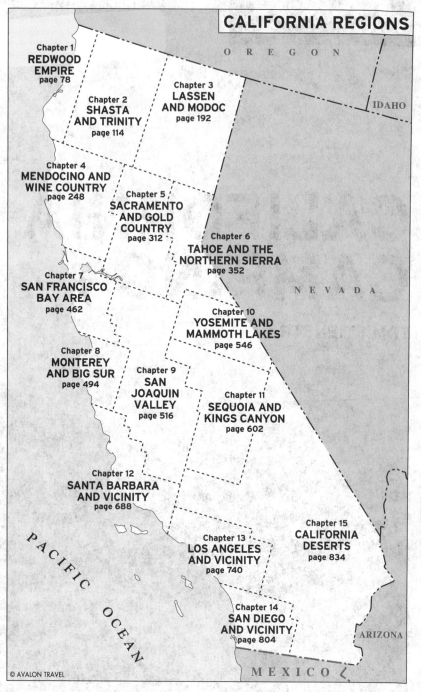

CALIFORNIA REGIONS

O R E G O N

IDAHO

Chapter 1
REDWOOD EMPIRE
page 78

Chapter 2
SHASTA AND TRINITY
page 114

Chapter 3
LASSEN AND MODOC
page 192

Chapter 4
MENDOCINO AND WINE COUNTRY
page 248

Chapter 5
SACRAMENTO AND GOLD COUNTRY
page 312

Chapter 6
TAHOE AND THE NORTHERN SIERRA
page 352

Chapter 7
SAN FRANCISCO BAY AREA
page 462

N E V A D A

Chapter 10
YOSEMITE AND MAMMOTH LAKES
page 546

Chapter 8
MONTEREY AND BIG SUR
page 494

Chapter 9
SAN JOAQUIN VALLEY
page 516

Chapter 11
SEQUOIA AND KINGS CANYON
page 602

Chapter 12
SANTA BARBARA AND VICINITY
page 688

Chapter 15
CALIFORNIA DESERTS
page 834

PACIFIC

Chapter 13
LOS ANGELES AND VICINITY
page 740

OCEAN

Chapter 14
SAN DIEGO AND VICINITY
page 804

ARIZONA

M E X I C O

© AVALON TRAVEL

Contents

How to Use This Book

ABOUT THE CAMPGROUND PROFILES

The campgrounds are listed in a consistent, easy-to-read format to help you choose the ideal camping spot. If you already know the name of the specific campground you want to visit, or the name of the surrounding geological area or nearby feature (town, national or state park, forest, mountain, lake, river, etc.), look it up in the index and turn to the corresponding page. Here is a sample profile:

Campground name and number →

Icons noting activities and facilities at or nearby the campground

1 SOMEWHERE USA CAMPGROUND

General location of the campground in relation to the nearest major town or landmark →

Scenic rating: 10

Rating of scenic beauty on a scale of 1-10 with 10 the highest rating

south of Somewhere USA Lake

Map 1.2, page 4   **BEST (**

Map the campground can be found on and page number the map can be found on →

Symbol indicating that the campground is listed among the author's top picks

Each campground in this book begins with a brief overview of its setting. The description typically covers ambience, information about the attractions, and activities popular at the campground.

Campsites, facilities: This section notes the number of campsites for tents and RVs and indicates whether hookups are available. Facilities such as restrooms, picnic areas, recreation areas, laundry, and dump stations will be addressed, as well as the availability of piped water, showers, playgrounds, stores, and other amenities. The campground's pet policy and wheelchair accessibility is also mentioned here.

Reservations, fees: This section notes whether reservations are accepted, and provides rates for tent sites and RV sites. If there are additional fees for parking or pets, or discounted weekly or seasonal rates, they will also be noted here.

Directions: This section provides mile-by-mile driving directions to the campground from the nearest major town or highway.

Contact: This section provides an address, phone number, and website, if available, for the campground.

ABOUT THE ICONS

The icons in this book are designed to provide at-a-glance information on activities, facilities, and services available on-site or within walking distance of each campground.

- 🏃 Hiking trails
- 🚴 Biking trails
- 🏊 Swimming
- 🎣 Fishing
- 🚤 Boating
- 🛶 Canoeing and/or kayaking
- ❄ Winter sports

- ♨ Hot springs
- 🐕 Pets permitted
- 🛝 Playground
- ♿ Wheelchair accessible
- 5️⃣ 5 Percent Club
- 🚐 RV sites
- ⛺ Tent sites

ABOUT THE SCENIC RATING

Each campground profile employs a scenic rating on a scale of 1 to 10, with 1 being the least scenic and 10 being the most scenic. A scenic rating measures only the overall beauty of the campground and environs; it does not take into account noise level, facilities, maintenance, recreation options, or campground management. The setting of a campground with a lower scenic rating may simply not be as picturesque that of as a higher rated campground, however other factors that can influence a trip, such as noise or recreation access, can still affect or enhance your camping trip. Consider both the scenic rating and the profile description before deciding which campground is perfect for you.

MAP SYMBOLS

Symbol	Name	Symbol	Name	Symbol	Name
═══════	Expressway	(80)	Interstate Freeway	✕	Airfield
───────	Primary Road	(101)	U.S. Highway	✈	Airport
┄┄┄┄┄	Secondary Road	(21)	State Highway	○	City/Town
⋯⋯⋯⋯	Unpaved Road	66	County Highway	▲	Mountain
··············	Ferry		Lake	▲	Park
─··─··─·	National Border		Dry Lake	⟩(	Pass
──··──	State Border		Seasonal Lake	◉	State Capital

ABOUT THE MAPS

This book is divided into chapters based on major regions in the state; an overview map of these regions precedes the table of contents. Each chapter begins with a map of the region, which is further broken down into detail maps. Campgrounds are noted on the detail maps by number.

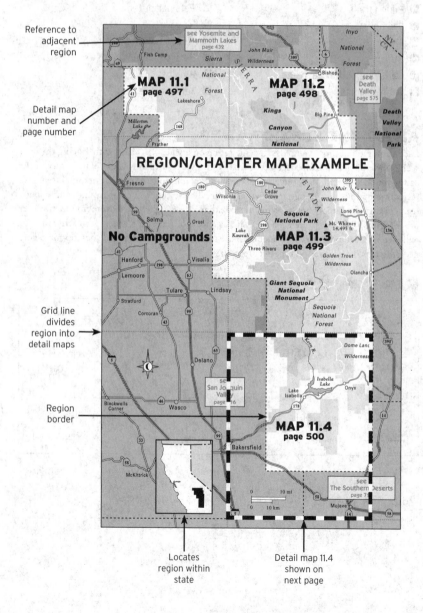

Reference to adjacent region

Detail map number and page number

REGION/CHAPTER MAP EXAMPLE

No Campgrounds

Grid line divides region into detail maps

Region border

Locates region within state

Detail map 11.4 shown on next page

Indicates adjacent detail maps within region

Locates detail map within region

Map number → **Map 11.4**

Sites shown on detail map and the page range where those sites are listed → **Sites 105-117**
Pages 564-570

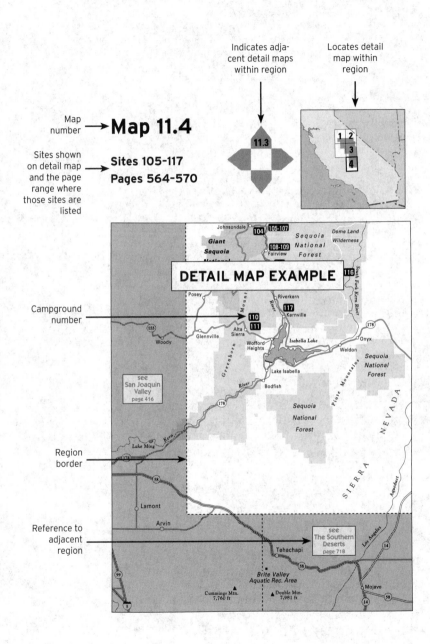

Campground number

Region border

Reference to adjacent region

INTRODUCTION

For Buddy and Pooch

Author's Note

Going on a camping trip can be like trying to put hiking boots on an octopus. You've tried it too, eh? Instead of a relaxing and fun trip full of adventure, it turns into a scenario called "You Against the World." You might as well try to fight a volcano.

But it doesn't have to be that way, and that's what this book is all about. If you give it a chance, the information herein can put the mystery, excitement, and fun back into your camping vacations—and remove the snarls, confusion, and occasional, volcanic temper explosions that keep people at home, locked away from the action.

Mystery? There are hundreds of hidden, rarely used campgrounds listed and mapped in this book that most people have never dreamed of. *Excitement?* At many of them, you'll find the sizzle with the steak: the hike to a great lookout or the big fish at the end of your line. *Fun?* The *Camping Tips* section of this book can help you take the futility out of your trips and put the fun back in. Add it up, put it in your cash register, and you can turn a camping trip into the satisfying adventure it's meant to be, whether it's just an overnight quickie or a monthlong expedition.

It's estimated that 95 percent of American vacationers use only 5 percent of the country's available recreation areas. With this book, you can leave the herd, wander, and be free. You can join the inner circle, the 5 Percenters who know the great hidden areas used by so few people. To join the 5 Percent Club, take a hard look at the maps for the areas you wish to visit and the corresponding campground listings. As you study the camps, you'll start to feel a sense of excitement building, a feeling that you are about to unlock a door and venture into a world that is rarely viewed. When you feel that excitement, act on it. Parlay that energy into a great trip.

The campground maps and listings can serve in two ways: 1) If you're on the road late in the day and you're stuck for a spot for the night, you can likely find one nearby; or 2) if you are planning a trip, you can tailor a vacation to fit exactly into your plans rather than heading off and hoping—maybe praying—it turns out all right.

For the latter, you may wish to obtain additional maps, particularly if you are venturing into areas governed by the U.S. Forest Service or Bureau of Land Management. Both are federal agencies that offer low-cost maps detailing all hiking trails, lakes, streams, and backcountry camps reached via logging roads. The *Resources* section at the back of this book details how to obtain these and other maps.

Backcountry camps listed in this book are often in primitive and rugged settings but provide the sense of isolation that you may want from a trip. They also provide good jump-off points for backpacking trips, if that's your calling. These camps are often free, and I have listed hundreds of them.

At the other end of the spectrum are the developed parks for RVs. They offer a home away from home, with everything from full hookups to a grocery store and laundry room. These spots are just as important as the remote camps with no facilities. Instead of isolation, an RV park provides a place to shower and get outfitted for food and clean clothes. For RV cruisers, it's a place to stay in high style while touring the area. RV parks range in price from $12 to $25 per night, depending on location, and an advance deposit may be necessary in summer.

Somewhere between the two extremes—the remote, unimproved camps and the lavish RV parks—are hundreds and hundreds of campgrounds that provide a compromise: beautiful settings and some facilities, with a small overnight fee. Piped water, vault toilets, and picnic tables tend to come with the territory. Fees for these sites are usually in the $6–15 range, with the higher-priced sites located near population centers. Because they offer a bit of both worlds, they are in high demand. Reservations are usually advised, and at state parks, particularly during the summer season, you can expect company. This doesn't mean you need to forgo them in hopes of a less confined environment. For one thing, most state parks have set up quotas so that visitors don't feel as if they've been squeezed in with a shoehorn. For another, the same parks are often uncrowded during the off-season and on weekdays.

Before your trip, you'll want to get organized, and that's when you must start putting boots on that giant octopus. The trick to organization for any task is breaking it down to its key components and then solving each element independent of the others. Remember the octopus. Grab a moving leg, jam on a boot, and make sure it's on tight before reaching for another leg. Do one thing at a time, in order, and all will get done quickly and efficiently.

In the *Camping Tips* section that follows, I have isolated the different elements of camping, and you should do the same when planning for your trip. There are separate sections on each of the primary ingredients for a successful trip: 1) Food and cooking gear; 2) Clothing and weather protection; 3) Hiking and foot care and how to choose the right boots and socks; 4) Sleeping gear; 5) Combating bugs and some commonsense first-aid; 6) Catching fish, avoiding bears, and camp fun; 7) Outdoors with kids; and 8) Weather prediction. I've also included sections on boat-in and desert camping and ethics in the outdoors, as well as a camping gear checklist.

Now you can become completely organized for your trip in just one week, spending just a little time each evening on a given component. Getting organized is an unnatural act for many. By splitting up the tasks, you take the pressure out of planning and put the fun back in.

As a full-time outdoors writer, the question I am asked more than any other is: "Where are you going this week?" All of the answers are in this book.

KEEP IT WILD

"Enjoy America's country and leave no trace." That's the motto of the Leave No Trace program, and I strongly support it. Promoting responsible outdoor recreation through education, research, and partnerships is its mission. Look for the Keep It Wild Tips, developed from the policies of Leave No Trace, throughout the Camping Tips portion of this book. This copyrighted information has been reprinted with permission from the Leave No Trace Center for Outdoor Ethics. For more information or materials, please visit www.LNT.org or call 303/442-8222 or 800/332-4100.

Best Campgrounds

The most common emails I get are those from readers asking me to plan their adventures and to rate campgrounds as launch points for specific activities. While I can't respond to all emails, I do often rate the top 10 campgrounds in California for scenery, hiking, fishing, boating, water sports, rafting, and family activities.

I've organized the following selections by activity, then rated them 1 through 10, starting with my pick for the best. These are among America's preeminent campgrounds, so if you plan a trip to any of them, be sure to plan your stay far in advance.

◖ Best Scenic Campgrounds
1. **Bridalveil Creek and Equestrian and Group Camp,** Yosemite and Mammoth Lakes, page 558.
2. **Emerald Bay State Park and Boat-In,** Tahoe and the Northern Sierra, page 454.
3. **Upper Hell Hole Walk-In/Boat-In,** Tahoe and the Northern Sierra, page 403.
4. **Donner Memorial State Park,** Tahoe and the Northern Sierra, page 447.
5. **Sardine Lakes,** Tahoe and the Northern Sierra, page 369.
6. **Santa Rosa Island,** Santa Barbara and Vicinity, page 734.
7. **Convict Lake,** Yosemite and Mammoth Lakes, page 589.
8. **Manresa Uplands State Beach Walk-In,** Monterey and Big Sur, page 498.
9. **Steep Ravine Environmental Campsites,** San Francisco Bay Area, page 471.
10. **Salt Point State Park,** Mendocino and Wine Country, page 292.

◖ Best Boat-In Campgrounds
1. **Emerald Bay State Park and Boat-In,** Tahoe and the Northern Sierra, page 454.
2. **Santa Rosa Island,** Santa Barbara and Vicinity, page 734.
3. **Englebright Lake Boat-In,** Sacramento and Gold Country, page 332.
4. **Bullards Bar Reservoir,** Sacramento and Gold Country, pages 328 and 329.
5. **Stone Lagoon Boat-In,** Redwood Empire, page 93.
6. **Mesa,** Los Angeles and Vicinity, page 765.
7. **Gaviota State Park,** Santa Barbara and Vicinity, page 709.
8. **Lake Sonoma Recreation Area,** Mendocino and Wine Country, page 291.
9. **Captains Point Boat-In,** Shasta and Trinity, page 164.
10. **Sarah Totten,** Shasta and Trinity, page 121.

◖ Best for Easy Backpacking
1. **Goldfield,** Shasta and Trinity, page 143
2. **Toad Lake Walk-In,** Shasta and Trinity, page 134
3. **Mill Creek Falls,** Lassen and Modoc, page 209.
4. **Van Damme State Park,** Mendocino and Wine Country, page 265.
5. **Pomo Canyon/Willow Creek Walk-In,** Mendocino and Wine Country, page 296.
6. **Wildcat Camp Hike-In,** San Francisco Bay Area, page 469.
7. **Woods Lake,** Tahoe and the Northern Sierra, page 418.
8. **Tuolumne Meadows,** Yosemite and Mammoth Lakes, page 555.
9. **Onion Valley,** Sequoia and Kings Canyon, page 663.
10. **Buckhorn,** Los Angeles and Vicinity, page 759.

◖ Best for Families
1. **Vermillion,** Sequoia and Kings Canyon, page 614.
2. **Serrano,** Los Angeles and Vicinity, page 783.

3. **Pine Cliff Resort,** Yosemite and Mammoth Lakes, page 576.

4. **Lake Siskiyou Resort & Camp,** Shasta and Trinity, page 136.

5. **Silver Lake West,** Tahoe and the Northern Sierra, page 419.

6. **Lake Alpine Campground,** Tahoe and the Northern Sierra, page 438.

7. **El Capitan Canyon,** Santa Barbara and Vicinity, page 710.

8. **Rancho Seco Recreation Area,** Sacramento and Gold Country, page 337

9. **Dorst Creek,** Sequoia and Kings Canyon, page 651.

10. **Historic Camp Richardson Resort,** Tahoe and the Northern Sierra, page 457.

◖ Best for Fishing

1. **Campland on the Bay,** San Diego and Vicinity, page 812.

2. **North Shore/South Shore San Antonio,** Santa Barbara and Vicinity, pages 695 and 696.

3. **Snug Harbor Resort,** Sacramento and Gold Country, page 339.

4. **Hirz Bay,** Shasta and Trinity, page 172.

5. **Panther Flat,** Redwood Empire, page 84.

6. **Cachuma Lake Recreation Area,** Santa Barbara and Vicinity, page 720.

7. **Almanor North, South, and Legacy,** Lassen and Modoc, page 231.

8. **Agnew Meadows and Equestrian Camp,** Yosemite and Mammoth Lakes, page 579.

9. **Convict Lake,** Yosemite and Mammoth Lakes, page 589.

10. **Dillon Creek,** Shasta and Trinity, page 124.

◖ Best for Hikes with Views

1. **Yosemite Creek (hike to Yosemite Point in Yosemite National Park),** Yosemite and Mammoth Lakes, page 554.

2. **Canyon View Group Camp (hike to Lookout Peak in Kings Canyon National Park),** Sequoia and Kings Canyon, page 649.

3. **Wilderness Walk-In Camps (climb San Jacinto Peak),** Los Angeles and Vicinity, page 792.

4. **Whitney Trailhead Walk-In (climb Mount Whitney),** Sequoia and Kings Canyon, page 665.

5. **Angel Island State Park Walk-In/Boat-In (hike to Mount Livermore),** San Francisco Bay Area, page 475.

6. **Manker Flats (climb Mount Baldy in Angeles National Forest),** Los Angeles and Vicinity, page 764.

7. **D. L. Bliss State Park (hike Rubicon Trail),** Tahoe and the Northern Sierra, page 453.

8. **Panther Meadows Walk-In (climb Mount Shasta),** Shasta and Trinity, page 137.

9. **Tuolumne Meadows (hike the Pacific Crest Trail to Grand Canyon of the Tuolumne),** Yosemite and Mammoth Lakes, page 555.

10. **Summit Lake: North, South, and Stock Corral (climb Lassen Peak),** Lassen and Modoc, page 221.

◖ Best Island Retreats

1. **Catalina Island Boat-In,** Los Angeles and Vicinity, page 756.

2. **Santa Cruz Island,** Santa Barbara and Vicinity, page 734.

3. **Two Harbors,** Los Angeles and Vicinity, page 754.

4. **Santa Rosa Island,** Santa Barbara and Vicinity, page 734.

5. **Angel Island State Park Walk-In/Boat-In,** San Francisco Bay Area, page 475.

6. **Anacapa Island,** Santa Barbara and Vicinity, page 735.

7. **San Miguel Island,** Santa Barbara and Vicinity, page 733.

8. **Little Harbor Hike-In,** Los Angeles and Vicinity, page 755.

9. **Parson's Landing Hike-In,** Los Angeles and Vicinity, page 753.
10. **Brannan Island State Recreation Area,** Sacramento and Gold Country, page 339.

〔 Best for Waterskiing

1. **Havasu Landing Resort and Casino,** California Deserts, page 855.
2. **Eddos Harbor and RV Park,** Sacramento and Gold Country, page 341.
3. **Moabi Regional Park,** California Deserts, page 849.
4. **Holiday Harbor Resort,** Shasta and Trinity, page 172.
5. **Lake Nacimiento Resort,** Santa Barbara and Vicinity, page 696.
6. **Lake Perris State Recreation Area,** Los Angeles and Vicinity, page 775.
7. **Lake Piru Recreation Area,** Los Angeles and Vicinity, page 744.
8. **La Laguna Resort,** Los Angeles and Vicinity, page 780.
9. **Los Alamos,** California Deserts, page 850.
10. **Snug Harbor Resort,** Sacramento and Gold Country, page 339.

〔 Best for White-Water Rafting

1. **Lumsden,** San Joaquin Valley, page 528.
2. **Matthews Creek,** Shasta and Trinity, page 128.
3. **Fairview,** Sequoia and Kings Canyon, page 670.
4. **Tree of Heaven,** Shasta and Trinity, page 131.
5. **Camp Lotus,** Sacramento and Gold Country, page 342.
6. **Kirch Flat,** Sequoia and Kings Canyon, page 641.
7. **Merced Recreation Area,** Yosemite and Mammoth Lakes, page 559.
8. **Elk Creek Campground and RV Park/Dillon Creek,** Shasta and Trinity, pages 120 and 124.
9. **Auburn State Recreation Area,** Sacramento and Gold Country, pages 333 and 334.
10. **Hobo,** Sequoia and Kings Canyon, page 681.

〔 BEST STATE PARK CAMPGROUNDS

Our state parks are in need of your support. In 2012, budget cuts threatened to close more than 70 state parks—and that includes their campgrounds. Thanks to numerous donor agreements and non-profits, many state park campgrounds will remain open—for now. But that means reduced services and fewer sites, while others still face the chopping block. Lend your support by pitching a tent and voting with your dollars and sense to keep California's natural treasures open to all.

Jedediah Smith Redwoods State Park, Redwood Empire, page 82.
Del Norte Coast Redwoods State Park, Redwood Empire, page 87.
Castle Crags State Park, Shasta and Trinity, page 144.
McArthur-Burney Falls Memorial State Park and Headwaters Horse Camp, Lassen and Modoc, page 203.
Portola Redwoods State Park, San Francisco Bay Area, page 484.
Henry W. Coe State Park, San Francisco Bay Area, page 488.
Andrew Molera State Park Walk-In, Monterey and Big Sur, page 505.
Palomar Mountain State Park, San Diego and Vicinity, page 815.
Red Rock Canyon State Park, California Deserts, page 842.
Borrego Palm Canyon, California Deserts, page 872.

Camping Tips

SLEEPING GEAR

On an eve long ago in the mountain pines, my dad, brother, and I had rolled out our sleeping bags and were bedded down for the night. After the pre-trip excitement, a long drive, an evening of trout fishing and a barbecue, we were like three tired doggies who had played too much.

But as I looked up at the stars, I was suddenly wide awake. I was still wired. A half hour later? No change. Wide awake.

And as little kids can do, I had to wake up ol' Dad to tell him about it. "Hey, Dad, I can't sleep."

After the initial grimace, he said: "This is what you do. Watch the sky for a shooting star and tell yourself that you cannot go to sleep until you see at least one shooting star. As you wait and watch, you will start getting tired, and it will be difficult to keep your eyes open. But tell yourself, you must keep watching. Then you'll start to really feel tired. When you finally see a shooting star, you'll go to sleep so fast you won't know what hit you."

Well, I tried it that night and I don't even remember seeing a shooting star, I went to sleep so fast.

It's a good trick, and along with having a good sleeping bag, ground insulation, maybe a tent, or a few tricks for bedding down in a pickup truck or RV, you can get a great night's sleep on every camping trip.

More than 20 years after that camping episode with my dad and brother, we made a trip to the planetarium at the Academy of Sciences in San Francisco to see a show. The lights dimmed, and the ceiling turned into a night sky, filled with stars and a setting moon. A scientist began explaining the phenomena of the heavens.

After a few minutes, I began to feel drowsy. Just then, a shooting star zipped across the planetarium ceiling. I went into such a deep sleep, it was like I was in a coma. I didn't wake up until the show was over, the lights were turned back on, and the people were leaving.

Feeling drowsy, I turned to see if Dad had liked the show. Oh yeah? Not only had he gone to sleep too, but he apparently had no intention of waking up, no matter what. Just like a camping trip.

Sleeping Bags

The first rule of a good nights' sleep is that you must be dry, warm and safe. A good sleeping bag can help plenty. A sleeping bag is a shell filled with heat-retaining insulation. By itself, it is not warm. Your body provides the heat, and the sleeping bag's ability to retain that heat is what makes it warm or cold.

The cheap cotton bags are heavy, bulky, cold, and, when wet, useless. With other options available, their function is limited. Anybody who sleeps outdoors or backpacks

---

KEEP IT WILD TIP 1: CAMP WITH CARE

1. Choose an existing, legal site. Restrict activities to areas where vegetation is compacted or absent.
2. Camp at least 75 steps (200 feet) from lakes, streams, and trails.
3. Always choose sites that won't be damaged by your stay.
4. Preserve the feeling of solitude by selecting camps that are out of view when possible.
5. Don't dig trenches or build structures or furniture.

should choose otherwise. Use a sleeping bag filled with down or one of the quality poly-fills. Down is light, warm, and aesthetically pleasing to those who don't think camping and technology mix. If you choose a down bag, be sure to keep it double wrapped in plastic garbage bags on your trips to keep it dry. Once it's wet, you'll spend your nights howling at the moon.

The polyfiber-filled bags are not necessarily better than those filled with down, but they can be. Their one key advantage is that even when wet, some poly-fills can retain up to 85 percent of your body heat. This allows you to sleep and get valuable rest even in miserable conditions. In my camping experience, no matter how lucky you may be, there will come a time when you will get caught in an unexpected, violent storm and everything you've got will get wet, including your sleeping bag. That's when a poly-fill bag becomes priceless. You have one and can sleep. Or you don't have one and suffer. It is that simple. Of the synthetic fills, Quallofil made by DuPont is the industry leader.

But just because a sleeping bag uses a high-tech poly-fill doesn't necessarily make it a better bag. There are other factors.

The most important are a bag's temperature rating and weight. The temperature rating of a sleeping bag refers to how cold it can get outside before you start actually feeling cold. Many campers make the mistake of thinking, "I only camp in the summer, so a bag rated at 30 or 40°F should be fine." Later, they find out it isn't so fine, and all it takes is one cold night to convince them of that. When selecting the right temperature rating, visualize the coldest weather you might ever confront, and then get a bag rated for even colder weather.

For instance, if you are a summer camper, you may rarely experience a night in the low 30s or high 20s. A sleeping bag rated at 20°F would be appropriate, keeping you snug, warm, and asleep. For most campers, I advise bags rated at 0 or 10°F.

But guess how the companies come up with their temperature ratings? Usually it's a guy like me field-testing a bag before it is commercially released, and then saying, "Well, it got down to 40°F and I was pretty warm." So they rate it at 30 degrees. Obviously, testers can have different threshold levels for cold, while others base their ratings on how much fill is used.

If you buy a poly-filled sleeping bag, try not to leave it squished in your stuff sack between camping trips. Instead, keep it on a hanger in a closet or use it as a blanket. One thing that can reduce a poly-filled bag's heat-retaining qualities is if the tiny hollow fibers that make up the fill lose their loft. You can avoid this with proper storage.

The weight of a sleeping bag can also be a key factor, especially for backpackers. When you have to carry your gear on your back, every ounce becomes important. Sleeping bags that weigh just 2–3 pounds are available, although they are expensive. But if you hike much, it's worth the price to keep your weight to a minimum. For an overnighter, you can get away with a 4- or 4.5-pound bag without much stress. However, bags weighing five pounds and up should be left back at the car.

I have several sleeping bags; they range from a seven-pounder that feels like a giant sponge to a three-pounder. The heavy-duty model is for pickup-truck camping in cold weather and doubles as a blanket at home. The lightweight bag is for expeditions.

Insulation Pads

Even with the warmest sleeping bag in the world, if you just lay it down on the ground and try to sleep, you will likely get as cold as a winter cucumber. That is because the cold ground will suck the warmth right out of your body. The solution is to have a layer of insulation between you and the ground. For this, you can use a thin Insulite pad, a lightweight Therm-a-Rest inflatable pad, a foam pad or mattress, an airbed, or a cot. Here is a capsule summary of each:

• **Insulite pads:** They are light, inexpensive,

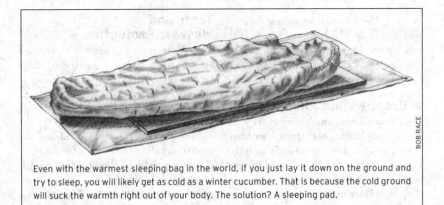

BOB RACE

Even with the warmest sleeping bag in the world, if you just lay it down on the ground and try to sleep, you will likely get as cold as a winter cucumber. That is because the cold ground will suck the warmth right out of your body. The solution? A sleeping pad.

roll up quickly for transport, and can double as a seat pad at your camp. The negative side is that in one night, they will compress, making you feel like you are sleeping on granite. But they are light and they help keep you warm in the wilderness.

• **Therm-a-Rest pads:** These are a real luxury for wilderness travel because they do everything an Insulite pad does, but they also provide a cushion. The negative side is that they are expensive by comparison, and if they get a hole in them, they become worthless without a patch kit. Most wilderness campers carry one "bonus item"—and a full-length Therm-A-Rest is often what they choose.

• **Foam mattresses, air beds, and cots:** These are excellent for car campers. The new line of air beds, especially the thicker ones, are outstanding and inflate quickly with an electric motor inflator that plugs into a power plug or cigarette lighter in your vehicle. Foam mattresses are also excellent; I think they are the most comfortable of all, but their size precludes many from considering them. I've found that cots work great, too. I've always had one and they're great for drive-in tent sites. For camping in the back of a pickup truck with a camper shell, the cots with three-inch legs are best, of course. Here's the trick: Put a blanket over the sleeping surface, then add a Therm-A-Rest pad; you need insulation to keep the cold air beneath you from sucking out the warmth.

A Few Tricks

When surveying a camp area, the most important consideration should be to select a good spot for sleeping. Everything else is secondary. Ideally, you want a flat area that is wind-sheltered and on ground soft enough to drive stakes into. Yeah, and I want to win the lottery, too.

Sometimes, the ground will have a slight slope to it. In that case, always sleep with your head on the uphill side. If you sleep parallel to the slope, every time you roll over, you'll find yourself rolling down the hill. If you sleep with your head on the downhill side, you'll get a headache that feels as if an ax is embedded in your brain.

When you've found a good spot, clear it of all branches, twigs, and rocks, of course. A good tip is to dig a slight indentation in the ground where your hip will fit. Since your body is not flat, but has curves and edges, it will not feel comfortable on flat ground. Some people even get severely bruised on the sides of their hips when sleeping on flat, hard ground. For that reason alone, they learn to hate camping. What a shame, especially when the problem is solved easily with a Therm-a-Rest pad, foam insulation, an air bed, or a cot.

After the ground is prepared, throw a ground cloth over the spot, which will keep much of the morning dew off you. In some areas, particularly where fog is a problem, morning dew can be heavy and get the outside of your sleeping bag quite wet. In that case, you need overhead protection, such as a tent or some kind of roof, like a poncho or tarp with its ends tied to trees.

A Great Nights' Sleep

Some people sleep seven, eight hours at camp, but it comes in 10 installments. They keep waking up. They wake up and half their body is paralyzed. Heh, heh, heh. They can't get comfortable. To solve this, practice camp-style sleeping at home until you get it perfect. At home, you have flexibility and complete control over your sleeping surface. Get it right. Get it just how you like it.

For wilderness travel, my bonus item is an extra inflatable pillow; that's right, I carry two, not one. I inflate them about half full. It puts my head at a perfect comfort zone for deep sleep. Whatever it takes, know how to get a great night's sleep and your entire trip has the chance to feel epic, no matter what you do.

Tents and Weather Protection

All it takes is to get caught in the rain once without a tent and you will never go anywhere without one again. A tent provides protection from rain, wind, and mosquito attacks. In exchange, you can lose a starry night's view, though some tents now even provide moon roofs.

A tent can be as complex as a four-season, tubular-jointed dome with a rain fly or as simple as a tarp roped up to a tree. They can be as cheap as a $10 tube tent, which is nothing more than a hollow piece of plastic, or as expensive as a $500 five-person deluxe expedition, multi-room dome. They vary greatly in size, price, and assembly time. For those who camp infrequently and want to buy a tent without paying much, off-brand models are available at considerable price discounts. My experience in field-testing outdoor gear, though, is that cheap tents often rip at the seams if subjected to regular use. If you plan on getting a good one, plan on doing plenty of shopping and asking lots of questions. With

© SABRINA YOUNG

Tents vary in complexity, size, and price. Be sure to buy the one that's right for you.

a little bit of homework, you can get the right answers to these questions:

WILL IT KEEP ME DRY?

On many one-person and two-person tents, the rain fly does not extend far enough to keep water off the bottom sidewalls of the tent. In a driving rain, water can also drip from the rain fly and onto those sections of the tent. Eventually, the water can leak through to the inside, particularly through the seams.

You must be able to stake out your rain fly so it completely covers all of the tent. If you are tent shopping and this does not appear possible, then don't buy the tent. To prevent potential leaks, use a seam water-proofer, such as Seam Lock, a glue-like substance that can close potential leak areas on tent seams. For large umbrella tents, keep a patch kit handy. Coleman tents, by the way, are guaranteed to keep campers dry.

Another way to keep water out of your tent is to store all wet garments outside the tent, under a poncho. Moisture from wet clothes stashed in the tent will condense on the interior tent walls. If you bring enough wet clothes into the tent, by the next morning you'll feel as if you're camping in a duck blind.

HOW HARD IS IT TO PUT UP?

If a tent is difficult to erect in full sunlight, you can just about forget it at night, especially the first night out if you arrive late to camp. Some tents can go up in just a few minutes, without requiring help from another camper. This might be the kind of tent you want.

The way to compare put-up times when shopping for tents is to count the number of connecting points from the tent poles to the tent and the number of stakes required. The fewer, the better. Think simple. My two-person-plus-a-dog tent has seven connecting points and, minus the rain fly, requires no stakes. It goes up in a few minutes.

My bigger family tent, which has three rooms with walls (so we can keep our two kids isolated on each side if necessary), takes about a half hour to put up. That's without anybody's help. With their help, add about 15 minutes. Heh, heh.

Another factor is the tent poles themselves. Always make sure the poles are connected by an interior bungee cord. It takes only an instant to convert them to a complete pole.

Some outdoor shops have tents on display on their showroom floors. Before buying the tent, have the salesperson take the tent down and put it back up. If it takes him more than five minutes, or he says he doesn't have time, then keep looking.

IS IT ROOMY ENOUGH?

Don't judge the size of a tent on floor space alone. Some tents that are small on floor space can give the illusion of roominess with a high ceiling. You can be quite comfortable and snug in them.

But remember that a one-person or two-person tent is just that. A two-person tent has room for two people plus gear. That's it. Don't buy a tent expecting it to hold more than it is intended to.

HOW MUCH DOES IT WEIGH?

If you're a hiker, this becomes the preeminent question. If it's much more than six or seven pounds, forget it. A 12-pound tent is bad enough, but get it wet and it's like carrying a piano on your back. On the other hand, weight is scarcely a factor if you camp only where you can take your car. My dad, for instance, used to have this giant canvas umbrella tent that folded down to a neat little pack that weighed about 500 pounds.

Family Tents

It is always worth spending the time and money to buy a tent you and your family will be happy with.

Many excellent family tents are available for $125–175, particularly from Cabela's, Coleman, Eureka!, North Face, Remington, and Sierra Designs. Guide-approved expedition tents for groups cost more, generally

$350–600. Here is a synopsis of some of best tents available:

CABELA'S TWO- OR THREE-ROOM CABIN
800/237-4444
www.cabelas.com

This beautiful tent features two to three rooms, a 10- by 16-foot floor available in different configurations with removable interior walls. Three doors mean everybody doesn't tromp through the center room for access to the side rooms. It will stand up to wind, rain, and frequent use.

COLEMAN MODIFIED DOME
800/835-3278
www.coleman.com

Coleman Modified Dome tents are available in six different single- and multi-room designs. The pole structure is unique, with all four upright poles and one ridgepole shock-corded together for an integrated system that makes setup extremely fast and easy. Yet, because of the ridgepole's engineering, the tent has passed tests in high winds. Mesh panels in the ceiling are a tremendous plus for ventilation.

COLEMAN WEATHERMASTER
800/835-3278
www.coleman.com

The Weathermaster series features tents with multiple rooms, walls, and ample headroom, and they are guaranteed to keep rain out. The 17- by 9-foot model sleeps six to eight, has a 76-inch ceiling, and has zippered dividers. Since the dividers are removable, you can configure the tent in multiple layouts. The frame is designed with poles adjustable to three different heights to accommodate uneven ground.

KELTY
800/423-2320
www.kelty.com

Kelty offers top-of-the-line tents based on a sleek dome profile. This is a great package, with mesh sides, tops, and doors, along with a full awning fly and coverage for weather protection. Clip sleeves and rubber-tipped poles for easy slide during setup are nice bonuses.

REI
800/423-2320
www.rei.com

REI has 94 backpacking tents and 27 tents available for car camping, including their own designs as well as those from other manufacturers. A great backpacking tent for two is the REI Half Dome 2 Plus. The Eureka Copper Canyon 6 ($249) is one of the better family values.

Bivouac Bags

If you like going light or solo, and choose not to own a tent at all, a bivy bag or tarp can be the way to go. Bivy is short for bivouac bag and pronounced "bivvy" as in dizzy, not "bivy" as in ivy, and can provide the extremely lightweight weather protection you require. A bivy bag is a water-repellent shell in which your sleeping bag fits. It is light and tough, and for some is the perfect alternative to a heavy tent. My own bivy weighs 31 ounces and cost around $250; it's made by OR (Outdoor Research), and I just plain love the thing on expeditions. On the downside, however, some say it can be a bit difficult getting settled just right in it, and others say they feel claustrophobic in such close quarters. Once you get used to a bivy, spend a night in a tent; the tent will feel like a room at the Mirage. For me, not a problem.

The idea of riding out a storm in a bivy can be quite worrisome for some. You can hear the rain hitting you, and sometimes even feel the pounding of the drops through the bivy bag. For some, it can be unsettling to try to sleep under such circumstances. On the other hand, I've always looked forward to it. In cold weather, a bivy also helps keep you warm. I've had just one miserable night in mine. That was when my sleeping bag was a bit wet when I started the night. By the middle of the night, the water was condensing from the sleeping bag on the interior walls of the bivy, and then soaking the bag, like a storm cycle. The night hit only about 45°F but I just about froze to death anyway. Otherwise, I've used it on more than 100 expeditions with great results: warm, dry quarters and deep, restful sleeps by night, and a pack lightened without carrying a tent by day.

Many long-distance hikers are switching to light tarps in the continuing mission to minimize weight. They work great in rain and the spacious feel beneath them is fantastic. You just need a tree to tie to and soft enough ground for stakes, so they don't work above tree line. Tarps are great, except when there are bug problems; then you need some kind of mosquito netting. A bivy or tent solves that, of course.

Pickup Truck Campers

If you own a pickup truck with a camper shell, you can turn it into a self-contained campground with a little work. This can be an ideal way to go: It's fast, portable, and you are guaranteed a dry environment.

But that does not necessarily mean it is a warm environment. In fact, without insulation from the metal truck bed, it can be like trying to sleep on an iceberg. The metal truck bed will get as cold as the air temperature, which is often much colder than the ground temperature. Without insulation, it can be much colder in your camper shell than it would be on the open ground.

When I camp in my rig, I use a large piece of foam for a mattress and insulation. The foam measures four inches thick, 48 inches wide, and 76 inches long. It makes for a bed as comfortable as anything one might ask for. In fact, during the winter, if I don't go camping for a few weeks because of writing obligations, I sometimes will throw the foam on the floor, lay down the old sleeping bag, light a fire, and camp right in my living room. It's in my blood, I tell you. Airbeds and cots are also extremely comfortable and I've used both many times. Whatever you choose, just make sure you have a comfortable sleeping unit. Good sleep makes for great camping trips.

RVs

The problems RVers encounter come from two primary sources: lack of privacy and light intrusion.

The lack of privacy stems from the natural restrictions of where a land yacht can go. Without careful use of the guide section of this book, owners of RVs can find themselves in parking-lot settings, jammed in with plenty of neighbors. Because RVs often have large picture windows, you lose your privacy, causing some late nights; then, come daybreak, light intrusion forces an early wake up. As a result, you get shorted on your sleep.

The answer is to carry inserts to fit over the inside of your windows. These close off the

---

KEEP IT WILD TIP 2: KEEP THE WILDERNESS WILD

1. Let nature's sound prevail. Avoid loud voices and noises.
2. Leave radios and tape players at home. At drive-in camping sites, never open car doors with music playing.
3. Careful guidance is necessary when choosing any games to bring for children. Most toys, especially any kind of gun toys with which children simulate shooting at each other, shouldn't be allowed on a camping trip.
4. Control pets at all times or leave them with a sitter at home.
5. Treat natural heritage with respect. Leave plants, rocks, and historical artifacts where you find them.

outside and retain your privacy. And if you don't want to wake up with the sun at daybreak, you don't have to. It will still be dark.

Many campgrounds and RV parks enforce a quiet time. If that is important to you, make sure you don't end up somewhere where a quiet time is optional.

HIKING AND FOOT CARE

We had set up a nice little camp in the woods, and my buddy, Foonsky, was strapping on his hiking boots, sitting against a big Douglas fir.

"New boots," he said with a grin. "But they seem pretty stiff."

We decided to hoof it down the trail for a few hours, exploring the mountain wildlands that are said to hide Bigfoot and other strange creatures. After just a short while on the trail, a sense of peace and calm seemed to settle in. The forest provides the chance to be purified with clean air and the smell of trees, freeing you from all troubles.

But it wasn't long before a look of trouble was on Foonsky's face. And no, it wasn't from seeing Bigfoot.

"Got a hot spot on my toe," he said.

Immediately, we stopped. He pulled off his right boot, then his sock, and inspected the left side of his big toe. Sure enough, a blister had bubbled up, filled with fluid, but hadn't popped. From his medical kit, Foonsky cut a small piece of moleskin to fit over the blister and taped it to hold it in place. In a few minutes we were back on the trail.

A half hour later, there was still no sign of Bigfoot. But Foonsky stopped again and pulled off his other boot. "Another hot spot." On the little toe of his left foot was another small blister, over which he taped a Band-Aid to keep it from further chafing against the inside of his new boot.

In just a few days, ol' Foonsky, a strong, 6-foot-5, 200-plus-pound guy, was walking around like a sore-hoofed horse that had been loaded with a month's worth of supplies and ridden over sharp rocks. Well, it wasn't the distance that had done Foonsky in; it was those blisters. He had them on eight of his 10 toes and was going through Band-Aids, moleskin, and tape like a walking emergency ward. If he'd used any more tape, he would've looked like a mummy from an Egyptian tomb.

If you've ever been in a similar predicament, you know the frustration of wanting to have a good time, wanting to hike and explore the area where you have set up a secluded camp, only to be held up by several blisters. No one is immune—all are created equal before the blister god. You can be forced to bow to it unless you get your act together.

What causes blisters? In almost all cases, it is the simple rubbing of a foot against the rugged interior of a boot. That can be worsened by several factors:

1. A very stiff boot or one in which your foot moves inside as you walk, instead of a boot that flexes as if it were another layer of skin.

2. Thin, ragged, or dirty socks. This is the fastest route to blisters. Thin socks will allow your feet to move inside your boots, ragged socks will allow your skin to chafe directly against the boot's interior, and dirty socks will wrinkle and fold, also rubbing against your feet instead of cushioning them.

3. Soft feet. By themselves, soft feet will not cause blisters, but in combination with a stiff boot or thin socks, they can cause terrible problems. The best way to toughen up your feet is to go barefoot. In fact, some of the biggest, toughest-looking guys you'll ever see, from Hells Angels to pro football players, have feet that are as soft as a baby's butt. Why? Because they never go barefoot and don't hike much.

The Perfect Boot

Every hiker eventually conducts a search for the perfect boot in the mission for ideal foot comfort and freedom from blisters. While there are many entries in this search—in fact, so many that it can be confusing—there is a way to find that perfect boot for you.

To stay blister-free, the most important factors are socks and boot flexibility. If there is any foot slippage from a thin sock or a stiff boot, you can rub up a blister in minutes. For instance, I never wear stiff boots and I sometimes wear two fresh sets of SmartWools.

My search for the perfect boot included discussions with the nation's preeminent long-distance hikers, Brian Robinson of Mountain View (7,200 miles in 2001) and Ray Jardine of Oregon (2,700 miles of Pacific Crest Trail in three months). Both believe that the weight of a shoe is the defining factor when selecting hiking footwear. They both go as light as possible, believing that heavy boots will eventually wear you out by forcing you to pick up several pounds on your feet over and over again.

It is absolutely critical to stay away from very stiff boots and thin socks. Always wear the right style boots for what you have in mind and then protect your feet with carefully selected socks. If you are still so unfortunate as to get a blister or two, it means knowing how to treat them fast so they don't turn your walk into a sore-footed endurance test.

Selecting the Right Boots

The first time we did the John Muir Trail, I hiked 400 miles in three months; that is, 150 miles in a two-month general-training program, then 250 miles in three weeks from Mount Whitney to Yosemite Valley. In that span, I got just one blister, suffered on the fourth day of the 250-miler. I treated it immediately and suffered no more. One key is wearing the right boot, and for me, that means a boot that acts as a thick layer of skin that is flexible and pliable to my foot. I want my feet to fit snugly in them, with no interior movement.

There are four kinds of hiking footwear, most commonly known as: 1. Hiking boots; 2. Hunting boots; 3. Mountaineering boots; 4. Athletic shoes. Select the right one for you or pay the consequences.

One great trick when on a hiking vacation is to bring all four, and then for each hike, wear different footwear. This has many benefits. By changing boots, you change the points of stress for your feet and legs, greatly reducing soreness and the chance of creating a hot spot on a foot. It also allows you to go light on flat trails and heavy on steep trails, where

© SABRINA YOUNG

Spend your time admiring the scenery instead of tending to blisters.

additional boot weight can help with traction in downhill stretches.

Hiking Boots

Lightweight hiking boots are basically Gore-Tex walking shoes. They are designed for day walks or short backpacking trips and look like rugged, lightweight athletic shoes, designed with a Gore-Tex top for lightness and a Vibram sole for traction. These are perfect for people who like to walk but rarely carry a heavy backpack. Because they are flexible, they are easy to break in, and with fresh socks, they rarely cause blister problems. Because they are light, general hiking fatigue is greatly reduced. Like many, I've converted over 100 percent to them.

On the negative side, because hiking boots are light, traction can be far from great on steep, gravelly surfaces. In addition, they provide less than ideal ankle support, which can be a problem in rocky areas, such as along a stream where you might want to go trout fishing.

Regardless of the distance you anticipate, they are the footwear of choice. My personal preference is Merrell's, but New Balance, Salomon, Asolo, Zamberlan, Vasque, and others make great hiking boots. Many of the greatest long-distance hikers in America wear trail running shoes.

Hunting Boots

Hunting boots are also called backpacking boots, super boots, or wilderness boots. They feature high ankle support, deep Vibram lug sole, built-in orthotics and arch support, and waterproof exterior.

They have fallen out of favor among campers and backpackers. On the negative side, hunting boots can be quite hot, weigh a ton, and if they get wet, take days to dry. Because they are heavy, they can wear you out. Often, the extra weight can add days to long-distance expeditions, cutting into the number of miles a hiker is capable of on a daily basis.

They are still popular among mountaineers who hunt. Their weight and traction make them good for trekking off-trail or for carrying

heavy packs because they provide additional support. They also can stand up to hundreds of miles of wilderness use, constantly being banged against rocks and walked through streams while supporting 200 pounds.

My favorite hunting boot is made by Mendl, out of Germany. I have also used Danner, Cabela's and RedWing.

Mountaineering Boots

Mountaineering boots are identified by mid-range tops, laces that extend almost as far as the toe area, and ankle areas that are as stiff as a board. The lack of "give" is what endears them to mountaineers. Their stiffness is preferred when rock-climbing, walking off-trail on craggy surfaces, or hiking along the edge of streambeds where walking across small rocks can cause you to turn your ankle. Because these boots don't give on rugged, craggy terrain, they reduce ankle injuries and provide better traction.

The drawback to stiff boots is that if you don't have the proper socks and your foot starts slipping around in the boot, blisters will inevitably follow. If you just want to go for a walk or a good tromp with a backpack, then hiking shoes or hunting boots will serve you better.

Vasque makes my favorite mountaineering boots for rock climbing.

At the Store

There are many styles, brands, and price ranges to choose from. If you wander about comparing all their many features, you will get as confused as a kid in a toy store.

Instead, go into the store with your mind clear about what you want, find it, and buy it. If you want the best, expect to spend $85–200 for hiking boots, $100–250 for hunting boots, $250–300 for mountaineering boots. If you go much cheaper, well, then you are getting cheap footwear.

This is one area where you don't want to scrimp, so try not to yelp about the high cost. Instead, walk into the store believing

KEEP IT WILD TIP 3: TRAVEL LIGHTLY

1. Visit the backcountry in small groups.
2. Below tree line, always stay on designated trails.
3. Don't cut across switchbacks.
4. When traveling cross-country where no trails are available, follow animal trails or spread out with your group so no new routes are created.
5. Read your map and orient yourself with landmarks, a compass, and an altimeter. Avoid marking trails with rock cairns, tree scars, or ribbons.

you deserve the best, and that's exactly what you'll pay for.

You don't always get what you pay for, though. Once, I spent $200-plus on some hunting boots that turned out to be miserable blister-makers and I had to throw them out. Even after a year of trying to get my money's worth, I never felt they worked right on the trail. Adios. Move on to what works.

If you plan to use the advice of a shoe salesperson, first look at what kind of boots he or she is wearing. If the salesperson isn't even wearing boots, then their advice may not be worth much. Most people I know who own quality boots, including salespeople, wear them almost daily if their jobs allow, since boots are the best footwear available. However, even these well-meaning folks can offer sketchy advice. Plenty of hikers claim to wear the world's greatest boot! Instead of asking how great the boot is, ask, "How many blisters did you get when you hiked 12 miles a day for a week?"

Enter the store with a precise use and style in mind. Rather than fish for suggestions, tell the salesperson exactly what you want, try two or three brands of the same style, and always try on both boots in a pair simultaneously so you know exactly how they'll feel. If possible, walk up and down stairs with them. Are they too stiff? Are your feet snug yet comfortable, or do they slip? Do they have that "right" kind of feel when you walk?

If you get the appropriate answers to those questions, then you're on your way to blister-free, pleasure-filled days of walking.

Socks

People can spend so much energy selecting the right kind of boots that they virtually overlook wearing the right kind of socks. One goes with the other.

Your socks should be thick enough to cushion your feet as well as fit snugly. Without good socks, you might tie your bootlaces too tight—and that's like putting a tourniquet on your feet. You should have plenty of clean socks on hand, or plan on washing what you have on your trip. As socks are worn, they become compressed, dirty, and damp. If they fold over, you'll rub up a blister in minutes.

My companions believe I go overboard when it comes to socks, that I bring too many and wear too many. But it works, so that's where the complaints stop. So how many do I wear? Well, it varies. On day hikes, I have found a sock called a SmartWool that makes my size 13s feel as if they're walking on pillows. I often wear two of them; that is, two on each foot. Several manufacturers now produce socks that are the equivalent of SmartWools, but are a lot less expensive. SmartWool socks and other similar socks are a synthetic composite. They can partially wick moisture away from the skin.

Some hikers wear multiple socks and it works for them—a comfortable cotton-poly blend sock on the interior and wool sock on the exterior. This will cushion your foot, provide that just-right snug fit in your boot, and give you some additional warmth and insulation in cold weather. It is critical to keep the interior sock clean. If you wear a sock over and over again, it will compact, lose its cushion, and start wrinkling or folding over while you hike and a blister will be born.

Do not wear thin cotton socks. Your foot can get damp and mix with dirt, which can cause a hot spot to start on your foot. Eventually, you get blisters, lots of them.

Inner Sole

If you are like most folks, the bottoms of your feet are rarely exposed and can be quite soft. You can take additional steps in their care. The best tip is keeping a fresh inner sole footpad in your boot. I prefer Dr. Scholl's gel pad or the equivalent. Some new inner soles can be slippery for a few days, which, if your foot slides around while you're hiking, can cause blisters. Just like new boots and new socks, they need to be broken in before an expedition.

Another cure for soft feet is to get out and walk or jog on a regular basis before your camping trip. On one trip on the Pacific Coast Trail, I ran into the long-distance master Jardine. He swore that going barefoot regularly is the best way to build up foot strength and arch support, while toughening up the bottom of your feet.

If you plan to use a foot pad and wear two heavy socks, you will need to use these items when sizing boots. Do not buy shoes if you're wearing thin cotton socks; wear the socks you're planning to wear when hiking, insert the inner sole, and then see how they feel. That's the only right way to size a hiking boot.

Treating Blisters

The key to treating blisters is fast work at the first sign of a hot spot. If you feel a hot spot, never keep walking, figuring that the problem will go away or that you will work through it. Wrong! Stop immediately and go to work.

Before you remove your socks, check to see if the sock has a wrinkle in it, a likely cause of the problem. If so, either change socks or pull them tight, removing the tiny folds, after taking care of the blister.

To take care of the blister, forget Moleskin. (They changed how they manufacture it and I've found it will slide off the blister while hiking.) Instead, use "Second Skin," which adheres over the top of the blister and does not dislodge. For small blisters, Band-Aids can do the job, but these have to be replaced daily, and sometimes with even more frequency. At night, clean your feet and sleep without socks. That will allow your feet to dry and heal.

Tips in the Field

Three other items that can help your walking are an Ace bandage, a pair of gaiters, and hiking poles.

For sprained ankles and twisted knees, an Ace bandage can be like an insurance policy to get you back on the trail and out of trouble. In many cases, a hiker with a twisted ankle or sprained knee has relied on a good wrap with a four-inch bandage for the added support to get home. Always buy the Ace bandages that come with the clips permanently attached, so you don't have to worry about losing them.

Gaiters are leggings made of Gore-Tex that fit from just below your knees, over your calves, and attach under your boots. They are of particular help when walking in damp areas or in places where rain is common. As your legs brush against ferns or low-lying plants, gaiters deflect the moisture. Without them, pants can get soaked wet in short order.

Many hikers would never hit the trail without hiking poles. Personally, they are not for me; I like to hike in rhythm and keeping my arms swinging effortlessly. I don't like to have to watch where I'm putting my poles all the time. But for those who have trouble with footing, a cranky knee or ankle, or want the upper body workout, poles can be a good fit. If it floats your boat, bring 'em.

Another tip: Should your boots become wet, never try to force-dry them. Some well-meaning folks will try to dry them quickly at the edge of a campfire, or at home, actually put the boots in an oven. While this may dry the boots, it can also loosen the glue that holds them together, ultimately weakening them until one day they fall apart in a heap.

A better bet is to treat the leather so the boots become water-repellent. Silicone-based liquids are the easiest to use and least greasy of the treatments available.

A final tip is to have another pair of lightweight shoes or moccasins that you can wear around camp and, in the process, give your feet the rest they deserve.

CLOTHING AND WEATHER PROTECTION

What started as an innocent pursuit of the perfect campground evolved into one heck of a predicament for Foonsky and me.

We had parked at the end of a logging road and then bushwhacked our way down a canyon to a pristine trout stream. On my first cast—a little flip into the plunge pool of a waterfall—I caught a 16-inch rainbow trout, a real beauty that jumped three times. Magic stuff.

Then, just across the stream, we saw it: The Perfect Camping Spot. On a sandbar on the edge of the forest, there lay a flat spot, high and dry above the river. Nearby was plenty of downed wood collected by past winter storms that we could use for firewood. And, of course, this beautiful trout stream was bubbling along just 40 yards from the site.

But nothing is perfect, right? To reach it, we had to wade across the river, although it didn't appear to be too difficult. The cold water tingled a bit, and the river came up surprisingly high, just above the belt. But it would be worth it to camp at The Perfect Spot.

Once across the river, we put on some dry clothes, set up camp, explored the woods, and fished the stream, catching several nice trout for dinner. But late that afternoon, it started raining. What? Rain in the summertime? Nature makes its own rules. By the next morning, it was still raining, pouring like a Yosemite waterfall from a solid gray sky.

That's when we noticed The Perfect Spot wasn't so perfect. The rain had raised the river level too high for us to wade back across. We were marooned, wet, and hungry.

"Now we're in a heck of a predicament," said Foonsky, the water streaming off him.

Getting cold and wet on a camping trip with no way to warm up is not only unnecessary and uncomfortable, it can be a fast ticket to hypothermia, the number one killer of campers in the woods. By definition, hypothermia is a condition in which body temperature is lowered to the point that it causes illness. It is particularly dangerous because the afflicted are usually unaware it is setting in. The first sign is a sense of apathy, then a state of confusion, which can lead eventually to collapse (or what appears to be sleep), then death.

You must always have a way to get warm and dry in short order, regardless of any conditions you may face. If you have no way of getting dry, then you must take emergency steps to prevent hypothermia. (See the steps detailed in *First Aid and Insect Protection* in this chapter.)

But you should never reach that point. For starters, always have spare sets of clothing tucked away so no matter how cold and wet you might get, you have something dry to put on. On hiking trips, I always carry a second set of clothes, sealed to stay dry, in a plastic garbage bag. I keep a third set waiting back at the truck.

If you are car camping, your vehicle can cause an illusory sense of security. But with an extra set of dry clothes stashed safely away, there is no illusion. The security is real. And remember, no matter how hot the weather is when you start your trip, always be prepared for the worst. Foonsky and I learned the hard way.

So both of us were soaking wet on that sandbar. With no other choice, we tried holing up in the tent for the night. A sleeping bag with Quallofil or another polyester fiberfill can retain warmth even when wet, because the fill is hollow and retains its loft. So as miserable as it was, the night passed without incident.

The rain stopped the next day and the river dropped a bit, but it was still rolling big and angry. Using a stick as a wading staff, Foonsky crossed about 80 percent of the stream before he was dumped, but he made a jump for it and managed to scramble to the riverbank. He waved for me to follow. "No problem," I thought.

It took me 20 minutes to reach nearly the same spot where Foonsky had been dumped. The heavy river current was above my belt and pushing hard. Then, in the flash of an instant, my wading staff slipped on a rock. I teetered in the river current and was knocked over like a bowling pin. I became completely submerged. I went tumbling down the river, heading right toward the waterfall. While underwater, I looked up at the surface, and I can remember how close it seemed yet how out of control I was. Right then, this giant hand appeared, and I grabbed it. It was Foonsky. If it weren't for that hand, I would have sailed right over the waterfall.

My momentum drew Foonsky right into the river, and we scrambled in the current, but I suddenly sensed the river bottom under my knees. On all fours, the two of us clambered ashore. We were safe.

"Thanks, ol' buddy," I said.

"Man, we're wet," he responded. "Let's get to the rig and get some dry clothes on."

The Art of Layering

The most important element for enjoying the outdoor experience in any condition is to stay dry and warm. There is no substitute. You must stay dry and you must stay warm.

Thus comes the theory behind layering, which suggests that as your body temperature fluctuates or the weather shifts, you simply peel off or add available layers as needed—and have a waterproof shell available in case of rain.

The introduction of a new era of outdoor clothing has made it possible for campers to turn choosing clothes into an art form. Like art, it's much more expensive than throwing on a pair of blue jeans, a T-shirt, and some flannel, but, for many, it is worth the price.

In putting together your ideal layering system, there are some general considerations. What you need to do is create a system that effectively combines elements of breathability, durability, insulation, rapid drying, water repellence, wicking, and wind resistance, while still being lightweight and offering the necessary freedom of movement, all with just a few garments.

The basic intent of a base layer is to manage moisture. Your base layer will be the first article of clothing you put on and the last to come off. Since your own skin will be churning out the perspiration, the goal of this second skin is to manage the moisture and move it away from you. The best base layers are made of bicomponent knits, that is, blends of polyester and cotton, which provide wicking and insulating properties in one layer.

The way it works is that the side facing your skin is water-hating, while the side away from your skin is water-loving; thus, it pulls or "wicks" moisture through the material. You'll stay dry and happy, even with only one layer on, something not possible with old single-function weaves. The best include Capilene, Driclime, Lifa, Polartec 100, and Thermax. The only time that cotton should become a part of your base layer is if you wish to keep cool, not warm, such as in a hot desert climate where evaporative cooling becomes your friend, not your enemy.

Stretch fleece and microdenier pile also provide a good base layer, though they can be used as a second layer as well. Microdenier pile can be worn alone or layered under or over other pieces; it has excellent wicking capability as well as more windproof potential.

The next layer should be a light cotton shirt or a long-sleeved cotton/wool shirt, or both, depending on the coolness of the day. For pants, many just wear blue jeans when camping, but blue jeans can be hot and tight, and once wet, they tend to stay that way. Putting on wet blue jeans on a cold morning is a torturous way to start the day. A better choice is pants made from nylon with detachable leggings; these are light, have a lot of give, and dry quickly. If the weather is quite warm, nylon shorts that have some room to them can be the best choice. My preference is for The North Face dark-green expedition hiking shorts.

Finally, you should top the entire ensemble off with a thin, windproof, water-resistant layer. You want this layer to breathe, yet not be so porous that rain runs through it. Patagonia's Velocity shell is one of the best; its outer fabric is treated with DWR (Durable Water Repellent finish) and the coating is by Goretex. Patagonia, Marmot, and The North Face and others all offer their own versions. Though condensation will still build up inside, it manages to get rid of enough moisture.

Note: It is critical to know the difference between "water-resistant" and "waterproof." (This is covered under the *Rain Gear* section in this chapter.)

But hey, why does anybody need all this fancy stuff just to go camping? Fair question. You don't have to opt for this aerobic-function fashion statement. It is unnecessary on many camping trips. The fact is that you must be ready for anything when you venture into the outdoors. The new era of outdoor clothing works, and it works better than anything that has come before. Regardless of what you choose, weather should never be a nuisance or cause discomfort. There is no such thing as bad weather, so the saying goes, only bad gear.

Hats

Another word of advice: Always pack along a warm hat for those times when you need to seal in warmth. You lose a large percentage of heat through your head. At night in cold weather, I wear a skullcap. During the day, I almost always wear a wide-brimmed hat, something like those that the legendary outlaws wore 150 years ago. There's actually logic behind it: My hat is made of waterproof canvas, is rigged with a lariat (it can be cinched down when it's windy), and has a wide brim that keeps the tops of my ears from being sunburned. If you're outside a lot, do not wear baseball hats—the tops of your ears will burn to a red crisp. Years ago, that's how an old friend of mine lost his ears to skin cancer.

Head Light

I've tried many head lights and the Trail Torch Hat Light is my favorite by a mile (www.halibut.net, $9.95). It comes with five white and green LED lights in a horizontal row that clips under the bill of your hat. For the best option, order the set with three green lights (for night vision) and two white lights. (At night you'll look like a jet coming in for a landing.)

Vests and Parkas

In cold weather, you should take the layer system one step further with a warm vest and a parka jacket. Vests are especially useful because they provide warmth without the bulkiness of a parka. The warmest vests and parkas are either filled with down or Quallofil, or they are made with a cotton/wool mix. Each has its respective merits and problems. Down fill provides the most warmth for the amount of weight, but becomes useless when wet, closely resembling a wet dishrag. Quallofil keeps much of its heat-retaining quality even when wet, but it is expensive. Vests made of cotton/wool mixes are the most attractive and also are quite warm, but they can be as heavy as a ship's anchor when wet.

Sometimes, the answer is combining a parka with a vest. One of my best camping companions wears a good-looking cotton/wool vest and a parka filled with Quallofil. The vest never gets wet, so weight is not a factor.

Rain Gear

One of the most miserable nights of my life was on a camping trip for which I hadn't brought my rain gear or a tent. Hey, it was early August, the temperature had been in the 90s for weeks, and if anybody had said it was going to rain, I would have told him to consult a brain doctor. But rain it did. And as I got wetter and wetter, I kept saying to myself, "Hey, it's summer, it's not supposed to rain." Then I remembered one of the 10 commandments of camping: Forget your rain gear and you can guarantee it will rain.

To stay dry, you need some form of water-repellent shell. It can be as simple as a $5 poncho made out of plastic or as elaborate as a $300 Gore-Tex jacket-and-pants set. What counts is not how much you spend, but how dry you stay.

The most important thing to realize is that waterproof and water-resistant are completely different things. In addition, there is no such thing as rain gear that is both waterproof and breathable. The more waterproof a jacket is, the less it breathes. Conversely, the more breathable a jacket is, the less waterproof it becomes.

If you wear water-resistant rain gear in a sustained downpour, you'll get soaked. Water-resistant rain gear is appealing because it breathes and will keep you dry in the light stuff, such as mist, fog, even a little splash from a canoe paddle. But in rain? Forget it.

So what is the solution?

I've decided that the best approach is a set of fairly light but 100 percent–waterproof rain gear. I recently bought a hooded jacket and pants from Coleman, and my assessment is that it is the most cost-efficient rain gear I've ever had. All I can say is, hey, it works: I stay dry, it doesn't weigh much, and it didn't cost a fortune.

The absolute best foul weather gear made is by Simms, both jacket and bib. While it is expensive, you will stay dry and warm in any condition but that in which you need a survival suit.

You can also stay dry with any of the waterproof plastics and even heavy-duty rubber-coated outfits made for commercial fishermen. But these are uncomfortable during anything but a heavy rain. Because they are heavy and don't breathe, you'll likely get soaked anyway

(that is, from your own sweat), even if it isn't raining hard.

On backpacking trips, I still stash a super-lightweight, water-repellent slicker for day hikes and a poncho, which I throw over my pack at night to keep it dry. But, otherwise, I never go anywhere—*anywhere*—without my rain gear.

Some do just fine with a cheap poncho, and note that ponchos can serve other uses in addition to a raincoat. Ponchos can be used as a ground tarp, as a rain cover for supplies or a backpack, or can be snapped together and roped up to trees in a pinch to provide a quick storm ceiling if you don't have a tent. The problem with ponchos is that in a hard rain, you just don't stay dry. First your legs get wet, then they get soaked. Then your arms follow the same pattern. If you're wearing cotton, you'll find that once part of the garment gets wet, the water spreads until, alas, you are dripping wet, poncho and all. Before long, you start to feel like a walking refrigerator.

One high-cost option is to buy a Gore-Tex rain jacket and pants. Gore-Tex is actually not a fabric, as is commonly believed, but a laminated film that coats a breathable fabric. The result is lightweight, water-repellent, breathable jackets and pants. They are perfect for campers, but they cost a fortune.

Some hiking buddies of mine have complained that the older Gore-Tex rain gear loses its water-repellent quality over time. However, manufacturers insist that this is the result of water seeping through seams, not leaks in the jacket. At each seam, tiny needles have pierced the fabric, and as tiny as the holes are, water will find a way through. An application of Seam Lock, especially at major seams around the shoulders of a jacket, can usually fix the problem.

If you don't want to spend the big bucks for Gore-Tex rain gear but want more rain protection than a poncho affords, a coated nylon jacket is the compromise that many choose. They are inexpensive, have the highest water-repellency of any rain gear, and are warm, providing a good outer shell for your layers of clothing. But they are not without fault. These jackets don't breathe at all, and if you zip them up tight, you can sweat a river.

My brother Rambob gave me a nylon jacket before a mountain-climbing expedition. I wore that cheap special all the way to the top with no complaints; it's warm and 100 percent waterproof. The one problem with nylon comes when temperatures drop below freezing. It gets so stiff that it feels as if you are wearing a straitjacket.

There's one more jacket-construction term to know: DWR, or Durable Water-Repellent finish. All of the top-quality jackets these days are DWR-treated. The DWR causes water to bead up on the shell. When the DWR wears off, even a once-waterproof jacket will feel like a wet dishrag.

Also note that ventilation is the key to coolness. The only ventilation on most shells is often the zipper. But waterproof jackets need additional openings. Look for mesh-backed pockets and underarm zippers, as well as cuffs, waists, and hems that can be adjusted to open wide. Storm flaps (the baffle over the zipper) that close with hook-and-loop material or snaps let you leave the zipper open for airflow into the jacket.

Other Gear

What are the three items most commonly forgotten on a camping trip? A hat, sunglasses, and lip balm.

A hat is crucial, especially when you are visiting high elevations. Without one you are constantly exposed to everything nature can give you. The sun will dehydrate you, sap your energy, sunburn your head, and in worst cases, cause sunstroke. Start with a comfortable hat. Then finish with sunglasses, lip balm, and sunscreen for additional protection. They will help protect you from extreme heat.

To guard against extreme cold, it's a good idea to keep a pair of thin ski gloves stashed away with your emergency clothes, along with a wool ski cap, or a skull cap. The gloves

should be thick enough to keep your fingers from stiffening up, but pliable enough to allow full movement so you don't have to take them off to complete simple tasks, like lighting a stove. An alternative to gloves is glovelets, which look like gloves with no fingers. In any case, just because the weather turns cold doesn't mean that your hands have to.

FOOD AND COOKING GEAR

It was a warm, crystal clear day, a perfect day for skydiving. That was exactly the case for my old pal Foonsky, who had never before tried the sport. But a funny thing happened after he jumped out of the plane and pulled on the rip cord: His parachute didn't open.

In total free fall, Foonsky watched the earth below getting closer and closer. Not one to panic, he calmly pulled the ripcord on the emergency parachute. Again, nothing happened. No parachute, no nothing.

The ground was getting ever closer, and as he tried to search for a soft place to land, Foonsky detected a small object shooting up toward him, growing larger as it approached. It looked like a camper.

Figuring this was his last chance, Foonsky shouted as they passed in midair, "Hey, do you know anything about parachutes?"

The other fellow just yelled back as he headed off into space, "Do you know anything about lighting camping stoves?"

Well, Foonsky got lucky and his parachute opened. As for the other guy, well, he's probably in orbit like a NASA weather satellite. If you've ever had a mishap while lighting a camping stove, you know exactly what I'm talking about.

When it comes to camping, all gear is not created equal. Nothing is more important than lighting your stove easily and having it reach full heat without feeling as if you're playing with a short fuse to a miniature bomb. If your stove does not work right, your trip can turn into a disaster, regardless of how well you have planned the other elements. In addition, a bad stove will add an underlying sense of foreboding to your day. You will constantly have the inner suspicion that your darn stove is going to foul up again.

Camping Stoves

If you are buying a camping stove, remember this one critical rule: Do not leave the store with a new stove unless you have been shown exactly how to use it.

Know what you are getting. Many stores that specialize in outdoor recreation equipment now staff experienced campers/employees who will demonstrate the use of every stove they sell. While they're at it, they'll also describe the stoves' respective strengths and weaknesses.

An innovation by Peak 1 is a two-burner butane-powered backpacking stove that allows you to boil water and heat a pot of food simultaneously. While that has long been standard for car campers using Coleman's legendary camp stove, it was previously unheard of for wilderness campers in high-elevation areas. It's a fantastic stove.

The standard Coleman car camping stove, the green one with the two burners, is a legend around the world. Electronic ignition has solved all the old lighting problems.

A stove that has developed a cult-like following is the little Sierra, which burns small twigs and pinecones, then uses a tiny battery-driven fan to develop increased heat and cooking ability. It's an excellent alternative for long-distance backpacking trips, as it solves the problem of carrying a fuel bottle, especially on expeditions for which large quantities of fuel would otherwise be needed. Some tinkering with the flame (a very hot one) is required, and they are legal and functional only in the alpine zone where dry wood is available. Also note that in years with high fire danger, the U.S. Forest Service enacts rules prohibiting open flames, and fires are also often prohibited above an elevation of 10,000 feet.

The MSR Whisperlite is an icon among backpackers. I've gone through several of them. It uses white gas in a separate fuel container so you can easily monitor fuel consumption. The one flaw is the connector links from the fuel line. After a few years of heavy use,

a standard Coleman propane stove

© SABRINA YOUNG

they can develop leaks; ignite and you've got meltdown.

For heavy, long-term use, ease of cleaning the burner is the most important. If you camp often, especially with a smaller stove, the burner holes will eventually become clogged. Some stoves have a built-in cleaning needle: a quick twist of the knob and you're in business. Others require disassembly and a protracted cleaning session using special tools. If a stove is difficult to clean, you will tend to put off the tiresome chore, and your stove will sputter and pant while you watch that pot of water sitting there, staying cold.

Before making a purchase, have the salesperson show you how to clean the burner head. Except in the case of large, multi-burner family-style camping stoves, which rarely require cleaning, this run-through can do more to determine the long-term value of a stove than any other factor.

Fuels for Camping Stoves

White gas and butane have long been the most popular camp fuels, but a newly developed fuel could dramatically change that.

LPG (liquid petroleum gas) comes in cartridges for easy attachment to a stove or lantern. At room temperature, LPG is delivered in a combustible gaseous form. When you shake the cartridge, the contents sound liquid; that is because the gas liquefies under pressure, which is why it is so easy to use. Large amounts of fuel can be compressed into small canisters.

The following summaries detail the benefits and drawbacks of other available fuels:

• **Butane:** You don't have to worry about explosions when using stoves that burn bottled butane fuel. Butane requires no pouring, pumping, or priming, and butane stoves are the easiest to light. Just turn a knob and light—that's it. On the minus side, because it comes in bottles, you never know precisely how much fuel you have left. And when a bottle is empty, you have a potential piece of litter. (Never litter. Ever.)

The other problem with butane is that it just plain does not work well in cold weather or when there is little fuel left in the cartridge. Since you cannot predict mountain weather in spring or fall, you might wind up using more fuel than originally projected. That can be frustrating, particularly if your stove starts wheezing when there are still several days left to go. In addition, with most butane cartridges, if there is any chance of the temperature falling below freezing, you often have to sleep with the cartridge to keep it warm. Otherwise, forget about using it come morning.

• **Butane/Propane:** This blend offers higher octane performance than butane alone, solving the cold temperature doldrums somewhat. However, propane burns off before butane, so there's a performance drop as the fuel level in the cartridge lowers.

• **Coleman Max Performance Fuel:** This fuel offers a unique approach to solving the consistent burn challenge facing all pressurized gas cartridges: operating at temperatures at or below 0°F. Using a standard propane/butane blend for high-octane performance, Coleman gets around the drop-off in performance other cartridges experience by using a version of fuel injection. A hose inside the cartridge pulls liquid fuel into the stove, where it vaporizes—a switch from the standard approach of pulling only a gaseous form of the fuel into a stove. By drawing liquid out of the cartridge, Coleman gets around the tendency of propane to burn off first and allows each cartridge to deliver a consistent mix of propane and butane to the stove's burners throughout the cartridge's life.

• **Denatured alcohol:** Though this fuel burns cleanly and quietly and is virtually explosion-proof, it generates much less heat than pressurized or liquid gas fuels.

• **Kerosene:** Never buy a stove that uses kerosene for fuel. Kerosene is smelly and messy, generates low heat, needs priming, and is virtually obsolete as a camp fuel in the United States. As a test, I once tried using a kerosene stove. I could scarcely boil a pot of water. In addition, some kerosene leaked out when the stove was packed, ruining everything it touched. The smell of kerosene never did go away. Kerosene remains popular in Europe only because most campers there haven't yet heard much about white gas. When they do, they will demand it.

• **Primus Tri-Blend:** This blend is made up of 20 percent propane, 70 percent butane, and 10 percent isobutane and is designed to burn with more consistent heat and efficiency than standard propane/butane mixes.

• **Propane:** Now available for single-burner stoves using larger, heavier cartridges to accommodate higher pressures, propane offers the very best performance of any of the pressurized gas canister fuels.

• **White gas:** White gas is the most popular camp fuel in the United States because it is inexpensive and effective—not to mention, sold at most outdoor recreation stores and many supermarkets. It burns hot, has virtually no smell, and evaporates quickly when spilled. If you are caught in wet, miserable weather and can't get a fire going, you can use white gas as an emergency fire starter; however, if you do so, use it sparingly and never on an open flame.

White gas is a popular fuel both for car campers who use the large, two-burner stoves equipped with a fuel tank and a pump and for hikers who carry a lightweight backpacking stove. On the latter, lighting can require priming with a gel called priming paste, which some people dislike. Another problem with white gas is that it can be extremely explosive.

As an example, I once almost burned my beard completely off in a mini-explosion while lighting one of the larger stoves designed for car camping. I was in the middle of cooking dinner when the flame suddenly shut down. Sure enough, the fuel tank was empty, and after refilling it, I pumped the tank 50 or 60 times to regain pressure. When I lit a match, the sucker ignited from three feet away. The resulting explosion was like a stick of dynamite going off, and immediately the smell of burning beard was in the air. In a flash, my once

thick, dark beard had been reduced to a mass of little, yellow, burned curlicues.

My error? After filling the tank, I forgot to shut the fuel cock off while pumping up the pressure in the tank. As a result, the stove burners were slowly emitting the gas/air mixture as I pumped the tank, filling the air above the stove. Then, strike a match from even a few feet away and ka-boom!

Building Fires

One summer expedition took me to the Canadian wilderness in British Columbia for a 75-mile canoe trip on the Bowron Lake Circuit, a chain of 13 lakes, six rivers, and seven portages. It is one of the greatest canoe trips in the world, a loop that ends just a few hundred feet from its starting point. But at the first camp at Kibbee Lake, my stove developed a fuel leak at the base of the burner, and the nuclear-like blast that followed just about turned Canada into a giant crater.

As a result, we had to complete the final 70 miles of the trip without a stove, cooking instead on open fires each night. The problem was compounded by the weather. It rained eight of the 10 days. Rain? In Canada, raindrops the size of silver dollars fall so hard they actually bounce on the lake surface. We had to stop paddling a few times to empty the rainwater out of the canoe. At the end of the day, we'd make camp and then face the critical decision: either make a fire or go to bed cold and hungry.

Equipped with an ax, at least we had a chance for success. Although the downed wood was soaked, I was able to make my own fire-starting tinder from the chips of split logs; no matter how hard it rains, the inside of a log is always dry.

In miserable weather, matches don't stay lit long enough to get tinder started. Instead, we used either a candle or the little waxlike fire-starter cubes that remain lit for several minutes. From those, we could get the tinder going. Then we added small, slender strips of wood that had been axed from the interior of

KEEP IT WILD TIP 4: CAMPFIRES

1. Fire use can scar the backcountry. If a fire ring is not available, use a lightweight stove for cooking.
2. Where fires are permitted, use existing fire rings away from large rocks or over-hangs.
3. Don't char rocks by building new rings.
4. Gather sticks from the ground that are no larger than the diameter of your wrist.
5. Don't snap branches of live, dead, or downed trees, which can cause personal injury and also scar the natural setting.
6. Put the fire "dead out" and make sure it's cold before departing. Remove all trash from the fire ring and sprinkle dirt over the site.
7. Remember that some forest fires can be started by a campfire that appears to be out. Hot embers burning deep in the pit can cause tree roots to catch fire and burn underground. If you ever see smoke rising from the ground, seemingly from nowhere, dig down and put the fire out.

the logs. When the flame reached a foot high, we added the logs, their dry interior facing in. By the time the inside of the logs had caught fire, the outside was drying from the heat. It wasn't long before a royal blaze was brightening the rainy night.

That's a worst-case scenario, and I hope you will never face anything like it. Nevertheless, being able to build a good fire and cook on it can be one of the more satisfying elements of a camping trip. At times, just looking into the flames can provide a special satisfaction at the end of a good day.

However, never expect to build a fire for every meal or, in some cases, even to build one at all. Many state and federal campgrounds have been picked clean of downed wood. During the fire season, the danger of forest fires can force rangers to prohibit fires altogether. In either case, you must use your camp stove or go hungry.

But when you can build a fire and the resources for doing so are available, it will enhance the quality of your camping experience. Of the campgrounds listed in this book, those where you are permitted to build fires will usually have fire rings. In primitive areas where you can make your own fire, you should dig a ring eight inches deep, line the edges with

rock, and clear all the needles and twigs in a five-foot radius. The next day, when the fire is dead, you can scatter the rocks, fill over the black charcoal with dirt, and then spread pine needles and twigs over it. Nobody will even know you camped there. That's the best way I know to keep a secret spot a real secret.

When you start to build a campfire, the first thing you will notice is that no matter how good your intentions, your fellow campers will not be able to resist moving the wood around. Watch. You'll be getting ready to add a key piece of wood at just the right spot, and your companion will stick his mitts in, confidently believing he has a better idea. He'll shift the fire around and undermine your best-thought-out plans.

So I enforce a rule on camping trips: One person makes the fire while everybody else stands clear or is involved with other camp tasks, such as gathering wood, getting water, putting up tents, or planning dinner. Once the fire is going strong, then it's fair game; anyone adds logs at his or her discretion. But in the early, delicate stages of the campfire, it's best to leave the work to one person.

Before a match is ever struck, you should gather a complete pile of firewood. Then, start small, with the tiniest twigs you can find, and slowly add larger twigs as you go, crisscrossing them like a miniature tepee. Eventually, you will get to the big chunks that produce high heat. The key is to get one piece of wood burning into another, which then burns into another, setting off what I call the chain of flame. Conversely, single pieces of wood set apart from each other will not burn.

On a dry summer evening at a campsite where plenty of wood is available, about the only way you can blow the deal is to get impatient and try to add the big pieces too quickly. Do that and you'll get smoke, not flames, and it won't be long before every one of your fellow campers is poking at your fire. It will drive you crazy, but they just won't be able to help it.

Cooking Gear

I like traveling light, and I've found that all I need for cooking is a pot, small frying pan, metal pot grabber, fork, knife, cup, and matches. If you want to keep the price of food low and also cook customized dinners each night, a small pressure cooker can be just the ticket. (See *Keeping the Price Down* in this chapter.) I store all my gear in one small bag that fits into my pack. If I'm camping out of my four-wheel-drive rig, I can easily keep track of the little bag of cooking gear. Going simple, not complicated, is the key to keeping a camping trip on the right track.

You can get more elaborate by buying complete kits with plates, a coffeepot, large pots, and other cookware, but what really counts is having a single pot that makes you happy. It needs to be just the right size, not too big or small, and stable enough so it won't tip over, even if it is at a slight angle on a fire, filled with water at a full boil. Mine is just six inches wide and 4.5 inches deep. It holds better than a quart of water and has served me well for several hundred camp dinners.

The rest of your cook kit is easy to complete. The frying pan should be small, light-gauge aluminum, and Teflon-coated, with a fold-in handle so it's no hassle to store. A pot grabber is a great addition. This little aluminum

gadget clamps to the edge of pots and allows you to lift them and pour water with total control and without burning your fingers. For cleanup, take along a plastic scrubber and a small bottle filled with dish soap, and you're in business.

A sierra cup, a wide aluminum cup with a wire handle, is an ideal item to carry because you can eat out of it as well as use it for drinking. This means no plates to scrub after dinner, so washing up is quick and easy. In addition, if you go for a hike, you can clip its handle to your belt. Some people bring a giant cup called a "Fair Share." In expeditions where food has to be rationed, they manage to get a lot more than their "fair share" because a cup of food looks so small in these giant vessels.

If you opt for a more formal setup, complete with plates, glasses, silverware, and the like, you can end up spending more time preparing and cleaning up after meals than enjoying the country you are exploring. In addition, the more equipment you bring, the more loose ends you will have to deal with, and loose ends can cause plenty of frustration. If you have a choice, go simple.

Remember what Thoreau said: "A man is rich in proportion to what he can do without."

Food and Cooking Tricks

On a trip to the Bob Marshall Wilderness in western Montana, I woke up one morning, yawned, and said, "What've we got for breakfast?"

The silence was ominous. "Well," finally came the response, "we don't have any food left."

"What!?"

"Well, I figured we'd catch trout for meals every other night."

On the return trip, we ended up eating wild berries, buds, and, yes, even roots (not too tasty). When we finally landed the next day at a suburban pizza parlor, we nearly ate the wooden tables.

Running out of food on a camping trip can

do more to turn reasonable people into violent grumps than any other event. There's no excuse for it, not when figuring meals can be done precisely and with little effort. You should not go out and buy a bunch of food, throw it in your rig, and head off for yonder. That leaves too much to chance. And if you've ever been really hungry in the woods, you know it's worth a little effort to guard against a day or two of starvation. Here's a three-step solution:

1. Draw up a general meal-by-meal plan and make sure your companions like what's on it.

2. Tell your companions to buy any specialty items (such as a special brand of coffee) on their own and not to expect you to take care of everything.

3. Put all the food on your living room floor and literally plan out every day of your trip, meal by meal, putting the food in plastic bags as you go. That way, you will know exact food quotas and you won't go hungry.

Fish for your dinner? There's one guarantee as far as that goes: If you expect to catch fish for meals, you will most certainly get skunked. If you don't expect to catch fish for meals, you will probably catch so many they'll be coming out of your ears. I've seen it a hundred times.

Keeping the Price Down

"There must be some mistake," I said with a laugh. "Whoever paid $750 for camp food?"

But the amount was as clear as the digital numbers on the cash register: $753.27.

"How is this possible?" I asked the clerk.

"Just add it up," she responded, irritated.

Then I started figuring. The freeze-dried backpack dinners cost $6 apiece. A small pack of beef jerky went for $2, the beef sticks for $0.75, granola bars for $0.50. Multiply it all by four hungry men, including Foonsky.

The dinners alone cost close to $500. Add in the usual goodies—candy, coffee, dried fruit, granola bars, jerky, oatmeal, soup, and Tang— and I felt as if an earthquake had struck when I saw the tab.

A lot of campers have received similar shocks. In preparation for their trips, campers shop with enthusiasm. Then they pay the bill in horror.

Well, there are solutions, lots of them. You can eat gourmet-style in the outback without having your wallet cleaned out. But it requires do-it-yourself cooking, more planning, and careful shopping. It also means transcending the push-button, I-want-it-now attitude that so many people can't leave behind when they go to the mountains.

Now when Foonsky, Mr. Furnai, Rambob, and I sit down to eat such a meal, we don't call it "eating." We call it "hodgepacking" or "time to pack your hodge." After a particularly long day on the trail, you can do some serious hodgepacking.

If your trip is a shorter one, say for a weekend, consider bringing more fresh food to add some sizzle to the hodge. You can design a hot soup/stew mix that is good enough to eat at home.

Start by bringing a pot of water to a full boil, and then add pasta, ramen noodles, or macaroni. While it simmers, cut in a potato, carrot, onion, and garlic clove, and cook for about 10 minutes. When the vegetables have softened, add in a soup mix or two, maybe some cheese, and you are just about in business. But you can still ruin it and turn your hodge into slodge. Make sure you read the directions on the soup mix to determine cooking time. It can vary widely. In addition, make sure you stir the whole thing up; otherwise, you will get those hidden dry clumps of soup mix that taste like garlic sawdust.

How do I know? Well, it was up near Kearsage Pass in the Sierra Nevada, where, feeling half-starved, I dug into our nightly hodge. I will never forget that first bite—I damn near gagged to death. Foonsky laughed at me, until he took his first bite (a nice big one) and then turned green.

Another way to trim food costs is to make your own beef jerky, the trademark staple of campers for more than 200 years. A tiny packet of beef jerky costs $2, and for that 250-mile

HOW TO MAKE BEEF JERKY IN YOUR OWN KITCHEN

Start with a couple of pieces of meat: lean top round, sirloin, or tri-tip. Cut them into 3/16-inch strips across the grain, trimming out the membrane, gristle, and fat. Marinate the strips for 24 hours in a glass dish. The fun begins in picking a marinade. Try two-thirds teriyaki sauce, one-third Worcestershire sauce. You can customize the recipe by adding pepper, ground mustard, bay leaf, red wine vinegar, garlic, and, for the brave, Tabasco sauce.

After a day or so, squeeze out each strip of meat with a rolling pin, lay them in rows on a cooling rack over a cookie sheet, and dry them in the oven at 125°F for 12 hours. Thicker pieces can take as long as 18–24 hours.

That's it. The hardest part is cleaning the cookie sheet when you're done. The easiest part is eating your own homemade jerky while sitting at a lookout on a mountain ridge. The do-it-yourself method for jerky may take a day or so, but it is cheaper and can taste better than any store-bought jerky.

–my thanks to Jeff Patty
for this recipe

You can supplement your eats with sweets, nuts, freeze-dried fruits, and drink mixes. In any case, make sure you keep the dinner menu varied. If you and your buddies look into your dinner cups and groan, "Ugh, not this again," you will soon start dreaming of cheeseburgers and french fries instead of hiking, fishing, and finding beautiful campsites.

If you are car camping and have a big ice chest, you can bring virtually anything to eat and drink. If you are on the trail and don't mind paying the price, the newest freeze-dried dinners provide another option.

Some of the biggest advances in the outdoors industry have come in the form of freeze-dried dinners. Some of them are almost good enough to serve in restaurants. Sweet-and-sour pork over rice, tostadas, Burgundy chicken—it sure beats the poopy goop we used to eat, like the old soupy chili-mac dinners that tasted bad and looked so unlike food that consumption was nearly impossible, even for my dog, Rebel. Foonsky usually managed to get it down, but just barely.

To provide an idea of how to plan a menu, consider what my companions and I ate while hiking 250 miles on California's John Muir Trail:

• Breakfast: instant soup, oatmeal (never get plain), one beef or jerky stick, coffee or hot chocolate.
• Lunch: one beef stick, two jerky sticks, one granola bar, dried fruit, half cup of pistachio nuts, Tang, one small bag of M&Ms.
• Dinner: instant soup, one freeze-dried dinner (split between two people), one milk bar, rainbow trout.

What was that last item? Rainbow trout? Right! Unless you plan on it, you can catch them every night.

Trout Dinner

If all this still doesn't sound like your idea of a gourmet but low-cost camping meal, well, you are forgetting the main course: rainbow trout. Remember: If you don't plan on catching them for dinner, you'll probably

expedition, I spent $150 on jerky alone. Never again. Now we make our own and get big strips of jerky that taste better than anything you can buy.

For a crew of four, you can get by with two freeze-dried dinners that you cook right in the container pouch. Liam Furniss discovered that by adding a separate bonus pack of garlic-seasoned mashed potatoes, which cook in 90 seconds; everybody has plenty of food. That goes even for his dad Mo, with his gigantic, crater-of-the-moon "Fair Share" cup.

land more than you can finish in one night's hodgepacking.

Some campers go to great difficulties to cook their trout, bringing along frying pans, butter, grills, tinfoil, and more, but all you need is some seasoned salt and a campfire.

Rinse the gutted trout, and while it's still wet, sprinkle on a good dose of seasoned salt, both inside and out. Clear any burning logs to the side of the campfire, then lay the trout right on the coals, turning it once so both sides are cooked. Sound ridiculous? Sound like you are throwing the fish away? Sound like the fish will burn up? Sound like you will have to eat the campfire ash? Wrong on all counts. The fish cooks perfectly, the ash doesn't stick, and after cooking trout this way, you may never fry trout again.

If you can't convince your buddies, who may insist that trout should be fried, then make sure you have butter to fry it in, not oil. Also make sure you cook them all the way through, so the meat strips off the backbone in two nice, clean fillets. The fish should end up looking like one that Sylvester the Cat just drew out of his mouth—only the head, tail, and a perfect skeleton.

FIRST AID AND INSECT PROTECTION

Mountain nights don't get any more perfect, I thought as I lay in my sleeping bag.

The sky looked like a mass of jewels and the air tasted sweet and smelled of pines. A shooting star fireballed across the sky, and I remember thinking, "It just doesn't get any better."

Just then, as I was drifting into sleep, a mysterious buzz appeared from nowhere and deposited itself inside my left ear. Suddenly awake, I whacked my ear with the palm of my hand, hard enough to cause a minor concussion. The buzz disappeared. I pulled out my flashlight and shined it on my palm, and there, lit in the blackness of night, lay the squished intruder: a mosquito, dead amid a stain of blood.

Satisfied, I turned off the light, closed my eyes, and thought of the fishing trip planned for the next day. Then I heard them. It was a squadron of mosquitoes making landing patterns around my head. I tried to grab them with an open hand, but they dodged the assault and flew off. Just 30 seconds later, another landed in my left ear. I promptly dispatched the invader with a rip of the palm.

Now I was completely awake, so I got out of my sleeping bag to retrieve some mosquito repellent. But en route, several of the buggers swarmed and nailed me in the back and arms. After I applied the repellent and settled snugly again in my sleeping bag, the mosquitoes would buzz a few inches from my ear. After getting a whiff of the poison, they would fly off. It was like sleeping in a sawmill.

The next day, drowsy from little sleep, I set out to fish. I'd walked but 15 minutes when I brushed against a bush and felt a stinging sensation on the inside of my arm, just above the wrist. I looked down: A tick had his clamps in me. I ripped it out before he could embed his head into my skin.

After catching a few fish, I sat down against a tree to eat lunch and just watch the water go by. My dog, Rebel, sat down next to me and stared at the beef jerky I was munching as if it were a T-bone steak. I finished eating, gave him a small piece, patted him on the head, and said, "Good dog." Right then, I noticed an itch on my arm where a mosquito had drilled me. I unconsciously scratched it. Two days later, in that exact spot, some nasty red splotches started popping up. Poison oak. By petting my dog and then scratching my arm, I had transferred the oil residue of the poison oak leaves from Rebel's fur to my arm.

When I returned home, Foonsky asked me about the trip.

"Great," I said. "Mosquitoes, ticks, poison oak. Can hardly wait to go back."

"Sorry I missed out," he answered.

Mosquitoes, No-See-Ums, Horseflies

On a trip to Canada, Foonsky and I were

fishing a small lake from the shore when suddenly a black horde of mosquitoes could be seen moving across the lake toward us. It was like when the French army looked across the Rhine and saw the Wehrmacht coming. There was a buzz in the air. We fought them off for a few minutes, then made a fast retreat to the truck and jumped in, content the buggers had been foiled. But in some way still unknown to us, the mosquitoes gained entry to the truck. In 10 minutes, we squished 15 of them as they attempted to plant their oil drills into our skins. Just outside the truck, the black horde waited for us to make a tactical error, such as rolling down a window. It finally took a miraculous hailstorm to squelch the attack.

When it comes to mosquitoes, no-see-ums, gnats, and horseflies, there are times when there is nothing you can do. However, in most situations, you can muster a defense to repel the attack.

When under heavy attack by mosquitoes, the first key is to wear clothing too heavy for them to drill through. Expose a minimum of skin, wear a hat, and tie a bandanna around your neck, preferably one that has been sprayed with repellent. If you try to get by with just a thin cotton T-shirt and nylon shorts, you will be declared a federal mosquito sanctuary.

So, first, your skin must be well covered, with only your hands and face exposed. Second, you should have your companion spray your clothes with repellent. (I prefer Deep Woods Off!) Third, you should dab liquid repellent directly on your skin.

At night, the easiest way to get a good sleep without mosquitoes buzzing in your ear is to sleep in a bug-proof tent. If the nights are warm and you want to see the stars, new tent models are available that have a skylight covered with mosquito netting. If you don't like tents on summer evenings, mosquito netting rigged with an air space at your head can solve the problem. Otherwise, prepare to get bitten, even with the use of mosquito repellent.

A newer option is a battery-powered, clip-on mosquito repellent made by Off! that is also portable. It includes a canister that lasts 12 hours and a small fan, so you can set right next to you. That's right, you don't spray it on.

If your problems are with no-see-ums or biting horseflies, then you need a slightly different approach. No-see-ums are tiny black insects that look like nothing more than a sliver of dirt on your skin. Then you notice something stinging, and when you rub the area, you scratch up a little no-see-um. The results are similar to mosquito bites, making your skin itch, splotch, and, when you get them bad, swell. In addition to using the techniques described to repel mosquitoes, you should go one step further.

The problem is that no-see-ums are tricky little devils. Somehow, they can actually get under your socks and around your ankles, where they will bite to their hearts' content all night long while you sleep, itch, sleep, and itch some more. The best solution is to apply a liquid repellent to your ankles, then wear clean socks.

Horseflies are another story. They are rarely a problem, but when they get their dander up, they can cause trouble you'll never forget.

Always wear sunglasses when you hike. If you enter an area with flies, the moisture from your eyes will attract them. The sunglasses will keep them from getting in your eyes.

On one trip, Foonsky and I were paddling a canoe along the shoreline of a Lake Quesnel in British Columbia. This giant horsefly, about the size of a fingertip, started dive-bombing the canoe. After 20 minutes, it landed on Foonsky's thigh. He immediately slammed it with an open hand, then let out a blood-curdling "Yeeeee-ow!" that practically sent ripples across the lake. When Foonsky whacked it, the horsefly had somehow turned around and bit him on the hand, leaving a huge red welt.

In the next 10 minutes, that big fly strafed the canoe on more dive-bomb runs. I finally got my canoe paddle, swung it as if it were a baseball bat, and nailed that horsefly as if I'd hit a home run. It landed about 15 feet from the boat, still alive and buzzing in the water. While I was trying to figure what it would take to kill this bugger, a large rainbow trout surfaced and snatched it out of the water, finally avenging the assault.

If you have horsefly or yellow jacket problems, you'd best just leave the area. One, two, or a few can be dealt with. More than that and your fun camping trip will be about as fun as being roped to a tree and stung by an electric shock rod.

On most trips, you will spend time doing everything possible to keep from getting bitten by mosquitoes or no-see-ums. When your attempts fail, you must know what to do next, and fast, especially if you are among those ill-fated campers who get big, red lumps from a bite inflicted from even a microscopic mosquito.

A fluid called After Bite or a dab of ammonia should be applied immediately to the bite. To start the healing process, apply a first-aid gel (not a liquid), such as the one made by Campho-Phenique.

DEET

What is DEET? You're not likely to find the word DEET on any repellent label. That's because DEET stands for N,N diethyl-m-toluamide. If the label contains this scientific name, the repellent contains DEET. Despite fears of DEET-associated health risks and the increased attention given natural alternatives, DEET-based repellents are still acknowledged as by far the best option when serious insect protection is required.

On one trip, I had a small bottle of mosquito repellent in the same pocket as a Swiss army knife. Guess what happened? The mosquito repellent leaked a bit and literally melted the insignia right off the knife. DEET will also melt synthetic clothes. That is why, in bad mosquito country, I'll expose a minimum of skin, just hands and face (with full beard), apply the repellent only to my cheeks and the back of my hands, and perhaps wear a bandanna sprinkled with a few drops as well. That does the trick, with a minimum of exposure to the repellent.

"NATURAL" REPELLENTS

Are natural alternatives a safer choice than DEET? Some are potentially hazardous if ingested, and most are downright painful if they find their way into the eyes or onto mucus membranes. For example, pennyroyal is perhaps the most toxic of the essential oils used to repel insects and can be deadly if taken internally. Other oils used include cedarwood, citronella, and perhaps the most common, eucalyptus and peppermint.

How effective are natural repellents? The average effective repelling time of a citronella product appears to range from 1.5–2 hours, so it must be reapplied to be effective.

What other chemical alternatives are there? Another line of defense against insects is the chemical permethrin, used on clothing, not on skin. Permethrin-based products are designed to repel and kill arthropods or crawling insects, making them a preferred repellent for ticks. The currently available products remain effective—repelling and killing chiggers, mosquitoes, and ticks—for two weeks and through two launderings.

Ticks

Ticks are nasty little vermin that will wait in ambush, jump on unsuspecting prey, and then crawl to a prime location before filling their bodies with their victim's blood.

I call them Dracula bugs, but by any name they can be a terrible camp pest. Ticks rest on grass and low plants and attach themselves to those who brush against the vegetation (dogs are particularly vulnerable). Typically, they can be found no more than 18 inches above ground, and if you stay on the trails, you can usually avoid them.

There are two common species of ticks. The common coastal tick is larger, brownish in color, and prefers to crawl around before putting its clamps on you. The feel of any bug crawling on your skin can be creepy, but consider it a forewarning of assault; you can just pick the tick off and dispatch it. The coastal tick's preferred destination is usually the back of your neck, just where the hairline starts. The other species, the wood tick, is small and black, and when he puts his clamps in, it's immediately painful. When a wood tick gets into a dog for a few days, it can cause a large red welt. In either case, ticks should be removed as soon as possible.

If you have hiked in areas infested with ticks, it is advisable to shower as soon as possible, washing your clothes immediately. If you just leave your clothes in a heap, a tick can crawl out and invade your home. They like warmth, and one way or another, they can end up in your bed. Waking up in the middle of the night with a tick crawling across your chest can be unsettling, to put it mildly.

Once a tick has its clampers in your skin, you must determine how long it has been there. If it has been a short time, the most painless and effective method for removal is to take a pair of sharp tweezers and grasp the little devil, making certain to isolate the mouth area, then pull him out. Reader Johvin Perry sent in the suggestion to coat the tick with Vaseline, which will cut off its oxygen supply, after which it may voluntarily give up the hunt.

If the tick has been in longer, you may wish to have a doctor extract it. Some people will burn a tick with a cigarette or poison it with lighter fluid, but neither is advisable. No matter how you do it, you must take care to remove all of the tick, especially its clawlike mouth.

The wound, however small, should then be cleansed and dressed. First, apply liquid peroxide, which cleans and sterilizes, and then apply a dressing coated with a first-aid gel, such as First-Aid Cream, Campho-Phenique, or Neosporin.

Lyme disease, which can be transmitted by the bite of a deer tick, is rare but common enough to warrant some attention. To prevent tick bites, some people tuck their pant legs into their hiking socks and spray tick repellent, called Permamone, on their pants.

The first symptom of Lyme disease is a bright red, splotchy rash that develops around the bite area. Other possible early symptoms include headache, nausea, fever, and/or a stiff neck. If any of these happen, or if you have any doubts, you should see your doctor immediately. If you do get Lyme disease, don't panic. Doctors say it is easily treated in the early stages with simple antibiotics. If you are nervous about getting Lyme disease, carry a small plastic bag with you when you hike. If a tick manages to get his clampers into you, put the tick in the plastic bag after you pull it out. Then give it to your doctor for analysis to see if the tick is a carrier of the disease.

During the course of my hiking and camping career, I have removed ticks from my skin hundreds of times without any problems. However, if you are worried about ticks, you can buy a tick removal kit from any outdoors store. These kits allow you to remove ticks in such a way that their toxins are guaranteed not to enter your bloodstream.

If you are particularly wary of ticks or perhaps even have nightmares of them, wear long pants that are tucked into your socks, as well as a long-sleeved shirt tucked securely into your pants and held with a belt. Clothing should be light in color, making it easier to see ticks, and tightly woven so ticks have trouble hanging on. On one hike with my mom, Eleanor, I brushed more than 100 ticks off my blue jeans in less than an hour, while she did not pick up a single one on her polyester pants.

Perform tick checks regularly, especially on the back of the neck. The combination of DEET insect repellents applied to the skin and permethrin repellents applied directly to clothing is considered to be the most effective line of defense against ticks.

Poison Oak

After a nice afternoon hike, about a five-miler, I was concerned about possible exposure to poison oak, so I immediately showered and put on clean clothes. Then I settled into a chair with my favorite foamy elixir to watch the end of a baseball game. But the game went on for hours, 18 innings; meanwhile, my dog, tired from the hike, went to sleep on my bare ankles.

A few days later, I had a case of poison oak. My feet looked as though they had been on fire and put out with an ice pick. The lesson? Don't always trust your dog, give him a bath as well, and beware of extra-inning ball games.

You can get poison oak only from direct contact with the oil residue from the plant's leaves. It can be passed in a variety of ways, as direct as skin-to-leaf contact or as indirect as leaf to dog, dog to sofa, sofa to skin. Once you have it, there is little you can do but feel horribly itchy. Applying Caladryl lotion or its equivalent can help because it contains antihistamines, which attack and dry the itch.

My pal Furniss offers a tip that may sound crazy but seems to work. You should expose the afflicted area to the hottest water you can stand, then suddenly immerse it in cold water. The hot water opens the skin pores and gets the "itch" out, and the cold water then quickly seals the pores.

In any case, you're a lot better off if you don't get poison oak to begin with. Remember that poison oak can disguise itself. In the spring, it is green; then it gradually turns reddish in the summer. By fall, it becomes a bloody, ugly-looking red. In the winter, it loses its leaves altogether and appears to be nothing more than the barren, brown sticks of a small plant. However, at any time and in any form, its contact with skin can quickly lead to infection.

Some people are more easily afflicted than others, but if you are one of the lucky few who aren't, don't cheer too loudly. While some people can be exposed to the oil residue of poison oak with little or no effect, the body's resistance can gradually be worn down with repeated exposure. At one time, I could practically play in the stuff and the only symptom would be a few little bumps on the inside of my wrist. Now, more than 15 years later, my resistance has broken down. If I merely brush

against poison oak now, in a few days the exposed area can look as if it were used for a track meet.

So regardless of whether you consider yourself vulnerable or not, you should take heed to reduce your exposure. That can be done by staying on trails when you hike and making sure your dog does the same. Remember, the worst stands of poison oak are usually brush-infested areas just off the trail. Also protect yourself by dressing so your skin is completely covered, wearing long-sleeved shirts, long pants, and boots. If you suspect you've been exposed, immediately wash your clothes and then wash yourself with aloe vera, rinsing with a cool shower.

And don't forget to give your dog a bath as well.

Sunburn

The most common injury suffered on camping trips is sunburn, yet some people wear it as a badge of honor, believing that it somehow enhances their virility. Well, it doesn't. Neither do suntans. Too much sun can lead to serious burns or sunstroke.

Both are easy enough to avoid. Use a high-level sunscreen on your skin, apply lip balm, and wear sunglasses and a hat. If any area gets burned, apply first-aid cream, which will soothe and provide moisture to the parched skin.

The best advice is not to get even a suntan. Those who tan are involved in a practice that can eventually ruin their skin and possibly lead to cancer.

Giardia and Cryptosporidium

You have just hiked in to your backwoods spot, you're thirsty and a bit tired, but you smile as you consider the prospects. Everything seems perfect—there's not a stranger in sight, and you have nothing to do but relax with your pals.

You toss down your gear, grab your cup, dip it into the stream, and take a long drink of that ice-cold mountain water. It seems crystal pure and sweeter than anything you've ever tasted.

It's not till later that you find out it can be just like drinking a cup of poison.

Whether you camp in the wilderness or not, if you hike, you're going to get thirsty. And if your canteen runs dry, you'll start eyeing any water source. Stop! Do not pass Go. Do not drink.

By drinking what appears to be pure mountain water without first treating it, you can ingest a microscopic protozoan called *Giardia lamblia*. The ensuing abdominal cramps can make you feel like your stomach and intestinal tract are in a knot, ready to explode. With that comes long-term diarrhea that is worse than even a bear could imagine.

Doctors call the disease giardiasis, or giardia for short, but it is difficult to diagnose. One friend of mine who contracted giardia was told he might have stomach cancer before the proper diagnosis was made.

Drinking directly from a stream or lake does not mean you will get giardia, but you are taking a giant chance. There is no reason to assume such a risk, potentially ruining your trip and enduring weeks of misery.

A lot of people are taking that risk. I made a personal survey of campers in the Yosemite National Park wilderness, and found that roughly only one in 10 was equipped with some kind of water-purification system. The result, according to the Public Health Service, is that an average of 4 percent of all backpackers and campers suffer giardiasis. According to the Parasitic Diseases Division of the Center for Infectious Diseases, the rates range from 1 percent to 20 percent across the country.

But if you get giardia, you are not going to care about the statistics. "When I got giardia, I just about wanted to die," said Henry McCarthy, a California camper. "For about 10 days, it was the most terrible thing I have ever experienced. And through the whole thing, I kept thinking, 'I shouldn't have drunk that water, but it seemed all right at the time.'"

KEEP IT WILD TIP 5: SANITATION

If no refuse facility is available:

1. Deposit human waste in "cat holes" dug 6-8 inches deep. Cover and disguise the cat hole when finished.

2. Deposit human waste at least 75 paces (200 feet) from any water source or camp.

3. Use toilet paper sparingly. When finished, carefully burn it in the cat hole, then bury it.

4. If no appropriate burial locations are available, such as in popular wilderness camps above tree line in granite settings, then all human refuse should be double-bagged and packed out.

5. At boat-in campsites, chemical toilets are required. Chemical toilets can also solve the problem of larger groups camping for long stays at one location where no facilities are available.

6. To wash dishes or your body, carry water away from the source and use small amounts of biodegradable soap. Scatter dishwater after all food particles have been removed.

7. Scour your campsites for even the tiniest piece of trash and any other evidence of your stay. Pack out all the trash you can, even if it's not yours. Finding cigarette butts, for instance, provides special irritation for most campers. Pick them up and discard them properly.

8. Never litter. Never. Or you become the enemy of all others.

© PUTT SAKDHNAGOOL/123RF.COM

No matter how clean and refreshing the water looks, don't drink unless you purify it.

That is the mistake most campers make. The stream might be running free, gurgling over boulders in the high country, tumbling into deep, oxygenated pools. It looks pure. Then in a few days, the problems suddenly start. Drinking untreated water from mountain streams is a lot like playing Russian roulette. Sooner or later the gun goes off.

SteriPEN

We would never do another wilderness trip without one and I keep mine with me all the time. By using UV light, the SteriPEN destroy viruses, bacteria and protozoa (like Giardia) that can make you sick. Dip your water bottle in a cold stream, purify the water with the UV light in under two minutes, and drink all the cold, clean mountain water you can. It's like having a cooler full of ice-cold water with you all the time. On expeditions of more than four days, make sure you bring extra batteries.

Filters

Handheld filters are getting more compact, lighter, easier to use, and often less expensive. Having to boil water or endure chemicals that leave a bad taste in the mouth has been all but eliminated.

With a filter, you just pump and drink. Filtering strains out microscopic contaminants, rendering the water clear and somewhat pure. How pure? That depends on the size of the filter's pores—what manufacturers call pore-size efficiency. A filter with a pore-size efficiency of one micron or smaller will remove protozoa, such as *Giardia lamblia* and cryptosporidium, as well as parasitic eggs and larva, but it takes a pore-size efficiency of less than 0.4 micron to remove bacteria. All but one of the filters recommended here do that.

A good backcountry water filter weighs less than 20 ounces, is easy to grasp, simple to use, and a snap to clean and maintain. At the very least, buy one that will remove protozoa and bacteria. (A number of cheap, pocket-sized filters remove only *Giardia lamblia* and cryptosporidium. That, in my book, is risking your health to save money.) Consider the flow rate, too: A liter per minute is good.

All filters will eventually clog—it's a sign that they've been doing their job. If you force water through a filter that's becoming difficult to pump, you risk injecting a load of microbial nasties into your bottle. Some models can be back-washed, brushed, or, as with ceramic elements, scrubbed to extend their useful lives. And if the filter has a pre-filter to screen out the big stuff, use it: It will give your filter a boost in mileage, which can then top out at about 100 gallons per disposable element. Any of the filters reviewed here will serve well on an outing into the wilds, providing you always play by the manufacturer's rules.

• **First Need Deluxe:** The filter pumps smoothly and puts out more than a liter per minute. The 15-ounce First Need Deluxe from General Ecology does something no other handheld filter will do: It removes protozoa, bacteria, and viruses without using chemicals. Such effectiveness is the result of a fancy three-stage matrix system. The First Need has been around since 1982. Additional cartridges mean you just replace the cartridge, not the entire unit. If you drop the filter and unknowingly crack the cartridge, all the little nasties can get through. A small point worth noting.

• **Basic Designs Ceramic:** It clogs quickly and therefore is not a good choice for long trips. The Basic Designs Ceramic Filter Pump weighs eight ounces and is as stripped-down a filter as you'll find. The pump is simple, easy to use, and quite reliable. The ceramic filter effectively removes protozoa and bacteria, making it ideal and cost effective for backpacking—but it won't protect against viruses. Also, the filter element is too bulbous to work directly from a shallow water source; as with the PentaPure, you'll have to decontaminate a pot, cup, or bottle to transfer your unfiltered water.

• **Katadyn Hiker Pro:** The Katadyn effectively removes protozoa and bacteria. I found it challenging to put any kind of power behind the pump's tiny handle, and the filtered water comes through at a paltry half-liter per minute. It also requires more cleaning than most filters—though the good news is that the element is made of long-lasting ceramic.

• **MSR MiniWorks:** The 14-ounce Mini-Works looks similar to the more expensive WaterWorks, and, like the WaterWorks, is fully field-maintainable, while guarding against protozoa, bacteria, and chemicals. It attaches directly to a standard one-quart Nalgene water bottle. Takes about 90 seconds to filter that quart.

• **MSR WaterWorks II Ceramic:** At 17.4 ounces, the WaterWorks II isn't light. You get a better flow rate (90 seconds per liter), an easy pumping action, and—like the original Mini Filter—a long-lasting ceramic cartridge. This filter is a good match for the person who encounters a lot of dirty water—its three-stage filter weeds out protozoa, bacteria, and chemicals. The MSR can be completely disassembled in the field for troubleshooting and cleaning.

• **SweetWater WalkAbout:** The WalkAbout is perfect for the day hiker or backpacker who obsesses on lightening the load. The filter weighs just 8.5 ounces, is easily cleaned in the field, and removes both protozoa and bacteria: a genuine bargain. There are some trade-offs, however, for its diminutiveness. Water delivery is a tad slow at just under a liter per minute, but filter cartridges are now good for up to 100 gallons.

The big drawback with filters is that if you pump water from a mucky lake, the filter can clog in a few days. Therein lies the weakness. Once plugged up, it is useless, and you have to replace it or take your chances. One trick to extend the filter life is to fill your cook pot with water, let the sediment settle, then pump from there. As an insurance policy, always have a spare filter canister on hand.

BOILING WATER

Except for water filtration, this is the only treatment that you can use with complete confidence. According to the federal Parasitic Diseases Division, it takes a few minutes at a rolling boil to be certain you've killed *Giardia lamblia*. At high elevations, boil for 3–5 minutes. A side benefit is that you'll also kill other dangerous bacteria that live undetected in natural waters.

But to be honest, boiling water is a thorn for most people on backcountry trips. For one thing, if you boil water on an open fire, what should taste like crystal-pure mountain water tastes instead like a mouthful of warm ashes. If you don't have a campfire, it wastes stove fuel. And if you are thirsty *now,* forget it. The water takes hours to cool.

The only time boiling always makes sense, however, is when you are preparing dinner. The ash taste will disappear in whatever freeze-dried dinner, soup, or hot drink you make.

WATER-PURIFICATION PILLS

I bring water-purification pills for back-up use only. They are cheap and, in addition, they kill most of the bacteria, regardless of whether you use iodine crystals or potable aqua iodine tablets. The problem is they just don't always kill *Giardia lamblia,* and that is the one critter worth worrying about on your trip. That makes water-treatment pills unreliable and dangerous.

Another key element is the time factor. Depending on the water's temperature, organic content, and pH level, these pills can take a long time to do the job. A minimum wait of 20 minutes is advised. Most people don't like waiting that long, especially when they're hot and thirsty after a hike and thinking, "What the heck, the water looks fine."

And then there is the taste. On one trip, my water filter clogged and we had to use the iodine pills instead. It doesn't take long to get tired of iodine-tinged water. Mountain water should be one of the greatest tasting beverages of the world, but the iodine kills that.

NO TREATMENT

This is your last resort and, using extreme care, can be executed with success. Michael Furniss, the renowned hydrologist, has shown me the difference between safe and dangerous water sources.

When I was in the Boy Scouts, I remember a scoutmaster actually telling me if you could find water running over a rock for at least five feet, it was a guarantee of its purity. Imagine that. What we've learned is that the safe water sources are almost always small springs in high, craggy mountain areas. The key is making sure no one has been upstream from where you drink. We drink untreated water only when we can see the source, such as a spring.

Furniss mentioned that another potential problem in bypassing water treatment is that even in settings free of *Giardia lamblia,* you can still ingest other bacteria that cause stomach problems.

Hypothermia

No matter how well planned your trip might be, a sudden change in weather can turn it into a puzzle for which there are few answers. Bad weather or an accident can set in motion a dangerous chain of events.

Such a chain of episodes occurred for my brother Rambob and me on a fishing trip one fall day just below the snow line. The weather had suddenly turned very cold, and ice was forming along the shore of the lake. Suddenly, the canoe became terribly imbalanced, and, just that quickly, it flipped. The little life vest seat cushions were useless, and using the canoe as a paddleboard, we tried to kick our way back to shore where my dad was going crazy at the thought of his two sons drowning before his eyes.

It took 17 minutes in that 38-degree water, but we finally made it to shore. When they pulled me out of the water, my legs were dead, not strong enough even to hold up my weight. In fact, I didn't feel so much cold as tired, and I just wanted to lie down and go to sleep.

I closed my eyes, and my brother-in-law, Lloyd Angal, slapped me in the face several times, then got me on my feet and pushed and pulled me about.

In the celebration over our making it to shore, only Lloyd had realized that hypothermia was setting in. Hypothermia is the condition in which the temperature of the body is lowered to the point that it causes poor reasoning, apathy, and collapse. It can look like the afflicted person is just tired and needs to sleep, but that sleep can be the first step toward a coma.

Ultimately, my brother and I shared what little dry clothing remained. Then we began hiking around to get muscle movement, creating internal warmth. We ate whatever munchies were available because the body produces heat by digestion. But most important, we got our heads as dry as possible. More body heat is lost through wet hair than any other single factor.

A few hours later, we were in a pizza parlor replaying the incident, talking about how only a life vest can do the job of a life vest. We decided never again to rely on those little flotation seat cushions that disappear when the boat flips.

We had done everything right to prevent hypothermia: Don't go to sleep, start a physical activity, induce shivering, put dry clothes on, dry your head, and eat something. That's how you fight hypothermia. In a dangerous situation, whether you fall in a lake or a stream or get caught unprepared in a storm, that's how you can stay alive.

After being in that ice-bordered lake for almost 20 minutes and then finally pulling ourselves to the shoreline, we discovered a strange thing. My canoe was flipped right-side up and almost all of its contents were lost: tackle box, flotation cushions, and cooler. But remaining were one paddle and one fishing rod, the trout rod my grandfather had given me for my 12th birthday.

Lloyd gave me a smile. "This means that you are meant to paddle and fish again," he said with a laugh.

Getting Unlost

I could not have been more lost. There I was, a guy who is supposed to know about these things, transfixed by confusion, snow, and hoofprints from a big deer.

I discovered that it is actually quite easy to

get lost. If you don't get your bearings, getting found is the difficult part. This occurred on a wilderness trip where I'd hiked in to a remote lake and then set up a base camp for a deer hunt.

"There are some giant bucks up on that rim," confided Mr. Furnai, who lives near the area. "But it takes a mountain man to even get close to them."

That was a challenge I answered. After four-wheeling it to the trailhead, I tromped off with pack and rifle, gut-thumped it up 100 switchbacks over the rim, then followed a creek drainage up to a small but beautiful lake. The area was stark and nearly treeless, with bald granite broken only by large boulders. To keep from getting lost, I marked my route with piles of small rocks to act as directional signs for the return trip.

But at daybreak the next day, I stuck my head out of my tent and found eight inches of snow on the ground. I looked up into a

Rock cairns (small piles of rocks) can act as directional signs to keep you from getting lost.

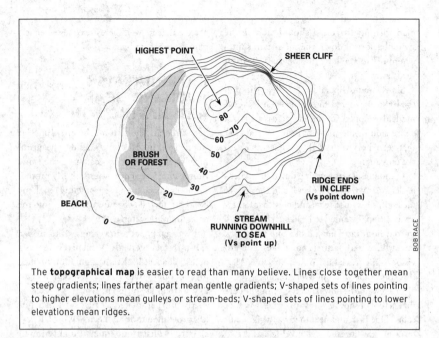

HIGHEST POINT

SHEER CLIFF

80
70
60
50
40
30
20
10
0

BRUSH
OR FOREST

BEACH

RIDGE ENDS
IN CLIFF
(Vs point down)

STREAM
RUNNING DOWNHILL
TO SEA
(Vs point up)

BOB RACE

The **topographical map** is easier to read than many believe. Lines close together mean steep gradients; lines farther apart mean gentle gradients; V-shaped sets of lines pointing to higher elevations mean gulleys or stream-beds; V-shaped sets of lines pointing to lower elevations mean ridges.

gray sky filled by huge, cascading snowflakes. Visibility was about 50 yards, with fog on the mountain rim. "I better get out of here and get back to my truck," I said to myself. "If my truck gets buried at the trailhead, I'll never get out."

After packing quickly, I started down the mountain. But after 20 minutes, I began to get disoriented. You see, all the little piles of rocks I'd stacked to mark the way were now buried in snow, and I had only a smooth white blanket of snow to guide me. Everything looked the same, and it was snowing even harder now.

Five minutes later, I started chewing on some jerky to keep warm, then suddenly stopped. Where was I? Where was the creek drainage? Isn't this where I was supposed to cross over a creek and start the switchbacks down the mountain?

Right then, I looked down and saw the tracks of a huge deer, the kind Mr. Furnai had talked about. What a predicament: I was lost and snowed in and seeing big hoofprints in the snow. Part of me wanted to abandon all

safety and go after that deer, but a little voice in the back of my head won out. "Treat this as an emergency," it said.

The first step in any predicament is to secure your present situation, that is, to make sure it does not get any worse. I unloaded my rifle (too easy to slip, fall, and have a misfire), took stock of my food (three days' worth), camp fuel (plenty), and clothes (rain gear keeping me dry). Then I wondered, "Where the hell am I?"

I took out my map, compass, and altimeter, then opened the map and laid it on the snow. It immediately began collecting snowflakes. I set the compass atop the map and oriented it to north. Because of the fog, there was no way to spot landmarks, such as prominent mountaintops, to verify my position. Then I checked the altimeter, which read 4,900 feet. Well, the elevation at my lake was 5,320 feet. That was critical information.

I scanned the elevation lines on the map and was able to trace the approximate area of my position, somewhere downstream from the lake, yet close to a 4,900-foot elevation. "Right here," I said, pointing to a spot on the map with my finger. "I should pick up the switchback trail down the mountain somewhere off to the left, maybe just 40 or 50 yards away."

Slowly and deliberately, I pushed through the light, powdered snow. In five minutes, I suddenly stopped. To the left, across a 10-foot depression in the snow, appeared a flat spot that veered off to the right. "That's it! That's the crossing."

In minutes, I was working down the switchbacks, on my way, no longer lost. I thought of the hoofprints I had seen, and now that I knew my position, I wanted to head back and spend the day hunting. Then I looked up at the sky, saw it filled with falling snowflakes, and envisioned my truck buried deep in snow. Alas, this time logic won out over dreams.

In a few hours, now trudging through more than a foot of snow, I was at my truck at a spot called Doe Flat, and next to it was a giant, all-terrain U.S. Forest Service vehicle and two rangers.

"Need any help?" I asked them.

They just laughed. "We're here to help you," one answered. "It's a good thing you filed a trip plan with our district office in Gasquet. We wouldn't have known you were out here."

"Winter has arrived," said the other. "If we don't get your truck out now, it will be stuck here until next spring. If we hadn't found you, you might have been here until the end of time."

They connected a chain from the rear axle of their giant rig to the front axle of my truck and started towing me out, back to civilization. On the way to pavement, I figured I had gotten some of the more important lessons of my life. Always file a trip plan and have plenty of food, fuel, and a camp stove you can rely on. Make sure your clothes, weather gear, sleeping bag, and tent will keep you dry and warm. Always carry a compass, altimeter, and map with elevation lines, and know how to use them, practicing in good weather to get the feel of it.

And if you get lost and see the hoofprints of a giant deer, well, there are times when it is best to pass them by.

CATCHING FISH, AVOIDING BEARS, AND HAVING FUN

Feet tired and hot, stomachs growling, we stopped our hike for lunch beside a beautiful little river pool that was catching the flows from a long but gentle waterfall. My brother Rambob passed me a piece of jerky. I took my boots off, then slowly dunked my feet into the cool, foaming water.

I was gazing at a towering peak across a canyon when suddenly, Wham! There was a quick jolt at the heel of my right foot. I pulled my foot out of the water to find that, incredibly, a trout had bitten it.

My brother looked at me as if I had antlers growing out of my head. "Wow!" he exclaimed. "That trout almost caught himself an outdoors writer!"

It's true that in remote areas trout sometimes bite on almost anything, even feet. On one high-country trip, I caught limits of trout using nothing but a bare hook. The only problem is that the fish will often hit the splitshot sinker instead of the hook. Of course, fishing isn't usually that easy. But it gives you an idea of what is possible.

America's wildlands are home to a remarkable abundance of fish and wildlife. Deer browse with little fear of man, bears keep an eye out for your food, and little critters, such as squirrels and chipmunks, are daily companions. Add in the fishing, and you've got yourself a camping trip.

Your camping adventures will evolve into premium outdoor experiences if you can work in a few good fishing trips, avoid bear problems, and occasionally add a little offbeat fun with some camp games.

Trout and Bass

He creeps up on the stream as quietly as an Indian scout, keeping his shadow off the water.

brother Rambob's big Almanor trout

With his little spinning rod he'll zip his lure within an inch or two of its desired mark, probing along rocks, the edges of riffles, pocket water, or wherever he can find a change in river habitat. Rambob is trout fishing, and he's a master at it.

In most cases, he'll catch a trout on his first or second cast. After that, it's time to move up the river, giving no spot much more than five minutes' due. Stick and move, stick and move, stalking the stream like a bobcat zeroing in on an unsuspecting rabbit. He might keep a few trout for dinner, but mostly he releases what he catches. Rambob doesn't necessarily fish for food. It's the feeling that comes with it.

You don't need a million dollars' worth of fancy gear to catch fish. What you need is the right outlook, and that can be learned. That goes regardless of whether you are fishing for trout or bass, the two most popular fisheries in the United States. Your fishing tackle selection should be as simple and clutter-free as possible.

At home, I've got every piece of fishing tackle you might imagine, more than 30 rods and many tackle boxes, racks and cabinets filled with all kinds of stuff. I've got one lure that looks like a chipmunk and another that resembles a miniature can of beer with hooks. If I hear of something new, I want to try it and usually do. It's a result of my lifelong fascination with the sport.

But if you just want to catch fish, there's an easier way to go. And when I go fishing, I take that path. I don't try to bring everything. It would be impossible. Instead, I bring a relatively small amount of gear. At home, I scan my tackle boxes for equipment and lures, make my selections, and bring just the essentials. Rod, reel, and tackle will fit into a side pocket of my backpack or a small carrying bag.

So what kind of rod should be used on an outdoor trip? For most camper/anglers, I suggest the use of a light, multi-piece spinning rod that will break down to a small size. The lowest-priced, quality six-piece rod on the market is the Daiwa 6.5-foot pack rod, number 6752, which is made of a graphite/glass composite that gives it the quality of a much more expensive model. And it comes in a hard plastic carrying tube for protection. Other major rod manufacturers, such as Fenwick, offer similar premium rods. It's tough to miss with any of them.

The use of graphite/glass composites in fishing rods has made them lighter and more sensitive, yet stronger. The only downside to graphite as a rod material is that it can be brittle. If you rap your rod against something, it can crack or cause a weak spot. That weak spot can eventually snap under even light pressure, like setting a hook or casting. Of course, a bit of care will prevent that from ever occurring.

If you haven't bought a fishing reel in some time, you will be surprised at the quality and price of micro spinning reels on the market. The reels come tiny and strong, with rear-control drag systems. Among others, Abu, Cardinal, Shimano, Sigma all make premium

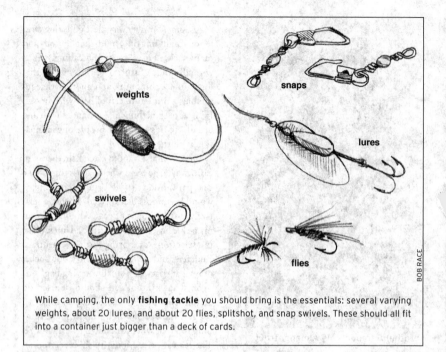

BOB RACE

While camping, the only **fishing tackle** you should bring is the essentials: several varying weights, about 20 lures, and about 20 flies, splitshot, and snap swivels. These should all fit into a container just bigger than a deck of cards.

reels. They're worth it. With your purchase, you've just bought a reel that will last for years and years.

The one downside to spinning reels is that after long-term use, the bail spring will weaken. As a result, after casting and beginning to reel, the bail will sometimes not flip over and allow the reel to retrieve the line. Then you have to do it by hand. This can be incredibly frustrating, particularly when stream fishing, where instant line pickup is essential. The solution is to have a new bail spring installed every few years. This is a cheap, quick operation for a tackle expert.

You might own a giant tackle box filled with lures but, on your fishing trip, you are better off to fit just the essentials into a small container. One of the best ways to do that is to use the Plano Micro-Magnum 3414, a tiny two-sided tackle box for trout anglers that fits into a shirt pocket. In mine, I can fit 20 lures in one side of the box and 20 flies, split-shot weights, and snap swivels in the other. For

bass lures, which are bigger, you need a slightly larger box, but the same principle applies.

There are more fishing lures on the market than you can imagine, but a few special ones can do the job. I make sure these are in my box on every trip. For trout, I carry a small black Panther Martin spinner with yellow spots, a small gold Kastmaster, a yellow Roostertail, a gold Z-Ray with red spots, a Super Duper, and a Mepps Lightning spinner.

You can take it a step further using insider's wisdom. My old pal Ed "the Dunk" showed me his trick of taking a tiny Dardevle spoon, spray painting it flat black, and dabbing five tiny red dots on it. It's a real killer, particularly in tiny streams where the trout are spooky.

The best trout catcher I've ever used on rivers is a small metal lure called a Met-L Fly. On days when nothing else works, it can be like going to a shooting gallery. The problem is that the lure is nearly impossible to find. Rambob and I consider the few we have remaining so valuable that if the lure is snagged on a rock, a cold swim is deemed mandatory for its retrieval. I've been able snag about five of these and they only get pulled out when fishing turns into Mission Impossible.

For bass, you can also fit all you need into a small plastic tackle box. I have fished with many bass pros, and all of them actually use just a few lures: twist-tail grubs, Senkos, Brush Hog, a white spinner bait, a surface plug called a Zara Spook, and AC plug. At times, like when the bass move into shoreline areas during the spring, shad minnow imitations like those made by Rebel or Rapala can be dynamite. My favorite is the one-inch, blue-silver Rapala. Every spring as the lakes begin to warm and the fish snap out of their winter doldrums, I like to float and paddle around in my small raft. I'll cast that little Rapala along the shoreline and catch and release hundreds of bass, bluegill, and sunfish. The fish are usually sitting close to the shoreline, awaiting my offering.

Fishing Tips

There's an old angler's joke about how you need to think like a fish. But if you're the one getting zilched, you may not think it's so funny.

The irony is that it is your mental approach, what you see and what you miss, that often determines your fishing luck. Some people will spend a lot of money on tackle, lures, and fishing clothes, and that done, just saunter up to a stream or lake, cast out, and wonder why they are not catching fish. The answer is their mental outlook. They are not attuning themselves to their surroundings.

You must live on nature's level, not your own. Try this and you will become aware of things you never believed even existed. Soon you will see things that will allow you to catch fish. You can get a head start by reading about fishing, but to get your degree in fishing, you must attend the University of Nature.

On every fishing trip, regardless of what you fish for, try to follow three hard-and-fast rules:

1. Always approach the fishing spot so you will be undetected.
2. Present your lure, fly, or bait in a manner so it appears completely natural, as if no line was attached.
3. Stick and move, hitting one spot, working it the best you can, then moving to the next.

Approach

No one can just walk up to a stream or lake, cast out, and start catching fish as if someone had waved a magic wand. Instead, give the fish credit for being smart. After all, they live there.

Your approach must be completely undetected by the fish. Fish can sense your presence through sight and sound, though these factors are misinterpreted by most people. By sight, fish rarely actually see you; more often, they see your shadow on the water or the movement of your arm or rod while casting. By sound, they don't necessarily hear you talking, but they do detect the vibrations of your footsteps along the shore, a rock being kicked, or the unnatural plunking sound of a heavy cast hitting the water. Any of these elements can spook them off the bite. In order to fish undetected, you must walk softly, keep your shadow off the water, and keep your casting motion low. All of these key elements become easier at sunrise or sunset, when shadows are on the water. At midday, the sun is at its peak, causing a high level of light penetration in the water. This can make the fish skittish to any foreign presence.

Like a hunter, you must stalk the spots. When my brother Rambob sneaks up on a fishing spot, he is like a burglar sneaking through an unlocked window.

Presentation

Your lure, fly, or bait must appear in the water as if no line were attached, so it looks as natural as possible. My pal Mo Furniss has skin-dived in rivers to watch what the fish see when somebody is fishing.

"You wouldn't believe it," he said. "When

BOB RACE

The rule of the wild is that wildlife will congregate wherever there is a distinct change in habitat. To find where fish are hiding, look where a riffle pours into a small pond, where a rapid plunges into a deep hole and flattens, and around submerged trees, rock piles, and boulders in the middle of a long riffle.

the lure hits the water, every trout within 40 feet, like 15, 20 trout, will do a little zigzag. They all see the lure and are aware something is going on. Meanwhile, onshore the guy casting doesn't get a bite and thinks there aren't any fish in the river."

If your offering is aimed at fooling a fish into striking, it must appear as part of the natural habitat, like an insect just hatching or a small fish looking for a spot to hide. That's where you come in.

After you have sneaked up on a fishing spot, you should zip your cast upstream and start your retrieval as soon as it hits the water. If you let the lure sink to the bottom and then start the retrieval, you have no chance. A minnow, for instance, does not sink to the bottom, then start swimming. On rivers, the retrieval should be more of a drift, as if the "minnow" is in trouble and the current is sweeping it downstream.

When fishing on trout streams, always hike and cast upriver and retrieve as the offering drifts downstream in the current. This is effective because trout will sit almost motionless, pointed upstream, finning against the current. This way, they can see anything coming their direction, and if a potential food morsel arrives, all they need to do is move over a few inches, open their mouths, and they've got an easy lunch. Thus, you must cast upstream.

Conversely, if you cast downstream, your retrieval will bring the lure from behind the fish, where he cannot see it approaching. And I've never seen a trout that had eyes in its tail. In addition, when retrieving a downstream lure, the river current will tend to sweep your lure inshore to the rocks.

FINDING SPOTS

A lot of anglers don't catch fish, and a lot of hikers never see any wildlife. The key is where they are looking.

The rule of the wild is that fish and wildlife will congregate wherever there is a distinct change in the habitat. This is where you

should begin your search. To find deer, for instance, forget probing a thick forest, but look for where it breaks into a meadow or a clearcut has splayed a stand of trees. That's where the deer will be.

In a river, it can be where a riffle pours into a small pool, a rapid plunges into a deep hole and flattens, a big boulder in the middle of a long riffle, a shoreline point, a rock pile, a submerged tree. Look for the changes. Conversely, long, straight stretches of shoreline will not hold fish—the habitat is lousy.

On rivers, the most productive areas are often where short riffles tumble into small oxygenated pools. After sneaking up from the downstream side and staying low, you should zip your cast so the lure plops gently into the white water just above the pool. Start your retrieval instantly; the lure will drift downstream and plunk into the pool. Bang! That's where the trout will hit. Take a few more casts and then head upstream to the next spot.

With a careful approach and lure presentation and by fishing in the right spots, you have the ticket to many exciting days on the water.

Of Bears and Food

The first time you come nose-to-nose with a bear can make your skin quiver.

Even the sight of mild-mannered black bears, the most common bear in America, can send shock waves through your body. They weigh 250–400 pounds and have large claws and teeth that are made to scare campers. When they bound, the muscles on their shoulders roll like ocean breakers. But in California, you don't have to be scared of them. They aren't interested in you, just your food.

Bears in camping areas are accustomed to sharing the mountains with hikers and campers. They have become specialists in the food-raiding business. As a result, you must be able to bear-proof your camp or be able to scare the fellow off. Many campgrounds provide bear- and raccoon-proof food lockers. In most

© CELSO DINIZ/123RF.COM

Use bear-proof containers to protect your campsite.

wilderness areas, bear-proof food canisters are required. Never leave your food or trash in your car!

Bear-proof food canisters are so effective in wilderness areas at Yosemite, Kings Canyon-Sequoia, and Mount Whitney that I never see bears on trips there anymore—they've given up on backpackers. Instead, they head to the drive-in campgrounds where they can walk right in and often find food sitting out on top of picnic tables.

No problem. Use the bear-proof food lockers. The bear will just move on to the next site on his daily mooching round.

Food Hangs

If you are staying at one of the backpack sites listed in this book, it is unlikely that there will be food lockers available. Your car will not be there, either. The solution is to make a bear-proof food hang, suspending all of your food wrapped in a plastic garbage bag from a rope in midair, 10 feet from the trunk of a tree and 20 feet off the ground. (Counterbalancing two bags with a rope thrown over a tree limb is very effective, but finding an appropriate limb can be difficult.)

The food hang is accomplished by tying a rock to a rope, then throwing it over a high but sturdy tree limb. Next, tie your food bag to the rope and hoist it in the air. When you are satisfied with the position of the food bag, tie off the end of the rope to another tree. In an area frequented by bears, a good food bag is a necessity—nothing else will do.

I've been there. On one trip, my pal Foonsky and my brother Rambob left to fish. I was stoking up an evening campfire when I felt the eyes of an intruder on my back. I turned around and saw a big bear heading straight for our camp. In the next half hour, I scared the bear off twice, but then he got a whiff of something sweet in my brother's pack.

The bear rolled into camp like a truck, grabbed the pack, ripped it open, and plucked out the Tang and the Swiss Miss. The 350-pounder then sat astride a nearby log and lapped at the goodies like a thirsty dog drinking water.

Once a bear gets his mitts on your gear, he considers it his. I took two steps toward the pack, and that bear jumped off the log and galloped across the camp right at me.

Scientists say a man can't outrun a bear, but they've never seen how fast I can go up a granite block with a bear on my tail.

Shortly thereafter, Foonsky returned to find me perched on top of the rock and demanded to know how I could let a bear get our Tang. It took all three of us, Foonsky, Rambob, and me, charging at once and shouting like madmen, to clear the bear out of camp and send him off over the ridge. We learned never to let food sit unattended.

The Grizzly

When it comes to grizzlies, well, my friends, you need what we call an attitude adjustment. Or that big ol' bear may just decide to adjust your attitude for you, making your stay at the park a short one.

Grizzlies are nothing like black bears. They are bigger, stronger, have little fear, and take what they want. Some people believe there are many different species of this critter, such as Alaskan brown, silvertip, cinnamon, and Kodiak, but the truth is they are all grizzlies. Any difference in appearance has to do with diet, habitat, and life habits, not speciation. By any name, they all come big.

The first thing you must do is determine if there are grizzlies in the area where you are camping. That can usually be done by asking local rangers. If you are heading into Yellowstone or Glacier National Park, or the Bob Marshall Wilderness of Montana, well, you don't have to ask. They're out there, and they're the biggest and potentially most dangerous critters you could run into.

One general way to figure the size of a bear is from his footprint. Take the width of the footprint in inches, add one to it, and you'll have an estimated length of the bear in feet. For instance, a nine-inch footprint equals a 10-foot bear. Any bear that big is a grizzly. In fact, most grizzly footprints average about 9–10 inches across, and black bears (though they may be brown in color) tend to have footprints only 4.5–6 inches across.

Most encounters with grizzlies occur when hikers fall into a silent march in the wilderness with the wind in their faces, and they walk around a corner and right into a big, unsuspecting grizzly. If you do this and see a big hump just behind its neck, don't think twice. It's a grizzly.

And then what should you do? Get up a tree, that's what. Grizzlies are so big that their claws cannot support their immense weight, and thus they cannot climb trees. And although young grizzlies can climb, they rarely want to get their mitts on you.

If you do get grabbed, every instinct in your

GRIZZLY BEAR TERRITORY

If you are hiking in a wilderness area in Canada or Alaska that may have grizzlies, it is necessary to wear bells on your pack (grizzlies are not a problem in California, but you do not want to attract the native bears either). That way the bear will hear you coming and likely get out of your way. Keep talking, singing, or maybe even debating the country's foreign policy, but do not fall into a silent hiking vigil. And if a breeze is blowing in your face, you must make even more noise (a good excuse to rant and rave about the government's domestic affairs). Noise is important because your smell will not be carried in the direction you are hiking. As a result, the bear will not smell you coming.

If a bear can hear you and smell you, it will tend to get out of the way and let you pass without your knowing it was even close by. The exceptions are if you are carrying fish or lots of sweets in your pack or if you are wearing heavy, sweet deodorants or makeup. All of these are bear attractants.

body will tell you to fight back. Don't believe it. Play dead. Go limp. Let the bear throw you around a little. After awhile, you'll become unexciting play material and the bear will get bored. My grandmother was grabbed by a grizzly in Glacier National Park and, after a few tosses and hugs, was finally left alone to escape.

Some say it's a good idea to tuck your head under his chin, since that way the bear will be unable to bite your head. I'll take a pass on that one. If you are taking action, any action, it's a signal that you are a force to be reckoned with, and he'll likely respond with more aggression. And bears don't lose many wrestling matches.

What grizzlies really like to do, believe it or not, is to pile a lot of sticks and leaves on you. Just let them, and keep perfectly still. Don't fight them; don't run. And when you have a 100 percent chance (not 98 or 99) to dash up a nearby tree, that's when you let fly. Once safely in a tree, you can hurl down insults and let your aggression out.

In a wilderness camp, there are special precautions you should take. Always hang your food at least 100 yards downwind of camp and get it high; 30 feet is reasonable. In addition, circle your camp with rope and hang the bells from your pack on it. Thus, if a bear walks into your camp, he'll run into the rope, the bells will ring, and everybody will have a chance to get up a tree before ol' griz figures out what's going on. Often, the unexpected ringing of bells is enough to send him off in search of a quieter environment.

You see, more often than not, grizzlies tend to clear the way for campers and hikers. So be smart, don't act like bear bait, and always have a plan if you are confronted by one.

My pal Foonsky had such a plan during a wilderness expedition in Montana's northern Rockies. On our second day of hiking, we started seeing scratch marks on the trees 13–14 feet off the ground.

"Mr. Griz made those," Foonsky said. "With spring here, the grizzlies are coming out of hibernation and using the trees like a cat uses a scratch board to stretch the muscles."

The next day, I noticed Foonsky had a pair of track shoes tied to the back of his pack. I just laughed.

"You're not going to outrun a griz," I said. "In fact, there's hardly any animal out here in the wilderness that man can outrun."

Foonsky just smiled.

"I don't have to outrun a griz," he said. "I just have to outrun you!"

Fun and Games

"Now what are we supposed to do?" the young boy asked his dad.

"Yeah, Dad, think of something," said another son.

Well, Dad thought hard. This was one of the first camping trips he'd taken with his sons and one of the first lessons he received was that kids don't appreciate the philosophic release of mountain quiet. They want action and lots of it. With a glint in his eye, Dad searched around the camp and picked up 15 twigs, breaking them so each was four inches long. He laid them in three separate rows, three twigs in one row, five twigs in another, and seven in the other.

"OK, this game is called 3-5-7," said Dad. "You each take turns picking up sticks. You are allowed to remove all or as few as one twig from a row, but here's the catch: You can pick only from one row per turn. Whoever picks up the last stick left is the loser."

I remember this episode well because those two little boys were my brother Bobby, as in Rambobby, and I. And to this day, we still play 3-5-7 on campouts, with the winner getting to watch the loser clean the dishes. What I have learned in the span of time since that original episode is that it does not matter what your age is: Campers need options for camp fun.

Some evenings, after a long hike or ride, you feel too worn out to take on a serious romp downstream to fish or a climb up to a ridge for a view. That is especially true if you have been in the outback for a week or more. At that point, a lot of campers will spend their time resting and gazing at a map of the area, dreaming of the next day's adventure, or just take a seat against a rock, watching the colors of the sky and mountain panorama change minute by minute. But kids in the push-button video era, and a lot of adults too, want more. After all, "I'm on vacation. I want some fun."

There are several options, such as the 3-5-7 twig game, and they should be just as much a part of your trip planning as arranging your gear.

For kids, plan on games, the more physically challenging the competition, the better. One of the best games is to throw a chunk of wood into a lake and challenge the kids to hit it by throwing rocks. It wreaks havoc on the fishing, but it can keep kids totally absorbed for some time. Target practice with a wrist-rocket slingshot—firing rocks at small targets, like pinecones set on a log—is also all-consuming for kids.

You can also set kids off on little missions near camp, such as looking for the footprints of wildlife, searching out good places to have a "snipe hunt," picking up twigs to get the evening fire started, or having them take the water purifier to a stream to pump some drinking water into a canteen. The latter is an easy, fun, yet important task that will allow kids to feel a sense of equality they often don't get at home.

For adults, the appeal should be more to the intellect. A good example is star and planet identification, and while you are staring into space, you're bound to spot a few asteroids or shooting stars. A star chart can make it easy to find and identify many distinctive stars and constellations, such as Pleiades (the Seven Sisters), Orion, and others from the zodiac, depending on the time of year. With a little research, this can add a unique perspective to your trip. You could point to Polaris, one of the most easily identified of all stars, and note that navigators in the 1400s used it to find their way. Polaris, of course, is the North Star and is at the end of the handle of the Little Dipper. Pinpointing Polaris is quite easy. First find the Big Dipper and then find the outside stars of the ladle of the Big Dipper. They are called the "pointer stars" because they point right at Polaris.

A tree identification book can teach you a few things about your surroundings. It is also a good idea for one member of the party to research the history of the area you have chosen and another research the geology. With shared knowledge, you end up with a deeper love of wild places.

Another way to add some recreation into your trip is to bring a board game, a number of which have been miniaturized for campers. The most popular are chess, checkers, and cribbage. The latter comes with an equally miniature set of playing cards. And if you bring those little cards, that opens a vast set of other possibilities. With kids along, for instance, just take three queens out of the deck and you can play Old Maid.

But there are more serious card games, and they come with high stakes. Such occurred on one high-country trip where Foonsky, Rambob, and I sat down for a late-afternoon game of poker. In a game of seven-card stud, I caught a straight on the sixth card and felt like a dog licking on a T-bone. Already, I had bet several Skittles and peanut M&Ms on this promising hand.

Then I examined the cards Foonsky had face up. He was showing three sevens, and acting as happy as a grizzly with a pork chop—or a full house. He matched my bet of two peanut M&Ms, then raised me three SweetTarts, one Starburst, and one sour apple Jolly Rancher. Rambob folded, but I matched Foonsky's bet and hoped for the best as the seventh and final card was dealt.

Just after Foonsky glanced at that last card, I saw him sneak a look at my grape stick and beef jerky stash.

"I raise you a grape stick," he said.

Rambob and I both gasped. It was the highest bet ever made, equivalent to a million dollars laid down in Las Vegas. Cannons were going off in my chest. I looked hard at my cards. They looked good, but were they good enough?

Even with a great hand like I had, a grape stick was too much to gamble, my last one with 10 days of trail ahead of us. I shook my head and folded my cards. Foonsky smiled at his victory.

But I still had my grape stick.

Old Tricks Don't Always Work

Most people are born honest, but after a few camping trips, they usually get over it.

I remember some advice I got from Rambob, normally an honest soul, on one camping trip. A giant mosquito had landed on my arm and he alerted me to an expert bit of wisdom.

"Flex your arm muscles," he commanded, watching the mosquito fill with my blood. "He'll get stuck in your arm, then he'll explode."

For some reason, I believed him. We both proceeded to watch the mosquito drill countless holes in my arm.

Alas, the unknowing face sabotage from their most trusted companions on camping trips. It can arise at any time, usually in the form of advice from a friendly, honest-looking face, as if to say, "What? How can you doubt me?" After that mosquito episode, I was a little more skeptical of my dear old brother. Then the next day, when another mosquito was nailing me in the back of the neck, out came this gem:

"Hold your breath," he commanded. I instinctively obeyed. "That will freeze the mosquito," he said, "then you can squish him."

But in the time I wasted holding my breath, the little bugger was able to fly off without my having the satisfaction of squishing him. When he got home, he probably told his family, "What a dummy I got to drill today!"

Over the years, I have been duped numerous times with dubious advice:

On a grizzly bear attack: "If he grabs you, tuck your head under the grizzly's chin; then he won't be able to bite you in the head." This made sense to me until the first time I saw a nine-foot grizzly 40 yards away. In seconds, I was at the top of a tree, which suddenly seemed to make the most sense.

On coping with animal bites: "If a bear bites you in the arm, don't try to jerk it away. That will just rip up your arm. Instead, force your arm deeper into his mouth. He'll lose his grip and will have to open it to get a firmer hold, and right then you can get away." I was told this in the Boy Scouts. When I was 14, I had a chance to try it out when a friend's dog bit me as I tried to pet it. What happened? When I shoved my arm deeper into his mouth, he bit me three more times.

On cooking breakfast: "The bacon will curl up every time in a camp frying pan. So make sure you have a bacon stretcher to keep it flat." As a 12-year-old Tenderfoot, I spent two hours looking for the bacon stretcher until I figured out the camp leader had forgotten it. It wasn't for several years that I learned that there is no such thing.

On preventing sore muscles: "If you haven't hiked for a long time and you are facing a rough climb, you can keep from getting sore muscles in your legs, back, and shoulders by practicing the ?Dead Man's Walk.' Simply let your entire body go slack, and then take slow, wobbling steps. This will clear your muscles of lactic acid, which causes them to be so sore after a rough hike." Foonsky pulled this one on me. Rambob and I both bought it and tried it while we were hiking up Mount Whitney, which requires a 6,000-foot elevation gain in six miles. In one 45-minute period, about 30 other hikers passed us and looked at us as if we were suffering from some rare form of mental aberration.

Fish won't bite? No problem: "If the fish are not feeding or will not bite, persistent anglers can still catch dinner with little problem. Keep casting across the current, and eventually, as they hover in the stream, the line will feed across their open mouths.

Keep reeling and you will hook the fish right in the side of the mouth. This technique is called 'lining.' Never worry if the fish will not bite, because you can always line 'em." Of course, heh, heh, heh, that explains why so many fish get hooked in the side of the mouth.

On keeping bears away: "To keep bears away, urinate around the borders of your campground. If there are a lot of bears in the area, it is advisable to go right on your sleeping bag." Yeah, surrrrrre.

On disposing of trash: "Don't worry about packing out trash. Just bury it. It will regenerate into the earth and add valuable minerals." Bears, raccoons, skunks, and other critters will dig up your trash as soon as you depart, leaving one huge mess for the next camper. Always pack out everything.

Often the advice comes without warning. That was the case after a fishing trip with a female companion, when she outcaught me two to one, the third such trip in a row. I explained this to a shopkeeper, and he nodded, then explained why.

"The male fish are able to detect the female scent on the lure, and thus become aroused into striking."

Of course! That explains everything!

Getting Revenge

I was just a lad when Foonsky pulled the old snipe-hunt trick on me. It took nearly 30 years to get revenge.

You probably know about snipe hunting. The victim is led out at night in the woods by a group, and then is left holding a bag.

"Stay perfectly still and quiet," Foonsky explained. "You don't want to scare the snipe. The rest of us will go back to camp and let the woods settle down. Then when the snipe are least expecting it, we'll form a line and charge through the forest with sticks, beating bushes and trees, and we'll flush the snipe out right to you. Be ready with the bag. When we flush the snipe out, bag it. But until we start our charge, make sure you don't move or make a

sound or you will spook the snipe and ruin everything."

I sat out there in the woods with my bag for hours, waiting for the charge. I waited, waited, and waited. Nothing happened. No charge, no snipe. It wasn't until well past midnight that I figured something was wrong. When I finally returned to camp, everybody was sleeping.

Well, I tell ya, don't get mad at your pals for the tricks they pull on you. Get revenge. About 25 years later, on the last day of a camping trip, the time finally came.

"Let's break camp early," Foonsky suggested to Mr. Furnai and me. "Get up before dawn, eat breakfast, pack up, and be on the ridge to watch the sun come up. It will be a fantastic way to end the trip."

"Sounds great to me," I replied. But when Foonsky wasn't looking, I turned his alarm clock ahead three hours. So when the alarm sounded at the appointed 4:30 A.M. wake-up time, Mr. Furnai and I knew it was actually only 1:30 A.M.

Foonsky clambered out of his sleeping bag and whistled with a grin. "Time to break camp."

"You go ahead," I answered. "I'll skip breakfast so I can get a little more sleep. At the first sign of dawn, wake me up, and I'll break camp."

"Me, too," said Mr. Furnai.

Foonsky then proceeded to make some coffee, cook a breakfast, and eat it, sitting on a log in the black darkness of the forest, waiting for the sun to come up. An hour later, with still no sign of dawn, he checked his clock. It now read 5:30 A.M. "Any minute now we should start seeing some light," he said.

He made another cup of coffee, packed his gear, and sat there in the middle of the night, looking up at the stars, waiting for dawn. "Anytime now," he said. He ended up sitting there all night long.

Revenge is sweet. Before a fishing trip at a lake, I took Foonsky aside and explained that the third member of the party, Jimbobo, was hard of hearing and very sensitive about it. "Don't mention it to him," I advised. "Just talk real loud."

Meanwhile, I had already told Jimbobo the same thing. "Foonsky just can't hear very good."

We had fished less than 20 minutes when Foonsky got a nibble.

"GET A BITE?" shouted Jimbobo.

"YEAH!" yelled back Foonsky, smiling. "BUT I DIDN'T HOOK HIM!"

"MAYBE NEXT TIME!" shouted Jimbobo with a friendly grin.

Well, they spent the entire day yelling at each other from the distance of a few feet. They never did figure it out. Heh, heh, heh.

That is, I thought so, until we made a trip salmon fishing. I got a strike that almost knocked my fishing rod out of the boat. When I grabbed the rod, it felt as if Moby Dick were on the other end. "At least a 25-pounder," I said. "Maybe bigger."

The fish dove, ripped off line, and then bulldogged. "It's acting like a 40-pounder," I announced, "Huge, just huge. It's going deep. That's how the big ones fight."

Some 15 minutes later, I finally got the "salmon" to the surface. It turned out to be a coffee can that Foonsky had clipped on the line with a snap swivel. By maneuvering the boat, he made the coffee can fight like a big fish.

This all started with a little old snipe hunt years ago. You never know what your pals will try next. Don't get mad. Get revenge.

CAMPING OPTIONS
Boat-In Seclusion

Most campers would never think of trading in their cars, pickup trucks, or RVs for a boat, but people who go by boat on a camping trip enjoy virtually guaranteed seclusion and top-quality outdoor experiences.

Camping with a boat is a do-it-yourself venture in living under primitive circumstances. Yet at the same time, you can bring along

any luxury item you wish, from giant coolers, stoves, and lanterns to portable gasoline generators. Weight is almost never an issue.

Many outstanding boat-in campgrounds in beautiful surroundings are available. The best are on the shores of lakes accessible by canoe or skiff, and at offshore islands reached by saltwater cruisers. Several boat-in camps are detailed in this book.

If you want to take the adventure a step further and create your own boat-in camp, perhaps near a special fishing spot, this is a go-for-it deal that provides the best way possible to establish your own secret campsite. But most people who set out freelance style forget three critical items for boat-in camping: a shovel, a sunshade, and an ax. Here is why these items can make a key difference in your trip:

• **Shovel:** Many lakes and virtually all reservoirs have steep, sloping banks. At reservoirs subject to drawdowns, what was lake bottom in the spring can be a campsite in late summer. If you want a flat area for a tent site, the only answer is to dig one out yourself. A shovel gives you that option.

• **Sunshade:** The flattest spots to camp along lakes often have a tendency to support only sparse tree growth. As a result, a natural shield from sun and rain is rarely available. What? Rain in the summer? Oh yeah, don't get me started. A light tarp, set up with poles and staked ropes, solves the problem.

• **Ax:** Unless you bring your own firewood, which is necessary at some sparsely wooded reservoirs, there is no substitute for a good, sharp ax. With an ax, you can almost always find dry firewood, since the interior of an otherwise wet log will be dry. When the weather turns bad is precisely when you will most want a fire. You may need an ax to get one going.

In the search to create your own personal boat-in campsite, you will find that the flattest areas are usually the tips of peninsulas and points, while the protected back ends of coves are often steeply sloped. At reservoirs,

© TOM STIENSTRA

Claim your own boat-in island on Shasta Lake.

the flattest areas are usually near the mouths of the feeder streams and the points are quite steep. On rivers, there are usually sandbars on the inside of tight bends that make for ideal campsites.

Almost all boat-in campsites developed by government agencies are free of charge, but you are on your own. Only in extremely rare cases is piped water available.

Any way you go, by canoe, skiff, or power cruiser, you end up with a one-in-a-million campsite you can call your own.

Desert Outings

It was a cold, snowy day in Missouri when 10-year-old Rusty Ballinger started dreaming about the vast deserts of the West.

"My dad was reading aloud from a Zane Grey book called *Riders of the Purple Sage*," Ballinger said. "He would get animated when he got to the passages about the desert. It wasn't long before I started to have the same feelings."

That was in 1947. Since then Ballinger has spent a good part of his life exploring the West, camping along the way. "The deserts are the best part. There's something about the uniqueness of each little area you see," Ballinger said. "You're constantly surprised. Just the time of day and the way the sun casts a different color. It's like the lady you care about. One time she smiles, the next time she's pensive. The desert is like that. If you love nature, you can love the desert. After awhile, you can't help but love it."

A desert adventure is not just an antidote for a case of cabin fever in the winter. Whether you go by RV, pickup truck, car, or on foot, it provides its own special qualities.

If you go camping in the desert, your approach has to be as unique as the setting. For starters, don't plan on any campfires, but bring a camp stove instead. And unlike in the mountains, do not camp near a water hole. That's because an animal, such as a badger, coyote, or desert bighorn, might be desperate for water, and if you set up camp in the animal's way, you may be forcing a confrontation.

In some areas, there is a danger of flash floods. An intense rain can fall in one area, collect in a pool, then suddenly burst through a narrow canyon. If you are in its path, you could be injured or drowned. The lesson? Never camp in a gully.

"Some people might wonder,?What good is this place?'" Ballinger said. "The answer is that it is good for looking at. It is one of the world's unique places."

CAMP ETHICS AND POLITICS

The perfect place to set up a base camp turned out to be not so perfect. In fact, according to Doug Williams of California, it did not even exist.

Williams and his son, James, had driven deep into Angeles National Forest, prepared to set up camp and then explore the surrounding area on foot. But when they reached their destination, no campground existed.

"I wanted a primitive camp in a national forest where I could teach my son some basics," said the senior Williams. "But when we got there, there wasn't much left of the camp, and it had been closed. It was obvious that the area had been vandalized."

It turned out not to be an isolated incident. A lack of outdoor ethics practiced by a few people using the unsupervised campgrounds available on national forestland has caused the U.S. Forest Service to close a few of them and make extensive repairs to others.

"There have been sites closed, especially in Angeles and San Bernardino National Forests in Southern California," said David Flohr, regional campground coordinator for the U.S. Forest Service. "It's an urban type of thing, affecting forests near urban areas, and not just Los Angeles. They get a lot of urban users and they bring with them a lot of the same ethics they have in the city. They get drinking and they're not afraid to do things. They vandalize and run. Of course, it is a public facility, so they think nobody is getting hurt."

But somebody is getting hurt, starting with the next person who wants to use the campground. And if the ranger district budget doesn't have enough money to pay for repairs, the campground is then closed for the next arrivals. Just ask Doug and James Williams.

In an era of considerable fiscal restraint for the U.S. Forest Service, vandalized campgrounds could face closure instead of repair. Williams had just a taste of it, but Flohr, as camping coordinator, gets a steady diet.

"It starts with behavior," Flohr said. "General rowdiness, drinking, partying, and then vandalism. It goes all the way from the felt-tip pen things (graffiti) to total destruction, blowing up toilet buildings with dynamite. I have seen toilets destroyed totally with shotguns. They burn up tables, burn barriers. They'll burn up signs for firewood, even the shingles right off the roofs of the bathrooms. They'll shoot anything, garbage cans, signs. It can get a little hairy. A favorite is to remove the stool out of a toilet building. We've had people fall in the open hole."

The National Park Service had similar problems some years back, especially with rampant littering. Park Director Bill Mott responded by creating an interpretive program that attempts to teach visitors the wise use of natural areas,

---

KEEP IT WILD TIP 6: PLAN AHEAD AND PREPARE

1. Learn about the regulations and issues that apply to the area you're visiting.
2. Avoid heavy-use areas.
3. Obtain all maps and permits.
4. Bring extra garbage bags to pack out any refuse you come across.

and to have all park workers set examples by picking up litter and reminding others to do the same.

The U.S. Forest Service has responded with a similar program, making brochures available that detail the wise use of national forests. The four most popular brochures are titled: "Rules for Visitors to the National Forest," "Recreation in the National Forests," "Is the Water Safe?" and "Backcountry Safety Tips." These include details on campfires, drinking water from lakes or streams, hypothermia, safety, and outdoor ethics.

Flohr said even experienced campers sometimes cross over the ethics line unintentionally. The most common example, he said, is when campers toss garbage into the outhouse toilet, rather than packing it out in a plastic garbage bag.

"They throw it in the vault toilet bowls, which just fills them up," Flohr said. "That creates an extremely high cost to pump it. You know why? Because some poor guy has to pick that stuff out piece by piece. It can't be pumped."

At most backcountry sites, the U.S. Forest Service has implemented a program called "Pack it in, pack it out," even posting signs that remind all visitors to do so. But a lot of people don't do it, and others may even uproot the signs and burn them for firewood.

On a trip to a secluded lake near Carson Pass in the Sierra Nevada, I arrived at a small, little-known camp where the picnic table had been spray painted and garbage had been strewn about. A pristine place, the true temple of God, had been defiled.

Getting Along with Fellow Campers

The most important thing about a camping, fishing, or hunting trip is not where you go, how many fish you catch, or how many shots you fire. It often has little to do with how beautiful the view is, how easily the campfire lights, or how sunny the days are.

Oh yeah? Then what is the most important factor? The answer: The people you are with. It is that simple.

Who would you rather camp with? Your enemy at work or your dream mate in a good mood? Heh, heh. You get the idea. A camping trip is a fairly close-knit experience, and you can make lifetime friends or lifelong enemies in the process. That is why your choice of companions is so important. Your own behavior is equally consequential.

Yet most people spend more time putting together their camping gear than considering why they enjoy or hate the company of their chosen companions. Here are 10 rules of behavior for good camping mates:

1. **No whining:** Nothing is more irritating than being around a whiner. It goes right to the heart of adventure, since often the only difference between a hardship and an escapade is simply whether or not an individual has the spirit for it. The people who do can turn a rugged day in the outdoors into a cherished memory. Those who don't can ruin it with their incessant sniveling.

2. **Activities must be agreed upon:** Always have a meeting of the minds with your companions over the general game plan. Then everybody will possess an equal stake in the outcome of the trip. This is absolutely critical. Otherwise they will feel like merely an addendum to your trip, not an equal participant, and a whiner will be born (see number one).

3. **Nobody's in charge:** It is impossible to be genuine friends if one person is always telling another what to do, especially if the orders involve simple camp tasks. You need to share the space on the same emotional plane, and the only way to do that is to have a semblance of equality, regardless of differences in experience. Just try ordering your mate around at home for a few days. You'll quickly see the results, and they aren't pretty.

4. **Equal chances at the fun stuff:** It's fun to build the fire, fun to get the first cast at the best fishing spot, and fun to hoist the bagged

KEEP IT WILD TIP 7: RESPECT OTHER USERS

1. Horseback riders have priority over hikers. Step to the downhill side of the trail and talk softly when encountering horseback riders.
2. Hikers and horseback riders have priority over mountain bikers. When mountain bikers encounter other users even on wide trails, they should pass at an extremely slow speed. On very narrow trails, they should dismount and get off to the side so hikers or horseback riders can pass without having their trip disrupted.
3. Mountain bikes aren't permitted on most single-track trails and are expressly prohibited in designated wilderness areas and all sections of the Pacific Crest Trail. Mountain bikers breaking these rules should be confronted and told to dismount and walk their bikes until they reach a legal area.
4. It's illegal for horseback riders to break off branches that may be in the path of wilderness trails.
5. Horseback riders on overnight trips are prohibited from camping in many areas and are usually required to keep stock animals in specific areas where they can do no damage to the landscape.

food for a bear-proof food hang. It is not fun to clean the dishes, collect firewood, or cook every night. So obviously, there must be an equal distribution of the fun stuff and the not-fun stuff, and everybody on the trip must get a shot at the good and the bad.

5. **No heroes:** No awards are bestowed for achievement in the outdoors, yet some guys treat mountain peaks, big fish, and big game as if they are prizes in a trophy competition. Actually, nobody cares how wonderful you are, which is always a surprise to trophy chasers. What people care about is the heart of the adventure, the gut-level stuff.

6. **Agree on a wake-up time:** It is a good idea to agree on a general wake-up time before closing your eyes for the night, and that goes regardless of whether you want to sleep in late or get up at dawn. Then you can proceed on course regardless of what time you crawl out of your sleeping bag in the morning, without the risk of whining (see number one).

7. **Think of the other guy:** Be self-aware instead of self-absorbed. A good test is to count the number of times you say, "What do you think?" A lot of potential problems can be solved quickly by actually listening to the answer.

8. **Solo responsibilities:** There are a number of essential camp duties on all trips, and while they should be shared equally, most should be completed solo. That means that when it is time for you to cook, you don't have to worry about me changing the recipe on you. It means that when it is my turn to make the fire, you keep your mitts out of it.

9. **Don't let money get in the way:** Of course everybody should share equally in trip expenses, such as the cost of food, and it should be split up before you head out yonder. Don't let somebody pay extra, because that person will likely try to control the trip. Conversely, don't let somebody weasel out of paying a fair share.

10. **Accordance on the food plan:** Always have complete agreement on what you plan to eat each day. Don't figure that just because you like Steamboat's Sludge, everybody else will, too, especially youngsters. Always, always, always check for food allergies, such as nuts, onions, or cheese, and make sure each person brings his or her own personal coffee brand.

Some people drink only decaffeinated; others might gag on anything but Burma monkey beans.

Obviously, it is difficult to find companions who will agree on all of these elements. This is why many campers say that the best camping buddies they'll ever have are their mates, who know all about them and like them anyway.

OUTDOORS WITH KIDS

How do you get a youngster excited about the outdoors? How do you compete with the television and remote control? How do you prove to a kid that success comes from persistence, spirit, and logic, which the outdoors teaches, and not from pushing buttons?

The answer is in the Ten Camping Commandments for Kids. These are lessons that will get youngsters excited about the outdoors and that will make sure adults help the process along, not kill it. I've put this list together with the help of my own kids, Jeremy and Kris,

and their mother, Stephani. Some of the commandments are obvious, some are not, but all are important:

1. Take children to places where there is a guarantee of action. A good example is camping in a park where large numbers of wildlife can be viewed, such as squirrels, chipmunks, deer, and even bears. Other good choices include fishing at a small pond loaded with bluegill or hunting in a spot where a kid can shoot a .22 at pinecones all day. Boys and girls want action, not solitude.

2. Enthusiasm is contagious. If you aren't excited about an adventure, you can't expect a child to be. Show a genuine zest for life in the outdoors, and point out everything as if it is the first time you have ever seen it.

3. Always, always, always be seated when talking to someone small. This allows the adult and child to be on the same level. That is why fishing in a small boat is perfect for adults and kids. Nothing is worse for youngsters than having a big person look down

© TOM STIENSTRA

at them and give them orders. What fun is that?

4. Always *show* how to do something, whether it is gathering sticks for a campfire, cleaning a trout, or tying a knot. Never tell—always show. A button usually clicks to "off" when a kid is lectured. But kids can learn behavior patterns and outdoor skills by watching adults, even when the adults are not aware they are being watched.

5. Let kids be kids. Let the adventure happen, rather than trying to force it within some preconceived plan. If they get sidetracked watching pollywogs, chasing butterflies, or sneaking up on chipmunks, let them be. A youngster can have more fun turning over rocks and looking at different kinds of bugs than sitting in one spot, waiting for a fish to bite.

6. Expect short attention spans. Instead of getting frustrated about it, use it to your advantage. How? By bringing along a bag of candy and snacks. Where there is a lull in the camp activity, out comes the bag. Don't let them know what goodies await, so each one becomes a surprise.

7. Make absolutely certain the child's sleeping bag is clean, dry, and warm. Nothing is worse than discomfort when trying to sleep, but a refreshing sleep makes for a positive attitude the next day. In addition, kids can become quite scared of animals at night. A parent should not wait for any signs of this, but always play the part of the outdoor guardian, the one who will take care of everything.

8. Kids quickly relate to outdoor ethics. They will enjoy eating everything they kill, building a safe campfire, and picking up all their litter, and they will develop a sense of pride that goes with it. A good idea is to bring extra plastic garbage bags to pick up any trash you come across. Kids long remember when they do something right that somebody else has done wrong.

9. If you want youngsters hooked on the outdoors for life, take a close-up photograph of them holding up fish they have caught, blowing on the campfire, or completing other camp tasks. Young children can forget how much fun they had, but they never forget if they have a picture of it.

10. The least important word you can ever say to a kid is "I." Keep track of how often you are saying "Thank you" and "What do you think?" If you don't say them very often, you'll lose out. Finally, the most important words of all are: "I am proud of you."

PREDICTING WEATHER

Foonsky climbed out of his sleeping bag, glanced at the nearby meadow, and scowled hard.

"It doesn't look good," he said. "Doesn't look good at all."

I looked at my adventure companion of 20 years, noting his discontent. Then I looked at the meadow and immediately understood why: *"When the grass is dry at morning light, look for rain before the night."*

"How bad you figure?" I asked him.

"We'll know soon enough, I reckon," Foonsky answered. *"Short notice, soon to pass. Long notice, long it will last."*

When you are out in the wild, spending your days fishing and your nights camping, you learn to rely on yourself to predict the weather. It can make or break you. If a storm hits the unprepared, it can quash the trip and possibly endanger the participants. But if you are ready, a potential hardship can be an adventure.

You can't rely on TV weather forecasters, people who don't even know that when all the cows on a hill are facing north, it will rain that night for sure. God forbid if the cows are all sitting. But what do you expect from TV?

Foonsky made a campfire, started boiling some water for coffee and soup, and we started to plan the day. In the process, I noticed the smoke of the campfire: It was sluggish, drifting and hovering.

"You notice the smoke?" I asked, chewing on a piece of homemade jerky.

"Not good," Foonsky said. "Not good." He knew that sluggish, hovering smoke indicates rain.

"You'd think we'd have been smart enough to know last night that this was coming," Foonsky said. "Did you take a look at the moon or the clouds?"

"I didn't look at either," I answered. "Too busy eating the trout we caught." You see, if the moon is clear and white, the weather will be good the next day. But if there is a ring around the moon, the number of stars you can count inside the ring equals the number of days until the next rain. As for clouds, the high, thin ones—called cirrus—indicate a change in the weather.

We were quiet for a while, planning our strategy, but as we did so, some terrible things happened: A chipmunk scampered past with his tail high, a small flock of geese flew by very low, and a little sparrow perched on a tree limb quite close to the trunk.

"We're in for trouble," I told Foonsky.

"I know, I know," he answered. "I saw 'em, too. And come to think of it, no crickets were chirping last night either."

"Damn, that's right!"

These are all signs of an approaching storm. Foonsky pointed at the smoke of the campfire and shook his head as if he had just been condemned. Sure enough, now the smoke was blowing toward the north, a sign of a south wind. *"When the wind is from the south, the rain is in its mouth."*

"We'd best stay hunkered down until it passes," Foonsky said.

I nodded. "Let's gather as much firewood now as we can, get our gear covered up, then plan our meals."

"Then we'll get a poker game going."

As we accomplished these camp tasks, the sky clouded up, then darkened. Within an hour, we had gathered enough firewood to make a large pile, enough wood to keep a fire going no matter how hard it rained. The day's meals had been separated out of the food bag so it wouldn't have to be retrieved during the storm. We buttoned two ponchos together, staked two of the corners with ropes to the ground, and tied the other two with ropes to different tree limbs to create a slanted roof/shelter.

As the first raindrop fell with that magic sound on our poncho roof, Foonsky was just starting to shuffle the cards.

"Cut for deal," he said.

Just as I did so, it started to rain a bit harder. I pulled out another piece of beef jerky and started chewing on it. It was just another day in paradise.

Weather lore can be valuable. Here is the list I have compiled over the years:

When the grass is dry at morning light,
Look for rain before the night.

Short notice, soon to pass.
Long notice, long it will last.

When the wind is from the east,
'Tis fit for neither man nor beast.

When the wind is from the south,
The rain is in its mouth.

When the wind is from the west,
Then it is the very best.

Red sky at night, sailors' delight.
Red sky in the morning, sailors take warning.

When all the cows are pointed north,
Within a day rain will come forth.

Onion skins very thin, mild winter coming in.
Onion skins very tough, winter's going to be
very rough.

When your boots make the squeak of snow,
Then very cold temperatures will surely show.

If a goose flies high, fair weather ahead.
If a goose flies low, foul weather will come
instead.

CAMPING GEAR CHECKLIST

Cooking Gear
- Camp stove and fuel
- Dish soap and scrubber
- Fire-starter cubes
- Heavy-duty paper plates
- Ice chest and drinks
- Itemized food, separated by groups
- Knife, fork, cup
- Large, heavy-duty garbage bags
- Matches stored in resealable (such as Ziploc) bags
- One lighter for each camper
- Paper towels
- Plastic spatula and stir spoon
- Pot grabber or pot holder
- Salt, pepper, spices
- Two pots and no-stick pan
- Water jug or lightweight plastic "cube"

Optional Cooking Gear
- Aluminum foil
- Ax or hatchet
- Barbecue tongs
- Can opener
- Candles
- Dustpan
- Grill or hibachi
- Plastic clothespins
- Tablecloth
- Whisk broom
- Wood or charcoal for barbecue

Clothing
- Cotton/canvas pants
- Gore-Tex parka or jacket
- Gore-Tex rain pants
- Lightweight, breathable shirt
- Lightweight fleece jacket
- Medium-weight fleece vest
- Polypropylene underwear
- Rain jacket and pants, or poncho
- Sunglasses
- Waterproofed, oilskin wide-brimmed hat

Optional Clothing
- Gloves
- Shorts
- Ski cap
- Swimsuit

Hiking Gear
- Backpack or daypack
- Hiking boots
- Fresh bootlaces
- Innersole or foot cushion (for expeditions)
- Moleskin and medical tape
- SmartWool (or equivalent) socks
- Water-purification system

Optional Hiking Gear
- Backup lightweight shoes or moccasins
- Gaiters
- Water-repellent boot treatment

Sleeping Gear
- Ground tarp
- Sleeping bag
- Tent or bivy bag
- Therm-a-Rest pad

Optional Sleeping Gear
- Air bed
- Cot
- Catalytic heater
- Foam pad for truck bed
- Mosquito netting

- Mr. Heater and propane tank (for use in pickup truck camper shell)
- Pillow (even in wilderness)
- RV windshield light screen
- Seam Lock for tent stitching

First Aid
- Ace bandage
- After-Bite for mosquito bites (before you scratch them)
- Aspirin
- Biodegradable soap
- Caladryl for poison oak
- Campho-Phenique gel for bites (after you scratch them)
- Mosquito repellent
- Lip balm
- Medical tape to affix pads
- Neosporin for cuts
- Roller gauze
- Sterile gauze pads
- Sunscreen
- Tweezers

Optional First Aid
- Athletic tape for sprained ankle
- Cell phone or coins for phone calls
- Extra set of matches
- Mirror for signaling
- Thermometer

Recreation Gear
- All required permits and licenses
- Fishing reel with fresh line
- Fishing rod
- Knife
- Leatherman tool or needle-nose pliers
- Small tackle box with flies, floats, hooks, lures, snap swivels, and splitshot

Optional Recreation Gear
- Backpacking cribbage board
- Deck of cards
- Folding chairs
- Guidebooks
- Hammock
- Mountain bike
- Reading material

Other Necessities
- Duct tape
- Extra plastic garbage bags
- Flashlight and batteries
- Lantern and fuel
- Maps
- Nylon rope for food hang
- Spade for cat hole
- Toilet paper
- Toothbrush and toothpaste
- Towelettes
- Wristwatch

Other Optional Items
- Altimeter
- Assorted bungee cords
- Binoculars
- Camera with fresh battery and digital card or film
- Compass
- Feminine hygiene products
- GPS unit
- Handkerchief
- Notebook and pen

Small signs provided by nature and wildlife can also be translated to provide a variety of weather information:

• A thick coat on a woolly caterpillar means a big, early snow is coming.

• Chipmunks will run with their tails up before a rain.

• Bees always stay near their hives before a rainstorm.

• When the birds are perched on large limbs near tree trunks, an intense but short storm will arrive.

• On the coast, if groups of seabirds are flying a mile inland, look for major winds.

• If crickets are chirping very loudly during the evening, the next day will be clear and warm.

• If the smoke of a campfire at night rises in a thin spiral, good weather is assured for the next day.

• If the smoke of a campfire at night is sluggish, drifting and hovering, it will rain the next day.

• If there is a ring around the moon, count the number of stars inside the ring, and that is how many days until the next rain.

• If the moon is clear and white, the weather will be good the next day.

• High, thin clouds, or cirrus, indicate a change in the weather.

• Oval-shaped lenticular clouds indicate high winds.

• Two levels of clouds moving in different directions indicate changing weather soon.

• Huge, dark, billowing clouds, called cumulonimbus, suddenly forming on warm afternoons in the mountains mean that a short but intense thunderstorm with lightning can be expected.

• When squirrels are busy gathering food for extended periods, it means good weather is ahead in the short term, but a hard winter is ahead in the long term.

And God forbid if all the cows are sitting down....

© JOERG HACKEMANN/123RF.COM

REDWOOD EMPIRE

© ARUN S/123RF.COM

BEST CAMPGROUNDS

Visitors come from around the world to the

Redwood Empire for one reason: to see the groves of giant redwoods, the tallest trees in the world. On a perfect day in the redwoods, refracted sunlight beams through the forest canopy, creating a solemn, cathedral-like effect. It feels as if you are standing in the center of the earth's pure magic.

But the redwood forests are only one of the attractions in this area. The Smith River canyon, Del Norte and Humboldt Coasts, and the remote edge of the Siskiyou Wilderness in Six Rivers National Forest all make this region like none other in the world.

On sunny days in late summer, some visitors are incredulous that so few people live in the Redwood Empire. The reason is the same one that explains why the trees grow so tall: rain in the winter – often for weeks at a time – and fog in the summer. If the sun does manage to appear, it's an event almost worthy of calling the police to say you've spotted a large, yellow Unidentified Flying Object. So most folks are content to just visit.

Three stellar areas should be on your must-see list for outstanding days of adventure here: the redwood parks from Trinidad to Klamath River, the Smith River Recreation Area, and the Lost Coast.

I've hiked every trailhead from Trinidad to Crescent City, and I believe that the hikes here feature some of the best adventuring day trips in Northern California. A good place to start is Prairie Creek Redwoods State Park, where you can see fantastic herds of Roosevelt elk. Then head over to the beach by hiking Fern Canyon, where you'll walk for 20 minutes at the bottom of a canyon adjacent to vertical walls covered with ferns before heading north on the Coastal Trail and its pristine woodlands and fantastic expanses of untouched beaches. All the trails through the redwoods north of the Klamath River are winners; it's just a matter of matching your level of ambition to the right hike.

The Smith River Recreation Area is equally gorgeous. The Smith is one of the last major free-flowing rivers in America. Wild, pristine, and beautiful, it's set in a series of gorges and bordered by national forest. The centerpiece is Jedediah Smith Redwoods State Park and its grove of monster-sized redwoods. South Fork Road provides an extended tour into Six Rivers National Forest along the South Fork Smith River, with the option of visiting many of the largest trees in Jedediah Smith Redwoods State Park. The turnoff is on U.S. 199 just northeast of the town of Hiouchi. Turn right, cross two bridges, and you will arrive at a fork in the road. Turning left at the fork will take you along the South Fork Smith River and deep into Six Rivers National Forest. Turning right at the fork will take you to a series of trailheads for hikes into redwoods. Of these, the best is the Boy Scout Tree Trail.

The Lost Coast is often overlooked by visitors because of the difficulty in reaching it; your only access is via a slow, curvy road through the Mattole River Valley, past Petrolia, and out to a piece of coast. The experience is like being in suspended animation – your surroundings peaceful and pristine, with a striking lack of people. One of the best ways to capture the sensation is to drive out near the mouth of the Mattole, then hike south on the Coastal Trail long enough to get a feel for the area.

Compared to other regions in California, this corner of the state is somewhat one-dimensional. The emphasis here is primarily on exploring the redwoods and the coast, and to some extent, the Smith River. Most of the campgrounds here are designed with that in mind.

Many private campgrounds are set on U.S. 101 as well as near the mouths of the Smith and Klamath Rivers. These make fine base camps for fishing trips when the salmon are running. The state and national park campgrounds in the redwoods are in high demand, and reservations are often necessary in the peak vacation season. On the opposite end of the spectrum are primitive and remote settings, in Six Rivers National Forest, the Lost Coast, and even a few surprise nuggets in Redwood National Park.

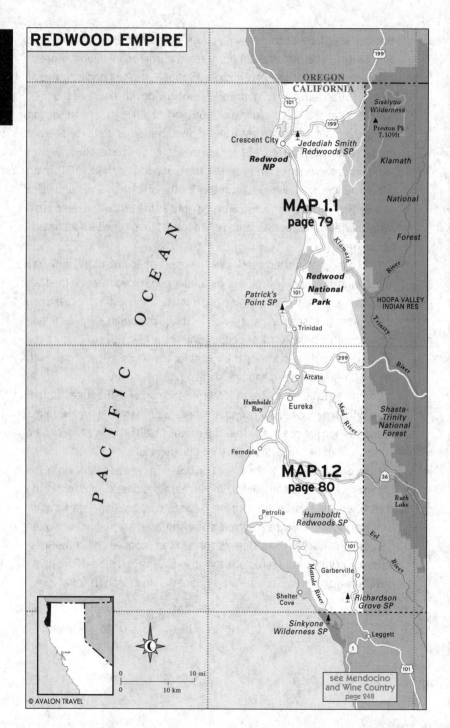

Map 1.1

Sites 1-34
Pages 81-97

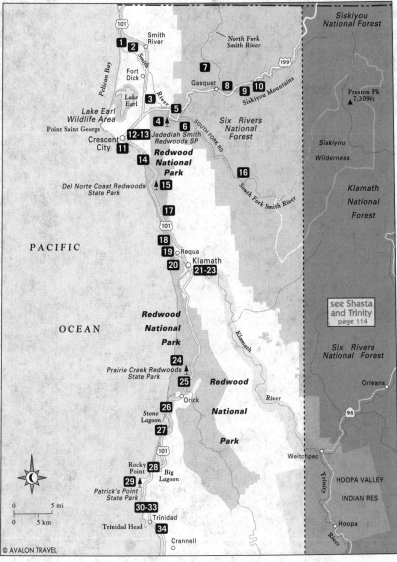

Map 1.2

Sites 35-59
Pages 98-110

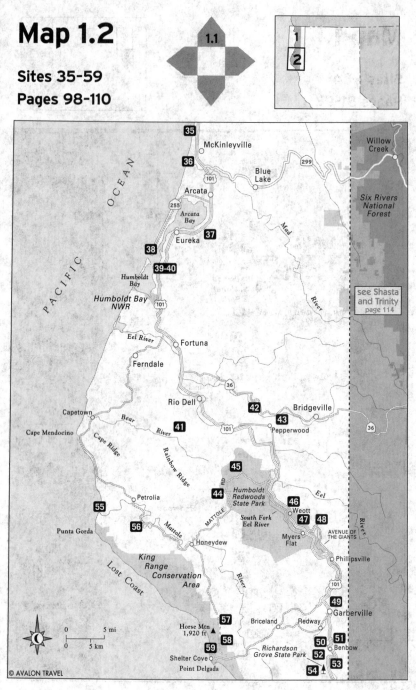

1 SALMON HARBOR RV RESORT

🛶 🚤 🏕 🚐 ⛺

Scenic rating: 6

on the Smith River

Map 1.1, page 79

If location is everything, this privately operated campground rates high for salmon and steelhead anglers in the fall. It is set near the mouth of the Smith River, where salmon enter and school in the deep river holes in October. The fish are big, often in the 20-pound range, occasionally surpassing even 40 pounds. Year-round this is a good layover for RV cruisers looking for a spot near the Oregon border. It is actually an RV parking area with hookups, set within a mobile home park. Salmon Harbor RV Resort overlooks the ocean, with good beachcombing and driftwood and agate hunting nearby. Note that most sites are filled for the entire summer, but several sites are kept open for overnight campers.

Campsites, facilities: There are 93 sites for tents or RVs up to 40 feet; most sites have full hookups (30 and 50 amps) and some are pull-through. Picnic tables and fire grills are provided. Drinking water, restrooms with flush toilets and showers, cable TV, coin laundry, storage sheds, WiFi (some sites) and modem access, and a recreation room are available. A grocery store, ice, gas, propane, a restaurant, boat ramp, fish cleaning station, RV storage, snack bar, and a bar are available within three miles. Leashed pets are permitted.

Reservations, fees: Reservations are accepted at 800/332-6139. Sites are $38 per night, $3 per person for more than two people. Monthly rates are available. Open year-round.

Directions: From Crescent City, drive north on U.S. 101 for 13 miles to the town of Smith River. Continue three miles north on U.S. 101 to the Salmon Harbor Road exit. Turn left on Salmon Harbor Road, drive a short distance, and look for Salmon Harbor Resort at the end of the road.

Contact: Salmon Harbor RV Resort, 707/487-3341, www.salmonharborrvresort.com.

2 SHIP ASHORE RESORT

🛶 🚤 🏕 🚐 ⛺

Scenic rating: 7

on the Smith River

Map 1.1, page 79

This is a famous spot for Smith River anglers in late fall and all through winter, when the tales get taller as the evening gets late. In the summer, the resort has become quite popular with people cruising the coast on U.S. 101. The park is set on five acres of land adjacent to the lower Smith River. Note that in addition to the 120 RV sites, another 80 sites have mobile homes. The salmon and steelhead seem to come in one size here—big—but they can be as elusive as Bigfoot. If you want to hear how big these fish can be, just check into the Captain's Galley restaurant any fall or winter evening. Salmon average 15–25 pounds, occasionally bigger, with 50-pounders caught each year, and steelhead average 10–14 pounds, with bigger fish occasionally hooked as well.

Campsites, facilities: There are 200 sites for RVs, and a separate area for 10–15 tents. Most RV sites have full hookups (30 amps); some sites are pull-through. Two houses and motel rooms are also available. Picnic tables are provided. Restrooms with flush toilets and showers, boat dock, boat ramp, coin laundry, propane, and a restaurant are available. A grocery store is two miles away. Leashed pets are permitted, with a maximum of two pets.

Reservations, fees: Reservations are not accepted. Tent sites are $13 per night; RV sites are $22 per night, $2 per person per night for more than two people. Weekly rates available. Some credit cards accepted. Open year-round.

Directions: From Crescent City, drive north on U.S. 101 for 16 miles, three miles past the town of Smith River, to the Ship Ashore sign at Chinook Street. At Chinook Street, turn left and drive a short distance (less than half a block) to the motel lobby to register.

Contact: Ship Ashore Resort, 707/487-3141, www.ship-ashore.com.

3 CRESCENT CITY REDWOODS KOA

🚶 🏊 🐕 ♿ 🎣 🚐 ⛺

Scenic rating: 6

five miles north of Crescent City

Map 1.1, page 79

This KOA camp is on the edge of a recreation wonderland, a perfect jump-off spot for a vacation. The park covers 17 acres, with 11 acres of redwood forest. A few farm animals live here, and guests are allowed to feed them. In addition, there are three golf courses nearby. The camp is only two miles from Redwood National Park, Jedediah Smith Redwoods State Park, and the Smith River National Recreation Area. It is also only a 10-minute drive to the beach and Tolowa Dunes Wildlife Area to the east, and to Crescent City Harbor to the south.

Campsites, facilities: There are 12 sites for tents and small RVs with partial hookups, 28 sites with full hookups (30 and 50 amps) including some pull-through sites for RVs of any length, and 35 sites with no hookups. Seventeen cabins and one lodge are also available. Picnic tables and fire grills are provided. A dump station, restrooms with flush toilets and showers, a coin laundry, free Wi-Fi, cable TV, playground, propane, convenience store, ice, firewood, recreation room, pool table, tetherball, table tennis, horseshoes, go-carts, and volleyball are available. Some facilities are wheelchair accessible. Leashed pets are permitted.

Reservations, fees: Reservations for RV sites are accepted at 800/562-5754. RV sites are $30–45 per night, tent sites are $25–35, $3–4 per person per night for more than two people. Some credit cards accepted. Open mid-March–mid-November.

Directions: From Crescent City, take U.S. 101 north for five miles to the campground entrance on the right (east) side of the road.

Contact: Crescent City Redwoods KOA, 707/464-5744, www.crescentcitykoa.com.

4 JEDEDIAH SMITH REDWOODS STATE PARK

🚶 🚴 🏊 🎣 🐕 ♿ 🚐 ⛺

Scenic rating: 10

on the Smith River

Map 1.1, page 79   BEST (

This is a beautiful park set along the Smith River, where the campsites are sprinkled amid a grove of old-growth redwoods. Reservations are usually a necessity during the summer. This park covers 10,000 acres on both sides of the Smith River, a jewel and California's last major free-flowing river. There are 20 miles of hiking and nature trails. The park has hiking trails that lead right out of the campground; one is routed along the beautiful Smith River, and another heads through forest, across U.S. 199, and hooks up with Simpson-Reed Interpretive Trail. In the summer, interpretive programs are available. There is also a good put-in spot at the park for river access in a drift boat, canoe, or raft. The fishing is best for steelhead from mid-January through March. In the summer, a seasonal footbridge connects the campground with more extensive trails. The best hikes are on the south side of the Smith River, accessible via Howland Hill Road, including the Boy Scout Tree Trail and Stout Grove (for access, see listing for Hiouchi RV Resort). Note that in winter, 100 inches of cumulative rainfall is common.

Campsites, facilities: There are 86 sites for tents or RVs up to 36 feet (no hookups) and trailers up to 31 feet, five hike-in/bike-in sites, and one group site for up to 15 vehicles and 50 people. Picnic tables, fire grills, and food lockers are provided. Drinking water, showers, flush toilets, and a dump station are available. There is a visitors center with exhibits and a nature store. Propane gas and groceries are available within one mile. Some facilities are wheelchair-accessible. Leashed pets are permitted only in the campground and on roads.

Reservations, fees: Reservations are accepted May through early September at 800/444-7275 (800/444-PARK) or www.reserveamerica.com

($8 reservation fee). Sites are first-come, first-served September through May. Sites are $35 per night, $8 per night for each additional vehicle, $300 per night for the group site, and $5 per person per night for hike-in/bike-in sites. Open year-round.

Directions: From Crescent City, drive north on U.S. 101 for four miles to the junction with U.S. 199. Turn east at U.S. 199 and drive five miles. Turn right at the well-signed entrance station.

Contact: Jedediah Smith Redwoods State Park, 707/465-7335, www.parks.ca.gov.

5 HIOUCHI RV RESORT

🏃 🛶 🐕 ♿ 🚐 ⛺

Scenic rating: 7

near the Smith River

Map 1.1, page 79

This camp is out of the wind and fog you get on the coast and set instead in the heart of the forest country. It makes a good base camp for a steelhead trip in winter. Insiders know that right next door, the fried chicken at the Hamlet's market is always good for a quick hit. An excellent side trip is to drive just east of Hiouchi on U.S. 199, turn right, and cross over two bridges, where you will reach a fork in the road. Turn left for a great scenic drive along the South Fork Smith River or turn right to get backdoor access to Jedediah Smith Redwoods State Park and three great trailheads for hiking in the redwoods. My favorite of the latter is the Boy Scout Tree Trail. Note that about one-fourth of the RV sites are filled with long-term renters, and many other sites fill up quickly with summer vacationers.

Campsites, facilities: There are 120 sites with full hookups (30 and 50 amps) for RVs of any length, six tent sites, and one yurt. Some sites are pull-through. Two park-model cabins and six furnished apartments are also available. Restrooms with flush toilets and showers, a dump station, coin laundry, Wi-Fi, high-speed modem hookups, cable TV, recreation room, fish cleaning station, horseshoe pits, grocery store, propane, and deli are available. A motel and café are nearby. A golf course is available within four miles. Some facilities are wheelchair-accessible. Leashed pets are permitted.

Reservations, fees: Reservations are accepted at 800/722-9468. RV sites are $33–45 per night, $2 per person per night for more than two people; tent sites are $22–25 per night; and the yurt is $60 per night. Some credit cards accepted. Open year-round.

Directions: From Crescent City, drive five miles north on U.S. 101 to U.S. 199. Turn east (right) on U.S. 199 and drive about five miles (just past the entrance to Jedediah Smith Redwoods State Park) to the town of Hiouchi. In Hiouchi, turn left at the well-signed campground entrance.

Contact: Hiouchi RV Resort, 707/458-3321, www.hiouchirv.com.

6 LITTLE BALD HILLS

🏃 🚴 5% ⛺

Scenic rating: 8

in Jedediah Smith Redwoods State Park

Map 1.1, page 79

Little Bald Hills is a little-known campground located in the backcountry at Jedediah Smith. The camp, set in a deep forest, is very quiet and is often overlooked because of its location off Howland Hill Road on the far side of the Smith River (not at the main entrance along Highway 199). Reaching the camp requires a 3.3-mile trip, accessible for hikers, mountain bikers, and horseback riders. For newcomers, the drive to the trailhead can seem circuitous and remote compared to other state and national parks. Nearby Stout Grove and the Boy Scout Tree Trail provide excellent side-trips. Bears are occasional visitors at night, so be sure to use the food lockers provided.

Campsites, facilities: There are four tent sites and one group site for up to 20 people. Picnic tables and fire rings are provided. Pit toilets, bear-proof lockers, a horse corral, and a water trough are available. Drinking water is not available, but there is a spigot for stock water. Garbage must be packed out.

Reservations, fees: Reservations are not accepted. A free backcountry permit is required (available at visitors centers in Crescent City and Hiouchi). There is no fee for camping.

Directions: From Crescent City, drive north on U.S. 101 for four miles to the junction with U.S. 199. Turn east at U.S. 199 and drive just past Hiouchi to the turnoff on the right for South Fork Road. Turn right and drive over two bridges to the junction with South Fork Road (on the left) and Howland Hill Road (on the right). Turn right and drive a short distance to the Little Bald Hills Trailhead on the left (just before Stout Grove).

Contact: Redwood National and State Parks, 707/465-2144, www.nps.gov/redw.

7 NORTH FORK

Scenic rating: 7

on the North Fork of the Smith River in Six Rivers National Forest

Map 1.1, page 79

This remote and primitive camp is a put-in for rafting and kayaking the North Fork Smith River in winter. Since there is no dam it can only be run in the rainy season, but this is a sensational Class III rafting trip in a rainstorm, including a spot at an overhanging rock along the northern shore where you can raft right through a waterfall. In the summer, the flows on the North Fork turn into a trickle and you can virtually walk down the stream. The campsites are primitive, open, and located within view of the river—not in the forest. Though there is space for RVs at the camp, the road in can be impassable for RVs during wet weather.

Campsites, facilities: There are five sites for tents or RVs up to 18 feet (no hookups). Large RVs are not advised. Picnic tables and fire rings are provided. Vault toilets are available, but there is no drinking water. Garbage must be packed out.

Reservations, fees: Reservations are not accepted. Sites are $8 per night; $5 per night per additional vehicle. Open year-round.

Directions: From Crescent City, drive north on U.S. 101 (straight ahead past the Hwy. 199 turnoff) to Rowdy Creek Road. Turn right on Rowdy Creek Road (it becomes Forest Road 308) and drive about 4.5 miles on Rowdy Creek Road/FR 308 to Forest Road 305. Turn left on Forest Road 305 (a dirt road) and drive 11 miles to the campground.

Contact: Smith River Recreation Area, Six Rivers National Forest, 707/457-3131, www.fs.usda.gov/srnf.

8 PANTHER FLAT

Scenic rating: 8

on the Smith River in Six Rivers National Forest

Map 1.1, page 79   BEST (

This is an ideal alternative to the often-crowded Jedediah Smith Redwoods State Park. The park provides easy road access since it is set right along U.S. 199, the two-laner that runs beside the Smith River. This is one of the featured campgrounds in the Smith River Recreation Area, with excellent prospects for salmon and steelhead fishing in the fall and winter respectively, and outstanding hiking and backpacking in the summer. A 0.25-mile interpretive trail and viewing area is one mile north of the campground, off U.S. 199. A great nearby hike is Stony Creek Trail, an easy walk along the North Fork Smith River; the trailhead is in nearby Gasquet on Stoney Creek Road. Redwood National Park is a short drive to the west. The Siskiyou Wilderness is a short drive to the southeast via forest roads detailed on Forest Service maps. The wild and scenic Smith River system provides fishing, swimming, sunbathing, kayaking for experts, and beautiful scenery.

Campsites, facilities: There are 38 sites for tents or RVs up to 40 feet (no hookups). Picnic tables and fire grills are provided. Drinking water, restrooms with flush toilets and coin showers, a visitor center, and horseshoe pits are available. Propane gas, groceries, and coin laundry are nearby. Some facilities are wheelchair-accessible. Leashed pets are permitted.

Reservations, fees: Reservations are accepted at 877/444-6777 or www.recreation.gov ($9 reservation fee). Sites are $15–30 per night, $5 per night for each additional vehicle. Open year-round.

Directions: From Crescent City, drive north on U.S. 101 for three miles to the junction with U.S. 199. At U.S. 199, turn east and drive 14.5 miles to Gasquet. From Gasquet, continue for 2.3 miles east on U.S. 199 and look for the entrance to the campground on the left side of the highway.

Contact: Smith River Recreation Area, Six Rivers National Forest, 707/457-3131, www. fs.usda.gov/srnf.

9 GRASSY FLAT

Scenic rating: 4

on the Smith River in Six Rivers National Forest
Map 1.1, page 79

This is one in a series of three easy-to-reach Forest Service camps set near U.S. 199 along the beautiful Middle Fork of the Smith River. It's a classic wild river, popular in the summer with kayakers, and the steelhead come huge in the winter for the crafty few. The camp itself is set directly across from a CalTrans waste area, and if you hit it when the crews are working, it can be noisy here. Most of the time, however, it is peaceful and quiet.

Campsites, facilities: There are 15 sites for tents or RVs up to 30 feet (no hookups) and four walk-in tent sites. Picnic tables and fire grills are provided. Drinking water and vault toilets are available. Propane gas and groceries are available nearby. Some facilities are wheelchair-accessible. Leashed pets are permitted.

Reservations, fees: Reservations are accepted at 877/444-6777 or www.recreation.gov ($9 reservation fee). Sites are $10 per night, $5 per night for each additional vehicle. Open June through September.

Directions: From Crescent City, drive north on U.S. 101 for three miles to the junction with U.S. 199. Turn east on U.S. 199 and drive 14.5 miles to Gasquet. From Gasquet, continue east on U.S. 199 for 4.4 miles and look for the campground entrance on the right side of the road.

Contact: Smith River Recreation Area, Six Rivers National Forest, 707/457-3131, www. fs.usda.gov/srnf.

10 PATRICK CREEK

Scenic rating: 8

in Six Rivers National Forest
Map 1.1, page 79

This is one of the prettiest spots along U.S. 199, where Patrick Creek enters the upper Smith River. It is also a historic California Conservation Corps site that was built in the 1930s. This section of the Smith looks something like a large trout stream, rolling green past a boulder-lined shore, complete with forest canopy. There are small cutthroat trout in summer and salmon and steelhead in fall and winter. A big plus for this camp is its nearby access to excellent hiking in the Siskiyou Wilderness, especially the great day hike to Buck Lake. It is essential to have a map of Six Rivers National Forest, both for driving directions to the trailhead and for the hiking route. You can buy maps at the information center for the Smith River National Recreation Area on the north side of U.S. 199 in Gasquet. Patrick Creek Lodge, on the opposite side of the highway from the campground, has a restaurant and bar. A paved trail connects the campground to Patrick Creek Lodge.

Campsites, facilities: There are 13 sites for tents or RVs up to 35 feet (no hookups). Picnic tables and fire grills are provided. Drinking water and flush toilets are available. Some facilities are wheelchair-accessible, including a fishing area. Leashed pets are permitted.

Reservations, fees: Reservations are accepted for individual sites and are required for group sites at 877/444-6777 or www.recreation.gov ($9 reservation fee). Sites are $14 per night, $5 per night for each additional vehicle. Open May through September.

Directions: From Crescent City, drive north on U.S. 101 for three miles to the junction with U.S. 199. Turn east on U.S. 199 and drive 14.5 miles to Gasquet. From Gasquet, continue east on U.S. 199 for 7.5 miles and look for the campground entrance on the right side of the road.

Contact: Smith River Recreation Area, Six Rivers National Forest, 707/457-3131, www.fs.usda.gov/srnf.

11 BAYSIDE RV PARK

Scenic rating: 6

in Crescent City

Map 1.1, page 79

If you are towing a boat, you just found your personal heaven: This RV park is directly adjacent to the boat docking area in Crescent City Harbor. There are several walks in the immediate area, including exploring the harbor and ocean frontage. For a quick change of scenery, it is only a 15-minute drive to Redwood National Park and Jedediah Smith Redwoods State Park along U.S. 199 to the north. Note that about 20 sites are filled with long-term renters, and most of the spaces book up for the entire season.

Campsites, facilities: There are 110 sites for RVs up to 34 feet. Most sites have full hookups (30 amps) and/or are pull-through. No tents. Picnic tables are provided. Restrooms with flush toilets and showers, cable TV, Wi-Fi, and a coin laundry are available. A restaurant is adjacent to the park. Leashed pets are permitted.

Reservations, fees: Reservations are accepted at 800/446-9482. Sites are $28–33 per night, $5 per person per night for more than two people. Open year-round.

Directions: From U.S. 101 at the southern end of Crescent City, drive to Citizen Dock Road and continue one-half block south to the park office.

Contact: Bayside RV Park, 750 U.S. 101, Crescent City, 707/464-9482.

12 VILLAGE CAMPER INN RV PARK

Scenic rating: 7

in Crescent City

Map 1.1, page 79

Woods and water, that's what attracts visitors to California's north coast. Village Camper Inn provides nearby access to big woods and big water. This RV park is on 20 acres of wooded land, about a 10-minute drive away from the giant redwoods along U.S. 199. In addition, you'll find some premium beachcombing for driftwood and agates a mile away on the spectacular rocky beaches just west of town. Note that about half of the sites fill up for the entire summer season.

Campsites, facilities: There are 135 sites for RVs of any length, and a separate area for tents. Most RV sites have full hookups (30 and 50 amps); some sites are pull-through. Picnic tables are provided. Drinking water, a dump station, restrooms with flush toilets and showers, coin laundry, WiFi, and cable TV are available. Leashed pets are permitted, with certain restrictions.

Reservations, fees: Reservations are accepted at 800/470-3544. Sites are $23.50–32.50 per night, $2 per person per night for more than two people. Monthly rates available. Some credit cards accepted. Open year-round.

Directions: From Crescent City, drive north on U.S. 101 to the Parkway Drive exit. Take that exit and drive 0.5 mile to the campground on the right.

On U.S. 101, driving south in Crescent City: Drive south on U.S. 101 to the Washington Boulevard exit. Turn left on

Washington Boulevard and drive one block to Parkway Drive. Turn left on Parkway and drive one block to the campground on the right.

Contact: Village Camper Inn RV Park, 707/464-3544, www.villagecamperinn.com.

13 SUNSET HARBOR RV PARK

Scenic rating: 4

in Crescent City

Map 1.1, page 79

People camp here with their RVs to be close to the action in Crescent City and to the nearby harbor and beach frontage. For starters, drive a few minutes to the northwest side of town, where the sea is sprinkled with gigantic rocks and boulders, for dramatic ocean views and spectacular sunsets. For finishers, go down to the west side of town for great walks along the ocean parkway or south to the harbor and adjacent beach, which is long and expansive. About half of the sites are filled with long-term renters.

Campsites, facilities: There are 69 sites with full hookups (30 and 50 amps) for RVs up to 45 feet. No tents. Picnic tables are provided at some sites. Restrooms with flush toilets and showers, cable TV, WiFi, coin laundry, and a recreation room are available. A grocery store is available nearby. Some facilities are wheelchair-accessible. Leashed pets are permitted.

Reservations, fees: Reservations are accepted. Sites are $28–31 per night, $3 per person per night for more than two people. Monthly rates are available. Some credit cards accepted. Open year-round.

Directions: In Crescent City on U.S. 101, drive to King Street. At King Street, turn east and drive one block to the park entrance at the end of the road.

Contact: Sunset Harbor RV Park, 707/464-3423, http://sunsetharborrv.com.

14 NICKEL CREEK

Scenic rating: 8

in Redwood National Park

Map 1.1, page 79

This camp is set 100 yards from the beach on a bluff, right near the mouth of Nickel Creek. One of the least-known national park campgrounds in the whole state, Nickel Creek Walk-In provides a backpacking-type experience, yet it requires only a short walk. In return for the effort, you get seclusion and beach frontage, with seashore walks and tidepool exploration available.

Campsites, facilities: There are five hike-in tent sites. There is no drinking water. Picnic tables, food lockers, and fire pits are provided. Composting toilets are available. Garbage must be packed out. No pets are allowed.

Reservations, fees: Reservations are not accepted, but a free backcountry permit is required (available from visitor centers). There is no fee for camping. Open year-round.

Directions: From Crescent City, drive south on U.S. 101 for two miles to Enderts Beach Road. Turn right on Enderts Beach Road and drive about a mile to the trailhead at the end of the road. From the trailhead, hike in 0.5 mile to the campground.

Contact: Crescent City Information Center, 707/465-7306; Redwood National and State Parks, 707/465-7306, www.nps.gov/redw.

15 DEL NORTE COAST REDWOODS STATE PARK

Scenic rating: 8

near Crescent City

Map 1.1, page 79   BEST (

The campsites are set in a series of loops in the forest, so while there are a lot of camps, you still feel a sense of privacy here. In addition to redwoods, there are also good stands of alders, along with a rambling stream fed by several creeks. It makes for a very pretty setting, with four loop trails available right out of the camp. This park covers 6,400 acres, featuring 50 percent old-growth coastal redwoods and eight miles of wild coastline. Topography is fairly steep, with elevations ranging from sea level to 1,277 feet. This range is oriented in a north-to-south direction, with steep cliffs adjacent to the ocean. That makes most of the rocky seacoast generally inaccessible except by Damnation Trail and Footsteps Rock Trail. The best coastal access is at Wilson Beach or False Klamath Cove, where there is a half-mile of sandy beach bordered by excellent tide pools.

The forest interior is dense, with redwoods and tanoaks, madrones, red alders, bigleaf maples, and California bay. One reason for the lush growth is what rangers call the "nurturing" coastal climate. Nurturing, in this case, means rain like you wouldn't believe in the winter—often more than 100 inches in a season—and lots of fog in the summer. Interpretive programs are conducted here. Insider's note: Hike-in and bike-in campers beware. There is a 900-foot elevation change over the course of two miles between the U.S. 101 access road and the campground.

Note: Del Norte Coast Redwoods was on the state park closure list. It is currently being managed cooperatively by the National Park Service and the California Department of Parks through Spring 2013.

Campsites, facilities: There are 145 sites for tents or RVs up to 31 feet (no hookups). Hike-in/bike-in sites are also available. Picnic tables, fire pits, and food lockers are provided. Drinking water, a dump station, and restrooms with flush toilets and coin showers are available. Some facilities are wheelchair-accessible. Leashed pets are permitted only in the campground.

Reservations, fees: Reservations are accepted at 800/444-7275 (800/444-PARK) or www.reserveamerica.com ($8 reservation fee); search

for Del Norte Coast Redwoods. Sites are $35 per night, $8 per night for each additional vehicle, $5 per person per night for hike-in/bike-in sites. Open May through September.

Directions: From Crescent City, drive seven miles south on U.S. 101 to a signed access road for Mill Creek Campground/Del Norte Coast Redwoods State Park. Turn east at the park entrance and continue 1.5 miles to the campground entrance.

Contact: Del Norte Coast Redwoods State Park, 707/465-2146, www.parks.ca.gov; Redwood National and State Parks, 707/464-6101, www.nps.gov/redw.

16 BIG FLAT

Scenic rating: 7

on Hurdygurdy Creek in
Six Rivers National Forest

Map 1.1, page 79

This camp provides an ideal setting for those who know of it, which is why it gets quite a bit of use for a relatively remote camp. Set along Hurdygurdy Creek, near where the creek enters the South Fork of the Smith River, it provides nearby access to South Kelsey Trail, an outstanding hiking route whether you are walking for a few hours or backpacking for days. In the summer, it is a good layover for rafters or kayakers paddling the South Fork of the Smith River.

Campsites, facilities: There are 25 sites for tents or RVs up to 22 feet (no hookups). Picnic tables and fire grills are provided. Vault toilets and food lockers are available. There is no drinking water and garbage must be packed out. Some facilities are wheelchair-accessible. Leashed pets are permitted.

Reservations, fees: Reservations are not accepted. Sites are $8 per night, $5 per night for each additional vehicle. Open May through mid-September.

Directions: From Crescent City, drive north

on U.S. 101 for three miles to the junction with U.S. 199. Turn east on U.S. 199 and drive five miles to Hiouchi. Continue just past Hiouchi to South Fork Road. Turn right and cross two bridges. At the Y, turn left on South Fork Road and drive about 14 miles to Big Flat Road/County Road 405. Turn left and drive 0.25 mile to the campground entrance road (Forest Road 15N59) on the left. Turn left and drive a short distance to the camp on the left.

Contact: Smith RiverRecreation Area, Six Rivers National Forest, 707/457-3131, www.fs.usda.gov/srnf.

17 DEMARTIN
🏃‍♂️ ⛺

Scenic rating: 9

in Redwood National Park

Map 1.1, page 79

For hikers on the Pacific Coastal Trail, this camp is ideal for an overnight spot. It is set in a grassy prairie area on a bluff overlooking the ocean along the DeMartin section of the trail, aside Wilson Creek. Sound good? You can chase the waves, hike the Coastal Trail, or just hunker down and let the joy of a peaceful spot renew your spirit.

Campsites, facilities: There are 10 tent sites. Picnic tables, fire pits, and food storage lockers are provided. Composting toilets are available. There is no drinking water. Garbage must be packed out. No pets are allowed.

Reservations, fees: Reservations are not accepted. A free backcountry permit is required (available from visitor centers). There is no fee for camping. Open year-round.

Directions: From Crescent City, drive south for approximately 18 miles on U.S. 101 to Wilson Creek Road. At Wilson Creek Road, turn left and drive 0.25 mile to the trailhead at the end of the road. From the trailhead, marked Coastal Trail, hike in about 3.5 miles to the campground.

Contact: Redwood National and State Parks, 707/465-7335, www.nps.gov/redw.

18 MYSTIC FOREST RV PARK
🏃‍♂️ 🏊 🐕 🚣 ♿ 🚐 ⛺

Scenic rating: 6

near the Klamath River

Map 1.1, page 79

The park features gravel roads, redwood trees, and grassy sites amid a 50-acre park designed primarily for RVs with a separate area for tents. A bonus here is the 18-hole miniature golf course. The Trees of Mystery is less than a mile away and features a nearly 50-foot-tall Paul Bunyan and his blue ox, Babe. (In the winter of 2008, you may recall the tale of Babe's head falling off in a storm. Have no fear—Babe again has a head.) The park is about 1.5 miles away from the ocean and 3.5 miles from the Klamath River. Jet-boat tours are available on the Klamath River.

Campsites, facilities: There are 30 sites with full hookups (30 amps) for RVs of any length and 14 tent sites. Some of the RV sites are pull-through. Picnic tables and fire rings are provided. Drinking water, restrooms with flush toilets and showers, Wi-Fi, cable TV, playground, recreation room, horseshoes, miniature golf, a coin laundry, convenience store and gift shop, group facilities, and firewood are available. Some facilities are wheelchair-accessible. Leashed pets are permitted.

Reservations, fees: Reservations are accepted. RV sites are $32 per night, tent sites are $18 per night, $4 per person per night for more than two people. Group rates available. Some credit cards accepted. Open year-round.

Directions: From Eureka, drive north on U.S. 101 to Klamath and continue north for five miles. Look for the entrance sign on the left side of the road. If you reach the Trees of Mystery, you have gone a mile too far north.

Contact: Mystic Forest RV Park, 707/482-4901, www.mysticforestrv.com.

19 CHINOOK RV RESORT

Scenic rating: 7

on the Klamath River

Map 1.1, page 79

The camping area at this park consists of grassy RV sites that overlook the Klamath River. Chinook RV Resort is one of the more well-known parks on the lower Klamath. A boat ramp and fishing supplies are available.

Campsites, facilities: There are 70 sites with full hookups (30 and 50 amps) for RVs of any length and a grassy area for tents. Some RV sites are pull-through. An apartment is also available. Picnic tables and fire grills are provided. Restrooms with flush toilets and showers, cable television, WiFi, coin laundry, fish cleaning station, recreation room, propane, convenience store, RV supplies, boat ramp, boat rentals, and a tackle shop are available. Leashed pets are permitted.

Reservations, fees: Reservations are accepted at 866/482-3511. RV sites are $27–33 per night, tent sites are $20 per night, $3 per person per night for more than two people, $3 per night for each additional vehicle. Some credit cards accepted. Open year-round.

Directions: From Eureka, drive north on U.S. 101 to Klamath. After crossing the bridge at the Klamath River, continue north on U.S. 101 for a mile to the campground on the left.

Contact: Chinook RV Resort, 707/482-3511, www.chinookrvresort.com.

20 FLINT RIDGE HIKE-IN

Scenic rating: 7

in Redwood National Park

Map 1.1, page 79

This little-known camp is on a grassy bluff overlooking the ocean along the Flint Ridge section of the Pacific Coastal Trail. From the parking area at the trailhead, it's only a five-minute walk to reach a meadow surrounded by a thicket of wild blackberries, alders, and redwoods, with the ocean looming huge to the west, but there is no trail to the beach from here. The parking area, by the way, is an excellent perch to watch for the "puff-of-smoke" spouts from passing whales. A hike out of camp is routed into the forest; it's a two-mile climb to reach a hill filled solid with redwoods. The only problem is that there is no real destination—just in and out with your friend. It's the "Trail to Nowhere."

Campsites, facilities: There are eight tent sites. Picnic tables, fire pits, and food lockers are provided. Composting toilets are available. There is no drinking water. Garbage must be packed out. No pets are allowed.

Reservations, fees: Reservations are not accepted. A free backcountry permit is required (available from visitor centers). There is no fee for camping. Open year-round.

Directions: From Eureka, drive north on U.S. 101 to the Klamath River. Just before reaching the bridge at the Klamath River, take the Coastal Drive exit and head west up the hill for four miles to a dirt parking area on the right side of the road. Park here. The campground trailhead is adjacent to the parking area on the east side of the road. Hike 0.25 mile to the camp.

Contact: Crescent City Information Center, 707/465-7354. Redwood National and State Parks, 707/465-7354, www.nps.gov/redw.

21 KLAMATH'S CAMPER CORRAL RV PARK AND CAMPGROUND

Scenic rating: 6

on the Klamath River

Map 1.1, page 79

This 50-acre resort offers 3,000 feet of Klamath River frontage, grassy tent sites, berry picking, access to the ocean, and hiking trails nearby. And, of course, in the fall it has salmon and steelhead, the main attraction on the lower Klamath. A boat launch is about 1.5 miles from the resort. Nature trails are on the property, and there is room for bike riding. River swimming is popular in summer. A nightly campfire is usually available. Organized recreation is available in summer. A free pancake breakfast is offered to campers on Sundays.

Campsites, facilities: There are 134 sites for RVs of any length and 50 tent sites. Many RV sites have full or partial hookups (30 amps) and are pull-through. Picnic tables and fire rings are provided at the tent sites. Drinking water, restrooms with flush toilets and showers, seasonal heated swimming pool, recreation hall, general store, playground, dump station, coin laundry, cable TV, ice, firewood, bait and tackle, fish-cleaning station, fishing guide service, group facilities, arcade, basketball, volleyball, badminton, shuffleboard, horseshoes, table tennis, croquet, and tetherball are available. Leashed pets are permitted.

Reservations, fees: Reservations are accepted at 800/701-7275. RV sites are $32.50–39.50 per night, tent sites are $24.50–29.50 per night; $4 per night for each additional vehicle, $4 per person per night for more than two people. Weekly and monthly rates are available. Some credit cards accepted. Open April through October.

Directions: From Eureka, drive north on U.S. 101 to Klamath. Just after crossing the Klamath River/Golden Bear Bridge, take the Terwer Valley/Highway 169 exit. At the stop sign, turn left, drive under the highway and continue a short distance west to the campground.

Contact: Klamath's Camper Corral, 707/482-5741, www.campercorral.net.

22 STEELHEAD LODGE

Scenic rating: 6

on the Klamath River

Map 1.1, page 79

Many anglers use this park as headquarters when the salmon and steelhead get going in August. The park has grassy sites near the Klamath River.

Campsites, facilities: There are 24 sites for tents or RVs of any length (full hookups); some sites are pull-through. Picnic tables are provided. Drinking water, restrooms with flush toilets and showers, and ice are available. A bar, restaurant, and motel are also available. Some facilities are wheelchair-accessible. Leashed pets are permitted.

Reservations, fees: Reservations are required. RV sites are $30 per night, tent sites are $15 per night. Weekly and monthly rates available. Some credit cards accepted. Open February through October.

Directions: From Eureka, drive north on U.S. 101 to Klamath and the junction with Highway 169. Turn east on Highway 169 and drive 3.2 miles to Terwer Riffle Road. Turn right (south) on Terwer Riffle Road and drive one block to Steelhead Lodge on the right.

Contact: Steelhead Lodge, 330 Terwer Riffle Rd., Klamath, 707/482-8145.

23 TERWER PARK

Scenic rating: 7

on the Klamath River

Map 1.1, page 79

This RV park is situated near the Terwer Riffle, one of the better shore-fishing spots for steelhead and salmon on the lower Klamath River. You'll find grassy sites, river access, and some fair trails along the Klamath. When the salmon arrive in late August and September, Terwer Riffle can be loaded with fish, as well as boaters and shore anglers—a wild scene. Note that at this park, tent campers are separated from the RV park, with tent camping at a grassy area near the river. Some sites are taken by monthly renters.

Campsites, facilities: There are 35 sites with full hookups (30 amps) for RVs up to 34 feet, and a separate tent area. Several sites are pull-through. Five cabins are also available.

Picnic tables are provided. Restrooms with flush toilets and showers are available. A pulley boat launch is nearby. Leashed pets are permitted.

Reservations, fees: Reservations are accepted. RV sites are $25 per night, tent sites are $20 per night, $5 per night for each additional vehicle. Weekly and monthly rates available. Open April through October.

Directions: From Eureka, drive north on U.S. 101 to Klamath and the junction with Highway 169. Turn east on Highway 169 and drive 3.5 miles to Terwer Riffle Road. Turn right on Terwer Riffle Road and drive two blocks, then bear right on Terwer Riffle Road and continue five blocks (about 0.5 mile) to the park at the end of the road.

Contact: Terwer Park, 641 Terwer Riffle Road, Klamath, 707/482-3855.

24 GOLD BLUFFS BEACH

Scenic rating: 8

in Prairie Creek Redwoods State Park

Map 1.1, page 79

The campsites here are set in a sandy, exposed area with windbreaks and with a huge, expansive beach on one side and a backdrop of 100- to 200-foot cliffs on the other side. You can walk for miles at this beach, often without seeing another soul, and there is a great trail routed north through forest, with many hidden little waterfalls. In addition, Fern Canyon Trail, one of the best 30-minute hikes in California, is at the end of Davison Road. Hikers walk along a stream in a narrow canyon, its vertical walls covered with magnificent ferns. There are some herds of elk in the area, often right along the access road. These camps are rarely used in the winter because of the region's heavy rain and winds. The expanse of beach here is awesome, covering 10 miles of huge, pristine ocean frontage. (See Elk Prairie in this chapter for more information about Prairie Creek Redwoods.)

Campsites, facilities: There are 26 sites for tents or RVs up to 24 feet (no hookups). There is one backcountry site (#25). No trailers or vehicles wider than eight feet. Fire grills, food lockers, and picnic tables are provided. Drinking water and restrooms with flush toilets and showers are available. Leashed pets are permitted.

Reservations, fees: Reservations are not accepted. Sites are $35 per night, $8 per night for each additional vehicle. The backcountry site is $5 per night; a free permit is required. Open year-round, weather permitting.

Directions: From Eureka, drive north on U.S. 101 for 45 miles to Orick. At Orick, continue north on U.S. 101 for three miles to Davison Road. Turn left (west) on Davison Road and drive six miles to the campground on the left. Note: No vehicles more than 24 feet long or eight feet wide are permitted on gravel Davison Road, which is narrow and very bumpy.

Contact: Redwood National and State Parks, 707/465-2146 or 707/464-6101, www.nps.gov/redw; Prairie Creek Redwoods State Park, 707/465-7347, Visitors Center 707/465-7354, www.parks.ca.gov.

25 ELK PRAIRIE

Scenic rating: 9

in Prairie Creek Redwoods State Park

Map 1.1, page 79

A small herd of Roosevelt elk wander free in this remarkable 14,000-acre park. Great opportunities for photographs abound, including a group of about five elk often found right along the highway and access roads. Where there are meadows, there are elk; it's about that simple. An elky here, an elky there, making this one of the best places to see wildlife in California. Remember that these are wild animals, they are huge, and they can be unpredictable; in other words, enjoy them, but don't harass them or get too close.

This park consists of old-growth coastal

redwoods, prairie lands, and 10 miles of scenic, open beach (Gold Bluff Beach). The interior of the park can be reached by 70 miles of hiking, biking, and nature trails, including a trailhead for a great bike ride at the visitors center. There are many additional trailheads and a beautiful tour of giant redwoods along the Drury Scenic Parkway. A visitors center and summer interpretive programs with guided walks and junior ranger programs are available. On the James Irvine Trail (trailhead near the visitor center), you can see world-class redwoods, Sitka spruce, western hemlock and Douglas fir in the span of a few miles. The forest understory is very dense due to moisture from coastal fog. Western azalea and rhododendron blooms, peaking in May and June, are best seen from the Rhododendron Trail. November through May, always bring your rain gear. Summer temperatures range 40–75°F; winter temperatures range 35–55°F.

Campsites, facilities: There are 76 sites for tents or RVs up to 27 feet (no hookups), and one hike-in/bike-in site. Picnic tables, fire rings, and bear-proof food lockers are provided. Drinking water and restrooms with flush toilets and coin showers are available. Some facilities are wheelchair-accessible. Leashed pets are permitted.

Reservations, fees: Reservations are accepted January–September at 800/444-7275 (800/444-PARK) or www.reserveamerica.com ($8 reservation fee). Sites are first-come, first-served September–January. Sites are $35 per night, $8 per night for each additional vehicle, $5 per person per night for hike-in/bike-in site. Open year-round.

Directions: From Eureka, drive 45 miles north on U.S. 101 to Orick. At Orick, continue north on U.S. 101 for five miles to the Newton B. Drury Scenic Parkway. Take the exit for the Newton B. Drury Scenic Parkway and drive north for a mile to the park. Turn left at the park entrance.

Contact: Redwood National and State Parks, 707/465-2146 or 707/464-6101, www.nps.gov/redw; Prairie Creek Redwoods State Park, 707/465-7347 or Visitors Center 707/465-7354, www.parks.ca.gov.

26 STONE LAGOON BOAT-IN

🚶 🏊 ⛵ 🎣 5% ⛺

Scenic rating: 10

in Humboldt Lagoons State Park

Map 1.1, page 79   **BEST (**

Virtually nobody knows about this ideal spot for canoeists. While Stone Lagoon is directly adjacent to U.S. 101, the camp is set in a cove that is out of sight of the highway. That makes it a secret spot for a lucky few. It is a great place to explore by canoe or kayak, especially paddling upstream to the lagoon's inlet creek. After setting up camp, it is possible to hike to a secluded sand spit and stretch of beachfront. You may see elk in this area on the rare occasion. The water is usually calm in the morning but often gets choppy from afternoon winds. Translation: Get your paddling done early on Stone Lagoon. There is also good fishing for cutthroat trout here. The early 1900s saw several dairy ranches established along Stone Lagoon's shore; however, today's regenerated marshland habitat is home to a wide range of marsh flora, as well as birdlife and other creatures.

Campsites, facilities: There are six primitive tent sites accessible by boat only. There is no drinking water. Picnic tables, food lockers, and fire rings are provided. Pit toilets are available. Garbage must be packed out. No pets are allowed.

Reservations, fees: Reservations are not accepted. Sites are $20 per night. All campers must register at the Patrick's Point State Park entrance station to obtain the combination to the gate lock. Open year-round.

Directions: From Eureka, drive 41 miles north on U.S. 101 (15 miles north of Trinidad) to Stone Lagoon. At Stone Lagoon, turn left at the visitors information center. The boat-in campground is in a cove directly across the lagoon from the visitors center. The campsites are dispersed in an area covering about 300 yards in the landing area.

Contact: Humboldt Lagoons State Park, Trinidad Sector, 707/677-3132 or 707/488-2169, www.parks.ca.gov; Patrick's Point State Park, 4150 Patrick's Point Dr., 707/677-3570.

27 DRY LAGOON WALK-IN
🚶 🚐 5% ⛺

Scenic rating: 8

in Humboldt Lagoons State Park

Map 1.1, page 79

This is a walk-in camp; that is, you need to walk about 200 yards from the parking area to reach the campsites. (Insider's tip: To find out if space is available, call Patrick's Point State Park.) This makes it a dream for members of the 5 Percent Club, because many tourists are unwilling to walk at all. It is beautiful here, set in the woods, with ocean views and beach access. In the early 1900s, Dry Lagoon was drained by farmers and several types of crops were attempted. The farming projects were colossal failures and the lagoon was allowed to refill. This spot receives 60 inches of rain, on average, in winter; spring and fall are pleasant. In summer, it can be foggy, cool, and damp, so bring warm, layered clothing. The park has a visitors center and bookstore. A highlight here is a three-mile segment of the Coastal Trail.

Note: This park is on the closure list developed by the California Department of Parks, pending final state budget decisions or the possible transfer of park management to other park agencies or volunteer groups.

Campsites, facilities: There are six primitive tent sites. Picnic tables, fire rings, and food lockers are provided. Pit toilets are available. There is no drinking water. Garbage must be packed out. No pets are allowed.

Reservations, fees: Reservations are not accepted. Sites are $20 per night. All campers must register at the Patrick's Point State Park entrance station to obtain the combination to the gate lock. Open year-round.

Directions: From Eureka, drive north on U.S. 101 for 22 miles to Trinidad. At Trinidad, continue north on U.S. 101 for 13 miles to Dry Lagoon Road. Turn left and drive approximately one mile to the gate at the end of the road. Open gate combination (register at entrance station) and drive 0.25 mile to the trailhead. Park and walk 200 yards to the camp.

Contact: Humboldt Lagoons State Park, Trinidad Sector, 707/677-3132 or 707/488-2169, www.parks.ca.gov; Patrick's Point State Park, 4150 Patrick's Point Dr., 707/677-3570.

28 BIG LAGOON COUNTY PARK
🚣 🎣 🚐 🛥 🐕 🏕 ♿ 🚐 ⛺

Scenic rating: 7

north of Trinidad overlooking the Pacific Ocean

Map 1.1, page 79

This is a remarkable, huge lagoon that borders the Pacific Ocean. It provides good boating, excellent exploring, fair fishing, and good duck hunting in the winter. It's a good spot to paddle a canoe around on a calm day. A lot of out-of-towners cruise by, note the lagoon's proximity to the ocean, and figure it must be saltwater. Wrong! Not only is it freshwater, but it provides a long shot for anglers trying for rainbow trout. One reason not many RV drivers stop here is that most of them are drawn farther north (another eight miles) to Freshwater Lagoon.

Campsites, facilities: There are 25 sites for tents or small RVs (no hookups). Picnic tables and fire grills are provided. Drinking water and restrooms with flush toilets and showers are available. A boat ramp is also available. Some facilities are wheelchair-accessible. Leashed pets are permitted.

Reservations, fees: Reservations are not accepted. Sites are $20 per night per vehicle, $5 per night for additional vehicle, $2 per pet per night. Maximum stay is 10 days. Open year-round.

Directions: From Eureka, drive 22 miles north on U.S. 101 to Trinidad. At Trinidad, continue north on U.S. 101 for eight miles to Big Lagoon Park Road. Turn left (west) at Big Lagoon Park Road and drive two miles to the park.

Contact: Humboldt County Public Works, 707/445-7651, www.co.humboldt.ca.us; Humboldt Lagoons State Park Visitor Center, 707/488-2041.

29 PATRICK'S POINT STATE PARK

Scenic rating: 9

near Trinidad

Map 1.1, page 79

This pretty park covers 640 acres of coastal headlands and is filled with Sitka spruce, dramatic ocean lookouts, and several beautiful beaches, including one with agates, one with tidepools, and another with an expansive stretch of beachfront leading to a lagoon. You can see it best on the Rim Trail, which has many little cut-off routes to the lookouts and down to the beaches. The campground is sheltered in the forest, and while it is often foggy and damp in the summer, it is always beautiful. A Native American village, constructed by the Yurok tribe, is also here. At the north end of the park, a short hike to see the bizarre "Octopus Trees" is a good side trip, with trees that are growing atop downed logs, their root systems exposed like octopus tentacles; the trail here loops through a grove of old-growth Sitka spruce. In addition, there are several miles of pristine beach to the north that extends to the lagoons. Interpretive programs are available. The forest here is dense, with spruce, hemlock, pine, fir, and red alder covering an ocean headland. Night and morning fog are common almost year-round, and there are periods when it doesn't lift for days. This area gets 60 inches of rain per year on average. For camping, plan on making reservations.

Campsites, facilities: There are 85 sites for tents or RVs (no hookups), 39 sites for RVs up to 31 feet, and two group sites for up to 100 people. Fire grills, storage lockers, and picnic tables are provided. Drinking water and restrooms with flush toilets and coin showers are available. Some facilities are wheelchair-accessible. Leashed pets are permitted at campsites, but not on trails or beaches.

Reservations, fees: Site-specific reservations are accepted at 800/444-7275 (800/444-PARK) or www.reserveamerica.com ($8 reservation fee). Abalone and Penn Creek sites are $35 per night, Agate Campground sites are $35–45 per night, $8 per night for each additional vehicle, $300 per night for the group sites. Open year-round.

Directions: From Eureka, drive north on U.S. 101 for 22 miles to Trinidad. At Trinidad, continue north on U.S. 101 for 5.5 miles to Patrick's Point Drive. Take that exit and at the stop sign turn left and drive 0.5 mile to the park entrance.

Contact: Patrick's Point State Park, 707/677-3570, www.parks.ca.gov.

30 SOUNDS OF THE SEA RV PARK

Scenic rating: 6

in Trinidad

Map 1.1, page 79

The Trinidad area, about 20 miles north of Eureka, is one of the great places on this planet. Nearby Patrick's Point State Park is one of the highlights, with a Sitka spruce forest, beautiful coastal lookouts, a great easy hike on the Rim Trail, and access to several secluded beaches. To the nearby south at Trinidad Head is a small harbor and dock, with deep-sea and salmon fishing trips available. A breezy beach is to the immediate north of the Seascape Restaurant. A bonus at this privately operated RV park is good berry picking in season.

Campsites, facilities: There are 52 sites with

full hookups (30 and 50 amps) for tents or RVs of any length; some sites are pull-through. RV rentals and four park-model cabins are also available. Picnic tables and fire rings are provided at most sites. Restrooms with showers, cable TV, Wi-Fi, exercise room and indoor spa (fee), bicycle rentals, dump station, coin laundry, convenience store, gift shop, propane, firewood, and ice are available. Leashed pets are permitted with certain restrictions.

Reservations, fees: Reservations are accepted at 800/598-0600. RV sites are $30–45 per night, tent sites are $30–38 per night, $3–5 per person per night for more than two people. Some credit cards accepted. Open year-round.

Directions: From Eureka, drive north on U.S. 101 for 28 miles to Trinidad. In Trinidad, continue north on U.S. 101 for five miles to the Patrick's Point exit. Take the Patrick's Point exit, turn left, and drive 0.5 mile to the park.

Contact: Sounds of the Sea RV Park, 707/677-3271, www.soundsofthesea.us.

31 SYLVAN HARBOR RV PARK AND CABINS

Scenic rating: 8

in Trinidad

Map 1.1, page 79

This park is designed as an RV park and fish camp, with cleaning tables and canning facilities available on-site. It is a short distance from the boat hoist at the Trinidad pier. Beauty surrounds Sylvan Harbor on all sides for miles. Visitors come to enjoy the various beaches, go agate hunting, or look for driftwood on the beach. Nearby Patrick's Point State Park is an excellent side-trip getaway. This is one of several privately operated parks in the Trinidad area, offering a choice of shaded or open sites. (For more information about recreation options nearby, see Sounds of the Sea RV Park listing.)

Campsites, facilities: There are 73 sites with full hookups (30 amps) for RVs up to 35 feet. No tents. A storage shed and cable TV are provided. Three cabins are available. Restrooms with showers, fish-cleaning stations, fish smokers, canning facilities, coin laundry, and propane are available. Leashed pets are permitted.

Reservations, fees: Reservations are accepted for cabins only. Sites are $28 per night, $5 per person per night for more than two people. Weekly and monthly rates available during the summer. Open year-round, weather permitting.

Directions: From Eureka, drive north on U.S. 101 for 28 miles to the Trinidad exit. Take that exit to Main Street. Turn left on Main Street and drive 0.1 mile under the freeway to Patrick's Point Drive. Turn right on Patrick's Point Drive and drive one mile to the campground on the right at 875 Patrick's Point Drive.

Contact: Sylvan Harbor RV Park and Cabins, 707/677-9988, www.sylvanharbor.com.

32 VIEW CREST LODGE

Scenic rating: 8

in Trinidad

Map 1.1, page 79

View Crest Lodge is one of the premium spots in Trinidad, with pretty cottages available as well as campsites for RVs and tents. A bonus here is the remarkable flights of swallows, many of which have nests at the cottages. Recreation options include deep-sea and salmon fishing at Trinidad Harbor to the nearby south, and outstanding easy hiking at Patrick's Point State Park to the nearby north.

Campsites, facilities: There are 36 sites with full hookups (20 and 30 amps) for RVs of any length and a separate area for 12 tent sites. Some sites are pull-through. Twelve cottages are also available. Picnic tables and fire rings are provided. Restrooms with showers, cable

TV, WiFi, a coin laundry, fish cleaning station, and firewood are available. Leashed pets are permitted only in the campground.

Reservations, fees: Reservations are accepted. RV sites are $27–38 per night, tent sites are $27, $3 per person per night for more than two people over age 12. Monthly rates available. Some credit cards accepted. Open year-round.

Directions: From Eureka, drive north on U.S. 101 for 28 miles to Trinidad. Take the Patrick's Point State Park exit. Continue north for five miles to Patrick's Point Drive. Turn left and drive 0.9 mile to the lodge on the left.

Contact: View Crest Lodge, 707/677-3393, www.viewcrestlodge.com.

33 EMERALD FOREST

Scenic rating: 5

in Trinidad

Map 1.1, page 79

This campground is set on 12 acres of redwoods, often dark and wet, with the ocean at Trinidad Head only about a five-minute drive away. The campground owners emphasize that they are a vacation and overnight park only, and not a mobile home or long-term park.

Campsites, facilities: There are 46 sites with full or partial hookups (30 amps) for RVs up to 45 feet and 30 tent sites. Some sites are pull-through. There are also 19 cabins. Picnic tables, fire rings, and barbecues are provided. Restrooms, showers, free cable TV in RV sites, playground, convenience store, ice, firewood, coin laundry, group facilities, fish-cleaning station, dump station, propane, telephone and modem hookups, Wi-Fi, volleyball, horseshoes, badminton, and video arcade are available. Leashed pets are permitted, except in the tent sites or cabins.

Reservations, fees: Reservations are recommended in the summer. RV sites are $24–43 per night, $3 per person per night for more than two people; tent sites are $24–30 per

night. Winter rates available. Some credit cards accepted. Open year-round.

Directions: From Eureka, drive north on U.S. 101 for 28 miles to the Trinidad exit. Take that exit to Main Street. Turn left on Main Street and drive 0.1 mile under the freeway to Patrick's Point Drive. Turn right on Patrick's Point Drive and drive 0.9 mile north to the campground.

Contact: Emerald Forest, 753 Patrick's Point Drive, 707/677-3554, www.rvintheredwoods.com.

34 HIDDEN CREEK

Scenic rating: 5

in Trinidad

Map 1.1, page 79

To tell you the truth, there really isn't much hidden about this RV park, but you might be hard-pressed to find year-round Parker Creek. Regardless, it is still in a pretty location in Trinidad, with the Trinidad pier, adjacent harbor, restaurants, and beach all within a drive of just a minute or two. Deep-sea fishing for salmon, lingcod, and rockfish is available on boats out of Trinidad Harbor. Crab and albacore tuna are also caught here, and there's beachcombing for agates and driftwood on the beach to the immediate north. Note that half of the sites are filled with long-term renters.

Campsites, facilities: There are 56 sites with full or partial hookups (30 and 50 amps) for RVs up to 40 feet, and a grassy area for tents. Six park-model cabins are also available. Picnic tables are provided. Cable TV, restrooms with showers, fish-cleaning station, ice, picnic area, and a dump station are available. Leashed pets are permitted.

Reservations, fees: Reservations are recommended in the summer. RV sites are $30 per night, tent sites are $20 per night, $2 per person per night for more than two people. Long-term rates available. Open year-round.

Directions: From Eureka, drive north on

U.S. 101 for 28 miles to Trinidad. Take the Trinidad exit to the stop sign. Turn right at Westhaven Drive and drive a short distance to the RV park on the left.

Contact: Hidden Creek RV Park, 199 North Westhaven, 707/677-3775, www.hidden-creekrvpark.com.

35 CLAM BEACH COUNTY PARK

Scenic rating: 7

near McKinleyville

Map 1.2, page 80

Here awaits a beach that seems to stretch on forever, one of the great places to bring a lover, dog, children, or, hey, all three. While the campsites are a bit exposed, making winds out of the north a problem in the spring, the direct beach access largely makes up for it. The park gets its name from the fair clamming that is available, but you must come equipped with a clam gun or special clam shovel, and then be out when minus low tides arrive at daybreak. Most people just enjoy playing tag with the waves, taking long romantic walks, or throwing sticks for the dog.

Campsites, facilities: There are nine tent sites and a parking lot for nine RVs of any length (no hookups). Picnic tables and fire rings are provided. Drinking water and vault toilets are available. Propane gas, grocery store, and a coin laundry are available in McKinleyville. Some facilities are wheelchair-accessible. Leashed pets are permitted.

Reservations, fees: Reservations are not accepted. Sites are $15 per night per vehicle, $5 per night for one additional vehicle, $8 per person per night for hike-in/bike-in, $2 per pet per night. Maximum stay is three days. Open year-round.

Directions: From Eureka, drive north on U.S. 101 to McKinleyville. Continue past McKinleyville to the Clam Beach Park exit. Take that exit and turn west at the sign for Clam Beach.

Drive two blocks to the campground, which is adjacent to Little River State Beach.

Contact: Humboldt County Public Works, 707/445-7651, www.co.humboldt.ca.us.

36 MAD RIVER RAPIDS RV PARK

Scenic rating: 7

in Arcata

Map 1.2, page 80

This park is near the farmlands on the outskirts of town, in a pastoral, quiet setting. There is a great bike ride nearby on a trail routed along the Mad River, and it is also excellent for taking a dog for a walk. Nearby Arcata is a unique town, a bit of the old and a bit of the new, and the Arcata Marsh at the north end of Humboldt Bay provides a scenic and easy bicycle trip, as well as an excellent destination for hiking, sightseeing, and bird-watching. About half of the sites are filled with long-term renters.

Campsites, facilities: There are 92 sites with full hookups (30 and 50 amps) for RVs of any length; some sites are pull-through. Picnic tables are provided. Fire grills are provided at two sites. Cable TV, Wi-Fi, a dump station, restrooms with showers, a recreation room, tennis courts, fitness room, playground, basketball courts, jogging trail, arcade, table tennis, horseshoe pits, heated seasonal swimming pool, spa, group facilities, restaurant and bar, convenience store, RV supplies, and coin laundry are available. A motel is adjacent to the park. Some facilities are wheelchair-accessible. Leashed pets are permitted.

Reservations, fees: Reservations are accepted at 800/822-7776. Sites are $36–45 per night, $3 per night per additional vehicle, $3 per person per night for more than two people. Some credit cards accepted. Weekly and monthly rates available. Open year-round.

Directions: From the junction of U.S. 101 and Highway 299 in Arcata, drive 0.25 mile north on U.S. 101 to the Giuntoli Lane/Janes Road exit. Take that exit and turn left (west) on Janes Road and drive two blocks to the park on the left.

Contact: Mad River Rapids RV Park, 707/822-7275, www.madriverrv.com.

37 EUREKA KOA

Scenic rating: 2

in Eureka

Map 1.2, page 80

This is a year-round KOA camp for U.S. 101 cruisers looking for a layover spot in Eureka. A bonus here is a few of those little KOA Kamping Kabins, the log-style jobs that win on cuteness alone. The closest significant recreation option is the Arcata Marsh on Humboldt Bay, a richly diverse spot with good trails for biking and hiking or just parking and looking at the water. Another option is excellent salmon fishing in June, July, and August.

Campsites, facilities: There are 140 sites with full or partial hookups (30 and 50 amps) for RVs of any length, 30 tent sites, and three hike-in/bike-in sites. Most RV sites are pull-through. Ten camping cabins and two cottages are also available. Picnic tables and fire pits are provided. Drinking water, restrooms with flush toilets and showers, cable TV, playground, recreation room, seasonal heated swimming pool, two spas, convenience store, coin laundry, horseshoe pits, volleyball and basketball court, dump station, propane, ice, firewood, fax machine, and Wi-Fi are available. Some facilities are wheelchair-accessible. Leashed pets are permitted.

Reservations, fees: Reservations are accepted at 800/562-3136. RV sites are $40–45 per night, tent sites are $28–35 per night, $3 per person per night for more than two people, $17 per night for hike-in/bike-in sites, $3 per pet per night, $2 per night for each additional vehicle. Some credit cards accepted. Open year-round.

Directions: From Eureka, drive north on U.S.

101 for four miles to KOA Drive (well signed on east side of highway). Turn right on KOA Drive and drive a short distance to the end of the road.

Contact: Eureka KOA, 707/822-4243, http://koa.com/campgrounds/eureka.

38 SAMOA BOAT RAMP COUNTY PARK

Scenic rating: 7

on Humboldt Bay near Eureka

Map 1.2, page 80

The nearby vicinity of the boat ramp, with access to Humboldt Bay and the Pacific Ocean, makes this a star attraction for campers towing their fishing boats. Near the campground you'll find good beachcombing and clamming at low tides, and a chance to see a huge variety of seabirds, highlighted by egrets and herons. There's a reason: Directly across the bay is the Humboldt Bay National Wildlife Refuge. Adjacent to the park is the Samoa Dunes Recreation Area, which is popular with ATV enthusiasts who are allowed to ride on the beach. This park is set near the famed all-you-can-eat, logger-style Samoa Cookhouse. The park is on the bay, not on the ocean.

Campsites, facilities: There are 25 sites for tents or RVs of any length (no hookups). Overflow camping for tents or RVs of any length is also available in a parking lot. Picnic tables and fire grills are provided. Drinking water and restrooms with flush toilets and coin showers are available. A boat ramp, grocery store, propane, and a coin laundry are available in Eureka (about five miles away). Leashed pets are permitted.

Reservations, fees: Reservations are not accepted. Sites are $20 per night per vehicle, $5 per night for each additional vehicle, $8 per person per night for hike-in/bike-in, $2 per pet per night. Maximum stay is seven days. Open year-round.

Directions: From U.S. 101 in Eureka, turn

west on Highway 255 and drive two miles until it dead-ends at New Navy Base Road. At New Navy Base Road, turn left and drive five miles to the end of the Samoa Peninsula and the campground entrance.

Contact: Humboldt County Public Works, 707/445-7651, www.co.humboldt.ca.us.

39 E-Z LANDING RV PARK AND MARINA

Scenic rating: 6

on Humboldt Bay

Map 1.2, page 80

In July and August, big schools of king salmon often teem just west of the entrance of Humboldt Bay. E-Z Landing provides a good base camp for salmon fishing, with a nearby boat ramp with access to Humboldt Bay. It's not the prettiest camp in the world, with quite a bit of asphalt, but most people use this camp as a simple parking spot for sleeping and getting down to the business of the day: fishing. This spot is ideal for ocean fishing, clamming, beachcombing, and boating. There are a few long-term and seasonal renters here.

Campsites, facilities: There are 45 RV sites with full hookups (30 amps); some sites are pull-through. Restrooms with flush toilets and showers, marine gas, ice, coin laundry, bait, and boat slips are available. Some facilities are wheelchair-accessible. Leashed pets are permitted.

Reservations, fees: Reservations are accepted. RV sites are $20 per night. Some credit cards accepted. Open year-round.

Directions: From Eureka, drive 3.5 miles south on U.S. 101 to King Salmon Avenue. Turn west (right) on King Salmon Avenue (it becomes Buhne Dr.) and drive for 0.5 mile to where the road turns. Turn left (south) on Buhne Drive and go 0.5 mile to the park on the left.

Contact: E-Z Landing RV Park and Marina, 1875 Buhne Dr., 707/442-1118.

40 JOHNNY'S MARINA AND RV PARK

Scenic rating: 5

on Humboldt Bay near Eureka

Map 1.2, page 80

This is a good base camp for salmon fishing during the peak season—always call, since the season changes each year as set by the Department of Fish and Game. Mooring for private boats is available, a nice plus for campers trailering boats. Other recreation activities include beachcombing, clamming, and perch fishing from shore. The owners have run this place since 1948. Note that a number of sites are filled with long-term renters, usually anglers who come for the season. So when the fishing is good, more space is tied up.

Campsites, facilities: There are 53 sites with full hookups (30 and 50 amps) for self-contained RVs up to 38 feet. There are no toilets or showers. Coin laundry and a boat dock are available. Leashed pets are permitted.

Reservations, fees: Reservations are accepted. Sites are $25 per night, $1 per person per night for more than two people. Open year-round.

Directions: From Eureka, drive 3.5 miles south on U.S. 101 to King Salmon Avenue. Turn west (right) on King Salmon Avenue (it becomes Buhne Drive). Continue about 0.5 mile to the park on the left.

Contact: Johnny's Marina and RV Park, 1821 Buhne Drive, 707/442-2284.

41 HONEYDEW CREEK

Scenic rating: 6

in the King Range National Conservation Area

Map 1.2, page 80

This little known and little used camp is located on Honeydew Creek, a tributary to the Mattole River in California's "Lost Coast." In summer, it's a hideaway that you can use as base camp to explore the Lost Coast and the

King Range. In late winter, steelhead fishing can be good on the Mattole River between Honeydew and Petrolia, providing for good access and stream flows. One problem is rain. It can pound here and the river can get too high to fish; winters with 100 inches of rain are typical in average-to-wet years.

Campsites, facilities: There are five sites for tents or RVs (no hookups). Picnic tables and fire rings are provided. Vault toilets are available, but there is no drinking water; creek water is available but must be purified before drinking. Some facilities are wheelchair accessible.

Reservations, fees: Reservations are not accepted. Sites are $8 per night.

Directions: From Garberville, drive north on U.S. 101 to the South Fork-Honeydew exit. Turn west on South Fork-Honeydew Road and drive to Wilder Ridge Road in Honeydew. Turn left (south) on Wilder Ridge Road and drive one mile to the campground.

Contact: Bureau of Land Management, Arcata Field Office, 707/825-2300, www.blm.gov/ca.

42 VAN DUZEN COUNTY PARK: SWIMMER'S DELIGHT

Scenic rating: 6

on the Van Duzen River

Map 1.2, page 80

This campground is set near the headwaters of the Van Duzen River, one of the Eel River's major tributaries. The river is subject to tremendous fluctuations in flows and height, so low in the fall that it is often temporarily closed to fishing by the Department of Fish and Game, so high in the winter that only fools would stick their toes in. For a short period in late spring, it provides a benign run for rafting and canoeing, putting in at Grizzly Creek and taking out at Van Duzen. In October, you'll find an excellent salmon fishing spot where the Van Duzen enters the Eel.

Campsites, facilities: There are 30 sites for tents or small RVs; some sites have partial hookups (30 amps). Picnic tables and fire grills are provided. Drinking water and restrooms with flush toilets and coin showers are available. A grocery store and coin laundry are available nearby. Some facilities are wheelchair-accessible. Leashed pets are permitted in the campground, but not on the beach.

Reservations, fees: Reservations are not accepted. Sites are $20 per night, $8 per person per night for hike-in/bike-in, $5 per night for each additional vehicle, $2 per pet per night. Maximum stay is 10 days. Open year-round.

Directions: From Eureka, drive south on U.S. 101 to the junction of Highway 36 at Alton. Turn east on Highway 36 and drive 12 miles to the campground.

Contact: Humboldt County Public Works, 707/445-7651, www.co.humboldt.ca.us.

43 GRIZZLY CREEK REDWOODS STATE PARK

Scenic rating: 8

near Bridgeville

Map 1.2, page 80

Most summer vacationers hit the campgrounds on the Redwood Highway, that is, U.S. 101. However, this camp is just far enough off the beaten path to provide some semblance of seclusion. It is set in redwoods, quite beautiful, with fair hiking and good access to the adjacent Van Duzen River. The park encompasses only a few acres, yet it is very intimate. There are 4.5 miles of hiking trails, a visitors center with exhibits, and a bookstore. The Cheatham Grove in this park is an exceptional stand of coast redwoods. Fishing is catch-and-release only with barbless hooks. Nearby attractions include the Victorian village of Ferndale and Fort Humboldt to the north, Humboldt Redwoods State Park to the south, and Ruth Lake to the more distant east. Insider's tip: Half of the park borders Highway 36, and you can hear highway noise from some campsites.

Note: Grizzly Creek Redwoods was on the state park closure list, however it will remain open until at least May 15, 2013 thanks to a donation from the Save the Redwoods League.

Campsites, facilities: There are 10 tent sites, nine sites for tents or small RVs, 11 sites for RVs up to 30 feet or trailers up to 24 feet, one hike-in/bike-in site, and one group site. No hookups. Picnic tables, food lockers, and fire grills are provided. Drinking water and restrooms with flush toilets and showers are available. A grocery store is available within 3.5 miles. Some facilities are wheelchair-accessible. Leashed pets are permitted in the campground, but not on trails or beach area.

Reservations, fees: Reservations are not accepted; the group site may be reserved by calling 707/777-3683. Sites are $35 per night, $8 per night for each additional vehicle, $5 per person per night for hike-in/bike-in site, $90 per night for the group site. Open year-round.

Directions: From Eureka, drive south on U.S. 101 to the junction of Highway 36 at Alton. Turn east on Highway 36 and drive about 17 miles to the campground on the right.

Contact: Humboldt County Parks and Recreation, 707/445-7651, http://co.humboldt.ca.us; Grizzly Creek Redwoods State Park, 707/777-3683, www.parks.ca.gov.

44 CUNEO CREEK HORSE CAMP
🥾 🚴 🏊 ⛵ 🎣 🚐 ⛺

Scenic rating: 7

in Humboldt Redwoods State Park

Map 1.2, page 80

This is a horse camp set within Humboldt Redwoods State Park near the South Fork Eel River. The site is woodsy and far enough away from other camps in the park to often make it feel all your own. Though it is primarily a camp set up for equestrians, you can also use it as a base camp for kayak trips on the nearby South Fork Eel, or for hiking and biking trips nearby.

Campsites, facilities: There are five individual and two group sites for tents and RVs for up to 25 and 65 people, with parking space for horse trailers. Picnic tables and fire rings are provided. Drinking water, coin showers, and flush toilets are available. There are water troughs and corrals for horses. Some facilities are wheelchair accessible. Leashed pets are permitted.

Reservations, fees: Reservations are accepted May–September at 800/444-7275 (800/444-PARK) or www.reserveamerica.com ($8 reservation fee). Individual sites are $35 per night, $8 per night for each additional vehicle, $135–200 for group sites. Open mid-April to mid-October.

Directions: From Eureka, drive south on U.S. 101 about 43 miles to the Honeydew exit (if you reach Weott, you have gone two miles too far). At Mattole Road, turn west and drive eight miles to the Cuneo Creek Horse Campground sign. Turn right onto the entrance road and continue to the campground.

Contact: Humboldt Redwoods State Park, 707/946-2472; Visitor Center, 707/946-2263, fax 707/946-2326, www.parks.ca.gov.

45 ALBEE CREEK
🥾 🏊 🚣 🐕 ♿ 🚐 ⛺

Scenic rating: 8

in Humboldt Redwoods State Park

Map 1.2, page 80

Humboldt Redwoods State Park is a massive sprawl of forest that is known for some unusual giant trees in the Federation Grove and Big Tree Area. The park covers nearly 53,000 acres, including more than 17,000 acres of old-growth coast redwoods. It has 100 miles of hiking trails, many excellent, both short and long. The camp is set in a redwood grove, and the smell of these trees has a special magic. Nearby Albee Creek, a benign trickle most of the year, can flood in the winter after heavy rains. Seasonal interpretive programs, campfire talks, nature walks, and junior ranger programs are available.

Campsites, facilities: There are 37 sites for tents or RVs up to 33 feet and trailers up to 24 feet (no hookups); five environmental sites; and a hike-in/bike-in site. Picnic tables, fire grills, and food lockers are provided. Drinking water, restrooms with flush toilets and showers, and firewood are available. Some facilities are wheelchair-accessible. Leashed pets are permitted.

Reservations, fees: Reservations are accepted at 800/444-7275 (800/444-PARK) or www. reserveamerica.com ($8 reservation fee). Sites are $35 per night. Open Memorial Day weekend through mid-October.

Directions: From Eureka, drive south on U.S. 101 about 43 miles to the Honeydew exit (if you reach Weott, you have gone two miles too far). At Mattole Road, turn west and drive five miles to the campground on the right.

Contact: Humboldt Redwoods State Park, 707/946-2472 or 707/946-2409; Visitor Center 707/946-2263, www.parks.ca.gov.

46 BURLINGTON

Scenic rating: 7

in Humboldt Redwoods State Park

Map 1.2, page 80

This camp is one of the centerpieces of Humboldt Redwoods State Park. Humboldt is California's largest redwood state park and also includes the largest remaining contiguous old-growth coastal redwood forest in the world: the Rockefeller Forest. The trees here are thousands of years old and have never been logged; they are as pristine now as 200 years ago. The park has hundreds of miles of trails, but it is little 0.5-mile Founders Grove Nature Trail that has the quickest payoff and requires the least effort. The average rainfall here is 65 inches per year, with most occurring between October and May. Morning and evening fog in the summer keeps the temperature cool in the river basin.

At Burlington, you get shady sites with big redwood stumps that kids can play on. There's good hiking on trails routed through the redwoods, and in winter, steelhead fishing is often good on the nearby Eel River. However, this camp is often at capacity during the tourist months and sites tend to be packed close together with plenty of RVs and road noise from Avenue of the Giants a few feet away.

Campsites, facilities: There are 58 sites for tents or RVs up to 33 feet (no hookups) and trailers up to 24 feet, and three hike-in/bike-in sites. Picnic tables, fire grills, and food lockers are provided. Drinking water, restrooms with flush toilets and showers, and firewood are available. Some facilities are wheelchair-accessible. Leashed pets are permitted.

Reservations, fees: Reservations are accepted at 800/444-7275 (800/444-PARK) or www. reserveamerica.com ($8 reservation fee). Sites are $35 per night, $8 per night for each additional vehicle, $5 per person per night for hike-in/bike-in sites. Open year-round.

Directions: From Eureka, drive south on U.S. 101 for 45 miles to the Weott/Newton Road exit. Turn right on Newton Road and continue to the T junction where Newton Road meets the Avenue of the Giants. Turn left on the Avenue of the Giants and drive two miles to the campground entrance on the left.

Contact: Humboldt Redwoods State Park, 707/946-1811 or 707/946-2409; Visitor Center 707/946-2263, www.parks.ca.gov.

47 HIDDEN SPRINGS

Scenic rating: 7

in Humboldt Redwoods State Park

Map 1.2, page 80

This camp gets heavy use from May through September, but the campsites have been situated in a way that offers relative seclusion. Side trips include good hiking on trails routed through redwoods and a touring drive on Avenue of the Giants. The park has more than 100 miles of hiking trails, many of them amid spectacular giant redwoods, including Bull Creek Flats Trail and Founders Grove Nature Trail. Bears are occasionally spotted by mountain bikers on rides out to the park's outskirts. In winter, nearby High Rock on the Eel River is one of the better shoreline fishing spots for steelhead. (For more information on Humboldt Redwoods, see Albee Creek and Burlington listings.)

Campsites, facilities: There are 155 sites for tents or RVs up to 33 feet (no hookups) and trailers up to 24 feet. Picnic tables, fire grills, and food lockers are provided. Drinking water, restrooms with flush toilets and showers, and firewood are available. A grocery store and coin laundry are available within one mile in Myers Flat. Leashed pets are permitted.

Reservations, fees: Reservations are accepted at 800/444-7275 (800/444-PARK) or www. reserveamerica.com ($8 reservation fee). Sites are $35 per night, $8 per night for each additional vehicle. Open mid-April through Labor Day weekend.

Directions: From Eureka, drive south 50 miles on U.S. 101 to the Myers Flat/Avenue of the Giants exit. Continue south and drive less than a mile to the campground entrance on the left.

Contact: Humboldt Redwoods State Park, 707/943-3177 or 707/946-2409; Visitor Center 707/946-2263, www.parks.ca.gov.

48 GIANT REDWOODS RV AND CAMP

Scenic rating: 8

on the Eel River near Myers Flat

Map 1.2, page 80

This privately operated park is set in a grove of redwoods and covers 23 acres, much of it fronting the Eel River. Trip options include the scenic drive on Avenue of the Giants.

Campsites, facilities: There are 26 tent sites and 55 sites for RVs of any length. RV sites have full or partial hookups (30 amps) and some are pull-through. Picnic tables and fire rings are provided. Restrooms with showers, free Wi-Fi, cable TV, a convenience store, ice, coin laundry, playground, volleyball court, horseshoe

pits, boat launch, dog "freedom area," and a recreation room are available. A camp host is on-site. Leashed pets are permitted.

Reservations, fees: Reservations are recommended in the summer. RV sites are $35–40 per night, tent sites are $25 per night, $3 per person per night for more than two people, $5 per night for additional vehicle. Discounted winter rates. Weekly rates available. Some credit cards accepted. Open year-round, with limited facilities in winter.

Directions: From Eureka, drive south 50 miles on U.S. 101 to the Myers Flat/Avenue of the Giants exit. Turn right on Avenue of the Giants and make a quick left onto Myers Avenue. Drive 0.25 mile on Myers Avenue to the campground entrance.

Contact: Giant Redwoods RV and Camp, 351 Myers Ave., 707/943-9999, http://giantredwoodsrv.com.

49 DEAN CREEK RESORT

Scenic rating: 7

on the South Fork of the Eel River

Map 1.2, page 80

This year-round RV park is set on the South Fork of the Eel River. This is a very family-oriented resort. In the summer, it makes a good base camp for a redwood park adventure, with Humboldt Redwoods State Park (well north of here) providing 100 miles of hiking trails, many routed through awesome stands of giant trees. In the winter heavy rains feed the South Fork Eel, inspiring steelhead upstream on their annual winter journey. Fishing is good in this area, best by shore at nearby High Rock. Bank access is good at several other spots. Note that there is catch-and-release fishing only; check fishing regulations. Contact information for fishing guides is available at the resort, and they offer winter steelhead fishing specials. An excellent side trip is to drive three miles south to the Avenue of the Giants, a tour through giant redwood trees. The campground also offers volleyball, shuffleboard, badminton, and horseshoes. You get the idea.

Campsites, facilities: There are 64 sites for tents or RVs of any length with full or partial hookups (30 and 50 amps); some sites are pull-through. Picnic tables and fire grills are provided. Restrooms with showers, recreation room, coin laundry, motel, convenience store, modem and Wi-Fi access, RV supplies, firewood, ice, giant spa, sauna, seasonal heated swimming pool, dump station, amphitheater, group facilities, arcade, basketball, tetherball, shuffleboard, volleyball, mini golf, and a playground are available. Some facilities are wheelchair-accessible. Leashed pets are permitted.

Reservations, fees: Reservations are recommended in the summer at 877/923-2555. RV sites are $39–41 per night, tent sites are $32 per night, $5 per person per night for more than two people, $1.50 per night for each additional vehicle. Some credit cards accepted. Open year-round.

Directions: From Eureka, drive 60 miles south on U.S. 101 to the Redwood Drive exit. Exit onto Redwood Drive and continue about one-half block to the motel/campground entrance on the right; check in at the motel.

Contact: Dean Creek Resort, 707/923-2555, www.deancreekresort.com.

50 BENBOW LAKE STATE RECREATION AREA

🥾 ♒ 🛶 🏊 🛥️ 🐕 ♿ 🚐 ⛺

Scenic rating: 6

on the Eel River

Map 1.2, page 80

Note: This park is on the closure list developed by the California Department of Parks, pending final state budget decisions or the possible transfer of park management to other park agencies or volunteer groups. As this book went to press, it remained closed but was open to bids for concessions.

The campground is set along the South Fork of the Eel River, with easy access from U.S. 101. A seasonal dam on the South Fork Eel used to create a 26-acre lake in summer for swimming and paddling in small boats. The dam is no longer installed in order to provide passage of downstream migrating juvenile steelhead and salmon. The lake is now a trickle of a creek in summer. In the winter, this stretch of river can be quite good for catch-and-release steelhead fishing.

Campsites, facilities: There are 77 sites for tents or RVs up to 30 feet; two sites have full hookups (30 amps). Picnic tables, food lockers, and fire grills are provided. Drinking water and restrooms with flush toilets and coin showers are available. A boat ramp (no motors) and seasonal boat rentals are available nearby. There is a dump station at the park entrance. Some facilities are wheelchair accessible. Leashed pets are permitted at campsites only.

Reservations, fees: Reservations are no longer accepted pending current park status. Check online at www.reserveamerica.com ($8 reservation fee). Sites were $35 per night, RV sites with hookups are $45 per night, $6 per night for each additional vehicle. Previously open May–September, weather permitting.

Directions: From the junction of U.S. 101 and Highway 1 in Leggett, drive north on U.S. 101 past Richardson Grove State Park to the Benbow Drive exit (two miles south of Garberville). Take that exit and drive 2.7 miles to the park entrance.

Contact: Benbow Lake State Recreation Area, 707/923-3238; Richardson Grove State Park, 707/247-3318; www.parks.ca.gov.

51 BENBOW VALLEY RV RESORT AND GOLF COURSE

🏊 🛶 🚐 🐕 ⛳ 🚐

Scenic rating: 7

on the Eel River

Map 1.2, page 80

This is an RV park with a pretty nine-hole regulation golf course set along U.S. 101 and the South Fork Eel River. It takes on a dramatically different character in the winter, when the highway is largely abandoned, the river comes up, and steelhead migrate upstream to the stretch of water here. Cooks Valley and Benbow provide good shore fishing access. Note that fishing restrictions for steelhead are extremely severe and subject to constant change; always check with DFG before fishing for steelhead.

Campsites, facilities: There are 112 sites with full hookups (30 and 50 amps), including four "VIP" sites for RVs of any length. Many sites are pull-through. No tents. Cottages, park-model cabins, and trailer rentals are also available. Picnic tables and cable TV are provided. Restrooms with showers, coin laundry, convenience store, snack bar, playground, recreation room, seasonal heated swimming pool, seasonal spa, Wi-Fi, fax and copy services, group facilities, organized activities, shuffleboard, table tennis, horseshoes, game room, RV supplies, and a nine-hole golf course are available. Some facilities are wheelchair accessible. Leashed pets are permitted. A doggy playground and pet wash are available.

Reservations, fees: Reservations are accepted at 866/236-2697. Sites are $47–60 per night, $6 per person per night for more than two people, $3 per pet per night. Discounted rates fall–spring. Some credit cards accepted. Open year-round.

Directions: From the junction of U.S. 101 and Highway 1 in Leggett, drive north on U.S. 101 past Richardson Grove State Park to the Benbow Drive exit (two miles south of Garberville). Take that exit and turn right at the stop sign. Drive a short distance to the end of the road and Benbow Drive. Bear left on Benbow Drive and continue a short distance to the resort on the left.

Contact: Benbow Valley RV Resort and Golf Course, 7000 Benbow Dr., 707/923-2777, www.benbowinn.com.

52 MADRONE, HUCKLEBERRY, AND DAWN REDWOOD

🏕️🏊🛶🐕♿🚐⛺

Scenic rating: 8

in Richardson Grove State Park

Map 1.2, page 80

The highway cuts a swath right through Richardson Grove State Park, and everyone slows to gawk at the tallest trees in the world, one of the most impressive groves of redwoods you can drive through in California. To explore further, there are several campgrounds available at the park, as well as a network of outstanding hiking trails, and the Eel River runs through the park, providing swimming holes in summer. The best of these are the short Exhibit Trail, Settler's Trail, and Toumey Trail. Richardson Grove is one of the prettiest and most popular state parks, making reservations a necessity from Memorial Day through Labor Day weekend. When arriving from points south on U.S. 101, this is the first park in the Redwood Empire where you will encounter significant old-growth redwood. There are nine miles of hiking trails, fishing in the winter for steelhead, and several trees of significant note.

Campsites, facilities: At Madrone Camp, there are 40 sites for tents or RVs up to 30 feet. At Huckleberry, there are 36 sites for tents or RVs up to 30 feet (no hookups). Dawn Redwood is a group camp (9–40 people) open in summer only. Picnic tables, food lockers, and fire grills are provided. Drinking water and restrooms with flush toilets and coin showers are available. WiFi is available near the ranger station. A dump station is three miles away. Some facilities are wheelchair-accessible. Leashed pets are permitted at campsites only.

Reservations, fees: Reservations are accepted January–September at 800/444-7275 (800/444-PARK) or www.reserveamerica.com ($8 reservation fee). September–January sites are first-come, first-served. Sites are $35 per night, $8 per night for each additional vehicle.

The group camp is $150 per night and a special-use permit is required. Open year-round, but subject to occasional winter closures.

Directions: From the junction of U.S. 101 and Highway 1 in Leggett, drive north on U.S. 101 for 16 miles (past Piercy) to the park entrance along the west (left) side of the road (eight miles south of Garberville).

Contact: Richardson Grove State Park, 707/247-3318, www.parks.ca.gov.

53 OAK FLAT

Scenic rating: 8

in Richardson Grove State Park

Map 1.2, page 80

Oak Flat is on the eastern side of the Eel River in the shade of forest and provides easy access to the river. The campground is open only in the summer. (For side-trip information, see the listing for Madrone, Huckleberry, and Dawn Redwood in this chapter.)

Campsites, facilities: There are 94 sites for tents or RVs up to 24 feet (no hookups) and trailers up to 18 feet. Picnic tables, food lockers, and fire grills are provided. Drinking water, restrooms with flush toilets and coin showers, and Wi-Fi are available. A grocery store and propane gas are available nearby. Leashed pets are permitted.

Reservations, fees: Reservations are accepted at 800/444-7275 (800/444-PARK) or www.reserveamerica.com ($8 reservation fee). Sites are $45 per night, $8 per night for each additional vehicle. Open mid-June through mid-September, weather permitting.

Directions: From the junction of U.S. 101 and Highway 1 in Leggett, drive north on U.S. 101 for 16 miles (past Piercy) to the park entrance on the west (left) side of the road (eight miles south of Garberville).

Contact: Richardson Grove State Park, 707/247-3318, www.parks.ca.gov.

54 RICHARDSON GROVE CAMPGROUND AND RV PARK

Scenic rating: 7

on the Eel River

Map 1.2, page 80

This private camp provides a nearby alternative to Richardson Grove State Park, complete with cabin rentals. The state park, with its grove of giant redwoods and excellent hiking, is the primary attraction. The RV park is family-oriented, with volleyball and basketball courts and horseshoe pits. The adjacent South Fork Eel River may look like a trickle in the summer, but there are some good swimming holes. It also provides good steelhead fishing in January and February, with especially good shore fishing access here as well as to the south in Cooks Valley (check DFG regulations before fishing). This campground is owned and operated by the Northern California/Nevada District Assemblies of God.

Campsites, facilities: There are 98 sites for tents or RVs; some sites are pull-through and many have full or partial hookups (30 amps). Two log cabins are also available. Picnic tables and fire rings are provided. Restrooms with showers, dump station, Wi-Fi, playground, coin laundry, convenience store, group facilities, propane, and ice are available. Leashed pets are permitted.

Reservations, fees: Reservations are recommended in the summer. RV sites are $28–33 per night, tent sites are $22 per night. Weekly, winter, and group rates available. Some credit cards accepted. Open year-round.

Directions: From the junction of U.S. 101 and Highway 1 in Leggett, drive north on U.S. 101 for 15 miles (one mile before reaching Richardson Grove State Park) to the camp entrance on the west (left) side of the road.

Contact: Richardson Grove Campground and RV Park, 707/247-3380, www.redwoodfamilycamp.com.

55 MATTOLE
🥾 🛶 🐕 ♿ 5% 🚐 🏕

Scenic rating: 8

north of Garberville

Map 1.2, page 80

This is a little-known camp set at the mouth of the Mattole River, right where it pours into the Pacific Ocean. It is beautiful and isolated. An outstanding hike leads to the Punta Gorda Lighthouse. Hike from the campground to the ocean and head south. It's a level walk, and at low tide, there's a chance to observe tidepool life. Perch fishing is good where the Mattole flows into the ocean, best during low tides. In the winter, the Mattole often provides excellent steelhead fishing. Check the Department of Fish and Game regulations for closed areas. Be sure to have a full tank on the way out—the nearest gas station is quite distant.

Campsites, facilities: There are 14 sites for tents or RVs up to 16 feet (no hookups). Picnic tables and fire rings are provided. Drinking water and vault toilets are available. Some facilities are wheelchair-accessible. Leashed pets are permitted.

Reservations, fees: Reservations are not accepted. Sites are $8 per night. Open year-round.

Directions: From U.S. 101 north of Garberville, take the South Fork-Honeydew exit and drive west to Honeydew. At Honeydew and Mattole Road, turn right on Mattole Road and drive toward Petrolia. At the second bridge over the Mattole River, one mile before Petrolia, turn west on Lighthouse Road and drive five miles to the campground at the end of the road.

Contact: Bureau of Land Management, Arcata Field Office, 707/825-2300, www.blm.gov/ca; Department of Fish & Game, Low-Flow Fishing Information, 707/442-4502.

56 A. W. WAY COUNTY PARK
🥾 🛶 🐕 🚐 🏕

Scenic rating: 8

on the Mattole River

Map 1.2, page 80

This secluded camp provides a home for visitors to the "Lost Coast," the beautiful coastal stretch of California far from any semblance of urban life. The highlight here is the Mattole River, a great steelhead stream when flows are suitable between January and mid-March. Nearby is excellent hiking in the King Range National Conservation Area. For the great hike out to the abandoned Punta Gorda Lighthouse, drive to the trailhead on the left side of Lighthouse Road (see the Mattole listing in this chapter). This area is typically bombarded with monsoon-level rains in winter.

Campsites, facilities: There are 30 sites for tents or small RVs (no hookups). Overflow camping is also available. Picnic tables and fire grills are provided. Drinking water, restrooms with flush toilets, and coin showers are available. A grocery store, coin laundry, and propane gas are available nearby. Leashed pets are permitted.

Reservations, fees: Reservations are not accepted. Sites are $20 per night, $8 per person per night for hike-in/bike-in, $5 per night for each additional vehicle, $2 per pet per night. Maximum stay is 10 days. Open year-round.

Directions: From Garberville, drive 22 miles north on U.S. 101 to the South Fork-Honeydew exit. Turn west on South Fork-Honeydew Road and drive 31 miles (the road changes between pavement, gravel, and dirt, and is steep and curvy) to the park entrance on the left side of the road. The park is 7.5 miles east of the town of Petrolia. (South Fork-Honeydew Road can be difficult for larger vehicles.)

Contact: Humboldt County Public Works, 707/445-7651, www.co.humboldt.ca.us.

57 HORSE MOUNTAIN

Scenic rating: 6

in the King Range

Map 1.2, page 80

Few people know of this spot. The campground is set along the northwest flank of Horse Mountain. A primitive road (Saddle Mountain Road) leads west from the camp and then goes left at the Y, up to Horse Mountain (1,929 feet), which offers spectacular ocean and coastal views on clear days. If you turn right at the Y, the road leads to the trailhead for the King Crest Trail near Saddle Mountain (3,290 feet). This hike is an ambitious climb to King Peak (4,087 feet), rewarding hikers with a fantastic panorama, including Mount Lassen poking above the Yolla Bolly Wilderness to the east.

Campsites, facilities: There are nine sites for tents only. Picnic tables and fire rings are provided. Vault toilets are available. No drinking water is available. Leashed pets are permitted.

Reservations, fees: Reservations are not accepted. Sites are $5 per night. Open year-round.

Directions: From Eureka, drive 60 miles south on U.S. 101 to the Redway/Shelter Cove exit. Take that exit and drive 2.5 miles north on Redwood Road to Briceland-Thorne Road. Turn right on Briceland-Thorne Road (which will become Shelter Cove Road) and drive 17 miles to King Peak Road (Horse Mountain). Turn right and continue six miles to the campground on the right.

Contact: Bureau of Land Management, Arcata Field Office, 707/825-2300, www.blm.gov/ca.

58 TOLKAN

Scenic rating: 6

in the King Range

Map 1.2, page 80

This remote camp is set at 1,840 feet, a short drive south of Horse Mountain. (For nearby side-trip options, see the listing for Horse Mountain in this chapter.)

Campsites, facilities: There are nine sites for tents or RVs up to 20 feet (no hookups). Picnic tables and fire rings are provided. Drinking water and vault toilets and are available. Some facilities are wheelchair-accessible. Leashed pets are permitted.

Reservations, fees: Reservations are not accepted. Sites are $8 per night. Open year-round.

Directions: From Eureka, drive 60 miles south on U.S. 101 to the Redway exit. Take the Redway/Shelter Cove exit onto Redwood Drive into the town of Redway. Drive 2.5 miles (look on the right for the King Range Conservation Area sign) to Briceland-Thorne Road. Turn right on Briceland-Thorne Road (which will become Shelter Cove Road) and drive 17 miles to King Peak (Horse Mountain) Road. Turn right on King Peak Road and continue 3.5 miles to the campground on the right.

Contact: Bureau of Land Management, Arcata Field Office, 707/825-2300, www.blm.gov/ca.

59 SHELTER COVE RV AND CAMPGROUND

Scenic rating: 8

in Shelter Coven

Map 1.2, page 80

This is a prime oceanside spot to set up a base camp for deep-sea fishing, whale-watching, tidepool gazing, beachcombing, and hiking. While this is a prime recreation area, the campground itself is rather uninspiring. Long-term renters occupy some of the campsites. A wide boat ramp makes it perfect for campers who have trailered boats and don't mind the long drive. Reservations are strongly advised here. The park's backdrop is the King Range National Conservation Area, offering spectacular views. The deli is well known for its fish-and-chips. The salmon, halibut, and rockfish fishing is quite good here in the summer; always call first for current regulations and seasons, which change every year. Clamming is best during winter's low tides; hiking is best in the King Mountain Range during the summer. Seasonal abalone diving and shore fishing for redtail perch are also available. There is heavy rain in winter. Insider's tip: Two miles north is one of the only black-sand beaches in the continental United States.

Campsites, facilities: There are 103 sites for tents or RVs; many have full hookups (30 amps); some sites are pull-through. Picnic tables and fire rings are provided. Restrooms with showers, dump station, coin laundry, grocery store, deli, propane, ice, and RV supplies are available. A boat ramp and marina are across the street. Leashed pets are permitted.

Reservations, fees: Reservations are recommended. Sites are $36–46 per night, $10 per person per night for more than two people, $1 per pet per night, $1 per night for additional vehicle. Some credit cards accepted. Open year-round.

Directions: From Eureka, drive 60 miles south on U.S. 101 to the Redway/Shelter Cove exit. Take that exit and drive 2.5 miles north on Redwood Road to Briceland-Thorne Road (which will become Shelter Cove Road). Turn right (west) and drive 18 miles (following the truck/RV route signs) to Upper Pacific Drive. Turn left (south) on Upper Pacific Drive and proceed (it becomes Machi Road) 0.5 mile to the park on the right.

Contact: Shelter Cove RV and Campground, 492 Machi Rd., 707/986-7474, http://sheltercoverv.com.

SHASTA AND TRINITY

© KARIN LAU/123RF.COM

BEST CAMPGROUNDS

At 14,162 feet, Mount Shasta rises like a diamond

in a field of coal. Its sphere of influence spans a radius of 125 miles, and its shadow is felt everywhere in the region. This area has much to offer with giant Shasta Lake, the Sacramento River above and below the lake, the McCloud River, and the wonderful Trinity Divide with its dozens of pretty backcountry lakes and several wilderness areas. This is one of the best regions anywhere for an outdoor adventure – especially hiking, fishing, powerboating, rafting, and exploring.

In this area, you can find campgrounds that are truly remote, set near quiet wilderness, and that offer the potential for unlimited adventures. Of all the regions in this book, this is the easiest one in which to find a campground in a secluded setting near great recreation opportunities. That is the main reason people visit.

There are hundreds of destinations, but the most popular are Shasta Lake, the Trinity Alps and their surrounding lakes and streams, and the Klamath Mountains, known by the locals as "Bigfoot Country."

Shasta Lake is one of America's top recreation lakes and the boating capital of the West. It is big enough to handle all who love it. The massive reservoir boasts 370 miles of shoreline; more than a dozen each of campgrounds, boat launches, and marinas; lakeshore lodging; and 400 houseboat and cabin rentals. A remarkable 22 species of fish live in the lake. Many of the campgrounds feature lake views. In addition, getting here is easy — a straight shot off I-5.

At the charmed center of this beautiful region are the Trinity Alps, where lakes are sprinkled everywhere. It's also home to the headwaters for feeder streams to the Trinity River, Klamath River, New River, Wooley Creek, and others. Trinity Lake provides outstanding boating and fishing, and just downstream, smaller Lewiston Lake offers a quiet alternative. One advantage to Lewiston Lake is that it is always full of water, even all summer long, making for a very pretty scene. Downstream of Lewiston, the Trinity River provides low-cost rafting and outstanding shoreline access along Highway 299 for fishing for salmon and steelhead.

The neighboring Klamath Mountains are well known as Bigfoot Country. If you drive up the Forest Service road at Bluff Creek, just off Highway 96 upstream of Weitchpec, you can even find the spot where the famous Bigfoot movie was shot in the 1960s. Well, I haven't seen Bigfoot, but I have discovered tons of outdoor recreation. This remote region features miles of the Klamath and Salmon Rivers, as well as the Marble Mountain Wilderness. Options include canoeing, rafting, and fishing for steelhead on the Klamath River, or hiking to your choice of more than 100 wilderness lakes.

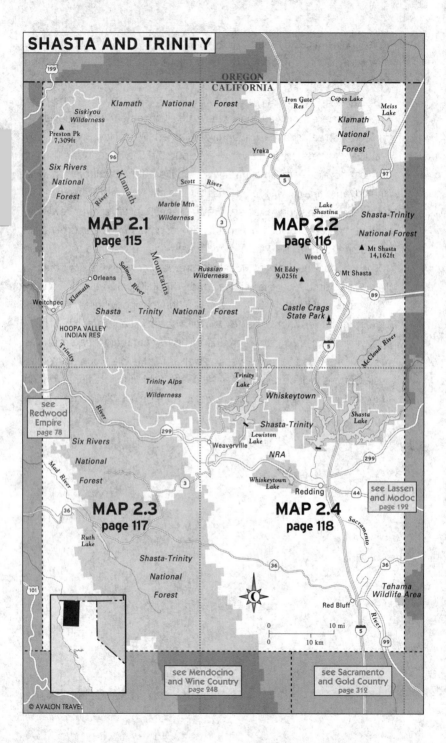

SHASTA AND TRINITY

199

OREGON
CALIFORNIA

Klamath National Forest

Siskiyou
Wilderness

▲
Preston Pk
7,309ft

Iron Gate
Res

Copco Lake

Meiss
Lake

Klamath

National

Forest

Six Rivers
National
Forest

96

Klamath

River

Scott   River

Yreka

5

97

Marble Mtn
Wilderness

3

MAP 2.1
page 115

Lake
Shastina

Shasta-Trinity

MAP 2.2
page 116

National Forest

▲ Mt Shasta
14,162ft

Mountains

Russian
Wilderness

Weed

89

Orleans

Salmon River

Mt Eddy
9,025ft ▲

○ Mt Shasta

Weitchpec

Klamath

Shasta - Trinity National Forest

Castle Crags
State Park ▲

HOOPA VALLEY
INDIAN RES

Trinity

5

McCloud River

**see
Redwood
Empire**
page 78

Trinity Alps
Wilderness

Trinity
Lake

Whiskeytown

Shasta
Lake

River

299

Shasta-Trinity

Six Rivers

Weaverville

Lewiston
Lake

NRA

299

National

Mad River

36

Forest

3

Whiskeytown
Lake

Redding

44

**see Lassen
and Modoc**
page 192

MAP 2.3
page 117

MAP 2.4
page 118

Sacramento

101

Ruth
Lake

36

36

Shasta-Trinity

National

Forest

Tehama
Wildlife Area

Red Bluff

River

0   10 mi

0   10 km

5

99

© AVALON TRAVEL

**see Mendocino
and Wine Country**
page 248

**see Sacramento
and Gold Country**
page 312

Map 2.1

**Sites 1-23
Pages 120-130**

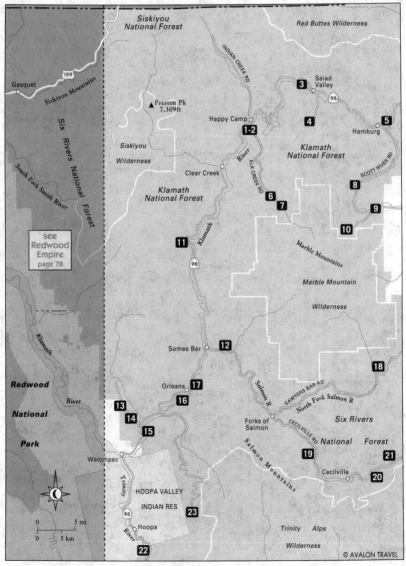

Map 2.2

Sites 24-55
Pages 130-146

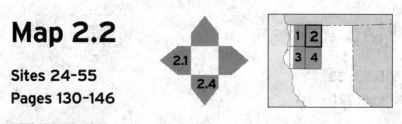

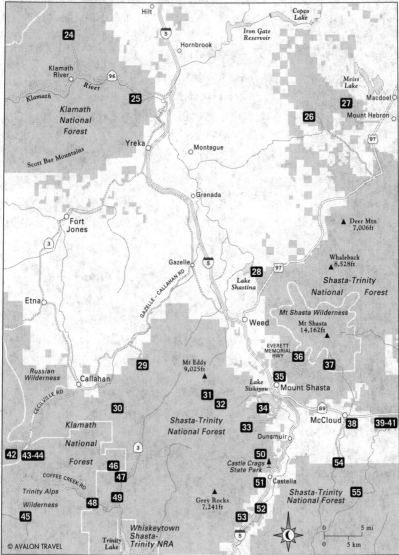

Map 2.3

Sites 56-76
Pages 147-156

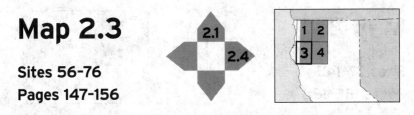

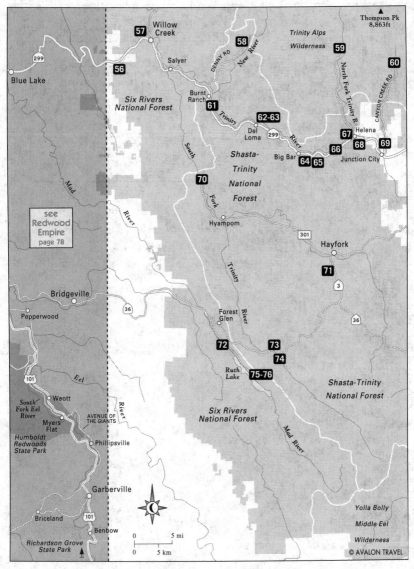

Thompson Pk
8,863ft

Trinity Alps
Wilderness

57 Willow
Creek

58

New River

DENNY RD

59

North Fork Trinity R.

60

CANYON CREEK RD

56

Salyer

299

Blue Lake

Six Rivers
National Forest

Burnt
Ranch

61

Trinity

62-63

Del
Loma

299

River

Helena

67

68

69

66

Big Bar

64 **65**

Junction City

South

Shasta-
Trinity

National

Forest

70

Fork

Hyampom

301

Hayfork

Mad

River

see
Redwood
Empire
page 78

Trinity

River

71

3

Bridgeville

36

Pepperwood

Forest
Glen

River

72

73

74

36

Eel

101

Ruth
Lake

75-76

Shasta-Trinity
National Forest

South
Fork Eel
River

Weott

Myers
Flat

AVENUE OF
THE GIANTS

River

Six Rivers
National Forest

Mad River

Humboldt
Redwoods
State Park

Phillipsville

Garberville

Yolla Bolly

Middle Eel

Briceland

101

Benbow

Wilderness

Richardson Grove
State Park

0   5 mi

0   5 km

© AVALON TRAVEL

Map 2.4

Sites 77-145
Pages 156-188

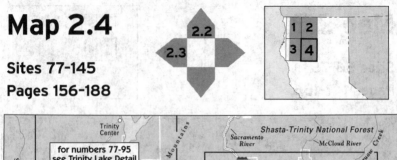

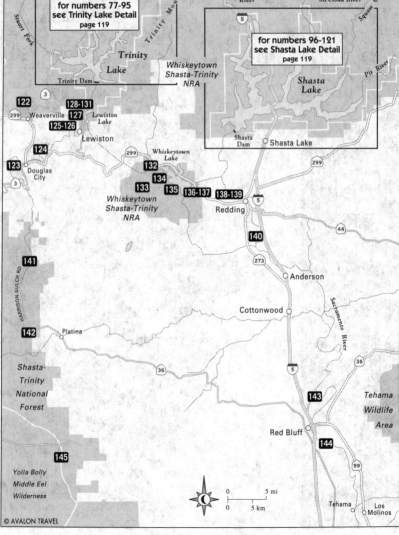

for numbers 77-95
see Trinity Lake Detail
page 119

for numbers 96-121
see Shasta Lake Detail
page 119

© AVALON TRAVEL

TRINITY LAKE DETAIL

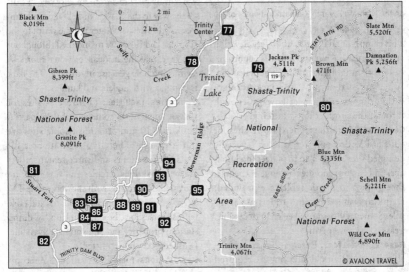

SHASTA LAKE DETAIL

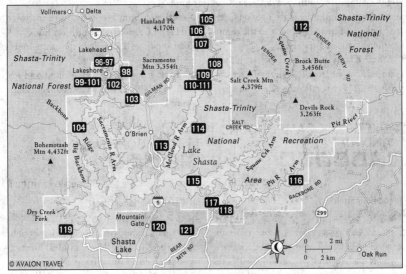

■1 CURLY JACK

Scenic rating: 7

on the Klamath River in Klamath National Forest

Map 2.1, page 115

This campground is set at 1,000 feet elevation on the Klamath River and provides opportunities for fishing, light rafting, and kayaking. What's special about Curly Jack, though, is that the water is generally warm enough through the summer for swimming.

Campsites, facilities: There are 12 sites for tents or RVs up to 42 feet, with two specially designed sites for RVs up to 60 feet (no hookups) and three group sites for up to 30 people. Fire grills and picnic tables are provided. Drinking water and vault toilets are available. Some facilities are wheelchair-accessible. Leashed pets are permitted.

Reservations, fees: Reservations are not accepted for individual sites but are required for group sites at 877/444-6777 or www.recreation.gov ($9 reservation fee). Sites are $15 per night, $50 per night for a group site. Open May–October.

Directions: From the town of Happy Camp on Highway 96, turn south on Elk Creek Road and drive about one mile. Turn right on Curly Jack Road and drive one block to the campground entrance on the right.

Contact: Klamath National Forest, Happy Camp and Oak Knoll Ranger Districts, 530/493-2243, www.fs.usda.gov/klamath.

■2 ELK CREEK CAMPGROUND AND RV PARK

Scenic rating: 8

on the Klamath River

Map 2.1, page 115   BEST

Elk Creek Campground is a year-round RV park set where Elk Creek pours into the Klamath River. It is a beautiful campground, with sites right on the water in a pretty, wooded setting.

The section of the Klamath River nearby is perfect for inflatable kayaking and rafting. Guided trips are available, with a wide scope of white water available, rated from the easy Class I stuff all the way to the Class V to-hell-and-back rapids. In addition, the water is quite warm in the summer and flows are maintained throughout the year, making it ideal for water sports. A swimming hole gets use in summer. The park is popular with anglers and hunters.

Campsites, facilities: There are 34 sites for RVs of any length, some with full or partial hookups (30 and 50 amps); some sites are pull-through. There is a separate area for tents. Three cabins and three rental trailers are available. Picnic tables and fire grills are provided. Restrooms with showers, cable TV, Wi-Fi, recreation room with billiards and table tennis, horseshoes, beach, coin laundry, dump station, propane, and firewood are available. Leashed pets are permitted.

Reservations, fees: Reservations are recommended. RV sites are $22–25 per night, tent sites are $15 per night, $6 per night for each additional person for more than four people. Weekly, monthly, and group rates are available. Some credit cards accepted. Open year-round.

Directions: From Highway 96 in the town of Happy Camp, turn south on Elk Creek Road and drive 0.75 mile to the campground on the right.

Contact: Elk Creek Campground and RV Park, 530/493-2208, www.elkcreekcampground.com.

■3 FORT GOFF WALK-IN

Scenic rating: 7

in Klamath National Forest

Map 2.1, page 115

This small, primitive campground is set right along the Klamath River, an ideal location for both fishing and rafting. Many productive shoreline fishing spots on the Klamath

River are in this area, with fair trout fishing in summer, good steelhead fishing in the fall and early winter, and a wild card for salmon in late September. There are pullouts along Highway 96 for parking, with short trails/scrambles down to the river. This is also a good spot for rafting, especially in inflatable kayaks, and commercial rafting operations have trips (Class II+ and III) available on this stretch of river. On the opposite side of Highway 96 (within walking distance, to the west) is a trailhead for a hike that is routed along Little Fort Goff Creek, an uphill tromp for five miles to Big Camp and Boundary National Recreation Trail. The creek also runs near the camp, and the elevation is 1,300 feet.

Campsites, facilities: There are five walk-in tent sites. Picnic tables and fire grills are provided. Vault toilets are available. There is no drinking water and garbage must be packed out. Supplies are available in Seiad Valley. Leashed pets are permitted.

Reservations, fees: Reservations are not accepted. There is no fee for camping. Open May through October.

Directions: From Yreka, drive north on I-5 to the junction with Highway 96. At Highway 96, turn west and drive to Seiad Valley. At Seiad Valley, continue west on Highway 96 for five miles to the campground on the left side of the road. Walk a very short distance (20–75 feet) to the campsites.

Contact: Klamath National Forest, Happy Camp and Oak Knoll Ranger Districts, 530/493-2243, www.fs.usda.gov/klamath.

4 GRIDER CREEK

Scenic rating: 6

in Klamath National Forest

Map 2.1, page 115

This obscure little camp is used primarily by hikers, since a trailhead for the Pacific Crest Trail is available, and by deer hunters in the fall. The camp is set at 1,400 feet along Grider Creek. Access to the Pacific Crest Trail is provided from a bridge across the creek. From here, the PCT is routed uphill along Grider Creek into the Marble Mountain Wilderness, about an 11-mile ripper to Huckleberry Mountain at 6,303 feet. There are no lakes along the route, only small streams and feeder creeks.

Campsites, facilities: There are 10 sites for tents or RVs up to 16 feet (no hookups). Picnic tables and fire grills are provided. Vault toilets, horse corrals, and a loading ramp are available. No drinking water is provided, but there is water for stock horses. Garbage must be packed out. Leashed pets are permitted.

Reservations, fees: Reservations are not accepted. There is no fee for camping. Two vehicles maximum per site. Open May–October.

Directions: From Yreka, drive north on I-5 to the junction with Highway 96. At Highway 96, turn west and drive to Walker Creek Road/Forest Road 46N64, one mile before Seiad Valley. Turn left to enter Walker Creek Road and stay to the right as it runs adjacent to the Klamath River to Grider Creek Road. At Grider Creek Road, turn left and drive south for three miles to the camp entrance.

Contact: Klamath National Forest, Happy Camp and Oak Knoll Ranger Districts, 530/493-2243, www.fs.usda.gov/klamath.

5 SARAH TOTTEN

Scenic rating: 7

on the Klamath River in Klamath National Forest

Map 2.1, page 115   BEST (

This is one of the more popular Forest Service camps on the Klamath River, and it's no mystery why. In the summer, its placement is perfect for rafters (Class II+ and III), who camp here and use it as a put-in spot. In fall and winter, anglers arrive for the steelhead run. It's in the "banana belt," or good-weather area of the Klamath, in a pretty grove of oak trees. Fishing is often good here for salmon in early

October and for steelhead from November through spring, providing there are fishable water flows.

Campsites, facilities: There are eight sites for tents or RVs up to 28 feet, and two group sites for tents or RVs up to 22 feet that can accommodate up to 30 people each. No hookups. Picnic tables and fire grills are provided. Drinking water and vault toilets are available. A small grocery store is nearby. Some facilities are wheelchair-accessible. Leashed pets are permitted.

Reservations, fees: Reservations are not accepted for individual sites but are required for the group sites at 877/444-6777 or www.recreation.gov ($9 reservation fee). Sites are $10 per night, $50 per night for group sites. Open May through October.

Directions: From Yreka, drive north on I-5 to the junction with Highway 96. At Highway 96, turn west and drive to Horse Creek, continuing west for five miles to the campground on the right side of the road. If you reach the town of Hamburg, you have gone one mile too far.

Contact: Klamath National Forest, Happy Camp and Oak Knoll Ranger Districts, 530/493-2243, www.fs.usda.gov/klamath.

6 SULPHUR SPRINGS
Scenic rating: 8

on Elk Creek in Klamath National Forest

Map 2.1, page 115

This hidden spot is set along Elk Creek on the border of the Marble Mountain Wilderness. The camp is at a trailhead that provides access to miles and miles of trails that follow streams into the backcountry of the wilderness area. It is a 12-mile backpack trip one-way and largely uphill to Spirit Lake, one of the prettiest lakes in the entire wilderness. The nearby hot springs (which are actually lukewarm) provide a side attraction. There are also some swimming

holes nearby in Elk Creek, but these aren't hot springs, so expect the water to be cold. Sulphur Springs Camp is set at 2,300 feet.

Campsites, facilities: There are six walk-in tent sites. Picnic tables and fire grills are provided. Vault toilets are available. No drinking water is available. Garbage must be packed out. Leashed pets are permitted.

Reservations, fees: Reservations are not accepted. There is no fee for camping. Open late May through early October.

Directions: From Yreka, drive north on I-5 to the junction with Highway 96. At Highway 96, turn west and drive to Happy Camp. In Happy Camp, turn south on Elk Creek Road and drive 12 miles to the campground.

Contact: Klamath National Forest, Happy Camp and Oak Knoll Ranger Districts, 530/493-2243, www.fs.usda.gov/klamath.

7 NORCROSS
Scenic rating: 7

near Happy Camp in Klamath National Forest

Map 2.1, page 115

The Forest Service closed this campground in 2010, renovated it, and then reopened it in 2011. The camp is set at 2,400 feet in elevation and serves as a staging area for various trails that provide access into the Marble Mountain Wilderness. There is also access to the popular Kelsey Trail and to swimming and fishing activities.

Campsites, facilities: There are six sites for tents or RVs up to 25 feet (no hookups). Picnic tables and fire pits are provided. Vault toilets, a horse corral, stock water, and a loading ramp are available. No drinking water is available. Garbage must be packed out. Some facilities are wheelchair-accessible. Leashed pets are permitted.

Reservations, fees: Reservations are not accepted. There is no fee for camping. Open May through October.

Directions: From Yreka on I-5, drive north on I-5 to the junction with Highway 96. Drive west on Highway 96 to the town of Happy Camp. In Happy Camp, turn south onto Elk Creek Road and drive 16 miles to the campground.

Contact: Klamath National Forest, Happy Camp and Oak Knoll Ranger Districts, 530/493-2243, www.fs.usda.gov/klamath.

8 BRIDGE FLAT

Scenic rating: 7

in Klamath National Forest

Map 2.1, page 115

This camp is set at 2,000 feet along the Scott River. Though commercial rafting trips are only rarely available here, the river is accessible during the early spring for skilled rafters and kayakers, with a good put-in and take-out spot four miles downriver; others begin their trip at the Buker Bridge or the Kelsey Creek Bridge (popular swimming hole here). For backpackers, a trailhead for the Kelsey Trail is nearby, leading into the Marble Mountain Wilderness. A fish-spawning area is located on Kelsey Creek, upriver from camp.

Campsites, facilities: There are four sites for tents or RVs up to 22 feet (no hookups). Picnic tables and fire grills are provided. Vault toilets are available. There is no drinking water and garbage must be packed out. Some facilities are wheelchair-accessible. Leashed pets are permitted.

Reservations, fees: Reservations are not accepted. There is no fee for camping. Open May through September.

Directions: From Redding, drive north on I-5 to Yreka. In Yreka, turn southwest on Highway 3 and drive 16.5 miles to Fort Jones. In Fort Jones, turn right on Scott River Road and drive 17 miles to the campground on the right side of the road, just after crossing a bridge.

Contact: Klamath National Forest, Scott River and Salmon River Ranger Districts, 530/468-5351, www.fs.usda.gov/klamath.

9 INDIAN SCOTTY

Scenic rating: 7

on the Scott River in Klamath National Forest

Map 2.1, page 115

This popular camp provides direct access to the adjacent Scott River. Because it is easy to reach (no gravel roads) and shaded, it gets a lot of use. The camp is set at 2,400 feet. The levels, forces, and temperatures on the Scott River fluctuate greatly from spring to fall. In the spring, it can be a raging cauldron, but cold from snowmelt. Come summer it quiets, with some deep pools providing swimming holes. By fall, it can be reduced to a trickle. Keep your expectations flexible according to the season.

Campsites, facilities: There are 28 sites and a group site (parking lot) for tents or RVs up to 30 feet (no hookups). Picnic tables and fire grills are provided. Drinking water and vault toilets are available. There is a playground in the group-use area. Some facilities are wheelchair accessible. Leashed pets are permitted.

Reservations, fees: Reservations are not accepted for individual sites but are required for the group site at 877/444-6777 or www.recreation.gov ($9 reservation fee). Individual sites are $10 per night, and the group site is $50 per night. Open May through October.

Directions: From Redding, drive north on I-5 to Yreka. In Yreka, turn southwest on Highway 3 and drive 16.5 miles to Fort Jones. In Fort Jones, turn right on Scott River Road and drive 14 miles to a concrete bridge and the adjacent signed campground entrance on the left.

Contact: Klamath National Forest, Scott River and Salmon River Ranger Districts, 530/468-5351, www.fs.usda.gov/klamath.

🔟 LOVERS CAMP
🚶 🐴 ⛺

Scenic rating: 5

in Klamath National Forest

Map 2.1, page 115

Lovers Camp isn't set up for lovers at all, but for horses and backpackers. This is a trailhead camp set at 4,300 feet at the edge of the Marble Mountain Wilderness, one of the best in the entire wilderness for packers with horses. The trail here is routed up along Canyon Creek to the beautiful Marble Valley at the foot of Black Marble Mountain. The most common destination is Sky High Lakes, a good one-day huff-and-puff away. Now there's a place for lovers.

Campsites, facilities: There are eight walk-in tent sites. Picnic tables and fire grills are provided. Vault toilets are available. There are also facilities for stock unloading and a corral. There is no drinking water, but water is available for stock. Garbage must be packed out. Leashed pets are permitted.

Reservations, fees: Reservations are not accepted. There is no fee for camping. Open May through October.

Directions: From Redding, drive north on I-5 to Yreka. In Yreka, turn southwest on Highway 3 and drive to Fort Jones and Scott River Road. Turn right on Scott River Road and drive 14 miles to Forest Road 44N45. Turn left (south) on Forest Road 44N45 and drive eight miles to the campground at the end of the road.

Contact: Klamath National Forest, Scott River and Salmon River Ranger Districts, 530/468-5351, www.fs.usda.gov/klamath.

🔟🔟 DILLON CREEK
🚶 🏊 🛶 🐴 ♿ 🚐 ⛺

Scenic rating: 7

on the Klamath River in
Six Rivers National Forest

Map 2.1, page 115   **BEST (**

This is a prime base camp for rafting or a steelhead fishing trip. A put-in spot for rafting is adjacent to the camp, with an excellent river run available from here on down past Presidio Bar to the takeout at Ti-Bar. If you choose to go on, make absolutely certain to pull out at Green Riffle river access and take-out, or risk death at Ishi Pishi Falls. The water is warm here in the summer, and there are also many excellent swimming holes in the area. In addition, this is a good stretch of water for steelhead fishing from September to February, best in early winter from Dillon Creek to Ti-Bar, with shoreline access available at Dillon Beach. The elevation is 1,780 feet.

Campsites, facilities: There are 21 sites for tents or RVs up to 30 feet (no hookups). Picnic tables, food lockers, and fire grills are provided. Drinking water and vault toilets are available. There is a dump station in Happy Camp 25 miles north of the campground, and at Aikens Creek nine miles west of the town of Orleans. Some facilities are wheelchair-accessible. Leashed pets are permitted.

Reservations, fees: Reservations are accepted for some sites three days in advance at 877/444-6777 or www.recreation.gov ($9 reservation fee). Sites are $10 per night, $5 per night for each additional vehicle. Open mid-May through early November.

Directions: From Yreka, drive north on I-5 to the junction with Highway 96. At Highway 96, turn west and drive to Happy Camp. Continue south from Happy Camp for 35 miles and look for the campground on the right side of the road.

Coming from the west, from Somes Bar, drive 15 miles northeast on Highway 96.

Contact: Six Rivers National Forest, Orleans Ranger District, 530/627-3291, www.fs.usda.gov.

12 OAK BOTTOM

Scenic rating: 7

on the Salmon River in
Six Rivers National Forest

Map 2.1, page 115

This camp is just far enough off Highway 96 that it gets missed by zillions of out-of-towners every year. It is set across the road from the lower Salmon River, a pretty, clean, and cold stream that pours out of the surrounding wilderness high country. Swimming is very good in river holes, though the water is cold, especially when nearby Wooley Creek is full of snowmelt pouring out of the Marble Mountains to the north. In the fall, there is good shoreline fishing for steelhead, though the canyon bottom is shaded almost all day and gets very cold.

Campsites, facilities: There are 26 sites for tents or RVs up to 25 feet (no hookups). Picnic tables and fire grills are provided. Drinking water and vault toilets are available. There is a dump station at the Elk Creek Campground in Happy Camp and at Aikens Creek, 13 miles southwest of the town of Orleans. Supplies are available in Somes Bar. Some facilities are wheelchair-accessible. Leashed pets are permitted.

Reservations, fees: Reservations are not accepted. Sites are $10 per night, $5 per night for each additional vehicle. Open April through mid-October, weather permitting.

Directions: From the junction of U.S. 101 and Highway 299 near Arcata, turn east on Highway 299 and drive to Willow Creek. In Willow Creek, turn north (left) on Highway 96 east and drive to Salmon River Road (0.25 mile before Somes Bar). Turn right on Salmon River Road and drive 2.3 miles to the campground on the left side of the road.

Contact: Six Rivers National Forest, Orleans Ranger District, 530/627-3291, www.fs.usda.gov.

13 FISH LAKE

Scenic rating: 8

in Six Rivers National Forest

Map 2.1, page 115

This is a pretty little lake that provides good fishing for stocked rainbow trout from the season opener on Memorial Day weekend through July. The camp gets little pressure in other months. It's in the heart of Bigfoot Country, with numerous Bigfoot sightings reported near Bluff Creek. No powerboats are permitted on the lake, but it's too small for that anyway, being better suited for a canoe, float tube, raft, or pram. The elevation is 1,780 feet. The presence here of Port-Orford-cedar root disease, spread by spores in the mud, forces closure from October through May in some years; call for current status.

Campsites, facilities: There are 24 sites for tents or RVs up to 20 feet (no hookups). Picnic tables and fire grills are provided. Drinking water, vault toilets, and a boat ramp are available. Some facilities are wheelchair-accessible. Leashed pets are permitted.

Reservations, fees: Reservations are required three days in advance at 877/444-6777 or www.recreation.gov ($9 reservation fee). Sites are $10 per night, $5 per night for each additional vehicle. Open late May through September, weather permitting.

Directions: From I-5 in Redding, turn west on Highway 299 and drive to Willow Creek. In Willow Creek, turn north (left) on Highway 96 east and drive to Weitchpec, continuing seven miles north on Highway 96 to Fish Lake Road/Bluff Creek Road. Turn left on Fish Lake Road/Bluff Creek Road and drive five miles (stay to the right at the Y) to Fish Lake.

Contact: Six Rivers National Forest, Orleans Ranger District, 530/627-3291, www.fs.usda.gov.

14 E-NE-NUCK

Scenic rating: 7

in Six Rivers National Forest

Map 2.1, page 115

The campground gets its name from a Karuk chief who lived in the area in the late 1800s. It's a popular spot for anglers; Bluff Creek and the Klamath are within walking distance and Fish Lake is eight miles to the west. Bluff Creek is the legendary site where the Bigfoot film of the 1960s was shot. While it was finally admitted that the film was a phony, it still put Bluff Creek on the map. A unique feature at this campground is a smokehouse for lucky anglers.

Campsites, facilities: There are 10 sites for tents or RVs up to 30 feet (no hookups). Picnic tables, fire rings, and cast-iron firebox stoves are provided. Drinking water, vault toilets, and a smokehouse are available. Some facilities are wheelchair-accessible. Leashed pets are permitted.

Reservations, fees: Reservations are not accepted. Sites are $10 per night, $5 for each additional vehicle. Open late June through October.

Directions: From the junction of U.S. 101 and Highway 299 near Arcata, turn east on Highway 299 and drive to Willow Creek. In Willow Creek, turn north (left) on Highway 96 east and drive to Weitchpec, continuing on Highway 96 for about five miles to the campground. E-Ne-Nuck is located just beyond Aikens Creek West campground.

Contact: Six Rivers National Forest, Orleans Ranger District, 530/627-3291, www.fs.usda.gov.

15 AIKENS CREEK WEST

Scenic rating: 7

on the Klamath River in
Six Rivers National Forest

Map 2.1, page 115

The Klamath River is warm and green here in summer, and this camp provides an ideal put-in spot for a day of easy rafting, especially for newcomers in inflatable kayaks. The camp is set at 340 feet in elevation along the Klamath. From here to Weitchpec is an easy paddle, with the take-out on the right side of the river just below the confluence with the Trinity River. The river is set in a beautiful canyon with lots of birds, and enters the Yurok Indian Reservation. The steelhead fishing can be good in this area from August through mid-November. Highway 96 is a scenic but slow cruise.

Campsites, facilities: There are dispersed sites for tents or RVs up to 35 feet (no hookups). Picnic tables and fire grills are provided. Vault toilets and a dump station are available, but there is no drinking water. There are reduced services in winter, and all garbage must be packed out. Leashed pets are permitted.

Reservations, fees: Reservations are not accepted. Sites are $8 per night, $5 per night for each additional vehicle; no fees during winter. Open year-round, weather permitting.

Directions: From the junction of U.S. 101 and Highway 299 near Arcata, turn east on Highway 299 and drive to Willow Creek. In Willow Creek, turn north (left) on Highway 96 east and drive to Weitchpec, continuing on Highway 96 for five miles to the campground on the right side of the road.

Contact: Six Rivers National Forest, Orleans Ranger District, 530/627-3291, www.fs.usda.gov.

16 KLAMATH RIVERSIDE RV PARK

Scenic rating: 8

on the Klamath River

Map 2.1, page 115

Klamath Riverside RV Park and Campground is an option for RV cruisers touring Highway 96—designated the Bigfoot Scenic Byway—and looking for a place in Orleans. The camp has large grassy sites set amid pine trees, right on the river. There are spectacular views of

Mount Orleans and the surrounding hills. A 12-foot Bigfoot statue is on the property. Through the years, I've seen many changes at this park. It has been transformed from a dusty fishing spot to a park more resembling a rural resort that attracts hikers, cyclists, gold panners, river enthusiasts, anglers, and hunters. One big plus is that the park offers guided fishing trips during the season.

Campsites, facilities: There are 45 sites with full hookups (30 and 50 amps) for RVs of any length. Two cabins and three rental trailers are also available. Picnic tables and fire rings are provided. Restrooms with showers, seasonal swimming pool, a spa, group pavilion, fish-cleaning station, coin laundry, horseshoes, playground, WiFi, pay phone, and RV storage are available. Guided drift-boat fishing in season is available. Leashed pets are permitted.

Reservations, fees: Reservations are accepted. RV sites are $35 per night, $6 per person per night for more than four people. Group, weekly, and monthly rates available. Open year-round.

Directions: From the junction of U.S. 101 and Highway 299 near Arcata, drive east on Highway 299 to Willow Creek, turn north (left) on Highway 96 east and drive past Weitchpec to Orleans. This campground is at the west end of the town of Orleans on Highway 96 on the right.

Contact: Klamath Riverside RV Park and Campground, 530/627-3239, www.krrvp. com.

17 PEARCH CREEK
Scenic rating: 7

on the Klamath River
in Six Rivers National Forest

Map 2.1, page 115

This is one of the premium Forest Service camps on the Klamath River because of its easy access from the highway and easy access to the river. The camp is set on Pearch Creek,

about a quarter mile from the Klamath at a deep bend in the river. Indeed, the fishing is often excellent for one- to five-pound steelhead from August through November. The elevation is 400 feet.

Campsites, facilities: There are 10 sites for tents or RVs up to 30 feet (no hookups). Picnic tables and fire grills are provided. Drinking water and vault toilets are available. A grocery store, coin laundry, and propane gas are available within one mile. Some facilities are wheelchair accessible. Leashed pets are permitted.

Reservations, fees: Reservations are accepted at 877/444-6777 or www.recreation.gov ($9 reservation fee). Sites are $10 per night, $5 per night for each additional vehicle. Open late May through October.

Directions: From I-5 in Redding, turn west on Highway 299 and drive to Willow Creek. In Willow Creek, turn north (left) on Highway 96 east, drive past Weitchpec, and continue to Orleans. In Orleans, continue for one mile and look for the campground entrance on the right side of the road.

Contact: Six Rivers National Forest, Orleans Ranger District, 530/627-3291, www.fs.usda. gov.

18 IDLEWILD
Scenic rating: 8

on the North Fork of the Salmon River
in Klamath National Forest

Map 2.1, page 115

This is one of the prettiest drive-to camps in the region, set on the North Fork of the Salmon River, a beautiful, cold, clear stream and a major tributary to the Klamath River. Most campers use the camp for its nearby trailhead (two miles north on a dirt Forest Service road out of camp). The hike here is routed to the north, climbing alongside the Salmon River for miles into the Marble Mountain Wilderness (wilderness permits are required). It's a rugged 10-mile, all-day climb to Lake of the

Island, with several other lakes (highlighted by Hancock Lake) to the nearby west, accessible on weeklong trips. The elevation is 2,560 feet.

Campsites, facilities: There are 18 sites for tents or RVs up to 24 feet (no hookups). Picnic tables and fire grills are provided. Vault toilets are available. Drinking water is unreliable, especially in the off-season. Some facilities are wheelchair-accessible. Leashed pets are permitted.

Reservations, fees: Reservations are not accepted. Sites are $10 per night, with no fee during the winter. Open May through October.

Directions: From Yreka, turn southwest on Highway 3 and drive to Etna. In Etna, turn west on Etna-Somes Bar Road (Main Street in town) and drive about 16 miles to the campground on the right side of the road. Note: A shorter, more scenic, and more complex route is available from Gazelle (north of Weed on Old Highway 99). Take Gazelle-Callahan Road west over the summit and continue north to Etna.

Contact: Klamath National Forest, Salmon River and Scott River Ranger Districts, 530/468-5351, www.fs.usda.gov/klamath.

19 MATTHEWS CREEK

🏊 🎣 🐕 🚐 ⛺

Scenic rating: 8

on the Salmon River in
Klamath National Forest

Map 2.1, page 115   **BEST (**

This camp is set in a dramatic river canyon, with the beautiful South Fork of the Salmon River nearby. Rafters call it the "Cal Salmon," and good put-in and take-out spots are found every few miles all the way to the confluence with the Klamath. In early summer the water is quite cold from snowmelt, but by midsummer it warms up significantly. The best fishing for steelhead on the Salmon is in December and January in the stretch of river downstream

from the town of Forks of Salmon or upstream in the South Fork (check regulations for closed areas). In winter the mountain rims shield the canyon floor from sunlight and it gets so cold you'll feel like a human glacier. The elevation is 1,760 feet.

Campsites, facilities: There are 11 sites for tents or RVs up to 24 feet (no hookups). Picnic tables and fire grills are provided. Drinking water and vault toilets are available, with limited winter facilities. Leashed or controlled pets are permitted.

Reservations, fees: Reservations are not accepted. Sites are $10 per night. Open May through October.

Directions: From the junction of U.S. 101 and Highway 299 near Arcata, head east on Highway 299 and drive to Willow Creek. In Willow Creek, turn north on Highway 96 and drive past Orleans to Somes Bar. At Somes Bar, turn east on Salmon River Road/Forest Road 2B01 and drive to the town of Forks of Salmon. Turn right on Cecilville Road/Forest Road 1002 and drive about nine miles to the campground. Cecilville Road is very narrow.

Contact: Klamath National Forest, Salmon River and Scott River Ranger Districts, 530/468-5351, www.fs.usda.gov/klamath.

20 EAST FORK

🏊 🎣 🐕 ♿ 🚐 ⛺

Scenic rating: 6

on the Salmon River in
Klamath National Forest

Map 2.1, page 115

This is one of the more spectacular areas in the fall when the leaves turn different shades of gold. It's set at 2,600 feet along the Salmon River, just outside the town of Cecilville. Directly adjacent to the camp is Forest Road 37N02, which leads to a Forest Service station four miles away, and to a trailhead for the Trinity Alps Wilderness three miles beyond that. Note to steelhead anglers: Check the

Department of Fish and Game regulations for closed areas on the Salmon River.

Campsites, facilities: There are six sites for tents or RVs up to 16 feet (no hookups). Picnic tables and fire grills are provided. Vault toilets are available. No drinking water is available. Garbage must be packed out. Some facilities are wheelchair accessible. Leashed pets are permitted.

Reservations, fees: Reservations are not accepted. There is no fee for camping. Open May through October.

Directions: From Weed, drive north on I-5 to the Edgewood exit. Take the Edgewood exit, turn left at the stop sign, and drive a short distance under the freeway to another stop sign at Old Highway 99. Turn right (north) and drive six miles to Gazelle and Gazelle-Callahan Road. Turn left (west) on Gazelle-Callahan Road, and drive to Callahan and Cecilville Road. Turn left (southwest) on Cecilville Road and drive about 30 miles to the campground on the right side of the road. If you reach the town of Cecilville, you have gone two miles too far.

Contact: Klamath National Forest, Salmon River and Scott River Ranger Districts, 530/468-5351, www.fs.usda.gov/klamath.

Long Gulch, and Trail Gulch. Note: The river adjacent to the campground is a spawning area and is closed to salmon and steelhead fishing, but you can take trout.

Campsites, facilities: There are five sites for tents or RVs up to 16 feet (no hookups). Picnic tables and fire grills are provided. Vault toilets are available. No drinking water is available. Garbage must be packed out. Some facilities are wheelchair accessible. Leashed pets are permitted.

Reservations, fees: Reservations are not accepted. There is no fee for camping. Open May through October.

Directions: From Weed, drive north on I-5 to the Edgewood exit. Take the Edgewood exit, turn left at the stop sign, and drive a short distance under the freeway to another stop sign at Old Highway 99. Turn right (north) and drive six miles to Gazelle and Gazelle-Callahan Road. Turn left (west) and drive to Callahan and Cecilville Road. Turn left (southwest) on Cecilville Road and drive about 23 miles to the campground on the left side of the road.

Contact: Klamath National Forest, Salmon River and Scott River Ranger Districts, 530/468-5351, www.fs.usda.gov/klamath.

21 SHADOW CREEK

Scenic rating: 7

in Klamath National Forest

Map 2.1, page 115

This tiny spot, secluded and quiet, is along little Shadow Creek where it enters the East Fork Salmon River, adjacent to a deep bend in the road. An unusual side trip is to take the Forest Service road out of camp (turn north off Cecilville Road) and follow it as it winds back and forth, finally arriving at Grouse Point, 5,409 feet elevation, for a view of the western slopes of the nearby Russian and Trinity Alps Wilderness Areas. There are three trailheads six miles to the east of the camp: Fish Creek,

22 TISH TANG

Scenic rating: 8

in Six Rivers National Forest

Map 2.1, page 115

This campground is adjacent to one of the best swimming holes in all of Northern California. By late July the adjacent Trinity River is warm and slow, perfect for tubing, a quick dunk, and paddling a canoe. There is a large gravel beach, and some people will bring along their short lawn chairs and just take a seat on the edge of the river in a few inches of water. Though Tish Tang is a good put-in spot for rafting in the late spring and early summer, the flows are too slow and quiet for most rafters to even ruffle a feather during the summer. The elevation is 300 feet.

Campsites, facilities: There are 40 sites for tents or RVs up to 22 feet (no hookups). Picnic tables and fire grills are provided. Drinking water and vault toilets are available, and there is a camp host. Leashed pets are permitted. Some facilities are wheelchair-accessible.

Reservations, fees: Reservations are accepted at 530/625-4284. Single sites are $15 per night, $5 per night for each additional vehicle, $20 per night for double sites. Open late May through September.

Directions: From the junction of U.S. 101 and Highway 299 near Arcata, turn east on Highway 299 and drive to Willow Creek. In Willow Creek, turn north (left) on Highway 96 east and drive eight miles north to the campground entrance on the right side of the road.

Contact: Hoopa Valley Tribal Council, Forestry Department, 530/625-4284, www.hoopa-nsn.gov.

23 MILL CREEK LAKE HIKE-IN

Scenic rating: 4

on the border of the Trinity Alps Wilderness

Map 2.1, page 115

Mill Creek Lake is a secret three-acre lake set at 5,000 feet on the edge of the Trinity Alps Wilderness. Reaching it requires a two-mile hike from the wilderness boundary, with the little lake set just north of North Trinity Mountain (6,362 feet). This is a rare chance to reach a wilderness lake with such a short walk, backpacking without having to pay the penalty of days of demanding hiking. The lake features excellent swimming, with warmer water than in higher and more remote wilderness lakes, and decent fishing for rainbow trout.

Campsites, facilities: There are three primitive tent sites at locations around the lake. Fire rings and a corral are provided. No drinking water or toilets are available. Garbage must be packed out. Leashed pets are permitted.

Reservations, fees: Reservations are not accepted. There is no fee for camping. A free wilderness permit is required from the U.S. Forest Service. Open year-round, weather permitting.

Directions: From the junction of U.S. 101 and Highway 299 near Arcata, turn east on Highway 299 and drive to Willow Creek. In Willow Creek turn north (left) on Highway 96 east and drive into the Hoopa Valley to Mill Creek Road. Turn east (right) on Mill Creek Road, and drive approximately 12 miles to the national forest boundary and Forest Road 10N02. Turn right on Forest Road 10N02 and drive about 3.5 miles, where you will reach another junction. Turn left at the signed junction to the Mill Creek Lake Trailhead and drive a short distance to the parking area. A one-hour walk is then required to reach the lake.

Contact: Six Rivers National Forest, Lower Trinity Ranger District, 530/629-2118, www.fs.usda.gov.

24 BEAVER CREEK

Scenic rating: 8

in Klamath National Forest

Map 2.2, page 116

This camp is set along Beaver Creek, a feeder stream to the nearby Klamath River, with two small creeks entering Beaver Creek on the far side of the river near the campground. It is quiet and pretty. There are several historic mining sites in the area; you'll need a map of Klamath National Forest (available for a fee at the district office) to find them. In the fall, this campground is usually taken over by deer hunters. The elevation is 2,400 feet.

Campsites, facilities: There are eight sites for tents or RVs up to 28 feet (no hookups). Picnic tables and fire grills are provided. Vault toilets are available. There is no drinking water. Garbage must be packed out. Leashed pets are permitted.

Reservations, fees: Reservations are not

accepted. There is no fee for camping. Open June through October.

Directions: From Yreka, drive north on I-5 to Highway 96. Turn west on Highway 96 and drive approximately 15 miles to Beaver Creek Road (if you reach the town of Klamath River, you have gone 0.5 mile too far). Turn right on Beaver Creek Road/Forest Road 11 and drive five miles to the campground.

Contact: Klamath National Forest, Happy Camp and Oak Knoll Ranger Districts, 530/493-2243, www.fs.usda.gov/klamath.

25 TREE OF HEAVEN

Scenic rating: 7

in Klamath National Forest

Map 2.2, page 116   **BEST**

This outstanding riverside campground provides excellent access to the Klamath River for fishing, rafting, and hiking. The best deal is to put in your raft, canoe, or drift boat upstream at the ramp below Iron Gate Reservoir, then make the all-day run down to the take-out at Tree of Heaven. This section of river is an easy paddle (Class II, II+, and III) and also provides excellent steelhead fishing in the winter. A 0.25 mile paved interpretive trail is near the camp. On the drive in from the highway, you can watch the landscape turn from high chaparral to forest.

Campsites, facilities: There are 21 sites for tents or RVs up to 35 feet (no hookups). Picnic tables and fire grills are provided. Drinking water and vault toilets are available. A river access spot for put-in and take-out for rafts and drift boats is available. Some facilities are wheelchair-accessible. Leashed pets are permitted.

Reservations, fees: Reservations are accepted at 877/444-6777 or www.recreation.gov ($9 reservation fee). Sites are $15 per night. Open May through October.

Directions: From Yreka, drive north on I-5 to Highway 96. Turn west on Highway 96 and

drive seven miles to the campground entrance on the left side of the road.

Contact: Klamath National Forest, Happy Camp and Oak Knoll Ranger Districts, 530/493-2243, www.fs.usda.gov/klamath.

26 MARTINS DAIRY

Scenic rating: 8

on the Little Shasta River
in Klamath National Forest

Map 2.2, page 116

This camp is set at 6,000 feet, where the deer get big and the country seems wide open. A large meadow is nearby, directly across the road from this remote camp, with fantastic wildflower displays in late spring. This is one of the prettiest camps around in the fall, with dramatic color from aspens, elderberries, and willows. It also makes a good base camp for hunters in the fall. Before heading into the surrounding backcountry, obtain a map (fee) of Klamath National Forest at the Goosenest Ranger Station on Highway 97, on your way in to camp.

Campsites, facilities: There are six sites for tents or RVs up to 30 feet (no hookups) and four horse campsites with four small corrals and a shared water tank. Picnic tables and fire grills are provided. Drinking water and vault toilets are available. Leashed pets are permitted.

Reservations, fees: Reservations are not accepted. Sites are $10 per night. Open June through October, weather permitting.

Directions: From I-5 in Weed, turn north on U.S. 97 (Klamath Falls exit) and drive to Grass Lake. Continue about seven miles to Forest Road 70/46N10 (if you reach Hebron Summit, you have driven about a mile too far). Turn left, drive about 10 miles to a Y, take the left fork, and drive three miles (including a very sharp right turn) to the campground on the right side of the road. A map of Klamath National Forest is advised.

Contact: Klamath National Forest, Goosenest Ranger District, 530/398-4391, www.fs.usda.gov/klamath.

27 JUANITA LAKE

🥾 🚴 ⚓ 🛶 🚤 🐴 ♿ 🚍 ⛺

Scenic rating: 7

in Klamath National Forest

Map 2.2, page 116

Small and relatively unknown, this camp is set along the shore of Juanita Lake at 5,100 feet. Swimming is not recommended because the water is cold and mucky, and mosquitoes can be abundant as well. It is stocked with rainbow trout, brown trout, bass, and catfish, but a problem with golden shiners has cut into the lake's fishing productivity. It's a small lake and forested, set near the Butte Valley Wildlife Area in the plateau country just five miles to the northeast. The latter provides an opportunity to see waterfowl and, in the winter, bald eagles. Campers will discover a network of Forest Service roads in the area, providing an opportunity for mountain biking. There are designated fishing areas and a paved trail around the lake that is wheelchair-accessible and spans approximately 1.25 miles.

Campsites, facilities: There are 22 sites for tents or RVs up to 42 feet (no hookups), and a group tent site that can accommodate up to 50 people. Picnic tables and fire grills are provided. Drinking water and vault toilets are available. Boating is allowed, but no motors are permitted on the lake. Many facilities are wheelchair-accessible. Leashed pets are permitted.

Reservations, fees: Reservations are not accepted for individual sites but are required for the group site at 530/398-4391. Individual sites are $15 per night, the double site is $20 per night, and the group site is $50 per night. Open late May through mid-October, weather permitting.

Directions: From Weed and I-5, turn north on U.S. 97 (Klamath Falls exit) and drive approximately 37 miles to Ball Mountain Road.

Turn left on Ball Mountain Road and drive 2.5 miles, veer right at the fork, and continue to the campground entrance at the lake.

Contact: Klamath National Forest, Goosenest Ranger District, 530/398-4391, www.fs.usda.gov/klamath.

28 LAKE SHASTINA

⚓ 🛶 🚤 🐴 ♿ 🚍 ⛺

Scenic rating: 5

near Klamath National Forest and Weed

Map 2.2, page 116

Lake Shastina is set at the northern foot of Mount Shasta at 3,000 feet in elevation. The campground is located on the access road to the boat ramp, about 0.25 mile from the lake. It offers sweeping views, good swimming on hot summer days, waterskiing, and all water sports. There is fishing for catfish and bass in the spring and summer, an occasional opportunity for crappie, and a chance for trout in late winter and spring. The lake level is often low, with the water drained for hay farmers to the north. One reason the views of Mount Shasta are so good is that this is largely high sagebrush country with few trees. As such, it can get very dusty, windy, and, in the winter, nasty cold. Since this campground is remote (yet not far from I-5), provides free access, and there is no campground host, the nearby lakeshore can be the site of late night parties with bonfires, drinking, and worse—amplified music from open car doors. This is one of the few lakes in Northern California that has property with lakeside housing (not near the campground). Locals often run their dogs off-leash. Lake Shastina Golf Course is nearby.

Campsites, facilities: There is a small primitive area for tents or RVs of any length (no hookups). There is one faucet, but you should bring your own water in case it is not turned on. A vault toilet is available and a boat launch is nearby; the boat ramp is nonfunctional when the lake level drops below the concrete ramp. Garbage service available May to September only. There is a 14-

day limit for camping. Supplies can be obtained five miles away in Weed. Some facilities are wheelchair accessible. Pets are permitted.

Reservations, fees: Reservations are not accepted. There is no fee for camping. Open May through September.

Directions: From Redding, take I-5 north to the central Weed exit and U.S. 97. Take the exit to the stop sign, turn right, drive through Weed, exiting for U.S. 97/Klamath Falls. Merge right (north) on U.S. 97 and drive about five miles to Big Springs Road. Turn left (west) on Big Springs Road and drive about two miles to Jackson Ranch Road. Turn left (west) on Jackson Ranch Road and drive about one mile to Emerald Isle Road (watch for the signed turnoff). Turn right and drive one mile to the campground.

Contact: Siskiyou County Public Works, 530/842-8250, www.co.siskiyou.ca.us.

29 KANGAROO LAKE
🏕 🏊 🎣 🐕 ♿ 🚐 🏕

Scenic rating: 9

in Klamath National Forest

Map 2.2, page 116

A remote paved road leads to the parking area for Kangaroo Lake, set at 6,500 feet. This provides a genuine rarity: a beautiful and pristine mountain lake with a campground, good fishing for brook and rainbow trout, and an excellent trailhead for hikers. The walk to the walk-in campsites is very short, 1–3 minutes, with many sites very close. Campsites are in a forested setting with no lake view. Reaching the lake requires another five minutes, but a paved wheelchair-accessible trail is available. In addition, a switchback ramp for wheelchairs makes it one of the best wheelchair-accessible fishing areas in California. The lake is small, 25 acres, but deep at 100 feet. No boat motors are allowed. A hiking trail rises steeply out of the campground and connects to the Pacific Crest Trail, from which you turn left to gain a dramatic lookout of Northern California peaks as well as the lake below.

Campsites, facilities: There are 13 sites for tents or RVs up to 30 feet (no hookups), plus five walk-in sites that require a short walk. Picnic tables and fire grills are provided. Drinking water and vault toilets are available. Some facilities are wheelchair-accessible, including a nearby fishing pier. Leashed pets are permitted.

Reservations, fees: Reservations are not accepted. Sites are $15 per night. Open June through October, weather permitting.

Directions: From Weed, drive north on I-5 and take the Edgewood exit. At the stop sign, turn left and drive a short distance under the freeway to the stop sign at Old Highway 99. Turn right (north) on Old Highway 99 and drive six miles to Gazelle and Gazelle-Callahan Road. Turn left at Gazelle-Callahan Road and drive over the summit. From the summit, continue about five miles to Rail Creek Road. Turn left at Rail Creek Road and drive approximately eight miles to where the road dead-ends near the campground. Walk approximately 30–150 yards to reach the campsites.

Contact: Klamath National Forest, Scott River and Salmon River Ranger Districts, 530/468-5351, www.fs.usda.gov/klamath.

30 SCOTT MOUNTAIN
🏕 🐕 🚐 🏕

Scenic rating: 7

in Shasta-Trinity National Forest

Map 2.2, page 116

This camp is a jump-off point for hikers, with the Pacific Crest Trail passing right by here. If you hike southwest, it leads into the Scott Mountains and skirts the northern edge of the Trinity Alps Wilderness. Another option here is driving on Forest Road 40N08, which begins directly across from camp and Highway 3. On this road, it's only two miles to Big Carmen Lake, a small, largely unknown and pretty little spot. Campground elevation is 5,400 feet. A Forest Service map is advisable.

Campsites, facilities: There are seven sites for tents or RVs up to 15 feet. Picnic tables and fire grills are provided. Vault toilets are available.

No drinking water is available. Garbage must be packed out. Leashed pets are permitted.

Reservations, fees: Reservations are not accepted. There is no fee for camping. Open year-round, weather permitting.

Directions: From Weed, drive north on I-5 and take the Edgewood exit. At the stop sign, turn left and drive a short distance under the freeway to the stop sign at Old Highway 99. Turn right (north) and drive six miles to Gazelle and Gazelle-Callahan Road. Turn left at Gazelle-Callahan Road and drive to Callahan and Highway 3. Turn south on Highway 3 and drive to Scott Mountain Summit and look for the campground on the right side of the road.

Contact: Shasta-Trinity National Forest, Weaverville Ranger District, 530/623-2121, www.fs.usda.gov/stnf.

31 TOAD LAKE WALK-IN

Scenic rating: 9

in Shasta-Trinity National Forest

Map 2.2, page 116   **BEST (**

Some people think this site is closed, since the Forest Service no longer lists it as an active campground. Nope. There are six primitive campsites at Toad Lake, including two with picnic tables. Because it is a free site with no maintenance provided, it is off the mainstream grid. So if you want the remote beauty and splendor of an alpine lake on the Pacific Crest Trail, yet you don't want to walk far to get there, this is the place. Toad Lake is no easy trick to get to, with a bone-jarring ride for the last half hour followed by a 15-minute walk, but it's worth the effort. It's a beautiful little lake, just 23.5 acres, set at 6,900 feet in the Mount Eddy Range, with lakeside sites, excellent swimming, fair fishing for small trout, and great hiking. The best hike is a 45-minute trail out of the Toad Lake Basin to pristine Porcupine Lake. To get there, follow the trail to the head of the lake. There it rises up the slope and to the top of the ridge, intersecting

with the Pacific Crest Trail. Turn left and walk a short distance to a spur trail junction on the right, which leads to Porcupine Lake.

Campsites, facilities: There are six walk-in tent sites. A vault toilet is available. No drinking water is available. Garbage must be packed out. Leashed pets are permitted.

Reservations, fees: Reservations are not accepted. There is no fee for camping. Open May through October, weather permitting.

Directions: From the town of Mount Shasta on I-5, take the Central Mount Shasta exit and drive to the stop sign. Turn west and drive less than a mile to Old Stage Road. Turn left and drive 0.25 mile to a Y intersection at W. A. Barr Road. Bear right and drive past Box Canyon Dam and the entrance to Lake Siskiyou, and continue up the mountain (the road becomes Forest Road 26). Just past a concrete bridge, turn right on Forest Road 41N53 and drive 0.2 mile to a fork and Toad Lake Road. Turn left onto Toad Lake Road (a dirt road) and continue for 11 miles to the parking area. The road is bumpy and twisty, and the final half-mile to the trailhead is rocky and rough. High-clearance or four-wheel-drive vehicles are recommended. Walk in about 0.5 mile to the lake and campsites. Note: Access roads may be closed because of flooding; call ahead for status.

Contact: Shasta-Trinity National Forest, Mount Shasta Ranger District, 530/926-4511, www.fs.usda.gov/stnf.

32 GUMBOOT

Scenic rating: 9

in Shasta-Trinity National Forest

Map 2.2, page 116

Gumboot Campground was once one of the great hideaways in the Trinity Divide, but little Gumboot Lake has had some troubled years. The problem is that some young locals have used the campsites as a party pad, with arrests for underage drinking and drug use, as well as some disreputable types living here for weeks in trailers. Too bad, because this pretty spot at 6,080 feet elevation provides a few small campsites set beside a small yet beautiful high mountain lake—the kind of place many think can only be reached only a long hike. The fishing has been good here, suited for a pram, raft, or float tube, but Fish and Game stopped stocking trout here after a lawsuit over... frogs. No motors of any kind are permitted, including electric motors. Floating in a pram or inflatable to the far end of the lake and flyfishing with black leeches and a sink-tip line is one of the best possibilities. Another option is hiking 10 minutes through forest to Upper Gumboot Lake, which is more of a pond with small trout. Another excellent hike is available here, tromping off-trail beyond Upper Gumboot Lake and up the back slope of the lake to the Pacific Crest Trail, then turning left and scrambling to a great lookout of Mount Shasta in the distance and Gumboot in the foreground.

Campsites, facilities: There are four sites for tents or RVs up to 16 feet (no hookups), and across the creek there are four walk-in tent sites. One unmaintained vault toilet is available. There is no drinking water. Garbage must be packed out. Some facilities are wheelchair-accessible. Leashed pets are permitted.

Reservations, fees: Reservations are not accepted. There is no fee for camping. Open June through October, weather permitting.

Directions: From the town of Mount Shasta on I-5, take the Central Mount Shasta exit and drive to the stop sign. Turn west and continue less than a mile to Old Stage Road. Turn left and drive 0.25 mile to a Y intersection at W. A. Barr Road. Bear right on W. A. Barr Road and drive two miles past Box Canyon Dam and the Lake Siskiyou Campground entrance. Continue 10 miles to a fork, signed for Gumboot Lake. Bear left and drive 0.5 mile to the lake and campsites. Note: Access roads may be closed because of flooding; call for current status.

Contact: Shasta-Trinity National Forest, Mount Shasta Ranger District, 530/926-4511, www.fs.usda.gov/stnf.

33 CASTLE LAKE

Scenic rating: 10

in Shasta-Trinity National Forest

Map 2.2, page 116

Castle Lake is a beautiful spot, a deep blue lake set in a granite bowl with a spectacular wall on the far side. The views of Mount Shasta are great, fishing is decent (especially ice fishing in winter), canoeing or floating around on a raft is a lot of fun, and there is a terrific hike that loops around the left side of the lake, rising to the ridge overlooking the lake for dramatic views. Locals use this lake for ice-skating in winter. The campground is not right beside the lake, to ensure the pristine clear waters remain untouched, but is rather just a short distance downstream along Castle Lake Creek. The lake is only 47 acres, but 120 feet deep. The elevation is 5,280 at the camp, and 5,450 feet at the lake.

Campsites, facilities: There are six sites for tents or RVs up to 10 feet (no hookups). Picnic tables and fire grills are provided. Vault toilets are available. No drinking water is available. Garbage must be packed out. Leashed pets are permitted.

Reservations, fees: Reservations are not accepted. There is no fee for camping. Open May through October, weather permitting.

Directions: From the town of Mount Shasta on I-5, take the Central Mount Shasta exit and drive to the stop sign. Turn west and drive less than a mile to Old Stage Road. Turn left and drive 0.25 mile to a Y intersection at W. A. Barr Road. Bear right on W. A. Barr Road and drive two miles past Box Canyon Dam. Turn left at Castle Lake Road and drive seven miles to the campground access road on the left. Turn left and drive a short distance to the campground. Note: Castle Lake is another 0.25 mile up the road; there are no legal campsites along the lake's shoreline.

Contact: Shasta-Trinity National Forest, Mount Shasta Ranger District, 530/926-4511, www.fs.usda.gov/stnf.

34 LAKE SISKIYOU RESORT & CAMP

Scenic rating: 9

near Mount Shasta

Map 2.2, page 116 **BEST (**

This is a true gem of a lake, a jewel set at the foot of Mount Shasta at 3,181 feet, the prettiest lake on the I-5 corridor in California. The lake level is almost always full (because it was built for recreation, not water storage) and offers a variety of quality recreation options, with great swimming, low-speed boating, and fishing. The campground complexes are huge, yet they are tucked into the forest so visitors don't get their styles cramped. The water in this 435-acre lake is clean and fresh. There is an excellent beach and swimming area, the latter protected by a buoy line. In spring, the fishing is good for trout, and then as the water warms, for smallmouth bass. A good boat ramp and boat rentals are available, and a 10-mph speed limit is strictly enforced, keeping the lake pristine and quiet. The City of Mount Shasta holds its Fourth of July fireworks display above the lake. The campgrounds are huge, and often fill on weekends and summer holidays.

Campsites, facilities: There are 150 sites with full or partial hookups (30 and 50 amps) for RVs of any length, including some pull-through sites, and 225 additional sites for tents, seven of which are group areas. There are also 30 cabins and five park-model cabins. Picnic tables and fire pits are provided. Drinking water, restrooms with flush toilets and showers, playground, propane, convenience store, gift shop, coin laundry, and a dump station are available. There are also a marina, boat rentals (canoes, kayaks, pedal boats, motorized boats), free boat launching, fishing dock, fish-cleaning station, boat slips, swimming beach, horseshoes, volleyball, group facilities, and a recreation room. A free movie plays every night in the summer. Some facilities are wheelchair-accessible. Leashed pets are permitted at the campground only.

Reservations, fees: Reservations are accepted. RV sites are $26–29 per night, $3 per person per night for more than two people, $5 per night for each additional vehicle, $2 per pet per night; tent sites are $20 per night. Some credit cards accepted. Open April through October, weather permitting.

Directions: From the town of Mount Shasta on I-5, take the Central Mount Shasta exit and drive to the stop sign. Turn west and drive less than a mile to Old Stage Road. Turn left and drive 0.25 mile to a Y intersection at W. A. Barr Road. Bear right on W. A. Barr Road and drive past Box Canyon Dam. Two miles farther, turn right at the entrance road for Lake Siskiyou Campground and Marina and drive a short distance to the entrance station.

Contact: Lake Siskiyou Resort & Camp, 530/926-2610 or 888/926-2618, http://reynoldsresorts.com/LakeSiskiyou.html.

35 KOA MOUNT SHASTA

Scenic rating: 7

in Mount Shasta City

Map 2.2, page 116

Despite this KOA camp's relative proximity to the town of Mount Shasta, the extended driveway, wooded grounds, and view of Mount Shasta offer some feeling of seclusion. There are many excellent side trips. The best is driving up Everitt Memorial Highway, which rises up the slopes of Mount Shasta to the tree line at Bunny Flat, where you can take outstanding, short day hikes with great views to the south of the Sacramento River Canyon and Castle Crags. In the winter, you can play in the snow, including heading up to Bunny Flat for snowplay or to the Mount Shasta Board and Ski Park for developed downhill and cross-country skiing. An ice skating rink is in Mount Shasta. One of the biggest events of the year in Mount Shasta is the Fourth of July Run for Fun (billed as the largest small-town foot race anywhere) and associated parade and fireworks display at nearby Lake Siskiyou.

Campsites, facilities: There are 35 sites with full hookups (20, 30, and 50 amps) for RVs of any length, 42 additional sites with partial hookups (water only) for tents or RVs, and seven camping cabins. All sites are pull-through. Picnic tables are provided, and fire grills are provided at tent sites only. Restrooms with showers, a playground, propane gas, a convenience store, recreation room with arcade, horseshoe pit, shuffleboard, a seasonal swimming pool, Wi-Fi, and coin laundry are available. Some facilities are wheelchair accessible. Leashed pets are permitted.

Reservations, fees: Reservations are accepted at 800/562-3617. RV sites are $37.40–39.60 per night, tent sites are $25.30 per night, $3–4 per person per night for more than two people, $3.50 per night for each additional vehicle, and a $5 site guarantee fee. Some credit cards accepted. Open year-round.

Directions: From Redding, drive north on I-5 to the town of Mount Shasta. Continue past the first Mount Shasta exit and take the Central Mount Shasta exit. At the stop sign, turn right (east) on Lake Street and drive 0.6 mile to Mount Shasta Boulevard. Turn left and drive 0.5 mile to East Hinckley Boulevard. Turn right (signed KOA) on East Hinckley, drive a very short distance, then turn left at the entrance to the extended driveway for KOA Mount Shasta.

Contact: KOA Mount Shasta, 530/926-4029, http://koa.com/campgrounds/mount-shasta.

36 McBRIDE SPRINGS

Scenic rating: 8

on Mount Shasta in
Shasta-Trinity National Forest

Map 2.2, page 116

This camp is set at 4,880 feet on the slopes of the awesome Mount Shasta (14,179 feet), California's most majestic mountain. Stargazing is fantastic here, and during full moons, an eerie glow is cast on the adjoining high mountain slopes. A good side trip is to drive to the end of Everitt Memorial Highway to Bunny Flat Trailhead at 6,950 feet; or continue beyond to the Old Ski Bowl at 7,800 feet (below towering

Green Butte). You'll find great lookouts to the west, and a jump-off point for a Shasta expedition or day hike to Panther Meadows.

In 2009, a root disease decimated the white fir trees in this campground. Infected trees were removed in 2011 and the campground has since reopened. The Forest Service has replanted disease-free native species and eventually nature will do the rest.

Campsites, facilities: There are 10 sites for tents or RVs up to 16 feet (no hookups). Picnic tables and fire grills are provided. Drinking water (from a single well with a hand pump at the north end of the campground) and vault toilets are available. Supplies and a coin laundry are available in the town of Mount Shasta. Some facilities are wheelchair-accessible. Leashed pets are permitted.

Reservations, fees: Reservations are not accepted. Sites are $10 per night; pay at the self-registration fee station at the entrance. Open Memorial Day weekend through October, weather permitting.

Directions: From Redding drive north on I-5 to the town of Mount Shasta and the Central Mount Shasta exit. Take that exit and drive to the stop sign and Lake Street. Turn right and continue on Lake Street through town; once out of town, the road becomes Everitt Memorial Highway. Continue on Everitt Memorial Highway for four miles to the campground entrance on the left side of the road.

Contact: Shasta-Trinity National Forest, Mount Shasta Ranger District, 530/926-4511, www.fs.usda.gov/stnf.

37 PANTHER MEADOWS WALK-IN

Scenic rating: 9

on Mount Shasta in
Shasta-Trinity National Forest

Map 2.2, page 116   BEST (

This quiet site, on the slopes of Mount Shasta at 7,500 feet, features access to the pristine Panther

Meadows, a high mountain meadow set just below tree line. It's a sacred place, regardless of your religious orientation. The hiking is excellent hike nearby, with a short hike out to Gray Butte (8,119 feet) for a view to the south of Castle Crags, Lassen Peak, and the Sacramento River Canyon. A three-night maximum stay is enforced to minimize long-term impacts.

Campsites, facilities: There are 10 walk-in tent sites (trailers not allowed). Picnic tables and fire grills are provided. Vault toilets are available. No drinking water is available. Garbage must be packed out. Supplies are available in the town of Mount Shasta. Leashed pets are permitted.

Reservations, fees: Reservations are not accepted. There is no fee for camping. Open mid-June through mid-October, weather permitting.

Directions: From Redding, drive north on I-5 to the town of Mount Shasta and the Central Mount Shasta exit. Take that exit and drive to the stop sign and Lake Street. Turn right and continue on Lake Street through town; once out of town, Lake Street becomes Everitt Memorial Highway. Continue on Everitt Memorial Highway for about 12 miles (passing the Bunny Flat parking area) to the campground parking area on the right. Park and walk a short distance to the campsites. Note: When the gate is closed just past Bunny Flat, the walk in is 1.5 miles from the gate to the campground.

Contact: Shasta-Trinity National Forest, Mount Shasta Ranger District, 530/926-4511, www.fs.usda.gov/stnf.

38 MCCLOUD DANCE COUNTRY RV PARK

Scenic rating: 6

in McCloud

Map 2.2, page 116

McCloud Dance Country RV Park has became a draw for RV travelers. The park is sprinkled with old-growth pine trees and bordered by Squaw Valley Creek, a pretty stream. The RV sites are grassy and manicured; many are shaded. (Note that some RV campers have complained about early morning highway noise from logging trucks.) The town of McCloud is the home of McCloud Dance Country Hall, a large dance hall dedicated to square and round dancing. The park used to be affiliated with the dance hall, but now it is open to the public. McCloud River's three waterfalls are accessible from the McCloud River Loop, five miles south of the park on Highway 89. Mount Shasta Board and Ski Park also offers summer activities such as biking, a rock-climbing structure, and chairlift rides to great views of the surrounding forests. The ski park access road is six miles west of McCloud off Highway 89 at Snowman's Hill Summit. (For more information, see the listing for Fowler's Camp in this chapter.)

Campsites, facilities: There are 136 sites with full or partial hookups (30 and 50 amps) for RVs of any length, a grassy area for dispersed tent camping, and seven cabins. There are a few long-term rentals. Large groups are welcome. Picnic tables are provided. Drinking water, restrooms with hot showers and a heated bathhouse, a central barbecue and campfire area, cable TV, pay telephone, coin laundry, dump station, propane, horseshoes, two trout ponds, fish-cleaning station, and two pet walks are available. Some facilities are wheelchair-accessible. Leashed pets are permitted, except in cabins.

Reservations, fees: Reservations are recommended. RV sites are $27–51 per night, tent sites are $20–28 per night, $7 per person per night for more than two people. Weekly and monthly rates available. Some credit cards accepted. Open May through October.

Directions: From Redding, drive north on I-5 and continue just past Dunsmuir to the junction with Highway 89. Turn east on Highway 89 and drive nine miles to McCloud and Squaw Valley Road. Turn right on Squaw

Valley Road and then turn immediately left into the park entrance.

Contact: McCloud Dance Country RV Park, 530/964-2252, www.mccloudrvpark.com.

39 FOWLERS CAMP

🚶 🏊 ⛵ 🏕 🐕 ♿ 🚐 ⛺

Scenic rating: 10

on the McCloud River in
Shasta-Trinity National Forest

Map 2.2, page 116

This campground is set beside the beautiful McCloud River at 3,400 feet. Nearby are three distinct waterfalls, including Middle Falls, one the stellar sights in Northern California. From the camp, the trail is routed upstream through forest, a near-level walk of only 15 minutes; it then arrives at awesome Middle Falls, a wide-sweeping curtain-like cascade. By summer, the flows subside and warm to the point that some people will swim in the pool at the base of the falls. The trail is also routed from camp downstream to Lower Falls, a chute-like fall and an outstanding swimming hole in midsummer. Above Middle Falls is Upper Falls, a stair-step falls with a trail that runs nearby. Fishing the McCloud River here is fair, with trout stocks made from Lakim Dam on downstream to the camp. If this camp is full, Cattle Camp and Algoma (see listings in this chapter) offer overflow areas.

Campsites, facilities: There are 38 sites and one double site for tents or RVs up to 30 feet (no hookups). Picnic tables and fire grills are provided. Drinking water and vault toilets are available. Some facilities are wheelchair-accessible. Leashed pets are permitted.

Reservations, fees: Reservations are not accepted. Sites are $15 per night. Open year-round, weather permitting.

Directions: From Redding, drive north on I-5 and continue just past Dunsmuir to the junction with Highway 89. Turn east on Highway 89 and drive 12 miles to McCloud. From McCloud, continue driving on Highway 89 for five miles to the campground entrance road on the right. Turn right and drive a short distance to a Y intersection, then turn left into the campground.

Contact: Shasta-Trinity National Forest, McCloud Ranger District, 530/964-2184, www.fs.usda.gov/stnf.

40 ALGOMA

🚶 🏊 ⛵ 🏕 🐕 🚐 ⛺

Scenic rating: 7

on the McCloud River in
Shasta-Trinity National Forest

Map 2.2, page 116

This little-known, undeveloped spot is an alternative to Fowler's Camp and Cattle Camp (see listings in this chapter). Algoma sits along the McCloud River at 3,800 feet elevation; note it can get quite dusty here in August. It A dirt road out of Algoma (turn right at the junction) follows the headwaters of the McCloud River past Cattle Camp to Upper Falls. There is a parking area for a short walk to view Middle Falls, and then on to Fowler's Camp and Lower Falls.

Campsites, facilities: There are eight sites for tents or RVs up to 24 feet (no hookups). Picnic tables and fire grills are provided. Vault toilets are available, but there is no drinking water. Leashed pets are permitted.

Reservations, fees: Reservations are not accepted. There is no fee for camping. Open year-round, weather permitting.

Directions: From Redding, drive north on I-5 and continue just past Dunsmuir to the junction with Highway 89. Turn east on Highway 89 and drive to McCloud. From McCloud, continue driving on Highway 89 for 13 miles to the campground entrance road on the right (signed). Turn right and drive one mile to the campground by the bridge.

Contact: Shasta-Trinity National Forest, McCloud Ranger District, 530/964-2184, www.fs.usda.gov/stnf.

41 CATTLE CAMP

Scenic rating: 5

on the McCloud River in
Shasta-Trinity National Forest

Map 2.2, page 116

This campground is set at 3,700 feet and is best suited for RV campers who want a rustic setting, or as an overflow area when the more attractive and popular Fowler's Camp (see listing in this chapter) is filled. A small swimming hole in the McCloud River is near the camp, although the water is typically cold. There are several good side trips in the area, including fishing on the nearby McCloud River, visiting the three waterfalls near Fowler's Camp, and exploring the north slopes of Mount Shasta (a map of Shasta-Trinity National Forest details the back roads).

Campsites, facilities: There are 19 individual sites and four double sites for tents or RVs up to 32 feet (no hookups). Picnic tables and fire grills are provided. Drinking water and vault toilets are available. Some facilities are wheelchair-accessible. Leashed pets are permitted.

Reservations, fees: Reservations are not accepted. Sites are $15 per night. Open year-round, weather permitting.

Directions: From Redding, drive north on I-5 and continue just past Dunsmuir to the junction with Highway 89. Turn east on Highway 89 and drive to McCloud. From McCloud, continue driving on Highway 89 for 11 miles to the campground entrance road on the right. Turn right and drive 0.5 mile to the campground on the left side of the road.

Contact: Shasta-Trinity National Forest, McCloud Ranger District, 530/964-2184, www.fs.usda.gov/stnf.

42 TRAIL CREEK

Scenic rating: 7

in Klamath National Forest

Map 2.2, page 116

This simple and quiet camp is set beside Trail Creek, a small tributary to the upper Salmon River, at an elevation of 4,700 feet. A trailhead is about a mile to the south, accessible via a Forest Service road, that provides access to a two-mile trail routed along Fish Creek and leads to little Fish Lake. From Fish Lake the trail climbs steeply, with switchbacks at times, for another two miles to larger Trail Gull Lake, a very pretty spot set below Deadman Peak (7,741 feet).

Campsites, facilities: There are 13 sites for tents or RVs up to 20 feet (no hookups). Picnic tables and fire grills are provided. Drinking water and vault toilets are available. Some facilities are wheelchair accessible. Leashed pets are permitted.

Reservations, fees: Reservations are not accepted. Sites are $10 per night. Open May through October.

Directions: From Weed, drive north on I-5 to the Edgewood exit. Take the Edgewood exit, turn left at the stop sign, and drive a short distance under the freeway to another stop sign at Old Highway 99. Turn right (north) and drive six miles to Gazelle and Gazelle-Callahan Road. Turn left (west) on Gazelle-Callahan Road and continue to Callahan and Cecilville Road. Turn left (southwest) on Cecilville Road (becomes narrow) and drive 17 miles to the campground. Those with RVs should bear right upon entering the campground to align properly with aprons.

Contact: Klamath National Forest, Scott River Ranger District, 530/468-5351, www.fs.usda.gov/klamath.

43 HIDDEN HORSE

Scenic rating: 7

in Klamath National Forest

Map 2.2, page 116

Hidden Horse provides an alternate horse camp to nearby Carter Meadows (see listing in this chapter). The horse camps are in close proximity to the Pacific Crest Trail, which passes through the area and serves as access to the Russian Wilderness to the north and the Trinity Alps Wilderness to the south. Trail Creek and East Fork campgrounds are nearby. The elevation is 6,000 feet.

Campsites, facilities: There are six sites for tents or RVs up to 35 feet (no hookups). Picnic tables and fire grills are provided. Drinking water and vault toilets are available. A horse-mounting ramp and corrals are also available. There is no designated water for stock available, so bring a bucket. Some facilities are wheelchair-accessible. Leashed pets are permitted.

Reservations, fees: Reservations are not accepted. Sites are $10 per night. Open June through October, weather permitting.

Directions: From Weed, drive north on I-5 to the Edgewood exit. Take the Edgewood exit, turn left at the stop sign, and drive a short distance under the freeway to Old Highway 99. Turn right (north) and drive six miles to Gazelle and Gazelle-Callahan Road. Turn left (west) on Gazelle-Callahan Road, and continue to Callahan and Cecilville Road. Turn left (southwest) on Cecilville Road (becomes narrow) and drive 11 miles to Carter Meadows Horse Camp. Continue 0.25 mile to the campground on the left.

Contact: Klamath National Forest, Scott River and Salmon River Ranger Districts, 530/468-5351, www.fs.usda.gov/klamath.

44 CARTER MEADOWS GROUP HORSE CAMP

Scenic rating: 7

in Klamath National Forest

Map 2.2, page 116

Carter Meadows offers an extensive trail network for riding and hiking. The Pacific Crest Trail passes through the area and serves as access to the Russian Wilderness to the north and the Trinity Alps Wilderness to the south. Stream fishing is another option here. Trail Creek and East Fork campgrounds are nearby.

Campsites, facilities: There is one dispersed group equestrian site for tents or RVs up to 35 feet (no hookups) that can accommodate up to 25 people and 25 horses. Group barbecues and picnic tables are provided. Drinking water, vault toilets, and three horse corrals are available. Leashed pets are permitted.

Reservations, fees: Reservations are required at 877/444-6777 or www.recreation.gov ($9 reservation fee). The camp is $50 per night. Open June through October, weather permitting.

Directions: From Weed, drive north on I-5 to the Edgewood exit. Take the Edgewood exit, turn left at the stop sign, and drive a short distance under the freeway to Old Highway 99. Turn right (north) and drive six miles to Gazelle and Gazelle-Callahan Road. Turn left (west) on Gazelle-Callahan Road, and continue to Callahan and Cecilville Road. Turn left (southwest) on Cecilville Road and drive 11 miles to the campground on the left.

Contact: Klamath National Forest, Scott River and Salmon River Ranger Districts, 530/468-5351, www.fs.usda.gov/klamath.

45 BIG FLAT

🚶 🛶 🐾 🚙 ⛺

Scenic rating: 8

on Coffee Creek in Klamath National Forest

Map 2.2, page 116

This is a great jump-off spot for a wilderness backpacking trip into the adjacent Trinity Alps. An 11-mile hike will take you into the beautiful Caribou Lakes Basin for lakeside campsites, excellent swimming, dramatic sunsets, and fair trout fishing. The trail is routed out of camp, crosses the stream, then climbs a series of switchbacks to the ridge. From here it gets easier, rounding a mountain and depositing you in the basin. Bypass Little Caribou, Lower Caribou, and Snowslide Lakes, and instead head all the way to Caribou, the biggest and best of the lot. Big Flat is set at 5,800 feet elevation along Coffee Creek, and on the drive in, you'll see big piles of boulders along the stream, evidence of past gold mining activity.

Campsites, facilities: There are nine sites for tents or RVs up to 24 feet (no hookups). Picnic tables and fire grills are provided. Vault toilets and a small corral are available. No drinking water is available, but there is stock water for horses. Garbage must be packed out. Leashed pets are permitted.

Reservations, fees: Reservations are not accepted. There is no fee for camping. Open June through October, weather permitting.

Directions: From Redding, turn east on Highway 299 and drive to Weaverville. In Weaverville, turn right (north) on Highway 3 and drive just past the north end of Trinity Lake to Coffee Creek Road/Forest Road 104, adjacent to a Forest Service ranger station. Turn left on Coffee Creek Road and drive 21 miles to the campground at the end of the road.

Contact: Klamath National Forest, Salmon River Ranger District, 530/468-5351, www.fs.usda.gov.

46 HORSE FLAT

🚶 🐾 🚙 ⛺

Scenic rating: 6

on Eagle Creek in
Shasta-Trinity National Forest

Map 2.2, page 116

This camp is used by commercial pack operations as well as horse owners preparing for trips into the Trinity Alps. A trail leads out of camp and is routed deep into the Trinity Alps Wilderness. The trail starts at 3,200 feet in elevation, then climbs all the way along Eagle Creek to Eagle Peak, where it intersects with the Pacific Crest Trail, then drops over the ridge to little Telephone Lake, a nine-mile hike. Note: Horse owners should call for the conditions of the corral and trail before making the trip.

Campsites, facilities: There are 13 sites for tents or RVs up to 16 feet (no hookups). Picnic tables and fire grills are provided. Vault toilets are available. No drinking water is available. Horse corrals are available. Garbage must be packed out. Leashed pets are permitted.

Reservations, fees: Reservations are not accepted. There is no fee for camping. Open mid-May through October.

Directions: From Redding, drive west on Highway 299 to Weaverville and Highway 3. Turn right (north) on Highway 3 and drive to Trinity Center at the north end of Trinity Lake. From Trinity Center, continue north on Highway 3 for 16.5 miles to Eagle Creek Campground (on the left) and Forest Road 38N27. Turn left on Forest Road 38N27 and drive two miles to the campground.

Contact: Shasta-Trinity National Forest, Weaverville Ranger Station, 530/623-2121, www.fs.usda.gov/stnf.

47 EAGLE CREEK

Scenic rating: 7

in Shasta-Trinity National Forest

Map 2.2, page 116

This campground is set where little Eagle Creek enters the north Trinity River. Some campers use it as a base camp for a fishing trip, with the rainbow trout often abundant but predictably small in this stretch of water. The elevation is 2,800 feet.

Campsites, facilities: There are 17 sites for tents or RVs up to 35 feet (no hookups). Picnic tables and fire grills are provided. Drinking water and vault toilets are available. Leashed pets are permitted.

Reservations, fees: Reservations are not accepted. Sites are $10 per night, $5 per night for an additional vehicle. Open mid-May through October.

Directions: From Redding, drive west on Highway 299 to Weaverville and Highway 3. Turn right (north) on Highway 3 and drive to Trinity Center at the north end of Trinity Lake. From Trinity Center, continue north on Highway 3 for 16.5 miles to the campground on the left side of the road.

Contact: Shasta-Trinity National Forest, Weaverville Ranger Station, 530/623-2121, www.fs.usda.gov/stnf.

48 GOLDFIELD

Scenic rating: 6

in Shasta-Trinity National Forest

Map 2.2, page 116

For hikers, this camp makes a perfect first stop after a long drive. You wake up, get your gear organized, and then take the trailhead to the south. The trail is routed along Boulder Creek, and a left turn at the junction (about four miles in) will take you to Boulder Lake (another two miles), set inside the edge of the Trinity Alps Wilderness. Back in the

day, former 49er coach George Seifert told me about the beauty of this place, and how perfectly this campground is situated for the hike. The elevation is 3,000 feet.

Campsites, facilities: There are six sites for tents or RVs up to 16 feet (no hookups). Picnic tables and fire grills are provided. Vault toilets and hitching posts for horses are available. No drinking water is available. Garbage must be packed out. Leashed pets are permitted.

Reservations, fees: Reservations are not accepted. There is no fee for camping. Open year-round.

Directions: From Redding, head east on Highway 299 and drive to Weaverville. Turn right (north) on Highway 3 and drive about 36 miles, just past the north end of Trinity Lake to Coffee Creek Road/Forest Road 104 (a Forest Service ranger station is nearby). Turn left on Coffee Creek Road/Forest Road 104 and drive 4.7 miles to the campground on the left side of the road.

Contact: Shasta-Trinity National Forest, Weaverville Ranger Station, 530/623-2121, www.fs.usda.gov/stnf.

49 TRINITY RIVER

Scenic rating: 7

in Shasta-Trinity National Forest

Map 2.2, page 116

This camp offers easy access off Highway 3, yet it is fairly secluded and provides streamside access to the upper Trinity River. It's a good base camp for a fishing trip when the upper Trinity is loaded with small trout. The elevation is 2,500 feet.

Campsites, facilities: There are seven sites for tents or RVs up to 35 feet (no hookups). Picnic tables and fire grills are provided. Drinking water and vault toilets are available. Leashed pets are permitted.

Reservations, fees: Reservations are not accepted. Sites are $10 per night, $5 for an additional vehicle. Open May through October.

Directions: From Redding, drive west on Highway 299 to Weaverville and Highway 3. Turn right (north) on Highway 3 and drive to Trinity Center at the north end of Trinity Lake. From Trinity Center, continue north on Highway 3 for 9.5 miles to the campground on the left side of the road.

Contact: Shasta-Trinity National Forest, Weaverville Ranger Station, 530/623-2121, www.fs.usda.gov/stnf.

50 CASTLE CRAGS STATE PARK

Scenic rating: 9

on the Sacramento River

Map 2.2, page 116 — BEST

This park is named for the awesome granite spires that tower 6,000 feet above the park. Beyond to the north is giant Mount Shasta (14,179 feet), which encompasses a spectacular natural setting. The campsites are set in forest, shaded, very pretty, and sprinkled along a paved access road. But not a year goes by when people don't write in complaining of the highway noise from I-5 echoing in the Sacramento River Canyon, as well as of the occasional passing freight trains in the night. Pristine and quiet, this campground is not. If state park funding is secured, the campground location may be moved farther up the canyon for a quieter setting. At the end of the access road is a parking area for the two-minute walk to the Crags Lookout, a beautiful view. Nearby is the trailhead (at 2,500 feet elevation) for hikes up the Crags, featuring a 5.4-mile round-trip that rises to the base of Castle Dome at 4,800 feet, the leading spire on the crag's ridge. Again, road noise echoing up the canyon provides a background once you clear the tree line. Trout fishing is good in the nearby Sacramento River and requires driving, walking, and exploring to find the best spots. There are also some good swimming holes, but the water is cold.

Note: Castle Crags State Park was on the state park closure list. It is currently in negotiations for management through a donor agreement, but this status may change. Contact the park prior to planning a trip.

Campsites, facilities: There are 52 sites for tents only, three sites for RVs up to 27 feet (no hookups), six walk-in environmental sites (100-yard walk required) with limited facilities, and a hike-in/bike-in site. The Riverside Campground is an overflow area with 12 sites and limited facilities. Picnic tables, food lockers, and fire grills or fire rings are provided. Drinking water, restrooms with flush toilets and showers, and firewood are available. Some facilities are wheelchair accessible. Leashed pets are permitted at campsites only.

Reservations, fees: Reservations are accepted seasonally at 800/444-7275 (800/444-PARK) or www.reserveamerica.com ($8 reservation fee). Tent and RV sites are $25–30 per night, $8 per night for each additional vehicle; primitive drive-in tent sites are $15 per night; hike-in/bike-in sites are $5 per person per night. Open year-round, pending state park budget changes.

Directions: From Redding, drive north on I-5 for 45 miles to the Castle Crags State Park exit. Take that exit, turn west, and drive a short distance to the well-signed park entrance on the right side of the road.

Contact: Castle Crags State Park, 530/235-2684, www.parks.ca.gov.

51 RAILROAD PARK RV AND CAMPGROUND

Scenic rating: 7

south of Dunsmuir

Map 2.2, page 116

The resort adjacent to the RV park and campground was designed in the spirit of the railroad, when steam trains ruled the rails. The property features old stage cars (available for overnight lodging) and a steam locomotive. The railroad theme does not extend to the campground, however. What you'll find at the park is a classic campground set amid tall trees. There is a swimming hole in Little Castle Creek alongside the park. Many good side trips are available in the area, including excellent hiking and sightseeing at Castle Crags State Park (where there is a series of awesome granite spires) and outstanding trout fishing on the upper Sacramento River. At night, the sound of occasional passing trains soothes some, wakes others.

Campsites, facilities: There are 21 sites with full or partial hookups (30 amps) for RVs of any length, 31 sites with no hookups for tents or RVs. Some sites are pull-through. Cabins and a motel are next door at the resort. Picnic tables and fire rings are provided. Restrooms with showers, ice, coin laundry, group barbecue pit, game room, and horseshoes are available. A restaurant and lounge are within walking distance. Some facilities are wheelchair-accessible. Leashed pets are permitted.

Reservations, fees: Reservations are accepted. RV sites are $36 per night, tent sites are $28 per night, $3 per person per night for more than two people, $3 per night for each additional vehicle. Some credit cards accepted. Open April through November, weather permitting.

Directions: From Redding, drive north on I-5 for 45 miles to Exit 728 for Cragview Drive/Railroad Park Road. Take that exit and drive to the stop sign and Railroad Park Road. Turn left and drive under the freeway and continue to the campground on the left.

Contact: Railroad Park RV and Campground, 530/235-0420, www.rrpark.com.

52 SIMS FLAT

🥾 🏊 🚴 🛶 🔥 ♿ 🚐 ⛺

Scenic rating: 7

on the Sacramento River

Map 2.2, page 116

The upper Sacramento River is one of the best trout streams in the West, with easy and direct access off an interstate highway, and this camp is a good example. Sitting beside the upper Sacramento River at an elevation of 1,600 feet, it provides access to some of the better spots for trout fishing, particularly from late April through July. In the spring, this is a good put-in for rafting down through Pollard Flat. There is also a wheelchair-accessible interpretive trail. If you want to literally get away from it all, there is a trailhead about three miles east on Sims Flat Road that climbs along South Fork, including a terrible, steep, one-mile section near the top, eventually popping out at Tombstone Mountain. The noise from passing trains can be a shock, even when you know it's coming.

Campsites, facilities: There are 19 sites for tents or RVs up to 16 feet (no hookups). Picnic tables and fire grills are provided. Drinking water and flush and vault toilets are available. A nearby seasonal grocery store is open intermittently. Supplies are available to the north in Castella and Dunsmuir. Some facilities are wheelchair-accessible. Leashed pets are permitted.

Reservations, fees: Reservations are not accepted. Sites are $15 per night. Open late April through October.

Directions: From Redding, drive north on I-5 for about 40 miles to the Sims Road exit. Take the Sims Road exit (on the east side of the highway) and drive south for a mile (crossing the railroad tracks and a bridge) to the campground on the right.

Contact: Shasta-Trinity National Forest, Mount Shasta Ranger District, 530/926-4511, www.fs.usda.gov/stnf.

53 BEST IN THE WEST RESORT

🥾 🏊 🚴 🛶 🚐 ⛺

Scenic rating: 5

near Dunsmuir

Map 2.2, page 116

This is a good layover spot for RV cruisers looking to take a break. The proximity to Castle Crags State Park, the Sacramento River, and Mount Shasta make the location a winner.

Meers Creek runs through the property, and the local area has outstanding swimming holes on the Sacramento River. Trains make regular runs every night in the Sacramento River Canyon and the noise is a problem for some visitors.

Campsites, facilities: There are 15 sites with full hookups (30 and 50 amps) for RVs, a separate grassy area for dispersed tent camping, eight cabins, and a lodge. Picnic tables are provided. Coin laundry, cable TV, and restrooms with showers are available. Leashed pets are permitted.

Reservations, fees: Reservations are recommended. Sites are $25 per night. Weekly and monthly rates available. Open year-round.

Directions: From Redding, drive north on I-5 for about 40 miles to the Sims Road exit. Take the Sims Road exit and drive one block west on Sims Road to the resort on the left.

Contact: Best in the West Resort, 530/235-2603, www.eggerbestwest.com.

54 FRIDAY'S RV RETREAT & McCLOUD FLY FISHING RANCH

🚶 ⛵ 🎣 🐕 ♿ 🚐 ⛺

Scenic rating: 7

near McCloud

Map 2.2, page 116

Friday's RV Retreat and McCloud Fly Fishing Ranch offers great recreation opportunities across 400 wooded and grassy acres. The property features a small private fishing lake, two casting ponds, 1.5 miles of Squaw Valley Creek frontage, and five miles of hiking trails. The ranch specializes in fly-fishing packages, with both lodging and fly-fishing for one price. In addition, the McCloud River's wild trout section is a 45-minute drive to the south, the beautiful McCloud Golf Course (nine holes, play it twice at different tee boxes) is within a five-minute drive, and a trailhead for the Pacific Crest Trail is also only five minutes away.

Owner Bob Friday is quite a character, and he figured out that if he planted giant rainbow trout in the ponds for catch-and-release fishing, fly fishers would stop to catch a monster, take a photograph, and then tell people they caught the fish on the McCloud River, where they are smaller and elusive. (Weeds are occasionally a problem at the ponds; call ahead if that is a concern.) The park also has an area for miniature radio-controlled airplanes, a subject of fascination for Bob.

Campsites, facilities: There are 30 sites with full hookups (30 and 50 amps) for RVs of any length, a large, grassy area for dispersed tent camping, and two cabins. Most RV sites are pull-through. Picnic tables and fire pits are provided. Drinking water, restrooms with showers and flush toilets, coin laundry, pay phone, propane gas, and a recreation room are available. A fly-fishing school is available by arrangement. Some facilities are wheelchair-accessible. Leashed pets are permitted.

Reservations, fees: Reservations are recommended. RV sites are $28 per night, tent sites are $19 per night, $4 per person per night for more than two people. Monthly rates available for RVs. Open early May through September.

Directions: From Redding, drive north on I-5 and continue just past Dunsmuir to the junction with Highway 89. Bear right on Highway 89 and drive nine miles to McCloud and Squaw Valley Road. Turn right at Squaw Valley Road and drive six miles to the park entrance on the right.

Contact: Friday's RV Retreat and McCloud Fly Fishing Ranch, 530/964-2878, www.wix.com/edit30/fridaysrvretreat.

55 AH-DI-NA

🚶 ⛵ 🎣 🐕 ⛺

Scenic rating: 9

on the McCloud River in Shasta-Trinity National Forest

Map 2.2, page 116

This is the base camp for trout fishing on the lower McCloud River, with campsites just a cast away from one of the prettiest streams in California. You get access to the McCloud, which includes a special two-mile stretch of river governed by the Nature Conservancy, where all fish must be released, no bait is permitted, single, barbless hooks are mandated, and only 10 rods are allowed on the river at any one time. Wildlife is abundant in the area, the Pacific Crest Trail passes adjacent to the camp, and an excellent nature trail is also available along the river in the McCloud Nature Conservancy.

Campsites, facilities: There are 16 sites for tents. Picnic tables and fire grills are provided. Drinking water, flush toilets, and garbage bins are available. Leashed pets are permitted.

Reservations, fees: Reservations are not accepted. Sites are $10 per night. Open late April through October, weather permitting.

Directions: From Redding, drive north on I-5 past Dunsmuir to the junction with Highway 89. Turn right and drive nine miles to McCloud and Squaw Valley Road. Turn right on Squaw Valley Road and drive to Lake McCloud. Turn right at Lake McCloud and continue along the lake to a signed turnoff on the right side of the road (at a deep cove in the lake). Turn right (the road turns to dirt) and drive four miles to the campground entrance on the left side of the road. Turn left and drive a short distance to the campground. The road in is dusty and winding—RVs and trailers are not advised.

Contact: Shasta-Trinity National Forest, McCloud Ranger District, 530/964-2184, www.fs.usda.gov/stnf.

56 EAST FORK

Scenic rating: 8

on Willow Creek

Map 2.3, page 117

This is a beautiful spot along Willow Creek. Set at a 2,000-foot elevation, it's one of the prettiest campgrounds in the area. While you can dunk into the cold creek, it's not really a good swimming area. Fishing is prohibited here.

Campsites, facilities: There are 11 sites for tents or RVs up to 20 feet (no hookups). Picnic tables and fire rings are provided. Vault toilets are available. No drinking water is available. Some facilities are wheelchair accessible. Leashed pets are permitted.

Reservations, fees: Reservations are not accepted. Sites are $8 per night, $5 per night for each additional vehicle. Open late May through September, weather permitting.

Directions: From the junction of U.S. 101 and Highway 299 near Arcata, turn east on Highway 299 and drive 32 miles (six miles west of Willow Creek) and look for the camp's entrance road (well signed) on the right (south) side of the road.

Contact: Six Rivers National Forest, Lower Trinity Ranger District, 530/629-2118, www.fs.usda.gov/stnf.

57 BOISE CREEK

Scenic rating: 7

in Six Rivers National Forest

Map 2.3, page 117

This camp features a 0.25-mile trail down to Willllow Creek and nearby access to the Trinity River. If you have ever wanted to see Bigfoot, you can do it while camping here—there's a giant wooden Bigfoot on display in nearby Willow Creek. After your Bigfoot experience, your best bet during summer is to head north on nearby Highway 96 (turn north in Willow Creek) to the campground at Tish Tang, where there is excellent river access, swimming, and rafting in the late summer's warm flows. The Trinity River also provides good salmon and steelhead fishing during fall and winter, respectively. Note that fishing is prohibited in nearby Willow Creek.

Campsites, facilities: There are 17 sites for tents or RVs up to 35 feet (no hookups). Picnic

tables and fire grills are provided. Drinking water and vault toilets are available. A camp host is on-site. A grocery store, gas station, restaurant, and propane gas are available nearby. Some facilities are wheelchair-accessible. Leashed pets are permitted.

Reservations, fees: Reservations accepted at 877/444-6777 or www.recreation.gov ($9 reservation fee). Sites are $10 per night, $5 per night for each additional vehicle. Open year-round.

Directions: From the intersection of U.S. 101 and Highway 299 near Arcata, drive 38 miles east on Highway 299 and look for the campground entrance on the left side of the road. If you reach the town of Willow Creek, you have gone 1.5 miles too far.

Contact: Six Rivers National Forest, Lower Trinity Ranger District, 530/629-2118, www.fs.usda.gov/stnf.

58 DENNY

Scenic rating: 6

on the New River in
Shasta-Trinity National Forest

Map 2.3, page 117

This is a secluded and quiet campground along the New River, a tributary to the Trinity River and a designated Wild and Scenic River. The stream here is OK for swimming but too cold to even dip a toe in until late summer. If you drive north from the camp on Denny Road, you will find several trailheads for trips into the Trinity Alps Wilderness. The best of them is at the end of the road, where there is a good parking area, with a trail that is routed along the East Fork New River up toward Limestone Ridge. Note that the stretch of river near the camp is closed to fishing year-round. The campground is set at 1,400 feet.

Campsites, facilities: There are five sites for tents or RVs up to 22 feet (no hookups). Picnic tables and fire grills are provided. Vault toilets are available. No drinking water is available.

Garbage must be packed out. Leashed pets are permitted. Supplies are available about one hour away in Salyers Bar.

Reservations, fees: Reservations are not accepted. There is no fee for camping. Open year-round.

Directions: From the junction of U.S. 101 and Highway 299 near Arcata, turn east on Highway 299 and drive to Willow Creek. In Willow Creek, continue east on Highway 299 and, after reaching Salyer, continue for four miles to Denny Road/County Road 402. Turn north (left) on Denny Road and drive about 14 miles on a paved but very windy road to the campground.

Contact: Shasta-Trinity National Forest, Big Bar Ranger Station, 530/623-6106, www.fs.usda.gov/stnf.

59 HOBO GULCH

Scenic rating: 7

on the North Fork of the Trinity River in
Shasta-Trinity National Forest

Map 2.3, page 117

Only the ambitious need apply. This is a trailhead camp set on the edge of the Trinity Alps Wilderness, and the reason only the ambitious show up is that it is a 20-mile uphill haul all the way to Grizzly Lake, set at the foot of the awesome Thompson Peak (8,663 feet), with no other lakes available en route. The camp is set at 2,200 feet along the North Fork of the Trinity River. The adjacent slopes of the wilderness are known for little creeks, woods, and a few pristine meadows, and are largely devoid of lakes.

Campsites, facilities: There are 10 sites for tents only. Picnic tables and fire grills are provided. Vault toilets are available. No drinking water is available. Garbage must be packed out. Supplies can be obtained in Junction City, about one hour away. Leashed pets are permitted.

Reservations, fees: Reservations are not

accepted. There is no fee for camping. Open year-round.

Directions: From Redding, turn on Highway 299 west and drive west past Weaverville, and continue 13 miles to Helena and County East Fork Road. Turn right on County East Fork Road and drive four miles to Hobo Gulch Road. At Hobo Gulch Road, turn left (north) and drive 16 miles (very rough road) to the end of the road at the campground.

Contact: Shasta-Trinity National Forest, Big Bar Ranger Station, 530/623-6106, www.fs.usda.gov/stnf.

60 RIPSTEIN

Scenic rating: 8

on Canyon Creek in
Shasta-Trinity National Forest

Map 2.3, page 117

This is one of the great trailhead camps for the neighboring Trinity Alps. It is set at 3,000 feet on the southern edge of the wilderness and is a popular spot for a late-night arrival followed by a backpacking trip the next morning. The Canyon Creek Lakes await you via a six-mile uphill hike along Canyon Creek. The destination is extremely beautiful—two alpine lakes set in high granite mountains. The route passes Canyon Creek Falls, a set of two different waterfalls, about 3.5 miles out. This is one of the most popular backpacking destinations in Northern California. Seasonal guided rafting trips on Canyon Creek are also available.

Campsites, facilities: There are 10 sites for tents only. Picnic tables and fire grills are provided. Vault toilets are available. No drinking water is available. Garbage must be packed out. Supplies can be obtained 25 minutes away in Junction City. Leashed pets are permitted.

Reservations, fees: Reservations are not accepted. There is no fee for camping. Open year-round.

Directions: From Redding, turn on Highway 299 west and drive west to Junction City and Canyon Creek Road. Turn right on Canyon Creek Road and drive 10 miles to the campground on the left side of the road.

Contact: Shasta-Trinity National Forest, Big Bar Ranger Station, 530/623-6106, www.fs.usda.gov/stnf; Trinity River Rafting Company, 530/623-3033 or 800/307-4837, www.trinityriverrafting.com.

61 BURNT RANCH

Scenic rating: 7

on the Trinity River in
Shasta-Trinity National Forest

Map 2.3, page 117

This campground is set on a bluff above the Trinity River and is one of its most compelling spots. This section of river is very pretty, with deep, dramatic canyons nearby. The elevation is 1,000 feet. Note that the trail to Burnt Ranch Falls is not maintained and is partially on private land—the landowners will not take kindly to anyone trespassing.

Campsites, facilities: There are 15 sites for tents or RVs up to 25 feet (no hookups). Picnic tables and fire grills are provided. Drinking water and vault toilets are available. Garbage must be packed out. Supplies can be obtained in Hawkins Bar about one hour away. Leashed pets are permitted.

Reservations, fees: Reservations are not accepted. Sites are $8 per night. Open year-round, weather permitting.

Directions: From Redding, take Highway 299 west and drive past Weaverville to Burnt Ranch. In Burnt Ranch, continue 0.5 mile and look for the campground entrance on the right side of the road.

Contact: Shasta-Trinity National Forest, Big Bar Ranger Station, 530/623-6106, www.fs.usda.gov/stnf; Trinity River Rafting Company, 530/623-3033 or 800/307-4837, www.trinityriverrafting.com.

62 DEL LOMA RV PARK AND CAMPGROUND

Scenic rating: 7

on the Trinity River

Map 2.3, page 117

RV cruisers looking for a layover spot near the Trinity River will find just that at Del Loma. Shady sites and sandy beaches are available here along the Trinity. Rafting and tubing trips are popular in this area during the summer. Salmon fishing is best in the fall, steelhead fishing in the winter. This camp is popular for family reunions and groups. Salmon fishing can be sensational on the Trinity in the fall, and some anglers will book a year in advance to make certain they get a spot. About two-thirds of the sites are rented for extended periods.

Campsites, facilities: There are 41 sites, including two pull-through, with full hookups (50 amps) for RVs and tents, five park-model cabins, and two apartments. Picnic tables and fire grills are provided. Restrooms with flush toilets and showers, dump station, convenience store, clubhouse, heated pool, deli, Wi-Fi, RV supplies, firewood, coin laundry, recreation room, volleyball, tetherball, 18-hole mini golf, and horseshoe pits are available. Some facilities are wheelchair accessible. Leashed pets are permitted.

Reservations, fees: Reservations are accepted at 800/839-0194. Sites are $28 per night, $2 per person per night for more than two people. Group and monthly rates available. Some credit cards accepted. Open year-round.

Directions: From the junction of U.S. 101 and Highway 299 in Arcata, turn east on Highway 299 and drive to Burnt Ranch. From Burnt Ranch, continue 10 miles east on Highway 299 to the town of Del Loma and look for the campground entrance on the right.

Contact: Del Loma RV Park and Campground, 530/623-2834 or 800/839-0194, www.dellomarv.com.

63 HAYDEN FLAT CAMPGROUND

Scenic rating: 7

on the Trinity River in Shasta-Trinity National Forest

Map 2.3, page 117

This campground is split into two pieces, with most of the sites grouped in a large, shaded area across the road from the river and a few on the river side. A beach is available along the river; it is a good spot for swimming as well as a popular put-in and take-out spot for rafters. The elevation is 1,200 feet.

Campsites, facilities: There are 35 sites for tents or RVs up to 25 feet (no hookups); it can also be used as a group camp with a three-site minimum. Picnic tables and fire grills are provided. Drinking water and vault toilets are available. Some facilities are wheelchair-accessible. Leashed pets are permitted.

Reservations, fees: Reservations are required for groups (minimum of three sites) at 530/623-2121. Single sites are $12 per night, $30 per night for groups. Open year-round.

Directions: From the junction of U.S. 101 and Highway 299 in Arcata, head east on Highway 299 and drive to Burnt Ranch. From Burnt Ranch, continue 10 miles east on Highway 299 and look for the campground entrance. If you reach the town of Del Loma, you have gone 0.5 mile too far.

Contact: Shasta-Trinity National Forest, Big Bar Ranger Station, 530/623-6106, www.fs.usda.gov/stnf.

64 BIG BAR

Scenic rating: 6

near the Trinity River in Shasta-Trinity National Forest

Map 2.3, page 117

You name it, you got it—a quiet, small campground with easy access, and good fishing nearby (in the fall). In addition, there is a good put-in spot for inflatable kayaks and rafts. It is an ideal piece of water for newcomers, with Trinity River Rafting offering inflatable rentals for as low as $40. The elevation is 1,200 feet. If the shoe fits…

Campsites, facilities: There are three sites for tents only. Picnic tables and fire grills are provided. Vault toilets are available. No drinking water is available. Garbage must be packed out. Supplies are available one mile away in Big Bar. Leashed pets are permitted.

Reservations, fees: Reservations are not accepted. There is no fee for camping. Open year-round.

Directions: From Redding, turn on Highway 299 west and drive west to Weaverville. Continue on Highway 299 for 25 miles to the ranger station one mile east of Big Bar, and look for Corral Bottom Road (across from the ranger station). Turn left on Corral Bottom Road and drive 0.25 mile to the campground on the left.

Contact: Shasta-Trinity National Forest, Big Bar Ranger Station, 530/623-6106, www.fs.usda.gov/stnf; Trinity River Rafting Company, 530/623-3033 or 800/307-4837, www.trinityriverrafting.com.

65 SKUNK POINT GROUP CAMP

Scenic rating: 7

on the Trinity River in
Shasta-Trinity National Forest

Map 2.3, page 117

This is an ideal site for groups on rafting trips. You get easy access to the nearby Trinity River with a streamside setting and privacy for the group. A beach on the river is nearby. In the spring, this section of river offers primarily Class II rapids (only more difficult during high water), but most of it is rated Class I. By late summer, the water is warm and benign, ideal for families. Guided rafting trips and inflatables are available for hire and rent in nearby Big Flat. The camp elevation is 1,200 feet.

Campsites, facilities: There are two group sites that can accommodate up to 50 people each. Picnic tables and fire grills are provided. Vault toilets are available. No drinking water is available. Some facilities are wheelchair-accessible. Leashed pets are permitted.

Reservations, fees: Reservations are accepted at 877/444-6777 or www.recreation.gov ($9 reservation fee). The camp is $40 per night per site. Open year-round.

Directions: From Redding, turn on Highway 299 west, and drive west past Weaverville, Junction City, and Helena, and continue for about seven miles. Look for the campground entrance on the left side of the road. If you reach the town of Big Bar, you have gone two miles too far.

Contact: Shasta-Trinity National Forest, Big Bar Ranger Station, 530/623-6106, www.fs.usda.gov/stnf; Trinity River Rafting Company, 530/623-3033 or 800/307-4837, www.trinityriverrafting.com.

66 BIG FLAT

Scenic rating: 6

on the Trinity River in
Shasta-Trinity National Forest

Map 2.3, page 117

This level campground is set off Highway 299, just across the road from the Trinity River. The sites are close together, and it can be hot and dusty in midsummer. No problem. That is when you will be on the Trinity River, taking a rafting or kayaking trip—as low as $40 to rent an inflatable kayak from Trinity River Rafting in nearby Big Bar. It's fun, exciting, and easy (newcomers are welcome).

Campsites, facilities: There are 10 sites for tents or RVs up to 22 feet (no hookups). Picnic tables and fire grills are provided. Drinking water and vault toilets are available. Some facilities are wheelchair-accessible. Leashed pets are permitted.

Reservations, fees: Reservations are not accepted. Sites are $8 per night. Open year-round.

Directions: From Redding, turn on Highway 299 west, and drive west past Weaverville, Junction City, and Helena, and continue for about seven miles. Look for the campground entrance on the right side of the road. If you reach the town of Big Bar, you have gone three miles too far.

Contact: Shasta-Trinity National Forest, Big Bar Ranger Station, 530/623-6106, www.fs.usda.gov/stnf; Trinity River Rafting Company, 530/623-3033 or 800/307-4837, www.trinityriverrafting.com.

67 PIGEON POINT AND GROUP

Scenic rating: 7

on the Trinity River in
Shasta-Trinity National Forest

Map 2.3, page 117

In the good old days, huge flocks of band-tail pigeons flew the Trinity River Canyon, swooping and diving in dramatic shows. Nowadays you don't see too many pigeons, but this camp still keeps its namesake. It is better known for its access to the Trinity River, with a large beach for swimming. The elevation is 1,100 feet.

Campsites, facilities: There are six sites for tents or RVs up to 22 feet, two multi-family sites, and one group site that can accommodate up to 50 people with tents or RVs up to 16 feet. No hookups. Picnic tables and fire grills are provided. Vault toilets are available. No drinking water is available. Supplies can be obtained within 10 miles in Big Bar or Junction City. Some facilities are wheelchair-accessible. Leashed pets are permitted.

Reservations, fees: Reservations are not accepted for individual sites but are required

for the group site at 530/623-2121. Sites are $12 per night, $15 for multi-family sites, and $75 per night for the group site. Open year-round.

Directions: From Redding, turn on Highway 299 west and drive west to Weaverville. Continue west on Highway 299 to Helena and continue 0.5 mile to the campground on the left (south) side of the road.

Contact: Shasta-Trinity National Forest, Big Bar Ranger Station, 530/623-6106, www.fs.usda.gov/stnf.

68 BIGFOOT CAMPGROUND AND RV PARK

Scenic rating: 8

on the Trinity River

Map 2.3, page 117

This private RV park is set along the Trinity River and has become one of the most popular spots on the Trinity River. Rafting and fishing trips are featured, along with cabin rentals. It is also a popular layover for Highway 299 cruisers but provides the option for longer stays with rafting, gold panning, and in the fall and winter, fishing for salmon and steelhead, respectively. RV sites are exceptionally large, and a bonus is that a storage area is available. A three-acre site for tent camping is set along the river.

Campsites, facilities: There are 46 sites with full or partial hookups (30 and 50 amps) for RVs of any length, a separate area for tent camping, and four cabins. Tent camping is not allowed during the winter. Picnic tables and barbecues are provided. Restrooms with flush toilets and coin showers, coin laundry, convenience store, dump station, propane gas, solar-heated swimming pool (summer only), and horseshoe pits are available. TV hookups and a tackle shop are also available. Some facilities are wheelchair-accessible. Leashed pets are permitted.

Reservations, fees: Reservations are recommended from June through October. RV sites are $26–32 per night, tent sites are $23 per night, $2.50 per night per person for more than two people at RV sites. Some credit cards accepted. Open year-round.

Directions: From Redding, turn on Highway 299 west and drive west to Junction City. Continue west on Highway 299 for three miles to the camp on the left.

Contact: Bigfoot Campground and RV Park, 530/623-6088 or 800/422-5219, www.bigfootrvcabins.com.

69 JUNCTION CITY

Scenic rating: 7

on the Trinity River

Map 2.3, page 117

Some of the Trinity River's best fall salmon fishing is in this area in September and early October, with steelhead following from mid-October into the winter. That makes it an ideal base camp for a fishing or camping trip.

Campsites, facilities: There are 22 sites for tents or RVs up to 40 feet (no hookups). Picnic tables, fire grills, and bearproof food lockers are provided. Drinking water and vault toilets are available. Groceries and propane gas are available within two miles in Junction City. Some facilities are wheelchair-accessible. Leashed pets are permitted.

Reservations, fees: Reservations are not accepted. Sites are $10 per night per vehicle, $5 per additional vehicle. Open May through November.

Directions: From Redding, turn on Highway 299 west and drive west to Junction City. At Junction City, continue west on Highway 299 for 1.5 miles to the camp on the right.

Contact: Bureau of Land Management, Redding Field Office, 530/224-2100, www.blm.gov/ca.

70 BIG SLIDE

Scenic rating: 7

on the South Fork of the Trinity River in Shasta-Trinity National Forest

Map 2.3, page 117

This camp is literally out in the middle of nowhere, a tiny, secluded, little-visited spot set along the South Fork of the Trinity River. Free? Of course it's free. Otherwise, someone would actually have to show up now and then to collect. The elevation is 1,250 feet.

Campsites, facilities: There are eight sites for tents only. Picnic tables and fire grills are provided. Vault toilets are available. No drinking water is available. Leashed pets are permitted.

Reservations, fees: Reservations are not accepted. There is no fee for camping. Open late May to early October, weather permitting.

Directions: From Redding, turn on Highway 299 west and drive west over the Buckhorn Summit to the junction with Highway 3 near Douglas City. Turn south on Highway 3 and drive to Hayfork. From Hayfork, turn right on County Road 301 and drive about 20 miles to the town of Hyampom. In Hyampom, turn right on Lower South Fork Road/County Road 311 and drive five miles on County Road 311 to the campground on the right.

Contact: Shasta-Trinity National Forest, Hayfork Ranger Station, 530/628-5227, www.fs.usda.gov/stnf.

71 PHILPOT

Scenic rating: 7

on the North Fork of Salt Creek in Shasta-Trinity National Forest

Map 2.3, page 117

It's time to join the 5 Percent Club; that is, the 5 percent of the people who know the little-used, beautiful spots in California. This is one of those places, set on the North Fork of Salt Creek on national forest land at an elevation of 2,600 feet. Remember: 95 percent of the people use just 5 percent of the available open space. Why would anyone come here? To join the 5 Percent Club, that's why. Note: The road is too rough for many vehicles, and the sites are too small for most RVs. Trailers and RVs are not recommended.

Campsites, facilities: There are six sites for tents only. Picnic tables and fire grills are provided. Vault toilets are available. No drinking water is available. Garbage must be packed out. Leashed pets are permitted.

Reservations, fees: Reservations are not accepted. There is no fee for camping. Open late May to early November, weather permitting.

Directions: From Redding, turn on Highway 299 west and drive west over the Buckhorn Summit, and continue to the junction with Highway 3 near Douglas City. Turn left (south) on Highway 3 and drive to Hayfork. From Hayfork, continue southwest on Highway 3 for eight miles to County Road 353 (Rattlesnake Creek Road). Turn right and drive one mile to Forest Road 30N31. Turn right and drive 0.5 mile to the campground on the left. Trailers and RVs are not recommended.

Contact: Shasta-Trinity National Forest, Hayfork Ranger Station, 530/628-5227, www.fs.usda.gov/stnf.

2,600 feet. The headwaters of the Mad River pour right past the campground, about two miles downstream from the Ruth Lake Dam. People making weekend trips to Ruth Lake sometimes end up at this little-used camp. Ruth Lake is a designated Watchable Wildlife Site and is the only major recreation lake within decent driving range of Eureka, offering a small marina with boat rentals and a good boat ramp for access to trout and bass fishing and waterskiing. Swimming and all water sports are allowed at Ruth Lake. Note: All boats must be certified mussel-free before launching.

Campsites, facilities: There are 40 sites for tents or RVs up to 22 feet (no hookups). Picnic tables and fire grills are provided. Drinking water and vault toilets are available. Some facilities are wheelchair accessible. Leashed pets are permitted.

Reservations, fees: Reservations are accepted at 877/444-6777 or www.recreation.gov ($9 reservation fee). Sites are $12 per night, $5 per night for each additional vehicle. Open late May through mid-September.

Directions: From Eureka, drive south on U.S. 101 to Alton. Turn east on Highway 36 and drive about 50 miles to the town of Mad River. Turn southeast on Lower Mad River Road and drive four miles to the camp on the right side of the road.

Contact: Six Rivers National Forest, Mad River Ranger District, 707/574-6233, www.fs.usda.gov/srnf.

72 MAD RIVER

Scenic rating: 7

in Six Rivers National Forest

Map 2.3, page 117

This Forest Service campground is set along an alluvial flood terrace, a unique landscape for this region, featuring a forest of manzanita and Douglas fir. It is often hot, always remote, in a relatively unknown section of Six Rivers National Forest at an elevation of

73 FOREST GLEN

Scenic rating: 7

on the South Fork of the Trinity River in Shasta-Trinity National Forest

Map 2.3, page 117

If you get stuck for a spot in this region, this camp almost always has sites open, even during three-day weekends. It is on the edge of a forest near the South Fork of the Trinity

River. If you hit it during a surprise storm, a primitive shelter is available at the nearby Forest Glen Guard Station, a historic cabin that sleeps eight and rents out from the Forest Service.

Campsites, facilities: There are 15 sites for tents or RVs up to 16 feet (no hookups). Picnic tables and fire grills are provided. Drinking water and vault toilets are available. Some facilities are wheelchair-accessible. Leashed pets are permitted.

Reservations, fees: Reservations are not accepted. Sites are $12 per night. Reservations are accepted for the cabin at 877/444-6777 or www.recreation.gov ($9 reservation fee). The cabin is $35–75 per night. Open late May through early November, weather permitting.

Directions: From Red Bluff, turn west on Highway 36 (very twisty) and drive past Platina to the junction with Highway 3. Continue west on Highway 36 for 12 miles to Forest Glen. The campground is at the west end of town on the right side of the road.

Contact: Shasta-Trinity National Forest, Hayfork Ranger Station, 530/628-5227, www.fs.usda.gov/stnf.

74 HELLS GATE

Scenic rating: 7

on the South Fork of the Trinity River in Shasta-Trinity National Forest

Map 2.3, page 117

This is a pretty spot bordering the South Fork of the Trinity River. The prime feature is for hikers. The South Fork National Recreation Trail begins at the campground and follows the river for many miles. Additional trails branch off and up into the South Fork Mountains. This area is extremely hot in summer. The elevation is 2,300 feet. It gets moderate use and may even fill on three-day weekends. Insider's note: If Hells Gate is full, there are seven primitive campsites at Scott's Flat

Campground, 0.5 mile beyond Hells Gate, that can accommodate RVs up to 20 feet.

Campsites, facilities: There are 17 sites for tents or RVs up to 16 feet (no hookups). Picnic tables and fire grills are provided. Drinking water and vault toilets are available. Some facilities are wheelchair-accessible. Leashed pets are permitted.

Reservations, fees: Reservations are not accepted. Sites are $12 per night. Open late May through early November, weather permitting.

Directions: From Red Bluff, turn west on Highway 36 (very twisty) and drive past Platina to the junction with Highway 3. Continue west on Highway 36 for 10 miles to the campground entrance on the left side of the road. If you reach Forest Glen, you have gone a mile too far.

Contact: Shasta-Trinity National Forest, Hayfork Ranger Station, 530/628-5227, www.fs.usda.gov/stnf.

75 FIR COVE

Scenic rating: 7

on Ruth Lake in Six Rivers National Forest

Map 2.3, page 117

This spot is situated along Ruth Lake adjacent to Bailey Cove. The elevation is 2,600 feet, and the lake covers 1,200 acres. Swimming and all water sports are allowed on Ruth Lake, and there are three boat ramps. In the summer the warm water makes this an ideal place for families to spend some time swimming. Fishing is decent for rainbow trout in the spring and for bass in the summer. Note: All boats must be certified mussel-free before launching.

Campsites, facilities: There 19 sites for tents or RVs up to 22 feet (no hookups). Picnic tables and fire grills are provided. Drinking water and vault toilets are available. Some facilities are wheelchair-accessible. Leashed pets are permitted.

Reservations, fees: Reservations are accepted at 877/444-6777 or www.recreation.gov ($9 reservation fee). Sites are $12 per night, $5 per night for each additional vehicle. Open late May through mid-September.

Directions: From Eureka, drive south on U.S. 101 to Alton and the junction with Highway 36. Turn east on Highway 36 and drive about 50 miles to the town of Mad River. Turn right at the sign for Ruth Lake/Lower Mad River Road and drive 12 miles to the campground on the right side of the road.

Contact: Six Rivers National Forest, Mad River Ranger District, 707/574-6233, www.fs.usda.gov/stnf.

76 BAILEY CANYON

Scenic rating: 7

on Ruth Lake in Six Rivers National Forest

Map 2.3, page 117

Ruth Lake is the only major lake within a reasonable driving distance of U.S. 101, although some people might argue with you over how "reasonable" this twisty drive is. Regardless, you end up at a camp along the east shore of Ruth Lake, where fishing for trout or bass and waterskiing are popular. What really wins out is that it is hot and sunny all summer, the exact opposite of the fogged-in Humboldt coast. The elevation is 2,600 feet. Note: All boats must be certified mussel-free before launching.

Campsites, facilities: There are 25 sites for tents or RVs up to 22 feet (no hookups). Picnic tables and fire grills are provided. Drinking water and vault toilets are available. A boat ramp and small marina are available nearby. Some facilities are wheelchair-accessible. Leashed pets are permitted.

Reservations, fees: Reservations are not accepted. Sites are $12 per night, $5 per night for each additional vehicle. Open late May through mid-September.

Directions: From Eureka, drive south on U.S. 101 to Alton and the junction with Highway 36. Turn east on Highway 36 and drive about 50 miles to the town of Mad River. Turn right at the sign for Ruth Lake/Lower Mad River Road and drive 13 miles to the campground on the right side of the road.

Contact: Six Rivers National Forest, Mad River Ranger District, 707/574-6233, www.fs.usda.gov/stnf.

77 TRINITY LAKE KOA

Scenic rating: 8

on Trinity Lake

Map 2.4 Trinity Lake detail, page 119

This huge resort (some may remember this as the former Wyntoon Resort) is an ideal family vacation destination. Set in a wooded area covering 90 acres on the north shore of Trinity Lake, it provides opportunities for fishing, boating, swimming, and waterskiing, with access within walking distance. The lake boasts a wide variety of fish, including smallmouth bass and rainbow trout. The tent sites are spread out on 20 forested acres. The lake sits at the base of the dramatic Trinity Alps, one of the most beautiful regions in the state.

Campsites, facilities: There are 97 tent sites, 136 sites with full hookups (30 and 50 amps) for RVs of any length, two group sites for 12–48 people, and 19 cottages. Some RV sites are pull-through. Picnic tables and fire rings are provided. Drinking water, restrooms with showers, coin laundry, two playgrounds, miniature golf, summer recreation program for kids, seasonal heated pool, dump station, gasoline, convenience store, ice, snack bar, fish-cleaning area, boat rentals, and slips are available. Some facilities are wheelchair-accessible. Leashed pets are permitted, with certain restrictions.

Reservations, fees: Reservations are accepted. RV sites are $43–56 per night, tent sites are $36–46 per night, $3–6 per person per night for more than two people. Some credit cards accepted. Open year-round.

Directions: From Redding, drive west 40 miles on Highway 299 to Weaverville and Highway 3. Turn right (north) on Highway 3 and drive approximately 30 miles to Trinity Lake. At Trinity Center, continue 0.5 mile north on Highway 3 to the resort on the right.

Contact: Trinity Lake KOA, 530/266-3337 or 800/562-7706, www.trinitylakekoa.com or www.koa.com.

78 PREACHER MEADOW
🏃 🏠 ♿ 🚐 ⛺

Scenic rating: 7

in Shasta-Trinity National Forest

Map 2.4 Trinity Lake detail, page 119

From the right vantage point, the view of the Trinity Alps can be excellent here. Otherwise, compared to all the other camps in the area so close to Trinity Lake, it has trouble matching up in the quality department. If the lakeside camps are full, this camp provides an overflow option.

Campsites, facilities: There are 45 sites for tents or RVs up to 40 feet (no hookups). Picnic tables and fire rings are provided. Drinking water and vault toilets are available. Supplies, a coin laundry, and a small airport are available nearby. Some facilities are wheelchair accessible. Leashed pets are permitted.

Reservations, fees: Reservations are not accepted. Sites are $12 per night. Open mid-May through October.

Directions: From Redding, drive west on Highway 299 for 30 miles to Weaverville and Highway 3. Turn right (north) on Highway 3 and drive 27 miles to Trinity Lake. Continue toward Trinity Center and look for the campground entrance on the left side of the road (if

you reach Trinity Center you have gone two miles too far).

Contact: Shasta-Trinity National Forest, Weaverville Ranger Station, 530/623-2121, www.fs.usda.gov/stnf.

79 JACKASS SPRINGS
🏃 🏊 ⛵ 🚣 🐴 🚐 ⛺

Scenic rating: 6

near Trinity Lake in
Shasta-Trinity National Forest

Map 2.4 Trinity Lake detail, page 119

If you're poking around for a more secluded campsite on this end of the lake, halt your search and pick the best spot you can find at this campground, since it's the only one in this area of Trinity Lake. The campground is 0.5 mile from Trinity Lake, but you can't see the lake from the camp. It is most popular in the fall as a base camp for deer hunters. The elevation is 2,500 feet.

Campsites, facilities: There are 21 sites for tents or RVs up to 32 feet (no hookups). Picnic tables and fire grills are provided. Vault toilets are available. No drinking water is available. Garbage must be packed out. Leashed pets are permitted.

Reservations, fees: Reservations are not accepted. There is no fee for camping. Open year-round, weather permitting.

Directions: From Redding, drive west on Highway 299 to Weaverville and the junction with Highway 3. Turn right (north) on Highway 3 and drive 29 miles to Trinity Center. Continue five miles past Trinity Center to County Road 106. Turn right on County Road 106 and drive 12 miles to the Jackass Springs/County Road 119 turnoff. Turn right on County Road 119 and drive five miles to the campground near the end of the road.

Contact: Shasta-Trinity National Forest, Weaverville Ranger Station, 530/623-2121, www.fs.usda.gov/stnf.

80 CLEAR CREEK

Scenic rating: 6

in Shasta-Trinity National Forest

Map 2.4 Trinity Lake detail, page 119

This is a primitive, little-known camp that gets little use. It is set near Clear Creek at 3,400 feet elevation. In fall hunters will occasionally turn it into a deer camp, with the adjacent slopes of Blue Mountain and Damnation Peak in the Trinity Divide country providing fair numbers of large bucks three points or better. Trinity Lake is only seven miles to the west, but it seems as if it's in a different world.

Campsites, facilities: There are six sites for tents or RVs up to 22 feet (no hookups). Picnic tables and fire grills are provided. Vault toilets are available. No drinking water is available. Garbage must be packed out. Leashed pets are permitted.

Reservations, fees: Reservations are not accepted. There is no fee for camping. Open year-round.

Directions: From Redding, drive west on Highway 299 for 17 miles to Trinity Mountain Road. Turn right (north) on Trinity Mountain Road and continue past the town of French Gulch for about 12 miles to East Side Road/County Road 106. Turn right on the gravel road and drive north for about 11 miles to the campground access road (dirt) on right. Turn right on the access road and drive two miles to the campground.

Contact: Shasta-Trinity National Forest, Weaverville Ranger District, 530/623-2121, www.fs.usda.gov/stnf.

81 BRIDGE CAMP

Scenic rating: 8

on Stuarts Fork in
Shasta-Trinity National Forest

Map 2.4 Trinity Lake detail, page 119

This remote spot is an ideal jump-off point for backpackers. It's at the head of Stuarts Fork Trail, about 2.5 miles from the western shore of Trinity Lake. The trail leads into the Trinity Alps Wilderness, along Stuarts Fork, past Oak Flat and Morris Meadows, and up to Emerald Lake and the Sawtooth Ridge. It is a long and grueling climb, but fishing is excellent at Emerald Lake as well as at neighboring Sapphire Lake. There's a great view of the Alps from this camp. It is set at 2,700 feet and remains open year-round, but there's no piped water in the winter and it gets mighty cold up here.

Campsites, facilities: There are 10 sites for tents or RVs up to 20 feet (no hookups). Picnic tables and fire grills are provided. Drinking water (summer season), vault toilets, and horse corrals are available. Leashed pets are permitted.

Reservations, fees: Reservations are not accepted. Sites are $12 per night in the summer, $5 per night in the winter. Open year-round.

Directions: From Redding, drive west on Highway 299 to Weaverville. In Weaverville, turn right (north) on Highway 3 and drive 17 miles to Trinity Alps Road (at Stuarts Fork of Trinity Lake). Turn left at Trinity Alps Road and drive about two miles to the campground on the right side of the road.

Contact: Shasta-Trinity National Forest, Weaverville Ranger Station, 530/623-2121, www.fs.usda.gov/stnf.

82 RUSH CREEK

Scenic rating: 4

in Shasta-Trinity National Forest,
north of Weaverville

Map 2.4 Trinity Lake detail, page 119

This small, primitive camp provides overflow space during busy holiday weekends when the camps at Lewiston and Trinity Lakes are near capacity. It may not be much, but hey, at least if you know about Rush Creek you'll never get stuck for a spot. The camp borders Rush Creek and is secluded, but again, it's nearly five miles to the nearest access point to Trinity Lake.

Campsites, facilities: There are 11 sites for tents or RVs up to 20 feet (no hookups). Picnic tables and fire pits are provided. Vault toilets are available. No drinking water is available. Leashed pets are permitted.

Reservations, fees: Reservations are not accepted. Sites are $10 per night. Open mid-May through mid-September.

Directions: From Redding, drive west on Highway 299 to Weaverville. In Weaverville, turn right (north) on Highway 3 and drive about eight miles to the signed turnoff on the left side of the road. Turn left and drive 0.25 mile on the short spur road to the campground on the left side of the road. If you get to Forest Road 113, you've gone too far.

Contact: Shasta-Trinity National Forest, Weaverville Ranger Station, 530/623-2121, www.fs.usda.gov/stnf.

83 STONEY POINT

Scenic rating: 7

on Trinity Lake in
Shasta-Trinity National Forest

Map 2.4 Trinity Lake detail, page 119

This camp is located at Trinity Lake, easily discovered and easily reached, near the outlet of Stuarts Fork. The elevation is 2,400 feet. Some of you may remember that this campground was closed in 2010, with low water; it reopened when the lake filled up in 2011.

Campsites, facilities: There are 21 sites for tents only. Picnic tables and fire grills are provided. Drinking water and flush toilets are available, with limited facilities during the winter season. Leashed pets are permitted.

Reservations, fees: Reservations are not accepted. Sites are $13 per night. Open May through October.

Directions: From Redding, drive west on Highway 299 to Weaverville. In Weaverville, turn right (north) on Highway 3 and drive 14 miles (about 0.25 mile past the Stuarts Fork Bridge) to the campground.

Contact: Shasta-Trinity National Forest, Weaverville Ranger Station, 530/623-2121, www.fs.usda.gov/stnf.

84 PINEWOOD COVE

Scenic rating: 7

on Trinity Lake

Map 2.4 Trinity Lake detail, page 119

This is a privately operated camp with full boating facilities at Trinity Lake. If you don't have a boat but want to get on Trinity Lake, this can be a good starting point. A reservation is advised during the peak summer season. The elevation is 2,300 feet.

Campsites, facilities: There are 45 sites with full or partial hookups (30 and 50 amps) for RVs up to 40 feet, including 10 RV sites rented for the entire season and wait-listed. There are also 28 tent sites and 15 park-model cabins. Picnic tables and fire grills are provided. Restrooms with showers, a coin laundry, dump station, RV supplies, seasonal heated swimming pool, playground, children's treehouse, volleyball, badminton, free movies three nights a week in summer, modem access, video rentals, recreation room with billiards and video arcade, convenience store, ice, fishing tackle, library, boat dock with 32 slips, beach, and canoe and kayak rentals are available. Some facilities are wheelchair-accessible. Leashed pets are permitted.

Reservations, fees: Reservations are recommended in the summer. RV sites are $36–46 per night, tent sites are $19.50–28.50 per night, $4 per person per night for more than six people, $4 per pet per night. Some credit cards accepted. Open mid-May through September.

Directions: From Redding, drive west on Highway 299 to Weaverville. In Weaverville, turn north (right) on Highway 3 and drive 14 miles to the campground entrance on the right.

Contact: Pinewood Cove Resort, 45110 Hwy. 3, Trinity Center, 530/286-2201, www.pinewoodcove.com.

85 STONEY CREEK GROUP CAMPGROUND

🚶 🏊 🛶 ⛵ 🐾 ⛺

Scenic rating: 7

on Trinity Lake in Shasta-Trinity National Forest

Map 2.4 Trinity Lake detail, page 119

A couple of camps sit on the northern shore of the Stuarts Fork arm of Trinity Lake. This is one of two designed for groups (the other is Fawn), and it is clearly the better. It is set along the Stoney Creek arm, a cove with a feeder creek, with the camp large but relatively private. A swimming beach nearby is a bonus. The elevation is 2,400 feet.

Campsites, facilities: This group tent site can accommodate up to 50 people. Picnic tables and fire grills are provided. Drinking water and flush toilets are available. Leashed pets are permitted.

Reservations, fees: Reservations are required (find Stoney Group) at 877/444-6777 or www.recreation.gov ($9 reservation fee). The camp is $75 per night. Open early May through late September.

Directions: From Redding, drive west on Highway 299 to Weaverville. In Weaverville, turn right (north) on Highway 3 and drive 14.5 miles (about a mile past the Stuarts Fork Bridge) to the campground on the left.

Contact: Shasta-Trinity National Forest, Weaverville Ranger Station, 530/623-2121, www.fs.usda.gov/stnf; Shasta Recreation Company, 530/623-1203.

86 TANNERY GULCH

🚶 🏊 🛶 ⛵ 🐾 🚐 ⛺

Scenic rating: 8

on Trinity Lake in Shasta-Trinity National Forest

Map 2.4 Trinity Lake detail, page 119

This is one of the more popular Forest Service camps on the southwest shore of huge Trinity Lake. There's a nice beach near the campground, provided the infamous Bureau of Reclamation hasn't drawn the lake level

down too far. It can be quite low in the fall. The elevation is 2,400 feet. Side note: This campground was named by the tannery that once operated in the area; bark from local trees was used in the tanning process.

Campsites, facilities: There are 82 sites for tents or RVs up to 40 feet (no hookups). Picnic tables and fire grills are provided. Drinking water, flush and vault toilets, and a boat ramp are available. In summer, programs are held in the amphitheater. Leashed pets are permitted.

Reservations, fees: Reservations are accepted (find Tannery) at 877/444-6777 or www.recreation.gov ($9 reservation fee). Single sites are $17 per night, double sites are $23 per night, $5 per night for each additional vehicle. Open early May through late September.

Directions: From Redding, drive west on Highway 299 to Weaverville. In Weaverville, turn right (north) on Highway 3 and drive 13.5 miles north to County Road 172. Turn right on County Road 172 and drive 1.5 miles to the campground entrance.

Contact: Shasta-Trinity National Forest, Weaverville Ranger Station, 530/623-2121, www.fs.usda.gov/stnf; Shasta Recreation Company, 530/623-1203.

87 FAWN GROUP CAMP

🏊 🛶 ⛵ 🐾 🚐 ⛺

Scenic rating: 7

on Trinity Lake in Shasta-Trinity National Forest

Map 2.4 Trinity Lake detail, page 119

If you want Trinity Lake all to yourself, one way to do it is to get a group together and then reserve this camp near the shore of Trinity Lake. The elevation is 2,500 feet.

Campsites, facilities: There are two group sites for tents or RVs up to 40 feet (no hookups) that can accommodate up to 100 people each. Picnic tables and fire grills are provided. Drinking water and flush toilets are available. A marina is nearby. Leashed pets are permitted.

Reservations, fees: Reservations are required at 877/444-6777 or www.recreation.gov ($9 reservation fee). Sites are $100 per night. Open early May through late September.

Directions: From Redding, drive west on Highway 299 to Weaverville. In Weaverville, turn right (north) on Highway 3 and drive about 15 miles to Fawn Road. Turn right and drive 0.25 mile to the campground.

Contact: Shasta-Trinity National Forest, Weaverville Ranger Station, 530/623-2121, www.fs.usda.gov/stnf; Shasta Recreation Company, 530/623-1203.

88 MINERSVILLE

Scenic rating: 7

on Trinity Lake in Shasta-Trinity National Forest

Map 2.4 Trinity Lake detail, page 119

The setting is near lakeside, quite beautiful when Trinity Lake is fullest in the spring and early summer. This is a good camp for boaters, with a boat ramp in the cove a short distance to the north. But note that the boat ramp is not always functional. When the lake level drops to 65 feet below full, the ramp is not usable. The elevation is 2,400 feet.

Campsites, facilities: There are 17 sites for tents or RVs up to 36 feet (no hookups). Picnic tables and fire grills are provided. Drinking water, flush toilets, and a low-water boat ramp are provided. Leashed pets are permitted.

Reservations, fees: Reservations are not accepted. Single sites are $16 per night, double sites are $24 per night, and walk-in sites are $13 per night. Open year-round, with limited winter services.

Directions: From Redding, drive west on Highway 299 to Weaverville. Turn right (north) on Highway 3 and drive about 18 miles (if you reach the Mule Creek Ranger Station, you have gone 0.5 mile too far). Turn right at the signed campground access road and drive 0.5 mile to the camp.

Contact: Shasta-Trinity National Forest, Weaverville Ranger Station, 530/623-2121, www.fs.usda.gov/stnf; Shasta Recreation Company, 530/623-1203.

89 RIDGEVILLE BOAT-IN CAMP

Scenic rating: 9

on Trinity Lake in Shasta-Trinity National Forest

Map 2.4 Trinity Lake detail, page 119

This is one of the ways to get a camping spot to call your own—go by boat. The camp is exposed on a peninsula, providing beautiful views. Prospects for waterskiing and trout or bass fishing are often outstanding. The early part of the season is the prime time here for boaters, before the furnace heat of full summer. A great view of the Trinity Alps is a bonus. The only downer is the typical lake drawdown at the end of summer and beginning of fall, when this boat-in camp becomes a long traipse from water's edge.

Campsites, facilities: There are 21 tent sites. Picnic tables and fire grills are provided. Vault toilets are available. No drinking water is available. Garbage must be packed out. Boat ramps can be found near Clark Springs, Alpine View, or farther north at Trinity Center. Leashed pets are permitted.

Reservations, fees: Reservations are not accepted. There is no fee for camping. Open year-round.

Directions: From Redding, drive west on Highway 299 to Weaverville. In Weaverville, turn right (north) on Highway 3 and drive seven miles to the Stuarts Fork arm of Trinity Lake. You'll find boat launches at Stuarts Fork. After launching, drive your boat to the mouth of Stuarts Fork. The campground is set on the western shore at the end of a peninsula at the entrance to that part of the lake.

Contact: Shasta-Trinity National Forest, Weaverville Ranger Station, 530/623-2121, www.fs.usda.gov/stnf.

90 CLARK SPRINGS

Scenic rating: 7

on Trinity Lake in Shasta-Trinity National Forest

Map 2.4 Trinity Lake detail, page 119

This used to be a day-use-only picnic area, but because of popular demand, the Forest Service opened it for camping. That makes sense because people were bound to declare it a campground anyway, since it has a nearby boat ramp and a beach. The elevation is 2,400 feet.

Campsites, facilities: There are 20 sites for tents or RVs up to 21 feet (no hookups). Picnic tables and fire grills are provided. Drinking water and flush toilets are available, with limited facilities in the winter. Supplies are available in Weaverville. Leashed pets are permitted.

Reservations, fees: Reservations are not accepted. Sites are $12 per night. Open early April through October.

Directions: From Redding, drive west on Highway 299 to Weaverville. In Weaverville, turn right (north) on Highway 3 and drive 16.5 miles (about four miles past the Stuarts Fork Bridge) to the campground entrance road on the right.

Contact: Shasta-Trinity National Forest, Weaverville Ranger Station, 530/623-2121, www.fs.usda.gov/stnf.

91 RIDGEVILLE ISLAND BOAT-IN CAMP

Scenic rating: 9

on Trinity Lake in Shasta-Trinity National Forest

Map 2.4 Trinity Lake detail, page 119

How would you like to be on a deserted island? You'll learn the answer at this tiny, little-known island with a great view of the Trinity Alps. Located at 2,400 feet, it is one of several boat-in camps in the Trinity Lake region. Note that the lake level at Trinity Lake typically drops significantly from September through October.

Campsites, facilities: There are three tent sites. Picnic tables and fire grills are provided. Vault toilets are available. No drinking water is available. Garbage must be packed out. Several boat ramps are available at campgrounds and private resorts at Trinity Lake. Leashed pets are permitted.

Reservations, fees: Reservations are not accepted. There is no fee for camping. Open year-round.

Directions: From Redding, drive west on Highway 299 to Weaverville. In Weaverville, turn right (north) on Highway 3 and drive seven miles to the Stuarts Fork arm of Trinity Lake. You'll find boat launches at Stuarts Fork. After launching, drive your boat to the campground set on a small island near Estrelita Marina, between Minersville and Mariner's Roost.

Contact: Shasta-Trinity National Forest, Weaverville Ranger Station, 530/623-2121, www.fs.usda.gov/stnf.

92 MARINERS ROOST BOAT-IN CAMP

Scenic rating: 8

on Trinity Lake in Shasta-Trinity National Forest

Map 2.4 Trinity Lake detail, page 119

A perfect boat camp? This comes close at Trinity because it's positioned perfectly for boaters, with spectacular views of the Trinity Alps to the west, and it is an ideal spot for water-skiers. That is because it is on the western side of the lake's major peninsula, topped by Bowerman Ridge. Secluded and wooded, this area is set at 2,400 feet elevation.

Campsites, facilities: There are seven tent sites. Picnic tables and fire grills are provided. Vault toilets are available. No drinking water is available. Garbage must be packed out. Several boat ramps are available at campgrounds and private resorts at Trinity Lake. Leashed pets are permitted.

Reservations, fees: Reservations are not accepted. There is no fee for camping. Open year-round.

Directions: From Redding, drive west on Highway 299 to Weaverville. In Weaverville, turn right (north) on Highway 3 and drive seven miles to the Stuarts Fork arm of Trinity Lake. You'll find boat launches at Stuarts Fork. After launching, drive your boat to West Bowerman Ridge (near the point of the main arm of the lake) and look for the camp on the peninsula, just east and on the opposite shore of Ridgeville Island Boat-In Camp.

Contact: Shasta-Trinity National Forest, Weaverville Ranger Station, 530/623-2121, www.fs.usda.gov/stnf.

93 HAYWARD FLAT

Scenic rating: 7

on Trinity Lake in Shasta-Trinity National Forest

Map 2.4 Trinity Lake detail, page 119

When giant Trinity Lake is full of water, Hayward Flat is one of the prettiest places you could ask for. The camp has become one of the most popular Forest Service campgrounds on Trinity Lake because it sits right along the shore and offers a beach. The elevation is 2,400 feet.

Campsites, facilities: There are 98 sites for tents or RVs up to 40 feet (no hookups) and six double sites. Picnic tables and fire grills are provided. Drinking water, flush toilets, and a dump station are available, and there is usually a camp host. Supplies and a boat ramp are nearby. Some facilities are wheelchair-accessible. Leashed pets are permitted.

Reservations, fees: Reservations are accepted at 877/444-6777 or www.recreation.gov ($9 reservation fee). Sites are $17–23 per night, $5 per night for each additional vehicle. Open mid-May through mid-September.

Directions: From Redding, drive west on Highway 299 to Weaverville. In Weaverville, turn right (north) on Highway 3 and drive 19.5 miles, approximately three miles past the Mule Creek Ranger Station. Turn right at the signed access road for Hayward Flat and drive about three miles to the campground at the end of the road.

Contact: Shasta-Trinity National Forest, Weaverville Ranger Station, 530/623-2121, www.fs.usda.gov/stnf; Shasta Recreation Company, 530/623-1203.

94 ALPINE VIEW

Scenic rating: 9

on Trinity Lake in Shasta-Trinity National Forest

Map 2.4 Trinity Lake detail, page 119

This is an attractive area, set on the shore of Trinity Lake at a creek inlet. The boat ramp nearby provides a bonus. It's a very pretty spot, with views to the west across the lake arm and to the Trinity Alps, featuring Granite Peak. The Forest Service occasionally runs tours from the campground to historic Bowerman Barn, which was built in 1894. The elevation is 2,400 feet.

Campsites, facilities: There are 54 sites for tents or RVs up to 32 feet (no hookups). Picnic tables and fire grills are provided. Drinking water and flush toilets are available. Some facilities are wheelchair-accessible. The Bowerman boat ramp is nearby. Leashed pets are permitted.

Reservations, fees: Reservations are not accepted. Sites are $17–23 per night, $5 per night for each additional vehicle. Open mid-May through mid-September.

Directions: From Redding, drive west on Highway 299 to Weaverville. In Weaverville, turn right (north) on Highway 3 and drive 22.5 miles to Covington Mill (south of Trinity Center). Turn right (south) on Guy Covington Drive and drive three miles to the camp (one mile past Bowerman boat ramp) on the right side of the road.

Contact: Shasta-Trinity National Forest, Weaverville Ranger Station, 530/623-2121, www.fs.usda.gov/stnf; Shasta Recreation Company, 530/623-1203.

95 CAPTAINS POINT BOAT-IN

Scenic rating: 7

on Trinity Lake in Shasta-Trinity National Forest

Map 2.4 Trinity Lake detail, page 119 BEST (

The Trinity River arm of Trinity Lake is a massive piece of water, stretching north from the giant Trinity Dam for nearly 20 miles. This camp is the only boat-in camp along this entire stretch of shore, and it is situated at a prominent spot, where a peninsula juts well into the main lake body. This is a perfect boat-in site for water-skiers or anglers. The fishing is often excellent for smallmouth bass in the cove adjacent to Captain's Point, using grubs. The elevation is 2,400 feet.

Campsites, facilities: There are three tent sites. Picnic tables and fire grills are provided. Vault toilets are available. No drinking water is available. Garbage must be packed out. Several boat ramps are available at campgrounds and private resorts at Trinity Lake. Leashed pets are permitted.

Reservations, fees: Reservations are not accepted. There is no fee for camping. Open year-round.

Directions: From Redding, drive west on Highway 299 to Weaverville. In Weaverville, turn right (north) on Highway 3 and drive about seven miles to the signed turnoff on the right side of the road for the Trinity Alps Marina. Turn right and drive approximately 10 miles to the marina and boat ramp. Launch your boat and cruise north about four miles up the main Trinity River arm of the lake. Look for Captains Point on the left side of the lake.

Contact: Shasta-Trinity National Forest, Weaverville Ranger Station, 530/623-2121, www.fs.usda.gov/stnf.

96 ANTLERS RV PARK & CAMPGROUND

Scenic rating: 7

on Shasta Lake

Map 2.4 Shasta Lake detail, page 119

Antlers Park is set along the Sacramento River arm of Shasta Lake at 1,116 feet. The park is set on 20 acres and has shady sites. This is a full-service spot for campers, boaters, and anglers, with access to the beautiful Sacramento River arm. The camp often fills in summer, including on weekdays.

Campsites, facilities: There are 70 sites with full hookups (30 and 50 amps) for RVs of any length (several are pull-through), 40 sites for tents, and several rental trailers. Picnic tables and fire rings or fire grills are provided. Tent sites also have food lockers. Restrooms with showers, seasonal convenience store and snack bar, ice, coin laundry, Sunday pancake breakfasts, cable TV hookups, video games, playground, volleyball court, table tennis, horseshoes, basketball, WiFi, and seasonal swimming pool. Boat rentals, houseboats, moorage, and a complete marina with recreation room are adjacent to the park. Some facilities are wheelchair-accessible. Leashed pets are permitted, with a limit of two.

Reservations, fees: Reservations are recommended. RV sites are $25–41.65 per night, tent sites are $18–28.35 per night, $4.40 per person per night for more than two people, $2 per pet per night. Some credit cards accepted. Open year-round.

Directions: From Redding, drive north on I-5 for 24 miles to the Lakeshore Drive/Antlers Road exit in Lakehead. Take that exit, turn right at the stop sign, and drive a short distance to Antlers Road. At Antlers Road, turn right and drive 1.5 miles south to the campground on the left.

Contact: Antlers RV Park & Campground, 20682 Antlers Rd., Lakehead, 530/238-2322 or 800/642-6849, www.antlersrvpark.com.

97 ANTLERS

Scenic rating: 7

on Shasta Lake in Shasta-Trinity National Forest

Map 2.4 Shasta Lake detail, page 119

This spot is set on the primary Sacramento River inlet of giant Shasta Lake. Antlers is a well-known spot that attracts returning campers and boaters year after year. It is the farthest upstream marina/camp on the lake. Lake levels can fluctuate greatly from spring through fall, and the operators will move their docks to compensate. Easy access off I-5 is a big plus for boaters.

Note: Through 2015, Caltrans will be replacing Antlers Bridge on I-5 over the Sacramento River arm of Shasta Lake near Lakehead. Another 0.4-mile section of I-5 south of the bridge will be realigned (thanks to a high accident rate). Traffic will continue on Antlers Bridge during construction with a new "parallel alignment," so expect some inconvenience and plan your time accordingly. Antlers Boat Ramp will remain open, as will lake access.

Campsites, facilities: There are 41 individual sites and 18 double sites for tents or RVs up to 30 feet (no hookups). Picnic tables, food lockers, and fire grills are provided. Drinking water and flush and vault toilets are available. A boat ramp, amphitheater with summer interpretive programs, grocery store, and coin laundry are nearby. Some facilities are wheelchair-accessible. Leashed pets are permitted.

Reservations, fees: Reservations are accepted May through September at 877/444-6777 or www.recreation.gov ($9 reservation fee). Sites are $18 per night, $30 per night for a double site, $5 per night for each additional vehicle. Open year-round.

Directions: From Redding, drive north on I-5 for 24 miles to the Lakeshore Drive/Antlers Road exit in Lakehead. Take that exit, turn right at the stop sign, and drive a short distance to Antlers Road. At Antlers Road, turn right and drive one mile south to the campground.

Contact: Shasta-Trinity National Forest, Shasta Lake Ranger District, 530/275-1587, www.fs.usda.gov/stnf; Shasta Lake Visitor Center, 530/275-1589; Shasta Recreation Company, 530/275-8113.

98 GREGORY CREEK

Scenic rating: 7

on Shasta Lake in Shasta-Trinity National Forest

Map 2.4 Shasta Lake detail, page 119

Gregory Creek Campground closes every year from late winter through early summer for bald eagle nesting. Until the birds leave the nest, the campground remains closed. When open, it is one of the more secluded Forest Service campgrounds on Shasta Lake, and it has become extremely popular with the younger crowd. It is set just above lakeside, on the eastern shore of the northern Sacramento River arm of the lake. When the lake is fullest in the spring and early summer, this is a great spot.

Campsites, facilities: There are 18 sites for tents or RVs up to 16 feet (no hookups). Picnic tables and fire grills are provided. Drinking water and flush toilets are available. Leashed pets are permitted.

Reservations, fees: Reservations are not accepted. Sites are $14 per night, $5 per night for each additional vehicle. Usually open July through September; call to verify current status.

Directions: From Redding, drive north on I-5 for 21 miles to the Salt Creek/Gilman Road exit. Take that exit and drive over the freeway to Gregory Creek Road. Turn right and drive 10 miles to the campground at the end of the road.

Contact: Shasta-Trinity National Forest, Shasta Lake Ranger District, 530/275-1587, www.fs.usda.gov/stnf; Shasta Lake Visitor Center, 530/275-1589; Shasta Recreation Company, 530/275-8113.

99 LAKESHORE VILLA RV PARK

🏊 ⛵ 🚤 🐕 🚶 ♿ 🚐 ⛰️

Scenic rating: 7

on Shasta Lake

Map 2.4 Shasta Lake detail, page 119

This is a large campground with level, shaded sites for RVs, set near the northern Sacramento River arm of giant Shasta Lake. Most of the campers visiting here are boaters coming for the water sports—waterskiing, wakeboarding, or tubing. The sites are level and graveled.

Campsites, facilities: There are 91 sites for tents or RVs up to 45 feet with full or partial hookups (20, 30, and 50 amps); some sites are pull-through. There are also two RV rentals. Restrooms with showers, ice, dump station, cable TV, WiFi, playground, group facilities, and a boat dock are available. Boat ramp, store, restaurant, and bar are nearby. Some facilities are wheelchair-accessible. Leashed pets are permitted (bring proof of current rabies shot).

Reservations, fees: Reservations are accepted. RV sites are $25–38 per night, tent sites are $18–25 per night, $2 per additional vehicle, $1.50 per dog per day. Some credit cards accepted. Open year-round.

Directions: From Redding, drive north on I-5 for 24 miles to Exit 702 for Lakeshore Drive/Antlers Road in Lakehead. Take that exit, turn left at the stop sign, and drive under the freeway to Lakeshore Drive. Turn left on Lakeshore Drive and drive 0.5 mile to the campground on the right.

Contact: Lakeshore Villa RV Park, 20672 Lakeshore Dr., Lakehead, 530/238-8688, www.lakeshorevillarvpark.com.

100 LAKESHORE INN & RV

🏊 ⛵ 🚤 🐕 🚶 ♿ 🚐 ⛰️

Scenic rating: 7

on Shasta Lake

Map 2.4 Shasta Lake detail, page 119

Shasta Lake is a boater's paradise and an ideal spot for campers with boats. The nearest marina is 2.75 miles away. It is on the Sacramento River arm of Shasta Lake. Shasta Lake Caverns are 10 miles away, and Shasta Dam tours are available about 20 miles away.

Campsites, facilities: There are 40 sites with full or partial hookups (30 and 50 amps) for tents or RVs of any length; some sites are pull-through. Ten cabins are also available. Picnic tables are provided. Restrooms with showers, cable TV, dump station, seasonal swimming pool, playground, video arcade, coin laundry, seasonal bar and restaurant, and a small seasonal convenience store are available. Family barbecues are held on Sunday in season, 5 P.M.–9 P.M. Live music is scheduled most Friday and Saturday nights. Some facilities are wheelchair-accessible. Leashed pets are permitted in the campground only.

Reservations, fees: Reservations are recommended at 530/238-2003. Sites are $20–37 per night, $2.50 per person per night for more than two people, $1 per pet per night. Some credit cards accepted. Open year-round, with limited winter facilities.

Directions: From Redding, drive north on I-5 for 24 miles to Exit 702 for Lakeshore Drive/Antlers Road in Lakehead. Take that exit, turn left at the stop sign, and drive under the freeway to Lakeshore Drive. Turn left on Lakeshore Drive and drive one mile to the campground.

Contact: Lakeshore Inn & RV, 20483 Lakeshore Dr., Lakehead, 530/238-2003, www.shastacamping.com.

101 SHASTA LAKE RV RESORT AND CAMPGROUND

🏊 ⛵ 🏕 🚣 🐕 🎣 🚐 ⛺

Scenic rating: 7

on Shasta Lake

Map 2.4 Shasta Lake detail, page 119

Shasta Lake RV Resort and Campground is one of a series on the upper end of Shasta Lake with easy access off I-5 by car, then easy access by boat to premium trout or bass fishing as well as waterskiing and water sports.

Campsites, facilities: There are 50 sites with full hookups (30 amps) for RVs up to 40 feet, 19 tent sites, one trailer rental, and three cabins. Some sites are pull-through. Picnic tables, barbecues, and fire rings are provided. Restrooms with showers, seasonal convenience store, firewood, bait, coin laundry, playground, table tennis, horseshoes, trailer and boat storage, WiFi, and a seasonal swimming pool are available. There is also a private dock with 36 boat slips. Leashed pets are permitted.

Reservations, fees: Reservations are accepted at 800/374-2782. RV sites are $35 per night, tent sites are $25 per night, $4 per person per night for more than three people, $2 per pet per night. Some credit cards accepted. Open year-round.

Directions: From Redding, drive north on I-5 for 24 miles to the Lakeshore Drive/Antlers Road exit in Lakehead. Take that exit, turn left at the stop sign, and drive under the freeway to Lakeshore Drive. Turn left on Lakeshore Drive and drive 1.5 miles to the campground on the right.

Contact: Shasta Lake RV Resort and Campground, 20433 Lakeshore Dr., 530/238-2370 or 800/374-2782, www.shastalakerv.com.

102 LAKESHORE EAST

🏃 🏊 ⛵ 🏕 🚣 🐕 ♿ 🚐 ⛺

Scenic rating: 7

on Shasta Lake in Shasta-Trinity National Forest

Map 2.4 Shasta Lake detail, page 119

Lakeshore East is near the full-service community of Lakehead and is on the Sacramento arm of Shasta Lake. It's a nice spot, with a good boat ramp and marina nearby at Antlers or Sugarloaf.

Campsites, facilities: There are 17 individual sites and six double sites for tents or RVs up to 30 feet (no hookups). Three of the single sites include yurts. Picnic tables and fire grills are provided. Drinking water and flush toilets are available. A boat ramp, grocery store, and coin laundry are available nearby. Some facilities are wheelchair-accessible. Leashed pets are permitted.

Reservations, fees: Reservations are accepted May through September at 877/444-6777 or www.recreation.gov ($9 reservation fee). Sites are $18 per night for a single site, $30 for a double site, $50 per night per yurt, $5 per night for each additional vehicle. Open year-round.

Directions: From Redding, drive north on I-5 for 24 miles to the Lakeshore Drive/Antlers Road exit at Lakehead. Take the Antlers exit, turn left at the stop sign, and drive under the freeway to Lakeshore Drive. Turn left on Lakeshore Drive and drive three miles. Look for the campground entrance on the left side of the road.

Contact: Shasta-Trinity National Forest, Shasta Lake Ranger District, 530/275-1587, www.fs.usda.gov/stnf; Shasta Lake Visitor Center, 530/275-1589; Shasta Recreation Company, 530/275-8113.

103 NELSON POINT AND GROUP CAMP

Scenic rating: 7

on Shasta Lake in Shasta-Trinity National Forest

Map 2.4 Shasta Lake detail, page 119

This is an easy-to-reach campground, only a few minutes from I-5. It's set beside the Salt Creek inlet of Shasta Lake, deep in a cove. In low-water years, or when the lake level is low in the fall and early winter, this camp can seem quite distant from water's edge. This campground can be reserved as a group camp July through September; the rest of the year, sites are available "as-needed."

Campsites, facilities: There are eight individual sites for tents or RVs up to 16 feet. No hookups. When used as a group site, it can accommodate up to 60 people. Vault toilets, picnic tables, and fire grills are provided. No drinking water is available. A grocery store and coin laundry are nearby in Lakehead. Leashed pets are permitted.

Reservations, fees: Reservations are required for group sites at 877/444-6777 or www.recreation.gov ($9 reservation fee). Individual sites are $10 per night, $5 per night for each additional vehicle. The groups site is $80 per night. Open May through early September.

Directions: From Redding, drive north on I-5 for about 20 miles to the Salt Creek Road/Gilman Road exit. Take that exit, turn left and drive 0.25 mile to Gregory Creek Road. Turn right and drive one mile to Conflict Point Road. Turn left and drive one mile to the campground on the left.

Contact: Shasta-Trinity National Forest, Shasta Lake Ranger District, 530/275-1587, www.fs.usda.gov/stnf; Shasta Lake Visitor Center, 530/275-1589; Shasta Recreation Company, 530/275-8113.

104 GOOSENECK COVE BOAT-IN

Scenic rating: 4

on Shasta Lake in Shasta-Trinity National Forest

Map 2.4 Shasta Lake detail, page 119

You want a camp all to yourself? There's a good chance of that here at Gooseneck Cove. One reason is because it is well hidden, set back in a cove on the west side of the Sacramento River arm of giant Shasta Lake:. The fishing on the Sacramento River arm of Shasta Lake is very good, both trolling for trout all summer, especially at the headwaters in midsummer, or in the spring, casting with Senkos or grubs (on darthead jigs or rigged Texas-style) for bass. Waterskiing is also excellent here, with water temperatures in the high 70s for most of summer.

Campsites, facilities: There are eight boat-in sites for tents. Picnic tables and fire grills are provided. Vault toilets are available. No drinking water is available. Garbage must be packed out. Small stores with supplies are available at Antlers. Leashed pets are permitted.

Reservations, fees: Reservations are not accepted. There is no fee for camping. An $8 fee is charged for boat launching. Open year-round.

Directions: From Redding, drive north on I-5 for 24 miles to the Lakeshore Drive/Antlers Road exit in Lakehead. Take that exit, turn left at the stop sign, and drive a short distance to Antlers Road. At Antlers Road, turn right and drive one mile south to the campground and nearby boat launch. Launch your boat and cruise seven miles south to the boat-in campground.

Contact: Shasta-Trinity National Forest, Shasta Lake Ranger District, 530/275-1587, www.fs.usda.gov/stnf; Shasta Lake Visitor Center, 530/275-1589.

105 MCCLOUD BRIDGE

🎣🏊🛶🐕♿🚐⛺

Scenic rating: 7

on Shasta Lake in Shasta-Trinity National Forest

Map 2.4 Shasta Lake detail, page 119

Even though reaching this camp requires a long drive, it remains popular. That is because the best shore-fishing access at the lake is available at nearby McCloud Bridge. It is common to see 15 or 20 people shore fishing here for trout on summer weekends. In the fall, big brown trout migrate through this section of lake en route to their upstream spawning grounds.

Campsites, facilities: There are 11 individual sites and three double sites for tents or RVs up to 16 feet (no hookups). Picnic tables and fire grills are provided. Drinking water, vault toilets, and a group picnic area are available. Some facilities are wheelchair-accessible. Leashed pets are permitted.

Reservations, fees: Reservations are not accepted. Single sites are $18 per night, $30 per night for double sites, $5 per night for each additional vehicle. Open early May through September.

Directions: From Redding, drive north on I-5 for about 20 miles to the Salt Creek/Gilman exit. Turn right on Gilman Road/County Road 7H009 and drive northeast for 18.5 miles. Cross the McCloud Bridge and drive one mile to the campground entrance on the right.

Contact: Shasta-Trinity National Forest, Shasta Lake Ranger District, 530/275-1587, www.fs.usda.gov/stnf; Shasta Lake Visitor Center, 530/275-1589; Shasta Recreation Company, 530/275-8113.

106 PINE POINT AND GROUP CAMP

🏊🛶🚤🐕🚐⛺

Scenic rating: 7

on Shasta Lake in Shasta-Trinity National Forest

Map 2.4 Shasta Lake detail, page 119

Pine Point is a pretty little camp, set on a ridge above the McCloud arm of Shasta Lake amid oak trees and scattered ponderosa pines. The view is best in spring, when lake levels are generally highest. Boat-launching facilities are available at Hirz Bay; boaters park their boats on shore below the camp while the rest of their party arrives at the camp by car. That provides a chance not only for camping, but also for boating, swimming, waterskiing, and fishing. Note: From July through September, this campground can be reserved as a group site only. It is also used as a summer overflow camping area on weekends and holidays.

Campsites, facilities: There are 14 sites for tents or RVs up to 24 feet (no hookups), which can also be used as a group camp for up to 100 people. Picnic tables, food lockers, and fire rings are provided. Drinking water and vault toilets are available. Leashed pets are permitted.

Reservations, fees: Reservations are required for the group site at 877/444-6777 or www.recreation.gov ($9 reservation fee). Single sites are $14 per night, double sites are $30 per night, $5 per night for each additional vehicle, and $110 per night for the group site. Open May through early September.

Directions: From Redding, drive north on I-5 for about 20 miles to the Salt Creek/Gilman exit. Turn right on Gilman Road/County Road 7H009 and drive northeast for 17 miles to the campground entrance road on the right.

Contact: Shasta-Trinity National Forest, Shasta Lake Ranger District, 530/275-1587, www.fs.usda.gov/stnf; Shasta Lake Visitor Center, 530/275-1589; Shasta Recreation Company, 530/275-8113.

107 ELLERY CREEK

Scenic rating: 7

on Shasta Lake in Shasta-Trinity National Forest

Map 2.4 Shasta Lake detail, page 119

This camp is set at a pretty spot where El-lery Creek empties into the upper McCloud arm of Shasta Lake. Several sites are set on the pavement with an unobstructed view of the beautiful McCloud arm. This stretch of water is excellent for trout fishing in the summer, with bank-fishing access available two miles upstream at the McCloud Bridge. In the spring, there are tons of small spotted bass along the shore from the camp continuing upstream to the inlet of the McCloud River. Boat-launching facilities are available five miles south at Hirz Bay.

Campsites, facilities: There are 19 sites for tents or RVs up to 30 feet (no hookups). Picnic tables, food lockers, and fire grills are provided. Drinking water and vault toilets are available. Leashed pets are permitted.

Reservations, fees: Reservations are accepted at 877/444-6777 or www.recreation.gov ($9 reservation fee). Sites are $16 per night, $5 per night for each additional vehicle. Open early May through September.

Directions: From Redding, drive north on I-5 for about 20 miles to the Salt Creek/Gilman exit. Turn right on Gilman Road/County Road 7H009 and drive northeast for 15 miles to the campground on the right side of the road.

Contact: Shasta-Trinity National Forest, Shasta Lake Ranger District, 530/275-1587, www.fs.usda.gov/stnf; Shasta Lake Visitor Center, 530/275-1589; Shasta Recreation Company, 530/275-8113.

108 MOORE CREEK AND GROUP CAMP

Scenic rating: 8

on Shasta Lake in Shasta-Trinity National Forest

Map 2.4 Shasta Lake detail, page 119

The McCloud arm of Shasta Lake is the most beautiful of the five arms at Shasta, with its emerald-green waters and limestone canyon towering overhead to the east. That beautiful setting is taken advantage of at this camp, with a good view of the lake and limestone, along with good trout fishing on the adjacent section of water. Moore Creek is rented as a group camp most of the summer, except during holidays when individual sites are available on a first-come, first-served basis.

Campsites, facilities: There are 12 sites for tents or RVs up to 16 feet (no hookups) that are usually rented as one group site for up to 90 people. Picnic tables and fire grills are provided. Drinking water and vault toilets are available. Leashed pets are permitted.

Reservations, fees: Reservations are required for the group site at 877/444-6777 or www.recreation.gov ($9 reservation fee). Sites are $14 per night for individual sites, $5 per night for each additional vehicle, $110 per night for group site. Open late May through early September.

Directions: From Redding, drive north on I-5 for about 20 miles to the Salt Creek/Gilman exit. Take that exit and turn right on Gilman Road/County Road 7H009 and drive northeast for 14 miles to the campground on the right side of the road.

Contact: Shasta-Trinity National Forest, Shasta Lake Ranger District, 530/275-1587, www.fs.usda.gov/stnf; Shasta Lake Visitor Center, 530/275-1589; Shasta Recreation Company, 530/275-8113.

109 DEKKAS ROCK GROUP CAMP

🚶 🏊 🛶 🎣 🐕 🚐 ⛺

Scenic rating: 8

on Shasta Lake in Shasta-Trinity National Forest

Map 2.4 Shasta Lake detail, page 119

The few people who know about this camp love this little spot. It is an ideal group camp, set on a flat above the McCloud arm of Shasta Lake, shaded primarily by bays and oaks, with a boat ramp two miles to the south at Hirz Bay. The views are pretty here, looking across the lake at the limestone ridge that borders the McCloud arm. In late summer and fall when the lake level drops, it can be a hike from the camp down to water's edge.

Campsites, facilities: There is one group site for tents or RVs up to 16 feet (no hookups) that can accommodate up to 60 people. A central meeting area with preparation tables, picnic tables, two pedestal grills, and a large barbecue is provided. Drinking water and vault toilets are available. Leashed pets are permitted.

Reservations, fees: Reservations are required at 877/444-6777 or www.recreation.gov ($9 reservation fee). The camp is $110 per night.

Directions: From Redding, drive north on I-5 for about 20 miles to the Salt Creek/Gilman exit. Turn right on Gilman Road/County Road 7H009 and drive northeast for 11 miles to the campground on the right side of the road.

Contact: Shasta-Trinity National Forest, Shasta Lake Ranger District, 530/275-1587, www.fs.usda.gov/stnf; Shasta Lake Visitor Center, 530/275-1589; Shasta Recreation Company, 530/275-8113.

110 HIRZ BAY 1 AND 2 GROUP CAMPS

🚶 🏊 🛶 🎣 🐕 🚐 ⛺

Scenic rating: 8

on Shasta Lake in Shasta-Trinity National Forest

Map 2.4 Shasta Lake detail, page 119

This is the spot for your own private party, provided you get a reservation, and is set on a point at the entrance of Hirz Bay on the McCloud River arm of Shasta Lake. A boat ramp is only 0.5 mile away on the camp access road, giving access to the McCloud River arm. This is an excellent spot to make a base camp for a fishing trip, with great trolling for trout in this stretch of the lake.

Campsites, facilities: There are two group sites for tents or RVs up to 30 feet (no hookups). Hirz Bay 1 can accommodate 120 people; Hirz Bay 2 can accommodate 80 people. Picnic tables and fire grills are provided. Drinking water, vault toilets, and a group picnic area are available. Leashed pets are permitted.

Reservations, fees: Reservations are required at 877/444-6777 or www.recreation.gov ($9 reservation fee). Hirz Bay 1 is $110 per night; Hirz Bay 2 is $80 per night. Open April through late September.

Directions: From Redding, drive north on I-5 for about 20 miles to the Salt Creek/Gilman exit. Turn right on Gilman Road/County Road 7H009 and drive northeast for 10 miles to the campground/boat launch access road. Turn right and drive 0.5 mile to the camp on the left side of the road. The group camp is past the family campground.

Contact: Shasta-Trinity National Forest, Shasta Lake Ranger District, 530/275-1587, www.fs.usda.gov/stnf; Shasta Lake Visitor Center, 530/275-1589; Shasta Recreation Company, 530/275-8113.

111 HIRZ BAY

Scenic rating: 8

on Shasta Lake in Shasta-Trinity National Forest

Map 2.4 Shasta Lake detail, page 119 BEST (

This camp is set on a point at the entrance of Hirz Bay and is an excellent spot to make a base camp for a fishing trip, with great trolling for trout in this stretch of the lake. This is one of three camps in the immediate area (the others are Hirz Bay 1 and 2 Group Camps; see listing in this chapter). All provide nearby access to a boat ramp (0.5 mile down the road) and the McCloud River arm of Shasta Lake.

Campsites, facilities: There are 37 individual sites and 11 double sites for tents or RVs up to 30 feet (no hookups). Picnic tables and fire grills are provided. Drinking water and flush toilets are available. A camp host is usually available in the summer. A boat ramp is nearby. Some facilities are wheelchair-accessible. Leashed pets are permitted.

Reservations, fees: Reservations are accepted May through September at 877/444-6777 or www.recreation.gov ($9 reservation fee). Sites are $18 per night, $30 per night for a double site, $5 per night for each additional vehicle. Open year-round.

Directions: From Redding, drive north on I-5 for about 20 miles to the Salt Creek/Gilman exit. Turn right on Gilman Road/County Road 7H009 and drive northeast for 10 miles to the campground/boat launch access road. Turn right and drive 0.5 mile to the camp on the left side of the road.

Contact: Shasta-Trinity National Forest, Shasta Lake Ranger District, 530/275-1587, www.fs.usda.gov/stnf; Shasta Lake Visitor Center, 530/275-1589; Shasta Recreation Company, 530/275-8113.

112 MADRONE CAMP

Scenic rating: 7

on Squaw Creek in
Shasta-Trinity National Forest

Map 2.4 Shasta Lake detail, page 119

Tired of people? Then you've come to the right place. This remote camp is set along Squaw Creek, a feeder stream of Shasta Lake, which lies to the southwest. It's way out there, far away from anybody. Even though Shasta Lake is relatively close, about 10 miles away, this is another world. A network of four-wheel-drive roads provides a recreation option, detailed on a map of Shasta-Trinity National Forest.

Campsites, facilities: There are 10 sites for tents or RVs up to 16 feet (no hookups). Picnic tables and fire grills are provided. Vault toilets are available. No drinking water is available. Garbage must be packed out. Leashed pets are permitted.

Reservations, fees: Reservations are not accepted. There is no fee for camping. Open year-round.

Directions: From Redding, drive 31 miles east on Highway 299 to the town of Montgomery Creek. Turn left on Fenders Ferry Road/Forest Road 27 and drive 18 miles to the camp (the road starts as gravel and then becomes dirt). Note: The access road is rough and RVs are not advised.

Contact: Shasta-Trinity National Forest, Shasta Lake Ranger District, 530/275-1587, www.fs.usda.gov/stnf; Shasta Lake Visitor Center, 530/275-1589.

113 HOLIDAY HARBOR RESORT

Scenic rating: 7

on Shasta Lake

Map 2.4 Shasta Lake detail, page 119 BEST (

This camp is one of the more popular family-oriented, all-service resorts on Shasta Lake, which has the second-largest dam in the United States. It is set on the lower McCloud arm of the lake, which is extremely beautiful, with a limestone mountain ridge off to the east. It is an ideal jump-off point for all water sports, especially waterskiing, houseboating and boating, and fishing. A good boat ramp, boat rentals, and store with all the goodies are bonuses. The place is full service and even offers boat-launching service. Campers staying here also get a 15 percent discount on boat rentals. Another plus is the nearby side trip to Shasta Caverns, a privately guided adventure (fee charged) into limestone caves. This camp often fills in summer, even on weekdays.

Campsites, facilities: There are 27 sites with full hookups (50 amps) for RVs up to 40 feet, with tents allowed in several sites. Picnic tables and barbecues are provided. Restrooms with showers, general store, seasonal café, gift shop, coin laundry, marina, marine repair service, boat moorage, swim area, playground, propane gas, and houseboat and boat and personal watercraft rentals are available. Some facilities are wheelchair-accessible. Leashed pets are permitted.

Reservations, fees: Reservations are recommended. Sites are $22.75–36 per night, $5.75–6 per person per night for more than two people, $4.50–6 per night for each additional vehicle, $7.75–12.50 per night for boat moorage, $1 per pet per night. Some credit cards accepted. Open April through October.

Directions: From Redding, drive 18 miles north on I-5 to Exit 695 and the O'Brien Road/Shasta Caverns Road exit. Turn right (east) at Shasta Caverns Road and drive one mile to the resort entrance on the right; check in at the store.

Contact: Holiday Harbor Resort, 20061 Shasta Caverns Rd., Shasta Lake, 530/238-2383 or 800/776-2628, www.lakeshasta.com.

114 GREENS CREEK BOAT-IN

Scenic rating: 10

on Shasta Lake in
Shasta-Trinity National Forest

Map 2.4 Shasta Lake detail, page 119

This is one of my favorite spots on the planet on a warm spring day, maybe mid-April, but it is always special. This boat-in campsite provides an exceptional base camp and boat-in headquarters for a recreation paradise. The camp is set at the foot of dramatic limestone formations on the McCloud arm of Shasta Lake. By boat, this is one of the best fishing spots. The campsites are in a region well wooded and little traveled, with good opportunities in the evening to see wildlife.

Campsites, facilities: There are nine boat-in sites for tents. Picnic tables, bear lockers, and fire grills are provided. Vault toilets are available. No drinking water is available. Garbage must be packed out. Supplies are available at Holiday Harbor. Leashed pets are permitted.

Reservations, fees: Reservations are not accepted. There is no fee for camping. An $8 fee is charged for boat launching. Open year-round.

Directions: From Redding, drive north on I-5 over the Pit River Bridge at Shasta Lake to the O'Brien Road/Shasta Caverns Road exit. Turn east (right) on Shasta Caverns Road and drive 0.25 mile to a signed turnoff for Bailey Cove. Turn right and drive one mile to Bailey Cove boat ramp. Launch your boat and cruise four miles northeast up the McCloud Arm. Land your boat and pick your campsite. Note: The Bailey Cove boat ramp is not usable when the lake level drops more than 50 feet.

Contact: Shasta-Trinity National Forest, Shasta Lake Ranger District, 530/275-1587, www.fs.usda.gov/stnf; Shasta Lake Visitor Center, 530/275-1589.

115 SKI ISLAND BOAT-IN

🏊 🚣 🛶 🐕 ⛺

Scenic rating: 8

on Shasta Lake in
Shasta-Trinity National Forest

Map 2.4 Shasta Lake detail, page 119

Could there be any secrets left about Shasta Lake? You bet, with boat-in campsites providing the best of all worlds for people willing to rough it just a little. Ski Island is an outstanding place to set up camp and then boat, fish, ski, or explore this giant lake. It is on the Pit River arm of the lake about three miles upstream from the Pit River (I-5) bridge. The closest boat ramp to Ski Island is at Silverthorn Resort, which is in a cove on the Pit River arm of the lake. The closest public boat ramp is at Jones Valley, also on the Pit River arm. Here you will find this three-acre island with a boat-in campground and several little trails. It is well out of sight, and out of mind for most campers as well. One note: In wet weather, the reddish, iron-based soil on the island will turn the bottom of your boat rust-colored with even a minimum of tracking in.

Campsites, facilities: There are 23 boat-in sites for tents. Picnic tables and fire grills are provided. Vault toilets are available. No drinking water is available. Garbage must be packed out. Small stores with supplies are available at Silverthorn Resort and Jones Valley Resort. Leashed pets are permitted.

Reservations, fees: Reservations are not accepted. There is no fee for camping. An $8 fee is charged for boat launching. Open year-round.

Directions: From Redding, drive north on I-5 for three miles to Exit 682 for Oasis Road. Take that exit and drive to Oasis Road. Turn right on Oasis Road and drive 3.5 miles to Bear Mountain Road. Turn right and drive to Dry Creek Road. Turn left on Dry Creek Road and drive seven miles to a fork in the road. Bear right at the fork and drive to Jones Valley Boat Ramp (a left at the fork takes you to Silverthorn Resort). Launch your boat and head west (to the left) for four miles to Ski Island. Land and pick your campsite.

Contact: Shasta-Trinity National Forest, Shasta Lake Ranger District, 530/275-1587, www.fs.usda.gov/stnf; Shasta Lake Visitor Center, 530/275-1589.

116 ARBUCKLE FLAT BOAT-IN

🏊 🚣 🛶 🐕 ⛺

Scenic rating: 9

on Shasta Lake in
Shasta-Trinity National Forest

Map 2.4 Shasta Lake detail, page 119

How could anything be secluded on Northern California's most popular recreation lake? Well, here is your answer. Arbuckle Flat is a truly secluded boat-in campground well up the Pit River arm of the lake, set far back in a deep cove. You will feel a million miles away from all the fast traffic back at the main lake body. Specifically, it is five miles east of the Jones Valley Boat Ramp, set on the right (south) side. You pay a small price for this seclusion. After landing your boat, you must then carry your gear up a hill to the campsites. When the lake is low, this is like a march up Cardiac Hill. In the spring, when the lake is full, there isn't an issue. The landscape surrounding the campsites is peppered with oak. Fishing in the area is often good in spring for the beautiful Pit River strain of rainbow trout, trolling along the shore. It's also good for bass and crappie in a nearby cove, where so many submerged trees stick up out of the water, that the lake looks like it needs a shave.

Campsites, facilities: There are 11 boat-in sites for tents. Picnic tables and fire grills are provided. Vault toilets are available. No drinking water is available. Garbage must be packed out. Small stores with supplies are available at Silverthorn Resort and Jones Valley Resort. Leashed pets are permitted.

Reservations, fees: Reservations are not accepted. There is no fee for camping. An $8 fee is charged for boat launching. Open year-round.

Directions: From Redding, drive north on I-5 for three miles to Exit 682 for Oasis Road. Take that exit and drive to Oasis Road. Turn right on Oasis Road and drive 3.5 miles to Bear Mountain Road. Turn right and drive to Dry Creek Road. Turn left on Dry Creek Road and drive seven miles to a fork in the road. Bear right at the fork and drive to Jones Valley Boat Ramp (a left at the fork takes you to Silverthorn Resort). Launch your boat and head east (to the right) for five miles. The last major arm off to your right hides the campground at the back of the cove, in the oaks above the shore. Land and pick your campsite.

Contact: Shasta-Trinity National Forest, Shasta Lake Ranger District, 530/275-1587, www.fs.usda.gov/stnf; Shasta Lake Visitor Center, 530/275-1589.

117 JONES VALLEY INLET

Scenic rating: 4

on Shasta Lake in
Shasta-Trinity National Forest

Map 2.4 Shasta Lake detail, page 119

This is one of the few primitive camp areas on Shasta Lake, set on the distant Pit River arm of the lake. It is an ideal camp for hiking and biking, with nearby Clickapudi Trail routed for miles along the lake's shore, in and out of coves, and then entering the surrounding foothills and oak/bay woodlands. The camp is pretty, if a bit exposed, with two nearby resorts, Jones Valley and Silverthorn, providing boat rentals and supplies.

Campsites, facilities: There is an area for dispersed, primitive camping for tents or RVs up to 30 feet (no hookups). Drinking water, portable toilets, and trash service are available. During fire season, a free California campfire permit is required. A boat ramp at Jones Valley is two miles from camp. Groceries are available nearby. Leashed pets are permitted.

Reservations, fees: Reservations are not accepted. Sites are $8 per vehicle per night. Open March 1 to October 31.

Directions: From Redding, turn east on Highway 299 and drive 7.5 miles just past the town of Bella Vista. At Dry Creek Road turn left and drive nine miles to a Y intersection. Bear right at the Y (left will take you to Silverthorn Resort) and drive a short distance to the campground entrance on the left side of the road.

Contact: Shasta-Trinity National Forest, Shasta Lake Ranger District, 530/275-1587, www.fs.usda.gov/stnf; Shasta Lake Visitor Center, 530/275-1589; Shasta Recreation Company, 530/275-8113.

118 UPPER AND LOWER JONES VALLEY CAMPS

Scenic rating: 3

on Shasta Lake in
Shasta-Trinity National Forest

Map 2.4 Shasta Lake detail, page 119

Lower Jones is a small camp set along a deep cove in the remote Pit River arm of Shasta Lake. The advantage of Lower Jones Valley is that it is closer to the lake than Upper Jones Valley. There is a trailhead at the camp that provides access to Clickapudi Trail, a great hiking and biking trail that traces the lake's shore, routed through woodlands. Two nearby resorts, Jones Valley and Silverthorn, provide boat rentals and supplies.

Note that the Bear Fire of 2004 burned the trees and vegetation around these campgrounds and the area is still recovering.

Campsites, facilities: There are 18 sites and three double sites for tents or RVs up to 16 feet (no hookups) in two adjacent campgrounds. Picnic tables and fire grills are provided. Drinking water, food lockers, and vault toilets are available. A boat ramp at Jones Valley is two miles from camp. Some facilities are wheelchair-accessible. Leashed pets are permitted.

Reservations, fees: Reservations are not accepted. Upper Jones sites are $14 per night. Lower Jones single sites are $18 per night and $30 per night for a double site, $5 per night for each additional vehicle. Lower Jones is open year-round. Upper Jones is open May through September.

Directions: From Redding, turn east on Highway 299 and drive 7.5 miles just past the town of Bella Vista. At Dry Creek Road, turn left and drive nine miles to a Y intersection. Bear right at the Y (left will take you to Silverthorn Resort) and drive a short distance to the campground entrances, on the left side for Lower Jones and the right side for Upper Jones.

Contact: Shasta-Trinity National Forest, Shasta Lake Ranger District, 530/275-1587, www.fs.usda.gov/stnf; Shasta Lake Visitor Center, 530/275-1589; Shasta Recreation Company, 530/275-8113.

119 SHASTA

Scenic rating: 6

on the Sacramento River in
Shasta-Trinity National Forest

Map 2.4 Shasta Lake detail, page 119

You cross Shasta Dam to reach this site, which doubles as a staging area for the nearby Chapple-Shasta OHV Area, one of the few in the north of the state. Expect to see lots of quads and dirt bikes—loud and wild and hey, it's a perfect spot for them. Because of past mining in the area, it's barren with almost no shade, but the views of the river and Shasta Dam are incredible. Nearby dam tours are unique and memorable.

Campsites, facilities: There are 22 sites for tents or RVs up to 30 feet (no hookups). Picnic tables and fire rings are provided. Drinking water and vault toilets are available. A boat ramp is nearby. Groceries and bait are available in Shasta Lake City. Leashed pets are permitted.

Reservations, fees: Reservations are not accepted. Sites are $10 per night, $5 per night for each additional vehicle. Open year-round.

Directions: From I-5 in Redding, drive north for three miles to the exit for the town of Shasta Lake City and Shasta Dam Boulevard. Take that exit and bear west on Shasta Dam Boulevard and drive three miles to Lake Boulevard. Turn right on Lake Boulevard and drive two miles. Cross Shasta Dam and continue four miles to the signed campground.

Contact: Bureau of Reclamation, Shasta Dam Visitor Center, 530/275-4463, www.blm.gov/ca; Shasta-Trinity National Forest, Shasta Lake Ranger District, 530/275-1587, www.fs.usda.gov/stnf; Shasta Lake Visitor Center, 530/275-1589.

120 FAWNDALE OAKS RV PARK

Scenic rating: 5

near Shasta Lake

Map 2.4 Shasta Lake detail, page 119

This RV park sits on 40 acres with shaded sites. It is midway between Shasta Lake and Redding, so it's close to many recreational activities. Toward Redding, the options include Turtle Bay Exploration Park, WaterWorks Park, public golf courses, and Sacramento River trails, which are paved, making them accessible for wheelchairs and bicycles. Toward Shasta Lake, there are tours of Shasta Caverns, via a short drive to Holiday Harbor.

Campsites, facilities: There are 10 tent sites and 15 sites with full hookups (30 and 50 amps) and cable TV for RVs up to 45 feet. Some sites are pull-through. A cabin and trailer are also available for rent. Picnic tables are provided and some sites have barbecues. Phone hookups, WiFi, coin laundry, boat and RV storage, a general store, picnic area, playground, seasonal swimming pool, club room, game room, propane, and group facilities are available. Some facilities are wheelchair-accessible. Leashed pets are permitted.

Reservations, fees: Reservations are accepted by telephone or online. RV sites are $26–28 per night for two people, tent sites are $19 per night for a family of four, $2 per person per night for any additional people, $1 per pet per night, $3 per night for each additional vehicle. Weekly and monthly rates are available. Some credit cards accepted. Open year-round.

Directions: From Redding, drive north on I-5 for nine miles to the Fawndale Road exit (Exit 689). Take that exit and turn right (east) on Fawndale Road. Drive 0.5 mile to the second RV park at the end of the road at 15015 Fawndale Road.

Contact: Fawndale Oaks RV Park, 15015 Fawndale Rd., Redding, 530/275-0764 or 888/838-2159, www.fawndaleoaks.com.

121 BEAR MOUNTAIN RV RESORT AND CAMPGROUND

🏃 🏊 ⛵ 🚤 🐕 🚲 🚐 ⛺

Scenic rating: 5

near Shasta Lake

Map 2.4 Shasta Lake detail, page 119

This is a privately operated park in the remote Jones Valley area five miles from Shasta Lake. It is set on 52 acres. A hiking trail leaves from the campground, rises up a hill, and provides a great view of Redding. The resort emphasizes that there is no train noise here, as there often is at campgrounds closer to Shasta Lake.

Campsites, facilities: There are 70 sites with full or partial hookups (30 amps) for RVs up to 40 feet, 14 tent sites, and four park-model cabins. Some RV sites are pull-through. Picnic tables and fire rings are provided. Drinking water, restrooms with flush toilets and coin showers, coin laundry, dump station, a seasonal swimming pool, table tennis, playground, volleyball, and horseshoe pit are available. A boat ramp is within three miles. Leashed pets are permitted.

Reservations, fees: Reservations are accepted. RV sites are $18–24 per night, tent sites are $14 per night, $2 per person per night for more than two people. Weekly and monthly rates available. Some credit cards accepted. Open year-round.

Directions: From Redding, drive north on I-5 for three miles to Exit 682 for Oasis Road. Take that exit and drive to Oasis Road. Turn right on Oasis Road and drive 3.5 miles to Bear Mountain Road. Turn right on Bear Mountain Road and drive 3.5 miles to the campground on the left.

Note: Do not use GPS or mapping sites to reach this area.

Contact: Bear Mountain RV Resort and Campground, 14216 Bear Mtn. Rd., Redding, 530/275-4728, www.campshasta.com.

122 EAST WEAVER

🏃 🏊 🐕 🚐 ⛺

Scenic rating: 6

on the east branch of Weaver Creek in Shasta-Trinity National Forest

Map 2.4, page 118

This camp is set along East Weaver Creek. Another mile to the west on East Weaver Road, the road dead-ends at a trailhead, a good side trip. From here, the hiking trail is routed four miles, a significant climb, to tiny East Weaver Lake, set to the southwest of Monument Peak (7,771 feet elevation). The elevation at East Weaver is 2,700 feet.

Campsites, facilities: There are 10 sites for tents or RVs up to 25 feet (no hookups). Picnic tables and fire grills are provided. Drinking water and vault toilets are available. Supplies and a coin laundry are available in Weaverville. Leashed pets are permitted.

Reservations, fees: Reservations are not accepted. Sites are $11 per night, $5 per night in the winter, $5 for additional vehicle. Open year-round.

Directions: From Redding, drive west on Highway 299 to Weaverville. In Weaverville, turn right (north) on Highway 3 and drive about two miles to East Weaver Road. Turn left on East Weaver Road and drive 3.5 miles to the campground.

Contact: Shasta-Trinity National Forest, Weaverville Ranger Station, 530/623-2121, www.fs.usda.gov/stnf.

123 DOUGLAS CITY AND STEINER FLAT

🏊 🛶 🚤 🐕 🚐 ⛺

Scenic rating: 7

on the Trinity River

Map 2.4, page 118

If you want to camp along this stretch of the main Trinity River, these camps are your best bet (they're along the river about two miles from each other). They are set off the main road, near the river, with good bank fishing access (the prime season is from mid-August through winter for salmon and steelhead). There's paved parking, a group picnic site, and two beaches at Douglas City. Steiner Flat, a more primitive camp, provides better access for fishing. This can be a good base camp for an off-season fishing trip on the Trinity River or a lounging spot during the summer. The elevation is 1,700 feet.

Campsites, facilities: Douglas City has 20 sites for tents or RVs up to 28 feet. No hookups. Picnic tables and fire grills are provided. Drinking water and restrooms with sinks and flush toilets are available. Steiner Flat has dispersed camping for 22 tents and RVs up to 40 feet. No hookups. Picnic tables and fire grills are provided. Vault toilets are available. There is no drinking water. Supplies are available within one mile in the town of Douglas City. Leashed pets are permitted at both sites.

Reservations, fees: Reservations are not accepted. Sites at Douglas City are $10 per night, $5 per additional vehicle. There is no fee for camping at Steiner Flat. Douglas City is open mid-May through November;

Steiner Flat is open year-round, weather permitting.

Directions: From Redding, turn on Highway 299 west and drive west (toward Weaverville). Continue over the bridge at the Trinity River near Douglas City to Steiner Flat Road. Turn left on Steiner Flat Road and drive 0.5 mile to Douglas City campground on the left. To reach Steiner Flat, continue two more miles and look for the campground on the left.

Contact: Bureau of Land Management, Redding Field Office, 530/224-2100, www.blm.gov/ca.

124 STEEL BRIDGE

🏊 🛶 🐕 ♿ 🚐 ⛺

Scenic rating: 7

on the Trinity River

Map 2.4, page 118

Very few people know of this camp, yet it can be a prime spot for anglers and campers; it's one of the better stretches of water in the area for steelhead, with good shore-fishing access (the prime time is from October through December). In the summer, the shade of conifers will keep you cool. Don't forget to bring your own water. The elevation is 1,700 feet.

Campsites, facilities: There are 12 sites for tents or RVs up to 20 feet (no hookups). Picnic tables and fire grills are provided. Vault toilets are available. No drinking water is available. Supplies are available within three miles in Douglas City. Some facilities are wheelchair-accessible. Leashed pets are permitted.

Reservations, fees: Reservations are not accepted. Sites are $5 per night, $5 per additional vehicle. Open mid-May through winter, weather permitting.

Directions: From Redding, turn west on Highway 299 and drive over Buckhorn Summit. Continue toward Douglas City to Steel Bridge Road (if you reach Douglas City, you have gone 2.3 miles too far). At Steel Bridge Road, turn right and drive about two miles to the campground at the end of the road.

Contact: Bureau of Land Management, Redding Field Office, 530/224-2100, www.blm.gov/ca.

125 OLD LEWISTON BRIDGE RV RESORT

Scenic rating: 7

on the Trinity River

Map 2.4, page 118

This is a popular spot for calm-water kayaking, rafting, and fishing. Though much of the water from Trinity and Lewiston Lakes is diverted via tunnel to Whiskeytown Lake (en route to the valley and points south), enough escapes downstream to provide a viable stream here near the town of Lewiston. This upstream section below Lewiston Lake is prime in the early summer for trout, particularly the chance for a huge brown trout (special regulations in effect). A fishing shuttle service is available. The campground is in a hilly area but has level sites, with nearby Lewiston Lake also a major attraction. Some sites are occupied by long-term renters.

Campsites, facilities: There are 52 sites with full hookups (30 amps) for RVs up to 45 feet, a separate area for tents, and five rental trailers. Picnic tables and fire rings are provided. Restrooms with showers, coin laundry, grocery store, modem access, ice, bait and tackle, and propane gas refills are available. A group picnic area is available by reservation. A restaurant is within 0.5 mile. Leashed pets are permitted.

Reservations, fees: Reservations are accepted by phone or website. Sites are $28 per night for RVs, $15 per night per vehicle for tent campers, $2 per person per night for more than two people. Weekly and monthly rates available. Some credit cards accepted. Open year-round.

Directions: From Redding, turn on Highway 299 and drive west over Buckhorn Summit, and continue for five miles to Trinity Dam Boulevard. Turn right on Trinity Dam Boulevard and drive four miles to Lewiston, and continue north to Rush Creek Road. Turn left (west) on Rush Creek Road and drive 0.25 mile to the resort on the left.

Contact: Old Lewiston Bridge RV Resort, Rush Creek Rd., Lewiston, 530/778-3894 or 800/922-1924, www.lewistonbridgerv.com.

126 TRINITY RIVER RESORT AND RV PARK

Scenic rating: 7

on the Trinity River

Map 2.4, page 118

For many, this privately operated park has an ideal location. You get level, grassy sites with shade trees along the Trinity River, yet it is just a short drive north to Lewiston Lake or a bit farther to giant Trinity Lake. Lake or river, take your pick. The resort covers nearly 14 acres, and about half the sites are rented for the entire summer.

Campsites, facilities: There are 60 sites with full hookups (30 and 50 amps) for RVs up to 40 feet, five tent sites, and one rental travel trailer. Restrooms with showers, a coin laundry, cable TV, WiFi, recreation room, lending library, clubhouse, athletic field, propane gas, camp store, ice, firewood, boat and trailer storage, horseshoes, and picnic area are available. Some facilities are wheelchair-accessible. Leashed pets are permitted.

Reservations, fees: Reservations are recommended. RV sites are $32 per night, tent sites are $22 per night. Weekly and monthly rates available. Some credit cards accepted. Open year-round.

Directions: From Redding, turn on Highway 299 west and drive west over Buckhorn Summit. Continue for five miles to Trinity Dam Boulevard. Turn right on Trinity Dam Boulevard and drive four miles to Lewiston. Continue on Trinity Dam Boulevard to Rush Creek Road. Turn left on Rush Creek Road and drive 2.3 miles to the campground on the left.

Contact: Trinity River Lodge RV Resort, 7420 Rush Creek Rd., Lewiston, 530/778-3791, www.trinityriverresort.com.

127 MARY SMITH

🧗 🛶 🚤 🚣 🎣 🏕️

Scenic rating: 10

on Lewiston Lake in
Shasta-Trinity National Forest

Map 2.4, page 118

This is one of the prettiest spots you'll ever see, set along the southwestern shore of Lewiston Lake. When you wake up and peek out of your sleeping bag, the natural beauty of this serene lake can take your breath away. Hand-launched boats, such as kayaks and canoes, are ideal here, and the lake speed limit is 10 mph. The lake has 15 miles of shoreline. Although swimming is allowed, the water is too cold for most people. Birdwatching is good in this area. The best fishing is from Lakeview Terrace and the tules upstream to just below Trinity Dam. The elevation is 2,000 feet.

Campsites, facilities: There are 17 sites for tents only, some requiring a very short walk. Picnic tables and fire grills are provided. Drinking water and flush and vault toilets are available. Boat launching and rentals are available nearby at Pine Cove Marina. Supplies and a coin laundry are available in Lewiston. Leashed pets are permitted.

Reservations, fees: Reservations are not accepted. Sites are $11 per night. Open early May through mid-September.

Directions: From Redding, turn on Highway 299 west and drive west over Buckhorn Summit. Continue for five miles to Trinity Dam Boulevard. Turn right on Trinity Dam Boulevard and drive four miles to Lewiston, and then continue on Trinity Dam Boulevard for 2.5 miles to the campground.

Contact: Shasta-Trinity National Forest,

Weaverville Ranger Station, 530/623-2121, www.fs.usda.gov/stnf; Hodge Management, 530/623-1203; Pine Cove Marina, 530/778-3770.

128 COOPER GULCH

🧗 🛶 🚤 🚣 🎣 ♿ 🚗 🏕️

Scenic rating: 8

on Lewiston Lake in
Shasta-Trinity National Forest

Map 2.4, page 118

Here is a nice spot along a beautiful lake, featuring a short trail to Baker Gulch, where a pretty creek enters Lewiston Lake. The trout fishing is good on the upper end of the lake (where the current starts) and upstream. The lake speed limit is 10 mph. Swimming is allowed, although the water is cold because it flows in from the bottom of Trinity Lake. The lake is designated a wildlife-viewing area, with large numbers of waterfowl and other birds often spotted near the tules off the shore of Lakeview Terrace. Bring all of your own supplies and plan on hunkering down here for a while.

Campsites, facilities: There are five sites for tents or RVs up to 16 feet (no hookups). Picnic tables and fire grills are provided. Drinking water and vault toilets are available. Boat launching and rentals are nearby at Pine Cove Marina. Supplies and a coin laundry are available in Lewiston. Some facilities are wheelchair-accessible. Leashed pets are permitted.

Reservations, fees: Reservations are not accepted. Sites are $13 per night, $5 per night per additional vehicle. Open early April through late October.

Directions: From Redding, turn on Highway 299 west and drive west over Buckhorn Summit. Continue for five miles to Trinity Dam Boulevard. Turn right on Trinity Dam Boulevard, drive four miles to Lewiston, and then continue on Trinity Dam Boulevard another four miles north to the campground.

Contact: Shasta-Trinity National Forest, Weaverville Ranger Station, 530/623-2121, www.fs.usda.gov/stnf; Hodge Management, 530/623-1203; Pine Cove Marina, 530/778-3770.

129 LAKE VIEW TERRACE RESORT

Scenic rating: 8

on Lewiston Lake

Map 2.4, page 118

This might be your Golden Pond. It's a terraced RV park—with cabin rentals also available—that overlooks Lewiston Lake, one of the prettiest drive-to lakes in the region. Fishing for trout is excellent from Lakeview Terrace continuing upstream toward the dam. Lewiston Lake is perfect for fishing, with a 10-mph speed limit in effect (all the hot boats go to nearby Trinity Lake), along with excellent prospects for rainbow and brown trout. Other fish species include brook trout and kokanee salmon. The topper is that Lewiston Lake is always full to the brim, just the opposite of the up-and-down nightmare of its neighboring big brother, Trinity.

Campsites, facilities: There are 40 sites with full hookups (50 amps) for tents or RVs up to 40 feet; some sites are pull-through. Cabins are also available. Picnic tables and barbecues are provided. Restrooms with showers, coin laundry, seasonal heated pool, propane gas, ice, horseshoes, playground, boat, kayak, and patio-boat rentals are available. Supplies are available within five miles. Leashed pets are permitted.

Reservations, fees: Reservations are recommended. Sites are $30 per night, $3 per person per night for more than two people, $2 per additional vehicle per night. Weekly and monthly rates available. Some credit cards accepted. Open year-round.

Directions: From Redding, turn on Highway 299 west and drive west over Buckhorn Summit. Continue for five miles to Trinity Dam Boulevard. Turn right on Trinity Dam Boulevard and drive 10 miles (five miles past Lewiston) to the resort on the left side of the road.

Contact: Lake View Terrace Resort, 530/778-3803, www.lakeviewterraceresort.com.

130 TUNNEL ROCK

Scenic rating: 7

on Lewiston Lake in
Shasta-Trinity National Forest

Map 2.4, page 118

This is a very small, primitive alternative to Ackerman (see listing in this chapter), which is more developed and another mile up the road to the north. The proximity to the Pine Cove boat ramp and fish-cleaning station, less than two miles to the south, is a primary attraction. Pine Cove Marina is full service and rents fishing boats. The elevation is 1,700 feet.

Campsites, facilities: There are six sites for tents or RVs up to 15 feet (no hookups). Picnic tables and fire grills are provided. Drinking water and vault toilets are available. Leashed pets are permitted.

Reservations, fees: Reservations are not accepted. Sites are $10 per night, $5 per additional vehicle. Open year-round.

Directions: From Redding, turn on Highway 299 west and drive over Buckhorn Summit. Continue for five miles to County Road 105/Trinity Dam Road. Turn right on Trinity Dam Road and drive four miles to Lewiston, and then continue another seven miles north on Trinity Dam Boulevard to the campground.

Contact: Shasta-Trinity National Forest, Weaverville Ranger Station, 530/623-2121, www.fs.usda.gov/stnf; Shasta Recreation Company, 530/623-1203.

131 ACKERMAN

Scenic rating: 7

on Lewiston Lake in
Shasta-Trinity National Forest

Map 2.4, page 118

Of the camps and parks at Lewiston Lake, Ackerman is closest to the lake's headwaters. This stretch of water below Trinity Dam is the best area for trout fishing on Lewiston Lake. Nearby Pine Cove boat ramp, two miles south of the camp, offers the only boat launch on Lewiston Lake with docks and a fish-cleaning station—a popular spot for anglers. When the Trinity powerhouse is running, trout fishing is excellent in this area. The elevation is 2,000 feet.

Campsites, facilities: There are 64 sites for tents or RVs up to 40 feet (no hookups). Picnic tables and fire grills are provided. Drinking water, flush toilets, and a dump station are available. Leashed pets are permitted.

Reservations, fees: Reservations are not accepted. Sites are $13 per night; $10 per night during the winter. Open year-round.

Directions: From Redding, turn on Highway 299 west and drive west over Buckhorn Summit. Continue for five miles to Trinity Dam Boulevard. Turn right on Trinity Dam Boulevard and drive four miles to Lewiston. Continue north on Trinity Dam Boulevard for eight miles to the campground.

Contact: Shasta-Trinity National Forest, Weaverville Ranger Station, 530/623-2121, www.fs.usda.gov/stnf; Shasta Recreation Company, 530/623-1203.

132 OAK BOTTOM

Scenic rating: 7

on Whiskeytown Lake in
Whiskeytown National Recreation Area

Map 2.4, page 118

The prettiest hiking trails at Whiskeytown Lake are at the far western end of the reservoir, and this camp provides excellent access to them. One hiking and biking trail skirts the north shoreline of the lake and is routed to the lake's inlet at the Judge Carr Powerhouse. The other, with the trailhead just a short drive to the west, is routed along Mill Creek, a pristine, clear-running stream with the trail jumping over the water many times. The campground sites seem a little close, but the camp is next to a beach area. There are junior ranger programs, and evening ranger programs at the Oak Bottom Amphitheater are available several nights per week from mid-June through Labor Day. A self-guided nature trail is five miles away at the visitors center.

Campsites, facilities: There are 98 walk-in tent sites and 22 sites for RVs up to 32 feet (no hookups) in a large parking area near the launch ramp. Picnic tables and fire grills are provided. Drinking water, restrooms with flush toilets and coin showers, storage lockers, convenience store, ice, firewood, dump station, boat ramp, and boat rentals are available. Some facilities are wheelchair-accessible. Leashed pets are permitted.

Reservations, fees: Reservations accepted at 530/359-2269. RV sites are $10–18 per night, tent sites are $10–22 per night, $2 per night per pet, plus a park-use permit of $5 per day, $10 per week, or $25 per year. Open year-round.

Directions: From Redding, turn on Highway 299 west and drive west for 15 miles (past the visitors center) to the campground entrance road on the left. Turn left and drive a short distance to the campground.

Contact: Forever Resorts, 530/359-2269, www.whiskeytownmarinas.com; Whiskeytown National Recreation Area, 530/242-3400 or 530/242-3412, www.nps.gov/whis; Whiskeytown Visitor Center, 530/246-1225; Oak Bottom Campground Store, 530/359-2269.

133 SHEEP CAMP

Scenic rating: 8

in Whiskeytown National Recreation Area

Map 2.4, page 118

Sheep Camp is a tiny, primitive camp often overlooked in Whiskeytown National Recreation Area. It is set near a cliff with great views; you will likely have it to yourself. One of the highlights here is the nearby hike to Brandy Creek Falls, a series of pool-and-drops that pours into a big pool. From the trailhead, it's a 1.5-mile one-way trip.

Campsites, facilities: There are four sites for tents only. Picnic tables, food lockers, and fire pits are provided. Vault toilets are available, but there is no drinking water except at the Whiskeytown Visitor Center. Garbage must be packed out.

Reservations, fees: Reservations are not accepted. Sites are $10 per night. A Backcountry Use Permit is required and may be obtained from the visitor center. A Whiskeytown annual pass is also required ($5 per day, $10 per week, or $25 annually). Open seasonally, weather permitting.

Directions: From Redding, turn west on Highway 299 and drive west for 10 miles to the visitor center on the left and get your permits. From the visitor center, continue south on Kennedy Memorial Drive to a fork. Bear right at the fork, cross over the dam, and continue pass the Brandy Creek campground area to Shasta Bally Road. Turn left and drive about eight miles to the campground.

Contact: Whiskeytown National Recreation Area, 530/242-3412, www.nps.gov/whis; Whiskeytown Visitor Center, 530/246-1225.

134 DRY CREEK GROUP CAMP

Scenic rating: 7

on Whiskeytown Lake in
Whiskeytown National Recreation Area

Map 2.4, page 118

If you're in a group and take the time to reserve this spot, you'll be rewarded with some room and the quiet that goes along with it. This is the most remote drive-to camp at Whiskeytown Lake. A boat ramp is about two miles away (to the east) at Brandy Creek. You'll pass it on the way in. Note: Reservations are an absolute must, and can be made five months in advance.

Campsites, facilities: There are two tent-only group sites that can accommodate up to 50 people each. Picnic tables and fire grills are provided. Drinking water, food storage lockers, and vault toilets are available. Leashed pets are permitted.

Reservations, fees: Reservations accepted during summer at 877/444-6777 or www.recreation.gov ($9 reservation fee). Sites are $75 per night. A Whiskeytown day use pass is required ($5 per day, $10 per week, $25 annually). Open early April through October.

Directions: From Redding, drive west on Highway 299 for 10 miles to the visitors center and Kennedy Memorial Drive. Turn left and drive six miles to the campground on the right side of the road.

Contact: Whiskeytown National Recreation Area, 530/242-3400 or 530/242-3412, www.nps.gov/whis; Whiskeytown Visitor Center, 530/246-1225.

135 BRANDY CREEK

Scenic rating: 7

on Whiskeytown Lake in
Whiskeytown National Recreation Area

Map 2.4, page 118

For campers with boats, this is the best place to stay at Whiskeytown, as there is a boat ramp less than 0.25 mile away. Whiskeytown Lake has 36 miles of shoreline and is popular for sailing and sailboarding; it gets a lot more wind than other lakes in the region. (Personal watercraft have been banned from this lake.) Fishing for kokanee salmon is good in the early morning before the wind comes up; trout fishing is pretty good as well.

Campsites, facilities: There are 37 sites for RVs up to 35 feet (no hookups). Drinking water and a dump station are available. There are no restrooms. Leashed pets are permitted.

Reservations, fees: Reservations are not accepted. Sites are $14 per night, $7 per night during off-season. A Whiskeytown day use pass is required ($5 per day, $10 per week, $25 annually). Open year-round.

Directions: From Redding, drive west on Highway 299 for eight miles to the visitors center and Kennedy Memorial Drive. Turn left at the visitors center (Kennedy Memorial Drive) and drive five miles to the campground entrance road on the right. Turn right and drive a short distance to the camp.

Contact: Whiskeytown National Recreation Area, 530/242-3400 or 530/242-3412, www.nps.gov/whis; Whiskeytown Visitor Center, 530/246-1225.

136 PELTIER BRIDGE

Scenic rating: 7

below the dam on Clear Creek in Whiskeytown National Recreation Area

Map 2.4, page 118

This is a small, pretty, and virtually secret campground located on Clear Creek in Whiskeytown National Recreation Area. Secret? That's right—rangers request its exact location not be revealed. Only when you get your permit at the visitor center overlooking Whiskeytown Lake will they provide specific directions. The camp is set in the woods and requires a short hike to get there. I can tell you that Clear Creek is stocked with rainbow trout in the 6- to 8-inch class.

Campsites, facilities: There are seven sites for tents only. Picnic tables, food lockers, and fire pits are provided. Vault toilets are available, but there is no drinking water except at the Whiskeytown Visitor Center. Garbage must be packed out.

Reservations, fees: Reservations are not accepted. Sites are $10 per night. A Backcountry Use Permit is required and may be obtained from the visitor center. A Whiskeytown day use pass is also required ($5 per day, $10 per week, $25 annually). Open seasonally, weather permitting.

Directions: From Redding, turn on Highway 299 west and drive west for 10 miles to the visitor center. Rangers will provide specific directions to the campground at that time.

Contact: Whiskeytown National Recreation Area, 530/242-3412, www.nps.gov/whis; Whiskeytown Visitor Center, 530/246-1225.

137 HORSE CAMP

Scenic rating: 6

in Whiskeytown National Recreation Area

Map 2.4, page 118

This is the only campground in Whiskeytown National Recreation Area where horse camping is permitted. Horse Camp is located on a well-maintained dirt road and is accessible to vehicles pulling horse trailers.

Campsites, facilities: There are two sites for tents only. Picnic tables, food lockers, and fire pits are provided. Vault toilets and drinking water (summer only) are available. Garbage must be packed out.

Reservations, fees: Reservations are required at 530/242-3412. Sites are $10 per night. A Backcountry Use Permit is required and may be obtained from the visitor center. A Whiskeytown day use pass is also required ($5 per day, $10 per week, $25 annually). Open seasonally, weather permitting.

Directions: From Redding, turn west on Highway 299 and drive west for 10 miles to the visitor center. Note that campers with horses must register at the visitor center to get permits and directions to the horse camp.

Contact: Whiskeytown National Recreation Area, 530/242-3412, www.nps.gov/whis; Whiskeytown Visitor Center, 530/246-1225.

138 PREMIER RV RESORTS

Scenic rating: 2

in Redding

Map 2.4, page 118

If you're stuck with no place to go, this large park could be your savior. Nearby recreation options include a waterslide park and the Turtle Bay Museum and Exploration Park on the Sacramento River. Sundial Bridge, with its glass walkway that allows users to look down into the river, is a stunning feat of architecture where the experience simulates walking on air. In addition, Whiskeytown Lake is nearby to the west, and Shasta Lake to the north. A casino and several golf courses are nearby.

Campsites, facilities: There are 120 sites with full or partial hookups (30 and 50 amps) for RVs of any length, a cabin, and two yurts. A flat cut-out area on a hillside provides space for dispersed tent sites. Picnic tables and fire grills are provided. Drinking water, restrooms with flush toilets and showers, playground, seasonal swimming pool, coin laundry, dump station, satellite TV hookups, WiFi, a convenience store, propane gas, and recreation room are available. Some facilities are wheelchair accessible. Leashed pets are permitted.

Reservations, fees: Reservations are accepted. RV sites are $36–44 per night; tent sites are $35 per night; yurts are $47 per night; $3 per person per night for more than two people over age five. Weekly and monthly rates, as well as group rates, are available. Some credit cards accepted. Open year-round.

Directions: In Redding, drive north on I-5

to the Lake Boulevard/Burney-Alturas exit. Turn west (left) on Lake Boulevard and drive 0.25 mile to North Boulder Drive. Turn right (north) on North Boulder Drive and drive one block to the resort on the left.

Contact: Premier RV Resorts, 530/246-0101 or 888/710-8450, www.premierrvresorts.com.

139 MARINA RV PARK

Scenic rating: 6

on the Sacramento River

Map 2.4, page 118

The riverside setting is a highlight here, with the Sacramento River providing relief from the dog days of summer. An easy, paved walking and bike trail is available nearby at the Sacramento River Parkway, providing river views and sometimes a needed breeze on hot summer evenings. It is also two miles away from the Turtle Bay Museum, and close to a movie theater. A golf driving range is nearby. This park includes an area with long-term RV renters.

Campsites, facilities: There are 42 sites with full or partial hookups (30 amps) for RVs up to 40 feet. Picnic tables, restrooms with showers, a coin laundry, small store, WiFi, seasonal swimming pool, spa, boat ramp, and a dump station are available. Leashed pets are permitted.

Reservations, fees: Reservations are accepted. Sites are $31.90 per night, $2 per person per night for more than two people. Weekly and monthly rates available. Open year-round.

Directions: In Redding, turn west on Highway 44 and drive 1.5 miles to the exit for Convention Center/Marina Park Drive. Take that exit, turn left, and drive over the highway to a stoplight and Marina Park Drive. Turn left (south) on Marina Park Drive and drive 0.8 mile to the park on the left.

Contact: Marina RV Park, 530/241-4396, www.marinarvpark.com.

140 SACRAMENTO RIVER RV PARK

Scenic rating: 7

south of Redding

Map 2.4, page 118

This makes a good headquarters for a fall fishing trip on the Sacramento River, where the salmon come big from August through October. In the summer, trout fishing is very good from this area as well, but a boat is a must. No problem; there's a boat ramp at the park. In addition, you can hire fishing guides who launch from here daily. The park is open year-round, and if you want to stay close to home, a three-acre pond with bass, bluegill, and perch is also available at the resort. You also get great long-distance views of Mount Shasta and Mount Lassen.

Campsites, facilities: There are 140 sites with full hookups (30 and 50 amps) for RVs of any length and 10 sites for tents in a shaded grassy area. Some RV sites are pull-through. Picnic tables, restrooms with showers, coin laundry, dump station, cable TV, Wi-Fi, bait, boat launch, playground, two tennis courts, basketball hoops, horseshoes, golf driving range, and a large seasonal swimming pool are available. A clubhouse is available by reservation. Some facilities are wheelchair-accessible. Leashed pets are permitted.

Reservations, fees: Reservations are accepted. RV sites are $26–32 per night, tent sites are $17 per night. Some credit cards accepted. Open year-round.

Directions: From Redding, drive south on I-5 for five miles to the Knighton Road exit. Turn west (right) and drive a short distance to Riverland Drive. Turn left on Riverland Drive and drive two miles to the park at the end of the road.

Contact: Sacramento River RV Resort, 530/365-6402, www.sacramentoriverrvresort.com.

141 DEERLICK SPRINGS

Scenic rating: 7

on Browns Creek in
Shasta-Trinity National Forest

Map 2.4, page 118

It's a long, twisty drive to this remote and primitive camp set on the edge of the Chanchelulla Wilderness in the transition zone where the valley's oak grasslands give way to conifers. This quiet little spot is set along Browns Creek. A trailhead just north of camp provides a streamside walk. The elevation is 3,100 feet.

Campsites, facilities: There are 13 sites for tents only. Picnic tables and fire grills are provided. Vault toilets are available. No drinking water is available. Garbage must be packed out. Leashed pets are permitted.

Reservations, fees: Reservations are not accepted. There is no fee for camping. Open May through October.

Directions: From Red Bluff, turn west on Highway 36 (very twisty) and drive to the Forest Service ranger station in Platina. In Platina, turn right (north) on Harrison Gulch Road and drive 10 miles to the campground on the left.

Contact: Shasta-Trinity National Forest, Yolla Bolly Ranger Station, 530/352-4211, www.fs.usda.gov/stnf.

142 BASIN GULCH

Scenic rating: 5

in Shasta-Trinity National Forest

Map 2.4, page 118

This is one of two little-known campgrounds in the vicinity that rarely gets much use. A trail out of this camp climbs Noble Ridge, eventually rising to a good lookout at 3,933 feet, providing sweeping views of the north valley. Of course, you could also just drive there, taking a dirt road out of Platina. There are many backcountry Forest Service roads in the area, so your best bet is to get a Shasta-Trinity National Forest map, which details the roads. The elevation is 2,700 feet.

Campsites, facilities: There are 13 sites for tents or RVs up to 20 feet (no hookups). Picnic tables and fire grills are provided. Vault toilets are available. No drinking water is available. Leashed pets are permitted.

Reservations, fees: Reservations are not accepted. Sites are $12 per night. Open May through October.

Directions: From Red Bluff, drive about 45 miles west on Highway 36 to the Yolla Bolly District Ranger Station. From the ranger station, turn south on Stuart Gap Road and drive two miles to the campground on the left.

Contact: Shasta-Trinity National Forest, Yolla Bolly Ranger Station, 530/352-4211, www.fs.usda.gov/stnf.

143 BEND RV PARK AND FISHING RESORT

Scenic rating: 7

on the Sacramento River

Map 2.4, page 118

Here's a spot for RV cruisers to rest their rigs for a while. Bend RV Park and Fishing Resort is open year-round and is set beside the Sacramento River. The salmon average 15–25 pounds in this area, and anglers typically have the best results from mid-August through October. In recent years, the gates of the Red Bluff Diversion Dam have been raised in early September. When that occurs, huge numbers of salmon charge upstream from Red Bluff to Anderson, holding in each deep river hole. Expect very hot weather in July and August.

Campsites, facilities: There are 14 sites with full or partial hookups (30 amps) for RVs up to 40 feet. In addition, there is a separate area for tents only. Picnic tables are provided. Drinking water, restrooms with showers and flush

toilets, convenience store, bait and tackle, boat ramp, boat dock, coin laundry, and a dump station are available. Leashed pets are permitted.

Reservations, fees: Reservations are accepted. RV sites are $33 per night, tent sites are $20 per night, $3.50 per person per night for more than two people. Open year-round.

Directions: From I-5 in Red Bluff, drive four miles north on I-5 to the Jelly's Ferry Road exit. Take that exit and turn northeast on Jelly's Ferry Road and drive 2.5 miles to the resort.

Contact: Bend RV Park and Fishing Resort, 21795 Bend Ferry Rd., Red Bluff, 530/527-6289.

144 SYCAMORE GROVE AND CAMP DISCOVERY

Scenic rating: 6

on the Sacramento River in Red Bluff Recreation Area

Map 2.4, page 118

Lake Red Bluff is a seasonal lake created by the Red Bluff Diversion Dam on the Sacramento River, and waterskiing, bird-watching, hiking, and fishing are the most popular activities. A three-mile-long paved trail parallels the river, and cycling and skating are allowed on the trail. It has become a backyard swimming hole for local residents in the summer when the temperatures reach the high 90s and low 100s almost every day. In early September, the Bureau of Reclamation raises the gates at the diversion dam to allow migrating salmon an easier course on the upstream journey, and in the process, Lake Red Bluff reverts to its former self as the Sacramento River.

Campsites, facilities: The Sycamore Grove Camp has 30 sites for tents or RVs up to 40 feet, some with partial hookups. Camp Discovery is a group sites with 11 screened cabins and can accommodate up to 100 people and RVs to 35 feet. Drinking water, restrooms with coin showers, flush and vault toilets, picnic areas, visitors center, two boat ramps, and a fish-viewing plaza are available. There are two large barbecues, electrical outlets, lockable storage, five large picnic tables, restroom with showers and sinks, and an amphitheater in the group camp area. Some facilities are wheelchair-accessible. Leashed pets are permitted.

Reservations, fees: Reservations for Sycamore Grove are accepted at 877/444-6777 or www.recreation.gov ($9 reservation fee). Sites are $16–30 per night. Reservations for Camp Discovery are required at 530/527-1196. The group camp is $175 per night. Open March through November.

Directions: From I-5 at Red Bluff, turn east on Highway 36 and drive 100 yards to the first turnoff at Sale Lane. Turn right (south) on Sale Lane and drive 2.5 miles to the campground at the end of the road.

Contact: Mendocino National Forest, Red Bluff Recreation Area, 530/527-2813, www.fs.fed.us; Discovery Center, 530/527-1196.

145 TOMHEAD SADDLE

Scenic rating: 4

in Shasta-Trinity National Forest

Map 2.4, page 118

This one is way out there in remote wildlands. Little known and rarely visited, it's primarily a jump-off point for ambitious backpackers. The camp is on the edge of the Yolla Bolly-Middle Eel Wilderness. A trailhead here is routed to the South Fork of Cottonwood Creek, a trek that entails hiking eight miles in dry, hot terrain. The elevation is 5,700 feet.

Campsites, facilities: There are five sites for tents only. Picnic tables and fire grills are provided. Vault toilets are available. No drinking water is available. Garbage must be packed out. Leashed pets are permitted.

Reservations, fees: Reservations are not accepted. There is no fee for camping. Open late June through mid-September, weather permitting.

Directions: From I-5 in Red Bluff, turn west on Highway 36 and drive about 13 miles to Cannon Road. Turn left on Cannon Road and drive about five miles to Pettyjohn Road. Turn west on Pettyjohn Road, drive to Saddle Camp and Forest Road 27N06. Turn south on Forest Road 27N06 and drive three miles to the campground on the left. It is advisable to obtain a map of Shasta-Trinity National Forest.

Contact: Shasta-Trinity National Forest, Yolla Bolly Ranger Station, 530/352-4211, www.fs.usda.gov/stnf.

LASSEN AND MODOC

© GARY WHITTON/123RF.COM

BEST CAMPGROUNDS

❰ Easy Backpacking
Mill Creek Falls, page 209.

❰ Fishing
Almanor North, South, and Legacy, page 231.

❰ Hikes with Views
Summit Lake: North, South, and Stock Corral, page 221.

❰ State Parks
McArthur-Burney Falls Memorial State Park and Headwaters Horse Camp, page 203.

Mount Lassen and its awesome volcanic past

seem to cast a shadow everywhere you go in this region. At 10,457 feet, the mountain's domed summit is visible for more than 100 miles in all directions. It blew its top in 1914, with continuing eruptions through 1918. Although now dormant, the volcanic-based geology dominates the landscape everywhere you look.

Of all the areas covered in this book, this region has the least number of romantic getaway spots. Instead it caters primarily to outdoors enthusiasts. And Lassen Volcanic National Park is one of the best places to lace up the hiking boots or spool new line on the reel. It's often off the radar of vacationers, making it one of the few national parks where you can enjoy the wilderness in relative solitude.

The national park is easily explored along the main route, the Lassen Park Highway. Along the way, you can pick a few trails for adventure. The best hikes are the Summit Climb (moderate to challenging), best done first thing in the morning, and Bumpass Hell (easy and great for kids) to see the sulfur vents and boiling mud pots. Another favorite for classic alpine beauty is the Shadow Lake Trail.

Unique features of the region include its pumice boulders, volcanic rock, and spring-fed streams from underground lava tubes. Highlights include the best still-water canoeing and fly-fishing at Fall River, Big Lake, and Ahjumawi State Park. Ahjumawi is reached by canoe or powerboat only — a great boat-in campground with access to a matrix of clear, cold waters with giant trout.

Nearby is Burney Falls State Park, along with the Pit River and Lake Britton, which together make up one of Northern California's best recreation destinations for families. This is also one of the best areas for fly-fishing, especially at Hat Creek, Pit River, Burney Creek, and Manzanita Lake. For more beautiful settings, you can visit Lake Almanor and Eagle Lake, both of which provide lakeside campgrounds and excellent fishing and boating recreation.

And there's more. In remote Modoc County, you'll find Lava Beds National Monument and the South Warner Wilderness. Lava Beds is a stark, pretty, and often lonely place. It's sprinkled with small lakes full of trout, is home to large-antlered deer that migrate in after the first snow (and after the hunting season has closed), and features a unique volcanic habitat with huge flows of obsidian (dark, smooth, natural glass formed by the cooling of molten lava) and dacite (gray, craggy, volcanic flow). Lava Beds National Monument boasts about 500 caves and lava tubes, including the 6,000-foot Catacomb Tunnel. Nearby is pretty Medicine Lake, formed in a caldera, which provides good trout fishing, hiking, and exploring.

There are so many campgrounds that, no matter where you go, it seems you can always find a match for what you desire.

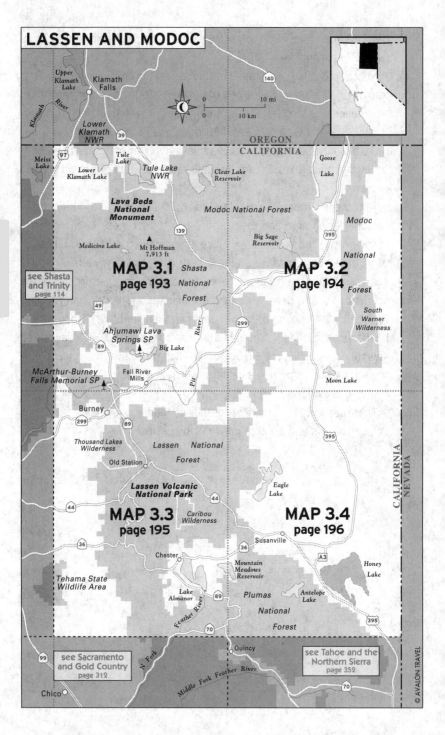

LASSEN AND MODOC

Upper Klamath Lake
Klamath Falls
140
Lower Klamath NWR
39
OREGON
CALIFORNIA

Meiss Lake
97
Lower Klamath Lake
Tule Lake
Tule Lake NWR
Clear Lake Reservoir
Goose Lake

Lava Beds National Monument
Modoc National Forest
Modoc

139
Big Sage Reservoir
395

Medicine Lake
Mt Hoffman 7,913 ft
Shasta
National

MAP 3.1
page 193

MAP 3.2
page 194

National Forest

South Warner Wilderness

see Shasta and Trinity page 114

49
299

Ahjumawi Lava Springs SP
Big Lake

River
Pit

Moon Lake

McArthur-Burney Falls Memorial SP
Fall River Mills

89

Burney
299
89
395

Thousand Lakes Wilderness
Lassen National Forest

Old Station
Eagle Lake

Lassen Volcanic National Park
44

MAP 3.3
page 195
Caribou Wilderness

MAP 3.4
page 196

44
36
Susanville
36
A3

Chester
Mountain Meadows Reservoir
Honey Lake

Tehama State Wildlife Area

Lake Almanor
89
Antelope Lake
Plumas
National
Forest
395

Feather River

70

CALIFORNIA
NEVADA

99
see Sacramento and Gold Country page 312

N. Fork

Quincy

see Tahoe and the Northern Sierra page 352

Middle Fork Feather River

70

Chico

© AVALON TRAVEL

0   10 mi
0   10 km

Map 3.1

Sites 1-16
Pages 197-204

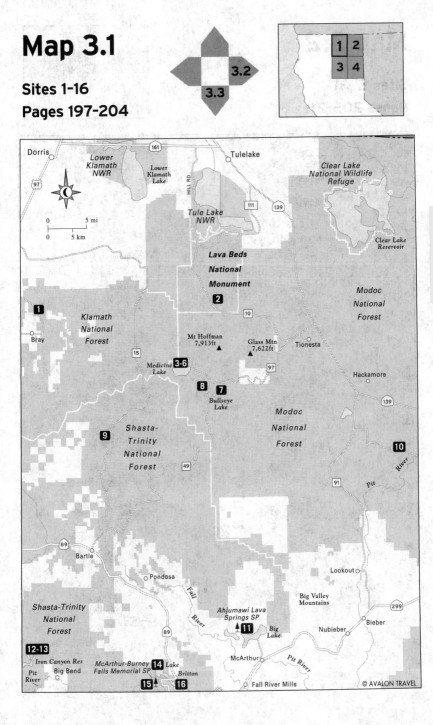

© AVALON TRAVEL

Map 3.2

Sites 17-31
Pages 205-211

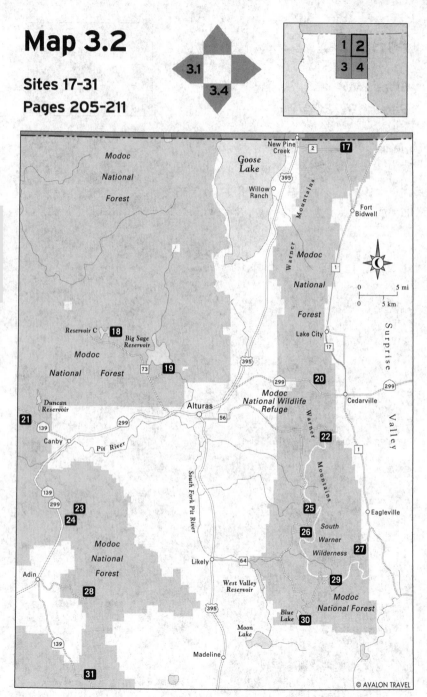

Map 3.3

Sites 32-84
Pages 211-236

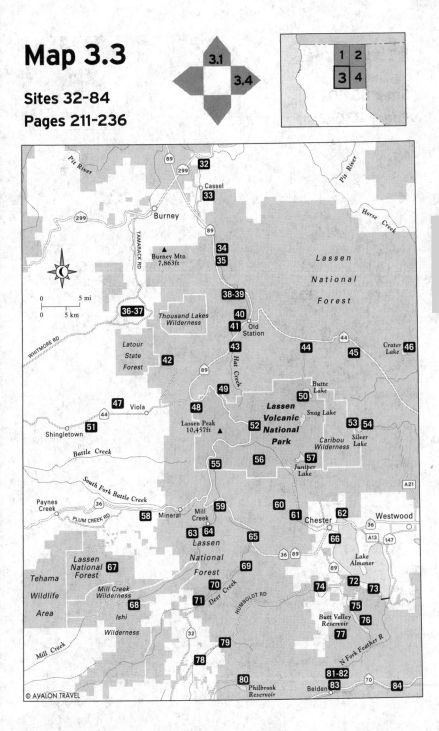

Map 3.4

**Sites 85-102
Pages 236-244**

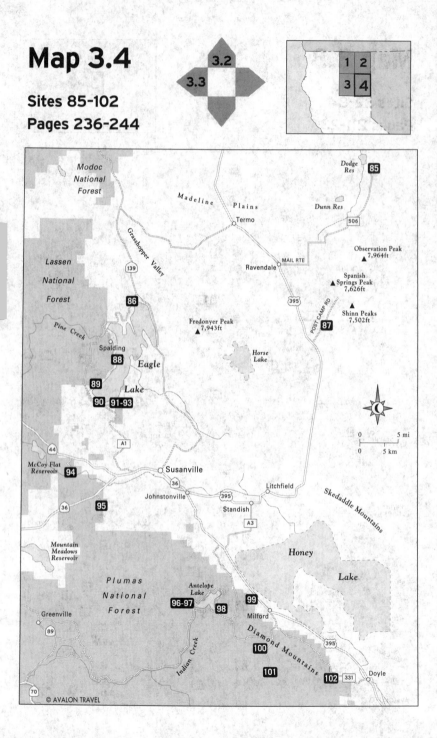

1 SHAFTER

🏃 🏊 🎣 🐕 5% 🚐 ⛺

Scenic rating: 4

in Klamath National Forest

Map 3.1, page 193

This is a little-used camp, with trout fishing at nearby Butte Creek for small rainbows, primarily six- to eight-inchers. Little Orr Lake, about a 10-minute drive away on the southwest flank of Orr Mountain, provides fishing for bass and larger rainbow trout, 10- to 12-inchers, as well as a sprinkling of smaller brook trout. This camp is primitive and not well known, set in a juniper- and sage-filled landscape. The elevation is 4,300 feet. A great side trip is to the nearby Orr Mountain Lookout, where there are spectacular views of Mount Shasta. The road adjacent to the campground is paved, keeping the dust down—a Forest Service touch that is like gold in the summer.

Campsites, facilities: There are 10 sites for tents or RVs up to 28 feet (no hookups). Picnic tables and fire grills are provided. Drinking water and vault toilets are available. A boat ramp is available at Orr Lake. Garbage must be packed out. Leashed pets are permitted.

Reservations, fees: Reservations are not accepted. Sites are $10 per night. Open year-round, with limited services in winter.

Directions: From Redding, drive north on I-5 to Weed and the exit for Central Weed/Highway 97. Take that exit, turn right at the stop sign, drive through Weed and bear right (north) on Highway 97 and drive 40 miles to Ball Mountain Road. Turn right at Ball Mountain Road and drive 2.5 miles to a T with Old State Highway 97. Turn right and drive 4.25 miles (crossing railroad tracks) to the campground on the right side of the road.

Contact: Klamath National Forest, Goosenest Ranger District, 530/398-4391, www.fs.usda.gov/klamath.

2 INDIAN WELL

🏃 🐕 ♿ 🚐 ⛺

Scenic rating: 9

in Lava Beds National Monument

Map 3.1, page 193

Lava Beds National Monument is a one-in-a-million spot, with more than 500 lava-tube caves, Schonchin Butte (a cinder cone with a hiking trail), Mammoth Crater, Native American petroglyphs and pictographs, battlefields and campsites from the Modoc War, and wildlife overlooks of Tule Lake. After winter's first snow, this is one of the best places in the West to photograph deer. Nearby is Klamath National Wildlife Refuge, the largest bald eagle wintering area in the lower 48. If you are new to the outdoors, an interpretive center is available to explain it all to you through informative displays. The visitors center is open year-round.

Campsites, facilities: There are 43 sites for tents or RVs up to 30 feet (no hookups) and a group site for up to 40 people. Picnic tables, fire rings, and cooking grills are provided. Drinking water and flush toilets are available. Some facilities are wheelchair-accessible. Supplies are available in the town of Tulelake (30 miles north). Leashed pets are permitted in the campground and on the roads only.

Reservations, fees: Reservations are not accepted for the individual sites, but are required for the group site at 530/667-8113. Individual sites are $10 per night, with a maximum of eight campers per site. The group site is $3 per person per night ($45–60 total per night). The park entrance fee is $10. Free backcountry camping is allowed; check at the visitor center. Open year-round.

Directions: From Redding, drive north on I-5 to the Central Weed/Highway 97 exit. Take that exit, turn right and continue for one mile to U.S. 97. Drive north on U.S. 97 for 54 miles to Highway 161. Turn east on Highway 161 and drive 20 miles to Hill Road.

Turn right (south) and drive 18 miles to the visitors center and the campground entrance on the left. Turn left and drive 0.25 mile to the campground.

Contact: Lava Beds National Monument Visitor Center, 530/667-8113, www.nps.gov/labe.

3 MEDICINE
🧍🏊🚣⛴🏕🐾♿🚐🏕

Scenic rating: 7

on Medicine Lake in Modoc National Forest

Map 3.1, page 193

Lakeside campsites tucked away in conifers make this camp a winner. Medicine Lake, at 640 acres, was formed in the crater of an old volcano and is surrounded by lodgepole pine and fir trees. The lake is stocked with rainbow and brook trout in the summer, gets quite cold in the fall, and freezes over in winter. All water sports are permitted. Many side trips are possible, including nearby Bullseye and Blanche Lakes and Ice Caves (both signed and off the access road) and Lava Beds National Monument just 15 miles north. At 6,700 feet, temperatures can drop in summer and the season is short.

Campsites, facilities: There are 22 sites for tents or RVs up to 30 feet (no hookups). Picnic tables and fire grills are provided. Drinking water and vault toilets are available. Ranger-guided cave tours, walks, and talks are available during the summer. A boat ramp is nearby. A café and bar are in Bartle; otherwise, no supplies are available within an hour's drive. Some facilities are wheelchair-accessible. Leashed pets are permitted.

Reservations, fees: Reservations are not accepted. Sites are $7 per vehicle per night. Open late May through early October, weather permitting.

Directions: From Redding, drive north on I-5 past Dunsmuir to Highway 89. Turn east on Highway 89 and drive 28 miles (just past Bartle) to Forest Road 15/Harris Springs Road. Turn left on Forest Road 15 and drive approximately five miles to the Y intersection with Forest Road 49/Medicine Lake Road. Turn right on Forest Road 49 and drive approximately 26 miles to the lake and campground access road.

Contact: Modoc National Forest, Doublehead Ranger District, 530/667-2246, www.fs.usda.gov/modoc.

4 A. H. HOGUE
🧍🏊🚣⛴🏕🐾♿🚐🏕

Scenic rating: 7

on Medicine Lake in Modoc National Forest

Map 3.1, page 193

This camp was created in 1990 when the original Medicine Lake Campground was divided in half. (For more information, see the Medicine listing.)

Campsites, facilities: There are 24 sites for tents or RVs up to 30 feet (no hookups). Picnic tables and fire grills are provided. Drinking water and vault toilets are available. A boat ramp is nearby. Some facilities are wheelchair-accessible. Leashed pets are permitted. A café and bar are in Bartle; otherwise, no supplies are available within an hour's drive.

Reservations, fees: Reservations are not accepted. Sites are $7 per vehicle per night. Open late May through early October, weather permitting.

Directions: From Redding, drive north on I-5 past Dunsmuir to Highway 89. Turn east on Highway 89 and drive 28 miles (just past Bartle) to Forest Road 15/Harris Springs Road. Turn left on Forest Road 15 and drive approximately five miles to the Y intersection with Forest Road 49/Medicine Lake Road. Turn right on Forest Road 49 and drive approximately 26 miles to the lake and campground access road.

Contact: Modoc National Forest, Doublehead Ranger District, 530/667-2246, www.fs.usda.gov/modoc.

5 HEMLOCK

🚶 🏊 🛶 🎣 🚣 🐴 ♿ 🚐 ⛺

Scenic rating: 7

on Medicine Lake in Modoc National Forest

Map 3.1, page 193

This is one in a series of campgrounds on Medicine Lake operated by the Forest Service. A special attraction at Hemlock is the natural sand beach. (For more information, see the Medicine listing in this chapter.)

Campsites, facilities: There are 19 sites for tents or RVs up to 22 feet (no hookups). Picnic tables and fire grills are provided. Drinking water and vault toilets are available. A boat ramp is available nearby. Some facilities are wheelchair-accessible. Leashed pets are permitted. A café and bar are in Bartle; otherwise, no supplies are available within an hour's drive.

Reservations, fees: Reservations are not accepted. Sites are $7 per vehicle per night. Open late May through early October, weather permitting.

Directions: From Redding, drive north on I-5 past Dunsmuir to Highway 89. Turn east on Highway 89 and drive 28 miles (just past Bartle) to Forest Road 15/Harris Springs Road. Turn left on Forest Road 15 and drive approximately five miles to the Y intersection with Forest Road 49/Medicine Lake Road. Turn right on Forest Road 49 and drive approximately 26 miles to the lake and campground access road.

Contact: Modoc National Forest, Doublehead Ranger District, 530/667-2246, www.fs.usda.gov/modoc.

6 HEADQUARTERS

🚶 🏊 🛶 🚣 🐴 ♿ 🚐 ⛺

Scenic rating: 7

on Medicine Lake in Modoc National Forest

Map 3.1, page 193

This is one of four campgrounds set beside Medicine Lake. There is no lake access from this camp because of private property between the lake and campground. The elevation is 6,700 feet. (For more information, see the Medicine listing in this chapter.)

Campsites, facilities: There are 16 sites for tents or RVs up to 18 feet (no hookups). Picnic tables and fire grills are provided. Drinking water and vault toilets are available. A boat ramp is nearby. A café and bar are in Bartle; otherwise, no supplies are available within an hour's drive. Some facilities are wheelchair accessible. Leashed pets are permitted.

Reservations, fees: Reservations are not accepted. Sites are $7 per vehicle per night. Open late May through early October, weather permitting.

Directions: From Redding, drive north on I-5 past Dunsmuir to Highway 89. Turn east on Highway 89 and drive 28 miles (just past Bartle) to Forest Road 15/Harris Springs Road. Turn left on Forest Road 15 and drive approximately five miles to the Y intersection with Forest Road 49/Medicine Lake Road. Turn right on Forest Road 49 and drive approximately 26 miles to the lake and campground access road.

Contact: Modoc National Forest, Doublehead Ranger District, 530/667-2246, www.fs.usda.gov/modoc.

7 BULLSEYE LAKE

🚶 🛶 🐴 🚐 ⛺

Scenic rating: 7

near Medicine Lake in Modoc National Forest

Map 3.1, page 193

This tiny lake gets overlooked every year, mainly because of its proximity to nearby Medicine Lake. Bullseye Lake is shallow, but because snow keeps it locked up until late May or early June, the water stays plenty cold for small trout through July. It is stocked with just 750 six- to eight-inch rainbow trout, not much to crow about—or to catch, for that matter. No boat motors are allowed. Nearby are some ice caves, created by ancient volcanic action. The place is small, quiet, and pretty, but most of all, small. This camp is set at an elevation of 6,500 feet.

Campsites, facilities: There are six sites for tents or RVs up to 22 feet (no hookups). Picnic tables and fire grills are provided. A vault toilet is available. Thre is no drinking water. Garbage must be packed out. Supplies are available in McCloud. A café and bar are in Bartle; otherwise, no supplies are available within an hour's drive. Leashed pets are permitted.

Reservations, fees: Reservations are not accepted. There is no fee for camping. Open late May through October, weather permitting.

Directions: From Redding, drive north on I-5 past Dunsmuir to Highway 89. Turn east on Highway 89 and drive 28 miles (just past Bartle) to Forest Road 15/Harris Springs Road. Turn left on Forest Road 15 and drive approximately five miles to the Y intersection with Forest Road 49/Medicine Lake Road. Turn right on Forest Road 49 and drive approximately 24 miles to the Bullseye Lake access road (if you reach Medicine Lake, you have gone about two miles too far). Turn right at the Bullseye Lake access road and drive a short distance past Blanche Lake, then turn right and drive a short distance to the lake.

Contact: Modoc National Forest, Doublehead Ranger District, 530/667-2246, www.fs.usda.gov.modoc.

8 PAYNE SPRINGS

Scenic rating: 8

near Medicine Lake in Modoc National Forest

Map 3.1, page 193

This camp is set by a small spring in a very pretty riparian area. It's small, but it is special.

Campsites, facilities: There are five dispersed sites for tents or RVs up to 20 feet (no hookups). Picnic tables and fire grills are provided. A vault toilet is available. No drinking water is available. Garbage must be packed out. A café and bar are in Bartle. Supplies are available in Tionesta, a 30-minute drive, or McCloud. Leashed pets are permitted.

Reservations, fees: Reservations are not

accepted. There is no fee for camping. Open late May through October, weather permitting.

Directions: From Redding, drive north on I-5 drive past Dunsmuir to Highway 89. Turn east on Highway 89 and drive 28 miles (just past Bartle) to Forest Road 15/Harris Springs Road. Turn left on Forest Road 15 and drive approximately five miles to the Y intersection with Forest Road 49/Medicine Lake Road. Turn right on Forest Road 49 and drive 30 miles (0.2 mile past the Bullseye Lake access road) to the Payne Springs access road (if you reach Medicine Lake, you have gone too far). Turn left on the Payne Springs access road and drive a short distance to the campground.

Contact: Modoc National Forest, Doublehead Ranger District, 530/667-2246, www.fs.usda.gov/modoc.

9 HARRIS SPRINGS

Scenic rating: 3

in Shasta-Trinity National Forest

Map 3.1, page 193

This camp is a hidden spot in remote Shasta-Trinity National Forest, nestled in the long, mountainous ridge that runs east from Mount Shasta to Lava Beds National Monument. The camp is set at 4,800 feet, with a part-time fire station within a quarter mile on the opposite side of the access road. The area is best explored by four-wheel drive, venturing to a series of small buttes, mountaintops, and lookouts in the immediate area. A map of Shasta-Trinity National Forest is a must.

Campsites, facilities: There are 15 sites for tents or RVs up to 32 feet (no hookups). Picnic tables and fire grills are provided. There is no drinking water. Vault toilets are available. Garbage must be packed out. Leashed pets are permitted.

Reservations, fees: Reservations are not accepted. There is no fee for camping. Open late May through early October, weather permitting.

Directions: From Redding, drive north on I-5 past Dunsmuir to the junction with Highway 89. Turn east on Highway 89 and drive 28 miles (just past Bartle) to Forest Road 15/Harris Springs Road. Bear left on Forest Road 15 and drive five miles to the Y intersection with Harris Springs Road and Medicine Lake Road/Forest Road 49. Bear left at the Y, staying on Harris Springs Road/Forest Road 15, and drive 12 miles to a junction with a forest road signed for the Harris Springs Ranger Station. Turn right and drive a short distance, and look for the campground entrance on the right side of the road.

Contact: Shasta-Trinity National Forest, McCloud Ranger District, 530/964-2184, www.fs.usda.gov/stnf.

10 COTTONWOOD FLAT
🏃🐕🚐⛺

Scenic rating: 6

in Modoc National Forest

Map 3.1, page 193

The camp is wooded and shady, set at 4,700 feet elevation in the rugged and remote Devil's Garden area of Modoc National Forest. The region is known for large mule deer, and Cottonwood Flat is well situated as a base camp for a hunting trip in the fall. The weather can get extremely cold early and late in the season.

Campsites, facilities: There are 10 sites for tents or RVs up to 16 feet (no hookups). Picnic tables and fire grills are provided. There is no drinking water. Vault toilets are available. Garbage must be packed out. Supplies are available within 10 miles in Canby. Leashed pets are permitted.

Reservations, fees: Reservations are not accepted. There is no fee for camping. Open May through October, weather permitting.

Directions: From Redding, drive east on Highway 299 for about 100 miles to the town of Adin. Continue on Highway 299 for about 20 miles to the Canby Bridge at the Pit River and the junction with Forest Road 84. Turn left on

Forest Road 84 and drive about eight miles to Forest Road 42N95. Turn right and drive 0.5 mile to the campground entrance on the left side of the road. Note: The access road is not recommended for RVs longer than 16 feet.

Contact: Modoc National Forest, Devil's Garden Ranger District, 530/233-5811, www.fs.usda.gov/modoc.

11 AHJUMAWI LAVA SPRINGS BOAT-IN
🏃🏊🛶⛵🐕⛺

Scenic rating: 8

at Big Lake

Map 3.1, page 193

This is a one-of-a-kind boat-in camp set on Big Lake and connecting Horr Pond in the Fall River matrix of streams. Ahjumawi means "where the waters come together," named by the Pit River Native Americans who inhabit the area near the confluence of Big Lake, Tule River, Ja She Creek, Lava Creek, and Fall River. Together the waters form one of the largest freshwater springs in the world. Springs flowing from the lava are prominent along the shoreline. This is a place of exceptional and primeval scenery. Much of the land is covered by lava flows, including vast areas of jagged black basalt, along with lava tubes and spattercone and conic depressions. There are brilliant aqua bays and, for campers, peace and quiet. However, you may be joined on land by armies of mosquitoes in the spring; they're not so bad while you're on the water.

Access is by boat only, ideal for canoes, and, in addition, the lake is not well known outside of the region. Expert fly fishers try for giant but elusive rainbow trout, best in the early morning at the springs. Because of high water clarity, long leaders and perfect casts are essential. There are also nesting areas around the lake for bald eagles, ospreys, and blue herons, and this park is considered a stellar habitat for bird-watching. A series of connecting trails are accessible from camp. The park is a wilderness area, covering 6,000 acres, and most of it is extremely rugged lava rock. There are many signs of this area's ancient past, with bedrock mortars, ceremonial sites, and prehistoric rockfish traps. There are also herds of large mule deer that forage through much of the park. Bears also roam this area. Finally, there are magnificent views of Mount Shasta, Lassen Peak, and other mountains.

Campsites, facilities: There are nine boat-in sites. Picnic tables, food lockers, and fire pits are provided. Vault toilets are available. No drinking water is available. Garbage must be packed out. Leashed pets are permitted.

Reservations, fees: Reservations are not accepted. Sites are $15 per night. Open year-round, weather permitting.

Directions: From Redding, drive east on Highway 299 for 73 miles to McArthur. Turn left on Main Street and drive 3.5 miles (becomes a dirt road) to the Rat Farm boat launch at Big Lake. Launch boat and proceed by boat one to three miles to one of the nine boat-in campsites. (As you head out from Rat Farm, the campsites are on the right side of the lake, tucked along the shore).

Contact: Ahjumawi Lava Springs State Park, c/o McArthur-Burney Falls Memorial State Park, 530/335-2777, www.parks.ca.gov.

12 DEADLUN
♿ 🏖 🎣 🚣 🐕 🚐 ⛺

Scenic rating: 7

on Iron Canyon Reservoir in
Shasta-Trinity National Forest

Map 3.1, page 193

Deadlun is a pretty campground set in the forest, shaded and quiet, with a five-minute walk or one-minute drive to the Deadlun Creek arm of Iron Canyon Reservoir. Drive. If you have a canoe to launch or fishing equipment to carry, driving is the choice. Trout fishing is good here, both in April and May, then again in October and early November. One downer is that the shoreline is often very muddy here

in March and early April. Because of an engineering error with the dam, the lake never fills completely, causing the lakeshore to be strewn with stumps and quite muddy after spring rains and snowmelt.

Campsites, facilities: There are 25 sites for tents or RVs up to 24 feet (no hookups). Picnic tables and fire grills are provided. Vault toilets are available. No drinking water is available. A small boat ramp is available one mile from the camp. Garbage must be packed out. Leashed pets are permitted.

Reservations, fees: Reservations are not accepted. There is no fee for camping. Open year-round.

Directions: From Redding, drive east on Highway 299 for 37 miles to Big Bend Road/County Road 7M01. Turn left and drive 17 miles to the town of Big Bend. Continue for five miles to the lake, bearing right at the T intersection, and continue for two miles (past the boat-launch turnoff) to the campground turnoff on the left side of the road. Turn left and drive one mile to the campground.

Contact: Shasta-Trinity National Forest, Shasta Lake Ranger District, 530/275-1587, www.fs.usda.gov/recarea/stnf; Shasta Lake Visitor Center, 530/275-1589.

13 HAWKINS LANDING
♿ 🏖 🎣 🚣 🏊 🐕 🚐 ⛺

Scenic rating: 7

on Iron Canyon Reservoir

Map 3.1, page 193

The adjacent boat ramp makes Hawkins Landing the better of the two camps at Iron Canyon Reservoir for campers with trailered boats (though Deadlun is far more secluded). Iron Canyon, with 15 miles of shoreline, provides good fishing for trout, has a resident bald eagle or two. One problem with this lake is the annual drawdown in late fall, which causes the shoreline to be extremely muddy in the spring. The lake usually rises high enough to make the boat ramp functional by mid-April. The best spot for swimming is near the earth dam, which is also a good put-in area for kayaks and canoes. This camp is set at an elevation of 2,700 feet.

Campsites, facilities: There are 10 sites for tents or RVs up to 30 feet (no hookups). Picnic tables and fire grills are provided. Drinking water, vault toilets, and a small boat ramp are available. Supplies can be obtained in Big Bend. Leashed pets are permitted.

Reservations, fees: Reservations are not accepted. Sites are $10 per night, $1 per pet per night, $3 per night for each additional vehicle, $8 per night for additional RV. Open mid-April through Labor Day weekend, weather permitting.

Directions: From Redding, drive east on Highway 299 for 37 miles to Big Bend Road. At Big Bend Road turn left and drive 15.2 miles to the town of Big Bend. Continue for 2.1 miles to Forest Road 38N11. Turn left and drive 3.3 miles to the Iron Canyon Reservoir Spillway. Turn right and drive 1.1 miles to a dirt road. Turn left and drive 0.3 mile to the campground.

Contact: PG&E Land Projects, 916/386-5164, www.pge.com/recreation.

14 NORTHSHORE

Scenic rating: 8

on Lake Britton

Map 3.1, page 193

After closing for improvements in 2012, Northshore reopened in the spring of 2013. This peaceful campground is set among the woodlands near the shore of Lake Britton, directly across the lake from McArthur-Burney Falls Memorial State Park. Boating and fishing are popular here, and once the water warms up in midsummer, swimming is also a winner. Boat rentals are available near the boat ramp. The lake has fair prospects for trout and smallmouth bass and is sometimes excellent for crappie. For side trips, the best trout

fishing in the area is on the Pit River near Powerhouse Number Three. A hot spring is available in Big Bend, about a 30-minute drive from camp. The elevation is 2,800 feet. Note: This is a bald eagle nesting area, and some areas are closed in spring when an active nest is verified.

Campsites, facilities: There are 30 sites for tents or RVs up to 30 feet (no hookups). Picnic tables and fire grills are provided. Drinking water and vault toilets are available. An unimproved boat ramp is available near the camp and an improved boat ramp is available in McArthur-Burney Falls State Park (about four miles away). Supplies can be obtained in Fall River Mills or Burney. Leashed pets are permitted.

Reservations, fees: Reservations are not accepted. Sites are $22 per night, $3 per night for each additional car, $8 per night per additional RV, $1 per pet per night. There is a $7 boat launch fee. Open mid-May through mid-September, weather permitting.

Directions: From Redding, drive east on Highway 299 to Burney and then continue for five miles to Highway 89. Turn left (north) and drive 9.7 miles (past the state park entrance and over the Lake Britton Bridge) to Clark Creek Road. Turn left (west) and drive about a mile to the camp access road. Turn left and drive one mile to the camp.

Contact: PG&E Land Projects, 916/386-5164, www.pge.com/recreation.

15 McARTHUR-BURNEY FALLS MEMORIAL STATE PARK AND HEADWATERS HORSE CAMP

Scenic rating: 9

in McArthur-Burney Falls Memorial State Park

Map 3.1, page 193   BEST (

McArthur-Burney Falls Memorial State Park was originally formed by volcanic activity and features 910 acres of forest and five miles of stream and lake shore. The Headwaters horse camp is three miles from the main campground. (Non-equestrian campers may stay at the horse camp, but only tents are allowed.) The campground is pretty and set amid large ponderosa pines. Camping-style cabins were installed in 2008 and have been a hit here since.

Burney Falls is a 129-foot waterfall, a beautiful cascade split at the top by a little grove of trees, with small trickles oozing and falling out of the adjacent moss-lined wall. Since it is fed primarily by a spring, it runs strong and glorious most of the year, producing 100 million gallons of water every day. The Headwaters Trail provides an outstanding hike, both to see the waterfall and Burney Creek, as well as for an easy adventure and fishing access to the stream. An excellent fly-fishing section of the Pit River is available below the dam. There are other stellar recreation options at this state park. At the end of the campground access road is a boat ramp for Lake Britton, with rentals available for canoes and paddleboats. This is a beautiful lake, with pretty canyon walls on its upper end, and good smallmouth bass (at rock piles) and crappie fishing (near the train trestle). Bald eagles and ospreys nest on tall snags along the lake. There is also a good swimming beach. The Pacific Crest Trail is routed right through the park and provides an additional opportunity for a day hike, best explored downstream from the dam. Reservations for sites are essential during the summer.

Campsites, facilities: There are 128 sites for tents or RVs up to 32 feet (no hookups), six horse-camp sites, one hike-in/bike-in site, and 24 wood camping cabins. Picnic tables, food lockers, and fire grills are provided. Drinking water, restrooms with flush toilets and showers, and a dump station are available. Vault toilets and a small horse corral are available at the horse camp. WiFi is available within 150 feet of the visitor center. A grocery/gift store and boat rentals are available in the summer. Some facilities are wheelchair-accessible.

Leashed pets are permitted, except on the trails and the beach.

Reservations, fees: Reservations are accepted seasonally for RV sites, tent sites, and camping cabins at 800/444-7275 (800/444-PARK) or www.reserveamerica.com ($8 reservation fee). Sites are $35 per night, $10 per night for each additional vehicle, $15–30 per night for primitive sites, $5 per person per night for hike-in/bike-in site. Camping cabins start at $71.50 per night. Reservations are not accepted for equestrian sites. The horse camp is $15 per night, $10 per night per additional vehicle and $2 per night per horse. Boat launching is $8 per day. Open year-round.

Directions: From Redding, drive east on Highway 299 to Burney and then continue for five miles to the junction with Highway 89. At Highway 89, turn north (left) and drive six miles to the campground entrance on the left side of the road.

Contact: McArthur-Burney Falls State Park, 530/335-2777, www.parks.ca.gov.

16 DUSTY CAMPGROUND

Scenic rating: 8

on Lake Britton

Map 3.1, page 193

This is one in a series of campgrounds near the north shore of Lake Britton. The lake has 18 miles of shoreline. (See Northshore listing in this chapter for more information.) The camp is set at an elevation of 2,800 feet. It provides an alternative to nearby McArthur-Burney Falls Memorial State Park, which is far more popular.

Campsites, facilities: There are seven sites for tents or RVs up to 30 feet (no hookups); two of the sites can accommodate groups of up to 12 people each. Fire rings are provided. Vault toilets are available. Drinking water is not available. Garbage must be packed out in winter. Some facilities are wheelchair-accessible. Leashed pets are permitted.

Reservations, fees: Reservations are not accepted. Single sites are $8 per night, $16 for double sites, $3 per night for each additional vehicle, $8 per night per additional RV, $1 per pet per night. Fees are collected mid-April through the week after Labor Day Weekend. Open year-round.

Directions: From Redding, drive east on Highway 299 to Burney and continue for five miles to the junction with Highway 89. Turn left (north) and drive 7.5 miles (past the state park entrance and over the Lake Britton Bridge) to the campground access road on the right (it will be confusing because the campground is on the left). Turn right and drive 0.75 mile (in the process crossing the highway) to the campground.

Contact: PG&E Land Projects, 916/386-5164, www.pge.com/recreation.

17 CAVE LAKE

Scenic rating: 8

in Modoc National Forest

Map 3.2, page 194

A pair of lakes can be discovered out here in the middle of nowhere, with Cave Lake on one end and Lily Lake on the other. Together they make a nice set, very quiet, extremely remote, with good fishing for rainbow trout and brook trout. A canoe, pram, or float tube can be ideal. No motors are permitted. Of the two lakes, it is nearby Lily Lake that is prettier and provides the better fishing. Cave Lake is set at 6,600 feet. By camping here, you become a member of the 5 Percent Club; that is, the 5 percent of campers who know of secret, isolated little spots such as this one.

Campsites, facilities: There are six sites for tents or RVs up to 15 feet (no hookups); trailers are not advised because of the steep access road. Picnic tables and fire grills are provided. Drinking water and vault toilets are available. Garbage must be packed out. Motors (including electric) are prohibited on the lake.

Supplies are available in New Pine Creek and Davis Creek. Leashed pets are permitted.

Reservations, fees: Reservations are not accepted. There is no fee for camping. Open July through October, weather permitting.

Directions: From Redding, drive east on Highway 299 for 146 miles to Alturas and U.S. 395. Turn north on U.S. 395 and drive 40 miles to Forest Road 2 (if you reach the town of New Pine Creek on the Oregon/California border, you have driven a mile too far). Turn right on Forest Road 2 (a steep dirt road—trailers are not recommended) and drive six miles to the campground entrance on the left side of the road, just beyond the Lily Lake picnic area.

Contact: Modoc National Forest, Warner Mountain Ranger District, 530/279-6116, www.fs.usda.gov/modoc.

18 RESERVOIR C

Scenic rating: 6

near Alturas in Modoc National Forest

Map 3.2, page 194

It is one great adventure to explore the "alphabet lakes" in the remote Devil's Garden area of Modoc County. Reservoir C and Reservoir F provide the best of the lot, but the success can go up and down like a yo-yo, just like the water levels in the lakes. Reservoir C is stocked with both Eagle Lake trout and brown trout. A sidelight to this area is the number of primitive roads that are routed through Modoc National Forest, perfect for four-wheel-drivers. The elevation is 4,900 feet.

Campsites, facilities: There are six sites for tents or RVs up to 22 feet (no hookups). Picnic tables and fire grills are provided. Vault toilets and a primitive boat ramp are available. No drinking water is available. Garbage must be packed out. Leashed pets are permitted.

Reservations, fees: Reservations are not accepted. There is no fee for camping. Open May through September.

Directions: From Alturas drive west on

Highway 299 for three miles to Crowder Flat Road/County Road 73. Turn right on Crowder Flat Road and drive 9.5 miles to Triangle Ranch Road/Forest Road 43N18. Turn left on Triangle Ranch Road and drive seven miles to Forest Road 44N32. Turn right on Forest Road 44N32, drive 0.5 mile, turn right on the access road for the lake and campground, and drive 0.5 mile to the camp at the end of the road.

Contact: Modoc National Forest, DevilÕs Garden Ranger District, 530/233-5811, www.fs.usda.gov/modoc.

19 BIG SAGE RESERVOIR

Scenic rating: 5

in Modoc National Forest

Map 3.2, page 194

This is a do-it-yourself camp; that is, pick your own spot, bring your own water, and don't expect to see anybody else. This camp is set along Big Sage Reservoir—that's right, sagebrush country at 5,100 feet elevation. It is a big lake, covering 5,000 surface acres, and a boat ramp is adjacent to the campground. This is one of the better bass lakes in Modoc County. Catfish and crappie are also here. Water sports are allowed, except for personal watercraft. Swimming is not recommended because of algae growth in midsummer, murky water, and muddy shoreline. Water levels can fluctuate greatly.

Campsites, facilities: There are 11 sites for tents or RVs up to 22 feet (no hookups). Picnic tables and fire grills are provided. Vault toilets are available. There is no drinking water. Some facilities are wheelchair-accessible. Garbage must be packed out. A boat ramp is available nearby. Leashed pets are permitted. Supplies can be obtained in Alturas, about eight miles away.

Reservations, fees: Reservations are not accepted. There is no fee for camping. Open May through September.

Directions: From Alturas, drive west on Highway 299 for three miles to Crowder Flat Road/County Road 73. Turn right on Crowder Flat Road and drive about five miles to County Road 180. Turn right on County Road 180 and drive four miles. Turn left at the access road for the campground and boat ramp and drive a short distance to the camp on the left side of the road.

Contact: Modoc National Forest, Doublehead Ranger District, 530/667-2246, www.fs.usda.gov/modoc.

20 STOUGH RESERVOIR

Scenic rating: 8

in Modoc National Forest

Map 3.2, page 194

Stough Reservoir looks like a large country pond where cattle might drink. You know why? Because it once actually was a cattle pond on a family ranch that has since been converted to Forest Service property. It is in the north Warner Mountains (not to be confused with the South Warner Wilderness), which features many back roads and remote four-wheel-drive routes. The camp is set at an elevation of 6,200 feet. Note that you may find this campground named "Stowe Reservoir" on some maps and in previous editions of this book. The name is now officially spelled "Stough Reservoir," after the family that originally owned the property.

Campsites, facilities: There are 14 sites for tents or RVs up to 22 feet (no hookups). Picnic tables and fire grills are provided. Drinking water and vault toilets are available. Garbage must be packed out. Leashed pets are permitted. Supplies can be obtained in Cedarville, six miles away.

Reservations, fees: Reservations are not accepted. There is no fee for camping. Open late May through early October, weather permitting.

Directions: From Redding, drive east on

Highway 299 to Alturas. In Alturas, continue north on Highway 299/U.S. 395 for five miles to the split-off for Highway 299. Turn right on Highway 299 and drive about 12 miles (just past Cedar Pass). Look for the signed entrance road on the left side of the road. Turn left and drive one mile to the campground on the left side of the road.

Contact: Modoc National Forest, Warner Mountain Ranger District, 530/279-6116, www.fs.usda.gov/modoc.

21 HOWARD'S GULCH

Scenic rating: 6

near Duncan Reservoir in Modoc National Forest

Map 3.2, page 194

This is the nearest campground to Duncan Reservoir, three miles to the north and stocked with trout each year by the Department of Fish and Game. The camp is set in the typically sparse woods of Modoc National Forest, but a beautiful grove of aspen is three miles to the west on Highway 139, on the left side of the road. By the way, Highway 139 isn't much of a highway at all, but it is paved and will get you there. The elevation is 4,700 feet.

Campsites, facilities: There are 11 sites for tents or RVs up to 22 feet (no hookups). Picnic tables and fire grills are provided. Drinking water and vault toilets are available. Some facilities are wheelchair-accessible. Supplies are available within five miles in Canby. Leashed pets are permitted.

Reservations, fees: Reservations are not accepted. Sites are $6 per night. Open May through October, weather permitting.

Directions: From Redding, drive east on Highway 299 for about 100 miles to Adin. Continue on Highway 299 for about 25 miles to Highway 139. Turn left (northwest) on Highway 139 and drive six miles to the campground on the left side of the road.

Contact: Modoc National Forest, Devil's Garden Ranger District, 530/233-5811, www.fs.usda.gov/modoc.

22 PEPPERDINE AND HORSE CAMP

Scenic rating: 5

in Modoc National Forest

Map 3.2, page 194

This camp is outstanding for hikers planning a backpacking trip into the adjacent South Warner Wilderness. The camp is at 6,680 feet, set along the south side of tiny Porter Reservoir, with horse corrals within walking distance. A trailhead out of camp provides direct access to the Summit Trail, the best hike in the South Warner Wilderness.

Campsites, facilities: There are four sites for tents or RVs up to 16 feet (no hookups) in the family camp and space for RVs up to 25 feet (no hookups) in the horse camp. Picnic tables and fire grills are provided. Drinking water and vault toilets are available. Corrals are available with water for stock. Garbage must be packed out. Supplies are available in Cedarville or Alturas. Some facilities are wheelchair accessible. Leashed pets are permitted.

Reservations, fees: Reservations are not accepted. There is no fee for camping. Open July through October, weather permitting.

Directions: In Alturas, drive south on U.S. 395 to the southern end of town and County Road 56. Turn left on County Road 56 and drive 13 miles to the Modoc Forest boundary and the junction with Parker Creek Road. Bear left on Parker Creek Road and continue for six miles to the signed campground access road on the right. Turn right and drive 0.5 mile to the campground on the left side of the road.

Contact: Modoc National Forest, Warner Mountain Ranger District, 530/279-6116, www.fs.usda.gov/modoc.

23 UPPER RUSH CREEK
🏃 🚣 🐕 🚐 ⛺

Scenic rating: 8

in Modoc National Forest

Map 3.2, page 194

Upper Rush Creek is a pretty campground, set along Rush Creek, a quiet, wooded spot that gets little use. It sits in the shadow of nearby Manzanita Mountain (7,036 feet elevation) to the east, where there is a Forest Service lookout for a great view. To reach the lookout, drive back toward Highway 299 and when you reach the paved road, County Road 198, turn left and drive 0.5 mile to Forest Road 22. Turn left on Forest Road 22 and head up the hill. One mile from the summit, turn left at a four-way junction and drive to the top. You get dramatic views of the Warm Springs Valley to the north and the Likely Flats to the east, looking across miles and miles of open country.

Campsites, facilities: There are 13 sites for tents or RVs up to 22 feet (no hookups), but Lower Rush Creek (see listing in this chapter) is better for trailers. Picnic tables and fire grills are provided. Vault toilets are available, but there is no drinking water. Garbage must be packed out. Supplies can be obtained about nine miles away in Adin or Canby. Leashed pets are permitted.

Reservations, fees: Reservations are not accepted. There is no fee for camping. Open May through October, weather permitting.

Directions: From Redding, turn east on Highway 299 and drive to Adin. Continue east on Highway 299 for about seven miles to a signed campground turnoff on the right side of the road. Turn right and drive to the junction with Forest Road 40N05. Turn left and drive 2.5 miles to the campground at the end of the road.

Contact: Modoc National Forest, Big Valley Ranger District, 530/299-3215, www.fs.usda.gov/modoc.

24 LOWER RUSH CREEK
🚣 🐕 🚐 ⛺

Scenic rating: 6

on Rush Creek in Modoc National Forest

Map 3.2, page 194

This is one of two obscure campgrounds set a short distance from Highway 299 on Rush Creek in southern Modoc County. Lower Rush Creek is the first camp you will come to, with flat campsites surrounded by an outer fence and set along Rush Creek. This little-known and little-used camp is better suited for trailers than the one at Upper Rush Creek. It's set at 4,400 feet elevation.

Campsites, facilities: There are 10 sites for tents or RVs up to 22 feet (no hookups). Picnic tables and fire grills are provided. Vault toilets are available, but there is no drinking water. Garbage must be packed out. Supplies are available in Adin or Canby. Leashed pets are permitted.

Reservations, fees: Reservations are not accepted. There is no fee for camping. Open May through October, weather permitting.

Directions: From Redding, turn east on Highway 299 and drive to Adin. Continue east on Highway 299 for about seven miles to a signed campground turnoff on the right side of the road. Turn right and drive to the junction with Forest Road 40N05. Turn left and drive one mile to the campground on the right.

Contact: Modoc National Forest, Big Valley Ranger District, 530/299-3215, www.fs.usda.gov/modoc.

25 SOUP SPRINGS
🏃 🐕 🚐 ⛺

Scenic rating: 8

in Modoc National Forest

Map 3.2, page 194

This is a beautiful, quiet, wooded campground at a trailhead into the South Warner Wilderness. Soup Creek originates at Soup Springs in the meadow adjacent to the campground.

The trailhead here is routed two miles into the wilderness, where it junctions with the Mill Creek Trail. From here, turn left for a beautiful walk along Mill Creek and into Mill Creek Meadow, an easy yet pristine stroll that can provide a serene experience. The elevation is 6,800 feet.

Campsites, facilities: There are eight sites for tents or RVs up to 22 feet (no hookups). Picnic tables and fire grills are provided. Drinking water and vault toilets are available. Corrals and stock water are also available. Supplies can be obtained in Likely. Leashed pets are permitted.

Reservations, fees: Reservations are not accepted. Sites are $6 per night. Open June through October, weather permitting.

Directions: From Alturas, drive south on U.S. 395 for 17 miles to the town of Likely, where you'll come to Jess Valley Road. Turn left on Jess Valley Road/County Road 64 and drive nine miles to the fork. Bear left on West Warner Road/Forest Road 5 and go 4.5 miles to Soup Loop Road. Turn right on Soup Loop Road/Forest Road 40N24 and continue on that gravel road for six miles to the campground entrance on the right.

Contact: Modoc National Forest, Warner Mountain Ranger District, 530/279-6116, www.fs.usda.gov/modoc.

26 MILL CREEK FALLS

Scenic rating: 9

in Modoc National Forest

Map 3.2, page 194   **BEST**

This nice, wooded campground is a good base camp for a backpacking trip into the South Warner Wilderness. The camp is set on Mill Creek at 5,700 feet elevation. To see Mill Creek Falls, take the trail out of camp and bear left at the Y. To enter the interior of the South Warner Wilderness, bear right at the Y, after which the trail passes Clear Lake, heads to Poison Flat and Poison Creek, and

then reaches a junction. Left will take you to the Mill Creek Trail; right will take you up to the Summit Trail. Take your pick. You can't go wrong.

Campsites, facilities: There are 19 sites for tents or RVs up to 22 feet (no hookups). Picnic tables and fire grills are provided. Drinking water and vault toilets are available. Supplies are available in Likely. Some facilities are wheelchair accessible. Leashed pets are permitted.

Reservations, fees: Reservations are not accepted. Sites are $6 per night. Open June through October, weather permitting.

Directions: From Alturas drive 17 miles south on U.S. 395 to the town of Likely, where you'll come to Jess Valley Road. Turn left on Jess Valley Road/County Road 64 and drive nine miles to the fork. Bear left on West Warner Road/Forest Road 5 and drive 2.5 miles to Forest Road 40N46. Turn right on Forest Road 40N46 and drive two miles to the campground entrance at the end of the road.

Contact: Modoc National Forest, Warner Mountain Ranger District, 530/279-6116, www.fs.usda.gov/modoc.

27 EMERSON

Scenic rating: 6

in Modoc National Forest

Map 3.2, page 194

This tiny camp is virtually unknown, nestled at 6,000 feet on the eastern boundary of the South Warner Wilderness. Big alkali lakes and miles of the Nevada flats can be seen on the other side of the highway as you drive along the entrance road to the campground. A trailhead at this primitive setting is used by hikers and backpackers. Note that hitting the trail is a steep, sometimes wrenching climb for 4.5 miles to North Emerson Lake (poor to fair fishing). For many, this hike is a true butt-kicker.

Campsites, facilities: There are four sites for

tents or RVs up to 16 feet (no hookups). Picnic tables and fire grills are provided. A campfire permit is required to use a camp stove or barbecue. Vault toilets are available. No drinking water is available. Garbage must be packed out. Supplies can be obtained in Eagleville. Leashed pets are permitted.

Reservations, fees: Reservations are not accepted. There is no fee for camping. Open July through October, weather permitting.

Directions: From Alturas, drive north on U.S. 395/Highway 299 for about five miles to the junction with Highway 299. Turn right on Highway 299 and drive to Cedarville and County Road 1. Turn south on County Road 1 and drive to Eagleville. From Eagleville, continue south on County Road 1 for 1.5 miles to Forest Road 40N43/County Road 40. Turn right and drive three miles to the campground at the end of the road. The access road is steep, narrow, and very slick in wet weather. Trailers are not recommended.

Contact: Modoc National Forest, Warner Mountain Ranger District, 530/279-6116, www.fs.usda.gov/modoc.

28 ASH CREEK

Scenic rating: 7

in Modoc National Forest

Map 3.2, page 194

This remote camp has stark beauty and is set at 4,800 feet along Ash Creek, a stream with small trout. This region of Modoc National Forest has an extensive network of backcountry roads, popular with deer hunters in the fall. The Ash Creek Wildlife Area is about 10 miles west of camp. Summer comes relatively late out here, and it can be cold and wet even in early June. Stash some extra clothes, just in case. That will probably guarantee nice weather.

Campsites, facilities: There are five sites for tents or RVs up to 22 feet (no hookups). Picnic tables and fire grills are provided. Vault toilets are available. No drinking water is available.

Garbage must be packed out. Supplies can be obtained in Adin. Leashed pets are permitted.

Reservations, fees: Reservations are not accepted. There is no fee for camping. Open May through October, weather permitting.

Directions: From Redding, turn east on Highway 299 and drive to Adin and Ash Valley Road. Turn right on Ash Valley Road/County Road 88/527 and drive eight miles. Turn left at the signed campground turnoff and drive a mile to the campground on the right side of the road.

Contact: Modoc National Forest, Big Valley Ranger District, 530/299-3215, www.fs.usda.gov/modoc; Ash Creek Wildlife Area, 530/294-5824.

29 PATTERSON

Scenic rating: 4

in Modoc National Forest

Map 3.2, page 194

Patterson is set at 7,200 feet amid a landscape recovering from a big forest fire. The 2001 Blue Fire enveloped 35,000 acres in the South Warners. Since then, vegetation growth has improved and the area is now recovering.

There are both positives and negatives to the burn of 2001. The positives are a chance for much wider and longer views, as well as the opportunity to watch the evolution of the landscape in a post-fire setting. The negatives are the tree skeletons. The most affected area is to the east, especially on East Creek Trail, which rises through the burned area to a high, barren mountain rim.

Campsites, facilities: There are 15 sites for tents or RVs up to 16 feet (no hookups). Picnic tables and fire grills are provided. Vault toilets are available. Drinking water may be available seasonally; call to confirm. Garbage must be packed out. Supplies are available in Likely or Cedarville. Leashed pets are permitted.

Reservations, fees: Reservations are not accepted. There is no fee for camping. Open mid-May through October, weather permitting.

Directions: From Alturas drive 17 miles south on U.S. 395 to the town of Likely. Turn left on Jess Valley Road/County Road 64 and drive nine miles to the fork. Bear right on Forest Road 64 and drive for 16 miles to the campground on the left.

Contact: Modoc National Forest, Warner Mountain Ranger District, 530/279-6116, www.fs.usda.gov/modoc.

30 BLUE LAKE

Scenic rating: 6

in Modoc National Forest

Map 3.2, page 194

This is a strange scene: a somewhat wooded campground (with some level campsites) near the shore of Blue Lake, with nearby slopes still showing damage from a 2001 forest fire. The lake covers 160 acres and provides fishing for large brown trout and rainbow trout. A 5-mph speed limit assures quiet water for small boats and canoes. A trail circles the lake and takes less than an hour to hike. The elevation is 6,000 feet. Bald eagles have been spotted here. While their presence negates year-round use of six campsites otherwise available, the trade-off is an unprecedented opportunity to view the national bird. The Blue Fire of 2001 burned 35,000 acres in this area, including the east and west slopes adjoining Blue Lake. Yet get this: The campground was untouched.

Campsites, facilities: There are 48 sites for tents or RVs up to 32 feet (no hookups). Picnic tables and fire grills are provided. Drinking water and vault toilets are available. Some facilities are wheelchair-accessible, including a paved boat launch and fishing pier. Supplies are available in Likely. Leashed pets are permitted.

Reservations, fees: Reservations are not accepted. Sites are $7 per night. Open mid-May through October, weather permitting.

Directions: From Alturas, drive south on U.S. 395 for seven miles to the town of Likely, where you'll come to Jess Valley Road. Turn left on Jess Valley Road/County Road 64 and drive nine miles to the fork. At the fork, bear right on Forest Road 64 and drive seven miles to Forest Road 38N30. Turn right on Forest Road 38N30 and drive two miles to the campground.

Contact: Modoc National Forest, Warner Mountain Ranger District, 530/279-6116, www.fs.usda.gov/modoc.

31 WILLOW CREEK

Scenic rating: 7

in Modoc National Forest

Map 3.2, page 194

This remote camp and picnic area is set at 5,200 feet along little Willow Creek amid pine, aspen, and willows. On the north side of the campground is Lower McBride Springs.

Campsites, facilities: There are eight sites for tents or RVs up to 32 feet (no hookups). Picnic tables and fire grills are provided. Drinking water and vault toilets are available. Some facilities are wheelchair-accessible. Leashed pets are permitted.

Reservations, fees: Reservations are not accepted. Sites are $6 per night. Open May through October, weather permitting.

Directions: From Redding, drive east on Highway 299 to Adin and Highway 139. Turn right on Highway 139 and drive 14 miles to the campground on the left side of the road.

Contact: Modoc National Forest, Big Valley Ranger District, 530/299-3215, www.fs.usda.gov/modoc.

32 PIT RIVER

Scenic rating: 6

on the Pit River

Map 3.3, page 195

Very few out-of-towners know about this hidden campground set along the Pit River. It can provide a good base camp for a fishing trip adventure. The best stretch of trout water on the Pit is near Powerhouse Number Three. In addition to fishing there are many other recreation options. A parking area and trail along Hat Creek are available where the Highway 299 bridge crosses Hat Creek. Baum Lake, Crystal Lake, and the Cassel section of Hat Creek are all within five miles of this camp.

Campsites, facilities: There are seven sites for tents or RVs up to 40 feet (no hookups), and one double site for up to eight people. Picnic tables and fire rings are provided. Vault toilets, wheelchair-accessible fishing pier, and small-craft launch ramp are available. No drinking water is available. Garbage must be packed out. There are supplies and a coin laundry in Fall River Mills. Some facilities are wheelchair-accessible. Leashed pets are permitted.

Reservations, fees: Reservations are not accepted. Sites are $8 per night, and $12 per night for the double site. Open May through November.

Directions: From Redding, drive east on Highway 299 to Burney and continue for five miles to the junction with Highway 89. At the junction, continue straight on Highway 299, cross the Pit River Bridge, and drive about three miles to Pit One Powerhouse Road. Turn right and drive down the hill to the Pit River Lodge. Turn right and drive 0.5 mile to the campground.

Contact: Bureau of Land Management, Alturas Field Office, 530/233-4666, www.blm.gov/ca.

33 CASSEL

Scenic rating: 8

on Hat Creek

Map 3.3, page 195

This camp is set at 3,200 feet in the beautiful Hat Creek Valley. It is an outstanding location for a fishing trip base camp, with nearby Crystal Lake, Baum Lake, and Hat Creek (all set in the Hat Creek Valley) providing trout fishing. This section of Hat Creek is well known for its challenging fly-fishing. A good source of fishing information is Vaughn's Sporting Goods in Burney. Baum Lake is ideal for cartop boats with electric motors.

Campsites, facilities: There are 27 sites for tents or RVs up to 30 feet (no hookups). Picnic tables and fire grills are provided. Drinking water and vault toilets are available. Some facilities are wheelchair-accessible. Leashed pets are permitted.

Reservations, fees: Reservations are not accepted. Sites are $22 per night, $3 per night for each additional vehicle, $11 per night per additional RV, $1 per pet per night. Open mid-April through mid-November, weather permitting.

Directions: From Redding, drive east on Highway 299 to Burney and continue for five miles to the junction with Highway 89. At the junction, continue straight on Highway 299 for two miles to Cassel Road. At Cassel Road, turn right and drive 3.6 miles to the campground entrance on the left.

Contact: PG&E Land Projects, 916/386-5164, www.pge.com/recreation.

34 HAT CREEK HEREFORD RANCH RV PARK AND CAMPGROUND

Scenic rating: 8

near Hat Creek

Map 3.3, page 195

This privately operated campground is set in a working cattle ranch. Campers are not allowed near the cattle pasture or cattle. Fishing is available in Hat Creek or in the nearby stocked trout pond. Swimming is also allowed in the pond. Sightseeing is excellent with Burney Falls, Lassen Volcanic National Park, and Subway Caves all within 30 miles.

Campsites, facilities: There are 40 tent sites and 50 RV sites with full or partial hookups

(30 amps); some sites are pull-through. Picnic tables and fireplaces are provided. Restrooms with showers, a dump station, coin laundry, playground, swimming beach, horseshoes, group pavilion, stocked fishing pond, WiFi, and a convenience store are available. Some facilities are wheelchair-accessible. Leashed pets are permitted.

Reservations, fees: Reservations are recommended and can be made by telephone or online. RV sites are $34 per night, tent sites are $24–27 per night, $3 per night for more than two people, $1 per night per pet. Some credit cards accepted. Open April through October.

Directions: From Redding, drive east on Highway 299 to Burney and continue for five miles to the junction with Highway 89. Turn right (south) on Highway 89 and drive 12 miles to the second Doty Road Loop exit. Turn left and drive 0.5 mile to the park entrance on the right.

Contact: Hat Creek Hereford Ranch RV Park and Campground, 530/335-7171 or 877/459-9532, www.hatcreekrv.com.

35 HONN

Scenic rating: 7

on Hat Creek in Lassen National Forest

Map 3.3, page 195

This primitive, tiny campground is set near the point where Honn Creek enters Hat Creek, at 3,400 feet elevation in Lassen National Forest. The creek is extremely pretty here, shaded by trees and flowing emerald green. The camp provides streamside access for trout fishing, though this stretch of creek is sometimes overlooked by the Department of Fish and Game in favor of stocking the creek at the more popular Cave Camp and Bridge Camp. (See listings in this chapter for more information.)

Campsites, facilities: There are six tent sites. Picnic tables and fire grills are provided.

Vault toilets are available. Drinking water is not available. A grocery store, coin laundry, and propane gas are nearby. Leashed pets are permitted.

Reservations, fees: Reservations are not accepted. Sites are $10 per night, $5 per night for each additional vehicle. Open late April through October, weather permitting.

Directions: From Redding, drive east on Highway 299 to Burney and continue for five miles to the junction with Highway 89. Turn right (south) on Highway 89 and drive 15 miles to the campground entrance on the left side of the road.

Contact: Lassen National Forest, Hat Creek Ranger District, 530/336-5521, www.fs.usda.gov/lassen; Department of Fish and Game fishing information, 530/225-2146.

36 OLD COW MEADOWS

Scenic rating: 7

in Latour Demonstration State Forest

Map 3.3, page 195

Nobody finds this campground without this book. You want quiet? You don't want to be bugged by anyone? This tiny camp, virtually unknown, is set at 5,900 feet in a wooded area along Old Cow Creek. Recreation options include all-terrain-vehicle use on existing roads and walking the dirt roads that crisscross the area.

Campsites, facilities: There are three sites for tents or RVs up to 25 feet (no hookups). Picnic tables and fire grills are provided. Vault toilets and drinking water are available. Garbage must be packed out. Some facilities are wheelchair-accessible. Leashed pets are permitted.

Reservations, fees: Reservations are not accepted. There is no fee for camping. Open June through October, weather permitting.

Directions: In Redding, turn east on Highway 44 and drive about 9.5 miles to Millville Road. Turn left on Millville Road and drive 0.5 mile to the intersection of Millville Road and Whitmore Road. Turn right on Whitmore Road and drive 13 miles, through Whitmore, until Whitmore Road becomes Tamarac Road. Continue for one mile to a fork at Bateman Road. Take the right fork on Bateman Road, drive 3.5 miles (where the road turns to gravel), and then continue 10 miles to Huckleberry Road. Turn right on Huckleberry Road and drive two miles to the campground.

Contact: Latour Demonstration State Forest, 530/225-2438, www.fire.ca.gov.

37 SOUTH COW CREEK

Scenic rating: 6

in Latour Demonstration State Forest

Map 3.3, page 195

This camp is set at 5,600 feet in a pretty, wooded area next to a small meadow along South Cow Creek. It's used mostly in the fall for hunting, with off-highway-vehicle use on the surrounding roads in the summer. If you want to get away from it all without leaving your vehicle, this is one way to do it. The creek is a reliable water source, providing you use a water filtration pump.

Latour has two other small, little-known campgrounds: Old Station, with three campsites; and Butcher Gulch, with two campsites.

Campsites, facilities: There are four sites for tents or RVs up to 30 feet (no hookups). Picnic tables and fire grills are provided. Vault toilets and drinking water are available. Garbage must be packed out. Some facilities are wheelchair-accessible. Leashed pets are permitted.

Reservations, fees: Reservations are not accepted. There is no fee for camping. Open June through October, weather permitting.

Directions: In Redding, turn east on Highway 44 and drive about 9.5 miles to Millville Road. Turn left on Millville Road and drive 0.5 mile to the intersection of Millville Road and Whitmore Road. Turn right on Whitmore Road and drive 13 miles, through Whitmore,

until Whitmore Road becomes Tamarac Road. Continue for one mile to the fork at Bateman Road. Take the right fork on Bateman Road, drive 3.5 miles (where the road turns to gravel), and then continue for 11 miles to South Cow Creek Road. Turn right (east) and drive one mile to the campground.

Contact: Latour Demonstration State Forest, 530/225-2438, www.fire.ca.gov.

38 BRIDGE CAMP

Scenic rating: 7

on Hat Creek in Lassen National Forest

Map 3.3, page 195

This camp is one of four along Highway 89 in the area along Hat Creek. It is set at 4,000 feet elevation, with shaded sites and the stream within very short walking distance. Trout are stocked on this stretch of the creek, with fishing access available out of camp, as well as at Rocky and Cave Camps to the south and Honn to the north. In one weekend, anglers might hit all four.

Campsites, facilities: There are 25 sites for tents or RVs up to 22 feet (no hookups). Picnic tables and fire grills are provided. There is no drinking water. Vault toilets are available. A grocery store and propane gas are nearby. Leashed pets are permitted.

Reservations, fees: Reservations are not accepted. Sites are $10 per night, $5 per night for each additional vehicle. Open late April to mid-October, weather permitting.

Directions: From Redding, drive east on Highway 299 to Burney and continue for five miles to the junction with Highway 89. Turn right (south) on Highway 89 and drive 19 miles to the campground entrance on the right side of the road. If you reach Old Station, you have gone five miles too far.

Contact: Lassen National Forest, Hat Creek Ranger District, 530/336-5521, www.fs.usda.gov/lassen; Department of Fish and Game fishing information, 530/225-2146.

39 ROCKY CAMP

Scenic rating: 7

on Hat Creek in Lassen National Forest

Map 3.3, page 195

This is a small, primitive camp along Hat Creek on Highway 89. It's usually a second choice for campers if nearby Cave and Bridge Camps are full. Streamside fishing access is a plus here, with this section of stream stocked with rainbow trout. The elevation is 4,000 feet. (See the Cave Camp listing for more information.)

Campsites, facilities: There are eight tent sites. Picnic tables and fire grills are provided. Vault toilets are available. No drinking water is available. A grocery store and propane gas are nearby. Leashed pets are permitted.

Reservations, fees: Reservations are not accepted. Sites are $10 per night, $5 per night for each additional vehicle. Open late April through October, weather permitting.

Directions: From Redding, drive east on Highway 299 to Burney and continue for five miles to the junction with Highway 89. Turn right (south) on Highway 89 and drive 20 miles to the campground entrance on the right side of the road. If you reach Old Station, you have gone four miles too far.

Contact: Lassen National Forest, Hat Creek Ranger District, 530/336-5521, www.fs.usda. gov/lassen.; Department of Fish and Game fishing information, 530/225-2146.

40 CAVE CAMP

Scenic rating: 7

on Hat Creek in Lassen National Forest

Map 3.3, page 195

Cave Camp is set right along Hat Creek, with easy access off Highway 89 and an anglers' trail available along the stream. This stretch of Hat Creek is planted with rainbow trout twice per month by the Department of Fish and Game, starting with the opening of trout season on the last Saturday of April. Nearby side trips include Lassen Volcanic National Park, about a 15-minute drive to the south on Highway 89, and Subway Caves (turn left at the junction just across the road from the campground). A rare bonus at this camp is that wheelchair-accessible fishing is available.

Campsites, facilities: There are 46 sites for tents or RVs up to 22 feet (no hookups). Picnic tables and fire grills are provided. Drinking water and flush and vault toilets are available. Supplies can be obtained in Old Station. Some facilities are wheelchair-accessible. Leashed pets are permitted.

Reservations, fees: Reservations are not accepted. Sites are $16 per night, $5 per night for each additional vehicle; $10 per night during winter season. Of the 46 campsites, 16 are open year round; the remaining 30 sites are open late April through mid-October, weather permitting.

Directions: From Redding, drive east on Highway 299 to Burney and continue for five miles to the junction with Highway 89. Turn right (south) on Highway 89 and drive 23 miles to the campground entrance on the right side of the road. If you reach Old Station, you have gone one mile too far.

Contact: Lassen National Forest, Hat Creek Ranger District, 530/336-5521, www.fs.usda. gov/lassen; Department of Fish and Game fishing information, 530/225-2146.

41 HAT CREEK

Scenic rating: 7

on Hat Creek in Lassen National Forest

Map 3.3, page 195

This is one in a series of Forest Service camps set beside beautiful Hat Creek, a good trout stream stocked regularly by the Department of Fish and Game. The elevation is 4,300 feet. The proximity to Lassen Volcanic National Park to the south is a big plus. Supplies are available in the little town of Old Station one mile to the north.

Campsites, facilities: There are 75 sites for tents or RVs up to 30 feet, and three group camps for tents or RVs up to 30 feet that can accommodate up to 50 people each. No hookups. Picnic tables and fire grills are provided. Drinking water and flush and vault toilets are available. A grocery store, dump station, coin laundry, and propane gas are nearby. There is an accessible fishing platform. Leashed pets are permitted.

Reservations, fees: Tent and RV sites are first-come, first-served. Reservations are required for group sites at 877/444-6777 or www.recreation.gov ($9 reservation fee). Tent and RV sites are $16 per night, $5 per night for each additional vehicle, $80 per night for group camps. Open late April through October, weather permitting.

Directions: From Redding, drive east on Highway 44 to the junction with Highway 89 (near the entrance to Lassen Volcanic National Park). Turn left (north) on Highway 89 and drive about 12 miles to the campground entrance on the left side of the road. Turn left and drive a short distance to the campground.

Contact: Lassen National Forest, Hat Creek Ranger District, 530/336-5521, www.fs.usda.gov/lassen; Department of Fish and Game fishing information, 530/225-2146.

42 NORTH BATTLE CREEK RESERVOIR

Scenic rating: 7

on Battle Creek Reservoir

Map 3.3, page 195

This little-known lake is at 5,600 feet in elevation, largely surrounded by Lassen National Forest. No gas engines are permitted on the lake, making it ideal for canoes, rafts, and car-top aluminum boats equipped with electric motors. When the lake level is up in early summer, it is a pretty setting with good trout fishing.

Campsites, facilities: There are 15 sites for tents or RVs up to 30 feet (no hookups) and five walk-in tent sites. Picnic tables and fire grills are provided. Drinking water and vault toilets are available. A car-top boat launch is available nearby. Leashed pets are permitted.

Reservations, fees: Reservations are not accepted. Sites are $18 per night, $3 per night for each additional vehicle, $9 per additional RV per night, $1 per pet per night. Open mid-May through mid-September, weather permitting.

Directions: From Redding, drive east on Highway 44 to Viola. From Viola, continue east for 3.5 miles to Forest Road 32N17. Turn left on Forest Road 32N17 and drive five miles to Forest Road 32N31. Turn left and drive four miles to Forest Road 32N18. Turn right and drive 0.5 mile to the reservoir and the campground on the right side of the road.

Contact: PG&E Land Projects, 916/386-5164, www.pge.com/recreation.

43 BIG PINE CAMP

Scenic rating: 7

on Hat Creek in Lassen National Forest

Map 3.3, page 195

This campground is set on the headwaters of Hat Creek, a pretty spot amid ponderosa pines. The elevation is 4,500 feet. A dirt road out of camp parallels Hat Creek, providing access for trout fishing. A great vista point is set on the highway, a mile south of the campground entrance road. It is only a 10-minute drive south to the Highway 44 entrance station for Lassen Volcanic National Park.

Campsites, facilities: There are 19 sites for tents or RVs up to 22 feet (no hookups). Picnic tables and fire grills are provided. Drinking water (at two hand pumps) and vault toilets are available. A dump station, grocery store, and propane gas are nearby. Leashed pets are permitted.

Reservations, fees: Reservations are not

accepted. Sites are $12 per night, $5 per night for each additional vehicle. Open May through October, weather permitting.

Directions: From Redding, drive east on Highway 44 to the junction with Highway 89 (near the entrance to Lassen Volcanic National Park). Turn left (north) on Highway 89 and drive about eight miles (one mile past the vista point) to the campground entrance on the right side of the road. Turn right and drive 0.5 mile to the campground.

Contact: Lassen National Forest, Hat Creek Ranger District, 530/336-5521, www.fs.usda. gov/lassen; Department of Fish and Game fishing information, 530/225-2146.

44 BUTTE CREEK

Scenic rating: 6

in Lassen National Forest

Map 3.3, page 195

This primitive, little-known spot is just three miles from the northern boundary of Lassen Volcanic National Park, set on little Butte Creek. The elevation is 5,600 feet. It is a four-mile drive south out of camp on Forest Road 18 to Butte Lake in Lassen Park and to the trailhead for a great hike up to the Cinder Cone (6,907 feet), with dramatic views of the Lassen wilderness.

Campsites, facilities: There are 10 dispersed camping sites for tents or RVs up to 22 feet (no hookups). There is no drinking water and there are no restrooms available. Garbage must be packed out. Leashed pets are permitted.

Reservations, fees: Reservations are not accepted. There is no fee for camping. Open May through October, weather permitting.

Directions: From Redding, drive east on Highway 44 to the junction with Highway 89 (near the entrance to Lassen Volcanic National Park). Turn north on Highway 89 and drive to Highway 44. Turn east (right) on Highway 44 and drive 11 miles to Forest Road 18. Turn right at Forest Road 18 and

drive three miles to the campground on the left side of the road.

Contact: Lassen National Forest, Eagle Lake Ranger District, 530/257-4188, www.fs.usda. gov/lassen.

45 BOGARD

Scenic rating: 6

in Lassen National Forest

Map 3.3, page 195

This little camp is set along Pine Creek, which flows through Pine Creek Valley at the foot of the Bogard Buttes. It is a relatively obscure camp that gets missed by many travelers. A bonus here are the beautiful aspens, breathtaking in fall. To the nearby west is a network of Forest Service roads, and beyond is the Caribou Wilderness.

Campsites, facilities: There are 11 dispersed camping sites for tents or RVs up to 25 feet (no hookups). Picnic tables and fire grills are provided. Drinking water (hand pumped) and vault toilets are available. Leashed pets are permitted.

Reservations, fees: Reservations are not accepted. Sites are $15 per night. Open May through October, weather permitting.

Directions: From Redding, drive east on Highway 44 to the junction with Highway 89 (near the entrance to Lassen Volcanic National Park). Turn north on Highway 89 and drive to Highway 44. Turn east on Highway 44 and drive to the Bogard Work Center (about seven miles past Poison Lake) and the adjacent rest stop. Continue east on Highway 44 for two miles to a gravel road on the right side of the road (Forest Road 31N26). Turn right on Forest Road 31N26 and drive two miles. Turn right on Forest Road 31N21 and drive 0.5 mile to the campground at the end of the road.

Contact: Lassen National Forest, Eagle Lake Ranger District, 530/257-4188, www.fs.usda. gov/lassen.

46 CRATER LAKE

🚶 🏊 🛶 🚤 🎣 🐕 5°/₀ ⛺

Scenic rating: 8

in Lassen National Forest

Map 3.3, page 195

This hideaway is set near Crater Lake at 6,800 feet elevation in remote Lassen National Forest, just below Crater Mountain (that's it up there to the northeast at 7,420 feet). This 27-acre lake provides trout fishing, boating, and, if you can stand the ice-cold water, a quick dunk on warm summer days.

Campsites, facilities: There are 17 sites for tents. Picnic tables and fire grills are provided. Drinking water (hand pumped) and vault toilets are available. No gas motors are allowed on the lake. Leashed pets are permitted.

Reservations, fees: Reservations are not accepted. Sites are $15 per night. Open June through October, weather permitting.

Directions: From Redding, drive east on Highway 44 to the junction with Highway 89 (near the entrance to Lassen Volcanic National Park). Turn north on Highway 89 and drive to Highway 44. Turn east on Highway 44 (right) and drive to the Bogard Work Center and adjacent rest stop. Turn left at Forest Road 32N08 (signed Crater Lake) and drive one mile to a T intersection. Bear right and continue on Forest Road 32N08 for six miles (including two hairpin left turns) to the campground on the left side of the road. Note: Forest Road 32N08 is a rough washboard road.

Contact: Lassen National Forest, Eagle Lake Ranger District, 530/257-4188, www.fs.usda.gov/lassen.

47 MACCUMBER RESERVOIR

🏊 🛶 🚤 🎣 🐕 🚐 ⛺

Scenic rating: 7

on MacCumber Reservoir

Map 3.3, page 195

Here's a small lake, easy to reach from Redding, that is little known and rarely visited. MacCumber Reservoir is set at 3,500 feet and is stocked with rainbow trout each year, providing fair fishing. No gas motors are permitted here. That's fine—it guarantees quiet, calm water, ideal for car-top boats: prams, canoes, rafts, and small aluminum boats.

Campsites, facilities: There are nine sites for tents or RVs up to 30 feet (no hookups) and five walk-in tent sites. Picnic tables and fire grills are provided. Drinking water and vault toilets are available. Leashed pets are permitted.

Reservations, fees: Reservations are not accepted. Sites are $18 per night, $3 per night for each additional vehicle, $9 per night per additional RV, $1 per pet per night. Open mid-April through mid-September, weather permitting.

Directions: In Redding, turn east on Highway 44 and drive toward Viola to Lake Mac-Cumber Road (if you reach Viola, you have gone four miles too far). Turn left at Lake MacCumber Road and drive two miles to the reservoir and campground.

Contact: PG&E Land Projects, 916/386-5164, www.pge.com/recreation.

48 MANZANITA LAKE

🚶 🏊 🛶 🚤 🎣 🐕 ♿ 🚐 ⛺

Scenic rating: 9

in Lassen Volcanic National Park

Map 3.3, page 195

Manzanita Lake, set at 5,890 feet, is one of the prettiest lakes in Lassen Volcanic National Park, and evening walks around the lake are beautiful. The campground, set among towering Ponderosa pines, is often crowded due to this great natural beauty. Manzanita Lake provides good catch-and-release trout fishing for experienced fly fishers in prams and other nonpowered boats. Fishing regulations prohibit bait and lures with barbs. This is no place for a dad, mom, and a youngster to fish from shore with Power Bait; you'll end up with a citation. Swimming is permitted, but there are few takers.

Campsites, facilities: There are 179 sites for tents or RVs up to 35 feet (no hookups) and five group sites (in Loop B) for up to 25 people each. Note that Loop D is tent-only. There are also 20 rustic cabins that sleep two to six people each. Picnic tables, fire grills, and bear-proof food lockers are provided. Drinking water (until mid-October) and flush and vault toilets are available. A museum, visitors center, and small store, as well as propane gas, groceries, coin showers, dump station, and coin laundry are nearby. Ranger programs are offered in the summer. A boat launch is also nearby (no motors are permitted on boats at Manzanita Lake). Some facilities are wheelchair-accessible. Leashed pets are permitted at campsites only.

Reservations, fees: Reservations for individual sites (Loops A and C) are accepted May to October and are required for group sites at 877/444-6777 or www.recreation. gov ($9 reservation fee). Sites in Loops B and D are first-come, first-served. Sites are $18 per night, $50 per night for the group sites, $57–81 per night for the cabins, $10 per vehicle park entrance fee. Some credit cards accepted. Open late May through late September, weather permitting. (In fall, it's open without drinking water at a reduced rate until the camp is closed by snow).

Directions: From Redding, drive east on Highway 44 to the junction with Highway 89. Turn right (south) on Highway 89 and drive one mile to the entrance station to Lassen Volcanic National Park (the state highway becomes Lassen Park Highway/Main Park Road). Continue a short distance on Lassen Park Highway/Main Park Road to the campground entrance road. Turn right and drive 0.5 mile to the campground.

Contact: Lassen Volcanic National Park, 530/595-4444, www.nps.gov/lavo.

49 CRAGS

Scenic rating: 8

in Lassen Volcanic National Park

Map 3.3, page 195

Crags is sometimes overlooked as a prime spot at Lassen Volcanic National Park because there is no lake nearby. No problem, because even though this campground is small compared to the giant complex at Manzanita Lake, the campsites are more spacious, do not fill up as quickly, and many are backed by forest. In addition, Emigrant Trail runs out of camp, routing east and meeting pretty Lost Creek after a little more than a mile, a great short hike. Directly across from Crags are the towering Chaos Crags, topping out at 8,503 feet. The elevation here is 5,720 feet.

Campsites, facilities: There are 45 sites for tents or RVs up to 35 feet (no hookups). Picnic tables, fire rings, and bear-proof food lockers are provided. Drinking water and vault toilets are available. Leashed pets are permitted in the campground and on paved roads only.

Reservations, fees: Reservations are not accepted. Sites are $12 per night, $10 per vehicle park entrance fee. Open late June through early September.

Directions: From Redding, drive east on Highway 44 for 42 miles to the junction with Highway 89. Turn right and drive one mile to the entrance station at Lassen Volcanic National Park (the state highway becomes Lassen Park Highway/Main Park Road). Continue on Lassen Park Highway/Main Park Road for about five miles to the campground on the left side of the road.

Contact: Lassen Volcanic National Park, 530/595-4444, www.nps.gov/lavo.

50 BUTTE LAKE

Scenic rating: 9

in Lassen Volcanic National Park

Map 3.3, page 195

Butte Lake campground is situated in an open, volcanic setting with a sprinkling of lodgepole pine. The contrast of the volcanics against the emerald green of the lake is beautiful and memorable; the Cinder Cone Trail can provide an even better look. The trailhead is near the boat launch area, and it's a strenuous hike involving a climb of 800 feet over the course of two miles to the top of the Cinder Cone. The footing is often loose because of volcanic pebbles. At the rim, you can peer inside the Cinder Cone, as well as be rewarded with lake views and a long-distance vista. Trout fishing is poor at Butte Lake, as at nearly all the lakes at this park, because trout have not been planted for years. The elevation is 6,100 feet, and the lake covers 212 acres.

Campsites, facilities: There are 101 sites for tents or RVs up to 35 feet (no hookups), one equestrian camp for up to 10 people, and six group tent sites that can accommodate 10–25 people each. Some sites are pull-through. Picnic tables, fire rings, and bear-proof food lockers are provided. Drinking water (through mid-September) and flush and vault toilets are available. Corrals and watering stations are available at the equestrian camp. A boat ramp is nearby. No motors are permitted on the lake. Some facilities are wheelchair-accessible. Leashed pets are permitted at campsites only.

Reservations, fees: Reservations are accepted for individual sites (Loop B) and are required for group and equestrian sites at 877/444-6777 or www.recreation.gov ($9 reservation fee). Sites in Loop A are first-come, first-served. Tent and RV sites are $16 per night; the equestrian camp is $35 per night; group sites are $50 per night; and the park entrance fee is $10 per vehicle. Open mid-June through October, weather permitting.

Directions: From Redding, drive east on Highway 44 to the junction with Highway 89. Bear north on Highway 89/44 and drive 13 miles to Old Station. Just past Old Station, turn right (east) on Highway 44 and drive 10 miles to Forest Road 32N21/Butte Lake Road. Turn right and drive six miles on a gravel road to the campground.

Contact: Lassen Volcanic National Park, 530/595-4444, www.nps.gov/lavo.

51 MOUNT LASSEN/ SHINGLETOWN KOA

Scenic rating: 6

near Lassen Volcanic National Park

Map 3.3, page 195

This popular KOA camp is 14 miles from the entrance of Lassen Volcanic National Park and has pretty, wooded sites. Location is always the critical factor on vacations, and this park is set up perfectly for launching trips into Lassen Volcanic National Park. Hat Creek provides trout fishing along Highway 89, and just inside the Highway 44 entrance station at Lassen is Manzanita Lake, providing good fishing and hiking.

Campsites, facilities: There are 30 sites with full or partial hookups (30 and 50 amps) for tents or RVs up to 60 feet, including some pull-through sites, and 10 cabins. Picnic tables and fire grills are provided. Restroom with flush toilets and showers, playground, basketball and volleyball half-courts, tether ball, heated pool (summer only), dump station, convenience store, ice, firewood, coin laundry, video arcade and recreation room, WiFi, dog run, and propane gas are available. Leashed pets are permitted, with certain restrictions.

Reservations, fees: Reservations are accepted with a deposit at 800/562-3403. RV sites are $38–44 per night, tent sites are $30–32 per night, $5 per person per night for more than two people. Some credit cards accepted. Open mid-March through November.

Directions: From Redding, turn east on Highway 44 and drive to Shingletown. In Shingletown, continue east for four miles and look for the park entrance on the right (signed KOA).

Contact: Mount Lassen/Shingletown KOA, 530/474-3133, www.koa.com.

52 SUMMIT LAKE: NORTH, SOUTH, AND STOCK CORRAL

🚶 🏊 🛶 🚐 🐴 ♿ 🧺 ⛺

Scenic rating: 9

in Lassen Volcanic National Park

Map 3.3, page 195   BEST (

Summit Lake is a beautiful spot where deer often visit in the evening on the adjacent meadow just east of the campgrounds. The lake is small, just 15 acres, and since trout plants were suspended it has been fished out. Summit Lake is the most popular lake for swimming in the park. Evening walks around the lake are perfect for families. A more ambitious trail is routed out of camp and leads past lavish wildflower displays in early summer to a series of wilderness lakes. The campgrounds are set at an elevation of 6,695 feet.

Campsites, facilities: There are 46 sites for tents or RVs up to 35 feet at North Summit; 48 sites for tents or RVs up to 30 feet at South Summit (Loop E is tent-only); and one equestrian site for tents or RVs up to 35 feet that can accommodate up to 10 people and eight horses. No hookups. Picnic tables, fire rings, and bear-proof food lockers are provided. Drinking water and toilets (flush toilets at North Summit; pit toilets at South Summit; vault toilets at the equestrian site) are available. Water for stock corral campers is available at both Summit Lake campgrounds. Ranger programs are sometimes offered in summer. Some facilities are wheelchair-accessible. Leashed pets are permitted at campsites only.

Reservations, fees: Reservations are accepted at 877/444-6777 or www.recreation.gov ($9 reservation fee). North Summit sites are $18 per night. Loop A sites are first-come, first-served; Loop B sites are available by reservation. South Summit sites are $16 per night. Loop C and D sites are available by reservation; Loop A sites are first-come, first-served for tents only. South Summit is first-come, first-served after mid-September, when sites are $10 per night. The equestrian site is $35 per night. There is a $10 park entrance fee per vehicle. Some credit cards accepted. Open late June through October, weather permitting.

Directions: From Redding, drive east on Highway 44 to the junction with Highway 89. Turn south on Highway 89 and drive one mile to the entrance station to Lassen Volcanic National Park (where the state highway becomes Lassen Park Highway/Main Park Road). Continue on Lassen Park Highway/Main Park Road for 12 miles to the campground entrance on the left side of the road. The horse camp is located across the street from the other campsites.

Contact: Lassen Volcanic National Park, 530/595-4444, www.nps.gov/lavo.

53 SILVER BOWL

🚶 🛶 🚐 🐴 🚙 ⛺

Scenic rating: 7

on Silver Lake in Lassen National Forest

Map 3.3, page 195

Silver Lake is a pretty lake set at 6,400 feet elevation at the edge of the Caribou Wilderness. There is an unimproved boat ramp at the southern end of the lake. It is occasionally planted by the Department of Fish and Game with Eagle Lake trout and brown trout, which provide a summer fishery for campers. A trailhead from adjacent Caribou Lake is routed west into the wilderness, with routes available both to Emerald Lake to the northwest, and Betty, Trail, and Shotoverin Lakes nearby to the southeast.

Campsites, facilities: There are 18 sites for tents or RVs up to 25 feet (no hookups). Picnic tables and fire grills are provided. Drinking water and vault toilets are available. Leashed pets are permitted.

Reservations, fees: Reservations are not accepted. Sites are $10 per night, $3 per night for each additional vehicle. Open late May through October, weather permitting.

Directions: From Red Bluff, drive east on Highway 36 to the junction with Highway 89. Continue east on Highway 36 past Lake Almanor to Westwood. In Westwood, turn left on County Road A21 and drive 12.5 miles to Silver Lake Road. Turn left on Silver Lake Road/County Road 110 and drive 8.5 miles north to Silver Lake. At Silver Lake, turn right and drive 0.75 mile to the campground.

Contact: Lassen National Forest, Almanor Ranger District, 530/258-2141, www.fs.usda.gov/lassen.

54 ROCKY KNOLL
🏃‍♂️ 🏊 🚣 🛶 🎣 🐎 🚐 ⛺

Scenic rating: 7

on Silver Lake in Lassen National Forest

Map 3.3, page 195

This is one of two camps at pretty Silver Lake, set at 6,400 feet elevation at the edge of the Caribou Wilderness. The other camp is Silver Bowl to the nearby north, which is larger and provides better access for hikers. This camp, however, is closer to the boat ramp, which is set at the south end of the lake. Silver Lake provides a good summer fishery for campers.

Campsites, facilities: There are 18 sites for tents or RVs up to 27 feet (no hookups). Picnic tables and fire grills are provided. Vault toilets are available, but there is no drinking water. Leashed pets are permitted.

Reservations, fees: Reservations are not accepted. There is no fee for camping. Open late May through early November, weather permitting.

Directions: From Red Bluff, drive east on Highway 36 to the junction with Highway 89. Continue east on Highway 36 past Lake

Almanor to Westwood. In Westwood, turn left on County Road A21 and drive 12.5 miles to Silver Lake Road. Turn left (west) on Silver Lake Road/County Road 110 and drive 8.5 miles to Silver Lake. At Silver Lake, turn left and drive 300 yards to the campground.

Contact: Lassen National Forest, Almanor Ranger District, 530/258-2141, www.fs.usda.gov/lassen.

55 SOUTHWEST WALK-IN
🏃‍♂️ 🐎 🚐 ⛺

Scenic rating: 8

in Lassen Volcanic National Park

Map 3.3, page 195

This pretty campground is located at 6,700 feet elevation, east of the Kohm Yah-mah-nee Visitors Center parking area near the southwest entrance station. Just taking the short walk required to reach the camp will launch you into an orbit beyond most of the highway cruisers visiting Lassen. The 4.6-mile hike to Mill Creek Falls, the park's highest waterfall, begins at the campground. The Sulphur Works and Brokeoff Mountain trailheads are nearby, as is the new visitors center. One must-see is Bumpass Hell. The trail is about seven miles north of the campground on the right side of the Lassen Park Highway/Main Park Road. This easy hike takes you past steam vents and boiling mud pots, all set in prehistoric-looking volcanic rock. Ranger-led programs are sometimes offered.

Campsites, facilities: There are 21 walk-in tent sites, and a large parking lot available for RVs of any length (no hookups). Picnic tables, fire rings, and bear-proof food lockers are provided. Drinking water and restrooms with flush toilets (in the visitors center) are available in summer. Leashed pets are permitted in campground only.

Reservations, fees: Reservations are not accepted. Sites are $14 per night for tent campers, $10 per night for RV parking, plus $10 per vehicle park entrance fee. Open year-round, weather permitting.

Directions: From Red Bluff, take Highway 36 east for 48 miles to the junction with Highway 89. Turn left on Highway 89 (becomes Lassen Park Highway/Main Park Road) and drive to the park's entrance. Just after passing through the park entrance gate, look for the camp parking area on the right side of the road.

Contact: Lassen Volcanic National Park, 530/595-4444, www.nps.gov/lavo.

56 WARNER VALLEY
🚶 🖑 🐾 ⛺

Scenic rating: 7

on Hot Springs Creek in
Lassen Volcanic National Park

Map 3.3, page 195

Lassen is one of the great national parks of the West, yet it gets surprisingly little use compared to Yosemite, Sequoia, and Kings Canyon National Parks. This campground gets overlooked because of its remote access out of Chester. The camp is set along Hot Springs Creek at 5,650 feet. The best hike here is the 2.5-mile walk out to the unique Devil's Kitchen geothermal area. Other options are a 2.5-mile hike—with an 800-foot climb—to Drake Lake, and a three-mile hike to Boiling Springs Lakes. It's also a good horseback-riding area. The Drakesbad Resort, where securing reservations is about as difficult as finding Bigfoot, is near the campground.

Campsites, facilities: There are 18 tent sites. RVs and trailers are not recommended because of road conditions. Picnic tables, food lockers, and fire rings are provided. Drinking water (until mid-September) and pit toilets are available. Leashed pets are permitted in the campground only.

Reservations, fees: Reservations are not accepted. Sites are $14 per night, $10 per night after mid-September. There is a park entrance fee of $10 per vehicle. Open June through late September, weather permitting (with no water from mid-September due to snow closure).

Directions: From Red Bluff, take Highway 36 east for 44 miles to the junction with Highway 89 (do not turn left, or north, on Highway 89 to Lassen Volcanic National Park entrance, as signed). Continue east on Highway 36/89 to Chester and Feather River Drive. Turn left (north) on Feather River Drive (Warner Valley Road) and drive 0.75 mile to County Road 312. Bear left and drive six miles to Warner Valley Road. Turn right and drive 11 miles to the campground on the right. Note: The last 3.5 miles are unpaved, and there is one steep hill that can be difficult to climb for large or underpowered RVs, or if you are towing a trailer.

Contact: Lassen Volcanic National Park, 530/595-4444, www.nps.gov/lavo.

57 JUNIPER LAKE
🚶 🏊 🖑 🐾 ⛺

Scenic rating: 10

in Lassen Volcanic National Park

Map 3.3, page 195

This pretty spot is on the eastern shore of Juniper Lake, at an elevation of 6,792 feet. It is far from the busy Lassen Park Highway/Main Park Road (Highway 89) corridor that is routed through central Lassen Volcanic National Park. From the north end of the lake, a great side trip is to make the 0.5-mile, 400-foot climb to Inspiration Point, which provides a panoramic view of the park's backcountry. A two-mile hike up Mount Harkness begins from camp. Since no drinking water is provided, it is critical to bring a water purification pump or plenty of bottled water.

Campsites, facilities: There are 18 tent sites, an equestrian site, and two group tent sites that can accommodate 10–15 people each. No hookups. Picnic tables, fire rings, and bear-proof food lockers are provided. Vault toilets are available. Drinking water is not available. Leashed pets are permitted in the campground only.

Reservations, fees: Reservations are not accepted for individual sites, but are required for the group site at 877/444-6777 or www. recreation.gov ($9 reservation fee). Reservations are also required for the equestrian site at 530/335-7029. Single sites are $10 per night, $30 per night for group sites, $10 per night for the equestrian site plus $4 per horse per night, $10 park entrance fee per vehicle. Open late June through late September, weather permitting.

Directions: From Red Bluff, take Highway 36 east for 44 miles to the junction with Highway 89 (do not turn left, or north, on Highway 89 to Lassen Volcanic National Park entrance, as signed). Continue east on Highway 36/89 to Chester and Feather River Drive. Turn left (north) on Feather River Drive and drive 0.75 mile to the Y and the junction for County Road 318. Bear right (marked for Juniper Lake) on County Road 318 and drive 11 miles to the campground on the right, set along the east side of the lake. Note: This is a very rough dirt road; RVs and trailers are not recommended.

Contact: Lassen Volcanic National Park, 530/595-4444, www.nps.gov/lavo.

58 BATTLE CREEK

Scenic rating: 7

on Battle Creek in Lassen National Forest

Map 3.3, page 195

This pretty spot offers easy access and streamside camping along Battle Creek. The trout fishing can be good in May, June, and early July, when the creek is stocked with trout by the Department of Fish and Game. Many people drive right by without knowing there is a stream here and that the fishing can be good. The elevation is 4,800 feet.

Campsites, facilities: There are 50 sites for tents or RVs up to 30 feet (no hookups). Picnic tables and fire grills are provided. Drinking water, flush and vault toilets, and a day-use picnic area are available. Supplies can be obtained in the town of Mineral. Leashed pets are permitted.

Reservations, fees: Reservations are not accepted. Sites are $18 per night, $3 per night for each additional vehicle. Open late April through early November, weather permitting.

Directions: From Red Bluff, turn east on Highway 36 and drive 39 miles to the campground (if you reach Mineral, you have gone two miles too far).

Contact: Lassen National Forest, Almanor Ranger District, 530/258-2141, www.fs.usda. gov/lassen; Department of Fish and Game fishing information, 530/225-2146.

59 CHILDS MEADOW RESORT

Scenic rating: 7

near Mill Creek

Map 3.3, page 195

Childs Meadow Resort is an 18-acre resort set at 5,000 feet elevation. It features many recreation options, including catch-and-release fishing one mile away at Mill Creek. There are also a number of trails nearby for horseback riding. The trailhead for Spencer Meadow Trail is just east of the resort along Highway 36. The trail provides a 12-mile route (one-way) to Spencer Meadow and an effervescent spring that is the source of Mill Creek.

Campsites, facilities: There are eight tent sites and 24 sites with full hookups (50 amps) for RVs of any length; most are pull-through. Cabins, park-model cabins, and a motel are also available. Picnic tables and fire rings are provided. Drinking water and restrooms with flush toilets and showers are available. A coin laundry, store, restaurant, WiFi, group picnic area, meeting room, and horseshoes are on-site. Groups can be accommodated. Leashed pets are permitted.

Reservations, fees: Reservations are accepted at 888/595-3383. RV sites are $30 per night, tent sites are $20 per night with limit of one tent per night. Some credit cards accepted. Open mid-May through October, weather permitting.

Directions: From Red Bluff, drive east on Highway 36 for 43 miles to the town of Mineral. Continue east on Highway 36 for 10 miles to the resort on the left.

Contact: Childs Meadow Resort, 530/595-3383 or 888/595-3383, www.childsmeadow-resort.com.

60 DOMINGO SPRINGS
🏃 🚣 🐕 🚐 ⛺

Scenic rating: 7

in Lassen National Forest

Map 3.3, page 195

This camp is named after a spring adjacent to the site. It is a small fountain that pours into the headwaters of the North Fork Feather River, a good trout stream. The Pacific Crest Trail is routed from this camp north for four miles to Little Willow Lake and the southern border of Lassen Volcanic National Park. The elevation is 5,060 feet.

Campsites, facilities: There are 18 sites for tents or RVs up to 27 feet (no hookups). Picnic tables and fire grills are provided. Drinking water and vault toilets are available. Leashed pets are permitted.

Reservations, fees: Reservations are not accepted. Sites are $14 per night, $3 per night for each additional vehicle. Open late May through early November, weather permitting.

Directions: From Red Bluff, take Highway 36 east to Chester and Feather River Drive. Turn left on Feather River Drive and drive 0.75 mile to County Road 312. Bear left and drive five miles to the Y with County Road 311 and County Road 312. Bear left on County Road 311 and drive two miles to the campground entrance road on the left.

Contact: Lassen National Forest, Almanor

Ranger District, 530/258-2141, www.fs.usda.gov/lassen.

61 HIGH BRIDGE
🏃 🚣 🐕 🚐 ⛺

Scenic rating: 8

on the North Fork of the Feather River in Lassen National Forest

Map 3.3, page 195

This camp is set at an elevation of 5,200 feet, near where the South Cascades meet the North Sierra, and is ideal for many people. The result is that it is often full in July and August. The payoff includes a pretty, adjacent trout stream, the headwaters of the North Fork Feather. Trout fishing is often good here, including some rare large brown trout, a surprise considering the relatively small size of the stream. Nearby access to the Warner Valley/Drakesbad entrance of Lassen Volcanic National Park provides a must-do side trip. The area is wooded and the road dusty.

Campsites, facilities: There are 11 sites for tents and one site that can accommodate an RV up to 20 feet (no hookups). Picnic tables and fire grills are provided. Drinking water and vault toilets are available. Groceries and propane gas are available in Chester. Leashed pets are permitted.

Reservations, fees: Reservations are not accepted. Sites are $14 per night, $3 per night for each additional vehicle. Open late May through early November, weather permitting.

Directions: From Red Bluff, take Highway 36 east to Chester and Feather River Drive. Turn left on Feather River Drive and drive 0.75 mile to County Road 312. Bear left and drive five miles to the campground entrance road on the left.

Contact: Lassen National Forest, Almanor Ranger District, 530/258-2141, www.fs.usda.gov/lassen; Department of Fish and Game fishing information, 530/225-2146.

62 LAST CHANCE CREEK

Scenic rating: 7

near Lake Almanor
Map 3.3, page 195

This secluded camp is set at 4,500 feet, adjacent to where Last Chance Creek empties into the north end of Lake Almanor. It is an unpublicized PG&E camp that is known primarily by locals and gets missed almost every time by out-of-towners. The adjacent lake area is a breeding ground in the spring for white pelicans, and the beauty of these birds in large flocks can be extraordinary.

Campsites, facilities: There are 12 sites for tents or RVs up to 30 feet (no hookups), and three group camps that can accommodate up to 100 people (total). Picnic tables and fire grills are provided. Drinking water and vault toilets are available. Some facilities are wheelchair accessible. Leashed pets are permitted.

Reservations, fees: Reservations are not accepted for individual sites but are required for the group camps at 916/386-5164. Sites are $22 per night for individual sites, $3 per night for each additional vehicle, $11 per night for each additional RV, $81–162 per night for group sites, $1 per pet per night. Group sites require a two-night minimum stay and a three-night minimum on holidays. Open mid-May through September, weather permitting.

Directions: From Red Bluff, take Highway 36 east to Chester and continue for two miles over the causeway (at the north end of Lake Almanor). About 0.25 mile after crossing the causeway, turn left on the campground access road and drive 3.5 miles to the campground.

Contact: PG&E Land Projects, 916/386-5164, www.pge.com/recreation.

63 HOLE-IN-THE-GROUND

Scenic rating: 8

on Mill Creek in Lassen National Forest
Map 3.3, page 195

This is one of two campgrounds set along Mill Creek at 4,300 feet. Take your pick. The highlight here is a trail that follows along Mill Creek for many miles; it provides good fishing access. Rules mandate the use of artificials with a single barbless hook, and catch-and-release; check current fishing regulations. The result is a challenging but quality wild-trout fishery. Another option is to drive 0.5 mile to the end of the Forest Service road, where there is a parking area for a trail that is routed downstream along Mill Creek and into a state game refuge. To keep things easy, obtain a map of Lassen National Forest that details the recreational opportunities.

Campsites, facilities: There are 13 sites for tents or RVs up to 24 feet (no hookups). Picnic tables and fire grills are provided. Drinking water and vault toilets are available. Supplies are available in Mineral. Leashed pets are permitted.

Reservations, fees: Reservations are not accepted. Sites are $12 per night, $3 per night for each additional vehicle. Open late April through early November, weather permitting.

Directions: From Red Bluff, drive 43 miles east on Highway 36 to the town of Mineral and the junction with Highway 172. Turn right on Highway 172 and drive six miles to the town of Mill Creek. In Mill Creek, turn south onto Forest Road 28N06 (signed) and drive five miles to the campground access road. Turn left and drive 0.25 mile to the camp.

Contact: Lassen National Forest, Almanor Ranger District, 530/258-2141, www.fs.usda.gov/lassen.

64 MILL CREEK RESORT

Scenic rating: 7

on Mill Creek near Lassen National Forest

Map 3.3, page 195

This is a great area, surrounded by Lassen National Forest and within close range of the southern Highway 89 entrance to Lassen Volcanic National Park. It is set at 4,800 feet along oft-bypassed Highway 172. A highlight here is Mill Creek (to reach it, turn south on the Forest Service road in town and drive to a parking area at the end of the road along the stream), where there is a great easy walk along the stream and fair trout fishing. Note that about half the campsites are taken by long-term renters.

Campsites, facilities: There are 14 sites for tents or self-contained RVs up to 35 feet and eight RV sites with full hookups (30 amps). Nine one- and two-bedroom cabins are also available. Picnic tables and fire rings are provided. Drinking water, vault toilets, seasonal showers, coin laundry, playground, a small grocery store, and a restaurant are also available. Some facilities are wheelchair-accessible. Leashed pets are permitted.

Reservations, fees: Reservations are recommended. RV sites are $25 per night, tent sites are $16 per night. Campsites are open May through October. Cabins are available year-round.

Directions: From Red Bluff, drive 43 miles east on Highway 36 to the town of Mineral and the junction with Highway 172. Turn right and drive six miles to the town of Mill Creek. In Mill Creek, look for the sign for Mill Creek Resort on the right side of the road.

Contact: Mill Creek Resort, 530/595-4449 or 888/595-4449, www.millcreekresort.net.

65 GURNSEY AND GURNSEY CREEK GROUP CAMPS

Scenic rating: 7

in Lassen National Forest

Map 3.3, page 195

This camp is set at 5,000 feet elevation in Lassen National Forest, with extremely easy access off Highway 36. The camp is on the headwaters of little Gurnsey Creek, a highlight of the surrounding Lost Creek Plateau. Gurnsey Creek runs downstream and pours into Deer Creek, a good trout stream with access along narrow, winding Highway 32 to the nearby south. The group camps are ideal spots for a Scout troop.

Campsites, facilities: There are 30 sites for tents or RVs up to 30 feet (no hookups). There are two group camps that can accommodate up to 56 people and 112 people respectively with tents or RVs up to 30 feet (no hookups); larger groups may reserve both camps together. Picnic tables and fire grills are provided. Drinking water and vault toilets are available. Supplies are available in Mineral. Some facilities are wheelchair accessible. Leashed pets are permitted.

Reservations, fees: Reservations are not accepted for individual sites, but are required for the group site at 877/444-6777 or www.recreation.gov ($9 reservation fee). Tent and RV sites are $14 per night, $3 per night for each additional vehicle. Gurnsey Creek Group Site 1 is $56 per night and Rainbow Group Camp is $112 per night, with a two-night minimum stay required on weekends. Open May through October, weather permitting.

Directions: From Red Bluff, drive east on Highway 36 for 55 miles (five miles east of Childs Meadow). Turn left at the campground entrance road and drive a short distance to the campground.

Contact: Lassen National Forest, Almanor Ranger District, 530/258-2141, www.fs.usda.gov/lassen.

66 NORTH SHORE CAMPGROUND

Scenic rating: 7

on Lake Almanor

Map 3.3, page 195

This is a large, privately developed park on the northern shoreline of beautiful Lake Almanor. The park has 37 acres and a mile of shoreline. The camp is set amid pine tree cover, and most of the sites are lakefront or lake-view. About half of the sites are filled with seasonal renters. The lending library here was once the original Chester jail, built in 1925. Alas, the jail itself busted out during a storm a few years ago and was found washed ashore at this campground, which converted it to its new use.

Campsites, facilities: There are 34 tent sites and 94 sites with partial hookups (30 amps) for RVs up to 40 feet; a few are pull-through. Three log cabins are also available. Picnic tables and fire rings are provided. Drinking water, restrooms with showers and flush toilets, coin laundry, general store, playground, lending library, modem access, Wi-Fi, propane, dump station, fish-cleaning station, horseshoes, boat ramp, boat dock, boat slips, and boat rentals are available. Leashed pets are permitted.

Reservations, fees: Reservations are accepted. RV sites are $40–52 per night, tent sites are $36 per night, $5 per person per night for more than two people at tent sites, $5 per night per additional vehicle, $2 per pet per night. Monthly and seasonal rates available. Some credit cards accepted. Open May through October.

Directions: From Red Bluff, take Highway 36 east for 44 miles to the junction with Highway 89. Drive east on Highway 36/89; the camp is two miles past Chester on the right.

Contact: North Shore Campground, 530/258-3376, www.northshorecampground.com.

67 SOUTH ANTELOPE

Scenic rating: 6

near the eastern edge of the Ishi Wilderness

Map 3.3, page 195

This primitive campsite is for visitors who want to explore the Ishi Wilderness without an extensive drive (compared to other camps in the wilderness here). The South Fork of Antelope Creek runs west from the camp and provides an off-trail route for the ambitious. For easier hikes, trailheads along Ponderosa Way provide access into the eastern flank of the Ishi. The best nearby trail is Lower Mill Creek Trail, with the trailhead eight miles south at Black Rock.

Campsites, facilities: There is dispersed camping for tents only. Picnic tables and fire pits are provided. There is no drinking water and there are no toilets. Garbage must be packed out. Leashed pets are permitted.

Reservations, fees: Reservations are not accepted. There is no fee for camping. A campfire permit is required. Open year-round.

Directions: From Red Bluff, drive east on Highway 36 for about 35 miles to the town of Paynes Creek and Plum Creek Road. Turn right (south) on Plum Creek Road and drive two miles to Ponderosa Way. Turn right (south) and continue for nine miles to the campground on the right. Note: The road is rough and only vehicles with high clearance are advised. No RVs or trailers are allowed.

Contact: Lassen National Forest, Almanor Ranger District, 530/258-2141, www.fs.usda.gov/lassen.

68 BLACK ROCK

Scenic rating: 7

on the eastern edge of the Ishi Wilderness

Map 3.3, page 195

This remote, primitive camp is set at the base of the huge, ancient Black Rock, one of the oldest geological points in Lassen National Forest. A bonus is that Mill Creek runs adjacent to the sites, providing a water source. This is the edge of the Ishi Wilderness, where remote hiking in solitude is possible without venturing to high mountain elevations; a campfire permit is required for overnight use by backpackers. A trailhead is available right out of the camp. The trail here is routed downstream along Mill Creek, extending five miles into the Ishi Wilderness, downhill all the way. Be prepared when hiking in this area because the heat can be almost intolerable at times, often passing the 100°F mark for days on end.

Campsites, facilities: There are six tent sites. Picnic tables and fire pits are provided. A vault toilet is available. No drinking water is available. Mill Creek is adjacent to the camp and is a viable water source; remember to filter stream water. Garbage must be packed out. Leashed pets are permitted.

Reservations, fees: Reservations are not accepted. There is no fee for camping. Open year-round, weather permitting.

Directions: From Red Bluff, drive east on Highway 36 for about 35 miles to the town of Paynes Creek and Plum Creek Road. Turn right (south) on Plum Creek Road and drive two miles to Ponderosa Way. Turn right (south) and continue for 16 miles to the campground on the right. Note: The road is rough and only vehicles with high clearance are advised. No RVs or trailers are allowed.

Contact: Lassen National Forest, Almanor Ranger District, 530/258-2141, www.fs.usda.gov/lassen.

69 ELAM

Scenic rating: 7

on Deer Creek in Lassen National Forest

Map 3.3, page 195

Of the campgrounds set on Deer Creek along Highway 32, Elam gets the most use. It is the first stopping point visitors arrive at while heading west on narrow, curvy Highway 32, and it has an excellent day-use picnic area available. The stream here is stocked with rainbow trout in late spring and early summer, with good access for fishing. It is a pretty area, set where Elam Creek enters Deer Creek. A Forest Service Information Center is nearby in Chester. If the camp has too many people to suit your style, consider other more distant and primitive camps downstream on Deer Creek. The elevation here is 4,600 feet.

Campsites, facilities: There are 15 sites for tents or RVs up to 30 feet (no hookups). Picnic tables and fire grills are provided. Drinking water and vault toilets are available. Leashed pets are permitted.

Reservations, fees: Reservations are not accepted. Sites are $14 per night, $3 per night for each additional vehicle. Open mid-April through October, weather permitting.

Directions: From Red Bluff, take Highway 36 east for 44 miles to the junction with Highway 89. Continue east on Highway 36/89 to the junction with Highway 32. Turn south on Highway 32 and drive three miles to the campground on the right side of the road. Trailers are not recommended.

Contact: Lassen National Forest, Almanor Ranger District, 530/258-2141, www.fs.usda.gov/lassen.

70 ALDER CREEK

Scenic rating: 7

on Deer Creek in Lassen National Forest

Map 3.3, page 195

Deer Creek is a great little trout stream that runs along Highway 32. Alder Creek is one of three camps set along Highway 32 with streamside access; this one is at 3,900 feet elevation, set near where both Alder Creek and Round Valley Creek pour into Deer Creek. The stream's best stretch of trout water is from here to Elam, upstream.

Campsites, facilities: There are six tent sites. Trailers and RVs are not recommended. Picnic tables and fire grills are provided. Vault toilets are available. No drinking water is available; stream water should be purified before use. Leashed pets are permitted.

Reservations, fees: Reservations are not accepted. Sites are $10 per night, $3 for each additional vehicle. Open mid-May through mid-October, weather permitting.

Directions: From Red Bluff, take Highway 36 east for 44 miles to the junction with Highway 89. Continue east on Highway 36/89 to the junction with Highway 32. Turn south on Highway 32 and drive eight miles to the campground on the right side of the road.

Contact: Lassen National Forest, Almanor Ranger District, 530/258-2141, www.fs.usda. gov/lassen.

71 POTATO PATCH

Scenic rating: 7

on Deer Creek in Lassen National Forest

Map 3.3, page 195

You get good hiking and fishing at this camp. It is set beside Deer Creek at 3,400 feet elevation, with good access for trout fishing. This is a wild trout stream in this area, and the use of artificials with a single barbless hook and catch-and-release are required along most of the river; check DFG regulations. An excellent anglers'/swimmers' trail is available along the river.

Campsites, facilities: There are 32 sites for tents or RVs up to 27 feet (no hookups). Picnic tables and fire grills are provided. Drinking water and vault toilets are available. Some facilities are wheelchair accessible. Leashed pets are permitted.

Reservations, fees: Reservations are not accepted. Sites are $14 per night, $3 per night for each additional vehicle. Open early April through early November, weather permitting.

Directions: From Red Bluff, take Highway 36 east for 44 miles to the junction with Highway 89. Continue east on Highway 36/89 to the junction with Highway 32. Turn south on Highway 32 and drive 11 miles to the campground on the right side of the road.

Contact: Lassen National Forest, Almanor Ranger District, 530/258-2141, www.fs.usda. gov/lassen; Department of Fish and Game, 530/225-2146.

72 ROCKY POINT CAMPGROUND

Scenic rating: 7

on Lake Almanor

Map 3.3, page 195

What you get here is a series of four campgrounds along the southwest shore of Lake Almanor, provided by PG&E as mitigation for its hydroelectric activities on the Feather River system. The camps are set upstream from the dam, with boat ramps available on each side of the dam. This is a pretty spot, with giant Almanor ringed by lodgepole pine and firs. The lake is usually full, or close to it, well into summer, with Mount Lassen set in the distance to the north—bring your camera. The lake is 13 miles long and all water sports are permitted. The lake level remains full most of the year and much of the shoreline is wooded. Though it can take a day or two to find the fish, once that effort is made, fishing is good for large trout and salmon in the spring and fall and for smallmouth bass in the summer. Oldtimers will recall this camp was once called "Lake Almanor Campground."

Campsites, facilities: There are 131 sites for tents or RVs up to 30 feet (no hookups), five overflow units, and two group sites (North and South) with 5 and 19 sites respectively. Picnic tables and fire grills are provided. Drinking water, vault toilets, and a dump station are available. Some facilities are wheelchair-accessible. Leashed pets are permitted.

Reservations, fees: Reservations are not accepted for individual sites, but are required for the group sites at 916/386-5164. Sites are $25 per night, the North group site is $135 per night, South group site is $515 per night, $3 per night for each additional vehicle, $10 per night per additional RV, $1 per pet per night. Weekend and weekly rates available. Open May through September.

Directions: From Red Bluff, take Highway 36 east for 44 miles to the junction with Highway 89. Continue east on Highway 36/89 to Lake Almanor and the next junction with Highway 89 (two miles before reaching Chester). Turn right on Highway 89 and drive eight miles to the southwest end of Lake Almanor. Turn left at your choice of four campground entrances.

Contact: PG&E Land Projects, 916/386-5164, www.pge.com/recreation.

73 ALMANOR NORTH, SOUTH, AND LEGACY

Scenic rating: 8

on Lake Almanor in Lassen National Forest

Map 3.3, page 195   **BEST (**

This is one of Lake Almanor's best-known and most popular Forest Service campgrounds, set along the western shore of beautiful Almanor at 4,550 feet elevation directly across from the beautiful Almanor Peninsula. There are two linked campgrounds—North and South—and a new first-come, first-served campground at Legacy. There is an excellent view of Mount Lassen to the north, along with gorgeous sunrises. A 10-mile recreation trail runs right through the campground and is excellent for biking or hiking. This section of the lake provides good fishing for smallmouth bass in the summer. Fishing in this lake is also good for rainbow trout, brown trout, and lake-raised salmon.

Campsites, facilities: There are 104 sites for tents or RVs up to 25 or 40 feet (no hookups)

at Almanor North and South. Almanor Legacy has 13 sites for tents or RVs (partial hookups). There is also a group camp for tents or RVs up to 60 feet that can accommodate up to 100 people. Picnic tables and fire grills are provided. Drinking water and vault toilets are available. A dump station, boat ramp and beach area are nearby. Some facilities are wheelchair-accessible. Leashed pets are permitted.

Reservations, fees: Reservations are accepted for individual sites at Almanor North and South and are required for the group camp at 877/444-6777 or www.recreation.gov ($9 reservation fee). Reservations are not accepted for Almanor Legacy. North and South sites are $18 per night for dingle sites, $36 per night for the double site, $30 per night for Almanor Legacy sites, $3 per night for each additional vehicle, and $100 per night for the group camp. Open May through September, weather permitting.

Directions: From Red Bluff, take Highway 36 east for 44 miles to the junction with Highway 89. Continue east on Highway 36/89 to Lake Almanor and the next junction with Highway 89 (two miles before reaching Chester). Turn right on Highway 89 and drive six miles to County Road 310. Turn left on County Road 310 and drive 0.25 mile to the campground.

Contact: Lassen National Forest, Almanor Ranger District, 530/258-2141, www.fs.usda.gov/lassen.

74 SOLDIER MEADOWS

Scenic rating: 7

on Soldier Creek in Lassen National Forest

Map 3.3, page 195

This primitive camp is little known and is used primarily by anglers and hunters in season. The campsites here are shaded, set in forest on the edge of meadows, and near a stream. The latter is Soldier Creek, which is stocked with trout by the Department of

Fish and Game; check fishing regulations. In the fall, early storms can drive deer through this area on their annual migration to their wintering habitat in the valley, making this a decent base camp for hunters. However, no early storms often mean no deer. The elevation is 4,890 feet.

Campsites, facilities: There are 15 sites for tents or RVs up to 25 feet (no hookups). Picnic tables and fire rings are provided. Vault toilets are available. No drinking water is available. Leashed pets are permitted.

Reservations, fees: Reservations are not accepted. Sites are $10 per night, $3 per night for each additional vehicle. Open late May through early November, weather permitting.

Directions: From Chester, drive south on Highway 89 for approximately six miles to Humboldt Road. Turn right on Humboldt Road and drive one mile, bear right at the fork, and continue five more miles to the intersection at Fanani Meadows. Turn right and drive one mile to the campground on the left.

Contact: Lassen National Forest, Almanor Ranger District, 530/258-2141, www.fs.usda.gov/lassen.

75 PONDEROSA FLAT

Scenic rating: 7

on Butt Valley Reservoir

Map 3.3, page 195

This camp is set at the north end of Butt Valley Reservoir (more commonly called Butt Lake), the little brother to nearby Lake Almanor. It is a fairly popular camp, with the boat ramp a prime attraction, allowing campers/anglers a lakeside spot with easy access. Technically, Butt is the "afterbay" for Almanor, fed by a four-mile-long pipe with water from Almanor. What occurs is that pond smelt from Almanor get ground up in the Butt Lake powerhouse, providing a large amount of feed for trout at the head of the lake; that's why the trout often get huge at Butt Lake. The one downer here is that lake drawdowns are common, exposing tree stumps. In 2012, a large forest fire burned the slopes above the far side of the lake.

Campsites, facilities: There are 63 sites, including three double sites, for tents or RVs up to 30 feet (no hookups), and an overflow camping area. Picnic tables and fire grills are provided. Drinking water, vault toilets, and a boat ramp are available. Some facilities are wheelchair-accessible. Leashed pets are permitted.

Reservations, fees: Reservations are not accepted. Sites are $25 per night, $3 per night for each additional vehicle, $1 per pet per night. Open May through October, weather permitting.

Directions: From Red Bluff, take Highway 36 east for 44 miles to the junction with Highway 89. Continue east on Highway 36/89 to Lake Almanor and the next junction with Highway 89 (two miles before reaching Chester). Turn right on Highway 89 and drive about seven miles to Butt Valley Road. Turn right on Butt Valley Road and drive 3.2 miles to the campground on the right side of the road.

Contact: PG&E Land Projects, 916/386-5164, www.pge.com/recreation.

76 COOL SPRINGS

Scenic rating: 7

on Butt Valley Reservoir

Map 3.3, page 195

One of two camps at Butt Lake (officially known as Butt Valley Reservoir), Cool Springs is set about midway down the lake on its eastern shore, 2.5 miles south of Ponderosa Flat. Cool Springs Creek enters the lake near the camp. (See the Ponderosa Flat listing for more information about Butt Lake.)

Campsites, facilities: There are 25 sites for tents or RVs up to 30 feet (no hookups), and

five walk-in tent sites. Picnic tables and fire grills are provided. Drinking water, vault toilets, and a boat ramp are available. Some facilities are wheelchair-accessible. Leashed pets are permitted.

Reservations, fees: Reservations are not accepted. Sites are $22 per night, $3 per night for each additional vehicle, $10 per night per additional RV, $1 per pet per night. Open mid-May to mid-September, weather permitting.

Directions: From Red Bluff, take Highway 36 east for 44 miles to the junction with Highway 89. Continue east on Highway 36/89 to Lake Almanor and the next junction with Highway 89 (two miles before reaching Chester). Turn right on Highway 89 and drive about seven miles to Butt Valley Road. Turn right on Butt Valley Road and drive 5.7 miles to the campground on the right side of the road.

Contact: PG&E Land Projects, 916/386-5164, www.pge.com/recreation.

77 YELLOW CREEK

Scenic rating: 8

in Humbug Valley

Map 3.3, page 195

Yellow Creek is one of Cal Trout's pet projects. It's a beautiful stream for fly fishers, demanding the best from skilled anglers. This camp is set at 4,400 feet in Humbug Valley and provides access to this stretch of water. Another option is to fish Butt Creek, much easier fishing for small, planted rainbow trout, with access along the road on the way in.

Campsites, facilities: There are 11 sites for tents or RVs up to 30 feet (no hookups). Picnic tables and fire grills are provided. Drinking water and vault toilets are available. Leashed pets are permitted.

Reservations, fees: Reservations are not accepted. Sites are $22 per night, $3 per night for each additional vehicle, $10 per night per additional RV, $1 per pet per night. Open mid-May to mid-September.

Directions: From Red Bluff, take Highway 36 east for 44 miles to the junction with Highway 89. Continue east on Highway 36/89 for eight miles to Humbug Road. Turn right and drive 0.6 mile and bear left to stay on Humbug Road. Continue for 1.2 miles and bear right (signed for Longville) to stay on Humbug Road. Continue for 5.4 miles to Humbug Valley and a road intersection. Turn left to stay on Humbug Road and drive 1.2 miles (passing the Soda Springs Historic Site) to a fork. Bear right to stay on Humbug Road and drive 0.3 mile to the campground.

Contact: PG&E Land Projects, 916/386-5164, www.pge.com/recreation.

78 BUTTE MEADOWS

Scenic rating: 6

on Butte Creek in Lassen National Forest

Map 3.3, page 195

On hot summer days, when a cold stream sounds even better than a cold drink, Butte Meadows provides a hideout in the national forest east of Chico. This is a summer camp situated along Butte Creek, which is stocked with rainbow trout by the Department of Fish and Game. Nearby Doe Mill Ridge and the surrounding Lassen National Forest can provide good side-trip adventures. The camp elevation is 4,600 feet.

Campsites, facilities: There are 13 sites for tents or RVs up to 25 feet (no hookups). Fire grills and picnic tables are provided. Drinking water and vault toilets are available. Supplies are available in Butte Meadows. Leashed pets are permitted.

Reservations, fees: Reservations are not accepted. Sites are $12 per night, $3 per night for each additional vehicle. Open late April through early November, weather permitting.

Directions: From Chico, drive about 15 miles northeast on Highway 32 to the town of Forest Ranch. Continue on Highway 32 for another nine miles. Turn right on Humboldt Road and drive five miles to Butte Meadows.

Contact: Lassen National Forest, Almanor Ranger District, 530/258-2141, www.fs.usda. gov/lassen; Department of Fish and Game fishing information, 530/225-2146.

79 CHERRY HILL
🏃 🛶 🏕 🚙 ⛺

Scenic rating: 7

on Butte Creek in Lassen National Forest

Map 3.3, page 195

The camp is set along little Butte Creek at the foot of Cherry Hill, just downstream from the confluence of Colby Creek and Butte Creek. It is also on the western edge of the alpine zone in Lassen National Forest. A four-mile drive to the north, much of it along Colby Creek, will take visitors to the Colby Mountain Lookout at 6,002 feet for a dramatic view of the Ishi Wilderness to the west. Nearby to the south is Philbrook Reservoir.

Campsites, facilities: There are six walk-in tent sites and 19 sites for tents or RVs up to 30 feet (no hookups). Picnic tables and fire grills are provided. Drinking water and vault toilets are available. Supplies are available in the town of Butte Meadows. Leashed pets are permitted.

Reservations, fees: Reservations are not accepted. Sites are $14 per night, $3 per night for each additional vehicle. Open late April through early November, weather permitting.

Directions: From Chico, drive northeast on Highway 32 for approximately 24 miles to the junction with Humboldt Road (well past the town of Forest Ranch). Turn right and drive five miles to Butte Meadows. Continue on Humboldt Road for three miles to the campground on the right side of the road.

Contact: Lassen National Forest, Almanor Ranger District, 530/258-2141, www.fs.usda. gov/lassen.

80 PHILBROOK RESERVOIR
🏊 🛶 🏕 🏕 ♿ 🚙 ⛺

Scenic rating: 7

in Lassen National Forest

Map 3.3, page 195

Philbrook Reservoir is set at 5,600 feet on the western mountain slopes above Chico, on the southwest edge of Lassen National Forest. It is a pretty lake, though subject to late-season drawdowns, with a scenic lookout a short distance from camp. Swimming beaches and a picnic area are bonuses. The lake is loaded with small trout—a dink here, a dink there, a dink everywhere.

Campsites, facilities: There are 20 sites for tents or RVs up to 30 feet (no hookups), and an overflow camping area. Picnic tables and fire grills are provided. Drinking water and vault toilets are available. Trailer and car-top boat launches are available. Some facilities are wheelchair-accessible. Leashed pets are permitted.

Reservations, fees: Reservations are not accepted. Sites are $22 per night, $3 per night for each additional vehicle, $10 per night per additional RV, $1 per pet per night. Open May through September.

Directions: At Orland on I-5, take the Highway 32/Chico exit and drive to Chico and the junction with Highway 99. Turn south on Highway 99 and drive to Skyway Road/ Paradise (in south Chico). Turn east on Skyway Road, drive through Paradise, and continue for 27 miles to Humbug Summit Road. Turn right and drive two miles to Philbrook Road. Turn right and drive 3.1 miles to the campground entrance road. Turn right and drive 0.5 mile to the campground. Note: Access roads are unpaved and often rough.

Contact: PG&E Land Projects, 916/386-5164, www.pge.com/recreation.

81 QUEEN LILY

Scenic rating: 7

on the North Fork of the Feather River in
Plumas National Forest

Map 3.3, page 195

The North Fork Feather River is a prime destination for camping and trout fishing, especially for families. This is one of three camps along the river on Caribou Road. This stretch of river is well stocked. Insider's note: The first 150 yards of river below the dam at Caribou typically have large but elusive trout.

Campsites, facilities: There are 12 sites for tents or RVs up to 30 feet (no hookups). Picnic tables, bear-proof lockers, and fire grills are provided. Drinking water and flush toilets are available. A grocery store and coin laundry are available within three miles. Leashed pets are permitted.

Reservations, fees: Reservations are not accepted. Sites are $23 per night. Open May through September.

Directions: From Oroville, drive north on Highway 70 to Caribou Road (two miles past Belden). Turn left on Caribou Road and drive about three miles to the campground on the left side of the road.

Contact: Plumas National Forest, Mt. Hough Ranger District, 530/283-0555, www.fs.usda.gov/plumas.

82 NORTH FORK

Scenic rating: 7

on the North Fork of the Feather River in
Plumas National Forest

Map 3.3, page 195

This camp is between Queen Lily to the nearby north and Gansner Bar camp to the nearby south, all three set on the North Fork Feather River. The elevation is 2,600 feet. Fishing access is good and trout plants are decent, making for a good fishing/camping trip. Note: All three camps are extremely popular on summer weekends.

Campsites, facilities: There are 20 sites for tents or RVs up to 32 feet (no hookups). Picnic tables, bear-proof lockers, and fire grills are provided. Drinking water and flush toilets are available. A grocery store and coin laundry are available within three miles. Leashed pets are permitted.

Reservations, fees: Reservations are not accepted. Sites are $23 per night. Open May through September.

Directions: From Oroville, drive north on Highway 70 to Caribou Road (two miles past Belden at Gansner Ranch Ranger Station). Turn left on Caribou Road and drive about two miles to the campground on the left side of the road.

Contact: Plumas National Forest, Mt. Hough Ranger District, 530/283-0555, www.fs.usda.gov.

83 GANSNER BAR

Scenic rating: 7

on the North Fork of the Feather River in
Plumas National Forest

Map 3.3, page 195

Gansner Bar is the first of three camps along Caribou Road, which runs parallel to the North Fork Feather River. Of the three, this one receives the highest trout stocks of rainbow trout in the 10- to 12-inch class. Caribou Road runs upstream to Caribou Dam, with stream and fishing access along almost all of it. The camps often fill on summer weekends.

Campsites, facilities: There are 14 sites for tents or RVs up to 30 feet (no hookups). Picnic tables, bear-proof lockers, and fire grills are provided. Drinking water and flush toilets are available. A grocery store and coin laundry are available within one mile. Some facilities are wheelchair-accessible. Leashed pets are permitted.

Reservations, fees: Reservations are not

accepted. Sites are $23 per night. Open April through October.

Directions: From Oroville, drive northeast on Highway 70 to Caribou Road (two miles past Belden). Turn left on Caribou Road and drive a short distance to the campground on the left side of the road.

Contact: Plumas National Forest, Mt. Hough Ranger District, 530/283-0555, www.fs.usda. gov/plumas.

84 HALLSTED

Scenic rating: 7

on the North Fork of the Feather River in Plumas National Forest

Map 3.3, page 195

Easy highway access and a pretty trout stream right alongside have made this an extremely popular campground. It typically fills on summer weekends. Hallsted is set on the East Branch North Fork Feather River at 2,800 feet elevation. The river is stocked with trout by the Department of Fish and Game. This campground closed in 2012 for major construction, reopening in 2013 with new restrooms with showers and with partial hookups available at some campsites.

Campsites, facilities: There are 20 sites for tents or RVs up to 30 feet (some hookups for water and electricity). Picnic tables and fire grills are provided. Drinking water and flush toilets are available. A grocery store is within a quarter mile. Some facilities are wheelchair-accessible. Leashed pets are permitted.

Reservations, fees: Reservations are not accepted. Sites are $23 per night. Open May through September.

Directions: From Oroville, drive northeast on Highway 70 to Belden. Continue past Belden for about 12 miles to the campground entrance on the right side of the road. Turn right and drive 0.25 mile to the campground.

Contact: Plumas National Forest, Mt. Hough

Ranger District, 530/283-0555, www.fs.usda. gov/plumas.

85 DODGE RESERVOIR

Scenic rating: 6

near Ravendale

Map 3.4, page 196

This camp is set at 5,735 feet elevation near Dodge Reservoir, remote and little used. The lake covers 400 acres and is stocked with Eagle Lake trout. Those who know of this lake feel as if they know a secret, because the limit is two at Eagle Lake itself, but it is five here. Small boats can be launched from the shoreline, and though it can be windy, mornings are usually calm, ideal for canoes. The surrounding hillsides are sprinkled with sage and juniper. This camp is also popular with hunters who get drawn in the annual DFG lottery for tags for this zone. There is a very good chance that, along the entire length of road from the Madeline Plain into Dodge Reservoir, you'll see some wild horses. There's no sight quite like them. They are considered to be wild, but some will stay close to the road, while others will come no closer then 300 yards.

Campsites, facilities: There are 11 sites for tents or RVs up to 35 feet (no hookups). Picnic tables and fire pits are provided. A vault toilet is available. No drinking water is available. Garbage must be packed out. There is no developed boat ramp, but hand-launched boats are permitted. Some facilities are wheelchair accessible. Leashed pets are permitted.

Reservations, fees: Reservations are not accepted. There is no fee for camping, but donations are encouraged. Open year-round, weather permitting.

Directions: From Susanville, drive north on U.S. 395 for 54 miles to Ravendale and County Road 502. Turn right on County Road 502 (Mail Route) and drive four miles, then bear left to stay on County Road 502. Continue four miles, then bear right to stay on County Road 502. Drive two miles to County Road 526. Continue straight onto County Road 526 and drive 4.5 miles to County Road 504. Turn left and drive two miles to County Road 506. Turn right and drive 7.5 miles to the access road for Dodge Reservoir. Turn left on the access road and drive one mile to the lake and camp. Note: The last mile of road before the turnoff to Dodge Reservoir can become impassable with just a small amount of rain or snow.

Contact: Bureau of Land Management, Eagle Lake Field Office, 530/257-0456, www.blm. gov/ca.

86 NORTH EAGLE LAKE

Scenic rating: 7

on Eagle Lake

Map 3.4, page 196

This camp provides direct access in the fall to the fishing area of Eagle Lake. When the weather turns cold, the population of Eagle Lake trout migrates to its favorite haunts just outside the tules, often in water only 5–8 feet deep. A boat ramp is about 1.5 miles to the southwest on Stone Road. In the summer this area is quite exposed and the lake can be hammered by west winds, which can howl from midday to sunset. A recent drawdown has also left boat ramps and marinas high and dry. The elevation is 5,100 feet.

Campsites, facilities: There are 20 sites for tents or RVs up to 35 feet (no hookups). Picnic tables and fire grills are provided. Drinking water and vault toilets are available. A boat ramp is nearby. A private dump station is within 1.5 miles. Leashed pets are permitted.

Reservations, fees: Reservations are not accepted. Sites are $8 per night. Open Memorial Day through mid-November, weather permitting.

Directions: From Red Bluff, drive east on Highway 36 to Susanville. In Susanville, turn left (north) on Highway 139 and drive 29 miles to County Road A1. Turn left at County Road A1 and drive 0.5 mile to the campground on the right.

Contact: Bureau of Land Management, Eagle Lake Field Office, 530/257-0456, www.blm. gov/ca.

87 RAMHORN SPRINGS

Scenic rating: 3

south of Ravendale

Map 3.4, page 196

This camp is not even three miles off the biggest state highway in northeastern California, yet it feels remote and is little known. It is way out in Nowhere Land, near the flank of Shinn Peak (7,562 feet). There are large numbers of antelope in the area, along with a sprinkling of large mule deer. Hunters lucky enough to get a deer tag can use this camp for their base in the fall. It is also popular for upland game hunters in search of sage grouse and chukar.

Campsites, facilities: There are 10 sites for tents or RVs up to 35 feet (no hookups). Picnic tables and fire grills are provided. Vault toilets and a horse corral are available. There is no drinking water, although spring water, which can be filtered, is available. Some facilities are wheelchair accessible. Leashed pets are permitted.

Reservations, fees: Reservations are not accepted. There is no fee for camping, but donations are encouraged. Open year-round, weather permitting.

Directions: From Red Bluff, drive east on Highway 36 to Susanville. In Susanville, turn north on U.S. 395 and drive 45 miles to Post Camp Road. Turn right on Post Camp Road (unmarked except for small recreation sign) and drive 2.5 miles east to the campground.

Contact: Bureau of Land Management, Eagle Lake Field Office, 530/257-0456, www.blm. gov/ca.

88 EAGLE LAKE RV PARK

Scenic rating: 7

near Susanville

Map 3.4, page 196

Eagle Lake RV Park has become something of a headquarters for anglers in pursuit of Eagle Lake trout, which typically range 18–22 inches. A nearby boat ramp provides access to Pelican Point and Eagle Point, where the fishing is often best in the summer. In the fall, the north end of the lake provides better prospects (see the North Eagle Lake listing in this chapter). This RV park has all the amenities, including a small store. That means no special trips into town, just vacation time, lounging beside Eagle Lake, maybe catching a big trout now and then. One downer: The wind typically howls here most summer afternoons. When the whitecaps are too big to deal with and surface conditions become choppy, get off the water; it can be dangerous here. Resident deer, including bucks with spectacular racks, can be like pets here on late summer evenings.

Campsites, facilities: There are 65 RV sites with full hookups (30 amps), including some pull-through sites, a separate grassy area for tents only, and cabin and RV rentals. Picnic tables and fire grills are provided. Restrooms with showers, coin laundry, satellite TV hookups, WiFi, dump station, convenience store, propane gas, diesel, bait and tackle, video rentals, RV supplies, firewood, and recreation room are available. A boat ramp, dock, and boat slips are nearby. Some facilities are wheelchair-accessible. Leashed pets are permitted.

Reservations, fees: Reservations are recommended. RV sites are $36.50–$38.50 per night, tent sites are $25 per night, $5 per night for each additional person for more than four people, $1 per pet per night. Some credit cards accepted. Open late May through early November, weather permitting.

Directions: From Red Bluff, drive east on Highway 36 toward Susanville. Just before reaching Susanville, turn left on County Road A1 and drive approximately 25 miles to County Road 518 near Spalding Tract. Turn right on County Road 518 and drive through a small neighborhood to The Strand (the lake frontage road). Turn right on The Strand and drive about eight blocks to Palmetto Way and the entrance to the store and the park entrance at 687-125 Palmetto Way. Register at the store.

Contact: Eagle Lake RV Park, 530/825-3133, www.eaglelakeandrv.com.

89 CHRISTIE

Scenic rating: 7

on Eagle Lake in Lassen National Forest

Map 3.4, page 196

This camp is set along the southern shore of Eagle Lake at 5,100 feet. Eagle Lake, with 100 miles of shoreline, is well known for its big trout (hooray) and big winds (boo). The camp offers some protection from the north winds. Its location is also good for seeing osprey in the Osprey Management Area, which covers a six-mile stretch of shoreline just two miles to the north above Wildcat Point. A nearby resort is a bonus. The nearest boat ramp is at Gallatin Marina. A five-mile-long paved trail runs from Christie to Aspen Grove Walk-In (see listing in this chapter), perfect for hiking, cycling, and horseback riding.

Campsites, facilities: There are 69 individual sites and 10 double sites for tents or RVs up to 50 feet. No hookups. Picnic tables and fire grills are provided. Drinking water and restrooms with electricity and flush toilets are available. Some facilities are wheelchair-accessible. A grocery store is nearby. A dump station is 2.5 miles away at Merrill Campground. Leashed pets are permitted. A campground host is on site.

Reservations, fees: Reservations are accepted at 877/444-6777 or www.recreation.gov ($9 reservation fee). Single sites are $20 per night, $30 per night for double sites, $5 per night for each additional vehicle. Open May through October, weather permitting.

Directions: From Red Bluff, drive east on Highway 36 toward Susanville. Three miles before Susanville turn left on Eagle Lake Road/County Road A1 and drive 19.5 miles to the campground on the right side of the road.

Contact: Lassen National Forest, Eagle Lake Ranger District, 530/257-4188, www.fs.usda.gov/lassen.

90 MERRILL

Scenic rating: 8

on Eagle Lake in Lassen National Forest

Map 3.4, page 196

This is one of the largest, most developed Forest Service campgrounds in the entire county. It is set along the southern shore of Eagle Lake at 5,100 feet. The nearest boat launch is at Gallatin Marina, where there is a developed swim beach.

Campsites, facilities: There are 300 individual sites and two double sites with full or partial hookups (30 and 50 amps) for tents or RVs up to 50 feet. Picnic tables and fire rings are provided. Drinking water and flush toilets are available. A dump station is nearby. Some facilities are wheelchair-accessible. A grocery store, Wi-Fi access, and boat ramp are nearby. Leashed pets are permitted. A camp host is on site.

Reservations, fees: Reservations are accepted at 877/444-6777 or www.recreation.gov ($9 reservation fee). Single sites are $20 per night, $30 per night for double sites (no hookups); $30 per night for sites with partial hookups, $35 per night for sites with full hookups, and $5 per night for each additional vehicle. Open May through October, weather permitting.

Directions: From Red Bluff, drive east on Highway 36 toward Susanville. Three miles before Susanville, turn left on Eagle Lake Road/County Road A1 and drive 17.5 miles to the campground on the right side of the road.

Contact: Lassen National Forest, Eagle Lake Ranger District, 530/257-4188, www.fs.usda.gov/lassen; camp host, 530/825-3450.

91 ASPEN GROVE WALK-IN

Scenic rating: 7

on Eagle Lake in Lassen National Forest

Map 3.4, page 196

Eagle Lake is known as one of the great trout lakes in California, producing the fast-growing and often huge Eagle Lake rainbow trout. All water sports are allowed and, with 100 miles of shoreline, there's plenty of room for everyone—just be prepared for cold water. This camp is one of four at the south end of the lake and is a popular choice for anglers, with a boat ramp adjacent to the campground. A bonus here is a good chance to see bald eagles and osprey. A five-mile-long paved, wheelchair-accessible recreation trail runs from this campground to Christie Campground, and then continues to other campgrounds.

One problem with Eagle Lake is the wind, which can whip the shallow lake into a froth in the early summer. (It is imperative that anglers/boaters get on the water early, and then get back to camp early, with the fishing for the day often done by 10:30 A.M.). A newer problem is the recent drawdown; the lake has been drawn down to the point that several boat ramps and marinas are high and dry.

Campsites, facilities: There are 28 tent sites. Picnic tables and fire grills are provided. Drinking water and flush toilets are available. A boat ramp is nearby. There are no wheelchair facilities for campers. Leashed pets are permitted.

Reservations, fees: Reservations are not accepted. Sites are $20 per night. Open May through September.

Directions: From Red Bluff, drive east on Highway 36 toward Susanville. Three miles before Susanville, turn left on Eagle Lake Road/County Road A1 and drive 15.5 miles to County Road 231. Turn right on County Road 231 and drive two miles to the campground on the left side of the road. Walk a short distance to the campsites.

Contact: Lassen National Forest, Eagle Lake Ranger District, 530/257-4188, www.fs.usda. gov/lassen; Aspen Grove Campground information, 530/825-3212 (May through October), 530/257-6952 (November through April).

92 WEST EAGLE GROUP CAMPS

🚶 🏊 ⛵ 🚣 🏕 🚻 ♿ 🚐 ⛺

Scenic rating: 9

on Eagle Lake in Lassen National Forest

Map 3.4, page 196

If you are coming in a big group to Eagle Lake, you'd better get on the telephone first and reserve this camp. Then you can have your own private slice of solitude along the southern shore of Eagle Lake. Bring your boat; the Gallatin Marina and a swimming beach are only about a mile away. The elevation is 5,100 feet.

Campsites, facilities: There are two group camps for tents or RVs up to 35 feet (no hookups) that can accommodate 75–100 people respectively. Picnic tables and fire grills are provided. Drinking water, flush toilets, electricity, and picnic areas are available. A grocery store, dump station, and boat ramp are nearby. Some facilities are wheelchair accessible. Leashed pets are permitted.

Reservations, fees: Reservations are required at 877/444-6777 or www.recreation. gov ($9 reservation fee). Sites are $125 per night. Open May through October, weather permitting.

Directions: From Red Bluff, drive east on Highway 36 toward Susanville. Three miles before Susanville, turn left on Eagle Lake Road/County Road A1 and drive 15.5 miles to County Road 231. Turn right on County Road 231 and drive 0.25 mile to the campground on the left side of the road.

Contact: Lassen National Forest, Eagle Lake Ranger District, 530/257-4188, www.fs.usda. gov/lassen.

93 EAGLE

🚶 🏊 ⛵ 🚣 🏕 🐕 ♿ 🚐 ⛺

Scenic rating: 8

on Eagle Lake in Lassen National Forest

Map 3.4, page 196

Eagle is set just up the road from Aspen Grove Walk-In, which is more popular because of the boat ramp nearby. The elevation is 5,100 feet. (See the Aspen Grove Walk-In listing in this chapter for information about Eagle Lake.)

Campsites, facilities: There are 50 individual sites and two double sites for tents or RVs up to 25 feet (no hookups). Picnic tables and fire grills are provided. Drinking water and flush toilets are available. Some facilities are wheelchair-accessible. There is a boat launch nearby at Gallatin Marina. Leashed pets are permitted.

Reservations, fees: Reservations are accepted at 877/444-6777 or www.recreation.gov ($9 reservation fee). Single sites are $20 per night, double sites are $30 per night, $5 per night for each additional vehicle. Open May through October, weather permitting.

Directions: From Red Bluff, drive east on Highway 36 toward Susanville. Three miles before Susanville, turn left on Eagle Lake Road/County Road A1 and drive 15.5 miles to County Road 231. Turn right and drive 0.5 mile to the campground on the left side of the road.

Contact: Lassen National Forest, Eagle Lake Ranger District, 530/257-4188, www.fs.usda. gov/lassen.

94 GOUMAZ

🚶 🚴 🚣 🚐 ❄ 🐕 🚐 ⛺

Scenic rating: 7

on the Susan River in Lassen National Forest

Map 3.4, page 196

This camp is set beside the Susan River, adjacent to historic Bizz Johnson Trail, a former route for a rail line that has been converted to a 25-mile trail. The trail runs from Susanville to

Westwood, but this section provides access to many of its prettiest and most remote stretches as it runs in a half-circle around Pegleg Mountain (7,112 feet) to the east. It is an outstanding route for biking, hiking, and horseback riding in the summer and cross-country skiing in the winter. Equestrian campers are welcome here. The elevation is 5,200 feet.

Campsites, facilities: There are five sites for tents or RVs up to 25 feet (no hookups). Picnic tables and fire grills are provided. Drinking water and vault toilets are available. Leashed pets are permitted.

Reservations, fees: Reservations are not accepted. Sites are $15 per night, $5 per night for each additional vehicle. Open May through October, weather permitting.

Directions: From Red Bluff, drive east on Highway 36 past Lake Almanor to the junction with Highway 44. Turn west on Highway 44 and drive six miles (one mile past the Worley Ranch) to Goumaz Road/Forest Road 30N08. Turn left on Goumaz Road and drive about five miles to the campground entrance road on the right.

Contact: Lassen National Forest, Eagle Lake Ranger District, 530/257-4188, www.fs.usda.gov/lassen.

95 ROXIE PECONOM WALK-IN

Scenic rating: 5

in Lassen National Forest

Map 3.4, page 196

This small camp, at 4,800 feet elevation, is set next to Willard Creek, a seasonal stream in eastern Lassen National Forest. It's shaded and quiet. The camp requires only about a 100-foot walk from the parking area. The best nearby recreation is the Bizz Johnson Trail, with a trailhead on Highway 36 (two miles east) at a parking area on the left side of the highway. This is an outstanding biking and hiking route.

Campsites, facilities: There are 10 walk-

in tent sites. Picnic tables and fire rings are provided. Drinking water and vault toilets are available. Garbage must be packed out. Leashed pets are permitted.

Reservations, fees: Reservations are not accepted. There is no fee for camping. Open May through October, weather permitting.

Directions: From Red Bluff, drive east on Highway 36 past Lake Almanor and continue past Fredonyer Pass for three miles to Forest Road 29N03 on the right. Turn right and drive two miles to the campground parking area on the right. Park and walk 100 feet to the campground.

Contact: Lassen National Forest, Eagle Lake Ranger District, 530/257-4188, www.fs.usda.gov/lassen.

96 BOULDER CREEK

Scenic rating: 7

at Antelope Lake in Plumas National Forest

Map 3.4, page 196

Antelope Lake is a pretty mountain lake circled by conifers, with nice campsites and good trout fishing. It is set at 5,000 feet elevation in remote eastern Plumas National Forest, far enough away so the marginally inclined never make the trip. Campgrounds are at each end of the lake (this one is just north of Lone Rock at the north end), with a boat ramp at Lost Cove on the east side of the lake. All water sports are permitted, and swimming is best near the campgrounds. The lake isn't huge, but it is big enough, with 15 miles of shoreline and little islands, coves, and peninsulas to give it an intimate feel.

Campsites, facilities: There are 70 sites for tents or RVs up to 40 feet (no hookups). Picnic tables and fire grills are provided. Drinking water and vault toilets are available. Some facilities are wheelchair-accessible. Leashed pets are permitted.

Reservations, fees: Reservations are accepted at 877/444-6777 or www.recreation.gov ($9

reservation fee). Sites are $23 per night. There is a $7 boat launch fee. Open May through early September.

Directions: From Red Bluff, drive east on Highway 36 to Susanville and U.S. 395. Turn south on U.S. 395 and drive about 10 miles (one mile past Janesville) to County Road 208. Turn right on County Road 208 (signed Antelope Lake) and drive about 15 miles to a Y (one mile before Antelope Lake). Turn left at the Y and drive four miles to the campground entrance on the right side of the road (on the northwest end of the lake).

Contact: Plumas National Forest, Mt. Hough Ranger District, 530/283-0555, www.fs.usda. gov/plumas.

97 LONE ROCK
🏃 🏊 🚣 ⛴ 🚤 🐕 ♿ 🚐 ⛺

Scenic rating: 9

at Antelope Lake in Plumas National Forest

Map 3.4, page 196

This camp provides an option to nearby Boulder Creek, to the immediate north at the northwest shore of Antelope Lake. (See the Boulder Creek listing for more information.) The elevation is 5,000 feet. Campfire programs are offered in the summer at the on-site amphitheater.

Campsites, facilities: There are 87 sites for tents or RVs up to 40 feet (no hookups). Picnic tables and fire grills are provided. Drinking water and vault toilets are available. Some facilities are wheelchair-accessible. Leashed pets are permitted.

Reservations, fees: Reservations are accepted at 877/444-6777 or www.recreation.gov ($9 reservation fee). Sites are $23–25 per night. There is a $7 boat launch fee. Open May through October.

Directions: From Red Bluff, drive east on Highway 36 to Susanville and U.S. 395. Go south on U.S. 395 and drive about 10 miles (one mile past Janesville) to County Road 208. Turn right on County Road 208 (signed

Antelope Lake) and drive about 15 miles to a Y (one mile before Antelope Lake). Turn left at the Y and drive three miles to the campground entrance on the right side of the road (on the northwest end of the lake).

Contact: Plumas National Forest, Mt. Hough Ranger District, 530/283-0555, www.fs.usda. gov/plumas.

98 LONG POINT
🏃 🏊 🚣 ⛴ 🚤 🐕 ♿ 🚐 ⛺

Scenic rating: 7

at Antelope Lake in Plumas National Forest

Map 3.4, page 196

Long Point is a pretty camp set on a peninsula that extends well into Antelope Lake, facing Lost Cove. The lake's boat ramp is at Lost Cove, a three-mile drive around the northeast shore. Trout fishing is often good here for both rainbow and brown trout, and there is a nature trail. A group campground is set within this campground.

Campsites, facilities: There are 38 sites for tents or RVs up to 30 feet, and four group sites for tents or RVs up to 35 feet that can accommodate up to 25 people each. No hookups. Picnic tables and fire grills are provided. Drinking water and vault toilets are available. A boat ramp is nearby. Some facilities are wheelchair-accessible. Leashed pets are permitted.

Reservations, fees: Reservations are accepted for individual sites and required for the group sites at 877/444-6777 or www.recreation.gov ($9 reservation fee). Single sites are $23 per night, double sites are $40 per night, $75 per night for group sites. Open May through October.

Directions: From Red Bluff, drive east on Highway 36 to Susanville and U.S. 395. Go south on U.S. 395 and drive about 10 miles (one mile past Janesville) to County Road 208. Turn right on County Road 208 (signed Antelope Lake) and drive about 15 miles to a Y (one mile before Antelope Lake). Turn right at the Y and drive one mile to the campground entrance on the left side of the road.

Contact: Plumas National Forest, Mt. Hough Ranger District, 530/283-0555, www.fs.usda. gov/plumas.

99 HONEY LAKE CAMPGROUND

Scenic rating: 4

near Milford

Map 3.4, page 196

For newcomers, Honey Lake is a strange-looking place—a vast, shallow lake set on the edge of the desert of the Great Basin. The campground is set at 4,385 feet elevation and covers 30 acres, most of it overlooking the lake. There are a few pine trees in the campground, and a waterfowl management area is along the north shore of the lake. This campground is popular with hunters. Equestrian facilities, including a corral and exercise ring, are available. The lake is 26 miles across, and on rare flat calm evenings, the sunsets are spectacular here.

Campsites, facilities: There are 44 pull-through sites for tents or RVs of any length, most with full or partial hookups (30 amps), plus 25 mobile homes and trailers. Picnic tables are provided. Restrooms with showers, coin laundry, dump station, propane gas, restaurant, gift and grocery store, playground, ice, video rentals, and a recreation room are available. Some facilities are wheelchair-accessible. Leashed pets are permitted.

Reservations, fees: Reservations are not accepted. RV sites are $16.95–19.95 per night, tent sites are $16.95 per night, $3.50 per person per night for more than two people. Long-term rentals are available. Some credit cards accepted. Open year-round.

Directions: From Susanville on U.S. 395, drive 17 miles south (if you reach Milford, you have gone two miles too far) to the campground on the west side of the highway. It is 65 miles north of Reno.

Contact: Honey Lake Campground, 530/253-2508.

100 LAUFMAN

Scenic rating: 5

in Plumas National Forest

Map 3.4, page 196

Laufman is an extremely remote and little-known campground set along little Willow Creek at an elevation of 5,100 feet. Though U.S. 395 is a high-use highway between Susanville and Reno, this small camp is overlooked. The shoulder seasons in spring and fall are cold, while spring and early summer can be windy.

Campsites, facilities: There are six sites for tents or RVs up to 25 feet (no hookups). Picnic tables and fire grills are provided. Vault toilets are available. No drinking water is available. Garbage must be packed out. Leashed pets are permitted.

Reservations, fees: Reservations are not accepted. There is no fee for camping. Open May through September, weather permitting.

Directions: From Susanville on U.S. 395, drive south for 24 miles to Milford. In Milford turn right (east) on County Road 336 and drive about four miles to the campground on the right.

Contact: Plumas National Forest, Beckwourth Ranger District, 530/836-2575, www.fs.usda. gov/plumas.

101 CONKLIN PARK

Scenic rating: 4

on Willow Creek in Plumas National Forest

Map 3.4, page 196

This camp is along little Willow Creek on the northeastern border of the Dixie Mountain State Game Refuge. The campground is little known, primitive, rarely used, and is not likely to change any time soon. The elevation is 5,900 feet.

Campsites, facilities: There are nine sites for tents or RVs up to 25 feet (no hookups). Picnic tables and fire grills are provided. Vault toilets are available. No drinking water is available.

Garbage must be packed out. Leashed pets are permitted.

Reservations, fees: Reservations are not accepted. There is no fee for camping. Open May through October, weather permitting.

Directions: From Susanville on U.S. 395, drive south for 24 miles to Milford. In Milford turn right (east) on County Road 336 and drive about four miles to a Y. Bear to the right on Forest Road 70/26N70 and drive three miles. Turn right at the bridge at Willow Creek, turn left on Forest Road 70 (now paved), and drive three miles to the camp entrance road on the left side.

Contact: Plumas National Forest, Beckwourth Ranger District, 530/836-2575, www.fs.usda.gov/plumas.

102 MEADOW VIEW EQUESTRIAN

Scenic rating: 6

near Little Last Chance Creek in Plumas National Forest

Map 3.4, page 196

This little-known, primitive camp is set along the headwaters of Little Last Chance Creek, along the eastern border of the Dixie Mountain State Game Refuge. The access road continues along the creek and connects with primitive roads that enter the interior of the game refuge. Side-trip options include Frenchman Lake to the south and the drive up to Dixie Mountain, at 8,323 feet elevation. The camp elevation is 6,100 feet.

Campsites, facilities: There are six sites for tents or RVs up to 30 feet (no hookups). Picnic tables and fire grills are provided. Vault toilets are available. No drinking water is available. A horse corral is available across the road from the campground. Garbage must be packed out. Leashed pets are permitted.

Reservations, fees: Reservations are not accepted. There is no fee for camping. Open May through October, weather permitting.

Directions: From Reno, drive north on U.S. 395 for 43 miles to Doyle. At Doyle, turn west on Doyle Grade Road/County Road 331 (a dirt road most of the way) and drive seven miles to the campground.

Contact: Plumas National Forest, Beckwourth Ranger District, 530/836-2575, www.fs.usda.gov/plumas.

MENDOCINO AND WINE COUNTRY

© JOERG HACKEMANN/123RF.COM

BEST CAMPGROUNDS

For many people, this region offers the best possible combination of geography, weather, and outdoor activities. The Mendocino coast is dramatic and remote, with several stellar state parks, while Sonoma Valley, in the heart of wine country, produces some of the most popular wines in the world. Add in the self-indulgent options of mud baths and hot springs at Calistoga and a dash of mainstream recreation at Clear Lake, Lake Berryessa, or any of the other area lakes, and you have a capsule summary of why the Mendocino coast and the wine country have turned into getaway favorites.

But they are like two worlds, and the twain do not meet.

For many, this area is where people go for romance, fine cuisine, great wine, mineral springs, and anything else that comes to mind spur-of-the-moment. Such is a vacation in the Napa and Sonoma wine country, or on the beautiful Sonoma and Mendocino coast.

This region wouldn't be the best of both worlds if there weren't options on the other end of the spectrum. Campgrounds set up primarily for family recreation are available at Clear Lake, Lake Berryessa, and Blue Lakes. If the shoe fits – and for many, it does – you can have a great time fishing, boating, and waterskiing.

The coast features a series of romantic hideaways and excellent adventuring and hiking. The Fort Bragg area alone has three state parks, all with outstanding recreation, including several easy hikes, many amid redwoods and along pretty streams. Reservations are always required far in advance for a campsite at a state park on a summer weekend. Fort Bragg also offers excellent fishing out of Noyo Harbor.

The driving tour of Highway 1 along this section of the coast is the fantasy of many, and it can live up to that fantasy if you don't mind the twists and turns of the road. Along the way, there are dozens of hidden beaches and untouched coastline where you can stop and explore and maybe play tag with the waves. The prize spots are MacKerricher State Park, Salt Point State Park, and Anchor Bay.

MENDOCINO AND WINE COUNTRY

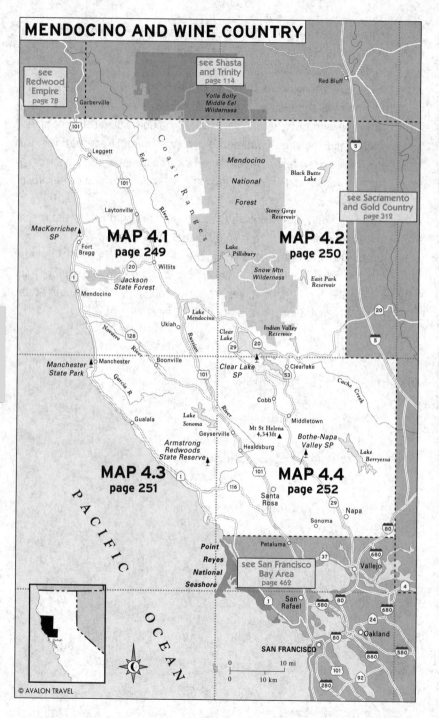

see Redwood Empire page 78

see Shasta and Trinity page 114

Yolla Bolly Middle Eel Wilderness

Red Bluff

Garberville

101

Leggett

Mendocino

National

Forest

Black Butte Lake

5

Stony Gorge Reservoir

101

Coast Ranges

Eel River

Laytonville

MacKerricher SP

Fort Bragg

20

Willits

1

Jackson State Forest

Mendocino

MAP 4.1 page 249

Lake Pillsbury

Snow Mtn Wilderness

MAP 4.2 page 250

East Park Reservoir

see Sacramento and Gold Country page 312

20

5

Navarro River

128

Ukiah

Russian River

Lake Mendocino

Clear Lake

29

20

Indian Valley Reservoir

Manchester State Park

Manchester

Boonville

101

Clear Lake SP

Clearlake

53

Cache Creek

Garcia R

Gualala

Lake Sonoma

River

Cobb

Mt St Helena 4,343ft ▲

Middletown

Bothe-Napa Valley SP

Lake Berryessa

Geyserville

Armstrong Redwoods State Reserve ▲

Healdsburg

MAP 4.3 page 251

1

101

116

MAP 4.4 page 252

29

Napa

Santa Rosa

Sonoma

80

PACIFIC

Point Reyes National Seashore

Petaluma

37

680

Vallejo

see San Francisco Bay Area page 462

4

OCEAN

1

San Rafael

580

80

680

24

Oakland

SAN FRANCISCO

880

580

0   10 mi
0   10 km

101

92

280

© AVALON TRAVEL

Map 4.1

Sites 1-37
Pages 253-271

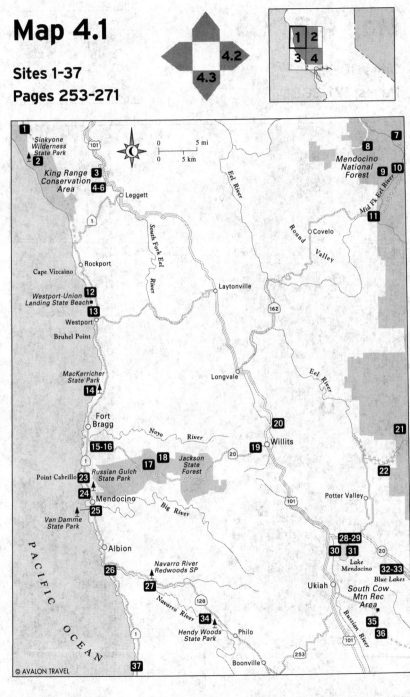

Map 4.2

Sites 38-73
Pages 271-288

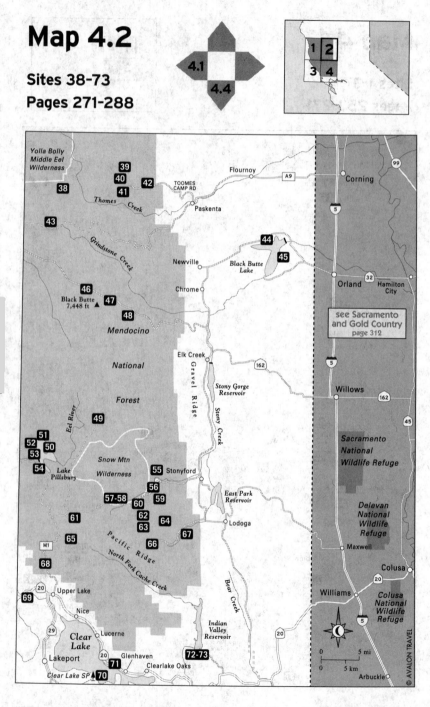

Map 4.3

Sites 74-93
Pages 288-299

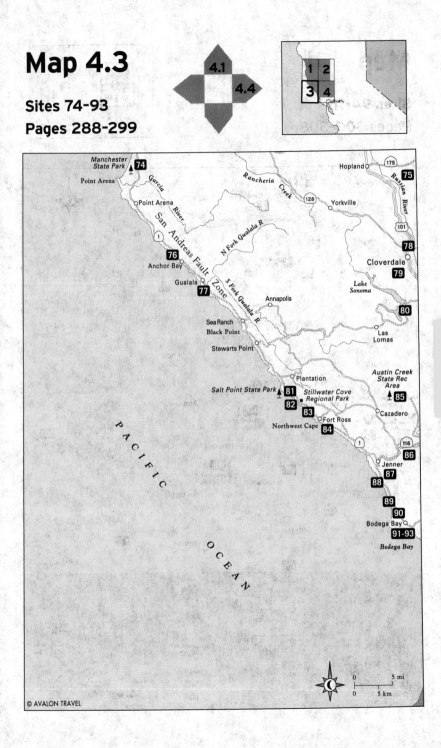

Map 4.4

Sites 94-111
Pages 300-308

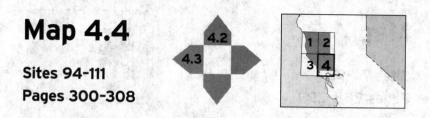

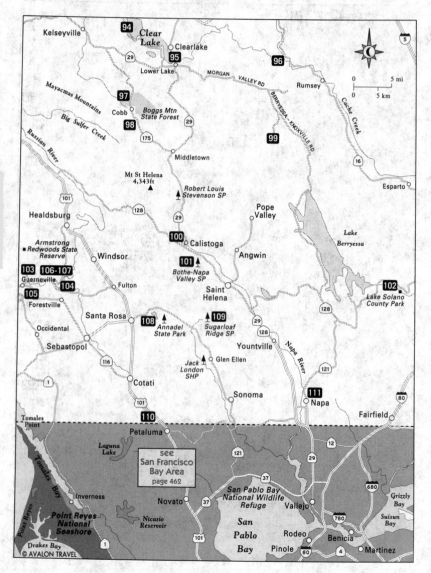

1 NADELOS AND WAILAKI

Scenic rating: 7

in the King Range

Map 4.1, page 249

Nadelos and Wailaki campgrounds are set a short distance apart at 1,840 feet elevation near the South Fork Bear Creek at the southern end of the King Range National Conservation Area. This provides access to a rare geographic dynamic, where mountains and coast adjoin. Nearby Chemise Mountain, elevation 2,598 feet, is one of the highest points in California within two miles of the sea, and it provides a dramatic lookout on clear days. Nadelos is also one of the few camps with individual sites that can be reserved by a group.

Campsites, facilities: There are eight tent sites at Nadelos, which is also available as a group site for 20–60 people. There are 13 sites for tents or RVs up to 20 feet (no hookups) at Wailaki. Picnic tables and fire grills are provided. Drinking water and vault toilets are available. Some facilities are wheelchair-accessible. Leashed pets are permitted.

Reservations, fees: Reservations for individual sites are not accepted. Reservations for group camping at Nadelos are accepted at 707/986-5400. Individual sites are $8 per night; group sites are $85 per night. Open year-round.

Directions: From Eureka, drive 60 miles south on U.S. 101 to the Redway exit. Take the Redway/Shelter Cove exit onto Redwood Drive into the town of Redway. Drive 2.5 miles (look on the right for the King Range Conservation Area sign) to Briceland-Thorne Road. Turn right on Briceland-Thorne Road (which will become Shelter Cove Road) and drive 17 miles to Chemise Mountain Road. Turn left (south) on Chemise Mountain Road and drive one mile to Nadelos Campground on the right. To reach Wailaki Campground from Nadelos, continue 0.4 mile to the camp on the right.

Contact: Bureau of Land Management, Arcata Field Office, 707/825-2300, www.blm.gov/ca.

2 SINKYONE WILDERNESS

Scenic rating: 10

in Sinkyone Wilderness State Park

Map 4.1, page 249

This is a great jump-off point for a backpacking trip in the Sinkyone Wilderness on the Lost Coast, one of the few wilderness areas where a trip can be made any month of the year. The terrain is primitive, steep, and often wet, but it provides a rare coastal wilderness experience. Starting at the northern trailhead at Orchard Camp, or the southern trailhead at the Usal Beach campground, it's an ambitious weekend tromp of 17 miles. This is a unique 7,367-acre park that is named after the Sinkyone tribe, who once lived in this area. It is called the Lost Coast because there are no highways that provide direct access. Regardless, it has become surprisingly popular for backpackers on the Coastal Trail. Annual rainfall is up to 80 inches per year, mostly between November and May. Summer temperatures range 45–75°F, with morning and evening fog common.

Campsites, facilities: At Usal Beach, there are 35 tent sites. Picnic tables and fire rings are provided. Pit toilets are provided. No drinking water is available and garbage must be packed out. Between Bear Harbor and Jones Beach there are 23 tent sites with picnic tables, fire rings, and pit toilets (bring your own toilet paper). Drinking water is available at the Needle Rock Visitor Center (see Directions) where there is a single developed campsite. Leashed pets are not permitted at campsites.

Reservations, fees: Reservations are not accepted. Sites are $25 per night, the site at Needle Rock Visitor Center is $30 per night, $3 per night for each additional vehicle, and walk-in trail sites are $5 per night. Open year-round, weather permitting (but roads may be impassable in wet weather).

Directions: To reach the northern boundary of the Sinkyone Wilderness from U.S. 101 north of Garberville, take the Redway exit, turn west on

Briceland Road, and drive 17 miles to Whitethorn. From Whitethorn continue six more miles to the four-corners fork. Drive straight ahead to the middle left fork and continue 3.5 miles on a dirt road to the Needle Rock Visitor Center (the last nine miles are unpaved).

To reach the southern boundary of the Sinkyone Wilderness from Leggett on U.S. 101, turn southwest on Highway 1 (toward Fort Bragg) and drive 14.66 miles to Mile Marker 90.88 at County Road 431. Turn right on County Road 431 (a dirt road, often unsigned) and drive six miles to the Usal Beach Campground. Note: The roads can be quite rough and impassable in wet weather. Trailers and RVs are not recommended.

Contact: Sinkyone Wilderness State Park, 707/986-7711 or 707/247-3318, www.parks.ca.gov.

3 REDWOODS RIVER RESORT

Scenic rating: 8

on the Eel River

Map 4.1, page 249

This resort is situated in a 21-acre grove of redwoods on U.S. 101 and features 1,500 feet of river access, including a sandy beach and two swimming holes. Many of the campsites are shaded. A hiking trail leads from the resort to the Eel River, a walk of just over a quarter mile. This is one in a series of both public and private campgrounds along the highway between Leggett and Garberville. Steelhead and salmon fishing are popular here in the winter, and the resort provides nearby access to state parks. The elevation is 700 feet.

Campsites, facilities: There are 14 tent sites and 27 sites with full hookups (30 amps) for RVs of any length; some sites are pull-through. Eight cabins and eight lodge rooms are also available. At campsites, picnic tables and fire rings are provided. Restrooms with showers, seasonal heated swimming pool, playground, recreation room, WiFi, minimart, coin laundry, group kitchen, dump station, table tennis, basketball, volleyball, badminton, horseshoes, shuffleboard, group facilities, seasonal organized activities, and a seasonal evening campfire are available. Some facilities are wheelchair-accessible. Leashed pets are permitted, with breed restrictions, except in buildings.

Reservations, fees: Reservations are recommended in the summer. RV sites with full hookups are $40–47 per night, RV sites with partial hookups are $36 per night, tent sites are $27 per night, $5 per person per night for more than two people, $2 per pet per night. Off-season discounts available. Some credit cards accepted. Open year-round.

Directions: From the junction of U.S. 101 and Highway 1 in Leggett, drive north on U.S. 101 for seven miles to the campground entrance on the left.

Contact: Redwoods River Resort, 707/925-6249, www.redwoodriverresort.com.

4 REDWOOD CAMPGROUND

Scenic rating: 8

in Standish-Hickey State Recreation Area

Map 4.1, page 249

Standish-Hickey covers 1,012 acres set in an inland river canyon; the South Fork Eel provides two miles of river frontage. The park is known as "the gateway to the tall trees country" and the Grove Trail contains one of the few virgin stands of redwoods in this area. This is one of three camps in Standish-Hickey State Recreation Area, and it is by far the most unusual. Reaching Redwood Campground requires driving over a temporary "summer bridge," which provides access to a pretty spot along the South Fork Eel River. In early September, out comes the bridge and up comes the river. (Note: Some may remember that Redwood Campground did not open in 2010 due to the cost of installing a temporarily access bridge; the bridge reopened in 2011.) Redwood Campground is open only in summer and rangers consider it a "premium" camp. There are two other campgrounds available at this park (see listings for Rock Creek and Hickey in this chapter). The elevation is 800 feet.

Note: This park was on the state park closure list. Its status is currently in negotiation with Mendocino Area Parks Association (MAPA) and Team Standish for a donor agreement to remain open. Check the park status online prior to planning a trip here.

Campsites, facilities: There are 63 sites for tents or RVs up to 18 feet (no hookups). No trailers, including pop-up tent trailers, are permitted. Picnic tables, food lockers, and fire rings are provided. Drinking water and restrooms with coin showers and flush toilets are available. Some facilities are wheelchair-accessible. Leashed pets are permitted.

Reservations, fees: Reservations are not accepted at this time. Sites are $45 per night, $8 per night for each additional vehicle. Open July through Labor Day weekend.

Directions: From the junction of U.S. 101 and Highway 1 in Leggett, drive north on U.S. 101 for one mile. The park entrance is on the west (left) side of the road.

Contact: Standish-Hickey State Recreation Area, 707/925-6482, www.parks.ca.gov.

5 ROCK CREEK

Scenic rating: 8

in Standish-Hickey State Recreation Area

Map 4.1, page 249

This is one of two main campgrounds (the other is Hickey, see listing in this chapter) set in a mixed redwood grove at Standish-Hickey State Recreation Area. This is a classic state park camp, with numbered sites, flat tent spaces, picnic tables, and food lockers. There are 12 miles of hiking trails in the park. Hiking is only fair, but most people enjoy the short tromp down to the nearby South Fork Eel River. In the winter, steelhead migrate through the area. (See the Redwood Campground listing for more details on this park.)

Note: This park was on the state park closure list. Its status is currently in negotiation with Mendocino Area Parks Association (MAPA) and Team Standish for a donor agreement to remain open. Check the park status online prior to planning a trip here.

Campsites, facilities: There are 35 sites for tents or RVs up to 27 feet (no hookups) and for trailers up to 24 feet; there is one hike-in/bike-in site. Picnic tables, food lockers, and fire rings are provided. Drinking water and restrooms with coin showers and flush toilets are available. Some facilities are wheelchair-accessible. Leashed pets are permitted.

Reservations, fees: Reservations are not accepted at this time. Sites are $35 per night, $8 per night for each additional vehicle, $5 per person per night for the hike-in/bike-in site. Open year-round.

Directions: From the junction of U.S. 101 and Highway 1 in Leggett, drive north on U.S. 101 for one mile. The park entrance is on the west (left) side of the road.

Contact: Standish-Hickey State Recreation Area, 707/925-6482, www.parks.ca.gov.

6 STANDISH-HICKEY STATE RECREATION AREA: HICKEY

Scenic rating: 8

on the Eel River in
Standish-Hickey State Recreation Area

Map 4.1, page 249

This is an ideal layover for U.S. 101 cruisers yearning to spend a night in the redwoods. The park is best known for its campsites set amid redwoods and for the nearby South Fork Eel River with its steelhead fishing in the winter. The elevation is 800 feet. Insider's tip: There's a great swimming hole on the Eel River in the summer. (See details about Standish-Hickey State Recreation Area in the Redwood Campground listing in this chapter.)

Note: This park was on the state park closure

list. Its status is currently in negotiation with Mendocino Area Parks Association (MAPA) and Team Standish for a donor agreement to remain open. Check the park status online prior to planning a trip here.

Campsites, facilities: There are 63 sites for tents or RVs up to 16 feet (no hookups) and trailers up to 24 feet. Picnic tables, food lockers, and fire rings are provided. Drinking water and restrooms with showers and flush toilets are available. A grocery store is available nearby. Some facilities are wheelchair-accessible. Leashed pets are permitted.

Reservations, fees: Reservations are not accepted at this time. Sites are $35 per night, $8 per night for each additional vehicle. Hike-in/bike-in sites are $5 per night. Open year-round.

Directions: From the junction of U.S. 101 and Highway 1 in Leggett, drive north on U.S. 101 for one mile. The park entrance is on the west (left) side of the road.

Contact: Standish-Hickey State Recreation Area, 707/925-6482, www.parks.ca.gov.

🚻 HAMMERHORN
🚶🏊🎣🐕🦽🚐⛺

Scenic rating: 7

on Hammerhorn Lake in
Mendocino National Forest

Map 4.1, page 249

Hammerhorn Lake is obscure and hidden: a veritable dot of a lake, just five acres, set at 3,500 feet in Mendocino National Forest. The lake is too small for motorized boats, but swimming is allowed and the Department of Fish and Game stocks the tiny lake every June. There is a spring at the south end of the lake; if go out of the camp and hike along the edge of the lake, you can often hear the water running out of the pipe before you see it. The lake is set near the border of the Yolla Bolly Wilderness, with Green Springs Trailhead a few miles away to the northeast. A great side trip is the drive up to Anthony Peak.

Campsites, facilities: There are nine sites for tents or RVs up to 16 feet (no hookups). Picnic tables and fire grills are provided. Drinking water, vault toilets, and fishing piers are available. Garbage must be packed out. Supplies are available in Covelo. Some facilities are wheelchair-accessible, including two fishing piers. Leashed pets are permitted.

Reservations, fees: Reservations are not accepted. Sites are $8 per night. Open May through December.

Directions: From Willits, drive north on U.S. 101 for 13 miles to Longvale and the junction with Highway 162. Turn northeast on Highway 162 and drive to Covelo. Continue east on Highway 162 for nine miles to the Eel River Bridge. After crossing the bridge, turn left on Forest Road M1 and drive about 17 miles to Forest Road M21. Turn right and drive one mile to the campground entrance.

Contact: Mendocino National Forest, Covelo Ranger District, 707/983-6118, www.fs.usda.gov/mendocino.

🚻 RATTLESNAKE CREEK
🚶🏊🐕5%⛺

Scenic rating: 7

in Mendocino National Forest

Map 4.1, page 249

This camp is so small and secret that it is not even listed on the Forest Service website. It has only two tent sites and is located relatively near Green Springs Camp (at the southern end of the Yolla Bolly Wilderness). The secret at Rattlesnake Creek is that a swimming hole is located just upstream of the bridge near the campground. Very few people know about this, or the campground either. The elevation is 4,000 feet.

Campsites, facilities: There are two primitive sites for tents only. There is no drinking water, and garbage must be packed out.

Reservations, fees: Reservations are not accepted. There is no fee for camping.

Directions: From Willits, drive north on U.S. 101 for 13 miles to Longvale and the junction with Highway 162. Turn northeast on Highway 162 and drive to Covelo. Continue east on Highway 162 for nine miles to the Eel River Bridge. Drive across the bridge and turn left on Forest Service Road M1/Indian Dick Road. Drive about 17 miles on Forest Service Road M1/Indian Dick Road to FS Road M21. From that junction, drive north on Indian Dick Road for five miles. Cross the cement bridge at Rattlesnake Creek and turn left to camp.

Contact: Mendocino National Forest, Covelo Ranger District, 707/983-6118, www.fs.usda.gov/mendocino.

9 HOWARDS MEADOWS AND HOWARD LAKE

Scenic rating: 8

near Howard Lake in
Mendocino National Forest

Map 4.1, page 249

Howard Lake is a small lake located deep in Mendocino National Forest. It is pretty and larger than Hammerhorn Lake to the north. Some years it is stocked with small trout. If the tiny campground at Howard Lake is occupied, the camp at Howard Meadows is within walking distance. The elevation is 3,500 feet.

Campsites, facilities: There are five sites for tents or small RVs at Howard Lake; one site is wheelchair accessible. There are 10 sites for tents or small RVs at Howard Meadows. Picnic tables and fire rings are provided. Vault toilets are available, but there is no drinking water. Garbage must be packed out.

Reservations, fees: Reservations are not accepted. Sites are $6 per night. Open April to November.

Directions: From Willits, drive north on U.S. 101 for 13 miles to Longvale and the junction with Highway 162. Turn northeast on Highway 162 and drive for nine miles to the Eel River Bridge. After crossing the bridge, turn left on Forest Service Road M1/Indian Dick

Road. Drive 22 miles on Forest Service Road M1/Indian Dick Road to the campground.

Contact: Mendocino National Forest, Covelo Ranger District, 707/983-6118, www.fs.usda.gov/mendocino.

10 LITTLE DOE

Scenic rating: 5

near Howard Lake in
Mendocino National Forest

Map 4.1, page 249

Little Howard Lake is tucked deep in the interior of Mendocino National Forest between Espee Ridge to the south and Little Doe Ridge to the north, at an elevation of 3,600 feet. For a drive-to lake, it is surprisingly remote and provides fair trout fishing, primitive camping, and an opportunity for car-top boating. The lake covers 15–20 acres, and swimming is allowed. Side trips include Hammerhorn Lake, about six miles away, and several four-wheel-drive roads that allow you to explore the area. A Forest Service map is recommended.

Campsites, facilities: There are 13 sites for tents or RVs up to 16 feet (no hookups). Picnic tables and fire pits are provided. Vault toilets are available. No drinking water is available. Garbage must be packed out. No gas motors allowed. Supplies are available in Covelo, 12 miles away. Leashed pets are permitted.

Reservations, fees: Reservations are not accepted. Sites are $6 per night. Open April through December.

Directions: From Willits, drive north on U.S. 101 for 13 miles to Longvale and the junction with Highway 162. Turn northeast on Highway 162 and drive to Covelo. Continue east on Highway 162 and drive for nine miles to the Eel River Bridge. After crossing the bridge, turn left on Forest Road M1 and drive about 11 miles to the campground.

Contact: Mendocino National Forest, Covelo Ranger District, 707/983-6118, www.fs.usda.gov/mendocino.

11 EEL RIVER

Scenic rating: 8

in Mendocino National Forest

Map 4.1, page 249

This is a little-known spot, set in oak woodlands at the confluence of the Middle Fork of the Eel River and Black Butte River. The elevation is 1,500 feet, and it's often extremely hot in summer. Eel River is an ancient Native American campsite and a major archaeological site. For this reason restoration has been limited and at times the camp is overgrown and weedy. Who cares, though? After all, you're camping.

Campsites, facilities: There are 15 sites for tents or RVs up to 21 feet (no hookups). Picnic tables and fire grills are provided. Drinking water and vault toilets are available. Garbage must be packed out. Leashed pets are permitted.

Reservations, fees: Reservations are not accepted. Sites are $8 per night. Open March through December.

Directions: From Willits, drive north on U.S. 101 for 13 miles to Longvale and the junction with Highway 162. Turn northeast on Highway 162 and drive to Covelo. Continue east on Highway 162 for 13 miles to the campground.

Contact: Mendocino National Forest, Covelo Ranger District, 707/983-6118, www.fs.usda.gov/mendocino.

12 WESTPORT–UNION LANDING STATE BEACH

Scenic rating: 8

near Westport overlooking the Pacific Ocean

Map 4.1, page 249

By state park standards, this campground, with sites set on an ocean bluff, is considered primitive. It can get windy here, but the reward is the view. This park covers more than three miles of rugged and scenic coastline. Splendid views, colorful sunsets, and tree-covered mountains provide great photo opportunities. Several small sandy beaches, and one large beach at the mouth of Howard Creek, provide some good spots for surf fishing. Several species of rockfish and abalone can be taken when tides and ocean conditions are right. But note that the surf here can surge, discouraging all but the hardy. The park was named for two early-day communities, Westport and Union Landing, settlements well known for lumber and rail ties. The northern Mendocino coast is remote, beautiful, and gets far less people pressure than the Fort Bragg area. That is the key to its appeal.

Note: This park is on the closure list developed by the California Department of Parks, pending final state budget decisions or the possible transfer of park management to other park agencies or volunteer groups. Westport Union Landing State Beach was scheduled for closure on July 1, 2012, but received funding at the last minute. Abalone Point Campground was closed as the book went to press but could reopen if funding comes through. Check online prior to planning your trip.

Campsites, facilities: There are 85 sites for tents or RVs of any length (no hookups); eight people maximum per site. Dispersed hike-in/bike-in sites are also available. Picnic tables and fire rings are provided. Drinking water and chemical flush toilets are available. A grocery store is nearby. Leashed pets are permitted.

Reservations, fees: Reservations are not accepted. Sites are $25 per night, $8 per night for each additional vehicle, hike-in/bike-in sites are $5 per night. Open year-round.

Directions: From Fort Bragg, drive north on Highway 1 to Westport. In Westport, continue north on Highway 1 for three miles to the campground entrance on the west side of the road.

Contact: California State Parks, Mendocino District, 707/937-5804, www.parks.ca.gov.

13 WESTPORT BEACH/N MENDOCINO COAST KOA

Scenic rating: 8

near Westport overlooking the Pacific Ocean

Map 4.1, page 249

Westport Beach RV and Camping is set above the beach near the mouth of Wages Creek, with both creekside and beach sites available. The 30-acre campground has a quarter mile of beach frontage. You will notice as you venture north from Fort Bragg that the number of vacationers in the area falls way off, providing a chance for quiet beaches and serene moments. The best nearby hiking is to the north out of the trailhead for the Sinkyone Wilderness.

Campsites, facilities: There are 75 sites for RVs of any length with full hookups (20, 30, and 50 amps), seven sites for RVs of any length (no hookups), 50 sites for tents only, and five group sites for tents or RVs (no hookups) that can accommodate 12–50 people each. Some RV sites are pull-through. Two cabins are also available. Picnic tables and fire rings are provided at most sites. Drinking water, restrooms with flush toilets and coin showers, convenience store, coin laundry, telephone, WiFi, playground, volleyball, shuffleboard, horseshoes, firewood, and ice are available. Some facilities are wheelchair-accessible. Leashed pets are permitted.

Reservations, fees: Reservations are accepted at 888/562-3427 or 707/964-2964. RV sites are $48–62 per night; tent sites, group sites, and RV sites (no hookups) are $25–45 per night per vehicle; $5–7 per night per person for more than two people Some credit cards accepted. Open year-round.

Directions: From Fort Bragg, drive north on Highway 1 to Westport. In Westport, continue north on Highway 1 for 0.5 mile to the campground entrance on the west side of the highway.

Contact: Westport Beach/N Mendocino Coast KOA, 707/964-2964, http://koa.com/campgrounds/westport-beach.

14 MACKERRICHER STATE PARK

Scenic rating: 9

north of Fort Bragg overlooking the Pacific Ocean

Map 4.1, page 249

MacKerricher is a beautiful park on the Mendocino coast, a great destination for adventure and exploration. The camps are set in a coastal forest, with gorgeous walk-in sites. Nearby is a small beach, great tidepools, a rocky point where harbor seals hang out in the sun, a small lake (Cleone) with trout fishing, a great bike trail, and outstanding short hikes. The short jaunt around little Cleone Lake has many romantic spots, often tunneling through vegetation, then emerging for lake views. The coastal walk to the point to see seals and tidepools is equally captivating. For wheelchair users, there is a wheelchair-accessible trail to Laguna Point and also a route on a raised boardwalk that runs halfway around Cleone Lake, a former tidal lagoon. This park covers more than 1,530 acres of beach, bluff, headlands, dune, forest, and wetlands. That diverse landscape provides habitat for more than 90 species of bird, most in the vicinity of Cleone Lake. The headland supplies a prime vantage point for whale-watching in winter and spring.

Campsites, facilities: There are 140 sites for tents or RVs up to 35 feet (no hookups), 10 walk-in sites, and two group sites for up to 40–60 people each. Picnic tables, fire rings, and food lockers are provided. Drinking water, restroom with flush toilets and coin showers, picnic area, Wi-Fi, and a dump station are available. A seasonal junior ranger program with nature walks, campfire programs, and exhibits is offered. Some facilities are wheelchair-accessible. Leashed pets are not permitted on Virgin Creek Beach, the northern half of Ten Mile Beach, the Seal Rocks Harbor seal nursery, or in the Surfwood Walk-In campground.

Reservations, fees: Reservations are accepted at 800/444-7275 (800/444-PARK) or www.reserveamerica.com ($8 reservation fee); family campsites are now site-specific. Drive-in sites are $35 per night, $8 per night for each additional vehicle, walk-in tent sites are $25 per night, hike-in/bike-in sites are $5 per night. Group sites are $200–260 per night. Open year-round.

Directions: From Fort Bragg, drive north on Highway 1 for three miles to the campground entrance on the left side of the road.

Contact: MacKerricher State Park, 707/964-9112; Mendocino District, 707/937-5804, www.parks.ca.gov.

15 FORT BRAGG LEISURE TIME RV PARK

Scenic rating: 5

in Fort Bragg

Map 4.1, page 249

This privately operated park adjoins Jackson State Forest, with easy access for hiking and cycling trails. The park offers horseshoes, badminton, and a covered group picnic area. The drive from Willits to Fort Bragg on Highway 20 is always a favorite, a curving two-laner through redwoods, not too slow, not too fast, best seen from the saddle of a Harley-Davidson. At the end of it is the coast, and just three miles inland is this campground in the sunbelt, said to be out of the fog by breakfast. Within short drives are Noyo Harbor in Fort Bragg, Russian Gulch State Park, Mendocino to the south, and MacKerricher State Park to the north. In fact, there's so much in the area, you could explore for days. Note that about 10 percent of the sites are filled with permanent or long-term renters.

Campsites, facilities: There are 70 sites, many with full or partial hookups (30 amps), for tents or RVs up to 40 feet; some sites are pull-through. Picnic tables and fire rings are provided. Restrooms with coin showers, satellite TV, WiFi, dump station, fish-cleaning station, horseshoes, RV storage, and a coin laundry are available. Some facilities are wheelchair-accessible. Leashed pets are permitted.

Reservations, fees: Reservations are accepted at 800/700-8542. RV sites with full hookups are $35 per night, partial hookup sites are $34 per night, tent sites are $25 per night, $5 per person per night for more than two people, $1 per night for each additional vehicle, $2 per night for first pet, and $1 per night for additional pet. Group rates are available. Monthly and seasonal rates available. Some credit cards accepted. Open year-round.

Directions: In Fort Bragg at the junction of Highway 1 and Highway 20, turn east on Highway 20 and drive 2.5 miles to the campground entrance on the right side of the road at 30801 Highway 20.

Contact: Fort Bragg Leisure Time RV Park, 707/964-5994, www.fortbraggltrvpark.com.

16 POMO RV PARK AND CAMPGROUND

Scenic rating: 7

in Fort Bragg

Map 4.1, page 249

This park covers 17 acres of lush, native vegetation, including rhododendrons, near the ocean. It is one of several camps on the Fort Bragg and Mendocino coast, and groups are welcome. Nearby Noyo Harbor offers busy restaurants, deep-sea fishing, a boat ramp, harbor, and a nice walk out to the Noyo Harbor jetty. Huckleberry picking is also an option. Many of the RV spaces are quite wide at this park.

Campsites, facilities: There are 94 sites with full or partial hookups (30 and 50 amps) for RVs of any length, and 30 sites for tents. Some sites are pull-through. Picnic tables and fire rings are provided. Restrooms with coin showers, cable TV hookups, Wi-Fi, convenience store, firewood, ice, RV supplies, propane gas, coin laundry, dump station, fish-cleaning table, group meeting room, horseshoe pits, and large grass playing field are available. Some facilities are wheelchair accessible. Leashed pets are permitted.

Reservations, fees: Reservations are recommended in the summer. RV sites with hookups are $43–45 per night, tent sites are $30 per night, $3–15 per person per night for more than two people, $1 per pet per night. Open year-round.

Directions: In Fort Bragg at the junction of Highway 1 and Highway 20, drive south on Highway 1 for one mile to Tregoning Lane. Turn left (east) and drive a short distance to the park at the end of the road (17999 Tregoning Lane).

Contact: Pomo RV Park and Campground, 707/964-3373, www.pomorv.com.

17 JACKSON DEMONSTRATION STATE FOREST, CAMP 1

Scenic rating: 7

near Fort Bragg

Map 4.1, page 249

Primitive campsites set in a vast forest of redwoods and Douglas fir are the prime attraction at Jackson Demonstration State Forest. Even though Highway 20 is a major connecting link to the coast in the summer, these camps get bypassed because they are primitive and largely unknown. Why? Because reaching them requires driving on dirt roads sometimes frequented by logging trucks, and there are few campground signs along the highway. This camp features lots of tree cover, with oaks, redwoods, and madrones. Most of the campsites are adjacent to the south fork of the north fork of the Noyo River, well known among locals, but completely missed by most others. A one-mile trail circles the campground; the trailhead is at the day-use area. A DFG hatchery is next to

the campground, but note that no fishing is permitted in the river.

Campsites, facilities: There are 32 sites for tents or RVs up to 27 feet (no hookups) and Tilley, a group site for tents or RVs up to 45 feet that can accommodate 25–150 people. Picnic tables and fire pits are provided. Pit toilets are available. No drinking water is available. A camp host is on site. Some facilities are wheelchair accessible. Leashed pets are permitted.

Reservations, fees: Reservations are only accepted for the group site at 707/964-5674; advance payment is required. Sites are $15 per night, $5 per night for additional vehicle, $50 per night for the group site. A camping permit is required and can be obtained from the camp host. Campers are limited to 30 days per year and no more than 14 consecutive days. Open late May through September.

Directions: From Willits on U.S. 101, turn west on Highway 20 and drive 27 miles to Forest Road 350 (at Mile Marker 5.9). Turn right (north) and drive 1.3 miles to the campground.

Contact: Jackson Demonstration State Forest, 707/964-5674, www.fire.ca.gov.

18 JACKSON DEMONSTRATION STATE FOREST, CAMP 20

Scenic rating: 6

near Fort Bragg

Map 4.1, page 249

A highlight of Jackson Demonstration Forest is a 50-foot waterfall on Chamberlain Creek. Set in a steep canyon at the east end of the forest, amid giant firs and redwoods, it can be reached with a 10-minute walk. There are also extensive logging roads that are good yet challenging for mountain biking. What to do first? Get a map from the State Forestry Department. For driving, the roads are extremely dusty in summer and muddy in winter.

Campsites, facilities: There are 30 sites for tents or RVs up to 16 feet (no hookups) and two group sites: Redtail and Horse Camp. Picnic tables and fire rings are provided. Vault toilets are available. No drinking water is available. Corrals are available only at Horse Camp. A camp host is on site. Leashed pets are permitted.

Reservations, fees: Reservations are not accepted for individual sites, but are required for group sites at 707/964-5674. Sites are $15 per night, $5 per night for additional vehicle, $50 per night for the group sites. A camping permit is required and can be obtained from the camp host or the State Department of Forestry and Fire Protection office (802 N. Main St./Hwy. 1, Fort Bragg, CA). Campers are limited to 30 days per year and no more than 14 consecutive days. Open late May through September.

Directions: From Willits on U.S. 101, turn west on Highway 20 and drive 17 miles. At Mile Marker 16.9 (just past the Chamberlain Bridge) continue driving for about 0.25 mile to the Dunlap camp entrance on the left.

Contact: Jackson Demonstration State Forest, 707/964-5674, www.fire.ca.gov.

19 WILLITS-UKIAH KOA

Scenic rating: 3

near Willits

Map 4.1, page 249

This is an ideal spot to park your RV if you plan on taking the Skunk Train west to Fort Bragg. A depot for the train is within walking distance of the campground, and tickets are available at KOA. The campground, which has a western theme, also offers nightly entertainment in summer. The elevation is 1,377 feet.

Campsites, facilities: There are 21 sites for tents and 50 sites with full or partial hookups (30 and 50 amps) for RVs of any length. Many sites are pull-through. Twelve cabins and two lodges are also available, as are tepees and rental RVs. Groups can be accommodated. Picnic tables and fire rings are provided.

Drinking water, restrooms with flush toilets and showers, Wi-Fi, a playground, seasonal heated swimming pool, mini golf, basketball, volleyball, fishing pond, convenience store, RV supplies, coin laundry, and a dump station are available. Hot tubs are available. Some facilities are wheelchair accessible. Leashed pets are permitted, with certain restrictions.

Reservations, fees: Reservations are accepted at 800/562-8542. RV sites with full hookups are $56–62, RV sites with partial hookups are $50–55, tent sites are $37–42 per night, $3–4 per person per night for more than two people. Teepees are $60 per night, cabins are $70–80 per night, camping lodges are $160–180 per night. Off-season and other discounts available. Monthly rates available off-season. Some credit cards accepted. Open year-round.

Directions: From Willits at the junction of U.S. 101 and Highway 20, turn west on Highway 20 and drive 1.5 miles to the campground on the right at 1600 Highway 20.

Contact: Willits-Ukiah KOA, 707/459-6179, www.willitskoa.com or www.koa.com.

20 CREEKSIDE CABINS AND RV RESORT

Scenic rating: 5

north of Willits

Map 4.1, page 249

The privately operated park is in a pretty valley, primarily oak/bay woodlands with a sprinkling of conifers. It was previously known as Hidden Valley Campground. The most popular nearby recreation option is taking the Skunk Train in Willits for the ride out to the coast at Fort Bragg. There are also two golf courses within six miles. Note that about half of the sites are occupied by long-term renters.

Campsites, facilities: There are 50 sites, including 35 with full or partial hookups (20, 30, 50 amps), for tents or RVs up to 50 feet. Picnic tables and fire grills are provided, and some sites provide satellite TV, telephone, and Wi-Fi access. Restrooms with showers, ice, a coin laundry, and a dump station are available. Some facilities are wheelchair accessible. Leashed pets are permitted.

Reservations, fees: Reservations are accepted. RV sites with full hookups are $45 per night, RV sites with partial hookups are $35 per night, tent sites are $25 per night, $3 per person per night for more than two people. Open year-round.

Directions: From Willits on U.S. 101, drive north for 6.5 miles on U.S. 101 to the campground on the east (right) side of the road.

Contact: Creekside Cabins and RV Resort, 29801 N. Highway 101, Willits, 707/459-2521.

21 POGIE POINT

Scenic rating: 7

on Lake Pillsbury in Mendocino National Forest

Map 4.1, page 249

This camp is set beside Lake Pillsbury in Mendocino National Forest, in the back of a cove at the lake's northwest corner. When the lake is full, this spot is quite pretty. A boat ramp is about a quarter mile to the south, a bonus. The elevation is 1,900 feet. (For more information about Lake Pillsbury, see the Fuller Grove listing in this chapter.)

Campsites, facilities: There are 42 sites for tents or RVs up to 16 feet (no hookups). Picnic tables and fire grills are provided. Drinking water and vault toilets are available. Some facilities are wheelchair-accessible. Leashed pets are permitted.

Reservations, fees: Reservations are not accepted. Sites are $16 per night, $3 per night for each additional vehicle, $1 per pet per night. Open May through October.

Directions: From Ukiah on U.S. 101, drive north to the junction with Highway 20. Turn east (right) on Highway 20 and drive five miles. Turn northwest on East Potter Valley

Road toward Lake Pillsbury. Drive 5.9 miles to the town of Potter Valley. Continue on East Potter Valley Road to Eel River Road. Turn right and drive 15 miles to the Eel River Information Kiosk at Lake Pillsbury. Continue for two miles to the campground access road. Turn right and drive a short distance to the campground.

Contact: Mendocino National Forest, Upper Lake Ranger District, 707/275-2361, www.fs.usda.gov/mendocino; PG&E Land Services, 916/386-5164, www.pge.com/recreation.

22 TROUT CREEK

Scenic rating: 7

near East Van Arsdale Reservoir

Map 4.1, page 249

Relatively few campers know about this spot. Most others looking over this area are setting up shop at nearby Lake Pillsbury to the east. But if you like to watch the water roll by, this could be your port of call since it sits at the confluence of Trout Creek and the Eel River (not far from the East Van Arsdale Reservoir). Boats can be hand-launched. Insider's tip: Nearby in Potter Valley to the south, the East Fork Russian River (Cold Creek) is stocked with trout during the summer. The elevation is 1,500 feet.

Campsites, facilities: There are 15 single sites for tents or RVs up to 30 feet (no hookups), one double site, and three walk-in tent sites. Fire grills and picnic tables are provided. Drinking water and vault toilets are available. Leashed pets are permitted.

Reservations, fees: Reservations are not accepted. Sites are $16 per night, $3 per night for each additional vehicle, $1 per pet per night. Open mid-April through September, weather permitting.

Directions: From Ukiah on U.S. 101, drive north to the junction with Highway 20. Turn east (right) on Highway 20 and drive five miles to East Potter Valley Road (M8/Eel River

Road). Turn northwest on East Potter Valley Road toward Lake Pillsbury and drive 5.9 miles to the town of Potter Valley. Continue on east Potter Valley Road to Eel River Road. Turn right and drive 4.5 miles to the Eel River Bridge. From the bridge, continue two miles to the campground entrance.

Contact: PG&E Land Services, 916/386-5164, www.pge.com/recreation.

23 CASPAR BEACH RV PARK

Scenic rating: 8

near Mendocino

Map 4.1, page 249

This privately operated park has opportunities for beachcombing, kayaking, fishing, abalone and scuba diving, and good lookouts for whale-watching. The park is across the road from the ocean and somewhat wooded, with a small, year-round creek running behind it. The park is about midway between Fort Bragg and Mendocino, with Fort Bragg five miles to the north. Note that some of the sites are filled with long-term renters.

Campsites, facilities: There are 59 sites with full or partial hookups (30 amps) for RVs up to 50 feet, 30 tent sites, and two group tent sites that can accommodate up to 20 people each. Some sites are pull-through. Picnic tables and fire rings are provided. Cable TV, Wi-Fi, restrooms with flush toilets and coin showers, dump station, fish cleaning station, convenience store, firewood, propane, playground, video arcade, video rentals, and a coin laundry are available. Some facilities are wheelchair accessible. Leashed pets are permitted.

Reservations, fees: Reservations are accepted. RV sites with full hookups are $42–50 per night, RV sites with partial hookups are $35 per night, tent sites are $28–32 per night, $3–5 per person per night for more than two people, $2 per pet per night. Group tent sites are $70 per night and $3–5 per person per

night for more than six people. Monthly rates available. Some credit cards accepted. Open year-round.

Directions: From Mendocino on Highway 1, drive north for 3.5 miles to the Point Cabrillo exit. Turn west on Point Cabrillo Drive and continue 0.75 mile to the campground on the left at 14441 Point Cabrillo Drive.

From Fort Bragg on Highway 1, drive south for 4.5 miles to Point Cabrillo Drive (Mile Marker 54.6). Turn right and continue 0.75 mile to the campground.

Contact: Caspar Beach RV Park, 707/964-3306, www.casparbeachrvpark.com.

24 RUSSIAN GULCH STATE PARK

Scenic rating: 9

north of Mendocino near the Pacific Ocean

Map 4.1, page 249

Russian Gulch State Park is set near some of California's most beautiful coastline, but the camp speaks to the woods, not the water, with the campsites set in a wooded canyon. They include some of the prettiest and most secluded drive-in sites available on the Mendocino coast. There is a great hike here, an easy hour-long walk to Russian Gulch Falls, a wispy 36-foot waterfall that cascades into a rock basin. While it's always pretty, it's awesome in late winter. Much of the route is accessible by bicycle, with a bike rack available where the trail narrows and turns to dirt. In addition, there are many more miles of hiking trails and a few miles of trails for cycling. The park covers more than 1,100 acres with about 1.5 miles of ocean frontage, its rugged headlands thrusting into the Pacific. It rivals Point Lobos for coastal beauty. And yet the park is better known for its heavily forested canyon, Russian Gulch Creek Canyon, and a headland that features the Devil's Punchbowl, a 100-foot-wide and 60-foot-deep blowhole where one can look right in and watch the sea surge.

Swim, dive, deep-sea fishing for rockfish, or explore the tidepools on the beach.

Note: This park is on the closure list developed by the California Department of Parks, pending final state budget decisions or the possible transfer of park management to other park agencies or volunteer groups. It is currently open with reduced services.

Campsites, facilities: There are 27 sites for tents or RVs up to 24 feet (no hookups), one hike-in/bike-in site, four equestrian sites, and one group site for up to 40 people. Picnic tables, fire grills, and food lockers are provided. Drinking water, coin showers, and flush toilets are available. A seasonal junior ranger program with nature walks, campfire programs and exhibits is also available. A day-use picnic area, beach access, and recreation hall are nearby. Some facilities are wheelchair-accessible. Leashed pets are permitted in the campground and on some trails.

Reservations, fees: Reservations are not accepted at this time. Call 707/937-5804 to confirm if equestrian sites can be reserved. Individual and equestrian sites are $35 per night, $8 per night for each additional vehicle, hike-in/bike-in site is $5 per night per person, the group site is $140 per night. Open mid-March through October, weather permitting, with a two-night maximum stay for hike-in/bike-in campers.

Directions: From Mendocino, drive two miles north on Highway 1 to the campground entrance on the west side of the highway.

Contact: Russian Gulch State Park, 707/937-4296; Mendocino District, 707/937-5804, www.parks.ca.gov.

25 VAN DAMME STATE PARK

Scenic rating: 10

near Mendocino

Map 4.1, page 249   BEST (

The campsites at Van Damme are extremely popular, usually requiring reservations, but with a bit of planning your reward is a base of operations in a beautiful park with redwoods and a remarkable fern understory. The hike-in site (about 1.75 miles) on Fern Canyon Trail are perfectly situated for those wishing to take one of the most popular hikes in the Mendocino area, with the trail crossing the Little River several times and weaving among old trees. Just across from the entrance to the park is a small but beautiful coastal bay with a pretty beach, ideal for launching sea kayaks. The park covers 1,831 acres. A sidelight is the Pygmy Forest, where mature cone-bearing cypress and pine trees are only six inches to eight feet tall. Another favorite is the Bog Trail, where skunk cabbage grows in abundance, most striking when seen in May and June. Ten miles of trails extend through the Little River's fern-rich canyon, and a paved road is popular with cyclists and joggers. Abalone divers explore the waters off the beach. Kayak tours may be available at the beach parking lot in the summer.

Campsites, facilities: There are 64 sites for tents or RVs up to 35 feet (no hookups), nine primitive environmental sites, one hike-in/bike-in site, and one group campsite for up to 50 people. Picnic tables, food lockers, and fire grills are provided. Drinking water, restrooms with flush toilets and coin showers, Wi-Fi, and a dump station are available. A seasonal junior ranger program with nature walks, campfire programs, and exhibits is also available. A grocery store and propane gas are available nearby. Some facilities are wheelchair-accessible. Leashed pets are permitted at campsites, but not in environmental sites.

Reservations, fees: Reservations are recommended at 800/444-7275 (800/444-PARK) or www.reserveamerica.com ($8 reservation fee). Sites are $35 per night, $8 per night for each additional vehicle, special environmental sites are $25 per night, hike-in/bike-in site is $5 per night per person, group site is $160 per night. Open year-round for family camping; group sites are open mid-March through August only.

Directions: From Mendocino on Highway 1, drive south for three miles to the town of Little River and the park entrance road on the left (east) side of the road.

Contact: Van Damme State Park, 707/937-0851; Mendocino District, 707/937-5804, www.parks.ca.gov.

26 NAVARRO BEACH CAMPGROUND

Scenic rating: 6

near the mouth of the Navarro River in Navarro River Redwoods State Park

Map 4.1, page 249

Navarro Beach is a primitive campground that can bail out drivers stuck for a night without a spot. It is small and open, with no tree cover, set near the ocean and the Navarro River. The camp is just south of the Navarro River Bridge.

Campsites, facilities: There are 10 sites for tents or RVs up to 30 feet (no hookups). Picnic tables and fire grills are provided. Pit toilets are available, but there is no drinking water. Leashed pets are permitted.

Reservations, fees: Reservations are not accepted. Sites are $25 per night, $8 per night for each additional vehicle. Open year-round.

Directions: Drive on U.S. 101 to the turnoff for Highway 128 (two miles north of Cloverdale). Turn west on Highway 128 and drive 55 miles to Highway 1. Turn south on Highway 1 and, almost immediately, take the exit for Navarro Bluffs Road. Drive a short distance on Navarro Bluffs Road to the campground (on the south side of the Navarro River Bridge).

Contact: Navarro River Redwoods State Park, c/o Hendy Woods State Park, 707/895-3141; Mendocino District, 707/937-5804, www. parks.ca.gov.

27 PAUL M. DIMMICK CAMPGROUND

Scenic rating: 7

on the Navarro River in Navarro River Redwoods State Park

Map 4.1, page 249

A pretty grove of second-growth redwood trees and the nearby Navarro River are the highlights of this campground at Navarro River Redwoods State Park. It's a nice spot but, alas, lacks any significant hiking trails that could make it an overall spectacular destination; all the trailheads along Highway 128 turn out to be just little spur routes from the road to the river. That is because the park consists of an 11-mile "redwood tunnel" along the Navarro River in its course to the ocean. The river provides swimming in summer, but is better suited for easy kayaking and canoeing in later winter and early spring.

Campsites, facilities: There are 26 sites for tents or RVs up to 30 feet (no hookups) and trailers up to 24 feet. Picnic tables and fire grills are provided. Pit toilets are available, but there is no drinking water. Leashed pets are permitted.

Reservations, fees: Reservations are not accepted. Sites are $25 per night, $8 per night for each additional vehicle. Open year-round, weather permitting.

Directions: From Cloverdale on U.S. 101, drive north for two miles to Highway 128. Turn west on Highway 128 and drive approximately 50 miles. Look for the signed campground entrance on the left side of the road at Mile Marker 8.

Contact: Navarro River Redwoods State Park, c/o Hendy Woods State Park, 707/895-3141; Mendocino District, 707/987-5804, www. parks.ca.gov.

28 BUSHAY

Scenic rating: 7

at Lake Mendocino

Map 4.1, page 249

Bushay, on the northeast end of Lake Mendocino, is set on a point that provides a pretty southern exposure when the lake is full. The lake is five miles long and one mile wide. It offers fishing for striped bass, largemouth bass, smallmouth bass, crappie, catfish, and bluegill, as well as waterskiing and powerboating. A nearby visitors center features exhibits of local Native American history. The elevation is 750 feet, and the lake covers 1,750 acres and has 15 miles of shoreline. (For more information about Lake Mendocino, see the Chekaka listing in this chapter.)

Campsites, facilities: There are 130 sites for tents or RVs up to 35 feet (no hookups). There are three group sites for 80–120 people. Picnic tables, fire rings, and lantern holders are provided. Drinking water, restrooms with showers and flush toilets, playground (in the adjacent day-use area), group facilities, dump station, and horse staging facilities are available. The boat ramp is two miles from camp near Kyen Campground. Some facilities are wheelchair-accessible. Leashed pets are permitted.

Reservations, fees: Reservations are accepted at 877/444-6777 or www.recreation.gov ($9 reservation fee). Sites are $25–30 per night, group sites are $235 per night. Boat launching is free with a camping pass. Open May through September.

Directions: From Ukiah, drive north on U.S. 101 for five miles to the Highway 20 turnoff. Drive five miles east on Highway 20. Just after crossing the Russian River bridge, turn left (Inlet Road) and drive approximately one mile to the campground.

Contact: U.S. Army Corps of Engineers, Lake Mendocino, 707/467-4200 or 707/462-7581.

29 KYEN

Scenic rating: 7

at Lake Mendocino

Map 4.1, page 249

This camp is on the north shore of Lake Mendocino. With the access road off Highway 20 instead of U.S. 101 (as with Chekaka), Kyen can be overlooked by newcomers. A nearby boat ramp makes it especially attractive. (For more information, see the Bushay and Chekaka listings in this chapter.)

Campsites, facilities: There are 93 sites for tents or RVs up to 30 feet (no hookups). Picnic tables, fire grills, and lantern holders are provided. Restrooms with showers and flush toilets, playground (in the adjacent day-use area), dump station, and boat ramp are available. Some facilities are wheelchair-accessible. Leashed pets are permitted, except in some day-use areas.

Reservations, fees: Reservations are accepted at 877/444-6777 or www.recreation. gov ($9 reservation fee). Sites are $22–30 per night. Boat launching is free with a camping pass. Open year-round with limited winter facilities.

Directions: From Ukiah, drive north on U.S. 101 for five miles to the Highway 20 turnoff. Drive east on Highway 20 to Marina Drive. Turn right and drive 200 yards (past the boat ramp) to the campground.

Contact: U.S. Army Corps of Engineers, Lake Mendocino, 707/462-7581.

30 CHEKAKA

Scenic rating: 7

at Lake Mendocino

Map 4.1, page 249

Lake Mendocino is known for good striped-bass fishing, waterskiing, and boating. Nearby, upstream of the lake, is Potter Valley and the East Fork Russian River (also called Cold Creek), which provides trout fishing in the summer. A boat ramp adjacent to the dam is a bonus. The elevation is 750 feet. This campground sits beside the dam at the south end of Lake Mendocino, and the Kaweyo trailhead is nearby. Insider's tip: A newly installed 18-hole Frisbee-golf course is at the Chekaka overlook.

Campsites, facilities: There are 22 sites for tents or RVs up to 35 feet (no hookups), and one group site for up to 50 people. Picnic tables, lantern hangers, and fire grills are provided. Drinking water, vault toilets, disc golf, a horse staging area, and a playground are available. A boat ramp is nearby. Some facilities are wheelchair-accessible. Leashed pets are permitted.

Reservations, fees: Reservations are accepted at 877/444-6777 or www.recreation.gov ($9 reservation fee). Single sites are $20 per night; the group site is $40 per night. Boat launching is free with a camping pass. Open early April through September.

Directions: From Ukiah, drive north on U.S. 101 to Lake Mendocino Drive. Exit right on Lake Mendocino Drive and continue to the first stoplight. Turn left on North State Street and drive to the next stoplight. Turn right (which will put you back on Lake Mendocino Drive) and drive about two miles to the signed entrance to the campground at Coyote Dam.

Contact: U.S. Army Corps of Engineers, Lake Mendocino, 707/462-7581.

31 MITI BOAT-IN/HIKE-IN

Scenic rating: 7

on Lake Mendocino

Map 4.1, page 249

This is one of several campgrounds on the north end of Lake Mendocino. Boat ramps are at Kyen at the north end of the lake and at Chekaka at the south end of the lake. The north ramp (Marina Drive off Highway 20) is open 24 hours; the south ramp closes at night.

Campsites, facilities: There are 15 boat-in/ hike-in sites for tents only. Picnic tables, fire rings, and lantern holders are provided. Vault toilets are available. No drinking water is available. Garbage must be packed out. Leashed pets are permitted.

Reservations, fees: Reservations are not accepted. Sites are $8 per night, one-time $3 boat launch fee. Open April through September, weather permitting. (Some sites may be flooded in the spring.)

Directions: From Ukiah, drive north on U.S. 101 to the Highway 20 turnoff. For boat-in campers: Drive east on Highway 20 to Marina Drive. Turn right and drive to the north boat ramp of the lake. The campground is approximately one mile by water.

For hike-in campers: Drive five miles east on Highway 20. Just after crossing the Russian River bridge, turn left (Inlet Road) and drive approximately one mile to the Bu-Shay Ranger Station. Park and hike two miles to the campground.

Contact: U.S. Army Corps of Engineers, Lake Mendocino, 707/462-7581.

32 PINE ACRES BLUE LAKES RESORT

Scenic rating: 8

on Upper Blue Lake

Map 4.1, page 249

The Blue Lakes are often overlooked because of their proximity to Clear Lake. These lovely lakes offer good fishing for trout, especially in spring and early summer on Upper Blue Lake. (Note: All boats must be certified mussel-free before launching.) Other fish species are bass, crappie, catfish, and bluegill. With a 5-mph speed limit in place, quiet boating is the rule. Lake frontage sites are available, and other bonuses are a sandy beach and a good swimming area. A lawn area is available for tent camping. Note that the RV sites are spaced very close together.

Campsites, facilities: There are 17 sites with

full or partial hookups (30 amps) for RVs up to 40 feet, a lawn area for dispersed tent camping, six cabins, and four lodge rooms. Two RV sites are pull-through. Picnic tables and barbecues are provided. Restrooms with flush toilets and coin showers, dump station, group facilities, boat rentals, boat launching, moorings, boat ramp, fish-cleaning station, horseshoes, convenience store, fishing supplies, and lake frontage sites are available. Leashed pets are permitted, with certain restrictions.

Reservations, fees: Reservations are recommended. RV sites with full hookups are $38–42 per night, tent sites are $33 per night, $6 per person per night for more than two people, $6 per night for each additional vehicle, $2 per pet per night. Boat launching is free for campers. Two-night minimum on weekends. Some credit cards accepted. Open year-round.

Directions: From Ukiah, drive north on U.S. 101 for five miles to the junction with Highway 20. Turn east on Highway 20 and drive about 13 miles to Irvine Avenue. Turn right on Irvine Avenue and drive one block to the end of the road and Blue Lakes Road. Turn right and drive a short distance to the resort on the right at 5328 Blue Lakes Road.

Contact: Pine Acres Blue Lakes Resort, 707/275-2811, www.bluelakepineacres.com.

33 NARROWS LODGE RESORT

🏊 ⛵ 🚤 🐴 🚐 ⛺

Scenic rating: 8

on Upper Blue Lake

Map 4.1, page 249

One of several campgrounds in the immediate vicinity at Blue Lakes, this is a good fish camp with boat docks and a fish-cleaning station. (Note: All boats must be certified mussel-free before launching.) The Blue Lakes are often overlooked because of their proximity to Clear Lake, but they are a quiet and pretty alternative, with good trout fishing in the spring and early summer, and decent prospects year-

round. The lakes are long and narrow with a primarily forested shoreline, and the elevation is 1,400 feet.

Campsites, facilities: There are 30 sites with full or partial hookups (50 amps) for tents or RVs of any length, three park-model cabins, two cabins, and 14 motel rooms. Picnic tables are provided. Restrooms with flush toilets and showers, dump station, WiFi, recreation room, boat rentals, pier, boat ramp, boat slips, fishing supplies, picnic area, and ice are available. Leashed pets are allowed.

Reservations, fees: Reservations are accepted at 800/476-2776. RV sites with full hookups are $30–35 per night, RV sites with partial hookups and tent sites are $28 per night, $5 per person per night for more than two people, $3 per night for each additional vehicle, $3 per pet per night. Some credit cards accepted. Open year-round.

Directions: From Ukiah, drive north on U.S. 101 for five miles to the junction with Highway 20. Turn east on Highway 20 and drive about 13 miles to Blue Lakes Road. Turn right and drive one mile to the resort (5690 Blue Lakes Road).

Contact: Narrows Lodge Resort, 707/275-2718 or 800/476-2776, www.thenarrowsresort.com.

34 HENDY WOODS STATE PARK

🥾 🚲 🏊 🐴 ♿ 🚐 ⛺

Scenic rating: 7

near Boonville

Map 4.1, page 249

This is a remarkable setting where the flora changes from open valley grasslands and oaks to a cloaked redwood forest with old growth, as if you had waved a magic wand. The campsites are set in the forest, with a great trail routed amid the old redwoods and up to the Hermit Hut (a fallen redwood stump covered with branches), where a hobo lived for 18 years. No, it wasn't me. There are two virgin redwood groves in the park: Big Hendy (80 acres with a self-guided discovery trail available) and Little Hendy (20 acres). The Navarro River runs the park's length, but note that fishing is forbidden in the park and that catch-and-release fishing is the law from the bridge at the park entrance on downstream; check regulations. The park is in the middle of the Anderson Valley wine district, which will at first seem an unlikely place to find an 845-acre redwood park, and is not as cold and foggy as the coastal redwood parks.

Note: This park was on the closure list developed by the California Department of Parks, pending final state budget decisions or the possible transfer of park management to other park agencies or volunteer groups. It is currently operating via a new non-profit donor agreement and reservation information may change.

Campsites, facilities: There are 92 sites for tents or RVs up to 35 feet (no hookups), two hike-in/bike-in sites, and three cabins. Picnic tables, food lockers, and fire grills are provided. Drinking water, flush toilets, coin showers, and a dump station are available. A seasonal junior ranger program with nature walks, campfire programs, and exhibits are also available. A grocery store and propane gas station are available nearby. Some facilities are wheelchair-accessible. Leashed pets are permitted.

Reservations, fees: Reservations are accepted April through late September at 800/444-7275 (800/444-PARK) or www.reserveamerica.com ($8 reservation fee). October through May, sites are first-come, first-served. Sites are $35 per night, $8 per night for each additional vehicle, hike-in/bike-in site is $5 per person per night, a cabin is $50 per night. Open year-round.

Directions: From Cloverdale on U.S. 101, turn northwest on Highway 128 and drive about 35 miles to Philo Greenwood Road. Turn left on Philo Greenwood Road and drive 0.5 mile to the park entrance on the left.

Contact: Hendy Woods State Park, 707/895-3141; Mendocino District, 707/937-5804, www.parks.ca.gov.

35 RED MOUNTAIN

Scenic rating: 3

near Ukiah

Map 4.1, page 249

Like Mayacmus (see listing in this chapter), this camp is set in the Cow Mountain area east of Ukiah. But be forewarned: It is a popular spot for off-highway motorcycles. If you don't like bikes, go to the other camp. Besides motorcycle trails, there are opportunities for hiking and hunting. Horseback riding is an option in the northern part of the recreation area.

Campsites, facilities: There are 11 tent sites. Picnic tables and fire grills are provided. Vault toilets are available, but there is no drinking water. Leashed pets are permitted.

Reservations, fees: Reservations are not accepted. There is no fee for camping. There is a 14-day stay limit. Open year-round, weather permitting.

Directions: From U.S. 101 in Ukiah, turn east on Talmage Road and drive 1.5 miles to Eastside Road. Turn right and drive a short distance to Mill Creek Road. Turn left and drive seven miles to the campground entrance road on the right. Turn right and drive 0.25 mile to the campground.

Contact: Bureau of Land Management, Ukiah Field Office, 707/468-4000, www.blm.gov/ca.

36 MAYACMUS

Scenic rating: 5

near Ukiah

Map 4.1, page 249

This campground is set within the Cow Mountain Recreation Area on the slopes of Cow Mountain, the oft-overlooked wild region east of Ukiah. The primitive area is ideal for hiking and horseback riding. In the fall, it is a popular hunting area as well, for the few who know of it. This section of the recreation area is quiet, with hiking on Mayacmus

Trail providing access to Willow Creek, Mill Creek, and several overlooks of Clear Lake to the south. The flora is chaparral and oak/bay grasslands, and the weather is extremely hot in the summer. By the way, off-highway vehicles frequent the southern part of the recreation area, but are prohibited in this immediate region.

Campsites, facilities: There are six tent sites. Picnic tables and fire grills are provided (sometimes stolen or vandalized). Pit toilets are available. No drinking water is available, but there is water for animals. Garbage must be packed out. Leashed pets are permitted.

Reservations, fees: Reservations are not accepted. There is no fee for camping. Stay limit is 14 days. Open year-round, weather permitting.

Directions: From U.S. 101 in Ukiah, turn east on Talmage Road and drive 1.5 miles to Eastside Road. Turn right and drive 0.25 mile to Mill Creek Road. Turn left and drive three miles (just beyond Mill Creek County Park) to the sign for North Cow Mountain at Mendo Rock Road. Turn left and drive five miles to a Y intersection with the campground access road. Bear left and drive one mile to the campground.

Contact: Bureau of Land Management, Ukiah Field Office, 707/468-4000, www.blm.gov/ca.

37 MANCHESTER BEACH KOA

🏃 🏊 🛶 🐕 🎣 ♿ 🚐 ⛺

Scenic rating: 7

north of Point Arena at Manchester State Beach

Map 4.1, page 249

This is a privately operated KOA park set beside Highway 1 and near the beautiful Manchester State Beach. A great plus here is the cute little log cabins, complete with electric heat. They can provide a great sense of privacy, and after a good sleep, campers are ready to explore the adjacent state park.

Campsites, facilities: There are 57 tent sites

and 43 sites with full or partial hookups (30 and 50 amps) for tents or RVs of any length. There are also two cottages and 27 cabins. Picnic tables, barbecues, and fire rings are provided. Drinking water, restrooms with flush toilets and showers, Wi-Fi, modem access, cable TV, heated seasonal pool, spa, recreation room, playground, dump station, convenience store, group facilities, ice, firewood, coin laundry, and propane gas are available. Some facilities are wheelchair-accessible. Leashed pets are permitted, with certain breeds prohibited; call for details.

Reservations, fees: Reservations are accepted at 800/562-4188. RV sites are $52–63 per night, tent sites are $28–40 per night, $3–5 per person per night for more than two people. Groups of 18 or more can reserve sites for $4–13 per person per night, $3 per pet per night. Hike-in/bike-in sites are $10 per night. Some credit cards accepted. Open year-round.

Directions: From U.S. 101 in Petaluma, take the Washington Street exit. Turn west on Washington Street and drive through Petaluma (Washington Street becomes Bodega Highway) and continue for 17 miles to Highway 1. Continue straight (west) on Highway 1 for eight miles to Bodega Bay. Turn north on Highway 1 and drive 66 miles to Point Arena. Continue north on Highway 1 for about six miles to Kinney Road. Turn west (toward the ocean) and drive one mile to the campground at 44330 Kinney Road.

Contact: Manchester Beach KOA, 707/882-2375, www.manchesterbeachkoa.com.

38 GREEN SPRINGS FAMILY AND EQUESTRIAN CAMP

🏃 🐕 5⁰ 🚐 ⛺

Scenic rating: 7

in Mendocino National Forest

Map 4.2, page 250

Green Springs is a wilderness trailhead camp and staging area, located at the southern border for the Yolla Bolly Wilderness. Green

Springs is not a destination camp, but rather a launch point. From here, you can head north along the ridge into the Yolla Bolly, what is called the Eel Divide: All water running off the slope to the west runs into the Eel River watershed; all water running to the east runs into the Sacramento River watershed. This is a land of little-known peaks, small creeks, and few people. The elevation is 6,000 feet. There is a good swimming hole at nearby Rattlesnake Creek Camp (see listing in this chapter).

Campsites, facilities: There are four primitive sites for tents or small RVs. Picnic tables and fire rings are provided. Vault toilets are available, but there is no drinking water. Water is available from a spring but must be boiled or treated before use. Horse corrals are available on a first-come first-served basis. Garbage must be packed out.

Reservations, fees: Reservations are not accepted. There is no fee for camping.

Directions: From Willits, drive north on U.S. 101 for 13 miles to Longvale and the junction with Highway 162. Turn northeast on Highway 162 and drive to Covelo. Continue east on Highway 162 for nine miles to the Eel River Bridge. Drive across the bridge and turn left on Forest Service (FS) Road M1/Indian Dick Road. Drive about 17 miles on Forest Service Road M1/Indian Dick Road to FS Road M21. Turn right and drive seven miles to FS Road M2. Turn left on FS Road M2 and drive 1.5 miles to the Green Springs Trailhead on the left.

Contact: Mendocino National Forest, Yolla Bolly-Middle Eel Wilderness, 707/983-6118, www.fs.usda.gov/mendocino.

39 THREE PRONG
🏃 🏕 5% 🚐 ⛺

Scenic rating: 6

in Mendocino National Forest

Map 4.2, page 250

Three Prong is a remote and primitive campground. The camp is situated near a large

meadow and you'll have a view of fir and pine trees. It gets little use, except in fall as a base camp for hunters. That's about it. The elevation is 5,800 feet.

Campsites, facilities: There are six sites for tents or small RVs. Picnic tables and fire rings are provided. Vault toilets are available, but there is no drinking water. Garbage must be packed out.

Reservations, fees: Reservations are not accepted. There is no fee for camping. Open June through October, weather permitting.

Directions: From Corning, take County Road A9 west for 20 miles to Paskenta and Forest Road 23N01. Turn west on Forest Road 23N01 and drive to Forest Road 24N13. Turn left on Forest Road 24N13 and drive to the campground.

Contact: Mendocino National Forest, Grindstone Ranger District, 530/934-3316; Paskenta Work Center, 530/833-5544, www.fs.usda.gov/mendocino.

40 KINGSLEY GLADE
🏃 🏕 5% 🚐 ⛺

Scenic rating: 6

in Mendocino National Forest

Map 4.2, page 250

Kingsley Grade is located west of Paskenta and Red Bluff. You know what that means, right? Right—it gets smoking hot out here in summer. Like nearby Sugarfoot to the south, this is primarily a base camp for hunters working the eastern slopes of the Eel Divide in the fall. It is set in the transition zone where oaks give way to pines. The elevation is 4,500 feet.

Campsites, facilities: There are six sites for tents or small RVs. Picnic tables and fire rings are provided. Vault toilets are available, but there is no drinking water. Garbage must be packed out.

Reservations, fees: Reservations are not accepted. There is no fee for camping. Open June through October, weather permitting.

Directions: From Corning, take County Road

A9 west for 20 miles to Paskenta and Forest Road M2/Thomes Road. Turn west on Forest Road M2/Thomes Road (Forest Road 23N01) and drive 18 miles to Forest Road 24N01. Turn left on Forest Road 24N01 and drive 4.3 miles to the campground.

Contact: Mendocino National Forest, Grindstone Ranger District, 530/934-3316; Paskenta Work Station, 530/833-5544, www.fs.usda.gov/mendocino.

41 SUGARFOOT GLADE

Scenic rating: 6

in Mendocino National Forest

Map 4.2, page 250

On the east-facing slopes of the Eel Divide, there are a series of tiny campgrounds sprinkled in national forest land west of Paskenta and the Sacramento Valley. This one is small, primitive, and so remote that it seems to be in the middle of nowhere. Actually, that is perfect in the fall when hunters use it as a base camp. A small seasonal creek runs through the camp amid a landscape of ponderosa pines and oak trees.

Campsites, facilities: There are six sites for tents or small RVs. Picnic tables and fire rings are provided. Vault toilets are available, but there is no drinking water. Garbage must be packed out.

Reservations, fees: Reservations are not accepted. There is no fee for camping. Open mid-May to mid-November.

Directions: From Corning, take County Road A9 west for 20 miles to Paskenta and Forest Road 23N01. Turn west on Forest Road 23N01 and drive to Forest Road 24N01. Turn left on Forest Road 24N01 and drive past Kingsley Glade Campground to Sugarfoot Glade Campground.

Contact: Mendocino National Forest, Grindstone Ranger Center, 530/934-3316; Paskenta Work Center, 530/833-5544, www.fs.usda.gov/mendocino.

42 WHITLOCK

Scenic rating: 4

in Mendocino National Forest

Map 4.2, page 250

This obscure Forest Service camp is often empty or close to it. It is set at 4,300 feet elevation, where conifers have taken over from the valley grasslands to the nearby east. The camp is situated amid good deer range and makes a good hunting base camp in the fall, with a network of Forest Service roads in the area. It is advisable to obtain a Forest Service map.

Campsites, facilities: There are three sites for tents or RVs up to 16 feet (no hookups). Picnic tables, fire rings, and stoves are provided. Vault toilets are available. Drinking water is not available. Garbage must be packed out. Leashed pets are permitted.

Reservations, fees: Reservations are not accepted. There is no fee for camping. Open late May through October.

Directions: From Corning on I-5, turn west onto County Road A9/Corning Road and drive 20 miles to Paskenta and Toomes Camp Road/County Road 122. Turn right (north) on Toomes Camp Road/County Road 122 and drive 14 miles to the campground on the right.

Contact: Mendocino National Forest, 530/934-3316, www.fs.usda.gov/mendocino; Paskenta Work Center, 530/833-5544.

43 WELLS CABIN

Scenic rating: 6

in Mendocino National Forest

Map 4.2, page 250

You'll join the 5 Percent Club when you reach this spot. It is one mile from Anthony Peak Lookout (6,900 feet) where, on a clear day, you can get great views all the way to the Pacific Ocean and sweeping views of the Sacramento Valley to the east. This campground is hardly used during the summer and often provides a cool escape from the heat of the valley. The elevation is 6,300 feet.

Campsites, facilities: There are 25 sites for tents or small RVs up to 16 feet (no hookups). Picnic tables, stoves, and fire rings are provided. Vault toilets are available. Drinking water is not available. Garbage must be packed out. Leashed pets are permitted.

Reservations, fees: Reservations are not accepted. There is no fee for camping. Open late June through October, weather permitting.

Directions: From Corning on I-5, turn west on County Road A9 and drive 20 miles to Paskenta and Forest Road M4. Turn west on Forest Road M4 and drive to the junction with Forest Road 23N16. Turn right (north) and drive three miles to the campground.

Contact: Mendocino National Forest, Grindstone Ranger District; Paskenta Work Center, 530/833-5544, www.fs.usda.gov/mendocino.

44 BUCKHORN

Scenic rating: 5

on Black Butte Lake

Map 4.2, page 250

Black Butte Lake is set in the foothills of the north Sacramento Valley at 500 feet. The bad news: In summer, the lack of trees and shade coupled with very hot weather equal temps capable of hitting 100°F for days on end. The good news: The lake is one of the 10 best lakes in Northern California for crappie, best in spring. There can also be good fishing for largemouth, smallmouth, and spotted bass, channel catfish, bluegill, and sunfish. Recreation options include powerboating, sailboating, and sailboarding. A one-mile-long interpretive trail is available.

Campsites, facilities: There are 87 sites for tents or RVs up to 35 feet (no hookups), five walk-in sites, and a group site for 25–80 people. Picnic tables and fire grills are provided. Drinking water, restrooms with flush toilets and showers, dump station, fish-cleaning station, and a playground are available. A boat ramp is nearby. Some facilities are wheelchair-accessible. Leashed pets are permitted.

Reservations, fees: Reservations are accepted at 877/444-6777 or www.recreation.gov ($9 reservation fee). Individual sites, including walk-in sites, are $16–18 per night. The group site is $120–150 per night. Open year-round.

Directions: From I-5 in Orland, take the Black Butte Lake exit. Drive about 15 miles west on Road 200/Newville Road to Buckhorn Road. Turn left and drive a short distance to the campground on the north shore of the lake.

Contact: Black Butte Lake, U.S. Army Corps of Engineers, 530/865-4781.

45 ORLAND BUTTES

Scenic rating: 5

on Black Butte Lake

Map 4.2, page 250

Black Butte Lake isn't far from I-5, but a lot of campers zoom right by it. The lake has 40 miles of shoreline at 500 feet in elevation. All water sports are allowed. The prime time to visit is in late spring and early summer, when the bass and crappie fishing can be quite good. Three self-guided nature trails are in the immediate area, including Paul Thomas Trail, a short 0.25-mile walk to an overlook. (See the Buckhorn listing for more information.) Note: In late winter and early spring, this area is delightful as spring arrives. But from mid-June through August, expect very hot, dry weather.

Campsites, facilities: There are 35 sites for tents or RVs up to 35 feet (no hookups) and a group site for 15–50 people. Picnic tables and fire grills are provided. Drinking water, flush toilets, showers, boat ramp, fish-cleaning station, disc golf course, and a dump station are available. Leashed pets are permitted.

Reservations, fees: Reservations are accepted at 877/444-6777 or www.recreation.gov ($9 reservation fee). Sites are $15–18 per night, the group site is $100 per night. Open April through early September.

Directions: From I-5 in Orland, take the Black Butte Lake exit. Drive west on Road 200/Newville Road for six miles to Road 206. Turn left and drive three miles to the camp entrance on the right.

Contact: Black Butte Lake, U.S. Army Corps of Engineers, 530/865-4781.

46 MASTERSON GROUP CAMP

Scenic rating: 5

near Plaskett Lakes in Mendocino National Forest

Map 4.2, page 250

This is a group camp only. It is just 0.5 mile away from the Plaskett Lakes, two small lakes of three and four acres set at 6,000 feet and surrounded by a mixed conifer forest. No motors are permitted at either lake, and swimming is not recommended because it is mucky and weedy. It is advisable to obtain a map of Mendocino National Forest, which details nearby streams, lakes, and hiking trails. One notable trail is the Black Butte Trail. (For more information, see the Plaskett Meadows listing.)

Campsites, facilities: This group camp has 20 tent or RV sites (no hookups) for up to 75 people. Fire grills and picnic tables are provided. Drinking water and vault toilets are available. Leashed pets are permitted.

Reservations, fees: Reservations are required at at 877/444-6777 or www.recreation.gov ($9 reservation fee). Sites are $75 per night. Open mid-May through mid-October.

Directions: In Willows on I-5, turn west on Highway 162 and drive toward the town of Elk Creek. Just after crossing the Stony Creek Bridge, turn north on County Road 306 and

drive four miles to Alder Springs Road/Forest Highway 7. Turn left and drive 31 miles to the camp on the right.

Contact: Mendocino National Forest, Grindstone Ranger District, Stonyford Work Center, 530/963-3128, www.fs.usda.gov/mendocino.

47 PLASKETT MEADOWS

Scenic rating: 7

in Mendocino National Forest

Map 4.2, page 250

This is a little-known camp in the mountains near Plaskett Lakes, a pair of connected dot-sized mountain lakes that form the headwaters of little Plaskett Creek. Trout fishing is best at the westernmost of the two lakes. No motors are permitted in the lakes and swimming is not recommended. The camp is set at an elevation of 6,000 feet.

Campsites, facilities: There are 31 sites for tents or RVs up to 26 feet (no hookups). Fire grills and picnic tables are provided. Drinking water and vault toilets are available. Garbage must be packed out. Some facilities are wheelchair-accessible. Leashed pets are permitted.

Reservations, fees: Reservations are not accepted. Sites are $10 per night. Open mid-May through mid-October.

Directions: In Willows on I-5, turn west on Highway 162 and drive toward the town of Elk Creek. Just after crossing the Stony Creek Bridge, turn north on County Road 306 and drive four miles to Alder Springs Road/Forest Highway 7. Turn left and drive 31 miles to the campground on the left.

Contact: Mendocino National Forest, Grindstone Ranger District, 530/934-3316; Stonyford Work Center, 530/963-3128, www.fs.usda.gov/mendocino.

48 ATCHISON CAMP

Scenic rating: 5

in Mendocino National Forest

Map 4.2, page 250

Very few people know about this little spot. Atchison Camp is set at an elevation of 3,900 feet in a remote national forest in an area that is hot and dry all summer long. There is a network of four-wheel-drive roads in the area. Hunters will use this camp as a base in the fall, then drive around in ATVs or pick-ups trucks looking for deer or places to hunt.

Campsites, facilities: There are three sites for tents or small RVs. Picnic tables and fire rings are provided. Vault toilets are available, but there is no drinking water. Garbage must be packed out.

Reservations, fees: Reservations are not accepted. There is no fee for camping.

Directions: In Willows, take Highway 162 west to the town of Elk Creek. Just after crossing the Stony Creek Bridge, turn north on County Road 306 and drive four miles to Alder Springs Road/Forest Highway 7. Turn left (east) onto Alder Springs Road/Forest Highway 7 and drive about 26 miles to the campground.

Contact: Mendocino National Forest, Covelo Ranger District, 707/983-6118, www.fs.usda. gov/mendocino.

49 LOWER NYE

Scenic rating: 8

in Mendocino National Forest

Map 4.2, page 250

This camp is on the northern border of the Snow Mountain Wilderness. It is a good jump-off point for backpackers, or a spot for folks who don't want to be bugged by anybody. It is set at 3,300 feet on Skeleton Creek near the Eel River. It is advisable to obtain a detailed USGS topographic map.

Campsites, facilities: There are six sites for tents or RVs up to 16 feet (no hookups). There are no tables, grills, toilets or drinking water available. Garbage must be packed out. Leashed pets are permitted.

Reservations, fees: Reservations are not accepted. There is no fee for camping. Open May to November, weather permitting.

Directions: From Ukiah on U.S. 101, drive north to the junction of Highway 20. Turn east on Highway 20 and drive to the town of Upper Lake and to Elk Mountain Road. Turn left on Elk Mountain Road (which becomes Forest Road M1) and drive 17 miles to Forest Road M-10/Bear Creek Road. Turn right (dirt road) on Forest Road M-10/Bear Creek Road and drive seven miles to Forest Road 18N04/Rice Creek Road. Turn north on Forest Road 18N04/Rice Creek Road and drive 14 miles to the campground.

Contact: Mendocino National Forest, Upper Lake Ranger District, 707/275-2361, www. fs.usda.gov/mendocino.

50 SUNSET CAMPGROUND

Scenic rating: 7

on Lake Pillsbury in Mendocino National Forest

Map 4.2, page 250

This camp is on the northeast corner of Lake Pillsbury, and Pillsbury Pines boat launch and picnic area are less than a quarter mile to the south. Lakeshore Trail, an adjacent designated nature trail along the shore of the lake here, is accessible to hikers, equestrians, and bicyclists. However, a section of the trail is covered with water when the lake is full. The surrounding national forest offers side-trip possibilities.

Campsites, facilities: There are 54 sites, including 14 double sites, for tents or small-to-medium RVs (no hookups). Picnic tables, stoves, and some fire grills are provided. Drinking water and vault toilets are available. A boat ramp is nearby. Leashed pets are permitted.

Reservations, fees: Reservations are not accepted. Sites are $16 per night, $3 per night for each additional vehicle, $1 per pet per night. Open May through October.

Directions: From Ukiah on U.S. 101, drive north to the junction with Highway 20. Turn east (right) on Highway 20 and drive five miles. Turn northwest on East Potter Valley Road toward Lake Pillsbury. Drive 5.9 miles to the town of Potter Valley. Continue on East Potter Valley Road to Eel River Road. Turn right and drive 15 miles to the Eel River Information Kiosk at Lake Pillsbury. Continue east for 4.1 miles to Lake Pillsbury and the junction with Hall Mountain Road. Turn right and drive three miles to the camp entrance.

Contact: Mendocino National Forest, Upper Lake Ranger District, 707/275-2361, www.fs.usda.gov/mendocino; PG&E Land Services, 916/386-5164, www.pge.com/recreation.

51 OAK FLAT

🏃 🏊 🥤 🛶 🐾 🚐 ⛺

Scenic rating: 6

near Lake Pillsbury in
Mendocino National Forest

Map 4.2, page 250

This primitive camp provides an option if Lake Pillsbury's other camps are full. It is set at 1,850 feet elevation near the north shore of Lake Pillsbury in the heart of Mendocino National Forest. Nearby trails leading into the backcountry are detailed on a Forest Service map.

Campsites, facilities: There are 18 sites for tents or RVs up to 16 feet (no hookups). Picnic tables and fire grills are provided. Drinking water and vault toilets are available. Garbage must be packed out. A campfire permit is required. A boat ramp is at the lake. Leashed pets are permitted.

Reservations, fees: Reservations are not accepted. Sites are $10 per night. Open year-round.

Directions: From Ukiah on U.S. 101, drive north to the junction with Highway 20. Turn

east (right) on Highway 20 and drive five miles to East Potter Valley Road. Turn northwest on East Potter Valley Road toward Lake Pillsbury and drive 5.9 miles to the town of Potter Valley. Continue on East Potter Valley Road to Eel River Road. Turn right and drive 15 miles to the Eel River Information Kiosk at Lake Pillsbury. Continue for four miles around the north end of the lake and look for the camp entrance on the right side of the road.

Contact: Mendocino National Forest, Upper Lake Ranger District, 707/275-2361, www.fs.usda.gov/mendocino.

52 NAVY CAMP

🏃 🏊 🥤 🛶 🍖 🐾 ♿ 🚐 ⛺

Scenic rating: 7

on Lake Pillsbury in
Mendocino National Forest

Map 4.2, page 250

This camp is used primarily as an overflow area, and is usually open on busy weekends and holidays. When Lake Pillsbury is full of water, this is an attractive camp. However, when the lake level is down, as is common in the fall, it can seem as if the camp is on the edge of a dust bowl. The camp is set in the lake's north cove, sheltered from north winds. Although the camp is in a pretty setting, there is little shade and a lot of poison oak.

Campsites, facilities: There are 20 sites for tents or RVs up to 16 feet (no hookups). Picnic tables are provided. Drinking water and vault toilets are available. A boat ramp is nearby at Fuller Grove. Some facilities are wheelchair-accessible. Leashed pets are permitted.

Reservations, fees: Reservations are not accepted. Sites are $16 per night, $3 per night for each additional vehicle, $1 per pet per night. Open Memorial Day weekend through October for overflow camping.

Directions: From Ukiah on U.S. 101, drive north to the junction with Highway 20. Turn east (right) on Highway 20 and drive five miles to East Potter Valley Road. Turn northwest on

East Potter Valley Road toward Lake Pillsbury and drive 5.9 miles to the town of Potter Valley. Continue on East Potter Valley Road to Eel River Road. Turn right and drive 15 miles to the Eel River Information Kiosk at Lake Pillsbury. Continue for four miles around the north end of the lake and look for the campground entrance on the right side of the road. The campground is on the north shore, just west of Oak Flat Camp.

Contact: Mendocino National Forest, Upper Lake Ranger District, 707/275-2361, www.fs.usda.gov/mendocino.

53 FULLER GROVE AND FULLER GROVE GROUP CAMP

Scenic rating: 7

on Lake Pillsbury in Mendocino National Forest

Map 4.2, page 250

This is one of several campgrounds bordering Lake Pillsbury, which, at 2,000 acres, is by far the largest lake in Mendocino National Forest. Set at an elevation of 1,800 feet, Pillsbury is big and pretty when full, with 65 miles of shoreline. It has lakeside camping, good boat ramps, and, in the spring, good fishing for trout, and in the warmer months, for bass. This camp is set along the northwest shore of the lake, with a boat ramp only about a quarter mile away to the north. There are numerous backcountry roads in the area, which provide access to a state game refuge to the north and the Snow Mountain Wilderness to the east.

Campsites, facilities: There are 30 sites for tents or RVs up to 22 feet (no hookups), and a group tent area for up to 60 people. Picnic tables, food lockers, and fire grills are provided. Drinking water and vault toilets are available. A boat ramp is nearby. Leashed pets are permitted.

Reservations, fees: Reservations are not accepted for individual sites but are required for the group site at 916/386-5164. Sites are $16 per night for individual sites, $3 per night for each additional vehicle, $1 per pet per night, and $133 per night for the group site with a two-night minimum stay required. Weekly rates are available. Open May through October.

Directions: From Ukiah on U.S. 101, drive north to the junction with Highway 20. Turn east (right) on Highway 20 and drive five miles to East Potter Valley Road. Turn northwest on East Potter Valley Road toward Lake Pillsbury and drive 5.9 miles to the town of Potter Valley. Continue on East Potter Valley Road to Eel River Road. Turn right and drive 15 miles to the Eel River Information Kiosk at Lake Pillsbury. Continue for 2.2 miles to the campground access road. Turn right and drive 0.25 mile to the campground; the group camp is adjacent to the boat ramp.

Contact: Mendocino National Forest, Upper Lake Ranger District, 707/275-2361, www.fs.usda.gov/mendocino; PG&E Land Services, 916/386-5164.

54 LAKE PILLSBURY RESORT

Scenic rating: 6

on Lake Pillsbury in Mendocino National Forest

Map 4.2, page 250

This is a pretty spot beside the shore of Lake Pillsbury in the heart of Mendocino National Forest. It can be headquarters for a vacation involving boating, fishing, waterskiing, or exploring the surrounding national forest. A boat ramp, small marina, and full facilities make this place a prime attraction in a relatively remote location. This is the only resort on the lake that accepts reservations, and it has some lakefront sites.

Campsites, facilities: There are 39 sites for tents or RVs up to 26 feet (no hookups) and two sites with full hookups (30 amps). Eight cabins are also available. Picnic tables and fire pits are provided. Drinking water, restrooms with flush toilets and coin showers, playground, boat rentals, fuel, boat dock, fishing supplies, and small marina are available. Leashed pets are permitted.

Reservations, fees: Reservations are recommended. RV sites with full hookups are $50 per night, tent sites are $26 per night, $7 per person per night for more than two people, $7 per night for each additional vehicle, $9 per pet per night. Boat launching is $7 per day. Weekly rates available. Some credit cards accepted. Open May through October.

Directions: From Ukiah on U.S. 101, drive north to the junction with Highway 20. Turn east (right) on Highway 20 and drive five miles to East Potter Valley Road (toward Lake Pillsbury). Turn left (northwest) on East Potter Valley Road and drive 5.9 miles to the town of Potter Valley. Continue on East Potter Valley Road to Eel River Road. Turn right and drive 11 miles (unpaved road) to the stop sign. Turn right (still Eel River Road) and drive 0.2 mile to Kapranos Road. Turn left and drive about 1.5 miles to the resort at 2756 Kapranos Road.

Contact: Lake Pillsbury Resort, 707/743-9935, www.lprandm.com.

55 NORTH FORK
🚶 🐕 ⛺

Scenic rating: 2

on Stony Creek in Mendocino National Forest
Map 4.2, page 250

This primitive camp is set at 1,700 feet elevation at the confluence of the north, south, and middle forks of Stony Creek. There are many trailheads for hiking in the area, within a few miles of the Snow Mountain Wilderness, but none at this camp. There are great views of St. John Mountain and Snow Mountain. (See the Mill Creek listing in this chapter for additional information.) OHV use is available from camp.

Campsites, facilities: There are 10 tent sites. Picnic tables and stoves are provided. Vault toilets are available. No drinking water is available. Garbage must be packed out. Leashed pets are permitted.

Reservations, fees: Reservations are not accepted. Sites are $5 per night. Open May through October.

Directions: From I-5 at Maxwell, turn west on Maxwell-Sites Road and drive to Sites. Turn left on Sites-Lodoga Road and continue to Lodoga and Lodoga-Stonyford Road. Turn right on Lodoga-Stonyford Road and loop around East Park Reservoir to reach Stonyford and Fouts Springs Road. Turn west on Fouts Springs Road/Forest Road M10 and drive about nine miles to Forest Road 18N03. Turn right on Forest Road 18N03 and drive two miles to the campground on the right.

Contact: Mendocino National Forest, Grindstone Ranger District, Stonyford Work Center, 530/963-3128, www.fs.usda.gov/mendocino.

56 FOUTS AND SOUTH FORK
🚶 🐕 🚶 ♿ 🚐 ⛺

Scenic rating: 1

on Stony Creek in Mendocino National Forest
Map 4.2, page 250

These two adjoining camps are in a designated off-highway-vehicle (OHV) area and are used primarily by dirt bikers. So if you're looking for quiet, these camps are not for you. Several OHV trails are nearby—North Fork, South Fork, and Mill Creek—and campers can ride their OHVs directly out of camp. To the west is the Snow Mountain Wilderness and excellent hiking trails; to the south is an extensive Forest Service road and OHV trail network. The elevation is 1,700 feet.

Campsites, facilities: There are nine sites for tents or RVs up to 16 feet at Fouts (no hookups); there are several dispersed sites at South Fork. Picnic tables and fire grills are provided. Vault toilets are available, but there is no drinking water. Garbage must be packed out. Some facilities are wheelchair-accessible. Leashed pets are permitted.

Reservations, fees: Reservations are not accepted. Sites are $5 per night. Open year-round, although trails may be closed during wet weather.

Directions: From I-5 at Maxwell, turn west on Maxwell-Sites Road and drive to Sites. Turn left on Sites-Lodoga Road and continue to Lodoga. Turn right on Lodoga-Stonyford Road and loop around East Park Reservoir to reach Stonyford. From Stonyford, turn west on Fouts Springs Road/County Road M10 and drive about eight miles. Turn right (north) on Forest Road 18N03 and drive one mile to the campgrounds on your right.

Contact: Mendocino National Forest, Grindstone Ranger District, 530/934-3316; Stonyford Work Center, 530/963-3128, www.fs.usda.gov/mendocino.

57 GRAY PINE GROUP CAMP

Scenic rating: 1

in Mendocino National Forest

Map 4.2, page 250

Similar to Fouts Campground, Gray Pine is set in a forest area with many OHV trails nearby. It is near (but not on) Stony Creek. (See the Fouts and South Fork listing for additional information.)

Campsites, facilities: There is one group site for tents or RVs up to 26 feet (no hookups) that can accommodate up to 75 people. Picnic tables and fire rings are provided. Drinking water, vault toilets, and a group barbecue grill are available. Leashed pets are permitted.

Reservations, fees: Reservations are required at 877/444-6777 or www.recreation.gov ($9 reservation fee). The fee is $75 per night. Open year-round, weather permitting.

Directions: From I-5 at Maxwell, turn west on Maxwell-Sites Road and drive to Sites. Turn left on Sites-Lodoga Road and continue to Lodoga. Turn right on Lodoga-Stonyford Road and loop around East Park Reservoir to reach Stonyford. From Stonyford, turn west on Fouts Springs Road/County Road M10 and drive about nine miles. Turn right on Forest Road 18N03 and drive less than a mile to the campground on your right.

Contact: Mendocino National Forest, Grindstone Ranger District, 530/934-3316; Stonyford Work Center, 530/963-3128, www.fs.usda.gov/mendocino.

58 DAVIS FLAT

Scenic rating: 1

in Mendocino National Forest

Map 4.2, page 250

Davis Flat is across the road from Fouts and South Fork campgrounds. All three campgrounds are in a designated off-highway-vehicle area, so expect OHVers, especially in the winter; campers are allowed to ride their OHVs from the campground. This isn't the quietest camp around, but there is some good hiking in the area to the immediate west in the Snow Mountain Wilderness. The elevation is 1,700 feet.

Campsites, facilities: There is dispersed camping for tents or RVs of any length (no hookups). Twenty picnic tables and fire grills are provided. Vault toilets are available, but there is no drinking water. Garbage must be packed out. Some facilities are wheelchair-accessible. Leashed pets are permitted.

Reservations, fees: Reservations are not accepted. Sites are $5 per night. Open year-round, weather permitting.

Directions: From I-5 at Maxwell, turn west on Maxwell-Sites Road and drive to Sites. Turn left on Sites-Lodoga Road and continue to Lodoga. Turn right on Lodoga-Stonyford

Road and loop around East Park Reservoir to reach Stonyford. From Stonyford, turn west on Fouts Springs Road/County Road M10 and drive about nine miles to Forest Road 18N03. Turn right and drive one mile to the campground on your left.

Contact: Mendocino National Forest, Grindstone Ranger District, 530/934-3316, Stonyford Work Center, 530/963-3128, www.fs.usda.gov/mendocino.

59 MILL CREEK

Scenic rating: 3

in Mendocino National Forest

Map 4.2, page 250

This campground is set beside Mill Creek near Fouts Springs at the southeastern boundary of the Snow Mountain Wilderness. A nearby trailhead, a mile to the west, provides a hiking route into the wilderness that connects along Trout Creek, a great little romp. Mill Creek is quite pretty in the late spring, but by late summer the flow drops way down. The elevation is 1,700 feet. Expect heavy off-highway-vehicle use from October through May. Fouts Springs/Davis Flat is an OHV staging area. OHV riders are allowed to ride from camp.

Campsites, facilities: There are six tent sites. Picnic tables and fire rings are provided. Vault toilets are available. No drinking water is available. Garbage must be packed out. Leashed pets are permitted.

Reservations, fees: Reservations are not accepted. Sites are $5 per night. Open year-round, weather permitting.

Directions: From I-5 at Maxwell, turn west on Maxwell-Sites Road and drive to Sites. Turn left on Sites-Lodoga Road and continue to Lodoga. Turn right on Lodoga-Stonyford Road and loop around East Park Reservoir to reach Stonyford. From Stonyford, turn west on Fouts Springs Road/Forest Road M10

and drive about 8.5 miles to the campground entrance on the right.

Contact: Mendocino National Forest, Grindstone Ranger District, Stonyford Work Center, 530/963-3128, www.fs.usda.gov/mendocino.

60 DIXIE GLADE HORSE CAMP

Scenic rating: 6

near the Snow Mountain Wilderness in Mendocino National Forest

Map 4.2, page 250

Got a horse who likes to tromp? No? Then take a pass on this one. Yes? Then sign right up, because this is a trailhead camp for people preparing to head north by horseback into the adjacent Snow Mountain Wilderness.

Campsites, facilities: There are seven sites for tents or RVs up to 26 feet (no hookups). Picnic tables and fire grills are provided. Vault toilets are available. No drinking water is available. Garbage must be packed out. A horse corral and hitching rack are available. Water in horse troughs is usually available; check current status. Leashed pets are permitted.

Reservations, fees: Reservations are not accepted. Sites are $5 per night. Open April through November, weather permitting.

Directions: From I-5 at Maxwell, turn west on Maxwell-Sites Road and drive to Sites and Sites-Lodoga Road. Turn left on Sites-Lodoga Road and continue to Lodoga and Lodoga-Stonyford Road. Turn right on Lodoga-Stonyford Road and loop around East Park Reservoir to reach Stonyford and Fouts Springs Road. Turn west on Fouts Springs Road/County Road M10 and drive 13 miles to the camp on the right side of the road.

Contact: Mendocino National Forest, Grindstone Ranger District, 530/934-3316; Stonyford Work Center, 530/963-3128, www.fs.usda.gov/mendocino.

61 BEAR CREEK CAMPGROUND

Scenic rating: 7

in Mendocino National Forest

Map 4.2, page 250

This campground is a primitive spot out in the boondocks of Mendocino National Forest, set at 2,000 feet elevation. It's a pretty spot, too, set beside Bear Creek near its confluence with Blue Slides Creek. Trout fishing can be good here. It's about a 10-minute drive to Summit Springs trailhead at the southern end of the Snow Mountain Wilderness. There are also numerous OHV roads in this region.

Campsites, facilities: There are 16 sites for tents or RVs up to 22 feet (no hookups). Picnic tables and fire grills are provided. Vault toilets are available. No drinking water is available. Garbage must be packed out. Leashed pets are permitted.

Reservations, fees: Reservations are not accepted. There is no fee for camping. Open year-round, weather permitting, but the camp closes when the creek is too high to ford.

Directions: From Ukiah on U.S. 101, drive north to the junction with Highway 20 at Calpella. Turn east on Highway 20 and drive to the town of Upper Lake and Mendenhall Avenue. Turn left on Mendenhall Avenue (which becomes Forest Road M1) and drive one mile to the stop sign and Forest Road M-1/ Elk Mountain Road. Bear left on Forest Road M-1/Elk Mountain Road and drive 16 miles (the latter stretch is extremely twisty) to Forest Road M-10. Turn right (east) and drive eight miles to the campground entrance road on the left. Turn left and continue 0.5 mile to the camp. Note: Approximately five miles along Forest Road M-10, the Rice Fork of the Eel River must be forded. Access can be dangerous and sometimes impossible when the water is high; call for road conditions. High-clearance vehicles are recommended.

Contact: Mendocino National Forest, Upper Lake Ranger District, 707/275-2361, www.fs.usda.gov/mendocino.

62 MILL VALLEY

Scenic rating: 5

near Letts Lake in Mendocino National Forest

Map 4.2, page 250

This camp is set beside Lily Pond, a little, teeny guy, with larger Letts Lake just a mile away. Since Lily Pond does not have trout and Letts Lake does, this camp gets far less traffic than its counterpart. The area is crisscrossed with numerous creeks, OHV routes, and Forest Service roads, making it a great adventure for owners of four-wheel drives who are allowed to drive their OHVs from the campground. The elevation is 4,200 feet.

Campsites, facilities: There are 15 sites for tents or RVs up to 18 feet (no hookups). Picnic tables and fire stoves are provided. Vault toilets and drinking water are available. Garbage must be packed out. Leashed pets are permitted.

Reservations, fees: Reservations are not accepted. Sites are $10 per night. Open mid-May through November, weather permitting.

Directions: From I-5 at Maxwell, turn west on Maxwell-Sites Road and drive to Sites and Sites-Lodoga Road. Turn left on Sites-Lodoga Road and continue to Lodoga and Lodoga-Stonyford Road. Turn right on Lodoga-Stonyford Road and loop around East Park Reservoir to reach Stonyford and Fouts Springs Road. Turn west on Fouts Springs Road/County Road M10 and drive about 16 miles into national forest (where the road becomes Forest Service 17N02) to the camp access road on the left. Turn left and drive 0.25 mile to the camp.

Contact: Mendocino National Forest, Grindstone Ranger District, 530/934-3316; Stonyford Work Center, 530/963-3128, www.fs.usda.gov/mendocino.

63 LETTS LAKE COMPLEX

Scenic rating: 9

in Mendocino National Forest

Map 4.2, page 250

An increasingly popular spot is Letts Lake, a 35-acre, spring-fed lake set in a mixed conifer forest at 4,500 feet just south of the Snow Mountain Wilderness. There are four main loops, each with a separate campground: Main, Stirrup, Saddle, and Spillway. The complex is set on the east side of the lake. No motors are allowed at Letts Lake, making it ideal for canoes, rafts, and float tubes. Swimming is allowed, although the shoreline is rocky. This lake is stocked with rainbow trout in early summer and is known also for black bass. It's a designated historical landmark, the site where the homesteaders known as the Letts brothers were murdered. While that may not impress you, the views to the north of the Snow Mountain Wilderness will. In addition, there are several natural springs that can be fun to hunt up. By the way, after such a long drive to get here, don't let your eagerness cause you to stop at Lily Pond (on the left, one mile before reaching Letts Lake), because there are no trout in it.

Campsites, facilities: There are four campgrounds with 42 sites for tents or RVs up to 24 feet (no hookups). Picnic tables and fire rings are provided. Drinking water and vault toilets are available. A picnic area is nearby. Some facilities, including a fishing pier, are wheelchair-accessible. Leashed pets are permitted.

Reservations, fees: Reservations are not accepted. Sites are $12 per night and there is a 14-day limit. Open May through October.

Directions: From I-5 at Maxwell, turn west on Maxwell-Sites Road and drive to Sites and Sites-Lodoga Road. Turn left on Sites-Lodoga Road and continue to Lodoga and Lodoga-Stonyford Road. Turn right on Lodoga-Stonyford Road and loop around East Park Reservoir to reach Stonyford and Fouts Springs Road. Turn west on Fouts Springs Road/County Road M10 and drive about 18 miles into national forest (where the road becomes Forest Service 17N02) to the campground on the east side of Letts Lake.

Contact: Mendocino National Forest, Grindstone Ranger District, Stonyford Work Center, 530/963-3128, www.fs.usda.gov/mendocino.

64 OLD MILL

Scenic rating: 5

near Mill Creek in Mendocino National Forest

Map 4.2, page 250

Little known and little used, this camp is set at 3,700 feet amid a mature stand of pine and fir on Trough Spring Ridge. It's at the site of—guess what?—an old mill. Expect some OHV company as drivers of OHVs are allowed to ride from camp.

Campsites, facilities: There are 10 sites for tents or RVs up to 16 feet (no hookups). Note that the access road is poor for RVs. Picnic tables and fire rings are provided. Vault toilets are available. No drinking water is available. Garbage must be packed out. Leashed pets are permitted.

Reservations, fees: Reservations are not accepted. There is no fee for camping. Open May through October.

Directions: From I-5 at Maxwell, turn west on Maxwell-Sites Road and drive to Sites and Sites-Lodoga Road. Turn left on Sites-Lodoga Road and continue to Lodoga and Lodoga-Stonyford Road. Turn right on Lodoga-Stonyford Road and loop around East Park Reservoir to reach Stonyford and Fouts Springs Road. Turn west on Fouts Springs Road/County Road M10 and drive about six miles to Forest Road M5. Turn left on Forest Road M5/Trough Springs Road and drive 7.5 miles on a narrow road to the campground on your right. (The access road is not recommended for RVs.)

Contact: Mendocino National Forest, Grindstone Ranger District, Stonyford Work Center, 530/963-3128, www.fs.usda.gov/mendocino.

65 DEER VALLEY CAMPGROUND

Scenic rating: 4

in Mendocino National Forest

Map 4.2, page 250

This one is way out there. It is used primarily in summer by OHV enthusiasts and in the fall by deer hunters. It is set at 3,700 feet in Deer Valley, about five miles from the East Fork of Middle Creek.

Campsites, facilities: There are 13 sites for tents or RVs up to 16 feet (no hookups). Picnic tables and fire grills are provided. Vault toilets are available. No drinking water is available. Garbage must be packed out. Leashed pets are permitted.

Reservations, fees: Reservations are not accepted. Sites are $6 per night. Open April through October, weather permitting.

Directions: From Ukiah on U.S. 101, drive north to the junction with Highway 20. Turn east on Highway 20 and drive to the town of Upper Lake and Mendenhall Avenue. Turn left on Mendenhall Avenue (which becomes Forest Road M1) and drive 17 miles (the latter stretch is extremely twisty) to Forest Road 16N01. Turn right on Forest Road 16N01 and drive about four miles to the campground.

Contact: Mendocino National Forest, Upper Lake Ranger District, 707/275-2361, www.fs.usda.gov/mendocino.

66 CEDAR CAMP

Scenic rating: 6

in Mendocino National Forest

Map 4.2, page 250

This camp is set at 4,300 feet elevation, just below Goat Mountain (6,121 feet) to the west about a mile away. Why did anybody decide to build a campground way out here? Because a small spring starts nearby, creating a trickle that runs into the nearby headwaters of Little Stony Creek.

Campsites, facilities: There are five sites for tents or RVs up to 16 feet (no hookups). Note that the access road is poor for trailers. Picnic tables and fire grills are provided. A vault toilet is available. No drinking water is available. Garbage must be packed out. Leashed pets are permitted.

Reservations, fees: Reservations are not accepted. There is no fee for camping. Open May to November, weather permitting.

Directions: From I-5 at Maxwell, turn west on Maxwell-Sites Road and drive to Sites and Sites-Lodoga Road. Turn left on Sites-Lodoga Road and continue to Lodoga and Lodoga-Stonyford Road. Turn right on Lodoga-Stonyford Road and loop around East Park Reservoir to reach Stonyford and Fouts Springs Road. Turn west on Fouts Springs Road/County Road M10 and drive about six miles to County Road M5. Turn left on County Road M5 (Trough Springs Road) and drive 13 miles to the campground on your right.

Contact: Mendocino National Forest, Grindstone Ranger District, Stonyford Work Center, 530/963-3128, www.fs.usda.gov/mendocino.

67 LITTLE STONY CAMPGROUND

Scenic rating: 7

on Little Stony Creek in Mendocino National Forest

Map 4.2, page 250

This pretty spot is set in Little Stony Canyon, beside Little Stony Creek at 1,500 feet. Very few people know of the place, and you will find it is appropriately named: It is little, it is stony, and the little trout amid the stones fit right in. The camp provides streamside access and, with Goat Mountain Road running along most of the stream, it is easy to fish much of this creek in an evening. Expect heavy OHV use from fall through spring.

Campsites, facilities: There are eight sites for tents or RVs up to 16 feet (no hookups). Picnic tables and fire grills are provided. Vault toilets are available. No drinking water is available. Garbage must be packed out. A day-use area is nearby. Leashed pets are permitted.

Reservations, fees: Reservations are not accepted. Sites are $5 per night. Open year-round.

Directions: From I-5 at Maxwell, turn west on Maxwell-Sites Road and drive to Sites. Turn left on Sites-Lodoga Road and continue to where the road crosses Stony Creek. Just after the bridge, turn left on Goat Mountain Road and drive four miles (a rough county road) to the campground on the left.

Contact: Mendocino National Forest, Grindstone Ranger District, 530/934-3316; Stonyford Work Center, 530/963-3128, www. fs.usda.gov/mendocino.

68 MIDDLE CREEK CAMPGROUND

Scenic rating: 6

in Mendocino National Forest

Map 4.2, page 250

Middle Creek campground—some call it CC Camp—is not widely known, but it's known well enough as an off-highway-vehicle staging area. An easy track for beginners on dirt bikes and OHVs is located here. The camp is set at 2,000 feet at the confluence of the West and East Forks of Middle Creek.

Campsites, facilities: There are 23 sites, including two double sites, for tents or RVs up to 30 feet (no hookups). Picnic tables and fire grills are provided. Drinking water and vault toilets are available. Leashed pets are permitted.

Reservations, fees: Reservations are not accepted. Sites are $8 per night, $12 per night for a double site, and $2 per night for each additional vehicle. Open year-round.

Directions: From Ukiah on U.S. 101, drive north to the junction with Highway 20. Turn east on Highway 20 and drive to the town of Upper Lake and Mendenhall Avenue. Turn left on Mendenhall Avenue (which becomes Forest Road M1) and drive eight miles to the camp on the right side of the road.

Contact: Mendocino National Forest, Upper Lake Ranger District, 707/275-2361, www. fs.usda.gov/mendocino.

69 KELLY'S FAMILY KAMPGROUND AND RV PARK

Scenic rating: 6

on Scotts Creek near Clear Lake

Map 4.2, page 250

This privately operated park is set beside Scotts Creek, within short driving range of Blue Lakes to the north on Highway 20 and the north end of Clear Lake to the south. The staff is friendly here, and the owner has been running the place for more than 30 years. A bonus is a 1.5-acre pond that can be used for swimming. Fishing is available 1.5 miles away at Blue Lakes. Note: All boats must be certified mussel-free before launching.

Campsites, facilities: There are 48 sites for tents or RVs up to 40 feet, many with partial hookups (30 amps). Picnic tables, fire pits, and barbecues are provided. Restrooms with flush toilets and coin showers, dump station, coin laundry, ice, volleyball, basketball, horseshoes, and a small camp store are available. Leashed pets are permitted.

Reservations, fees: Reservations are accepted. Sites are $25–31 per night, $6 per each additional person, $3 per night for each additional vehicle, $2 per pet per night. Open April through October.

Directions: From Ukiah on U.S. 101, drive north to the junction with Highway 20. Turn east and drive 14 miles (five miles from Upper Lake) to Scotts Valley Road. Turn right (south) and drive 1.5 miles to the park on the left (at 8220 Scotts Valley Road).

Contact: Kelly's Family Kampground and RV Park, 707/263-5754.

70 CLEAR LAKE STATE PARK

Scenic rating: 9

in Kelseyville at Clear Lake

Map 4.2, page 250

If you have fallen in love with Clear Lake and its surrounding oak woodlands, it is difficult to find a better spot than at Clear Lake State Park. It is set on the western shore of Clear Lake, and though the oak woodlands flora means you can seem quite close to your camping neighbors, the proximity to quality boating, water sports, and fishing makes the lack of privacy worth it. Reservations are a necessity in summer. That stands to reason, with excellent bass fishing from boats beside a tule-lined shoreline near the park and good catfishing in the sloughs that run through the park. Some campsites have water frontage. The elevation is 1,500 feet. Clear Lake is the largest natural freshwater lake within California state borders, and it has 150 miles of shoreline. Despite its name, the lake is not clear but green, and in late summer, rather soupy with algae and water grass in certain areas. The high nutrients in the lake give rise to a flourishing aquatic food chain. With that comes the highest number of large bass of any lake in Northern California. A few short hiking trails are also available at the park. The self-guided Indian Nature Trail passes through the site of what was once a Pomo village. Rangers here are friendly, helpful, and provide reliable fishing information. Junior ranger programs and guided walks for bird and flower identification are also available. Note: All boats must be certified mussel-free before launching.

Campsites, facilities: There are 147 sites for tents or RVs up to 35 feet (no hookups), two group sites for up to 40 people each, and two hike-in/bike-in sites. Eight cabins are also available. Picnic tables and fire rings are provided. Drinking water, restrooms with coin showers and flush toilets, and a dump station are available. A boat ramp, dock, fish-cleaning stations, boat battery charging station, visitors center, Wi-Fi, and swimming beach are nearby. A grocery store, coin laundry, propane gas, restaurant, and gas station are available within three miles. Some facilities, including the boat ramp, are wheelchair-accessible. Leashed pets are permitted in the campgrounds.

Reservations, fees: Reservations are accepted at 800/444-7275 (800/444-PARK) or www.reserveamerica.com ($8 reservation fee). Drive-in sites at Cole Creek are $30 per night, drive-in sites at Kelsey Creek are $30 per night, premium sites at Lakeview are $35 per night, premium sites at Kelsey Creek and Lakeside are $45 per night, $5 per night for each additional vehicle, $75 per night for group sites, and hike-in/bike-in sites are $5 per person per night. Boat launching is $5 per day. Open year-round.

Directions: From Vallejo, drive north on Highway 29 to Lower Lake. Turn left on Highway 29 and drive seven miles to Soda Bay Road. Turn right on Soda Bay Road and drive 11 miles to the park entrance on the right side of the road.

From Kelseyville on Highway 29, take the Kelseyville exit and turn north on Main Street. Drive a short distance to State Street. Turn right and drive 0.25 mile to Gaddy Lane. Turn right on Gaddy Lane and drive about two miles to Soda Bay Road. Turn right and drive one mile to the park entrance on the left.

Contact: Clear Lake State Park, 707/279-4293 or 707/279-2267, www.parks.ca.gov.

71 GLENHAVEN BEACH CAMP AND MARINA

Scenic rating: 6

on Clear Lake

Map 4.2, page 250

This makes a good base camp for boaters, water-skiers, and anglers. It is set on a peninsula on the eastern shore of Clear Lake, with nearby Indian Beach providing a good recreation and water-play spot. In addition, it is a short boat ride out to Anderson Island, Weekend Island, and Buckingham Point, where bass fishing can be excellent along shaded tules. Note that in addition to the campsites listed, there are another 22 sites occupied by long-term or permanent renters. Note: All boats must be certified mussel-free before launching.

Campsites, facilities: There are 15 sites with full or partial hookups (30 amps) for RVs up to 35 feet and tents. Picnic tables and fire rings are provided. Drinking water, restrooms with showers and flush toilets, marina with gas, pier, mooring, convenience store, bait and tackle, boat ramp, boat and personal watercraft rentals, WiFi, and recreation room are available. A boat ramp and boat rentals are nearby. Some facilities are wheelchair accessible. Leashed pets are permitted.

Reservations, fees: Reservations are accepted. RV sites with partial hookups are $35 per night, tent sites are $25–35 per night, $5 per person per night for more than two people. Some credit cards accepted. Open year-round.

Directions: From north of Ukiah on U.S. 101 (or I-5 at Williams), turn on Highway 20 and drive to Clear Lake and the town of Glenhaven (four miles northwest of Clearlake Oaks). In Glenhaven, continue on Highway 20 to the camp (lakeside) at 9625 East Highway 20.

Contact: Glenhaven Beach Camp and Marina, 707/701-6000, www.glenhavenbeach.net.

72 BLUE OAK

Scenic rating: 7

at Indian Valley Reservoir

Map 4.2, page 250

Indian Valley Reservoir is kind of like an ugly dog that you love more than anything because inside beats a heart that will never betray you. The camp is out in the middle of nowhere in oak woodlands, about a mile from the dam. It is primitive and little known. For many, that kind of isolation is perfect. The lake has 41 miles of shoreline, is long and narrow, and is set at 1,500 feet elevation. The boat speed limit is 10 mph. While there are good trails nearby, it is the outstanding fishing for bass, bluegill, and some kokanee salmon at the lake every spring and early summer that is the key reason to make the trip. In addition, in the spring, there is a great variety of wildflowers in and around the campground. A detailed map is available from the BLM. Note: All boats must be certified mussel-free before launching. Inspections are not available at the reservoir; they are instead available at Clear Lake.

Campsites, facilities: There are six sites for tents or RVs up to 20 feet (no hookups). Picnic tables and fire grills are provided. Vault toilets are available, but there is no drinking water. Leashed pets are permitted.

Reservations, fees: Reservations are not accepted. There is no fee for camping. There is a 14-day stay limit. Open year-round, weather permitting.

Directions: From Williams on I-5, turn west on Highway 20 and drive 25 miles into the foothills to Walker Ridge Road. Turn north (right) on Walker Ridge Road (a dirt road) and drive north for about four miles to a "major" intersection of two dirt roads. Turn left and drive about 2.5 miles toward the Indian Valley Dam. The Blue Oak campground is just off the road on the right, about 1.5 miles from Indian Valley Reservoir.

Contact: Bureau of Land Management, Ukiah Field Office, 707/468-4000, www.blm.gov/ca; Yolo County Flood Control, 530/662-0265.

73 INDIAN VALLEY CAMPGROUND

🏊 🚤 🏄 🐾 🚐 ⛺

Scenic rating: 7

at Indian Valley Reservoir

Map 4.2, page 250

Of the lakes nestled in the foothills of the western Sacramento Valley, Indian Valley Reservoir is the most remote and often provides the best fishing. The drive in is long and slow, especially if you are towing a boat. In recent years, trolling for kokanee salmon has been excellent. In the spring, bass fishing can be better than at Clear Lake (to the west), with tons of submerged trees providing good structure. Lake draw-downs are a frequent problem from mid-summer to fall, and there have been several fires in the wilderness near the lake. Note: All boats must be certified mussel-free before launching. Inspections are not available at the reservoir; they are instead available at Clear Lake.

Campsites, facilities: There are 20 sites for tents and small RVs. Picnic tables and fire rings are provided. Drinking water and flush toilets are available. Leashed pets are permitted.

Reservations, fees: Reservations are not accepted. Sites are $13 per vehicle per night.

Directions: In Williams, take Highway 20 west for 15 miles to Walker Ridge Road. Turn north (right) on Walker Ridge Road (a dirt road) and continue north for about four miles to a "major" intersection of two dirt roads. Turn left and drive about five miles to the campground at the dam.

Contact: Yolo County Flood Control, 530/662-0265, www.ycfcwcd.org.

74 MANCHESTER STATE PARK

🚶 🚤 🏄 🚐 ⛺

Scenic rating: 8

near Point Arena

Map 4.3, page 251

Manchester State Park is a beautiful park on the Sonoma coast, set near the Garcia River with the town of Point Arena to the nearby north providing a supply point. If you hit it during one of the rare times when the skies are clear and the wind is down, the entire area will seem aglow in magical sunbeams. The park features 760 acres of beach, sand dunes, and grasslands, with 18,000 feet of ocean frontage and five miles of gentle sandy beach stretching southward toward the Point Arena Lighthouse. The curved beach catches a large amount of driftwood and other debris. Alder Creek Trail is a great hike, routed north along beachfront to the mouth of Alder Creek and its beautiful coastal lagoon. This is where the San Andreas Fault heads off from land into the sea. In winter, the main attraction is steelhead fishing in the Garcia River. Spring and early summer see a variety of coastal wildflowers. The park provides habitat for tundra swans. The region near the park is grazing land for sheep and cattle. Sixteen campsites were closed in 2004 to protect an endangered species, the Point Arena mountain beaver.

Note: This park was on the closure list developed by the California Department of Parks, pending final state budget decisions or the possible transfer of park management to other park agencies or volunteer groups. It is currently open via an operating agreement, but service reductions are in place.

Campsites, facilities: There are 18 sites for tents or RVs up to 30 feet, 10 environmental sites (a one-mile walk in), and one group site for up to 40 people and RVs up to 30 feet. No hookups. Picnic tables and fire grills are provided. Drinking water, vault toilets, and a dump station are available. The environmental sites have pit toilets, picnic tables and fire rings, but no drinking water, and garbage must be packed out. Leashed pets are permitted. Some facilities are wheelchair accessible. No dogs in environmental sites.

Reservations, fees: Reservations are not accepted at this time. Individual and environmental sites are $25 per night, $8 per night for each additional vehicle, the group site is $100 per night. Open year-round.

Directions: On U.S. 101 north of Santa Rosa, turn west on River Road and drive 16 miles to Guerneville and Highway 116. Continue west on Highway 116 and drive about 20 miles to Highway 1 at Jenner. Turn north on Highway 1 and drive 55 miles to Point Arena. From Point Arena, continue north about five miles to Kinney Lane. Turn left and drive one mile to the campground entrance on the right.

Contact: Manchester State Park, 707/882-2463; Mendocino District, 707/937-5804, www.parks.ca.gov.

75 SHELDON CREEK

Scenic rating: 3

near Hopland

Map 4.3, page 251

Only the locals know about this spot, and hey, there aren't a lot of locals around. The camp is set amid rolling hills, grasslands, and oaks along little Sheldon Creek. It is pretty and quiet in the spring when the hills have greened up, but hot in the summer. Recreational possibilities include hiking and, in the fall, hunting.

Campsites, facilities: There are five sites for tents only. Picnic tables and fire grills are provided. Vault toilets are available. No drinking water is available. Garbage must be packed out. Leashed pets are permitted.

Reservations, fees: Reservations are not accepted. There is no fee for camping. There is a 14-day stay limit. Open year-round, weather permitting.

Directions: From Santa Rosa on U.S. 101,

drive north to Hopland and the junction with Highway 175. Turn east on Highway 175 and drive three miles to Old Toll Road. Turn right on Old Toll Road and drive eight miles to the camp.

Contact: Bureau of Land Management, Ukiah Field Office, 707/468-4000, www.blm.gov/ca.

76 ANCHOR BAY CAMPGROUND

Scenic rating: 8

near Gualala

Map 4.3, page 251

This is a quiet and beautiful stretch of California coast. The six-acre campground is on the ocean side of Highway 1 north of Gualala, with sites set at ocean level as well as amid trees—take your pick. Nearby Gualala Regional Park, six miles to the south, provides an excellent easy hike, the headlands-to-beach loop with coastal views, a lookout of the Gualala River, and many giant cypress trees. In winter, the nearby Gualala River attracts large but elusive steelhead.

Campsites, facilities: There are 30 sites for tents or RVs up to 40 feet; 12 sites have partial hookups (15 amps). Picnic tables and fire pits are provided. Drinking water, restrooms with flush toilets and coin showers, Wi-Fi, fish-cleaning room, dive-gear washroom, ice, bait, firewood, picnic area, and a dump station are available. Some facilities are wheelchair accessible. Leashed pets are permitted, with certain restrictions, at a maximum of two per site.

Reservations, fees: Reservations are recommended at 707/884-4222 ($10 reservation fee). Base rates for all sites are $40–45 per night, plus $20 per night for a second vehicle (free if towed by RV), $3–5 per person per night for more than two people, $3 per pet per stay. Boat launching is $5 per day. Some credit cards accepted. Off-season and senior discounts available. Open year-round.

Directions: From San Francisco, take U.S. 101

north to Cotati/Rhonert Park and the exit for Highway 116. Take that exit to Highway 116 west and drive 14 miles to River Road/Main Street (still Highway 116). Turn left and drive 12 miles to Highway 1 at Jenner. Turn north on Highway 1 and drive 38 miles to Gualala. Continue four miles north on Highway 1 to the campground on the left (west) side of the road.

Contact: Anchor Bay Campground, 707/884-4222, www.abcamp.com.

77 GUALALA POINT REGIONAL PARK

🥾 🚲 ⛵ 🎣 ♿ 🚐 ⛺

Scenic rating: 8

at Sonoma County Regional Park

Map 4.3, page 251

This is a dramatic spot near the ocean, close to the mouth of the Gualala River. The campground is on the east side of the highway, about 0.3 mile from the ocean. A trail along the bluff provides an easy hiking adventure; on the west side of the highway other trails to the beach are available.

Campsites, facilities: There are 23 sites for tents or RVs up to 25 feet (no hookups) and one hike-in/bike-in site. Picnic tables and fire rings are provided. Drinking water, restrooms with flush toilets and coin showers, dump station, and firewood are available. Some facilities are wheelchair-accessible. Leashed pets are permitted with valid rabies certificate.

Reservations, fees: Reservations are accepted on weekdays at 707/565-2267 ($8.50 reservation fee). Sites are $28–32 per night, $6 per night for each additional vehicle, the hike-in/bike-in site is $5 per night, $2 per pet per night. Open year-round.

Directions: On U.S. 101 north of Santa Rosa, turn west on River Road and drive 16 miles to Guerneville and Highway 116. Continue west on Highway 116 and drive about 20 miles to Highway 1 at Jenner. Turn north on Highway

1 and drive 38 miles to Gualala. Turn right at the park entrance (a day-use area is on the west side of the highway).

Contact: Gualala Point Regional Park 707/785-2377, www.sonoma-county.org.

78 CLOVERDALE/ HEALDSBURG KOA

🥾 ⛵ 🛶 🎣 🦌 ♿ 🚐 ⛺

Scenic rating: 7

near the Russian River

Map 4.3, page 251

This KOA campground is set just above the Russian River in the Alexander Valley wine country, just south of Cloverdale. The park is both rustic and tidy. The hillside pool has a nice view. In addition, a fishing pond is stocked with largemouth bass, bluegill, and catfish. On moonless nights, this is a great place for stargazing. Bird-watching is another pastime in this area. The nearby Russian River is an excellent beginner's route in an inflatable kayak or canoe. The nearby wineries in Asti make for a popular side trip.

Campsites, facilities: There are 64 sites with full hookups (30 and 50 amps) for RVs of any length, 42 sites for tents, 18 cabins, and 12 lodges. Some sites are pull-through. Picnic tables and fire grills are provided. Restrooms with flush toilets and showers, Wi-Fi, solar-heated swimming pool, gymnastic playground, dump station, coin laundry, recreation room, mini golf, spa and hot tub, nature trails, catch-and-release fish pond, weekend entertainment in the summer, and a convenience and gift store are available. Some facilities are wheelchair-accessible. Leashed pets are permitted, with certain restrictions.

Reservations, fees: Reservations are accepted at 800/562-4042. RV sites with full hookups are $55–70 (pull-thru, view and 50-amps), tent sites are $45–50 (with electricity), $10 per person per night for more than two people, $10 per night for each additional vehicle. Camping cabins are $80–100 per night, lodges are $190–260 per night. Some credit cards accepted. Open year-round.

Directions: From Cloverdale on U.S. 101, take the Central Cloverdale exit, which puts you on Asti Road. Drive straight on Asti Road to 1st Street. Turn right (east) and drive a short distance to River Road. Turn right (south) and drive four miles to Asti Ridge Road. Turn left and drive to the campground entrance.

In summer/fall: South of Cloverdale on U.S. 101, take the Asti exit to Asti Road. Turn right (south) on Asti Road and drive 1.5 miles to Washington School Road. Turn left (east) and drive 1.5 miles to Asti Ridge Road. Turn right and drive to the campground entrance. Note: This route is usually open Memorial Day Weekend through late November, when a seasonal bridge is in place. Both routes are well signed.

Contact: Cloverdale KOA, 707/894-3337 or 800/562-4042, www.winecountrykoa.com.

79 DUTCHER CREEK RV PARK & CAMPGROUND

🏊 🏕 🚐 ⛺

Scenic rating: 6

in the Alexander Valley

Map 4.3, page 251

This RV park is set in foothill-style oak woodlands and provides a layover spot for those touring the Alexander Valley wine country. The Russian River is nearby, running north to south through Cloverdale, the valley, and on to Healdsburg.

Campsites, facilities: There are 38 RV sites with full hookups (30 and 50-amp) and a limited number of tent sites. There is one pull-through site. Picnic tables are provided. Drinking water, a swimming pool, a coin laundry, and restrooms with flush toilets and showers are available. Leashed pets are permitted.

Reservations, fees: Reservations are accepted online. Sites are $35 per night with weekly and monthly rates available. Credit cards accepted online only. Open year-round.

Directions: From Highway 101 south of Cloverdale, take the Dutcher Creek Road exit and drive 0.2 mile to Theresa Drive. Turn west on Theresa Drive and drive 0.3 mile to the campground.

Contact: Dutcher Creek RV Park & Campground, 707/894-4829, www.dutchercreekrv.com.

80 LAKE SONOMA RECREATION AREA

🚶 🏊 🛶 🚐 🐴 ♿ 🚙 ⛺

Scenic rating: 8

near Healdsburg

Map 4.3, page 251   BEST (

Lake Sonoma is one of the best weekend vacation sites for Bay Area campers. The developed campground (Liberty Glen) is fine for car campers, but the boat-in sites are ideal for folks who desire a quiet and pretty lakeside setting. This is a big lake, extending nine miles north on the Dry Creek arm and four miles west on the Warm Springs Creek arm. There is an adjacent 8,000-acre wildlife area that was set aside to protect nesting peregrine falcons, as well as 40 miles of hiking trails. The lake is set at an elevation of 450 feet, with 53 miles of shoreline and hundreds of hidden coves. A sandy swimming beach is available at Yorty Creek, but there is no lifeguard. The water-skier versus angler conflict has been resolved by limiting high-speed boats to specified areas. Laws are strictly enforced, making this lake excellent for either sport. Wildlife-watching includes wild pigs, wild turkeys, blacktail deer, and river otters. The best fishing is in the protected coves of the Warm Springs and Dry Creek arms of the lake. Fish species include bass, catfish, rainbow trout, crappie, and sunfish. The visitors center is adjacent to a public fish hatchery. Steelhead come to spawn from the Russian River between late December and late March.

Campsites, facilities: There are 103 primitive

boat-in/hike-in sites around the lake and 95 tent and RV sites (no hookups). There are also five group sites, including two boat-in, one equestrian, and two drive-in at Liberty Glen Campground (2.5 miles from the lake). Picnic tables, fire grills, vault toilets, lantern poles, and garbage bins are provided at the primitive sites, but no drinking water is available. Picnic tables, fire rings, and lantern holders are provided at Liberty Glen, and showers and flush toilets are also available. A boat ramp and houseboat and boat rentals are nearby. Saturday night campfire talks are held at an amphitheater during the summer. Campsites have limited facilities in winter. Some facilities are wheelchair-accessible. Leashed pets are permitted.

Reservations, fees: Reservations for the boat-in sites and group sites only are accepted at 877/444-6777 or www.recreation.gov ($9 reservation fee). Reservations for equestrian sites are accepted at 707/431-4590. Single sites are $14 per night, double sites are $28 per night, and group and equestrian group sites are $56 per night. A camping permit is required from the visitors center for boat-in sites. Open year-round.

Directions: From Santa Rosa, drive north on U.S. 101 to Healdsburg. In Healdsburg, take the Dry Creek Road exit, turn left, and drive northwest for 11 miles. After you cross a small bridge, the visitors center will be on your right.

To reach the Yorty Creek Boat Ramp: On U.S. 101 at the south end of Cloverdale, take the Cloverdale Boulevard exit to Cloverdale Boulevard. Turn right on Cloverdale Boulevard and drive one block to Treadway Street. Turn left and drive two blocks to Foothill Boulevard. Turn right and drive 0.75 mile to Hot Springs Road. Turn left and drive about five miles to the boat launch. Note: Hot Springs Road is narrow with many hairpin turns. Trailers are prohibited, but the launch provides access for canoes, kayaks, and car-top boats to boat-in sites nearby.

Contact: U.S. Army Corps of Engineers,

Lake Sonoma Visitor Center, 707/431-4533; headquarters, 707/431-4590; Lake Sonoma Marina, 707/433-2200.

81 SALT POINT STATE PARK

Scenic rating: 9

near Fort Ross

Map 4.3, page 251   BEST

This is a gorgeous piece of Sonoma coast, highlighted by Fisk Mill Cove, inshore kelp beds, outstanding short hikes, and abalone diving. In fact, this is one of the finest diving areas for red abalone in the state. There is also an underwater reserve for divers, which is a protected area. Unfortunately there are also diving accidents that are due to the occasional large surf, strong currents, and rocky shoreline. There are two campgrounds here, Gerstle Cove Campground and the much larger Woodside Campground. Great hikes include Bluff Trail and Stump Beach Trail (great views). During abalone season, this is one of the best and most popular spots on the Northern California coast; note that new regulations require a review to ensure no diving in closed areas. The Kruse Rhododendron Reserve is within the park and definitely worth the stroll. This is a 317-acre conservation reserve that features second-growth redwoods, Douglas firs, tan oak, and many rhododendrons, with five miles of hiking trails. After the fall rains, this area is popular for mushroom hunters (the Kruse Rhododendron Reserve is closed to mushroom picking). Mushroom hunters must park in the area open to picking and be limited to five pounds per day. Of course, this can be a dangerous hobby; only eat mushrooms you can identify as safe. But you knew that, right?

Campsites, facilities: At Gerstle Cove Campground, there are 30 sites for tents or RVs up to 31 feet (no hookups). At Woodside Campground, there are 79 sites for tents or RVs up to 31 feet (no hookups), 20 walk-in tent sites (about a 300-yard walk), 10 hike-in/bike-in sites, a group site that can accommodate up to 40 people, and a primitive overflow area for self-contained vehicles. Picnic tables and fire rings are provided. Drinking water and flush toilets are available. Summer interpretive programs are offered; firewood is available for purchase. The picnic area and one hiking trail are wheelchair-accessible. Leashed pets are permitted, except on trails.

Reservations, fees: Reservations are accepted at 800/444-7275 (800/444-PARK) or www.reserveamerica.com ($8 reservation fee). Sites at Gerstle Cove and Woodside are $35 per night, $8 per night for each additional vehicle, Woodside's tent-only sites are $25 per night, hike-in/bike-in sites are $5 per person per night, the group site is $200 per night. Open year-round.

Directions: On U.S. 101 north of Santa Rosa, turn west on River Road and drive 16 miles to Guerneville and Highway 116. Continue west on Highway 116 and drive 13.1 miles to Highway 1 at Jenner. Turn north on Highway 1 and drive about 20 miles to the park entrance; Woodside Campground on the right and Gerstle Cove on the left.

Contact: Salt Point State Park, 707/847-3221; Russian River District, 707/865-2391, www.parks.ca.gov.

82 OCEAN COVE CAMPGROUND

Scenic rating: 8

near Fort Ross

Map 4.3, page 251

The highlights here are the campsites on a bluff overlooking the ocean. Alas, it can be foggy during the summer. A good side trip is to Fort Ross, with a stellar easy hike available on the Fort Ross Trail, which features a walk through an old colonial fort as well as great coastal views, excellent for whale-watching. There is also excellent hiking at Stillwater Cove Regional Park, just a mile to the south off Highway 1.

Campsites, facilities: There are 125 pull-through sites for tents or RVs of any length (no hookups) and three large group sites. Picnic tables and fire grills are provided. Drinking water, chemical toilets, and coin showers are available. A boat launch, grocery store, fishing supplies, and diving-gear sales are nearby. Leashed pets are permitted.

Reservations, fees: Reservations are not accepted for individual sites, but are required for group sites. Sites are $20 per night per vehicle, $2 per pet per night, $8 per day for boat launching. The group site is $200 per night for up to 10 vehicles, $20 per night per each additional vehicle. Some credit cards accepted. Open April through November.

Directions: From San Francisco, take U.S. 101 north to Cotati/Rhonert Park and the exit for Highway 116. Take that exit to Highway 116 west and drive 14 miles to River Road/Main Street (still Highway 116). Turn left and drive 12 miles to Highway 1 at Jenner. Turn north on Highway 1 and drive 17 miles north on Highway 1 (five miles north of Fort Ross) to the campground entrance on the left.

Contact: Ocean Cove Campground, 707/847-3422, www.oceancove.org.

83 STILLWATER COVE REGIONAL PARK

Scenic rating: 8

near Fort Ross

Map 4.3, page 251

Stillwater Cove has a dramatic rock-strewn cove and sits on a classic chunk of Sonoma coast. The campground is sometimes overlooked, since it is a county-operated park and not on the state park reservation system. One of the region's great hikes is available here: Stockoff Creek Loop, with the trailhead at the day-use parking lot. In a little more than a mile, the trail is routed through forest with both firs and redwoods, and then along a pretty stream. To get beach access, you will need to cross Highway 1 and then drop to the cove.

Campsites, facilities: There are 20 sites for

tents or RVs up to 30 feet (no hookups), and a hike-in/bike-in site. Picnic tables and fire rings are provided. Drinking water, restrooms with flush toilets and coin showers, firewood, and a dump station are available. Supplies can be obtained in Ocean Cove (one mile north) and Fort Ross. Some facilities are wheelchair-accessible. Leashed pets are permitted with a valid rabies certificate.

Reservations, fees: Reservations are accepted at 707/565-2267 on weekdays ($8.50 reservation fee). Sites are $28 –32 per night, $6 per night for each additional vehicle, hike-in/bike-in site is $5 per night, $2 per pet per night. Open year-round.

Directions: From San Francisco, take U.S. 101 north to Cotati/Rhonert Park and the exit for Highway 116. Take that exit to Highway 116 west and drive 14 miles to River Road/Main Street (still Highway 116). Turn left and drive 12 miles to Highway 1 at Jenner. Turn north on Highway 1 and drive 16 miles north on Highway 1 (four miles north of Fort Ross) to the park entrance.

Contact: Stillwater Cove Regional Park, Sonoma County, 707/847-3245; Sonoma County Regional Parks, 707/565-2041, www.sonoma-county.org.

84 REEF

Scenic rating: 8

at Fort Ross State Historic Park

Map 4.3, page 251

The campground at Fort Ross is two miles south of the north entrance station, less than 0.25 mile from the ocean. The privacy and beauty of the campsites vary as much as in any state park in California. Some redwoods and pines provide cover, and some sites are open. The sites at the end of the road fill up very quickly. Though the weather is relatively benign, tents are needed for protection against moisture from fog. From camp, a trail leads down to a beach, more rocky than sandy, and a one-mile trail leads to the fort.

Fort Ross is just as its name announces: an old fort, in this case, an old Russian fort from 1812. As a destination site, Fort Ross is known as a popular abalone diving spot, with the best areas below the campground and at nearby Reef Terrace. It also provides good, easy hikes amid its 3,386 acres. The park features a museum in the visitors center, which is always a must-see for campers making the tour up Highway 1. Note: Mushroom picking is prohibited in this park.

Campsites, facilities: There are 21 sites for tents or RVs up to 18 feet (no hookups). Picnic tables, food lockers, and fire rings are provided. Drinking water and flush toilets are available. Supplies can be obtained nearby. A visitor center and guided tours and programs are available. Some facilities are wheelchair-accessible. Leashed pets are permitted.

Reservations, fees: Reservations are not accepted. Sites are $15 per night, $6 per night for each additional vehicle. Senior discounts available. Open April through November, weather permitting.

Directions: On U.S. 101 north of Santa Rosa, turn west on River Road and drive 16 miles to Guerneville and Highway 116. Continue west on Highway 116 and drive about 13 miles to Highway 1 at Jenner. Turn north on Highway 1 and drive 10 miles to the (Fort Ross Reef) campground entrance. To reach the main state park entrance, drive north for two miles.

Contact: Fort Ross State Historic Park, 707/847-3286 or 707/847-3708, www.parks.ca.gov.

85 BULLFROG POND

Scenic rating: 7

in Austin Creek State Recreation Area
near the Russian River

Map 4.3, page 251

Austin Creek State Recreation Area and Armstrong Redwoods State Reserve together form

7,000 acres of continuous parkland. Bullfrog Pond is in Austin Creek SRA, set near a pond and in an open landscape featuring woodlands and foothills; the rugged topography provides a sense of isolation. The highlight here is a system of 22 miles of hiking trails that lead to a series of small creeks: Schoolhouse Creek, Gilliam Creek, and Austin Creek. The hikes involve pretty steep climbs, and in the summer it's hot—with temperatures occasionally exceeding 100°F—so plan accordingly. All of the park's trails are open to horses, and horseback-riding rentals are available in adjacent Armstrong Redwoods State Park. There are many attractive side-trip possibilities, including Armstrong Redwoods, of course, but also canoeing on the Russian River (3.5 miles away), fishing (smallmouth bass in summer, steelhead in winter), and wine-tasting. Annual winter rainfall often exceeds 50 inches. Elevations range 150–1,900 feet on Marble Mine Ridge.

Note: This park was on the closure list developed by the California Department of Parks, pending final state budget decisions or the possible transfer of park management to other park agencies or volunteer groups. It is currently open thanks to an operating agreement with the Stewards of the Coast and Redwoods.

Campsites, facilities: There are 23 sites for tents or RVs up to 20 feet (no hookups or trailers). Three backcountry campsites (requiring a hike of 3.5–5.1 miles) are scheduled to open; call the park for information. Picnic tables and fire grills are provided. Drinking water and flush toilets are available. Some facilities are wheelchair-accessible. Leashed pets are permitted at the main campground only.

Reservations, fees: Reservations are not accepted. Sites are $25 per night, $8 per night for each additional vehicle. Group reservations are available for $35 per night. Open year-round, but expect occasional fire closures during summer.

Directions: On U.S. 101 north of Santa Rosa, turn west on River Road and drive 15 miles to Guerneville and Armstrong Woods Road. Turn right and drive 2.5 miles to the entrance of Armstrong Redwoods State Park. Check in at the kiosk, and continue 3.5 miles through Armstrong Redwoods to Austin Creek State Recreation Area and the campground. The final 2.5 miles are steep and narrow, and no trailers, towed vehicles, or vehicles over 20 feet are permitted.

Contact: Austin Creek State Recreation Area, 707/869-2015 or 707/865-2391, www.parks.ca.gov; Stewards of the Coast and Redwoods, 707/869-9177, www.stewardsofthecoastandredwoods.org.

86 CASINI RANCH FAMILY CAMPGROUND

Scenic rating: 8

on the Russian River

Map 4.3, page 251

Woods and water—this campground has both, with sites set near the Russian River in both sun-filled and shaded areas. Its location on the lower river makes a side trip to the coast easy, with Sonoma Coast State Beach about a 15-minute drive to the nearby west. No long-term rentals available.

Campsites, facilities: There are 225 sites for tents or RVs of any length; many have full or partial hookups (30 amps); some sites are pull-through. Group and youth group camping is also available. Picnic tables and fire grills are provided. Restrooms with flush toilets and showers, playground, dump station, coin laundry, cable TV, Wi-Fi, game arcade, boat and canoe rentals, propane gas, group facilities, seasonal activities, and convenience store are available. Some facilities are wheelchair-accessible. Leashed pets are permitted.

Reservations, fees: Reservations are accepted at 800/451-8400. RV sites with full hookups are $49–52 per night, RV sites with partial hookups are $46–54 (riverfront) per night, tent sites are $41–48 per night, group camping is $204 per night, $3–12 per person per night for more than two people, $1 per pet per night. Weekly and monthly rates available. Discounts available weekdays and in off-season. Some credit cards accepted. Open year-round.

Directions: On U.S. 101 north of Santa Rosa, turn west on River Road and drive 16 miles to Guerneville and Highway 116. Continue west on Highway 116 and drive eight miles to Duncan Mills and Moscow Road. Turn left (southeast) on Moscow Road and drive 0.6 mile to the campground on the left.

Contact: Casini Ranch Family Campground Store, 707/865-2255, www.casiniranch.com.

87 POMO CANYON/ WILLOW CREEK WALK-IN

Scenic rating: 10

in Sonoma Coast State Beach

Map 4.3, page 251   BEST (

Sonoma Coast State Beach is on Reserve AmericaÕs list of Top 100 family campgrounds nationwide. Pomo Canyon is a gorgeous camp, well hidden, and offering a great trailhead and nearby beach access. The camp is actually not on the coast at all, but on the east-facing slope of Pomo Canyon (just over the ridge from the coast), where the campsites are set within a beautiful second-growth redwood forest and among fern understory. A trail is routed through the redwoods (with many cathedral trees) and up to the ridge, where there are divine views of the mouth of the Russian River, Goat Rock, and the beautiful Sonoma coast. The trail continues for three miles, all the way to Shell Beach, where you can spend hours poking around and beachcombing. The camp's seclusion and proximity to the Bay Area make it a rare winner. Now get this: A camping option is provided at nearby Willow Creek hike-in sites. Willow Creek Campground is nestled in trees, adjacent to open meadow, next to the Russian River.

Campsites, facilities: At Pomo Canyon, there

are 20 walk-in tent sites. Picnic tables, food lockers, and fire rings are provided. Drinking water and pit toilets are available. Some facilities are wheelchair-accessible. No pets are permitted. At Willow Creek, there are 11 hike-in sites. No drinking water. Pit toilets are available, otherwise no facilities. Some facilities are wheelchair accessible. No pets are permitted.

Reservations, fees: Reservations are not accepted. Sites are $25 per night, $8 per night for each additional vehicle. Open April through November, weather permitting.

Directions: In Petaluma on U.S. 101, take the East Washington exit and turn west (this street becomes Bodega Avenue). Drive west through Petaluma and continue for 17 miles to Highway 1. Turn right (north) on Highway 1 and drive nine miles to Bodega Bay, then continue north for nine miles to Willow Creek Road. To reach Pomo Canyon Campground, turn right on Willow Creek Road and drive about three miles to the campground parking. Park and walk to the campsites, a one- to five-minute walk. To reach Willow Creek Campground, turn right on Willow Creek Road and drive 1.5 miles to the campground parking on the left. Hike up to 0.25 mile to reach the campsites.

Contact: Sonoma Coast State Beach, 707/875-3483, www.parks.ca.gov.

88 WRIGHTS BEACH

Scenic rating: 8

in Sonoma Coast State Beach

Map 4.3, page 251

This park provides more than its share of heaven and hell. This state park campground is at the north end of a beach that stretches south for about a mile, yet to the north it is steep and rocky. The campsites are considered a premium because of their location next to the beach. Because the campsites are often full, a key plus is an overflow area available for self-contained vehicles. Sonoma Coast State Beach stretches from Bodega Head to Vista Trail for 17 miles, separated by rock bluffs and headlands that form a series of beaches. More than a dozen access points from the highway allow you can reach the beach. There are many excellent side trips. The best is to the north, where you can explore dramatic Shell Beach (the turnoff is on the west side of Highway 1), or take Pomo Trail (the trailhead is on the east side of the highway, across from Shell Beach) up the adjacent foothills for sweeping views of the coast. That's the heaven. Now for the hell: Dozens of people have drowned here. Wrights Beach is not for swimming; rip currents, heavy surf, and surprise rogue waves can make even playing in the surf dangerous. Many rescues are made each year. The bluffs and coastal rocks can also be unstable and unsafe for climbing. Got it? 1. Stay clear of the water. 2. Don't climb the bluffs. Now it's up to you to get it right.

Campsites, facilities: There are 29 sites for tents or RVs up to 27 feet (no hookups), with a limit of eight people per site, and an overflow area for self-contained vehicles. Picnic tables, food lockers, and fire rings are provided. Drinking water and flush toilets are available. Showers and a dump station are available at nearby Bodega Dunes Campground. Some facilities are wheelchair accessible. Leashed pets are permitted in the campground and on the beach.

Reservations, fees: Reservations are recommended at 800/444-7275 (800/444-PARK) or www.reserveamerica.com ($8 reservation fee). Developed sites are $35 per night, premium sites are $45 per night, $8 per night for each additional vehicle. Open year-round, weather permitting.

Directions: In Petaluma on U.S. 101, take the East Washington exit and turn west (this street becomes Bodega Avenue). Drive west through Petaluma and continue for 17 miles to Highway 1. Turn right (north) on Highway 1 and drive nine miles to Bodega Bay. From Bodega Bay, continue north for six miles to the campground entrance.

Contact: Sonoma Coast State Beach, 707/875-3483, www.parks.ca.gov.

89 BODEGA BAY RV PARK

Scenic rating: 8

in Bodega Bay

Map 4.3, page 251

Bodega Bay RV Park is one of the oldest RV parks in the state, and there are few north-state coastal destinations better than Bodega Bay. Excellent seafood restaurants are available within five minutes, and some of the best deep-sea fishing is available out of Bodega Bay Sportfishing. In addition, there is a great view of the ocean at nearby Bodega Head to the west. It is a 35-minute walk from the park to the beach.

Campsites, facilities: There are 72 sites, most with full hookups (30 and 50 amps), for RVs of any length; some sites are pull-through. No tents. Picnic tables are provided. Drinking water and restrooms with flush toilets and showers are available. Coin laundry, restaurant, group facilities, fish cleaning station, horseshoes, video arcade, bocce ball, Wi-Fi, and cable TV are available. Some facilities are wheelchair-accessible. Leashed pets are permitted.

Reservations, fees: Reservations are recommended at 800/201-6864. RV sites with full hookups are $41 per night, RV sites without hookups are $28 per night, $5 per person per night for more than two people. Group discounts available. Some credit cards accepted. Open year-round.

Directions: In Petaluma on U.S. 101, take the East Washington exit and turn west (this street becomes Bodega Avenue). Drive west through Petaluma and continue for 17 miles to Highway 1. Turn right (north) on Highway 1 and drive nine miles to Bodega Bay. In Bodega Bay, continue north for two miles to the RV park on the left at 2001 Highway 1.

Contact: Bodega Bay RV Park, 707/875-3701, www.bodegabayrvpark.com.

90 BODEGA DUNES

Scenic rating: 8

in Sonoma Coast State Beach

Map 4.3, page 251

Sonoma Coast State Beach features several great campgrounds, and if you like beaches, this one rates high. Bodega Dunes campground is set near Salmon Creek Beach, the closest beach to the campground and far safer than Wrights Beach. The beach stretches for miles, providing stellar beach walks and excellent beachcombing during low tides. For some campers, a foghorn sounding repeatedly through the night can make sleep difficult. The quietest sites here are among the dunes. A day-use area includes a wheelchair-accessible boardwalk that leads out to a sandy beach. In summer, campfire programs and junior ranger programs are often offered. To the nearby south is Bodega Bay, with a major deep-sea sportfishing operation—crowned by often excellent salmon fishing; check current fishing regulations. The town of Bodega Bay offers a full marina and restaurants.

Campsites, facilities: There are 98 sites for tents or RVs up to 31 feet (no hookups), and one hike-in/bike-in site. Picnic tables, food lockers, and fire grills are provided. Drinking water, restrooms with flush toilets and free showers, and a dump station are available. Laundry facilities, supplies, and horse rentals are available within one mile. Some facilities, including a boardwalk to the beach, are wheelchair-accessible. Leashed pets are permitted at the campsites only.

Reservations, fees: Reservations are accepted at 800/444-7275 (800/444-PARK) or www.reserveamerica.com ($8 reservation fee). Sites are $35 per night, $8 per night for each additional vehicle, hike-in/bike-in site is $5 per person per night. Open year-round.

Directions: In Santa Rosa on U.S. 101, turn west on Highway 12 and drive 10 miles to Sebastopol (Highway 12 becomes Bodega Highway). Continue straight (west) for 10 miles to Bodega. Continue for 0.5 mile to Highway 1. Turn right (north) on Highway 1 and drive five miles to Bodega Bay. Continue 0.5 mile north to the campground entrance on the left (west).

Contact: Sonoma Coast State Beach, 707/875-3483, www.parks.ca.gov.

91 WESTSIDE REGIONAL PARK

Scenic rating: 7

on Bodega Bay

Map 4.3, page 251

This campground is on the west shore of Bodega Bay. One of the greatest boat launches on the coast is adjacent to the park on the south, providing access to prime fishing waters. Salmon fishing is excellent from mid-June through August; check current fishing regulations. A small, protected beach (where kids can dig in the sand and wade) is available at the end of the road beyond the campground. Hiking trails can be found at the state beach nearby.

Campsites, facilities: There are 45 sites for tents or RVs of any length (no hookups); most sites are pull-through. Picnic tables and fire grills are provided. Drinking water, restrooms with flush toilets and coin showers, fish-cleaning station, boat rinsing station, firewood, dump station, and boat ramp are available. Supplies can be obtained in Bodega Bay. Some facilities are wheelchair-accessible. Leashed pets are permitted with valid rabies certificate.

Reservations, fees: Reservations are accepted on weekdays at 707/565-2267 ($8.50 reservation fee). Sites are $30–32 per night, $6 per night for each additional vehicle, $2 per pet per night. Open year-round.

Directions: In Petaluma on U.S. 101, take the East Washington exit and turn west (this street becomes Bodega Avenue). Drive west through Petaluma and continue for 17 miles to

Highway 1 north. Merge right onto Highway 1 and drive north nine miles to Bodega Bay. In Bodega Bay, continue north to Eastshore Road. Turn left and drive one block to Bay Flat Road. Turn right and drive (becomes Westshore Road) two miles to the park on the left, 0.5 mile past Spud Point Marina.

Contact: Westside Regional Park, Sonoma County Parks Department, 707/875-3540 or 707/565-2041, www.sonoma-county.org.

92 PORTO BODEGA MARINA & RV PARK

Scenic rating: 7

in Bodega Bay

Map 4.3, page 251

This RV park is located a short distance from Bodega Bay. The sites are open, most with full hookups, and the park is designed as a base to launch getaways. Fishing is often excellent out of Bodega Bay, and charter boat operations and an excellent marina and boat ramp are nearby. Nearby Bodega Head is an excellent spot for short walks or to watch the sunset. Note that new owners acquired this RV park in 2008.

Campsites, facilities: There are 58 sites for RVs to 42 feet, 18 of which have full hookups (20, 30, and 50-amp). Picnic tables and fire pits are provided. Drinking water, restrooms with flush toilets, showers, boat launch, cable TV hookups, and a dump station are available. Restaurants and grocery stores are nearby. Leashed pets are permitted.

Reservations, fees: Reservations are recommended at 707/875-2354. Sites are $40–43 with hookups, $28 without, per night.

Directions: From Highway 101 in Santa Rosa, drive west on Highway 12 to Sebastopol, where Highway 12 becomes Bodega Highway. Continue west on Bodega Highway 11 miles to where Bodega Highway ends at Highway 1. Turn right and drive five miles into Bodega Bay. Turn left on Eastshore Road and drive one block to the intersection with Bay Flat Road. Drive straight through the intersection and bear right to the campground.

Contact: Porto Bodega Marina & RV Park, 1500 Bay Flat Road, 707/875-2354, www.portobodega.com.

93 DORAN REGIONAL PARK

Scenic rating: 7

on Bodega Bay

Map 4.3, page 251

This campground is set beside Doran Beach on Bodega Bay, which offers complete fishing and marina facilities. In season, it's also a popular clamming and crabbing spot. This park has a wide, somewhat sheltered sandy beach. Salmon fishing is often excellent during the summer at the Whistle Buoy offshore from Bodega Head, and rock fishing is good year-round offshore. Fishing is also available off the rock jetty in the park.

Campsites, facilities: There are 132 sites for tents or RVs of any length (no hookups), one group tent site for up to 50 people, and one hike-in/bike-in site. Picnic tables and fire grills are provided. Drinking water, restrooms with flush toilets and coin showers, dump stations, fish-cleaning station, and boat ramp are available. Some facilities are wheelchair-accessible. Supplies can be obtained in Bodega Bay. Leashed pets are permitted with a valid rabies certificate.

Reservations, fees: Reservations are accepted on weekdays at 707/565-2267 ($8.50) reservation fee. Sites are $30–32 per night, $6 per night for each additional vehicle, the hike-in/bike-in site is $5 per night, $2 per pet per night. The group site is $150 per night. Open year-round.

Directions: In Petaluma on U.S. 101, take the East Washington exit and turn west (this street becomes Bodega Avenue). Drive west through Petaluma and continue for 17 miles to

Highway 1. Merge right (north) on Highway 1 and drive toward Bodega Bay and Doran Park Road. Turn left onto the campground entrance road. If you reach the town of Bodega Bay, you have gone a mile too far.

Contact: Sonoma County Parks Department, 707/875-3540 or 707/565-2041, www.sonoma-county.org.

94 EDGEWATER RESORT AND RV PARK

Scenic rating: 7

on Clear Lake

Map 4.4, page 252

Soda Bay is one of Clear Lake's prettiest and most intimate spots, and this camp provides excellent access. It also provides friendly, professional service. Both waterskiing and fishing for bass and bluegill are excellent in this part of the lake. The resort has 600 feet of lake frontage, including a 300-foot swimming beach and a 230-foot fishing pier. This resort specializes in groups and family reunions. Wine-tasting, casinos, and golfing are nearby. Insider's tip: This park is very pet friendly and has occasional doggie socials. Note: All boats must be certified mussel-free before launching.

Campsites, facilities: There are 61 sites with full hookups (20, 30, and 50 amps) for tents or RVs of any length, and eight cabins. Picnic tables and fire grills are provided. Restrooms with showers, cable TV, WiFi, clubhouse, group facilities, general store, coin laundry, seasonal heated swimming pool, horseshoes, volleyball, and table tennis are available. A seasonal swimming beach, pet station, dog run, bait and tackle, boat ramp, fishing pier, boat docking, fish-cleaning station, and watercraft rentals are available on the premises. Firewood is available for purchase. Leashed pets are permitted.

Reservations, fees: Reservations are accepted at 800/396-6224. Gold sites for RVs or tents are $45 per night, Silver sites are $40 per night, standard sites are $35 per night, $5 per person per night for more than two people, $5 per pet per night. Boat launching is $10 per day and includes slip and trailer parking. RVs and tents cannot occupy same site. Group rates are available. Holiday rates are higher. Winter discounts and weekly rates are available. Some credit cards accepted. Open year-round.

Directions: In Kelseyville on Highway 29, take the Merritt Road exit and drive on Merritt Road for two miles (it becomes Gaddy Lane) to Soda Bay Road. Turn right on Soda Bay Road and drive three miles to the campground entrance on the left at 6420 Soda Bay Road.

Contact: Edgewater Resort and RV Park, 707/279-0208, www.edgewaterresort.net.

95 SHAW'S SHADY ACRES

Scenic rating: 7

on Cache Creek

Map 4.4, page 252

Shaw's Shady Acres is set beside Cache Creek, just south of Clear Lake. Canoeing and kayaking are popular. The fishing for catfish is often quite good on summer nights in Cache Creek, a deep, green, slow-moving water that looks more like a slough in a Mississippi bayou than a creek. Waterfront campsites with scattered walnut, ash, and oak trees are available. Clear Lake (the lake, not the town) is a short drive to the north, and a state park is across the creek, an excellent destination for kayaking. In addition to the campsites mentioned, there are an additional 36 long-term or permanent sites. Note: All boats must be certified mussel-free before launching.

Campsites, facilities: There are six RV sites with full hookups (30 amps) and 10 tent sites. Picnic tables and barbecues are provided. Restrooms with showers, a fishing dock, fishing boat rentals, boat ramp, coin laundry, swimming pool (seasonal), fishing supplies, and convenience store are available. Leashed pets are allowed, with certain restrictions.

Reservations, fees: Reservations are recommended. Sites are $30 per night, $4 per person per night for more than two people. Boat launching is free for campers. Open year-round.

Directions: From the town of Lower Lake, drive north on Highway 53 for 1.3 miles to Old Highway 53. Turn left on Old Highway 53 and then almost immediately you will arrive at Cache Creek Way. Turn left and drive 0.25 mile to the park entrance at 7805 Cache Creek Way.

Contact: Shaw's Shady Acres, 707/994-2236.

96 CACHE CREEK REGIONAL PARK

Scenic rating: 7

near Rumsey

Map 4.4, page 252

This is the best campground in Yolo County, yet it's known by few out-of-towners. It is set at 1,300 feet elevation beside Cache Creek, which is the closest river to the Bay Area that provides white-water rafting opportunities. This section of river features primarily Class I and II water, ideal for inflatable kayaks and overnight trips. One rapid, Big Mother, is sometimes considered Class III, though that might be a stretch. Huge catfish are occasionally caught in this area.

Campsites, facilities: There are 45 sites for tents or RVs up to 42 feet (no hookups), including some pull-through sites, and four group sites that can accommodate 20–30 people. Picnic tables, barbecue pits, and fire rings are provided. Drinking water, restrooms with flush toilets, playground, and dump station are available. Some facilities are wheelchair-accessible. Leashed pets are permitted.

Reservations, fees: Reservations are accepted for the group sites and for some of the individual sites at 530/406-4880. Sites are $25 per night, $6 per night for each additional vehicle, $2 per pet per night. Group sites are $165 per night. Hike-in/bike-in sites are $25. Off-season discounts available. Discount for Yolo County residents. Open year-round.

Directions: From Vacaville on I-80, turn north on I-505 and drive 21 miles to Madison and the junction with Highway 16 west. Turn northwest on Highway 16 and drive northwest for about 35 miles to the town of Rumsey. From Rumsey, continue west on Highway 16 for five miles to the park entrance on the left at 1475 State Highway 16.

Contact: Cache Creek Regional Park, Yolo County, 530/406-4880, www.yolocounty. org.

97 BOGGS MOUNTAIN DEMONSTRATION STATE FOREST

Scenic rating: 5

near Middletown

Map 4.4, page 252

This overlooked spot is set in a state forest that covers 3,500 acres of pine and Douglas fir. There are two adjoining campgrounds here. This is a popular destination for the region's equestrians. There are numerous trails for horses, hikers, and bikers. Remember: Equestrians have the right of way over hikers and bikers, and hikers have the right of way over bikers. Got it? The International Mountain Biking Association has chosen this as one of the top 10 riding areas in the country. There is a 14-mile trail system available that started as a series of hand-built fire lines. Note that in early fall, this area is open to deer hunting. Boggs is one of nine state forests managed with the purpose of demonstrating economical forest management, which means there is logging along with compatible recreation.

Campsites, facilities: There are 19 sites for tents or RVs up to 22 feet (no hookups). No drinking water is available. Picnic tables and fire pits are provided. Vault toilets are available. Garbage must be packed out. Coin laundry, pizza parlor, and gas station are available within two miles. Horses and leashed pets are permitted.

Reservations, fees: Reservations are not accepted. Sites are $10 per night. Self-registration required. Open year-round.

Directions: From Vallejo, drive north on Highway 29 past Calistoga to Middletown and the junction with Highway 175. Turn left (north) on Highway 175 and drive seven miles (through the town of Cobb) to Forestry Road. Turn right and drive one mile to the campgrounds on the left.

Contact: Boggs Mountain Demonstration State Forest, 707/928-4378, boggsmountain. net.

98 JELLYSTONE RV PARK

Scenic rating: 7

near Cobb Mountain

Map 4.4, page 252

Kelsey Creek runs through this campground which has a trout creek, a pond with canoe and kayak rentals in summer, plus plenty of hiking and bird-watching opportunities. In addition, horseback riding and hot-air balloon rides are available nearby. The camp is set near Highway 175 between Middletown and Clear Lake, and while there is a parade of vacation traffic on Highway 29, relatively few people take the longer route on Highway 175. Cobb Mountain looms nearby. Golf courses are in the vicinity. (Those familiar with this area may remember this camp was formerly called Beaver Creek RV Park.)

Campsites, facilities: There are 97 sites with full hookups (30 and 50 amps) for RVs up to 40 feet, 10 tent sites, and four cabins. Most sites are pull-through. Picnic tables and fire rings are provided. Drinking water, restrooms with showers, group facilities, coin laundry, Wi-Fi, seasonal swimming pool, kayak and paddleboat rentals, boating pond, playground, horseshoes, miniature golf, recreation hall, picnic area, athletic field, basketball, volleyball, horseshoes, firewood, ice, propane, and camp store are available. Some facilities are wheelchair-accessible. Leashed pets are permitted.

Reservations, fees: Reservations are accepted. Sites are $35–45 per night, $5–10 per person per night for more than two people, $10 per pet. Some credit cards accepted. Open year-round.

Directions: From Vallejo, drive north on Highway 29 past Calistoga to Middletown and the junction with Highway 175. Turn north on Highway 175 (to Cobb) and drive 12 miles to Bottle Rock Road. Turn left and drive three miles to the campground entrance on the left side of the road at 14117 Bottle Rock Road.

Contact: Jellystone RV Park, 707/928-4322 or 800/928-4322, www.jellystonecobbmtn. com.

99 LOWER HUNTING CREEK

Scenic rating: 4

near Lake Berryessa

Map 4.4, page 252

This little-known camp might seem, to the folks who wind up here accidentally, as if it's out in the middle of nowhere, and it turns out that it is. If you plan on spending a few days here, it's advisable to get information or a map of the surrounding area from the Bureau of Land Management before your trip. There are about 25 miles of trails for off-highway-vehicle exploration on the surrounding lands. In the fall, the area provides access for deer hunting with generally poor to fair results.

Campsites, facilities: There are five sites for tents or RVs up to 20 feet (no hookups) and an overflow area. Picnic tables and fire grills are provided. Shade shelters, garbage cans, and vault toilets are available, but there is no drinking water. Leashed pets are permitted.

Reservations, fees: Reservations are not accepted. There is no fee for camping. There is a 14-day stay limit. Open year-round.

Directions: In Lower Lake on Highway 29,

turn southeast on Morgan Valley Road/Ber-ryessa-Knoxville Road and drive 15 miles to Devilhead Road. Turn south and drive two miles to the campground.

Contact: Bureau of Land Management, Ukiah District, 707/468-4000, www.blm.gov/ca.

100 CALISTOGA RV AND CAMPGROUND

Scenic rating: 3

in Calistoga

Map 4.4, page 252

What this really is, folks, is just the Napa County Fairgrounds converted into an RV park. It is open year-round, except when the county fair is in progress. Who knows, maybe you can win a stuffed bear. What is more likely, of course, is that you have come here for the health spas, with great natural hot springs, mud baths, and assorted goodies at the resorts in Calistoga. Downtown Calistoga is within walking distance and nearby parks include Bothe–Napa Valley and Robert Louis Stevenson State Parks. Cycling, wine-tasting, and hot-air balloon rides are also popular.

Campsites, facilities: There are 72 sites with partial or full hookups (30 and 50 amps) for RVs. Some sites are pull-through. Group sites are available by reservation only with a 10-vehicle minimum. Restrooms with flush toilets and showers, picnic area, WiFi, and dump station are available. No fires are permitted. Picnic tables are available for a fee ($10). A nine-hole golf course is adjacent to the campground area. Some facilities are wheelchair-accessible. Leashed pets are permitted.

Reservations, fees: Reservations are accepted and are required for groups at 707/942-5221 or online. RV sites with full hookups are $37 per night, RV sites with partial hookups are $34 per night, $5 per person for more than two people, $5 per night per additional vehicle, $2 per pet per night. Some credit cards accepted. Open year-round.

Directions: From Napa on Highway 29, drive north to Calistoga, turn right on Lincoln Avenue, and drive four blocks to Fairway. Turn left and drive about four blocks to the end of the road to the campground.

Contact: Calistoga RV and Campground, 707/942-5221, www.calistogacampground.org.

101 BOTHE–NAPA VALLEY STATE PARK

Scenic rating: 7

near Calistoga

Map 4.4, page 252

It's always a stunner for newcomers to discover this beautiful park with redwoods and a pretty stream so close to the Napa Valley wine and spa country. Though the campsites are relatively exposed, they are set beneath a pretty oak/bay/madrone forest, with trailheads for hiking nearby. One trail is routed south from the day-use parking lot for 1.8 mile to the restored Bale Grist Mill, a giant waterwheel on a pretty creek. Weekend tours of the Bale Grist Mill are available in summer. Another, more scenic, route, the Redwood Trail, heads up Ritchey Canyon, amid redwoods and towering Douglas fir, and along Ritchey Creek, all of it beautiful and intimate. The park covers 2,000 acres. Most of it is rugged, with elevations ranging from 300 to 2,000 feet. In summer, temperatures can reach the 100s, which is why finding a redwood grove can be stunning. The park has more than 10 miles of trails. Those who explore will find that the forests are on the north-facing slopes while the south-facing slopes tend to be brushy. The geology here is primarily volcanic, yet the vegetation hides most of it. Bird-watchers will note that this is one of the few places where you can see six species of woodpeckers, including the star of the show, the pileated woodpecker (the size of a crow).

Campsites, facilities: There are 30 sites for tents or a few RVs up to 31 feet and trailers up to 24 feet (no hookups). There are also nine walk-in (up to 50 feet) tent sites, one hike-in/bike-in site, one group tent site for up to 30 people, and three yurts. Picnic tables and fire rings are provided. Drinking water, restrooms with flush toilets and coin showers, and seasonal swimming pool are available. Supplies can be obtained four miles away in Calistoga. Some facilities are wheelchair-accessible. Leashed pets are permitted, but not on trails.

Reservations, fees: Reservations are recommended at 800/444-7275 (800/444-PARK) or www.reserveamerica.com ($8 reservation fee). Sites are $35 per night, $8 per night for each additional vehicle, the group site is $100 per night, hike-in/bike-in sites are $3 per person, and yurts are $70 per night. Open year-round.

Directions: From Napa on Highway 29, drive north to St. Helena and continue north for five miles (one mile past the entrance to Bale Grist Mill State Park) to the park entrance road on the left.

Contact: Bothe–Napa Valley State Park, 707/942-4575, www.parks.ca.gov.

102 LAKE SOLANO PARK

Scenic rating: 6

near Lake Berryessa

Map 4.4, page 252

Lake Solano provides a low-pressure option to nearby Lake Berryessa. It is a long, narrow lake set below the outlet at Monticello Dam at Lake Berryessa, technically called the after-bay. Compared to Berryessa, life here moves at a much slower pace and some people prefer it. The water temperature at Lake Solano is also much cooler than at Berryessa. The lake has fair trout fishing in the spring, and it is known among Bay Area anglers as the closest fly-fishing spot for trout in the region. No motors, including electric motors, are permitted on boats at the lake. The park covers 177 acres along the river. A swimming pond is available in summer, and a children's fishing pond (trout and bass) is open year-round. The gate closes at night; check in before dusk.

Campsites, facilities: There are 47 sites for tents or RVs (no hookups), and 36 sites with for tents or RVs (water and electricity, 30 amps) up to 38 feet; some sites are pull-through. Picnic tables and fire grills are provided. Drinking water, restrooms with flush toilets and showers, one dump station, picnic area, boat ramp, and boat rentals (summer weekends only) are available. A grocery store is within walking distance, and firewood and ice are sold on the premises. Some facilities are wheelchair-accessible. Leashed pets are permitted in the campground only.

Reservations, fees: Reservations are recommended and are allowed at least 14 days in advance at 530/795-2990. Tent sites are $21 per night, RV sites with water and electricity are $30 per night, $10 per night for each additional vehicle, $1 per pet per night. Some credit cards accepted. Open year-round.

Directions: In Vacaville, turn north on I-505 and drive 11 miles to the junction of Highway 128. Turn west on Highway 128 and drive about five miles (past Winters) to Pleasant Valley Road. Turn left on Pleasant Valley Road and drive to the park at 8685 Pleasant Valley Road (well signed).

Contact: Lake Solano Park, 530/795-2990, www.co.solano.ca.us.

103 JOHNSON'S BEACH & RESORT

Scenic rating: 7

on the Russian River in Guerneville

Map 4.4, page 252

Johnson's is located on the north bank of the Russian River in Guerneville. The resort offers canoes, kayaks, and paddleboats for rent, as well as beach chairs and a boat launch. This is often a good fishing spot for steelhead in early winter.

Campsites, facilities: There are 35 tent sites and six sites with partial 20-amp hookups for

RVs to 32 feet. Picnic tables and fire rings are provided. Restrooms with flush toilets, coin showers, dump station, laundry room, game room and a sandy beach are available. Dogs are not permitted; you will be turned away if you bring a dog.

Reservations, fees: Reservations are not accepted; sites are first-come, first-served. RV sites with hookups are $30–40 per night, tent sites are $25 per night, $5 per night per additional person. Open mid-May to mid-October, weather permitting.

Directions: From Santa Rosa, take Highway 101 north to River Road. Turn left (west) on River Road and drive 15 miles to Church Street in Guerneville. Turn left (south) on Church Street and drive one block to the campground at the corner of Church and First Streets.

Contact: Johnson's Beach & Resort, 707/869-2022, www.johnsonsbeach.com (click on resort).

104 SCHOOLHOUSE CANYON PARK

Scenic rating: 7

near Guerneville on the Russian River

Map 4.4, page 252

Schoolhouse Canyon Park offers a step back in time on the banks of the Russian River. Just two miles outside Guerneville, this 30-acre heritage park rolls out the welcome mat for families.

Campsites, facilities: There are 25 sites for tents or RVs up to 25 feet (some partial hookups). Picnic tables and fire pits are provided. Restrooms with flush toilets and coin showers are available. Leashed pets are permitted with some restrictions.

Reservations, fees: Reservations are accepted. RV sites (with hookups) are $37 per night, tent sites are $30 per night for two people, $5 for each additional person, $5 per night for each additional vehicle, $5 per pet per night. Cash only. Open May to September.

Directions: From Santa Rosa, take Highway 101 north to River Road. Turn left (west) on River Road and drive about 11.5 miles to Schoolhouse Canyon Park.

Contact: Schoolhouse Canyon Park, 12600 River Road, Guerneville, 707/869-2311, www.schoolhousecanyon.com.

105 HILTON PARK FAMILY CAMPGROUND

Scenic rating: 6

on the Russian River

Map 4.4, page 252

This lush, wooded park is set on the banks of the Russian River, with a choice of open or secluded sites. The highlight of the campground is a large, beautiful beach that offers access for swimming, fishing, and canoeing. You get a choice of many recreation options in the area.

Campsites, facilities: There are 30 sites for tents, 10 sites with partial hookups (30 amps) for RVs up to 35 feet, three group sites for 10–150 people, eight camping cottages, and a "magic bus." Picnic tables and fire rings are provided. Restrooms with coin showers, dishwashing area, arcade, WiFi, horseshoe pits, playground, coin laundry, camp store, firewood, and ice are available. A beach is nearby. Boat rentals are available within three miles. Leashed pets are permitted, with certain restrictions.

Reservations, fees: Reservations are recommended. RV sites are $45 per night, tent sites are $35 per night, $12 per person over age 17 per night for more than two people, $6 per person age 6–17 per night for more than two people, $5 per night for each additional vehicle, $5 per night per pet. Some credit cards accepted. Open May through October.

Directions: From U.S. 101 north of Santa Rosa, take the River Road/Guerneville exit. Drive west on River Road for 11.5 miles (one mile after the metal bridge) to the campground on the left side of the road (just before the Russian River Pub).

Contact: Hilton Park Family Campground, 10750 River Road, 707/887-9206, www.hiltonparkcampground.com.

106 BURKE'S CANOE TRIPS

Scenic rating: 7

on the Russian River near Guerneville

Map 4.4, page 252

Burke's Canoe Trips is one of the major canoe rental businesses on the Russian River. Their campground is set amid redwoods along the Russian River and provides a great base for canoe trips, including shuttle rides. Canoe rentals ($60 per trip) includes shuttle and equipment, for a great paddle through the redwoods to Guerneville. For RV camping, try Mirabel Trailer Park (707/887-2383) next door, but be aware there are a high number of permanent residents, not always a positive thing (and because of that, they do not qualify as a true campground for this book). Because groups come to Burke's for canoe trips, at times they can turn camping into a loud party into the night.

Campsites, facilities: There are 30 sites for tents only and a group site for 75 people. Picnic tables and fire rings are provided. Drinking water and restrooms with flush toilets and showers are available. Canoe and kayak rentals are available, with shuttle provided for easy return to camp.

Reservations, fees: Reservations are recommended. Tent sites are $10 per person per night. Call for rates for the group site. Open seasonally until September, weather permitting.

Directions: From Santa Rosa, take Highway 101 north to River Road. Turn left (west) on River Road and drive 8.2 miles to Burke's, just past the Mirabel Trailer Park.

Contact: Burke's Canoe Trips, 8600 River Road, 707/887-1222, www.burkescanoetrips.com.

107 RIVER BEND RESORT

Scenic rating: 7

on the Russian River near Guerneville

Map 4.4, page 252

River Bend Resort provides direct access to the Russian River and has a small beach for swimming. Burke's Canoe Trips is located nearby and Korbel Champagne Cellars is adjacent to the property. Guerneville is four miles away.

Campsites, facilities: There are 26 tent sites and 62 RV sites (most with full hookups). Picnic tables, fire pits, water, and electricity are provided. Restrooms with flush toilets, showers, a dog walk, a general store, propane, playground, WiFi, and a sport court are available. Leashed pets are permitted with some restrictions.

Reservations, fees: Reservations are required. RV sites with full hookups are $45–55 (riverfront) per night, tent sites are $32–43 per night for two people, $5 for each additional person, $5 per night for additional vehicle, $3 per pet per night. Open year-round.

Directions: From Santa Rosa, take Highway 101 north to River Road. Turn left (west) on River Road and drive about 11 miles to River Bend Resort.

Contact: River Bend Resort, 11820 River Road, 707/887-7662, www.riverbendresort.net.

108 SPRING LAKE REGIONAL PARK

Scenic rating: 6

at Spring Lake near Santa Rosa

Map 4.4, page 252

Spring Lake is one of the few lakes in the greater Bay Area that provides lakeside camping. No gas-powered boats are permitted on this small, pretty lake, which keeps things fun and quiet for everybody. An easy trail along the west shore of the lake to the dam, then into adjoining Howarth Park, provides a pleasant evening stroll. This little lake is where a 24-

pound world-record bass was reportedly caught, a story taken as a hoax by nearly all anglers.

Campsites, facilities: There are 26 sites for tents or RVs up to 40 feet (no hookups), four hike-in sites, and one group site for up to 75 people and 15 vehicles. Several sites are pull-through. Picnic tables and fire grills are provided. Drinking water, restrooms with flush toilets and showers, dump station, boat ramp (no gas-powered motorboats), and boat rentals (in summer) are available. A grocery store, coin laundry, firewood, and propane gas are available within five minutes. Some facilities are wheelchair-accessible. Leashed pets are permitted.

Reservations, fees: Reservations are accepted on weekdays at 707/565-2267 ($8.50 reservation fee). Sites are $30–32 per night, $6 per night for each additional vehicle, hike-in/bike-in sites are $5 per night, $2 per pet per night. The group site is $200 per night. There is a 10-day camping limit. Open daily from May through September and on weekends and holidays only during off-season.

Directions: From Santa Rosa on U.S. 101, turn east on Highway 12 and drive two miles to the junction with Hoen Avenue. Continue straight (east) onto Hoen Avenue and drive one mile (crossing Summerfield Road) to Newanga Avenue. Turn left and drive 0.5 mile to the park entrance at 5585 Newanga Avenue.

Contact: Spring Lake Regional Park, 707/539-8092; Sonoma County Parks, 707/565-2041, www.sonoma-county.org.

109 SUGARLOAF RIDGE STATE PARK

🚶 🚴 🐴 🚐 ⛺

Scenic rating: 5

near Santa Rosa

Map 4.4, page 252

Sugarloaf Ridge State Park is a perfect example of a place that you can't make a final judgment about from your first glance. Your first glance will lead you to believe that this is just hot foothill country, with old ranch roads set in oak woodlands for horseback riding and sweaty hiking or biking. A little discovery here, however, is that a half-mile walk off the Canyon Trail will lead you to a 25-foot waterfall, beautifully set in a canyon, complete with a redwood canopy. A shortcut to this waterfall is available off the south side of the park's entrance road. Otherwise, it can be a long, hot, and challenging hike. In all, there are 25 miles of trails here for hikers and equestrians. Hikers planning for a day of it should leave early, wear a hat, and bring plenty of water. Rangers report that some unprepared hikers have suffered heat stroke in summer, and many others have just plain suffered. In the off-season, when the air is cool and clear, the views from the ridge are eye-popping—visitors can see the Sierra Nevada, Golden Gate, and a thousand other points of scenic beauty from the top of Bald Mountain at 2,769 feet. For the less ambitious, a self-guided nature trail along Sonoma Creek begins at the campground.

Note: This park was on the closure list developed by the California Department of Parks, pending final state budget decisions or the possible transfer of park management to other park agencies or volunteer groups. It is currently being operated by Team Sugarloaf, a nonprofit organization.

Campsites, facilities: There are 49 sites for tents or RVs up to 27 feet (no hookups), and one group site for tents only for up to 30 people. Picnic tables, food lockers and fire grills are provided. Drinking water, coin showers, and flush toilets are available. Leashed pets are permitted in campsites only.

Reservations, fees: Reservations are recommended at 800/444-7275 (800/444-PARK) or www.reserveamerica.com ($8 reservation fee). Sites are $35 per night, $8 per night for each additional vehicle, the group site is $165 per night. Open year-round.

Directions: From Santa Rosa on U.S. 101, turn east on Highway 12 and drive seven miles to Adobe Canyon Road. Turn left and drive 3.5

miles to the park entrance at the end of the road.

Contact: Sugarloaf Ridge State Park, 707/833-5712, www.parks.ca.gov or http://sugarloaf-park.org.

110 SAN FRANCISCO NORTH/ PETALUMA KOA

Scenic rating: 3

near Petaluma

Map 4.4, page 252

This campground is less than a mile from U.S. 101, yet it has a rural feel in a 60-acre farm setting. It's a good base camp for folks who require some quiet mental preparation before heading south to the Bay Area or to the nearby wineries, redwoods, and Russian River. The big plus here is that this KOA has the cute log cabins called "Kamping Kabins," providing privacy for those who want it. There are recreational activities and live music on Saturdays in summer. During October, a pumpkin patch and corn maze are open across the street from the park.

Campsites, facilities: There are 312 sites, most with full or partial hookups (30 and 50 amps) for RVs or tents, 34 cabins, 11 lodges, and four studio lodges. Most sites are pull-through. Picnic tables and fire pits are provided. Restrooms with flush toilets and showers, cable TV hookups, free Wi-Fi, dump station, playground, recreation rooms, basketball, volleyball, heated seasonal swimming pool, spa, petting farm, horseshoes, bocce ball, coin laundry, propane gas, and convenience store are available. Some facilities are wheelchair-accessible. Leashed pets are permitted, with certain restrictions.

Reservations, fees: Reservations are accepted at 800/562-1233 or through the website. RV sites with full hookups are $66–75 per night, RV sites with partial hookups are $56 per night, tent sites are $52 per night, $5–7 per person per night for more than two people. Camping cabins are $90 per night, lodges are $207 per night. Some credit cards accepted. Open year-round.

Directions: From Petaluma on U.S. 101 north, take the Penngrove exit and drive west for 0.25 mile on Petaluma Boulevard to Stony Point Road. Turn right (north) on Stony Point Road and drive 0.25 mile to Rainsville Road. Turn left (west) on Rainsville Road and drive a short distance to the park entrance at 20 Rainsville Road.

Contact: San Francisco North/Petaluma KOA, 707/763-1492, www.petalumakoa.com.

111 NAPA VALLEY EXPOSITION RV PARK

Scenic rating: 2

in Napa

Map 4.4, page 252

This RV park is directly adjacent to the Napa Valley Exposition. When the fair is in operation in late July and early August, it is closed. The rest of the year it is simply a RV parking area, and it can come in handy.

Campsites, facilities: There are 28 sites with full hookups (30 and 50 amps) for RVs of any length and a grassy area for at least 100 self-contained RVs. Some sites are pull-through. Picnic tables, restrooms with showers, coin laundry, free WiFi, and a dump station are available. A camp host is on-site. A restaurant is within walking distance. Some facilities are wheelchair-accessible. Leashed pets are permitted.

Reservations, fees: Reservations are recommended for individual sites and are required for groups at 707/253-4900, ext. 102. RV sites with full hookups are $45 per night. Open year-round, except during the fair.

Directions: From Napa on Highway 29, drive to the Napa/Lake Berryessa exit. Take that exit and turn right (east) and drive about one mile to Silverado/Highway 121. Turn right and drive less than one mile to the fairgrounds entrance on the left.

Contact: Napa Valley Exposition, 707/253-4900, www.napavalleyexpo.com.

SACRAMENTO AND GOLD COUNTRY

© ROBERT KEENAN/123RF.COM

BEST CAMPGROUNDS

From a distance, this section of the Sacramento

Valley looks like flat farmland extending into infinity, with a sprinkling of cities and towns interrupting the view. But a closer look reveals a landscape filled with Northern California's most significant rivers – the Sacramento, Feather, Yuba, American, and Mokelumne. All of these provide water recreation, in both lakes and rivers, as well as serve as the lifeblood for a series of wildlife refuges.

This is an area for California history buffs, with Placerville KOA and nearby Malakoff Diggins State Historic Park in the center of some of the state's most extraordinary history: the gold rush era. Another good deal is the Lake Oroville Floating Camps, which can sleep 15 and cost $100 a night.

The highlight of foothill country is its series of great lakes – Camanche, Rollins, Oroville, and many others – for water sports, fishing, and any lake recreation. Note that the mapping I use for this region extends up to Bucks Lake, which is set high in Plumas National Forest, the northern start to the Gold Country.

Timing is everything in love and the great outdoors, and so it is in the Central Valley and the nearby foothills. Spring and fall are gorgeous, as are many summer evenings. But there are always periods of 100°F-plus temperatures in the summer.

But that's what gives the lakes and rivers such appeal, and in turn, why they are treasured. Take your pick: Lake Oroville in the northern Sierra, Folsom Lake outside Sacramento... the list goes on. On a hot day, jumping into a cool lake makes water more valuable than gold, a cold drink on ice worth more than silver. These have become top sites for boating-based recreation and fantastic areas for water sports and fishing.

In the Mother Lode country, three other lakes – Camanche, Amador, and Pardee – are outstanding for fishing. Lake Oroville and Camanche Lake are best for bass while Lake Amador makes it for bluegill and catfish. Lake Pardee rates high for rainbow trout and salmon.

For touring, the state capital and nearby Old Sacramento are favorites. Others prefer reliving the gold-mining history of California's past or exploring the foothill country, including Malakoff Diggins State Historic Park.

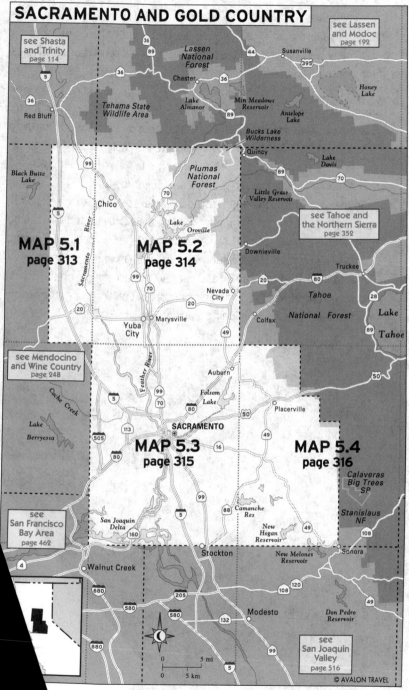

SACRAMENTO AND GOLD COUNTRY

see Shasta and Trinity
page 114

see Lassen and Modoc
page 192

Lassen National Forest

Susanville

Chester

36

89

44

395

Honey Lake

36

Red Bluff

Tehama State Wildlife Area

Lake Almanor

Mtn Meadows Reservoir

Antelope Lake

89

Bucks Lake Wilderness

Black Butte Lake

99

Plumas National Forest

Quincy

Lake Davis

89

70

Chico

70

Lake Oroville

Little Grass Valley Reservoir

see Tahoe and the Northern Sierra
page 352

MAP 5.1
page 313

MAP 5.2
page 314

Downieville

Truckee

99

70

20

80

28

Nevada City

20

Tahoe National Forest

Lake Tahoe

20

Yuba City

Marysville

Colfax

89

49

see Mendocino and Wine Country
page 248

Feather River

Auburn

50

Cache Creek

99

70

Folsom Lake

80

Placerville

Lake Berryessa

113

SACRAMENTO

50

49

505

80

MAP 5.3
page 315

16

MAP 5.4
page 316

Calaveras Big Trees SP

see San Francisco Bay Area
page 462

San Joaquin Delta

5

88

Camanche Res

Stanislaus NF

108

160

New Hogan Reservoir

49

Stockton

New Melones Reservoir

Sonora

4

Walnut Creek

680

205

108

120

49

580

580

132

Modesto

Don Pedro Reservoir

880

99

5

see San Joaquin Valley
page 516

0   5 mi
0   5 km

© AVALON TRAVEL

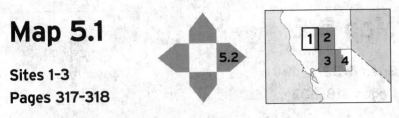

Map 5.1

Sites 1-3
Pages 317-318

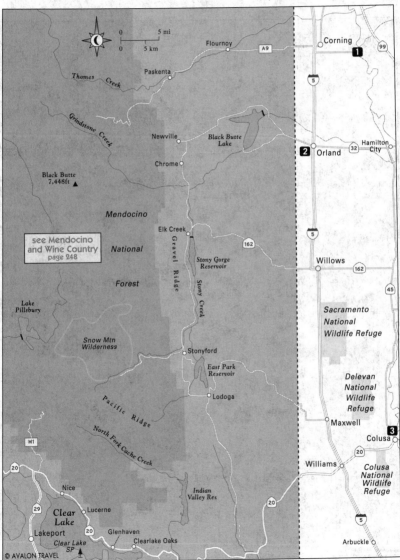

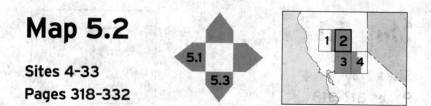

Map 5.2

Sites 4-33
Pages 318-332

5.1

5.3

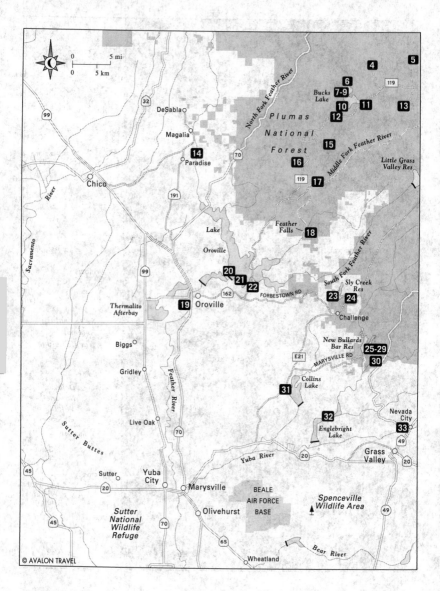

Map 5.3

Sites 34-50
Pages 333-341

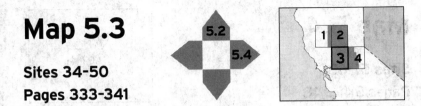

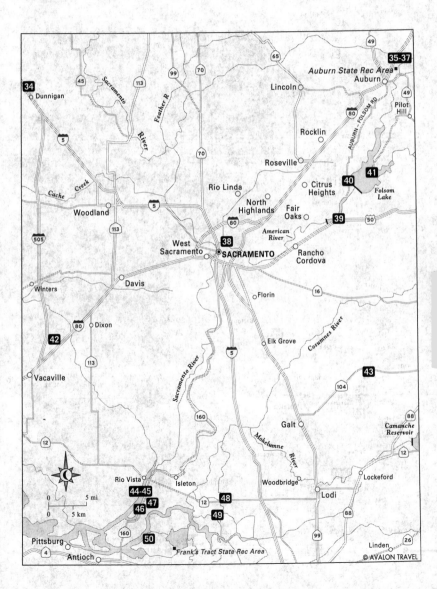

© AVALON TRAVEL

Map 5.4

**Sites 51-63
Pages 341-348**

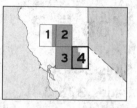

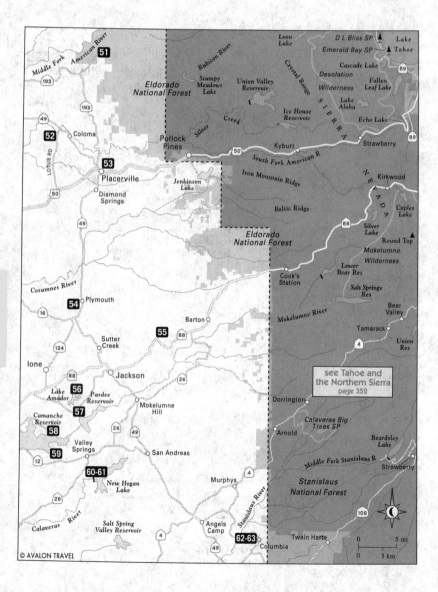

1 WOODSON BRIDGE STATE RECREATION AREA

Scenic rating: 7

on the Sacramento River

Map 5.1, page 313

The campground at Woodson Bridge features direct access to the Sacramento River. The preserve itself is 328-acres of thick, riparian forest, including some of the only virgin habitat left on this 400-mile length of the Sacramento River. Boat-in sites, designed as camping spots for kayakers and canoeists, and a nearby boat ramp provide easy access for water sports, making this an ideal spot for campers with trailered boats. Note that waterskiing and personal watercraft are discouraged on this section of the river.

There are about two miles of hiking trails in the park; a beach is nearby. In June, the nearby Tehama Riffle is one of the best spots on the entire river for shad fishing. By mid-August, salmon start arriving, en route to their spawning grounds. Summer weather here is hot, with high temperatures commonly 85–100°F. In winter, look for bald eagles; in summer, the yellow-billed cuckoo builds nests here.

Note: This park was on the closure list developed by the California Department of Parks, pending final state budget decisions or the possible transfer of park management to other park agencies or volunteer groups. It is currently open following a concession agreement with American Land and Leisure.

Campsites, facilities: There are 37 sites for tents or RVs up to 31 feet (no hookups) and one boat-in site. One group site for up to 40 people is available. Picnic tables and fire grills are provided. Drinking water, coin showers, flush toilets, and boat launch (across the street) are available, and there is a camp host. Leashed pets are permitted.

Reservations, fees: Reservations are accepted May through September at 800/444-7275 (800/444-PARK) or www.reserveamerica.com ($8 reservation fee). In April and October sites are first-come, first-served. Sites are $25 per night, $8 per night for each additional vehicle, $135 per night for the group camp. Open April through October.

Directions: From Corning, take the South Avenue exit off I-5 and drive six miles east to the campground on the left.

Contact: Woodson Bridge State Recreation Area, 530/839-2112, www.parks.ca.gov; American Land and Leisure, 800/342-2267, www.americanll.com.

2 OLD ORCHARD RV PARK

Scenic rating: 4

near Orland

Map 5.1, page 313

Most folks use this as a layover spot while on long trips up or down I-5 in the Central Valley. If you're staying longer than a night, there are two side trips that have appeal for anglers. Nearby Black Butte Lake to the west, with crappie in the early summer, and the Sacramento River to the east, with salmon in the late summer and early fall, can add some spice to your trip. The elevation is 250 feet. Some sites are filled with long-term renters.

Campsites, facilities: There are 52 pull-through sites with partial or full hookups (30 and 50 amps) for RVs up to 60 feet, and six tent sites. Restrooms with showers, dump station, coin laundry, and WiFi are available. All facilities are wheelchair-accessible. Leashed pets are permitted.

Reservations, fees: Reservations are accepted. RV sites are $26 per night, tent sites are $15 per night, $2 per person per night for more than two adults, $2 per night for 50-amp full hookup. Some credit cards accepted. Open year-round.

Directions: From Orland, take the Chico/Highway 32 exit west (Exit 619) off I-5. Drive west one block to County Road HH. Turn right on County Road HH and drive north one block to the park on the right at 4490 County Road HH.

Contact: Old Orchard RV Park, 530/865-5335 or 877/481-9282.

3 COLUSA-SACRAMENTO RIVER STATE RECREATION AREA

Scenic rating: 5

near Colusa

Map 5.1, page 313

This region of the Sacramento Valley is well known as a high-quality habitat for birds. This park covers 67 acres and features great bird-watching opportunities. Nearby Delevan and Colusa National Wildlife Refuges are outstanding destinations for wildlife-viewing as well, and they provide good duck hunting in December. In summer the nearby Sacramento River is a bonus, with shad fishing in June and July, salmon fishing from August through October, sturgeon fishing in the winter, and striped-bass fishing in the spring. The landscape here features cottonwoods and willows along the Sacramento River.

Note: This park was on the closure list developed by the California Department of Parks, pending final state budget decisions or the possible transfer of park management to other park agencies or volunteer groups. It is currently being operated by the City of Colusa.

Campsites, facilities: There are 10 sites for tents, four sites for tents or RVs up to 30 feet, and one group site for 10–100 people. No hookups. Picnic tables and barbecues are provided. Drinking water, restrooms with flush toilets and coin showers, boat ramp, Wi-Fi, and a dump station are available. Some facilities are wheelchair-accessible. A grocery store, restaurant, gas station, tackle shop, and coin laundry are nearby (within three blocks). Leashed pets are permitted.

Reservations, fees: Reservations for individual sites are accepted at 800/444-7275

(800/444-PARK) or www.reserveamerica.com ($8 reservation fee). Group reservations are accepted at Colusa City Hall 530/458-4740, ex. 106. Sites are $28 per night, $6 per night for each additional vehicle. The group site is $135 per night, $6 per vehicle for more than 10 vehicles. Open year-round.

Directions: In Williams, at the junction of I-5 and Highway 20, drive east on Highway 20 for nine miles to the town of Colusa. Turn north (straight ahead) on 10th Street and drive two blocks, just over the levee, to the park.

Contact: Colusa City Hall, 530/458-4740, ext. 106, www.cityofcolusa.com; Colusa–Sacramento River State Recreation Area, 530/458-4927, www.parks.ca.gov.

4 SILVER LAKE

Scenic rating: 8

in Plumas National Forest

Map 5.2, page 314

While tons of people go to Bucks Lake for the great trout fishing and lakeside camps, nearby Silver Lake gets little attention despite great natural beauty, good hiking, decent trout fishing, and a trailhead to the Bucks Lake Wilderness. The camp is at the north end of the lake, at 5,800 feet elevation, a primitive and secluded spot. No powerboats (or swimming) is allowed on Silver Lake, which makes it ideal for canoes and rafts. The lake has lots of small brook trout. The Pacific Crest Trail is routed on the ridge above the lake, skirting past Mount Pleasant (6,924 feet) to the nearby west.

Campsites, facilities: There are seven tent sites. Picnic tables and fire grills are provided. Vault toilets are available. Garbage must be packed out. No drinking water is available. Leashed pets are permitted.

Reservations, fees: Reservations are not accepted. There is no fee for camping. Open May through October, weather permitting.

Directions: From Oroville, drive north on Highway 70 to the junction with Highway 89. Turn south on Highway 89/70 and drive 11 miles to Quincy and Bucks Lake Road. Turn right at Bucks Lake Road and drive west for nine miles to Silver Lake Road. Turn right and drive seven miles to the campground at the north end of the lake.

Contact: Plumas National Forest, Mt. Hough Ranger District, 530/283-0555, www.fs.usda. gov/plumas.

5 SNAKE LAKE

Scenic rating: 8

in Plumas National Forest

Map 5.2, page 314

Snake Lake is a rarity in the northern Sierra, a mountain lake that has bass, catfish, and bluegill. That is because it is a shallow lake, set at 5,800 feet elevation in Plumas National Forest. The camp is on the west shore. Motors of up to 5 horsepower are allowed. A road that circles the lake provides a good bicycle route for youngsters. A side trip to the nearby north is Smith Lake, about a five-minute drive, with the Butterfly Valley Botanical Area bordering it.

Campsites, facilities: There are nine sites for tents only. Picnic tables and fire grills are provided. Campfire permits are required when campfires are allowed. Vault toilets are available. No drinking water is available. Garbage must be packed out. Leashed pets are permitted.

Reservations, fees: Reservations are not accepted. There is no fee for camping. Open May through October, weather permitting.

Directions: From Oroville, drive north on Highway 70 to the junction with Highway 89. Turn south on Highway 89/70 and drive 11 miles to Quincy and Bucks Lake Road. Turn right at Bucks Lake Road and drive five miles to County Road 422. Turn right and drive two miles to the Snake Lake access road. Turn

right and drive one mile to the campground on the right.

Contact: Plumas National Forest, Mt. Hough Ranger District, 530/283-0555, www.fs.usda. gov/plumas.

6 MILL CREEK

Scenic rating: 7

at Bucks Lake in Plumas National Forest

Map 5.2, page 314

When Bucks Lake is full, this is one of the prettiest spots on the lake. The camp is set deep in Mill Creek Cove, adjacent to where Mill Creek enters the northernmost point of Bucks Lake. A boat ramp is 0.5 mile away to the south, providing boat access to one of the better trout fishing spots at the lake. Unfortunately, when the lake level falls, this camp is left high and dry, some distance from the water. All water sports are permitted on this 1,800-acre lake. The elevation is 5,200 feet.

Campsites, facilities: There are eight sites for tents or RVs up to 27 feet (no hookups) and two walk-in tent sites. Picnic tables, food lockers, and fire grills are provided. Drinking water and vault toilets are available. Groceries are available within five miles. Leashed pets are permitted.

Reservations, fees: Reservations are not accepted. Sites are $23–25 per night. Open mid-May through September, weather permitting.

Directions: From Oroville, drive north on Highway 70 to the junction with Highway 89. Turn south on Highway 89/70 and drive 11 miles to Quincy. In Quincy, turn right at Bucks Lake Road and drive 17 miles to Bucks Lake and the junction with Bucks Lake Dam Road/Forest Road 33. Turn right, drive around the lake, cross over the dam, and continue for about three miles to the campground.

Contact: Plumas National Forest, Mt. Hough Ranger District, 530/283-0555, www.fs.usda. gov/plumas.

7 SUNDEW

Scenic rating: 7

on Bucks Lake in Plumas National Forest

Map 5.2, page 314

Sundew Camp is set on the northern shore of Bucks Lake, just north of Bucks Lake Dam. A boat ramp is about two miles north at Sandy Point Day Use Area at the Mill Creek Cove, providing access to one of the better trout spots on the lake. You want fish? At Bucks Lake you can get fish—it's one of the state's top mountain trout lakes. Fish species include rainbow, brown, and Mackinaw trout. Sunrises are often spectacular from this camp, with the light glowing on the lake's surface.

Campsites, facilities: There are 19 sites for tents or RVs up to 35 feet (no hookups). Picnic tables, food lockers, and fire grills are provided. Drinking water and vault toilets are available. Leashed pets are permitted. There is a boat ramp two miles north of the camp.

Reservations, fees: Reservations are not accepted. Sites are $23–24 per night. Open mid-May through September, weather permitting.

Directions: From Oroville, drive north on Highway 70 to the junction with Highway 89. Turn south on Highway 89/70 and drive 11 miles to Quincy. In Quincy, turn right at Bucks Lake Road and drive 17 miles to Bucks Lake and the junction with Bucks Lake Dam Road/Forest Road 33. Turn right, drive around the lake, cross over the dam, continue for 0.5 mile, and turn right at the campground access road.

Contact: Plumas National Forest, Mt. Hough Ranger District, 530/283-0555, www.fs.usda. gov/plumas.

8 HUTCHINS GROUP CAMP

Scenic rating: 6

near Bucks Lake in Plumas National Forest

Map 5.2, page 314

This is a prime spot for a Scout outing or for any other large group that would like a pretty spot. An amphitheater is available. It is set at 5,200 feet elevation near Bucks and Lower Bucks Lakes. (For more information, see the Sundew, Lower Bucks, and Haskins Valley listings in this chapter.)

Campsites, facilities: There are three group sites for tents or RV up to 35 feet (no hookups) that can accommodate up to 25 people each. Picnic tables, food lockers, and fire grills are provided. Drinking water and vault toilets are available. A boat ramp is available. Some facilities are wheelchair accessible. Leashed pets are permitted.

Reservations, fees: Reservations are required at 877/444-6777 or www.recreation.gov ($9 reservation fee). The group camp is $70–75 per night. Open May through October.

Directions: From Oroville, drive north on Highway 70 to the junction with Highway 89. Turn south on Highway 89/70 and drive 11 miles to Quincy and Bucks Lake Road. Turn right at Bucks Lake Road and drive 17 miles to Bucks Lake and the junction with Bucks Lake Dam Road/Forest Road 33. Turn right, drive around the lake, cross over the dam, continue for a short distance, and turn right. Drive 0.5 mile, cross the stream (passing an intersection), and continue straight for 0.5 mile to the campground.

Contact: Plumas National Forest, Mt. Hough Ranger District, 530/283-0555, www.fs.usda. gov/plumas.

9 LOWER BUCKS

Scenic rating: 7

on Lower Bucks Lake in
Plumas National Forest

Map 5.2, page 314

This camp is on Lower Bucks Lake, which is actually the afterbay for Bucks Lake, set below the Bucks Lake Dam. It is a small, primitive, and quiet spot that is often overlooked because it is not on the main lake. If you end up here, there's a piece of bad news: no water or bathrooms.

Campsites, facilities: There are seven sites for tents or self-contained RVs up to 26 feet (no hookups). Picnic tables and fire rings are provided. There is no drinking water. Leashed pets are permitted.

Reservations, fees: Reservations are not accepted. Sites are $19 per night. Open May through October.

Directions: From Oroville, drive north on Highway 70 to the junction with Highway 89. Turn south on Highway 89/70 and drive 11 miles to Quincy and Bucks Lake Road. Turn right at Bucks Lake Road and drive 17 miles to Bucks Lake and the junction with Bucks Lake Dam Road/Forest Road 33. Turn right and drive four miles around the lake, cross over the dam, drive 0.25 mile, and then turn left on the campground entrance road.

Contact: Plumas National Forest, Mt. Hough Ranger District, 530/283-0555, www.fs.usda.gov/plumas.

10 HASKINS VALLEY

Scenic rating: 7

on Bucks Lake

Map 5.2, page 314

This is the biggest and most popular of the campgrounds at Bucks Lake, a pretty alpine lake with excellent trout fishing and clean campgrounds. A boat ramp is available to the nearby north, along with Bucks Lodge. This camp is set deep in a cove at the extreme south end of the lake, where the water is quiet and sheltered from north winds. Bucks Lake, at 5,200 feet elevation, is well documented for excellent fishing for rainbow and Mackinaw trout, with high catch rates of rainbow trout and lake records in the 16-pound class. Insider's tip: This is the best lake in the region for sailboarding.

Campsites, facilities: There are 65 sites for tents or RVs up to 40 feet (no hookups). Picnic tables and fire grills are provided. Drinking water and vault toilets are available. A dump station and boat ramp are available nearby. Some facilities are wheelchair-accessible. Leashed pets are permitted.

Reservations, fees: Reservations are not accepted. Sites are $25 per night, $3 per night for each additional vehicle, $1 per pet per night, $10 boat launch fee. Open May to early October, weather permitting.

Directions: From Oroville, drive north on Highway 70 to the junction with Highway 89. Turn south on Highway 89/70 and drive 11 miles to Quincy. In Quincy, turn right at Bucks Lake Road and drive 16.5 miles to the campground entrance on the right side of the road.

Contact: PG&E Land Services, 916/386-5164, www.pge.com/recreation.

11 WHITEHORSE

Scenic rating: 7

near Bucks Lake in Plumas National Forest

Map 5.2, page 314

This campground is set along Bucks Creek, about two miles from the boat ramps and south shore concessions at Bucks Lake. The trout fishing can be quite good at Bucks Lake. The elevation is 5,200 feet. (For more information, see the Haskins Valley listing.)

Campsites, facilities: There are 20 sites for tents or RVs up to 27 feet (no hookups). Picnic

tables and fire grills are provided. Drinking water and vault toilets are available. A grocery store and coin laundry are available within five miles. Leashed pets are permitted.

Reservations, fees: Reservations are not accepted. Sites are $20 per night. Open June through September.

Directions: From Oroville, drive north on Highway 70 to the junction with Highway 89. Turn south on Highway 89/70 and drive 11 miles to Quincy and Bucks Lake Road. Turn right at Bucks Lake Road and drive 14.5 miles to the campground entrance on the right side of the road.

Contact: Plumas National Forest, Mt. Hough Ranger District, 530/283-0555, www.fs.usda. gov/plumas.

12 GRIZZLY CREEK

Scenic rating: 4

near Bucks Lake in Plumas National Forest

Map 5.2, page 314

This is an alternative to the more developed, more crowded campgrounds at Bucks Lake. It is a small, primitive camp set near Grizzly Creek at 5,400 feet elevation. Nearby Bucks Lake provides good trout fishing, resorts, and boat rentals.

Campsites, facilities: There are eight sites for tents or RVs up to 35 feet (no hookups). Picnic tables and fire grills are provided. Vault toilets are available. There is no drinking water. A boat ramp is available at Bucks Lake. Leashed pets are permitted.

Reservations, fees: Reservations are not accepted. Sites are $20 per night. Open June through October.

Directions: From Oroville, drive north on Highway 70 to the junction with Highway 89. Turn south on Highway 89/70 and drive 11 miles to Quincy and Bucks Lake Road. Turn right at Bucks Lake Road and drive 17 miles to Bucks Lake and the junction with Bucks Lake Dam Road/Forest Road 33. Turn

right and drive one mile to the junction with Oroville-Quincy Road/Forest Road 36. Bear left and drive one mile to the campground on the right side of the road.

Contact: Plumas National Forest, Mt. Hough Ranger District, 530/283-0555, www.fs.usda. gov/plumas.

13 DEANES VALLEY

Scenic rating: 5

on Rock Creek in Plumas National Forest

Map 5.2, page 314

This secret spot is set on South Fork Rock Creek, deep in a valley at an elevation of 4,400 feet in Plumas National Forest. The trout here are very small natives. If you want a pure, quiet spot, great; if you want good fishing, not so great. The surrounding region has a network of backcountry roads, including routes passable only by four-wheel-drive vehicles; to explore these roads, get a map of Plumas National Forest.

Campsites, facilities: There are seven sites for tents or RVs up to 24 feet (no hookups). Picnic tables and fire grills are provided. A campfire permit is required when campfires are allowed. Vault toilets are available. No drinking water is available. Garbage must be packed out. Leashed pets are permitted.

Reservations, fees: Reservations are not accepted. There is no fee for camping. Open April through October, weather permitting.

Directions: From Oroville, drive north on Highway 70 to the junction with Highway 89. Turn south on Highway 89/70 and drive 11 miles to Quincy and Bucks Lake Road. Turn right at Bucks Lake Road and drive 3.5 miles to Forest Road 24N28. Turn left and drive seven miles to the campground on the left.

Contact: Plumas National Forest, Mt. Hough Ranger District, 530/283-0555, www.fs.usda. gov/plumas.

14 QUAIL TRAILS VILLAGE RV AND MOBILE HOME PARK

Scenic rating: 4

near Paradise

Map 5.2, page 314

This is a rural motor-home campground, set near the west branch of the Feather River, with nearby Lake Oroville as the feature attraction. The Lime Saddle section of the Lake Oroville State Recreation Area is three miles away, with a beach, boat-launching facilities, and concessions. Note: About one-third of the sites are taken by long-term rentals.

Campsites, facilities: There are 20 pull-through sites with full hookups (30 amps) for RVs of any length, and five tent sites. Picnic tables are provided. Restrooms with showers and coin laundry are available. WiFi is available. All facilities are wheelchair-accessible. Leashed pets up to 30 pounds are permitted.

Reservations, fees: Reservations are accepted. RV sites are $32 per night, tent sites are $20 per night. Weekly and monthly rates available. Open year-round.

Directions: From Oroville, drive north on Highway 70 for six miles to Pentz Road. Turn left and drive six miles south to the park on the left (5110 Pentz Road).

Contact: Quail Trails Village RV and Mobile Home Park, 530/877-6581, www.quailtrails-village.com.

15 LITTLE NORTH FORK

Scenic rating: 7

on the Middle Fork of the Feather River in Plumas National Forest

Map 5.2, page 314

Guaranteed quiet? You got it. This is a primitive camp in the outback that few know of. It is set along the Little North Fork of the Middle Fork of the Feather River at 4,000 feet elevation. The surrounding backcountry of Plumas National Forest features an incredible number of roads, giving four-wheel-drive owners a chance to get so lost they'll need this camp. Instead, get a map of Plumas National Forest before venturing out.

Campsites, facilities: There are six sites for tents or RVs up to 16 feet (no hookups). Picnic tables and fire grills are provided. A campfire permit is required when campfires are allowed. Drinking water and vault toilets are available. Garbage must be packed out. Some facilities are wheelchair accessible. Leashed pets are permitted.

Reservations, fees: Reservations are not accepted. There is no fee for camping. Open May through October.

Directions: From Oroville, turn east on Highway 162/Oroville-Quincy Highway and drive 26.5 miles to the Brush Creek Work Center. Continue northeast on Oroville-Quincy Highway for about six miles to County Road 60. Turn right and drive about eight miles to the campground entrance road on the left side of the road. Turn left and drive 0.25 mile to the campground. Note: This route is long, twisty, bumpy, and narrow for most of the way.

Contact: Plumas National Forest, Feather River Ranger District, 530/534-6500, www.fs.usda.gov/plumas.

16 ROGERS COW CAMP

Scenic rating: 4

in Plumas National Forest

Map 5.2, page 314

This remote camp is set in Plumas National Forest at 4,000 feet elevation near the headwaters of Coon Creek. The drive to get here is along the Oroville-Quincy "Highway," a long and curvy but paved Forest Service road; this backcountry route connects Oroville to Quincy and passes Lake Oroville and Bucks Lake in the process. It can still put you way out there in no-man's land. You want quiet, you got it. You want water, you bring it yourself. There are no other natural destinations in the area, and I'm not saying Coon Creek is anything to see. It's advisable to obtain a map of Plumas National Forest, which details all backcountry roads. There has also been logging activity in the area.

Campsites, facilities: There are six sites for tents or RVs up to 16 feet (no hookups). Picnic tables and fire grills are provided. Vault toilets are available. No drinking water is available. Garbage must be packed out. Some facilities are wheelchair accessible. Leashed pets are permitted.

Reservations, fees: Reservations are not accepted. There is no fee for camping. Open year-round, weather permitting.

Directions: In Oroville, drive east on Highway 162/Oroville-Quincy Highway for 26.5 miles to the Brush Creek Work Center. Continue on Oroville-Quincy Highway for eight miles to the campground entrance road on the left side of the road. Turn left and drive a short distance to the camp.

Contact: Plumas National Forest, Feather River Ranger District, 530/534-6500, www.fs.usda.gov/plumas.

17 MILSAP BAR
🏃 🏊 🛶 🐕 🚐 ⛺

Scenic rating: 8

on the Middle Fork of the Feather River in Plumas National Forest

Map 5.2, page 314

Milsap Bar is a well-known access point to the Middle Fork Feather River. This river country features a deep canyon and beautiful surroundings. Access is excellent for flyfishing for trout. Your best bet is heading upstream from the bridge; you'll see a tributary that enters the main stem on the left, that's the best spot to start. On the far side of the campground is a feeder stream with pool-and-drop. Insider's note: Locals often turn this campground into a party pad on Friday or Saturday nights; weeknights in spring and fall best. The elevation is 1,600 feet.

Campsites, facilities: There are five sites for tents or RVs up to 16 feet (no hookups). Picnic tables and fire grills are provided. Vault toilets are available. No drinking water is available. Garbage must be packed out. Leashed pets are permitted.

Reservations, fees: Reservations are not accepted. There is no fee for camping. Open May through September.

Directions: In Oroville, drive east on Highway 162/Oroville-Quincy Highway for 26.5 miles to the Brush Creek Work Center and Bald Rock Road. Turn right on Bald Rock Road and drive for about 0.5 mile to Forest Road 22N62/Milsap Bar Road. Turn left and drive eight miles to the campground (a narrow, steep, mountain dirt road).

Contact: Plumas National Forest, Feather River Ranger District, 530/534-6500, www.fs.usda.gov/plumas.

18 FEATHER FALLS TRAILHEAD CAMPGROUND
🏃 🏊 🛶 🐕 🚐 ⛺

Scenic rating: 7

Feather Falls Scenic Area in Plumas National Forest

Map 5.2, page 314

This small campground is located at the trailhead for the fantastic hike to 410-foot Feather Falls. This is one of California's greatest hikes, a 9.5-mile round-trip loop leading past Native American grinding mortars to a viewing deck perched on a knife-edge outcrop for a full frontal view of the waterfall. In addition, the creek canyon is the winter home for millions of ladybugs.

Campsites, facilities: There are five sites for tents or RVs up to 16 feet (no hookups). Picnic tables and fire grills are provided. Drinking water and vault toilets are available. Garbage service is available; but when cans are full, garbage must be packed out. Leashed pets are permitted.

Reservations, fees: Reservations are not

accepted. There is no fee for camping. A 14-day maximum stay rule is in place. Open May through September, weather permitting.

Directions: From Oroville, drive east on Oroville Dam Boulevard to Olive Highway. Turn right on Olive Highway and drive 5 miles to Forbestown Road. Turn right on Forbestown Road and drive 7 miles to Lumpkin Road. Turn left on Lumpkin Road and drive 12 miles to the trailhead turnoff. Turn left at the turnoff and drive 1.5 miles to the parking area. Campsites are at the beginning of the parking area, while the trailhead is at the far end.

Contact: Plumas National Forest, Feather River Ranger District, 530/534-6500, www.fs.usda.gov/plumas.

19 DINGERVILLE USA

Scenic rating: 3

near Oroville

Map 5.2, page 314

You're right, they thought of this name all by themselves, needed no help. It is an RV park set in the Oroville foothill country—hot and dry in the summer, but with a variety of side trips nearby. It is adjacent to a wildlife area and the Feather River and within short range of Lake Oroville and the Thermalito Afterbay for boating, water sports, and fishing. The RV park is a clean, quiet campground with easy access from the highway. Some of the sites are occupied by long-term renters.

Campsites, facilities: There are 29 pull-through sites with full hookups (30 amps) for RVs of any length. No tents. Picnic tables are provided. Restrooms with showers, cable TV, seasonal swimming pool, coin laundry, horseshoe pit, and a nine-hole executive golf course are available. Some facilities are wheelchair-accessible. Leashed pets are permitted.

Reservations, fees: Reservations are recommended. Sites are $32 per night. Some credit cards accepted. Open year-round.

Directions: From Oroville, drive south on Highway 70 to the second Pacific Heights Road turnoff. Turn right at Pacific Heights Road and drive less than one mile to the campground on the left.

From Marysville, drive north on Highway 70 to Palermo-Welsh Road. Turn left on Palermo-Welsh Road and drive to Pacific Heights Road. Turn left (north) on Pacific Heights Road and drive 0.5 mile to the campground entrance on the right.

Contact: Dingerville USA, 530/533-9343.

20 LAKE OROVILLE BOAT-IN AND FLOATING CAMPS

Scenic rating: 10

on Lake Oroville

Map 5.2, page 314

It doesn't get any stranger than this, and for those who have tried, it doesn't get any better. We're talking about the double-decker floating camps at Lake Oroville, along with the great boat-in sites. The floating camps look like giant patio boats. They sleep 15 people and they include picnic table, sink, food locker, garbage can, vault toilet, and propane barbecue. There are also a series of dispersed boat-in camps around the lake, which are particularly excellent in the spring and early summer, when the water level at the lake is high. In late summer, when the lake level drops, it can be a fair hike up the bank to the campsites, and, in addition, if the water drops quickly, your boat can be left sitting on the bank; it can be quite an effort to get it back in the water. Oroville is an outstanding lake for water sports, with warm water and plenty of room, and also with excellent bass fishing, especially in the spring.

Campsites, facilities: There are four dispersed boat-in camps, one group boat-in site (Bloomer) for up to 75 people, and 10 boat-in floating camps for up to 15 people. Picnic tables and fire grills are provided. Vault toilets are available. No drinking water is provided.

Some facilities are wheelchair accessible. Leashed pets are permitted, except on trails or beaches.

Reservations, fees: Reservations are accepted at 800/444-7275 (800/444-PARK) or www.reserveamerica.com ($8 reservation fee). Floating camps are $175 per night, individual boat-in sites are $20 per night, and the group boat-in site is $135 per night. Open year-round.

Directions: From Oroville, drive east on Oroville Dam Boulevard/Highway 162 (becomes the Olive Highway) for 5.5 miles to Canyon Drive. Turn left and drive two miles to Oroville Dam. Turn left and drive over the dam to the spillway parking lot at the end of the road. Register at the entrance station. Boats can be launched from this area.

Contact: Lake Oroville State Recreation Area, 530/538-2200; Lake Oroville Visitor Center, 530/538-2219, www.parks.ca.gov.

21 BIDWELL CANYON

Scenic rating: 7

on Lake Oroville

Map 5.2, page 314

Bidwell Canyon is a major destination at giant Lake Oroville as the campground is near a major marina and boat ramp. It is set along the southern shore of the lake, on a point directly adjacent to the massive Oroville Dam to the west. Many campers use this spot for boating headquarters. Lake Oroville is created from the tallest earth-filled dam in the country, rising 770 feet above the streambed of the Feather River. It creates a huge reservoir when full. It is popular for waterskiing, as the water is warm enough in the summer for all water sports, and there is enough room for both anglers and water-skiers. Fishing is excellent for spotted bass. What a lake—there are even floating toilets here (imagine that!). It is very hot in midsummer, with high temperatures ranging from the mid-80s to the low 100s. The area has four distinct seasons—spring is quite

beautiful with many wildflowers and greenery. A must-see is the view from the 47-foot tower using the high-powered telescopes, where there is a panoramic view of the lake, Sierra Nevada, valley, foothills, and the Sutter Buttes. The Feather River Hatchery is nearby.

Campsites, facilities: There are 75 sites with full hookups (30 amps) for tents or RVs up to 40 feet and trailers up to 31 feet (including boat trailers). Picnic tables and fire grills are provided. Drinking water, flush toilets, and coin showers are available. Boat rentals are available on the lake. A grocery store, boat ramp, marina with fuel and boat pumping station, snack bar, and propane gas are available within two miles. Leashed pets are permitted, except on trails or beaches.

Reservations, fees: Reservations are accepted at 800/444-7275 (800/444-PARK) or www.reserveamerica.com ($8 reservation fee). Sites are $45 per night, $4 per night for each additional vehicle. Open year-round.

Directions: From Oroville, drive east on Oroville Dam Boulevard/Highway 162 (becomes the Olive Highway) for 6.8 miles to Kelly Ridge Road. Turn left (north) on Kelly Ridge Road and drive 1.5 miles to Arroyo Drive. Turn right and drive 0.25 mile to the campground.

Contact: Lake Oroville State Recreation Area, 530/538-2200; Lake Oroville Visitor Center, 530/538-2219, www.parks.ca.gov.

22 LOAFER CREEK FAMILY, GROUP, AND EQUESTRIAN CAMPS

Scenic rating: 7

on Lake Oroville

Map 5.2, page 314

These are three different campground areas that are linked, designed for individual use, groups, and equestrians, respectively. The camps are just across the water at Lake Oroville from Bidwell Canyon, but campers come here for more spacious sites. It's also a primary option for campers with boats, with the Loafer Creek boat ramp one mile away. So hey, this spot is no secret. A bonus here includes an extensive equestrian trail system right out of camp.

Campsites, facilities: There are 137 sites for tents or RVs up to 40 feet (no hookups) and trailers to 31 feet (including boat trailers), 15 equestrian sites with a two-horse limit per site, and six group sites for up to 25 people each. Picnic tables and fire grills are provided. Drinking water, restrooms with flush toilets and coin showers, laundry tubs, Wi-Fi, and a dump station are available. A tethering and feeding station is near each site for horses, and a horse-washing station is provided. Some facilities are wheelchair-accessible. Propane, groceries, boat rentals, and a boat ramp are available nearby. Leashed pets are permitted, but not on trails or beaches.

Reservations, fees: Reservations are accepted at 800/444-7275 (800/444-PARK) or www. reserveamerica.com ($8 reservation fee). Sites are $30 per night for single sites, $4 per night for each additional vehicle, $100 per night for group sites, $40 per night for equestrian sites. Open year-round.

Directions: From Oroville, drive east on Oroville Dam Boulevard/Highway 162 (becomes the Olive Highway) for approximately eight miles to the signed campground entrance on the left.

Contact: Lake Oroville State Recreation Area, 530/538-2200; Lake Oroville Visitor Center, 530/538-2219, www.parks.ca.gov.

23 SLY CREEK
🏊 🎣 🚤 🐕 ♿ � ⛺

Scenic rating: 7

on Sly Creek Reservoir in Plumas National Forest

Map 5.2, page 314

Sly Creek Camp is set on Sly Creek Reservoir's southwestern shore near Lewis Flat, with a boat ramp about a mile to the north. Both camps at this lake are well situated for campers and anglers. This camp provides direct access to the lake's main body, with good trout fishing well upstream on the main lake arm. You get quiet water and decent fishing. The elevation is 3,530 feet.

Campsites, facilities: There are 25 sites for tents or RVs up to 40 feet (no hookups). Picnic tables and fire grills are provided. Drinking water and vault toilets are available. A cartop boat launch and fish-cleaning stations are available on Sly Creek Reservoir. Some facilities are wheelchair-accessible. Leashed pets are permitted.

Reservations, fees: Reservations are not accepted. Sites are $22 per night. Open late April through mid-October, weather permitting.

Directions: From Oroville, drive east on Highway 162/Oroville Dam Boulevard for about eight miles (becomes the Olive Highway) to Forbestown Road. Turn right and drive through Forbestown to Challenge and LaPorte Road. Turn left on LaPorte Road and drive 15 miles to Forest Road 16 (signed for Sly Creek Reservoir). Turn left on Forest Road 16 and drive 4.5 miles to the campground on the eastern end of the lake.

Contact: Plumas National Forest, Feather River Ranger District, 530/534-6500, www. fs.usda.gov/plumas.

24 STRAWBERRY
🏊 🎣 🚤 🐕 � ⛺

Scenic rating: 7

on Sly Creek Reservoir in Plumas National Forest

Map 5.2, page 314

Sly Creek Reservoir is a long, narrow lake set in western Plumas National Forest. There are two campgrounds on opposite ends of the lake, with different directions to each. This camp is set in the back of a cove on the lake's eastern arm at an elevation of 3,530 feet, with a boat ramp nearby. This is a popular lake for trout fishing in the summer. You must bring your own drinking water. The water source (such as at the fish-cleaning station) has a high mineral content and strong smell.

Campsites, facilities: There are 17 sites for tents or RVs up to 40 feet (no hookups). Picnic tables and fire grills are provided. Drinking water and vault toilets are available. A car-top boat launch and fish-cleaning station are available on Sly Creek Reservoir. Leashed pets are permitted.

Reservations, fees: Reservations are not accepted. Sites are $22 per night. Open mid-May to early October, weather permitting.

Directions: From Oroville, drive east on Highway 162/Oroville Dam Boulevard for about eight miles (becomes the Olive Highway) to Forbestown Road. Turn right and drive through Forbestown to Challenge and LaPorte Road. Turn left on LaPorte Road and drive 15 miles to Forest Road 16 (signed for Sly Creek Reservoir). Turn left on Forest Road 16 and drive two miles to the campground on the eastern end of the lake.

Contact: Plumas National Forest, Feather River Ranger District, 530/534-6500, www.fs.usda.gov/plumas.

25 GARDEN POINT BOAT-IN
🏊 🛶 🚤 🐕 5% ⛺

Scenic rating: 8

on Bullards Bar Reservoir

Map 5.2, page 314   BEST (

Bullards Bar Reservoir is one of the few lakes in the Sierra Nevada to offer boat-in camping at developed boat-in sites and to allow boaters to create their own primitive sites anywhere along the lake's shoreline when permitted. A chemical toilet is required gear for boat-in shoreline camping at some sites. Garden Point Boat-In is on the western shore of the northern Yuba River arm. This lake provides plenty of recreation options, including good fishing for kokanee salmon and small spotted bass, waterskiing, and many coves for playing in the water. All water sports are allowed.

Campsites, facilities: There are 12 single and four double tent sites accessible by boat only. Picnic tables and fire grills are provided. Vault toilets are available. No drinking water is available. Garbage must be packed out. Supplies and boat rentals are available at the Emerald Cove Marina. Leashed pets are permitted.

Reservations, fees: Reservations and a camping permit are required from Emerald Cove Marina at 530/692-3200 ($8 reservation fee). Single sites are $22 per night, double sites are $44 per night. Open mid-April to mid-October, weather permitting.

Directions: From Marysville, drive northeast on Highway 20 to Marysville Road. Turn north at Marysville Road (signed "Bullards Bar Reservoir") and drive about 12 miles to Old Marysville Road. Turn right and drive 14 miles to reach the Cottage Creek launch ramp and the marina (turn left just before the dam).

To reach the Dark Day boat ramp, continue over the dam and drive four miles, turn left on Dark Day Road, and continue to the ramp. From the boat launch, continue to the campground on the northwest side.

Contact: Emerald Cove Marina, 530/692-3200; Tahoe National Forest, Yuba River Ranger District, North, 530/288-3231, www.bullardsbar.com, www.fs.usda.gov/plumas.

26 DARK DAY WALK-IN
🥾 🏊 🛶 🚤 🐕 ⛺

Scenic rating: 8

on Bullards Bar Reservoir

Map 5.2, page 314

Along with Schoolhouse, this is a car-accessible camping area at Bullards Bar Reservoir with direct shoreline access. You park in a central area and then walk a short distance to the campground. The lake is a very short walk beyond that. Bullards Bar is a great camping lake, pretty, with 55 miles of shoreline and several lake arms and good fishing for kokanee salmon (as long as you have a boat) and bass.

It is set at 2,000 feet elevation in the foothills, like a silver dollar in a field of pennies. A bonus at Bullards Bar is that there is never a charge for day use, parking, or boat launching.

Campsites, facilities: There are 10 walk-in tent sites (some are double or triple sites). Picnic tables and fire pits are provided. Drinking water and vault toilets are available. Garbage must be packed out. A boat ramp is available nearby, and supplies and boat rentals are available at Emerald Cove Marina. Leashed pets are permitted.

Reservations, fees: Reservations and a camping permit are required from Emerald Cove Marina at 530/692-3200 ($8 reservation fee). Sites are $22 per night, $44 per night for a double site, and $66 per night for a triple site. Open mid-April through mid-October, weather permitting.

Directions: From Marysville, drive northeast on Highway 20 to Marysville Road. Turn north at Marysville Road (signed "Bullards Bar Reservoir") and drive about 12 miles to Old Marysville Road. Turn right, drive 14 miles, and continue over the dam for four miles to Dark Day Road. Turn left and drive past the boat launch to the campground on the northwest side of the lake.

Contact: Emerald Cove Marina, 530/692-3200; Tahoe National Forest, Yuba River Ranger District, North, 530/288-3231, www.bullardsbar.com, www.fs.usda.gov/plumas.

27 SHORELINE CAMP BOAT-IN

Scenic rating: 8

on Bullards Bar Reservoir

Map 5.2, page 314

There are two boat-in campgrounds on Bullards Bar Reservoir, but another option is to throw all caution to the wind and just head out on your own, camping wherever you want. It is critical to bring a shovel to dig a flat site for sleeping, a large tarp for sun protection, and, of course, plenty of water or a water purification pump. This is a big, beautiful lake, with good trolling for kokanee salmon. Rainbow trout are also here. Note: A portable chemical toilet and camping permit are required.

Campsites, facilities: Boaters may choose their own primitive campsite anywhere on the shore of Bullards Bar Reservoir, with a maximum of six people per site. Garbage must be packed out. Supplies and boat rentals are available at Emerald Cove Marina. Leashed pets are permitted.

Reservations, fees: Reservations and a camping permit are required from Emerald Cove Marina at 530/692-3200 ($8 reservation fee). Sites are $22 per night. Open mid-April through mid-October, weather permitting.

Directions: From Marysville, drive east on Highway 20 for 12 miles to Marysville Road. Turn left on Marysville Road (signed "Bullards Bar Reservoir") and drive 12 miles to Old Marysville Road. Turn right on Old Marysville Road and drive 14 miles to the Cottage Creek Launch Ramp (turn left just before the dam). To reach the boat launch, continue to the campgrounds on the west side.

Contact: Emerald Cove Marina, 530/692-3200; Tahoe National Forest, Yuba River Ranger District, North, 530/288-3231, www.bullardsbar.com, www.fs.usda.gov/plumas.

28 MADRONE COVE BOAT-IN

Scenic rating: 8

on Bullards Bar Reservoir

Map 5.2, page 314   BEST (

This is one of two boat-in campgrounds at Bullards Bar Reservoir. It is set on the main Yuba River arm of the lake, along the western shore. This is a premium boat-in site. The elevation is 2,000 feet.

Campsites, facilities: There are 10 tent sites, accessible by boat only. Picnic tables and fire grills are provided. Vault toilets are available. No drinking water is available. Garbage must be packed out. Supplies and boat rentals are available at the marina. Leashed pets are permitted.

Reservations, fees: Reservations and a camping permit are required from Emerald Cove Marina at 530/692-3200 ($8 reservation fee). Sites are $22 per night. Open mid-April through mid-October.

Directions: From Marysville, drive east on Highway 20 for 12 miles to Marysville Road (signed "Bullards Bar Reservoir"). Turn left at Marysville Road and drive 12 miles to Old Marysville Road. Turn right on Old Marysville Road and drive 14 miles to reach the Cottage Creek Launch Ramp and the marina (turn left just before the dam). To reach the ramp, continue over the dam, drive four miles to Dark Day Road, turn left, and continue to the ramp. From the boat launch, continue to the campground on the west side.

Contact: Emerald Cove Marina, 530/692-3200; Tahoe National Forest, Yuba River Ranger District, North, 530/288-3231, www.bullardsbar.com, www.fs.usda.gov/plumas.

29 SCHOOLHOUSE

🧍🏊🚴🛶🛥️🐕♿🚐⛺

Scenic rating: 7

on Bullards Bar Reservoir

Map 5.2, page 314

Bullards Bar Reservoir is one of the better lakes in the Sierra Nevada for camping, primarily because the lake level tends to be higher here than at many other lakes. The camp is set on the southeast shore, with a trail out of the camp to a beautiful lookout of the lake. Bullards Bar is known for good fishing for trout and kokanee salmon, waterskiing, and all water sports. A concrete boat ramp is to the south at Cottage Creek. Boaters should consider the special boat-in camps at the lake. The elevation is 2,200 feet.

Campsites, facilities: There are 56 sites for tents or RVs of any length (no hookups). Single sites accommodate six people, double sites accommodate 12 people, and triple sites hold up

to 18 people. Picnic tables, food lockers, and fire rings are provided. Drinking water and flush and vault toilets are available. A boat ramp and boat rentals are nearby. Some facilities are wheelchair-accessible. Supplies are available in North San Juan, Camptonville, Dobbins, and at the marina. Leashed pets are permitted.

Reservations, fees: Reservations and a camping permit are required from Emerald Cove Marina at 530/692-3200 ($8 reservation fee). Single sites are $22 per night, double sites are $44 per night, and triple sites are $66 per night. Open mid-April through mid-October.

Directions: From Marysville, drive east on Highway 20 for 12 miles to Marysville Road (signed "Bullards Bar Reservoir"). Turn left on Marysville Road and drive 12 miles to Old Marysville Road. Turn right on Old Marysville Road and drive 14 miles to the dam, then continue three miles to the campground entrance road on the left.

Contact: Emerald Cove Marina, 530/692-3200; Tahoe National Forest, Yuba River Ranger District, North, 530/288-3231, www.bullardsbar.com, www.fs.usda.gov/plumas.

30 HORNSWOGGLE GROUP CAMP

🏊🚴🛥️🐕🚐⛺

Scenic rating: 7

on Bullards Bar Reservoir in Tahoe National Forest

Map 5.2, page 314

This camp is designed for group use. A concrete boat ramp is one mile north at the Dark Day Picnic Area. (For information about family campgrounds and boat-in sites, see the listings in this chapter that are located on Bullards Bar Reservoir.)

Campsites, facilities: There are five 25-person group sites and one 50-person group site for tents or RVs up to 50 feet (no hookups). Picnic tables, food lockers, and fire grills are provided. Drinking water and flush and vault toilets are available. A boat ramp is nearby. Supplies and boat rentals are available at the marina. Leashed pets are permitted.

Reservations, fees: Reservations and a camping permit are required from Emerald Cove Marina at 530/692-3200 ($8 reservation fee). Sites are $80–140 per night. Open April to mid-October.

Directions: From Auburn, drive north on Highway 49 to Nevada City and continue for 17 miles through the town of North San Juan. Continue on Highway 49 for approximately eight miles to Marysville Road. Turn left on Marysville Road and drive approximately five miles to the campground on the left.

Contact: Emerald Cove Marina, 530/692-3200; Tahoe National Forest, Yuba River Ranger District, North, 530/288-3231, www.bullardsbar.com, www.fs.usda.gov/plumas.

31 COLLINS LAKE RECREATION AREA

Scenic rating: 8

near Marysville on Collins Lake

Map 5.2, page 314

Collins Lake is set in the foothill country east of Marysville at 1,200 feet elevation, ideal for the camper, boater, and angler. I counted 45 campsites set near the lakefront. This lake is becoming known as an outstanding destination for trophy-sized trout, especially in late spring through early summer, though fishing is often good year-round for know-hows. Other fish species are bass, crappie, bluegill, and catfish. Guide Larry Hemphill has made it a habit to catch big bass here. The lake has 12 miles of shoreline and is quite pretty. In summer, warm water makes the lake exceptional for waterskiing (permitted from May through mid-October). There is a marina adjacent to the campground, and farther south is a 60-foot-wide swimming beach and boat ramp. Bonuses for anglers: No personal watercraft are allowed on the lake. A weekly fishing report is available at the camp's website. Insider's tip: Lakefront sites fill quickly; book early.

Campsites, facilities: There are 150 sites with full or partial hookups (30 amps) for RVs or tents, 134 sites with no hookups for tents or RVs, four group tent sites, one group RV site, and a large overflow camping area. Some sites are pull-through. Four rental trailers and five cabins are also available. Picnic tables and barbecues are provided. Restrooms with flush toilets and coin showers, drinking water, portable toilets, dump station, playground, marina, boat ramp, boat rentals, berths, sandy swimming beach, beach volleyball, three group picnic areas, convenience store, coin laundry, firewood, ice, and propane gas are available. RV storage is also available. Some facilities are wheelchair-accessible. Leashed pets are permitted.

Reservations, fees: Reservations are accepted up to one year in advance (two-night minimum, $10 nonrefundable reservation deposit required). Tent sites are $28–35 per night, RV sites without hookups are $28–35 per night, RV sites with hookups are $40–56 per night, lakefront RV sites are $38 (no hookups) and $56 (full hookups) per night, $10 per night per additional vehicle, $4 per night per additional person age 13 and older. There is an open area for tent camping at $25 per night and an open parking area for self-contained RVs at $35 per night. Boat launching is $8 per day with campsite. Weekly and monthly rates available. Some credit cards accepted. Open year-round.

Directions: From Marysville, drive east on Highway 20 for about 12 miles to Marysville Road/Road E-21. Turn left (north) and drive approximately 10 miles to the recreation area entrance road on the right. Turn right, drive 0.3 mile to the entrance station and store, and then continue to the campground. (For detailed directions from other areas, visit the website.)

Contact: Collins Lake Recreation Area, 530/692-1600 or 800/286-0576, www.collinslake.com.

32 ENGLEBRIGHT LAKE BOAT-IN

Scenic rating: 8

near Marysville

| Map 5.2, page 314 | BEST (|

Englebright Lake is an outstanding destination for boat-in camping, fishing, and waterskiing. Remember this place. It always seems to have plenty of water, and there are more developed boat-in campsites along its 19 miles of shoreline than at any other lake in California. The lake looks like a huge water snake, long and narrow, set in the Yuba/Nevada Canyon at 520 feet elevation. In summer, it is a waterskiing mecca, with warm, calm water. All water sports are allowed. Trout fishing is good on the upper end of the lake, where waterskiing is prohibited year-round. Rangers say people show up every week with tents or RVs, but all sites are boat-in only!

Campsites, facilities: There are 96 boat-in sites (no hookups) along the shores of Englebright Lake. Picnic tables, fire grills, and lantern hangers are provided. Pit toilets are available. Two boat ramps are available on either side of Skippers Cove. Drinking water is available at the Narrows day-use area and at the marina. Boat rentals (including houseboats), mooring, fuel dock, and groceries are available at the marina. Leashed pets are permitted.

Reservations, fees: Reservations are not accepted. Sites are $15 per night. Open year-round.

Directions: From Auburn, drive north on Highway 49 to Grass Valley and the junction with Highway 20. Turn west on Highway 20 and drive to Mooney Flat Road (if you reach Smartville, you have gone a mile too far). Turn right on Mooney Flat Road and drive three miles to the entrance for the Narrows Recreation Area. Continue 0.5 mile to Joe Miller Road and the entrance to Skipper's Cove Marina on the left.

Contact: U.S. Army Corps of Engineers, Sacramento District, Englebright Lake, 530/432-6427 (reservations); Skippers Cove, concessionaire, 530/432-6302, www.englebrightlake.com.

33 NEVADA COUNTY FAIRGROUNDS

Scenic rating: 6

near Grass Valley

| Map 5.2, page 314 |

The motto here is "California's Most Beautiful Fairgrounds," and that's right. The area is set at 2,300 feet in the Sierra foothills, with a good number of pines sprinkled about. The park is adjacent to the fairgrounds, and even though the fair runs for a week every August, the park is open year-round. However, check status before planning a trip because the campground is sometimes closed for scheduled activities. A caretaker at the park is available to answer any questions. Kids can fish at a small lake nearby. The Draft Horse Classic is held here every September and a country Christmas Faire is held Thanksgiving weekend.

Campsites, facilities: There are 144 sites with full or partial hookups (50 amps) for RVs of any length, and an open dirt and grassy area with no hookups available as an overflow area. No tents. Two dump stations, drinking water, restrooms with showers and flush toilets, WiFi, and group facilities are available. Some facilities are wheelchair-accessible. Leashed pets are permitted.

Reservations, fees: Reservations are recommended. RV sites are $22–30 per night, showers are $5 per person. A seven-day limit is enforced. Some credit cards accepted. Open year-round.

Directions: From Auburn, drive north on Highway 49 to Grass Valley and the McKnight Way exit. Take that exit and turn left on McKnight Way and drive over the freeway to Freeman Lane (just past the shopping center on the left). Turn right on Freeman Lane and drive to the second stop sign and McCourtney Road. Continue straight on McCourtney Road and drive two blocks to the fairgrounds on the right. Continue to Gate 4.

Contact: Nevada County Fairgrounds, 530/273-6217, www.nevadacountyfair.com.

34 CAMPERS INN RV AND GOLF RESORT

Scenic rating: 3

near Dunnigan

Map 5.3, page 315

This private park has a rural valley atmosphere and provides a layover for drivers cruising I-5. The park has a par-three golf course (nine holes), and it specializes in golf tournaments and group outings. The Sacramento River to the east is the closest body of water, but this section of river is hardly a premium side-trip destination. There are no nearby lakes.

Campsites, facilities: There are three tent sites and 72 sites with full or partial hookups (30 and 50 amps) for RVs of any length. All sites are pull-through. Picnic tables are provided. Restrooms with flush toilets and showers, seasonal swimming pool, two clubhouses/meeting rooms, horseshoes, nine-hole golf course, coin laundry, propane gas, ice, and general store are available. Some facilities are wheelchair-accessible. Leashed pets are permitted.

Reservations, fees: Reservations are accepted. Sites are $19.80–36.50 per night. Some credit cards accepted. Open year-round.

Directions: From I-5 in Dunnigan, take the Dunnigan exit (Exit 556, just north of the I-505 cutoff). Drive west on County Road E4/Road 6 for a mile to County Road 88. Turn right and drive for 1.5 miles to the park.

Contact: Campers Inn RV and Golf Resort, 530/724-3350 or 800/79-GOLF3 (800/794-6533), www.campersinnrv.com.

35 LAKE CLEMENTINE BOAT-IN

Scenic rating: 8

in Auburn State Recreation Area near Auburn

Map 5.3, page 315   **BEST (**

This boat-in campground is on Lower Lake Clementine, a long and narrow 3.5-mile lake. It's a great destination for kayaking and boat-in camping, but no trout are stocked at this lake. All water sports are allowed on Lake Clementine, with a boat limit of 25 boats per day—and the quota is reached every day on summer weekends. Auburn State Recreation Area is a jewel in the valley foothill country, covering more than 42,000 acres along the North and Middle Forks of the American River. The Auburn SRA is composed of land set aside for the Auburn Dam, consisting of 40 miles along two forks of the American River. Formerly the domain of gold miners, the area is now home to wildlife as well as a wide variety of recreational opportunities. The American River runs through the park, offering visitors opportunities to fish, boat, kayak, and raft. In addition, there are more than 100 miles of hiking, biking, and horseback-riding trails.

Note that there is a very sharp hair-pin turn on the road in that makes it difficult to get trailered boats in, especially those towed by trucks with long wheelbases. Trailers over 24 feet are not advised.

Campsites, facilities: There are 15 boat-in sites (eight people per site). Picnic tables, fire grills, and pit toilets are provided. A marina and boat launch are available. There is no drinking water. Garbage must be packed out.

Reservations, fees: Reservations are accepted at 800/444-7275 (800/444-PARK) or www.reserveamerica.com ($8 reservation fee). Boat-in sites are $38 per night, $10 per extra vehicle, $8 fee for boat launch. Open May 15–September 15.

Directions: From I-80 at Auburn, take the Auburn Ravine/Foresthill exit to Foresthill Road. Turn right and drive on Foresthill Road for two miles to Lake Clementine Road. Turn left (road narrows) and drive 2.5 miles (with a

very sharp hair-pin turn that is very difficult to negotiate by trucks with trailered boats) to the boat launch. After launching, cruise by boat 1.5 miles northeast to the boat-in campgrounds.
Contact: Auburn State Recreation Area, 530/885-4527, www.parks.ca.gov; marina 530/885-5097.

36 MINERAL BAR

Scenic rating: 8

in Auburn State Recreation Area near Colfax

Map 5.3, page 315   BEST (

Mineral Bar is a primitive camp situated near the American River in the Auburn State Recreation Area, a 42,000-acre park. This recreational mecca is paradise for hikers and boaters, and is especially popular for whitewater rafting.
Campsites, facilities: There are 18 sites for tents or RVs up to 24 feet (no hookups). Picnic tables and fire grills are provided. Chemical toilets are available. No drinking water is available. Leashed pets are permitted.
Reservations, fees: Reservations are not accepted. Sites are $28 per night, $10 per night for each additional vehicle. Open year-round, with limited winter facilities.
Directions: From I-80 in Auburn, drive east for 15 miles to Colfax and the Canyon Way/ Placer Hills Drive exit. Take that exit and turn left on Canyon Way and drive one mile to Iowa Hill Road. Turn right and drive three miles on a narrow paved road to the campground.
Contact: Auburn State Recreation Area, 530/885-4527, www.parks.ca.gov.

37 RUCK-A-CHUCKY

Scenic rating: 8

in Auburn State Recreation Area near Auburn

Map 5.3, page 315   BEST (

Ruck-A-Chucky is a small primitive camp located in the Auburn State Recreation Area; it is one of two primitive camps at the park. Auburn State Recreation Area covers more than 42,000 acres along the North and Middle Forks of the American River and is home to wildlife as well as a wide variety of recreational opportunities.
Campsites, facilities: There are five sites for tents only. Picnic tables and fire grills are provided. Chemical toilets are available. No drinking water is available. Leashed pets are permitted.
Reservations, fees: Reservations are not accepted. Sites are $28 per night, $10 per night for each additional vehicle. Open spring through fall, weather permitting.
Directions: From I-80 in Auburn, take the Auburn Ravine/Foresthill Road exit to Foresthill Road. Turn right and drive for seven miles to Drivers Flat Road. Turn right and drive 2.8 miles on a dirt road to the campground on the right. Vehicles with high clearance are recommended.
Contact: Auburn State Recreation Area, 530/885-4527, www.parks.ca.gov.

38 PENINSULA

Scenic rating: 6

in Folsom Lake State Recreation Area

Map 5.3, page 315

This is one of the big camps at Folsom Lake, but it is also more remote than the other camps, requiring a circuitous drive. It is set on the peninsula on the northeast shore, right where the North Fork American River arm of the lake enters the main lake area. A nearby boat ramp, marina, and boat rentals make this a great weekend spot. Fishing for bass and trout is often quite good in spring and early summer, and other species include catfish and perch. Waterskiing and wakeboarding are popular in the hot summer, and all water sports are allowed.
Campsites, facilities: There are 100 sites for tents or RVs up to 32 feet (no hookups). Picnic tables and fire grills are provided. Drinking water and restrooms with flush toilets are

available. A bike path is nearby. Boat rentals, moorings, snack bar, ice, and bait and tackle are available at the Folsom Lake Marina. Some facilities, including the Oaks Nature Trail, are wheelchair accessible. Leashed pets are permitted.

Reservations, fees: Reservations are accepted at 800/444-7275 (800/444-PARK) or www. reserveamerica.com ($8 reservation fee). Sites are $30 per night, $8 per night for each additional vehicle. Open year-round.

Directions: From Placerville, drive east on U.S. 50 to the Spring Street/Highway 49 exit. Turn north on Highway 49 (toward the town of Coloma) and continue 8.3 miles into the town of Pilot Hill and Rattlesnake Bar Road. Turn left on Rattlesnake Bar Road and drive nine miles to the end of the road and the park entrance.

Contact: Folsom Lake State Recreation Area, 916/988-0205 or 916/933-6108 (kiosk), www. parks.ca.gov.

39 BEAL'S POINT

Scenic rating: 6

in Folsom Lake State Recreation Area

Map 5.3, page 315

Folsom Lake State Recreation Area is Sacramento's backyard vacation spot, a huge lake covering about 18,000 acres with 75 miles of shoreline, which means plenty of room for boating, waterskiing, fishing, and suntanning. This camp is set on the lake's southwest side, just north of the dam, with a boat ramp nearby at Granite Bay. The lake has a productive trout fishery in the spring, a fast-growing population of kokanee salmon, and good prospects for bass in late spring and early summer. By summer, wakeboarders and waterskiers usually take over the lake each day by about 10 A.M. One problem with this lake is that a minor water drawdown can cause major amounts of shoreline to become exposed on its upper arms. There are opportunities for

hiking, biking, running, picnics, and horseback riding. A paved 32-mile-long trail, the American River Parkway, connects Folsom Lake with many Sacramento County parks before reaching Old Sacramento. This trail is outstanding for family biking and inline skating. Summers are hot and dry.

Campsites, facilities: There are 64 sites for tents or RVs of any length; some sites have full hookups (30 and 50 amps). Picnic tables and fire grills are provided. Drinking water, restrooms with flush toilets and showers, and a dump station are available. A bike path and horseback-riding facilities are nearby. Some facilities are wheelchair-accessible. There are boat rentals, moorings, summer snack bar, ice, and bait and tackle available at the Folsom Lake Marina. Leashed pets are permitted.

Reservations, fees: Reservations are accepted April through September at 800/444-7275 (800/444-PARK) or www.reserveamerica. com ($8 reservation fee). Tent sites are $33 per night, RV sites (hookups) are $58 per night, $12 per night for each additional vehicle. Discounts available in off-season. Open year-round.

Directions: From Sacramento, drive east on U.S. 50 to the Folsom Boulevard exit. Take that exit to the stop sign and Folsom Boulevard. Turn left and continue north on Folsom Boulevard for 3.5 miles (road name changes to Folsom-Auburn Road) to the park entrance on the right.

Contact: Folsom Lake State Recreation Area, 916/988-0205; Beal's Point Campground, 916/791-1531 or 916/791-1531 (kiosk), www. parks.ca.gov.

40 NEGRO BAR GROUP CAMP

Scenic rating: 8

in Folsom Lake State Recreation Area

Map 5.3, page 315

Lake Natoma is pretty and quiet, compared to nearby Folsom, with no parties, mayhem, or water sports. Natoma is the afterbay for Folsom Lake, located directly below Folsom Dam. It is comparatively small with 13 miles of shoreline, very narrow instead of wide, with cold water instead of warm. This camp is set at the head of the lake on the northern shore, with an adjacent boat ramp available. Lake Natoma is popular for crew races, sailing, kayaking, and other aquatic sports. A 5-mph speed limit is enforced on the lake, and swimming is allowed. The Folsom Lake entrance is a 10-minute drive from Lake Natoma. The Sacramento River Parkway runs nearby.

Campsites, facilities: There are three group tent sites that can accommodate 25–50 people each. Picnic tables and fire grills are provided. Drinking water and restrooms with flush toilets are available. A bike path and canoe and kayak rentals are available nearby. Leashed pets are permitted.

Reservations, fees: Reservations are accepted at 800/444-7275 (800/444-PARK) or www.reserveamerica.com ($8 reservation fee). Negro Bar A and B are $175 per night, Negro Bar C is $95 per night. Open year-round.

Directions: From I-80 north of Sacramento, take the Douglas Boulevard exit and head east for five miles to Auburn-Folsom Road. Turn right on Auburn-Folsom Road and drive south for six miles to Greenback Lane. Turn right on Greenback Lane and merge immediately into the left lane. The park entrance is approximately 0.2 mile on the left.

Contact: Folsom Lake State Recreation Area, 916/988-0205 or 916/988-6923 (kiosk), www.parks.ca.gov.

41 SACRAMENTO WEST/ OLD TOWN KOA

Scenic rating: 2

in West Sacramento

Map 5.3, page 315

This is the choice of car and RV campers touring California's capital and looking for a layover spot. It is in West Sacramento not far from the Capitol building, the railroad museum, Sutter's Fort, Old Sacramento, Crocker Museum, and shopping.

Campsites, facilities: There are 95 pull-through sites with full or partial hookups (30 and 50 amps) for RVs of any length and 21 tent sites. Twelve cabins, three cottages, three park models, and a group camping area are also available. Restrooms with flush toilets and showers, Wi-Fi, cable TV, playground, fishing pond, seasonal swimming pool, coin laundry, dump station, propane gas, firewood, and convenience and gift store are available. Some facilities are wheelchair-accessible. Leashed pets are permitted, with certain restrictions.

Reservations, fees: Reservations are accepted at 800/562-2747. RV sites are $46–51 per night, tent sites are $36–40 per night. Off-season discounts are available. Some credit cards accepted. Open year-round.

Directions: From Sacramento, drive west on I-80 about four miles to the West Capitol Avenue exit. Exit and turn left onto West Capitol Avenue, going under the freeway to the second stoplight and the intersection with Lake Road. Turn left onto Lake Road and continue a half block to the camp on the right at 3951 Lake Road.

Contact: Sacramento West/Old Town KOA, 916/371-6771, www.sacramentokoa.com.

42 VINEYARD RV PARK

Scenic rating: 2

in Vacaville

Map 5.3, page 315

This is one of two privately operated parks in the area set up primarily for RVs. It is in a eucalyptus grove, with clean, well-kept sites. If you are heading to the Bay Area, it is late in the day, and you don't have your destination set, this spot offers a chance to hole up for the night and formulate your travel plans. Note that about half of the sites are long-term rentals.

Campsites, facilities: There are 110 sites with full hookups (30 and 50 amps) for RVs of any length. Some sites are pull-through. RV and tent cabin rentals are aalso available. Picnic tables are provided. Restrooms with flush toilets and showers, Wi-Fi, seasonal swimming pool, coin laundry, enclosed dog walk, and ice are available. Some facilities are wheelchair-accessible. Leashed pets are permitted, with certain restrictions.

Reservations, fees: Reservations are recommended at 866/447-8797. RV sites are $48 per night, tent sites are $20–25 per night, $1 per pet per night. Weekly and monthly rates available. Some credit cards accepted. Open year-round.

From Vacaville on I-80, turn north on I-505 and drive three miles to Midway Road. Turn right (east) on Midway Road and drive 0.5 mile to the second campground on the left at 4985 Midway Road.

Contact: Vineyard RV Park, 866/447-8797, www.vineyardrvpark.com.

43 RANCHO SECO RECREATION AREA

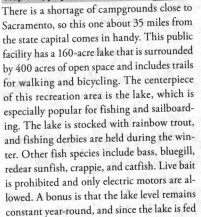

Scenic rating: 6

near Sacramento

Map 5.3, page 315   **BEST (**

There is a shortage of campgrounds close to Sacramento, so this one about 35 miles from the state capital comes in handy. This public facility has a 160-acre lake that is surrounded by 400 acres of open space and includes trails for walking and bicycling. The centerpiece of this recreation area is the lake, which is especially popular for fishing and sailboarding. The lake is stocked with rainbow trout, and fishing derbies are held during the winter. Other fish species include bass, bluegill, redear sunfish, crappie, and catfish. Live bait is prohibited and only electric motors are allowed. A bonus is that the lake level remains constant year-round, and since the lake is fed by the Folsom South Canal, the water is warm in summer. Swimming is popular and there is a large sandy beach with summer lifeguard service. Pedal boats and kayaks can also be rented on weekends in summer. Tent sites are situated along the lake and a seven-mile nature trail loop is also next to the lake. The Amanda Blake Memorial Wildlife Refuge is here, and visitors can observe exotic captive wildlife that has been rescued from circuses and other performing groups. Migratory birds, including bald eagles, winter at the lake. What are those two large towers? They're remnants of the now-closed Rancho Seco nuclear power–generating station.

Campsites, facilities: There are 12 tent sites, 18 sites with partial hookups (30 amps) for RVs of any length, and two group tent sites that can accommodate up to 200 people each. A couple of sites are pull-through. Picnic tables and fire grills are provided. Drinking water, restrooms with coin showers, dump station, swimming beach, six fishing piers, picnic areas, coin laundry, fish-cleaning station, horseshoe pit, recreation room, seasonal general store, weekend boat rentals, and boat launch are available. Supplies are available in Galt. Some facilities are wheelchair-accessible, including some fishing piers. Leashed pets are permitted.

Reservations, fees: Reservations are accepted at 916/732-4913. Tent sites are $25 per night, RV sites (hookups are) $40 per night, and the group tent site is $45 per night for the first 20 people, plus $1.50 per person per night for additional campers. Boat launch fee is $8. There is a 14-day maximum stay. Open April through October.

Directions: From Sacramento, drive south on Highway 99 for approximately 25 miles to the Twin Cities Road/Highway 104 exit. Take that exit and drive east for 13 miles, past the two towers, to the Rancho Seco Park exit. Turn right and continue to the lake and campground.

Contact: Rancho Seco Recreation Area, 916/732-4913, www.smud.org.

44 SANDY BEACH REGIONAL PARK

🎣 🚐 🐕 ♿ 🚗 ⛺

Scenic rating: 6

on the Sacramento River

Map 5.3, page 315

This is a surprisingly little-known park, especially considering it provides beach access to the Sacramento River. The actual campground consists of what are called "utility parking spots," that is, drive-in parking with water and electricity. The park has a sandy beach stretching for more than a half mile, fairly unique for the lower Delta and Sacramento River. In winter and spring, it is one of the few viable spots where you can fish from the shore for sturgeon. It also provides outstanding boating access to the Sacramento River, including one of the best fishing spots for striped bass in the fall, and again in spring (usually best near the Rio Vista Bridge). Windy summer days provide good windsurfing, though the water can be a bit choppy.

Campsites, facilities: There are 42 sites with partial hookups (30 amps) for tents or RVs of any length. Picnic tables and fire pits are provided. Drinking water, restrooms with flush toilets and showers, a dump station, picnic areas, volleyball, horseshoes, firewood, and a boat ramp are available. A camp host is on-site. Some facilities are wheelchair-accessible. Supplies can be obtained nearby (within a mile). Leashed pets are permitted in the campground only.

Reservations, fees: Reservations are accepted ($9 reservation fee). Tent and RV sites (water and electricity) are $30 per night, $10 per night for each additional vehicle, $1 per pet per night. Some credit cards accepted. Open year-round.

Directions: From I-80 in Fairfield, take the Highway 12 exit and drive southeast for 14 miles to Rio Vista and the intersection with Main Street. Turn right on Main Street and drive a short distance to 2nd Street. Turn right and drive 0.5 mile to Beach Drive. Turn left (west) and drive 0.5 mile to the park.

Contact: Sandy Beach Regional Park, 707/374-2097, www.solanocounty.com.

45 DELTA MARINA YACHT HARBOR AND RV PARK

🏊 🎣 🚐 🐕 ⛵ ♿ 🚗

Scenic rating: 6

on the Sacramento River Delta

Map 5.3, page 315

This is a prime spot for boat campers. Summers are hot and breezy, and waterskiing is popular on the nearby Sacramento River. From November to March, the striped-bass fishing is quite good, often as close as just a half mile upriver at the Rio Vista Bridge. The boat launch at the harbor is a bonus, especially with night lighting. Some campsites have river frontage, and some sites are filled with long-term renters.

Campsites, facilities: There are 25 sites with full hookups (30 and 50 amps) for RVs up to 40 feet. No tents. Picnic tables and fire grills are provided. Restrooms with showers, cable TV, WiFi, coin laundry, playground, boat ramp, fishing pier, marine repair service, pet restroom, restaurant, marine supplies and gift store, ice, and propane gas are available. Fuel is available 24 hours. Free boat launching for RV guests. Some facilities are wheelchair-accessible. Leashed pets are permitted.

Reservations, fees: Reservations are accepted at 866/774-2315. RV sites are $30–40 per night. Two-week maximum stay in summer. Some credit cards accepted. Open year-round.

Directions: From Fairfield on I-80, take the Highway 12 exit and drive southeast for 14 miles to Rio Vista and the intersection with Main Street. Take the Main Street exit and drive a short distance to 2nd Street. Turn right on 2nd Street and drive to Marina Drive. Turn left on Marina Drive, and continue another short distance to the harbor.

Contact: Delta Marina Yacht Harbor and RV Park, 707/374-2315, www.deltamarina.com.

46 BRANNAN ISLAND STATE RECREATION AREA

Scenic rating: 7

on the Sacramento River

Map 5.3, page 315   **BEST (**

This state park is perfectly designed for boaters, set in the heart of the Delta's vast waterways. You get year-round adventure: waterskiing, wakeboarding, and fishing for catfish are popular in the summer, and in the winter the immediate area is often good for striped-bass fishing. The proximity of the campgrounds to the boat launch deserves a medal. What many people do is tow a boat here, launch it, keep it docked, and then return to their site and set up; this allows them to come and go as they please, boating, fishing, and exploring in the Delta. There is a six-lane boat ramp that provides access to a maze of waterways amid many islands, marshes, sloughs, and rivers. Day-use areas include the Windy Cove sailboarding area. Though striped bass in winter and catfish in summer are the most favored fish here, sturgeon, bluegill, perch, bullhead, and bass are also caught. Some sections of the San Joaquin Delta are among the best bass fishing spots in California. A hiking/biking trail circles the park.

Note: This park was on the closure list developed by the California Department of Parks, pending final state budget decisions or the possible transfer of park management to other park agencies or volunteer groups. It will remain open through a concessionaire agreement with American Land and Leisure.

Campsites, facilities: There are 102 sites (12 sites with hookups) for tents or RVs up to 36 feet, 12 walk-in sites, and six group sites for up to 30 people each. Picnic tables and fire grills are provided. Drinking water, restrooms with coin showers (at campground and boat launch), boat berths, dump station, and a boat launch are available. Supplies can be obtained three miles away in Rio Vista. Some facilities are wheelchair-accessible. Leashed pets are permitted.

Reservations, fees: Reservations are accepted at 800/444-7275 (800/444-PARK) or www.reserveamerica.com ($8 reservation fee). Tent and RV sites (no hookups) are $25–30 per night, RV sites (with hookups) are $40 per night, $8 per night for each additional vehicle. Group camping is $100 per night. Boat launching is $5 per day. Open year-round.

Directions: In Fairfield on I-80, take the Highway 12 exit, drive southeast 14 miles to Rio Vista, and continue to Highway 160. Turn right on Highway 160 and drive three miles to the park entrance on the left.

Contact: Brannan Island State Recreation Area, 916/777-6671; Entrance Kiosk, 916/777-7701, www.parks.ca.gov; American Land and Leisure, 800/342-2267, www.americanll.com.

47 SNUG HARBOR RESORT

Scenic rating: 7

near Rio Vista

Map 5.3, page 315   **BEST (**

This year-round resort is an ideal resting place for families who enjoy waterskiing, wakeboarding, boating, biking, swimming, and fishing. After the ferry ride, it is only a few minutes to Snug Harbor, a gated marina resort on eight acres with a campground, RV hookups, and a separate area with cabins and cottages. Some say that the waterfront sites with docks give the place the feel of a Louisiana bayou, yet everything is clean and orderly, including a full-service marina, a store, and all facilities—and an excellent location to explore the boating paradise of the Delta. Anglers will find good prospects for striped bass, black bass, bluegill, steelhead, sturgeon, and catfish. The waterfront sites with docks are a bonus.

Campsites, facilities: There are 38 waterfront sites with docks available with full or partial hookups (30 and 50 amps) for RVs of any length, including four pull-through water-view sites with full or partial hookups for RVs. There are also 10 tent sites (tents are allowed at some RV sites), two double sites for RVs, and 12 park-model cabins. Barbecues or burn barrels are provided. Restrooms with key-accessible showers, dump station, Wi-Fi, small convenience store, swimming beach, children's play area, volleyball, croquet, bocce ball, badminton, horseshoes, boat launch, and a covered-berth marina are available. Some facilities are wheelchair-accessible. Dogs are permitted on leash at some sites.

Reservations, fees: Reservations are recommended. RV sites are $38–54 per night, double sites are $84–104, tent sites are $35–40 per night, $10 per night for each additional vehicle, $2 per pet per night. Boat launching is available for a one-time fee of $10. Some credit cards accepted. Open year-round.

Directions: From Fairfield, take Highway 12 east to Rio Vista and Front Street. Turn left on Front Street (before crossing the bridge) and drive under the bridge to River Road. Turn right on River Road and drive two miles to the Rio Vista/Real McCoy Ferry (signed Ryer Island). Take the ferry (free) across the Sacramento River to Ryer Island and Levee Road. Turn right on Levee Road and drive 4.5 miles to the Snug Harbor entrance on the right.

Contact: Snug Harbor Resort, 916/775-1455, www.snugharbor.net.

48 WESTGATE LANDING COUNTY PARK

Scenic rating: 6

on the San Joaquin River Delta near Stockton

Map 5.3, page 315

Summer temperatures typically reach the high 90s and low 100s here, and this county park provides a little shade and boating access to the South Fork Mokelumne River. On hot summer nights, some campers will stay up late and night fish for catfish. Between storms in winter, the area typically gets smothered in dense fog.

The sites are not pull-through but semicircles, which work nearly as well for RV drivers.

Campsites, facilities: There are 14 sites for tents or RVs up to 32 feet (no hookups). Picnic tables and barbecues are provided. Drinking water and flush toilets are available. Groceries and propane gas are nearby. A fishing pier, 24 boat slips, and boat docking are available. Some facilities are wheelchair-accessible. Leashed pets are permitted, with a limit of two.

Reservations, fees: Reservations are accepted at least two weeks in advance at 209/953-8800 ($10 reservation fee). Less than two weeks, sites are first come, first served. Sites are $20 per night, $5 per night for each additional vehicle, boat slips $20 per day, $1 per pet per night. Open year-round.

Directions: On I-5, drive to Lodi and Highway 12. Take Highway 12 west and drive about five miles to Glasscock Road. Turn right and drive about a mile to the park.

Contact: San Joaquin County Parks Department, 209/953-8800 or 209/331-7400, www.mgzoo.com.

49 STOCKTON DELTA KOA

Scenic rating: 6

near Stockton

Map 5.3, page 315

Some people may remember this campground by its previous name: Tower Park Resort. This huge resort is ideal for boat-in campers who desire a full-facility marina. The camp is set on Little Potato Slough near the Mokelumne River. In the summer, this is a popular waterskiing area. Some hot weekends are like a continuous party. Note that tents are now allowed here.

Campsites, facilities: There are 300 sites with full hookups (30 amps) for RVs up to 70 feet, 50 tent sites, and 21 park-model cabins. Picnic tables are provided. Restrooms with showers, dump station, pavilion, banquet room, boat rentals, overnight boat slips, boat storage, double boat launch, playground, swimming pool, spa, water slides, gas station, restaurant, coin laundry, WiFi, gift shop, store, ice, and propane gas are available. Leashed pets are permitted, with certain restrictions.

Reservations, fees: Reservations are available at 800/562-0913, with a three-night minimum on summer holidays. RV sites are $30–86 per night, tent sites are $49–59 per night, maximum six people per site. Some credit cards accepted. Open year-round.

Directions: On I-5, drive to Lodi and Highway 12. Take Highway 12 west and drive about five miles to Tower Park Way (before first bridge). Turn left and drive a short distance to the park.

Contact: Stockton Delta KOA, 209/369-1041, www.koa.com or http://koa.com/campgrounds/stockton.

50 EDDOS HARBOR AND RV PARK

🏊 🛶 🚣 🛥️ 🐕 ♿ 🚐

Scenic rating: 6

on the San Joaquin River Delta

Map 5.3, page 315   **BEST (**

This is an ideal spot for campers with boats. Eddos is set on the San Joaquin River and Gallagher Slough, upstream of the Antioch Bridge, in an outstanding region for fishing, powerboating, wakeboarding, and waterskiing. In summer, boaters have access to 1,000 miles of Delta waterways, with the best of them in a nearby spider web of rivers and sloughs off the San Joaquin to False River, Frank's Tract, and Old River. Hot weather and sheltered sloughs make this ideal for waterskiing. In the winter, a nearby fishing spot, as well as the mouth of the False River, attract striped bass. Many of the sites here are occupied by seasonal renters; plan well ahead for the summer.

Campsites, facilities: There are 42 sites with full hookups (30 and 50 amps) for RVs up to 40 feet. Picnic tables are provided. Restrooms with flush toilets and showers, launch ramp, boat storage, fuel dock, Wi-Fi, coin laundry, propane, and a small grocery store are available. Some facilities are wheelchair-accessible. Leashed pets are permitted, with some breed restrictions.

Reservations, fees: Reservations are recommended. Sites are $35–38 per night. Weekly and monthly rates available. Some credit cards accepted. Open year-round.

Directions: In Fairfield on I-80, take the Highway 12 exit and drive 14 miles southeast to Rio Vista and continue three miles to Highway 160 (at the signal just after the bridge). Turn right on Highway 160 and drive three miles to Sherman Island/East Levee Road, at the end of the drawbridge. Turn left on East Levee Road and drive 5.5 miles to the campground along the San Joaquin River. Note: If arriving by boat, look for the camp adjacent to Light 21.

Contact: Eddos Harbor and RV Park, 925/757-5314, www.eddosharbor.com.

51 DRU BARNER EQUESTRIAN CAMP

🚶 🐎 ♿ 🚐 ⛺

Scenic rating: 7

near Georgetown in Eldorado National Forest

Map 5.4, page 316

This camp, set at 3,200 feet elevation in an area of pine and fir, is ideal for horses; there are miles of equestrian trails. Please note that wheat straw is not allowed at this campground.

Campsites, facilities: There are 48 sites for tents or RVs up to 35 feet (no hookups). Picnic tables and fire rings are provided. Drinking water and flush and vault toilets are available. Five stock troughs and four hitching posts are also available. Some facilities are wheelchair-accessible. Leashed pets are permitted.

Reservations, fees: Reservations are not accepted. Sites are $8 per night, $8 per night for each additional vehicle. Open year-round.

Directions: From Sacramento on I-80, drive east to the north end of Auburn and the exit for

Elm Avenue. Take that exit and turn left on Elm Avenue and drive about 0.1 mile to High Street. Turn left on High Street and drive through the signal that marks the continuation of High Street as Highway 49 and drive 3.5 miles on Highway 49 to the bridge. Turn right over the bridge and drive 2.5 miles into the town of Cool and Georgetown Road/Highway 193. Turn left and drive 14 miles into Georgetown to a four-way stop at Main Street. Turn left on Main Street and drive 5.5 miles (the road becomes Georgetown–Wentworth Springs Road/Forest Road 1) to Bottle Hill Bypass Road. Turn left on Bottle Hill Bypass Road and drive about a mile to the campground on the left.

Contact: Eldorado National Forest, Georgetown Ranger District, 530/333-4312, www. fs.usda.gov/eldorado.

52 CAMP LOTUS

Scenic rating: 7

on the American River near Coloma

Map 5.4, page 316   BEST (

This is a great area with 0.5 mile of frontage on the South Fork of the American River. During spring and summer you'll see plenty of whitewater rafters and kayakers here because this is a popular place for outfitters to put in and take out. Several swimming holes are in the immediate vicinity. The camp is situated on 23 acres at 700 feet elevation. There are a variety of trees at Camp Lotus, including pines, oaks, willows, and cottonwoods. Coloma, two miles away, is where you'll find the Marshall Gold Discovery Site. Gold was discovered there in 1848, and the site features displays and exhibits on gold rush–era mining methods and the history of the California gold rush. Wineries are nearby, and gold panning, hiking, and fishing are also popular.

Campsites, facilities: There are 30 tent sites and 10 sites with partial hookups (20 and 30 amps) for tents or RVs of any length. A cabin and three lodge rooms are also available for rent. Picnic tables and fire grills are provided. Drinking water, restrooms with showers, Wi-Fi, dump station, general store with deli, volleyball, horseshoes, and raft and kayak put-in and take-out areas are available. Groups can be accommodated. Limited supplies are available in Coloma. Some facilities are wheelchair-accessible. Dogs are not permitted.

Reservations, fees: Reservations are accepted and required for weekends. Sites are $24–33 per night, $8–11 per person for more than three people. Credit cards accepted. Open February through October.

Directions: From Sacramento, drive east on Highway 50 for approximately 30 miles (past Cameron Park) to Exit 37, the Ponderosa Road exit. Take that exit and drive north over the freeway to North Shingle Road. Turn right and drive 10 miles (the road becomes Lotus Road) to Bassi Road. Turn left and drive one mile to the campground entrance on the right.

Contact: Camp Lotus, 530/622-8672, www. camplotus.com.

53 PLACERVILLE KOA

Scenic rating: 5

near Placerville

Map 5.4, page 316

This is a classic KOA campground, complete with the cute little log cabins KOA calls "Kamping Kabins." The location of this camp is ideal for many, set near U.S. 50 in the Sierra foothills, the main route up to South Lake Tahoe. Nearby is Apple Hill, where from September to November it is a popular tourist attraction, when the local ranches and orchards sell produce and crafts, often with live music. In addition, the Marshall Gold Discovery Site is 10 miles north, where gold was discovered in 1848, setting off the 1849 gold rush. Whitewater rafting and gold panning are popular on the nearby American River.

Campsites, facilities: There are 70 sites with full or partial hookups (30 and 50 amps) for

RVs of any length, 14 tent sites, including eight with electricity, 20 sites for tents or RVs, and eight cabins. Some sites are pull-through. Picnic tables and barbecues are provided. Restrooms with flush toilets and showers, drinking water, dump station, cable TV, modem access, Wi-Fi, recreation room, seasonal swimming pool, spa (some restrictions apply), playground, video arcade, basketball courts, 18-hole miniature golf course, convenience store, snack bar, dog run, petting zoo, fishing pond, bike rentals, pavilion cooking facilities, volleyball court, and horseshoe pits are available. Some facilities are wheelchair-accessible. Leashed pets are permitted, with certain restrictions.

Reservations, fees: Reservations are accepted at 800/562-4197. RV sites are $39–62, tent sites are $36–41, $3 per person per night for more than two people. Some credit cards accepted. Open year-round.

Directions: From U.S. 50 west of Placerville, take the exit for Shingle Springs Drive/Exit 39 (and not the Shingle Springs/Ponderosa Road exit). Drive one block to Rock Barn Road. Turn left and drive 0.5 mile to the campground at the end of the road.

Contact: Placerville KOA, 530/676-2267, www.koa.com.

54 FAR HORIZONS 49ER VILLAGE RV RESORT

Scenic rating: 4

in Plymouth

Map 5.4, page 316

This is the granddaddy of RV parks, set on 23 acres in the heart of the Gold Country 40 miles east of Stockton and Sacramento. It is rarely crowded and offers warm pools and a huge spa. A bonus is the year-round heated, covered swimming pool. This resort is pet-friendly, and dogs receive a free milk bone at check-in. Wineries are nearby. Note that renters occupy about one-fourth of the sites.

Campsites, facilities: There are 329 sites with full hookups (30 and 50 amps) for RVs up to 40 feet and 15 park model cabins. Some sites are pull-through. Restrooms with flush toilets and showers, cable TV, dump station, playground, two heated swimming pools, indoor spa, recreation room, TV lounge, recreation complex, modem access, Wi-Fi, business services, organized activities, café, gift shop, coin laundry, propane gas, and a general store are available. Some facilities are wheelchair-accessible. Leashed pets are permitted.

Reservations, fees: Reservations are recommended at 800/339-6981. Sites are $39–71 per night (holiday rates higher), $5 per night for additional person, $2 per night for each additional vehicle, $3 per night per pet. Winter discounts are available. Some credit cards accepted. Open year-round.

Directions: From Sacramento, drive east on U.S. 50 to Watt Avenue. Turn south on Watt Avenue and drive to Highway 16. Turn left (east) on Highway 16/Jackson Road and drive approximately 30 miles to Highway 49 north/Jackson Road. Merge north on Highway 49 and drive two miles to the resort on the left side of the road at 18265 Highway 49. Note: This is a mile south of Main Street in Plymouth.

Contact: Far Horizons 49er Village RV Resort, 209/245-6981, www.49ervillage.com.

55 INDIAN GRINDING ROCK STATE HISTORIC PARK

Scenic rating: 7

near Jackson

Map 5.4, page 316

This park is like a living history lesson. Indian Grinding Rock covers 135 acres in the Sierra foothills at an elevation of 2,400 feet. Set in a small valley of meadows and oaks, the park contains the most remarkable limestone bedrock mortars in California, as well as a reconstructed Miwok village with petroglyphs, a museum, and two nature trails; one massive table rock has hundreds of mortars. (If it looks familiar, you may recognize it from TV show I shot here.) Interpretive talks are offered for groups (by reservation).

Local Native Americans schedule several ceremonies each year, including the Acorn Harvest Thanksgiving in September. In summer, expect warm and dry temperatures, often exceeding 90°F. Spring and fall are ideal, with winters cool, often right on the edge of snow (a few times) and rain (mostly) during storms.

Campsites, facilities: There are 23 sites for tents or RVs up to 27 feet (no hookups), and a group camp for up to 44 people that includes bark houses. Picnic tables, fire grills, and food lockers are provided. Drinking water and restrooms with flush toilets and coin showers are available. Some facilities are wheelchair-accessible. Leashed pets are permitted.

Reservations, fees: Reservations are not accepted for individual sites, but are required for the group camp ($25 non-refundable deposit required), which includes the bark houses; call 209/296-7488. Tent and RV sites are $25 per night, $8 per night for each additional vehicle, $85 per night for the group camp. Open year-round.

Directions: From Jackson, drive east on Highway 88 for 11 miles to Pine Grove–Volcano Road. Turn left on Pine Grove–Volcano Road and drive 1.75 miles to the campground on the left.

Contact: Indian Grinding Rock State Historic Park, 209/296-7488, www.parks.ca.gov.

56 LAKE AMADOR RECREATION AREA

Scenic rating: 7

near Stockton

Map 5.4, page 316

Lake Amador is set in the foothill country east of Stockton at an elevation of 485 feet, covering 400 acres with 13 miles of shoreline. Everything here is set up for fishing, with large trout stocks from winter through late spring and the chance for huge bass. The lake record bass weighed 17 pounds, 1.25 ounces. The Carson Creek arm and Jackson Creek arm are the top spots. Night fishing is available. Waterskiing and personal watercraft are prohibited, and the speed limit is 5 mph. A bonus is a swimming pond. About half of the sites are lakefront with full hookups.

Campsites, facilities: There are 150 sites for tents or RVs of any length, and 13 group sites for 5–30 vehicles each; some sites have full hookups (30 and 50 amps). Picnic tables and fire grills are provided. Drinking water, restrooms with showers, dump station, boat ramp, boat rentals, fishing supplies (including bait and tackle), seasonal café, convenience store, propane gas, swimming pond with water slide, pool tables, horseshoe pits, and a playground are available. Some facilities are wheelchair-accessible. Leashed pets are permitted.

Reservations, fees: Reservations are accepted February through August ($5 reservation fee). Tent sites are $25 per night per vehicle, $1 per person for more than four people; RV sites are $30 per night. Boat launching is $7 per day and fishing is $8 per day. Some credit cards accepted. Open year-round.

Directions: From Stockton, turn east on Highway 88 and drive 24 miles to Clements. Just east of Clements, bear left on Highway 88 and drive nine miles to Jackson Valley Road. Turn right (well signed) and drive five miles to Lake Amador Drive. Turn right and drive over the dam to the campground office.

Contact: Lake Amador Recreation Area, 209/274-4739, www.lakeamador.com.

57 LAKE PARDEE MARINA

Scenic rating: 7

on Pardee Reservoir

Map 5.4, page 316

Many people think that Pardee is the prettiest lake in the Mother Lode country; it's a big lake covering 2,257 acres with 37 miles of shoreline. It is a beautiful sight in the spring when the lake is full and the surrounding hills are green and glowing. Waterskiing, personal watercraft, swimming, and all water/body contact are prohibited at the lake; it is set up expressly for fishing, with high catch rates for rainbow trout and kokanee salmon. During hot weather, attention turns to bass, both smallmouth and largemouth, as well as catfish and sunfish. The lake speed limit is 25 mph. All of the money collected from the daily $4 fishing fee is used to purchase and stock rainbow trout.

Campsites, facilities: There are 190 sites for tents or RVs up to 42 feet (no hookups) and 12 sites with full hookups (50 amps) for RVs. Picnic tables and fire grills are provided. Drinking water, restrooms with showers (in the hookup section), chemical toilets (in the no-hookup campground), dump station, full-service marina, fish-cleaning station, boat ramp, boat rentals, coin laundry, café, gas station, convenience store, propane gas, RV and boat storage, wading pool, and a seasonal swimming pool are available. Some facilities are wheelchair-accessible. Leashed pets are permitted.

Reservations, fees: Reservations are accepted ($8 registration fee). RV sites with full hookups are $31 per night, tent sites are $22–26 per night, $11 per night for each additional vehicle, $3 per pet per night. Boat launching is $7.50 per day. There is a daily fishing fee of $4. Monthly and seasonal rates available. Some credit cards accepted. Open February through October.

Directions: From Stockton, drive east on Highway 88/Waterloo Road for 17 miles to the town of Clements. One mile east of Clements, bear left on Highway 88 and drive 11 miles to Jackson Valley Road. Turn right and drive 3.4 miles to a four-way-stop sign at Buena Vista. Turn right and drive 3.1 miles to Stony Creek Road. Turn left and drive a mile to the campground on the right. (Driving directions from other areas are available on the marina's website.)

Contact: Lake Pardee Marina, 209/772-1472, www.pardeelakerecreation.com.

58 CAMANCHE LAKE NORTH

Scenic rating: 7

on Camanche Lake

Map 5.4, page 316

The sites at North Shore feature grassy spots with picnic tables set above the lake, and though there are few trees and the sites seem largely exposed, the lake view is quite pretty. In spring, this site rates much higher. The lake will beckon you and is excellent for boating and all water sports, with a full-service marina available. The warm, clean waters make for good waterskiing and wakeboarding (in specified areas), and fishing for trout in spring, bass in early summer, and crappie, bluegill, and catfish in summer. There are five miles of hiking and equestrian trails. Note: All boats must be certified mussel-free before launching.

Campsites, facilities: There are 219 sites for tents or RVs of any length (no hookups) and four group sites for 12–72 people. There are also seven boat-in sites at Eagle Beach Campground, nine cottages, four triplexes, and motel rooms available. Picnic tables and fire grills are provided. Restrooms with showers, drinking water, dump station, boat ramp, boat rentals, coin laundry, convenience store, café, and a playground are available. Some facilities are wheelchair-accessible. Leashed pets are permitted.

Reservations, fees: Reservations are accepted at 866/763-5121 ($9 reservation fee). Tent sites are $28 per night, premium tent sites and boat-in sites are $34 per night, RV sites are $45 per night, premium RV sites are $50 per night. Car and boat access is $16, fishing is $4 per day, boat launch is $8 per day, $4 per pet per day. Group rates are available on a sliding scale. Discounts available off-season. Some credit cards accepted. Open year-round.

Directions: From Stockton, drive east on

Highway 88/Waterloo Road for 17 miles to Clements. One mile east of Clements, bear left on Highway 88 and drive six miles to Liberty Road/North Camanche Parkway. Turn right and drive six miles to Camanche Road. Turn right and drive to the Camanche North Shore entrance gate.

Contact: Camanche Lake North, 209/763-5121, www.camancherecreation.com.

59 CAMANCHE LAKE SOUTH AND EQUESTRIAN

Scenic rating: 7

on Camanche Lake

Map 5.4, page 316

Camanche Lake is a huge, multifaceted facility, covering 7,700 acres with 53 miles of shoreline, set in the foothills east of Lodi at 325 feet elevation. It is the number-one recreation lake for waterskiing, wakeboarding, and personal watercraft (in specified areas), as well as swimming. In the spring and summer, it provides outstanding fishing for bass, trout, crappie, bluegill, and catfish. There are two campgrounds at the lake, and both have boat ramps nearby and full facilities. A new equestrian campground is open, and it's about one mile from the main campground area. This one at South Shore has a large, but exposed, overflow area for camping, a way to keep from getting stuck for a spot on popular weekends. Note: All boats must be certified mussel-free before launching.

Campsites, facilities: There are 149 sites for tents or RVs of any length (no hookups), including 35 double sites and 35 group sites for up to 16 people. Seven cottages are also available. Turkey Hill Equestrian Camp can accommodate groups of up to 32 people, as well as their horses and trailers. Picnic tables and fire grills are provided. Drinking water, restrooms with flush toilets and showers, chemical toilets, dump station, trout pond, marina, boat ramp, boat rentals, coin laundry, amphitheater with seasonal movies, basketball, tennis courts, and a convenience store are available. Some facilities are wheelchair-accessible. Leashed pets are permitted.

Reservations, fees: Reservations are accepted at 866/763-5178 ($9 reservation fee). Tent sites are $28 per night, premium tent sites are $34 per night, RV sites are $45 per night, premium RV sites are $50 per night, equestrian sites range $45–150 for 8–32 people. Car and boat access is $16, fishing is $4 per day, boat launch is $8 per day, $4 per pet per day. Group rates are available on a sliding scale. Monthly rates available with a six-month limit. Discounts available off-season. Some credit cards accepted. Open year-round.

Directions: From Stockton, drive east on Highway 88/Waterloo Road for 17 miles to Clements. One mile east of Clements, continue east on Highway 12 and drive six miles to South Camanche Parkway at Wallace. Continue straight and drive five miles to the entrance gate.

Contact: Camanche Lake South, 209/763-5178, www.camancherecreation.com.

60 OAK KNOLL CAMPGROUND AND COYOTE POINT GROUP CAMP

Scenic rating: 7

at New Hogan Lake

Map 5.4, page 316

This is one of two camps at New Hogan Lake. The reservoir was created by an Army Corps of Engineers dam project on the Calaveras River. (See the Acorn Campground listing for more information.)

Campsites, facilities: There are 49 sites for tents or RVs of any length, and a group site for tents or RVs of any length that can accommodate up to 50–60 people. No hookups. Fire grills and picnic tables are provided. Drinking water, vault toilets, and coin showers are available. A dump station, a fish cleaning station, and a four-lane boat ramp (at Fiddleneck) are nearby. A grocery store and propane gas are within five miles. Some facilities are wheelchair accessible. Leashed pets are permitted.

Reservations, fees: Reservations are accepted at 877/444-6777 or www.recreation.gov ($9 reservation fee). Sites are $14 per night, and the group site is $125 per night. Open May through early September.

Directions: From Stockton, drive east on Highway 26 for about 30 miles to Valley Springs and Hogan Dam Road. Turn right and drive 1.5 miles to Hogan Parkway. Turn left and drive one mile to South Petersburg Road. Turn left and drive 0.5 mile to the campground on the right (adjacent to Acorn Campground).

Contact: U.S. Army Corps of Engineers, Sacramento District, 209/772-1343.

61 ACORN CAMP AND DEER FLAT BOAT-IN

Scenic rating: 7

at New Hogan Lake

Map 5.4, page 316

New Hogan is a big lake in the foothill country east of Stockton, set at an elevation of 680 feet and covering 4,000 acres, with 50 miles of shoreline. Acorn is on the lake and operated by the Army Corps of Engineers. Boaters might also consider boat-in sites near Deer Flat on the eastern shore, and there is a group camp at Coyote Point. Boating and waterskiing are popular here, and all water sports are allowed. It's a decent lake for fishing, with a unique opportunity for striped bass, and it's OK for largemouth bass. Other species are crappie, bluegill, and catfish. There are bicycle trails and an eight-mile equestrian trail. An interpretive trail below the dam is worth checking out. Insider's tip: This is a wintering area for bald eagles.

Campsites, facilities: There are 127 sites for tents or RVs of any length (no hookups) and 30 boat-in sites. Fire pits and picnic tables

are provided. Drinking water, restrooms with flush toilets and coin showers, pay telephones, fish-cleaning station, amphitheater, and a dump station are available. A two-lane, paved boat ramp and an 18-hole disc golf course are nearby. Nature walks and ranger programs are sometimes available. Groceries, a restaurant, and propane gas are within two miles. Some facilities are wheelchair accessible. Leashed pets are permitted.

Reservations, fees: Reservations are accepted for the Acorn campsites at 877/444-6777 or www.recreation.gov ($9 reservation fee). Sites are $16–20 per night, and boat-in sites are $10 per night. Some credit cards accepted. Open year-round, with reduced number of sites in winter; boat-in sites are open May through September.

Directions: From Stockton, drive east on Highway 26 for about 30 miles to Valley Springs and Hogan Dam Road. Turn right and drive 1.5 miles to Hogan Parkway. Turn left and drive one mile to South Petersburg Road. Turn left and drive 0.25 mile to the campground on the right.

Contact: U.S. Army Corps of Engineers, Sacramento District, 209/772-1343.

62 49ER RV RANCH

Scenic rating: 6

near Columbia

Map 5.4, page 316

This historic ranch/campground was originally built in 1852 as a dairy farm. Several original barns are still standing. The place has been brought up to date, of course, with a small store on the property providing last-minute supplies. Location is a plus, with the Columbia State Historic Park only 0.5 mile away, and the Stanislaus River arm of New Melones Lake within a five-minute drive. Live theater and wineries are nearby. The elevation is 2,100 feet. Note that there is a separate mobile home park on the premises.

Campsites, facilities: There are 42 sites with full hookups (50 amps) for trailers and RVs up to 50 feet. No tents. Picnic tables and cable TV are provided. Restrooms with showers, drinking water, coin laundry, convenience store, dump station, Wi-Fi, propane gas, and a large barn for group or club activities are available. Some facilities are wheelchair-accessible. Leashed pets are permitted.

Reservations, fees: Reservations are accepted by phone or website. RV sites are $49 per night, $2.50 per night for additional person, $3 per night for each additional vehicle. Group and senior rates available. Open year-round.

Directions: From Sonora, turn north on Highway 49 and drive for 2.5 miles to Parrotts Ferry Road. Turn right and drive 1.7 miles to Columbia Street. Turn right and drive 0.4 mile to Pacific Street. Turn left and drive a block to Italian Bar Road. Turn right and drive 0.5 mile to the campground on the right.

Contact: 49er RV Ranch, 209/532-4978, www.49rv.com.

63 MARBLE QUARRY RV PARK

🏃 🏊 🚣 🐎 🚴 ♿ 🚐 ⛺

Scenic rating: 6

near Columbia

Map 5.4, page 316

This is a family-oriented RV park set at 2,100 feet elevation in the Gold Country, within nearby range of several adventures. A 0.25-mile trail leads directly to Columbia State Historic Park, and the Stanislaus River arm of New Melones Lake is only five miles away.

Campsites, facilities: There are 85 sites with full or partial hookups (30 and 50 amps) for RVs up to 40 feet, a small area for tents, and three cabins of different sizes, including mid-size and executive cabins with kitchenettes. A few sites are pull-through. Picnic tables are provided. Restrooms with showers, satellite TV, seasonal swimming pool, coin laundry, Wi-Fi, convenience store, dump station, playground, two clubhouses, reading/TV room, group facilities, and propane gas are available. Some facilities are wheelchair-accessible. Leashed pets are permitted.

Reservations, fees: Reservations are accepted at 866/677-8464 or www.marblequarry.com. RV sites are $44–52 per night, tent sites are $26–30 per night, $4 per person per night for more than two people over age 6, cabins are $70–168. Discounts available for seniors and military and off-season. Some credit cards accepted. Open year-round.

Directions: From Sonora, turn north on Highway 49 and drive 2.5 miles to Parrotts Ferry Road (stop sign). Bear right on Parrotts Ferry Road and drive 1.5 miles to Columbia Street. Turn right and drive a short distance to Jackson Street. Turn right on Jackson Street and drive 0.25 mile (becomes Yankee Hill Road) to the campground on the right (at 11551 Yankee Hill Road).

Contact: Marble Quarry RV Park, 866/677-8464 or 209/532-9539, www.marblequarry.com.

TAHOE AND THE NORTHERN SIERRA

© MARIUSZ BLACH/123RF.COM

BEST CAMPGROUNDS

❰ **Scenic Campgrounds**
Sardine Lakes, page 369.
Upper Hell Hole Walk-In/Boat-In, page 403.
Donner Memorial State Park, page 447.
Emerald Bay State Park and Boat-In, page 454.

❰ **Boat-In Campgrounds**
Emerald Bay State Park and Boat-In, page 454.

❰ **Easy Backpacking**
Woods Lake, page 418.

❰ **Families**
Silver Lake West, page 419.
Lake Alpine Campground, page 438.
Historic Camp Richardson Resort, page 457.

❰ **Hikes with Views**
D. L. Bliss State Park, page 453.

Mount Tallac affords a view across Lake Tahoe

like no other: a cobalt-blue expanse of water bordered by mountains that span miles of Sierra wildlands. The beauty is stunning. Lake Tahoe is one of the few places on earth where people feel an emotional response just by looking at it. Yosemite Valley, the giant sequoias, the Grand Canyon, a perfect sunset on the Pacific Ocean... these are a few other sights that occasionally can evoke the same response. But Tahoe often seems to strike the deepest chord. It can resonate inside you for weeks, even after a short visit.

This area has the widest range and number of campgrounds in California. "What about all the people?" you ask. It's true that people come here in droves. But I found many spots that I shared only with the chipmunks. You can enjoy these spots, too, if you're willing to read my books, hunt a bit, and, most important, time your trip to span Monday through Thursday.

Tahoe and the Northern Sierra feature hundreds of lakes, including dozens you can drive to. The best for scenic beauty are Echo Lakes, Donner, Fallen Leaf, Sardine, Caples, Loon, Union Valley — well, I could go on and on. It is one of the most beautiful regions anywhere on earth.

The north end of the Northern Sierra starts near Bucks Lake, a great lake for trout fishing, and extends to Bear River Canyon (and Caples Lake, Silver Lake, and Bear River Reservoir). In between are the Lakes Basin Recreation Area (containing Gold, Sardine, Packer, and other lakes) in southern Plumas County; the Crystal Basin (featuring Union Valley Reservoir and Loon Lake, among others) in the Sierra foothills west of Tahoe; Lake Davis (with the highest catch rates for trout) near Portola; and the Carson River Canyon and Hope Valley south of Tahoe.

You could spend weeks exploring any of these places, having the time of your life, and still not get to Tahoe's magic. But it is Tahoe where the adventure starts for many, especially in the surrounding Tahoe National Forest and Desolation Wilderness.

One of California's greatest day trips from Tahoe is to Echo Lakes, where you can take a hikers shuttle boat across the two lakes to the Pacific Crest Trail, then hike a few miles into Desolation Wilderness and Aloha Lakes. Yet with so many wonderful ways to spend a day in this area, this day trip is hardly a blip on the radar.

With so many places and so little time, this region offers what can be the ultimate adventureland.

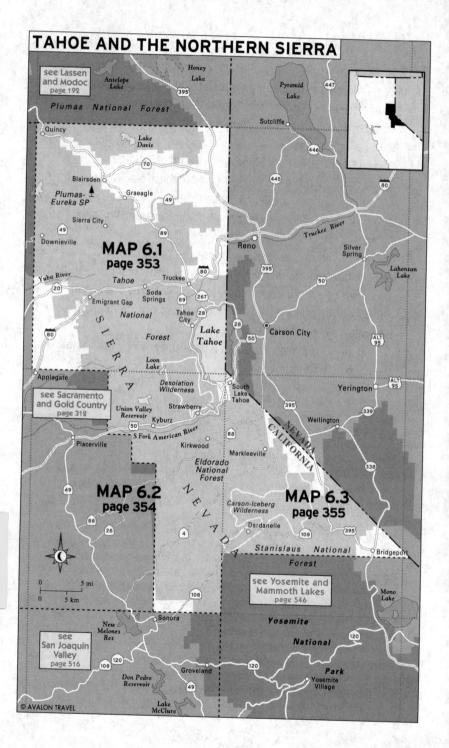

TAHOE AND THE NORTHERN SIERRA

Map 6.1

Sites 1-102
Pages 357-403

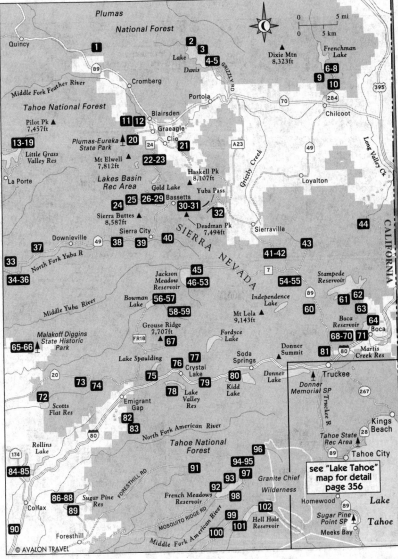

Map 6.2

Sites 103-156
Pages 404-428

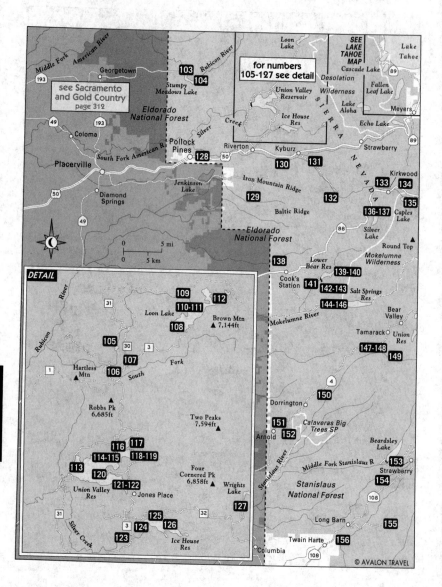

Map 6.3

Sites 157-199
Pages 428-447

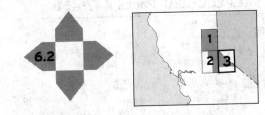

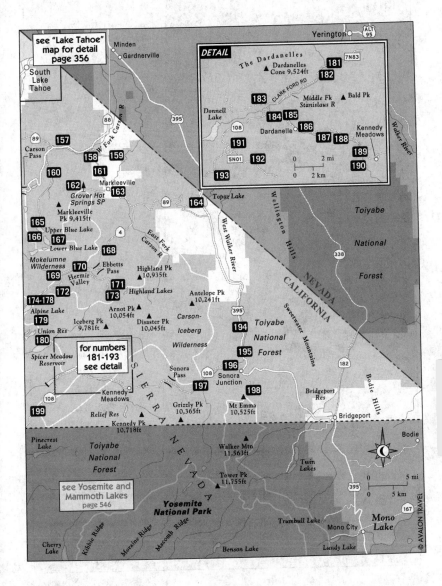

LAKE TAHOE
Sites 200-220 Pages 447-458

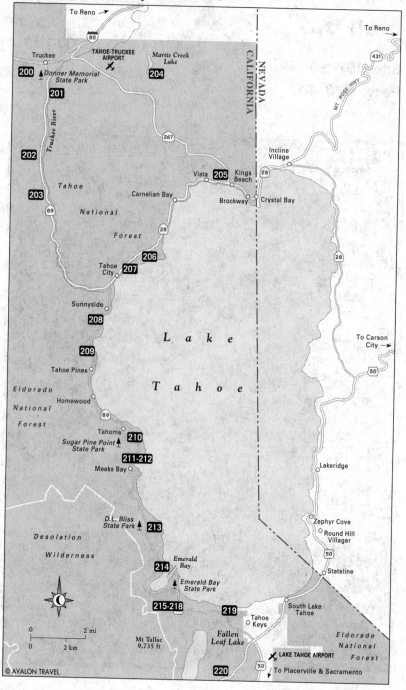

1 BRADY'S CAMP

Scenic rating: 4

on Pine Creek in Plumas National Forest

Map 6.1, page 353

Don't expect much company here. This is a tiny, little-known, primitive camp near Pine Creek, at roughly 7,000 feet elevation. A side trip is to make the half-mile drive up to Argentine Rock (7,209 feet) for a lookout onto this remote forest country. To the east are many miles of national forest accessible by vehicle.

Campsites, facilities: There are four tent sites. Picnic tables and fire grills are provided. Vault toilets are available. No drinking water is available. Garbage must be packed out. Leashed pets are permitted.

Reservations, fees: Reservations are not accepted. There is no fee for camping. Open May through October, weather permitting.

Directions: From Oroville, drive north on Highway 70 to the junction with Highway 89. Turn south on Highway 89/70 and drive 11 miles to Quincy. In Quincy, continue on Highway 89/70 for six miles to Squirrel Creek Road. Turn left and drive seven miles (after two miles bear right at the Y) to Forest Road 25N29. Turn left and drive one mile to the campground on the right side of the road.

Contact: Plumas National Forest, Mt. Hough Ranger District, 530/283-0555, www.fs.usda.gov/plumas.

2 LIGHTNING TREE

Scenic rating: 7

on Lake Davis in Plumas National Forest

Map 6.1, page 353

Lightning Tree campground is set near the shore of Lake Davis. Davis is a good-sized lake, with 32 miles of shoreline, set high in the northern Sierra at 5,775 feet. Lake Davis is one of the top mountain lakes in California for fishing, with large rainbow trout in the early summer and fall. This camp is perfectly situated for a fishing trip. It is at Lightning Tree Point on the lake's remote northeast shore, directly across the lake from Freeman Creek, one of the better spots for big trout. This lake is famous for pike; the Department of Fish and Game has twice poisoned the lake to kill them. In turn, the biggest trout plants in California history have been made here. There are three boat ramps on the lake.

Campsites, facilities: There are 40 sites (including several double sites) for tents or RVs up to 50 feet (no hookups). Vault toilets and drinking water are available. A dump station and a car-top boat launch are nearby. Some facilities are wheelchair-accessible. Leashed pets are permitted.

Reservations, fees: Reservations are accepted at 877/444-6777 or www.recreation.gov ($9 reservation fee). Sites are $20 per night, $40 per night for a double site. Open May through October, weather permitting.

Directions: From Truckee, turn north on Highway 89 and drive to Sattley and County Road A23. Turn right on County Road A23 and drive 13 miles to Highway 70. Turn left on Highway 70 and drive one mile to Grizzly Road. Turn right on Grizzly Road and drive about six miles to Lake Davis. Continue north on Lake Davis Road along the lake's east shore and drive about five miles to the campground entrance on the left side of the road.

Contact: Plumas National Forest, Beckwourth Ranger District, 530/836-2575, Lake Davis Recreation Area, www.fs.usda.gov/plumas; Thousand Trails, 530/258-7606.

3 GRASSHOPPER FLAT

Scenic rating: 7

on Lake Davis in Plumas National Forest

Map 6.1, page 353

Grasshopper Flat provides a nearby alternative to Grizzly at Lake Davis, with the boat ramp at adjacent Honker Cove a primary attraction for campers with trailered boats for fishing. The camp is on the southeast end of the lake, at 5,800 feet elevation. Lake Davis is known for its large rainbow trout that bite best in early summer and fall. Swimming and powerboats are allowed, but no waterskiing or personal watercraft are permitted.

Campsites, facilities: There are 69 sites for tents or RVs up to 35 feet (no hookups) and one group site for up to 25 people. Picnic tables and fire grills are provided. Drinking water and restrooms with flush toilets and coin showers are available. A boat ramp, grocery store, and a dump station are nearby. Some facilities are wheelchair-accessible. Leashed pets are permitted.

Reservations, fees: Reservations are accepted at 877/444-6777 or www.recreation.gov ($9 reservation fee). Sites are $21 per night for single sites, $90 per night for the group site. Open May through October, weather permitting.

Directions: From Truckee, turn north on Highway 89 and drive to Sattley and County Road A23. Turn right on County Road A23 and drive 13 miles to Highway 70. Turn left on Highway 70 and drive one mile to Grizzly Road. Turn right on Grizzly Road and drive about six miles to Lake Davis. Continue north on Lake Davis Road for a mile (just past Grizzly) to the campground entrance on the left side of the road.

Contact: Plumas National Forest, Beckwourth Ranger District, 530/836-2575, Lake Davis Recreation Area, www.fs.usda.gov/plumas; Thousand Trails, 530/258-7606.

◢ CROCKER

Scenic rating: 5

in Plumas National Forest

Map 6.1, page 353

Even though this camp is just four miles east of Lake Davis, it is little known and little used since there are three lakeside camps close by.

This camp is set in Plumas National Forest at 5,900 feet elevation, and it is about a 15-minute drive north to the border of the Dixie Mountain State Game Refuge.

Campsites, facilities: There are 10 sites for tents or RVs up to 16 feet (no hookups). Picnic tables and fire grills are provided. Vault toilets are available. No drinking water is available. Garbage must be packed out. Leashed pets are permitted.

Reservations, fees: Reservations are not accepted. There is no fee for camping. Open May through October, weather permitting.

Directions: From Reno, drive north on U.S. 395 to the junction with Highway 70. Turn west on Highway 70 and drive to Beckwourth and County Road 111/Beckwourth-Genessee Road. Turn right on County Road 111 and drive six miles to the campground on the left side of the road.

Contact: Plumas National Forest, Beckwourth Ranger District, 530/836-2575, www.fs.usda.gov/plumas; Thousand Trails, 530/258-7606.

◢ GRIZZLY

Scenic rating: 7

on Lake Davis in Plumas National Forest

Map 6.1, page 353

This is one of the better developed campgrounds at Lake Davis and is a popular spot for camping anglers. Its proximity to the Grizzly Store, just over the dam to the south, makes getting last-minute supplies a snap. In addition, a boat ramp is to the north in Honker Cove, providing access to the southern reaches of the lake, including the island area, where trout trolling is good in early summer and fall. The elevation is 5,800 feet.

Campsites, facilities: There are 56 sites for tents or RVs up to 35 feet (no hookups). Picnic tables and fire grills are provided. Drinking water and flush toilets are available. A boat ramp, grocery store, and a dump station are nearby. Some facilities are wheelchair-accessible. Leashed pets are permitted.

Reservations, fees: Reservations are accepted at 877/444-6777 or www.recreation.gov ($9 reservation fee). Sites are $21 per night. Open late May through mid-October, weather permitting.

Directions: From Truckee, turn north on Highway 89 and drive to Sattley and County Road A23. Turn right on County Road A23 and drive 13 miles to Highway 70. Turn left on Highway 70 and drive one mile to Grizzly Road. Turn right on Grizzly Road and drive about six miles to Lake Davis. Continue north on Lake Davis Road for less than a mile to the campground entrance on the left side of the road.

Contact: Plumas National Forest, Beckwourth Ranger District, Lake Davis Recreation Area, 530/836-2575, www.fs.usda.gov/plumas; Thousand Trails, 530/258-7606.

6 BIG COVE

🚶 ⛵ 🏊 🛥 🐕 ♿ 🚐 ⛺

Scenic rating: 7

at Frenchman Lake in Plumas National Forest

Map 6.1, page 353

Big Cove is one of four camps at the southeastern end of Frenchman Lake, with a boat ramp available about a mile away near the Frenchman and Spring Creek camps. (For more information, see the Frenchman listing in this chapter.) A trail from the campground leads to the lakeshore. Another trail connects to the Spring Creek campground, a walk of 0.5 mile. The elevation is 5,800 feet.

Campsites, facilities: There are 42 sites, including 10 doubles, for tents or RVs up to 50 feet (no hookups). Picnic tables and fire rings are provided. Drinking water and flush toilets are available. Some facilities are wheelchair-accessible. A boat ramp and dump station are nearby. A grocery store and propane gas are available seven miles away. Leashed pets are permitted.

Reservations, fees: Reservations are accepted at 877/444-6777 or www.recreation.gov ($9 reservation fee). Sites are $21–42 per night, $2

per pet per night. Open May through October, weather permitting.

Directions: From Reno, drive north on U.S. 395 to the junction with Highway 70. Turn west on Highway 70 and drive to Chilcoot and the junction with Frenchman Lake Road. Turn right on Frenchman Lake Road and drive nine miles to the lake and to a Y. At the Y, turn right and drive two miles to Forest Road 24N01. Turn left and drive a short distance to the campground entrance on the left side of the road (on the east side of the lake).

Contact: Plumas National Forest, Beckwourth Ranger District, 530/836-2575, www.fs.usda.gov/plumas; Thousand Trails, 530/258-7606.

7 SPRING CREEK

🚶 ⛵ 🏊 🛥 🐕 ♿ 🚐 ⛺

Scenic rating: 7

on Frenchman Lake in Plumas National Forest

Map 6.1, page 353

Frenchman Lake is set at 5,800 feet elevation, on the edge of high desert to the east and forest to the west. The lake has 21 miles of shoreline and is surrounded by a mix of sage and pines. All water sports are allowed. This camp is on the southeast end of the lake, where there are three other campgrounds, including a group camp and a boat ramp. The lake provides good fishing for stocked rainbow trout—best in the cove near the campgrounds. Trails lead out from the campground: One heads 0.25 mile to the Frenchman campground; the other a 0.5-mile route to Big Cove campground.

Campsites, facilities: There are 32 sites for tents or RVs up to 35 feet (no hookups). Picnic tables and fire grills are provided. Drinking water and vault toilets are available. Some facilities are wheelchair-accessible. A boat ramp and dump station are nearby. Leashed pets are permitted.

Reservations, fees: Reservations are accepted at 877/444-6777 or www.recreation.gov ($9

reservation fee). Sites are $21 per night. Open May through October, weather permitting.

Directions: From Reno, drive north on U.S. 395 to the junction with Highway 70. Turn west on Highway 70 and drive to Chilcoot and the junction with Frenchman Lake Road. Turn right on Frenchman Lake Road and drive nine miles to the lake and to a Y. At the Y, turn right and drive two miles to the campground on the left side of the road.

Contact: Plumas National Forest, Beckwourth Ranger District, 530/836-2575, www.fs.usda.gov/plumas; Thousand Trails, 530/258-7606.

8 FRENCHMAN

Scenic rating: 7

on Frenchman Lake in Plumas National Forest

Map 6.1, page 353

This camp is on the southeast end of the lake, where there are three other campgrounds, including a group camp and a boat ramp. The best trout fishing is in the cove near the campgrounds and the two inlets, one along the west shore and one at the head of the lake. The proximity to Reno, only 35 miles away, keeps gambling in the back of the minds of many anglers. Because of water demands downstream, the lake often drops significantly by the end of summer. A trail from camp is routed 0.25 mile to the Spring Creek campground.

Campsites, facilities: There are 38 sites for tents or RVs up to 35 feet (no hookups). Picnic tables and fire grills are provided. Drinking water and vault toilets are available. A dump station and boat ramp are nearby. Some facilities are wheelchair accessible. Leashed pets are permitted.

Reservations, fees: Reservations are accepted at 877/444-6777 or www.recreation.gov ($9 reservation fee). Sites are $21 per night, $2 per pet per night. Open May through October, weather permitting.

Directions: From Reno, drive north on U.S. 395 to the junction with Highway 70. Turn west on Highway 70 and drive to Chilcoot and the junction with Frenchman Lake Road. Turn right on Frenchman Lake Road and drive nine miles to the lake and to a Y. At the Y, turn right and drive 1.5 miles to the campground on the left side of the road.

Contact: Plumas National Forest, Beckwourth Ranger District, 530/836-2575, www.fs.usda.gov/plumas; Thousand Trails, 530/258-7606.

9 COTTONWOOD SPRINGS

Scenic rating: 7

near Frenchman Lake in Plumas National Forest

Map 6.1, page 353

Cottonwood Springs, elevation 5,800 feet, is largely an overflow camp at Frenchman Lake. It is the only camp at the lake with a group site. The more popular Frenchman, Big Cove, and Spring Creek camps are along the southeast shore of the lake near a boat ramp.

Campsites, facilities: There are 20 sites for tents or RVs up to 50 feet (no hookups) and two group sites for tents or RVs up to 35 feet that can accommodate up to 25 and 50 people respectively. Picnic tables and fire rings are provided. Drinking water and flush toilets are available. Some facilities are wheelchair-accessible. A boat ramp and dump station are nearby. Leashed pets are permitted.

Reservations, fees: Reservations are accepted for individual sites and are required for group sites at 877/444-6777 or www.recreation.gov ($9 reservation fee). Sites are $21 per night, $90–130 per night for groups, $2 per pet per night. Open May through October, weather permitting.

Directions: From Reno, drive north on U.S. 395 to the junction with Highway 70. Turn west on Highway 70 and drive to Chilcoot and the junction with Frenchman Lake Road. Turn right on Frenchman Lake Road and drive nine miles to the lake and to a Y. At the Y, turn left and drive 1.5 miles to the campground on the right side of the road.

Contact: Plumas National Forest, Beckwourth Ranger District, 530/836-2575, www.fs.usda. gov/plumas; Thousand Trails, 530/258-7606.

10 CHILCOOT

Scenic rating: 7

on Little Last Chance Creek in
Plumas National Forest

Map 6.1, page 353

This small camp is set along Little Last Chance Creek at 5,400 feet elevation, about three miles downstream from Frenchman Lake. The stream provides good trout fishing, but access can be difficult at some spots because of brush.

Campsites, facilities: There are 40 sites for tents or RVs up to 35 feet (no hookups), and five walk-in sites for tents only. Picnic tables and fire rings are provided. Drinking water and flush toilets are available. Some facilities are wheelchair-accessible. A boat ramp, grocery store, and dump station are nearby. Leashed pets are permitted.

Reservations, fees: Reservations are accepted at 877/444-6777 or www.recreation.gov ($9 reservation fee). Sites are $21 per night, $2 per pet per night. Open May through October, weather permitting.

Directions: From Reno, drive north on U.S. 395 to the junction with Highway 70. Turn west on Highway 70 and drive to Chilcoot and the junction with Frenchman Lake Road. Turn right on Frenchman Lake Road and drive six miles to the campground on the left side of the road.

Contact: Plumas National Forest, Beckwourth Ranger District, 530/836-2575, www.fs.usda. gov/plumas; Thousand Trails, 530/258-7606.

11 LITTLE BEAR RV PARK

Scenic rating: 7

on the Feather River

Map 6.1, page 353

This is a privately operated RV park set near the Feather River. Nearby destinations include Plumas-Eureka State Park and the Lakes Basin Recreation Area. The elevation is 4,300 feet. About half of the sites are taken by full-season rentals.

Campsites, facilities: There are 97 sites with full or partial hookups (30 amps) for RVs of any length, and 10 sleeping cabins. Picnic tables and fire rings are provided. Drinking water, restrooms with showers and flush toilets, coin laundry, convenience store, satellite TV, WiFi, RV storage, propane, and ice are available. A dump station, clubhouse, table tennis, shuffleboard, and horseshoes are also available. Leashed pets are permitted at campsites; but no pets in the cabins.

Reservations, fees: Reservations are recommended. RV sites with hookups are $33–36, $4–6 per person per night for more than two people, $1 per pet per night. Camping cabins are $45–55 per night. Weekly and monthly rates available. Open mid-April through late October.

Directions: In Truckee, drive north on Highway 89 to Graeagle. Continue north on Highway 89 for one mile to Little Bear Road. Turn left on Little Bear Road and drive a short distance to the campground on the right.

Contact: Little Bear RV Park, tel. 530/836-2774, www.littlebearrvpark.com.

12 MOVIN' WEST RV PARK

Scenic rating: 5

in Graeagle

Map 6.1, page 353

This RV park began life as a mobile home park. Approximately half of the sites are for permanent residents; the other half are for vacationers, with about half of those rented for the summer. The park has also become very popular with golfers. A nine-hole golf course is across the road and five other golf courses are within five miles. The elevation is 4,300 feet.

Campsites, facilities: There are 51 sites for RVs of any length with full (30 amps), partial, or no hookups, including five pull-through sites. There are also two tent sites and two cabins. Picnic tables and fire rings are provided. Drinking water, restrooms with flush toilets and showers, pay phone, cable TV, Wi-Fi, and a coin laundry are available. Propane gas, a nine-hole golf course, swimming pond, horse stable, and mini golf are nearby. Leashed pets are permitted.

Reservations, fees: Reservations are recommended. RV sites with hookups are $33–36 per night, tent sites are $30 per night, cabins are $40 per night, $4 per person per night for more than two people. Weekly rates available. Open May through October.

Directions: From Truckee, drive northwest on Highway 89 about 50 miles to Graeagle. Continue just past Graeagle to County Road A14 (Graeagle-Johnsville Road). Turn left and drive 0.25 mile northwest to the campground on the left.

Contact: Movin' West RV Park, 530/836-2614.

13 BLACK ROCK WALK-IN AND OVERFLOW

Scenic rating: 7

on Little Grass Valley Reservoir in Plumas National Forest

Map 6.1, page 353

This is the only campground on the west shore of Little Grass Valley Reservoir, with an adjacent boat ramp making it an attractive choice for anglers. The lake is set at 5,060 feet elevation in Plumas National Forest and provides lakeside camping and decent fishing for rainbow trout and kokanee salmon. If you don't like the company, there are seven other camps to choose from at the lake, all on the opposite eastern shore.

Campsites, facilities: There are 20 walk-in sites (a walk of a few yards to 0.1 mile) for tents or RVs up to 22 feet (no hookups). There is a parking lot for overflow camping for RVs up to 35 feet. Picnic tables and fire grills are provided. Drinking water, vault toilets, and a fish-cleaning station are available. A dump station, boat ramp, and grocery store are nearby. Some facilities are wheelchair accessible. Leashed pets are permitted.

Reservations, fees: Reservations are not accepted. Sites are $22 per night. Open May through September, weather permitting.

Directions: From Oroville, drive east on Highway 162/Oroville Dam Boulevard for about eight miles (becomes the Olive Highway) to Forbestown Road. Turn right and drive through Forbestown to Challenge and LaPorte Road. Turn left on LaPorte Road and drive to LaPorte. Continue two miles past LaPorte to the junction with County Road 514/Little Grass Valley Road. Turn left and drive about five miles to the campground access road on the west side of the lake. Turn right on the access road and drive 0.25 mile to the campground.

Contact: Plumas National Forest, Feather River Ranger District, 530/534-6500, www.fs.usda.gov/plumas.

14 HORSE CAMPGROUND

Scenic rating: 7

on Little Grass Valley Reservoir in Plumas National Forest

Map 6.1, page 353

This camp is reserved for equestrians only and thus it gets low use. This is a high-country forested campground set near Little Grass Valley Reservoir, but there is no lake view because of tree cover. Several trails are accessible from the campground, including the Pacific Crest Trail and Lakeshore Trail, as well as access to Bald Mountain (6,255 feet). The elevation at camp is 5,060 feet.

Campsites, facilities: There are 10 sites for tents or RVs up to 25 feet (no hookups) available for equestrian campers only. Picnic tables and fire grills are provided. Vault toilets are available. No drinking water is available. Hitching posts, a wheelchair-accessible mounting rack, and a fish-cleaning station are available. A restaurant and deli are available five miles away in LaPorte. Leashed pets are permitted.

Reservations, fees: Reservations are accepted at 877/444-6777 or www.recreation.gov ($9 reservation fee). Sites are $22 per night. Open June through September.

Directions: From Oroville, drive east on Highway 162/Oroville Dam Boulevard for about eight miles (becomes the Olive Highway) to Forbestown Road. Turn right and drive through Forbestown to Challenge and LaPorte Road. Turn left on LaPorte Road and drive to LaPorte. Continue on County Road 512 (which becomes County Road 514/Little Grass Valley Road) for three miles to Forest Road 22N57. Turn right and drive four miles (cross the bridge) to the campground on the left.

Contact: Plumas National Forest, Feather River Ranger District, 530/534-6500, www.fs.usda.gov/plumas.

15 PENINSULA TENT

🚶 🏊 ⛵ 🏕 🐾 🚐 ⛺

Scenic rating: 9

on Little Grass Valley Reservoir in Plumas National Forest

Map 6.1, page 353

This camp, at 5,060 feet in elevation, is exceptional in that most of the campsites provide views of Little Grass Valley Reservoir, a pretty lake in national forest. The fishing can be excellent, especially for rainbow trout, brown

trout, and kokanee salmon. The camp gets moderate use, and it is a pretty site with tents sprinkled amid white fir and pine. This is a good family campground. A 13.5-mile hiking trail circles the lake.

Campsites, facilities: There are 25 sites for tents. Picnic tables and fire rings are provided. Drinking water and flush toilets are available. A boat launch, fish-cleaning station, and a swimming beach are nearby. Some facilities are wheelchair accessible. Leashed pets are permitted.

Reservations, fees: Reservations are not accepted. Sites are $22 per night. Open Memorial Day weekend through September, weather permitting.

Directions: From Oroville, drive east on Highway 162/Oroville Dam Boulevard for about eight miles (becomes the Olive Highway) to Forbestown Road. Turn right and drive through Forbestown to Challenge and LaPorte Road. Turn left on LaPorte Road and drive to LaPorte. Continue on County Road 512 (which becomes County Road 514/Little Grass Valley Road) for three miles to Forest Road 22N57. Continue on Forest Road 514 for one mile to the campground entrance on right. Turn right and drive 0.25 mile to the campground.

Contact: Plumas National Forest, Feather River Ranger District, 530/534-6500, www.fs.usda.gov/plumas.

16 RUNNING DEER

🚶 🏊 ⛵ 🏕 🐾 🚐 ⛺

Scenic rating: 7

on Little Grass Valley Reservoir in Plumas National Forest

Map 6.1, page 353

Little Grass Valley Reservoir is a pretty mountain lake set at 5,060 feet elevation in Plumas National Forest, providing lakeside camping, boating, and fishing for rainbow trout and kokanee salmon. Looking straight north from the camp is a spectacular view, gazing across the water and up at Bald Mountain, at 6,255 feet elevation. One of seven campgrounds on the eastern shore, this one is on the far northeastern end of the lake. A trailhead for the Pacific Crest Trail is nearby at little Fowler Lake about four miles north of Little Grass Valley Reservoir. Note that fish-cleaning stations are not available at Running Deer, but there is one nearby at Little Beaver.

Campsites, facilities: There are 41 sites for tents or RVs up to 40 feet (no hookups). Picnic tables and fire rings are provided. Drinking water and flush toilets are available. A fish-cleaning station, boat ramp, grocery store, and a dump station are nearby. Leashed pets are permitted.

Reservations, fees: Reservations are accepted at 877/444-6777 or www.recreation.gov ($9 reservation fee). Sites are $22–24 per night. Open late May through September.

Directions: From Oroville, drive east on Highway 162/Oroville Dam Boulevard for about eight miles (becomes the Olive Highway) to Forbestown Road. Turn right and drive through Forbestown to Challenge and LaPorte Road. Turn left on LaPorte Road and drive to LaPorte. Continue on County Road 512 (which becomes County Road 514/Little Grass Valley Road) for three miles to Forest Road 22N57. Turn right and drive three miles to the campground on the left.

Contact: Plumas National Forest, Feather River Ranger District, 530/534-6500, www. fs.usda.gov/plumas.

17 WYANDOTTE

🚶 🏊 🚣 🚴 🚙 🦌 🚐 ⛺

Scenic rating: 8

on Little Grass Valley Reservoir in Plumas National Forest

Map 6.1, page 353

Of the eight camps on Little Grass Valley Reservoir, this is the favorite. It is set at 5,100 feet elevation on a small peninsula that extends well into the lake, with a boat ramp nearby. All water sports are allowed. (For more

information, see the Running Deer listing in this chapter.)

Campsites, facilities: There are 28 individual sites (including two double sites) for tents or RVs up to 40 feet (no hookups). Picnic tables and fire rings are provided. Drinking water and flush toilets are available. A dump station, boat ramp, fish-cleaning station, and grocery store are nearby. Leashed pets are permitted.

Reservations, fees: Reservations are not accepted. Single sites are $22 per night, $38 per night for a double site. Open late May through mid-October, weather permitting.

Directions: From Oroville, drive east on Highway 162/Oroville Dam Boulevard for about eight miles (becomes the Olive Highway) to Forbestown Road. Turn right and drive through Forbestown to Challenge and LaPorte Road. Turn left on LaPorte Road and drive to LaPorte. Continue two miles past LaPorte to the junction with County Road 514/Little Grass Valley Road. Turn left and drive one mile to a junction. Turn left and drive one mile to the campground entrance road on the right.

Contact: Plumas National Forest, Feather River Ranger District, 530/534-6500, www. fs.usda.gov/plumas.

18 LITTLE BEAVER

🚶 🏊 🚣 🚴 🚙 🦌 ♿ 🚐 ⛺

Scenic rating: 7

on Little Grass Valley Reservoir in Plumas National Forest

Map 6.1, page 353

This is one of eight campgrounds on Little Grass Valley Reservoir, set at 5,060 feet elevation. Take your pick. (For more information, see the Running Deer listing in this chapter.)

Campsites, facilities: There are 118 sites for tents or RVs up to 40 feet (no hookups). Picnic tables and fire rings are provided. Drinking water and flush toilets are available. A grocery store, dump station, fish-cleaning station, and boat ramp are nearby. Some facilities are wheelchair-accessible. Leashed pets are permitted.

Reservations, fees: Reservations are not accepted. Sites are $22–24 per night. Open June through mid-September, weather permitting.

Directions: From Oroville, drive east on Highway 162/Oroville Dam Boulevard for about eight miles (becomes the Olive Highway) to Forbestown Road. Turn right and drive through Forbestown to Challenge and LaPorte Road. Turn left on LaPorte Road and drive to LaPorte. Continue two miles past LaPorte to the junction with County Road 514/Little Grass Valley Road. Turn left and drive one mile to a junction. Turn right and drive two miles to the campground entrance road on the left.

Contact: Plumas National Forest, Feather River Ranger District, 530/534-6500, www. fs.usda.gov/plumas.

19 RED FEATHER CALIFORNIA

Scenic rating: 7

on Little Grass Valley Reservoir in Plumas National Forest

Map 6.1, page 353

This camp is well developed and popular, set on the eastern shore of Little Grass Valley Reservoir, just south of Running Deer and just north of Little Beaver. Bears frequent this area, so be sure to properly store your food and avoid scented products. (For more information, see the Running Deer listing in this chapter.)

Campsites, facilities: There are 58 sites for tents or RVs up to 40 feet (no hookups). Picnic tables and fire rings are provided. Drinking water and flush toilets are available. A dump station, boat ramp, fish-cleaning station, and grocery store are nearby. Leashed pets are permitted.

Reservations, fees: Reservations are accepted at 877/444-6777 or www.recreation.gov ($9 reservation fee). Sites are $22–24 per night. Open late June through September, weather permitting.

Directions: From Oroville, drive east on Highway 162/Oroville Dam Boulevard for about eight miles (becomes the Olive Highway) to Forbestown Road. Turn right and drive through Forbestown to Challenge and LaPorte Road. Turn left on LaPorte Road and drive to LaPorte. Continue two miles past LaPorte to the junction with County Road 514/Little Grass Valley Road. Turn left and drive one mile to a junction. Turn right and drive three miles to the campground entrance road on the left.

Contact: Plumas National Forest, Feather River Ranger District, 530/534-6500, www. fs.usda.gov/plumas.

20 PLUMAS-EUREKA STATE PARK

Scenic rating: 9

near Graeagle

Map 6.1, page 353

Plumas-Eureka State Park is a beautiful chunk of parkland, featuring great hiking, a pretty lake, and a well-maintained campground. For newcomers to the area, Jamison Camp at the southern end of the park makes for an excellent first stop. So does the nearby hike to Grass Lake, a first-class tromp that takes about two hours and features a streamside walk along Little Jamison Creek, with the chance to take a five-minute cutoff to see 40-foot Jamison Falls. A historic mine, park museum, blacksmith shop, stable, and stamp mill are also here, with campers allowed free admission to the museum. Other must-see destinations in the park include Eureka Lake, and from there, the 1,100-foot climb to 7,447-feet Eureka Peak (formerly known as Gold Mountain) for a dramatic view of all the famous peaks in this region. Camp elevation is 5,200 feet and the park covers 5,500 acres. Fishing opportunities include Madora and Eureka Lakes and Jamison Creek, best in May and June. The visitors center was originally constructed as a bunkhouse for miners; more than $8 million in gold was mined here.

Note: This park was on the closure list developed by the California Department of Parks, pending final state budget decisions or the possible transfer of park management to other park agencies or volunteer groups. It is open thanks to a donor agreement with the Plumas-Eureka State Park Association.

Campsites, facilities: Upper Jamison Creek Campground has 55 sites for tents or RVs up to 30 feet (no hookups). Picnic tables, food lockers, and fire rings are provided. Drinking water and restrooms with flush toilets and free showers are available. A dump station is nearby, and a grocery store, coin laundry, and propane gas are available within five miles. Some facilities are wheelchair-accessible. Leashed pets are permitted.

The group camp, Camp Lisa, is closed through April 2014 for repairs. When open it accommodates tents for up to 50 people.

Reservations, fees: Reservations are accepted at 800/444-7275 or www.reserveamerica.com ($8 reservation fee). Sites are $35 per night, $8 per night for each additional vehicle, $225 per night for the group site. Open mid-May through September, weather permitting.

Directions: In Truckee, drive north on Highway 89 to Graeagle. Just after passing Graeagle (one mile from the junction of Highway 70) turn left on County Road A14/Graeagle-Johnsville Road and drive west for about five miles to the park entrance on the left.

Contact: Plumas-Eureka State Park, 530/836-2380, www.parks.ca.gov; Plumas-Eureka State Park Association, www.plumas-eureka.org.

21 CLIO'S RIVERS EDGE RV PARK

Scenic rating: 7

on the Feather River

Map 6.1, page 353

This is a giant RV park set adjacent to a pretty and easily accessible stretch of the Feather River. There are many possible side-trip destinations, including Plumas-Eureka State Park, Lakes Basin Recreation Area, and several nearby golf courses and a horseback-riding facility. The elevation is about 4,500 feet. Many of the sites are rented for the entire summer season.

Campsites, facilities: There are 220 sites with full hookups (50 amps) for RVs of any length. Some sites are pull-through. Picnic tables are provided. Drinking water, restrooms with flush toilets and coin showers, coin laundry, Wi-Fi, and cable TV are available. A grocery store is within three miles. Some facilities are wheelchair-accessible. Leashed pets are permitted, with certain restrictions.

Reservations, fees: Reservations are accepted. RV sites with hookups are $34–40 per night, $5 per person per night for more than two people, $2 per night per additional vehicle. Weekly and monthly rates are available. Some credit cards accepted. Open mid-April through October.

Directions: From Truckee, drive north on Highway 89 toward Graeagle and Blairsden. Near Clio (4.5 miles south of Highway 70 at Blairsden), look for the campground entrance on the right (0.2 mile south of Graeagle).

Contact: Clio's River's Edge, 530/836-2375, www.riversedgervpark.net.

22 LAKES BASIN GROUP CAMP

Scenic rating: 8

in Plumas National Forest

Map 6.1, page 353

This is a Forest Service group camp that is ideal for Boy and Girl Scouts. It is set at 6,400 feet elevation, just a short drive from the trailhead to beautiful Frazier Falls, and also near Gold Lake, Little Bear Lake, and 15 lakes set below nearby Mount Elwell.

Campsites, facilities: This group camp is for tents only and can accommodate up to 25 people. Fire grills are provided, but there are no picnic tables. Drinking water and vault toilets are available. Supplies are available in Graeagle. Some facilities are wheelchair accessible. Leashed pets are permitted.

Reservations, fees: Reservations are required at 877/444-6777 or www.recreation. gov ($9 reservation fee). The group site is $70 per night, $2 per pet per night. Open June through October, weather permitting.

Directions: From Truckee, drive north on Highway 89 toward Graeagle to the Gold Lake Highway (one mile before reaching Graeagle). Turn left on the Gold Lake Highway and drive about seven miles to the campground.

Contact: Plumas National Forest, Beckwourth Ranger District, 530/836-2575, www.fs.usda. gov/plumas; Thousand Trails, 530/258-7606.

23 LAKES BASIN

Scenic rating: 8

in Plumas National Forest

Map 6.1, page 353

This camp is a great location for a base camp to explore the surrounding Lakes Basin Recreation Area. From nearby Gold Lake or Elwell Lodge, there are many short hikes to small pristine lakes. The trailhead to climb Mount Elwell is also at the camp, and there is a short hike to beautiful Long Lake. In early summer, a must-do trip is the easy hike to Frazier Falls, only a mile round-trip to see the spectacular 176-foot waterfall, though the trail is crowded during the middle of the day. The trail to this waterfall is paved and is wheelchair-accessible. The camp elevation is 6,400 feet.

Campsites, facilities: There are 23 sites for tents or RVs up to 30 feet (no hookups). Fire grills are provided, but there are no picnic tables. Drinking water and vault toilets are available. Supplies are available in Graeagle. Some facilities are wheelchair-accessible Leashed pets are permitted.

Reservations, fees: Reservations are accepted at 877/444-6777 or www.recreation.gov ($9 reservation fee). Single sites are $18 per night and double sites are $36 per night, $2 per pet per night. Open June through October, weather permitting.

Directions: From Truckee, drive north on Highway 89 toward Graeagle to the Gold Lake Highway (one mile before reaching Graeagle). Turn left on the Gold Lake Highway and drive about seven miles to the campground.

Contact: Plumas National Forest, Beckwourth Ranger District, 530/836-2575, www.fs.usda. gov/plumas; Thousand Trails, 530/258-7606.

24 PACKSADDLE

Scenic rating: 6

near Packer Lake in Tahoe National Forest

Map 6.1, page 353

Packsaddle is a Forest Service site about 0.5 mile from Packer Lake, with an additional 15 lakes within a five-mile radius. The trailhead to climb Sierra Buttes—one of America's truly great hiking trails—is just up the road. Sierra Buttes features a climb of 2,369 feet over the course of five miles, highlighted by a stairway with 176 steps that literally juts into open space. All of this is crowned by an astounding view for hundreds of miles in all directions. Packer Lake, at 6,218 feet elevation, is nearby and has log cabins, trout fishing, and low-speed boating. The campground elevation is 6,000 feet.

Campsites, facilities: There are 14 sites for tents or RVs up to 35 feet (no hookups). Vault toilets and drinking water are available. Pack and saddle animals are permitted and corrals and hitching rails are available. Supplies are available in Bassetts and Sierra City. Some facilities are wheelchair-accessible. Leashed pets are permitted.

Reservations, fees: Reservations are accepted at 877/444-6777 or www.recreation.gov ($9 reservation fee). Sites are $19.09–20.91 per night, $5 per night for each additional vehicle. Holiday rates are higher. Open late May through September, weather permitting.

Directions: From Truckee, turn north on Highway 89 and drive 22 miles to Sierraville and Highway 49. Turn left on Highway 49 and drive about 18 miles to the Bassetts Store and the Gold Lakes Highway. Turn right on Gold Lakes Highway and drive 1.5 miles to Packer Lake Road. Turn left, drive a short distance to a fork. Bear right at the fork (signed for Packer Lake) and drive 2.5 miles to the campground on the left.

Contact: Tahoe National Forest, Yuba River Ranger District, North, 530/288-3231, www.fs.usda.gov/tahoe; California Land Management, 530/862-1368.

25 BERGER
🏃‍♀️ 🏊 🐎 🚐 ⛺

Scenic rating: 6

in Tahoe National Forest

Map 6.1, page 353

Berger Creek provides an overflow alternative to nearby Diablo, which is also extremely primitive. On busy summer weekends, when an open campsite can be difficult to find at a premium location in the Lakes Basin Recreation Area, these two camps provide a safety valve to keep you from being stuck for the night. Nearby are Packer Lake, the trail to the Sierra Buttes, Sardine Lakes, and Sand Pond, all excellent destinations. The elevation is 5,900 feet.

Campsites, facilities: There are 10 sites for tents or RVs up to 16 feet (no hookups). Picnic tables and fire grills are provided. Vault toilets and garbage bins are available. No drinking water is available. Supplies are available in Bassetts and Sierra City. Leashed pets are permitted.

Reservations, fees: Reservations are accepted at 877/444-6777 or www.recreation.gov ($9 reservation fee). Sites are $16–18 per night, $5 per night for each additional vehicle. Open June through October, weather permitting.

Directions: From Truckee, turn north on Highway 89 and drive 22 miles to Sierraville and Highway 49. Turn left on Highway 49 and drive about 18 miles to the Bassetts Store and the Gold Lakes Highway. Turn right on Gold Lakes Highway and drive 1.5 miles to Packer Lake Road. Turn left, drive a short distance, bear right at the fork, and drive two miles to the campground on the left.

Contact: Tahoe National Forest, Yuba River Ranger District, North, 530/288-3231, www.fs.usda.gov/tahoe; California Land Management, 530/862-1368.

26 SNAG LAKE
🏃‍♀️ 🏊 🛶 🐎 🚐 ⛺

Scenic rating: 8

in Tahoe National Forest

Map 6.1, page 353

Snag Lake is an ideal little lake for camping anglers with canoes. There are no boat ramps and you can have the place virtually to yourself. It is set at 6,000 feet in elevation, an easy-to-reach lake in the Lakes Basin Recreation Area. Trout fishing is only fair, as in fair numbers and fair size, mainly rainbow trout in the 10- to 12-inch class. Note that campers here must provide their own drinking water.

Campsites, facilities: There are 12 sites for tents or RVs up to 16 feet (no hookups). Picnic tables and fire grills are provided. Vault toilets are available. No drinking water is available. Garbage must be packed out. Only hand boat launching is allowed. Supplies are available in Bassetts and Sierra City. Leashed pets are permitted.

Reservations, fees: Reservations are not accepted. There is no fee for camping. Open June through October, weather permitting.

Directions: From Truckee, turn north on Highway 89 and drive 22 miles to Sierraville and Highway 49. Turn left on Highway 49 and drive about 18 miles to the Bassetts Store and the Gold Lakes Highway. Turn right on

Gold Lakes Highway and drive five miles to the campground on the left.

Contact: Tahoe National Forest, Yuba River Ranger District, North, 530/288-3231, www.fs.usda.gov/tahoe; California Land Management, 530/862-1368.

27 DIABLO

Scenic rating: 8

on Packer Creek in Tahoe National Forest

Map 6.1, page 353

This is a developed camping area set on Packer Creek, about two miles from Packer Lake. This area is extremely beautiful with several lakes nearby, including the Sardine Lakes and Packer Lake, and this camp provides an overflow area when the more developed campgrounds have filled.

Campsites, facilities: There are 14 sites for tents or RVs up to 30 feet (no hookups). Picnic tables and fire rings are provided. Vault toilets are available. No drinking water is available. Supplies are available in Bassetts and Sierra City. Leashed pets are permitted.

Reservations, fees: Reservations are accepted at 877/444-6777 or www.recreation.gov ($9 reservation fee). Sites are $16–18 per night, $5 per night for each additional vehicle. Open June through October, weather permitting.

Directions: From Truckee, turn north on Highway 89 and drive 22 miles to Sierraville and Highway 49. Turn left on Highway 49 and drive about 18 miles to the Bassetts Store and the Gold Lakes Highway. Turn right on Gold Lakes Highway and drive 1.5 miles to Packer Lake Road. Turn left, drive a short distance, bear right at the fork, and drive one mile to the campground on the right side of the road.

Contact: Tahoe National Forest, Yuba River Ranger District, North, 530/288-3231, www.fs.usda.gov/tahoe; California Land Management, 530/862-1368.

28 SALMON CREEK

Scenic rating: 9

in Tahoe National Forest

Map 6.1, page 353

This campground is set at the confluence of Packer and Salmon Creeks, at 5,800 feet elevation, with easy access off the Gold Lakes Highway. It is near the Lakes Basin Recreation Area, with literally dozens of small lakes within five miles, plus great hiking, fishing, and low-speed boating.

Campsites, facilities: There are 27 sites for tents or RVs up to 30 feet (no hookups). Picnic tables and fire grills are provided. Drinking water and vault toilets are available. Supplies and a coin laundry are available in Sierra City. Leashed pets are permitted.

Reservations, fees: Reservations are accepted at 877/444-6777 or www.recreation.gov ($9 reservation fee). Sites are $20–21 per night, $5 per night for each additional vehicle. Open June through October.

Directions: From Truckee, turn north on Highway 89 and drive 22 miles to Sierraville and Highway 49. Turn left on Highway 49 and drive about 18 miles to the Bassetts Store and the Gold Lakes Highway. Turn right on Gold Lakes Highway and drive two miles to the campground on the left side of the road.

Contact: Tahoe National Forest, Yuba River Ranger District, North, 530/288-3231, www.fs.usda.gov/tahoe; California Land Management, 530/862-1368.

29 SARDINE LAKES

Scenic rating: 8

in Tahoe National Forest

Map 6.1, page 353   BEST (

This campground is set in the Tahoe National Forest near Sand Pond and about a mile from Lower Sardine Lake. Lower Sardine Lake is a jewel below the Sierra Buttes, one of the prettiest settings in California. A great hike is routed along the shore of Lower Sardine Lake to a hidden waterfall (in spring) that feeds the lake, and ambitious hikers can explore beyond and discover Upper Sardine Lake. Trout fishing is excellent in Lower Sardine Lake, with a primitive boat ramp available for small boats. The speed limit and small size of the lake keeps boaters slow and quiet. A small marina and boat rentals are available. Nearby is the beautiful Sand Pond Interpretive Trail.

Campsites, facilities: There are 29 sites for tents or RVs up to 22 feet (no hookups). Picnic tables and fire grills are provided. Drinking water and vault toilets are available. Limited supplies are available at the Sardine Lake Lodge or in Bassetts. Leashed pets are permitted.

Reservations, fees: Reservations are accepted at 877/444-6777 or www.recreation.gov ($9 reservation fee). Single sites are $20 per night, $5 per night for each additional vehicle, $40 per night for double sites. Holiday rates are higher. Open June through October, weather permitting.

Directions: From Truckee, turn north on Highway 89 and drive 22 miles to Sierraville and Highway 49. Turn left on Highway 49 and drive about 18 miles to the Bassetts Store and the Gold Lakes Highway. Turn right on Gold Lakes Highway and drive 1.5 miles to Packer Lake Road. Turn left, drive a short distance, then bear left at the fork (signed) and drive 0.5 mile to the campground on the left.

Contact: Tahoe National Forest, Yuba River Ranger District, North, 530/288-3231, www.fs.usda.gov/tahoe; California Land Management, 530/862-1368.

30 CHAPMAN
🚶 🏊 🛶 🐕 🚐 ⛺

Scenic rating: 8

on the North Yuba River in
Tahoe National Forest

Map 6.1, page 353

This campground is set along Chapman Creek at 6,000 feet, just across the highway from where it enters the North Yuba River. A good side trip is to hike Chapman Creek Trail, which leads out of camp to Beartrap Meadow or to Haskell Peak (8,107 feet).

Campsites, facilities: There are 21 sites for tents or RVs up to 22 feet (no hookups). Picnic tables and fire grills are provided. Drinking water and vault toilets are available. Supplies are available in Bassetts. Leashed pets are permitted.

Reservations, fees: Reservations are accepted at 877/444-6777 or www.recreation.gov ($9 reservation fee). Sites are $20–21 per night, $5 per night for each additional vehicle. Open June through October, weather permitting.

Directions: From Truckee, turn north on Highway 89 and drive 20 miles to Sierraville. At Sierraville, turn left on Highway 49, drive over Yuba Pass, and continue for four miles to the campground on the right.

Contact: Tahoe National Forest, Yuba River Ranger District, North, 530/288-3231, www.fs.usda.gov/tahoe; California Land Management, 530/862-1368.

31 SIERRA
🚶 🏊 🛶 🐕 🚐 ⛺

Scenic rating: 7

on the North Yuba River in
Tahoe National Forest

Map 6.1, page 353

This is an easy-to-reach spot set along the North Yuba River, used primarily as an overflow area from nearby Chapman Creek (a mile upstream). Nearby recreation options include Chapman Creek Trail, several waterfalls (see the Wild Plum listing in this chapter), and the nearby Lakes Basin Recreation Area to the north off the Gold Lake Highway. The elevation is 5,600 feet. Note: Bring your own drinking water.

Campsites, facilities: There are 16 sites for tents or RVs up to 22 feet (no hookups). Picnic tables and fire rings are provided. Vault toilets are available. No drinking water is available. Supplies are available in Bassetts. Leashed pets are permitted.

Reservations, fees: Reservations are accepted at 877/444-6777 or www.recreation.gov ($9 reservation fee). Sites are $16–18 per night, $5 per night for each additional vehicle. Holiday rates are higher. Open June through October, weather permitting.

Directions: From Truckee, turn north on Highway 89 and drive 20 miles to Sierraville. At Sierraville, turn left on Highway 49 and drive over Yuba Pass. Continue for five miles to the campground on the left side of the road.

Contact: Tahoe National Forest, Yuba River Ranger District, North, 530/288-3231, www.fs.usda.gov/tahoe; California Land Management, 530/862-1368.

32 YUBA PASS

Scenic rating: 6

in Tahoe National Forest

Map 6.1, page 353

This camp is set right at Yuba Pass at an elevation of 6,700 feet. In the winter, the surrounding area is a Sno-Park, which gives it an unusual look in summer. Yuba Pass is a popular bird-watching area in the summer.

Campsites, facilities: There are 19 sites for tents or RVs up to 22 feet (no hookups). Picnic tables and fire grills are provided. Drinking water and vault toilets are available. Supplies are available at Bassetts. Leashed pets are permitted.

Reservations, fees: Reservations are accepted at 877/444-6777 or www.recreation.gov ($9 reservation fee). Sites are $20–21 per night, $5 per night for each additional vehicle. Holiday rates are higher. Open late June through October, weather permitting.

Directions: From Truckee, drive north on Highway 89 past Sattley to the junction with Highway 49. Turn west on Highway 49 and drive about six miles to the campground on the left side of the road.

Contact: Tahoe National Forest, Yuba River Ranger District, North, 530/288-3231, www.fs.usda.gov/tahoe; California Land Management, 530/862-1368.

33 CARLTON/CAL-IDA

Scenic rating: 7

on the North Yuba River in Tahoe National Forest

Map 6.1, page 353

Carlton is on the North Yuba River, and Cal-Ida is across the road. Both are right next door to Fiddle Creek. (For more information, see the Fiddle Creek listing in this chapter.)

Campsites, facilities: There are 19 sites at Carlton and 18 sites at Cal-Ida for tents or RVs up to 28 feet (no hookups). Picnic tables and fire grills are provided. Drinking water and vault toilets are available. Some facilities are wheelchair-accessible. Some supplies are available at the Indian Valley Outpost nearby. Leashed pets are permitted.

Reservations, fees: Reservations are accepted at 877/444-6777 or www.recreation.gov ($9 reservation fee). Sites are $20–21 per night, $5 per night for each additional vehicle. Holiday rates are higher. Open mid-April through November, weather permitting.

Directions: From Auburn, take Highway 49 north to Nevada City and continue on Highway 49 (the road jogs left, then narrows) to Camptonville. Continue northeast for nine miles to the campground entrance. The camping area at Carlton is one mile northeast of the Highway 49 bridge at Indian Valley. The camping area at Cal-Ida is just east of the Indian Valley Outpost on the Cal-Ida Road.

Contact: Tahoe National Forest, Yuba River Ranger District, North, 530/288-3231, www.fs.usda.gov/tahoe; California Land Management, 530/862-1368.

34 FIDDLE CREEK

Scenic rating: 7

on the North Yuba River in
Tahoe National Forest

Map 6.1, page 353

This camp is situated on the North Yuba River along Highway 49 in a quiet, forested area. This is a beautiful river, one of the prettiest to flow westward out of the Sierra Nevada, with deep pools and miniature waterfalls. It is popular for rafting out of Goodyears Bar, and if you can stand the cold water, there are many good swimming holes along Highway 49. It's set at 2,200 feet elevation. There are a series of campgrounds on this stretch of the Yuba River. Fiddle Creek Ridge Trail starts across the highway on Cal-Ida Road and is routed out to Indian Rock.

Campsites, facilities: There are 13 tent sites. Picnic tables and fire rings are provided. Drinking water and vault toilets are available. Limited supplies are nearby at the Indian Valley Outpost. Some facilities are wheelchair-accessible, including a paved trail to the Yuba River. Leashed pets are permitted.

Reservations, fees: Reservations are accepted at 877/444-6777 or www.recreation.gov ($9 reservation fee). Sites are $20–21 per night, $5 per night for each additional vehicle. Holiday rates are higher. Open April to November, weather permitting.

Directions: From Auburn, take Highway 49 north to Nevada City and continue on Highway 49 (the road jogs left, then narrows) to Camptonville. Continue northeast for 9.5 miles to the campground entrance on the right.

Contact: Tahoe National Forest, Yuba River Ranger District, North, 530/288-3231, www. fs.usda.gov/tahoe; California Land Management, 530/862-1368.

35 INDIAN VALLEY

Scenic rating: 7

on the North Yuba River in
Tahoe National Forest

Map 6.1, page 353

This is an easy-to-reach spot set at 2,200 feet beside the North Yuba River. Highway 49 runs adjacent to the Yuba River for miles eastward, providing easy access to the river in many areas. There are several other campgrounds in the immediate area (see the listings in this chapter for Fiddle Creek and Carlton/Cal-Ida, both within a mile).

Campsites, facilities: There are 17 sites for tents or RVs up to 22 feet (no hookups). Picnic tables and fire grills are provided. Drinking water and vault toilets are available. Limited supplies are available nearby at the Indian Valley Outpost. Leashed pets are permitted.

Reservations, fees: Reservations are accepted at 877/444-6777 or www.recreation.gov ($9 reservation fee). Single sites are $20 per night, $40 for a double site, $5 per night for each additional vehicle. Holiday rates are higher. Open year-round.

Directions: From Auburn, take Highway 49 north to Nevada City and continue on Highway 49 (the road jogs left, then narrows) to Camptonville. Drive 10 miles to the camp entrance on the right.

Contact: Tahoe National Forest, Yuba River Ranger District, North, 530/288-3231, www. fs.usda.gov/tahoe; California Land Management, 530/862-1368.

36 ROCKY REST

Scenic rating: 7

on the North Yuba River in
Tahoe National Forest

Map 6.1, page 353

This is one in a series of campgrounds set at streamside on the North Yuba River. The elevation is 2,200 feet. A footbridge crosses the North Yuba River and provides an outstanding seven-mile hike.

Campsites, facilities: There are 10 dispersed camping sites for tents and RVs up to 16 feet (no hookups). Picnic tables and fire grills are provided. Drinking water and vault toilets are available. Limited supplies are nearby at the Indian Valley Outpost. Leashed pets are permitted.

Reservations, fees: Reservations are accepted at 877/444-6777 or www.recreation.gov ($9 reservation fee). Sites are $20–21 per night, $5 per night for each additional vehicle. Holiday rates are higher. Open mid-April through November, weather permitting.

Directions: From Auburn, take Highway 49 north to Nevada City and continue (the road jogs left, then narrows) to Camptonville. Continue on Highway 49 for 10 miles to the campground entrance on the right.

Contact: Tahoe National Forest, Yuba River Ranger District, North, 530/288-3231, www.fs.usda.gov/tahoe; California Land Management, 530/862-1368.

37 RAMSHORN

Scenic rating: 7

on the North Yuba River in
Tahoe National Forest

Map 6.1, page 353

This camp is set on Ramshorn Creek, just across the road from the North Yuba River. It's one in a series of camps on this stretch of the beautiful North Yuba River. One mile east is a well-known access point for white-water rafting trips on the Yuba. The camp's elevation is 2,200 feet.

Campsites, facilities: There are 15 sites for tents or RVs up to 22 feet (no hookups). Picnic tables and fire grills are provided. Vault toilets and drinking water are available. Supplies are available in Downieville. Leashed pets are permitted.

Reservations, fees: Reservations are accepted at 877/444-6777 or www.recreation.gov ($9 reservation fee). Sites are $20–21 per night, $5 per night for each additional vehicle per night. Holiday rates are higher. Open year-round.

Directions: From Auburn, take Highway 49 north to Nevada City and continue on Highway 49 (the road jogs left, then narrows) to Camptonville. Drive 15 miles north to the campground entrance on the left.

Contact: Tahoe National Forest, Yuba River Ranger District, North, 530/288-3231, www.fs.usda.gov/tahoe; California Land Management, 530/862-1368.

38 UNION FLAT

Scenic rating: 8

on the North Yuba River in
Tahoe National Forest

Map 6.1, page 353

Of all the campgrounds on the North Yuba River along Highway 49, Union Flat has the best swimming. The camp has a nice swimming hole next to it, and the water is cold. The Goodyear's Bar Run is a highly popular one-day eight-mile rafting trip, primarily Class III-IV, with an outrageous Class V rapid (Class VI means risk of death) that newcomers can portage. The put-in is at Union Flat Campground and the take-out is at Fiddle Creek Campground. Recreational mining is also an attraction here. The elevation is 3,400 feet.

Campsites, facilities: There are 11 sites for tents or RVs up to 35 feet (no hookups). Picnic tables and fire grills are provided. Drinking water and vault toilets are available. Some facilities are wheelchair-accessible. Supplies are available in Downieville. Leashed pets are permitted.

Reservations, fees: Reservations are accepted at 877/444-6777 or www.recreation.gov ($9 reservation fee). Single sites are $20 per night, $5 per night for each additional vehicle, $40 for double sites. Holiday rates are higher. Open May through October, weather permitting.

Directions: From Auburn, take Highway 49 north to Nevada City and continue (the road jogs left, then narrows) to Downieville. Drive six miles east to the campground entrance on the right.

Contact: Tahoe National Forest, Yuba River Ranger District, North, 530/288-3231, www. fs.usda.gov/tahoe; California Land Management, 530/862-1368.

39 LOGANVILLE

Scenic rating: 8

on the North Yuba River in Tahoe National Forest

Map 6.1, page 353

Sierra City is only two miles away, meaning you can make a quick getaway for a prepared meal or any food or drink you may need to add to your camp. Loganville is set on the North Yuba River, elevation 4,200 feet. It offers a good stretch of water in this region for trout fishing, with many pools set below miniature waterfalls.

Campsites, facilities: There are 17 sites for tents or RVs up to 22 feet (no hookups). Picnic tables and fire grills are provided. Drinking water and vault toilets are available. Supplies and a coin laundry are available in Sierra City. Leashed pets are permitted.

Reservations, fees: Reservations are accepted at 877/444-6777 or www.recreation.gov ($9 reservation fee). Sites are $20–21 per night, $5 per night for each additional vehicle. Rates are higher on holidays. Open May through October, weather permitting.

Directions: From Auburn, take Highway 49 north to Nevada City and continue on Highway 49 (the road jogs left, then narrows) to Downieville. Drive 12 miles east to the campground entrance on the right (two miles west of Sierra City).

Contact: Tahoe National Forest, Yuba River Ranger District, North, 530/288-3231, www. fs.usda.gov/tahoe; California Land Management, 530/862-1368.

40 WILD PLUM

Scenic rating: 8

on Haypress Creek in Tahoe National Forest

Map 6.1, page 353

This popular Forest Service campground is set on Haypress Creek at 4,400 feet. There are several hidden waterfalls in the area, which makes this a popular camp for the people who know of them. There's a scenic hike up Haypress Trail, which goes past a waterfall to Haypress Valley. Two other nearby waterfalls are Loves Falls (on the North Yuba on Highway 49 two miles east of Sierra City) and Hackmans Falls (remote, set in a ravine one mile south of Sierra City; no road access).

Campsites, facilities: There are 46 sites for tents or RVs up to 22 feet (no hookups). Picnic tables, food lockers, and fire grills are provided. Drinking water and vault toilets are available. Supplies and a coin laundry are available in Sierra City. Leashed pets are permitted.

Reservations, fees: Reservations are accepted at 877/444-6777 or www.recreation.gov ($9 reservation fee). Sites are $20–21 per night, $5 per night for each additional vehicle. Rates are higher on holidays. Open May through October, weather permitting.

Directions: From Auburn, take Highway 49 north to Nevada City and continue (the road jogs left, then narrows) past Downieville to Sierra City at Wild Plum Road. Turn right on Wild Plum Road and drive two miles to the campground entrance road on the right.

Contact: Tahoe National Forest, Yuba River Ranger District, North, 530/288-3231, www. fs.usda.gov/tahoe; California Land Management, 530/862-1368.

41 COLD CREEK

Scenic rating: 8

in Tahoe National Forest

Map 6.1, page 353

There are four small campgrounds along Highway 89 between Sierraville and Truckee, all within close range of side trips to Webber Lake, Independence Lake, and Sierra Hot Springs in Sierraville. Cold Creek is set just upstream of the confluence of Cottonwood Creek and Cold Creek, at 5,800 feet elevation.

Campsites, facilities: There are 11 sites for tents or RVs up to 22 feet (no hookups). Picnic tables and fire rings are provided. Drinking water and vault toilets are available. Supplies are available in Sierraville. Leashed pets are permitted.

Reservations, fees: Reservations are accepted at 877/444-6777 or www.recreation.gov ($9 reservation fee). Sites are $12–14 per night, $5 per night for each additional vehicle. Rates are higher on holidays. Open May through October.

Directions: From Truckee, drive north on Highway 89 for about 20 miles to the campground on the left side of the road. If you reach Sierraville, you have gone five miles too far.

Contact: Tahoe National Forest, Sierraville Ranger District, 530/994-3401, www.fs.usda.gov/tahoe; California Land Management, 480/209-7433.

42 COTTONWOOD CREEK

Scenic rating: 7

in Tahoe National Forest

Map 6.1, page 353

This camp sits beside Cottonwood Creek at 5,800 feet elevation. An interpretive trail starts at the upper camp and makes a short loop, and there are several nearby side-trip options, including trout fishing on the Little Truckee River to the nearby south, visiting the Sierra Hot Springs out of Sierraville to the nearby north, or venturing into the surrounding Tahoe National Forest.

Campsites, facilities: There are 57 sites for tents or RVs up to 22 feet (no hookups). Picnic tables and fire rings are provided. Drinking water and vault toilets are available. Supplies are available in Sierraville. Leashed pets are permitted.

Reservations, fees: Reservations are accepted at 877/444-6777 or www.recreation.gov ($9 reservation fee). Sites are $16–18 per night, $5 per night for each additional vehicle. Rates are higher on holidays. Open mid-May through early October, weather permitting.

Directions: From Truckee, drive north on Highway 89 for about 20 miles to the campground entrance road on the right (0.5 mile past Cold Creek Camp).

Contact: Tahoe National Forest, Sierraville Ranger District, 530/994-3401, www.fs.usda.gov/tahoe; California Land Management, 480/209-7433.

43 BEAR VALLEY

Scenic rating: 7

on Bear Valley Creek in Tahoe National Forest

Map 6.1, page 353

The surrounding national forest land was largely burned by the historic Cottonwood Fire of 1994, but the camp itself was saved. It is at 6,700 feet elevation, with a spring adjacent to the campground. The road leading southeast out of camp is routed to Sardine Peak Look-Out (8,134 feet), where there is a dramatic view of the region. There is an 18-mile loop OHV trail across the road from the campground.

Campsites, facilities: There are 10 sites for tents or RVs up to 16 feet (no hookups). Picnic tables and fire rings are provided. Vault toilets are available. There is no drinking water. Garbage must be packed out. Supplies are available in Sierraville. Leashed pets are permitted.

Reservations, fees: Reservations are not accepted. There is no fee for camping. Open May through October, weather permitting.

Directions: From Truckee, drive north on Highway 89 about 17 miles. Turn right on County Road 451 and drive northeast about six miles to the campground entrance on the right.

Contact: Tahoe National Forest, Sierraville Ranger District, 530/994-3401, www.fs.usda.gov/tahoe.

44 LOOKOUT

Scenic rating: 4

in Humboldt-Toiyabe National Forest

Map 6.1, page 353

This primitive camp is set in remote country near the California/Nevada border at 6,700 feet elevation. It is a former mining site, and the highlight here is a quartz crystal mine a short distance from the campground. Stampede Lake provides a side-trip option, about 10 miles to the southwest, over the rough dirt Henness Pass Road.

Campsites, facilities: There are 18 sites for tents or RVs up to 35 feet (no hookups). Picnic tables and fire grills are provided. Vault toilets are available. There is no drinking water. Garbage must be packed out. Leashed pets are permitted.

Reservations, fees: Reservations are accepted at 775/882-2766. Sites are $6 per night, $6 per night for extra vehicle. Open June through September.

Directions: From Truckee on I-80, drive east across the state line into Nevada to Verdi. Take the Verdi exit and drive north through town to Bridge Street and then to Old Dog Valley Road. Drive north on Old Dog Valley Road for 11 miles to the campground.

Contact: Humboldt-Toiyabe National Forest, Carson Ranger District, 775/882-2766, www.fs.usda.gov/tahoe.

45 LITTLE LASIER MEADOWS EQUESTRIAN

Scenic rating: 7

near Jackson Meadow Reservoir

Map 6.1, page 353

This is the best camp in the area for those with horses. Little Lasier Meadows has open sites in the forest, adjacent to a meadow, and has a horse corral. Best of all, there is direct access to the Pacific Crest Trail. Nearby Jackson Meadows Reservoir is very pretty and provides boating, fishing, and swimming.

Campsites, facilities: There are 11 sites for tents or RVs. Drinking water and vault toilets are available. Picnic tables, fire rings, horse corrals, and tie rails are provided. Water for horses is available.

Reservations, fees: Reservations are required at 877/444-6777 or www.recreation.gov ($9 reservation fee). Sites are $20–21, $5 each additional vehicle per night. Open year-round, weather permitting.

Directions: From Truckee, drive north 17.5 miles on Highway 89 to Forest Road 7/Fiberboard Road. Turn left and drive 15 miles to the East Meadows turnoff. Cross the metal bridge and take the first left turn. Drive approximately two miles to the campground.

Contact: Tahoe National Forest, Sierraville Ranger District, 530/994-3401, www.fs.usda.gov/tahoe; California Land Management, 480/209-7433.

46 SILVER TIP GROUP CAMP

Scenic rating: 7

at Jackson Meadow Reservoir in Tahoe National Forest

Map 6.1, page 353

This group camp is set on the southwest edge of Jackson Meadow Reservoir at 6,100 feet elevation, in a pretty area with pine forest, high meadows, and the trademark granite look of the Sierra Nevada. A boat ramp and swimming beach are nearby at Woodcamp. (For more information, see the Woodcamp listing in this chapter.)

Campsites, facilities: There are two group sites for tents or RVs up to 22 feet (no hookups) that can accommodate up to 25 people each. Picnic tables and fire rings are provided. Drinking water and vault toilets are available. Obtain supplies in Truckee or Sierraville. A boat ramp is nearby. Leashed pets are permitted.

Reservations, fees: Reservations are required at 877/444-6777 or www.recreation.gov ($9 reservation fee). The camps are $80 per night. Open June through October, weather permitting.

Directions: From Truckee, drive north on Highway 89 for 17 miles to Forest Road 7. Turn left on Forest Road 7 and drive 16 miles to Jackson Meadow Reservoir. At the lake, continue across the dam around the west shoreline and then turn left at the campground access road. The entrance is on the right just after the Woodcamp campground.

Contact: Tahoe National Forest, Sierraville Ranger District, 530/994-3401, www.fs.usda.gov/tahoe; California Land Management, 480/209-7433.

47 WOODCAMP

Scenic rating: 7

at Jackson Meadow Reservoir in
Tahoe National Forest

Map 6.1, page 353

Woodcamp and Pass Creek are the best camps for boaters at Jackson Meadow Reservoir because each is directly adjacent to a boat ramp. That is critical because fishing is far better by boat here than from shore, with a good mix of both rainbow and brown trout. The camp is set at 6,700 feet elevation along the lake's southwest shore, in a pretty spot with a swimming beach and short interpretive hiking trail nearby. All water sports are allowed. This is a beautiful lake in the Sierra Nevada,

complete with pine forest and a classic granite backdrop.

Campsites, facilities: There are 16 sites for tents or RVs up to 22 feet (no hookups). Picnic tables and fire rings are provided. Drinking water, flush and vault toilets, food lockers, and firewood (fee) are available. Supplies are available in Truckee or Sierraville. A boat ramp is adjacent to the camp and a dump station is nearby. Leashed pets are permitted.

Reservations, fees: Reservations are accepted at 877/444-6777 or www.recreation.gov ($9 reservation fee). Sites are $21–23 per night, $5 per night for each additional vehicle. Rates are higher on holidays. Open June through October, weather permitting.

Directions: From Truckee, drive north on Highway 89 for 17 miles to Forest Road 7. Turn left on Forest Road 7 and drive 16 miles to Jackson Meadow Reservoir. At the lake, continue across the dam around the west shoreline and then turn left at the campground access road. The entrance is on the right just before the Woodcamp boat ramp.

Contact: Tahoe National Forest, Sierraville Ranger District, 530/994-3401, www.fs.usda.gov/tahoe; California Land Management, 480/209-7433.

48 FIR TOP

Scenic rating: 7

at Jackson Meadow Reservoir in
Tahoe National Forest

Map 6.1, page 353

Jackson Meadow is a great destination for a short vacation, and that's why there are so many campgrounds available; it's not exactly a secret. This camp is set above the lake, less than a mile from a boat ramp near Woodcamp. (See the Woodcamp and Pass Creek listings in this chapter for more information.) The elevation is 6,200 feet.

Campsites, facilities: There are 12 sites for tents or RVs up to 22 feet (no hookups). Picnic

tables and fire rings are provided. Drinking water, flush and vault toilets, and food lockers are available. Supplies are available in Truckee or Sierraville. Leashed pets are permitted.

Reservations, fees: Reservations are accepted at 877/444-6777 or www.recreation.gov ($9 reservation fee). Sites are $21–23 per night, $5 per night for each additional vehicle. Rates are higher on holidays. Open June through November, weather permitting.

Directions: From Truckee, drive north on Highway 89 for 17.5 miles to Forest Road 7. Turn left on Forest Road 7 and drive 16 miles to Jackson Meadow Reservoir. Continue across the dam and around the lake to the west side. Turn left at the campground access road. The campground entrance is on the right across from the entrance to the Woodcamp Picnic Area.

Contact: Tahoe National Forest, Sierraville Ranger District, 530/994-3401, www.fs.usda. gov/tahoe; California Land Management, 480/209-7433.

49 FINDLEY

Scenic rating: 7

at Jackson Meadow Reservoir in
Tahoe National Forest

Map 6.1, page 353

Findley is set near Woodcamp Creek, 0.25 mile from where it pours into Jackson Meadow Reservoir. Though it is not a lakeside camp, it is quite pretty just the same, and within a mile of the boat ramp near Woodcamp. It is set at 6,300 feet elevation. This is one of several camps at the lake.

Campsites, facilities: There are 15 sites for tents or RVs up to 22 feet (no hookups). Picnic tables and fire rings are provided. Drinking water, flush and vault toilets, and food lockers are available. Supplies are available in Truckee or Sierraville. A boat ramp is nearby. Some facilities are wheelchair-accessible. Leashed pets are permitted.

Reservations, fees: Reservations are accepted at 877/444-6777 or www.recreation.gov ($9

reservation fee). Sites are $21–23 per night, $5 per night for each additional vehicle. Open May through October.

Directions: From Truckee, drive north on Highway 89 for 17 miles to Forest Road 7. Turn left on Forest Road 7 and drive 16 miles to Jackson Meadow Reservoir. Continue across the dam around the lake to the west side. Turn left at the campground access road and drive about 0.25 mile to the entrance on the left.

Contact: Tahoe National Forest, Sierraville Ranger District, 530/994-3401, www.fs.usda. gov/tahoe; California Land Management, 480/209-7433.

50 JACKSON POINT BOAT-IN

Scenic rating: 10

at Jackson Meadow Reservoir in
Tahoe National Forest

Map 6.1, page 353

This is one of the few boat-in camps available anywhere in the high Sierra. The gorgeous spot is situated on the end of a peninsula that extends from the east shore of Jackson Meadow Reservoir. Small and primitive, it's the one place at the lake where you can gain entry into the 5 Percent Club. From the point, there is a spectacular view of the Sierra Buttes. Because the lake levels are kept near full all summer, this boat-in camp is doubly appealing. The elevation is 6,200 feet.

Campsites, facilities: There are 12 tent sites. Picnic tables and fire rings are provided. Vault toilets are available. There is no drinking water available; reservoir water must be purified before drinking. Garbage must be packed out. Supplies are available in Truckee or Sierraville. Leashed pets are permitted.

Reservations, fees: Reservations are not accepted. There is no fee for camping. Open June through September, weather permitting.

Directions: From Truckee, drive north on Highway 89 for 17 miles to Forest Road 7. Turn left on Forest Road 7 and drive 16 miles to Jackson Meadow Reservoir. Drive to Pass Creek and boat launch (on the left at the north end of the lake). Launch your boat and cruise 0.5 mile south to Jackson Point and the boat-in campsites.

Contact: Tahoe National Forest, Sierraville Ranger District, 530/994-3401, www.fs.usda.gov/tahoe.

51 PASS CREEK

Scenic rating: 7

at Jackson Meadow Reservoir in Tahoe National Forest

Map 6.1, page 353

This is the premium campground at Jackson Meadow Reservoir, a developed site with water, concrete boat ramp, swimming beach nearby at Aspen Creek Picnic Area, and access to the Pacific Crest Trail 0.5 mile to the east (you'll pass it on the way in). This lake has the trademark look of the high Sierra, and the bonus here is that lake levels are often kept higher than at other reservoirs on the western slopes of the Sierra Nevada. Trout stocks are excellent, with rainbow and brown trout planted each summer after ice-out. The elevation is 6,100 feet.

Campsites, facilities: There are 30 sites for tents or RVs up to 22 feet (no hookups). Picnic tables and fire rings are provided. Drinking water, flush and vault toilets, and food lockers are available. A dump station is nearby. A boat ramp is nearby. Supplies are available in Truckee or Sierraville. Some facilities are wheelchair accessible. Leashed pets are permitted.

Reservations, fees: Reservations are accepted at 877/444-6777 or www.recreation.gov ($9 reservation fee). Sites are $20–21 per night, $5 per night for each additional vehicle. Rates are higher on holidays. Open May through October, weather permitting.

Directions: From Truckee, drive north on Highway 89 for 17 miles to Forest Road 7. Turn left on Forest Road 7 and drive 16 miles to Jackson Meadow Reservoir; the campground is on the left at the north end of the lake.

Contact: Tahoe National Forest, Sierraville Ranger District, 530/994-3401, www.fs.usda.gov/tahoe; California Land Management, 480/209-7433.

52 EAST MEADOWS

Scenic rating: 7

at Jackson Meadow Reservoir in Tahoe National Forest

Map 6.1, page 353

This camp is in a beautiful setting on the northeast side of Jackson Meadow Reservoir, on the edge of a sheltered cove. The Pacific Crest Trail passes right by camp, providing access for a day trip, though no stellar destinations are on this stretch of the PCT. The nearest boat ramp is at Pass Creek, two miles away. The elevation is 6,200 feet.

Campsites, facilities: There are 46 sites for tents or RVs up to 40 feet (no hookups). Picnic tables and fire rings are provided. Drinking water, flush and vault toilets, food lockers, a camp store, and firewood (fee) are available. A dump station and boat ramp are near Pass Creek. Supplies are available in Truckee or Sierraville. Some facilities are wheelchair-accessible. Leashed pets are permitted.

Reservations, fees: Reservations are accepted at 877/444-6777 or www.recreation.gov ($9 reservation fee). Single sites are $20 per night, $5 per night for each additional vehicle, $40 per night for double sites. Open May through October, weather permitting.

Directions: From Truckee, drive north on Highway 89 for 17 miles to Forest Road 7. Turn left on Forest Road 7 and drive 15 miles to the campground entrance road on the left (if you reach Pass Creek, you have gone too far). Turn left and drive a mile to the campground on the right.

Contact: Tahoe National Forest, Sierraville Ranger District, 530/994-3401, www.fs.usda.gov/tahoe; California Land Management, 480/209-7433.

53 ASPEN GROUP CAMP
🏊 🛶 🚐 🐂 �'❓' 🏕

Scenic rating: 7

at Jackson Meadow Reservoir in
Tahoe National Forest

Map 6.1, page 353

A boat ramp and easy access to adjacent Jackson Meadow Reservoir make this a premium group camp. The elevation is 6,100 feet.

Campsites, facilities: There are three group sites for tents or RVs up to 40 feet (no hookups) that can accommodate 25–50 people each. Picnic tables and fire grills are provided. Drinking water, vault toilets, food lockers, firewood (fee), and a campfire circle are available. Some facilities are wheelchair accessible. A dump station is nearby. There is a boat ramp nearby at Pass Creek. Supplies are available in Truckee or Sierraville. Leashed pets are permitted.

Reservations, fees: Reservations are required at 877/444-6777 or www.recreation.gov ($9 reservation fee). Sites are $73–120 per night. Open mid-May through October, weather permitting.

Directions: From Truckee, drive north on Highway 89 for 17.5 miles to Forest Road 7. Turn left on Forest Road 7 and drive 16 miles (a mile past Pass Creek) to the campground entrance on the right.

Contact: Tahoe National Forest, Sierraville Ranger District, 530/994-3401, www.fs.usda. gov/tahoe; California Land Management, 480/209-7433.

54 UPPER LITTLE TRUCKEE
🏃 🛶 🐂 🚐 🏕

Scenic rating: 7

on the Little Truckee River in
Tahoe National Forest

Map 6.1, page 353

This camp is set along the Little Truckee River at 6,100 feet. The Little Truckee is a pretty trout stream, with easy access not only from this campground, but also from another three miles northward along Highway 89, then from another seven miles to the west along Forest Road 7, the route to Webber Lake. It is only about a 10-minute drive from this camp to reach Stampede Lake to the east.

Campsites, facilities: There are 26 sites for tents or RVs up to 30 feet (no hookups). Picnic tables and fire rings are provided. Drinking water and vault toilets are available. Supplies are available in Sierraville. Leashed pets are permitted.

Reservations, fees: Reservations are accepted at 877/444-6777 or www.recreation.gov ($9 reservation fee). Sites are $16–18 per night, $5 per night for each additional vehicle. Rates are higher on holidays. Open mid-May through October, weather permitting.

Directions: From Truckee, drive north on Highway 89 for about 11 miles to the campground on the left, a short distance beyond Lower Little Truckee Camp.

Contact: Tahoe National Forest, Sierraville Ranger District, 530/994-3401, www.fs.usda. gov/tahoe; California Land Management, 480/209-7433.

55 LOWER LITTLE TRUCKEE
🛶 🐂 🚐 🏕

Scenic rating: 7

on the Little Truckee River in
Tahoe National Forest

Map 6.1, page 353

This pretty camp is set along Highway 89 and the Little Truckee River at 6,200 feet. (For more information, see the Upper Little Truckee listing in this chapter.)

Campsites, facilities: There are 15 sites for tents or RVs up to 20 feet (no hookups). Picnic tables and fire grills are provided. Drinking water and vault toilets are available. Supplies are available in Sierraville or Truckee. Leashed pets are permitted.

Reservations, fees: Reservations are accepted at 877/444-6777 or www.recreation.gov ($9 reservation fee). Sites are $16–18 per night, $5 per night for each additional vehicle. Rates are higher on holidays. Open May through October, weather permitting.

Directions: From Truckee, drive north on Highway 89 for about 12 miles to the campground on the left. If you reach Upper Little Truckee Camp, you have gone 0.5 mile too far.

Contact: Tahoe National Forest, Sierraville Ranger District, 530/994-3401, www.fs.usda. gov/tahoe; California Land Management, 480/209-7433.

56 JACKSON CREEK

Scenic rating: 7

near Bowman Lake in Tahoe National Forest

Map 6.1, page 353

This primitive campground is at 5,600 feet elevation, adjacent to Jackson Creek, a primary feeder stream to Bowman Lake to the nearby west. There are several lakes within a five-mile radius, including Bowman Lake, Jackson Meadow Reservoir, Sawmill Lake (private), and Faucherie Lake. A trailhead is available a mile south (on the right side of the road) at the north end of Sawmill Lake. The trail is routed to a series of pretty Sierra lakes to the west of Haystack Mountain (7,391 feet).

Campsites, facilities: There are 14 primitive tent sites. Picnic tables and fire grills are provided. Vault toilets are available. No drinking water is available; stream water must be purified before drinking. Garbage must be packed out. Leashed pets are permitted.

Reservations, fees: Reservations are not accepted. There is no fee for camping. Open June through October, weather permitting.

Directions: From Sacramento, drive east on I-80 past Emigrant Gap to Highway 20. Turn west on Highway 20 and drive to Bowman Road/Forest Road 18. Turn right and drive about 16 miles to Bowman Lake (much of the road is quite rough), then continue for four miles east of the lake to the campground. High-clearance vehicles are required and four-wheel-drive vehicles are recommended.

Contact: Tahoe National Forest, Yuba River Ranger District, South, 530/265-4531, www. fs.usda.gov/tahoe.

57 BOWMAN LAKE

Scenic rating: 8

in Tahoe National Forest

Map 6.1, page 353

Bowman is a sapphire jewel set in Sierra granite at 5,568 feet elevation, extremely pretty and ideal for campers with car-top boats. Pine trees surround the lake, and the shoreline is sprinkled with large granite slabs. Swimming is allowed, and the boat speed limit is 10 mph. There is no boat ramp (you wouldn't want to trailer a boat on the access road anyway), but there are lots of small rainbow trout that are eager to please during the evening bite. The camp is set on the eastern end of the lake, just below where Jackson Creek pours in. The lake is flanked by Bowman Mountain (7,392 feet) and Red Hill (7,075 feet) to the south and Quartz Hill (7,025 feet) to the north.

Campsites, facilities: There are seven primitive tent sites. Vault toilets are available. No drinking water is available. Garbage must be packed out. Leashed pets are permitted.

Reservations, fees: Reservations are not accepted. There is no fee for camping. Open mid-June through October, weather permitting.

Directions: From Sacramento, drive east on I-80 past Emigrant Gap to Highway 20. Turn west on Highway 20 and drive to Bowman Road/Forest Road 18. Turn right and drive about 16 miles (much of the road is quite rough) to Bowman Lake and the campground on the right side of the road at the head of the lake. High-clearance vehicles are required and four-wheel-drive vehicles are recommended.

Contact: Tahoe National Forest, Yuba River Ranger District, South, 530/265-4531, www. fs.usda.gov/tahoe; Big Bend Visitor Center, 530/426-3609.

58 FAUCHERIE GROUP CAMP

🧍‍♀️ 🏊 🛶 🚣 🐎 🚐 ⛺

Scenic rating: 7

near Bowman Lake in Tahoe National Forest

Map 6.1, page 353

Faucherie Lake is the kind of place that most people believe can be reached only by long, difficult hikes with a backpack. Guess again: Here it is, set in Sierra granite at 6,100 feet elevation, quiet and pristine, a classic alpine lake. It is ideal for car-top boating and has decent fishing for both rainbow and brown trout. This group camp is on the lake's northern shore, a prime spot, with the outlet creek nearby.

Campsites, facilities: There are two group camps for tents or RVs up to 22 feet (no hookups) that can accommodate up to 25 people each. Picnic tables and fire grills are provided. Vault toilets and garbage bins are available. No drinking water is available; stream water must be purified before drinking. A primitive boat ramp is nearby. Leashed pets are permitted.

Reservations, fees: Reservations are required at 877/444-6777 or www.recreation.gov ($9 reservation fee). The camp is $50 per night. Open June through October, weather permitting.

Directions: From Sacramento, drive east on I-80 past Emigrant Gap to Highway 20. Turn west on Highway 20 and drive to Bowman Road/Forest Road 18. Turn right and drive about 16 miles (much of the road is quite rough) to Bowman Lake and continue four miles to a Y. Bear right at the Y and drive about three miles to the campground at the end of the road. Four-wheel drive vehicles are advised.

Contact: Tahoe National Forest, Yuba River Ranger District, South, 530/265-4531, www.fs.usda.gov/tahoe; Big Bend Visitor Center, 530/426-3609.

59 CANYON CREEK

🧍‍♀️ 🛶 🐎 🚐 ⛺

Scenic rating: 6

near Faucherie Lake in Tahoe National Forest

Map 6.1, page 353

This pretty spot is at 6,000 feet elevation in Tahoe National Forest, a mile from Sawmill Lake (which you pass on the way in) and a mile from pretty Faucherie Lake. It is set along Canyon Creek, the stream that connects those two lakes. Of the two, Faucherie provides better fishing and, because of that, there are fewer people at Sawmill. Take your pick. A trailhead is available at the north end of Sawmill Lake with a hike to several small alpine lakes, a great day or overnight backpacking trip.

Campsites, facilities: There are 16 sites for tents or RVs up to 16 feet (no hookups). Picnic tables and fire grills are provided. Vault toilets and food-storage lockers are available. No drinking water is available; stream water must be purified before drinking. Garbage must be packed out. Leashed pets are permitted.

Reservations, fees: Reservations are not accepted. There is no fee for camping. Open June through October, weather permitting.

Directions: From Sacramento, drive east on I-80 to Emigrant Gap. Take the off-ramp and head north on the short connector road to Highway 20. Turn west on Highway 20 and drive four miles to Bowman Road/Forest Road 18. Turn right and drive about 16 miles (nine of these miles are paved, but the rest is quite rough) to Bowman Lake and continue four miles to a Y. Bear right at the Y and drive about two miles to the campground on the right side of the road. High-clearance vehicles are required and four-wheel-drive vehicles are recommended.

Contact: Tahoe National Forest, Yuba River Ranger District, South, 530/265-4531, www.fs.usda.gov/tahoe; Big Bend Visitor Center, 530/426-3609.

60 SAGEHEN CREEK

Scenic rating: 7

in Tahoe National Forest

Map 6.1, page 353

This is a small, primitive camp set at 6,500 feet beside little Sagehen Creek, just north of a miniature mountain range called the Sagehen Hills, which top out at 7,707 feet. Sagehen Creek provides an option when the camps along Highway 89 and at Stampede, Boca, and Prosser Creek have filled. In the fall, it is popular as a base camp.

Campsites, facilities: There are 11 sites for tents or RVs up to 16 feet (no hookups). Picnic tables and fire grills are provided. Vault toilets are available. No drinking water is available. Garbage must be packed out. Leashed pets are permitted.

Reservations, fees: Reservations are not accepted. There is no fee for camping. Open mid-May to mid-October, weather permitting.

Directions: From Truckee, drive 8.5 miles north on Highway 89 to Sagehen Summit Road on the left. Turn left and drive four miles to the campground.

Contact: Tahoe National Forest, Truckee Ranger District, 530/587-3558, www.fs.usda.gov/tahoe.

61 LOGGER

Scenic rating: 7

at Stampede Lake in Tahoe National Forest

Map 6.1, page 353

Covering 3,400 acres and with 25 miles of shoreline, Stampede Lake is a huge lake by Sierra standards—the largest in the region after Lake Tahoe. It is set at 6,000 feet, surrounded by Sierra granite mountains and pines, and is big, and on days when the wind is down, quite beautiful. The campground is also huge, set along the lake's southern shore, a few minutes' drive from the Captain Roberts boat ramp. This camp is ideal for campers, boaters, and anglers. The lake is becoming one of the top fishing lakes in California for kokanee salmon (which can be caught only by trolling), and it also has some large Mackinaw trout and a sprinkling of planter-sized rainbow trout. All water sports are allowed. One problem at Stampede is receding water levels from midsummer through fall, a real pain, which puts the campsites some distance from the lake. Even when the lake is full, there are only a few "lakeside" campsites. However, the boat ramp has been extended to assist boaters during drawdowns.

Campsites, facilities: There are 252 sites for tents or RVs up to 32 feet (no hookups). Picnic tables and fire rings are provided. Drinking water, vault toilets, and a dump station are available. A concrete boat ramp is available one mile from camp. Some facilities are wheelchair-accessible. Leashed pets are permitted.

Reservations, fees: Reservations are accepted at 877/444-6777 or www.recreation.gov ($9 reservation fee). Tent sites are $22–24 per night, RV sites are $22–43 per night, $5 per night for each additional vehicle. Rates are higher on holidays. Open May through October.

Directions: From Truckee, drive east on I-80 for seven miles to the Boca-Hirschdale/County Road 270 exit. Take that exit and drive north on County Road 270 for about seven miles (past Boca Reservoir) to the junction with County Road S261 on the left. Turn left and drive 1.5 miles to the campground on the right.

Contact: Tahoe National Forest, Truckee Ranger District, 530/587-3558, www.fs.usda.gov/tahoe; California Land Management, 530/587-9281.

62 EMIGRANT GROUP

Scenic rating: 7

at Stampede Lake in Tahoe National Forest

Map 6.1, page 353

Emigrant Group is set at a beautiful spot on Stampede Lake, near a point along a cove on the southeastern corner of the lake. There is a beautiful view of the lake from the point, and a boat ramp is two miles to the east. Elevation is 6,000 feet. (See the Logger listing in this chapter for more information.)

Campsites, facilities: There are four group sites for tents or RVs up to 32 feet (no hook-ups) that can accommodate 25–50 people each. Picnic tables and fire grills are provided. Drinking water and vault toilets are available. Bring your own firewood. Horseshoe pits and a three-lane concrete boat ramp are available. Some facilities are wheelchair-accessible. Leashed pets are permitted.

Reservations, fees: Reservations are required at 877/444-6777 or www.recreation.gov ($9 reservation fee). Group sites are $78–164 per night. Open May through September, weather permitting.

Directions: From Truckee, drive east on I-80 for seven miles to the Boca-Hirschdale/County Road 270 exit. Take that exit and drive north on County Road 270 for about seven miles (past Boca Reservoir) to the junction with County Road S261 on the left. Turn left and drive 1.5 miles to the campground access road on the right. Turn right and drive one mile to the camp on the left.

Contact: Tahoe National Forest, Truckee Ranger District, 530/587-3558, www.fs.usda.gov/tahoe; California Land Management, 530/587-9281 or 650/322-1181.

63 BOYINGTON MILL

🥾 ⛵ 🏕️ 🐕 🚐 ⛺

Scenic rating: 7

on the Little Truckee River in Tahoe National Forest

Map 6.1, page 353

Boyington Mill is a little Forest Service camp set between Boca Reservoir to the nearby south and Stampede Lake to the nearby north, along a small inlet creek to the adjacent Little Truckee River. Though open all summer, it is most often used as an overflow camp when lakeside campsites at Boca, Stampede, and Prosser have already filled. The elevation is 5,700 feet.

Campsites, facilities: There are 11 sites for tents or RVs up to 32 feet (no hookups). Picnic tables and fire rings are provided. Vault toilets are available. No drinking water is available. Leashed pets are permitted.

Reservations, fees: Reservations are accepted at 877/444-6777 or www.recreation.gov ($9 reservation fee). Sites are $17–19 per night, $5 per night for each additional vehicle. Open May through October, weather permitting.

Directions: From Truckee, drive east on I-80 for seven miles. Take the Boca-Hirschdale exit and drive north on County Road 270 for four miles (past Boca Reservoir) to the campground.

Contact: Tahoe National Forest, Truckee Ranger District, 530/587-3558, www.fs.usda.gov/tahoe; California Land Management, 530/587-9281.

64 BOCA REST CAMPGROUND

🏊 ⛵ 🛶 🏕️ 🐕 🚐 ⛺

Scenic rating: 7

on Boca Reservoir in Tahoe National Forest

Map 6.1, page 353

The Boca Dam faces I-80, so the lake is out of sight of the zillions of highway travelers who would otherwise certainly stop here. Those who do stop find that the lake is very pretty, set at 5,700 feet elevation and covering 1,000 acres with deep, blue water and 14 miles of shoreline. All water sports are allowed. This camp is on the lake's northeastern shore, not far from the inlet to the Little Truckee River. The boat ramp is some distance away.

Campsites, facilities: There are 34 sites for tents or RVs up to 22 feet (no hookups). Picnic tables and fire grills are provided. Drinking water and vault toilets are available. A hand-launch boat ramp is also available. A concrete boat ramp is three miles away on the southwest shore of Boca Reservoir. Leashed pets are permitted.

Reservations, fees: Reservations are accepted at 877/444-6777 or www.recreation.gov ($9 reservation fee). Sites are $17–19 per night, $5 per night for each additional vehicle. Open May through October, weather permitting.

Directions: From Truckee, drive east on I-80 for seven miles to the Boca-Hirschdale exit. Take that exit and drive north on County Road 270 for about 2.5 miles to the campground on the left side of the road.

Contact: Tahoe National Forest, Truckee Ranger District, 530/587-3558, www.fs.usda.gov/tahoe; California Land Management, 530/587-9281.

65 MALAKOFF DIGGINS STATE HISTORIC PARK

Scenic rating: 6

near Nevada City

Map 6.1, page 353

This camp is set at 3,400 feet elevation near a small lake in the park, but the main attraction of the area is its gold-mining past. A trip here is like a walk through history. Gold-mining efforts at this site washed away entire mountains with powerful streams of water, leaving behind enormous cliffs. This practice began in the 1850s and continued for many years. Several major gold-mining operations combined hydraulic mining with giant sluice boxes. Hydraulic mining was a scourge to the land, of course, and was eventually put to an end due to litigation between mine operators and landowners downstream. Though the remains of the state's biggest hydraulic mine are now closed to the public, visitors can view exhibits on mining life. The park also contains a 7,847-foot bedrock tunnel that served as a drain. Although this tunnel is not open to the public, a shorter tunnel is available for viewing.

Note: This park is on the closure list developed by the California Department of Parks, pending final state budget decisions or the possible transfer of park management to other park agencies or volunteer groups. The Chute Hill camp and the group camp remain closed as this book went to press.

Campsites, facilities: There are 30 sites for tents or RVs up to 24 feet (no hookups), three cabins, and one group tent site for up to 50 people. Picnic tables and fire grills are provided. Drinking water and flush toilets (March through mid-November) are available. Leashed pets are permitted.

Reservations, fees: Reservations are not accepted at this time. Sites are $35 per night, $8 per night for each additional vehicle, $165 per night for the group site. The cabins are $40 per night. The park is open year-round.

Directions: From Auburn, drive north on Highway 49 to Nevada City and continue 11 miles to the junction of Tyler Foote Crossing Road. Turn right and drive approximately 11 miles (in the process the road changes names to Cruzon Grade and Back Bone Road) to Der Bec Road. Turn right on Der Bec Road and drive one mile to North Bloomfield Road. Turn right and drive two miles to the entrance on the right. The route is well signed; the last two miles are quite steep.

Contact: California State Parks, 530/265-2740, www.parks.ca.gov.

66 SOUTH YUBA

Scenic rating: 7

near the Yuba River

Map 6.1, page 353

This little-known BLM camp is set next to where little Kenebee Creek enters the Yuba River. The Yuba is about a mile away, with some great swimming holes and evening trout-fishing spots to explore. A good side trip is to nearby Malakoff Diggins State Historic Park and the town of North Bloomfield (about a 10-minute drive to the northeast on North Bloomfield Road), which is being completely restored to its 1850s character. Twelve-mile-long South Yuba Trail begins at the state park and features outstanding spring wildflower blooms. The elevation is 2,600 feet.

Campsites, facilities: There are 16 sites for tents or RVs up to 27 feet (no hookups). Picnic tables and fire grills are provided. Drinking water and pit toilets are available. Some facilities are wheelchair-accessible. Leashed pets are permitted.

Reservations, fees: Reservations are not accepted. Sites are $5 per night. Open April through mid-October, weather permitting.

Directions: From Auburn, turn north on Highway 49, drive to Nevada City, and then continue on Highway 49 (the highway jogs left in town) a short distance to North Bloomfield Road. Turn right and drive 10 miles to the one-lane bridge at Edward's Crossing. Cross the bridge and continue 1.5 miles to the campground on the right side of the road (the road becomes quite rough). This route is not recommended for RVs or trailers.

Alternate route for RVs or vehicles with trailers: From Auburn turn north on Highway 49 to Nevada City and continue on Highway 49 (the highway jogs left in town) to Tyler Foote Crossing Road. Turn right and drive to Grizzly Hills Road (just past North Columbia). Turn right and drive two miles to North Bloomfield Road. Bear right on North Bloomfield Road and drive 0.5 mile to the campground on the left.

Contact: Bureau of Land Management, Mother Lode Field Office, 916/941-3101, www.blm.gov/ca.

67 GROUSE RIDGE

Scenic rating: 7

near Bowman Lake in Tahoe National Forest

Map 6.1, page 353

Grouse Ridge is set at 7,520 feet elevation at the gateway to beautiful hiking country filled with small high Sierra lakes. The camp is primarily used as a trailhead and jump-off point, not as a destination itself. The closest hike is the 0.5-mile tromp up to Grouse Ridge Lookout, at 7,707 feet, which provides a spectacular view to the north of this area and its many small lakes. As you hike north, the trail passes Round Lake (to the left) in the first mile and Middle Lake (on the right) two miles later, with opportunities to take cutoff trails on either side of the ridge to visit numerous other lakes.

Campsites, facilities: There are nine sites for tents only. Picnic tables and fire grills are provided. Vault toilets are available. No drinking water is available. Garbage must be packed out. Leashed pets are permitted.

Reservations, fees: Reservations are not accepted. There is no fee for camping. Open June through October, weather permitting.

Directions: From Sacramento, drive east on I-80 past Emigrant Gap to Highway 20. Turn west on Highway 20 and drive to Bowman Road/Forest Road 18. Turn north on Bowman Road and drive five miles to Grouse Ridge Road. Turn right on Grouse Ridge Road and drive six miles on rough gravel to the campground. High-clearance vehicles are required and four-wheel-drive vehicles are recommended.

Contact: Tahoe National Forest, Yuba River Ranger District, South, 530/265-4531, www.fs.usda.gov/tahoe; Big Bend Visitor Center, 530/426-3609.

68 LAKESIDE

Scenic rating: 7

on Prosser Creek Reservoir in Tahoe National Forest

Map 6.1, page 353

This primitive camp is in a deep cove in the northwestern end of Prosser Creek Reservoir, near the lake's headwaters. It is a gorgeous lake, set at 5,741 feet elevation, and a 10-mph speed limit keeps the fast boats out. The adjacent shore is decent for hand-launched, car-top boats, providing the lake level is up, and a concrete boat ramp is a mile down the road. Lots of trout are stocked here every year. The trout fishing is often quite good after the ice breaks up in late spring. Sound perfect? Unfortunately for many, the Prosser OHV Park is nearby and can be noisy.

Campsites, facilities: There are 32 sites for tents or RVs up to 33 feet (no hookups). Drinking water and vault toilets are available. A boat ramp is nearby. Some facilities are wheelchair accessible. Leashed pets are permitted.

Reservations, fees: Reservations are accepted at 877/444-6777 or www.recreation.gov ($9 reservation fee; search for Lakeside in Truckee). Sites are $17–19 per night, $5 per night for each additional vehicle. Rates are higher on holidays. Open June through October, weather permitting.

Directions: From Truckee, drive north on Highway 89 for three miles to the campground entrance road on the right. Turn right and drive less than a mile to the campground.

Contact: Tahoe National Forest, Truckee Ranger District, 530/587-3558, www.fs.usda.gov/tahoe; California Land Management, 530/587-9281.

69 PROSSER RANCH CAMPGROUND

🧍‍♂️🏊‍♀️🛶🚤🏊🚐🏕️

Scenic rating: 9

at Prosser Reservoir

Map 6.1, page 353

This camp is set at an elevation of 5,800 feet on the west shore peninsula of Prosser Reservoir. Though water levels can be an issue in late summer and fall, this campground is gorgeous in late spring and early summer. The landscape consists of Sierra granite sprinkled with pines, and the contrast of the emerald water, granite shore, and cobalt sky can be very special. In spring and fall, look for rainbow trout up to 18 inches. In summer, anglers have a shot a 10- to 12-inch planters. A 10-mph speed limit for boaters keeps it quiet.

Campsites, facilities: There are 29 sites for tents and small RVs, and one group site for up to 50 people. Drinking water and vault toilets are available. Picnic tables and fire grills are provided. A boat ramp is nearby.

Reservations, fees: Reservations are accepted for individual sites (search for Prosser Family) and are required for the group site (search for Prosser Ranch Group) at 877/444-6777 or www.recreation.gov ($9 reservation fee). Sites are $17–19, the group site is $120, $5 each additional vehicle per night. A maximum stay of 14 days is enforced. Open late May through early September.

Directions: From Truckee, drive north on Highway 89 for four miles and turn right onto access road to Prosser Reservoir. This campground is past Lakeside Campground.

Contact: Tahoe National Forest, Truckee Ranger District, 530/587-3558, www.fs.usda.gov/tahoe; California Land Management, 530/587-9281.

70 BOCA SPRING CAMPGROUND AND GROUP CAMP

🧍‍♂️🏊‍♀️🛶🚤🏊♿🚐🏕️

Scenic rating: 7

in Tahoe National Forest

Map 6.1, page 353

Boca Spring is located just past the north end of Boca Lake, near the Little Truckee River and a short way beyond Lakeside Campground. Boca is known for good trolling for trout and large kokanee salmon. A Forest Road provides access to a good stretch of the Little Truckee River, which can also provide good fishing for small trout. The elevation is 5,800 feet.

Campsites, facilities: There are seven tent sites, eight sites for tents or RVs, and one group site for up to 25 people. Some sites are pull-through. Drinking water and vault toilets are available. Fire grills are provided. Horses are permitted in the campground; a watering trough and horse corral are provided. Some facilities are wheelchair accessible.

Reservations, fees: Reservations are accepted at 877/444-6777 or www.recreation.gov ($9 reservation fee). Sites are $17–19, the group site is $50, $5 each additional vehicle fee. Rates are higher on holidays. A maximum stay of 14 days is enforced. Open mid-May through September.

Directions: From Truckee, drive north on Highway 89 for four miles and turn right onto access road to Prosser Reservoir. This campground is past Lakeside Campground.

Contact: Tahoe National Forest, Truckee Ranger District, 530/587-3558, www.fs.usda. gov/tahoe; California Land Management, 530/587-9281.

71 BOCA

Scenic rating: 7

on Boca Reservoir in Tahoe National Forest

Map 6.1, page 353

Boca Reservoir is known as a "big fish factory," with some huge but rare brown trout and rainbow trout sprinkled among a growing fishery for kokanee salmon. The lake is set at 5,700 feet amid a few sparse pines. While the surrounding landscape is not in the drop-dead beautiful class, the lake can still seem a Sierra gem on a windless dawn out on a boat. It is within a few miles of I-80. The camp is the best choice for anglers/boaters, with a launch ramp set just down from the campground.

Campsites, facilities: There are 23 sites for tents or RVs up to 16 feet (no hookups). Picnic tables and fire grills are provided. Vault toilets are available. No drinking water is available. A concrete boat ramp is north of the campground on Boca Reservoir. Truckee is the nearest place for telephones and supplies. Leashed pets are permitted.

Reservations, fees: Reservations are accepted at 877/444-6777 or www.recreation.gov ($9 reservation fee). Sites are $17–19 per night, $5 per night for each additional vehicle. Open May through October, weather permitting.

Directions: From I-80 in Truckee, take the exit for Highway 89-North. At the stoplight, turn left onto Highway 89-North and drive approximately one mile to Prosser Dam Road. Turn right and drive 4.5 miles to Prosser-Boca Road. Turn right and drive approximately four miles to the camp on the left.

Contact: Tahoe National Forest, Truckee Ranger District, 530/587-3558, www.fs.usda. gov/tahoe; California Land Management, 530/587-9281.

72 SCOTTS FLAT LAKE RECREATION AREA

Scenic rating: 8

near Grass Valley

Map 6.1, page 353

Set at 3,100 feet elevation, Scotts Flat Lake is shaped like a large teardrop and is one of the prettier lakes in the Sierra foothills, with 7.5 miles of shoreline circled by forest. Rules prohibiting personal watercraft keep the place sane. The camp is set on the lake's north shore, largely protected from spring winds and within short range of the marina and one of the lake's two boat launches. Trout fishing is good here in the spring and early summer. When the lake heats up, waterskiing and powerboating become more popular. Sailing and sailboarding are also good during afternoon winds.

Campsites, facilities: There are 187 sites for tents or RVs up to 35 feet (no hookups). Picnic tables and fire pits are provided. Restrooms with flush toilets and coin showers, coin laundry, and a dump station are provided. A general store, bait and tackle, boat rentals, boat ramp, and a playground are also available. Groups can be accommodated. Some facilities are wheelchair-accessible. Leashed pets are permitted.

Reservations, fees: Reservations are recommended in the summer at 530/265-5302. Tent sites are $19–21 per night, RV sites are $24–26 per night, lakefront sites are $30–35 per night, $10 per night for each additional vehicle, $2 per additional person per night, $3 per pet per night, $6 boat launch fee ($13 if not camping). Maximum stay 14 days. Discount rates are available mid-October to mid-April. Some credit cards accepted. Open year-round, weather permitting.

Directions: From Auburn, drive north on Highway 49 to Nevada City and the junction with Highway 20. Continue straight onto Highway 20 and drive five miles (east) to Scotts Flat Road. Turn right and drive four miles to the camp entrance road on the right (on the north shore of the lake).

Contact: Scotts Flat Lake Recreation Area, 530/265-5302 or 530/265-8861, www.scotts-flatlake.net.

73 WHITE CLOUD

Scenic rating: 5

in Tahoe National Forest

Map 6.1, page 353

This camp is set along historic Pioneer Trail, which has turned into one of the top mountain-bike routes in the Sierra Nevada, easy and fast. The trail traces the route of the first wagon road opened by emigrants and gold seekers in 1850. It is best suited for mountain biking, with a lot of bikers taking the one-way downhill ride (with an extra car for a shuttle ride) from Bear Valley to Lone Grave. The Omega Overlook is the highlight, with dramatic views of granite cliffs and the Yuba River. The elevation is 4,200 feet.

Campsites, facilities: There are 46 sites for tents or RVs of any length (no hookups). Picnic tables and fire grills are provided. Drinking water, flush toilets, and vault toilets are available. Leashed pets are permitted.

Reservations, fees: Reservations are accepted at 877/444-6777 or www.recreation. gov ($9 reservation fee). Sites are $21–23 per night, $5 per night for each additional vehicle. Open May through September, weather permitting.

Directions: From Sacramento, drive east on I-80 to Emigrant Gap. Take the off-ramp and then head north on the short connector road to Highway 20. Turn west on Highway 20 and drive about 15 miles to the campground entrance on the left.

Contact: Tahoe National Forest, Yuba River Ranger District, South, 530/265-4531, www. fs.usda.gov/tahoe; Big Bend Visitor's Center, 530/426-3609.

74 SKILLMAN FAMILY, EQUESTRIAN, AND GROUP CAMP

Scenic rating: 5

in Tahoe National Forest

Map 6.1, page 353

Skillman Group Camp is set at 4,400 feet, on a loop access road just off Highway 20, and historic Pioneer Trail runs right through it. (See the White Cloud listing in this chapter for more information.)

Campsites, facilities: There are 12 sites for tents or RVs up to 25 feet (no hookups). This campground can also be used as a group camp for tents or RVs up to 25 feet and can accommodate up to 36 people. Picnic tables and fire grills are provided. Vault toilets and drinking water are available. Horse corrals, tie rails, troughs, and stock water are available. Leashed pets are permitted.

Reservations, fees: Reservations are accepted at 877/444-6777 or www.recreation.gov ($9 reservation fee). Sites are $21 per night, the group camp is $120 per night. Open May through October, weather permitting.

Directions: From Sacramento, drive east on I-80 past Emigrant Gap to Highway 20. Turn west on Highway 20 and drive 12 miles to the campground entrance on the left.

Contact: Tahoe National Forest, Yuba River Ranger District, South, 530/265-4531, www. fs.usda.gov/tahoe; Big Bend Visitor Center, 530/426-3609.

75 LAKE SPAULDING

Scenic rating: 8

near Emigrant Gap

Map 6.1, page 353

Lake Spaulding is set at 5,000 feet elevation in the Sierra Nevada, complete with huge boulders and a sprinkling of conifers. Its clear, pure, very cold water has startling effects on swimmers. The 772-acre lake is extremely pretty, with the Sierra granite backdrop looking as if it has been cut, chiseled, and smoothed. Just one problem: There's not much of a lake view from the campground, although there are a few sites with filtered views. In fact, the lake is about a quarter mile from the campground. The drive here is nearly a straight shot up I-80, so there will be plenty of company at the campground. All water sports are allowed, except personal watercraft. Fishing for kokanee salmon and rainbow trout is often good, as well as fishing for trout at the nearby South Fork Yuba River. There are many other lakes set in the mountain country to the immediate north that can make for excellent side trips, including Bowman, Weaver, and Faucherie Lakes.

Campsites, facilities: There are 25 sites (13 are walk-in) for tents or RVs up to 30 feet (no hookups) and an overflow area. Picnic tables and fire grills are provided. Drinking water, vault toilets, and picnic areas are available. A boat ramp is nearby. Supplies are available in Nevada City. Some facilities are wheelchair-accessible. Leashed pets are permitted.

Reservations, fees: Reservations are not accepted. Sites are $22 per night, $3 per night for each additional vehicle, $1 per pet per night, $10 per day for boat launching. Open mid-May through September, weather permitting.

Directions: From Sacramento, drive east on I-80 past Emigrant Gap to Highway 20. Drive west on Highway 20 for 2.3 miles to Lake Spaulding Road. Turn right on Lake Spaulding Road and drive 0.5 mile to the campground.

Contact: PG&E Land Projects, 916/386-5164, www.pge.com/recreation; Big Bend Visitor Center, 530/426-3609.

76 INDIAN SPRINGS

Scenic rating: 8

near the Yuba River in Tahoe National Forest

Map 6.1, page 353

The camp is easy to reach from I-80 yet is in a beautiful setting at 5,600 feet along the South Fork Yuba River. This is a gorgeous stream, running deep blue-green and pure through a granite setting, complete with giant boulders and beautiful pools. Trout fishing is fair. There is a small beach nearby where you can go swimming, though the water is cold. There are also several lakes in the vicinity.

Campsites, facilities: There are 35 sites for tents or RVs up to 26 feet (no hookups). Picnic tables and fire grills are provided. Drinking water and vault toilets are available. A grocery store and propane gas are nearby. Leashed pets are permitted.

Reservations, fees: Reservations are accepted at 877/444-6777 or www.recreation.gov ($9 reservation fee). Sites are $21 per night, $5 per night for each additional vehicle. Open June through September, weather permitting.

Directions: From Sacramento, drive east on I-80 to Yuba Gap and continue for about three miles to the Eagle Lakes exit. Head north on Eagle Lakes Road for a mile to the campground on the left side of the road.

Contact: Tahoe National Forest, Yuba River Ranger District, South, 530/265-4531, www.fs.usda.gov/tahoe; Big Bend Visitor Center, 530/426-3609.

77 WOODCHUCK

Scenic rating: 8

on Rattlesnake Creek in Tahoe National Forest

Map 6.1, page 353

This small camp is only a few miles from I-80, but it is quite obscure and little known to most travelers. It is set on Rattlesnake Creek at 6,300 feet in Tahoe National Forest, at the threshold of some great backcountry and four-wheel-drive roads that lead to many beautiful lakes. To explore, a map of Tahoe National Forest is a must.

Campsites, facilities: There are eight sites for tents. Picnic tables and fire grills are provided. Vault toilets are available. No drinking water is available; stream water must be purified before drinking. Garbage must be packed out. A grocery store and propane gas are available nearby. Leashed pets are permitted.

Reservations, fees: Reservations are not accepted. Sites are $15 per night, $5 per night for each additional vehicle. Open June through October, weather permitting.

Directions: From Sacramento, drive east on I-80 to Yuba Gap and continue for about four miles to the Cisco Grove exit north. Take that exit, turn left on the frontage road, and drive a short distance to the stop sign and Rattlesnake Road/frontage road. Turn left on the frontage road/Rattlesnake Road and drive a short distance. Turn right and continue on Rattlesnake Road (gravel, steep, and curvy; trailers not recommended) and drive four miles to the campground on the right.

Contact: Tahoe National Forest, Yuba River Ranger District, South, 530/265-4531, www.fs.usda.gov/tahoe; Big Bend Visitor's Center, 530/426-3609; California Land Management, 530/862-1368.

78 LODGEPOLE
🥾 🏊 🎣 🛶 🐾 ♿ 🚐 ⛺

Scenic rating: 8

on Lake Valley Reservoir in
Tahoe National Forest

Map 6.1, page 353

Lake Valley Reservoir is set at 5,786 feet elevation and covers 300 acres. It is gorgeous when full, its shoreline sprinkled with conifers and boulders. The lake provides decent results for anglers, who have the best luck while trolling. A 15-mph speed limit prohibits waterskiing and personal watercraft, and that keeps the place quiet and peaceful. The camp is about a quarter mile from the lake's southwest shore and two miles from the boat ramp on the north shore. A trailhead from camp leads south up Monumental Ridge and to Monumental Creek (three miles, one-way) on the northwestern flank of Quartz Mountain (6,931 feet).

Campsites, facilities: There are 35 sites for tents or RVs up to 20 feet (no hookups). Picnic tables and fire grills are provided. Drinking water and vault toilets are available. A boat ramp is available nearby. Supplies can be obtained off I-80. Some facilities are wheelchair-accessible. Leashed pets are permitted.

Reservations, fees: Reservations are not accepted. Sites are $25 per night, $3 per night for each additional vehicle, $1 per pet per night. Open late May through September, weather permitting.

Directions: From I-80, take the Yuba Gap exit and drive south for 0.4 mile to Lake Valley Road. Turn right on Lake Valley Road and drive for 1.2 miles until the road forks. Bear right and continue for 1.5 miles to the campground entrance road to the right on another fork.

Contact: PG&E Land Projects, 916/386-5164, www.pge.com/recreation.

79 HAMPSHIRE ROCKS
🥾 🏊 🎣 🐾 🚐 ⛺

Scenic rating: 8

on the Yuba River in Tahoe National Forest

Map 6.1, page 353

This camp sits along the South Fork of the Yuba River at 5,800 feet elevation, with easy access off I-80 and a nearby Forest Service information center. Fishing for trout is fair. There are some swimming holes, but the water is often very cold. Nearby lakes that can provide side trips include Sterling and Fordyce Lakes (drive-to) to the north, and the Loch Leven Lakes (hike-to) to the south.

Campsites, facilities: There are 30 sites for tents or RVs up to 22 feet (no hookups) and four walk-in tent sites. Picnic tables and fire grills are provided. Drinking water and vault toilets are available. A convenience store, restaurant, and propane gas are available nearby. Leashed pets are permitted.

Reservations, fees: Reservations are accepted at 877/444-6777 or www.recreation.gov ($9 reservation fee). Sites are $21 per night, $5 per night for each additional vehicle. Open June through September, weather permitting.

Directions: From Sacramento, drive east on I-80 to Cisco Grove and continue for a mile to the Big Bend exit. Take that exit (remaining just south of the highway), then turn left on the frontage road and drive east for two miles to the campground on the right.

Contact: Tahoe National Forest, Yuba River Ranger District, South, 530/265-4531, www. fs.usda.gov/tahoe; Big Bend Visitor Center, 530/426-3609.

80 KIDD LAKE GROUP CAMP

Scenic rating: 7

west of Truckee

Map 6.1, page 353

Kidd Lake is one of four lakes bunched in a series along the access road just south of I-80. It is set in the northern Sierra's high country, at 6,750 feet, and gets loaded with snow every winter. In late spring and early summer, always call ahead for conditions on the access road. The fishing is frustrating, consisting of a lot of tiny brook trout. Only car-top boats are permitted on Kidd Lake, with a primitive area available for launching. The camp is set just northeast of the lake, within walking distance of the shore. It features 10 small group sites that can accommodate 100 people when reserved together.

Campsites, facilities: There are 10 group tent sites for up to 10 people each. Picnic tables and fire grills are provided. Drinking water and vault toilets are available. Supplies are available in Truckee. Leashed pets are permitted.

Reservations, fees: Reservations are required at 916/386-5164 and must be reserved in increments of at least two sites. Group sites are $50–175 per person per night, $1 per pet per night. Open June through mid-October, weather permitting.

Directions: From Sacramento, drive east on I-80 toward Truckee. Take the Norden/Soda Springs exit, drive a short distance, turn south on Soda Springs Road, and drive 0.8 mile to Pahatsi Road. Turn right and drive two miles. When the road forks, bear right and drive a mile to the campground entrance road on the left.

Contact: PG&E Land Projects, 916/386-5164, www.pge.com/recreation.

81 COACHLAND RV PARK

Scenic rating: 6

in Truckee

Map 6.1, page 353

Truckee is the gateway to recreation at North Tahoe. Within minutes are Donner Lake, Prosser Creek Reservoir, Boca Reservoir, Stampede Lake, the Truckee River, and ski resorts. Squaw Valley is a short distance to the south off Highway 89, and Northstar is just off Highway 267. The park is set in a wooded area near I-80, providing easy access. The downtown Truckee area (with restaurants) is a 0.5 mile away. This is one of the few parks in the area that is open year-round. The elevation is 6,000 feet. One problem: Only 25 of the 131 sites are available for overnighters, with the rest taken by long-term rentals.

Campsites, facilities: There are 131 pull-through sites with full hookups (30 amps, 13 sites provide 50 amps) for trailers or RVs up to 40 feet. No tents. Picnic tables are provided. Restrooms with showers, coin laundry, cable TV, Wi-Fi, playground, horseshoes, athletic field, tetherball, clubhouse, and propane are available. Some facilities are wheelchair-accessible. Leashed pets are permitted.

Reservations, fees: Reservations are

recommended. RV sites with hookups are $44 per night, $1.50–3 per person per night for more than two people, $2 per night for each additional vehicle, $5 for 50-amp electricity. Weekly and monthly rates available. Some credit cards accepted. Open year-round.

Directions: From eastbound I-80 in Truckee, take the 188A exit to Donner Pass Road. Turn north on Donner Pass Road and drive one block to Pioneer Trail. Turn left and drive a short distance to the park at 10100 Pioneer Trail on the left side of the road.

From westbound I-80 in Truckee, take the 188 exit to Highway 89. Turn right on Highway 89 and drive north one block to Donner Pass Road. Turn left and drive one block to Pioneer Trail. Turn right and continue to the park.

Contact: Coachland RV Park, 530/587-3071, www.coachlandrvpark.com.

82 NORTH FORK

🏃 🏊 🎣 🐕 🚐 ⛺

Scenic rating: 7

on the North Fork of the American River in Tahoe National Forest

Map 6.1, page 353

This is gold-mining country, and this camp is set along the Little North Fork of the North Fork American River at 4,400 feet in elevation, where you might still find a few magic gold flecks. Unfortunately, they will probably be fool's gold, not the real stuff. This feeder stream is small and pretty, and the camp is fairly remote and overlooked by most. It is set on the edge of a network of backcountry Forest Service roads. To explore them, a map of Tahoe National Forest is a must.

Campsites, facilities: There are 17 sites for tents or RVs up to 16 feet (no hookups). Picnic tables and fire grills are provided. Drinking water and vault toilets are available. Supplies are available at Emigrant Gap, Cisco Grove, and Soda Springs. Leashed pets are permitted.

Reservations, fees: Reservations are accepted at 877/444-6777 or www.recreation.gov ($9 reservation fee). Sites are $21–23 per night, $5 per night for each additional vehicle. Open June through October, weather permitting.

Directions: From Sacramento, drive east on I-80 to the Emigrant Gap exit. Take that exit and drive south a short distance to Texas Hill Road/Forest Road 19. Turn right and drive about seven miles to the camp on the right.

Contact: Tahoe National Forest, Yuba River Ranger District, South, 530/265-4531, www. fs.usda.gov/tahoe; Big Bend Visitor Center, 530/426-3609.

83 TUNNEL MILLS GROUP CAMP

🏃 🏊 🎣 🏕 🚐 ⛺

Scenic rating: 7

on the North Fork of the American River in Tahoe National Forest

Map 6.1, page 353

This is a good spot for a Boy or Girl Scout camp-out. It's a rustic, quiet group camp set all by itself along the (take a deep breath) East Fork of the North Fork of the North Fork of the American River (whew). (See the North Fork listing in this chapter for more recreation information.) The elevation is 4,400 feet.

Campsites, facilities: There are two group sites that can accommodate up to 30 people each: one site is for tents only and the other is for tents or RVs up to 40 feet (no hookups). Picnic tables and fire grills are provided. Vault toilets are available. No drinking water is available. Supplies are available at the Nyack exit near Emigrant Gap. Leashed pets are permitted.

Reservations, fees: Reservations are required at 877/444-6777 or www.recreation.gov ($9 reservation fee). The camp is $90 per night. Open June through September, weather permitting.

Directions: From Sacramento, drive east on I-80 to the Emigrant Gap exit. Drive south for a short distance to Texas Hill Road/Forest

Road 19. Turn right and drive about nine miles to the campground on the right side of the road.

Contact: Tahoe National Forest, Yuba River Ranger District, South, 530/265-4531, www.fs.usda.gov/tahoe; Big Bend Visitor Center, 530/426-3609.

84 ORCHARD SPRINGS RESORT

Scenic rating: 7

on Rollins Lake

Map 6.1, page 353

Orchard Springs Resort is set on the shore of Rollins Lake among pine, oak, and cedar trees in the Sierra Nevada foothills. The summer heat makes the lake excellent for waterskiing, boating, and swimming. Spring and fall are great for trout and bass fishing.

Campsites, facilities: There are 70 tent sites and 13 sites with full hookups (30 amps) for tents or RVs up to 40 feet. Two sites are pull-through. Four camping cabins are also available. Picnic tables, fire rings, and some barbecues are provided. Drinking water, restrooms with flush toilets and showers, launch ramp, boat rentals, slips, bait and tackle, swimming beach, group picnic area, and a convenience store are available. Some facilities are wheelchair-accessible. Leashed pets are permitted.

Reservations, fees: Reservations are accepted. RV sites (hookups) are $39 per night, water-view tent sites are $29–33 per night, $10 per night for each additional vehicle unless towed, $6.50 per boat per night, $3 per pet per night, $25 daily boat slip rental. Camping cabins are $59 per night. Some credit cards accepted. Open year-round.

Directions: From Auburn, drive northeast on I-80 for about 20 miles to the Colfax/Grass Valley exit. Take that exit and loop back over the freeway to the stop sign. Turn right and drive a short distance to Highway 174. Turn right and drive north on Highway 174 (a winding, two-lane road) for 3.7 miles (bear left at Giovanni's Restaurant) to Orchard Springs Road. Turn right on Orchard Springs Road and drive 0.5 mile to the road's end. Turn right at the gatehouse and continue to the campground.

Contact: Orchard Springs Resort, 530/346-2212, www.osresort.net.

85 PENINSULA CAMPING AND BOATING RESORT

Scenic rating: 8

on Rollins Lake

Map 6.1, page 353

Peninsula Campground is set on a point that extends into Rollins Lake, flanked on each side by two sprawling lake arms. The resort has 280 acres and 1.5 miles of lake frontage. A bonus is that you can boat directly from some of the lakefront sites. If you like boating, waterskiing, or swimming, you'll definitely like this place in the summer. All water sports are allowed. Fishing is available for rainbow and brown trout, small- and largemouth bass, perch, crappie, and catfish. This is a family-oriented campground with lots of youngsters on summer vacation. In summer, the lake is crowded and water sports dominate.

Campsites, facilities: There are 70 sites for tents or RVs up to 40 feet (no hookups), and two group sites for 24–40 people. Three cabins are also available. Picnic tables and fire pits are provided. Restrooms with flush toilets and showers, drinking water, Wi-Fi, dump station, boat rentals (fishing boats, patio boats, canoes, and kayaks), boat ramp, fish-cleaning station, swimming beach, horseshoes, volleyball, and a convenience store are available. Marine gas is available on the lake. Leashed pets are permitted, but call for current status.

Reservations, fees: Reservations are accepted by phone or online ($5–20 registration fee). Single sites are $32.50–36.50 per night, double sites are $65–80 per night, $10 per night for each additional vehicle, the group sites are $125–175 per night, cabins are $55 per night, $6 per pet per night. Maximum 14-day stay. Some credit cards accepted. Open mid-April through September.

Directions: From Auburn, drive northeast on I-80 for about 20 miles to the Colfax/Grass Valley exit. Take that exit and loop back over the freeway to the stop sign. Turn right and drive a short distance to Highway 174. Turn right and drive north on Highway 174 (a winding, two-lane road) for eight miles to You Bet Road. Turn right and drive 4.3 miles (turning right again to stay on You Bet Road), and continue another 3.1 miles to the campground entrance at the end of the road.

Contact: Peninsula Camping and Boating Resort, 530/477-9413 or 866/4MY-CAMP (866/469-2267), www.penresort.com.

86 GIANT GAP

🕺🏊🚣🛶🚤🐎♿🚐⛺

Scenic rating: 7

on Sugar Pine Reservoir in Tahoe National Forest

Map 6.1, page 353

This is a lakeside spot along the western shore of Sugar Pine Reservoir at 4,000 feet elevation in Tahoe National Forest. There is a ramp on the south shore for boaters. A 10-mph speed limit is the law, making this lake ideal for anglers in search of quiet water. Other recreation notes: There's a little less than a mile of paved trail, which goes through the day-use area. Big Reservoir (also known as Morning Star Lake), five miles to the east, is the only other lake in the region and also has a campground. The trout and bass fishing at Sugar Pine is fair—not usually great, not usually bad. Swimming is allowed; kayaking and canoeing are also popular.

Campsites, facilities: There are 30 sites for tents or RVs of any length (no hookups). Picnic tables and fire grills are provided. Drinking water and vault toilets are available. Some facilities are wheelchair-accessible. A dump station and boat ramp are on the south shore. Supplies can be obtained in Foresthill. Leashed pets are permitted.

Reservations, fees: Reservations are accepted at 877/444-6777 or www.recreation.gov ($9 reservation fee). Single sites are $21–23 per night, $40–42 per night for a double site, $5 per night for additional vehicle. Open May to mid-October, weather permitting.

Directions: From Sacramento, drive east on I-80 to the north end of Auburn and the Foresthill Road exit. Take that exit and drive east for 20 miles to Foresthill. Drive through Foresthill (road changes to Foresthill Divide Road) and continue for eight miles to Sugar Pine Road. Turn left and drive five miles to a fork. Turn right and drive one mile to the campground.

Contact: Tahoe National Forest, American River Ranger District, Foresthill Ranger Station, 530/367-2224, www.fs.usda.gov/tahoe; California Land Management, 530/478-0248.

87 SHIRTTAIL CREEK

🕺🏊🚣🛶🐎♿🚐⛺

Scenic rating: 7

on Sugar Pine Reservoir in Tahoe National Forest

Map 6.1, page 353

This camp is set near the little creek that feeds into the north end of Sugar Pine Reservoir. The boat ramp is all the way around the south side of the lake, near Forbes Creek Group Camp. (For recreation information, see the Giant Gap listing in this chapter.)

Campsites, facilities: There are 30 sites for tents or RVs of any length (no hookups, double and triple sites are available). Picnic tables and fire grills are provided. Drinking water and vault toilets are available. Some facilities are wheelchair-accessible. A dump station and boat ramp are on the south shore. Supplies can be obtained in Foresthill. Leashed pets are permitted.

Reservations, fees: Reservations are accepted at 877/444-6777 or www.recreation.gov ($9 reservation fee). Single sites are $21–23 per night, $42–46 for double sites, and $60–62 for triple sites. Open May through mid-October, weather permitting.

Directions: From Sacramento, drive east on I-80 to the north end of Auburn and the Foresthill Road exit. Take that exit and drive east for 20 miles to Foresthill. Drive through Foresthill (road changes to Foresthill Divide Road) and continue for eight miles to Sugar Pine Road. Turn left and drive five miles to the campground access road. Turn right (signed) and drive to the campground.

Contact: Tahoe National Forest, American River Ranger District, Foresthill Ranger Station, 530/367-2224, www.fs.usda.gov/tahoe; California Land Management, 530/478-0248.

88 BIG RESERVOIR/ MORNING STAR LAKE

Scenic rating: 7

on Big Reservoir in Tahoe National Forest

Map 6.1, page 353

Here's a quiet lake where only electric boat motors are allowed; no gas motors are permitted. That makes it ideal for canoeists, rowboaters, and tube floaters who don't like the idea of having to dodge water-skiers. The lake is stocked with rainbow trout; free fishing permits are required and can be obtained at the lake. Big Reservoir (also known as Morning Star Lake) is quite pretty with a nice beach and some lakefront campsites. The elevation is 4,000 feet.

Campsites, facilities: There are 106 sites for tents or RVs up to 40 feet (no hookups) and two group sites for 40–60 people. Picnic tables and fire grills are provided. Drinking water, vault toilets, showers, dump station,

and firewood (fee) are available. There is a small store near the campground and supplies are also available in Foresthill. Some facilities are wheelchair-accessible. Leashed pets are permitted.

Reservations, fees: Reservations are accepted at 530/367-2129. Single sites are $25–35 per night, $6 per night per extra vehicle, and the group sites are $100–160. Fishing fees are charged. Open May through October, weather permitting.

Directions: From Sacramento, drive east on I-80 to the north end of Auburn and the Foresthill Road exit. Take that exit and drive east for 20 miles to Foresthill. Drive through Foresthill (road changes to Foresthill Divide Road) and continue for eight miles to Sugar Pine Road. Turn left and drive about three miles to Forest Road 24 (signed Big Reservoir). Continue straight onto Forest Road 24 and drive about three miles to the campground entrance road on the right.

Contact: Tahoe National Forest, American River Ranger District, Foresthill Ranger Station, 530/367-2224, www.fs.usda.gov/tahoe; concessionaire: DeAnza Placer Gold Mining Company, 530/367-2129.

89 FORBES CREEK GROUP CAMP

Scenic rating: 7

on Sugar Pine Reservoir in Tahoe National Forest

Map 6.1, page 353

The boat launch is nearby, but note: A 10-mph speed limit is the law. That makes for quiet water, perfect for anglers, canoeists, and other small boats. A paved trail circles the 160-acre lake. (For more information see the Giant Gap listing in this chapter.)

Campsites, facilities: There are two group campsites, Madrone and Rocky Ridge, for tents or RVs up to 45 feet (no hookups) that can accommodate up to 50 people each. Picnic tables and fire grills are provided. Drinking water and vault toilets are available. Some facilities are wheelchair-accessible. A campfire circle, central parking area, dump station, and a boat ramp are available nearby. Supplies can be obtained in Foresthill. Leashed pets are permitted.

Reservations, fees: Reservations are accepted at 877/444-6777 or www.recreation.gov ($9 reservation fee). Sites are $120 per night. Open May through mid-October, weather permitting.

Directions: From Sacramento, drive east on I-80 to the north end of Auburn and the Foresthill Road exit. Take that exit and drive east for 20 miles to Foresthill. Drive through Foresthill (road changes to Forest-hill Divide Road) and continue for eight miles to Sugar Pine Road/Forest Road 10. Turn left and drive five miles to the fork in the road (still Sugar Pine Road/Forest Road 10). Bear left and drive approximately 4.5 miles to the boat ramp (still Sugar Pine Road/Forest Road 10). Turn right, head up the hill, and drive approximately seven miles to the camp.

Contact: Tahoe National Forest, American River Ranger District, Foresthill Ranger Station, 530/367-2224, www.fs.usda.gov/tahoe; California Land Management, 530/478-0248.

90 BEAR RIVER CAMPGROUND

🥾 🏊 🛶 🐾 🚐 ⛺

Scenic rating: 7

near Colfax on Bear River

Map 6.1, page 353

This RV park is set in the Sierra foothills at 1,800 feet, near Bear River, and features riverfront campsites. The park covers 200 acres, offers five miles of hiking trails, and is set right on the Placer and Nevada County lines. It fills up on weekends and is popular with both locals and out-of-towners. In the spring, when everything is green, it can be a gorgeous landscape. Fishing is OK for rainbow and brown trout, smallmouth bass, and bluegill. Noncommercial gold panning is permitted, and some rafting is popular on the river. A 14-day maximum stay is enforced. No amplified music is allowed at any time—yes!

Campsites, facilities: There are 23 sites for tents or small RVs up to 30 feet (no hookups), and two group sites for tents or RVs up to 35 feet for 50–100 people. Picnic tables and fire rings are provided. Vault toilets are available. There is no drinking water. Supplies are available within five miles in Colfax or Bowman. Leashed pets are permitted.

Reservations, fees: Reservations are accepted only for the group sites at 530/886-4901 ($5 reservation fee). Sites are $10 per night, $2 per night for each additional vehicle, $1 per pet per night, and $40–75 per night for group sites. A certificate of insurance and security deposit are required for group sites. Open April through October, weather permitting.

Directions: From Sacramento, drive east on I-80 east of Auburn to West Weimar Crossroads exit. Take that exit on to Weimar Cross Road and drive north for 1.5 miles to Placer Hills Road. Turn right and drive 2.5 miles to Plum Tree Road. Turn left and drive one mile to the campground on the left. The access road is steep and narrow.

Contact: Bear River Campground, Placer County Facilities Services, 530/886-4901, www.placer.ca.gov.

91 ROBINSONS FLAT

🥾 🐾 ♿ 🚐 ⛺

Scenic rating: 5

near French Meadows Reservoir in Tahoe National Forest

Map 6.1, page 353

This camp is set at 6,800 feet elevation in remote Tahoe National Forest, on the eastern flank of Duncan Peak (7,116 feet), with a two-mile drive south to Duncan Peak Lookout (7,182 feet). A trail out of camp follows along a small stream, a fork to Duncan Creek, in Little Robinsons Valley. French Meadows Reservoir is 15 miles southeast. An equestrian camp with seven sites is also available.

Campsites, facilities: There are seven sites for tents or RVs up to 25 feet, plus an equestrian camp with seven sites for tents or RVs up to 45 feet. No hookups. Picnic tables and fire grills are provided. Drinking water (from a hand pump in the equestrian section) and vault toilets are available. Garbage must be packed out. Supplies are available in Foresthill. Some facilities are wheelchair-accessible. Leashed pets are permitted.

Reservations, fees: Reservations are not accepted. There is no fee for camping. Open mid-May through October, weather permitting.

Directions: From Sacramento, drive east on I-80 to the north end of Auburn and the Foresthill Road exit. Take that exit and drive east to Foresthill (the road name changes to Foresthill Divide Road) and continue northeast (the road is narrow and curvy) for 27 miles to the junction with County Road 43. The campground is at the junction.

Contact: Tahoe National Forest, American River Ranger District, Foresthill Ranger Station, 530/367-2224, www.fs.usda.gov/tahoe.

92 POPPY HIKE-IN/BOAT-IN

Scenic rating: 10

on French Meadows Reservoir in Tahoe National Forest

Map 6.1, page 353

This camp is on the north side of French Meadows Reservoir, about midway along the lake's shore. It can be reached only by boat or on foot, supplying a great degree of privacy compared to the other camps on this lake. A trail that is routed along the north shore of the reservoir runs right through the camp, providing two different trailhead access points, as well as a good side-trip hike. The lake is

quite big, covering nearly 2,000 acres when full, at 5,300 feet elevation on a dammed-up section of the Middle Fork American River. It is stocked with rainbow trout but also has prime habitat for brown trout, and big ones are sometimes caught by surprise.

Campsites, facilities: There are 12 tent sites, accessible by boat or by a mile-long foot trail from McGuire boat ramp. Picnic tables and fire grills are provided. Vault toilets are available. No drinking water is available. Garbage must be packed out. Supplies are available in Foresthill. Leashed pets are permitted.

Reservations, fees: Reservations are not accepted. Sites are $15 per night. Open May through October, weather permitting.

Directions: From Sacramento, drive east on I-80 to the north end of Auburn and the Foresthill Road exit. Take that exit and drive east to Foresthill and Mosquito Ridge Road (Forest Road 96). Turn right (east) and drive 40 miles (curvy) to French Meadows Reservoir Dam and to a junction. Turn left (still Mosquito Ridge Road) and continue for three miles to the lake and campground.

Contact: Tahoe National Forest, American River Ranger District, Foresthill Ranger Station, 530/367-2224, www.fs.usda.gov/tahoe.

93 LEWIS AT FRENCH MEADOWS

Scenic rating: 7

on French Meadows Reservoir in Tahoe National Forest

Map 6.1, page 353

This camp is not right at lakeside but is just across the road from French Meadows Reservoir. It is still quite pretty, set along a feeder creek near the lake's northwest shore. A boat ramp is available only 0.5 mile to the south, and the adjacent McGuire boat ramp area has a trailhead that is routed along the lake's northern shoreline. This lake is big (2,000 acres) and pretty, created by a dam on the

Middle Fork American River, with good fishing for rainbow trout.

Campsites, facilities: There are 40 sites for tents or RVs up to 45 feet (no hookups). Picnic tables and fire grills are provided. Drinking water and flush and vault toilets are available. A concrete boat ramp is nearby. Supplies are available in Foresthill. Some facilities are wheelchair-accessible. Leashed pets are permitted.

Reservations, fees: Reservations are accepted at 877/444-6777 or www.recreation.gov ($9 reservation fee). Sites are $17–19 per night, $5 per night per additional vehicle. Open mid-May through early September.

Directions: From Sacramento, drive east on I-80 to the north end of Auburn and the Foresthill Road exit. Take that exit and drive east to Foresthill and Mosquito Ridge Road (Forest Road 96). Turn right (east) and drive 40 miles (curvy) to Anderson Dam and to a junction. Turn left (still Mosquito Ridge Road) and then continue along the southern shoreline of French Meadows Reservoir for five miles to a fork at the head of the lake. Bear left at the fork and drive 0.5 mile to the camp on the right side of the road.

Contact: Tahoe National Forest, American River Ranger District, Foresthill Ranger Station, 530/367-2224, www.fs.usda.gov/tahoe; California Land Management, 530/478-0248.

94 AHART

Scenic rating: 7

near French Meadows Reservoir in Tahoe National Forest

Map 6.1, page 353

This camp is a mile north of French Meadows Reservoir near where the Middle Fork of the American River enters the lake. It is on the Middle Fork and is primarily used for campers who would rather camp near this river than French Meadows Reservoir. Note: This is bear country in the summer.

Campsites, facilities: There are 12 sites for tents or RVs up to 40 feet (no hookups). Picnic tables and fire grills are provided. Vault toilets are available. No drinking water is available. Supplies are available in Foresthill. Leashed pets are permitted.

Reservations, fees: Reservations are not accepted. Sites are $17 per night, $5 per night per additional vehicle. Open late May through October, weather permitting.

Directions: From Sacramento, drive east on I-80 to the north end of Auburn and the Foresthill Road exit. Take that exit and drive east to Foresthill and Mosquito Ridge Road (Forest Road 96). Turn right (east) and drive 40 miles (curvy) to Anderson Dam and to a junction. Turn left (still Mosquito Ridge Road) and then continue along the southern shoreline of French Meadows Reservoir for seven miles.

Contact: Tahoe National Forest, American River Ranger District, Foresthill Ranger Station, 530/367-2224, www.fs.usda.gov/tahoe.

95 GATES GROUP CAMP

Scenic rating: 7

on the North Fork of the American River in Tahoe National Forest

Map 6.1, page 353

This group camp is well secluded along the North Fork American River, just upstream from where it pours into French Meadows Reservoir. (For recreation options, see the French Meadows, Lewis at French Meadows, and Coyote Group Camp listings in this chapter.)

Campsites, facilities: There are three group sites for tents or RVs of any length (no hookups) that can accommodate 25–75 people each. Picnic tables and fire grills are provided. Drinking water, vault toilets, central parking, and a campfire circle are available. Obtain supplies in Foresthill. Leashed pets are permitted.

Reservations, fees: Reservations are required

at 877/444-6777 or www.recreation.gov ($9 reservation fee). Sites are $75–150 per night. Open mid-May through October, weather permitting.

Directions: From Sacramento, drive east on I-80 to the north end of Auburn and the Foresthill Road exit. Take that exit and drive east to Foresthill and Mosquito Ridge Road (Forest Road 96). Turn right (east) and drive 40 miles (curvy) to Anderson Dam and to a junction. Turn left (still Mosquito Ridge Road) and continue along the southern shoreline of French Meadows Reservoir for five miles to a fork at the head of the lake. Bear left at the fork (Forest Road 68) and drive a mile to the camp at the end of the road.

Contact: Tahoe National Forest, American River Ranger District, Foresthill Ranger Station, 530/367-2224, www.fs.usda.gov/tahoe; California Land Management, 530/478-0248.

available in Foresthill. The camp is within a state game refuge and no firearms are permitted. Some facilities are wheelchair accessible. Leashed pets are permitted.

Reservations, fees: Reservations are not accepted. There is no fee for camping. Open June through October, weather permitting.

Directions: From Sacramento, drive east on I-80 to the north end of Auburn and the Foresthill Road exit. Take that exit and drive east to Foresthill and Mosquito Ridge Road (Forest Road 96). Turn right (east) and drive 40 miles (curvy) to Anderson Dam and to a junction. Turn left (still Mosquito Ridge Road) and then continue along the southern shoreline of French Meadows Reservoir for four miles (road turns into dirt) and continue four more miles to the campground.

Contact: Tahoe National Forest, American River Ranger District, Foresthill Ranger Station, 530/367-2224, www.fs.usda.gov/tahoe.

96 TALBOT

Scenic rating: 7

on the Middle Fork of the American River in Tahoe National Forest

Map 6.1, page 353

Talbot camp is set at 5,600 feet elevation along the Middle Fork of the American River, primarily used as a trailhead camp for backpackers heading into the Granite Chief Wilderness. The trail is routed along the Middle Fork American River, turning south into Picayune Valley, flanked by Needle Peak (8,971 feet), Granite Chief (9,886 feet), and Squaw Peak to the east, then beyond to connect with the Pacific Crest Trail. The nearby trailhead has stock trailer parking. Hitching rails are available at the trailhead.

Campsites, facilities: There are five tent sites. Picnic tables and fire grills are provided. Vault toilets are available. No drinking water is available; river water must be purified before drinking. Garbage must be packed out. Supplies are

97 COYOTE GROUP CAMP

Scenic rating: 6

on French Meadows Reservoir in Tahoe National Forest

Map 6.1, page 353

This group camp is set right at the head of French Meadows Reservoir, at 5,300 feet elevation. A boat ramp is two miles to the south, just past Lewis on the lake's north shore. (For recreation options, see the Poppy Hike-In/Boat-In and French Meadows listings in this chapter.)

Campsites, facilities: There are four group sites for tents or RVs of any length (no hookups) that can accommodate 25–50 people each. Black Bear is the largest camp and has wheelchair-accessible facilities. Picnic tables and fire grills are provided. Drinking water and vault toilets are available. A campfire circle and central parking area are also available. Supplies are available in Foresthill. Leashed pets are permitted.

Reservations, fees: Reservations are required at 877/444-6777 or www.recreation.gov ($9 reservation fee). Sites are $75–130 per night. Open mid-May through October.

Directions: From Sacramento, drive east on I-80 to the north end of Auburn and the Foresthill Road exit. Take that exit and drive east to Foresthill and Mosquito Ridge Road (Forest Road 96). Turn right (east) and drive 40 miles (curvy) to Anderson Dam and to a junction. Turn left (still Mosquito Ridge Road) and then continue along the southern shoreline of French Meadows Reservoir for five miles to a fork at the head of the lake. Bear left at the fork and drive 0.5 mile to the camp on the left side of the road.

Contact: Tahoe National Forest, American River Ranger District, Foresthill Ranger Station, 530/367-2224, www.fs.usda.gov/tahoe; California Land Management, 530/478-0248.

98 FRENCH MEADOWS

🥾 🏊 ⛵ 🛶 🎣 ♿ 🚐 ⛺

Scenic rating: 7

on French Meadows Reservoir in Tahoe National Forest

Map 6.1, page 353

The nearby boat launch makes this the choice for boating campers. The camp is on French Meadows Reservoir at 5,300 feet elevation. It is set on the lake's southern shore, with the boat ramp about a mile to the south (you'll see the entrance road on the way in). This is a big lake set in remote Tahoe National Forest in the North Fork American River Canyon with good trout fishing. All water sports are allowed. The lake level often drops in late summer, and then a lot of stumps and boulders start poking through the lake surface. This creates navigational hazards for boaters and water skiers, but it also makes it easier for the anglers to know where to find the fish. If the fish don't bite here, boaters should make the nearby side trip to pretty Hell Hole Reservoir to the south.

Campsites, facilities: There are 75 sites for tents or RVs up to 45 feet (no hookups). Picnic tables and fire grills are provided. Drinking water and vault toilets are available. Some facilities are wheelchair-accessible. A concrete boat ramp is nearby. Supplies are available in Foresthill. Leashed pets are permitted.

Reservations, fees: Reservations are accepted at 877/444-6777 or www.recreation.gov ($9 reservation fee). Sites are $21–23 per night, $5 per night for each additional vehicle. Open late May through October, weather permitting.

Directions: From Sacramento, drive east on I-80 to the north end of Auburn and the Foresthill Road exit. Take that exit and drive east to Foresthill and Mosquito Ridge Road (Forest Road 96). Turn right (east) and drive 40 miles (curvy) to Anderson Dam and to a junction. Turn left (still Mosquito Ridge Road) and then continue along the southern shoreline of French Meadows Reservoir for four miles to the campground.

Contact: Tahoe National Forest, American River Ranger District, Foresthill Ranger Station, 530/367-2224, www.fs.usda.gov/tahoe; California Land Management, 530/478-0248.

99 BIG MEADOWS

🥾 🏊 ⛵ 🛶 🎣 ♿ 🚐 ⛺

Scenic rating: 7

near Hell Hole Reservoir in Eldorado National Forest

Map 6.1, page 353

This camp sits on a meadow near the ridge above Hell Hole Reservoir, which is about two miles away. (For more information, see the Hell Hole listing in this chapter.)

Campsites, facilities: There are 54 sites available, including six tent sites and 45 sites for tents or RVs up to 50 feet (no hookups). Picnic tables are provided. Drinking water and flush and vault toilets are available. A boat ramp is nearby. Some facilities are wheelchair accessible. Leashed pets are permitted.

Reservations, fees: Reservations are not accepted. Single sites are $10 per night, double sites are $20, $5 per night for each additional vehicle. Open late May through early November, weather permitting.

Directions: From Sacramento, drive east on I-80 to the north end of Auburn. Take the Elm Avenue exit and turn left at the first stoplight onto Elm Avenue. Drive 0.1 mile, turn left on High Street, and continue through the signal where High Street merges with Highway 49. Continue on Highway 49 for about 3.5 miles, turn right over the bridge, and drive about 2.5 miles into the town of Cool. Turn left on Georgetown Road/Highway 193 and drive about 14 miles into Georgetown. At the four-way stop turn left on Main Street (which becomes Wentworth Springs/Forest Road 1) and drive about 25 miles. Turn left on Forest Road 2 and drive 21 miles to the campground on the left.

Contact: Eldorado National Forest, Georgetown Ranger District, 530/333-4312, www.fs.usda.gov/eldorado.

100 MIDDLE MEADOWS GROUP CAMP

Scenic rating: 7

on Long Canyon Creek in
Eldorado National Forest

Map 6.1, page 353

This group camp is within range of several adventures. To the nearby east is Hell Hole Reservoir (you'll need a boat here to do it right), and to the nearby north is French Meadows Reservoir (you'll drive past the dam on the way in). Unfortunately, there isn't a heck of a lot to do at this camp other than watch the water flow by on adjacent Long Canyon Creek.

Campsites, facilities: There are two group sites for tents or RVs up to 16 feet (no hookups), including one that can accommodate 50 people. Picnic tables and fire grills are provided. Drinking water and flush and vault

toilets are available. Supplies can be obtained in Foresthill. Some facilities are wheelchair accessible. Leashed pets are permitted.

Reservations, fees: Reservations are accepted at 877/444-6777 or www.recreation.gov ($9 reservation fee). The sites are $25–50 per night. Open mid-May through mid-September, weather permitting.

Directions: From Sacramento, drive east on I-80 to the north end of Auburn. Take the Elm Avenue exit and turn left at the first stoplight onto Elm Avenue. Drive 0.1 mile, turn left on High Street, and continue through the signal where High Street merges with Highway 49. Travel on Highway 49 for about 3.5 miles, turn right over the bridge, and drive about 2.5 miles into the town of Cool. Turn left on Georgetown Road/Highway 193 and drive about 14 miles into Georgetown. At the four-way stop turn left on Main Street (which becomes Wentworth Springs/Forest Road 1) and drive about 25 miles. Turn left on Forest Road 2 and drive 19 miles to the campground on the right.

Contact: Eldorado National Forest, Georgetown Ranger District, 530/333-4312, www.fs.usda.gov/eldorado.

101 HELL HOLE

Scenic rating: 8

near Hell Hole Reservoir in
Eldorado National Forest

Map 6.1, page 353

Hell Hole is a mountain temple with sapphire-blue water. For the most part, there is limited bank access because of its granite-sculpted shore, and that's why there are no lakeside campsites. This is the closest drive-to camp at Hell Hole Reservoir, about a mile away with a boat launch nearby. All water sports are allowed. Be sure to bring a boat and then enjoy the scenery while you troll for kokanee salmon, brown trout, Mackinaw trout, and a sprinkling of rainbow trout. This is a unique fishery compared to the put-and-take rainbow trout at so many other lakes. The lake has 15 miles of shoreline, and the elevation is 4,700 feet; the camp elevation is 5,200 feet. Note that afternoon winds can make the water choppy.

Campsites, facilities: There are 10 sites for tents only. Picnic tables and fire rings are provided. Drinking water and vault toilets are available. Supplies can be obtained in Georgetown. A boat launch is available nearby at the reservoir. Leashed pets are permitted.

Reservations, fees: Reservations are not accepted. Sites are $22 per night. Open late May through early November, weather permitting.

Directions: From Sacramento, drive east on I-80 to the north end of Auburn. Take the Elm Avenue exit and turn left at the first stoplight onto Elm Avenue. Drive 0.1 mile, turn left on High Street, and continue through the signal where High Street merges with Highway 49. Continue on Highway 49 for about 3.5 miles, turn right over the bridge, and drive about 2.5 miles into the town of Cool. Turn left on Georgetown Road/Highway 193 and drive about 14 miles into Georgetown. At the four-way stop turn left on Main Street (which becomes Wentworth Springs/Forest Road 1) and drive about 25 miles. Turn left on Forest Road 2 and drive about 22 miles to the campground on the left.

Contact: Eldorado National Forest, Georgetown Ranger District, 530/333-4312, www.fs.usda.gov/eldorado.

102 UPPER HELL HOLE WALK-IN/BOAT-IN

🏃 🏊 🛶 🚣 🐕 5% ⛺

Scenic rating: 10

on Hell Hole Reservoir in
Eldorado National Forest

Map 6.1, page 353   BEST (

When the lake is full, this is a beautiful spot, set on the southern shore at the upper end of Hell Hole Reservoir in remote national forest seen by relatively few people. Getting here requires a boat-in or five-mile walk on a trail routed along the southern edge of the lake overlooking Hell Hole. The trail's short rises and falls feel longer than five miles and can tire you out on a hot day—bring plenty of water. When the lake level is high, an access road on the opposite side of the lake leads to a put-in for kayaks and canoes that can shorten the trip. You'll arrive at this little trail camp, ready to explore onward the next day into the Granite Chief Wilderness, or just do nothing except enjoy adjacent Buck Meadow, the lake's headwaters, and the paradise you have discovered. Note that bears frequent this area, so store your food properly and avoid scented products.

Campsites, facilities: There are 15 tent sites, accessible by trail or boat only. Picnic tables and fire grills are provided. Vault toilets are available. No drinking water is available, so bring a water filter. Garbage must be packed out. A boat launch is at the reservoir and the camp can be reached by boat, but low water levels during August and September can make passage difficult or impossible; call for current status. Supplies can be obtained in Georgetown. Leashed pets are permitted.

Reservations, fees: Reservations are not accepted. There is no fee for camping. Campfire permits are required from the Forest Service. Open May to mid-September, weather permitting.

Directions: From Sacramento, drive east on I-80 to the north end of Auburn. Take the Elm Avenue exit and turn left at the first stoplight onto Elm Avenue. Drive 0.1 mile, turn left on High Street, and continue through the signal where High Street merges with Highway 49. Continue on Highway 49 for about 3.5 miles, turn right over the bridge, and drive about 2.5 miles into the town of Cool. Turn left on Georgetown Road/Highway 193 and drive about 14 miles into Georgetown. At the four-way stop turn left on Main Street (which becomes Wentworth Springs/Forest Road 1) and drive about 25 miles. Turn left on Forest Road 2 and drive about 23 miles (a mile past the Hell Hole Campground access road) to the parking area at the boat ramp. From the trailhead, hike 3.5 miles to the camp.

Contact: Eldorado National Forest, Georgetown Ranger District, 530/333-4312, www.fs.usda.gov/eldorado.

103 STUMPY MEADOWS

Scenic rating: 9

on Stumpy Meadows Lake in Eldorado National Forest

Map 6.2, page 354

This is the camp of choice for visitors to Stumpy Meadows Lake. The first things visitors notice are the huge ponderosa pine trees, noted for their distinctive, mosaic-like bark. The lake is set at 4,400 feet elevation in Eldorado National Forest and covers 320 acres with water that is cold and clear; this is one of the prettiest lakes you can reach on pavement in the region. The lake has both rainbow and brown trout, and in the fall provides good fishing for big browns (they move up into the head of the lake, near where Pilot Creek enters).

Campsites, facilities: There are 40 sites for tents or RVs up to 28 feet length (no hookups). Two of the sites are double units. Picnic tables and fire grills are provided. Drinking water and vault toilets are available. A boat ramp and a dump station are nearby. Some facilities are wheelchair accessible. Leashed pets are permitted.

Reservations, fees: Reservations are accepted at 877/444-6777 or www.recreation.gov ($9 reservation fee). Single sites are $17–19 per night, $38 per night for double sites, $6 per night for each additional vehicle, $2 per pet per night, boat launch is $7 per day. Open May through mid-October, weather permitting.

Directions: From Sacramento on I-80, drive east to the north end of Auburn. Turn left on Elm Avenue and drive about 0.1 mile. Turn left on High Street and drive through the signal that marks the continuation of High Street as Highway 49. Drive 3.5 miles on Highway 49, turn right over the bridge, and drive 2.5 miles into the town of Cool. Turn left on Georgetown Road/Highway 193 and drive 14 miles into Georgetown. At the four-way stop, turn left on Main Street, which becomes Georgetown–Wentworth Springs Road/Forest Road 1. Drive about 18 miles to Stumpy Meadows Lake. Continue about a mile and turn right into Stumpy Meadows campground.

Contact: Eldorado National Forest, Georgetown Ranger District, 530/333-4312, www.fs.usda.gov/eldorado.

104 BLACK OAK GROUP CAMP

Scenic rating: 8

near Stumpy Meadows Lake in Eldorado National Forest

Map 6.2, page 354

This group camp is set directly adjacent to Stumpy Meadows Campground. (See the Stumpy Meadows listing in this chapter for more information.) The boat ramp for the lake is just south of the Mark Edson Dam, near the picnic area. The elevation is 4,400 feet.

Campsites, facilities: There are three group sites for tents that can accommodate 10–50 people and one group site for RVs of any length (no hookups) that can accommodate 75 people. Picnic tables and fire grills are provided. Drinking water and vault toilets are available. A boat ramp and a dump station are nearby. Leashed pets are permitted.

Reservations, fees: Reservations are accepted at 877/444-6777 or www.recreation.gov ($9 reservation fee). Tent sites are $50–85 per night, the RV site is $100–110 per night, boat launch is $7 per day. Open mid-May through mid-September, weather permitting.

Directions: From Sacramento on I-80, drive east to the north end of Auburn. Turn left on

Elm Avenue and drive about 0.1 mile. Turn left on High Street and drive through the signal that marks the continuation of High Street as Highway 49. Drive 3.5 miles on Highway 49, turn right over the bridge, and drive 2.5 miles into the town of Cool. Turn left on Georgetown Road/Highway 193 and drive 14 miles into Georgetown. At the four-way stop, turn left on Main Street, which becomes Georgetown–Wentworth Springs Road/Forest Road 1. Drive about 18 miles to Stumpy Meadows Lake, and then continue for two miles to the north shore of the lake and the campground entrance road on the right.

Contact: Eldorado National Forest, Georgetown Ranger District, 530/333-4312, www.fs.usda.gov/eldorado.

105 GERLE CREEK

Scenic rating: 7

on Gerle Creek Reservoir in Eldorado National Forest

Map 6.2, page 354

This is a small, pretty, but limited spot set along the northern shore of little Gerle Creek Reservoir at 5,231 feet elevation. This camp was renovated in 2012. The lake is ideal for canoes or other small boats because no motors are permitted and no boat ramp is available. That makes for quiet water. It is set in the Gerle Creek Canyon, which feeds into the South Fork Rubicon River. No trout plants are made at this lake, and fishing can be correspondingly poor. A wild brown trout population lives here, though. A network of Forest Service roads to the north can provide great exploring. A map of Eldorado National Forest is a must.

Campsites, facilities: There are 50 sites for tents or RVs up to 40 feet (no hookups). Picnic tables and fire grills are provided. Drinking water and vault toilets are available. Wheelchair-accessible trails and fishing pier are available nearby. Leashed pets are permitted.

Reservations, fees: Reservations are accepted at 877/444-6777 or www.recreation.gov ($9 reservation fee). Sites are $22 per night, $7 per night for each additional vehicle. Open mid-May through mid-October, weather permitting.

Directions: From Placerville, drive east on U.S. 50 for 23 miles to Riverton and the junction with Ice House Road/Forest Road 3. Turn north and drive 27 miles (past Union Valley Reservoir) to a fork with Forest Road 30. Turn left, drive two miles, bear left on the campground entrance road, and drive a mile to the campground.

Contact: Eldorado National Forest, Pacific Ranger District, 530/644-2349, www.fs.usda.gov/eldorado.

106 SOUTH FORK GROUP CAMP

Scenic rating: 8

on the South Fork of the Rubicon River in Eldorado National Forest

Map 6.2, page 354

This primitive national forest camp sits alongside the South Fork Rubicon River, just over a mile downstream from the outlet at Gerle Creek Reservoir. Trout fishing is fair, the water tastes extremely sweet (always pump filter with a water purifier), and there are several side trips available. These include Loon Lake (eight miles to the northeast), Gerle Creek Reservoir (to the nearby north), and Union Valley Reservoir (to the nearby south). The elevation is 5,200 feet.

Campsites, facilities: There is a group camp for tents only that can accommodate up to 125 people. Picnic tables and fire grills are provided. Vault toilets are available. No drinking water is available; stream water must be purified before drinking. Garbage must be packed out. Leashed pets are permitted.

Reservations, fees: Reservations are required at 877/444-6777 or www.recreation.gov ($9 reservation fee). The camp is $100 per night. Open late May through early September.

Directions: From Placerville, drive east on U.S. 50 for 23 miles to Riverton and the junction with Ice House Road/Forest Road 3. Turn north and drive about 23 miles to the junction with Forest Road 13N28 (3.5 miles past Union Valley Reservoir). Bear left on Forest Road 13N28 and drive two miles to the campground entrance on the right.

Contact: Eldorado National Forest, Pacific Ranger District, 530/644-2349, www.fs.usda.gov/eldorado.

107 AIRPORT FLAT

Scenic rating: 6

near Loon Lake in Eldorado National Forest

Map 6.2, page 354

Loon Lake is a gorgeous mountain lake in the Crystal Basin. Airport Flat provides an overflow area when the camps at Loon Lake (see listing in this chapter) are full. Trout fishing is good and Loon Lake, along with Ice House Reservoir, is a favorite spot whether for a weekend or a week. Smaller Gerle Creek Reservoir and Union Valley Reservoir are also in the area. The elevation is 5,300 feet.

Campsites, facilities: There are 16 sites for tents or RVs. Vault toilets, picnic tables, fire rings, and bear-proof boxes are provided. No drinking water is available. Garbage must be packed out. All sites are wheelchair-accessible. Leashed pets are allowed.

Reservations, fees: Reservations are not accepted. There is no fee for camping. Open Memorial Day weekend to mid-October.

Directions: From Placerville, drive east on U.S. 50 for 23 miles to Riverton and the junction with Ice House Road/Forest Road 3. Turn north and drive 27 miles (past Union Valley Reservoir) to a fork with Forest Road 30. Turn left toward Gerle Creek Reservoir and the campground is about three miles from the fork, on the right.

Contact: Eldorado National Forest, Pacific Ranger District, 530/644-2349, www.fs.usda.gov/eldorado; Crystal Basin, 530/293-3510.

108 LOON LAKE

Scenic rating: 9

in Eldorado National Forest

Map 6.2, page 354

Loon Lake is set near the Sierra crest at 6,400 feet, covering 600 acres with depths up to 130 feet. This is the lake's primary campground, and it is easy to see why, with a picnic area, beach (includes a small unit for changing clothes), and boat ramp adjacent to the camp. The lake provides good trout fishing, and the lake is stocked on a regular basis once the access road is clear of snow. Afternoon winds drive anglers off the lake but are cheered by sailboarders. An excellent trail is also available here, with the hike routed along the lake's eastern shore to Pleasant Hike-In/Boat-In, where there's a trailhead for the Desolation Wilderness.

Campsites, facilities: There are 53 sites for tents or RVs up to 40 feet, nine equestrian sites, two group sites for 25 and 50 people respectively, and one group equestrian site for tents or RVs up to 40 feet that can accommodate up to 25 people. No hookups. Picnic tables and fire grills are provided. Drinking water and vault toilets are available. Tie lines are available for horses. A boat ramp and swimming beach are nearby. A dump station is two miles away. Some facilities are wheelchair-accessible. Leashed pets are permitted.

Reservations, fees: Reservations are accepted at 877/444-6777 or www.reserveamerica.com ($10 reservation fee). Single sites are $22 per night, $44 per night for a double site, $7 per night for each additional vehicle, $90–130 per night for group sites. Open June through mid-October, weather permitting.

Directions: From Placerville, drive east on U.S. 50 for 23 miles to Riverton and the junction with Ice House Road/Forest Road 3. Turn left and drive 34 miles to a fork at the foot of Loon Lake. Turn right and drive one mile to the Loon Lake Picnic Area or boat ramp.

Contact: Eldorado National Forest, Pacific Ranger District, 530/644-2349, www.fs.usda. gov/eldorado; American Land and Leisure, 530/293-0827.

109 WENTWORTH SPRINGS FOUR-WHEEL DRIVE

Scenic rating: 7

near Loon Lake in Eldorado National Forest

Map 6.2, page 354

There is one reason people come here: to set up a base camp for an OHV adventure, whether they are the owners of four-wheel drives, all-terrain vehicles, or dirt bikes. A network of roads leads from this camp, passable only by these vehicles; these roads would flat-out destroy your average car. The camp is set deep in Eldorado National Forest, at 6,200 feet elevation. While the north end of Loon Lake is a mile to the east, the road there is extremely rough (perfect, right?). The road is gated along the lake, preventing access to this camp for those who drive directly to Loon Lake.

Campsites, facilities: There are eight sites for tents only. Picnic tables and fire grills are provided. Vault toilets are available. No drinking water is available. Garbage must be packed out. Leashed pets are permitted.

Reservations, fees: Reservations are not accepted. There is no fee for camping. Open June through October, weather permitting.

Directions: From Placerville, drive east on U.S. 50 for 23 miles to Riverton and the junction with Ice House Road/Forest Road 3. Turn left and drive 30 miles to the junction with Forest Road 30. Bear left and drive 3.5 miles to Forest Road 33. Turn right and drive seven miles to the campground on the left side of the road. (The access road is suitable for four-wheel-drive vehicles and off-highway motorcycles only.)

Contact: Eldorado National Forest, Pacific Ranger District, 530/644-2349, www.fs.usda. gov/eldorado.

110 NORTHSHORE

Scenic rating: 9

on Loon Lake in Eldorado National Forest

Map 6.2, page 354

The waterfront sites are in an extremely pretty setting on the northwestern shore of Loon Lake. There are few facilities, though, and no boat ramp; the boat ramp is near the Loon Lake campground and picnic area at the south end of the lake. (For more information, see the Loon Lake and Pleasant Hike-In/Boat-In listings.)

Campsites, facilities: There are 15 sites for tents or RVs up to 35 feet (no hookups). Picnic tables and fire grills are provided. Vault toilets are available. There is no drinking water. Some facilities are wheelchair-accessible. Leashed pets are permitted.

Reservations, fees: Reservations are not accepted. Sites are $10 per night, $5 per night for each additional vehicle. Open June through September, weather permitting.

Directions: From Placerville, drive east on U.S. 50 for 23 miles to Riverton and the junction with Ice House Road/Forest Road 3. Turn left and drive 34 miles to a fork at the foot of Loon Lake. Turn left and drive three miles to the campground.

Contact: Eldorado National Forest, Pacific Ranger District, 530/644-2349, www.fs.usda. gov/eldorado.

111 RED FIR GROUP CAMP

Scenic rating: 6

on Loon Lake in Eldorado National Forest

Map 6.2, page 354

This is a pretty, wooded camp, ideal for medium-sized groups. It is across the road from the 600-acre lake, offering a secluded, quiet spot. Lake access is a short hike away. All water sports are allowed on Loon Lake. (See the Loon Lake and Northshore listings in this chapter for more information.) The elevation is 6,500 feet.

Campsites, facilities: This tent-only group site can accommodate up to 25 people. Drinking water, vault toilets, fire rings, and grills are available. Some facilities are wheelchair-accessible. Leashed pets are permitted.

Reservations, fees: Reservations are required at 877/444-6777 or www.recreation.gov ($9 reservation fee). The camp is $35 per night. Open mid-June through mid-October, weather permitting.

Directions: From Placerville, drive east on U.S. 50 for 23 miles to Riverton and the junction with Ice House Road/Forest Road 3. Turn left and drive 34 miles to a fork at the foot of Loon Lake. Turn left and drive three miles to the campground (just beyond the Loon Lake Northshore camp).

Contact: Eldorado National Forest, Pacific Ranger District, 530/644-2349, www.fs.usda.gov/eldorado.

112 PLEASANT HIKE-IN/ BOAT-IN

Scenic rating: 10

on Loon Lake in Eldorado National Forest

Map 6.2, page 354

This premium Sierra camp, hike-in or boat-in only, is set on the remote northeast shore of Loon Lake at 6,378 feet elevation. In many ways this makes for a perfect short vacation. A trail is routed east from the camp for four miles past Buck Island Lake (6,436 feet) and Rockbound Lake (6,529 feet), set just inside the northern border of the Desolation Wilderness. When the trail is clear of snow, this makes for a fantastic day hike; a wilderness permit is required if staying overnight inside the wilderness boundary.

Campsites, facilities: There are 10 boat-in or hike-in tent sites. Picnic tables and fire rings are provided. A free California Campfire permit, available at any Forest Service office, is required for campfires. No drinking water or toilets are available. Garbage must be packed out. The camp is accessible by boat or trail only. Leashed pets are permitted.

Reservations, fees: Reservations are not accepted. There is no fee for camping. Open mid-June to mid-October, weather permitting.

Directions: From Placerville, drive east on U.S. 50 for 23 miles to Riverton and the junction with Ice House Road/Forest Road 3. Turn left and drive 34 miles to a fork at the foot of Loon Lake. Turn right and drive a mile to the Loon Lake Picnic Area or boat ramp. Either hike or boat 2.5 miles to the campground on the northeast shore of the lake.

Contact: Eldorado National Forest, Pacific Ranger District, 530/644-2349, www.fs.usda.gov/eldorado.

113 WEST POINT

Scenic rating: 9

at Union Valley Reservoir in Eldorado National Forest

Map 6.2, page 354

West Point is a pretty, primitive campground on the northwest shore of little Union Valley Reservoir. This is a pretty spot in the Crystal Basin that sometimes gets overlooked in the shadow of Loon Lake and Ice House Reservoir. But the camping, low-speed boating, and trout fishing can be excellent. Some surprise giant mackinaw trout and brown trout can provide a fish of a lifetime when the lake first opens in late spring. The elevation is 4,875 feet.

Campsites, facilities: There are eight sites for tents or RVs. Vault toilet and a boat launch are available. Fire rings are provided, but there are no grills or picnic tables. Drinking water is not available.

Reservations, fees: Reservations are not accepted. There is no fee for camping.

Directions: From Placerville, drive east on Highway 50 for 23 miles to Riverton and the junction with Ice House Road/Forest Road 3. Turn north on Ice House Road, and drive 7 miles to Peavine Ridge Road. Turn left on Peavine Ridge Road and drive east for 3 miles to Bryant Springs Road. Turn right on Bryant Springs Road and drive north 5 miles to just past West Point Boat Ramp on the right.

Contact: Eldorado National Forest, Pacific Ranger District, 530/644-2349, www.fs.usda. gov/eldorado; Crystal Basin, 530/293-3510.

114 WOLF CREEK AND WOLF CREEK GROUP

🚶 🏊 🚣 🛶 ⛵ 🎣 🐾 ♿ 🚐 ⛺

Scenic rating: 9

on Union Valley Reservoir in
Eldorado National Forest

Map 6.2, page 354

Wolf Creek Camp is on the north shore of Union Valley Reservoir. Listen up. Notice that it's quieter? Yep. That's because there are not as many water-skiers in the vicinity. Why? The nearest boat ramp is three miles away. The view of the Crystal Range from the campground is drop-dead gorgeous. The elevation is 4,900 feet.

Campsites, facilities: There are 42 sites for tents or RVs up to 40 feet and three group sites for tents or RVs up to 40 feet that can accommodate up to 50 people. No hookups. Picnic tables and fire grills are provided. Drinking water and vault toilets are available. Some facilities are wheelchair-accessible. A boat ramp is three miles away at the campground at Yellowjacket. Leashed pets are permitted.

Reservations, fees: Reservations are accepted for individual sites and required for group sites at 877/444-6777 or www.recreation.gov ($9 reservation fee). Single sites are $22 per night for a single site, $44 per night for a double site, $7 per night for each additional vehicle. Group sites are $90–130 per night. Open mid-May through mid-September, weather permitting.

Directions: From Placerville, drive east on U.S. 50 for 23 miles to Riverton and the junction with Ice House Road/Forest Road 3. Turn left (north) and drive 19 miles to Forest Road 12N78/Union Valley Road (at the head of Union Valley Reservoir). Turn left (west) and drive two miles to the campground.

Contact: Eldorado National Forest, Pacific Ranger District, 530/644-2349, www.fs.usda. gov/eldorado.

115 CAMINO COVE

🚶 🏊 🚣 🛶 ⛵ 🎣 🐾 ♿ 🚐 ⛺

Scenic rating: 10

on Union Valley Reservoir in
Eldorado National Forest

Map 6.2, page 354

Camino Cove Camp is the nicest spot at Union Valley Reservoir, a slam dunk. It is set at the north end of the lake on a peninsula, absolutely beautiful, a tree-covered landscape and yet with sweeping views of the Crystal Basin. The nearest boat ramp is 1.5 miles to the west at West Point. If this camp is full, there is a small camp at West Point, with just eight sites. The elevation is 4,900 feet.

Campsites, facilities: There are 32 sites for tents or RVs up to 30 feet (no hookups). Fire rings are provided. Vault toilets are available. No drinking water is available. Garbage must be packed out. A swimming beach is nearby and a boat ramp is 1.5 miles away at the campground at West Point. Some facilities are wheelchair-accessible. Leashed pets are permitted.

Reservations, fees: Reservations are not accepted. There is no fee for camping.

Open early May through October, weather permitting.

Directions: From Placerville, drive east on U.S. 50 for 23 miles to Riverton and the junction with Ice House Road/Forest Road 3. Turn north on Ice House Road and drive seven miles to Peavine Ridge Road. Turn left and drive three miles to Bryant Springs Road. Turn right and drive five miles north past the West Point boat ramp, and continue 1.5 miles east to the campground entrance on the right.

Contact: Eldorado National Forest, Pacific Ranger District, 530/644-2349, www.fs.usda.gov/eldorado.

116 YELLOWJACKET

Scenic rating: 8

on Union Valley Reservoir in
Eldorado National Forest

Map 6.2, page 354

The camp is set at 4,900 feet elevation on the north shore of gorgeous Union Valley Reservoir. A boat launch adjacent to the camp makes this an ideal destination for trout-angling campers with boats. Union Valley Reservoir, a popular weekend destination for campers from the Central Valley, is stocked with brook trout and rainbow trout by the Department of Fish and Game.

Campsites, facilities: There are 40 sites for tents or RVs up to 30 feet (no hookups). Picnic tables and fire rings are provided. Drinking water and flush and vault toilets are available. A boat ramp and dump station are nearby. Leashed pets are permitted.

Reservations, fees: Reservations are accepted at 877/444-6777 or www.recreation.gov ($9 reservation fee). Sites are $22 per night, $7 per night for each additional vehicle. Open mid-May through mid-September, weather permitting.

Directions: From Placerville, drive east on

U.S. 50 for 23 miles to Riverton and the junction with Ice House Road/Forest Road 3. Turn left (north) and drive 19 miles to Forest Road 12N78/Union Valley Road (at the head of Union Valley Reservoir). Turn left (west) and drive one mile to Forest Road 12N33. Turn left (south) and drive 0.5 mile to the campground.

Contact: Eldorado National Forest, Pacific Ranger District, 530/644-2349, www.fs.usda.gov/eldorado.

117 WENCH CREEK AND WENCH CREEK GROUP

Scenic rating: 7

on Union Valley Reservoir in
Eldorado National Forest

Map 6.2, page 354

Wench Creek is on the northeast shore of Union Valley Reservoir. (For more information, see the Jones Fork and Peninsula Recreation Area listings in this chapter.) The elevation is 4,900 feet.

Campsites, facilities: There are 100 sites for tents or RVs up to 25 feet (no hookups), and two group tent sites for up to 50 people each. Picnic tables and fire grills are provided. Drinking water and vault toilets are available. A boat ramp is three miles away at the Yellowjacket campground. Leashed pets are permitted.

Reservations, fees: Reservations are not accepted for individual sites, but are accepted for group sites at 877/444-6777 or www.recreation.gov ($9 reservation fee). Sites are $22 per night, $7 per night for each additional vehicle. The group sites are $130 per night. Open mid-May through September.

Directions: From Placerville, drive east on U.S. 50 for 23 miles to Riverton and the junction with Ice House Road/Forest Road 3. Turn left and drive 15 miles to the campground entrance road (four miles past the turnoff for

Sunset Camp). Turn left and drive a mile to the campground at the end of the road.

Contact: Eldorado National Forest, Pacific Ranger District, 530/644-2349, www.fs.usda.gov/eldorado.

118 BIG SILVER GROUP CAMP

Scenic rating: 7

on Big Silver Creek in Eldorado National Forest

Map 6.2, page 354

This camp was built along the Union Valley bike trail, less than a mile from Union Valley Reservoir. The paved bike trail stretches for miles both north and south of the campground and is wheelchair-accessible. It's a classic Sierra forest setting, with plenty of ponderosa pine on the north side of Big Silver Creek.

Campsites, facilities: There is one group site for tents or RVs up to 50 feet (no hookups) that can accommodate up to 50 people. Picnic tables and fire grills are provided. Vault toilets are available. No drinking water is available; stream water must be purified before drinking. There is also a group kitchen area with pedestal grills. Some facilities are wheelchair-accessible. Leashed pets are permitted.

Reservations, fees: Reservations are required at 877/444-6777 or www.recreation.gov ($9 reservation fee). The camp is $45 per night. Open late May through mid-October, weather permitting.

Directions: From Placerville, drive east on U.S. 50 for 23 miles to Riverton and the junction with Ice House Road/Forest Road 3. Turn left (north) and drive about 16 miles to the campground.

Contact: Eldorado National Forest, Pacific Ranger District, 530/644-2349, www.fs.usda.gov/eldorado.

119 AZALEA COVE HIKE-IN/BOAT-IN

Scenic rating: 9

on Union Valley Reservoir in Eldorado National Forest

Map 6.2, page 354

Union Valley Reservoir, at 4,900 feet elevation, has 4.5 miles of bike trail on its shores, in addition to boating and fishing activities. The distance to the campsite is less than a half-mile by trail and approximately one mile by boat. (For additional information, see the Wench Creek and Peninsula Recreation Area listings in this chapter.)

Campsites, facilities: There are 10 sites for tents only. Picnic tables and fire rings are provided. Vault toilets are available. No drinking water is available. Garbage must be packed out. Some facilities are wheelchair-accessible. Leashed pets are permitted.

Reservations, fees: Reservations are not accepted. There is no fee for camping. Open mid-June through mid-October, weather permitting.

Directions: From Placerville, drive east on U.S. 50 for 23 miles to Riverton and the junction with Ice House Road/Forest Road 3. Turn left (north) and drive about 16 miles to the Big Silver Group Campground parking lot. Park and then hike or cycle approximately 0.5 mile to Azalea Cove Campground. To reach Azalea Cove Campground by boat, continue for three miles on Ice House Road to Forest Road 12N78. Turn left (west) and drive one mile to Forest Road 12N33. Turn left (south) and drive 0.5 mile to Yellowjacket Campground. Park and boat approximately one mile to Azalea Cove Campground.

Contact: Eldorado National Forest, Pacific Ranger District, 530/644-2349, www.fs.usda.gov/eldorado; Crystal Basin, 530/293-3510.

120 PENINSULA RECREATION AREA

Scenic rating: 8

on Union Valley Reservoir in
Eldorado National Forest

Map 6.2, page 354

The two campgrounds here, Sunset and Fashoda, are the prettiest of all the camps at Union Valley Reservoir, set at the eastern tip of the peninsula that juts into the lake at the mouth of Jones Fork. A nearby boat ramp (you'll see it on the left on the way in) is a big plus, along with a picnic area and beach. All water sports are allowed. The lake has decent trout fishing, with brook trout, brown trout, rainbow trout, Mackinaw, kokanee salmon, and smallmouth bass. The place is gorgeous, set at 4,900 feet elevation in the Sierra Nevada.

Campsites, facilities: There are 131 sites for tents or RVs up to 50 feet (no hookups) at Sunset Camp and 30 walk-in tent sites at Fashoda Camp. Picnic tables, fire rings, and fire grills are provided. Drinking water, coin showers (at Fashoda), vault toilets, boat ramp, and a dump station are available. Some facilities are wheelchair-accessible. Leashed pets are permitted.

Reservations, fees: Reservations are accepted at 877/444-6777 or www.recreation.gov ($9 reservation fee, look for Sunset-Union Valley or Fashoda). Single sites are $22 per night, $44 per night for a double site, $7 per night for each additional vehicle. Open late May through late September, weather permitting.

Directions: From Placerville, drive east on U.S. 50 for 23 miles to Riverton and the junction with Ice House Road/Forest Road 3. Turn left and drive 14 miles to the campground entrance road (a mile past the turnoff for Jones Fork Camp). Turn left and drive 1.5 miles to the campground at the end of the road.

Contact: Eldorado National Forest, Pacific Ranger District, 530/644-2349, www.fs.usda.gov/eldorado.

121 JONES FORK

Scenic rating: 7

on Union Valley Reservoir in
Eldorado National Forest

Map 6.2, page 354

The Crystal Basin Recreation Area is the most popular backcountry region for campers from the Sacramento area, and Union Valley Reservoir is the centerpiece. The area gets its name from the prominent granite Sierra ridge, which looks like crystal when it is covered with frozen snow. This is a big lake, set at 4,900 feet elevation, with numerous lakeside campgrounds and three boat ramps providing access. This is the first camp you will arrive at, set at the mouth of the Jones Fork Cove.

Campsites, facilities: There are 10 sites for tents or RVs up to 25 feet (no hookups). Picnic tables and fire rings are provided. Vault toilets are available. No drinking water is available. Some facilities are wheelchair accessible. Leashed pets are permitted.

Reservations, fees: Reservations are not accepted. Sites are $10 per night, $5 per night for each additional vehicle. Open June through October.

Directions: From Placerville, drive east on U.S. 50 for 23 miles to Riverton and the junction with Ice House Road/Forest Road 3. Turn left and drive 14 miles to the campground entrance road on the left (at the south end of Union Valley Reservoir). Turn left and drive 0.5 mile to the campground.

Contact: Eldorado National Forest, Pacific Ranger District, 530/644-2349, www.fs.usda.gov/eldorado.

122 LONE ROCK

Scenic rating: 9

near Union Valley Reservoir in
Eldorado National Forest

Map 6.2, page 354

This is a hike-in, bike-in, or boat-in spot at Union Valley Reservoir. It is little known, but once you claim it, it will always be on your list. Lake views and quiet tent sites in a primitive do-it-yourself setting makes this a winner for those who know of it. The elevation is 4,800 feet.

Campsites, facilities: There are five sites for tents only that can only be accessed by bike, trail, or boat. Vault toilets are available. Picnic tables, fire rings, and a bike rack are provided. There is no drinking water.

Reservations, fees: Reservations are not accepted. There is no fee for camping.

Directions: From Placerville, drive east on Highway 50 for 23 miles to Riverton and the junction with Ice House Road/Forest Road 3. If hiking or biking, turn left and drive 14 miles to the Jones Fork campground entrance and begin there. For boat-in camping, drive 14 miles to the Sunset Camp entrance to launch from there.

Contact: Eldorado National Forest, Pacific Ranger District, 530/644-2349, www.fs.usda.gov/eldorado; Crystal Basin, 530/293-3510.

123 SILVER CREEK GROUP

Scenic rating: 5

near Ice House Reservoir in
Eldorado National Forest

Map 6.2, page 354

Silver Creek is a pretty spot at 5,200 feet elevation. Ice House is only two miles north, and Union Valley Reservoir is four miles north. Either bring your own drinking water or bring a water filtration pump for stream water. Note: RVs and trailers are not allowed.

Campsites, facilities: There is one group tent site that can accommodate up to 40 people. Picnic tables and fire rings are provided. Vault toilets are available. No drinking water is available; stream water must be purified before drinking. Leashed pets are permitted.

Reservations, fees: Reservations are required at 877/444-6777 or www.recreation.gov ($9 reservation fee). The site is $100 per night. Open June through October, weather permitting.

Directions: From Placerville, drive east on U.S. 50 for 23 miles to Riverton and the junction with Ice House Road/Forest Road 3. Turn left and drive about nine miles to the campground entrance road on the left (if you reach the junction with Forest Road 3, you have gone 0.25 mile too far). Turn left and drive 0.25 mile to the campground.

Contact: Eldorado National Forest, Pacific Ranger District, 530/644-2349, www.fs.usda.gov/eldorado.

124 ICE HOUSE UPPER AND LOWER

Scenic rating: 8

on Ice House Reservoir in
Eldorado National Forest

Map 6.2, page 354

Along with Loon Lake and Union Valley Reservoir, Ice House Reservoir is a feature destination in the Crystal Basin Recreation Area. Ice House gets most of the anglers and Union Valley gets most of the campers. All water sports are allowed at Ice House, though. The camp is set on the lake's northwestern shore, at 5,500 feet elevation, just up from the dam and adjacent to the lake's boat ramp. The lake, created by a dam on South Fork Silver Creek, covers 650 acres with the deepest spot about 130 feet deep. It is stocked with rainbow trout, brook trout, and brown trout. A 2.5-mile bike trail connects Ice House to Northwind and Strawberry Point campgrounds.

Campsites, facilities: There are 83 sites for tents or RVs up to 30 feet (no hookups). Picnic tables and fire grills are provided. Drinking water, vault toilets, boat ramp, and a dump station are available. Some facilities are wheelchair-accessible. Leashed pets are permitted.

Reservations, fees: Reservations are accepted at 877/444-6777 or www.recreation.gov ($9 reservation fee). Single sites are $22 per night, $44 per night for a double site, $7 per night for each additional vehicle. Open late May through mid-October, weather permitting.

Directions: From Placerville, drive east on U.S. 50 for 23 miles to Riverton and the junction with Ice House Road/Forest Road 3. Turn left (north) and drive 11 miles to Forest Road 32/Ice House/Wrights Tie Road. Turn right (east) and drive 1.5 miles to the campground access road on the right.

Contact: Eldorado National Forest, Pacific Ranger District, 530/644-2349, www.fs.usda.gov/eldorado.

125 NORTHWIND

Scenic rating: 7

on Ice House Reservoir in Eldorado National Forest

Map 6.2, page 354

This camp sits on the north shore of Ice House Reservoir. It is slightly above the reservoir, offering prime views. A 2.5-mile bike trail connects Northwind with Ice House and Strawberry Point campgrounds. (See the Ice House listing for more information.)

Campsites, facilities: There are nine sites for tents or RVs up to 40 feet (no hookups). Picnic tables and fire grills are provided. Vault toilets are available. No drinking water is available; lake water must be purified before drinking. Some facilities are wheelchair-accessible. Leashed pets are permitted.

Reservations, fees: Reservations are not accepted. Sites are $10 per night, $5 per night for

each additional vehicle. Open May through mid-October, weather permitting.

Directions: From Placerville, drive east on U.S. 50 for 23 miles to Riverton and the junction with Ice House Road/Forest Road 3. Turn left (north) and drive 11 miles to Forest Road 32/Ice House/Wrights Tie Road. Turn right (east) and drive three miles (two miles past the boat ramp) to the campground access road on the right.

Contact: Eldorado National Forest, Pacific Ranger District, 530/644-2349, www.fs.usda.gov/eldorado.

126 STRAWBERRY POINT

Scenic rating: 7

on Ice House Reservoir in Eldorado National Forest

Map 6.2, page 354

This camp is set on the north shore of Ice House Reservoir, at 5,400 feet elevation. A 2.5-mile bike trail connects Strawberry Point with Northwind and Ice House campgrounds. (For more information, see the Ice House listing in this chapter.)

Campsites, facilities: There are 10 sites for tents or RVs up to 40 feet (no hookups). Picnic tables and fire grills are provided. Vault toilets are available. No drinking water is available; lake water must be purified before drinking. Some facilities are wheelchair-accessible. Leashed pets are permitted.

Reservations, fees: Reservations are not accepted. Sites are $10 per night, $5 per night for each additional vehicle. Open May through December, weather permitting.

Directions: From Placerville, drive east on U.S. 50 for 23 miles to Riverton and the junction with Ice House Road/Forest Road 3. Turn left (north) and drive 11 miles to Forest Road 32/Ice House/Wrights Tie Road. Turn right (east) and drive three miles (three miles past the boat ramp) to the campground access road on the road.

Contact: Eldorado National Forest, Pacific Ranger District, 530/644-2349, www.fs.usda.gov/eldorado.

127 WRIGHTS LAKE AND EQUESTRIAN

🏃 🚣 🏊 🎣 🏕 ♿ 🚐 ⛺

Scenic rating: 9

in Eldorado National Forest

Map 6.2, page 354

This high mountain lake (7,000 feet) has shoreline picnicking and good fishing and hiking. There is no boat ramp, and the rules do not permit motors, so it is ideal for canoes, rafts, prams, and people who like quiet. Swimming is allowed. Fishing is fair for both rainbow trout and brown trout. It is a classic alpine lake, though small (65 acres), with a trailhead for the Desolation Wilderness at its north end. From here it is only a three-mile hike to the beautiful Twin Lakes and Island Lake, set on the western flank of Mount Price (9,975 feet).

Campsites, facilities: There are 72 sites for tents or RVs up to 50 feet (no hookups) and 15 sites at the equestrian camp. Picnic tables and fire grills are provided. Drinking water and vault toilets are available. Some facilities are wheelchair-accessible, including a boat dock. Leashed pets are permitted.

Reservations, fees: Reservations are accepted and are required for some sites in July and August at 877/444-6777 or www.recreation.gov ($9 reservation fee). Single sites are $20 per night, $36 per night for a double site, $5 per night for each additional vehicle. Open late June through mid-October, weather permitting.

Directions: From Placerville, drive east on U.S. 50 for 23 miles to Riverton and the junction with Ice House Road/Forest Road 3. Turn left (north) and drive 11 miles to Forest Road 32/Ice House/Wrights Tie Road. Turn right (east) and drive nine miles to Forest Road 4/Wrights Lake Road. Turn left (north) and drive two

miles to the campground on the right side of the road.

Contact: Eldorado National Forest, Pacific Ranger District, 530/644-2349, www.fs.usda.gov/eldorado.

128 SLY PARK RECREATION AREA

🏃 🚴 🏊 🚣 🛶 🏕 ♿ 🚐 ⛺

Scenic rating: 7

on Jenkinson Lake

Map 6.2, page 354

Sly Park and Jenkinson Lake are set at 3,500 feet elevation in the lower reaches of Eldorado National Forest, with a climate that is perfect for summer camping, fishing and water sports. The best campsites are No. 10, 12, 14–16, 67–70, 133-134 and 140. Sly Park publishes a special reader on camping etiquette and I'd like to see more of that across the state. Jenkinson Lake covers 640 acres and features eight miles of forested shoreline. Participants of water sports get along, with most water-skiers/wakeboarders motoring around the lake's main body, while anglers head upstream into the Hazel Creek arm of the lake for trout (in the spring) and bass (in the summer). Good news for anglers: Personal watercraft are not permitted. More good news: This is one of the better lakes in the Sierra for brown trout. There is a boat ramp at the campground, and another one located on the southwest end of the lake. The area also has several hiking trails, and the lake is good for swimming. There are nine miles of trails available for hiking, biking, and equestrians; an equestrian trail also circles the lake. A group camp is available for visitors with horses, complete with riding trails, hitching posts, and corrals. Note: No pets or babies with diapers are allowed in the lake.

Campsites, facilities: There are 191 sites for tents or RVs up to 40 feet (no hookups). There are five group sites that can accommodate 50–100 people and an equestrian camp called Black Oak, which has 12 sites and two youth-group areas. Picnic tables, fire rings, and barbecues are provided. Drinking water, vault toilets, boat rentals, and firewood are available. Two boat ramps are available nearby. Some facilities are wheelchair-accessible. A grocery store, snack bar, dump station, bait, and propane gas are available nearby. Leashed pets are permitted.

Reservations, fees: Reservations are accepted at least seven days in advance at 866/759-7275 or 530/644-2792 ($8 reservation fee). Standard tent sites are $30 per night, Black Oak sites are $35 per night, premium sites are $45 per night, $15 per night per additional vehicle. A youth group camping area is $115 per night for up to 35 people, adult group sites are $265 per night, $4 per night for each additional person. Boat launching is $9 per day. Reduced rates available for seniors and in winter. Some credit cards accepted during the summer season. Open year-round.

Directions: From Sacramento, drive east on U.S. 50 to Pollock Pines and take the exit for Sly Park Road. Drive south for 4.5 miles to Jenkinson Lake and the campground entrance.

Contact: Sly Park Recreation Area, El Dorado Irrigation District, 530/295-6824, www.eid.org.

129 CAPPS CROSSING GROUP CAMP
🥾 🛶 🐕 5% 🏕

Scenic rating: 7

on the North Fork of the Cosumnes River in Eldorado National Forest

Map 6.2, page 354

This camp is set out in the middle of nowhere along the North Fork of the Cosumnes River. It's a primitive spot that doesn't get much use. This camp is in the western reaches of a vast number of backcountry Forest Service roads. A map of Eldorado National Forest is a must to explore them. The elevation is 5,200 feet.

Campsites, facilities: There is one group tent site for up to 42 people. Single sites are available if the camp is not reserved by a group.

Picnic tables and fire grills are provided. Drinking water and vault toilets are available. Leashed pets are permitted.

Reservations, fees: Reservations are required at 877/444-6777 or www.recreation.gov ($9 reservation fee). The group camp is $85 per night, single sites are $18 per night, $36 per night for double sites. Open mid-May through mid-September, weather permitting.

Directions: From Sacramento, drive east on U.S. 50 to Placerville and continue for 12 miles to the Sly Park Road exit. Turn right and drive about six miles to the Mormon Emigrant Trail/Forest Road 5. Turn left on Mormon Emigrant Trail and drive about 13 miles to North-South Road/Forest Road 6. Turn right (south) on North-South Road and drive about six miles to the campground on the left side of the road.

Contact: Eldorado National Forest, Placerville Ranger District, 530/644-2324, www.fs.usda.gov/eldorado.

130 SAND FLAT-AMERICAN RIVER
🏊 🛶 🐕 ♿ 🚙 🏕

Scenic rating: 7

on the South Fork of the American River in Eldorado National Forest

Map 6.2, page 354

This first-come, first-served campground often gets filled up by U.S. 50 travelers. And why not? You get easy access, a well-signed exit, and a nice setting on the South Fork of the American River. The elevation is 3,900 feet. The river is very pretty here, but fishing is often poor. In winter, the snow level usually starts just a few miles uphill.

Campsites, facilities: There are 29 sites for tents or RVs of any length (no hookups) and four walk-in tent sites. Picnic tables and fire grills are provided. Drinking water and vault toilets are available. Groceries, restaurant, and gas are nearby. Some facilities are wheelchair-accessible. Leashed pets are permitted.

Reservations, fees: Reservations are not

accepted. Single sites are $18 per night, $36 per night for a double site, $7 per night for each additional vehicle. Open May through late October, weather permitting.

Directions: From Sacramento, drive east on U.S. 50 to Placerville and then continue 28 miles to the campground on the right. (If you reach the Kyburz store, you have driven about one mile too far.)

Contact: Eldorado National Forest, Placerville Ranger District, 530/644-2324, www.fs.usda.gov/eldorado.

131 CHINA FLAT

Scenic rating: 7

on the Silver Fork of the American River in Eldorado National Forest

Map 6.2, page 354

China Flat sits across the road from the Silver Fork American River, with a nearby access road that is routed along the river for a mile. This provides access for fishing, swimming, gold panning, and exploring. The elevation is 4,800 feet. The camp feels far off the beaten path, even though it is only five minutes from that parade of traffic on U.S. 50.

Campsites, facilities: There are 19 sites for tents or RVs of any length (no hookups). Picnic tables and fire grills are provided. Drinking water and vault toilets are available. Some facilities are wheelchair-accessible. Leashed pets are permitted.

Reservations, fees: Reservations are not accepted. Single sites are $18 per night, $36 per night for double sites, $7 per night for each additional vehicle. Open May through October, weather permitting.

Directions: From Sacramento, drive east on U.S. 50 to Kyburz and Silver Fork Road. Turn right and drive three miles to the campground on the right side of the road.

Contact: Eldorado National Forest, Placerville Ranger District, 530/644-2324, www.fs.usda.gov/eldorado.

132 SILVER FORK

Scenic rating: 7

on the Silver Fork of the American River in Eldorado National Forest

Map 6.2, page 354

The tons of vacationers driving U.S. 50 along the South Fork American River always get frustrated when they try to fish or camp, because there are precious few opportunities for either. But, just 20 minutes off the highway, you can find both at Silver Fork Camp. The access road provides many fishing opportunities and the stream is stocked with rainbow trout by the state. The camp is set right along the river, at 5,500 feet elevation, in Eldorado National Forest.

Campsites, facilities: There are 35 sites for tents or RVs of any length (no hookups) and four double sites. Picnic tables and fire grills are provided. Drinking water and vault toilets are available. Some of the facilities are wheelchair-accessible. Leashed pets are permitted.

Reservations, fees: Reservations are not accepted. Single sites are $18 per night, $36 per night for double sites, $7 per night for each additional vehicle. Open May through October, weather permitting.

Directions: From Sacramento, drive east on U.S. 50 to Kyburz and Silver Fork Road. Turn right and drive eight miles to the campground on the right side of the road.

Contact: Eldorado National Forest, Placerville Ranger District, 530/644-2324, www.fs.usda.gov/eldorado.

133 KIRKWOOD LAKE

Scenic rating: 8

in Eldorado National Forest

Map 6.2, page 354

Little Kirkwood Lake is in a beautiful Sierra setting, with good shoreline access, fishing for small rainbow trout, and quiet water. Despite that, it is often overlooked in favor of nearby Silver Lake and Caples Lake along Highway 88. No boat motors are allowed, but swimming is permitted. Nearby Kirkwood Ski Resort stays open all summer and offers excellent opportunities for horseback riding, hiking, and meals. The elevation is 7,600 feet. Note: No trailers. The access road is too narrow.

Campsites, facilities: There are 12 sites for tents only. Picnic tables and fire grills are provided. Drinking water, vault toilets, and food lockers are available. Some facilities are wheelchair accessible. Leashed pets are permitted.

Reservations, fees: Reservations are not accepted. Sites are $22 per night, $5 per night for each additional vehicle. Open June through mid-October, weather permitting.

Directions: From Jackson, drive east on Highway 88 for 60 miles (four miles past Silver Lake) to the campground entrance road on the left (if you reach the sign for Kirkwood Ski Resort, you have gone 0.5 mile too far). Turn left and drive 0.25 mile (road not suitable for trailers or large RVs) to the campground on the left.

Contact: Eldorado National Forest, Amador Ranger District, 209/295-4251, www.fs.usda.gov/eldorado.

134 CAPLES LAKE

Scenic rating: 8

in Eldorado National Forest

Map 6.2, page 354

Caples Lake, in the high country at 7,800 feet, is a pretty lake right along Highway 88. It covers 600 acres, has a 5-mph speed limit, and provides good trout fishing and excellent hiking terrain. Swimming is allowed. The camp is set across the highway (a little two-laner) from the lake, with the Caples Lake Resort, boat rentals, and a boat launch nearby. There is a parking area at the west end of the lake, and from here you can begin a great 3.5-mile hike to Emigrant Lake, in the Mokelumne

Wilderness on the western flank of Mount Round Top (10,310 feet).

Campsites, facilities: There are 30 sites for tents or RVs up to 35 feet (no hookups), and seven walk-in tent sites (requiring a 200-foot walk). Picnic tables and fire grills are provided. Drinking water and vault toilets are available. Groceries, propane gas, boat ramp, and boat rentals are nearby. Some facilities are wheelchair-accessible. Leashed pets are permitted.

Reservations, fees: Reservations are not accepted. Single sites are $24 per night, double sites are $48 per night, $5 per night for each additional vehicle. Open June through mid-October, weather permitting.

Directions: From Jackson, drive east on Highway 88 for 63 miles (one mile past the entrance road to Kirkwood Ski Area) to the camp entrance road on the left.

Contact: Eldorado National Forest, Amador Ranger District, 209/295-4251, www.fs.usda.gov/eldorado; Caples Lake Resort, 209/258-8888, http://capleslakeresort.com.

135 WOODS LAKE

Scenic rating: 9

in Eldorado National Forest

Map 6.2, page 354 BEST (

Woods Lake is only two miles from Highway 88, yet it can provide campers the feeling of visiting a far-off land. It is a small but beautiful lake in the granite backdrop of the high Sierra, set at 8,200 feet elevation near Carson Pass. Boats with motors are not permitted, making it ideal for canoes and rowboats. Trout fishing is fair. A great trailhead is available here, a three-mile loop hike to little Round Top Lake and Winnemucca Lake (twice the size of Woods Lake) and back. They are set on the northern flank of Mount Round Top (10,310 feet).

Campsites, facilities: There are 25 tent sites. Picnic tables and fire rings are provided.

Drinking water and vault toilets are available. Groceries and propane gas are available within five miles. Some facilities are wheelchair-accessible. Leashed pets are permitted.

Reservations, fees: Reservations are not accepted. Single sites are $24 per night, $48 per night for double site, $5 per night for each additional vehicle. Open late June through October, weather permitting.

Directions: From Jackson, drive east on Highway 88 to Caples Lake and continue for a mile to the Woods Lake turnoff on the right (two miles west of Carson Pass). Turn south and drive a mile to the campground on the right (trailers and RVs are not recommended).

Contact: Eldorado National Forest, Amador Ranger District, 209/295-4251, www.fs.usda.gov/eldorado.

136 SILVER LAKE WEST

Scenic rating: 9

on Silver Lake in Eldorado National Forest

Map 6.2, page 354   BEST (

The Highway 88 corridor provides access to three excellent lakes: Lower Bear River Reservoir, Silver Lake, and Caples Lake. Silver Lake is difficult to pass by, with cabin rentals, pretty campsites, decent trout fishing, and excellent hiking. The lake is set at 7,200 feet elevation in a classic granite cirque just below the Sierra ridge. This camp is on the west side of Highway 88, across the road from the lake. A great hike starts at the trailhead on the east side of the lake, a two-mile tromp to little Hidden Lake, one of several nice hikes in the area. In addition, horseback-riding is available nearby at Plasse's Resort. Note that bears frequent this campground, so store food properly and avoid scented products.

Campsites, facilities: There are 42 sites for tents or RVs up to 24 feet (no hookups). Picnic tables, food lockers, and fire pits are provided. Vault toilets and drinking water are available. A boat ramp and boat rentals are nearby.

Leashed pets are permitted. There is a maximum of six people and two pets per site.

Reservations, fees: Reservations are not accepted. Sites are $20–25 per night, $10 per night for each additional vehicle, $3 per pet per night, boat launch is $10. Open Memorial Day Weekend through October, weather permitting.

Directions: From Jackson, drive east on Highway 88 for 50 miles (to the north end of Silver Lake) to the campground entrance road on the left.

Contact: Eldorado Irrigation District, 530/295-6824, www.eid.org.

137 SILVER LAKE EAST

Scenic rating: 7

in Eldorado National Forest

Map 6.2, page 354

Silver Lake is an easy-to-reach alpine lake set at 7,200 feet, providing a beautiful setting, good trout fishing, and hiking. This camp is on the northeast side of the lake, with a boat ramp nearby. (See the Silver Lake West listing in this chapter for more information.)

Campsites, facilities: There are 59 sites for tents or RVs up to 24 feet (no hookups). Picnic tables, food lockers, and fire grills are provided. Drinking water and flush and vault toilets are available. A grocery store, boat rentals, boat ramp, and propane gas are nearby. Leashed pets are permitted.

Reservations, fees: Reservations are accepted at 877/444-6777 or www.recreation.gov ($9 reservation fee). Single sites are $24 per night, $48 per night for a double site, $10 per night for each additional vehicle, $3 per pet per night. Open June through mid-October, weather permitting.

Directions: From Jackson, drive east on Highway 88 for 50 miles (to the north end of Silver Lake) to the campground entrance road on the right.

Contact: Eldorado National Forest, Amador

Ranger District, 209/295-4251, www.fs.usda.gov/eldorado; Silver Lake Resort, 209/258-8598.

138 PIPI

Scenic rating: 7

on the Middle Fork of the Cosumnes River in Eldorado National Forest

Map 6.2, page 354

PiPi (pronounced pie-pie) is far enough out of the way to get missed by most campers. It is beside the Middle Fork of the Cosumnes River at 4,100 feet elevation. There are some good swimming holes in the area, but the water is cold and swift in early summer (after all, it's snowmelt). A trail/boardwalk along the river is wheelchair-accessible. Several sites border a pretty meadow in the back of the camp. This is also a gateway to a vast network of Forest Service roads to the north in Eldorado National Forest.

Campsites, facilities: There are 51 sites for tents or RVs up to 42 feet (no hookups), including two double sites and one triple site. Picnic tables and fire grills are provided. Drinking water and vault toilets are available. Some facilities are wheelchair-accessible. Leashed pets are permitted.

Reservations, fees: Reservations are accepted at 877/444-6777 or www.recreation.gov ($9 reservation fee). Single sites are $22 per night, $44 per night for double sites, $66 per night for the triple site, $5 per night for each additional vehicle. Open May through mid-November, weather permitting.

Directions: From Jackson, drive east on Highway 88 to Pioneer and continue for nine miles to Omo Ranch Road. Turn left and drive 0.8 mile to North-South Road/Forest Road 6. Turn right and drive 5.9 miles to the campground on the right side of the road.

Contact: Eldorado National Forest, Amador Ranger District, 209/295-4251, www.fs.usda.gov/eldorado.

139 BEAR RIVER GROUP CAMP

Scenic rating: 6

on Bear River Reservoir in Eldorado National Forest

Map 6.2, page 354

This is a group camp set near Bear River Reservoir, a pretty lake that provides powerboating and trout fishing. (See the listing in this chapter for South Shore, which is just a mile from this camp.)

Campsites, facilities: There are four group sites for tents only that can accommodate 25–50 people each. Picnic tables, fire grills, and group cooking facilities are provided. Drinking water, vault toilets, coin showers, food lockers, and wash racks are available. A grocery store, boat ramp, boat rentals, and propane gas are available nearby. Leashed pets are permitted.

Reservations, fees: Reservations are required at 877/444-6777 or www.recreation.gov ($9 reservation fee). Sites are $75–150 per night. Open mid-June through mid-September, weather permitting.

Directions: From Stockton, drive east on Highway 88 for about 80 miles to the lake entrance on the right side of the road (well signed). Turn right and drive five miles (past the dam) to the campground entrance on the left side of the road.

Contact: Eldorado National Forest, Amador Ranger District, 209/295-4251, www.fs.usda.gov/eldorado.

140 BEAR RIVER LAKE RESORT

Scenic rating: 8

on Bear River Reservoir

Map 6.2, page 354

Bear River Lake Resort is a complete vacation service lodge, with everything you could ask for. A lot of people have been asking in recent years, making this a popular spot that often requires a reservation. The resort also sponsors fishing derbies in the summer and sweetens the pot considerably by stocking exceptionally large rainbow trout. Other fish species include brown trout and Mackinaw trout. The resort is set at 6,000 feet. The lake freezes over in the winter. (See the South Shore listing in this chapter for more information about Bear River Reservoir.)

Campsites, facilities: There are 152 sites with partial hookups (15 amps) for tents or RVs up to 35 feet, a group site for up to 60 people, and seven cabins. Picnic tables and fire pits are provided. Restrooms with flush toilets and coin showers, drinking water, dump station, boat ramp, boat rentals, berthing, bait and tackle, fishing licenses, video arcade, playground, firewood, ice, propane gas, coin laundry, WiFi, pay phone, restaurant and cocktail lounge, and grocery store are available. ATVs are permitted, but no motorcycles are allowed. Some facilities are wheelchair-accessible. Leashed pets are permitted at campsites, but not in lodging units.

Reservations, fees: Reservations are recommended. Tent and RV sites (water and electricity) are $33 per night, extra-large sites are $50 per night, $5 for each additional vehicle with a maximum of two vehicles, $255 per night for the group site, $5 one-time pet fee, and $117 per night for cabins. Monthly rates available. Some credit cards accepted. Open April through October.

Directions: From Stockton, drive east on Highway 88 for about 80 miles to the lake entrance on the right side of the road, 42 miles east of Jackson. Turn right and drive 2.5 miles to a junction (if you pass the dam, you have gone 0.25 mile too far). Turn left and drive 0.5 mile to the campground entrance on the right side of the road.

Contact: Bear River Lake Resort, 209/295-4868, www.bearrivercampground.com.

141 SUGAR PINE POINT

Scenic rating: 7

near Bear River Reservoir in Eldorado National Forest

Map 6.2, page 354

This camp is similar in nature to Pardoes Point (see listing in this chapter), with one exception: It is located directly across the lake, on the other shoreline, that is, from Pardoes.

Campsites, facilities: There are eight sites for tents only, including two double sites. Picnic tables and fire rings are provided. Vault toilets are available. Drinking water is not available; lake water must be purified before drinking. Some facilities are wheelchair accessible. Leashed pets permitted.

Reservations, fees: Reservations are not accepted. Single sites are $20 per night, double sites are $40 per night, $5 each additional vehicle per night. Open from May to mid-November.

Directions: From Stockton, drive east on Highway 88 for about 80 miles to Bear River Road. Turn right and drive 2.5 miles south on Bear River Road to Forest Road 8N20. Turn right on Forest Road 8N20 and drive three miles to the campground.

Contact: Eldorado National Forest, Amador Ranger District, 209/295-4251, www.fs.usda.gov/eldorado.

142 PARDOES POINT

Scenic rating: 7

in Eldorado National Forest

Map 6.2, page 354

There are several camps at Bear River Reservoir—Bear River Resort is the most popular because you can see the lake, it has a boat ramp, and you can get supplies. Pardoes Point is located near the lower end of the reservoir. It's not a true "lakeside" camp, though you can get glimpses of the lake from some sites. Bear River Reservoir often provides good fishing.

The elevation is 6,000 feet and ice-outs occur earlier than at Silver Lake and Caples Lake farther up Highway 88.

Campsites, facilities: There are 10 tent sites, including one double site. Picnic tables and fire rings are provided. Drinking water and vault toilets are available. Some facilities are wheelchair accessible. Leashed pets permitted.

Reservations, fees: Reservations are not accepted. Single sites are $22 per night, double sites are $44 per night, $5 per each additional vehicle per night. Open from May to mid-November.

Directions: From Stockton, drive east on Highway 88 for about 80 miles to Bear River Road. Turn right and drive south on Bear River Road for four miles to the campground.

Contact: Eldorado National Forest, Amador Ranger District, 209/295-4251, www.fs.usda.gov/eldorado.

143 SOUTH SHORE
Scenic rating: 7

on Bear River Reservoir in
Eldorado National Forest

Map 6.2, page 354

Bear River Reservoir is set at 5,900 feet, which means it becomes ice-free earlier in the spring than its uphill neighbors to the east, Silver Lake and Caples Lake. It is a good-sized lake—725 acres—and cold and deep, too. All water sports are allowed. It gets double-barreled trout stocks, receiving fish from the state and from the operator of the lake's marina and lodge. This campground is on the lake's southern shore, just east of the dam. Explorers can drive south for five miles to Salt Springs Reservoir, which has a trailhead and parking area on the north side of the dam for a great day hike along the lake.

Campsites, facilities: There are 22 sites for tents or RVs up to 35 feet (no hookups).

Picnic tables and fire grills are provided. Drinking water and vault toilets are available. A boat ramp, grocery store, boat rentals, and propane gas are available at nearby Bear River Lake Resort. Some facilities are wheelchair-accessible. Leashed pets are permitted.

Reservations, fees: Reservations are accepted at 877/444-6777 or www.recreation.gov ($9 reservation fee). Single sites are $22 per night, $44 per night for double sites, $66 for triple sites, $5 per each additional vehicle per night. Open mid-May through mid-October, weather permitting.

Directions: From Stockton, drive east on Highway 88 for about 80 miles to the lake entrance on the right side of the road (well signed). Turn right and drive four miles (past the dam) to the campground entrance on the right side of the road.

Contact: Eldorado National Forest, Amador Ranger District, 209/295-4251, www.fs.usda.gov/eldorado.

144 WHITE AZALEA
Scenic rating: 7

on the Mokelumne River in
Eldorado National Forest

Map 6.2, page 354

Out here in the remote Mokelumne River Canyon are three primitive camps set on the Mokelumne's North Fork. White Azalea, at 3,500 feet elevation, is the closest of the three to Salt Springs Reservoir, the prime recreation destination. It's about a three-mile drive to the dam and an adjacent parking area for a wilderness trailhead for the Mokelumne Wilderness. This trail makes a great day hike, routed for four miles along the north shore of Salt Springs Reservoir to Blue Hole at the head of the lake.

Campsites, facilities: There are six tent sites. Portable toilets are provided. No drinking water is available; river water must be purified before drinking. Garbage must be packed out. Leashed pets are permitted.

Reservations, fees: Reservations are not accepted. There is no fee for camping. Open year-round, weather permitting.

Directions: From Jackson, drive east on Highway 88 to Pioneer and then continue for 18 miles to Ellis Road/Forest Road 92 (78 miles from Jackson), at a signed turnoff for Lumberyard Campground. Turn right on Ellis Road and drive 12 miles to Salt Springs Road (Forest Road 9). Turn left, cross the Bear River, and continue for three miles to the campground on the right. The road is steep, narrow, and curvy in spots, not good for RVs or trailers.

Contact: Eldorado National Forest, Amador Ranger District, 209/295-4251, www.fs.usda.gov/eldorado.

145 MOORE CREEK

🏊 🚴 🐕 🏕

Scenic rating: 7

on the Mokelumne River in
Eldorado National Forest

Map 6.2, page 354

This camp is set at 3,200 feet elevation on little Moore Creek, a feeder stream to the nearby North Fork Mokelumne River. It's one of three primitive camps within two miles. (See the White Azalea listing for more information.)

Campsites, facilities: There are eight tent sites. Picnic tables are provided. Vault toilets are available. No drinking water is available; river water must be purified before drinking. Garbage must be packed out. Leashed pets are permitted.

Reservations, fees: Reservations are not accepted. There is no fee for camping. Open year-round, weather permitting.

Directions: From Jackson, drive east on Highway 88 to Pioneer and then continue for 18 miles to Ellis Road/Forest Road 92 (78 miles from Jackson), at a signed turnoff for Lumberyard Campground. Turn right on Ellis Road and drive 12 miles to Salt Springs Road (Forest

Road 9). Turn right and drive 2.5 miles, cross the bridge over the Mokelumne River, and turn right on the campground entrance road. Drive 0.25 mile to the campground on the right. The road is steep, narrow, and winding in spots—not good for RVs or trailers.

Contact: Eldorado National Forest, Amador Ranger District, 209/295-4251, www.fs.usda.gov/eldorado.

146 MOKELUMNE

🏊 🚴 🐕 🏕

Scenic rating: 7

on the Mokelumne River in
Eldorado National Forest

Map 6.2, page 354

This primitive spot is set beside the Mokelumne River at 3,200 feet elevation, one of three primitive camps in the immediate area. There are some good swimming holes nearby. Fishing is fair, with the trout on the small side. (See the White Azalea listing in this chapter for more information.)

Campsites, facilities: There are 13 sites for tents only. Vault toilets and some picnic tables are provided. No drinking water is available; river water must be purified before drinking. Garbage must be packed out (it is occasionally serviced in summer). Leashed pets are permitted.

Reservations, fees: Reservations are not accepted. There is no fee for camping. Open year-round, weather permitting.

Directions: From Jackson, drive east on Highway 88 to Pioneer and then continue for 18 miles to Ellis Road/Forest Road 92 (78 miles from Jackson), at a signed turnoff for Lumberyard Campground. Turn right on Ellis Road and drive 12 miles to Salt Springs Road (Forest Road 9). Turn right and drive 2.5 miles to the campground on the left side of the road (at the Mokelumne River).

Contact: Eldorado National Forest, Amador Ranger District, 209/295-4251, www.fs.usda.gov/eldorado.

147 BIG MEADOW AND BIG MEADOW GROUP CAMP

Scenic rating: 5

in Stanislaus National Forest

Map 6.2, page 354

Big Meadow is set at 6,460 feet elevation on the western slopes of the Sierra Nevada. There are a number of recreation attractions nearby, the most prominent being the North Fork Stanislaus River two miles to the south in a national forest (see the Sand Flat Four-Wheel Drive listing in this chapter), with access available from a four-wheel-drive road just east of camp, or on Spicer Reservoir Road (see the Stanislaus River listing in this chapter). Lake Alpine, a pretty lake popular for trout fishing, is nine miles east on Highway 4. Three mountain reservoirs—Spicer, Utica, and Union—are all within a 15-minute drive. Big Meadow is also a good base camp for hunting.

Campsites, facilities: There are 68 sites for tents or RVs up to 27 feet (no hookups), and one group tent site (requires a walk in of 100 feet) that can accommodate 25–50 people. Picnic tables and fire grills are provided. Drinking water and vault toilets are available. Groceries, coin laundry, and propane gas are within five miles. Leashed pets are permitted.

Reservations, fees: Reservations are accepted for individual sites and required for the group camp at 877/444-6777 or www.recreation.gov ($9 reservation fee). Sites are $19 per night, $50 per night for the group camp. Open June through October, weather permitting.

Directions: From Angels Camp on Highway 49, turn east on Highway 4 and drive about 30 miles (three miles past Ganns Meadows) to the campground on the right.

Contact: Stanislaus National Forest, Calaveras Ranger District, 209/795-1381, www.fs.usda/stanislaus.

148 SAND FLAT FOUR-WHEEL DRIVE

Scenic rating: 7

on the Stanislaus River in Stanislaus National Forest

Map 6.2, page 354

This one is for four-wheel-drive cowboys who want to carve out a piece of the Sierra Nevada wildlands for themselves. It is set at 5,900 feet elevation on the North Fork Stanislaus River, where there is decent fishing for small trout, with the fish often holding right where white water runs into pools. You won't get bugged by anyone at this tiny, primitive camp, named for the extensive sandy flat on the south side of the river. The access road is steep and often rough. Trailers are not allowed.

Campsites, facilities: There are 10 sites for tents only. Picnic tables and fire rings are provided. Pit toilets are available. No drinking water is available. Garbage must be packed out. Leashed pets are permitted.

Reservations, fees: Reservations are not accepted. There is no fee for camping. Free campfire permits are required. Open June through October, weather permitting.

Directions: From Angels Camp on Highway 49, turn east on Highway 4, drive about 25 miles (0.5 mile past Big Meadows) to a dirt/gravel road on the right. Turn right and drive two miles on a steep, unimproved road (four-wheel drive required).

Contact: Stanislaus National Forest, Calaveras Ranger District, 209/795-1381, www.fs.usda/stanislaus.

149 STANISLAUS RIVER

Scenic rating: 8

in Stanislaus National Forest

Map 6.2, page 354

As you might figure from its name, this camp provides excellent access to the adjacent North

Fork Stanislaus River. The elevation is 6,200 feet, with timbered sites and the river just south of camp.

Campsites, facilities: There are 25 sites for tents or RVs up to 35 feet (no hookups). Fire grills and picnic tables are provided. Drinking water and vault toilets are available. Garbage must be packed out. Supplies are available in Bear Valley. Leashed pets are permitted.

Reservations, fees: Reservations are not accepted. Sites are $8 per night. Open June through October, weather permitting.

Directions: From Angels Camp on Highway 49, turn east on Highway 4 and drive about 44 miles to Spicer Reservoir Road. Turn right and drive four miles to the campground on the right side of the road.

Contact: Stanislaus National Forest, Calaveras Ranger District, 209/795-1381, www.fs.usda.gov.

150 WA KA LUU HEP YOO

Scenic rating: 8

on the Stanislaus River in Stanislaus National Forest

Map 6.2, page 354

This is a riverside Forest Service campground that provides good trout fishing on the Stanislaus River and a put-in for white-water rafting. The highlight for most is the fishing here—one of the best spots on the Stanislaus, stocked by Fish and Game, and good for rainbow, brook, and brown trout. It is four miles downstream of Dorrington and was first opened in 1999 as part of the Sourgrass Recreation Complex. There are cultural sites and preserved artifacts, such as grinding rocks. It is a pretty streamside spot, with ponderosa pine and black oak providing good screening. A wheelchair-accessible trail is available along the stream. The camp is set at an elevation of 3,900 feet, but it feels higher. By the way, I was told that the name of the campground means "wild river."

Campsites, facilities: There are 49 sites for tents or RVs up to 50 feet (no hookups). Picnic tables and fire grills are provided. Drinking water and restrooms with hot showers and flush and vault toilets are available. Some facilities are wheelchair-accessible. Leashed pets are permitted.

Reservations, fees: Reservations are not accepted. Sites are $20 per night. Free campfire permits are required. Open Memorial Day weekend through October, weather permitting.

Directions: From Angels Camp, drive east on Highway 4, past Arnold to Dorrington and Board's Crossing-Sourgrass Road. Turn right and drive four miles to the campground on the left (just before the bridge that crosses the Stanislaus River).

Contact: Stanislaus National Forest, Calaveras Ranger District, 209/795-1381, www.fs.usda/stanislaus.

151 GOLDEN PINES RV RESORT AND CAMPGROUND

Scenic rating: 6

near Arnold

Map 6.2, page 354

This is a privately operated park set at 5,800 feet elevation on the slopes of the Sierra Nevada. The resort is surrounded by 400 acres of forest and has a self-guided nature trail. Nearby destinations include Stanislaus National Forest, the North Stanislaus River, and Calaveras Big Trees State Park (two miles away). The latter features 150 giant sequoias, along with the biggest stump you can imagine, and two easy hikes, one routed through the North Grove, another through the South Grove. The Bear Valley/Mount Reba ski resort is nearby. Note that about half the sites here are long-term vacation leases.

Campsites, facilities: There are 33 sites with full or partial hookups (30 amps) for RVs up to 42 feet, and 40 tent sites. Picnic tables, fire pits, and barbecues are provided. Drinking water, restrooms with showers, seasonal heated swimming pool, playground, horseshoes, table tennis, volleyball, group facilities, pay phone, coin laundry, and propane gas are available. Some facilities are wheelchair-accessible. Leashed pets are permitted.

Reservations, fees: Reservations are recommended. RV sites with full hookups are $40 per night, RV sites with partial hookups are $35 per night, tent sites are $25 per night, $2 per night for more than two people, $2.50 per night for each additional vehicle, $2.50 one-time charge per pet. Some credit cards accepted. Weekly and monthly rates available. Open year-round.

Directions: From Angels Camp, turn northeast on Highway 4 and drive 22 miles to Arnold. Continue for seven miles to the campground entrance on the left.

Contact: Golden Pines RV Resort and Campground, 209/795-2820, www.goldenpines-resort.com.

152 CALAVERAS BIG TREES STATE PARK

Scenic rating: 7

near Arnold

Map 6.2, page 354

Calaveras Big Trees State Park is known for its two groves of giant sequoias and an epic stump. (Giant sequoias are known for their massive diameter rather than height, as is the case with coast redwoods.) The park covers 6,500 acres, preserving the extraordinary North Grove of giant sequoias, which includes the Discovery Tree. Through the years, additional acreage surrounding the grove has been added, providing a mixed conifer forest as a buffer around the giant sequoias. The North Grove Loop is an easy 1.5-mile walk that is routed among 150 sequoias; the sweet fragrance of the huge trees fills the air. Another hike, a five-miler, is in the South Grove, where the park's two largest sequoias (the Agassiz Tree and the Palace Hotel Tree) can be seen on a spur trail. A visitors center is open during peak periods, offering exhibits on the giant sequoia and natural history. The North Fork Stanislaus River runs near Highway 4, providing trout-fishing access. The Stanislaus (near the bridge) and Beaver Creek (about 10 miles away) are stocked with trout in late spring and early summer. In the winter, this is a popular spot for cross-country skiing and snowshoeing. The elevation is 4,800 feet.

Campsites, facilities: The North Grove Campground has 51 sites for tents, 48 sites for RVs up to 30 feet (no hookups), five hike-in environmental sites, and two group sites for 40 and 60 people respectively. The Oak Hollow Campground has 23 sites for tents only and 18 sites for RVs up to 30 feet (no hookups). Picnic tables, fire rings, and food lockers are provided. Drinking water, restrooms with flush toilets and coin showers, and firewood are available. A dump station is available in North Grove. No bicycles are allowed on the paths, but they are permitted on fire roads and paved roads. Some facilities are wheelchair-accessible, including a nature trail and exhibits. Leashed pets are permitted, but not on trails.

Reservations, fees: Reservations are accepted May through September at 800/444-7275 (800/444-PARK) or www.reserveamerica.com ($8 reservation fee). Sites are first-come, first-served October through April. Sites are $35 per night, $8 per night for each additional vehicle, $135–200 per night for group sites, and $20 per night for environmental sites. Open year-round, with 12 sites available in winter.

Directions: From Angels Camp, drive east on Highway 4 for 23 miles to Arnold and then continue another four miles to the park entrance on the right.

Contact: Calaveras Big Trees State Park, 209/795-2334; Columbia State Park, 209/544-9128, www.parks.ca.gov.

153 BEARDSLEY

Scenic rating: 6

at Beardsley Reservoir in
Stanislaus National Forest

Map 6.2, page 354

This lake is set in a deep canyon with a paved
ramp, nice picnic area, and a fair beach. It is
often an outstanding fishery early in the season for brown trout, and then once planted,
good for catches of hatchery fish during the
evening bite. In winter and spring, as soon
as the gate is opened to the boat ramp access road, the fishing is best when the wind
blows. This lake allows powerboats and all
water sports. The water is generally warm
enough for swimmers by midsummer. The
camp is set at 3,400 feet elevation, but because it is near the bottom of the lake canyon, it actually feels much higher. Since
the lake is a reservoir, it is subject to severe
drawdowns in late summer. Bonus: There
is more fishing nearby on the Middle Fork
of the Stanislaus.

Campsites, facilities: There are 16 sites for
tents or RVs up to 22 feet (no hookups).
Fire rings are provided. Vault toilets are
available. No drinking water is available.
Garbage must be packed out. Leashed pets
are permitted.

Reservations, fees: Reservations are not accepted. There is no fee for camping. Open
May through October, weather permitting
(the road is often gated at the top of the canyon when the boat ramp road at lake level is
iced over).

Directions: From Sonora, drive east on Highway 108 for about 25 miles to Strawberry and
the turnoff for Beardsley Reservoir/Forest
Road 52. Turn left and drive seven miles to
Beardsley Dam. Continue for 0.25 mile past
the dam to the campground.

Contact: Stanislaus National Forest, Summit
Ranger District, 209/965-3434, www.fs.usda/
stanislaus.

154 FRASER FLAT

Scenic rating: 7

on the South Fork of the Stanislaus River in
Stanislaus National Forest

Map 6.2, page 354

This camp is set along the South Fork of the
Stanislaus River at an elevation of 4,800 feet.
If the fish aren't biting, a short side trip via
Forest Service roads will route you north into
the main canyon of the Middle Fork Stanislaus. A map of Stanislaus National Forest is
required for this adventure.

Campsites, facilities: There are 38 sites for
tents or RVs up to 30 feet (no hookups). Picnic
tables and fire grills are provided. Drinking
water, vault toilets, and a wheelchair-accessible
fishing pier are available. Some facilities are
wheelchair-accessible. A grocery store and
propane gas are nearby. Leashed pets are
permitted.

Reservations, fees: Reservations are not accepted. Sites are $18 per night, $5 per night for
each additional vehicle. Open May through
October, weather permitting.

Directions: From Sonora, drive east on Highway 108 to Long Barn. Continue east for six
miles to Spring Gap Road/Forest Road 4N01.
Turn left and drive three miles to the campground on the left side of the road.

Contact: Stanislaus National Forest, Mi-
Wok Ranger District, 209/586-3234, www.
fs.usda/stanislaus; Dodge Ridge Corporation,
209/965-3116.

155 HULL CREEK

Scenic rating: 7

in Stanislaus National Forest

Map 6.2, page 354

This obscure camp borders little Hull Creek
(too small for trout fishing) at 5,600 feet elevation in Stanislaus National Forest. This is a
good spot for those wishing to test out four-

wheel-drive vehicles, with an intricate set of Forest Service roads available to the east. To explore that area, a map of Stanislaus National Forest is essential.

Campsites, facilities: There are 19 sites for tents or RVs up to 22 feet (no hookups). Picnic tables and fire grills are provided. Drinking water and vault toilets are available. Some facilities are wheelchair accessible. Leashed pets are permitted.

Reservations, fees: Reservations are not accepted. Sites are $5 per night. Open May through October, weather permitting.

Directions: From Sonora, drive east on Highway 108 to Long Barn and the Long Barn Fire Station and a signed turnoff for the campground at Road 31/Forest Road 3N01. Turn right and drive 12 miles to the campground on the left side of the road.

Contact: Stanislaus National Forest, Mi-Wok Ranger District, 209/586-3234, www.fs.usda/stanislaus.

156 SUGAR PINE RV PARK
🚶 🏊 🐎 🎣 ♿ 🚐 ⛺

Scenic rating: 5

in Twain Harte

Map 6.2, page 354

Twain Harte is a beautiful little town, right at the edge of the snow line in winter, and right where pines take over the alpine landscape. This park is at the threshold of mountain country, with Pinecrest, Dodge Ridge, and Beardsley Reservoir nearby. It sits on 15 acres and features several walking paths. Note that only 17 of the RV sites are available for overnight campers; the other sites are rented as annual vacation leases. RVs and mobile homes are also for sale at the park.

Campsites, facilities: There are 78 sites with full hookups (20, 30, and 50 amps) for RVs up to 40 feet, 15 tent sites, and three park-model cabins. Picnic tables are provided. Restrooms with showers, cable TV, WiFi, playground, seasonal swimming pool, horseshoes, volleyball, badminton, tetherball, basketball, coin laundry, group facilities, and convenience store are available. Some facilities are wheelchair-accessible. Leashed pets are permitted.

Reservations, fees: Reservations are accepted. Sites are $28–42 per night, $1 per pet per night, $3.50 per night for each additional guest or vehicle. Some credit cards accepted. Open year-round.

Directions: From Sonora, drive east on Highway 108 for 17 miles to the park on the right side of the road, three miles east of Twain Harte.

Contact: Sugar Pine RV Park, 209/586-4631, www.sugarpinervpark.com.

157 KIT CARSON
🚶 🏊 🐎 🚐 ⛺

Scenic rating: 8

on the West Fork of the Carson River in Humboldt-Toiyabe National Forest

Map 6.3, page 355

This is one in a series of pristine, high-Sierra camps set along the West Fork of the Carson River. There's good trout fishing, thanks to regular stocks from the Department of Fish and Game. This is no secret, however, and the area from the Highway 89 bridge on downstream gets a lot of fishing pressure. The elevation is 6,900 feet.

Campsites, facilities: There are 10 sites for tents or RVs up to 22 feet (no hookups). Picnic tables and fire grills are provided. Drinking water and vault toilets are available. Leashed pets are permitted.

Reservations, fees: Reservations are not accepted. Sites are $16 per night, $6 per night for extra vehicle. Open late-May through mid-September, weather permitting.

Directions: From Sacramento, drive east on U.S. 50 to the junction with Highway 89. Turn south on Highway 89 and drive over Luther Pass to the junction with Highway 88. Turn left and drive a mile to the campground on the left side of the road.

From Jackson, drive east on Highway 88 over Carson Pass and to the junction with Highway 89 and then continue for a mile to the campground on the left side of the road.

Contact: Humboldt-Toiyabe National Forest, Carson Ranger District, 775/882-2766, www. fs.usda/htnf.

158 CRYSTAL SPRINGS

🚶 🏊 🐕 ♿ 🚐 ⛺

Scenic rating: 8

on the West Fork of the Carson River in Humboldt-Toiyabe National Forest

Map 6.3, page 355

For many people, this camp is an ideal choice. It is set at an elevation of 6,000 feet, right alongside the West Fork of the Carson River. This stretch of water is stocked with trout by the Department of Fish and Game. Crystal Springs is easy to reach, just off Highway 88, and supplies can be obtained in nearby Woodfords or Markleeville. Grover Hot Springs State Park makes a good side-trip destination.

Campsites, facilities: There are 19 sites for tents or RVs up to 22 feet (no hookups). Picnic tables and fire grills are provided. Drinking water and vault toilets are available. Some facilities are wheelchair-accessible. Leashed pets are permitted.

Reservations, fees: Reservations are not accepted. Sites are $16 per night, $6 per night for extra vehicle. Open late April to early October, weather permitting.

Directions: From Sacramento, drive east on U.S. 50 to the junction with Highway 89. Turn south on Highway 89 and drive over Luther Pass to the junction with Highway 88. Turn left (east) and drive 4.5 miles to the campground on the right side of the road.

From Jackson, drive east on Highway 88 over Carson Pass to the junction with Highway 89 and continue for 4.5 miles to the campground on the right side of the road.

Contact: Humboldt-Toiyabe National Forest, Carson Ranger District, 775/882-2766, www. fs.usda/htnf.

159 INDIAN CREEK RECREATION AREA

🚶 🏊 🛶 🏕 🚣 🐕 ♿ 🚐 ⛺

Scenic rating: 10

near Indian Creek Reservoir and Markleeville

Map 6.3, page 355

This beautiful campground is set amid sparse pines near Indian Creek Reservoir, elevation 5,600 feet. The campground is popular and often fills to capacity. This is an excellent lake for trout fishing, and the nearby Carson River is managed as a trophy trout fishery. The lake covers 160 acres, with a maximum speed for boats on the lake set at 5 mph. Sailing, sailboarding, and swimming are allowed. There are several good hikes in the vicinity as well. The best is a short trek, a one-mile climb to Summit Lake, with scenic views of the Indian Creek area. Summers are dry and warm here, with high temperatures typically in the 80s, and nights cool and comfortable. (There is little shade in the summer at the group site.) Bears provide an occasional visit. The lake freezes over in winter. It is about 35 miles to Carson City, Nevada, and two miles to Markleeville.

Campsites, facilities: There are 19 sites for tents or RVs up to 30 feet (no hookups), 10 walk-in sites for tents only, and a group tent site for up to 40 people. Picnic tables and fire grills are provided. Drinking water, restrooms with flush toilets and showers, and a dump station are available. A boat ramp is nearby. Some facilities are wheelchair-accessible. Leashed pets are permitted.

Reservations, fees: Reservations are not accepted for individual sites but are required for the group tent site at 775/885-6000. Single sites are $20 per night, double sites are $32 per night, $14 per night for walk-in sites, $50 per night for group site. Open late April through mid-November, weather permitting.

Directions: From Sacramento, drive east on U.S. 50 over Echo Summit to Meyers and Highway 89. Turn south on Highway 89 and drive to Highway 88. Turn left (east) on Highway 88/89 and drive six miles to Woodfords and Highway 89. Turn right (south) on Highway 89 and drive about four miles to Airport Road. Turn left on Airport Road and drive four miles to Indian Creek Reservoir. At the fork, bear left and drive to the campground on the west side of the lake.

From Markleeville, drive north on Highway 89 for about four miles to Airport Road. Turn right on Airport Road and drive about four miles to Indian Creek Reservoir. At the fork, bear left and drive to the campground on the west side of the lake.

Contact: Bureau of Land Management, Carson City Field Office, 775/885-6000, www.blm.gov/nv.

160 HOPE VALLEY

Scenic rating: 7

near the Carson River in
Humboldt-Toiyabe National Forest

Map 6.3, page 355

The West Fork of the Carson River runs right through Hope Valley, a pretty trout stream with a choice of four streamside campgrounds. Trout stocks are made near the campgrounds during summer. The campground at Hope Valley is just east of Carson Pass, at 7,300 feet elevation, in a very pretty area. A trailhead for the Pacific Crest Trail is three miles south of the campground. The primary nearby destination is Blue Lakes, about a 10-minute drive away. Insider's note: Little Tamarack Lake, set just beyond the turnoff for Lower Blue Lake, is excellent for swimming.

Campsites, facilities: There are 15 single sites for tents or RVs up to 22 feet and six group sites that can accommodate up to 12 people each. No hookups. Picnic tables and fire grills are provided. Drinking water and vault toilets

are available. Some facilities are wheelchair accessible. Leashed pets are permitted.

Reservations, fees: Reservations are accepted for individual sites and are required for the group site at 877/444-6777 or www.recreation.gov ($9 reservation fee). Sites are $16 per night, $32 per night for group sites, $6 per night for extra vehicle. Open June through September.

Directions: From Sacramento, drive east on U.S. 50 to the junction with Highway 89. Turn south on Highway 89 and drive over Luther Pass to the junction with Highway 88. Turn right (west) and drive two miles to Blue Lakes Road. Turn left (south) and drive 1.5 miles to the campground on the right side of the road.

From Jackson, drive east on Highway 88 over Carson Pass and continue east for five miles to Blue Lakes Road. Turn right (south) and drive 1.5 miles to the campground on the right side of the road.

Contact: Humboldt-Toiyabe National Forest, Carson Ranger District, 775/882-2766, www.fs.usda/htnf.

161 TURTLE ROCK PARK

Scenic rating: 5

near Woodfords

Map 6.3, page 355

Because it is administered at the county level, this pretty, wooded campground, set at 6,000 feet elevation, gets missed by a lot of folks. Most vacationers want the more pristine beauty of the nearby camps along the Carson River. But it doesn't get missed by mountain bikers, who travel here every July for the "Death Ride," a wild ride over several mountain passes. The camp always fills for this event. (If it snows, it closes, so call ahead if you're planning an autumn visit.) Nearby side trips include Grover Hot Springs and the hot springs in Markleeville.

Campsites, facilities: There are 26 sites for trailers or RVs up to 34 feet (no hookups) and 12 tent sites. Picnic tables and fire grills are provided. Drinking water, flush toilets, and showers are available. A camp host is on-site. A recreation building is available for rent; tennis and basketball courts, a disc golf course, and horseshoe pits are available. Coin laundry, groceries, and propane gas are available within two miles. Some facilities are wheelchair-accessible. Leashed pets are permitted.

Reservations, fees: Reservations are not accepted. Tent sites are $10 per night, drive-in sites are $15 per night, $3 per night for each additional vehicle. Monthly and senior rates are available. Open May through mid-October, weather permitting.

Directions: From Sacramento, drive east on U.S. 50 to the junction with Highway 89. Turn south on Highway 89 and drive over Luther Pass to the junction with Highway 88. Turn left (east) and drive to Woodfords and the junction with Highway 89. Turn south on Highway 89 and drive 4.5 miles to the park entrance on the right side of the road.

Contact: Alpine County Public Works, 530/694-2140, www.alpinecountyca.gov.

162 GROVER HOT SPRINGS STATE PARK

Scenic rating: 8

near Markleeville

Map 6.3, page 355

This is a famous spot for folks who like the rejuvenating powers of hot springs. Some say they feel a glow about them for weeks after soaking here. When touring the South Tahoe/Carson Pass area, many vacationers take part of a day to make the trip to the hot springs. This park is set in alpine meadow at 5,900 feet elevation on the east side of the Sierra at the edge of the Great Basin, and surrounded by peaks that top 10,000 feet. The hot springs are green because of the mineral deposits at the bottom of the pools. The landscape is primarily pine forest and sagebrush. It is well known for the great fluctuations in weather,

from serious blizzards to intense, dry heat, and from mild nights to awesome rim-rattling thunderstorms. High winds are occasional but legendary. During thunderstorms, the hot springs pools close because of the chance of lightning strikes. Yet they remain open in snow, even blizzards, when it can be a euphoric experience to sit in the steaming water. Note that the pools are closed for maintenance for two weeks in September. A 2.4-mile round-trip hike starts from the campground and continues to a series of small waterfalls. Side-trip options include a nature trail in the park and driving to the Carson River (where the water is a mite cooler) and fishing for trout.

Campsites, facilities: There are 26 sites for tents, and 50 sites for tents or RVs up to 27 feet (no hookups) and trailers up to 24 feet. Picnic tables, fire grills, and food lockers are provided. Restrooms with flush toilets and coin showers (summer only), drinking water, hot springs pool with wheelchair access, and heated swimming pool are available. A visitor center is opposite the campground entrance. A grocery store is four miles away, and a coin laundry is within 10 miles. Leashed pets are permitted.

Reservations, fees: Reservations are accepted at 800/444-7275 (800/444-PARK) or www.reserveamerica.com ($8 reservation fee). Sites are $35 per night, $8 per night for each additional vehicle, pool fees are $5–7 per person per day. Open year-round, with reduced facilities in winter.

Directions: From Sacramento, drive east on U.S. 50 to the junction with Highway 89. Turn south on Highway 89 and drive over Luther Pass to the junction with Highway 88. Turn left and drive to Woodfords and the junction with Highway 89. Turn right (south) and drive six miles to Markleeville and the junction with Hot Springs Road. Turn right and drive four miles to the park entrance.

Contact: Grover Hot Springs State Park, 530/694-2248; Sierra District, 530/525-7232, www.parks.ca.gov; pool information, 530/525-7232.

163 MARKLEEVILLE

Scenic rating: 7

on Markleeville Creek in
Humboldt-Toiyabe National Forest

Map 6.3, page 355

This is a pretty, streamside camp set at 5,500 feet along Markleeville Creek, a mile from the East Fork of the Carson River. The trout here are willing, but alas, are dinkers. This area is the transition zone where high mountains to the west give way to the high desert to the east. The hot springs in Markleeville and Grover Hot Springs State Park provide good side trips.

Campsites, facilities: There are 10 sites for tents or RVs up to 24 feet (no hookups). Trailers are not recommended because of road conditions. Picnic tables and fire grills are provided. Drinking water and vault toilets are available. A grocery store and restaurant are nearby. Leashed pets are permitted.

Reservations, fees: Reservations are not accepted. Sites are $16 per night, $6 per night for extra vehicle. Open late April through September, weather permitting.

Directions: From Sacramento, drive east on U.S. 50 to the junction with Highway 89. Turn south on Highway 89 and drive over Luther Pass to the junction with Highway 88. Turn left and drive to Woodfords and the junction with Highway 89. Turn south, drive six miles to Markleeville, and continue for 0.5 mile to the campground on the left side of the highway.

Contact: Humboldt-Toiyabe National Forest, Carson Ranger District, 775/882-2766, www.fs.usda/htnf.

164 TOPAZ LAKE RV PARK

Scenic rating: 6

on Topaz Lake, near Markleeville

Map 6.3, page 355

Topaz Lake, set at 5,000 feet elevation, is one of the hidden surprises for California anglers. The surprise is the size of the rainbow trout, with one of the highest rates of 15- to 18-inch trout of any lake in the mountain country. All water sports are allowed on this 2,400-acre lake, and there is a swimming area. The campground itself is attractive, with a number of shade trees. The setting is on the edge of barren high desert, which also serves as the border between California and Nevada. Wind is a problem for small boats, especially in the early summer. Some of the sites here are rented for the entire season.

Campsites, facilities: There are 50 sites with full hookups (30 amps) for RVs up to 42 feet. Some sites are pull-through. Tents are allowed with RVs only, though tent-only sites are allowed during non-peak season. Picnic tables and cable TV are provided. Restrooms with coin showers, coin laundry, propane gas, small grocery store, fish-cleaning station, horseshoe pit, and Wi-Fi are available. A 40-boat marina with courtesy launch and boat-trailer storage is available at lakeside. Some facilities are wheelchair-accessible. Leashed pets are permitted.

Reservations, fees: Reservations are recommended. RV sites (full hookups) are $35 per night, $3.50 per person for more than two people. Discounts available. Monthly rates available. Some credit cards accepted. Open March through early October, weather permitting.

Directions: From Carson City, drive south on U.S. 395 for 45 miles to Topaz Lake and the campground on the left side of the road.

From Bridgeport, drive north on U.S. 395 for 45 miles to the campground on the right side of the road (0.3 mile south of the California/Nevada border).

Contact: Topaz Lake RV Park, 530/495-2357, www.topazlakervpark.com.

165 UPPER BLUE LAKE DAM AND EXPANSION

🚶‍♂️ 🏊 🛶 🚤 🚣 🐕 🚗 ⛺

Scenic rating: 7

near Carson Pass

Map 6.3, page 355

These two camps are set across the road from each other along Upper Blue Lake, and are two of five camps in the area. The trout fishing is usually quite good here in early summer. (See the Lower Blue Lake listing in this chapter for more information.) These camps are three miles past the Lower Blue Lake campground. The elevation is 8,400 feet.

Campsites, facilities: There are 10 sites at Upper Blue Lake Dam and 15 sites at the expansion area for tents or RVs up to 25 feet. Picnic tables and fire grills are provided at Upper Blue Lake Dam only. Drinking water and vault toilets are available. Leashed pets are permitted.

Reservations, fees: Reservations are not accepted. Sites are $23 per night, $3 per night for each additional vehicle, $1 per pet per night. Open June through mid-September, weather permitting.

Directions: From Sacramento, drive east on U.S. 50 to the junction with Highway 89. Turn south on Highway 89 and drive over Luther Pass to the junction with Highway 88. Turn right and drive 2.5 miles to Blue Lakes Road. Turn left and drive 12 miles to the junction at the south end of Lower Blue Lake. Turn right and drive three miles to the Upper Blue Lake Dam campground on the left side of the road or the expansion area on the right.

From Jackson, drive east on Highway 88 over Carson Pass and continue east for five miles to Blue Lakes Road. Turn right (south) and drive 12 miles to a junction at the south end of Lower Blue Lake. Turn right and drive three miles to the Upper Blue Lake Dam campground on the left side of the road or the expansion area on the right.

Contact: PG&E Land Projects, 916/386-5164, www.pge.com/recreation.

166 MIDDLE CREEK AND EXPANSION

🚶‍♂️ 🛶 🐕 ♿ 🚗 ⛺

Scenic rating: 7

near Carson Pass and Blue Lakes

Map 6.3, page 355

This tiny, captivating spot, set along the creek that connects Upper and Lower Blue Lakes, provides a take-your-pick deal for anglers. PG&E has expanded this facility and now offers a larger camping area about 200 yards from the original campground. (See the Lower Blue Lake listing in this chapter for more information.) The elevation is 8,200 feet.

Campsites, facilities: There are five sites for tents or RVs up to 30 feet at Middle Creek and 35 sites for tents or RVs up to 45 feet at the expansion area. No hookups. Picnic tables and fire grills are provided. Drinking water and vault toilets are available at the expansion area. Some facilities are wheelchair-accessible. Leashed pets are permitted.

Reservations, fees: Reservations are not accepted. Sites are $23 per night, $3 per night for each additional vehicle, $1 per pet per night. Open late May to mid-October, weather permitting.

Directions: From Sacramento, drive east on U.S. 50 to the junction with Highway 89. Turn south on Highway 89 and drive over Luther Pass to the junction with Highway 88. Turn right and drive 2.5 miles to Blue Lakes Road. Turn left and drive 12 miles to a junction at the south end of Lower Blue Lake. Turn right and drive 1.5 miles to the Middle Creek campground on the left side of the road and continue another 200 yards to reach the expansion area.

From Jackson, drive east on Highway 88 over Carson Pass and continue east for five miles to Blue Lakes Road. Turn right (south) and drive 12 miles (road becomes dirt) to a junction at the south end of Lower Blue Lake. Turn right and drive 1.5 miles to the Middle Creek campground on the left side of the road and continue another 200 yards to reach the expansion area.

Contact: PG&E Land Projects, 916/386-5164, www.pge.com/recreation.

167 LOWER BLUE LAKE

🧍🏊🚴🚤🐕🚙🏕️

Scenic rating: 7

near Carson Pass

Map 6.3, page 355

This is the high country, at 8,400 feet, where the terrain is stark and steep and edged by volcanic ridgelines, and where the deep blue-green hue of lake water brightens the land-scape. Lower Blue Lake provides a popular trout fishery, with rainbow, brook, and cut-throat trout all stocked regularly. The boat ramp is adjacent to the campground. The access road crosses the Pacific Crest Trail, providing a route to a series of small, pretty, hike-to lakes just outside the edge of the Mokelumne Wilderness.

Campsites, facilities: There are 16 sites for tents or RVs up to 25 feet (no hookups). Picnic tables and fire grills are provided. Drinking water and vault toilets are available. Leashed pets are permitted.

Reservations, fees: Reservations are not accepted. Sites are $23 per night, $3 per night for each additional vehicle, $1 per pet per night, 14-day occupancy limit. Open June through September, weather permitting.

Directions: From Sacramento, drive east on U.S. 50 to the junction with Highway 89. Turn south on Highway 89 and drive over Luther Pass to the junction with Highway 88. Turn right and drive 2.5 miles to Blue Lakes Road. Turn left and drive 12 miles to a junction at the south end of Lower Blue Lake. Turn right and drive a short distance to the campground on the left side of the road.

From Jackson, drive east on Highway 88 over Carson Pass and continue east for five miles to Blue Lakes Road. Turn right (south) and drive 12 miles to a junction at the south end of Lower Blue Lake. Turn right and drive

a short distance to the campground on the left.

Contact: PG&E Land Projects, 916/386-5164, www.pge.com/recreation.

168 SILVER CREEK

🏊🐕🚙🏕️

Scenic rating: 6

in Humboldt-Toiyabe National Forest

Map 6.3, page 355

This pretty spot, set near Silver Creek, has easy access from Highway 4 and, in years without washouts, good fishing in early summer for small trout. It is in the remote high Sierra, east of Ebbetts Pass. A side trip to Ebbetts Pass features Kinney Lake, Pacific Crest Trail access, and a trailhead at the north end of the lake (on the west side of Highway 4) for a mile hike to Lower Kinney Lake. No bikes are permitted on the trails. The elevation is 6,800 feet.

Campsites, facilities: There are 21 sites for tents or RVs up to 22 feet (no hookups). Picnic tables and fire grills are provided. Drinking water and vault toilets are available. Leashed pets are permitted.

Reservations, fees: Reservations are accepted at 877/444-6777 or www.recreation. gov ($9 reservation fee). Sites are $14–17 per night, $6 per night for extra vehicle. Open late May through early September, weather permitting.

Directions: From Angels Camp, drive east on Highway 4 all the way over Ebbetts Pass and continue for about six miles to the campground.

From Markleeville, drive south on Highway 89 to the junction with Highway 4. Turn west on Highway 4 (steep and winding) and drive about five miles to the campground.

Contact: Humboldt-Toiyabe National Forest, Carson Ranger District, 775/882-2766, www.fs.usda/htnf.

169 MOSQUITO LAKE

🥾 🏊 🛶 🐎 🚙 ⛺

Scenic rating: 10

at Mosquito Lake in Stanislaus National Forest

Map 6.3, page 355

Mosquito Lake is in a pristine Sierra setting at 8,260 feet elevation, presenting remarkable beauty for a place that can be reached by car. Most people believe that Mosquito Lake is for day-use only, and that's why they crowd into nearby Lake Alpine Campground. But it's not just for day-use, and this camp is often overlooked because it is about a mile west of the little lake. The lake is small, a pretty emerald green, and even has a few small trout in it. The camp provides a few dispersed sites.

Campsites, facilities: There are 11 sites for tents or RVs up to 16 feet (no hookups). Picnic tables and fire grills are provided. Vault toilets are available. No drinking water is available. Garbage must be packed out. Leashed pets are permitted.

Reservations, fees: Reservations are not accepted. Sites are $5 per night. A free campfire permit is required from the district office. Open June through September, weather permitting.

Directions: From Angels Camp, drive east on Highway 4 to Lake Alpine and continue for about six miles to the campground on the left side of the road.

Contact: Stanislaus National Forest, Calaveras Ranger District, 209/795-1381, www.fs.usda.gov/stanislaus.

170 HERMIT VALLEY

🥾 🛶 🐎 🚙 ⛺

Scenic rating: 8

in Stanislaus National Forest

Map 6.3, page 355

This tiny, remote, little-known spot is set near the border of the Mokelumne Wilderness near where Grouse Creek enters the Mokelumne River, at 7,100 feet elevation. Looking north, there is a good view into Deer Valley. A primitive road, 0.5-mile west of camp, is routed through Deer Valley north for six miles to the Blue Lakes. On the opposite (south) side of the road from the camp there is a little-traveled hiking trail that is routed up Grouse Creek to Beaver Meadow and Willow Meadow near the border of the Carson-Iceberg Wilderness.

Campsites, facilities: There are 25 sites for tents or RVs of any length (no hookups). Vault toilets are available. No drinking water is available. Garbage must be packed out. Leashed pets are permitted.

Reservations, fees: Reservations are not accepted. There is no fee for camping. A free campfire permit is required from the district office. Open June through October, weather permitting.

Directions: From Angels Camp, drive east on Highway 4 to Lake Alpine and continue for about nine miles to the campground on the left side of the road (just east of the Mokelumne River Bridge). Note: Trailers are not recommended because of the steep access road.

Contact: Stanislaus National Forest, Calaveras Ranger District, 209/795-1381, www.fs.usda.gov/stanislaus.

171 BLOOMFIELD

🥾 🛶 🐎 5% 🚙 ⛺

Scenic rating: 7

in Stanislaus National Forest

Map 6.3, page 355

This is a primitive and little-known camp set at 7,800 feet elevation near Ebbetts Pass. The North Fork Mokelumne River runs right by the camp, with good stream access for about a mile on each side of the camp. The access road continues south to Highland Lakes, a destination that provides car-top boating, fair fishing, and trailheads for hiking into the Carson-Iceberg Wilderness.

Campsites, facilities: There are 20 sites for tents or RVs up to 16 feet (no hookups). Picnic tables and fire rings are provided. Drinking water and vault toilets are available. Garbage must be packed out. Facilities and supplies are available at Lake Alpine Lodge, 25 minutes away. Leashed pets are permitted.

Reservations, fees: Reservations are not accepted. Sites are $8 per night. A free campfire permit is required from the district office. Open June through October, weather permitting.

Directions: From Angels Camp, drive east on Highway 4 to Lake Alpine and continue for about 15 miles to Forest Road 8N01 on the right side of the road (1.5 miles west of Ebbetts Pass). Turn right and drive two miles to the campground on the right side of the road. Note: Access roads are rough and not recommended for trailers.

Contact: Stanislaus National Forest, Calaveras Ranger District, 209/795-1381, www.fs.usda. gov/stanislaus.

172 PACIFIC VALLEY
🥾 🐕 🚐 ⛺

Scenic rating: 7

in Stanislaus National Forest
overlooking Pacific Creek

Map 6.3, page 355

This is a do-it-yourself special; that is, more of a general area for camping than a campground, set up for backpackers heading out on expeditions into the Carson-Iceberg Wilderness to the south. It is set at 7,600 feet elevation along Pacific Creek, a tributary to the Mokelumne River. The landscape is an open lodgepole forest with nearby meadow and a small stream. The trail from camp is routed south and reaches three forks within two miles. The best is routed deep into the wilderness, flanking Hiram Peak (9,760 feet), Airola Peak (9,938 feet), and Iceberg Peak (9,720 feet).

Campsites, facilities: There are 15 sites for tents or RVs up to 16 feet (no hookups). Picnic tables and fire grills are provided. Vault toilets are available. There is no drinking water.

Equestrians with horse trailers may camp at the southern end of the campground, near the trailhead. Garbage must be packed out. Leashed pets are permitted.

Reservations, fees: Reservations are not accepted. There is no fee for camping. A free campfire permit is required from the district office. Open June through October, weather permitting.

Directions: From Angels Camp, drive east on Highway 4 to Lake Alpine and continue for eight miles to a dirt road. Turn right (south) and drive about 0.5 mile to the campground. Note: Trailers are not recommended because of the rough roads.

Contact: Stanislaus National Forest, Calaveras Ranger District, 209/795-1381, www.fs.usda. gov/stanislaus.

173 UPPER AND LOWER HIGHLAND LAKES
🥾 🏊 🚤 🛶 🎣 🐕 ♿ 🚐 ⛺

Scenic rating: 9

in Stanislaus National Forest

Map 6.3, page 355

This camp is set between Upper and Lower Highland Lakes, two beautiful alpine ponds that offer good fishing for small brook trout as well as spectacular panoramic views. The boat speed limit is 15 mph, and a primitive boat ramp is at Upper Highland Lake. Swimming is allowed, although the water is very cold. The elevation at this campground is 8,600 feet, with Hiram Peak (9,760 feet) looming to the nearby south. Several great trails are available from this camp. Day hikes include up Boulder Creek and Disaster Creek. For overnight backpacking, a trail that starts at the north end of Highland Lakes (a parking area is available) is routed east for two miles to Wolf Creek Pass, where it connects with the Pacific Crest Trail; from there, turn left or right—you can't lose. The access road is not recommended for trailers or large RVs.

Campsites, facilities: There are 35 sites for

tents or RVs up to 16 feet (no hookups). Picnic tables and fire grills are provided. Drinking water and vault toilets are available. Garbage must be packed out. Some facilities are wheelchair accessible. Leashed pets are permitted.

Reservations, fees: Reservations are not accepted. Sites are $8 per night. Open July through September, weather permitting.

Directions: From Angels Camp, drive east on Highway 4 to Arnold, past Lake Alpine, and continue for 14.5 miles to Forest Road 8N01 (one mile west of Ebbetts Pass). Turn right and drive 7.5 miles to the campground on the right side of the road. Note: The roads are rough and trailers are not recommended.

Contact: Stanislaus National Forest, Calaveras Ranger District, 209/795-1381, www.fs.usda.gov/stanislaus.

174 LODGEPOLE GROUP LAKE ALPINE

Scenic rating: 6

near Lake Alpine in Stanislaus National Forest

Map 6.3, page 355

What to do when all the campgrounds at Lake Alpine are full? Gather together your friends and family and head to this group site just two miles west of the lake. Set in an undeveloped plain at 7,290 feet, the camp is large, flat, and open; but with Lake Alpine so close, there are plenty of opportunities for hiking, fishing, and boating.

Campsites, facilities: There are two group sites for up to 50 people each with tents or RVs (no hookups). Picnic tables and fire grills are provided. Drinking water and vault toilets are available. A grocery store, restaurant, coin showers, and a coin laundry are nearby. Some facilities are wheelchair accessible. Leashed pets are permitted.

Reservations, fees: Reservations are required at 877/444-6777 or www.recreation.gov ($9 reservation fee) and must be made at least four days in advance. Sites are $73–80 per night. Open mid-June through early September, weather permitting.

Directions: From Angels Camp, drive east on Highway 4 for 50 miles to Lake Alpine. Lodgepole Group is two miles west of Lake Alpine, near Bear Valley.

Contact: Stanislaus National Forest, Calaveras Ranger District, 209/795-1381, www.fs.usda.gov/stanislaus.

175 SILVERTIP

Scenic rating: 6

near Lake Alpine in Stanislaus National Forest

Map 6.3, page 355

This camp is just over 0.5 mile from the shore of Lake Alpine at an elevation of 7,350 feet. Why then would anyone camp here when there are campgrounds right at the lake? Two reasons: One, those lakeside camps are often full on summer weekends. Two, Highway 4 is snowplowed to this campground entrance, but not beyond. So in big snow years when the road is still closed in late spring and early summer, you can park your rig here to camp, then hike in to the lake. In the fall, it also makes for a base camp for hunters. (See the Lake Alpine Campground listing in this chapter for more information.)

Campsites, facilities: There are 23 sites for tents or RVs up to 27 feet (no hookups). Picnic tables and fire grills are provided. Drinking water and restrooms with flush toilets are available. A boat launch is about a mile away. A grocery store, coin laundry, and coin showers are nearby. Some facilities are wheelchair-accessible. Leashed pets are permitted.

Reservations, fees: Reservations are not accepted. Sites are $22 per night. Open June through early October, weather permitting.

Directions: From Angels Camp, drive east on Highway 4 to Arnold and continue for 29 miles to Lake Alpine. A mile before reaching the lake (adjacent to the Bear Valley/Mount

Reba turnoff), turn right at the campground entrance on the right side of the road.

Contact: Stanislaus National Forest, Calaveras Ranger District, 209/795-1381, www.fs.usda.gov/stanislaus.

176 LAKE ALPINE CAMPGROUND

Scenic rating: 8

on Lake Alpine in Stanislaus National Forest

Map 6.3, page 355   **BEST (**

Lake Alpine is one of the prettiest lakes you can drive to, set at 7,303 feet elevation amid pines and Sierra granite. This is the campground that is in the greatest demand at Lake Alpine, and it is easy to see why. It is very small, a boat ramp is adjacent to the camp, you can get supplies at a small grocery store within walking distance, and during the evening rise you can often see the jumping trout from your campsite. A trailhead out of nearby Silver Valley Camp provides a two-mile hike to pretty Duck Lake and beyond into the Carson-Iceberg Wilderness.

Campsites, facilities: There are 25 sites for tents or RVs up to 27 feet (no hookups). Picnic tables and fire grills are provided. Drinking water, restrooms with flush toilets, and a boat launch are available. A grocery store, restaurant, coin showers, and a coin laundry are nearby. Some facilities are wheelchair-accessible. Leashed pets are permitted.

Reservations, fees: Reservations are not accepted. Sites are $22 per night. Open June through October, weather permitting.

Directions: From Angels Camp, drive east on Highway 4 to Arnold and continue east for 29 miles to Lake Alpine. Just before reaching the lake turn right and drive 0.25 mile to the campground on the left.

Contact: Stanislaus National Forest, Calaveras Ranger District, 209/795-1381, www.fs.usda.gov/stanislaus.

177 PINE MARTEN

Scenic rating: 8

near Lake Alpine in Stanislaus National Forest

Map 6.3, page 355

Lake Alpine is a beautiful Sierra lake surrounded by granite and pines and set at 7,320 feet, just above where the snowplows stop in winter. This camp is on the northeast side, about a quarter mile from the shore. Fishing for rainbow trout is good in May and early June, before the summer crush. Despite the long drive to get here, the lake is becoming better known for its beauty, camping, and hiking. Lake Alpine has 180 surface acres and a 10-mph speed limit. A trailhead out of nearby Silver Valley Camp provides a two-mile hike to pretty Duck Lake and beyond into the Carson-Iceberg Wilderness.

Campsites, facilities: There are 30 sites for tents or RVs up to 27 feet (no hookups). Picnic tables and fire grills are provided. Drinking water and flush are available. A boat ramp is nearby. A grocery store, propane gas, and coin laundry are nearby. Some facilities are wheelchair-accessible. Leashed pets are permitted.

Reservations, fees: Reservations are not accepted. Sites are $22 per night. Open June through early October, weather permitting.

Directions: From Angels Camp, drive east on Highway 4 to Arnold and continue east for 29 miles to Lake Alpine. Drive to the northeast end of the lake to the campground entrance on the right side of the road.

Contact: Stanislaus National Forest, Calaveras Ranger District, 209/795-1381, www.fs.usda.gov/stanislaus.

178 SILVER VALLEY

Scenic rating: 8

on Lake Alpine in Stanislaus National Forest

Map 6.3, page 355

This is one of four camps at Lake Alpine. Silver Valley is on the northeast end of the lake at 7,400 feet elevation, with a trailhead nearby that provides access to the Carson-Iceberg Wilderness. (For recreation information, see the Pine Marten listing in this chapter.)

Campsites, facilities: There are 20 sites for tents or RVs up to 16 feet (no hookups). Picnic tables and fire grills are provided. Drinking water and restrooms with flush toilets are available. Some facilities are wheelchair-accessible. A boat launch, grocery store, and coin laundry are nearby. Leashed pets are permitted.

Reservations, fees: Reservations are not accepted. Sites are $22 per night. A free campfire permit is required. Open June through October, weather permitting.

Directions: From Angels Camp, drive east on Highway 4 to Arnold and continue east for 29 miles to Lake Alpine. Drive to the northeast end of the lake to the campground entrance on the right side of the road. Turn right and drive 0.5 mile to the campground.

Contact: Stanislaus National Forest, Calaveras Ranger District, 209/795-1381, www.fs.usda. gov/stanislaus.

179 UNION RESERVOIR WALK-IN

Scenic rating: 10

northeast of Arnold in
Stanislaus National Forest

Map 6.3, page 355

Union Reservoir is set in Sierra granite at 6,850 feet. It's a beautiful and quiet lake that is kept that way with rules that mandate a 5-mph speed limit and walk-in camping only. Most of the sites provide lakeside views. Fishing is often good—trolling for kokanee salmon—but you need a boat. The setting is great, especially for canoes or other small boats. This camp was once a secret, but now it fills up quickly on weekends.

Campsites, facilities: There are 15 dispersed, primitive walk-in tent sites. Vault toilets are available. No drinking water is available.

Garbage must be packed out. A boat ramp is nearby. Leashed pets are permitted.

Reservations, fees: Reservations are not accepted. There is no fee for camping. Open June through September, weather permitting.

Directions: From Angels Camp, drive east on Highway 4 for about 32 miles to Spicer Reservoir Road. Turn right and drive east for about seven miles to Forest Road 7N75. Turn left and drive three miles to Union Reservoir. There are four designated parking areas for the walk-in camps along the road.

Contact: Stanislaus National Forest, Calaveras Ranger District, 209/795-1381, www.fs.usda. gov/stanislaus.

180 SPICER RESERVOIR AND GROUP CAMP

Scenic rating: 8

near Spicer Reservoir in
Stanislaus National Forest

Map 6.3, page 355

Set at 6,200 feet elevation and covering only 227 acres, Spicer Reservoir isn't big by reservoir standards, but it is surrounded by canyon walls and is quite pretty from a boat. Good trout fishing adds to the beauty. A boat ramp is available near the campground, and the lake speed limit is 10 mph. A trail links the east end of Spicer Reservoir to the Summit Lake trailhead, with the route bordering the north side of the reservoir. Note: This area can really get hammered with snow in big winters, so always check for access conditions in the spring and early summer before planning a trip.

Campsites, facilities: There are 60 sites for tents or RVs up to 50 feet (no hookups). There is also one group site for tents or RVs up to 28 feet (no hookups) that can accommodate up to 60 people. Picnic tables and fire grills are provided. Drinking water and vault toilets, group facilities, and a primitive amphitheater are available. A boat ramp is nearby. Some facilities are wheelchair-accessible. Leashed pets are permitted.

Reservations, fees: Reservations are not accepted for individual sites, but are required for the group site at 209/296-8895. Sites are $22 per night, the group site is $140 per night. Open June through October, weather permitting.

Directions: From Angels Camp, drive east on Highway 4 for about 32 miles to Spicer Reservoir Road/Forest Road 7N01. Turn right, drive seven miles, bear right at a fork with a sharp right turn, and drive a mile to the campground at the west end of the lake.

Contact: Stanislaus National Forest, Calaveras Ranger District, 209/795-1381, www.fs.usda.gov/stanislaus.

181 SAND FLAT-STANISLAUS RIVER

Scenic rating: 7

on the Clark Fork of the Stanislaus River in Stanislaus National Forest

Map 6.3, page 355

Sand Flat campground, at 6,200 feet, is only three miles (by vehicle on Clark Fork Road) from an outstanding trailhead for the Carson-Iceberg Wilderness. The camp is used primarily by late-arriving backpackers who camp for the night, get their gear in order, then head off on the trail. The trail is routed out of Iceberg Meadow, with a choice of heading north to Paradise Valley (unbelievably green and loaded with corn lilies along a creek) and onward to the Pacific Crest Trail, or east to Clark Fork and upstream to Clark Fork Meadow below Sonora Peak. Two choices, both winners.

Campsites, facilities: There are 68 sites for tents or RVs up to 22 feet (no hookups) and 15 walk-in tent sites. Picnic tables and fire grills are provided. Drinking water and vault toilets are available. You can buy supplies in Dardanelle. Some facilities are wheelchair-accessible. Leashed pets are permitted.

Reservations, fees: Reservations are not accepted. Sites are $17 per night per vehicle.

Open May through early October, weather permitting.

Directions: From Sonora, drive east on Highway 108 past the town of Strawberry to Clark Fork Road. Turn left on Clark Fork Road and drive six miles to the campground entrance on the right side of the road.

Contact: Stanislaus National Forest, Summit Ranger District, 209/965-3434, www.fs.usda.gov/stanislaus.

182 CLARK FORK AND CLARK FORK HORSE

Scenic rating: 8

on the Clark Fork of the Stanislaus River in Stanislaus National Forest

Map 6.3, page 355

Clark Fork borders the Clark Fork of the Stanislaus River and is used by both drive-in vacationers and backpackers. A trailhead for hikers is 0.25 mile away on the north side of Clark Fork Road (a parking area is available here). From here the trail is routed up along Arnot Creek, skirting between Iceberg Peak on the left and Lightning Mountain on the right, for eight miles to Wolf Creek Pass and the junction with the Pacific Crest Trail. (For another nearby trailhead, see the Sand Flat–Stanislaus River listing in this chapter.)

Campsites, facilities: There are 88 sites for tents or RVs up to 40 feet, and at an adjacent area, 14 equestrian sites for tents or RVs up to 22 feet. No hookups. Picnic tables and fire grills are provided. Drinking water, vault and flush toilets, accessible coin showers, and a dump station are available. At the equestrian site, no drinking water is available but there are water troughs. Supplies are available in Dardanelle. Some facilities are wheelchair-accessible. Leashed pets are permitted.

Reservations, fees: Reservations are not accepted. Single sites are $17–18 per night, double sites $34–36 per night, the horse camp is $15 per night, $5 per night for each additional vehicle. Open May through October, weather permitting.

Directions: From Sonora, drive east on Highway 108 past the town of Strawberry to Clark Fork Road. Turn left, drive five miles, turn right again, and drive 0.5 mile to the campground entrance on the right side of the road.

Contact: Stanislaus National Forest, Summit Ranger District, 209/965-3434, www.fs.usda. gov/stanislaus.

183 FENCE CREEK

Scenic rating: 4

near the Middle Fork of the Stanislaus River in Stanislaus National Forest

Map 6.3, page 355

Fence Creek is a feeder stream to Clark Fork, which runs a mile downstream and joins with the Middle Fork Stanislaus River en route to Donnells Reservoir. The camp sits along little Fence Creek, at 5,600 feet elevation. Fence Creek Road continues east for another nine miles to an outstanding trailhead at Iceberg Meadow on the edge of the Carson-Iceberg Wilderness.

Campsites, facilities: There are 37 sites for tents or RVs up to 22 feet (no hookups). Picnic tables and fire grills are provided. Vault toilets are available. No drinking water is available. Supplies are available in Pinecrest about 10 miles away. Some facilities are wheelchair accessible. Leashed pets are permitted.

Reservations, fees: Reservations are not accepted. Sites are $5 per night. Open May through mid-October, weather permitting.

Directions: From Sonora, drive east on Highway 108 about 50 miles to Clark Ford Road. Turn left and drive a mile to Forest Road 6N06. Turn left again and drive 0.5 mile to the campground on the right.

Contact: Stanislaus National Forest, Summit Ranger District, 209/965-3434, www.fs.usda. gov/stanislaus.

184 BOULDER FLAT

Scenic rating: 7

near the Middle Fork of the Stanislaus River in Stanislaus National Forest

Map 6.3, page 355

You want camping on the Stanislaus River? As you drive east on Highway 108, this is the first in a series of campgrounds along the Middle Fork Stanislaus. Boulder Flat is set at 5,600 feet elevation and offers easy access off the highway. Here's another bonus: This stretch of river is stocked with trout.

Campsites, facilities: There are 20 sites for tents or RVs up to 22 feet (no hookups). Picnic tables and fire grills are provided. Drinking water and vault toilets are available. You can buy supplies in Dardanelle. Some facilities are wheelchair-accessible. Leashed pets are permitted.

Reservations, fees: Reservations are not accepted. Sites are $16–18 per night, $5 per night for each additional vehicle. Open May through October, weather permitting.

Directions: From Sonora, drive east on Highway 108 past the town of Strawberry to Clark Fork Road. At Clark Fork Road, continue east on Highway 108 for a mile to the campground on the left side of the road.

Contact: Stanislaus National Forest, Summit Ranger District, 209/965-3434, www.fs.usda. gov/stanislaus; Dodge Ridge Corporation, 209/965-3116.

185 BRIGHTMAN FLAT

Scenic rating: 7

on the Middle Fork of the Stanislaus River in Stanislaus National Forest

Map 6.3, page 355

This camp is on the Middle Fork of the Stanislaus River at 5,700 feet elevation, a mile east of Boulder Flat and two miles west of

Dardanelle. (For recreation options, see the Pigeon Flat listing in this chapter.)

Campsites, facilities: There are 32 sites for tents or RVs up to 22 feet (no hookups). Picnic tables and fire grills are provided. Vault toilets are available. There is no drinking water, although untreated water may be available from the stream. You can buy supplies in Dardanelle. Some facilities are wheelchair-accessible. Leashed pets are permitted.

Reservations, fees: Reservations are not accepted. Sites are $13 per night, $5 per night for each additional vehicle. Open May through October, weather permitting.

Directions: From Sonora, drive east on Highway 108 past the town of Strawberry to Clark Fork Road. At Clark Fork Road continue east on Highway 108 for two miles to the campground entrance on the left side of the road.

Contact: Stanislaus National Forest, Summit Ranger District, 209/965-3434, www.fs.usda. gov/stanislaus; Dodge Ridge Corporation, 209/965-3116.

186 DARDANELLE

🥾 🏊 🐕 �t 🏕

Scenic rating: 7

on the Middle Fork of the Stanislaus River in Stanislaus National Forest

Map 6.3, page 355

This Forest Service camp is within walking distance of supplies in Dardanelle and is also right alongside the Middle Fork Stanislaus River. This section of river is stocked with trout by the Department of Fish and Game. The trail to see Columns of the Giants is just 1.5 miles to the east out of Pigeon Flat.

Campsites, facilities: There are 27 sites for tents or RVs up to 28 feet (no hookups). Picnic tables and fire grills are provided. Drinking water and vault toilets are available. You can buy supplies in Dardanelle. Leashed pets are permitted.

Reservations, fees: Reservations are not accepted. Sites are $18–22 per night, $5 per

night for each additional vehicle. Open May through October, weather permitting.

Directions: From Sonora, drive east on Highway 108 past Strawberry to Dardanelle and the campground on the left side of the road.

Contact: Stanislaus National Forest, Summit Ranger District, 209/965-3434, www.fs.usda. gov/stanislaus; Dodge Ridge Corporation, 209/965-3116.

187 PIGEON FLAT

🥾 🏊 🐕 🏕

Scenic rating: 7

on the Middle Fork of the Stanislaus River in Stanislaus National Forest

Map 6.3, page 355

The prime attraction at Pigeon Flat is the short trail to Columns of the Giants, a rare example of columnar hexagonal rock, similar to the phenomenon at Devils Postpile near Mammoth Lakes. In addition, the camp is adjacent to the Middle Fork Stanislaus River; trout are small here and get fished hard. Supplies are available within walking distance in Dardanelle. The elevation is 6,000 feet.

Campsites, facilities: There are seven walk-in tent sites. Picnic tables and fire grills are provided. Vault toilets are available. No drinking water is available. You can buy supplies in Dardanelle. Leashed pets are permitted.

Reservations, fees: Reservations are not accepted. Sites are $11 per night, $5 per night for each additional vehicle. Open May through October, weather permitting.

Directions: From Sonora, drive east on Highway 108 past the town of Strawberry to Dardanelle. Continue 1.5 miles east to the campground on the right side of the road, next to the Columns of the Giants Interpretive Site.

Contact: Stanislaus National Forest, Summit Ranger District, 209/965-3434, www.fs.usda. gov/stanislaus; Dodge Ridge Corporation, 209/965-3116.

188 EUREKA VALLEY

Scenic rating: 8

on the Middle Fork of the Stanislaus River in Stanislaus National Forest

Map 6.3, page 355

There are about a half-dozen campgrounds on this stretch of the Middle Fork Stanislaus River near Dardanelle, at 6,100 feet elevation. The river runs along two sides of this campground, making it quite pretty. This stretch of river is planted with trout by the Department of Fish and Game, but it is hit pretty hard despite its relatively isolated location. A good short and easy hike is to Columns of the Giants, accessible on a 0.25-mile-long trail out of Pigeon Flat, a mile to the west.

Campsites, facilities: There are 27 sites for tents or RVs up to 22 feet (no hookups). Picnic tables and fire grills are provided. Drinking water and vault toilets are available. You can buy supplies in Dardanelle. Leashed pets are permitted.

Reservations, fees: Reservations are not accepted. Sites are $18 per night, $5 per night for each additional vehicle. Open May through October, weather permitting.

Directions: From Sonora, drive east on Highway 108 past the town of Strawberry to Dardanelle. Continue three miles east to the campground on the right.

Contact: Stanislaus National Forest, Summit Ranger District, 209/965-3434, www.fs.usda.gov/stanislaus; Dodge Ridge Corporation, 209/965-3116.

189 BAKER

Scenic rating: 7

on the Middle Fork of the Stanislaus River in Stanislaus National Forest

Map 6.3, page 355

Baker lies at the turnoff for the well-known and popular Kennedy Meadow trailhead for the Emigrant Wilderness. The camp is set along the Middle Fork Stanislaus River, at 6,200 feet elevation, downstream a short way from the confluence with Deadman Creek. The trailhead, with a nearby horse corral, is another two miles farther on the Kennedy Meadow access road. From here it is a 1.5-mile hike to a fork in the trail; right will take you two miles to Relief Reservoir, 7,226 feet, and left will route you up Kennedy Creek for five miles to pretty Kennedy Lake, just north of Kennedy Peak (10,716 feet).

Campsites, facilities: There are 44 sites for tents or RVs up to 22 feet (no hookups). Picnic tables and fire grills are provided. Drinking water and vault toilets are available. You can buy supplies in Dardanelle. Leashed pets are permitted.

Reservations, fees: Reservations are not accepted. Sites are $18–36 per night, $5 per night for each additional vehicle. Open May through mid-October, weather permitting.

Directions: From Sonora, drive east on Highway 108 past Strawberry to Dardanelle. From Dardanelle, continue 5.5 miles east to the campground on the right side of the road at the turnoff for Kennedy Meadow.

Contact: Stanislaus National Forest, Summit Ranger District, 209/965-3434, www.fs.usda.gov/stanislaus.

190 DEADMAN

Scenic rating: 7

on the Middle Fork of the Stanislaus River in Stanislaus National Forest

Map 6.3, page 355

This is a popular trailhead camp and an ideal jump-off point for backpackers heading into the adjacent Emigrant Wilderness. The elevation is 6,200 feet. The camp is a short distance from Baker (see the Baker listing in this chapter for hiking destinations).

Campsites, facilities: There are 17 sites for tents or RVs up to 22 feet (no hookups). Picnic tables and fire grills are provided. Drinking water and vault toilets are available. You can buy supplies in Dardanelle. Some facilities are wheelchair-accessible. Leashed pets are permitted.

Reservations, fees: Reservations are not accepted. Sites are $18–36 per night, $5 per night for each additional vehicle. Open May through early October, weather permitting.

Directions: From Sonora, drive east on Highway 108 past the town of Strawberry to Dardanelle. From Dardanelle, continue 5.5 miles east to the Kennedy Meadow turnoff. Drive a mile on Kennedy Meadow Road to the campground, which is opposite the parking area for Kennedy Meadow Trail.

Contact: Stanislaus National Forest, Summit Ranger District, 209/965-3434, www.fs.usda.gov/stanislaus.

191 NIAGARA CREEK

Scenic rating: 6

in Stanislaus National Forest

Map 6.3, page 355

This camp is set beside Niagara Creek at 6,600 feet elevation, high in Stanislaus National Forest on the western slopes of the Sierra. It provides direct access to a network of roads in national forest, including routes to Double Dome Rock and another to Eagle Meadows. So if you have a four-wheel-drive vehicle or dirt bike, this is the place to come.

Campsites, facilities: There are 10 sites for tents or RVs up to 22 feet (no hookups); some are walk-in sites. Picnic tables and fire grills are provided. A vault toilet is available. No drinking water is available. You can buy supplies in Pinecrest about 10 miles away. Leashed pets are permitted.

Reservations, fees: Reservations are not accepted. Sites are $5 per vehicle per night. Open May through October, weather permitting.

Directions: From Sonora, drive east on Highway 108 to the town of Strawberry and continue for about 15 miles to Eagle Meadows Road/Forest Road 5N01 on the right. Turn

right and drive 0.5 mile to the campground on the left.

Contact: Stanislaus National Forest, Summit Ranger District, 209/965-3434, www.fs.usda.gov/stanislaus.

192 NIAGARA CREEK OFF-HIGHWAY VEHICLE

Scenic rating: 6

on Niagara Creek in Stanislaus National Forest

Map 6.3, page 355

This small, primitive camp along Niagara Creek is designed primarily for people with off-highway vehicles. Got it? It is set on Niagara Creek near Donnells Reservoir. The elevation is 6,600 feet.

Campsites, facilities: There are 10 sites for tents or RVs up to 22 feet (no hookups). Picnic tables and fire grills are provided. A vault toilet is available. No drinking water is available. You can buy supplies in Pinecrest about 10 miles away. Leashed pets are permitted.

Reservations, fees: Reservations are not accepted. Sites are $8 per vehicle per night. Open May through October, weather permitting.

Directions: From Sonora, drive east on Highway 108 to Strawberry and continue for about 15 miles to Eagle Meadows Road/Forest Road 5N01. Turn right and drive 1.5 miles to the campground on the left (just after crossing the bridge at Niagara Creek).

Contact: Stanislaus National Forest, Summit Ranger District, 209/965-3434, www.fs.usda.gov/stanislaus.

193 MILL CREEK

Scenic rating: 7

on Mill Creek in Stanislaus National Forest

Map 6.3, page 355

This pretty little camp is set along Mill Creek at 6,200 feet elevation, high in Stanislaus

National Forest, near a variety of outdoor recreation options. The camp is near the Middle Fork Stanislaus River, which is stocked with trout near Donnells. For hiking, there is an outstanding trailhead at Kennedy Meadow (east of Donnells). For fishing, both Beardsley Reservoir (boat necessary) and Pinecrest Lake (shoreline prospects fair) provide two nearby alternatives.

Campsites, facilities: There are 17 sites for tents or RVs up to 22 feet (no hookups). Picnic tables and fire grills are provided. Vault toilets and garbage service are available. There is no drinking water. Leashed pets are permitted.

Reservations, fees: Reservations are not accepted. Sites are $5 per night. Open May through mid-October, weather permitting.

Directions: From Sonora, drive east on Highway 108 to Strawberry. From Strawberry continue east on Highway 108 about 13 miles to Forest Road 5N21. Turn right on Forest Road 5N21 and drive 0.1 mile to the campground access road (Forest Road 5N26) on the left.

Contact: Stanislaus National Forest, Summit Ranger District, 209/965-3434, www.fs.usda.gov/stanislaus.

194 BOOTLEG

Scenic rating: 6

on the Walker River in
Humboldt-Toiyabe National Forest

Map 6.3, page 355

Location is always key, and easy access off U.S. 395, the adjacent West Walker River, and good trout stocks in summer make this a popular spot. Note that this camp is on the west side of the highway, and anglers will have to cross the road to gain fishing access. The elevation is 6,600 feet. (See the Chris Flat and Sonora Bridge listings in this chapter for more information.)

Campsites, facilities: There are 63 sites for tents or RVs up to 35 feet (no hookups). Picnic tables and fire grills are provided. Drinking

water and flush toilets are available. Leashed pets are permitted.

Reservations, fees: Reservations are not accepted. Sites are $20 per night, $5 per night for each additional vehicle. Open early May through mid-September, weather permitting.

Directions: From Carson City, drive south on U.S. 395 to Coleville and then continue south for 13 miles to the campground on the west side of the highway (six miles north of the junction of U.S. 395 and Highway 108).

Contact: Humboldt-Toiyabe National Forest, Bridgeport Ranger District, 760/932-7070, www.fs.usda.gov/htnf.

195 CHRIS FLAT

Scenic rating: 7

on the Walker River in
Humboldt-Toiyabe National Forest

Map 6.3, page 355

This is one of two campgrounds set along U.S. 395 next to the West Walker River, a pretty trout stream with easy access and good stocks of rainbow trout. The plants are usually made at two campgrounds, resulting in good prospects here at Chris Flat and west on Highway 108 at Sonora Bridge. The elevation is 6,600 feet.

Campsites, facilities: There are 14 sites for tents or RVs up to 30 feet (no hookups). Picnic tables and fire grills are provided. Drinking water (shut off during freezing temperatures) and vault toilets are available. Leashed pets are permitted.

Reservations, fees: Reservations are not accepted. Sites are $20 per night, $5 per night for each additional vehicle. Open April through mid-November, weather permitting.

Directions: From Carson City, drive south on U.S. 395 to Coleville and then continue south for 15 miles to the campground on the east side of the road (four miles north of the junction of U.S. 395 and Highway 108).

Contact: Humboldt-Toiyabe National Forest,

Bridgeport Ranger District, 760/932-7070, www.fs.usda.gov/htnf.

196 SONORA BRIDGE
🏃 ⛵ 🎣 🚐 ⛺

Scenic rating: 7

near the Walker River in
Humboldt-Toiyabe National Forest

Map 6.3, page 355

The West Walker River is a pretty stream, flowing over boulders and into pools, and each year this stretch of river is well stocked with rainbow trout by the Department of Fish and Game. One of several campgrounds near the West Walker, Sonora Bridge is set at 6,800 feet elevation, about 0.5 mile from the river. The setting is in the transition zone from high mountains to high desert on the eastern edge of the Sierra Nevada.

Campsites, facilities: There are 23 sites for tents or RVs up to 35 feet (no hookups). Picnic tables and fire grills are provided. Drinking water and vault toilets are available. Leashed pets are permitted.

Reservations, fees: Reservations are not accepted. Sites are $17 per night, $6 per night for each additional vehicle. Open mid-May through mid-October, weather permitting.

Directions: From north of Bridgeport, at the junction of U.S. 395 and Highway 108, turn west on Highway 108 and drive one mile to the campground on the left.

Contact: Humboldt-Toiyabe National Forest, Bridgeport Ranger District, 760/932-7070, www.fs.usda.gov/htnf.

197 LEAVITT MEADOWS
🏃 ⛵ 🎣 ♿ 🚐 ⛺

Scenic rating: 9

on the Walker River in
Humboldt-Toiyabe National Forest

Map 6.3, page 355

While Leavitt Meadows sits right beside Highway 108, a little winding two-laner, there are several nearby off-pavement destinations that make this camp a winner. The camp is set in the high eastern Sierra, east of Sonora Pass at 7,000 feet elevation, where Leavitt Creek and Brownie Creek enter the West Walker River. There is a pack station for horseback riding nearby. For four-wheel-drive owners, the most popular side trip is driving four miles west on Highway 108, then turning south and driving four miles to Leavitt Lake, where the trout fishing is sometimes spectacular, if you're trolling a gold Cripplure.

Campsites, facilities: There are 16 sites for tents or RVs up to 30 feet (no hookups). Picnic tables, food lockers, and fire grills are provided. Drinking water and vault toilets are available. Some facilities are wheelchair accessible. Leashed pets are permitted.

Reservations, fees: Reservations are not accepted. Sites are $17 per night, $5 per night for each additional vehicle. Open April through mid-October, weather permitting.

Directions: From the junction of Highway 108 and U.S. 395 north of Bridgeport, turn west on Highway 108 and drive approximately seven miles to the campground on the left side of the road.

Contact: Humboldt-Toiyabe National Forest, Bridgeport Ranger District, 760/932-7070, www.fs.usda.gov/htnf.

198 OBSIDIAN
🏃 ⛵ 🎣 🚐 ⛺

Scenic rating: 6

on Molybdenite Creek in
Humboldt-Toiyabe National Forest

Map 6.3, page 355

This primitive, little-known camp at 7,800 feet elevation is set up for backpackers, with an adjacent trailhead providing a jump-off point into the wilderness; wilderness permits are required. The trail is routed up the Molybdenite Creek drainage and into the Hoover Wilderness.

Campsites, facilities: There are 14 sites for

tents or RVs up to 30 feet (no hookups). Picnic tables and fire grills are provided. Vault toilets are available. No drinking water is available. Garbage must be packed out. Leashed pets are permitted.

Reservations, fees: Reservations are not accepted. Sites are $12 per night, $6 per night for each additional vehicle. Open June through October, weather permitting.

Directions: At the junction of U.S. 395 and Highway 108 (13 miles north of Bridgeport), drive south a short distance on U.S. 395 to an improved dirt road and a sign that reads "Little Walker River Road." Turn west and drive four miles to the campground.

Contact: Humboldt-Toiyabe National Forest, Bridgeport Ranger District, 760/932-7070, www.fs.usda.gov/htnf.

199 CASCADE CREEK

Scenic rating: 6

in Stanislaus National Forest

Map 6.3, page 355

This campground is set along Cascade Creek at an elevation of 6,000 feet. A Forest Service road about a quarter mile west of camp on the south side of the highway provides a side trip three miles up to Pikes Peak, at 7,236 feet.

Campsites, facilities: There are 13 sites for tents or RVs up to 22 feet (no hookups). Picnic tables and fire rings are provided. Vault toilets are available. No drinking water is available. Garbage must be packed out. Supplies are available in Dardanelle. Leashed pets are permitted.

Reservations, fees: Reservations are not accepted. Sites are $5 per night. Open May through October, weather permitting.

Directions: From Sonora, drive east on Highway 108 to Strawberry and continue for 11 miles to the campground on the left side of the road.

Contact: Stanislaus National Forest, Summit Ranger District, 209/965-3434, www.fs.usda.gov/stanislaus.

200 DONNER MEMORIAL STATE PARK

Scenic rating: 9

on Donner Lake

Lake Tahoe map, page 356   **BEST (**

The remarkable beauty of Donner Lake often evokes a deep, heartfelt response. Nearly everybody passing by from nearby I-80 has looked down and seen it. The lake is big, three miles long and 0.75-mile wide, gemlike blue, and set near the Sierra crest at 5,900 feet. The area is well developed, with a number of cabins and access roads, and this state park is the feature destination. Along the southeastern end of the lake, it is extremely pretty, but the campsites are set in forest, not along the lake. Fishing is good here (typically only in the early morning), trolling for kokanee salmon or rainbow trout, with big Mackinaw and brown trout providing wild cards. The park features more than three miles of frontage of Donner Creek and Donner Lake, with 2.5 miles of hiking trails. Donner Lake itself has 7.5 miles of shoreline. The lake is open to all water sports, but there is no boat launch at the park; a public ramp is available in the northwest corner of the lake. Campers get free admission to Emigrant Trail Museum. Note: All boats must be certified mussel-free before launching.

Campsites, facilities: There are 138 sites for tents or RVs up to 28 feet (no hookups) and trailers up to 24 feet, and two hike-in/bike-in sites. Picnic tables, food lockers, and fire pits are provided. Drinking water, coin showers, vault toilets, picnic area, and interpretive trail are available. Supplies are available about one mile away in Truckee. Some facilities are wheelchair-accessible. Leashed pets are permitted.

Reservations, fees: Reservations are accepted at 800/444-7275 (800/444-PARK) or www.reserveamerica.com ($8 reservation fee). Sites are $35 per night, $8 per night for each additional vehicle, $7 per person per night for hike-in/bike-in sites (two-night maximum).

Open late May to mid-September, weather permitting.

Directions: From Auburn, drive east on I-80 just past Donner Lake to the Donner State Park exit. Take that exit and turn south (right) on Donner Pass Road and drive 0.5 mile to the park entrance on the left at the southeast end of the lake.

Contact: Donner Memorial State Park, 530/582-7892 or 530/582-7894. For boat-launching info, call 530/582-7720, www.parks.ca.gov.

201 GRANITE FLAT

Scenic rating: 6

on the Truckee River in Tahoe National Forest

Lake Tahoe map, page 356

This camp is set along the Truckee River at 5,800 feet elevation. The area is known for a ton of traffic on adjacent Highway 89, as well as decent trout fishing and, in the spring and early summer, rafting. It is about a 15-minute drive to Squaw Valley or Lake Tahoe. A bike route is also available along the Truckee River out of Tahoe City.

Campsites, facilities: There are 58 sites for tents or RVs up to 40 feet (no hookups) and seven walk-in tent sites. Picnic tables and fire grills are provided. Drinking water and vault toilets are available. Some facilities are wheelchair-accessible. Leashed pets are permitted.

Reservations, fees: Reservations are accepted at 877/444-6777 or www.recreation.gov ($9 reservation fee). Sites are $19–21 per night, $5 per night for each additional vehicle. Open May through October, weather permitting.

Directions: From Truckee, drive south on Highway 89 for 1.5 miles to the campground entrance on the left.

Contact: Tahoe National Forest, Truckee Ranger District, 530/587-3558, www.fs.usda.gov/tahoe; California Land Management, 530/587-9281.

202 GOOSE MEADOWS

Scenic rating: 6

on the Truckee River in Tahoe National Forest

Lake Tahoe map, page 356

There are three campgrounds set along the Truckee River off Highway 89 between Truckee and Tahoe City. Goose Meadows provides good fishing access with decent prospects, despite the high number of vehicles roaring past on the adjacent highway. This stretch of river is also popular for rafting. The elevation is 5,800 feet.

Campsites, facilities: There are 21 sites for tents or RVs up to 30 feet (no hookups). Picnic tables and fire grills are provided. Drinking water and vault toilets are available. Supplies are available in Truckee and Tahoe City. Some facilities are wheelchair-accessible. Leashed pets are permitted.

Reservations, fees: Reservations are accepted at 877/444-6777 or www.recreation.gov ($9 reservation fee). Sites are $17–19 per night, $5 per night for each additional vehicle. Open May through October, weather permitting.

Directions: From Truckee, drive south on Highway 89 for four miles to the campground entrance on the left (river) side of the highway.

Contact: Tahoe National Forest, Truckee Ranger District, 530/587-3558, www.fs.usda.gov/tahoe; California Land Management, 530/587-9281.

203 SILVER CREEK

Scenic rating: 8

on the Truckee River in Tahoe National Forest

Lake Tahoe map, page 356

This pretty campground is set near where Silver Creek enters the Truckee River. The trout fishing is often good in this area. This is one of three campgrounds along Highway 89 and the

Truckee River, between Truckee and Tahoe City. The elevation is 6,000 feet.

Campsites, facilities: There are 23 sites for tents or RVs up to 40 feet (no hookups) and seven walk-in tent sites. Picnic tables and fire grills are provided. Drinking water and vault toilets are available. Supplies are available in Truckee and Tahoe City. Some facilities are wheelchair-accessible. Leashed pets are permitted.

Reservations, fees: Reservations are accepted at 877/444-6777 or www.recreation. gov ($9 reservation fee). Sites are $17–19 per night, $5 per night for each additional vehicle. Open June through September, weather permitting.

Directions: From Truckee, drive south on Highway 89 for six miles to the campground entrance on the river side of the highway.

Contact: Tahoe National Forest, Truckee Ranger District, 530/587-3558, www.fs.usda. gov/tahoe; California Land Management, 530/587-9281.

204 MARTIS CREEK LAKE

Scenic rating: 7

near Truckee

Lake Tahoe map, page 356

If only this lake weren't so often windy in the afternoon, it would be heaven to fly fishers in float tubes. To some it's heaven anyway, with Lahontan cutthroat trout growing to 25 inches here. This is a special catch-and-release fishery where anglers are permitted to use only artificial lures with single, barbless hooks. The setting is somewhat sparse and open—a small lake, 70 acres, on the eastern edge of the Martis Valley. No motors are permitted at the lake, making it ideal (when the wind is down) for float tubes or prams. Sailing, sailboarding, and swimming are permitted. There is no boat launch, but small boats can be hand-launched. The lake level can fluctuate daily, which, along with the wind, can be frustrating for those

who show up expecting automatic perfection; that just isn't the way it is out there. At times, the lake level can even be very low. The elevation is 5,800 feet.

Campsites, facilities: There are 25 sites for tents or RVs of any length feet (no hookups). Some sites are pull-through. Picnic tables and fire grills are provided. Drinking water, vault toilets, tent pads, firewood, and pay phones are available. Supplies are available in Truckee. Some facilities are wheelchair-accessible. Leashed pets are permitted.

Reservations, fees: Reservations accepted for wheelchair-accessible sites only at 530/587-8113. Sites are $18 per night. Open mid-May through mid-October, weather permitting.

Directions: From Truckee, drive south on Highway 267 for about three miles (past the airport) to the lake entrance road on the left. Turn left and drive another 2.5 miles to the campground at the end of the road.

Contact: U.S. Army Corps of Engineers, Sacramento District, 530/587-8113.

205 SANDY BEACH CAMPGROUND

Scenic rating: 8

on Lake Tahoe

Lake Tahoe map, page 356

Sandy Beach Campground is set at 6,200 feet elevation near the northwest shore of Lake Tahoe. This private park is located just across the street from "Sandy Beach." A nearby boat ramp provides access to one of the better fishing areas of the lake for Mackinaw trout. A public beach is across the road. But the water in Tahoe is always cold, and though a lot of people will get suntans on beaches next to the lake, swimmers need to be members of the Polar Bear Club. A short drive to the east will take you past the town of Kings Beach and into Nevada, where there are some small casinos near the shore of Crystal Bay. Sites often fill in summer. Note: All boats must be certified mussel-free before launching.

Campsites, facilities: There are 27 sites with full or partial hookups (30 amps) for tents or RVs up to 40 feet. Some sites are pull-through. Picnic tables, barbecues, and fire rings are provided. Drinking water, restrooms with showers and flush toilets, and a dump station are available. A boat ramp is half a block away. A grocery store and propane gas are available nearby. Leashed pets are permitted.

Reservations, fees: Reservations are recommended. RV sites (electricity and water) are $30 per night, tent sites are $25 per night for up to six people with two vehicles, two-dog limit. For weeklong stays, seventh night is free. Some credit cards accepted. Open May through October.

Directions: From Truckee, drive south on Highway 267 to Highway 28. Turn right and drive one mile to the park on the right side of the road (entrance well signed).

Contact: Sandy Beach Campground, Lake Tahoe Basin Management Unit, 530/543-2600, www.fs.usda.gov/ltmbu; Taylor Creek Visitor Center, 530/543-2674; California Land Management, 530/583-3642.

206 LAKE FOREST CAMPGROUND

Scenic rating: 8

on Lake Tahoe

Lake Tahoe map, page 356

The north shore of Lake Tahoe provides beautiful lookouts and excellent boating access. The latter is a highlight of this camp, with a boat ramp nearby. From here it is a short cruise to Dollar Point and around the corner north to Carnelian Bay, one of the better stretches of water for trout fishing. The elevation is 6,200 feet. There is a 10-day camping limit. Note: All boats must be certified mussel-free before launching.

Campsites, facilities: There are 20 sites for tents or RVs up to 20 feet (no hookups). Picnic tables and fire grills are provided. Drinking water and vault toilets are available. Some facilities are wheelchair-accessible. A grocery store, coin laundry, and propane gas are available within four miles. Leashed pets are permitted.

Reservations, fees: Reservations are not accepted. Sites are $20 per night. Open May through October, weather permitting.

Directions: From Truckee, drive south on Highway 89 through Tahoe City to Highway 28. Bear north on Highway 28 and drive four miles to the campground entrance road (Lake Forest Road) on the right.

Contact: Tahoe City Public Utility District, Parks and Recreation, 530/583-3440, ext. 10.

207 TAHOE STATE RECREATION AREA

Scenic rating: 9

on Lake Tahoe

Lake Tahoe map, page 356

This is a popular summer-only campground at the north shore of Lake Tahoe. The Tahoe State Recreation Area covers a large area just west of Highway 28 near Tahoe City. There are opportunities for hiking and horseback riding nearby (though not right at the park). It is also near shopping, restaurants, and, unfortunately, traffic jams in Tahoe City. A boat ramp is two miles to the northwest at nearby Lake Forest, and bike rentals are available in Tahoe City for rides along Highway 89 near the shore of the lake. For a more secluded site nearby at Tahoe, get reservations instead for Sugar Pine Point State Park, 11 miles south on Highway 89. Note: All boats must be certified mussel-free before launching.

Campsites, facilities: There are 25 sites for tents or RVs up to 27 feet (no hookups) and trailers up to 24 feet. Picnic tables, food lockers, barbecues, and fire pits are provided. Drinking water, vault toilets, and coin showers are available. Firewood, other supplies, and a coin laundry are available within walking distance. Leashed pets are permitted.

Reservations, fees: Reservations are accepted at 800/444-7275 (800/444-PARK) or www.reserveamerica.com ($8 reservation fee). Sites are $35 per night, $8 per night for each additional vehicle. Open May through October, weather permitting.

Directions: From Truckee, drive south on Highway 89 through Tahoe City. Turn north on Highway 28 and drive 0.9 mile to the campground entrance on the right side of the road.

Contact: Tahoe State Recreation Area, 530/583-3074 or 530/525-7982; Sierra District, 530/525-7232, www.parks.ca.gov.

208 WILLIAM KENT

Scenic rating: 8

near Lake Tahoe in the Lake Tahoe Basin

Lake Tahoe map, page 356

William Kent camp is a little pocket of peace set near the busy traffic of Highway 89 on the western shore corridor. It is on the west side of the highway, meaning visitors have to cross the highway to get lakeside access. The elevation is 6,300 feet, and the camp is wooded with primarily lodgepole pines. The drive here is awesome or ominous, depending on how you look at it, with the view of incredible Lake Tahoe to the east, the third-deepest blue lake in North America and the 10th-deepest lake in the world. But you often have a lot of time to look at it, since traffic rarely moves quickly. Note: All boats must be certified mussel-free before launching.

Campsites, facilities: There are 55 tent sites and 36 sites for RVs up to 40 feet (no hookups). Picnic tables, food lockers, and fire grills

are provided. Drinking water, flush toilets, and a dump station are available. A grocery store, coin laundry, and propane gas are available nearby. Some facilities are wheelchair-accessible. Leashed pets are permitted, but not on the beach.

Reservations, fees: Reservations are accepted at 877/444-6777 or www.recreation.gov ($9 reservation fee). Sites are $27–29 per night, $5 per night for each additional vehicle. Open late May through mid-October, weather permitting.

Directions: From Truckee, drive south on Highway 89 to Tahoe City. Turn south on Highway 89 and drive three miles to the campground entrance on the right side of the road.

Contact: Lake Tahoe Basin Management Unit, 530/543-2600, www.fs.usda.gov/ltmbu; Taylor Creek Visitor Center, 530/543-2674; California Land Management, 530/583-3642.

209 KASPIAN

Scenic rating: 7

on Lake Tahoe

Lake Tahoe map, page 356

As gorgeous and as huge as Lake Tahoe is, there are relatively few camps or even restaurants with lakeside settings. Kaspian is one of the few, set along the west shore of the lake at 6,235 feet elevation near the little town of Tahoe Pines. A Forest Service road (Barker Pass Road) is available adjacent to the camp that is routed west into national forest to trailheads for Ellis Peak, Twin Peaks, and the Pacific Crest Trail for incredible views of Lake Tahoe. Note: All boats must be certified mussel-free before launching.

Campsites, facilities: There are nine walk-in sites for tents only. RVs up to 20 feet may use the parking lot on a space-available basis. Picnic tables and fire grills are provided. Drinking water, food lockers, and flush toilets are available. A grocery store, coin laundry, and propane gas are nearby. Some facilities are wheelchair accessible. Leashed pets are permitted, but not on the beach.

Reservations, fees: Reservations are accepted at 877/444-6777 or www.recreation. gov ($9 reservation fee). Sites are $19–21 per night, $5 per night for each additional vehicle. Open May through September, weather permitting.

Directions: From Truckee, drive south on Highway 89 to Tahoe City. Turn south on Highway 89 and drive four miles to the campground (signed) on the west side of the road. The tent sites require a walk-in of 50–100 feet.

Contact: Lake Tahoe Basin Management Unit, 530/543-2600, www.fs.usda.gov/ltmbu; Taylor Creek Visitor Center, 530/543-2674; California Land Management, 530/583-3642.

210 ED Z'BERG SUGAR PINE POINT STATE PARK

Scenic rating: 10

on Lake Tahoe

Lake Tahoe map, page 356

This is one of three beautiful and popular state parks on the west shore of Lake Tahoe. It is just north of Meeks Bay on General Creek, with almost two miles of lake frontage available, though the campground is on the opposite side of Highway 89. General Creek, a feeder stream to Lake Tahoe, is one of the clearest streams imaginable. A pretty trail is routed seven miles along the creek up to Lost Lake, just outside the northern boundary of the Desolation Wilderness. This stream also provides trout fishing from mid-July to mid-September. This park contains one of the finest remaining natural areas at Lake Tahoe. The park features dense forests of pine, fir, aspen, and juniper, covering more than 2,000 acres of beautiful landscape. There are many hiking trails, a swimming beach, and, in winter, 20

kilometers of cross-country skiing trails and a heated restroom. There is also evidence of occupation by Washoe Indians, with bedrock mortars, or grinding rocks, near the Ehrman Mansion. The elevation is 6,200 feet. Note: All boats must be certified mussel-free before launching.

Campsites, facilities: There are 175 sites for tents or RVs up to 32 feet and trailers up to 26 feet (no hookups). There are also 10 group sites for up to 40 people each. Picnic tables and fire rings are provided. Drinking water, restrooms with flush toilets and coin showers (except in winter), dump station, a day-use area, WiFi, and nature center with bird display are available. A grocery store, coin laundry, and propane gas are available nearby. Some facilities are wheelchair-accessible. Leashed pets are permitted.

Reservations, fees: Reservations are accepted at 800/444-7275 (800/444-PARK) or www. reserveamerica.com ($8 reservation fee). Sites are $35 per night, $8 per night for each additional vehicle, $165 per night for a group site. Open year-round.

Directions: From Truckee, drive south on Highway 89 through Tahoe City. Continue south on Highway 89 and drive 9.3 miles to the campground (signed) on the right (west) side of the road.

Contact: Ed Z'berg Sugar Pine Point State Park, 530/525-7982; Sierra District, 530/525-7232, www.parks.ca.gov.

211 MEEKS BAY

Scenic rating: 9

on Lake Tahoe

Lake Tahoe map, page 356

Meeks Bay is a beautiful spot along the western shore of Lake Tahoe. A bicycle trail is available nearby and is routed along the lake's shore, but it requires occasionally crossing busy Highway 89. Note: All boats must be certified mussel-free before launching.

Campsites, facilities: There are 36 sites for tents or RVs up to 20 feet (no hookups). Picnic tables, food lockers, and fire grills are provided. Drinking water and flush toilets are available. Coin laundry and groceries are available nearby. Some facilities are wheelchair accessible. Leashed pets are permitted, but not on the beach.

Reservations, fees: Reservations are accepted at 877/444-6777 or www.recreation.gov ($9 reservation fee). Sites are $27–29 per night, $5 per night for each additional vehicle. Open mid-May through mid-October, weather permitting.

Directions: In South Lake Tahoe at the junction of Highway 89 and U.S. 50, turn north on Highway 89 and drive 17 miles to the campground (signed) on the east side of Highway 89.

Contact: Lake Tahoe Basin Management Unit, 530/543-2600; Taylor Creek Visitor Center, 530/543-2674; California Land Management, 530/583-3642.

212 MEEKS BAY RESORT AND MARINA

🚴 🏊 🛶 🚐 ⛺

Scenic rating: 7

on Lake Tahoe

Lake Tahoe map, page 356

Prime access for boating makes this a camp of choice for the boater/camper at Lake Tahoe. This campground is extremely popular and often booked well ahead of time for July and August. A boat launch is on the premises, and access to Rubicon Bay and beyond to breathtaking Emerald Bay is possible, a six-mile trip one-way for boats. The resort is adjacent to a 20-mile paved bike trail, with a swimming beach also nearby. A 14-day stay limit is enforced. Note: All boats must be certified mussel-free before launching.

Campsites, facilities: There are 22 sites with full hookups (50 amps) for RVs up to 60 feet and 14 sites for tents. Some sites are pull-through. Lodge rooms, cabins, and a house are also available. Picnic tables, bear lockers, and fire grills are provided. Restrooms with showers and flush toilets, snack bar, gift shop, and a camp store are available. A boat ramp, boat rentals (kayaks, canoes, and paddle boats), and boat slips are also available.

Reservations, fees: Reservations are accepted at 877/326-3357. RV sites are $45 per night, tent sites are $25 per night, $60 per night for boat slips, $25 to launch boats. Some credit cards accepted. Open May through September.

Directions: In South Lake Tahoe at the junction of Highway 89 and U.S. 50, turn north on Highway 89 and drive 17 miles to the campground on the right at 7941 Emerald Bay Road.

Contact: Meeks Bay Resort and Marina, 530/525-6946 or 988/326-3357, www.meeksbayresort.com.

213 D. L. BLISS STATE PARK

🚶 🚴 🏊 🛶 🐕 ♿ 🚐 ⛺

Scenic rating: 10

on Lake Tahoe

Lake Tahoe map, page 356   **BEST** (

D. L. Bliss State Park is set on one of Lake Tahoe's most beautiful stretches of shoreline, from Emerald Point at the mouth of Emerald Bay northward to Rubicon Point, spanning about three miles. The camp is at the north end of the park, the sites nestled amid pine trees, with 80 percent of the campsites within 0.5–1 mile of the beach. The park is named for a pioneering lumberman, railroad owner, and banker of the region, whose family donated this 744-acre parcel to California in 1929. There are two great easy hiking trails. Rubicon Trail is one of Tahoe's most popular easy hikes, a meandering path just above the southwest shore of Lake Tahoe, wandering through pine, cedar, and fir, with breaks for fantastic panoramas of the lake, as well as spots where you can see nearly 100 feet into the lake. Don't be surprised if you are joined by a chipmunk circus, many begging, sitting upright, hoping for their nut for the day. While this trail is beautiful and solitary at dawn, by noon it can be crowded with hikers and chipmunks alike. Another trail, a great hike for youngsters, is Balancing Rock Trail, just a 0.5-mile romp, where after about 40 yards you arrive at this 130-ton, oblong granite boulder that is set on a tiny perch, and the whole thing seems to defy gravity. Some day it has to fall, right? Not yet. Rubicon Trail runs all the way past Emerald Point to Emerald Bay. Note: All boats must be certified mussel-free before launching.

Campsites, facilities: There are 142 sites for tents or RVs up to 18 feet (no hookups) and trailers up to 15 feet, one hike-in/bike-in site, and a group site for up to 50 people. Picnic tables, fire grills, and food lockers are provided. Restrooms with coin showers and flush toilets and a dump station are available. All water must sometimes be pump-filtered or boiled before use, depending on current water conditions. Some facilities are wheelchair-accessible. Leashed pets are permitted at campsites only.

Reservations, fees: Reservations are accepted at 800/444-7275 (800/444-PARK) or www.reserveamerica.com ($8 reservation fee). Sites are $35 per night, premium lakefront sites are $45 per night, $8 per night for each additional vehicle, $165 per night for group site, $7 per night for hike-in/bike-in site (two-night maximum). Open late May through late September, weather permitting.

Directions: In South Lake Tahoe at the junction of Highway 89 and U.S. 50, turn north on Highway 89 and drive 10.5 miles to the state park turnoff on the right side of the road. Turn right (east) and drive to the park entrance. (If arriving from the north, drive from Tahoe City south on Highway 89 for 17 miles to the park entrance road.)

Contact: D. L. Bliss State Park, 530/525-7277; Sierra District, 530/525-7232, www.parks.ca.gov.

214 EMERALD BAY STATE PARK AND BOAT-IN

Scenic rating: 10

on Lake Tahoe

Lake Tahoe map, page 356   BEST (

Emerald Bay is a place of rare and divine beauty, one of the most striking and popular state parks on the planet. With its deep cobalt-blue waters, awesome surrounding ridgelines, glimpses of Lake Tahoe out the mouth of the bay, and even a little island, there may be no place more perfect to run a boat or kayak.

There are boat-in camps on the northern side of Emerald Bay, set in pine forest with water views. Even when Tahoe is packed, there are times when you can paddle right up and find a site—though reservations at one of the 22 boat-in sites makes for a sure thing, of course. Drive-in campsites are available near Eagle Point at the mouth of Emerald Bay. Sites are also accessible via the Rubicon Trail from D. L. Bliss State Park.

Emerald Bay is a designated underwater park featuring Fanette Island, Tahoe's only island, and Vikingsholm, one of the greatest examples of Scandinavian architecture in North America. Vikingsholm is located along the shore about a mile's hike from the campground and tours are very popular. The park also has several short hiking trails. Note: All boats must be certified mussel-free before launching.

Campsites, facilities: There are 94 sites for tents or RVs up to 21 feet (no hookups) and trailers up to 18 feet and 20 boat-in sites. Picnic tables and fire grills are provided. Drinking water and restrooms with flush toilets and coin showers are available. At boat-in sites, drinking water and vault toilets are available. Leashed pets are permitted in the campground and on asphalt, but not on trails.

Reservations, fees: Reservations are accepted at 800/444-7275 (800/444-PARK) or www.reserveamerica.com ($8 reservation fee). Sites are $35 per night, $8 per night for each additional vehicle, $35 per night for boat-in sites. Open early June through mid-September, weather permitting.

Directions: In South Lake Tahoe at the junction of Highway 89 and U.S. 50, turn north on Highway 89 and drive 6.5 miles to the state park entrance turnoff on the right side of the road.

Contact: Emerald Bay State Park, 530/541-3030, or D. L. Bliss State Park, 530/525-7277, www.parks.ca.gov.

215 CAMP SHELLY

Scenic rating: 7

near Lake Tahoe in the Lake Tahoe Basin

Lake Tahoe map, page 356

This campground is set near South Lake Tahoe within close range of an outstanding bicycle trail. The camp is set in the woods, with campfire programs available on Saturday night in summer. Nearby to the west is the drive to Inspiration Point and the incredible lookout of Emerald Bay, as well as the parking area for the short hike to Eagle Falls. Nearby to the east are Fallen Leaf Lake and the south shore of Lake Tahoe. Note: All boats must be certified mussel-free before launching.

Campsites, facilities: There are 25 sites for tents or RVs up to 24 feet long and 10.5 feet high (no hookups). Group camping is available; at least five sites must be reserved. Picnic tables, food lockers, and fire grills are provided. Drinking water, restrooms with free showers and flush toilets, horseshoes, ping-pong, volleyball, and basketball are available. Some facilities are wheelchair-accessible. Groceries, propane, and a boat ramp are available nearby at Camp Richardson. Leashed pets are permitted.

Reservations, fees: Reservations can be made in person at the Robert Livermore Community Center (4444 East Ave., Livermore, CA 94550, 9 A.M.–4 P.M. Mon.–Fri.). Reservations can also be made by mail, at the campground office (which is intermittently staffed during the season), or by calling 925/960-2400. A reservation form can be downloaded online. Sites are $35 per night, $5 per night for each additional vehicle; group sites are an extra $4 per site per night. Open mid-June through Labor Day weekend.

Directions: In South Lake Tahoe at the junction of U.S. 50 and Highway 89, turn north on Highway 89, drive 2.5 miles to Camp Richardson, and then continue for 1.3 miles to the sign for Mount Tallac. Turn left at the sign for Mount Tallac Trailhead/Camp Shelly and drive to the campground on the right.

Contact: Camp Shelly, 530/541-6985; Livermore Area Recreation and Park District, 925/373-5700 or 925/960-2400, www.larpd.dst.ca.us.

216 FALLEN LEAF CAMPGROUND

Scenic rating: 7

in the Lake Tahoe Basin

Lake Tahoe map, page 356

This is a large camp near the north shore of Fallen Leaf Lake, set at 6,337 feet elevation. The lake is big (three miles long), quite deep (430 feet at its deepest point), and almost as blue as nearby Lake Tahoe. A concessionaire operates the campground. There are a variety of recreational opportunities, including boat rentals at the marina and horseback-riding at Camp Richardson Resort. Fishing is best in the fall for kokanee salmon. Because Fallen Leaf Lake is circled by forest—much of it private property—you will need a boat to fish or explore the lake. A visitors center is north of the Fallen Leaf Lake turnoff on Highway 89. Note: All boats must be certified mussel-free before launching.

Campsites, facilities: There are 75 sites for

tents, 130 sites for tents or RVs up to 40 feet (no hookups), and six yurts. Picnic tables, food lockers, and fire grills are provided. Drinking water, vault toilets, and coin showers are available. A boat ramp, coin laundry, and supplies are nearby. Some facilities are wheelchair-accessible. Leashed pets are permitted.

Reservations, fees: Reservations are accepted at 877/444-6777 or www.recreation.gov ($9 reservation fee). Sites are $32–34 per night, $5 per night for each additional vehicle, $82–84 per night for yurts. Open mid-May through mid-October, weather permitting.

Directions: In South Lake Tahoe at the junction of U.S. 50 and Highway 89, turn north on Highway 89 and drive two miles to the Fallen Leaf Lake turnoff. Turn left and drive 1.5 miles to the campground.

Contact: Lake Tahoe Basin Management Unit, 530/543-2600, www.fs.usda.gov/ltmbu; Taylor Creek Visitor Center, 530/543-2674; California Land Management, 530/544-0426.

217 TAHOE VALLEY RV RESORT

🏕️ 🐕 🚴 ♿ 🚐 ⛺

Scenic rating: 5

near Lake Tahoe

Lake Tahoe map, page 356

This is a massive, privately operated park near South Lake Tahoe. The nearby attractions include five golf courses, horseback riding, casinos, and, of course, "The Lake." Note that about half of the sites are filled with seasonal renters. Note: All boats must be certified mussel-free before launching.

Campsites, facilities: There are 305 sites with full or partial hookups (30 and 50 amps) for RVs of any length, 77 sites for tents, and two group sites for up to 100 people. Some RV sites are pull-through. Picnic tables and fire grills are provided. Restrooms with showers, cable TV, Wi-Fi, dump station, coin laundry, seasonal heated swimming pool, playground, tennis courts, grocery store, RV supplies, propane gas, ice, firewood, and recreation room are available. Some facilities are wheelchair-accessible. Leashed pets are permitted.

Reservations, fees: Reservations are recommended at www.reserveamerica.com ($9 reservation fee). RV sites (with hookups) are $44–70, tent sites are $35–60 per night, $3 resort fee per day. Monthly rates available. Credit cards accepted. Open year-round.

Directions: From South Lake Tahoe on U.S. 50, drive east on U.S. 50 to Meyers. Continue on U.S. 50 about five miles beyond Meyers to the signed entrance on the right. Turn right on C Street and drive 1.5 blocks to the campground.

Contact: Tahoe Valley RV Resort, 530/541-2222 or 877/717-8737.

218 CAMPGROUND BY THE LAKE

🚴 🏊 🎣 🛶 🚤 🐕 🚴 ♿ 🚐 ⛺

Scenic rating: 5

near Lake Tahoe

Lake Tahoe map, page 356

This city-operated campground provides an option at South Lake Tahoe. It is set at 6,200 feet elevation, across the road from the lake, with pine trees and views of the lake. Note: All boats must be certified mussel-free before launching.

Campsites, facilities: There are 175 sites for tents or RVs up to 40 feet. Some sites have partial hookups (30 and 50 amps) and/or are pull-through. Five tent cabins are also available. Picnic tables, barbecues, and fire grills are provided. Drinking water, restrooms with flush toilets and showers, dump station, playground, and boat ramp (check current status) are available. An indoor ice-skating rink and a public indoor heated pool are nearby (fee for access). Some facilities are wheelchair-accessible. Supplies and a coin laundry are nearby. Leashed pets are permitted.

Reservations, fees: Reservations are accepted at 530/542-6096 ($7 reservation fee). Sites are $24–29 per night, RV sites (with electricity) are $35–40 per night, $6 per night for each additional person, $6 per night for each additional vehicle, tent cabins are $49–51 per night, $2 per pet per night. Weekly rates available. Some credit cards accepted. Open April through October, with a 14-day maximum stay.

Directions: If entering South Lake Tahoe on U.S. 50, drive east on U.S. 50 to Rufus Allen Boulevard. Turn right and drive 0.25 mile to the campground on the right side of the road.

Contact: Campground by the Lake, 530/542-6096; City of South Lake Tahoe, Parks and Recreation Department, 530/542-6055, www.cityslt.us.

219 HISTORIC CAMP RICHARDSON RESORT

Scenic rating: 7

on Lake Tahoe

Lake Tahoe map, page 356   BEST (

Camp Richardson Resort is within minutes of boating, biking, gambling, and, in the winter, skiing and snowboarding. It's a take-your-pick deal. It's a legendary spot, often called "Camp Rich." With cabins, restaurant, and live music (often nightly in summer) also on the property, this is a place that offers one big package. The campsites are set in the woods, not on the lake itself, but are within a short walking distance of the lake. From here you can gain access to an excellent bike route that runs for three miles, then loops around by the lake for another three miles, most of it flat and easy, all of it beautiful. You can also make the easy, beautiful ride to Fallen Leaf Lake. A marina for boating, water ski lessons (I actually did this!), an ice cream parlor, and year-round recreation make Camp Rich a

popular winner. The elevation is 6,300 feet. Note: All boats must be certified mussel-free before launching.

Campsites, facilities: There are 223 sites for tents, and 112 sites with full or partial hookups (30 amps) for RVs up to 35 feet, including two pull-through sites. Cabins, duplex units, inn rooms, and hotel rooms are also available. Picnic tables and fire pits are provided. Restrooms with showers and flush toilets, drinking water, dump station, group facilities, and playground are available. A full-service marina, boat ramp, boat rentals, swimming beach, bike rentals, general store, restaurant, ice cream parlor, and propane gas are nearby. Some facilities are wheelchair-accessible.

Reservations, fees: Reservations are accepted at 800/544-1801. RV sites (hookups) are $40–45 per night, tent sites are $35 per night, $5 per night for each additional vehicle. Cabins are rented by the week in summer Some credit cards accepted. Open June through October, with lodging available year-round.

Directions: In South Lake Tahoe at the junction of Highway 89 and U.S. 50, turn north on Highway 89 and drive 2.5 miles to the resort on the right side of the road.

Contact: Historic Camp Richardson Resort, 530/541-1801, www.camprichardson.com.

220 KOA SOUTH LAKE TAHOE

Scenic rating: 5

near Lake Tahoe

Lake Tahoe map, page 356

Like so many KOA camps, this one is on the outskirts of a major destination area, in this case, South Lake Tahoe. It is within close range of gambling, fishing, hiking, and bike rentals. The camp is set at 6,300 feet elevation. Note: All boats must be certified mussel-free before launching.

Campsites, facilities: There are 40 sites with

full hookups (30 amps) for RVs up to 36 feet, and 16 sites with no hookups for tents and RVs. Some sites are pull-through. A lodge, chalet, and chateau are also available. Picnic tables and fire grills are provided. Restrooms with showers, cable TV, Wi-Fi, dump station, recreation room, seasonal heated swimming pool, playground, coin laundry, convenience store, RV supplies, horseshoes, firewood, ice, and propane gas are available. Some facilities are wheelchair accessible. Leashed pets are permitted.

Reservations, fees: Reservations are recommended at 800/562-3477. RV sites (hookups) are $60–82 per night, tent sites are $45–55 per night, $5 per person per night for more than two people, $5 per night for each additional vehicle, $20 per boat per night, $5 per pet per night. Off-season prices are discounted; holiday rates are higher. Weekly and monthly rates available. Some credit cards accepted. Open April through mid-October.

Directions: From Sacramento, take U.S. 50 and drive east over the Sierra Nevada past Echo Summit to Meyers. As you enter Meyers, it will be the first campground on the right. Turn right and enter the campground.

Contact: KOA South Lake Tahoe, 530/577-3693, www.laketahoekoa.com.

SAN FRANCISCO BAY AREA

© JEFFREY BANKE/123RF.COM

BEST CAMPGROUNDS

€ **Scenic Campgrounds**
Steep Ravine Environmental Campsites, **page 471.**

€ **Easy Backpacking**
Wildcat Camp Hike-In, **page 469.**

€ **Hikes with Views**
Angel Island State Park Walk-In/Boat-In, **page 475.**

€ **Island Retreats**
Angel Island State Park Walk-In/Boat-In,
page 475.

€ **State Parks**
Portola Redwoods State Park, **page 484.**
Henry W. Coe State Park, **page 488.**

It's ironic that many people who have chosen to live in the Bay Area are often the ones who complain the most about it. We've even heard some say, "Some day I'm going to get out of here and start having a good time."

I wish I could take anyone who has ever had these thoughts on a little trip in my airplane and circle the Bay Area at 3,000 feet. What you see is that despite strips of roadways and pockets of cities where people are jammed together, most of the region is wild, unsettled, and beautiful. There is no metropolitan area in the world that offers better and more diverse recreation and open space so close to so many.

The Bay Area has 150 significant parks (including 12 with redwoods), 7,500 miles of hiking and biking trails, 45 lakes, 25 waterfalls, 100 miles of coast, mountains with incredible lookouts, bays with islands, and, in all, 1.2 million acres of greenbelt with hundreds of acres being added each year with land bought by money earmarked from property taxes. The land has no limit. Enjoy it.

Along with the unique recreation possibilities come unique camp-grounds. There are boat-in camps at Tomales Bay, ferry-in camps on

Angel Island, and hike-in camps at Point Reyes National Seashore, the Marin Headlands, Sunol-Ohlone Wilderness, Butano Redwoods State Park, and Big Basin Redwoods State Park – along with a sprinkling of the more traditional drive-in sites at state, county, and regional parks throughout the region.

Note that proximity to a metropolitan area means two things: The demand is higher, so plan ahead; and second, 85 percent of the park use occurs from 3 P.M. Friday to 5 P.M. Sunday, so if you visit at non-peak times it's like having the park to yourself. One shocker is that in spring and fall, there is a huge drop-off in use on weekdays, Sunday through Thursday.

There are many world-class landmarks to see while staying in the Bay Area. In San Francisco alone there are the Golden Gate Bridge, Fisherman's Wharf, Alcatraz, Ghirardelli Square, Chinatown, AT&T ballpark, the Crissy Field waterfront, cable cars, Fort Point, the Cliff House and Ocean Beach, and Fort Funston.

In fact, instead of going far away for a vacation, residents might consider what so many do from all over the world: Stay and discover the treasures in your own backyard.

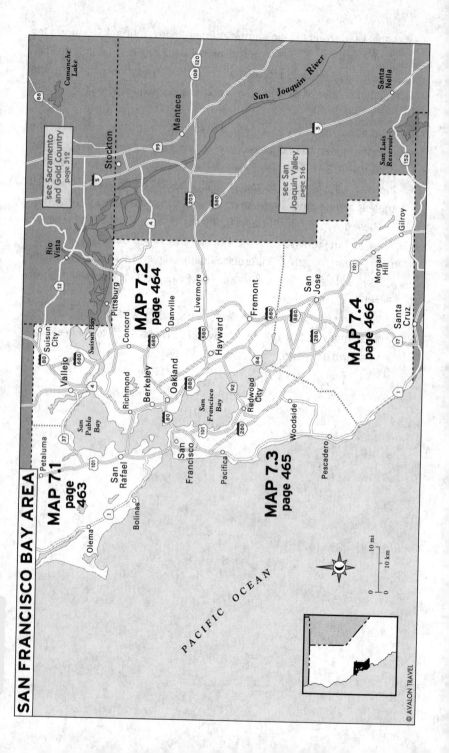

SAN FRANCISCO BAY AREA

MAP 7.1
page 463

MAP 7.2
page 464

MAP 7.3
page 465

MAP 7.4
page 466

see Sacramento and Gold Country
page 312

see San Joaquin Valley
page 516

PACIFIC OCEAN

San Joaquin River

Camanche Lake
Santa Nella
San Luis Reservoir
Manteca
Stockton
Rio Vista
Gilroy
Morgan Hill
San Jose
Santa Cruz
Suisun City
Vallejo
Pittsburg
Concord
Danville
Livermore
Fremont
Richmond
Berkeley
Oakland
Hayward
Redwood City
Woodside
Pescadero
San Pablo Bay
Suisun Bay
San Francisco Bay
Petaluma
San Rafael
San Francisco
Pacifica
Bolinas
Olema

0   10 mi
0   10 km

© AVALON TRAVEL

Map 7.1

Sites 1-16 Pages 467-475

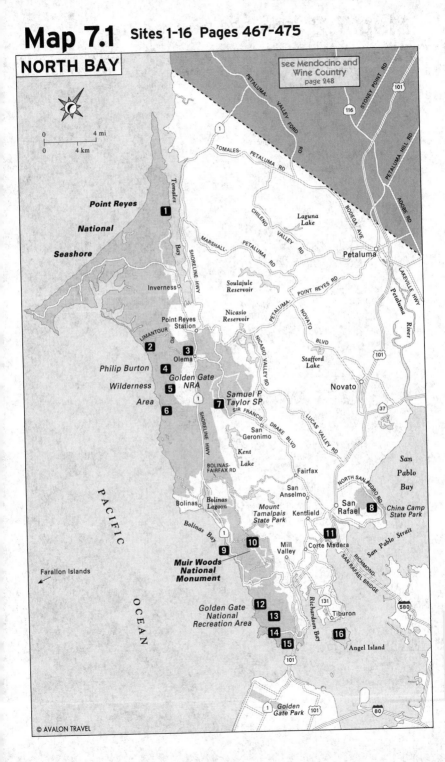

NORTH BAY

see Mendocino and
Wine Country
page 248

Point Reyes

National

Seashore

Inverness

Point Reyes
Station

Olema

Philip Burton

Wilderness

Area

Golden Gate
NRA

Samuel P
Taylor SP

SIR FRANCIS

San
Geronimo

Kent
Lake

BOLINAS-
FAIRFAX RD

Bolinas

Bolinas
Lagoon

Bolinas Bay

Fairfax

San
Anselmo

Mount
Tamalpais
State Park

Kentfield

Corte Madera

Mill
Valley

Muir Woods
National
Monument

Golden Gate
National
Recreation Area

Richardson Bay

Tiburon

Angel Island

Farallon Islands

PACIFIC

OCEAN

Tomales

Tomales Bay

SHORELINE HWY

LIMANTOUR RD

Laguna
Lake

Petaluma

Soulajule
Reservoir

Nicasio
Reservoir

Stafford
Lake

Novato

San Rafael

China Camp
State Park

San
Pablo
Bay

San Pablo Strait

RICHMOND-
SAN RAFAEL BRIDGE

Golden
Gate Park

TOMALES- PETALUMA RD

CHILENO VALLEY RD

MARSHALL- PETALUMA RD

POINT REYES RD

PETALUMA- POINT REYES RD

NICASIO VALLEY RD

NOVATO BLVD

LUCAS VALLEY RD

NORTH SAN PEDRO RD

DRAKE BLVD

PETALUMA VALLEY FORD RD

STONEY POINT RD

PETALUMA HILL RD

ADOBE RD

BODEGA AVE

LAKEVILLE HWY

Petaluma
River

101

116

37

101

131

580

80

1

1

1

1

101

101

© AVALON TRAVEL

Map 7.2 Sites 17-20 Pages 476-478

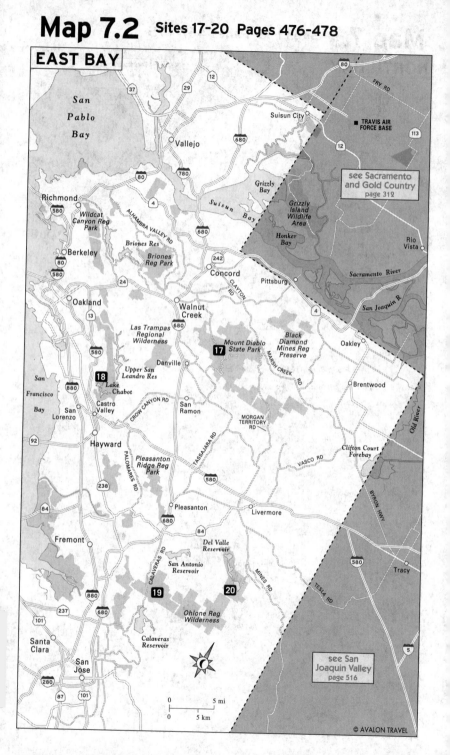

Map 7.3 Sites 21-27 Pages 479-482

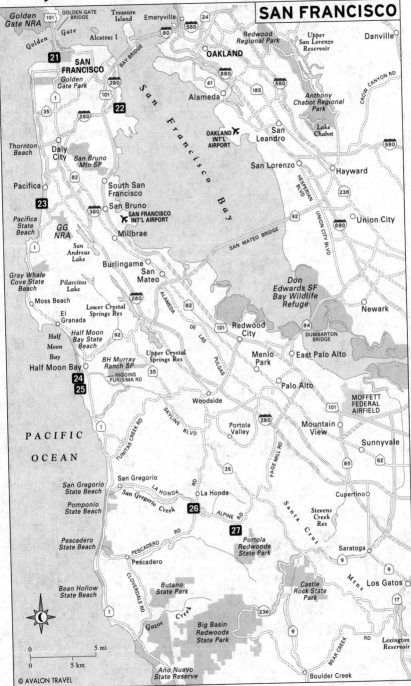

SAN FRANCISCO

Golden Gate NRA
GOLDEN GATE BRIDGE
Treasure Island
Emeryville
Alcatraz I
Golden Gate
Redwood Regional Park
Upper San Lorenzo Reservoir
Danville
OAKLAND
21 SAN FRANCISCO
Golden Gate Park
San Francisco Bay
Alameda
22
Anthony Chabot Regional Park
Lake Chabot
Thornton Beach
Daly City
San Bruno Mtn SP
OAKLAND INT'L AIRPORT
San Leandro
San Lorenzo
Hayward
Pacifica
South San Francisco
San Bruno
SAN FRANCISCO INT'L AIRPORT
23
Pacifica State Beach
GG NRA
Millbrae
Burlingame
San Mateo
SAN MATEO BRIDGE
Don Edwards SF Bay Wildlife Refuge
Newark
Union City
HESPERIAN BLVD
UNION CITY BLVD
Gray Whale Cove State Beach
San Andreas Lake
Pilarcitos Lake
Moss Beach
El Granada
Lower Crystal Springs Res
Half Moon Bay State Beach
DE LAS PULGAS
Redwood City
Menlo Park
East Palo Alto
DUMBARTON BRIDGE
Half Moon Bay
BH Murray Ranch SP
HIGGINS PURISIMA RD
Upper Crystal Springs Res
Palo Alto
MOFFETT FEDERAL AIRFIELD
24
25
Woodside
Portola Valley
Mountain View
Sunnyvale
PACIFIC OCEAN
TUNITAS CREEK RD
SKYLINE BLVD
PAGE MILL RD
San Gregorio State Beach
San Gregorio
LA HONDA RD
La Honda
26
ALPINE RD
Stevens Creek Res
Cupertino
Pomponio State Beach
San Gregorio Creek
Santa Cruz
Pescadero State Beach
PESCADERO RD
27
Portola Redwoods State Park
Saratoga
Pescadero
CLOVERDALE RD
Bean Hollow State Beach
Butano State Park
Castle Rock State Park
Mtns
Los Gatos
Gazos Creek
Big Basin Redwoods State Park
BEAR CREEK RD
Lexington Reservoir
Año Nuevo State Reserve
Boulder Creek

0   5 mi
0   5 km

© AVALON TRAVEL

Map 7.4 Sites 28-39 Pages 483-490

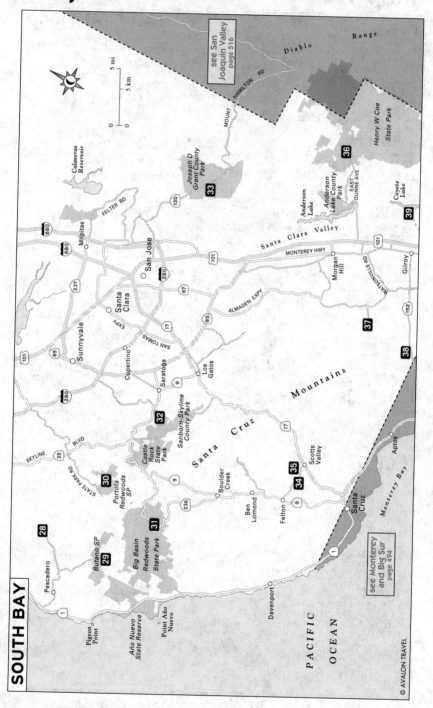

1 TOMALES BAY BOAT-IN

Scenic rating: 10

in Point Reyes National Seashore

Map 7.1, page 463

Here is a little slice of paradise secreted away along the west shore of Tomales Bay. A series of dispersed boat-in camps are set along small, sandy coves along the bases of steep cliffs, set from just north of Indian Beach at Tomales Bay State Park all the way north to Tomales Point. Boaters are required to bring portable toilets, and reservations are often a necessity, especially on weekends. Tomales Bay is pretty, quiet, protected from the onshore coastal winds, and offers outstanding sea kayaking. Note that some spots that appear gorgeous during low tides can be covered by water during high tides, so pick your spot above the tide line. Sightings of elk are common, with a herd of 500 on the Pierce Ranch section of Point Reyes National Seashore. Day hikes are sensational from Pierce Ranch to Tomales Point, and kayaking is outstanding.

Campsites, facilities: There are 20 permits issued daily for dispersed boat-in tent sites along the shore of Tomales Bay. Pit toilets are available only at Marshall Beach and Tomales/Kehoe Beach. No drinking water or other facilities are available. Garbage must be packed out. Boaters must bring portable toilets. No wood gathering permitted.

Reservations, fees: Reservations are accepted at 877/444-6777 or www.recreation.gov ($9 reservation fee). Camping permits are required from the Bear Valley Visitor Center at 415/663-8054 and must be picked up in person (for directions, see the Sky Camp Hike-In listing in this chapter). Single sites are $20 per night, group sites (7–25 people) are $40–50; four-day maximum stay. Open year-round, weather permitting.

Directions: To reach the boat launch, drive on U.S. 101 to Petaluma and the East Washington exit. Take that exit and drive west (this street becomes Bodega Avenue) through Petaluma and continue to Highway 1. Turn left (south) on Highway 1 and drive 3.5 miles to the Miller County Park boat launch on the right (0.5 mile before Blakes Landing). Launch your boat and paddle across Tomales Bay to the boat-in campsites along the Point Reyes National Seashore.

Contact: Point Reyes National Seashore, 415/464-5100, www.nps.gov/pore.

2 COAST CAMP HIKE-IN

Scenic rating: 7

in Point Reyes National Seashore

Map 7.1, page 463

This hike-in camp is set on an open ocean-bluff, just above Santa Maria Beach on the Point Reyes National Seashore. It is a 1.8-mile hike to get to this northernmost camp on Coast Trail. (The complete Coast Trail is a 19-mile trip and one of the best hikes in the Bay Area.) From Coast Camp, you can continue south, where the trail contours south along the bluffs above the beach for 1.4 miles to Sculptured Beach. You'll find a series of odd geologic formations, including caves, tunnels, and sea stacks. A backcountry permit is required. You can also hike up the Woodward Trail for sensational views of Drakes Bay and across the ocean.

Campsites, facilities: There are 12 individual and two group hike-in sites. Picnic tables and fire grills are provided. Drinking water is available. Vault toilets are available. Charcoal or gas stoves are allowed, with backpacking stoves recommended for cooking. No wood fires permitted. Garbage must be packed out. No vehicles or pets are permitted.

Reservations, fees: Reservations are accepted at 877/444-6777 or www.recreation.gov ($9 reservation fee). Camping permits are required from the Bear Valley Visitor Center at 415/663-8054 and must be picked up in person (for directions, see the Sky Camp Hike-In listing in this chapter). Single sites are $20 per night, group sites (7–25 people) are $40–50; four-day maximum stay. Open year-round.

Directions: From U.S. 101 in Marin, take the

Sir Francis Drake Boulevard/San Anselmo exit and drive about 20 miles to Highway 1 at Olema. Turn right on Highway 1 and drive a very short distance. Turn left at Bear Valley Road and drive north for two miles to Limantour Road. Turn left at Limantour Road and drive six miles to the access road for the Point Reyes Hostel. Turn left and drive 0.2 mile to the trailhead on the right side of the road. A parking area is a short distance ahead and to the right.

Contact: Point Reyes National Seashore, 415/464-5100, www.nps.gov/pore.

3 OLEMA RV RESORT & CAMPGROUND
🏃 🐕 🎣 ♿ 🚐 ⛺

Scenic rating: 4

in Olema

Map 7.1, page 463

If location is everything, then this 32-acre campground should be rated a 10. It is set in Olema, in a valley amid Marin's coastal foothills, an ideal jump-off spot for a Point Reyes adventure. It borders the Point Reyes National Seashore to the west and the Golden Gate National Recreation Area to the east, with Tomales Bay to the nearby north. There are several excellent trailheads available within a 10-minute drive along Highway 1 to the south. The campsites are small, tightly placed, and I have received a few complaint letters about the ambience of the place.

Campsites, facilities: There are 187 sites, some with full or partial hookups (30 and 50 amps), for tents or RVs of any length, and a large area for up to 175 tents. Picnic tables and fire rings are provided. Drinking water, restrooms with showers, dump station, coin laundry, post office, ATM, firewood, ice, playground, RV supplies, propane, horseshoes, volleyball, shuffleboard, ping-pong, badminton, tetherball, Wi-Fi, modem access, meeting facilities, amphitheater, and a recreation hall (for groups of 25 or more only) are available. Some

facilities are wheelchair-accessible. Leashed pets are permitted.

Reservations, fees: Reservations are accepted at 800/655-CAMP (800/655-2267). RV sites are $53–63 per night, $2 per night for each additional vehicle; tent sites are $44–49, $1.50–3 per person per night for more than two people. Rates are discounted fall through spring. Weekly rates available. No credit cards. Open year-round.

Directions: From U.S. 101 in Marin, take the San Anselmo/Sir Francis Drake Boulevard exit and drive west for about 22 miles to Highway 1 at Olema. Turn north (right) on Highway 1 and drive 0.25 mile to the campground on the left.

Contact: Olema RV Resort & Campground, 415/663-8106, www.olemarvresort.com.

4 SKY CAMP HIKE-IN
🏃 ⛺

Scenic rating: 7

in Point Reyes National Seashore

Map 7.1, page 463

Sky Camp is set on the western flank of Inverness Ridge at 1,025 feet elevation, with panoramic views of Drakes Bay, Point Reyes and the Farallon Islands. Hit it right and it will feel like a foothold in the sky. To reach the camp, start at the Sky Trail Trailhead off Limantour Road. The hike starts by climbing a service road then enters a forest to emerge at Sky Camp in 1.4 miles. Some sites are secluded for privacy, while others are out in the open. Wildflower blooms are exceptional in spring.

Campsites, facilities: There are 11 individual sites and a group site (walk-in only) which can accommodate up to 25 people. Permits must be obtained from the Bear Valley Visitor Center before camping. Vault toilets and fire grills (charcoal only, no wood fires) are provided. Drinking water is available intermittently; check for current status. Garbage must be packed out. No vehicles or pets are allowed.

Reservations, fees: Reservations are accepted

at 877/444-6777 or www.recreation.gov ($9 reservation fee). Camping permits are required from the Bear Valley Visitor Center at 415/663-8054 and must be picked up in person. Single sites are $20 per night, group sites (7–25 people) are $40–50; four-day maximum stay. Open year-round.

Directions: From U.S. 101 in Marin, take the Sir Francis Drake Boulevard/San Anselmo exit and drive west for about 20 miles to Highway 1 at Olema. Turn north on Highway 1 and drive a very short distance to Bear Valley Road. Turn left at Bear Valley Road and drive north for 0.7 mile to the visitors center road on the left (signed "Seashore Information"). Turn left and drive to the visitors center parking lot and Bear Valley Trailhead.

To reach the trailhead: From Bear Valley Visitor Center, exit the parking lot onto Bear Valley Road. Turn left on Bear Valley Road and drive two miles to Limantour Road. Turn left on Limantour and drive three miles to the signed spur road for Sky Trail trailhead on the left. Turn left and go a short distance to the parking area and trailhead.

Contact: Point Reyes National Seashore, 415/464-5100, www.nps.gov/pore.

5 GLEN CAMP HIKE-IN
🚶 ⛺

Scenic rating: 10

in Point Reyes National Seashore

Map 7.1, page 463

Glen Camp Hike-In is set in the coastal foothills of Point Reyes National Seashore and is surrounded by forest. The hike to it starts at the Bear Valley Visitor Center, where you can obtain your backcountry permits and hiking information, and is routed on popular Bear Valley Trail, a wide road made out of compressed rock. It is 1.6 miles to Divide Meadow, with a modest 215-foot climb, then another 1.6 miles through Bear Valley to Glen Trail. Turn left on Glen Loop Trail and hike 1.4 miles, with the trail moving laterally in and

out of two canyons to reach the camp. It is secluded and quiet. Get a map, a permit, and bring everything you need.

Campsites, facilities: There are 12 hike-in sites. Picnic tables and fire grills are provided. Vault toilets are available. Drinking water is available intermittently; check for current status. Charcoal or gas stoves are allowed, with backpacking stoves recommended for cooking. No wood fires permitted. Garbage must be packed out. No vehicles or pets are permitted.

Reservations, fees: Reservations are accepted at 877/444-6777 or www.recreation.gov ($9 reservation fee). Camping permits are required from the Bear Valley Visitor Center at 415/663-8054 and must be picked up in person (for directions, see the Sky Camp Hike-In listing in this chapter). Single sites are $20 per night, group sites (7–25 people) are $40–50; four-day maximum stay. Open year-round.

Directions: From U.S. 101 in Marin, take the Sir Francis Drake Boulevard/San Anselmo exit and drive west for about 20 miles to Highway 1 at Olema. Turn north on Highway 1 and drive a very short distance to Bear Valley Road. Turn left at Bear Valley Road and drive north for 0.7 mile to the visitors center road on the left (signed "Seashore Information"). Turn left and drive to the visitors center parking lot and Bear Valley Trailhead. It is a 4.6-mile hike to the camp.

Contact: Point Reyes National Seashore, 415/464-5100, www.nps.gov/pore.

6 WILDCAT CAMP HIKE-IN
🚶 ⛺

Scenic rating: 10

in Point Reyes National Seashore

Map 7.1, page 463   BEST (

This backpack camp sits in a grassy meadow near a small stream that flows to the ocean, just above remote Wildcat Beach. From the Palomarin Trailhead, getting to this camp takes you on a fantastic 5.5-mile hike that crosses some of the Bay Area's most beautiful wildlands. The trail is routed along the ocean for about a mile, heads up into the coastal hills, turns left, and skirts past Bass Lake, Crystal Lake, and Pelican Lake and, ultimately, heads past Alamere Creek to this beautiful camp set on an ocean bluff. A fantastic side trip is to hike along the beach from Wildcat Camp to the south, where you can get a full frontal view of Alamere Falls. It is a dramatic 40-foot free fall, one of the rare ocean bluff waterfalls anywhere.

Campsites, facilities: There are five individual and three group hike-in sites. Picnic tables and fire grills are provided. Vault toilets are available. Drinking water is available intermittently; check for current status. Charcoal or gas stoves are allowed, with backpacking stoves recommended for cooking. No wood fires permitted. Garbage must be packed out. No vehicles or pets are permitted.

Reservations, fees: Reservations are accepted at 877/444-6777 or www.recreation. gov ($9 reservation fee). Camping permits are required from the Bear Valley Visitor Center at 415/663-8054 and must be picked up in person (for directions, see the Sky Camp Hike-In listing in this chapter). Single sites are $20 per night, group sites (7–25 people) are $40–50; four-day maximum stay. Open year-round.

Directions: From U.S. 101 in Marin, take the Sir Francis Drake Boulevard/San Anselmo exit and drive about 20 miles west on Sir Francis Drake Boulevard to the town of Olema and Highway 1. Turn left on Highway 1 and drive 9.3 miles to Olema-Bolinas Road on the right (if the sign is missing—a common event—note that a white ranch house is opposite the turn). Turn right on Olema-Bolinas Road and drive 1.5 miles to Mesa Road. Turn right and drive six miles (past an area known as "The Towers" due to all the antennas) to the parking area and Palomarin Trailhead. It is a 5.6-mile hike to the campground on Coast Trail.

Contact: Point Reyes National Seashore, 415/464-5100 or 415/663-8054, www.nps. gov/pore.

7 SAMUEL P. TAYLOR STATE PARK

Scenic rating: 9

near San Rafael

Map 7.1, page 463

This is a beautiful park, with campsites set amid redwoods, complete with a babbling brook running nearby. The park covers more than 2,700 acres of wooded countryside in the steep and rolling hills of Marin County and features a unique contrast of coast redwoods with open grassland. Hikers will find 20 miles of trails, a hidden waterfall, and some good mountain-biking routes on service roads. The paved bike path that runs through the park and parallels Lagunitas Creek is a terrific, easy ride. Trees include redwood, Douglas fir, oak, and madrone, and native wildflowers include buttercups, milkmaids, and Indian paintbrush. The section of the park on the north side of Sir Francis Drake has the best hiking in the park. Campsites are on the south side of the park, except for three sites on the north side.

Note: This park is on the closure list developed by the California Department of Parks, pending final state budget decisions or the possible transfer of park management to other park agencies or volunteer groups. It is currently operating with limited facilities via an agreement with the National Park Service.

Campsites, facilities: There are 25 sites for tents, 35 sites for tents or RVs up to 27 feet (no hookups), one hike-in/bike-in camp, one group site at Madrone for 50 people, two primitive group sites for up to 10 people each at Devil's Gulch, and one equestrian site with corrals at Devil's Gulch Horse Camp. Cabins are also available. Picnic tables, food lockers, and fire grills are provided. Drinking water, coin showers, flush and pit toilets, and Wi-Fi are available. There is a small store and café two miles away in Lagunitas. Some facilities are wheelchair-accessible. Leashed pets are permitted in campsites only.

Reservations, fees: Reservations are not accepted at this time; all sites are first-come, first-served through March 2013. Sites are $35 per night, $8 per night for each additional vehicle, the equestrian camp is $75 per night, $5 per person per night for hike-in/bike-in sites. Devil's Gulch group sites are $35–75 per night; the Madrone group site is $225 per night. Cabins are $85 per night ($100 deposit). Open year-round.

Directions: From U.S. 101 in Marin, take the Sir Francis Drake Boulevard exit and drive west for about 15 miles to the park entrance on the left side of the road.

Contact: Samuel P. Taylor State Park, 415/488-9897, www.parks.ca.gov; Marin Sector, 415/898-4362.

8 CHINA CAMP STATE PARK

Scenic rating: 10

on San Pablo Bay near San Rafael

Map 7.1, page 463

This is one of the Bay Area's prettiest campgrounds, set in woodlands with a picturesque creek running past. The camps are shaded and sheltered. Directly adjacent to the camp is a meadow, marshland, and then San Pablo Bay. Deer can seem as tame as chipmunks. Hiking is outstanding here, either taking Shoreline Trail for a pretty walk near the edge of San Pablo Bay, or Bay View Trail for the climb up the ridge that borders the park, in the process gaining spectacular views of the bay and miles of charm. The landscape here includes an extensive intertidal salt marsh, and meadow and oak habitats. There are five miles of hiking trails, heavily used on spring and summer weekends. A highlight is the China Camp Village, which depicts an early Chinese settlement.

Campsites, facilities: There are 30 walk-in tent sites and one hike-in/bike-in site. Picnic tables, food lockers, and fire grills are provided. Drinking water and a restroom with flush toilets and showers are available. Some facilities are wheelchair accessible. Leashed pets are permitted at the campground and picnic areas.

Reservations, fees: Reservations are accepted at 800/444-7275 (800/444-PARK) or www.reserveamerica.com ($8 reservation fee). Sites are $35 per night, $8 per night for each additional vehicle, $5 per person per night for hike-in/bike-in site. Open year-round, weather permitting.

Directions: From San Francisco, drive north on U.S. 101 to San Rafael and take the North San Pedro Road exit. Drive east on North San Pedro Road for five miles to the Back Ranch Meadows Campground entrance on the right. Turn right and drive a short distance to the campground trailhead at the end of the road. Reaching the sites requires a one- to five-minute walk.

Contact: China Camp State Park, 415/456-0766, www.parks.ca.gov; Friends of China Camp, 415/488-5161, www.friendsofchina-camp.org.

9 STEEP RAVINE ENVIRONMENTAL CAMPSITES

Scenic rating: 10

in Mount Tamalpais State Park

Map 7.1, page 463   BEST (

This is one of the most remarkable spots on the California coast, with primitive cabins/wood shacks set on a bluff on Rocky Point overlooking the ocean. It is primitive but dramatic, with passing ships, fishing boats, lots of marine birds, occasionally even whales, and a chance for heart-stopping sunsets. There is an easy walk to the north down to Redrock Beach, which is secluded. Just across Highway

1 (with a short jog to the right) is a trailhead for Steep Ravine Trail on the slopes of Mount Tamalpais. After a while you'll feel like you're a million miles from civilization.

Campsites, facilities: There are seven walk-in sites for tents and 10 primitive cabins (also known as environmental sites), each with a wood stove, picnic table, and a flat wood surface for sleeping. At tent sites, picnic tables and fire grills are provided and pit toilets are available. Drinking water is nearby, and wood is available for purchase. No pets are permitted.

Reservations, fees: Reservations are accepted at 800/444-7275 (800/444-PARK) or www.reserveamerica.com ($8 reservation fee). Sites are $25 per night for tent sites, $100 per night for environmental cabins, one vehicle per cabin, five people maximum per site. Open year-round.

Directions: From U.S. 101 in Marin, take the Stinson Beach/Highway 1 exit. Drive west to the stoplight at the T intersection (Highway 1). Turn left on Highway 1 and drive about 11 miles to the gated access road on the left side of the highway at Rocky Point. (The gate lock combination will be provided when reservations are made, or by calling 415/388-2070 up to one week before your stay.)

Contact: Mount Tamalpais State Park, 415/388-2070; Marin Sector, 415/898-4362, www.parks.ca.gov.

10 PANTOLL WALK-IN, ALICE EASTWOOD, AND FRANK VALLEY

Scenic rating: 10

in Mount Tamalpais State Park

Map 7.1, page 463

When camping at Pantoll, you are within close range of the divine, including some of the best hiking, best lookouts, and just plain best places to be anywhere in the Bay Area. The camp is set in the woods on the western slopes of Mount Tamalpais, which some say is a place of special power, with sensational hiking and trailheads. The walk to the Pantoll Campground can be as short as 100 feet, and as long as just over a quarter mile. This landscape is a mix of redwood groves, oak woodlands, and grasslands, and provides both drop-dead beautiful views of the ocean nearby, as well as a trip into a lush redwood canyon with a stream. Steep Ravine Trail is routed out of camp to the west into a wondrous gorge filled with redwoods and a stream with miniature waterfalls. It is best seen after a good rain, when everything is dripping with moisture. Another great hike from this camp is on Matt Davis/Coastal Trail, which provides beautiful views of the coast. Another must is the nearby drive to the East Peak Lookout, where the entire world seems within reach. This park provides more than 50 miles of trails for hiking and biking, which in turn link to a network of 200 miles of other trails.

Campsites, facilities: There are 16 walk-in tent sites, two group sites for 25 and 75 people each, and one equestrian group site for up to 25 people. Picnic tables, food lockers, and fire grills are provided. Drinking water, flush toilets, and Wi-Fi are available. Firewood is available for purchase. Leashed pets are permitted at campsites only.

Reservations, fees: Reservations are accepted for group and equestrian sites at 800/444-7275 (800/444-PARK) or www.reserveamerica.com ($8 reservation fee). Walk-in sites are $25 per night, the Alice Eastwood Group Camps are $110 and $225 per night Frank Valley Horse Camp is $75 per night (horse required). Open year-round.

Directions: From U.S. 101 in Marin, take the Stinson Beach/Highway 1 exit. Drive west to the stoplight at the T intersection for Highway 1. Turn left and drive about four miles uphill to the Panoramic Highway. Bear to the right on Panoramic Highway and continue for 5.5 miles to the Pantoll parking area. Turn left at the Pantoll parking area and ranger station. A 100- to 500-foot walk is required to reach the campground.

Directions to the group site and the combination to the gate lock will be provided when reservations are made; or call 415/388-2070 up to one week before your stay.

Contact: Mount Tamalpais State Park, 415/388-2070; Marin Sector, 415/898-4362, www.parks.ca.gov.

11 MARIN RV PARK

Scenic rating: 2

in Greenbrae

Map 7.1, page 463

For out-of-towners with RVs, this can make an ideal base camp for Marin County adventures. To the west are Mount Tamalpais State Park, Muir Woods National Monument, Samuel P. Taylor State Park, and Point Reyes National Seashore. To the nearby east is the Loch Lomond Marina on San Pablo Bay, where fishing trips can be arranged for striped bass and sturgeon; phone Loch Lomond Bait Shop, 415/456-0321. The park offers complete sightseeing information and easy access to buses and ferry service to San Francisco.

Campsites, facilities: There are 86 sites with full hookups (30 and 50 amps) for tents or RVs. Restrooms with showers, coin laundry, Wi-Fi, swimming pool, dump station, and RV supplies are available. Some facilities are wheelchair-accessible. Leashed pets are permitted.

Reservations, fees: Reservations are recommended. Sites are $50 per night for two people, $45 per night in winter, $2 per person per night for more than two people, six people maximum per site. Weekly and monthly rates available in off-season. Some credit cards accepted. Open year-round.

Directions: From the south: From the Golden Gate Bridge, drive north on U.S. 101 for 10 miles to Lucky Drive (south of San Rafael). Exit and turn left on Redwood Highway (no sign) and drive three blocks north to the park entrance on the right.

From the north: From San Rafael, drive south on U.S. 101 to the Lucky Drive exit (450A). Take that exit to the first light at Tamal Vista. Turn left and drive to the next stoplight and Wornum Avenue. Turn left at Wornum Avenue and drive under the freeway to Redwood Highway (frontage road). Turn left and drive four blocks north to the park entrance.

Contact: Marin RV Park, 415/461-5199 or 888/461-5199, www.marinrvpark.com.

12 HAYPRESS HIKE-IN

Scenic rating: 9

on Marin Headlands

Map 7.1, page 463

Nope, your eyes aren't foolin' ya—this is one of three free(!) campgrounds in the Marin Headlands. Haypress campground is set on the northern outskirts of Tennessee Valley at the north end of the Marin Headlands. This is a primitive backpacking campground where you must bring everything you need. Reaching this camp is not difficult, just a 0.75-mile hike departing from one of Marin's most popular trailheads in Tennessee Valley. Yet in just 20–30 minutes, hikers can visit a world that seemingly belongs just to them.

Campsites, facilities: There are five tent sites, with a maximum of four people per site. Picnic tables are provided. Portable toilets and food lockers are available. No drinking water is available. No fires are permitted; backpacking stoves required for cooking. A map/brochure is available at the Marin Headlands Visitor Center or by contacting the Golden Gate National Recreation Area. A detailed hiking map of the area is available for a fee.

Reservations, fees: Reservations and a permit are required from the visitors center before camping. There is no fee. Groups up to 20 can reserve any site from November through March. Three sites can be reserved for groups up to 12 from April through October. Open year-round, weather permitting. Three-night maximum stay per season.

Directions: From U.S. 101 in Marin, take the Stinson Beach/Highway 1 exit. Drive 0.6 mile to Tennessee Valley Road. Turn left on Tennessee Valley Road and drive two miles until the road dead-ends at the parking area and trailhead. Take the trailhead for Tennessee Valley (see directions above and map/brochure) and hike 0.75 miles to the campground.

Contact: Marin Headlands Visitor Center, Golden Gate National Recreation Area, Building 948, Fort Barry, Sausalito, CA 94965, 415/331-1540, www.nps.gov/goga.

13 HAWK CAMP HIKE-IN
🏃🏕

Scenic rating: 10

on Marin Headlands

Map 7.1, page 463

This is the most remote of the campgrounds on the Marin Headlands. It is high above Gerbode Valley, requiring a hike of 3.5 miles, climbing much of the way from the parking lot and trailhead at Tennessee Valley. It is a small campground, with three sites and room for no more than four people per site. After parking at Tennessee Valley, take the trailhead for the Old Marincello Vehicle Road/Bobcat Trail. This route climbs in a counterclockwise direction around Mount Vortac; after 1.7 miles you will reach a junction with Mount Vortac Trail. Do not turn at that junction. Continue straight on Bobcat Trail for 0.7 mile to a junction with Hawk Trail. Turn right and hike on the trail for one mile to Hawk Camp, set at an elevation of 750 feet. Below you to the southeast is Gerbode Valley.

Campsites, facilities: There are three tent sites, with a maximum of four people per site. Picnic tables and food lockers are provided and chemical toilets are available. There is no drinking water and fires are not permitted. Backpacking stoves are required for cooking. A map/brochure is available at the Marin Headlands Visitor Center or by contacting the Golden Gate National Recreation Area. A detailed hiking map of the area is available for a fee.

Reservations, fees: Reservations and a permit are required from the visitors center before camping. There is no fee. All three sites can be reserved by groups of up to 12 from November through March. Open year-round, weather permitting, with a three-night maximum stay per season.

Directions: From U.S. 101 in Marin, take the Stinson Beach/Highway 1 exit. Drive 0.6 mile and turn left on Tennessee Valley Road. Drive two miles until the road dead-ends at the parking area and trailhead. Take the trailhead for Old Marincello Vehicle Road/Bobcat Trail and hike 3.5 miles.

Contact: Marin Headlands Visitor Center, Golden Gate National Recreation Area, Building 948, Fort Barry, Sausalito, CA 94965, 415/331-1540, www.nps.gov/goga.

14 BICENTENNIAL WALK-IN
🏃🏕

Scenic rating: 9

on Marin Headlands

Map 7.1, page 463

Of the hike-in campgrounds set on the Marin Headlands, it is Bicentennial Walk-In that is the easiest to reach. It is only a 100-yard walk northwest from the parking area near Battery Wallace. This is a small camp with space for just three tents, with a maximum of two people per site.

Campsites, facilities: There are three tent sites with no more than three people and one tent per site. Portable toilets and food lockers are available. Picnic tables and barbecue grills are available 100 yards away at Battery Wallace. Drinking water is available one mile away at the Marin Headlands Visitor Center. Backpacking stoves required for cooking. A map/brochure is available at the Marin Headlands Visitor Center or by contacting the Golden Gate National Recreation Area. A detailed hiking map of the area is available for a fee.

Reservations, fees: Reservations and a permit are required from the visitors center before camping. There is no fee. Open year-round, weather permitting, with a three-night maximum stay per season.

Directions: From San Francisco drive north on U.S. 101 over the Golden Gate Bridge, and into Marin to the Alexander Avenue exit. Take the Alexander Avenue exit and turn left underneath the highway. Take the wide paved road to the right (Conzelman Road, but there is no sign), and look for the Marin Headlands sign. Continue west for 3.5 miles (it becomes a one-way road) to the parking area on your left for Battery Wallace (on your right). Park and walk 100 yards north to the campground.

Contact: Marin Headlands Visitor Center, Golden Gate National Recreation Area, Building 948, Fort Barry, Sausalito, CA 94965, 415/331-1540, www.nps.gov/goga.

15 KIRBY COVE

Scenic rating: 10

on Marin Headlands

Map 7.1, page 463

Kirby Cove is nestled in a grove of cypress and eucalyptus trees in a stunning setting just west of the Golden Gate Bridge. It is small and pristine, with space for just four sites and restricted parking. Two campsites are perched on a bluff overlooking the beach; the views are drop-dead beautiful of the Golden Gate Bridge, San Francisco Headlands, and the mouth of the bay opening to the Pacific Ocean. Group sites are set amid eucalyptus trees and are a short walk inland. An old concrete military bunker provides curiosity for many.

Campsites, facilities: There are four tent sites for no more than 10 people per site. Picnic tables, food lockers, and fire rings/barbecue pits are provided. Vault toilets are available, but there is no drinking water. It is recommended that you bring a backpacking stove because of occasional fire restrictions; wood collecting is not permitted. A map/brochure is available at the Marin Headlands Visitor Center or by contacting the Golden Gate National Recreation Area. A detailed hiking map of the area is available for a fee.

Reservations, fees: Reservations are accepted at 877/444-6777 or www.recreation.gov ($9 reservation fee). Sites are $25 per night for up to three cars and 10 people. Maximum stay of three nights per year. Open April through October.

Directions: From San Francisco drive north on U.S. 101 over the Golden Gate Bridge and into Marin to the Alexander Avenue exit. Take the Alexander Avenue exit and turn left underneath the highway. Take the wide paved road to the right (Conzelman Road, but there is no sign), and look for the Marin Headlands sign. Continue west on Conzelman about 0.25 mile to Kirby Cove Road (the first turn on the left, a dirt road). Bear left and drive to the gate. When you get reservations, you will get the code for the gate. Unlock the gate and drive 0.9 mile to the campground.

Contact: Marin Headlands Visitor Center, Golden Gate National Recreation Area, Building 948, Fort Barry, Sausalito, CA 94965, 415/331-1540, www.nps.gov/goga.

16 ANGEL ISLAND STATE PARK WALK-IN/BOAT-IN

Scenic rating: 10

on Angel Island

Map 7.1, page 463   BEST (

Camping at Angel Island is one of the unique adventures in the Bay Area; the only catch is that getting to the campsites requires a ferry boat ride and then a walk of 1–2 miles, or a kayak or boat trip from the mainland directly to the camp. The payoff comes at the end of the day, when all of the park's day visitors depart for the mainland, leaving the entire island to you. Plan far ahead because the sites can book up months in advance. The group camp is popular with kayakers because of beach access. From start to finish, it's a great trip, featuring a private campsite, often with spectacular views of San Francisco Bay, the San Francisco waterfront and skyline, Marin Headlands, and Mount Tamalpais. The tromp up to 798-foot Mount Livermore includes a short, steep stretch, but in return furnishes one of the most spectacular urban lookouts in America. Be ready for cold, foggy weather at night in midsummer. The park features more than 13 miles of trails, including Perimeter Road, a must-do for all avid cyclists. Bikes are also permitted on the park's fire road system. Angel Island has a stunning history, including being used from 1910 to 1940 to process thousands of immigrants as they entered America; historic tram tours are available.

Campsites, facilities: There are 10 hike-in sites and one group hike-in/boat-in site for up to 20 people. Picnic tables, barbecues, and food lockers are provided. Drinking water and pit toilets are available. Garbage service is available. No open wood campfires permitted; only charcoal allowed. A seasonal café is on the island. Some facilities are wheelchair-accessible.

Reservations, fees: Reservations are accepted at 800/444-7275 (800/444-PARK) or www.reserveamerica.com ($8 reservation fee). Sites are $30 per night (limit eight people per site). The boat-in group site is $50 per night. To avoid park entrance fees, campers must check in at the Ayala Cove kiosk (at Angel Island) and show reservation vouchers to the ferry boat operator. Open year-round, with limited ferry service in winter.

Directions: Angel Island can be reached by ferry from San Francisco and Oakland/Alameda; for schedule information, call 415/773-1188, www.blueandgoldfleet.com. From Tiburon, contact 415/435-2131 or www.angelislandferry.com for schedule information.

Contact: Angel Island State Park, 415/435-191, www.parks.ca.gov; Marin District 707/769-5665; bike rentals and tram tours, www.angelisland.com.

17 MOUNT DIABLO STATE PARK

Scenic rating: 8

east of Oakland

Map 7.2, page 464

Mount Diablo, elevation 3,849 feet, provides one of the most all-encompassing lookouts anywhere in America, an awesome 360° on clear mornings. On crystal-clear days you can see the Sierra Nevada and its white, snow-bound crest. Some claim to have seen Half Dome in Yosemite with binoculars. The drive to the summit is a must-do trip, and the weekend interpretive center right on top of the mountain is one of the best in the Bay Area. The camps at Mount Diablo are set in foothill/oak grassland country, with some shaded sites. Winter and spring are good times to visit, when the weather is still cool enough for good hiking trips. Most of the trails require long hikes, often including significant elevation gains and losses. No alcohol is permitted in the park. The park offers extensive but challenging hiking, biking, and horseback riding. A museum, visitors center, and gift shop is perched on the Diablo summit. Summers are hot and dry, and in late summer the park can be closed because of fire danger. In winter, snow occasionally falls on the peak—according to my logbook, during the first full moon in February.

Campsites, facilities: There are 64 sites in three campgrounds for tents or RVs up to 20 feet long (no hookups) and five group sites for 20–50 people. Barbecue Terrace is a group site for equestrian use with hitching posts and a water trough. Picnic tables and fire grills are provided. Drinking water and flush and vault toilets are available. Showers are available at Juniper campground. Some facilities are wheelchair accessible. Leashed pets are permitted only in campgrounds and picnic areas.

Reservations, fees: Reservations are accepted at 800/444-7275 (800/444-PARK) or www.

reserveamerica.com ($8 reservation fee). Sites are $30 per night, $10 per night for each additional vehicle, group sites are $65–165 per night. Open year-round.

Directions: From Danville on I-680, take the Diablo Road exit. Turn east on Diablo Road and drive three miles to Mount Diablo Scenic Boulevard. Turn left and continue 3.5 miles (the road becomes South Gate Road) to the park entrance station. Register at the kiosk, obtain a park map, and drive to the designated campground.

Contact: Mount Diablo State Park, 925/837-2525 or 925/837-0904; Diablo Vista District, 707/769-5652, www.parks.ca.gov.

18 ANTHONY CHABOT REGIONAL PARK

Scenic rating: 7

near Castro Valley

Map 7.2, page 464

The campground at Chabot Regional Park is set on a hilltop sheltered by eucalyptus, with good views and trails available. The best campsites are the walk-in units, requiring a walk of only a minute or so. Several provide views of Lake Chabot to the south 0.5-mile away. The 315-acre lake provides good trout fishing in the winter and spring, and a chance for huge but elusive largemouth bass. Huckleberry Trail is routed down from the campground (near walk-in site 20) to the lake at Honker Bay, a good fishing area. There is also a good 12-mile bike ride around the lake. In all, this 5,000-acre park includes 31 miles of hiking, biking, and riding trails. East Bay Skyline Trail runs the length of the park. Boat rentals are available, but no swimming or water-body contact is permitted. Note: All boats must be certified mussel-free before launching. A weekend marksmanship range is available at the park, and a golf course is nearby.

Campsites, facilities: There are 75 sites for tents and small RVs, including 11 RV sites with full hookups (30 amps) and 10 walk-in tent sites. Group camping is available for a minimum of 11 people. Picnic tables and fire grills are provided. Restrooms with flush toilets and showers, drinking water, dump station, amphitheater, picnic area and naturalist-led campfire programs are available. A small marina, boat rentals, snack bar, and bait and tackle are available nearby at Lake Chabot Regional Park. There is no boat launch and gas motors and inflatables are prohibited; canoes and kayaks can be carried about 100 yards and hand launched. Some facilities are wheelchair accessible. Leashed pets are permitted.

Reservations, fees: Reservations are accepted at 888/327-2757, option 2, or http://ebparks.org ($8 reservation fee). Group sites cannot be reserved online. Sites are $22–30 per night, $8 per night for each additional vehicle, $2 per pet per night. Group sites are $100 per night. Some credit cards accepted. Open year-round.

Directions: From I-580 in the Oakland hills, drive to the 35th Avenue exit. Take that exit, and at the stop sign, turn east on 35th Avenue and drive up the hill and straight across Skyline Boulevard, where 35th Avenue becomes Redwood Road. Continue on Redwood Road for eight miles to the park and Marciel Road (campground entrance road) on the right.

Contact: Regional Park Headquarters, 888/327-2757; Anthony Chabot Regional Park, 510/639-4751; Chabot Equestrian Center, 510/569-4428, www.ebparks.org.

19 SUNOL REGIONAL WILDERNESS

Scenic rating: 7

south of Sunol

Map 7.2, page 464

Sunol's primary campground is closed until 2014. The hike-in backcountry campsites on the Ohlone Trail are still available and require a hike of 3.4 miles or more. Sunol Regional Wilderness is set in rolling oak and bay grasslands and is an outstanding park for off-season hiking, camping, wildlife-viewing, and wildflowers. In the spring and early summer, it is one of the best of the 150 parks in the Bay Area to see wildflowers. It is also the home of more nesting golden eagles than anywhere else in the world, with a chance to see falcons and hawks as well. In addition, Alameda Creek in Little Yosemite forms several miniature pool-and-drop waterfalls in the spring and early summer. The Little Yosemite area is a scenic gorge about two miles upstream from the visitors center. Dogs are allowed in the Ohlone Wilderness during the day, but are not permitted overnight. No alcohol is permitted in the park, and it is subject to confiscation. Bicycles and fires are prohibited at the trail and equestrian camps. Temporary closures can occur in late summer because of fire danger. Gates are locked at night; campers must arrive before dusk.

Campsites, facilities: There is a hike-in wilderness camping area for tents only requiring a hike of 3.4 miles and longer. There are no other facilities. There is no drinking water and garbage must be packed out.

Reservations, fees: Reservations are required one week in advance at 888/327-2757, option 2 or www.ebparks.org ($8 reservation fee). Sites are $5 per person per night; the equestrian camp is $7 per person per night; $2 per pet per night. A permit required for the wilderness camps. Some credit cards accepted. Open year-round, weather permitting.

Directions: From Walnut Creek, take I-680 to Sunol and take the Highway 84/Calaveras Road exit. Turn south on Calaveras and drive four miles to Geary Road. Turn left on Geary Road and drive two miles to the park entrance.

Contact: East Bay Regional Park District Headquarters, 888/327-2757; Sunol Regional Wilderness, 925/862-2244, www.ebparks.org/parks.htm.

20 DEL VALLE REGIONAL PARK

Scenic rating: 7

near Livermore

Map 7.2, page 464

Of the 65 parks in the East Bay Regional Park District, it is Del Valle that provides the greatest variety of recreation at the highest quality. Del Valle Reservoir is the centerpiece, a five-mile-long, narrow lake that fills a canyon with 16 miles of shoreline, providing a good boat launch for powerboats (10-mph speed limit) and good fishing for trout (stocked), striped bass, panfish, and catfish. Note: All boats must be certified mussel-free before launching. Two swimming beaches are popular in summer and an excellent mountain bike ride along the lake starts just north of the marina. The park offers boat tours of the natural history and lake ecology of the area.

The campsites are somewhat exposed because of the grassland habitat, but they fill anyway on most weekends and three-day holidays. Phase 2 campsites are closest to water in a more open area; Phase 4 campsites are set inland and are more wooded. A trailhead south of the lake provides access to Ohlone Wilderness Trail, and for the well conditioned, there is the 5.5-mile butt-kicker of a climb to Murietta Falls, gaining 1,600 feet in 1.5 miles. Murietta Falls is the Bay Area's highest waterfall, 100 feet tall, though its thin, silvery wisp is only full in late winter after heavy rains when the hills and aquifer are saturated. Riding trails are also available in this 4,000-acre park.

Campsites, facilities: There are 150 sites, including some with full or partial (50-amp) hookups, for tents or RVs of any length. There are also two walk-in group areas for 11–75 people, requiring a walk of 0.25–1 mile. Picnic tables and fire grills are provided. Drinking water, restrooms with flush toilets and showers, dump station, full marina, boat and sailboard rentals, seasonal campfire programs, swimming beaches, and a boat launch are available. Some facilities are wheelchair-accessible. Leashed pets are permitted.

Reservations, fees: Reservations are accepted at 888/327-2757, option 2 or ebparks.org ($8 reservation fee). Sites are $22–45 per night, $8 per night for each additional vehicle, $5 per day boat launch fee, $2 per pet per night. Some credit cards accepted. Open year-round.

Directions: From I-580 east in Livermore, take the North Livermore Avenue exit and turn south (right if driving from San Francisco). Drive south and proceed through Livermore (road becomes South Livermore Avenue). Continue for 1.5 miles (the road then becomes Tesla Road) to Mines Road. Turn right on Mines Road and drive 3.5 miles to Del Valle Road. Continue straight on Del Valle Road for four miles to the park entrance.

Contact: Del Valle Regional Park, 925/373-0332; East Bay Regional Park District, 888/327-2757, www.ebparks.org/parks.htm.

21 ROB HILL GROUP WALK-IN

Scenic rating: 8

in San Francisco Presidio

Map 7.3, page 465

Rob Hill campground reopened in 2010 with sparkling facilities and upgraded campsites. This is San Francisco's only campground with tent sites, well hidden in the Presidio beneath a canopy of cypress and eucalyptus trees and with a view of Immigrant Point. The Bay Area Ridge Trail passes directly by the camp and Presidio's roads offer popular bike routes. There are two group camps here—a great spot for a youth group camp—and they are always full. From the limited parking area, it is an uphill climb of 150 feet to the camp. Free shuttle service is available within the Presidio, which can connect you to Muni bus service.

Campsites, facilities: There are four group tent sites for up to 30 people each. Picnic tables, drinking water, restrooms with flush toilets, BBQ grills, and a community circle are available. Generators and amplified music are prohibited. Parking is limited (parking permit provided with reservation).

Reservations, fees: Reservations are required at 415/561-5444 (ask for reservations) or download an application online at www.presidio.gov/explore and fax it to 415/561-7604. Sites are $100 per night with a two-night maximum stay; credit cards only. Open April through October.

Directions: From the south: Take Highway 1 north into San Francisco. Highway 1 becomes 19th Avenue; stay on 19th Avenue and get in the far left lane as it enters Golden Gate Park (at Lincoln). Take the 25th Avenue exit to your left. Stay on 25th Avenue, continuing north for one mile. Turn right onto El Camino del Mar/Lincoln Boulevard. Turn right on Kobbe Avenue, then right onto Washington Avenue. Drive to Central Magazine and turn left; look for the first service road on the right. Turn right at that service road and park. Walk up the hill 150 feet to the campground.

From the north: Take U.S. 101/Highway 1 south over the Golden Gate Bridge and get in the right lane at the toll plaza ($7 toll). Immediately after the toll plaza, look for Merchant Street on the right. Turn right on Merchant Street and drive up the hill to the stop sign at Lincoln Boulevard. Turn right and drive to Kobbe Avenue. Turn left onto Kobbe Avenue and then right onto Washington Boulevard. Drive to Central Magazine and turn left; look for the first service road on the right. Turn right at that service road and park. Walk up the hill 150 feet to the campsites on the right.

Contact: The Presidio Trust, Rob Hill reservations 415/561-5444, www.presidio.gov/explore.

22 CANDLESTICK RV PARK

Scenic rating: 6

in San Francisco

Map 7.3, page 465

This RV park is set adjacent to Candlestick Park. It is five miles from downtown San Francisco and an ideal destination for out-of-towners who want to explore the city without having to drive, because the park offers tours and inexpensive shuttles to the downtown area. In addition, there are good hiking opportunities along the shoreline of the bay. On summer afternoons, when the wind howls at 20–30 mph here, sailboarders rip by. Rates are higher, much higher, on 49er game days, and the stadium is usually packed with 60,000 or more people.

Campsites, facilities: There are 165 sites with full hookups (30 and 50 amps) for trailers or RVs up to 42 feet, and 24 tent sites. Some sites are pull-through. Restrooms with showers, coin laundry, Wi-Fi, grocery store, game room, and RV washing are available. Shuttles and bus tours are also available. Some facilities are wheelchair-accessible. A security officer is posted at the entry station at night. Small leashed pets are permitted.

Reservations, fees: Reservations are recommended at 800/888-CAMP (800/888-2267). RV sites are $74–79 per night for two people, $5 per person per night for more than two people. Rates are higher on game days. Some credit cards accepted. Open year-round.

Directions: From San Francisco on U.S. 101, take the Candlestick Park exit (Exit 429A) to Gilman Road. Turn east on the stadium entrance road/Gilman Road and drive around the parking lot to the far end of the stadium (Gate 4).

Contact: Candlestick RV Park, 415/822-2299 or 800/888-2267, www.sanfranciscorvpark.com.

23 SAN FRANCISCO RV RESORT

Scenic rating: 8

in Pacifica

Map 7.3, page 465

This is one of the best RV parks in the Bay Area. It is set on the bluffs just above the Pacific Ocean in Pacifica, complete with beach access, nearby fishing pier, and sometimes excellent surf fishing. There is also a nearby golf course and the chance for dramatic ocean sunsets. The park is kept clean and in good shape, and though there is too much asphalt, the proximity to the beach overcomes it. It is only 20 minutes from San Francisco.

Campsites, facilities: There are 162 sites with full hookups (50 amps) for RVs up to 45 feet. No tents. Restrooms with showers, heated swimming pool, year-round spa, playground, game room, group facilities, cable TV, Wi-Fi, modem access, convenience store, coin laundry, and propane gas are available. Some facilities are wheelchair-accessible. Leashed pets are permitted, with some exceptions.

Reservations, fees: Reservations are recommended at 650/355-7093 or 800/822-1250. Sites are $56–95 per night. Weekly and monthly rates available. Some credit cards accepted. Open year-round.

Directions: From San Francisco, drive south on Highway 280 to Highway 1. Bear west on Highway 1 and drive into Pacifica to the Palmetto Drive exit. Take that exit and drive south to the stop sign (you will be on the west side of the highway). Continue straight ahead (the road becomes Palmetto Avenue) for about two blocks and look for the entrance to the park on the right side of the road at 700 Palmetto.

From the south, drive north on Highway 1 into Pacifica. Take the Manor Drive exit. At the stop sign, turn left on Oceana Avenue (you will be on the east side of the highway), and drive a block to another stop sign at Manor Drive. Turn left, drive a short distance over the highway to a stop sign at Palmetto Avenue. Turn left and drive about two blocks to the park on the right.

Contact: San Francisco RV Resort, 650/355-7093, www.sanfranciscorvresort.com.

24 HALF MOON BAY STATE BEACH

🧍 🚴 🏊 🛶 🎣 ♿ 🚐 ⛺

Scenic rating: 7

at Half Moon Bay

Map 7.3, page 465

In summer, this park often fills to capacity with campers touring Highway 1. The campground has level, grassy sites for tents, a clean parking area for RVs, and a state beach available just a short walk away. The feature here is four miles of broad, sandy beaches with three access points with parking. A visitors center is available. This can be the starting point for an outstanding bike ride seven miles north to Pillar Point Marina. Kayak rentals, fishing, and whale-watching trips are available at the harbor. Typical weather is fog in summer, clear days in spring and fall, and wet and windy in the winter—yet occasionally there are drop-dead beautiful days in winter between storms, warm, clear, and windless. Temperatures range from lows in the mid-40s in winter to highs in the mid-60s in fall. One frustrating point: The weekend traffic on Highway 1 up and down the coast here is often jammed, with absolute gridlock during festivals.

Campsites, facilities: There are 52 sites for tents or RVs up to 40 feet (no hookups), four hike-in/bike-in sites, and one group site (for 9–50 people) two miles north of the main campground. Picnic tables, food lockers, and fire grills are provided. Restrooms with flush toilets and coin showers, drinking water, Wi-Fi, pay telephone, and dump station are available. Some facilities are wheelchair-accessible. Leashed pets are permitted, except on the beach.

Reservations, fees: Reservations are required at 800/444-7275 (800/444-PARK) or www.reserveamerica.com ($8 reservation fee). Sites are $35–50 per night, $165 per night for group site, $7 per person per night for hike-in/bike-in sites, $8 per night for each additional vehicle. Open year-round.

Directions: Drive to Half Moon Bay to the junction of Highway 1 and Highway 92. Turn south on Highway 1 and drive two blocks to Kelly Avenue. Turn right on Kelly Avenue and drive 0.5 mile to the park entrance at the end of the road.

Contact: Half Moon Bay State Beach, 650/726-8820 or 650/726-8819; Santa Cruz District, 831/335-6318, www.parks.ca.gov.

25 PELICAN POINT RV PARK

🧍 🏊 🛶 🚐 🐕 🚐

Scenic rating: 7

in Half Moon Bay

Map 7.3, page 465

Pelican Point is set on an extended bluff near the ocean in a rural area on the southern outskirts Half Moon Bay. Fog is common on summer mornings. Sites consist of cement slabs with picnic tables; half of the RV sites are monthly rentals. The harbor has an excellent boat launch, a fish-cleaning station, party boat trips for salmon and rockfish and, in the winter, whale-watching trips. A beautiful golf course is nearby.

Campsites, facilities: There are 75 sites with full hookups (30 and 50 amps) for RVs up to 40 feet. Picnic tables are provided. Restrooms with showers, coin laundry, propane gas, small store, clubhouse, and dump station are available. All facilities are nearby, with restaurants in Half Moon Bay and 10 miles north in Princeton at Pillar Point Harbor. Leashed pets are permitted.

Reservations, fees: Reservations are accepted. Sites are $52–56 per night, $2 per night for each additional vehicle, $3.30 per person per night for more than two people, $1 per pet per night. Some credit cards accepted. Open year-round.

Directions: In Half Moon Bay, at the junction of Highway 1 and Highway 92, turn south on Highway 1 and drive 2.5 miles to Miramontes Point Road. Turn right and drive a short distance to the park entrance on the left.

Contact: Pelican Point RV Park, 650/726-9100.

26 JACK BROOK HORSE CAMPS

Scenic rating: 7

in Sam McDonald County Park
just outside La Honda

Map 7.3, page 465

This is a beautiful horse camp with access to a network of service roads. The park is filled with second-growth redwoods and then feeds north to rolling foothills. You get a mix of moist, cool redwoods in the canyons and rolling grassland foothills on the ridges. From the top, you also get views to the west across Butano Canyon to the coast.

Campsites, facilities: There are three group sites: two small sites for up to 10 people each and one larger site for up to 40 people. Some sites have 15 or 20-amp hookups. Picnic tables and barbecues are provided. Drinking water, flush toilets, showers, horse paddocks, tie posts, and a horse-wash rack are available. A shared outdoor kitchen is also provided.

Reservations, fees: Reservations are required at 650/363-4021 ($10 reservation fee) or www.eparks.net ($7 reservation fee). The two smaller sites are $125 per night on weekends, $75 per night Sunday through Thursday; the larger site is $275 per night on weekends, $150 per night Sunday through Thursday. Open May 1 through mid-November, weather permitting.

Directions: From the Peninsula, take Highway 101 or 280 to Redwood City/Woodside and Highway 84. Take Highway 84 (Woodside-La Honda-San Gregorio Rd.) west to La Honda and continue one mile to Alpine Road. Turn left on Alpine Road and drive 1.1 miles to a Y with Pescadero Road. Bear right at the Y and drive 0.5 mile to the park entrance on the right.

From Highway 1: Take the Pescadero Road exit. Drive east on Pescadero Creek Road about 11 miles to the Jack Brook entrance or continue to the Sam McDonald Park entrance where horse trailers can be parked for entrance on horseback.

Contact: San Mateo County Parks and Recreation, 650/879-0238 or 650/363-4021, www.co.sanmateo.ca.us.

27 MEMORIAL COUNTY PARK

Scenic rating: 8

near La Honda

Map 7.3, page 465

This beautiful 500-acre redwood park is set on the western slopes of the Santa Cruz Mountains, tucked in a pocket between the tiny towns of La Honda and Loma Mar. The park is known for its family camping areas and Tan Oak and Mount Ellen nature trails. The campground features access to a nearby network of 50 miles of trails, with the best hike along the headwaters of Pescadero Creek. In late winter, it is sometimes possible to see steelhead spawn (no fishing permitted, of course). The trails link with others in nearby Portola State Park and Sam McDonald County Park, providing access to a vast recreation land. A swimming hole on Pescadero Creek next to the campground is popular during the summer. The camp is often filled on summer weekends, but the sites are spaced so it won't cramp your style.

Campsites, facilities: There are 158 sites for tents or RVs up to 35 feet, two group sites for tents or RVs up to 35 feet (no hookups) that can accommodate up to 75 people, and two areas for youth groups of up to 50 people.

Picnic tables, food lockers, and fire grills are provided. Drinking water, restrooms with coin showers and flush toilets, amphitheater, picnic area, summer convenience store, visitors center, summer campfire programs, dump station, and firewood are available. No smoking is allowed.

Reservations, fees: Reservations are required at 650/363-4021 ($10 reservation fee) or www.eparks.net ($7 reservation fee). Sites are $25–40 per vehicle per night, $10 per night for each additional vehicle. Group sites are $150 –175 per night, plus $6 per vehicle per stay. Open year-round.

Directions: From Half Moon Bay at the junction of Highway 1 and Highway 92, drive south on Highway 1 for 18 miles to the Pescadero Road exit. Turn left (east) on Pescadero Road and drive about 10.5 miles to the park entrance on the right.

Contact: Memorial County Park, 650/879-0238; San Mateo County Parks and Recreation, 650/363-4021, www.eparks.net or www.co.sanmateo.ca.us.

28 PESCADERO CREEK COUNTY PARK

🚶 🚴 ⛺

Scenic rating: 7

near Pescadero

Map 7.4, page 466

The area that comprises Pescadero Creek Park's 8,020 acres includes Sam McDonald, Memorial, and Heritage Grove Parks. But it's Pescadero Creek Park itself that offers solitude and remote access like no other. There are 26 miles of trail suitable for hiking, biking, and horseback riding, but you'll rarely come across another soul. The reason? Pescadero Creek remains undeveloped. There are no paved roads in and access is only through one of the nearby parks or from the Tarwater Trailhead via a single-lane dirt road. So it gets overlooked. Beautiful coast redwoods line Pescadero Creek, but unfortunately there's no

fishing. Pescadero Creek is protected steelhead trout habitat. The hike-in backpacking campgrounds here are small and primitive, with no water, but plenty of solitude.

Campsites, facilities: There are two hike-in campgrounds available for drop-in camping. Shaw Flat offers 8 sites and Tarwater Trail has 6 sites. Drinking water is not provided. Campfires are not permitted, but backpacking stoves are allowed.

Reservations, fees: Reservations are not accepted. The Shaw Flat and Tarwater campgrounds are available first-come, first-served. Sites are $10 per night for up to four campers and one vehicle per site. Check in is at the Memorial State Park Ranger Station. Open year-round; closing times vary.

Directions: Take Highway 101 or 280 to Redwood City/Woodside and Highway 84. Take Highway 84 (Woodside-La Honda-San Gregorio Rd.) west to La Honda. Turn left at 0.5 mile past the village center in La Honda on Pescadero Road. Continue 6 miles on Pescadero Road to the park entrance.

Contact: San Mateo County Parks and Recreation, 650/879-0238 or 650/363-4021, www.co.sanmateo.ca.us/smc.

29 BUTANO REDWOODS STATE PARK

🚶 🐕 🚐 ⛺

Scenic rating: 9

near Pescadero

Map 7.4, page 466

The campground at Butano is set in a canyon filled with a redwood forest, so pretty and with such good hiking that it has become popular enough to make reservations a must. The reason for its popularity is a series of exceptional hikes, including one to the Año Nuevo Lookout (well, the lookout is now blocked by trees, but there are glimpses of the ocean elsewhere along the way), Mill Ox Loop, and, for the ambitious, 11-mile Butano Rim Loop. The latter has a backpack camp with eight trail campsites (primitive with pit toilets available) requiring a 5.5-mile hike in the park's most remote area, where no drinking water is available. Creek water is within 0.5 mile of the campsites; bring a water purifier. Año Nuevo State Reserve is about 10 miles away, and is an excellent side-trip during elephant seal mating season (Dec.–Feb.).

Campsites, facilities: There are 21 sites for tents or RVs up to 24 feet (no hookups), 18 walk-in sites, and eight hike-in sites (5.5 miles, with a pit toilet available); a camp stove is required. Picnic tables, food lockers, and fire grills are provided. Drinking water and restrooms with flush toilets are available. Leashed pets are permitted in campsites, picnic areas, and on paved roads.

Reservations, fees: Reservations are accepted May through October at 800/444-7275 (800/444-PARK) or www.reserveamerica.com ($8 reservation fee). Reservations are not available for hike-in trail sites. Sites are $35 per night, $10 per night for each additional vehicle. Open April through November.

Directions: In Half Moon Bay, at the junction of Highway 1 and Highway 92, drive south on Highway 1 for 18 miles to the Pescadero Road exit. Turn left on Pescadero Road and drive three miles past the town of Pescadero to Cloverdale Road. Turn right and drive 4.5 miles to the park entrance on the left.

Contact: Butano State Park, 650/879-2040; Half Moon Bay State Park, 650/726-8819, www.parks.ca.gov.

30 PORTOLA REDWOODS STATE PARK

Scenic rating: 9

near Skyline Ridge

Map 7.4, page 466　　　　**BEST (**

Portola Redwoods State Park is very secluded since getting here requires travel on an extremely slow and winding series of roads. The park features redwoods and a mixed evergreen and hardwood forest on the western slopes of the Santa Cruz Mountains, the headwaters of Pescadero Creek, and 18 miles of hiking trails. A literal highlight is a 300-foot-high redwood, one of the tallest trees in the Santa Cruz Mountains. In addition to redwoods, there are Douglas fir and live oak, as well as a riparian zone along the stream. A four-mile hike links up to nearby Pescadero Creek County Park (which, in turn, borders Memorial County Park). At times in the summer, a low fog will move in along the San Mateo coast, and from lookouts near Skyline, visitors can peer to the west at what seems like a pearlescent sea with little islands (hilltops) poking through (this view is available from the access road, not from campsites). Wild pigs are occasionally spotted here, with larger numbers at neighboring Pescadero Creek County Park. The Slate Creek Backpack Camp provides a little-known option.

Note: This park was on the closure list developed by the California Department of Parks, pending final state budget decisions or the possible transfer of park management to other park agencies or volunteer groups. It is currently operating via a donor agreement with Save the Redwoods League, Peninsula Open Space Trust, and Portola-Castle Rock Foundation.

Campsites, facilities: There are 53 sites for tents or RVs up to 24 feet (no hookups), four hike-in/bike-in sites, four walk-in sites, six hike-in backpack sites (three-mile hike), and four group sites for 25 or 50 people. Picnic tables, storage lockers, and fire grills are provided. Drinking water, restrooms with flush toilets and coin showers, and firewood are available. The nearest gas is 13 miles away. Some facilities are wheelchair accessible. Leashed pets are permitted on paved surfaces only.

Reservations, fees: Reservations are accepted April through October at 800/444-7275 (800/444-PARK) or www.reserveamerica.com ($8 reservation fee). Sites are $35 per night, $10 per night for each additional vehicle, $5 per person per night for hike-in/bike-in sites,

$35 per night for walk-in sites, $15 per night for hike-in backpack sites, $165–335 per night for group sites. Reservations for Slate Creek Backpack Camp are accepted through Big Basin Redwoods at 831/338-8861. Open April through November.

Directions: From Palo Alto on I-280, turn west on Page Mill Road and drive (slow and twisty) to Skyline Boulevard/Highway 35. Cross Skyline and continue west on Alpine Road (very twisty) for about three miles to Portola State Park Road. Turn left on Portola State Park Road and drive about three miles to the park entrance at the end of the road.

Contact: Portola Redwoods State Park, 650/948-9098, www.parks.ca.gov or www.santacruzstateparks.org.

31 BIG BASIN REDWOODS STATE PARK

Scenic rating: 10

near Santa Cruz

Map 7.4, page 466

Big Basin is one of the best state parks in California, featuring giant redwoods near the park headquarters, secluded campsites set in forest, and rare opportunities to stay in a tent cabin or a backpacking trail site. The park covers more than 18,000 acres of redwoods, much of it old-growth, including forest behemoths more than 1,000 years old. It is a great park for hikers, with four waterfalls making for stellar destinations. Sempervirens Falls, a long, narrow, silvery stream, is an easy 1.5-miles round-trip on Sequoia Trail. The famous Berry Creek Falls is a spectacular 70-foot cascade set in a beautiful canyon framed by redwoods. For hikers in good condition, figure two hours (4.7 miles) to reach Berry Creek Falls, five hours for the round-trip in and out, and six hours for the complete loop (12 miles) that extends into the park's most remote areas. Other spectacular waterfalls—Silver Falls and Golden Cascade—lie one mile up the canyon Berry Creek Falls.

There is also an easy nature loop trail near the park headquarters in the valley floor that routes past several mammoth redwoods. This is California's oldest state park, established in 1902. It is home to the largest continuous stand of ancient coast redwoods south of Humboldt State Park in far Northern California. There are more than 80 miles of trails with elevations varying from 2,000 feet at the eastern Big Basin Rim on down to sea level. Rainfall averages 60 inches per year, most arriving from December through mid-March.

Campsites, facilities: There are 31 sites for tents or RVs up to 27 feet or trailers up to 24 feet (no hookups), 69 sites for tents only, 38 walk-in sites, 36 tent cabins (reservations required), two hike-in/bike-in sites, 52 hike-in campsites, and four group sites for 40–50 people. Picnic tables, food lockers, and fire grills are provided. Drinking water, pit toilets, restrooms with flush toilets and coin showers, dump station, firewood, and groceries are available. Some facilities are wheelchair-accessible. Leashed pets are allowed in campsites and on paved roads only.

Reservations, fees: Reservations are accepted at 800/444-7275 (800/444-PARK) or www.reserveamerica.com ($8 reservation fee); search for Big Basin Tent Cabins to reserve a tent cabin. Sites are $35 per night for individual sites and walk-in sites, $10 per night for each additional vehicle, $35 per person for hike-in sites, $6 per person per night for hike-in/bike-in sites, $270–335 per night for group sites. The tent cabins are $75 per night. Open year-round.

Directions: From Santa Cruz, turn north on Highway 9 and drive 12 miles to Boulder Creek and Highway 236 (signed Big Basin). Turn west on Highway 236 and drive nine miles to the park headquarters.

Contact: Big Basin Redwoods State Park, 831/338-8860 or 831/338-8861; Santa Cruz District, 831/335-6318, www.santacruzstateparks.org, www.parks.ca.gov; Big Basin Tent Cabins, 831/338-4745, www.bigbasin-tentcabins.com.

32 SANBORN-SKYLINE COUNTY PARK

Scenic rating: 8

near Saratoga

Map 7.4, page 466

This is a pretty camp set in a redwood forest, semi-primitive, but like a world in a different orbit compared to the asphalt of San Jose and the rest of the Santa Clara Valley. These campgrounds get heavy use on summer weekends, of course. This is headquarters for a 3,688-acre park that stretches from the foothills of Saratoga up to the Skyline Ridge in the Santa Cruz Mountains. Fifteen miles of hiking trails are available, with a trailhead at camp. Most trails explore lush wooded slopes, with redwoods and tan oak. Dogs are prohibited at walk-in sites, but are allowed at the RV sites, the main park's grassy area, and day-use areas.

Campsites, facilities: There are 15 sites with full hookups (20 and 30 amps) for RVs up to 30 feet at Sanborn, a separate walk-in campground with 33 sites for tents, and a youth group area for up to 35 people. Picnic tables, food lockers, and fire pits are provided. Drinking water, restrooms with flush toilets and coin showers, dump station, a seasonal youth science center, and a one-mile nature trail are available. Some facilities are wheelchair-accessible. Leashed pets are permitted in RV campground and picnic areas only.

Reservations, fees: Reservations are required at 408/355-2201 (Mon.–Fri.) or at www.parkhere.org or www.gooutsideandplay.org ($6 reservation fee). Walk-in sites are $12 per night, tent sites are $24 per night, RV sites are $30 per night. The youth group area is $50 for up to 35 people the first night and then $10 per night. Check-in required before sunset; gates are locked at dusk. Some credit cards accepted. RV sites open year-round; walk-in sites open mid-March through mid-October.

Directions: From San Jose, take Highway 17 south for six miles to Highway 9/Saratoga Avenue. Turn west and drive to Saratoga, then continue on Highway 9 for two miles to Sanborn Road. Turn left and drive one mile to the park on the right. Walk-in sites require a 0.1- to 0.5-mile walk from the parking area.

Contact: Sanborn-Skyline County Park, 408/867-9959, www.parkhere.org.

33 JOSEPH D. GRANT COUNTY PARK

Scenic rating: 7

near San Jose

Map 7.4, page 466

Grant Ranch is a great, wild playland covering more than 9,000 acres in the foothills of nearby Mount Hamilton to the east. It features 52 miles of hiking trails (horses permitted), 20 miles of old ranch roads that are perfect for mountain biking, a pretty lake (Grant Lake), and miles of foothills, canyons, oaks, and grasslands. The campground is set amid oak grasslands, is shaded, and can be used as a base camp for planning the day's recreation. The best hikes are to Halls Valley, especially in the winter and spring when there are many secret little creeks and miniature waterfalls in hidden canyons; Hotel Trail; and Cañada de Pala Trail, which drops to San Felipe Creek, the prettiest stream in the park. Warm-water fishing is available in the lake and several smaller ponds. A great side trip is the slow, curvy drive east to the Mount Hamilton Summit and Lick Observatory for great views of the Santa Clara Valley. Wood fires are often banned in summer.

Campsites, facilities: There are 40 sites for tents or RVs up to 31 feet (no hookups). Picnic tables, food lockers, and fire pits are provided. Drinking water, restrooms with flush toilets and free showers, and dump station are available. Some facilities are wheelchair accessible. Leashed pets are permitted.

Reservations, fees: Reservations are required at 408/355-2201 (Mon.–Fri.) or at www.parkhere.org or www.gooutsideandplay.org ($6 reservation fee). Tent sites are $24 per night, RV sites are $30 per night. Off-season rates are lower. Check-in required before sunset;

gates are locked at dusk. The 22 Halls Valley sites are open year-round; the 18 Snell sites are available April through October.

Directions: In San Jose at the junction of I-680 and U.S. 101, take I-680 north to the Alum Rock Avenue exit. Turn east and drive four miles to Mount Hamilton Road. Turn right and drive eight miles to the park headquarters entrance on the right side of the road.

Contact: Joseph D. Grant County Park, 408/274-6121, www.parkhere.org.

34 HENRY COWELL REDWOODS STATE PARK

Scenic rating: 8

near Santa Cruz

Map 7.4, page 466

This state park near Santa Cruz has good hiking, good views, and a chance of fishing in the winter for steelhead. The 1,750-acre park features 20 miles of trails in the forest, where the old-growth redwoods are estimated at 1,400–1,800 years old. One great easy hike is a 15-minute walk to a lookout platform over Santa Cruz and the Pacific Ocean; the trailhead is near campsite 49. Another good hike is Eagle Creek Trail, a three-mile walk that heads along Eagle Creek and the San Lorenzo River, running through a classic redwood canyon. In winter, there is limited steelhead fishing in the San Lorenzo River. A side-trip option is taking the Roaring Camp Big Trees Railroad (831/335-4400), which is adjacent to camp. Insider's tips: Poison oak is prevalent in this park and around the campground. Alcohol is prohibited in the campground, but not in the day-use area.

Campsites, facilities: There are 111 sites for tents or RVs up to 35 feet (no hookups), and one hike-in/bike-in site for up to eight people. Picnic tables and fire grills are provided. Drinking water, restrooms with flush toilets and coin showers, and Wi-Fi are available. Some facilities are wheelchair-accessible. A nature center, bookstore, and picnic area are nearby. Leashed pets are permitted, but must be kept inside tents or vehicles at night.

Reservations, fees: Reservations accepted mid-March through October at 800/444-7275 (800/444-PARK) or www.reserveamerica.com ($8 reservation fee). Sites are $35 per night (maximum of eight people). The hike-in/bike-in site is first come, first served, $7 per person per night. Open March through October.

Directions: In Scotts Valley on Highway 17, take the Mount Hermon Road exit and drive west toward Felton to Lockwood Lane. Turn left on Lockwood Lane and drive about one mile to Graham Hill Road. Turn left on Graham Hill Road and drive 0.5 mile to the campground on the right.

Contact: Henry Cowell Redwoods State Park, 831/438-2396 or 831/335-4598, www.santacruzstateparks.org or www.parks.ca.gov.

35 SANTA CRUZ RANCH RV PARK

Scenic rating: 5

near Scotts Valley

Map 7.4, page 466

This camp is situated on 6.5 acres and is just a short hop from Santa Cruz and Monterey Bay. There are many side-trip options, making this a prime location for vacationers cruising the California coast. In Santa Cruz there are several quality restaurants, plus fishing trips and boat rentals at Santa Cruz Wharf, as well as the famous Santa Cruz Beach Boardwalk and amusement park. Discount tickets for local attractions are available in the office. Note that most of the sites are filled with long-term renters; a few sites are set aside for overnight vacationers.

Campsites, facilities: There are 27 pull-through sites with full hookups (30 amps) for RVs up to 45 feet and five sites for tents. Picnic tables are provided. Restrooms with showers, cable TV, coin laundry, free Wi-Fi, recreation and meeting room, hot tub, and seasonal heated swimming pool are available. No open fires. Leashed pets are permitted with approval.

Reservations, fees: Reservations are recommended. RV sites are $52–62 per night, tent sites are $40 per night. The first pet is free, a second pet is $1 per night. Weekly, monthly, and group rates available. Some credit cards accepted. Open year-round.

Directions: From Santa Cruz, at the junction of Highways 1 and 17, turn north on Highway 17 and drive three miles to the Mount Hermon/Big Basin exit. Take that exit north onto Mount Hermon Road and drive 0.5 mile to Scotts Valley Drive. Turn right and drive 0.7 mile to Disc Drive. Turn right and continue to 917 Disc Drive on the left. Note: Big rigs use Granite Creek exit, or call for best route.

Contact: Santa Cruz Ranch RV Park, 831/438-1288 or 800/546-1288, www.santacruzranchrv.com.

36 UVAS CANYON COUNTY PARK

🏃 🛶 🐾 ♿ ⛺

Scenic rating: 8

near Morgan Hill

Map 7.4, page 466

This lushly wooded park of 1,133 acres is nestled on the eastern side of the Santa Cruz Mountains. It has a stunning array of waterfalls that can be reached with short hikes, including Triple Falls, Black Rock Falls, and several others, making for stellar hikes in winter and spring. In all, the park has six miles of trails, including a self-guided interpretive trail. Note that the gate to the campground is locked at sunset. Uvas Reservoir (five miles away) is closed to all boating, including float tubes.

Campsites, facilities: There are 25 sites for tents and small RVs. There is also a youth group area with tent sites for up to 40 people. Picnic tables, food lockers, and fire grills (charcoal fires only) are provided; fires may be prohibited during fire season. Drinking water, showers, and flush toilets are available. Some facilities are wheelchair-accessible. Leashed pets are permitted.

Reservations, fees: Reservations are required at 408/355-2201 (Mon.–Fri.) or at www.parkhere.org or www.gooutsideandplay.org ($6 reservation fee). Sites are $24 per night, the youth group camp is $50 per night. Open year-round. Check-in required before sunset; gates close at sunset.

Directions: From San Jose, take U.S. 101 south through Coyote to the exit for Bailey Avenue. Take that exit, turn right (west) on Bailey and drive into the foothills to McKean Road. Turn left on McKean (after 2.2 miles the road becomes Uvas Road) and drive to Croy Road. Turn right on Croy Road and drive 4.4 miles (through Sveadal, drive slow) to the park entrance.

Contact: Uvas Canyon County Park, 408/779-9232, www.parkhere.org.

37 HENRY W. COE STATE PARK

🏃 🚴 🛶 🐾 5% 🚙 ⛺

Scenic rating: 8

near Gilroy

Map 7.4, page 466   **BEST (**

This is the Bay Area's backyard wilderness, with 87,000 acres of wildlands, including a 23,300-acre designated wilderness area. There are more than 100 miles of ranch roads and 300 miles of hiking trails, a remarkable network that provides access to 140 ponds and small lakes, hidden streams, and a habitat that is paradise for fish, wildlife, and wild flora. In 2007, a wildfire burned about half of the park, but this grassland country sprang back to life with heavy rains in spring of 2010. The backcountry lakes filled as well, with good bass fishing in the more remote lakes that see very little fishing pressure.

The best camping introduction is at the drive-in campsites at park headquarters (east of Morgan Hill), set on a hilltop at 2,600 feet elevation that is ideal for stargazing and watching meteor showers. That provides a taste. If you like it, then come back for the full meal. It is the wilderness hike-in and bike-in sites where you will get the full flavor of the park. Before setting out for the outback, always consult with the rangers here—the ambitious plans of many hikers cause them to suffer dehydration and heatstroke. For wilderness trips, the best jump-off point is Coyote Creek or Hunting Hollow trailheads upstream of Coyote Reservoir east of Gilroy. The park has excellent pond-style fishing but requires extremely long hikes (typically 10- to 25-mile round-trips) to reach the best lakes, including Mustang Pond, Jackrabbit Lake, Coit Lake, and Mississippi Lake. Expect hot weather in the summer; spring and early summer are the prime times. Even though the park may appear to be 120 square miles of oak foothills, the terrain is often steep, and making ridges often involves climbs of 1,500 feet. There are many great secrets to be discovered here, including Rooster Comb and Coyote Creek. At times on spring days, wild pigs seem to be everywhere. Golden eagles are also abundant. Bring a water purifier for hikes because there is no developed drinking water in the outback.

Note: This park is on the closure list developed by the California Department of Parks, pending final state budget decisions or the possible transfer of park management to other park agencies or volunteer groups. The Pine Ridge Association has put together a co-operative venture to run the campground.

Campsites, facilities: There are 10 sites for tents only and 10 sites for tents or RVs up to 24 feet (no hookups). There is also a drive-in equestrian camp with eight sites, 82 hike-in/bike-in sites, and 11 hike-in group sites for 9–50 people. Picnic tables and fire grills are provided. Drinking water and vault toilets are available. Restrooms with flush toilets are available at the visitors center. Some facilities are wheelchair accessible. Leashed pets are permitted at the campgrounds, on paved roads, and on the trail from the visitor center to the overflow parking lot.

Corrals are available at the equestrian camp. Vault toilets are provided a short walk from the hike-in/bike-in sites. No drinking water is available at hike-in/bike-in site and garbage must be packed out.

Reservations, fees: Reservations are accepted at 800/444-7275 or www.reserveamerica.com ($8 reservation fee). The hike-in/bike-in sites are first-come, first-served; a wilderness permit is required from park headquarters or at the day-use parking lot. Sites are $20 per night, $8 per night for each additional vehicle, $75 per night for group sites, $25 per night for horse sites, $5 per person per night for hike-in/bike-in sites. Open year-round.

Directions: From Morgan Hill on U.S. 101, take the East Dunne Avenue exit. Turn east and drive 13 miles (including over the bridge at Anderson Lake, then very twisty and narrow) to the park entrance.

Contact: Henry W. Coe State Park, 408/779-2728, www.coepark.org or www.parks.ca.gov.

38 MOUNT MADONNA COUNTY PARK

Scenic rating: 7

between Watsonville and Gilroy

Map 7.4, page 466

It's a twisty son-of-a-gun road to reach the top of Mount Madonna, but the views on clear days of Monterey Bay to the west and Santa Clara Valley to the east always make it worth the trip. In addition, a small herd of white deer are protected in a pen near the parking area for a rare chance to see unique wildlife. This 3,688-acre park is dominated by redwood forest, but at the lower slopes of Mount Madonna the landscape changes to oak woodland, dense chaparral, and grassy meadows. Ohlone Indians once lived here. There are many good hiking trails in the park; the best is Bayview Loop. The 20-mile trail system includes a one-mile self-guided nature trail. Elevation in the park reaches 1,896 feet. Free programs are offered at the amphitheater on Saturday evenings during the summer. Insider's note: Campsite 105 at Valley View is the only pull-through site. While no credit cards are accepted in person, there is a self-pay machine that accepts credit cards, a nice touch. The campsites are dispersed throughout four campgrounds.

Campsites, facilities: There are 118 sites with partial hookups (30 amps) for tents or RVs up to 30 feet, five yurts, and two group areas for up to 240 people. One site is pull-through. Five youth-group areas for 40–50 people each are also available; youth groups must have tax-exempt status. Picnic tables, food lockers, and fire pits are provided. Drinking water, restrooms with coin showers and flush toilets, dump station, seasonal live music, archery range, picnic areas, amphitheater, and visitors center are available. Some facilities are wheelchair-accessible. Leashed pets are permitted.

Reservations, fees: Reservations are required at 408/355-2201 (Mon.–Fri.) or at www.parkhere.org or www.gooutsideandplay.org ($6 reservation fee). RV sites are $30 per night, tent sites are $24 per night, yurts are $35–50 (sleeps 6), $55–70 (sleeps 8), $75–90 (sleeps 10) per nights. Group camps are $180–450 per night, the youth group area is $50 per night. Some credit cards accepted at self-serve machine. Open year-round.

Directions: From U.S. 101 in Gilroy, take the Hecker Pass Highway/Highway 152 exit west. Drive west seven miles to Pole Line Road and the park entrance on the right.

From Highway 1 in Watsonville, turn east onto Highway 152 and drive about 12 miles east to Pole Line Road and the park entrance on the left.

Contact: Mount Madonna County Park, 408/842-2341, www.parkhere.org.

39 COYOTE LAKE AND HARVEY BEAR COUNTY PARKS

Scenic rating: 8

near Gilroy

Map 7.4, page 466

Several campsites here are set on a bluff with a lake view. Where else in the greater Bay Area can you get that? The campground is nestled in oaks, among 796 acres of parkland, furnishing some much-needed shade. Coyote Lake, a long, narrow lake set in a canyon just over the ridge east of U.S. 101, is a pretty surprise to newcomers. It covers 635 acres and provides one of the best lakes for bass fishing in the Bay Area. Other species are bluegill and crappie. Both powerboating and non-motorized boating are allowed; the boat launch is one mile north of the visitors center. Swimming is prohibited. There are no longer hiking trails along the lakeshore, but more than 13 miles of multi-use trails (horses and mountain bikes are allowed) are available, along with trails on the adjacent Harvey Bear County Park to the west that overlooks the lake. Note: If you continue east about four miles on the access road that runs past the lake to the Coe State Park Hunting Hollow entrance, you'll come to two outstanding trailheads (one at a parking area, one at the Coyote Creek gate) into that park's wildlands. Wildlife, including deer and wild turkey, is abundant. Note: All boats must be certified mussel-free before launching.

Campsites, facilities: There are 73 pull-through sites for tents or RVs up to 31 feet; 18 sites have partial hookups. Picnic tables, food lockers, and fire pits are provided. Drinking water, flush toilets, showers, and a boat ramp are available. A visitor center is also available. Some facilities are wheelchair-accessible. Leashed pets are permitted.

Reservations, fees: Reservations are required at 408/355-2201 (Mon.–Fri.) or at www.parkhere.org or www.gooutsideandplay.org ($6 reservation fee). Tent sites are $24 per night, RV sites are $30 per night, $6 per day for boat launching plus an inspection fee. Some credit cards accepted. Open year-round.

Directions: Drive on U.S. 101 to Gilroy and Leavesley Road. Take that exit and drive east on Leavesley Road for 1.75 miles to New Avenue. Turn left on New Avenue and drive 0.6 mile to Roop Road. Turn right on Roop Road and drive three miles to Coyote Reservoir Road. Turn left on Coyote Reservoir Road and drive to the campground.

Contact: Coyote Lake County Park, 408/842-7800, www.parkhere.org; Coyote Discount Bait and Tackle, 408/463-0711.

MONTEREY AND BIG SUR

© PRASHANT RAGHU/123RF.COM

BEST CAMPGROUNDS

The scenic charm seems to extend to infinity

from the seaside towns of Santa Cruz, Monterey, Big Sur, and San Simeon. The primary treasure is the coast, which is rock-strewn and sprinkled with inshore kelp beds, where occasionally you can find sea otters playing Pop Goes the Weasel. The sea here is a color like no other, often more of a tourmaline than a straight green or blue.

From Carmel to Lucia alone, touring Big Sur on Highway 1 is one of the most captivating drives anywhere. The inland strip along Highway 1 provides access to state parks, redwoods, coastal streams, Los Padres National Forest, and the Ventana Wilderness. As you explore farther south on the Pacific Coast Highway, you will discover a largely untouched coast.

Most vacations to this region include several must-do trips, often starting in Monterey with a visit to Fisherman's Wharf and its domesticated sea lions, and then to the nearby Monterey Bay Aquarium.

From there, most head south to Big Sur to take in a few brush strokes of nature's canvas, easily realizing why this area is beloved around the world. At first glance, however, it's impossible not to want the whole painting. That is where the campgrounds come in. They provide both the ideal getaway and a launching point for adventure.

At Big Sur, the campgrounds are what many expect: small hideaways in the big redwoods. The campgrounds are in a variety of settings, some near Big Sur River, others in the forest.

Other good opportunities are available in Los Padres National Forest and the adjacent Ventana Wilderness, which provide outstanding camping and hiking in the off-season, when the Sierra is buried in snow.

One note of caution: The state park campgrounds on Highway 1 are among the most popular in North America. Reservations are required far in advance all summer, even on weekdays. They are always the first to fill on the state's reservation system. So get the game wired to get your site.

During the summer, only the fog on the coast and the intense heat just 10 miles inland keep this region from attaining perfection.

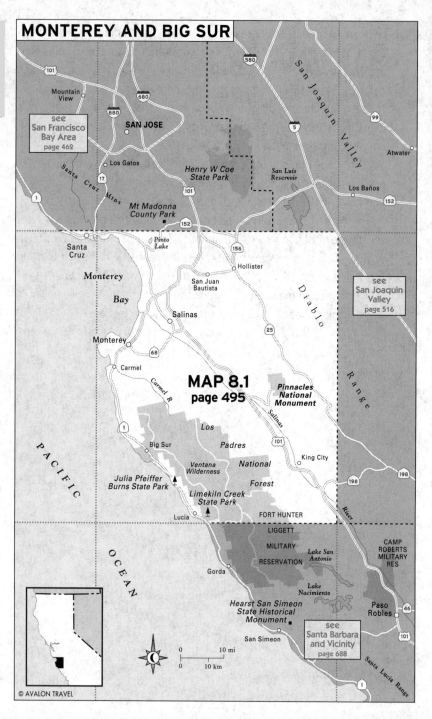

MONTEREY AND BIG SUR

see San Francisco Bay Area page 462

SAN JOSE

Mountain View

Los Gatos

Henry W Coe State Park

San Luis Reservoir

Los Baños

Santa Cruz Mtns

Mt Madonna County Park

Santa Cruz

Pinto Lake

Hollister

San Juan Bautista

Salinas

Monterey Bay

Monterey

Carmel

Carmel R

MAP 8.1 page 495

Los Padres National Forest

Ventana Wilderness

Big Sur

Julia Pfeiffer Burns State Park

Limekiln Creek State Park

Lucia

PACIFIC OCEAN

San Joaquin Valley

Atwater

see San Joaquin Valley page 516

Diablo Range

Pinnacles National Monument

Salinas

King City

FORT HUNTER LIGGETT MILITARY RESERVATION

Lake San Antonio

Gorda

Lake Nacimiento

CAMP ROBERTS MILITARY RES

Paso Robles

Hearst San Simeon State Historical Monument

San Simeon

see Santa Barbara and Vicinity page 688

Santa Lucia Range

0   10 mi
0   10 km

© AVALON TRAVEL

Map 8.1

Sites 1-34
Pages 496-511

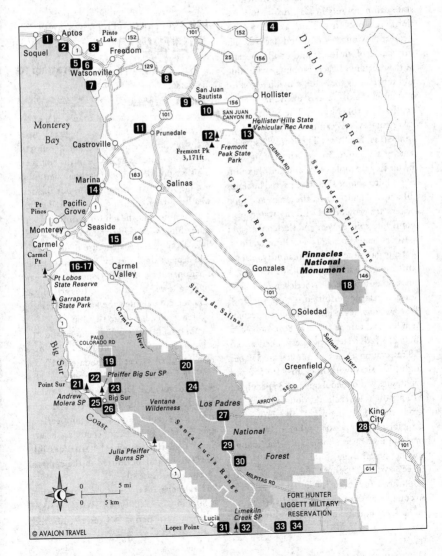

1 NEW BRIGHTON STATE BEACH

Scenic rating: 10

near Capitola

Map 8.1, page 495

This is one in a series of state park camps set on the bluffs overlooking Monterey Bay. They are among the most popular and in-demand state campgrounds in California. Reservations are a necessity. This camp is set near a forest of Monterey pine and live oak. The summer is often foggy and cool, especially in the morning. Beachcombing, swimming, and surf fishing for perch provide recreation options, and skiff rentals are available at the nearby Capitola Wharf. The San Lorenzo River enters the ocean nearby.

Campsites, facilities: There are 82 sites for tents or RVs up to 36 feet, three group sites for up to 25 people each, and four hike-in/bike-in sites. Some sites have partial hookups (30 amps). Picnic tables, fire rings, and food lockers are provided. Drinking water, restrooms with coin showers and flush toilets, and a visitors center are available. Dump stations, propane gas, groceries, coin laundry, restaurant, and gas station are available within 2.5 miles. Some facilities are wheelchair-accessible. Leashed pets are permitted.

Reservations, fees: Reservations are recommended and can be made at 800/444-7275 (800/444-PARK) or www.reserveamerica.com ($8 reservation fee). Premium sites are $50 per night, RV sites (with hookups) are $50 per night, sites without hookups are $35 per night, $10 per night for each additional vehicle, the group site is $185 per night, hike-in/bike-in camping is $5 per person per night. Two-night maximum stay per month. Open year-round, weather permitting.

Directions: From Santa Cruz, drive south on Highway 1 for about five miles to the Park Avenue exit. Take that exit and turn right on Park Avenue and drive a short distance to McGregor Drive (a four-way stop). Turn left and drive a short distance to the park entrance on the right.

Contact: New Brighton State Beach, 831/464-6329; California State Parks, Santa Cruz District, 831/335-6318 or 831/335- 3455, www.santacruzstateparks.org or www.parks.ca.gov; Pacific Migrations Visitor Center, 831/464-5620.

2 SEACLIFF STATE BEACH

Scenic rating: 10

near Santa Cruz

Map 8.1, page 495

Here is a very pretty spot on a beach along Monterey Bay. Beach walks are great, especially on clear evenings for dramatic sunsets. A visitors center is available in the summer. This is a popular layover for vacationers touring Highway 1 in the summer, but the best weather is from mid-August to early October. This is a popular beach for swimming and sunbathing, with a long stretch of sand backed by coastal bluffs. A structure many call the "old cement ship" nearby provides some fascination, but for safety reasons visitors are no longer allowed to walk on it. It is actually an old concrete freighter, the Palo Alto. Fishing is often good adjacent to the ship.

Campsites, facilities: There are 35 sites for self-contained RVs up to 40 feet, and an overflow area that can accommodate 21 RVs up to 34 feet (no hookups). Picnic tables and fire grills are provided. Drinking water, restrooms with flush toilets and coin showers, and picnic area are available. Propane gas, groceries, a coin laundry, and a visitor center are nearby. Some facilities are wheelchair-accessible. Leashed pets are permitted in the camping area and on the beach.

Reservations, fees: Reservations are accepted at 800/444-7275 (800/444-PARK) or www.reserveamerica.com ($8 reservation fee).

Premium sites are $65 per night, sites without hookups are $55 per night, $10 per night for each additional vehicle. Open year-round, weather permitting.

Directions: From Santa Cruz, drive south on Highway 1 about six miles to State Park Drive/Seacliff Beach exit. Take that exit, turn west (right), and drive a short distance to the park entrance.

Contact: Seacliff State Beach, 831/685-6442 or 831/685-6500; California State Parks, Santa Cruz District, 831/429-2851, www.santacruzstateparks.org or www.parks.ca.gov; visitor center, 831/685-6444.

3 PINTO LAKE PARK

Scenic rating: 7

near Watsonville

Map 8.1, page 495

Pinto Lake can be a real find. Of the nine lakes in the nine Bay Area counties that offer camping, it is the only one where the RV campsites are actually near the lake. For the few who know about it, it's an offer that can't be refused. But note that no tent camping is permitted. The lake is best known as a fishing lake, with trout stocks and a small resident population of crappie and bluegill. Rainbow trout are stocked twice monthly in season. A 5-mph speed limit has been established for boaters, and no swimming or wading is permitted. The leash law for dogs is strictly enforced here.

Campsites, facilities: There are 28 sites with full hookups (30 amps) for RVs of any length. No tents. Picnic tables, cable TV, and barbecues are provided. A boat ramp, boat rentals, WiFi, volleyball, and softball field are available nearby in the summer. Leashed pets are permitted. Most facilities are wheelchair-accessible. Open year-round.

Reservations, fees: Reservations are accepted at 831/728-6194. Sites are $34 per night, $2

per night per person for more than two people (children 12 and under are free), $2 per night for each additional vehicle, $2 per pet per night. Credit cards are not accepted.

Directions: From Santa Cruz, drive 17 miles south on Highway 1 to the exit for Watsonville/Gilroy–Highway 152. Take that exit onto Main Street, then immediately turn left on Green Valley Road and drive 2.7 miles (0.5 mile past Holohan intersection) to the entrance for the lake and campground on the left.

From Monterey, drive north on Highway 1 to the Green Valley Road exit. Take that exit and turn right at the Green Valley Road and drive 2.7 miles (0.5 mile past the Holohan intersection) to the entrance for the lake and campground.

Contact: Pinto Lake Park, 831/728-6194, www.pintolake.com.

4 CASA DE FRUTA RV ORCHARD RESORT

Scenic rating: 3

near Pacheco Pass

Map 8.1, page 495

This 80-acre RV park has a festival-like atmosphere to it, with country music and dancing every weekend in the summer and barbecues on Sunday. The resort is also busy during the Gilroy Garlic Festival in July and the Hollister Independence Rally, a motorcycle event held nearby during the Fourth of July weekend. Huge, but sparse, San Luis Reservoir is 20 miles to the east.

Campsites, facilities: There are 300 sites with full hookups (30 amps) for RVs; some sites are pull-through. Tent sites are also available. Picnic tables are provided. Restrooms with flush toilets and showers, dump station, Wi-Fi, satellite TV, coin laundry, playground, swimming pool, wading pool, outdoor dance floor, horseshoes, volleyball courts, baseball diamonds, wine- and cheese-tasting room, candy factory, bakery, fruit stand, 24-hour restaurant, motel, gift shop, carousel, narrow-gauge train ride through animal park, and a minimart are available. Some facilities are wheelchair-accessible. Leashed pets are permitted.

Reservations, fees: Reservations are accepted at 800/548-3813. RV sites are $40–45 per night, tent sites are $34 per night, $2 per person per night for more than two people, $3 per pet per stay. Some credit cards accepted. Open year-round.

Directions: Drive on U.S. 101 to the junction with Highway 152 (near Gilroy). Take Highway 152 east and drive 13 miles to Casa de Fruta Parkway. Take that exit and drive a short distance to the resort.

Contact: Casa de Fruta RV Orchard Resort, 408/842-9316 or 800/548-3813, www.casadefruta.com.

５ MANRESA UPLANDS STATE BEACH WALK-IN

Scenic rating: 10

south of Santa Cruz

Map 8.1, page 495 **BEST (**

This is a beautiful and extremely popular state park, with the campground set on uplands overlooking the Pacific Ocean. Many sites have ocean views; others are set back in a secluded grove of pine and cypress trees. The walk to the campsites is 20–150 yards from a vehicle-unloading zone. There is beach access for fishing, swimming, and surfing. Santa Cruz and Monterey are each a short drive away and offer endless recreation possibilities.

Campsites, facilities: There are 64 walk-in tent sites. Picnic tables, food lockers, and fire grills are provided. Drinking water, restrooms with flush toilets and coin showers, and firewood are available. Some facilities are wheelchair-accessible. Leashed pets are permitted in the campground and on the beach.

Reservations, fees: Reservations are accepted

at 800/444-7275 (800/444-PARK) or www.reserveamerica.com ($8 reservation fee). Sites are $35 per night. Open March through November.

Directions: From Santa Cruz, drive 12 miles southeast on Highway 1 to the San Andreas Road exit. Take that exit south and drive five miles to Sand Dollar Drive. Turn right and drive a short distance to the park entrance on the left. The parking area is about 1,000 yards from the camping area. A 20-minute unloading zone is available within 20–150 yards of the sites.

Contact: Manresa Uplands State Beach, 831/761-1795; California State Parks, Santa Cruz District, 831/335-6318, www.santacruzstateparks.org or www.parks.ca.gov.

６ SANTA CRUZ KOA

Scenic rating: 8

near Watsonville

Map 8.1, page 495

Bike rentals and nearby access to Manresa State Beach make this KOA campground a winner. The little log cabins are quite cute, and security is first class. It is a popular layover spot and weekend vacation destination. The only downer is the amount of asphalt. In 2012, Santa Cruz KOA won both the KOA President's Award and the Founders Award for exceptional service.

Campsites, facilities: There are 180 sites, including five pull-through sites, with full or partial hookups (30 and 50 amps) for RVs of any length, seven sites for tents only, 50 camping cabins, 21 camping lodges, and three Airstream trailers. Picnic tables and fire grills are provided. Restrooms with showers, two dump stations, free Wi-Fi, cable TV, swimming pool, spa, playground, two recreation rooms, bicycle rentals, miniature golf, basketball court, snack bar, convenience store, and propane gas are available. Some facilities are wheelchair-accessible. Leashed pets are permitted.

Reservations, fees: Reservations are advised at 800/562-7701. RV sites are $88–108, tent sites are $60–80, camping cabins are $130–145 per night, Airstreams are $180–200 per night, and camping lodges are $205–230 per night. Some credit cards accepted. Open year-round.

Directions: From Santa Cruz, drive 12 miles southeast on Highway 1. Take the San Andreas Road exit and head southwest for 3.5 miles to 1186 San Andreas Road.

Contact: Santa Cruz KOA, 831/722-0551, www.santacruzkoa.com or www.koa.com.

7 SUNSET STATE BEACH

🐕 🚴 🏊 🛶 🎣 ♿ 🚐 ⛺

Scenic rating: 9

near Watsonville

Map 8.1, page 495

On clear evenings, the sunsets here look as if they are imported from Hawaii. The camp is set on a bluff along Monterey Bay. While there are no ocean views from the campsites, the location makes for easy, short walks down to the beach for beautiful shoreline walks. The beachfront features pine trees, bluffs, and expansive sand dunes. Large agricultural fields border the park. This area was once a good spot for clamming, but the clams have just about been fished out. The best weather is in late summer and fall. Spring can be windy here, and early summer is often foggy. Reservations are often needed well in advance to secure a spot.

Campsites, facilities: There are 91 sites for tents or RVs up to 31 feet (no hookups), one hike-in/bike-in site, and one group site for 9–50 people. Picnic tables, food lockers, and fire grills are provided. Drinking water, restrooms with flush toilets and coin showers, and firewood are available. Some facilities are wheelchair-accessible. Leashed pets are permitted, except on the beach.

Reservations, fees: Reservations are accepted at 800/444-7275 (800/444-PARK) or www.reserveamerica.com ($8 reservation fee). Sites are $35 per night, $10 per night for each additional vehicle, $5 per person per night for hike-in/bike-in site, $335 per night for group site. South Camp and the group site are open year-round, but Dunes and Pine Hollow campgrounds are only open mid-March through October.

Directions: From Highway 1 near Watsonville, take the Riverside Drive exit toward the ocean to Beach Road. Drive 3.5 miles on Beach Road to the San Andreas Road exit. Turn right on San Andreas Road and drive about three miles to Sunset Beach Road. Turn left and drive a short distance to the park entrance.

Contact: Sunset State Beach, 831/763-7063; California State Parks, Santa Cruz District, 831/335-6318, www.santacruzstateparks.org or www.parks.ca.gov.

8 McALPINE LAKE AND PARK

🛶 🎣 ♿ 🚐 ⛺

Scenic rating: 5

near San Juan Bautista

Map 8.1, page 495

This is the only privately operated campground in the immediate region that has any spots for tent campers. The camping cabins here look like miniature log cabins, quite cute and comfortable. In addition, the park has a 40-foot-deep lake stocked with trout, bass, bluegill, sturgeon, and catfish; no fishing license is required. The swimming pool was recently transformed into a trout-fishing pond. Other highlights of the park are its proximity to Mission San Juan Bautista and the relatively short drive to the Monterey-Carmel area.

Campsites, facilities: There are 45 sites for tents only, 27 sites with partial hookups (30 amps) for tents or RVs, 14 sites with full hookups (30 amps) for RVs, and four cabins. Picnic tables and fire grills are provided. Restrooms with flush toilets and showers, dump station, group barbecue facilities, fishing pond, bait and tackle, gold panning, coin laundry, propane gas, and groceries are available. Some facilities are wheelchair-accessible. Leashed pets are permitted.

Reservations, fees: Reservations are accepted. RV sites are $40 per night, tent sites are $32 per night, $10 per person per night for more than four people, $5 per night for each additional vehicle. Some credit cards accepted. Weekly and monthly rates available. Open year-round.

Directions: On U.S. 101, drive to the Highway 129 exit. Take Highway 129 west and drive 100 feet to Searle Road (frontage road). Turn left onto Searle Road and drive to the stop sign at Anzar. Turn left again on Anzar and drive under the freeway to the park entrance on the left (900 Anzar Road).

Contact: McAlpine Lake and Park, 831/623-4263, www.mcalpinelake.com.

9 MONTEREY VACATION RV PARK

Scenic rating: 4

near San Juan Bautista

Map 8.1, page 495

This RV park has an ideal location for many vacationers. It's a 10-minute drive to San Juan Bautista, 15 minutes to winery tours, 30 minutes to the Monterey Bay Aquarium, and 40 minutes to Monterey's Fisherman's Wharf and Cannery Row. It's set in an attractive spot with some trees, but the nearby attractions are what make it a clear winner. The park is next to the old stagecoach trail where famous outlaw Joaquin Murrieta once ambushed travelers. Note that about half of the sites are occupied by long-term renters.

Campsites, facilities: There are 88 sites with full hookups (30 amps) for RVs up to 40 feet; many are pull-through. No tents. Picnic tables and barbecues are provided at some sites. Restrooms with flush toilets and showers, coin laundry, WiFi, and propane gas are available. Some facilities are wheelchair-accessible. Leashed pets up to 40 pounds are permitted, with certain restrictions.

Reservations, fees: Reservations are recommended for three-day holiday weekends; $27–35 per night, $3 per person per night for more than two people, $1 per pet per night. Some credit cards accepted (except on discounts). Open year-round.

Directions: On U.S. 101, drive toward San Juan Bautista (between Gilroy and Salinas). The park is on U.S. 101 two miles south of the Highway 156/San Juan Bautista exit at 1400 Highway 101.

Contact: Monterey Vacation RV Park, 831/726-9118.

10 MISSION FARM RV PARK

Scenic rating: 4

near San Juan Bautista

Map 8.1, page 495

The primary appeal of this RV park is that it is within easy walking distance of San Juan Bautista. The park is set beside a walnut orchard. Golfing and fishing are nearby.

Campsites, facilities: There are 144 sites with full hookups (30 amps) for RVs up to 33 feet and a grassy area for tents. Picnic tables are provided. Restrooms with flush toilets and showers, coin laundry, and propane gas are available. Some facilities are wheelchair-accessible. Leashed pets are permitted.

Reservations, fees: Reservations are recommended. Sites are $33 per night, $7 per person per night for more than two people, $5 per pet per night. Monthly rates available. Some credit cards accepted. Open year-round.

Directions: From U.S. 101 near San Juan Bautista, drive three miles east on U.S. 101/Highway 156. Merge onto Highway 156 East toward San Juan Bautista/Hollister and drive three miles to The Alameda. Turn right at The Alameda and drive one block to San Juan–Hollister Road. Turn left and drive 0.25 mile to the campground at 400 San Juan–Hollister Road.

Contact: Mission Farm RV Park, 831/623-4456.

11 SALINAS/MONTEREY KOA
🏊 🏕 🐕 ♿ 🚐

Scenic rating: 3

near Salinas

Map 8.1, page 495

If Big Sur, Monterey, and Carmel are packed, this RV park provides some overflow space. This KOA is located right by the highway, about a half-hour drive from the Monterey area.

Campsites, facilities: There are 79 sites with full or partial hookups (30 amps) for RVs up to 40 feet; some sites are pull-through. There are also 21 cabins. Picnic tables are provided. Restrooms with showers, recreation room, swimming pool (heated and open mid-May–mid-Oct.), playground, cable TV, clubhouse, basketball court, and coin laundry are available. Some facilities are wheelchair-accessible. Pets are permitted, with breed restrictions, and must be attended and leashed at all times.

Reservations, fees: Reservations are recommended. RV sites are $55–60 per night, $10 per night per each additional vehicle. Some credit cards accepted. Open year-round.

Directions: From Salinas, drive north on U.S. 101 for seven miles to Highway 156 West. Take the exit for Highway 156 West and drive over the overpass 0.2 mile to the Prunedale Road exit. Take that exit to Prunedale North Road. Turn right and drive a short distance to the campground entrance on the left.

Contact: Salinas/Monterey KOA, 831/663-2886 or 800/541-0085 (reservations), www.koa.com or www.reynoldsresorts.com.

12 FREMONT PEAK STATE PARK
🥾 🏕 🐕 ♿ 🚐 ⛺

Scenic rating: 7

near San Juan Bautista

Map 8.1, page 495

Most vacationers in this region are heading to Monterey Bay and the surrounding environs. That's why Fremont Peak State Park is missed by a lot of folks. It is on a ridge (2,900 feet) with great views of Monterey Bay available on the trail going up Fremont Peak (3,169 feet) in the Gavilan Range. An observatory with a 30-inch telescope at the park is open to the public on specified Saturday evenings. There are views of the San Benito Valley, Salinas Valley, and the Santa Lucia Mountains. A picnic is held in the park each April to commemorate Captain John C. Frémont, his expeditions, and his raising of the U.S. flag in defiance of the Mexican government. Note: There is no access from this park to the adjacent Hollister Hills State Vehicular Recreation Area.

Campsites, facilities: There are 21 primitive sites for tents or RVs up to 25 feet (no hookups), and one group site for up to 50 people. Picnic tables and fire rings are provided. Drinking water and pit toilets are available. Some facilities are wheelchair-accessible. Leashed pets are permitted.

Reservations, fees: Reservations are accepted at 800/444-7275 (800/444-PARK) or www.reserveamerica.com ($8 reservation fee). Sites are $25 per night, $10 per night for each additional vehicle, $100 per night for group site. The Valley View campground is open March through November; the Oak Point and the group campgrounds are open year-round.

Directions: From Highway 156 in San Juan Bautista, drive to San Juan Canyon Road. Turn south on San Juan Canyon Road (unsigned except for state park directional sign) and drive 11 miles (narrow, twisty, not recommended for vehicles longer than 25 feet) to the park.

Contact: Fremont Peak State Park, 831/623-4255; Monterey State Park District, Gavilan Sector, 831/623-4526, www.parks.ca.gov; observatory, 831/623-2465, www.fpoa.net.

13 HOLLISTER HILLS STATE VEHICULAR RECREATION AREA

Scenic rating: 4

near Hollister

Map 8.1, page 495

This unique park was designed for off-high-way-vehicle enthusiasts. It provides 80 miles of trails for motorcycles and 40 miles of trails for four-wheel-drive vehicles. Some of the trails are accessible directly from the campground. All trails close at sunset. Note that there is no direct access to Fremont Peak State Park, bordering directly to the west. Elevations at the park range 800–2,600 feet. Visitors are advised to always call in advance when planning a trip because the area is sometimes closed for special events. A sidelight is that a 288-acre area is set aside for hiking and mountain biking. In addition, a self-guided natural history walk is routed into Azalea Canyon and along the San Andreas Fault.

Campsites, facilities: There are seven campgrounds with a total of 125 sites for tents or RVs of any length (no hookups) and group sites for up to 300 people. Picnic tables and fire rings are provided. Drinking water, restrooms with flush toilets and showers, and a camp store are available. Some facilities are wheelchair-accessible. Leashed pets are permitted.

Reservations, fees: Reservations are not accepted. Sites are $10 per night per vehicle. Group sites are $250 per night. Open year-round.

Directions: From Highway 156 west of Hollister, drive east to Union Road. Turn right (south) on Union Road and drive three miles to Cienega Road. Turn right (south) on Cienega Road and drive five miles to the park on the right.

Contact: Hollister Hills State Vehicular Recreation Area, 831/637-3874 or 831/637-8186 (district office), www.parks.ca.gov or www.ohv.parks.ca.gov; Fault Line Power Sports, 831/637-9780, www.faultlinemc.com.

14 MARINA DUNES RV PARK

Scenic rating: 4

near Monterey Bay

Map 8.1, page 495

This is a popular park for RV cruisers who are touring Highway 1 and want a layover spot near Monterey. This place fills the bill, open all year and in Marina, just a short drive from the many side-trip opportunities available in Monterey and Carmel. It is set in the sand dunes, about 300 yards from the ocean. Horseback riding, boat rentals, and golfing are nearby.

Campsites, facilities: There are 65 sites, most with full hookups (30 and 50 amps), for RVs of any length and 10 sites for tents. Picnic tables and barbecue grills are provided. Restrooms with showers, drinking water, coin laundry, cable TV, Wi-Fi, recreation room, playground, volleyball, horseshoes, meeting room, picnic area, RV supplies, gift shop, dump station, and propane are available. Some facilities are wheelchair-accessible. Leashed pets are permitted.

Reservations, fees: Reservations are recommended. RV sites are $55–80 per night, tent sites are $35 per night. Credit cards accepted. Open year-round.

Directions: From Highway 1 in Marina, drive to the Reservation Road exit. Take that exit and drive west a short distance to Dunes Drive. Turn right on Dunes Drive and drive to the end of the road and the park entrance on the right.

Contact: Marina Dunes RV Park, 831/384-6914, www.marinadunesrv.com.

15 LAGUNA SECA RECREATION AREA

Scenic rating: 5

near Monterey

Map 8.1, page 495

This campground is just minutes away from the sights in Monterey and Carmel. It is situated in oak woodlands overlooking the world-famous Laguna Seca Raceway. There are three separate camping areas: Chaparral, Cam-Am Circle, and Grand Prix Campgrounds.

Campsites, facilities: There are 172 sites for tents or RVs up to 40 feet; most sites have partial hookups (30 amps). A large overflow area is also available for RVs and tents. Picnic tables and fire pits are provided. Restrooms with showers, dump station, pond, rifle and pistol range, clubhouse, and group camping and meeting facilities are available. Some facilities are wheelchair-accessible. Leashed pets are permitted.

Reservations, fees: Reservations are accepted at 888/588-2267 ($5 reservation fee). There are 70 tent and RV sites (no hookups) at Grand Prix for $30 per night. RV sites (water and electricity) are available at Chaparral and Cam-Am Circle for $35 per night, $10 per night for each additional vehicle, $2 per pet per night. Off-season and group rates available. Some credit cards accepted. Open year-round.

Directions: From Monterey and Highway 101, drive east on Highway 68 for 6.5 miles to the park entrance on the left.

Contact: Laguna Seca Recreation Area, 831/758-3604 or 888/588-2267, www.co.monterey.ca.us/parks.

16 CARMEL BY THE RIVER RV PARK

Scenic rating: 8

on the Carmel River

Map 8.1, page 495

Location, location, location. That's what vacationers want. Well, this park is set on the Carmel River, minutes away from Carmel, Cannery Row, the Monterey Bay Aquarium, golf courses, and the beach. Hedges and flowers separate each RV site.

Campsites, facilities: There are 35 sites with full hookups (30 and 50 amps) for RVs up to 45 feet. No tents. Restrooms with showers, cable TV, Wi-Fi, recreational cabana, game room with pool tables, barbecue area, and river access are available. A convenience store, laundromat, and propane gas are nearby. Some facilities are wheelchair-accessible. Leashed pets are permitted.

Reservations, fees: Reservations are accepted for two or more nights. Sites are $68–75 per night, $3 per person per night for more than two people over age 12, $5 per night for each additional vehicle, $2 per pet per night. Open year-round.

Directions: In Carmel on Highway 1 drive to Carmel Valley Road. Take Carmel Valley Road southeast and drive 4.5 miles to Schulte Road. Turn right and drive to the end of the road (27680 Schulte Road in Carmel).

Contact: Carmel by the River RV Park, 831/624-9329, www.carmelrv.com.

17 SADDLE MOUNTAIN RV PARK AND CAMPGROUND

Scenic rating: 6

near the Carmel River

Map 8.1, page 495

This pretty park is set about 100 yards from the Carmel River amid a grove of oak trees.

The park offers hiking trails, and if you want to make a buyer's swing into Carmel, it's only a five-mile drive. Note: The Carmel River is reduced to a trickle most of the year and can go dry in drought years.

Campsites, facilities: There are 28 tent sites and 23 sites with full hookups (30 amps) for RVs up to 40 feet. Picnic tables, cable TV, Wi-Fi, and barbecue grills are provided. Restrooms with flush toilets and showers are available. A seasonal swimming pool, playground, horseshoe pits, badminton, croquet, and a basketball court are available nearby. Some facilities are wheelchair-accessible. Leashed pets are permitted in the RV area only; check for current status of pet policy for campground.

Reservations, fees: Reservations are accepted. RV sites are $60 per night, tent sites are $35 per night, $5 per person per night for more than two people, $5 per night for each additional vehicle, $5 per pet. Weekly and monthly rates available. Group rates available. Open year-round.

Directions: In Carmel on Highway 1 drive to Carmel Valley Road. Take Carmel Valley Road southeast and drive 4.5 miles to Schulte Road. Turn right and drive to the park at the end of the road.

Contact: Saddle Mountain RV Park and Campground, 831/624-1617, www.saddlemountain-carmel.com.

18 PINNACLES CAMPGROUND

Scenic rating: 7

near Pinnacles National Monument

Map 8.1, page 495

This is the only camp at the Pinnacles National Monument, where there are more than 30 miles of hiking trails and two sets of talus caves. Pinnacles National Monument is like a different planet—it's a 24,000-acre park with volcanic clusters and strange caves, all great for exploring. The jagged pinnacles for which the park was named were formed by the erosion of an ancient volcanic eruption and are popular for rock climbing. This is a popular place for astronomy buffs—ranger-led dark sky viewings are offered occasionally—and condors can sometimes be seen flying in the monument and over the campground. Campfire programs are held in the amphitheater most of the year. If you are planning to stay a weekend in the spring, arrive early on Friday evening to be sure you get a campsite. In the summer, beware of temperatures in the 90s and 100s. Also note that the Bear Gulch Caves can be closed seasonally to protect nesting bat populations; always check with rangers.

Campsites, facilities: There are 99 sites for tents, 36 RV sites with partial hookups (30 amps), and 14 group sites for 20 people each. Picnic tables and fire grills are provided. Drinking water, restrooms with flush toilets and showers, dump station, amphitheater, convenience store, and a swimming pool (Apr.–Sept.) are available. Campfires are permitted, but are subject to change without warning. Although discouraged, leashed dogs are permitted in the campground. They are not permitted on trails.

Reservations, fees: Reservations are accepted at 877/444-6777 or www.recreation.gov ($9 reservation fee). Tent sites are $23 per night, RV sites are $36 per night. Group sites are $75 per night for 1–10 people, $110 for 11–20 people. Some credit cards accepted. There is a park entrance fee of $5. Open year-round, weather permitting.

Directions: From Hollister, drive south on Highway 25 for 32 miles to Highway 146 west (signed "Pinnacles"). Take Highway 146 and drive 2.5 miles to the campground on the left.

Contact: Pinnacles Campground, www.nps.gov/pinn; Pinnacles Campground Store (3–5 P.M. only), 831/389-4538.

19 BOTTCHER'S GAP WALK-IN

Scenic rating: 4

in Los Padres National Forest

Map 8.1, page 495

Here is a surprise for all the Highway 1 cruisers who never leave the highway. Just inland is this little-known camp, set in beautiful, redwood-filled Palo Colorado Canyon. It's a good jump-off spot for a hiking trip; the trail leading out of camp is routed all the way into the Ventana Wilderness. Compared to the RV parks near Monterey and Carmel, this place is truly a world apart. The elevation is 2,100 feet.

Campsites, facilities: There are 12 tent sites, including some walk-in sites. Picnic tables and fire grills are provided. Vault toilets are available. There is no drinking water. Bottled water is available from the campground manager. Leashed pets are permitted.

Reservations, fees: Reservations are not accepted. Sites are $12 per night. Open year-round.

Directions: From Carmel, drive south on Highway 1 for about 10 miles to Palo Colorado Road/County Road 5012. Turn left and drive nine miles to the campground.

Contact: Los Padres National Forest, Monterey Ranger District, 831/385-5434, www.fs.usda. gov/lpnf; Parks Management Company, 805/434-1996, www.campone.com.

20 WHITE OAKS

Scenic rating: 7

on Chews Ridge in Los Padres National Forest

Map 8.1, page 495

This camp is set at 4,000 feet elevation, near Anastasia Creek, and there's a surprisingly remote feel to the area despite its relative proximity to Carmel Valley. There is a good hike that starts about a mile from the camp and is routed into the Ventana Wilderness. Several backcountry trail camps are also available.

Campsites, facilities: There are seven sites for tents or RVs up to 20 feet. Picnic tables and fire grills are provided. Vault toilets are available. There is no drinking water. Campfire permits are required and are available free from the Forest Service. Leashed pets are permitted.

Reservations, fees: Reservations are not accepted. There is no fee for camping. Open year-round, weather permitting.

Directions: From Highway 1 in Carmel, drive to Carmel Valley road. Turn east on Carmel Valley Road and drive about 22 miles to Tassajara Road/County Road 5007. Turn right (south) on Tassajara Road/County Road 5007 and drive eight miles to the campground on the left.

From Salinas, drive south on Highway 101 to Soledad. Continue south for approximately one mile to the exit for Arroyo Road. Take that exit and drive west on Arroyo Road (becomes Arroyo Seco Road) for 16.5 miles to Carmel Valley Road. Turn right and drive 17.5 miles to Tassajara Road. Turn left and drive eight miles to the campground on the left.

Contact: Los Padres National Forest, Monterey Ranger District, 831/385-5434, www.fs.usda. gov/lpnf.

21 ANDREW MOLERA STATE PARK WALK-IN

Scenic rating: 7

in Big Sur

Map 8.1, page 495   BEST (

Considering the popularity and grandeur of Big Sur, some campers might find it hard to believe that any primitive campgrounds are available. Believe it. This park offers walk-in sites amid some beautiful coastal terrain. One of the highlights is a great trail that leads one mile to a beautiful beach. It is part of a trail system that features miles of trails routed through meadows, along beaches, and to hill-tops. Over the years, this campground has gone through several changes. At one time, the campsites here used to be overcrowded and too close together, but the campground has since been reorganized to provide more privacy for campers. It was on the reservation system for a short while, but campers demanded that it be changed back to first-come, first-served. They got their wish.

Campsites, facilities: There are 24 sites for tents limited to four people each. Picnic tables, food lockers and fire grills are provided. Drinking water and flush toilets are available. Bring your own firewood.

Reservations, fees: Reservations are not accepted. Sites are $25 per night. Open year-round, weather permitting.

Directions: From Carmel, drive 21 miles south on Highway 1 to the park camping lot on the right. Park and walk 150 yards to the camp.

Contact: Pfeiffer Big Sur State Park, 831/667-2315; California State Parks, Monterey District, 831/649-2836, www.parks.ca.gov.

22 BIG SUR CAMPGROUND AND CABINS

🕴️ 🏊 🛶 🦮 🏕️ 🚐 ⛺

Scenic rating: 8

on the Big Sur River

Map 8.1, page 495

This camp is in the redwoods near the Big Sur River. Campers can stay in the redwoods, hike on great trails through the forest at nearby state parks, or explore nearby Pfeiffer Beach. Nearby Los Padres National Forest and Ventana Wilderness in the mountains to the east provide access to remote hiking trails with ridge-top vistas. Cruising Highway 1 south to Lucia and back offers endless views of breathtaking coastal scenery.

Campsites, facilities: There are 35 sites with partial hookups (20 and 30 amps) for RVs up to 40 feet, 35 sites for tents and RVs (no hookups), 16 cabins, and four tent cabins. Picnic tables and fire grills are provided. Restrooms with flush toilets and showers, drinking water, dump station, playground, basketball, inner-tube rentals, convenience store, and coin laundry are available. Leashed pets are permitted at campsites, but not in cabins.

Reservations, fees: Reservations are recommended. RV sites are $50–80 per night, tent sites are $40–70 per night, $5 per person per night for more than two people, $15 per night for each additional vehicle with a maximum of two cars, $5 per pet per night. Some credit cards accepted. Open year-round.

Directions: From Carmel, drive 25 miles south on Highway 1 to the campground on the right side of the road (two miles north of the state park).

Contact: Big Sur Campground and Cabins, 831/667-2322, www.bigsurcamp.com.

23 PFEIFFER BIG SUR STATE PARK

🕴️ 🚲 🏊 🛶 🏕️ ♿ 🚐 ⛺

Scenic rating: 10

in Big Sur

Map 8.1, page 495

This stretch of coast is one of the most beautiful anywhere. This is one of the most popular state parks in California, and it's easy to see why. You can have it all: fantastic coastal vistas along Highway 1, redwood forests and waterfalls in the Julia Pfeiffer Burns State Park (11.5 miles to the south), expansive beaches with elusive sea otters playing on the edge of kelp beds in Andrew Molera State Park (4.5 miles north), great restaurants such as Ventana Inn (a few miles south), and private, patrolled sites. Reservations are a necessity. Some campsites in this park are set along the Big Sur River. The park features 800 acres of alders, conifers, cottonwoods, maples, oaks, redwoods, sycamores, and willows, plus open meadows—just about everything, in other words. Wildlife includes raccoons, skunk, deer, squirrels, occasional bobcats and mountain lions, and many birds, among them water ouzels and belted kingfishers. Wild boar are spotted infrequently. A number of loop trails provide spectacular views of the Pacific Ocean and the Big Sur Gorge (note that Pfeiffer Falls Trail remains closed due to damage from 2008 wildfires). Big Sur Lodge is also within the park.

Campsites, facilities: There are 204 sites for tents or RVs up to 32 feet and trailers up to 27 feet, two hike-in/bike-in sites, and two group sites for up to 35 people each. Picnic tables and fire grills are provided. Restrooms with flush toilets and showers, Wi-Fi, a coin laundry, and drinking water are available. Groceries, a café, a dump station, and propane gas are nearby. Some facilities are wheelchair-accessible. Leashed pets are permitted in the campground only.

Reservations, fees: Reservations are accepted at 800/444-7275 (800/444-PARK) or www.reserveamerica.com ($8 reservation fee). Tent and RV sites are $35 per night, premium sites are $50 per night, $10 per night for each additional vehicle, $125 per night for group sites, $5 per person per night for hike-in/bike-in sites. Open year-round.

Directions: From Carmel, drive 26 miles south on Highway 1 to the park on the left (east side of highway).

Contact: Pfeiffer Big Sur State Park, 831/667-2315; California State Parks, Monterey District, 831/649-2836, www.parks.ca.gov.

24 CHINA CAMP
🚶🏕️🐕🚐🏕️

Scenic rating: 6

on Chews Ridge in Los Padres National Forest

Map 8.1, page 495

A lot of folks might find it difficult to believe that a spot that feels so remote can be so close to the manicured Carmel Valley. But here it is, one of two camps on Tassajara Road at an elevation of 4,500 feet. This one has a trail out of camp that is routed into the Ventana Wilderness. Tassajara Hot Springs, a private

facility, is seven miles away at the end of Tassajara Road.

Campsites, facilities: There are six sites for tents or RVs up to 20 feet (no hookups). Picnic tables and fire grills are provided. Vault toilets are available. No drinking water is available. Leashed pets are permitted.

Reservations, fees: Reservations are not accepted. There is no fee for camping. Open April through November, weather permitting.

Directions: From Highway 1 in Carmel, turn east on Carmel Valley Road and drive about 22 miles. Turn right (south) on Tassajara Road/County Road 5007 and drive 11 miles to the campground on the right.

From Salinas, drive south on Highway 101 to Soledad. Continue south for approximately one mile to the exit for Arroyo Road. Take that exit and drive west on Arroyo Road (becomes Arroyo Seco Road) for 16.5 miles to Carmel Valley Road. Turn right and drive 17.5 miles to Tassajara Road. Turn left and drive 11 miles to the campground on the right.

Contact: Los Padres National Forest, Monterey Ranger District, 831/385-5434, www.fs.usda.gov/lpnf.

25 RIVERSIDE CAMPGROUND AND CABINS
🚶🏊🛶🐕🚐🏕️

Scenic rating: 8

on the Big Sur River

Map 8.1, page 495

This is one in a series of privately operated camps designed for Highway 1 cruisers touring the Big Sur area. This camp is set amid redwoods. Side trips include expansive beaches with sea otters playing on the edge of kelp beds (Andrew Molera State Park), redwood forests and waterfalls (Julia Pfeiffer Burns State Park), and several quality restaurants, including Nepenthe for those on a budget, and the Ventana Inn for those who can light cigars with $100 bills.

Campsites, facilities: There are 40 sites for tents or RVs up to 34 feet; 12 sites have partial hookups (20 amps). Twelve cabins are also available. Picnic tables and fire pits are provided. Restrooms with flush toilets and coin showers are available. A coin laundry and firewood are available. A store is on-site. Leashed pets are permitted at campsites and in most cabins.

Reservations, fees: Reservations are recommended at 831/667-2414 or reservations@riversidecampground.com. RV sites are $45–50 per night, tent sites are $40–45 per night, premiere sites are more, $5 per person per night for more than two people over age six, with a maximum of five people, $10 per night for each additional vehicle, with a maximum of two vehicles, $5 per pet per night at tent and RV sites, $20 per pet per night in cabins. Some credit cards accepted. Open year-round, weather permitting.

Directions: From Carmel, drive 22 miles south on Highway 1 to the campground on the right.

Contact: Riverside Campground and Cabins, tel. 831/667-2414, www.riversidecampground.com.

26 FERNWOOD RESORT
🏕️ 🏊 🛶 🐕 ♿ 🚐 ⛺

Scenic rating: 7

on the Big Sur River

Map 8.1, page 495

This resort is on the banks of the Big Sur River in the redwoods of the beautiful Big Sur coast. Many of the campsites are set along the river. There also are eight tent cabins and a roadside motel. A highlight is that there is live music on Saturday nights in season. You can crown your trip with a dinner at the on-site Redwood Grill or a hike at nearby Pfeiffer Big Sur State Park.

Campsites, facilities: There are 15 sites for tents only, 31 sites with partial hookups (30 amps) for RVs up to 36 feet, 11 tent cabins, and a motel. Fire grills and picnic tables are provided. Restrooms with showers, grocery store, restaurant, and a bar are available. Some facilities are wheelchair-accessible. Leashed pets are permitted.

Reservations, fees: Reservations are recommended. RV sites are $50 per night, tent sites are $45 per night, $5 per person per night for more than two people (maximum of six), $5 per night for each additional vehicle, $5 per pet per night. Tent cabins are $75 per night, $10 per person per night for more than two people. Discounts available in the off-season. Some credit cards accepted. Open year-round.

Directions: From Carmel, drive 26 miles south on Highway 1 to the campground on the right.

Contact: Fernwood Resort, 831/667-2422, www.fernwoodbigsur.com.

27 ARROYO SECO
🏕️ 🏊 🛶 🐕 ♿ 🚐 ⛺

Scenic rating: 5

along Arroyo Seco River in
Los Padres National Forest

Map 8.1, page 495

This pretty spot near the Arroyo Seco River is just outside the northern border of the Ventana Wilderness. The elevation is 900 feet. Arroyo Seco Group Camp is available to keep the pressure off this campground.

Campsites, facilities: There are 49 sites for tents or RVs up to 26 feet, plus a group site for 25–50 people. Picnic tables and fire grills are provided. Drinking water, restrooms with flush toilets and coin showers, and a dump station are available. Firewood is available from the camp host, and a grocery store is within five miles. Some facilities are wheelchair-accessible. Leashed pets are permitted.

Reservations, fees: Reservations are accepted for individual sites and required for group sites at 877/444-6777 or www.recreation.gov ($9 reservation fee). Single sites are $20 per night, double sites are $40 per night, primitive single sites are $15, primitive double sites are $30 per night, $5 per night for each additional vehicle, and the group site is $75 per night. Open year-round.

Directions: Drive on U.S. 101 to the town of Greenfield and the Arroyo Seco Road/Elm Avenue exit. Turn west on Elm Avenue/Road G16 and drive six miles to Arroyo Seco Road. Turn left and drive 6.5 miles to Carmel Valley Road. Turn right and drive 3.5 miles to the campground.

Contact: Los Padres National Forest, Monterey Ranger District, 831/385-5434, www.fs.usda. gov/lpnf; Rocky Mountain Recreation Company, 831/674-5726.

28 SAN LORENZO COUNTY PARK

Scenic rating: 3

in King City

Map 8.1, page 495

A lot of folks cruising up and down the state on U.S. 101 can underestimate their travel time and find themselves caught out near King City, a small city about midpoint between Northern and Southern California. Well, don't sweat it, because San Lorenzo County Park offers a spot to overnight. It's set near the Salinas River, which isn't exactly the Mississippi, but it'll do. A museum complex captures the rural agricultural life of the valley. The park covers 200 acres, featuring playgrounds and ball fields.

Campsites, facilities: There are 93 sites with full or partial hookups (30 amps) for tents or RVs of any length; some sites are pull-through. Picnic tables and fire pits are provided. A dump station, restrooms with flush toilets and showers, picnic area, coin laundry, meeting facilities, playgrounds, horseshoes, putting green, volleyball, softball fields, walking trail, and computer kiosks are available. Leashed pets are permitted.

Reservations, fees: Reservations are accepted at 831/385-5964 ($5 reservation fee; $15 for groups). Tent sites are $35 per night, RV sites (water and electricity) are $35 per night, RV sites (full hookups) are $40 per night, $10 per night for each additional vehicle, $2 per pet per night. Off-season and group rates available. Open year-round.

Directions: From King City on U.S. 101, take the Broadway exit, turn onto Broadway, and drive to the park at 1160 Broadway.

Contact: San Lorenzo County Park, 831/385-5964, www.co.monterey.ca.us/parks.

29 ESCONDIDO

Scenic rating: 6

in Los Padres National Forest

Map 8.1, page 495

This is a prime jump-off spot for backpackers heading into the Ventana Wilderness. The camp is set at an elevation of 2,300 feet at a trailhead that connects to a network of other trails. The only catch is you have to plan on an often-steep climb of more than 1,000 feet to reach the ridge.

Campsites, facilities: There are nine sites for tents only. Picnic tables and fire grills are provided. Vault toilets are available. There is no drinking water. Spring water is available; purify before use. Garbage must be packed out. Leashed pets are permitted.

Reservations, fees: Reservations are not accepted. There is no fee for camping. Open April through November, weather permitting.

Directions: From U.S. 101 in King City, turn south on County Route G14 and drive 18 miles. Turn north on Mission Road and drive six miles. Turn left on Del Venturi–Milpitas Road/Indian Road and drive 20 miles to the campground on the left.

Contact: Los Padres National Forest, Monterey Ranger District, 831/385-5434, www.fs.usda. gov/lpnf.

30 MEMORIAL PARK

🏃 ♨ 🏕 5% ⛺

Scenic rating: 6

in Los Padres National Forest

Map 8.1, page 495

This is one of two backcountry camps in the area. The highlights are a trailhead and the vicinity of the Arroyo Seco River. The camp has a trailhead that provides access to the Ventana Wilderness trail network. The elevation is 2,000 feet, which gives hikers a nice head start on the climb. Be sure to pack plenty of drinking water for the trail and, even in spring, expect warm, dry conditions.

Campsites, facilities: There are eight sites for tents only. Picnic tables and fire grills are provided. Vault toilets are available. No drinking water is available. Garbage must be packed out. Leashed pets are permitted.

Reservations, fees: Reservations are not accepted. There is no fee for camping. Open year-round, weather permitting.

Directions: From U.S. 101 in King City, turn south on County Route G14 and drive 18 miles. Turn north on Mission Road and drive six miles. Turn left on Del Venturi–Milpitas Road/County Road 4050 and drive 16 miles to the campground on the right.

Contact: Los Padres National Forest, Monterey Ranger District, 831/385-5434, www.fs.usda.gov/lpnf.

31 KIRK CREEK

🏃 🚴 ♨ ⚓ 🏕 🚐 ⛺

Scenic rating: 8

in Los Padres National Forest
near the Pacific Ocean

Map 8.1, page 495

This pretty camp is set along Kirk Creek where it empties into the Pacific Ocean. There is beach access through a footpath. Another trail from camp branches north through the Ventana Wilderness, which is sprinkled with little-used, hike-in, backcountry campsites.

For gorgeous scenery without all the work, a quaint little café in Lucia provides open-air dining on a cliff-top deck, with a dramatic sweeping lookout over the coast.

Campsites, facilities: There are 34 sites for tents or RVs up to 30 feet (no hookups). Picnic tables and fire grills are provided. Drinking water and flush toilets are available. A camp host has firewood for sale. Leashed pets are permitted.

Reservations, fees: Reservations are accepted for 50 percent of the sites at 877/444-6777 or www.recreation.gov ($9 reservation fee). Sites are $22 per night, hike-in/bike-in sites are $5 per night. Open year-round.

Directions: From Monterey, drive south on Highway 1 to Lucia. From Lucia, continue south on Highway 1 for four miles to the campground on the right.

Contact: Parks Management Company, 805/434-1996, www.campone.com; Los Padres National Forest, Monterey Ranger District, 831/385-5434, www.fs.usda.gov/lpnf.

32 LIMEKILN STATE PARK

🏃 🏕 ♿ 🚐 ⛺

Scenic rating: 9

south of Big Sur

Map 8.1, page 495

Limekiln State Park reopened in the summer of 2010 to near-full glory. It had closed in 2008 after the Chalk Fire, but the redwoods and the neighboring coastal grasslands are fire resilient. Limekiln provides spectacular views of the coast and is a layover spot for Highway 1 cruisers south of the Big Sur area. Drive-in campsites are set near both the beach and the redwoods—take your pick. Several hiking trails are nearby, including one that is routed past some historic lime kilns, which were used in the late 1800s to make cement and bricks. A short rock hop on a spur trail (just off the main trail) leads to gorgeous 100-foot Limekiln Falls. One problem: Parking is limited.

Campsites, facilities: There are 13 sites for tents and 11 sites for tents or RVs up to 24 feet (no hookups) and trailers up to 15 feet. Picnic tables and fire grills are provided. Drinking water, restrooms with showers and flush toilets, and firewood are available. Some facilities are wheelchair accessible. Leashed pets are allowed, except on trails.

Reservations, fees: Reservations are accepted at 800/444-7275 (800/444-PARK) or www. reserveamerica.com ($8 reservation fee). Sites are $35 per night, $10 per night for each additional vehicle. Some credit cards accepted for reservations, but not at the park. Open year-round, weather and road conditions permitting.

Directions: From Big Sur, drive south on Highway 1 for 32 miles (past Lucia) to the park on the left.

Contact: Limekiln State Park, 831/667-2403; California State Parks, Monterey District, 831/649-2836, www.parks.ca.gov; Parks Management Company, 805/434-1996, www. campone.com.

33 NACIMIENTO
🚶 ⛵ 🐕 🚐 ⛺

Scenic rating: 4

in Los Padres National Forest

Map 8.1, page 495

This little-known spot is set near the Nacimiento River at 1,600 feet elevation. Most campers will head up Nacimiento-Ferguson Road to camp on a Friday night and get up Saturday morning to head off on a hiking or backpacking trip in the nearby Ventana Wilderness.

Campsites, facilities: There are eight sites for tents or RVs up to 25 feet (no hookups). Picnic tables and fire grills are provided. Vault toilets are available. No drinking water is available. Leashed pets are permitted.

Reservations, fees: Reservations are not accepted. Sites are $10 per night. Open year-round.

Directions: From Monterey, drive south on Highway 1 to Lucia. From Lucia, continue south on Highway 1 for four miles to Nacimiento Road. Turn east (left) on Nacimiento Road and drive 11 winding miles to the campground on the right.

Contact: Parks Management Company, 805/434-1996, www.campone.com; Los Padres National Forest, Monterey Ranger District, 831/385-5434, www.fs.usda.gov/lpnf.

34 PONDEROSA
🚶 🐕 🚐 ⛺

Scenic rating: 4

in Los Padres National Forest

Map 8.1, page 495

As soon as you turn off Highway 1, you leave behind the crowds and enter a land that is largely unknown to people. This camp is set at 1,500 feet elevation in Los Padres National Forest, not far from the border of the Ventana Wilderness (good hiking and backpacking) and the Hunter Liggett Military Reservation (wild-pig hunting is allowed there with a permit). It is one in a series of small camps on Nacimiento-Ferguson Road.

Campsites, facilities: There are 23 sites for tents or RVs up to 35 feet. Picnic tables and fire grills are provided. Vault toilets and drinking water are available. Leashed pets are permitted.

Reservations, fees: Reservations accepted at 877/444-6777 or www.recreation.gov ($9 reservation fee). Sites are $15 per night. Open year-round.

Directions: From Monterey, drive south on Highway 1 to Lucia. From Lucia, continue south on Highway 1 for four miles to Nacimiento-Ferguson Road. Turn left on Nacimiento-Ferguson Road and drive about 12 miles to the campground on the right.

Contact: Parks Management Company, 805/434-1996, www.campone.com; Los Padres National Forest, Monterey Ranger District, 831/385-5434, www.fs.usda.gov/lpnf.

SAN JOAQUIN VALLEY

BEST CAMPGROUNDS

◖ **White-Water Rafting**
Lumsden, page 528.

The San Joaquin Valley is noted for its searing

weather all summer long. But that is also when the lakes in the foothills become something like a Garden of Eden for boating and water-sports enthusiasts. The region also offers many settings in the Sierra foothills, which can serve as launch points for short drives into the alpine beauty of Yosemite, Sequoia, and Kings Canyon National Parks.

Most of the campgrounds in this region are family-oriented. Many of them are on access roads to Yosemite. A bonus is that most have lower prices than their counterparts in the park, and are more hospitable to children.

The lakes are the primary recreation attraction, with the refreshing, clean water revered as a tonic against the valley heat all summer long. When viewed from the air, the closeness of these lakes to the Sierra Nevada mountain range is surprising to many. Their proximity to the high country results in cool, high-quality water – the product of snowmelt sent down river canyons on the western slope. Some of these lakes are among the best around for waterskiing and powerboat recreation, including Lake Don Pedro east of Modesto, Bass Lake near Oakhurst, Lake McClure near Merced, Pine Flat Lake east of Fresno, and Lake Kaweah near Visalia.

In addition, Lake Don Pedro, and Pine Flat Lake and Lake Kaweah in the nearby Sequoia and Kings Canyon region, are among the best fishing lakes in the entire Central Valley; some anglers rate Don Pedro as the number-one all-around fishing lake in the state. The Sierra rivers that feed these lakes (and others) also offer the opportunity to fly-fish for trout. In particular, the Kaweah and Kings Rivers boast many miles of ideal pocket water for fly fishers. While the trout on these streams are only occasionally large, the catch rates are often high and the rock-strewn beauty of the river canyons is exceptional.

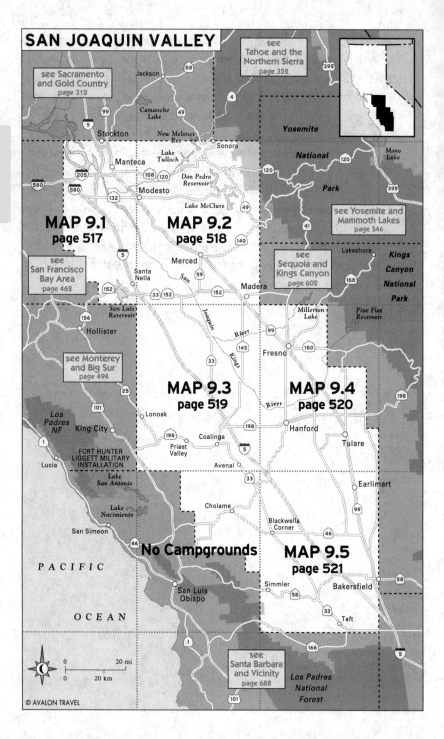

SAN JOAQUIN VALLEY

see Sacramento
and Gold Country
page 312

see Tahoe and the
Northern Sierra
page 352

MAP 9.1
page 517

MAP 9.2
page 518

see San Francisco
Bay Area
page 462

see Yosemite and
Mammoth Lakes
page 546

see Sequoia and
Kings Canyon
page 602

see Monterey
and Big Sur
page 494

MAP 9.3
page 519

MAP 9.4
page 520

No Campgrounds

MAP 9.5
page 521

PACIFIC

OCEAN

Los Padres NF

Kings Canyon National Park

Yosemite National Park

Los Padres National Forest

see Santa Barbara
and Vicinity
page 688

0   20 mi
0   20 km

© AVALON TRAVEL

Map 9.1

Sites 1-7
Pages 522-525

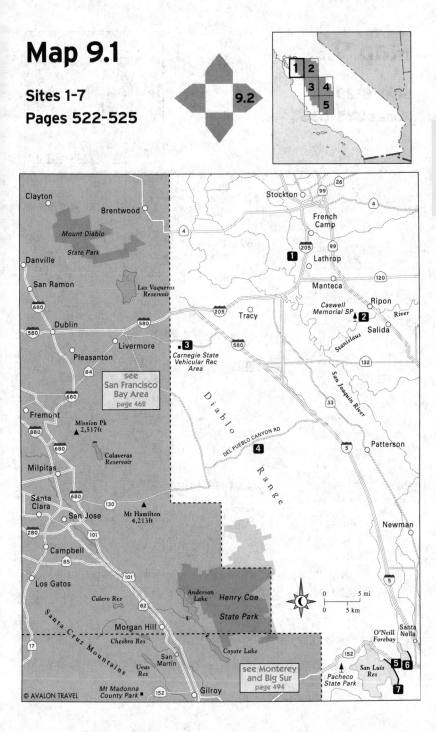

Map 9.2

Sites 8-29
Pages 525-536

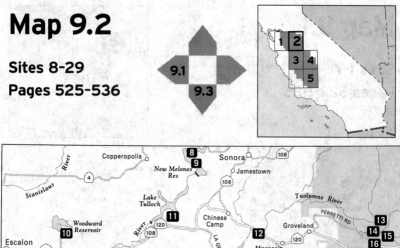

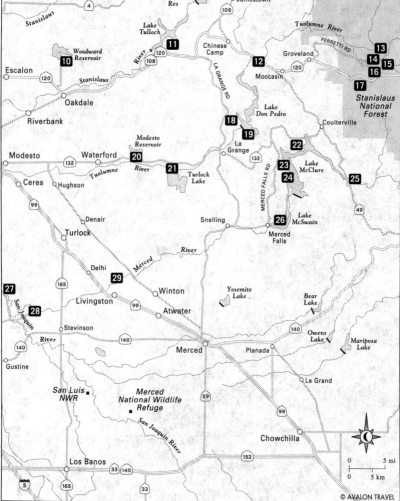

Map 9.3

Site 30
Page 537

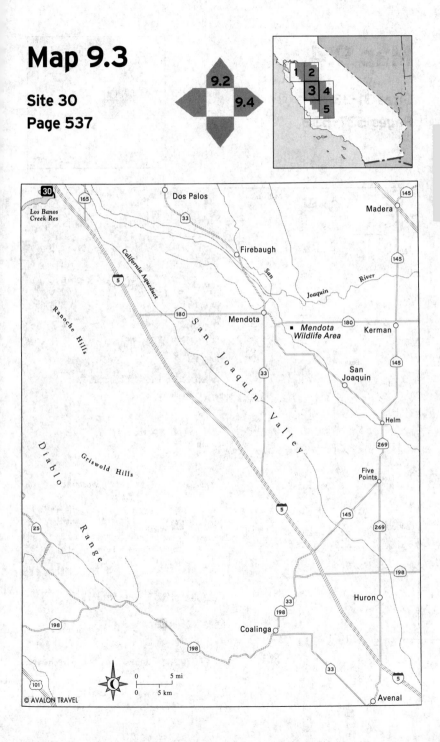

Map 9.4

Sites 31-33
Pages 537-538

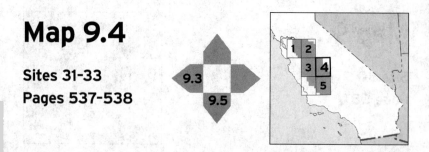

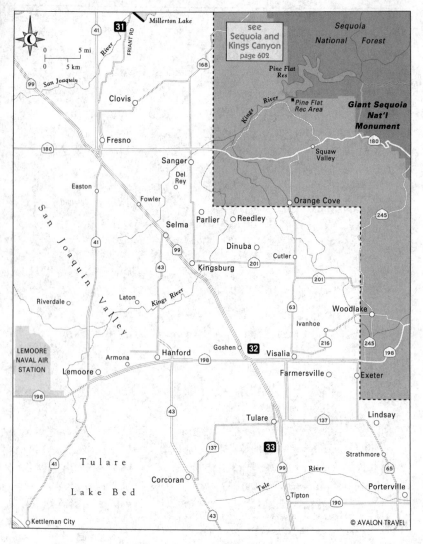

see Sequoia and Kings Canyon page 602

© AVALON TRAVEL

Map 9.5

Sites 34-37
Pages 539-541

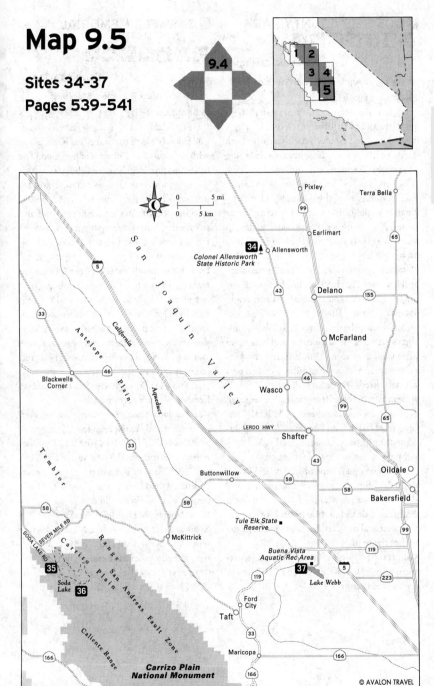

1 DOS REIS COUNTY PARK

Scenic rating: 6

on the San Joaquin River near Stockton

Map 9.1, page 517

This is a nine-acre county park that has a quarter mile of San Joaquin River frontage, boat ramp, and nearby access to the eastern Delta near Stockton. Note that tent camping is available on weekends and holidays only. The sun gets scalding hot here in the summer, branding everything in sight. That's why boaters make quick work of getting in the water, then cooling off with water sports. In the winter, this area often has zero visibility from tule fog.

Campsites, facilities: There are 26 sites with full hookups (20 and 30 amps) for RVs of any length and tents; some sites are pull-through. Picnic tables and fire grills are provided. Restrooms with showers and flush toilets, children's play area, horseshoe pits, and boat ramp are available. A store, coin laundry, and propane gas are within three miles. Leashed pets are permitted, with a limit of two.

Reservations, fees: Reservations are required at least two weeks in advance at 209/331-7400 ($10 reservation fee). Sites are $25 per night, $5 per night for each additional vehicle, $1 per pet per night. Open year-round.

Directions: From I-5 and Stockton, drive south to the Lathrop exit. Turn west on Lathrop and drive 1.5 blocks to Manthy Road. Turn north (right) and drive 0.5 mile to Dos Reis Road. Turn left and drive to the campground at the end of the road.

Contact: San Joaquin County Parks Department, 209/331-7400 or 209/953-8800, www.mgzoo.com/parks.

2 CASWELL MEMORIAL STATE PARK

Scenic rating: 7

on the Stanislaus River near Stockton

Map 9.1, page 517

Caswell Memorial State Park features shoreline frontage along the Stanislaus River, along with an additional 250 acres of parkland. The Stanislaus provides shoreline fishing for catfish on summer nights. Bass and crappie are also occasionally caught. Other recreation options here include an interpretive nature trail and swimming. Bird-watching is popular; look for red-shouldered and red-tail hawks. During warm months, bring mosquito repellent.

Campsites, facilities: There are 64 sites for tents or RVs up to 24 feet (no hookups), and one group site for up to 50 people. Picnic tables, food lockers, and fire grills are provided. Drinking water, flush toilets, showers, firewood, a swimming beach, and nature trails are available. Weekend interpretive programs and junior ranger programs are offered in the summer. Some facilities are wheelchair-accessible. Leashed pets are permitted.

Reservations, fees: Reservations are accepted in summer and are required for the group site at 800/444-7275 (800/444-PARK) or www.reserveamerica.com ($8 reservation fee). Sites are $30 per night, and $10 per night for each additional vehicle, and the group site is $165 per night. Open year-round.

Directions: From Highway 99, take the Austin Road exit (1.5 miles south of Manteca). Turn south on Austin Road and drive four miles to the park entrance at the end of the road.

Contact: Caswell Memorial State Park, 209/599-3810, www.parks.ca.gov.

3 CARNEGIE STATE VEHICULAR RECREATION AREA

Scenic rating: 2

near Tracy

Map 9.1, page 517

This is a major state-run OHV area, with mainly dirt bikes and all-terrain vehicles. Don't show up without one, or its equivalent. This area is barren, ugly, and extremely noisy on weekends. It can get hot, windy, and dusty as well. But that's just what dirt bikers want, and they have it all to themselves. The main campground fills on most weekends from October through May. The area covers 1,500 acres with challenging hill-type trail riding and a professionally designed motocross track. There is also a four-wheel-drive obstacle course. Elevations here rise to 1,800 feet, with summer temperatures peaking at 105°F. Winters are mild.

Campsites, facilities: There are 22 sites for tents or RVs of any length (no hookups). Picnic tables, shade ramadas, and fire rings are provided. Drinking water, coin showers, and flush toilets are available, but note that the drinking water (high in iron) might taste terrible, and you are advised to bring bottled water. Cell phone service is not available, but there is a pay phone. Nearest supplies are 14 miles away. Some facilities are wheelchair-accessible. Leashed pets are permitted.

Reservations, fees: Reservations are not accepted. Sites are $10 per night. Open year-round, weather permitting.

Directions: From I-580 (south of Tracy), drive to Corral Hollow Road. Take that exit and drive west for six miles to the campground on the left.

Contact: Carnegie State Vehicular Recreation Area, 925/447-9027; Carnegie Sector Office, 925/447-0426, www.parks.ca.gov.

4 DEER CREEK CAMPGROUND

Scenic rating: 4

in Frank Raines OHV Regional Park
near Modesto

Map 9.1, page 517

This park is primarily a riding area for folks with dirt bikes, all-terrain vehicles, and dune buggies who take advantage of the rough-terrain riding course. About 850 acres of this 1,500-acre park are reserved for OHV use. Deer and pig hunting in season are also a possibility. A side-trip option is to visit Minniear Park, directly to the east, which is a day-use wilderness park with hiking trails and a creek. This area is very pretty in the spring when the foothills are still green and many wildflowers are blooming.

Campsites, facilities: There are 34 sites with full hookups (30 amps) for RVs or tents and 20 sites for tents or RVs (no hookups). A few sites are pull-through. Fire grills and picnic tables are provided. Restrooms with showers and flush toilets, picnic area, baseball diamond, group facilities, nature trails, and a recreation hall with a full kitchen are available. Bring your own drinking water or be prepared to boil or treat water before use. Some facilities are wheelchair-accessible. Leashed pets are permitted.

Reservations, fees: Reservations are not accepted. Tent sites are $15 per night, RV sites (hookups) are $25 per night, $10 per night for each additional vehicle, $3 per pet per night, the OHV fee is $5 per day. OHV recreation is open mid-October through early June. Deer Creek Campground is open year-round, weather permitting.

Directions: On I-5, drive to the Patterson exit (south of the junction of I-5 and I-580). Turn west on the Patterson exit and drive onto Diablo Grande Parkway. Continue a short distance under the freeway to Del Puerto Canyon Road. Turn west (right) and drive 16 miles to the park and the campground on the right.

Contact: Stanislaus County Parks and Recreation Department, 866/648-7275, 209/525-6750, or 408/897-3127, www.stancounty.com.

5 SAN LUIS CREEK

Scenic rating: 5

on San Luis Reservoir

Map 9.1, page 517

San Luis Creek Campground is near San Luis Reservoir. It is one in a series of camps operated by the state in the San Luis Reservoir State Recreation Area, adjacent to the reservoir and O'Neill Forebay, home of many of the biggest striped bass in California, including the world record for landlocked stripers. Note: All boats must be certified mussel-free before launching.

Campsites, facilities: There are 53 sites with partial hookups (20 and 30 amps) for tents or RVs up to 35 feet and two group sites for up to 30 and 60 people each. Picnic tables and fire pits are provided. Drinking water, pit toilets, and a dump station are available. Flush toilets, coin showers, and shade ramadas are available in the group sites. A boat ramp is nearby. Some facilities are wheelchair accessible. Leashed pets are permitted.

Reservations, fees: Reservations are accepted at 800/444-7275 (800/444-PARK) or www.reserveamerica.com ($8 reservation fee). Sites are $40 per night, $10 per night for each additional vehicle, $100–200 per night for group sites. Open year-round.

Directions: Drive on Highway 152 to San Luis Reservoir (12 miles west of Los Banos) and the signed campground entrance road (15 miles west of Los Banos). Turn north and drive two miles to the campground on the left.

Contact: San Luis Reservoir State Recreation Area, 209/826-1196; Four Rivers Sector, 209/826-1197, www.parks.ca.gov.

6 MEDEIROS

Scenic rating: 5

on O'Neill Forebay near Santa Nella

Map 9.1, page 517

This is a vast, primitive campground set on the stark expanse of foothill country on O'Neill Forebay and near San Luis Reservoir. Some of the biggest striped bass in California history have been caught here at the forebay. It is best known for wind in the spring, hot weather in the summer, and low water levels in the fall. Striped-bass fishing is best in the fall when the wind is down and stripers will corral schools of bait fish near the lake surface. Sailboarding is decent. There's a large, developed, swimming beach on O'Neill Forebay, and boats can be launched four miles west of the campground at San Luis Creek. There used to be another boat ramp at Medeiros, but it's been closed since 9/11 and will not reopen. The closest boat launch is at San Luis Creek. In addition to security concerns, there were problems with launching in low water conditions. The forebay can get congested on weekends and holidays; the reservoir is less crowded. The campground elevation is 225 feet. (See the Basalt listing for more information about San Luis.) Note: All boats must be certified mussel-free before launching.

Campsites, facilities: There are 350 primitive sites for tents or RVs of any length (no hookups). Some shaded ramadas with fire grills and picnic tables are available. Drinking water and chemical toilets are available. A boat ramp is four miles away. Leashed pets are permitted.

Reservations, fees: Reservations are not accepted. Sites are $15 per night, and each additional vehicle is $10 per night. Boat launching is $6 per day. Open year-round.

Directions: Drive on Highway 152 to Highway 33 (about 10 miles west of Los Banos). Turn north (right) on Highway 33 and drive 0.25 mile to the campground entrance on the left.

Contact: San Luis Reservoir State Recreation Area, 209/826-1196; Four Rivers Sector, 209/826-1197, www.parks.ca.gov.

⑦ BASALT

Scenic rating: 5

on San Luis Reservoir

Map 9.1, page 517

San Luis Reservoir is a huge, man-made lake, covering 13,800 acres with 65 miles of shoreline, developed among stark foothills to provide a storage facility along the California Aqueduct. It fills by late winter and is used primarily by anglers, water-skiers, and sailboarders. When the Sacramento River Delta water pumps take the water, they also take the fish, filling this lake up with both. Striped-bass fishing is best in the fall when the stripers chase schools of bait fish on the lake surface. Spring and early summer can be quite windy, but that makes for good sailboarding. The adjacent O'Neill Forebay is the best recreation bet because of the boat launch and often good fishing. There is a visitors center at the Romero Overlook. The elevation is 575 feet. Summer temperatures can occasionally exceed 100°F, but evenings are usually pleasant. During winter, tule fog is common. Note that in spring and early summer, it can turn windy very quickly. Warning lights mark several spots at the reservoir and forebay. Note: All boats must be certified mussel-free before launching.

Campsites, facilities: There are 79 sites for tents or RVs up to 35 feet (no hookups). Picnic tables and fire grills are provided. Drinking water, restrooms with flush toilets and coin showers, dump station, picnic areas, and a boat ramp are available. A store, coin laundry, gas station, restaurant, and propane gas are nearby (about 1.5 miles away). Some facilities are wheelchair-accessible. Leashed pets are permitted.

Reservations, fees: Reservations are accepted at 800/444-7275 (800/444-PARK) or www.reserveamerica.com ($8 reservation fee). Sites are $30 per night, and $10 per night for each additional vehicle. Boat launching is $6 per day. Open year-round.

Directions: Drive on Highway 152 to San Luis Reservoir (12 miles west of Los Banos) and the Basalt campground entrance road. Turn south on Basalt Road and drive 2.5 miles to the campground on the left.

Contact: San Luis Reservoir State Recreation Area, 209/826-1196; Four Rivers Sector, 209/826-1197, www.parks.ca.gov.

⑧ GLORY HOLE

Scenic rating: 7

at New Melones Reservoir

Map 9.2, page 518

Glory Hole encompasses both Big Oak and Ironhorse campgrounds. This is one of two major recreation areas on New Melones Reservoir in the Sierra Nevada foothills, a popular spot with a boat ramp nearby for access to outstanding waterskiing and fishing. Campfire programs are often offered at the amphitheater in summer. Camp hosts are usually on-site year-round. (See the Tuttletown Recreation Area listing for more information.)

Campsites, facilities: Big Oak has 53 sites for tents or RVs up to 40 feet (no hookups). Ironhorse has 69 sites for tents or RVs of any length; 20 walk-in sites are for tents only. Picnic tables and fire grills are provided. Drinking water, restrooms with flush toilets and showers, marina, boat ramps, houseboat and boat rentals, swimming beach, amphitheater, and playground are available. Some facilities are wheelchair-accessible. Leashed pets are permitted.

Reservations, fees: Reservations are accepted at 877/444-6777 or www.recreation.gov ($9 reservation fee). Sites are $18–22 per night, $8 per night per additional vehicle. Open year-round.

Directions: From Sonora, drive north on Highway 49 for about 15 miles (Glory Hole Market will be on the left side of the road) to Whittle Ranch Road. Turn left and drive five miles to the campground, with sites on both sides of the road.

Contact: U.S. Bureau of Reclamation, New Melones Visitor Center, 209/536-9094; New

Melones Lake Marina, 209/785-3300; Glory Hole Sports, 209/736-4333.

9 TUTTLETOWN RECREATION AREA

Scenic rating: 7

at New Melones Reservoir

Map 9.2, page 518

Here is a mammoth camping area set on the giant New Melones Reservoir in the Sierra Nevada foothills, a beautiful sight when the lake is full. The lake is set in the valley foothills between the historic mining towns of Angels Camp and Sonora. New Melones is one of California's top recreation lakes. All water sports are permitted. Waterskiing and houseboating are particularly popular. Tuttletown encompasses three campgrounds (Acorn, Manzanita, and Chamise) and two group camping areas (Oak Knoll and Fiddleneck). New Melones is a huge reservoir that covers 12,500 acres and offers more than 100 miles of shoreline and good fishing. The elevation is 1,085 feet. A boat ramp is near camp. Although the lake's main body is huge, the better fishing is well up the lake's Stanislaus River arm (for trout) and in its coves (for bass and bluegill), where there are submerged trees providing perfect aquatic habitat. Trolling for kokanee salmon also has become popular. The lake level often drops dramatically in the fall.

Campsites, facilities: Acorn has 69 sites for tents or RVs of any length (no hookups); Chamise has 35 tent sites; Manzanita has 52 sites for tents or RVs of any length and 15 walk-in tent sites; Oak Knoll group site holds up to 50 people and Fiddleneck group site holds up to 60 people. Picnic tables and fire grills are provided. Drinking water, restrooms with flush toilets and showers, dump station, playground, and boat ramp are available. Some facilities are wheelchair-accessible. Leashed pets are permitted.

Reservations, fees: Reservations are accepted at 877/444-6777 or www.recreation.gov ($9 reservation fee). Sites are $18–22 per night, $8 per night per additional vehicle, and the group sites are $125–150 per night. Open year-round.

Directions: From Sonora, drive north on Highway 49 to Reynolds Ferry Road. Turn left and drive about two miles to the entrance road to the campgrounds.

Contact: U.S. Bureau of Reclamation, New Melones Visitor Center, 209/536-9094.

10 WOODWARD RESERVOIR COUNTY PARK

Scenic rating: 7

near Oakdale

Map 9.2, page 518

This is one of the best sailing lakes in Northern California. Regattas are held through the year, and it is also very popular for sailboarding. Woodward's nickname, in fact, is "Windward Reservoir." Woodward Reservoir is a large lake covering 2,900 acres with 23 miles of shoreline, set in the rolling foothills just north of Oakdale. It is a good lake for both waterskiing and fishing, with minimal conflict between the two sports. All boating is allowed, and speedboats have the main lake body to let her rip. Trout fishing has improved and they are stocked here in winter. In recent years, the county and local hatcheries began restocking the reservoir, planting redear sunfish, bluegill, largemouth bass, and channel catfish in addition to rainbow trout. Note that because this is one of the largest reservoirs near Modesto and Stockton, it gets lots of local traffic, especially on summer weekends. There are equestrian facilities at this park, and horse camping is permitted in undeveloped sites only (Area A to Area FF).

Note: Seasonally, all body-to-water contact at the reservoir is prohibited; call ahead to confirm.

Campsites, facilities: There are 180 sites for

tents and RVs, some with partial hookups, and 40 RV sites with full hookups (30 amps). Primitive camping is available in designated areas. Picnic tables and fire grills are provided. Drinking water, a dump station, picnic shelter, three boat ramps, fish cleaning station, dry boat storage, restrooms with flush toilets and showers, and some equestrian facilities are available. Some facilities are wheelchair-accessible. Leashed pets are permitted.

Reservations, fees: Reservations are not accepted. Primitive sites are $20 per night, RV sites (hookups) are $25 per night, $7 per day boat launch fee, $10 per night per additional vehicle, $3 per pet per night, $2 per horse per night. Holiday weekend rates are $2 higher. Open year-round.

Directions: Drive on Highway 120 to Oakdale (the road becomes Highway 108/120) and the junction with County Road J14/26 Mile Road. Turn left on 26 Mile Road and drive four miles to the park entrance at Woodward Reservoir (14528 26 Mile Road).

Contact: Woodward Reservoir County Park, 209/847-3304; Stanislaus County Parks, 209/525-6750, www.stancounty.com/parks.

11 LAKE TULLOCH RV CAMPGROUND AND MARINA

Scenic rating: 7

on the south shore of Lake Tulloch

Map 9.2, page 518

This camp features tons of waterfront on Lake Tulloch, a dispersed tent area, and cabins with direct beach access. Unlike so many reservoirs in the foothill country, this one is nearly always full of water. In addition, it is a place where anglers and water-skiers live in harmony. That is because of the many coves and a six-mile-long arm with an enforced 5-mph speed limit. It's a big lake, shaped like a giant X with extended lake arms adding up to 55 miles of shoreline. The campground features mature oak trees

that provide shade to most of the developed sites. A secret at Tulloch is that fishing is also good for crawdads. The elevation is 500 feet.

Campsites, facilities: There are 130 sites, including 31 boat sites and 30 with full or partial hookups (30 and 50 amps) for tents or RVs up to 35 feet, a large area for lakefront tent camping and self-contained RVs, and 12 waterfront cabins. Picnic tables and fire grills are provided. Drinking water, restrooms with flush toilets and showers, coin laundry, convenience store, dump station, playground, restaurant, volleyball, horseshoes, tetherball, ping pong, swimming beach, marina, boat rentals, boat slips, fuel dock, and a boat launch are available. Some facilities are wheelchair-accessible. Leashed pets are permitted.

Reservations, fees: Reservations are accepted. Sites are $23–35 per night, $15 per night for the first additional vehicle, $23 per each additional vehicle, and $3 per pet per night. Cabins are $100–150 per night. Group rates are available. Boat launch fee is $10 (once per weekend). Credit cards accepted. Open year-round.

Directions: From Manteca, drive east on Highway 120 (it becomes Highway 108/120) to Oakdale. Continue east for 13 miles to Tulloch Road on the left. Turn left and drive 4.6 miles to the campground entrance and gatehouse at the south shore of Lake Tulloch.

Contact: Lake Tulloch RV Campground and Marina, 209/881-0107 or 800/894-2267, www.laketullochcampground.com; Lake Tulloch Boat Rentals, 209/881-3410 or 866/979-2628.

12 MOCCASIN POINT

Scenic rating: 7

at Lake Don Pedro

Map 9.2, page 518

This camp is at the northeastern end of Lake Don Pedro, adjacent to a boat ramp. Moccasin Point juts well into the lake, directly across from where the major Tuolumne River arm enters the lake. Don Pedro is a giant lake, with extended lake arms and nearly 13,000 surface acres and 160 miles of shoreline. It is one of the best boating and recreation lakes in California, but subject to drawdowns from midsummer through early fall. At different times, fishing is excellent for salmon, trout, or bass. Other species are redear sunfish, catfish, crappie, and bluegill. Houseboating and boat-in camping (bring sunscreen) provide options. The elevation is 800 feet.

Campsites, facilities: There are 50 sites for tents, 18 sites with full hookups (20 and 30 amps) for RVs of any length, and an overflow camping area with 28 sites. Some sites are pull-through. Picnic tables, fire rings, food lockers, and barbecue units are provided at all sites. Drinking water, restrooms with showers, dump station, group picnic area, WiFi, fish-cleaning station, propane gas, ice, small store, boat ramp, motorboat and houseboat rentals, fuel, moorings, and bait and tackle are available. Some facilities are wheelchair-accessible.

Reservations, fees: Reservations are accepted for a minimum of two nights (three nights on holidays) and can be at 209/852-2396 or www.donpedrolake.com ($10 reservation fee). Tent sites are $24 per night, RV sites (partial hookups) are $30 per night, RV sites (full hookups) are $36 per night, $18 per night for each additional vehicle. Weekend rates are higher. Boat launch is $8 per day. Primitive boat-in camping is $8 per night. Some credit cards accepted. Open year-round.

Directions: From Manteca, drive east on Highway 120 (it becomes Highway 108/120) for 30 miles to the Highway 120/Yosemite exit. Bear right on Highway 120 and drive 11 miles to Jacksonville Road. Turn left on Jacksonville Road and drive a short distance to the campground on the right.

Contact: Don Pedro Recreation Agency, 209/852-2396; Moccasin Point Marina, 209/989-2206, www.donpedrolake.com.

13 LUMSDEN BRIDGE

Scenic rating: 7

on the Tuolumne River in
Stanislaus National Forest

Map 9.2, page 518   BEST (

This is one of three camps along this immediate stretch of the Tuolumne River, one of the best white-water-rafting rivers in California. Note that a permit is required for this activity; contact the Forest Service for details. The camp is set at 1,500 feet elevation on the north side of the river, accessible just after crossing the Lumsden Bridge, hence the name. (See the Lumsden listing for more information.)

Campsites, facilities: There are nine walk-in sites for tents only. Picnic tables and fire grills are provided. Vault toilets are available. No drinking water is available; river water must be purified before use. Garbage must be packed out. Leashed pets are permitted.

Reservations, fees: Reservations are not accepted. There is no fee for camping. Open April through October, weather permitting.

Directions: From Groveland, drive east on Highway 120 for about eight miles (just under a mile beyond County Road J132) to Ferretti Road. Turn left on Ferretti Road and drive to Lumsden Road. Turn right and continue for 5.5 miles to the camp on the left side of the road. (The road is not recommended for RVs or trailers.)

Contact: Stanislaus National Forest, Groveland Ranger District, 209/962-7825, www.fs.usda.gov.

14 LUMSDEN

Scenic rating: 8

on the Tuolumne River in
Stanislaus National Forest

Map 9.2, page 518   BEST (

This is one of the great access points for white-water rafting on the wild and scenic Tuolumne

River and its premium stretch between Hetch Hetchy Reservoir in Yosemite and Don Pedro Reservoir in the Central Valley foothills. This particular section of "The T" is one of the best in America. Unless you are an expert rafter, you are advised to attempt running this stretch of river only with a professional rafting company. Note that a permit is required for this activity; contact the Forest Service for details. The camp is set at 1,500 feet elevation, just across the road from the river. The access road down the canyon is steep and bumpy. There are two other camps within a mile, South Fork and Lumsden Bridge.

Campsites, facilities: There are eight sites for tents only. Picnic tables and fire grills are provided. Vault toilets are available. No drinking water is available; river water must be purified before use. Garbage must be packed out. Leashed pets are permitted.

Reservations, fees: Reservations are not accepted. There is no fee for camping. Open year round, weather permitting.

Directions: From Groveland, drive east on Highway 120 for about eight miles (just under a mile beyond County Road J132) to Ferretti Road. Turn left on Ferretti Road and drive to Lumsden Road. Turn right and continue for four miles to the camp on the left side of the road. (The road is not recommended for RVs or trailers.)

Contact: Stanislaus National Forest, Groveland Ranger District, 209/962-7825, www.fs.usda.gov.

15 SOUTH FORK
🏊 🐕 🏕

Scenic rating: 6

near the Tuolumne River in
Stanislaus National Forest

Map 9.2, page 518

South Fork camp is 0.5 mile upstream from Lumsden and about a mile downstream from Lumsden Bridge. Why do I say "upstream" and "downstream" instead of east and west? Because this is a camp for white-water rafters, featuring the spectacular Tuolumne River and access to its most exciting stretches. You should attempt to run this river only with a professional rafting company; a Forest Service permit is required. The elevation is 1,500 feet. A Forest Service map is advised when visiting this area.

Campsites, facilities: There are nine sites for tents only. Picnic tables and fire grills are provided. Vault toilets are available. No drinking water is available; treat any river water before drinking. Garbage must be packed out. Leashed pets are permitted.

Reservations, fees: Reservations are not accepted. There is no fee for camping. Open year-round, weather permitting.

Directions: From Groveland, drive east on Highway 120 for about eight miles (just under a mile beyond County Road J132) to Ferretti Road. Turn left on Ferretti and drive to Lumsden Road. Turn right and continue for five miles to the camp on the left side of the road. (The road is not recommended for RVs or trailers.)

Contact: Stanislaus National Forest, Groveland Ranger District, 209/962-7825, www.fs.usda.gov.

16 LOST CLAIM
🏊 🐕 🏕

Scenic rating: 4

near the Tuolumne River in
Stanislaus National Forest

Map 9.2, page 518

This is one in a series of easy-access camps off Highway 120 that provide overflow areas when all the sites are taken in Yosemite National Park to the east. A feeder stream to the Tuolumne River runs by the camp. The elevation is 3,100 feet.

Campsites, facilities: There are 10 sites for tents only. Picnic tables and fire grills are provided. Vault toilets and drinking water are available. A convenience store is nearby. Leashed pets are permitted.

Reservations, fees: Reservations are not accepted. Single sites are $16 per night, $32 per night for double sites. Open May through Labor Day.

Directions: From Groveland, drive east on Highway 120 for 12 miles (four miles past the Groveland District Office) to the campground on the left side of the road. (The access road is not recommended for RVs or trailers.)

Contact: Stanislaus National Forest, Groveland Ranger District, 209/962-7825, www. fs.usda.gov.

17 THE PINES AND PINES GROUP

Scenic rating: 4

in Stanislaus National Forest

Map 9.2, page 518

The Pines camp is set at 3,200 feet elevation on the western edge of Stanislaus National Forest, only 0.5 mile from the Groveland District Office and about five miles from the Tuolumne River (see the Lumsden listing in this chapter). A Forest Service road is routed south of camp for two miles, climbing to Smith Peak Lookout (3,877 feet) and providing sweeping views to the west of the San Joaquin Valley foothills.

Campsites, facilities: There are 11 sites for tents or RVs up to 22 feet (no hookups), and a group site for up to 50 people. Picnic tables and fire grills are provided. Drinking water and vault toilets are available. A convenience store is nearby. Some facilities are wheelchair accessible. Leashed pets are permitted.

Reservations, fees: Reservations are required for the group sites only at 877/444-6777 or www.recreation.gov ($9 reservation fee, look for Pines Group Stanislaus). Sites are $16 per night, $65 per night for the group site. Open year-round, weather permitting. There is no fee in winter (limited facilities).

Directions: From Groveland, drive east on Highway 120 for nine miles (about a mile past

the County Road J132 turnoff) to the signed campground entrance road on the right. Turn right onto the campground entrance road and drive a short distance to the camp.

Contact: Stanislaus National Forest, Groveland Ranger District, 209/962-7825, www. fs.usda.gov.

18 BLUE OAKS

Scenic rating: 7

at Lake Don Pedro

Map 9.2, page 518

Blue Oaks is between the dam at Lake Don Pedro and Fleming Meadows. The on-site boat ramp to the east is a big plus here. (See the Fleming Meadows and Moccasin Point listings in this chapter for more information.)

Campsites, facilities: There are 195 sites for tents or RVs of any length; some sites have partial hookups (20 and 30 amps) and one is pull-through. Group camping is available. Picnic tables, fire rings, food lockers, and barbecue units are provided. Drinking water, restrooms with flush toilets and showers, boat launch, fish-cleaning stations, WiFi, and a dump station are available. Some facilities are wheelchair-accessible. A store, coin laundry, and propane gas are nearby at Fleming Meadows Marina. No pets are permitted.

Reservations, fees: Reservations are accepted for a minimum of two nights (three nights on holidays) and can be made at 209/852-2396 or www.donpedrolake.com ($10 reservation fee). Tent sites are $24 per night, RV sites (partial hookups) are $30 per night, RV sites (full hookups) are $36 per night, $9 per night for each additional vehicle. Weekend rates are higher. Boat launch is $8 per day. The group site is $300 per night. Primitive boat-in camping is $8 per night. Some credit cards accepted. Open year-round.

Directions: From Manteca, take Highway 120 east to Oakdale (the road becomes Highway 120/108). Continue east on Highway 108 for

20 miles to La Grange Road/J59 (signed "Don Pedro Reservoir"). Turn right on La Grange Road and drive 10 miles to Bonds Flat Road. Turn left on Bonds Flat Road and drive 0.5 mile to the campground on the left.

Contact: Don Pedro Recreation Area, 209/852-2396, www.donpedrolake.com; Lake Don Pedro Marina, 209/852-2369.

19 FLEMING MEADOWS

Scenic rating: 7

on Lake Don Pedro

Map 9.2, page 518

Fleming Meadows is set on the shore of Lake Don Pedro, just east of the dam. A boat ramp is available in the campground on the southeast side of the dam. A sandy beach and concession stand are here. This is a big camp at the foot of a giant lake, where hot weather, warm water, waterskiing, and bass fishing make for weekend vacations. Don Pedro has many extended lake arms, providing 160 miles of shoreline and nearly 13,000 surface acres when full. (See the Moccasin Point listing in this chapter for more information.)

Campsites, facilities: There are 172 sites for tents or RVs of any length, including 51 walk-in sites for tents, and 90 sites with full hookups (20 and 30 amps) for RVs. A few sites are pull-through. Picnic tables, fire rings, food lockers, and barbecues are provided. Drinking water, restrooms with flush toilets and showers, and a dump station are available. A coin laundry, store, ice, snack bar, WiFi, group picnic areas, restaurant, swimming lagoon, amphitheater, softball field, volleyball, bait and tackle, motorboat and houseboat rentals, boat ramp, mooring, boat storage, engine repairs, and propane gas are nearby. Some facilities are wheelchair-accessible.

Reservations, fees: Reservations are accepted for a minimum of two nights (three nights on holidays) and can be made by phone at 209/852-2396 or www.donpedrolake.com ($10 reservation fee). Tent sites are $24 per night, RV sites (partial hookups) are $30 per night, RV sites (full hookups) are $36 per night, $9 per night for each additional vehicle. Weekend rates are higher. Boat launch is $8 per day. Primitive boat-in camping is $8 per night. Some credit cards accepted. Open year-round.

Directions: From Manteca, take Highway 120 east to Oakdale (the road becomes Highway 120/108). Continue east on Highway 108 for 20 miles to La Grange Road/J59 (signed "Don Pedro Reservoir"). Turn right on La Grange Road and drive 10 miles to Bonds Flat Road. Turn left on Bonds Flat Road and drive 2.5 miles to the campground on the left.

Contact: Don Pedro Recreation Area, 209/852-2396; Lake Don Pedro Marina, 209/852-2369, www.donpedrolake.com.

20 MODESTO RESERVOIR REGIONAL PARK AND BOAT-IN

Scenic rating: 7

on Modesto Reservoir

Map 9.2, page 518

Modesto Reservoir is a big lake, at 2,800 acres with 31 miles of shoreline, set in the hot foothill country. That's good because it is a popular place in the summer. Waterskiing is excellent in the main lake body. Sandy swimming beaches are available, and swimming is popular. Anglers head to the southern shore of the lake, which is loaded with submerged trees and coves and is also protected by a 5-mph speed limit. Fishing for bass is good, though the fish are often small. Wildlife viewing is good and waterfowl hunting is available in season. The elevation is 200 feet. All watercraft must be certified free of mussels.

Campsites, facilities: There are 134 sites with full hookups (30 amps) for RVs up to 36 feet and 36 tent sites. Picnic tables and fire grills are provided. Drinking water, restrooms with flush toilets and showers, dump station, two boat ramps, store, snack bar, propane, gas, archery range, and radio-controlled glider field are available. Some facilities are wheelchair-accessible. No gas cans are permitted.

Reservations, fees: Reservations are not accepted. RV sites (full hookups) are $25 per night, tent sites are $20 per night, $10 per night per additional vehicle. Holiday weekend rates are $2 higher. Boat launch is $7 per day. Open year-round.

Directions: From Modesto, drive east on Highway 132 for 16 miles past Waterford to Reservoir Road. Turn left and drive to the campground at 18143 Reservoir Road.

Contact: Modesto Reservoir Regional Park, 209/525-6750, www.stancounty.com/parks.

21 TURLOCK LAKE STATE RECREATION AREA

Scenic rating: 6

east of Modesto

Map 9.2, page 518

This campground is on the shady south shore of the Tuolumne River, about one mile from Turlock Lake. Turlock Lake warms to 65–74°F in the summer, cooler than many Central Valley reservoirs, since the water entering this lake is released from the bottom of Don Pedro Reservoir. It often seems just right for boating and all water sports on hot summer days. The lake covers 3,500 surface acres and offers 26 miles of shoreline. A boat ramp is available near the camp, making it ideal for boaters/campers. Bass fishing is fair in the summer. In the late winter and spring, the lake is quite cold, fed by snowmelt from the Tuolumne River. Trout fishing is good year-round as a result. The elevation is 250 feet. The park is bordered by ranches, orchards, and mining tailings along the river.

Note: This park was on the closure list developed by the California Department of Parks, pending final state budget decisions or the possible transfer of park management to other park agencies or volunteer groups. The park

is currently open through a concession agreement with American Land and Leisure.

Campsites, facilities: There are 48 sites for tents or RVs up to 27 feet (no hookups), 15 sites for tents, and one hike-in/bike-in site. Picnic tables, fire grills, and food lockers are provided. Drinking water and restrooms with flush toilets and coin showers are available. A swimming beach and boat ramp are available nearby. The boat facilities are wheelchair-accessible. Leashed pets are permitted.

Reservations, fees: Reservations are accepted May through October at 800/444-7275 (800/444-PARK) or www.reserveamerica.com ($8 reservation fee). Sites are $30 per night, $10 per night for each additional vehicle, $5 per person per night for hike-in/bike-in site. Boat launching is $6 per day. Open year-round.

Directions: From Modesto, drive east on Highway 132 for 14 miles to Waterford, then continue eight miles on Highway 132 to Roberts Ferry Road. Turn right (south) and drive one mile to Lake Road. Turn left and drive two miles to the campground on the left.

Contact: Turlock Lake State Recreation Area, 209/874-2056 or 209/874-2008, www.parks.ca.gov; American Land and Leisure, 800/342-2267, www.americanll.com.

22 McCLURE: HORSESHOE BEND RECREATION AREA

Scenic rating: 7

on Lake McClure

Map 9.2, page 518

Lake McClure is a unique, horseshoe-shaped lake in the foothill country west of Yosemite. It adjoins smaller Lake McSwain, connected by the Merced River. McClure is shaped like a giant H, with its lake arms providing 82 miles of shoreline, warm water for waterskiing, and fishing for bass (on the west half of the H near Cotton Creek) and for trout (on the east half of the H). There is a boat launch adjacent to the campground. It's one of four lakes in the immediate area; the others are Don Pedro Reservoir to the north and Modesto Reservoir and Turlock Lake to the west. The elevation is 900 feet.

Campsites, facilities: There are 100 sites for tents or RVs of any length, including 35 with partial hookups (30 amps). Picnic tables and barbecues are provided. Restrooms with showers, dump station, a boat ramp, fish-cleaning stations, picnic areas, swimming lagoon, store (seasonal), and coin laundry are available. Some facilities are wheelchair-accessible. Leashed pets are permitted.

Reservations, fees: Reservations are accepted at 855/800-2267. Tent sites are $22–23 per night, RV sites (hookups) are $28–30 per night, $14 per night for each additional vehicle, $4 per pet per night. Senior and extended-stay discounts are available. Boat launch is $7 per day. Some credit cards accepted. Open year-round.

Directions: From Modesto, drive east on Highway 132 for 31 miles to La Grange and then continue for about 17 miles (toward Coulterville) to the north end of Lake Mc-Clure and the campground entrance road on the right side of the road. Turn right and drive 0.5 mile to the campground.

Contact: Horseshoe Bend Recreation Area, 209/878-3452 or 209/378-2521; Merced Irrigation District, 209/378-2521, www.lakemcclure.com.

23 BARRETT COVE RECREATION AREA

Scenic rating: 7

on Lake McClure

Map 9.2, page 518

Lake McClure is shaped like a giant H, with its lake arms providing 82 miles of shoreline. The lake is popular for water sports, including skiing, wakeboarding, houseboating, and fishing. Although swimming is not prohibited in the lake, you'll rarely see people swimming or playing along the shore, mainly because of the typically steep drop-offs. This camp is on

the left side of the H, that is, on the western shore, within a park that provides a good boat ramp. This is the largest in a series of camps on Lake McClure. (See the Horseshoe Bend Recreation Area, McClure Point Recreation Area, and Bagby Recreation Area listings in this chapter for more information.)

Campsites, facilities: There are 275 sites for tents or RVs of any length, including 89 with full hookups (30 amps). Picnic tables and barbecues are provided. Restrooms with showers, boat ramps, dump station, swimming lagoon, and playground are available. A convenience store, coin laundry, marina, picnic areas, fish-cleaning stations, boat and houseboat rentals, and propane gas are also available onsite. Some facilities are wheelchair-accessible. Leashed pets are permitted.

Reservations, fees: Reservations are accepted at 855/800-2267. Tent sites are $22–23 per night, RV sites (hookups) are $28–30 per night, $14 per night for each additional vehicle, $4 per pet per night. Senior and extended-stay discounts are available. Boat launch is $7 per day. Some credit cards accepted. Open year-round.

Directions: From Modesto, drive east on Highway 132 for 31 miles to La Grange and then continue for about eight miles (toward Coulterville) to Merced Falls Road. Turn right and drive three miles to the campground entrance on the left. Turn left and drive a mile to the campground on the left side of the road.

Contact: Barrett Cove Recreation Area, 209/378-2611; Merced Irrigation District, 209/378-2521, www.lakemcclure.com.

24 McCLURE POINT RECREATION AREA

Scenic rating: 7

on Lake McClure

Map 9.2, page 518

McClure Point Recreation Area is the campground of choice for campers/boaters coming from the Turlock and Merced areas. It is a well-developed facility with an excellent boat ramp that provides access to the main body of Lake McClure. This is the best spot on the lake for waterskiing.

Campsites, facilities: There are 100 sites for tents or RVs up to 40 feet; 52 sites have partial hookups (30 amps). Picnic tables and barbecues are provided. Restrooms with showers, boat ramps, boat rentals, marina, fish-cleaning stations, picnic areas, swimming lagoon, and a coin laundry are available. A store is nearby. Leashed pets are permitted.

Reservations, fees: Reservations are accepted at 855/800-2267. Tent sites are $22–23 per night, RV sites (hookups) are $28–30 per night, $14 per night for each additional vehicle, $4 per pet per night. Senior and extended-stay discounts are available. Boat launch is $7 per day. Some credit cards accepted. Open year-round.

Directions: From Turlock, drive east on County Road J16 for 19 miles to the junction with Highway 59. Continue east on Highway 59/County Road J16 for 4.5 miles to Snelling and bear right at Lake McClure Road. Drive approximately two miles to Lake McSwain Dam and continue for seven miles to the campground at the end of the road.

Contact: McClure Point and Bagby Recreation Area, 209/378-2521, www.lakemcclure.com.

25 BAGBY RECREATION AREA

Scenic rating: 7

on upper Lake McClure

Map 9.2, page 518

This is the most distant and secluded camp on Lake McClure. It is set near the Merced River as it enters the lake, way up adjacent to the Highway 49 bridge, nearly an hour's drive from the dam. Trout fishing is good in the area, and it makes sense; when the lake

heats up in summer, the trout naturally congregate near the cool incoming flows of the Merced River.

Campsites, facilities: There are 30 sites for tents or RVs of any length, including 10 sites with partial hookups (30 amps). Drinking water, restrooms with flush toilets and coin showers, picnic areas, and fish-cleaning stations are available. A boat ramp is available unless the lake water level is too low. Some facilities are wheelchair accessible. Leashed pets are permitted.

Reservations, fees: Reservations are accepted at 855/800-2267. Tent sites are $22–23 per night, RV sites (hookups) are $28–30 per night, $14 per night for each additional vehicle, $4 per pet per night. Senior and extended-stay discounts are available. Boat launch is $7 per day. Some credit cards accepted. Open year-round.

Directions: From Turlock, drive east on County Road J16 for 19 miles to the junction with Highway 59. Continue east on Highway 59/County Road J16 for 4.5 miles to Snelling and Merced Falls Road (continue straight, well signed). Drive 0.5 mile to Hornitos Road. Turn right and drive eight miles (drive over the bridge) to Hornitos to a Y. Bear left at the Y in Hornitos (signed to Highway 49) and drive 10 miles to Highway 49. Turn left on Highway 49 and drive eight miles to the Bagby Bridge and entrance kiosk on the right.

Contact: McClure Point and Bagby Recreation Area, 209/378-2521, www.lakemcclure.com.

26 LAKE McSWAIN RECREATION AREA

Scenic rating: 7

near McSwain Dam on the Merced River

Map 9.2, page 518

Lake McSwain is actually the afterbay for adjacent Lake McClure, and this camp is near the McSwain Dam on the Merced River. Even though McClure and McSwain sit beside each other, each has its own identity. McSwain is low-key with a 10-mph speed limit. If you have a canoe or car-top boat, this lake is preferable to Lake McClure because waterskiing is not allowed. In terms of size, McSwain is like a pond compared to the giant McClure, but unlike McClure, the water levels are kept up almost year-round at McSwain. The water is cold here and trout stocks are good in the spring. The lake is used primarily by anglers, and several fishing derbies are held here each year. The shoreline is favorable for swimming, and there is even a good sandy beach.

Campsites, facilities: There are 100 sites for tents or RVs up to 40 feet, including 65 with partial hookups (30 amps). The best access sites for large RVs are the pull-through sites in the G Loop. Picnic tables, barbecues, and electrical connections are provided. Drinking water, dump station, restrooms with showers, boat ramp, boat rentals, coin laundry, and a playground are available. A convenience store, marina, snack bar, fish-cleaning stations, picnic area, and propane gas are available nearby. Some facilities are wheelchair-accessible. Leashed pets are permitted.

Reservations, fees: Reservations are accepted at 855/800-2267. Tent sites are $22–23 per night, RV sites (hookups) are $28–30 per night, $14 per night for each additional vehicle, $4 per pet per night. Senior and extended-stay discounts are available. Boat launch is $7 per day. Some credit cards accepted. Open year-round.

Directions: From Turlock, drive east on County Road J16 for 19 miles to the junction with Highway 59. Continue east on Highway 59/County Road J16 for 4.5 miles to Snelling. Continue straight ahead to Lake McClure Road and drive seven miles to the campground turnoff on the right.

Contact: Lake McSwain Recreation Area, 209/378-2521; Lake McSwain Marina, 209/378-2534, www.lakemcclure.com.

27 FISHERMAN'S BEND RIVER CAMPGROUND

Scenic rating: 5

on the San Joaquin River

Map 9.2, page 518

This small, privately operated campground is set along the San Joaquin River on the fork of the San Joaquin and Merced Rivers in the southern outskirts of the San Joaquin Delta country. The park offers shaded sites and direct river access for boaters. This section of river provides fishing for catfish, largemouth bass, and occasionally striped bass and sturgeon. Although many of the sites are rented seasonally or longer, about 10 sites are usually available for overnight campers.

Campsites, facilities: There are 38 pull-through sites with full hookups (30 amps) for RVs of any length, and 20 sites for tents only. Picnic tables are provided. Drinking water, restrooms with showers, coin laundry, boat ramp, horseshoes, basketball, convenience store, fish-cleaning station, and playground, are available. Some facilities are wheelchair-accessible. Leashed pets are permitted, with certain restrictions.

Reservations, fees: Reservations are accepted at 209/862-3731. Sites are $15–25 per night, $5 per night per extra vehicle. Weekly and monthly rates available. Open year-round.

Directions: Drive on I-5 to the exit for Newman/Stuhr Road (south of the junction of I-5 and I-580). Take that exit and turn east on County Road J18/Stuhr Road and drive 6.5 miles to Hills Ferry Road. Turn left and drive a mile to River Road. Turn left on River Road and drive to 26836 River Road on the right.

Contact: Fisherman's Bend River Campground, 209/862-3731.

28 GEORGE J. HATFIELD STATE RECREATION AREA WALK-IN

Scenic rating: 5

near Newman

Map 9.2, page 518

This is a small state park set in the heart of the San Joaquin Valley, near the confluence of the Merced River and the San Joaquin River, well known for hot summer days and foggy winter nights. The park has many trees. Swimming is popular in the summer. Fishing is good for catfish in the summer, and some folks will stay up late hoping a big channel catfish will take their bait. During the peak migration from late fall through winter and early spring, there can also be a good number of striped bass in the area. This park is more popular for day use than for camping. The campsites require a walk of about 100 feet.

Note: This park is on the closure list developed by the California Department of Parks, pending final state budget decisions or the possible transfer of park management to other park agencies or volunteer groups. It is operating via a donor agreement with limited facilities.

Campsites, facilities: There are 15 walk-in sites for tents and a large group site for tents or RVs up to 25 feet that can accommodate up to 40 people. Picnic tables and fire grills are provided. Chemical toilets are provided. There is no drinking water. Supplies can be obtained in Newman, five miles away. Leashed pets are permitted.

Reservations, fees: Reservations are accepted for the group site February through June 2013 at 800/444-7275 or www.reserveamerica.com ($8 reservation fee). Individual sites are first-come, first-served. Sites are $14 per night, $10 per night for each additional vehicle, $100 per night for group site. Open year-round, weather permitting.

Directions: Drive on I-5 to the exit for Newman/Stuhr Road (south of the junction of I-5 and I-580). Take that exit and turn east on County Road J18/Stuhr Road and drive to Newman and the junction with Highway 33. Continue straight on Stuhr Road for 1.5 miles to Hills Ferry Road. Turn left and drive three miles to the park entrance on the right (just past the bridge over the San Joaquin River).

Contact: George J. Hatfield State Recreation Area, 209/632-1852; Four Rivers Sector, 209/826-1197, www.parks.ca.gov.

29 McCONNELL STATE RECREATION AREA

Scenic rating: 6

on the Merced River

Map 9.2, page 518

The weather gets scorching hot around these parts in the summer, and a lot of out-of-towners would pay a bunch for a little shade and a river to sit next to. That's what this park provides, with the Merced River flowing past, along with occasional mermaids on the beach. The park covers 70 acres and has many trees. Fishing is popular for catfish, black bass, and panfish. In high-water years the Merced River attracts salmon (in the fall); check current fishing regulations.

Note: This park was on the closure list developed by the California Department of Parks, pending final state budget decisions or the possible transfer of park management to other park agencies or volunteer groups. It is currently open through a donor agreement.

Campsites, facilities: There are 20 sites for tents or RVs up to 30 feet (no hookups) and two group sites for tents only for 25–50 people. Group sites have an electrical hookup (20 amps). Picnic tables, fire grills, and food lockers are provided. Drinking water, restrooms with flush toilets and coin showers, and a swimming beach are available. Firewood is available for purchase. Supplies can be obtained in Delhi, five miles away. Some facilities are wheelchair-accessible. Leashed pets are permitted.

Reservations, fees: Reservations are accepted February through June 2013 at 800/444-7275 (800/444-PARK) or www.reserveamerica.com ($8 reservation fee). After June 2013, reservations will be accepted for group camping only. Sites are $25 per night, $10 per night for each additional vehicle, $90–145 per night for group sites. Open when reservations are accepted; call to confirm.

Directions: From Modesto, drive south on Highway 99 to Delhi. Continue south for five miles to the South Avenue exit. Take that exit and turn east on South Avenue and drive 2.7 miles to Pepper Street. Turn right and drive one mile to McConnell Road. Turn right and drive a short distance to the park entrance at the end of the road.

Contact: McConnell State Recreation Area, 209/394-7755; Four Rivers Sector, 209/826-1197, www.parks.ca.gov.

30 LOS BANOS CREEK RESERVOIR

Scenic rating: 6

near Los Banos

Map 9.3, page 519

Los Banos Creek Reservoir is set in a long, narrow valley, covering 410 surface acres with 12 miles of shoreline. It provides a smaller, more low-key setting (a 5-mph speed limit is enforced) compared to the nearby giant, San Luis Reservoir. In spring, it can be quite windy and is a popular spot for sailboarding and sailing. It is also stocked with trout in late winter and spring, and some large bass have been caught here. The elevation is 330 feet. Although drinking water is available, campers are advised to bring their own water, as the water supply is limited. Note: All boats must be certified mussel-free before launching.

Campsites, facilities: There are 14 sites for tents or RVs up to 30 feet (no hookups). Picnic tables, shade ramadas, and fire grills are provided. Drinking water, chemical toilets (one

with wheelchair accessibility), and picnic areas are available. A boat ramp is nearby. Leashed pets are permitted.

Reservations, fees: Reservations are not accepted. Sites are $15 per night, and $10 per night for each additional vehicle. Boat launching is $6 per day. Open year-round, weather permitting.

Directions: Drive on Highway 152 to Volta Road (five miles west of Los Banos). Turn south on Volta Road and drive about a mile to Pioneer Road. Turn left on Pioneer Road and drive a mile to Canyon Road. Turn south (right) onto Canyon Road and drive about five miles to the park.

Contact: San Luis Reservoir State Recreation Area, 209/826-1196; Four Rivers Sector, 209/826-1197, www.parks.ca.gov.

31 LOST LAKE

Scenic rating: 7

on the lower San Joaquin River

Map 9.4, page 520

Lost Lake campground is part of a Fresno County park. It is set in the foothills of the San Joaquin Valley, at an elevation of about 500 feet, along the lower San Joaquin River. The campground is broken out into two areas, with about half along the river. Many think this park is quite pretty. There is a lot of wildlife at this park, especially birds and deer. A self-guided hiking trail is routed into a nature study area. Easy kayaking and canoeing is a plus, with no powerboats permitted. Trout fishing is available; check fishing regulations.

Campsites, facilities: There are 42 sites for tents, with most accessible for self-contained RVs up to 36 feet, and one group site for up to 80 people. Picnic tables and barbecues are provided. Drinking water, flush toilets, volleyball, softball, and playground are available. A restaurant and store are two miles away in Friant. Some facilities, including a fishing dock, are wheelchair accessible. Leashed pets are permitted.

Reservations, fees: Reservations accepted for the group site only at 559/600-3004. Sites are $18 per night. $5 per night for each additional vehicle, and $110 per night for the group site (10 vehicle minimum). Open year-round.

Directions: From Fresno, drive north on Highway 41 for 24 miles to the first exit for Friant Road. Take that exit and drive 12 miles to the entrance road for Lost Lake. Turn left and drive a short distance to the campground.

Contact: Fresno County Parks Department, 559/488-3004.

32 VISALIA/FRESNO SOUTH KOA

Scenic rating: 3

west of Visalia

Map 9.4, page 520

This is a layover spot for Highway 99 cruisers. If you're looking for a spot to park your rig for the night, you can't get too picky around these parts. Most campers here are on their way to or from Sequoia and Kings Canyon National Parks. The swimming pool is a great bonus during the summer. Grassy shaded sites are available. Golf and tennis are nearby. Note that monthly renters occupy some of the sites and new owners took over operations for the 2011 season. (And by the way, Visalia is my favorite town in the San Joaquin Valley.)

Campsites, facilities: There are 48 pull-through RV sites with full or partial hookups (30 and 50 amps), 20 sites for tents or RVs with no hookups, 20 sites for tents only, and eight cabins. Restrooms with showers, seasonal heated swimming pool, laundry facilities, playground, recreation room, free Wi-Fi, dog walk, store, gift shop, dump station, and propane gas are available. Leashed pets are permitted, with certain restrictions.

Reservations, fees: Reservations are accepted at 800/562-0540. Pull-through RV sites with full hookups (50 amps) are $53–56 per night, pull-through RV sites with water and electricity are $46–48 per night; standard RV sites with full or partial hookups are $35–51 per night; tent sites are $30–33 per night, $5 per person per night for more than four people. Some credit cards accepted. Open year-round.

Directions: From Highway 99 near Visalia, take the Goshen Avenue exit and drive 0.2 mile to Betty Drive/County Road 332. Turn left and drive 0.5 mile to County Road 76. Turn left and drive 0.5 mile (becomes Avenue 308) to the campground.

Contact: Visalia-Fresno KOA, 559/651-0544, www.koa.com.

33 SUN AND FUN RV PARK

Scenic rating: 2

near Tulare

Map 9.4, page 520

This RV park is just off Highway 99, exactly halfway between San Francisco and Los Angeles. Are you having fun yet? Anybody making the long drive up or down the state on Highway 99 will learn what a dry piece of life the San Joaquin Valley can seem in summer. That's why the swimming pool at this RV park can be a lifesaver. The park has a number of mature trees, providing an opportunity for shade. Note that most of the sites are filled with long-term renters, but a few spaces are reserved for overnight campers.

Campsites, facilities: There are 59 sites with full hookups (30 and 50 amps) for RVs up to 45 feet. No tents. Picnic tables and barbecues are provided at some sites. Restrooms with showers, drinking water, cable TV, dump station, playground, swimming pool, spa, coin laundry, dog runs, and a recreation room are available. A golf course, restaurant, and store are nearby. Some facilities are wheelchair-accessible. Leashed pets are permitted.

Reservations, fees: Reservations are accepted.

Sites are $36 per night. Weekly and monthly rates available. Open year-round.

Directions: From Tulare, drive south on Highway 99 for three miles to the Avenue 200 exit. Take Avenue 200 west and drive a short distance to the park.

Contact: Sun and Fun RV Park, 1000 East Rankin, 559/686-5779, www.westernm.com/communities.

34 COLONEL ALLENSWORTH STATE HISTORIC PARK

Scenic rating: 2

near Earlimart

Map 9.5, page 521

What you have here is the old town of Allensworth, which has been restored as a historical park dedicated to the African American pioneers who founded it with Colonel Allen Allensworth. Allensworth is the sole town in California to be established, financed, and governed by African Americans and the Colonel was the highest-ranking army chaplain of his time. A museum is available at the school and the colonel's house offers a 30-minute movie on the history of Allensworth. Tours are available by appointment. One frustrating element is that railroad tracks run alongside the park and it can be disruptive. There can be other problems—very hot weather in the summer, and since it is an open area, the wind can blow dust and sand. Are we having fun yet? One nice touch is the addition of shade ramadas at some campsites, although campsites are on the primitive side.

Campsites, facilities: There are 15 sites for tents or RVs up to 35 feet (no hookups). Picnic tables and camp stoves are provided. Restrooms with flush toilets and coin showers, drinking water, dump station, a visitors center, and picnic area are available. A store and coin laundry are 12 miles away in Delano. Some facilities are wheelchair-accessible. Leashed pets are permitted.

Reservations, fees: Reservations are accepted at 800/444-7275 (800/444-PARK) or www.reserveamerica.com ($8 reservation fee). Sites are $20 per night. Open year-round, Friday and Saturday only.

Directions: From Fresno, drive south on Highway 99 about 60 miles to Earlimart and the Avenue 56 exit. Turn right (west) on Avenue 56 and drive seven miles to the Highway 43 turnoff. Turn left (south) on Highway 43 and drive two miles to Palmer Avenue. Turn right (and drive over the railroad tracks) to the park entrance.

Contact: Colonel Allensworth State Historic Park, 661/849-3433 or 661/849-2101, www.parks.ca.gov.

35 SELBY

Scenic rating: 6

at Carrizo Plain National Monument, northeast of San Luis Obispo

Map 9.5, page 521

The Carrizo Plain is California's largest nature preserve, but because of its remote location, primitive setting, and lack of recreational lakes and streams, it remains largely unknown and is explored by few people. The feature attraction is to visit Soda Lake in the winter to see flocks of the endangered sandhill crane; the lake is a nesting area for these huge birds with seven-foot wingspans. Selby is a primitive camping area at the base of the Caliente Mountain Range, known for its scorching hot temperatures (hey, after all, "Caliente") during the summer. The top hiking destination in the region is Painted Rock, a 55-foot rock with Chumash pictographs. Other hiking trails are available.

Campsites, facilities: This is a primitive camping area with 13 designated sites for tents or RVs up to 25 feet (no hookups). Picnic tables, shade ramadas, and fire rings are provided. Vault toilets and horse corrals are available. No drinking water is available, but there is usually water for livestock. Garbage must be packed out. Nearest services are about 50 miles away. Leashed pets are permitted.

Reservations, fees: Reservations are not accepted. There is no fee for camping, but donations are encouraged. Group camping must be authorized by calling 661/391-6048. Open year-round.

Directions: From Bakersfield, drive west on Highway 58 for about 30 miles to McKittrick (where Highway 33 merges with Highway 58). Bear left on Highway 58/33, continuing through town, and drive west for approximately 10 miles to Seven-Mile Road. Turn west on Seven-Mile Road, and drive seven miles (six miles will be on gravel/dirt road) to Soda Lake Road. Turn left on Soda Lake Road and drive about six miles to the Selby camping area on your right.

Contact: Bureau of Land Management, Bakersfield Field Office, 661/391-6000, www. blm.gov/ca.

36 KCL

Scenic rating: 6

at the Carrizo Plain National Monument, northeast of San Luis Obispo

Map 9.5, page 521

KCL is the name of the old ranch headquarters in the Carrizo, of which remain old broken-down outbuildings, a corral, and not much else. Note that the buildings are off-limits to visitors. At least there are some trees here (in comparison, there are none at nearby Selby camp). The Carrizo Plain is best known for providing a habitat for many rare species of plants, animals, and insects, in addition to furnishing the winter nesting sites at Soda Lake for the awesome migration of giant sandhill cranes. These birds are often spotted north of this area. This campground is popular with hunters and birders because of its easy access to Soda Lake Road for daily outings. Dispersed camping is allowed throughout the national monument.

Campsites, facilities: This is a primitive camping area with 12 sites for tents or RVs up to 25 feet (no hookups). Picnic tables and fire pits are provided. Vault toilets and corrals are available. No drinking water is available, but there is usually water for livestock. Garbage must be packed out. The nearest services are about 50 miles away. Some facilities are wheelchair-accessible. Leashed pets are permitted.

Reservations, fees: Reservations are not accepted. There is no fee for camping. Group camping must be authorized by calling 661/391-6048. Open year-round.

Directions: From Bakersfield, drive west on Highway 58 for about 30 miles to McKittrick (where Highway 33 merges with Highway 58). Bear left on Highway 58/33, continuing through town, and drive west for about 10 miles to Seven-Mile Road. Turn west on Seven-Mile Road, and drive seven miles (six miles will be on gravel/dirt road) to Soda Lake Road. Turn left on Soda Lake Road and drive 0.5 mile to the entrance of the Carrizo Plains National Monument. Continue about 15 miles to the KCL camping area on your right.

Contact: Bureau of Land Management, Bakersfield Field Office, 661/391-6000, www. blm.gov/ca.

37 BUENA VISTA AQUATIC RECREATION AREA

Scenic rating: 6

near Bakersfield

Map 9.5, page 521

This is the showpiece of Kern County recreation. Buena Vista is actually two connected lakes fed by the West Side Canal: little Lake Evans to the west and larger Lake Webb to the east. Be certain to know the difference between the two: Lake Webb (875 acres) is open to all boating including personal watercraft, and fast boats towing skiers are a common sight in designated ski areas. The speed limit is 45 mph. Lake Evans (85 acres) is small, quiet, and has a strictly enforced 5-mph speed limit, an ideal lake for family water play and fishing. Swimming is prohibited at both lakes, but is allowed in the lagoons. Lake Webb is a catfish lake, while Lake Evans is stocked in season with trout, and also has bass, bluegill, catfish, and crappie. The elevation is 330 feet.

Campsites, facilities: There are 112 sites, some with full hookups (30 and 50 amps) for RVs or tents, and an overflow camping area. Picnic tables and fire grills are provided. Restrooms with flush toilets and showers, drinking water, playground, four boat ramps, store, dump station, and picnic shelters are available. Two swimming lagoons, marina, snack bar, fishing supplies, and groceries are available nearby. A PGA-rated golf course is two miles west. Some facilities are wheelchair-accessible. Leashed pets are permitted.

Reservations, fees: Reservations are accepted Monday through Friday at 661/868-7050 ($7 reservation fee). Tent sites are $14–32 per night, RV sites (hookups) are $21–39 per night, $12–15 for each additional vehicle, $4 per night per pet, $7 per night for boats. Group discounts are available. Some credit cards accepted. Open year-round.

Directions: From I-5 just south of Bakersfield, take Highway 119 west and drive two miles to Highway 43. Turn south (left) on Highway 43 and drive two miles to the campground at road's end.

Contact: Buena Vista Aquatic Recreation Area, Kern County Parks, 661/868-7000, www.co.kern.ca.us/parks/index.htm; Buena Vista concession, 661/763-1526.

YOSEMITE AND MAMMOTH LAKES

© SABRINA YOUNG

BEST CAMPGROUNDS

Some of nature's most perfect artwork and the

most profound natural phenomena imaginable have been created in Yosemite and the adjoining eastern Sierra near Mammoth Lakes.

Yosemite Valley is the world's greatest showpiece. It is also among the most highly visited and well-known destinations on earth. Many of the campgrounds listed in this section are within close driving proximity of Yosemite National Park. When it comes to cabin rentals in this region, the variety is extraordinary.

Anything in Yosemite, or in its sphere of influence, is going to be in high demand almost year-round, and the same is true near Mammoth Lakes.

Many family recreation opportunities exist at lake-based settings, including at Lake Alpine, Pinecrest Lake on the western slopes of the Sierra, and June Lake, Silver Lake, Lake Mary, Twin Lakes, Convict Lake, and Rock Creek Lake on the eastern Sierra.

Of course, most visits to this region start with a tour of Yosemite Valley. It is framed on one side by El Capitan, the Goliath of Yosemite, and the three-spired Cathedral Rocks on the other. As you enter the valley, Bridalveil Fall comes to view, a perfect free fall over the south canyon rim, then across a meadow. To your left you'll see the two-tiered Yosemite Falls, and finally, Half Dome, the single most awesome piece of rock in the world.

The irony is that this is all most people ever see of the region, even though it represents but a fraction of the fantastic land of wonder, adventure, and unparalleled natural beauty. Though 24,000 people jam into five square miles of Yosemite Valley each summer day, the park is actually 90 percent wilderness. Other landmark areas you can reach by car include the Wawona Grove of Giant Sequoias, Tenaya Lake, Tuolumne Meadows, and Hetch Hetchy.

But that's still only scratching the surface. For those who hike, another world will open up: Yosemite has 318 lakes, dozens of pristine streams, the Grand Canyon of the Tuolumne River, Matterhorn Peak, Benson Lake (with the largest white-sand beach in the Sierra), and dozens of spectacular waterfalls.

If you explore beyond the park boundaries, the adventures just keep getting better. Over Tioga Pass, outside the park and just off Highway 120, are Tioga Lake, Ellery Lake, and Saddlebag Lake (10,087 feet), the latter of which is the highest lake in California accessible by car. To the east is Mono Lake and its weird tufa spires, which create a stark moonscape.

The nearby June Lake Loop and Mammoth Lakes area is a launch point to another orbit. Both have small lakes with on-site cabin rentals, excellent fishing, great hiking and mountain biking for all levels, and phenomenal skiing and winter sports. In addition, just east of Mammoth Lakes airport is a series of hot springs, including a famous spot on Hot Creek, something of a legend in these parts.

More hiking and fishing opportunities abound at Devils Postpile National Monument, where you can hike to Rainbow Falls. At nearby Agnew Meadows, you'll find a trail that hugs the pristine San Joaquin River up to Thousand Island Lake and leads to the beautiful view from Banner and Ritter Peaks in the Ansel Adams Wilderness. Horseback riding is also popular in this area, with pack trips available from Reds Meadow.

In case you didn't already know, many of California's best lakes for a chance to catch giant rainbow and brown trout are in this region. They include Bridgeport Reservoir, Twin Lakes, June Lake, Convict Lake, and Crowley Lake in the eastern Sierra.

This region has it all: beauty, variety, and a chance at the hike or fish of a lifetime. There is nothing else like it.

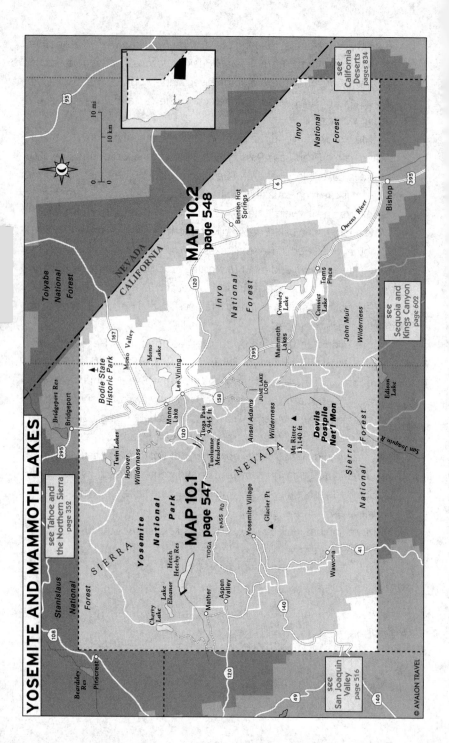

YOSEMITE AND MAMMOTH LAKES

see Tahoe and the Northern Sierra
page 352

MAP 10.2
page 548

MAP 10.1
page 547

see California Deserts
pages 834

see Sequoia and Kings Canyon
page 602

see San Joaquin Valley
page 516

Toiyabe National Forest

Stanislaus National Forest

Inyo National Forest

Hoover Wilderness

Ansel Adams Wilderness

John Muir Wilderness

Sierra National Forest

Yosemite National Park

Bodie State Historic Park

Mono Lake

Lee Vining

Mono Valley

Mammoth Lakes

Crowley Lake

Convict Lake

Toms Place

Benton Hot Springs

Bishop

Bridgeport Res

Bridgeport

Twin Lakes

Cherry Lake

Lake Eleanor

Hetch Hetchy Res

Mather

Aspen Valley

Yosemite Village

Glacier Pt

Wawona

Tuolumne Meadows

Tioga Pass 9,945 ft

Mt Ritter ▲ 13,140 ft

Devils Postpile Nat'l Mon

JUNE LAKE LOOP

Edison Lake

Beardsley Res

Pinecrest

Owens River

San Joaquin R.

TIOGA PASS RD

NEVADA

CALIFORNIA

108

95

6

395

120

167

158

395

41

140

120

49

140

10 mi

10 km

0

0

© AVALON TRAVEL

Map 10.1

Sites 1-72
Pages 549-583

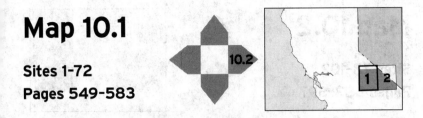

see Tahoe and the Northern Sierra page 352

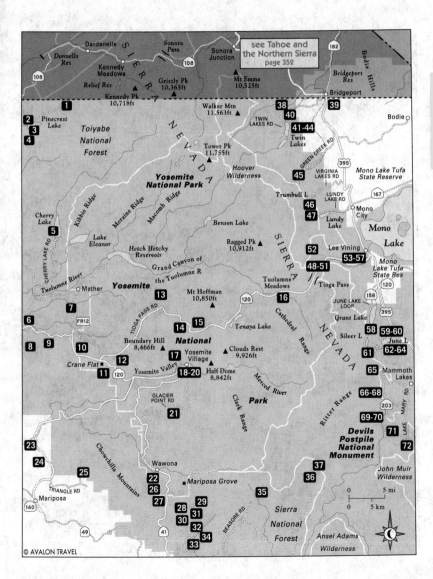

© AVALON TRAVEL

Map 10.2

Sites 73-102
Pages 583-597

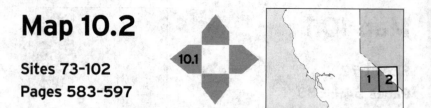

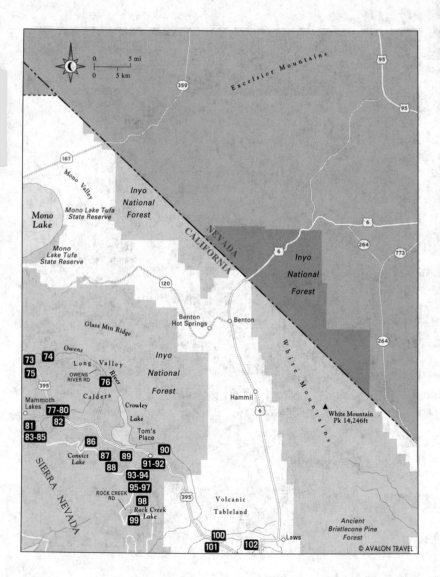

© AVALON TRAVEL

1 HERRING RESERVOIR

Scenic rating: 8

at Herring Lake in Stanislaus National Forest

Map 10.1, page 547

This is a pretty little spot, a rustic campground set near Herring Creek as it enters Herring Lake, set at an elevation of 7,350 feet. There is no boat ramp, but hand-launched boats, such as kayaks, canoes, rafts, prams, and float tubes, are ideal. The lake is shallow, with fair fishing for brook trout and rainbow trout. No horses are permitted.

Campsites, facilities: There are 42 sites for tents or RVs up to 22 feet (no hookups). Fire rings are provided. Vault toilets are available. No drinking water is available. Garbage must be packed out. Leashed pets are permitted.

Reservations, fees: Reservations are not accepted. There is no fee for camping, but donations are accepted. Open May through October, weather permitting.

Directions: From Sonora, drive east on Highway 108 for about 25 miles to Strawberry. Continue past Strawberry for two miles to Herring Creek Road/Forest Road 4N12. Turn right and drive seven miles to Hamill Canyon Road/Forest Road 4N12. Bear right and drive 0.25 mile to Herring Creek Reservoir. Continue another 0.25 mile (cross the bridge) and turn right and drive to the campground. The road is rough and not recommended for RVs or low-clearance vehicles.

Contact: Stanislaus National Forest, Summit Ranger District, 209/965-3434, www.fs.usda.gov/stanislaus.

2 PINECREST

Scenic rating: 7

near Pinecrest Lake in
Stanislaus National Forest

Map 10.1, page 547

This monster-sized Forest Service camp is set near Pinecrest Lake. A launch ramp is available, and a 20-mph speed limit is enforced on the lake. A trail circles the lake and also branches off to nearby Catfish Lake. In early summer, there is good fishing for stocked rainbow trout. The elevation is 5,600 feet. Winter camping is allowed near the Pinecrest Day-Use Area. (For details about Pinecrest Lake, see the Meadowview listing in this chapter.)

Campsites, facilities: There are 200 sites for tents or RVs up to 22 feet (no hookups). Picnic tables and fire grills are provided. Drinking water and flush toilets are available. Garbage must be packed out. A grocery store, coin laundry, coin showers, boat ramp, and propane gas are nearby at Pinecrest Lake Resort. Some facilities are wheelchair-accessible. Leashed pets are permitted.

Reservations, fees: Reservations are required mid-May–mid-September at 877/444-6777 or www.recreation.gov ($9 reservation fee). Sites are $21 per night. Open May through October, weather permitting.

Directions: From Sonora, drive east on Highway 108 for about 30 miles to the signed turn for Pinecrest Lake on the right. Turn right and drive to the access road (0.7 mile past the turnoff signed Pinecrest) for the campground. Turn right and drive a short distance to the campground.

Contact: Stanislaus National Forest, Summit Ranger District, 209/965-3434, www.fs.usda.gov/stanislaus; Dodge Ridge Corporation, 209/965-3475; Pinecrest campground, 209/965-3116.

3 PIONEER TRAIL GROUP CAMP

Scenic rating: 8

near Pinecrest Lake in
Stanislaus National Forest

Map 10.1, page 547

If you're going to Pinecrest Lake with a Scout troop, this is the spot, since it is set up specifically for groups. You get beautiful creek and lake views, with the camp set at an elevation of 5,700 feet. (For recreation information, see the Meadowview listing in this chapter.)

Campsites, facilities: There are three group areas for tents or RVs up to 22 feet (no hookups) that can accommodate 50–100 people each. Picnic tables and fire grills are provided. Drinking water and vault toilets are available. Garbage must be packed out. A grocery store, coin laundry, boat ramp, coin showers, and propane gas are nearby. Some facilities are wheelchair-accessible. Leashed pets are permitted.

Reservations, fees: Reservations are accepted at 877/444-6777 or www.recreation.gov ($9 reservation fee). Sites are $80–120 per night. Open May through October, weather permitting.

Directions: From Sonora, drive east on Highway 108 for about 30 miles to the signed road for Pinecrest Lake. Turn right at the sign and drive 0.5 mile to the signed road for Pinecrest/Dodge Ridge Road. Turn right and drive about a mile to the campground entrance on the left.

Contact: Stanislaus National Forest, Summit Ranger District, 209/965-3434, www.fs.usda.gov/stanislaus; Dodge Ridge Corporation, 209/965-3475.

4 MEADOWVIEW

Scenic rating: 7

near Pinecrest Lake in
Stanislaus National Forest

Map 10.1, page 547

No secret here, folks. This camp is one mile from Pinecrest Lake, a popular weekend vacation area (and there's a trail that connects the camp with the town). Pinecrest Lake is set at 5,621 feet elevation, covers 300 acres and 2.5 miles of shoreline, has a sandy swimming beach, and has a 20-mph speed limit for boaters. The lake is the centerpiece of a fully developed family vacation area; boat rentals at the small marina are a big bonus. The lake is stocked with rainbow trout and also has a small resident population of brown trout. The easy hike

around the lake is a popular walk. If you want something more ambitious, there is a cutoff on the north side of the lake that is routed one mile up to little Catfish Lake, which in reality is a set of shallow ponds surrounded by old-growth forest. The Dodge Ridge Ski Area is nearby, with many privately owned cabins in the area.

Campsites, facilities: There are 100 sites for tents or RVs up to 22 feet (no hookups). Picnic tables and fire grills are provided. Drinking water and flush toilets are available. A grocery store, coin laundry, boat ramp, boat rentals, coin showers, and propane gas are nearby. Garbage must be packed out. Some facilities are wheelchair-accessible. Leashed pets are permitted.

Reservations, fees: Reservations are not accepted. Sites are $19 per night. Open May through September, weather permitting.

Directions: From Sonora, drive east on Highway 108 for about 30 miles to the signed road for Pinecrest Lake. Turn right at the sign and drive 0.5 mile to Pinecrest/Dodge Ridge Road. Turn right and drive about 200 yards to the campground entrance on the right side of the road.

Contact: Stanislaus National Forest, Summit Ranger District, 209/965-3434, www.fs.usda.gov/stanislaus; Dodge Ridge Corporation, 209/965-3475.

5 CHERRY VALLEY AND BOAT-IN

Scenic rating: 9

on Cherry Lake in Stanislaus National Forest

Map 10.1, page 547

Cherry Lake is a mountain lake surrounded by national forest at 4,700 feet elevation, just outside the western boundary of Yosemite National Park. It is much larger than most people anticipate and provides much better trout fishing than anything in Yosemite. The camp is on the southwest shore of the lake, a very pretty spot, about a mile ride to the boat launch on the west side of the Cherry Valley Dam. A bonus is that dispersed boat-in camping is allowed on the lake's east side. All water sports are allowed, yet because it takes a considerable drive to reach the lake, you won't find nearly the waterskiing traffic as at other regional lakes. Water levels can fluctuate here. The lake is bordered to the east by Kibbie Ridge; just on the other side are Yosemite Park and Lake Eleanor. Insider's tip: During periods of campfire restrictions, which is often most of the summer in this national forest, this campground is the only one in the area where campfires are permitted. A fire permit is required from the Forest Service.

Campsites, facilities: There are 45 sites for tents or RVs up to 22 feet (no hookups). Primitive boat-in camping is permitted on the lake's east side. Picnic tables and fire grills are provided. Drinking water and vault toilets are available. A boat ramp is nearby. Leashed pets are permitted.

Reservations, fees: Reservations are not accepted. Single sites are $19 per night, $38 per night for double sites. There is no fee for camping for boat-in sites. A 14-day limit is enforced. Open April through October, weather permitting.

Directions: From Groveland, drive east on Highway 120 for about 15 miles to Forest Road 1N07/Cherry Lake Road. Turn left and drive 20 miles (narrow, curvy, steep in some spots) to Cottonwood Road/Forest Road 1N04. Turn left and drive one mile to the campground entrance road. Turn right and drive one mile to the campground.

Contact: Stanislaus National Forest, Groveland Ranger District, 209/962-7825, www. fs.usda.gov/stanislaus.

6 SWEETWATER

Scenic rating: 4

near the South Fork of the Tuolumne River in Stanislaus National Forest

Map 10.1, page 547

This camp is set at 3,000 feet elevation, near the South Fork Tuolumne River, one of several camps along Highway 120 that provide a

safety valve for campers who can't find space in Yosemite National Park to the east. Nearby, on the North Fork of the Tuolumne River, is a popular swimming area known as Rainbow Pools, with a waterfall and series of pools created by the river. Whitewater rafting and kayaking are also available a few miles from this camp; a Forest Service permit is required.

Campsites, facilities: There are 12 sites for tents or RVs up to 22 feet (no hookups). Picnic tables and fire grills are provided. Drinking water and vault toilets are available. Leashed pets are permitted.

Reservations, fees: Reservations are not accepted. Single sites are $19 per night, double sites are $28 per night. A 14-day limit is enforced. Open April through October, weather permitting.

Directions: From Groveland, drive east on Highway 120 for about 15 miles (five miles past the Groveland District Office) to the campground on the left side of the road.

Contact: Stanislaus National Forest, Groveland Ranger District, 209/962-7825, www. fs.usda.gov/stanislaus.

7 DIMOND "O"

Scenic rating: 7

in Stanislaus National Forest

Map 10.1, page 547

Dimond "O" is set at 4,400 feet elevation on the eastern side of Stanislaus National Forest—just two miles from the western border of Yosemite National Park.

Campsites, facilities: There are 36 sites for tents or RVs up to 22 feet (no hookups). Picnic tables and fire grills are provided. Drinking water and vault toilets are available. Some facilities are wheelchair-accessible. Leashed pets are permitted.

Reservations, fees: Reservations are accepted at 877/444-6777 or www.recreation.gov ($9 reservation fee). Single sites are $21 per night, double sites are $42 per night. Open April through October, weather permitting.

Directions: From Groveland, drive east on Highway 120 for 25 miles to Evergreen Road/Forest Road 12. Turn left on Evergreen Road and drive six miles to the campground.

Contact: Stanislaus National Forest, Groveland Ranger District, 209/962-7825, www.fs.usda.gov/stanislaus.

8 MOORE CREEK

Scenic rating: 6

in Stanislaus National Forest

Map 10.1, page 547

This camp is set at 3,100 feet elevation, just past where the Sierra alpine zone takes over from foothill oak woodlands. It is near the access route (Highway 120) to the Crane Flat entrance station of Yosemite National Park.

Campsites, facilities: This camp is for dispersed tent camping only. Vault toilets are available. There is no drinking water. Garbage must be packed out. A campfire permit is required. Leashed pets are permitted.

Reservations, fees: Reservations are not accepted. There is no fee for camping. Open year-round.

Directions: From Groveland, drive east on Highway 120 for about 12 miles to Buck Meadows Road. Turn right and drive 1.5 miles (the road becomes Forest Road 2S05) to the campground on the right.

Contact: Stanislaus National Forest, Groveland Ranger District, 209/962-7825, www.fs.usda.gov/stanislaus.

9 YOSEMITE LAKES

Scenic rating: 6

on Tuolumne River at Groveland

Map 10.1, page 547

This is a 400-acre park set at 3,600 feet elevation along the South Fork Tuolumne River in the Sierra foothills near Groveland. Its proximity to Yosemite National Park, just five miles from the west entrance station, makes it ideal for many. The park is an affiliate of Thousand Trails, whose facilities usually are open only to members, but in this case, it is open to the general public on a limited basis. It is a family-oriented park with a large variety of recreation options and seasonal organized activities. Fishing and swimming are popular, and the river is stocked with trout. A plus is 24-hour security.

Campsites, facilities: There are 20 sites with full hookups (30 amps) for RVs of any length and 25 sites for tents available to the public (more sites available to Thousand Trails members only), and cabins, yurts, and a hostel. Picnic tables and fire rings are provided. Restrooms, drinking water, showers, flush toilets, fish-cleaning station, and coin laundry are available. A store, gas station, propane, and firewood are available. Kayak rentals, pedalboats, inner tubes, and bicycles are available for rent. Some facilities are wheelchair accessible. Leashed pets are permitted.

Reservations, fees: Reservations are accepted at 800/533-1001. Sites are $48 per night. Credit cards accepted. Open year-round, weather permitting.

Directions: Drive east on Highway 120 to Groveland. From Groveland, continue east for 18 miles to the entrance road (signed) for Yosemite Lakes on the right. Turn right and drive a short distance to the park.

Contact: Yosemite Lakes, 209/962-0121, www.stayatyosemite.com.

10 HODGDON MEADOW

Scenic rating: 7

in Yosemite National Park

Map 10.1, page 547

Hodgdon Meadow is on the outskirts of Yosemite, just inside the park's borders at the Big Oak Flat (Highway 120) entrance station, at 4,900 feet in elevation. It is near a small feeder creek to the South Fork Tuolumne River. It is about a 20-minute drive on Highway 120 to a major junction, where a left turn takes you on Tioga Road and to Yosemite's high country, including Tuolumne Meadows, and where staying on Big Flat Road routes you toward Yosemite Valley (25 miles from the camp). Because of the presence of bears, use of food lockers is required.

Campsites, facilities: There are 105 sites for tents or RVs up to 35 feet (no hookups) and four group sites for 13–30 people each (no trailers in group sites). Picnic tables, fire rings, and food lockers are provided. Drinking water and flush toilets are available. Leashed pets are permitted in the campground, but not in group camps or on trails.

Reservations, fees: Reservations are accepted and are required mid-April through mid-October at 877/444-6777 or www.recreation.gov ($9 reservation fee). Sites are $20 per night May through October, $14 remainder of year, group campsite $40 per night, plus $20 park entrance fee per vehicle. Open year-round, except for group sites.

Directions: From Groveland, drive east on Highway 120 to the Big Oak Flat entrance station for Yosemite National Park. Just after passing the entrance station, turn left and drive a short distance to the campground on the right.

Contact: Yosemite National Park, 209/372-0200 for an automated menu of recorded information, www.nps.gov/yose.

11 CRANE FLAT

Scenic rating: 6

near Tuolumne Grove of Big Trees in Yosemite National Park

Map 10.1, page 547

Crane Flat is within a five-minute drive of the Tuolumne Grove of Big Trees and to the Merced Grove to the nearby west. This is the feature attraction in this part of Yosemite National Park, set near the western border in close proximity to the Big Oak Flat Entrance Station (Highway 120). The elevation is 6,200 feet. Yosemite Valley is about a 25-minute drive away.

Campsites, facilities: There are 166 sites for tents or RVs up to 35 feet (no hookups). Picnic tables, fire rings, and food lockers are provided. Drinking water and flush toilets are available. Groceries, propane gas, and a gas station are nearby. Some facilities are wheelchair-accessible. Leashed pets are allowed in the campground.

Reservations, fees: Reservations are required at 877/444-6777 or www.recreation.gov ($9 reservation fee). Sites are $20 per night, plus $20 park entrance fee per vehicle. Open July through September, weather permitting.

Directions: From Groveland, drive east on Highway 120 to the Big Oak Flat entrance station for Yosemite National Park. After passing through the entrance station, drive about 10 miles to the campground entrance road on the right. Turn right and drive 0.5 mile to the campground.

Contact: Yosemite National Park, 209/372-0200 for an automated menu of recorded information, www.nps.gov/yose.

12 TAMARACK FLAT

Scenic rating: 7

on Tamarack Creek in Yosemite National Park

Map 10.1, page 547

The road to this campground looks something like the surface of the moon. Then you arrive and find one of the few primitive drive-to camps in Yosemite National Park, at 6,300 feet elevation. From the trailhead at camp, you can link up with El Capitan Trail and then hike across Ribbon Meadow on up to the north valley rim at El Capitan, at 7,569 feet elevation. This is the largest single piece of granite in the world, and standing atop it for both the sensation and the divine view is a breathtaking experience. From camp, Yosemite Valley is 23 miles away. Note that the use of food lockers is required.

Campsites, facilities: There are 52 sites for tents. RVs and trailers are not recommended. Picnic tables, food lockers, and fire grills are provided. Vault toilets are available. No drinking water is available.

Reservations, fees: Reservations are not accepted. Sites are $10 per night, plus $20 park entrance fee per vehicle. Open June through September.

Directions: From Merced, drive east on Highway 140 to the Arch Rock entrance station. Continue east to the Big Oak Flat Road junction (0.5 mile before entering Yosemite Valley). Turn left and drive 14 miles to Tioga Road. Turn right on Tioga Road and drive three miles to the campground entrance on the right side of the road. Turn right and drive 2.5 miles to the campground at the end of the road. Note that the access road is difficult; trailers and RVs are not advised.

Contact: Yosemite National Park, 209/372-0200 for an automated menu of recorded information, www.nps.gov/yose.

13 WHITE WOLF
🏞️ 🛶 🦌 🚐 ⛺

Scenic rating: 8

in Yosemite National Park

Map 10.1, page 547

This is one of Yosemite National Park's prime mountain camps for people who like to hike, either for great day hikes in the immediate area and beyond, or for overnight backpacking trips. The day hike to Lukens Lake is an easy two-mile trip, the payoff being this pretty little alpine lake set amid a meadow, pines, and granite. Just about everybody who camps at White Wolf makes the trip. Backpackers (wilderness permit required) can make the overnight trip into the Ten Lakes Basin, set below Grand Mountain and Colby Mountain.

Bears are common at this camp, and campers are required to secure food in the bear-proof lockers. The elevation is 8,000 feet.

Campsites, facilities: There are 74 sites for tents or RVs up to 27 feet (no hookups). Tent cabins are also available. Picnic tables, food lockers, and fire grills are provided. Drinking water and flush toilets are available. Evening ranger programs are occasionally offered. A small store with a walk-up window and limited items is nearby. Leashed pets are permitted in the campground, but not on trails.

Reservations, fees: Reservations are not accepted. Sites are $14 per night, plus $20 park entrance fee per vehicle. Open July to early September, weather permitting.

Directions: From Merced, drive east on Highway 140 to the Arch Rock entrance station. Continue east to the Big Oak Flat Road junction (0.5 mile before entering Yosemite Valley). Turn left and drive 14 miles to Tioga Road. Turn right and drive 15 miles to White Wolf Road on the left. Turn left and drive a mile to the campground entrance road on the right.

Contact: Yosemite National Park, 209/372-0200 for an automated menu of recorded information, www.nps.gov/yose.

14 YOSEMITE CREEK
🏞️ 🛶 🦌 ⛺

Scenic rating: 9

on Yosemite Creek in Yosemite National Park

Map 10.1, page 547   **BEST (**

This is the most remote drive-to camp in Yosemite National Park, a great alternative to camping in the valley or at Tuolumne Meadows, and the rough, curvy access road keeps many visitors away. It is set along Yosemite Creek at 7,659 feet elevation, with poor trout fishing but a trailhead for a spectacular hike. If you arrange a shuttle ride, you can make a great one-way trip down to the north side of the Yosemite Canyon rim, skirting past the top of Yosemite Falls (a side trip to Yosemite

Point is a must!), then tackling the unbelievable descent into the valley, emerging at Camp 4 Walk-In. Note: The narrow entrance road is a remnant of "Old Tioga Road."

Campsites, facilities: There are 75 tent sites. RVs and trailers are not recommended. Picnic tables, food lockers (mandatory use), and fire grills are provided. Vault toilets are available. No drinking water is available. Leashed pets are permitted.

Reservations, fees: Reservations are not accepted. Sites are $10 per night, plus $20 park entrance fee per vehicle. A 14-day stay limit is enforced. Open July through early September, weather permitting.

Directions: From Merced, drive east on Highway 140 to the Arch Rock entrance station. Continue east to the Big Oak Flat Road junction (0.5 mile before entering Yosemite Valley). Turn left and drive 14 miles to Tioga Road. Turn right and drive about 30 miles (just beyond the White Wolf turnoff on the left) to Yosemite Creek Campground Road on the right. Turn right and drive five miles to the campground at the end of the road. RVs and trailers are not recommended.

Contact: Yosemite National Park, 209/372-0200 for an automated menu of recorded information, www.nps.gov/yose.

15 PORCUPINE FLAT
🏃 🚐 ⛺

Scenic rating: 6

near Yosemite Creek in
Yosemite National Park

Map 10.1, page 547

Porcupine Flat, set at 8,100 feet elevation, is southwest of Mount Hoffman, one of the prominent nearby peaks along Tioga Road in Yosemite National Park. The trailhead for a hike to May Lake, set just below Mount Hoffman, is about five miles away on a signed turnoff on the north side of the road. There are several little peaks above the lake where

hikers can gain great views, including one of the back side of Half Dome.

Campsites, facilities: There are 52 sites for tents or RVs up to 24 feet (no hookups). There is limited RV space. Picnic tables, fire rings, and food lockers (mandatory use) are provided. Vault toilets are available. No drinking water is available.

Reservations, fees: Reservations are not accepted. Sites are $10 per night, plus $20 park entrance fee per vehicle. Open July through mid-October, weather permitting.

Directions: From Merced, drive east on Highway 140 to the Arch Rock entrance station. Continue east to the Big Oak Flat Road junction (0.5 mile before entering Yosemite Valley). Turn left and drive 14 miles to Tioga Road. Turn right and drive about 25 miles to the campground on the left side of the road (16 miles west from Tuolumne Meadows).

Contact: Yosemite National Park, 209/372-0200 for an automated menu of recorded information, www.nps.gov/yose.

16 TUOLUMNE MEADOWS
🏃 🚣 🏠 🐕 🚐 ⛺

Scenic rating: 8

in Yosemite National Park

Map 10.1, page 547   BEST (

This is Yosemite's biggest camp, and for the variety of nearby adventures, it might also be the best. It is set in the high country, at 8,600 feet, and can be used as a base camp for fishing, hiking, and horseback riding, or as a start-up point for a backpacking trip (wilderness permits required). This is one of the top trailheads in North America. There are two outstanding and easy day hikes from here, one heading north on the Pacific Crest Trail for the near-level walk to Tuolumne Falls and Glen Aulin, the other heading south up Lyell Fork (toward Donohue Pass), with good fishing for small brook trout. With a backpack (wilderness permit required), either route can be extended for as long as desired into remote and beautiful country. The campground is huge, and neighbors are guaranteed, but it is well wooded and feels somewhat secluded even with all the RVs and tents. There are lots of food-raiding bears in the area, so use of the food lockers is required.

Campsites, facilities: There are 304 sites for tents or RVs up to 35 feet (no hookups), four horse camps, and seven group sites that can accommodate 30 people each. There are also an additional 25 hike-in sites available for backpackers (no parking is available for backpacker campsites, often reserved for those hiking the Pacific Crest Trail, for which a wilderness permit is required). Picnic tables, fire grills, and food lockers are provided. Drinking water, flush toilets, and dump station are available. Showers and groceries are nearby. Leashed pets are permitted, except in group sites, horse camps, and backpacker sites.

Reservations, fees: Reservations are accepted for half of the sites at 877/444-6777 or www.recreation.gov ($9 reservation fee); the other half are first come, first served; reservations are required for the group and horse camps. Tent and RV sites are $20 per night, $5 per night per person for walk-in (backpack) sites, $25 per night for horse campsites, and $40 per night for group sites, plus a $20 per vehicle park entrance fee. Open July through late September, weather permitting.

Directions: From Merced, drive east on Highway 140 to the Arch Rock entrance station. Continue east to the Big Oak Flat Road junction (0.5 mile before entering Yosemite Valley). Turn left and drive 14 miles to Tioga Road. Turn right and drive 46 miles to the campground on the right side of the road.

From just south of Lee Vining at the junction of U.S. 395 and Highway 120, turn west and drive to the Tioga Pass entrance station for Yosemite National Park. Continue for about eight miles to the campground entrance on the left.

Contact: Yosemite National Park, 209/372-0200 for an automated menu of recorded information, www.nps.gov/yose.

17 CAMP 4

Scenic rating: 8

in Yosemite Valley in Yosemite National Park

Map 10.1, page 547

The concept at Camp 4 was to provide a climber's bivouac near the base of El Capitan, and so it is. It has also worked as a walk-in alternative to drive-in camps that sometimes resemble combat zones. The sites here are jammed together, and six people will be placed in your site, whether you know them or not. Regardless, the camp is in a great location, within walking distance of Yosemite Falls. It has a view of Leidig Meadow and the southern valley rim, with Sentinel Rock directly across the valley. A trail is routed from camp to Lower Yosemite Fall. In addition, the trailhead for Yosemite Falls Trail is a short distance away, a terrible, butt-kicking climb up Columbia Rock to the rim adjacent to the top of the falls, but providing one of the most incredible views in all the world. Insider's note: After originally being named Camp 4, the park once renamed this campground as "Sunnyside Walk-In." The name was switched back to the original, because climbers never stopped calling it Camp 4.

Campsites, facilities: There are 35 walk-in tent sites. Six people are placed in each campsite, regardless of the number of people in each party. Picnic tables, fire pits, and food lockers (mandatory use) are provided. Drinking water and flush toilets are available. A parking area, showers, groceries, and a coin laundry are nearby. No pets are allowed.

Reservations, fees: Reservations are not accepted. Sites are $5 per person per night, plus $20 park entrance fee per vehicle. There is a seven-day limit during the summer. Open year-round.

Directions: From Merced, drive east on Highway 140 to the Arch Rock entrance station. Continue east to the Big Oak Flat Road junction (0.5 mile before entering Yosemite Valley). Continue into Yosemite Valley, and drive past the chapel to a stop sign. Turn left, cross Sentinel Bridge, and drive one mile to another stop sign. Continue 1.5 miles and look for the large sign marking the parking area for Camp 4 Walk-In on the right (near the base of El Capitan).

Contact: Yosemite National Park, 209/372-0200 for an automated menu of recorded information, www.nps.gov/yose.

18 LOWER PINES

Scenic rating: 9

in Yosemite Valley in Yosemite National Park

Map 10.1, page 547

Lower Pines sits right along the Merced River, quite pretty, in the center of Yosemite Valley. Of course, the tents and RVs are jammed in quite close together. Within walking distance is the trail to Mirror Lake (a zoo on parade), as well as the trailhead at Happy Isles for the hike up to Vernal Fall and Nevada Fall. The park's shuttle bus picks up riders near the camp entrance.

Campsites, facilities: There are 60 sites for tents or RVs up to 40 feet, one double site for tents or RVs up to 40 feet, and two group camps for up to 12 people each. No hookups. Fire rings, picnic tables, and food lockers (mandatory use) are provided. Drinking water and flush toilets are available. A grocery store, coin laundry, propane gas, recycling center, dump station and horse and bike rentals are nearby. Some facilities are wheelchair accessible. Leashed pets are permitted.

Reservations, fees: Reservations are required at 877/444-6777 or www.recreation.gov ($9 reservation fee). Sites are $20 per night, $30 per night for double or group sites, plus $20 park entrance fee per vehicle. There is a seven-day limit during the summer. Open late March through October, weather permitting.

Directions: From Merced, drive east on Highway 140 to the Arch Rock entrance station. Continue east to the Big Oak Flat Road

junction (0.5 mile before entering Yosemite Valley). Continue into Yosemite Valley, drive past Curry Village (on the right) to the campground entrance on the left side of the road (just before Clarks Bridge).

Contact: Yosemite National Park, 209/372-0200, for an automated menu of recorded information, www.nps.gov/yose.

19 UPPER PINES

Scenic rating: 9

in Yosemite Valley in Yosemite National Park

Map 10.1, page 547

Of the campgrounds in Yosemite Valley, Upper Pines is the closest trailhead to paradise, providing you can get a campsite at the far south end of the camp. From here it is a short walk to Happy Isles trailhead and with it the chance to hike to Vernal Fall on Mist Trail (steep), or beyond to Nevada Fall (very steep) at the foot of Liberty Cap. But crowded this camp is, and you'd better expect it. People come from all over the world to camp here. Sometimes it appears as if they are from other worlds as well. The elevation is 4,000 feet.

Campsites, facilities: There are 238 sites for tents or RVs up to 35 feet (no hookups). Fire rings, picnic tables, and food lockers (mandatory use) are provided. Drinking water, flush toilets, and dump station are available. A grocery store, coin laundry, propane gas, recycling center, and horse and bike rentals are nearby. Three sites provide wheelchair access. Leashed pets are permitted in the campgrounds, but not on trails.

Reservations, fees: Reservations are required March 15 through November at 877/444-6777 or www.recreation.gov ($9 reservation fee); sites are first-come, first-served December to March 15. Sites are $20 per night, plus $20 park entrance fee per vehicle. There is a seven-day limit during the summer. Open year-round.

Directions: From Merced, drive east on

Highway 140 to the Arch Rock entrance station. Continue east to the Big Oak Flat Road junction (0.5 mile before entering Yosemite Valley). Continue into Yosemite Valley, drive past Curry Village (on the right) to the campground entrance on the right side of the road (just before Clarks Bridge).

Contact: Yosemite National Park, 209/372-0200, for an automated menu of recorded information, www.nps.gov/yose.

20 NORTH PINES

🚶 🚴 🏊 🎣 🦌 ♿ 🚙 ⛺

Scenic rating: 9

in Yosemite Valley in Yosemite National Park

Map 10.1, page 547

North Pines is set along the Merced River. A trail out of camp heads east and links with the paved road/trail to Mirror Lake, a virtual parade of people. If you continue hiking past Mirror Lake you will get astounding views of Half Dome and then leave the masses behind as you enter Tenaya Canyon. The elevation is 4,000 feet.

Campsites, facilities: There are 81 sites for tents or RVs up to 40 feet (no hookups). Picnic tables, fire grills, and food lockers (mandatory use) are provided. Drinking water, flush toilets, and a dump station are available. A grocery store, coin laundry, recycling center, propane gas, and horse and bike rentals are nearby. Some facilities are wheelchair accessible. Leashed pets are allowed.

Reservations, fees: Reservations are required at 877/444-6777 or www.recreation.gov ($9 reservation fee). Sites are $20 per night, plus $20 park entrance fee per vehicle. Open April through September, weather permitting.

Directions: From Merced, drive east on Highway 140 to the Arch Rock entrance station. Continue east to the Big Oak Flat Road junction (0.5 mile before entering Yosemite Valley). Continue into Yosemite Valley, drive past Curry Village (on the right), continue past Upper and Lower Pines Campgrounds, and drive over Clarks Bridge to a junction at the horse stables. Turn left at the horse stables and drive a short distance to the campground on the right.

Contact: Yosemite National Park, 209/372-0200, for an automated menu of recorded information, www.nps.gov/yose.

21 BRIDALVEIL CREEK AND EQUESTRIAN AND GROUP CAMP

🚶 🎣 🐴 🚙 ⛺

Scenic rating: 10

near Glacier Point in Yosemite National Park

Map 10.1, page 547   **BEST (**

There may be no better view in the world than the one from Glacier Point, looking down into Yosemite Valley, where Half Dome stands like nature's perfect sculpture. Then there are the perfect views of Yosemite Fall, Nevada Fall, Vernal Fall, and several hundred square miles of Yosemite's wilderness backcountry. This is the closest camp to Glacier Point's drive-to vantage point, but it is also the closest camp to the best day hikes in the entire park. Along Glacier Point Road are trailheads to Sentinel Dome (incredible view of Yosemite Fall) and Taft Point (breathtaking drop, incredible view of El Capitan), and McGurk Meadow (one of the most pristine spots on Earth). At 7,200 feet, the camp is more than 3,000 feet higher than Yosemite Valley. A good day hike out of camp leads you to Ostrander Lake, just below Horse Ridge.

Campsites, facilities: There are 110 sites for tents or RVs up to 35 feet (no hookups), three equestrian sites, and two group sites for 13–30 people each. Picnic tables, fire rings, and food lockers (mandatory use) are provided. Drinking water and flush toilets are available. Leashed pets are permitted, except in group sites.

Reservations, fees: Reservations are not accepted for individual sites, but they are required for equestrian sites and group sites at 800/444-6777 or www.recreation.gov ($9 reservation fee). Sites are $14 per night, $25 per night for equestrian site, $40 per night for group site, plus $20 park entrance fee per vehicle. A 14-day stay limit is enforced. Open July through early September, weather permitting.

Directions: From Merced, drive east on Highway 140 to the Arch Rock entrance station. Continue east (past Big Oak Flat Road junction) to the junction with Wawona Road/Highway 41 (just before Yosemite Valley). Turn right on Highway 41/Wawona Road and drive about 10 miles to Glacier Point Road. Turn left on Glacier Point Road and drive about five miles (a few miles past Badger Pass Ski Area) to Peregoy Meadow and the campground access road on the right. Turn right and drive a short distance to the campground.

Contact: Yosemite National Park, 209/372-0200, for an automated menu of recorded information, www.nps.gov/yose.

22 WAWONA
🧗🏊🚣🏇🐕♿🚐⛺

Scenic rating: 9

on the South Fork of the Merced River in Yosemite National Park

Map 10.1, page 547

Wawona is an attractive alternative to the packed camps in Yosemite Valley, providing you don't mind the relatively long drives to the best destinations. The camp is pretty, set along the South Fork of the Merced River, with the sites more spacious than at most other drive-to camps in the park. The nearest attraction is the Mariposa Grove of Giant Sequoias, but get your visit in by 9 A.M., because after that it turns into a zoo, complete with shuttle train. The best nearby hike is a strenuous 10-mile round-trip to Chilnualna Falls, the prettiest sight in the southern region of the park; the trailhead is at the east end of Chilnualna Road in North Wawona. It's a 45-minute drive to either Glacier Point or Yosemite Valley.

Campsites, facilities: There are 93 sites for tents or RVs up to 35 feet (no hookups), one group tent site for 13–30 people each, and two horse camps. Picnic tables, fire grills, and food lockers (mandatory use) are provided. Drinking water and flush toilets are available. There are some stock-handling facilities for camping with pack animals; call for further information. A grocery store, dump station, propane gas, gas station, post office, restaurant, and seasonal horseback-riding facilities are nearby. Some facilities are wheelchair accessible. Leashed pets are permitted, but not in group sites, horse camps, or on trails.

Reservations, fees: From mid-April through September, reservations are required at 877/444-6777 or www.recreation.gov ($9 reservation fee). Online reservations are not accepted for horse sites. Reservations are not needed from October to April. Sites are $20 per night or $14 per night in off-season, horse campsites are $25 per night, the group site is $40 per night, $20 park entrance fee is per vehicle. A seven-day camping limit is enforced during the summer. Open year-round, and horse camp open April through October.

Directions: From Oakhurst, drive north on Highway 41 to the Wawona entrance of Yosemite National Park. Continue north on Highway 41 past Wawona (golf course on the left) and drive one mile to the campground entrance on the left.

Contact: Yosemite National Park, 209/372-0200, for an automated menu of recorded information, www.nps.gov/yose.

23 MERCED RECREATION AREA
🧗🚴🏊🚣🏊🐕♿🚐⛺

Scenic rating: 8

on the Merced River east of Briceburg

Map 10.1, page 547   BEST (

What a spot: The campsites are along one of the prettiest sections of the Merced River, where you can enjoy great hiking, swimming, rafting, kayaking, and fishing, all on the same day. There are three campgrounds here: McCabe Flat, Willow Placer, and Railroad Flat. The access road out of camp leads downstream to the Yosemite Railroad Grade, which has been converted into a great trail. One of the best wildflower blooms anywhere in the Sierra foothills is found near here at Red Hills (just outside Chinese Camp), usually best in April. If you don't mind the cold water, swimming in the Merced River's pools can provide relief from summer heat. Evening fly-fishing is good in many of the same spots through July. But the true attraction on the Merced River is rafting and kayaking. An extraordinarily long stretch of river, 29 miles, can be run from the put-in at Red Bud Day-Use Area to the take-out at Bagby. A number of whitewater guide companies work this stretch of river.

Campsites, facilities: There are 23 walk-in tent sites, nine sites for tents or RVs up to 18 feet (no hookups), and one large group site at Willow Placer campground. Picnic tables, fire grills, and garbage collection are provided. Vault and pit toilets are available. No drinking water is available at the campsites (drinking water is available across from the Briceburg Bridge). Supplies are available in Mariposa. Some facilities are wheelchair-accessible. Leashed pets are permitted.

Reservations, fees: Reservations are not accepted. Sites are $10 per night. There is a 14-day limit. Open April through October, weather permitting.

Directions: From Merced, turn east on Highway 140 and drive 40 miles to Mariposa. Continue another 15 miles to Briceburg and the Briceburg Visitor Center on the left. Turn left at a road that is signed "BLM Camping Areas" (the road remains paved for about 150 yards). Drive over the Briceburg suspension bridge and turn left, traveling downstream on the road, parallel to the river. Drive 2.5 miles to McCabe Flat, 3.8 miles to Willow Placer, and 4.8 miles to Railroad Flat.

Contact: Bureau of Land Management, Mother Lode Field Office, 916/941-3101, www.blm.gov/ca.

24 YOSEMITE WEST-MARIPOSA KOA

Scenic rating: 7

near Mariposa

Map 10.1, page 547

A little duck pond, swimming pool, and proximity to Yosemite National Park make this one a winner. A shuttle bus service (fee) to the national park is a great bonus. The RV sites are lined up along the entrance road. A 10 P.M. "quiet time" helps ensure a good night's sleep. It's a one-hour drive to Yosemite Valley, and your best bet is to get there early to enjoy the spectacular beauty before the park is packed with people.

Campsites, facilities: There are 49 sites with full or partial hookups (30 and 50 amps) for RVs up to 40 feet, 26 tent sites, 12 cabins, and three lodges. Picnic tables and barbecues are provided; no wood fires. Restrooms with showers, dump station, Wi-Fi, telephone/modem access, coin laundry, convenience store, propane gas, seasonal swimming pool, train caboose with arcade, and playground are available. Some facilities are wheelchair accessible. Leashed pets are permitted in RV and tent sites only, with certain restrictions.

Reservations, fees: Reservations are accepted at 800/562-9391. RV sites are $55–63 per night, tent sites are $40 per night, $6 per person per night for more than two people, $2 per pet per night. Call for cabin and lodge prices. Some credit cards accepted. Open March through October.

Directions: From Merced, drive east on Highway 140 to Mariposa. Continue on Highway 140 for seven miles to Midpines and the campground entrance on the left at 6323 Highway 140.

Contact: Yosemite-Mariposa KOA, 209/966-2201, www.yosemitekoa.com.

25 JERSEYDALE

Scenic rating: 5

in Sierra National Forest

Map 10.1, page 547

This little camp gets overlooked by many visitors shut out of nearby Yosemite National Park simply because they don't realize it exists. Jerseydale is set southwest of the national park in Sierra National Forest, with two good side trips nearby. If you continue north on Jerseydale Road to its end (about six miles), you will come to a Forest Service road/trailhead that provides access east along a portion of the South Fork of the Merced River, where there is often good fishing, swimming, and rafting. In addition, a dirt road from the camp is routed east for many miles into the Chowchilla Mountains.

Campsites, facilities: There are 10 sites for tents or RVs up to 24 feet (no hookups). Picnic tables and fire grills are provided. Vault toilets are available. Water is available but must be boiled before drinking. A few hitching posts are available and horses are permitted at these camps. Leashed pets are permitted.

Reservations, fees: Reservations are not accepted. There is no fee for camping. Open May through November.

Directions: From Mariposa, drive northeast on Highway 140 for about five miles to Triangle Road (if you reach Midpines, you have gone 1.5 miles too far). Turn right on Triangle Road and drive about six miles to Darrah and Jerseydale Road. Turn left and drive three miles to the campground on the left side of the road (adjacent to the Jerseydale Ranger Station).

Contact: Sierra National Forest, Bass Lake Ranger District, 559/877-2218, www.fs.usda.gov/sierra.

26 SUMMIT CAMP

Scenic rating: 5

in Sierra National Forest

Map 10.1, page 547

The prime attraction of tiny Summit Camp is its proximity to the Wawona entrance of Yosemite National Park. It sits along a twisty Forest Service road, perched in the Chowchilla Mountains at 5,800 feet, about three miles from Big Creek. It's a little-known alternative when the park campgrounds at Wawona are packed.

Campsites, facilities: There are sites for dispersed camping only. Picnic tables and fire grills are provided. Vault toilets are available. No drinking water is available. Garbage must be packed out. Leashed pets are permitted.

Reservations, fees: Reservations are not accepted. There is no fee for camping. A 14-day limit is enforced. Open June through October, weather permitting.

Directions: From Oakhurst, drive north on Highway 41 toward the town of Fish Camp and to the gravel Forest Road 5S09X a mile before Fish Camp on the left. Turn left and drive six twisty miles to the campground on the left side of the road. High-clearance vehicles are required. Trailers are not advised.

Contact: Sierra National Forest, Bass Lake Ranger District, 559/877-2218, www.fs.usda.gov/sierra.

27 SUMMERDALE

Scenic rating: 7

on the South Fork of the Merced River in Sierra National Forest

Map 10.1, page 547

You can't get much closer to Yosemite National Park. This camp is within a mile of the Wawona entrance to Yosemite, about a five-minute drive to the Mariposa Grove. If you don't mind its proximity to the highway, this is a pretty spot in its own right, set along Big Creek, a feeder stream to the South Fork Merced River. Some good swimming holes are in this area. The elevation is 5,000 feet.

Campsites, facilities: There are 29 sites for tents or RVs up to 24 feet (no hookups). Picnic tables and fire grills are provided. Vault toilets are available. Water is available but must be boiled before drinking. A grocery store is nearby (within one mile). Some facilities are wheelchair-accessible. Leashed pets are permitted.

Reservations, fees: Reservations are accepted at 877/444-6777 or www.recreation.gov ($9 reservation fee). Sites are $21–23 per night, $5 per night for each additional vehicle. Open May through October, weather permitting.

Directions: From Oakhurst, drive north on Highway 41 to Fish Camp and continue for one mile to the campground entrance on the left side of the road.

Contact: Sierra National Forest, Bass Lake Ranger District, 559/877-2218, www.fs.usda.gov/sierra.

28 BIG SANDY

Scenic rating: 7

on Big Creek in Sierra National Forest

Map 10.1, page 547

It's only six miles from the highway and just eight miles from the southern entrance to Yosemite National Park. Add that up: Right, when Wawona is full in southern Yosemite, this camp provides a much-needed option. It's a pretty camp set on Big Creek in the Sierra National Forest, one of two camps in the immediate area. The elevation is 5,800 feet. If you head into Yosemite for the tour of giant sequoias in Wawona, get there early, by 7:30 or 8:30 A.M., when the grove is still quiet and cool, and you will have the old, mammoth trees practically to yourself.

Campsites, facilities: There are 18 sites for tents or RVs up to 20 feet (no hookups). Picnic tables and fire grills are provided. Vault toilets are available. No drinking water is available. Leashed pets are permitted.

Reservations, fees: Reservations are not accepted. Single sites are $17 per night, double sites are $34 per night, $5 per night for each additional vehicle. Open May through September, weather permitting.

Directions: From Oakhurst drive north on Highway 41 for 15 miles to Forest Road 6S07 (one mile before reaching Marriotts). Turn right on Forest Road 6S07 and drive about six miles (a slow, rough road) to the camp.

Contact: Sierra National Forest, Bass Lake Ranger District, 559/877-2218, www.fs.usda.gov/sierra.

29 FRESNO DOME

Scenic rating: 7

on Big Creek in Sierra National Forest

Map 10.1, page 547

This camp is named after nearby Fresno Dome to the east, at 7,540 feet elevation the dominating feature in the surrounding landscape. The trailhead for a mile hike to its top is two miles curving down the road to the east. This camp is set at 6,400 feet on Big Creek in Sierra National Forest, a good option to nearby Yosemite National Park.

Campsites, facilities: There are 15 sites for tents or RVs up to 20 feet (no hookups). Picnic tables and fire grills are provided. Vault toilets are available. No drinking water is available. Garbage service is located near the entrance to the campground. Leashed pets are permitted.

Reservations, fees: Reservations are not accepted. Single sites are $17 per night, double sites are $34 per night, $5 per night for each additional vehicle. A 14-day limit is enforced. Open June through mid-October, weather permitting.

Directions: From Oakhurst, drive north on Highway 41 approximately five miles to Sky Ranch Road/Forest Road 6S10. Turn right and drive 12 miles to the campground on the left.

Contact: Sierra National Forest, Bass Lake Ranger District, 559/877-2218, www.fs.usda.gov/sierra.

30 NELDER GROVE

Scenic rating: 7

in Sierra National Forest

Map 10.1, page 547

Nelder Grove is a primitive spot, also pretty, yet it is a camp that is often overlooked. It is set amid the Nelder Grove of giant sequoias, the majestic mountain redwoods. There are two interpretive trails, each about a two-mile walk. Since the southern entrance to Yosemite National Park is just 10 miles away, Nelder Grove is overshadowed by Yosemite's Wawona Grove. The elevation is 5,300 feet.

Campsites, facilities: There are seven sites for tents or RVs up to 20 feet (no hookups). Picnic tables and fire grills are provided. Vault toilets are available. No drinking water is available. Garbage must be packed out. Leashed pets are permitted.

Reservations, fees: Reservations are not accepted. There is no fee for camping. Open May through October, weather permitting.

Directions: From Fresno, drive north on Highway 41 for 46 miles to the town of Oakhurst. Continue north on Highway 41 for five miles to Sky Ranch Road/Forest Road 6S10. Turn right (northeast) and drive about eight miles to Forest Road 6S47Y. Turn left and drive a short distance to the campground.

Contact: Sierra National Forest, Bass Lake Ranger District, 559/877-2218, www.fs.usda.gov/sierra.

31 KELTY MEADOW AND EQUESTRIAN CAMP

Scenic rating: 6

on Willow Creek in Sierra National Forest

Map 10.1, page 547

This primitive campground is often used by campers with horses. It is at Kelty Meadow by Willow Creek. Side-trip options feature nearby Fresno Dome, the Nelder Grove of giant sequoias and, of course, the southern entrance to nearby Yosemite National Park. The elevation is 5,800 feet.

Campsites, facilities: There are 11 sites for tents or RVs up to 20 feet. Fire grills and picnic tables are provided. Vault toilets and hitching posts are available. No drinking water is available. Garbage service is located near the entrance to the campground. Leashed pets are permitted.

Reservations, fees: Reservations are required at 877/444-6777 or www.recreation.gov ($9 reservation fee). Single sites are $17 per night, double sites are $34 per night, $5 per night for each additional vehicle. Open June through September, weather permitting.

Directions: From Oakhurst on Highway 41, drive five miles north to Sky Ranch Road/Forest Road 6S10. Turn left (northeast) and drive approximately 10 miles to the campground.

Contact: Sierra National Forest, Bass Lake Ranger District, 559/877-2218, www.fs.usda.gov/sierra.

32 SOQUEL

Scenic rating: 7

on the North Fork of Willow Creek in Sierra National Forest

Map 10.1, page 547

Soquel is at 5,400 feet elevation on the North Fork of Willow Creek, an alternative to nearby Grey's Mountain in Sierra National Forest. When the camps are filled at Bass Lake, these two camps provide overflow areas as well as more primitive settings for those who are looking for more of a wilderness experience.

Campsites, facilities: There are 11 sites for tents or RVs up to 20 feet (no hookups). Picnic tables and fire grills are provided. Vault toilets are available. No drinking water is available. Leashed pets are permitted.

Reservations, fees: Reservations are accepted at 877/444-6777 or www.recreation.gov ($9 reservation fee). Single sites are $17 per night, double sites are $34 per night, $5 per night for each additional vehicle. Open May through October, weather permitting.

Directions: From Fresno, drive north on Highway 41 for 46 miles to the town of Oakhurst. Continue north on Highway 41 for five miles to Sky Ranch Road/Forest Road 6S10. Turn right (east) and drive approximately five miles to Forest Road 6S40. Turn right and drive about three-quarters of a mile to the campground.

Contact: Sierra National Forest, Bass Lake Ranger District, 559/877-2218, www.fs.usda.gov/sierra.

33 GREY'S MOUNTAIN
🏊 🦌 🚗 ⛺

Scenic rating: 7

on Willow Creek in Sierra National Forest

Map 10.1, page 547

This is a small, primitive campground to keep in mind when all the campgrounds are filled at nearby Bass Lake. It is one of a series of campgrounds on Willow Creek. The elevation is 5,400 feet, set just below Sivels Mountain to the east at 5,813 feet.

Campsites, facilities: There are 26 sites for tents or RVs up to 20 feet (no hookups). Picnic tables and fire grills are provided. Vault toilets are available. No drinking water is available. Leashed pets are permitted.

Reservations, fees: Reservations are not accepted. Single sites are $17 per night, double sites are $34 per night, $5 per night for each

additional vehicle. Open May through November, weather permitting.

Directions: From Oakhurst, drive north on Highway 41 for approximately five miles to Sky Ranch Road/Forest Road 6S10. Turn right and drive five miles to Forest Road 6S40. Turn right and drive 0.75 mile to Forest Road 6S08 and the camp.

Contact: Sierra National Forest, Bass Lake Ranger District, 559/877-2218, www.fs.usda.gov/sierra.

34 TEXAS FLAT GROUP CAMP
🏊 🦌 🚗 ⛺

Scenic rating: 5

on the North Fork of Willow Creek in Sierra National Forest

Map 10.1, page 547

If you are on your honeymoon, this definitely ain't the place to be. Unless you like the smell of horses, that is. It's a pretty enough spot, set along the North Fork of Willow Creek, but the camp is primitive and designed for groups with horses. This camp is 15 miles from the south entrance of Yosemite National Park and 15 miles north of Bass Lake. The elevation is 5,400 feet.

Campsites, facilities: There are four group sites for tents or RVs up to 20 feet (no hookups) that can accommodate 25–100 people each. Fire grills and picnic tables are provided. Vault toilets and a corral are available. No drinking water is available. Leashed pets are permitted.

Reservations, fees: Reservations are accepted at 877/444-6777 or www.recreation.gov ($9 reservation fee). Sites are $60.50–90.20 per night. A 14-day limit is enforced. Open June through November.

Directions: From Fresno, drive about 52 miles north on Highway 41 to Sky Ranch Road/County Road 632. Turn right (east) on Sky Ranch Road/Forest Road 6S10 and drive approximately five miles to Forest Road 6S40.

Turn right and drive about three-quarters of a mile to Forest Road 6S08. Turn left and drive 2.5 miles to Forest Road 6S38 and the campground.

Contact: Sierra National Forest, Bass Lake Ranger District, 559/877-2218, www.fs.usda.gov/sierra.

35 UPPER CHIQUITO

Scenic rating: 7

on Chiquito Creek in Sierra National Forest

Map 10.1, page 547

Upper Chiquito is set at 6,800 feet elevation on a major access road to Sierra National Forest and the western region of the Ansel Adams Wilderness, about 15 miles to the east. The camp is set on Upper Chiquito Creek. About a mile down the road (southwest) is a Forest Service spur road (turn north) that provides access to a trail that is routed up Chiquito Creek for three miles to gorgeous Chiquita Lake (another route with a longer drive and shorter hike is available out of Fresno Dome).

Campsites, facilities: There are 20 sites for tents or RVs up to 20 feet (no hookups). Picnic tables and fire rings are provided. Vault toilets are available. No drinking water is available. Garbage service is located at the entrance to the campground. Leashed pets are permitted.

Reservations, fees: Reservations are not accepted. There is no fee for camping. Open July through October, weather permitting.

Directions: From Fresno, drive north on Highway 41 for 50 miles to Yosemite Forks and County Road 222. Turn right on County Road 222 (keeping to the right at each of two Y intersections) and drive six miles to Pines Village and Beasore Road. Turn left onto Beasore Road and drive 16 miles to the campground.

Contact: Sierra National Forest, Bass Lake Ranger District, 559/877-2218, www.fs.usda.gov/sierra.

36 CLOVER MEADOW

Scenic rating: 8

in Sierra National Forest

Map 10.1, page 547

This is one of two excellent jump-off camps in the area for backpackers; the other is Granite Creek. The camp is set at 7,000 feet elevation, adjacent to the Clover Meadow Ranger Station, where backcountry information is available. While a trail is available from camp heading east into the Ansel Adams Wilderness, most hikers drive about three miles farther northeast on Minarets Road to a trailhead for a five-mile hike to Cora Lakes.

Campsites, facilities: There are seven sites for tents or RVs up to 20 feet (no hookups). Picnic tables and fire rings are provided. Drinking water and vault toilets are available. Garbage must be packed out. Leashed pets are permitted.

Reservations, fees: Reservations are not accepted. There is no fee for camping. Open June through October, weather permitting.

Directions: From Fresno, drive north on Highway 41 for about 25 miles to North Fork Road/County Road 200. Turn right and drive northeast for 17.5 miles to Auberry Road/County Road 222. Turn left (north) and drive one mile to the town of North Fork and Mammoth Pool Road. Turn right and drive 1.5 miles to County Road 225 (still Mammoth Pool Road). Turn right and drive (the road eventually becomes Minarets Road) to the junction with Forest Road 4S81. Bear left (north) on Forest Road 4S81 and drive to the campground entrance road. Bear left (signed "Clover Meadow") and drive to the campground, adjacent to the Clover Meadow Ranger Station. The total distance from North Fork to the entrance road is about 63 miles; it's 20 miles north of the well-signed Mammoth Pool Reservoir on Minarets Road.

Contact: Sierra National Forest, Bass Lake Ranger District, 559/877-2218, www.fs.usda.gov/sierra.

37 GRANITE CREEK AND EQUESTRIAN CAMP

🏃 🏊 🎣 🐴 🚗 ⛺

Scenic rating: 6

in Sierra National Forest

Map 10.1, page 547

This camp is a good jump-off point for backpackers since a trail from camp leads north for five miles to Cora Lakes in the Ansel Adams Wilderness, with the option of continuing to more remote wilderness. Note that nearby Clover Meadow camp (see listing in this chapter) may be more desirable because it has both drinking water to tank up your canteens and a ranger station to obtain the latest trail information. In addition, the upper half of this campground is available for equestrians. The elevation is 6,900 feet.

Campsites, facilities: There are 20 sites for tents or RVs up to 20 feet (no hookups). Picnic tables and fire rings are provided. Vault toilets are available. A horse corral is available in the upper loop. No drinking water is available. Garbage must be packed out. Leashed pets are permitted.

Reservations, fees: Reservations are not accepted. There is no fee for camping. Open June through October, weather permitting.

Directions: From Fresno, drive north on Highway 41 for about 25 miles to North Fork Road/County Road 200. Turn right and drive northeast for 17.5 miles to Auberry Road/County Road 222. Turn left (north) and drive one mile to the town of North Fork and Mammoth Pool Road. Turn right and drive 1.5 miles to County Road 225 (still Mammoth Pool Road). Turn right and drive (the road eventually becomes Minarets Road) to the junction with Forest Road 4S81. Bear left (north) on Forest Road 4S81 and drive to the campground entrance road. Turn left (signed for Granite Creek) and drive 3.5 miles to the campground. (The total distance from North Fork to the entrance road is about 66.5 miles; it's 23.5 miles north of Mammoth Pool Reservoir on the well-signed Minarets Road.)

Contact: Sierra National Forest, Bass Lake Ranger District, 559/877-2218, www.fs.usda.gov/sierra.

38 BUCKEYE

🏃 🏊 ♨ 🐴 ♿ 🚗 ⛺

Scenic rating: 8

near Buckeye Creek in Humboldt-Toiyabe National Forest

Map 10.1, page 547

Here's a little secret: A two-mile hike out of camp heads to the undeveloped Buckeye Hot Springs. That is what inspires campers to bypass the fishing at nearby Robinson Creek (three miles away) and Twin Lakes (six miles away). The camp feels remote and primitive, set at 7,000 feet elevation on the eastern slope of the Sierra near Buckeye Creek. Another secret is that rainbow trout are planted at the little bridge that crosses Buckeye Creek near the campground. A trail that starts near camp is routed through Buckeye Canyon and into the Hoover Wilderness.

Campsites, facilities: There are 68 paved sites for tents or RVs up to 35 feet (no hookups). Picnic tables and fire grills are provided. Vault and flush toilets are available. There is no drinking water. Some facilities are wheelchair-accessible. Leashed pets are permitted.

Reservations, fees: Reservations are not accepted. Sites are $17 per night, $5 per night for each additional vehicle. Open May to mid-October, weather permitting.

Directions: On U.S. 395, drive to Bridgeport and the junction with Twin Lakes Road. Turn west and drive seven miles to Buckeye Road. Turn right (north) on Buckeye Road (dirt, often impassable when wet) and drive 3.5 miles to the campground.

Contact: Humboldt-Toiyabe National Forest, Bridgeport Ranger District, 760/932-7070, www.fs.usda.gov/htnf; West Rec, 760/932-7995.

39 WILLOW SPRINGS MOTEL AND RV PARK

Scenic rating: 6

near Bridgeport

Map 10.1, page 547

Willow Springs RV Park is set at 6,800 feet elevation along U.S. 395, which runs along the eastern Sierra from Carson City south to Bishop and beyond to Lone Pine. The park is one mile from the turnoff to Bodie ghost town. A nice touch to the place is a central campfire that has been in place for more than 50 years. The country is stark here on the edge of the high Nevada desert, but there are many side trips that give the area life. The most popular destinations are to the nearby south: Mono Lake, with its tufa towers and incredible populations of breeding gulls and waterfowl, and the Bodie ghost town. For trout fishing, there's Bridgeport Reservoir to the north (good trolling) and downstream to the East Walker River (fly-fishing), both excellent destinations, as well as Twin Lakes to the west (huge brown trout).

Campsites, facilities: There are 25 sites with full hookups (30 amps) for RVs of any length. A motel is also available. Picnic tables are provided. Restrooms with showers, coin laundry, and campfires are sometimes available. A restaurant is within walking distance. Leashed pets are permitted.

Reservations, fees: Reservations are accepted. Sites are $35 per night, $5 per person per night for more than two people. Open May through October.

Directions: From Bridgeport on U.S. 395, drive five miles south to the park, which is on the east side of the highway.

Contact: Willow Springs Motel and RV Park, 760/932-7725.

40 HONEYMOON FLAT

Scenic rating: 8

on Robinson Creek in Humboldt-Toiyabe National Forest

Map 10.1, page 547

The camp is set beside Robinson Creek at 7,000 feet elevation, in the transition zone between the Sierra Nevada range to the west and the high desert to the east. It is easy to reach on the access road to Twin Lakes, only three miles farther. The lake is famous for occasional huge brown trout. However, the fishing at Robinson Creek is also often quite good, thanks to large numbers of trout planted each year.

Campsites, facilities: There are 35 sites for tents or RVs up to 35 feet (no hookups). Picnic tables and fire grills are provided. Drinking water, food lockers, and vault toilets are available. Some facilities are wheelchair-accessible. Leashed pets are permitted.

Reservations, fees: Reservations are accepted at 877/444-6777 or www.recreation.gov ($9 reservation fee). Sites are $17 per night, double sites are $34, $5 per night for each additional vehicle. Open mid-April through October.

Directions: On U.S. 395, drive to Bridgeport and the junction with Twin Lakes Road. Turn west and drive eight miles to the campground.

Contact: Humboldt-Toiyabe National Forest, Bridgeport Ranger District, 760/932-7070, www.fs.usda.gov/htnf; West Rec, 760/932-7995.

41 PAHA

Scenic rating: 8

near Twin Lakes in Humboldt-Toiyabe National Forest

Map 10.1, page 547

This is one in a series of camps near Robinson Creek and within close range of Twin

Lakes. The elevation at the camp is 7,000 feet. (See the Lower Twin Lake and Honeymoon Flat listings in this chapter for more information.)

Campsites, facilities: There are 22 sites for tents or RVs up to 35 feet (no hookups). Picnic tables and fire grills are provided. Drinking water, flush toilets, garbage bins, and food lockers are available. Two boat launches, a store, coin showers, and a coin laundry are available nearby at Twin Lakes Resort. Some facilities are wheelchair accessible. Leashed pets are permitted.

Reservations, fees: Reservations are accepted at 877/444-6777 or www.recreation.gov ($9 reservation fee). Sites are $20 per night, double sites are $40 per night, $5 per night for each additional vehicle. Open May through October, weather permitting.

Directions: On U.S. 395, drive to Bridgeport and the junction with Twin Lakes Road. Turn west and drive 10 miles to the campground.

Contact: Humboldt-Toiyabe National Forest, Bridgeport Ranger District, 760/932-7070, www.fs.usda.gov/htnf; West Rec, 760/932-7995.

42 ROBINSON CREEK

Scenic rating: 9

near Twin Lakes in
Humboldt-Toiyabe National Forest

Map 10.1, page 547

This campground, one of a series in the area, is set at 7,000 feet elevation on Robinson Creek, not far from Twin Lakes. The campground is divided into two areas. (For recreation options, see the Lower Twin Lake and Honeymoon Flat listings in this chapter.)

Campsites, facilities: There are 54 paved sites for tents or RVs up to 35 feet (no hookups). Picnic tables, food lockers, and fire grills are provided. Drinking water and flush and vault toilets are available. Some facilities are wheelchair-accessible. An amphitheater is

nearby. Boat launches, a store, coin laundry, and coin showers are nearby at Twin Lakes Resort. Leashed pets are permitted.

Reservations, fees: Reservations are accepted at 877/444-6777 or www.recreation.gov ($9 reservation fee). Sites are $20 per night, double sites are $40, $5 per night for each additional vehicle. Open mid-April through October, weather permitting.

Directions: On U.S. 395, drive to Bridgeport and the junction with Twin Lakes Road. Turn west and drive 10 miles to the campground.

Contact: Humboldt-Toiyabe National Forest, Bridgeport Ranger District, 760/932-7070, www.fs.usda.gov/htnf; West Rec, 760/932-7995.

43 CRAGS CAMPGROUND

Scenic rating: 8

on Robinson Creek in
Humboldt-Toiyabe National Forest

Map 10.1, page 547

Crags Campground is set at 7,100 feet elevation in the Sierra, one of a series of campgrounds along Robinson Creek near Lower Twin Lake. While this camp does not offer direct access to Lower Twin, home of giant brown trout, it is very close. (See the Lower Twin Lake and Honeymoon Flat listings in this chapter.)

Campsites, facilities: There are 55 sites for tents or RVs up to 45 feet (no hookups) and a group site for up to 45 people. Picnic tables, food lockers, and fire grills are provided. Drinking water and flush toilets are available. Some facilities are wheelchair-accessible. A boat launch (at Lower Twin Lake), store, coin laundry, and coin showers are within a half mile. Leashed pets are permitted.

Reservations, fees: Reservations are accepted at 877/444-6777 or www.recreation.gov ($9 reservation fee). Single sites are $20 per night, double sites are $40 per night, triple sites are $50 per night, $5 per night for each additional vehicle. The group site is $110 per night. Open mid-May through September, weather permitting.

Directions: On U.S. 395, drive to Bridgeport and the junction with Twin Lakes Road. Turn west and drive 11 miles to South Twin Road (just before reaching Lower Twin Lake). Turn left and drive over the bridge at Robinson Creek to another road on the left. Turn left and drive a short distance to the campground.

Contact: Humboldt-Toiyabe National Forest, Bridgeport Ranger District, 760/932-7070, www.fs.usda.gov/htnf; West Rec, 760/932-7995.

44 LOWER TWIN LAKE
Scenic rating: 9

in Humboldt-Toiyabe National Forest

Map 10.1, page 547

The Twin Lakes are actually two lakes, set high in the eastern Sierra at 7,000 feet elevation. Each lake is unique. Lower Twin, known as the fishing lake, with a 5-mph speed limit, has a full resort, marina, boat ramp, and some of the biggest brown trout in the West. The state-record brown—26.5 pounds—was caught here in 1985. Of course, most of the trout are your typical 10- to 12-inch planted rainbow trout, but nobody seems to mind, with the chance of a true monster-sized fish always in the back of the minds of anglers. Upper Twin Lake, with a resort and marina, is a primary destination for boaters, personal watercraft, water-skiers, swimmers, and sailboarders. These lakes are very popular in summer. An option for campers is an excellent trailhead for hiking near Mono Village at the head of Upper Twin Lake. Here you will find Barney Lake Trail, which is routed up the headwaters of Robinson Creek, steeply at times, to Barney Lake, an excellent day hike.

Campsites, facilities: There are 24 paved sites for tents or RVs up to 35 feet (no hookups).

Picnic tables and fire grills are provided. Drinking water, flush toilets, and food lockers are available. A boat launch, store, coin showers, and a coin laundry are available nearby. Leashed pets are permitted.

Reservations, fees: Reservations are accepted at 877/444-6777 or www.recreation.gov ($9 reservation fee). Sites are $20 per night, $5 per night for each additional vehicle. Open early May through mid-October, weather permitting.

Directions: On U.S. 395, drive to Bridgeport and the junction with Twin Lakes Road. Turn west and drive 11 miles to South Twin Road (just before reaching Lower Twin Lake). Turn left and drive over the bridge at Robinson Creek and to the campground entrance road on the right.

Contact: Humboldt-Toiyabe National Forest, Bridgeport Ranger District, 760/932-7070, www.fs.usda.gov/htnf; West Rec, 760/932-7995.

45 GREEN CREEK
Scenic rating: 7

in Humboldt-Toiyabe National Forest

Map 10.1, page 547

This camp is ideal for backpackers or campers who like to fish for trout in streams. That is because it is set at 7,500 feet, with a trailhead that leads into the Hoover Wilderness and to several high mountain lakes, including Green Lake, West Lake, and East Lake; the ambitious can hike beyond in remote northeastern Yosemite National Park. The camp is set along Green Creek, a fair trout stream with small rainbow trout.

Campsites, facilities: There are 10 sites for tents or RVs up to 35 feet, three double sites, and two group sites for tents or RVs of any length that can accommodate 25–30 people each. No hookups. Picnic tables and fire grills are provided. Drinking water and vault toilets are available. Leashed pets are permitted.

Reservations, fees: Reservations are not accepted for individual sites but are required for group sites at 877/444-6777 or www.recreation.gov ($9 reservation fee). Sites are $17 per night, $5 per night for each additional vehicle, and the group site is $60–75 per night. Open mid-May through early October, weather permitting.

Directions: From Bridgeport, drive south on U.S. 395 for four miles to Green Lakes Road (dirt). Turn right and drive seven miles to the campground.

Contact: Humboldt-Toiyabe National Forest, Bridgeport Ranger District, 760/932-7070, www.fs.usda.gov/htnf; West Rec, 760/932-7995.

46 TRUMBULL LAKE

Scenic rating: 8

in Humboldt-Toiyabe National Forest

Map 10.1, page 547

This is a high-mountain camp (9,500 feet) at the gateway to a beautiful Sierra basin. Little Trumbull Lake is the first lake on the north side of Virginia Lakes Road, with Virginia Lakes set nearby, along with the Hoover Wilderness and access to many other small lakes by trail. A trail is available that is routed just north of Blue Lake, and then it leads west to Frog Lake, Summit Lake, and beyond into a remote area of Yosemite National Park. If you don't want to rough it, cabins, boat rentals, and a restaurant are available at Virginia Lakes Resort. No gas motors, swimming, and water/body contact is permitted at Virginia Lakes.

Campsites, facilities: There are 33 sites for tents or RVs up to 40 feet (no hookups) and a group camp for 20–50 people. Picnic tables and fire grills are provided. Drinking water, garbage bins, and vault toilets are available. A store is nearby at the resort. Some facilities are wheelchair-accessible. Leashed pets are permitted.

Reservations, fees: Reservations are accepted at 877/444-6777 or www.recreation.gov ($9 reservation fee). Single sites are $17 per night, double sites are $34 per night, triple sites are $51 per night, $5 per night for each additional vehicle. Open June through September, weather permitting.

Directions: From Bridgeport, drive south on U.S. 395 for 13.5 miles to Virginia Lakes Road. Turn right on Virginia Lakes Road and drive 6.5 miles to the campground entrance road.

Contact: Humboldt-Toiyabe National Forest, Bridgeport Ranger District, 760/932-7070, www.fs.usda.gov/htnf; West Rec, 760/932-7995.

47 LUNDY CANYON CAMPGROUND

Scenic rating: 7

near Lundy Lake

Map 10.1, page 547

This camp is set high in the eastern Sierra at 7,400 feet elevation along pretty Lundy Creek, the mountain stream that feeds Lundy Lake and then runs downhill, eventually joining other creeks on its trip to nearby Mono Lake. Nearby Lundy Lake (at 7,800 feet elevation) is a long, narrow lake with good fishing for rainbow trout and brown trout. The water is clear and cold, even through the summer. There is a trailhead just west of the lake that is routed steeply up into the Hoover Wilderness to several small pretty lakes, passing two waterfalls about two miles in. A must-do side trip is visiting Mono Lake and its spectacular tufa towers, best done at the Mono Lake Tufa State Reserve along the southern shore of the lake.

Campsites, facilities: There are 37 sites for tents or RVs up to 30 feet (no hookups). Picnic tables and fire rings are provided. Pit toilets are available. No drinking water is available. You can buy supplies in Lee Vining, 8.5 miles away. Some facilities are wheelchair accessible. Leashed pets are permitted.

Reservations, fees: Reservations are not accepted. Sites are $12 per night, with a limit of two vehicles and six people per site. Monthly rates available. Open May through mid-November.
Directions: From Lee Vining, drive north on U.S. 395 for seven miles to Lundy Lake Road. Turn left and drive a short distance to the campground.
Contact: Mono County Public Works, 760/932-5440.

48 TIOGA LAKE

Scenic rating: 9

in Inyo National Forest

Map 10.1, page 547

Tioga Lake is a dramatic sight, with gemlike blue waters encircled by Sierra granite at 9,700 feet elevation. Together with adjacent Ellery Lake, it makes a pair of gorgeous waters with near-lake camping, trout fishing (stocked with rainbow trout), and access to Yosemite National Park and Saddlebag Lake. Conditions here are much like those at neighboring Ellery. The only downers: It can get windy here (no foolin'!) and the camps fill quickly from the overflow crowds at Tuolumne Meadows. (See the Ellery Lake listing for more information.)
Campsites, facilities: There are 12 sites for tents or RVs up to 30 feet (no hookups). Picnic tables, food lockers, and fire grills are provided. Drinking water and pit toilets are available. Some facilities are wheelchair-accessible. Leashed pets are permitted.
Reservations, fees: Reservations are not accepted. Sites are $19 per night. Open early June through mid-October, weather permitting.
Directions: On U.S. 395, drive to just south of Lee Vining and the junction with Highway 120. Turn west on Highway 120 and drive about 11 miles (just past Ellery Lake) to the campground on the left side of the road.

From Merced, drive east on Highway 140

to the Arch Rock entrance station. Continue east to the Big Oak Flat Road junction (0.5 mile before entering Yosemite Valley). Turn left and drive 14 miles to Tioga Road. Turn right and drive about 65 miles (past Tuolumne Meadows) and through the Tioga Pass entrance station. Continue one mile to the campground entrance road on the right side of the road.
Contact: Inyo National Forest, Mono Basin Scenic Area Ranger Station and Visitor Center, 760/647-3044, www.fs.usda.gov/inyo; Inyo Recreation, 760/934-5795.

49 ELLERY LAKE

Scenic rating: 9

in Inyo National Forest

Map 10.1, page 547

Ellery Lake offers all the spectacular beauty of Yosemite but is two miles outside park borders. That means it is stocked with trout by the Department of Fish and Game (no lakes in Yosemite are planted, hence the lousy fishing). Just like neighboring Tioga Lake, here are deep-blue waters set in rock in the 9,500-foot-elevation range, one of the most pristine highway-access lake settings anywhere. Although there is no boat ramp, boats with small motors are allowed and can be hand-launched. Nearby Saddlebag Lake, the highest drive-to lake in California, is a common side trip. Whenever Tuolumne Meadows fills in Yosemite, this camp fills shortly thereafter. Camp elevation is 9,500 feet.
Campsites, facilities: There are 15 sites for tents or RVs up to 30 feet (no hookups). Picnic tables and fire grills are provided. Drinking water, food lockers, and pit toilets are available. A grocery store is nearby. Some facilities are wheelchair-accessible. Leashed pets are permitted.
Reservations, fees: Reservations are not accepted. Sites are $19 per night. Open early June through mid-October, weather permitting.

Directions: On U.S. 395, drive to just south of Lee Vining and the junction with Highway 120. Turn west on Highway 120 and drive about 10 miles to the campground on the left side of the road.

From Merced, drive east on Highway 140 to the Arch Rock entrance station. Continue east to the Big Oak Flat Road junction (0.5 mile before entering Yosemite Valley). Turn left and drive 14 miles to Tioga Road. Turn right and drive about 65 miles (past Tuolumne Meadows) and through the Tioga Pass entrance station. Continue four miles to the campground entrance road on the right.

Contact: Inyo National Forest, Mono Basin Scenic Area Ranger Station and Visitor Center, 760/647-3044, www.fs.usda.gov/inyo; Inyo Recreation, 760/934-5795.

50 JUNCTION

🏃 🏊 🐕 ♿ 🚐 ⛺

Scenic rating: 7

near Ellery and Tioga Lakes in
Inyo National Forest

Map 10.1, page 547

Which way do you go? From Junction, any way you choose, you can't miss. Two miles to the north is Saddlebag Lake, the highest drive-to lake (10,087 feet) in California. Directly across the road is Ellery Lake, and a mile to the south is Tioga Lake, two beautiful, pristine waters with trout fishing. To the east is Mono Lake, and to the west is Yosemite National Park. From camp, it is a one-mile hike to Bennetville, a historic camp. Take your pick. Camp elevation is 9,600 feet.

Campsites, facilities: There are 13 sites for tents or RVs up to 30 feet (no hookups). Picnic tables, food lockers, and fire grills are provided. Pit toilets are available. No drinking water is available. Some facilities are wheelchair-accessible. Leashed pets are permitted.

Reservations, fees: Reservations are not accepted. Sites are $14 per night. Open early June through mid-October, weather permitting.

Directions: On U.S. 395, drive to just south of Lee Vining and the junction with Highway 120. Turn west on Highway 120 and drive about 10 miles to Saddlebag Road and the campground on the right side of the road.

From Merced, drive east on Highway 140 to the Arch Rock entrance station. Continue east to the Big Oak Flat Road junction (0.5 mile before entering Yosemite Valley). Turn left and drive 14 miles to Tioga Road. Turn right and drive about 65 miles (past Tuolumne Meadows) and through the Tioga Pass entrance station. Continue two miles to Saddlebag Lake Road and the campground on the left side of the road.

Contact: Inyo National Forest, Mono Basin Scenic Area Ranger Station and Visitor Center, 760/647-3044, www.fs.usda.gov/inyo; Inyo Recreation, 760/934-5795.

51 SAWMILL WALK-IN

🏃 🐕 ⛺

Scenic rating: 8

near Ellery and Tioga Lakes in
Inyo National Forest

Map 10.1, page 547

This walk-in tent campground features sites peppered above Sawmill Valley and Lee Vining Creek. The first site is a 0.15-mile from the parking lot; sites 11 and 12 (next to the Harvey Monroe Hall National Area border) are 0.2 mile away. Solitude, breathtaking vistas, and hiking opportunities make a stay here an awesome experience. Yosemite National Park and Mono Basin Scenic Area offer nearby side trips. The elevation is 9,700 feet.

Campsites, facilities: There are 12 tent sites. Picnic tables, food lockers, and fire grills are provided. Pit toilets are available. No drinking water is available. Nearby Tioga Pass Resort has limited groceries and supplies. Leashed pets are permitted.

Reservations, fees: Reservations are not accepted. Sites are $14 per night. Open early June through mid-October, weather permitting.

Directions: From Lee Vining, take U.S. 395 south 0.3 mile to the sign for Tioga Pass. Turn right onto Highway 120 and drive west 10.2 miles to Saddlebag Road. Turn left onto Saddlebag Road (gravel) and drive 1.6 miles to campground on left.

Contact: Inyo National Forest, Mono Basin Scenic Area Ranger Station and Visitor Center, 760/647-3044, www.fs.usda.gov/inyo; Inyo Recreation, 760/934-5795.

52 SADDLEBAG LAKE AND TRAILHEAD GROUP

Scenic rating: 10

in Inyo National Forest

Map 10.1, page 547

This camp is set in spectacular high country above tree line, the highest drive-to camp and lake in California, at 10,087 feet elevation. The camp is about a quarter mile from the lake, within walking range of the little store, boat rentals, and a one-minute drive for launching a boat at the ramp. The scenery is stark; everything is granite, ice, or water, with only a few lodgepole pines managing precarious toeholds, sprinkled across the landscape on the access road. An excellent trailhead is available for hiking, with the best hike routed out past little Hummingbird Lake to Lundy Pass. A hikers shuttle boat, which will ferry you across the lake, is a nice plus. Note that with the elevation and the high mountain pass, it can be windy and cold here, and some people find it difficult to catch their breath on simple hikes. In addition, RV users should note that level sites are extremely hard to come by.

Campsites, facilities: There are 19 sites for tents or RVs up to 30 feet (no hookups) at Saddlebag Lake, and one group tent site for up to 25 people at Trailhead. Drinking water, fire grills, and picnic tables are provided. Flush toilets, boat rentals, and a primitive boat launch are available. A grocery store is nearby. Some facilities are wheelchair-accessible. Leashed pets are permitted.

Reservations, fees: Reservations are not accepted for individual sites, but are required for the group site (listed as Trailhead Group) at 877/444-6777 or www.recreation.gov ($9 reservation fee). Sites are $19 per night, $60 per night for the group site. Open late June through early September, weather permitting.

Directions: On U.S. 395, drive 0.5 mile south of Lee Vining and the junction with Highway 120. Turn west and drive about 11 miles to Saddlebag Lake Road. Turn right and drive 2.5 miles to the campground on the right.

From Merced, drive east on Highway 140 to the Arch Rock entrance station. Continue east to the Big Oak Flat Road junction (0.5 mile before entering Yosemite Valley). Turn left and drive 14 miles to Tioga Road. Turn right and drive about 65 miles (past Tuolumne Meadows) and through the Tioga Pass entrance station. Continue two miles to Saddlebag Lake Road. Turn left and drive 2.5 miles (rough road) to the campground on the right.

Contact: Inyo National Forest, Mono Basin Scenic Area Ranger Station and Visitor Center, 760/647-3044, www.fs.usda.gov/inyo; Inyo Recreation, 760/934-5795.

53 BIG BEND

Scenic rating: 8

on Lee Vining Creek in Inyo National Forest

Map 10.1, page 547

This camp is set in sparse but beautiful country along Lee Vining Creek at 7,800 feet elevation. Ancient pine trees are on site. It is an excellent bet for an overflow camp if Tuolumne Meadows in nearby Yosemite is packed. The view from the camp to the north features Mono Dome (10,614 feet) and Lee Vining Peak (11,691 feet).

Campsites, facilities: There are 17 sites for tents or RVs up to 30 feet (no hookups). Picnic

tables, food lockers, and fire grills are provided. Drinking water and vault toilets are available. Some facilities are wheelchair-accessible. Leashed pets are permitted.

Reservations, fees: Reservations are not accepted. Sites are $19 per night. A 14-day limit is enforced. Open late April through mid-October, weather permitting.

Directions: On U.S. 395, drive to just south of Lee Vining and the junction with Highway 120. Turn west on Highway 120 and drive about 3.5 miles to Poole Power Plant Road and the signed campground access road on the right. Turn right and drive a short distance to the camp.

Contact: Inyo National Forest, Mono Basin Scenic Area Ranger Station and Visitor Center, 760/647-3044, www.fs.usda.gov/inyo.

54 ASPEN

Scenic rating: 8

on Lee Vining Creek

Map 10.1, page 547

This high-country, primitive camp is set along Lee Vining Creek at 7,500 feet elevation, on the eastern slopes of the Sierra just east of Yosemite National Park. Take the side trip to moonlike Mono Lake, best seen at the south shore's Tufa State Reserve.

Campsites, facilities: There are 56 sites for tents or RVs up to 40 feet (no hookups). Picnic tables and fire rings are provided. Drinking water and vault toilets are available. You can buy supplies in Lee Vining. Leashed pets are permitted.

Reservations, fees: Reservations are not accepted. Sites are $14 per night. A 14-day limit is enforced. Open May through October, weather permitting.

Directions: On U.S. 395, drive to just south of Lee Vining and the junction with Highway 120. Turn west on Highway 120 and drive about 3.5 miles. Exit onto Poole Power Plant Road. Turn left and drive about four miles west to the campground on the left.

Contact: Inyo National Forest, Mono Basin Scenic Area Ranger Station and Visitor Center, 760/647-3044, www.fs.usda.gov/inyo.

55 MORAINE CAMP

Scenic rating: 7

near Lee Vining

Map 10.1, page 547

This camp provides an alternative to Yosemite National Park. (For more information, see the Lower Lee Vining Camp listing in this chapter.)

Campsites, facilities: There are 27 sites for tents or RVs up to 40 feet (no hookups). Picnic tables and fire rings are provided. Pit toilets are available. There is no drinking water. You can buy supplies in Lee Vining (about two miles away). Leashed pets are permitted.

Reservations, fees: Reservations are not accepted. Sites are $14 per night. Open May through October, weather permitting.

Directions: On U.S. 395, drive to just south of Lee Vining and the junction with Highway 120. Turn west on Highway 120 and drive 3.5 miles to Poole Power Plant Road. Exit left onto Poole Power Plant Road and drive 0.25 mile to the campground entrance at the end of the road.

Contact: Inyo National Forest, Mono Basin Scenic Area Ranger Station and Visitor Center, 760/647-3044, www.fs.usda.gov/inyo.

56 CATTLEGUARD CAMP

Scenic rating: 7

near Lee Vining

Map 10.1, page 547

The Forest Service only opens this campground during a busy camping season as an alternative to Yosemite National Park. Though primitive, it has several advantages: It is quiet, gets more sun than the two neighboring camps (Lower Lee Vining and Moraine), and provides the best views of Dana Plateau. (For more information, see the Lower Lee Vining Camp listing in this chapter.)

Campsites, facilities: There are 16 sites for tents or RVs up to 40 feet (no hookups). Picnic tables, food lockers, and fire rings are provided. Pit toilets are available. No drinking water is available. You can buy supplies in Lee Vining (about two miles away). Leashed pets are permitted.

Reservations, fees: Reservations are not accepted. Sites are $15 per night. A 14-day limit is enforced. Open May through October, weather permitting.

Directions: On U.S. 395, drive to just south of Lee Vining and the junction with Highway 120. Turn west on Highway 120 and drive about three miles. Turn left into the campground entrance.

Contact: Inyo National Forest, Mono Basin Scenic Area Ranger Station and Visitor Center, 760/647-3044, www.fs.usda.gov/inyo.

57 LOWER LEE VINING CAMP

Scenic rating: 7

near Lee Vining

Map 10.1, page 547

This former Mono County camp and its neighboring camps—Cattleguard, Moraine, Aspen, and Big Bend—can be a godsend for vacationers who show up at Yosemite National Park and make the discovery that there are no sites left, a terrible experience for some late-night arrivals. But these Forest Service campgrounds provide a great safety valve, even if they are extremely primitive, on the edge of timber. Lee Vining Creek is the highlight, flowing right past the campgrounds along Highway 120, bound for Mono Lake to the nearby east. It is stocked regularly during the fishing season. A must-do side trip is venturing to the south shore of Mono Lake to walk amid the bizarre yet beautiful tufa towers. There is good rock-climbing and hiking in the area. Although sunshine is the norm, be prepared for all kinds of weather: It can snow

every month of the year here. Short but lively thunderstorms are common in early summer. Other nearby trips are available to Mammoth Lakes, June Lake, and Bodie State Park.

Campsites, facilities: There are 54 sites for tents or RVs up to 40 feet (no hookups). Picnic tables, food lockers, and fire rings are provided. Vault toilets are available. No drinking water is available. You can buy supplies in Lee Vining (about two miles away). Leashed pets are permitted.

Reservations, fees: Reservations are not accepted. Sites are $14 per night. Open May through October, weather permitting.

Directions: On U.S. 395, drive to just south of Lee Vining and the junction with Highway 120. Turn west on Highway 120 and drive about 2.5 miles. Turn left into the campground entrance.

Contact: Inyo National Forest, Mono Basin Scenic Area Ranger Station and Visitor Center, 760/647-3044, www.fs.usda.gov/inyo.

58 SILVER LAKE

Scenic rating: 9

in Inyo National Forest

Map 10.1, page 547

Silver Lake is set at 7,200 feet elevation, an 80-acre lake in the June Lake Loop with Carson Peak looming in the background. Boat rentals, fishing for trout at the lake, a beautiful trout stream (Rush Creek) next to the camp, and a nearby trailhead for wilderness hiking and horseback riding (rentals available) are the highlights. The camp is largely exposed and vulnerable to winds, the only downer. Within walking distance to the south is Silver Lake, always a pretty sight, especially when afternoon winds cause the lake surface to sparkle in crackling silvers. The lake speed limit is 10 mph. Swimming is not recommended because of the rocky shoreline. Just across the road from the camp is a great trailhead for the Ansel Adams Wilderness, with a two-hour hike that climbs to pretty

Agnew Lake overlooking the June Lake basin; wilderness permit required for overnight use.

Campsites, facilities: There are 63 sites for tents or RVs up to 40 feet (no hookups). Picnic tables, food lockers, and fire rings are provided. Drinking water, flush toilets, and horseback-riding facilities are available. A grocery store, coin laundry, motorboat rentals, boat ramp, bait, café, boat fuel, and propane gas are nearby. Some facilities are wheelchair-accessible. Leashed pets are permitted.

Reservations, fees: Reservations are accepted at 877/444-6777 or www.recreation.gov ($9 reservation fee). Sites are $18–20 per night, $5 for each additional vehicle. A 14-day limit is enforced. Open late April through early November, weather permitting.

Directions: From Lee Vining on U.S. 395, drive south for six miles to the first Highway 158 north/June Lake Loop turnoff. Turn west (right) and drive nine miles (past Grant Lake) to Silver Lake. Just as you arrive at Silver Lake (a small store is on the right), turn left at the campground entrance.

Contact: Inyo National Forest, Mono Basin Scenic Area Ranger Station and Visitor Center, 760/647-3044, www.fs.usda.gov/inyo; Inyo Recreation, 760/934-5795.

59 OH! RIDGE

Scenic rating: 8

on June Lake in Inyo National Forest

Map 10.1, page 547

This is the largest of the campgrounds on June Lake. However, it is not the most popular since it is not right on the lakeshore, but back about a quarter mile or so from the north end of the lake. Regardless, it has the best views of the lake, with the ridge of the high Sierra providing a backdrop. The lake is a good one for trout fishing. The elevation is 7,600 feet.

Campsites, facilities: There are 147 sites for tents or RVs up to 40 feet (no hookups). Picnic tables and fire grills are provided. Drinking

water, flush toilets, and a swimming beach are available. A grocery store, coin laundry, volleyball, amphitheater, boat ramp, boat and tackle rentals, moorings, and propane gas are nearby. Some facilities are wheelchair-accessible. Leashed pets are permitted.

Reservations, fees: Reservations are accepted at 877/444-6777 or www.recreation.gov ($9 reservation fee). Sites are $21–23 per night. Open late April through early November, weather permitting.

Directions: From Lee Vining, drive south on U.S. 395 (past the first Highway 158/June Lake Loop turnoff) to June Lake Junction (a gas station/store is on the west side of the road) and Highway 158 south. Turn west on Highway 158 south and drive two miles to Oh! Ridge Road. Turn right and drive a mile to the campground access road (signed). Turn left and drive to the campground.

Contact: Inyo National Forest, Mono Basin Scenic Area Ranger Station and Visitor Center, 760/647-3044, www.fs.usda.gov/inyo; Inyo Recreation, 760/934-5795.

60 PINE CLIFF RESORT

Scenic rating: 7

at June Lake

Map 10.1, page 547   BEST (

You'll find "kid heaven" at Pine Cliff Resort. This camp is in a pretty setting along the north shore of June Lake (7,600 feet elevation), the feature lake among four in the June Lake Loop. The campsites are nestled in pine trees, designed so each site accommodates different-sized rigs and families, and the campground is set about a quarter mile from June Lake. This is the only camp at June Lake Loop that has a swimming beach. The landscape is a pretty one, with the lake set below snowcapped peaks. The bonus is that June Lake gets large numbers of trout plants each summer, making it extremely popular with anglers. Of the lakes in the June Lake Loop, this is the one that has the most of everything—the most beauty, the most fish, the most developed accommodations, and, alas, the most people. This resort has been operated as a family business for more than 50 years.

Campsites, facilities: There are 154 sites with full hookups (20 and 30 amps) for RVs, 17 sites with partial hookups (20 and 30 amps) for tents or RVs, and 55 sites for tents; a few sites are pull-through. There are also 14 rental trailers. Picnic tables and fire rings are provided. Restrooms with flush toilets and coin showers, drinking water, coin laundry, basketball, volleyball, tetherball, horseshoes, convenience store, and propane gas are available. Some facilities are wheelchair-accessible. A primitive boat ramp, fish-cleaning facilities, and fuel are nearby. Leashed pets are permitted, with a maximum of two pets per site.

Reservations, fees: Reservations are recommended. Sites are $18–28 per night, $5 per night for each additional vehicle, $1 per person per night for more than four people. The first pet is free, and the second pet is $1 per night. Open mid-April through October.

Directions: From Lee Vining, drive south on U.S. 395 (passing the first Highway 158 north/June Lake Loop turnoff) to June Lake Junction (a sign is posted for "June Lake Village") and Highway 158 south. Turn right (west) on Highway 158 south and drive two miles to North Shore Drive (a sign is nearby for Pine Cliff Resort). Turn right and drive 0.5 mile to Pine Cliff Road. Turn left and drive 0.5 mile to the resort store on the right (route is well signed).

Contact: Pine Cliff Resort, 760/648-7558, www.pinecliffresort.net.

61 GULL LAKE

Scenic rating: 8

in Inyo National Forest

Map 10.1, page 547

Little Gull Lake, just 64 acres, is the smallest of the lakes on the June Lake Loop, but to many it is the prettiest. It is set at 7,600 feet, just west of June Lake and, with Carson Peak looming on the Sierra crest to the west, it is a dramatic and intimate setting. The lake is stocked with trout each summer, providing good fishing. A boat ramp is on the lake's southwest corner. Insider's tip: There is a rope swing at Gull Lake that youngsters love.

Campsites, facilities: There are 11 sites for tents or RVs up to 30 feet (no hookups). Drinking water, fire grills, and picnic tables are provided, and flush toilets are available. A grocery store, coin laundry, boat ramp, and propane gas are nearby. Some facilities are wheelchair-accessible. Leashed pets are permitted.

Reservations, fees: Reservations are not accepted. Sites are $20 per night. Open late April through early November, weather permitting.

Directions: From Lee Vining, drive south on U.S. 395 (past the first Highway 158/June Lake Loop turnoff) to June Lake Junction (a gas station/store is on the west side of the road) and Highway 158. Turn west on Highway 158 and drive three miles to the campground entrance on the right side of the road.

Contact: Inyo National Forest, Mono Basin Scenic Area Ranger Station and Visitor Center, 760/647-3044, www.fs.usda.gov/inyo; Inyo Recreation, 760/934-5795.

62 REVERSED CREEK

Scenic rating: 6

in Inyo National Forest

Map 10.1, page 547

This camp is set at 7,600 feet elevation near pretty Reversed Creek, the only stream in the region that flows toward the mountains, not away from them. It is a small, tree-lined stream that provides decent trout fishing. The campsites are sheltered and set in a grove of aspen, but close enough to the road so you can still hear highway traffic. There are also cabins available for rent near here. Directly opposite the camp, on the other side of the road, is Gull Lake and the boat ramp. Two miles to the west, on the west side of the road, is the trailhead for the hike to Fern Lake on the edge of the Ansel Adams Wilderness, a little butt-kicker of a climb.

Campsites, facilities: There are 15 sites for tents or RVs up to 30 feet (no hookups). Picnic tables and fire grills are provided. Drinking water and flush toilets are available. A grocery store, coin laundry, and propane gas are nearby. Boating is available at nearby Silver Lake, two miles away. Some facilities are wheelchair-accessible. Leashed pets are permitted.

Reservations, fees: Reservations are accepted at 877/444-6777 or www.recreation.gov ($9 reservation fee). Sites are $20 per night. Open mid-May through October, weather permitting.

Directions: From Lee Vining, drive south on U.S. 395 (past the first Highway 158/June Lake Loop turnoff) to June Lake Junction (a gas station/store is on the west side of the road) and Highway 158 south. Turn right (west) on Highway 158 south and drive three miles to the campground on the left side of the road (across from Gull Lake).

Contact: Inyo National Forest, Mono Basin Scenic Area Ranger Station and Visitor Center, 760/647-3044, www.fs.usda.gov/inyo; Inyo Recreation, 760/934-5795.

This one is on the northeast shore of the lake at 7,600 feet elevation, a pretty spot with all supplies available just two miles to the south in the town of June Lake. The nearest boat launch is north of town. This is a good lake for trout fishing, receiving high numbers of stocked trout each year. A 10-mph speed limit is enforced.

Campsites, facilities: There are 28 sites for tents or RVs up to 32 feet (no hookups). Picnic tables, food lockers, and fire grills are provided. Drinking water, restrooms with flush toilets and coin showers, and boat ramp are available. A grocery store, coin laundry, boat and tackle rentals, moorings, and propane gas are nearby. Leashed pets are permitted.

Reservations, fees: Reservations are accepted at 877/444-6777 or www.recreation.gov ($9 reservation fee). Sites are $20 per night. Open late April through early November, weather permitting.

Directions: From Lee Vining, drive south on U.S. 395 (passing Highway 158 North) for 20 miles (six miles past Highway 158 north) to June Lake Junction (signed "June Lake Village") and Highway 158 south. Turn west (right) on Highway 158 south and drive two miles to June Lake. Turn right (signed) and drive a short distance to the campground.

Contact: Inyo National Forest, Mono Basin Scenic Area Ranger Station and Visitor Center, 760/647-3044, www.fs.usda.gov/inyo; Inyo Recreation, 760/934-5795.

63 JUNE LAKE

Scenic rating: 9

in Inyo National Forest

Map 10.1, page 547

June Lake gets the highest use of all the lakes in the June Lakes Loop, and it has the best swimming, best fishing, and best sailboarding. There are three campgrounds at pretty June Lake; this is one of the two operated by the Forest Service (the other is Oh! Ridge).

64 HARTLEY SPRINGS

Scenic rating: 8

in Inyo National Forest

Map 10.1, page 547

Even though this camp is only a five-minute drive from U.S. 395, those five minutes will take you into another orbit. It is set in a forest of Jeffrey pine and has the feel of a remote, primitive camp, set in a high-mountain environment at an elevation of 8,400 feet. About two miles to the immediate north, at 8,611 feet, is Obsidian Dome "Glass Flow," a craggy geologic formation that some people enjoy scrambling around and exploring; pick your access point carefully.

Campsites, facilities: There are 20 sites for tents or RVs up to 40 feet (no hookups). Picnic tables and fire grills are provided. Vault toilets are available. No drinking water is available. Garbage must be packed out. Leashed pets are permitted.

Reservations, fees: Reservations are not accepted. There is no fee for camping. Open late May through early November, weather permitting.

Directions: From Lee Vining, drive south on U.S. 395 (passing the first Highway 158/June Lake Loop turnoff) for 10 miles to June Lake Junction. Continue south on U.S. 395 for six miles to Glass Creek Road (a dirt road on the west side of the highway). Turn west (right) and drive two miles to the campground entrance road on the left.

Contact: Inyo National Forest, Mono Basin Scenic Area Ranger Station and Visitor Center, 760/647-3044, www.fs.usda.gov/inyo.

65 AGNEW MEADOWS AND EQUESTRIAN CAMP

Scenic rating: 9

in Inyo National Forest

Map 10.1, page 547   BEST (

This is a perfect camp to use as a launching pad for a backpacking trip or day of fly-fishing for trout. It is set along the Upper San Joaquin River at 8,400 feet, with a trailhead for the Pacific Crest Trail available near the camp. From here you can hike seven miles to the gorgeous Thousand Island Lake, a beautiful lake sprinkled with islands set below Banner and Ritter Peaks in the spectacular Minarets. For day hiking, walk the River Trail, which is routed from Agnew Meadows along the San Joaquin. The trail provides access to excellent fishing with a chance at the grand slam of California trout—four species in a single day (though the trout are small).

Campsites, facilities: There are 21 sites for tents or RVs up to 45 feet, and four group sites for tents or RVs that can accommodate 10–20 people each. No hookups. Picnic tables and fire grills are provided. Drinking water, vault toilets, and horseback-riding facilities are available (three family sites have hitching racks where horse camping is permitted). Supplies can be obtained at Red's Meadow store. Some facilities are wheelchair accessible. Leashed pets are permitted.

Reservations, fees: Reservations are not accepted for individual sites, but are required for equestrian sites and group sites at 877/444-6777 or www.recreation.gov ($9 reservation fee). Sites are $20 per night for individual sites, $31–63 per night group sites, $22 per night for equestrian site, plus $4–7 per person Reds Meadow/Agnew Meadows access fee. Open mid-June through mid-September, weather permitting.

Directions: On U.S. 395, drive to Mammoth Junction/Highway 203. Turn west on Highway 203 and drive four miles, through the town of Mammoth Lakes to Minaret Road (still Highway 203). Turn right and drive five miles to Minaret Station (past the Mammoth Mountain Ski Area). Continue for 2.6 miles to the campground entrance road on the right. Turn right and drive just under a mile to the campground. Note: The access road to the group sites is steep and narrow.

Note: Noncampers are required to use a shuttle bus (fee) from the shuttle bus terminal at Mammoth Mountain Main Lodge Gondola Station 7 A.M.–7:30 P.M. Space is available for leashed dogs, bikes, and backpacks.

Contact: Inyo National Forest, Mono Basin Scenic Area Ranger Station and Visitor Center, 760/647-3044, www.fs.usda.gov/inyo; Inyo Recreation, 760/934-5795.

66 PUMICE FLAT

Scenic rating: 8

on the San Joaquin River in
Inyo National Forest

Map 10.1, page 547

Pumice Flat (7,700 feet elevation) provides roadside camping within short range of several adventures. A trail out of camp links with the Pacific Crest Trail, where you can hike along the Upper San Joaquin River for miles, with excellent access for fly-fishing, and head north into the Ansel Adams Wilderness. Devils Postpile National Monument is just two miles south, along with the trailhead for Rainbow Falls.

Campsites, facilities: There are 17 sites for tents or RVs up to 45 feet (no hookups). Picnic tables and fire grills are provided. Drinking water, vault toilets, and horseback-riding facilities are available. Limited supplies are available at a small store, or buy full supplies in Mammoth Lakes. Leashed pets are permitted.

Reservations, fees: Reservations are not accepted. Sites are $20 per night, plus $4–7 per person Reds Meadow/Agnew Meadows access fee. Open mid-June through mid-September, weather permitting.

Directions: On U.S. 395, drive to Mammoth Junction/Highway 203. Turn west on Highway 203 and drive four miles, through the town of Mammoth Lakes to Minaret Road (still Highway 203). Turn right and drive five miles to Minaret Station (past the Mammoth Mountain Ski Area). Continue for 5.1 miles to the campground on the right.

Note: Noncampers are required to use a shuttle bus (fee) from the shuttle bus terminal at Mammoth Mountain Main Lodge Gondola Station 7 A.M.–7:30 P.M. Space is available for leashed dogs, bikes, and backpacks.

Contact: Inyo National Forest, Mono Basin Scenic Area Ranger Station and Visitor Center, 760/647-3044, www.fs.usda.gov/inyo; Inyo Recreation, 760/934-5795.

67 UPPER SODA SPRINGS

Scenic rating: 8

on the San Joaquin River in
Inyo National Forest

Map 10.1, page 547

This is a premium location within earshot of the Upper San Joaquin River and within minutes of many first-class recreation options. The river is stocked with trout at this camp, with several good pools within short walking distance. Farther upstream, accessible by an excellent trail, are smaller wild trout that provide good fly-fishing prospects. Devils Postpile National Monument, a massive formation of ancient columnar jointed rock, is only three miles to the south. The Pacific Crest Trail passes right by the camp, providing a trailhead for access to numerous lakes in the Ansel Adams Wilderness. The elevation is 7,700 feet.

Campsites, facilities: There are 26 sites for tents or RVs up to 36 feet (no hookups). Picnic tables and fire grills are provided. Drinking water, flush toilets, and horseback-riding facilities are available. Limited supplies can be obtained at Red's Meadow store. Leashed pets are permitted.

Reservations, fees: Reservations are not accepted. Sites are $20 per night, plus $4–7 per person Reds Meadow/Agnew Meadows access fee. Open mid-June through mid-September, weather permitting.

Directions: On U.S. 395, drive to Mammoth Junction/Highway 203. Turn west on Highway 203 and drive four miles, through the town of Mammoth Lakes to Minaret Road (still Highway 203). Turn right and drive five miles to Minaret Station (past the Mammoth Mountain Ski Area). Continue for 5.1 miles to the campground entrance road on the right. Turn right and drive 0.25 mile to the campground.

Note: Noncampers are required to use a shuttle bus (fee) from the shuttle bus terminal at Mammoth Mountain Main Lodge Gondola

Station 7 A.M.–7:30 P.M. Space is available for leashed dogs, bikes, and backpacks.

Contact: Inyo National Forest, Mono Basin Scenic Area Ranger Station and Visitor Center, 760/647-3044, www.fs.usda.gov/inyo; Inyo Recreation, 760/934-5795.

68 PUMICE FLAT GROUP CAMP
🏃 🛶 🏕 🚐 ⛺

Scenic rating: 6

on the San Joaquin River in
Inyo National Forest

Map 10.1, page 547

Pumice Flat Group Camp is set at 7,700 feet elevation near the Upper San Joaquin River, adjacent to Pumice Flat. (For recreation information, see the Pumice Flat listing in this chapter.)

Campsites, facilities: There are four group sites for tents or RVs up to 45 feet (no hookups) that can accommodate 20–50 people each. Picnic tables and fire grills are provided. Drinking water, flush toilets, and horseback-riding facilities are available. You can buy supplies in Mammoth Lakes. Leashed pets are permitted.

Reservations, fees: Reservations are accepted at 877/444-6777 or www.recreation.gov ($9 reservation fee). Sites are $61–134 per night per group, plus $4–7 per person Reds Meadow/Agnew Meadows access fee. Open mid-June through mid-September, weather permitting.

Directions: On U.S. 395, drive to Mammoth Junction/Highway 203. Turn west on Highway 203 and drive four miles, through the town of Mammoth Lakes to Minaret Road (still Highway 203). Turn right and drive five miles to Minaret Station (past the Mammoth Mountain Ski Area). Continue for 5.1 miles to the campground on the left side of the road.

Note: Noncampers are required to use a shuttle bus (fee) from the shuttle bus terminal at Mammoth Mountain Main Lodge Gondola

69 MINARET FALLS
🏃 🛶 🏕 ♿ 🚐 ⛺

Scenic rating: 8

on the San Joaquin River in
Inyo National Forest

Map 10.1, page 547

This camp has one of the prettiest settings of the series of camps along the Upper San Joaquin River and near Devils Postpile National Monument. It is set at 7,600 feet elevation near Minaret Creek, across from where beautiful Minaret Falls pours into the San Joaquin River. Devils Postpile National Monument, one of the best examples in the world of hexagonal, columnar jointed rock, is less than a mile from camp, where there is also a trail to awesome Rainbow Falls. The Pacific Crest Trail runs right through this area as well, and if you hike to the south, there is excellent streamside fishing access.

Campsites, facilities: There are 26 sites for tents or RVs up to 47 feet (no hookups). Picnic tables and fire grills are provided. Drinking water and vault toilets are available. Horse-back-riding facilities are nearby. You can buy limited supplies at Red's Meadow store, or all supplies in Mammoth Lakes. Some facilities are wheelchair-accessible. Leashed pets are permitted.

Reservations, fees: Reservations are not accepted. Sites are $20 per night, plus $4–7 per person Reds Meadow/Agnew Meadows access fee. Open mid-June through mid-September, weather permitting.

Directions: On U.S. 395, drive to Mammoth Junction/Highway 203. Turn west on Highway 203 and drive four miles, through the town of Mammoth Lakes to Minaret Road (still Highway 203). Turn right and drive five miles to Minaret Station (past the Mammoth Mountain Ski Area). Continue for six miles to the campground entrance road on the right. Turn right and drive 0.25 mile to the campground.

Note: Noncampers are required to use a shuttle bus from the shuttle bus terminal at Mammoth Mountain Main Lodge Gondola Station 7 A.M.–7:30 P.M. Space is available for leashed dogs, bikes, and backpacks.

Contact: Inyo National Forest, Mono Basin Scenic Area Ranger Station and Visitor Center, 760/647-3044, www.fs.usda.gov/inyo; Inyo Recreation, 760/934-5795.

70 DEVILS POSTPILE NATIONAL MONUMENT

Scenic rating: 9

near the San Joaquin River

Map 10.1, page 547

Devils Postpile is a spectacular and rare example of hexagonal, columnar jointed rock that looks like posts, hence the name. The camp is set at 7,600 feet elevation and provides nearby access for the easy hike to the Postpile. Guided walks are offered during the summer; call for details. If you keep walking, it is a 2.5-mile walk to Rainbow Falls, a breathtaking 101-foot cascade that produces rainbows in its floating mist, seen only from the trail alongside the waterfall looking downstream. The camp is also adjacent to the Middle Fork San Joaquin River and the Pacific Crest Trail.

Campsites, facilities: There are 21 sites for tents or RVs up to 25 feet (no hookups). Picnic tables, food lockers, and fire grills are provided. Drinking water and flush toilets are available. Some facilities are wheelchair-accessible. Leashed pets are permitted.

Reservations, fees: Reservations are not accepted. Sites are $14 per night, plus $4–7 per person Reds Meadow/Devils Postpile access fee. Open mid-June through mid-October, weather permitting, with a two-week maximum stay. Note: National Parks Pass and Golden Passport are not accepted.

Directions: On U.S. 395, drive to Mammoth Junction/Highway 203. Turn west on Highway 203 and drive four miles, through the town of Mammoth Lakes to Minaret Road (still Highway 203). Turn right and drive five miles to Minaret Station (past the Mammoth Mountain Ski Area). Continue for nine miles to the campground entrance road on the right.

Note: Noncampers are required to use a shuttle bus from the shuttle bus terminal at Mammoth Mountain Main Lodge Gondola Station 7 A.M.–7:30 P.M. Space is available for leashed dogs, bikes, and backpacks.

Contact: Devils Postpile National Monument, 760/934-2289, www.nps.gov/depo.

71 RED'S MEADOW

Scenic rating: 6

in Inyo National Forest

Map 10.1, page 547

Red's Meadow has long been established as one of the best outfitters for horseback-riding trips. To get the feel of it, three-mile round-trip rides are available to Rainbow Falls. Multiday trips into the Ansel Adams Wilderness on the Pacific Crest Trail are also offered. A small restaurant is a bonus here, always a must-stop for long-distance hikers getting a shot to chomp their first hamburger in weeks, something like a bear finding a candy bar, quite a sight for the drive-in campers. The nearby Devils Postpile National Monument, Rainbow Falls, Minaret Falls, and San Joaquin River provide recreation options. The elevation is 7,600 feet.

Campsites, facilities: There are 52 sites for tents or RVs up to 30 feet (no hookups). Picnic tables, food lockers, and fire grills are provided. Drinking water, flush toilets, horseback riding, and natural hot springs are available. You can buy limited supplies at a small store. Leashed pets are permitted.

Reservations, fees: Reservations are not accepted. Sites are $20 per night, plus $4–7 per person Reds Meadow/Agnew Meadows access fee. Open mid-June through mid-September, weather permitting.

Directions: On U.S. 395, drive to Mammoth Junction/Highway 203. Turn west on Highway 203 and drive four miles, through the town of Mammoth Lakes to Minaret Road (still Highway 203). Turn right and drive five miles to Minaret Station (past the Mammoth Mountain Ski Area). Continue for 7.4 miles to the campground entrance on the left.

Note: Noncampers are required to use a shuttle bus from the shuttle bus terminal at Mammoth Mountain Main Lodge Gondola Station 7 A.M.–7:30 P.M. Space is available for leashed dogs, bikes, and backpacks.

Contact: Inyo National Forest, Mono Basin Scenic Area Ranger Station and Visitor Center, 760/647-3044, www.fs.usda.gov/inyo; Inyo Recreation, 760/934-5795.

72 LAKE GEORGE
🚶‍♀️ 🛶 🎣 🏕️ 🐕 🚐 ⛺

Scenic rating: 8

in Inyo National Forest

Map 10.1, page 547

The sites here have views of Lake George, a beautiful lake in a rock basin set below the spectacular Crystal Crag. Lake George is at 9,000 feet elevation, a small lake fed by creeks coming from both Crystal Lake and TJ Lake. TJ Lake is only about a 20-minute walk from the campground, and Crystal Lake is about a 45-minute romp; both make excellent short hiking trips. Trout fishing at Lake George is decent—not great, not bad, but decent. Swimming is not allowed, but boats with small motors are permitted.

Campsites, facilities: There are 16 sites for tents or RVs up to 25 feet (no hookups). Picnic tables and fire grills are provided. Drinking water and flush toilets are available. A grocery store, coin laundry, coin showers, primitive

boat launch, and propane gas are nearby. Leashed pets are permitted.

Reservations, fees: Reservations are not accepted. Sites are $21 per night with a seven-day limit. Open mid-June through mid-September, weather permitting.

Directions: From Lee Vining on U.S. 395, drive south for 25 miles to Mammoth Junction and Highway 203/Minaret Summit Road. Turn west on Highway 203 and drive four miles to Lake Mary Road. Continue straight through the intersection and drive four miles to Lake Mary Loop Drive. Turn left and drive 0.3 mile to Lake George Road. Turn right and drive 0.5 mile to the campground.

Contact: Inyo National Forest, Mono Basin Scenic Area Ranger Station and Visitor Center, 760/647-3044, www.fs.usda.gov/inyo; Inyo Recreation, 760/934-5795.

73 GLASS CREEK
🚶‍♀️ 🛶 🎣 🐕 ♿ 🚐 ⛺

Scenic rating: 5

in Inyo National Forest

Map 10.2, page 548

This primitive camp is set along Glass Creek at 7,600 feet elevation, about a mile from Obsidian Dome to the nearby west. A trail follows Glass Creek past the southern edge of the dome, a craggy, volcanic formation that tops out at 8,611 feet elevation. That trail continues along Glass Creek, climbing to the foot of San Joaquin Mountain for a great view of the high desert to the east. Insider's tip: The Department of Fish and Game stocks Glass Creek with trout just once each June, right at the camp.

Campsites, facilities: There are 50 sites for tents or RVs up to 40 feet (no hookups). Picnic tables and fire grills are provided. Vault toilets are available. No drinking water is available. Some facilities are wheelchair-accessible. Leashed pets are permitted.

Reservations, fees: Reservations are not accepted. There is no fee for camping. A 42-

day limit is enforced. Open late April through early November, weather permitting.

Directions: From Lee Vining, drive south on U.S. 395 (past the first Highway 158/June Lake Loop turnoff) for 11 miles to June Lake Junction. Continue south on U.S. 395 for six miles to a Forest Service road (Glass Creek Road). Turn west (right) and drive 0.25 mile to the camp access road on the right. Turn right and continue 0.5 mile to the main camp at the end of the road. Two notes: 1. A primitive area with large RV sites can be used as an overflow area on the right side of the access road. 2. If arriving from the south on U.S. 395, a direct left turn to Glass Creek Road is impossible. Heading north you will pass the CalTrans Crestview Maintenance Station on the right. Continue north, make a U-turn when possible, and follow the above directions.

Contact: Inyo National Forest, Mono Basin Scenic Area Ranger Station and Visitor Center, 760/647-3044, www.fs.usda.gov/inyo.

74 BIG SPRINGS

Scenic rating: 5

on Deadman Creek in Inyo National Forest

Map 10.2, page 548

Big Springs, at 7,300 feet elevation, is set on the edge of the high desert on the east side of U.S. 395. The main attractions are Deadman Creek, which runs right by the camp, and Big Springs, which is set just on the opposite side of the river. There are several hot springs in the area, best reached by driving south on U.S. 395 to the Mammoth Lakes Airport and turning left on Hot Creek Road. As with all hot springs, use at your own risk.

Campsites, facilities: There are 26 sites for tents or RVs up to 40 feet (no hookups). Picnic tables and fire grills are provided. Vault toilets are available. No drinking water is available. Leashed pets are permitted.

Reservations, fees: Reservations are not accepted. There is no fee for camping. A 21-day limit is enforced. Open late April through early November, weather permitting.

Directions: From Lee Vining, drive south on U.S. 395 (past the first Highway 158/June Lake Loop turnoff) to June Lake Junction. Continue south for about seven miles to Owens River Road. Turn east (left) and drive two miles to a fork. Bear left at the fork and drive 0.25 mile to the camp on the left side of the road.

Contact: Inyo National Forest, Mono Basin Scenic Area Ranger Station and Visitor Center, 760/647-3044, www.fs.usda.gov/inyo.

75 DEADMAN AND OBSIDIAN FLAT GROUP

Scenic rating: 5

on Deadman Creek in Inyo National Forest

Map 10.2, page 548

This little-known camp is set at 7,800 feet elevation along little Deadman Creek. It is primitive and dusty in the summer, cold in the early summer and fall. From camp, hikers can drive west for three miles to the headwaters of Deadman Creek and to a trailhead for a route that runs past San Joaquin Mountain and beyond to little Yost Lake, a one-way hike of four miles.

Campsites, facilities: There are 30 sites for tents or RVs up to 30 feet. Nearby Obsidian Flat Group Camp can accommodate tents or RVs of any length and up to 50 people (no hookups). Picnic tables and fire grills are provided. Vault toilets are available. No drinking water is available. Garbage must be packed out. Leashed pets are permitted.

Reservations, fees: Reservations are not accepted at Deadman and there is no fee for camping. Reservations are required at Obsidian Flat Group at 877/444-6777 or www.recreation.gov ($9 reservation fee); the group site is $20 per night. Open late May through early November, weather permitting.

Directions: From Lee Vining, drive south on U.S. 395 (past the first Highway 158/June Lake Loop turnoff) to June Lake Junction. Continue south for 6.5 miles to a Forest Service road (Deadman Creek Road) on the west (right) side of the road. Turn west (right) and drive two miles to the camp access road on the right. Turn right and drive 0.5 mile to the camp. Note: If you are arriving from the south on U.S. 395 and you reach the CalTrans Crestview Maintenance Station on the right, you have gone one mile too far; make a U-turn when possible and return for access.

Contact: Inyo National Forest, Mono Basin Scenic Area Ranger Station and Visitor Center, 760/647-3044, www.fs.usda.gov/inyo.

76 BROWN'S OWENS RIVER CAMPGROUND
🚶 🚵 🏊 ⛴ 🐕 ♿ 🚐 ⛺

Scenic rating: 7

near the Owens River

Map 10.2, page 548

This camp is located along the upper Owens River, and is well situated for hiking, mountain biking, fishing, and swimming. The campground landscape is fairly sparse, so the campground can seem less intimate than those set in a forest. But this makes for great long-distance views of the White Mountains and for taking in those sunsets.

Campsites, facilities: There are 75 sites for tents or RVs up to any feet (no hookups). Some trailer rentals with full hookups are available. Picnic tables and fire rings are provided. Drinking water, flush and pit toilets, coin showers, coin laundry, a convenience store and cafe are available. Some facilities are wheelchair-accessible. Leashed pets are permitted.

Reservations, fees: Reservations are accepted. Sites are $20 per night.

Directions: From Mammoth Lakes on Highway 395/203, drive south on Highway 395 to Benton Crossing Road. Turn left and drive five miles to campground.

Contact: Brown's Owens River Campground, 760/920-0975, www.brownscampgrounds. com.

77 PINE GLEN
🚶 🐕 🚐 ⛺

Scenic rating: 6

in Inyo National Forest

Map 10.2, page 548

This is a well-situated base camp for several side trips. The most popular is the trip to Devils Postpile National Monument, with a shuttle ride from the Mammoth Ski Area. Other nearby trips include exploring Inyo Craters and Mammoth Lakes. The elevation is 7,800 feet.

Campsites, facilities: There are 10 sites (used as overflow from Old Shady Rest and New Shady Rest campgrounds) and nine group sites for tents or RVs up to 55 feet (no hookups) that can accommodate 15–30 people each. Picnic tables and fire grills are provided. Drinking water, flush toilets, and a dump station are available. A grocery store, coin laundry, propane gas, and horseback-riding facilities are nearby in Mammoth Lakes. Leashed pets are permitted.

Reservations, fees: Reservations are accepted for individual sites but are required for group sites at 877/444-6777 or www.recreation.gov ($9 reservation fee). Sites are $20 per night, group sites are $50–65 per night, $5 per night for each additional vehicle, Open late May through September, weather permitting.

Directions: From Lee Vining on U.S. 395, drive south for 25 miles to Mammoth Junction and Highway 203/Minaret Summit Road. Turn west on Highway 203 and drive about three miles to the Mammoth Lakes Visitor Center. Just past the visitor center, turn right on Old Sawmill Road and drive a short distance to the campground on the right.

Contact: Inyo National Forest, Mono Basin Scenic Area Ranger Station and Visitor Center, 760/647-3044, www.fs.usda.gov/inyo; Inyo Recreation, 760/934-5795.

78 NEW SHADY REST

Scenic rating: 6

in Inyo National Forest

Map 10.2, page 548

This easy-to-reach camp is set at 7,800 feet elevation, not far from the Mammoth Mountain Ski Area. The surrounding Inyo National Forest provides many side-trip opportunities, including Devils Postpile National Monument (by shuttle available from near the Mammoth Mountain Ski Area), Upper San Joaquin River, and the Inyo National Forest backcountry trails, streams, and lakes.

Campsites, facilities: There are 92 sites for tents or RVs up to 38 feet (no hookups) and nine group sites for 15–30 people each. Picnic tables and fire grills are provided. Drinking water and flush toilets are available. A dump station, playground, grocery store, coin laundry, and propane gas are nearby. Leashed pets are permitted.

Reservations, fees: Reservations are accepted for individual sites and are required for the group sites at 877/444-6777 or www.recreation.gov ($9 reservation fee). Sites are $20 per night, group sites are $50–65 per night, $5 per night for each additional vehicle. Open mid-May through October with a 14-day limit, weather permitting.

Directions: From Lee Vining on U.S. 395, drive south for 25 miles to Mammoth Junction and Highway 203/Minaret Summit Road. Turn west on Highway 203 and drive about three miles to the Mammoth Lakes Visitor Center. Just past the visitors center, turn right on Old Sawmill Road and drive

a short distance to the campground on the right.

Contact: Inyo National Forest, Mono Basin Scenic Area Ranger Station and Visitor Center, 760/647-3044, www.fs.usda.gov/inyo; Inyo Recreation, 760/934-5795.

79 OLD SHADY REST

Scenic rating: 6

in Inyo National Forest

Map 10.2, page 548

Names such as "Old Shady Rest" are usually reserved for mom-and-pop RV parks. The Forest Service respected tradition in officially naming this park what the locals have called it all along. Like New Shady Rest, this camp is near the Mammoth Lakes Visitor Center, with the same side trips available. It is one of three camps in the immediate vicinity. The elevation is 7,800 feet.

Campsites, facilities: There are 45 sites for tents or RVs up to 55 feet (no hookups). Picnic tables and fire grills are provided. Drinking water and flush toilets are available. A dump station, playground, grocery store, coin laundry, and propane gas are nearby. Leashed pets are permitted.

Reservations, fees: Reservations are accepted at 877/444-6777 or www.recreation.gov ($9 reservation fee). Sites are $20 per night, $5 per night for each additional vehicle, with a 14-day limit. Open mid-June through early September, weather permitting.

Directions: From Lee Vining on U.S. 395, drive south for 25 miles to Mammoth Junction and Highway 203/Minaret Summit Road. Turn west on Highway 203 and drive about three miles to the Forest Service Visitor Center. Just past the visitors center, turn right and drive 0.3 mile to the campground on the left.

Contact: Inyo National Forest, Mono Basin Scenic Area Ranger Station and Visitor Center), 760/647-3044, www.fs.usda.gov/inyo; Inyo Recreation, 760/934-5795.

80 MAMMOTH MOUNTAIN RV PARK

🏊 ✖️ 🐕 🏕️ ♿ 🚐 ⛺

Scenic rating: 6

near Mammoth Lakes

Map 10.2, page 548

This RV park is just across the street from the Forest Service Visitor Center. Got a question? Someone there has got an answer. This camp is open year-round, making it a great place to stay for a ski trip.

Campsites, facilities: There are 179 sites, some with full hookups (50 amps), for tents or RVs up to 45 feet, and two group tent sites for at least 15 people (minimum). Two cabins are also available. Picnic tables are provided. Fire pits are provided at some sites. Restrooms with showers, drinking water, cable TV, modem access, dump station, coin laundry, heated year-round swimming pool, seasonal recreation room, playground, RV supplies, and a spa are available. Some facilities are wheelchair-accessible. Supplies can be obtained in Mammoth Lakes, 0.25 mile away. Leashed pets are permitted, with certain restrictions.

Reservations, fees: Reservations are accepted at 800/582-4603. RV sites are $42–52 per night, tent sites are $27 per night, $3 per person per night for more than two people, $2 per night for each additional vehicle, $2 per pet per night. The group site is $25 per night with $5 per each additional person. Some credit cards accepted. Open year-round.

Directions: From Lee Vining on U.S. 395, drive south for 25 miles to Mammoth Junction and Highway 203. Turn west on Highway 203 and drive three miles to the park on the left.

From Bishop, drive 40 miles north on Highway 395 to Mammoth Lakes exit. Turn west on Highway 203, go under the overpass, and drive three miles to the park on the left.

Contact: Mammoth Mountain RV Park, 760/934-3822, www.mammothrv.com.

81 TWIN LAKES

🚶 🛶 🐕 ♿ 🚐 ⛺

Scenic rating: 8

in Inyo National Forest

Map 10.2, page 548

From Twin Lakes, you can look southwest and see pretty Twin Falls, a wide cascade that runs into the head of upper Twin Lake. There are actually two camps here, one on each side of the access road, at 8,600 feet. Lower Twin Lake is a favorite for fly fishers in float tubes. Powerboats, swimming, and sailboarding are not permitted. Use is heavy at the campground. Often there will be people lined up waiting for another family's weeklong vacation to end so theirs can start. Excellent hiking trails are in the area.

Campsites, facilities: There are 94 sites for tents or RVs up to 40 feet (no hookups). Picnic tables and fire grills are provided. Drinking water, flush toilets, and a boat launch are available. A grocery store, coin laundry, coin showers, and propane gas are nearby. Some facilities are wheelchair-accessible. Leashed pets are permitted.

Reservations, fees: Reservations are accepted at 877/444-6777 or www.recreation.gov ($9 reservation fee). Sites are $21 per night, $5 per night for each additional vehicle. Open mid-May through late October, weather permitting.

Directions: From Lee Vining on U.S. 395, drive south for 25 miles to Mammoth Junction and Highway 203/Minaret Summit Road. Turn west on Highway 203 and drive four miles to Lake Mary Road. Continue straight through the intersection and drive 2.3 miles to Twin Lakes Loop Road. Turn right and drive 0.5 mile to the campground.

Contact: Inyo National Forest, Mono Basin Scenic Area Ranger Station and Visitor Center, 760/647-3044, www.fs.usda.gov/inyo; Inyo Recreation, 760/934-5795.

82 SHERWIN CREEK

Scenic rating: 7

in Inyo National Forest

Map 10.2, page 548

This camp is set along little Sherwin Creek, at 7,600 feet elevation, a short distance from the town of Mammoth Lakes. If you drive a mile east on Sherwin Creek Road, then turn right at the short spur road, you will find a trailhead for a hike that is routed up six miles to Valentine Lake in the John Muir Wilderness, set on the northwest flank of Bloody Mountain.

Campsites, facilities: There are 70 sites for tents or RVs up to 34 feet (no hookups) and 15 walk-in tent sites. Picnic tables and fire grills are provided. Drinking water and flush toilets are available. Leashed pets are permitted.

Reservations, fees: Reservations are accepted at 877/444-6777 or www.recreation.gov ($9 reservation fee). Sites are $20 per night, $5 per night for each additional vehicle. Open early May through mid-September, weather permitting.

Directions: From Lee Vining on U.S. 395, drive south for 25 miles to Mammoth Junction and Highway 203/Minaret Summit Road. Turn west on Highway 203 and drive about three miles to the Mammoth Lakes Visitor Center and continue a short distance to Old Mammoth Road. Turn left and drive about a mile to Sherwin Creek. Turn south and drive two miles on largely unpaved road to the campground on the left side of the road.

Contact: Inyo National Forest, Mono Basin Scenic Area Ranger Station and Visitor Center, 760/647-3044, www.fs.usda.gov/inyo; Inyo Recreation, 760/934-5795.

83 LAKE MARY

Scenic rating: 9

in Inyo National Forest

Map 10.2, page 548

Lake Mary is the star of the Mammoth Lakes region. Of the 11 lakes in the area, this is the largest and most developed. It provides a resort, boat ramp, and boat rentals, and it receives the highest number of trout stocks. No water/body contact, including swimming, is allowed, and the speed limit is 10 mph. It is set at 8,900 feet elevation in a place of incredible natural beauty, one of the few spots that literally has it all. Of course, that often includes quite a few other people. If there are too many for you, an excellent trailhead is available at nearby Coldwater camp that routes you up to Emerald Lake.

Campsites, facilities: There are 41 sites for tents or RVs up to 30 feet (no hookups). Picnic tables, food lockers, and fire grills are provided. Drinking water and flush toilets are available. A grocery store, coin laundry, and propane gas are nearby. Leashed pets are permitted.

Reservations, fees: Reservations are not accepted. Sites are $21 per night, $5 per night for each additional vehicle. Open early June through mid-September with a 14-day limit, weather permitting.

Directions: Take U.S. 395 to Mammoth Junction and Highway 203. Turn west on Highway 203 and drive through the town of Mammoth Lakes to the junction of Minaret Road/Highway 203 and Lake Mary Road. Continue straight through the intersection and drive 3.6 miles to Lake Mary Loop Drive. Turn right and drive 0.5 mile to the campground entrance.

Contact: Inyo National Forest, Mono Basin Scenic Area Ranger Station and Visitor Center, 760/647-3044, www.fs.usda.gov/inyo; Inyo Recreation, 760/934-5795.

84 PINE CITY

Scenic rating: 7

near Lake Mary in Inyo National Forest

Map 10.2, page 548

This camp is at the edge of Lake Mary at an elevation of 8,900 feet. It's popular for both families and fly fishers with float tubes. Swimming is not permitted.

Campsites, facilities: There are 10 sites for tents or RVs up to 40 feet (no hookups). Picnic tables and fire grills are provided. Drinking water and flush toilets are available. A grocery store, coin laundry, boat launch, boat rentals, and propane gas are nearby. Some facilities are wheelchair-accessible. Leashed pets are permitted.

Reservations, fees: Reservations are not accepted. Sites are $21 per night. Open early June through mid-September.

Directions: Take U.S. 395 to Mammoth Junction and Highway 203. Turn west on Highway 203 and drive through the town of Mammoth Lakes to the junction of Minaret Road/Highway 203 and Lake Mary Road. Continue straight through the intersection and drive 3.6 miles to Lake Mary Loop Drive. Turn left and drive 0.25 mile to the campground.

Contact: Inyo National Forest, Mono Basin Scenic Area Ranger Station and Visitor Center, 760/647-3044, www.fs.usda.gov/inyo; Inyo Recreation, 760/934-5795.

85 COLDWATER

Scenic rating: 7

on Coldwater Creek in Inyo National Forest

Map 10.2, page 548

While this camp is not the first choice of many simply because there is no lake view, it has a special attraction all its own. First, it is a two-minute drive from the campground to Lake Mary, where there is a boat ramp, rentals, and good trout fishing. Second, at the end of the campground access road is a trailhead for two outstanding hikes. From the Y at the trailhead, if you head right, you will be routed up Coldwater Creek to Emerald Lake, a great little hike. If you head to the left, you will have a more ambitious trip to Arrowhead, Skelton, and Red Lakes, all within three miles. The elevation is 8,900 feet.

Campsites, facilities: There are 74 sites for tents or RVs up to 50 feet (no hookups). Picnic tables and fire grills are provided. Drinking water, flush toilets, and horse facilities are available. You can buy supplies in Mammoth Lakes. Leashed pets are permitted.

Reservations, fees: Reservations are accepted at 877/444-6777 or www.recreation.gov ($9 reservation fee). Sites are $21 per night, $5 per night for each additional vehicle, with a 14-day limit. Open mid-June through mid-September.

Directions: From Lee Vining on U.S. 395, drive south for 25 miles to Mammoth Junction and Highway 203/Minaret Summit Road. Turn west on Highway 203 and drive four miles to Lake Mary Road. Continue straight through the intersection and drive 3.6 miles to Lake Mary Loop Drive. Turn left and drive 0.6 mile to the camp entrance road.

Contact: Inyo National Forest, Mono Basin Scenic Area Ranger Station and Visitor Center, 760/647-3044, www.fs.usda.gov/inyo; Inyo Recreation, 760/934-5795.

86 CONVICT LAKE

Scenic rating: 7

in Inyo National Forest

Map 10.2, page 548   BEST (

This is the most popular camp in the Mammoth area and it is frequently full. While the lake rates a 10 for scenic beauty, the camp itself is in a stark desert setting, out of sight of the lake, and it can get windy and cold due to the exposed sites. After driving on U.S. 395 to get here, it is always astonishing to clear the rise and see Convict Lake (7,583 feet) and its gemlike waters set in a mountain bowl beneath a back wall of high, jagged wilderness peaks. The camp is right beside Convict Creek, about a quarter mile from Convict Lake. Both provide very good trout fishing, including some rare monster-sized brown trout below the Convict Lake outlet. Fishing is often outstanding in Convict Lake, with a chance of hooking a 10- or 15-pound trout. The lake speed limit is 10 mph, and although swimming is allowed, it is not popular because of the cold, often choppy water. A trail is routed around the lake, providing a nice day hike. A bonus is an outstanding resort with a boat launch, boat rentals, cabin rentals, small store, restaurant, and bar. Horseback rides and hiking are also available, with a trail routed along the north side of the lake, then along upper Convict Creek (a stream crossing is required about three miles in), and into the John Muir Wilderness.

Campsites, facilities: There are 48 sites for tents or RVs up to 40 feet (no hookups). Rental cabins are also available through Convict Lake Resort. Picnic tables and fire grills are provided. Drinking water, coin showers, and flush toilets are available. A dump station, boat ramp, store, restaurant, and horseback-riding facilities are available nearby. Some facilities are wheelchair-accessible. Leashed pets are permitted.

Reservations, fees: Reservations are accepted at 877/444-6777 or www.recreation.gov ($9 reservation fee). For cabin reservations, call 800/992-2260. Sites are $21 per night, $7 per night for each additional vehicle. Open mid-April through October, weather permitting; cabins open year-round.

Directions: From Lee Vining on U.S. 395, drive south for 31 miles (five miles past Mammoth Junction) to Convict Lake Road (adjacent to Mammoth Lakes Airport). Turn west (right) on Convict Lake Road and drive three miles to Convict Lake. Cross the dam and drive a short distance to the campground

entrance road on the left. Turn left and drive 0.25 mile to the campground.

From Bishop, drive north on U.S. 395 for 35 miles to Convict Lake Road. Turn west (left) and drive three miles to the lake and campground.

Contact: Inyo National Forest, Mono Basin Scenic Area Ranger Station and Visitor Center, 760/647-3044, www.fs.usda.gov/inyo; Convict Lake Resort and Cabins, 800/992-2260, www.convictlake.com.

87 McGEE CREEK RV PARK

Scenic rating: 6

near Crowley Lake

Map 10.2, page 548

This is a popular layover spot for folks visiting giant Crowley Lake. Crowley Lake is still one of the better lakes in the Sierra for trout fishing, with good prospects for large rainbow trout and brown trout, though the 20-pound brown trout that once made this lake famous are now mainly a legend. McGee Creek runs through the campground, and trout fishing is popular. Several trout ponds are also available; call for fees. Beautiful Convict Lake provides a nearby side-trip option. It is also about nine miles to Rock Creek Lake, a beautiful high-mountain destination. Note: All boats must be certified mussel-free before launching. The elevation is 7,000 feet.

Campsites, facilities: There are 40 sites with full, partial, or no hookups (50 amps) for tents or RVs up to 40 feet; some sites are pull-through. Picnic tables are provided and there are fire pits at some sites. Drinking water and restrooms with showers and flush toilets are available. Leashed pets are permitted.

Reservations, fees: Reservations are accepted. Sites are $22–32 per night, $3 per person per night for more than two people age 16 and over. Weekly and monthly rates available. Open late April through September, weather permitting.

Directions: From the junction of U.S. 395 and Highway 203 (the Mammoth Lakes turnoff), drive south on U.S. 395 for eight miles to the turnoff for McGee Creek Road. Take that exit and look for the park entrance on the left.

Contact: McGee Creek RV Park, 760/935-4233, www.mcgeecreekrv-campground.com.

88 McGEE CREEK

Scenic rating: 7

in Inyo National Forest

Map 10.2, page 548

This is a Forest Service camp at an elevation of 7,600 feet, set along little McGee Creek, a good location for fishing and hiking. There are few trees here. The stream is stocked with trout, and a trailhead is just up the road. From here you can hike along upper McGee Creek and into the John Muir Wilderness.

Campsites, facilities: There are 28 sites for tents or RVs up to 25 feet (no hookups). Picnic tables and fire grills are provided. Drinking water, flush and vault toilets, and shade structures are available. Horseback-riding facilities are available nearby. Some facilities are wheelchair-accessible. Leashed pets are permitted.

Reservations, fees: Reservations are accepted at 877/444-6777 or www.recreation.gov ($9 reservation fee). Sites are $20 per night, $7 per night for additional vehicle. Open mid-May through mid-October, weather permitting.

Directions: From Mammoth Lakes at the junction of U.S. 395 and Highway 203, drive south on U.S. 395 for 8.5 miles to McGee Creek Road (signed). Turn right (toward the Sierra) and drive 1.5 miles on a narrow, windy road to the campground.

Contact: Inyo National Forest, White Mountain Ranger District, 760/873-2500, www.fs.usda.gov/inyo; McGee Creek Pack Station, 760/935-4324.

89 CROWLEY LAKE

Scenic rating: 5

near Crowley Lake

Map 10.2, page 548

This large BLM camp is across U.S. 395 from the south shore of Crowley Lake. The surroundings are fairly stark and the elevation is 6,800 feet. For many, that is of little concern. Crowley is the trout-fishing capital of the eastern Sierra, with the annual opener (the last Saturday in April) a great celebration. Though the trout fishing can go through a lull in midsummer, it can become excellent again in the fall when the lake's population of big brown trout heads up to the top of the lake at the mouth of the Owens River. This is a large lake with 45 miles of shoreline. In the summer, water sports include swimming, waterskiing, wakeboarding, personal watercraft riding, and sailboarding. Note: All boats must be certified mussel-free before launching.

Campsites, facilities: There are 47 sites for tents or RVs of any length (no hookups). Picnic tables and fire grills are provided. Drinking water and vault toilets are available. Floating chemical toilets are available on the lake. A grocery store, boat ramp, boat rentals, and horseback-riding facilities are nearby. Leashed pets are permitted.

Reservations, fees: Reservations are not accepted. Sites are $5 per night, and season passes are available for $300. There is a 14-day limit. Open late April through October, weather permitting.

Directions: Drive on U.S. 395 to the Crowley Lake Road exit (30 miles north of Bishop). Take that exit west (toward the Sierra) to Crowley Lake Road. Turn right on Crowley Lake Road and drive northwest for three miles to the campground entrance on the left (well signed).

Contact: Bureau of Land Management, Bishop Field Office, 760/872-5008, www.blm.gov/ca; McGee Creek Pack Station, 760/935-4324.

90 TUFF

⬛ 🐕 ♿ 🚐 ⛺

Scenic rating: 5

near Crowley Lake in Inyo National Forest

Map 10.2, page 548

Easy access off U.S. 395 makes this camp a winner, though it is not nearly as pretty as those up Rock Creek Road to the west of Tom's Place. The fact that you can get in and out of here quickly makes it ideal for campers planning fishing trips to nearby Crowley Lake. The elevation is 7,000 feet. Note: All boats must be certified mussel-free before launching.

Campsites, facilities: There are 34 sites for tents or RVs up to 45 feet (no hookups). Picnic tables and fire grills are provided. Drinking water and flush toilets are available. Some facilities are wheelchair-accessible. Leashed pets are permitted.

Reservations, fees: Reservations are accepted at 877/444-6777 or www.recreation.gov ($9 reservation fee). Sites are $20 per night, $7 per additional vehicle. A 21-day limit is enforced. Open late April through mid-October, weather permitting.

Directions: From Mammoth Lakes at the junction of U.S. 395 and Highway 203, drive south on U.S. 395 for 15.5 miles (one mile north of Tom's Place) to Rock Creek Road. Turn left (east) on Rock Creek Road and drive 0.5 mile to the campground.

Contact: Inyo National Forest, White Mountain Ranger District, 760/873-2500, www. fs.usda.gov/inyo.

91 FRENCH CAMP

⬛ 🐕 🚐 ⛺

Scenic rating: 5

on Rock Creek near Crowley Lake in Inyo National Forest

Map 10.2, page 548

French Camp is just a short hop from U.S. 395 and Tom's Place, right where the high Sierra turns into high plateau country. Side-trip opportunities include boating and fishing on giant Crowley Lake and, to the west on Rock Creek Road, visiting little Rock Creek Lake 10 miles away. The elevation is 7,500 feet. Note: All boats must be certified mussel-free before launching at Crowley Lake.

Campsites, facilities: There are 85 sites for tents or RVs up to 40 feet (no hookups). Picnic tables and fire grills are provided. Drinking water, flush toilets, and dump station are available. Leashed pets are permitted.

Reservations, fees: Reservations are accepted at 877/444-6777 or www.recreation.gov ($9 reservation fee). Sites are $20 per night, $7 per additional vehicle. Open early May through October, weather permitting.

Directions: From Mammoth Lakes at the junction of U.S. 395 and Highway 203, drive south on U.S. 395 for 15 miles to Tom's Place and Rock Creek Road. Turn right (toward the Sierra) at Rock Creek Road and drive 0.25 mile to the campground on the right.

Contact: Inyo National Forest, White Mountain Ranger District, 760/873-2500, www. fs.usda.gov/inyo.

92 HOLIDAY CAMPGROUND

🥾 ⬛ 🐕 🚤 ♿ 🚐 ⛺

Scenic rating: 5

near Crowley Lake in Inyo National Forest

Map 10.2, page 548

There's a story behind every name. Holiday is a group camp that is opened as an overflow camp when needed. It is near Rock Creek, not far from Crowley Lake, with surroundings far more stark than the camps to the west on Rock Creek Road. The elevation is 7,500 feet. Note: All boats must be certified mussel-free before launching at Crowley Lake.

Campsites, facilities: There are 35 sites for tents or RVs up to 16 feet (no hookups) or groups up to 100 people. Picnic tables and fire grills are provided. Drinking water (summer only) and vault toilets are available. Some facilities are wheelchair-accessible. Leashed pets are permitted.

Reservations, fees: Reservations are not accepted. Sites are $20 per person per night (rate for group camping varies based on size). Open seasonally.

Directions: From Mammoth Lakes at the junction of U.S. 395 and Highway 203, drive south on U.S. 395 for 15 miles south to Tom's Place and Rock Creek Road. Turn right (toward the Sierra) and drive 0.5 mile to the campground on the left.

Contact: Inyo National Forest, White Mountain Ranger District, 760/873-2500, www.fs.usda.gov/inyo; Recreation Resource Management, www.camprm.com.

93 ASPEN GROUP CAMP
🎿 🛶 🏕 🐕 ♿ 🚐 ⛺

Scenic rating: 7

near Crowley Lake in Inyo National Forest

Map 10.2, page 548

This small group campground set on Rock Creek is used primarily as a base camp for anglers and campers heading to nearby Crowley Lake or venturing west to Rock Creek Lake. All boats must be certified mussel-free before launching at Crowley Lake. The elevation at the camp is 8,100 feet.

Campsites, facilities: There is one group camp for tents or RVs up to 25 feet (no hookups) that can accommodate up to 25 people. Picnic tables and fire grills are provided. Drinking water and flush toilets are available. Limited supplies are available in Tom's Place, three miles away. Some facilities are wheelchair-accessible. Leashed pets are permitted.

Reservations, fees: Reservations are required at 877/444-6777 or www.recreation.gov ($9 reservation fee). The group fee is $65 per night. Open mid-May through mid-October, weather permitting.

Directions: From Mammoth Lakes at the junction of U.S. 395 and Highway 203, drive south on U.S. 395 for 15 miles south to Tom's Place and Rock Creek Road. Turn right (toward the Sierra) at Rock Creek Road and drive three miles to the campground.

Contact: Inyo National Forest, White Mountain Ranger District, 760/873-2500, www.fs.usda.gov/inyo; Recreation Resource Management, camprm.com.

94 IRIS MEADOW
🎿 🛶 🚐 🏕 ♿ 🚐 ⛺

Scenic rating: 5

near Crowley Lake in Inyo National Forest

Map 10.2, page 548

Iris Meadow, at 8,300 feet elevation on the flank of Red Mountain (11,472 feet), is the first in a series of five Forest Service camps set near Rock Creek Canyon on the road leading from Tom's Place up to pretty Rock Creek Lake. A bonus is that some of the campsites are next to the creek. Rock Creek is stocked with trout, and nearby Rock Creek Lake also provides fishing and boating for hand-launched boats. Note: All boats must be certified mussel-free before launching at Crowley Lake. This camp also has access to a great trailhead for wilderness exploration.

Campsites, facilities: There are 14 sites for tents or RVs up to 40 feet (no hookups). Picnic tables and fire grills are provided. Drinking water and flush toilets are available. Limited supplies are available in Tom's Place, three miles away. Some facilities are wheelchair-accessible. Leashed pets are permitted.

Reservations, fees: Reservations are not accepted. Sites are $20 per night. Open late May through mid-September, weather permitting.

Directions: From Mammoth Lakes at the junction of U.S. 395 and Highway 203, drive south on U.S. 395 for 15 miles to Tom's Place and Rock Creek Road. Turn right (toward the Sierra) at Rock Creek Road and drive three miles to the campground.

Contact: Inyo National Forest, White

Mountain Ranger District, 760/873-2500, www.fs.usda.gov/inyo.

95 BIG MEADOW

Scenic rating: 8

near Crowley Lake in Inyo National Forest

Map 10.2, page 548

This is a smaller, quieter camp in the series of campgrounds along Rock Creek. Some of the campsites are along the creek. Beautiful Rock Creek Lake provides a nearby side trip. In the fall, turning aspens make for spectacular colors. The elevation is 8,600 feet.

Campsites, facilities: There are 11 sites for tents or RVs up to 22 feet (no hookups). Picnic tables and fire grills are provided. Drinking water and flush toilets are available. Limited supplies are available in Tom's Place, four miles away. Some facilities are wheelchair-accessible. Leashed pets are permitted.

Reservations, fees: Reservations are not accepted. Sites are $20 per night. Open early May through late October.

Directions: From Mammoth Lakes at the junction of U.S. 395 and Highway 203, drive south on U.S. 395 for 15 miles south to Tom's Place and Rock Creek Road. Turn right (toward the Sierra) at Rock Creek Road and drive four miles to the campground.

Contact: Inyo National Forest, White Mountain Ranger District, 760/873-2500, www.fs.usda.gov/inyo.

96 PALISADE GROUP

Scenic rating: 8

in Rock Creek Canyon in Inyo National Forest

Map 10.2, page 548

This shoe might just fit. Palisade, formerly a tiny family campground, now provides a pretty spot for group camping along Rock Creek at 8,600 feet elevation, with many side-trip options. The closest is fishing for small trout on Rock Creek and at pretty Rock Creek Lake up the road to the west. Another option is horseback riding, and horse rentals are in the area. The area is loaded with aspens. Some of the campsites are directly on the creek.

Campsites, facilities: There is a group site for tents or RVs up to 30 feet (no hookups). Picnic tables and fire grills are provided. Drinking water and flush toilets are available. Horseback-riding facilities are nearby. Limited supplies are available in Tom's Place, five miles away. Leashed pets are permitted.

Reservations, fees: Reservations are required at 877/444-6777 or www.recreation.gov ($9 reservation fee). The site is $100 per night. Open mid-May through mid-September, weather permitting.

Directions: From Mammoth Lakes at the junction of U.S. 395 and Highway 203, drive south on U.S. 395 for 15 miles south to Tom's Place and Rock Creek Road. Turn right (toward the Sierra) at Rock Creek Road and drive five miles to the campground.

Contact: Inyo National Forest, White Mountain Ranger District, 760/873-2500, www.fs.usda.gov/inyo; Rock Creek Pack Station, 760/935-4493, www.rockcreekpackstation.com; Recreation Resource Management, cam-prm.com.

97 EAST FORK

Scenic rating: 8

in Rock Creek Canyon in Inyo National Forest

Map 10.2, page 548

This is a beautiful, popular campground set along East Fork Rock Creek at 9,000 feet elevation. The camp is only three miles from Rock Creek Lake, where there's an excellent trailhead. Mountain biking is popular in this area, and Lower Rock Creek and Sand Canyon have two of the most difficult and desirable trails around; they're suggested for experienced riders only.

Campsites, facilities: There are 133 sites for tents or RVs up to 40 feet (no hookups). Picnic tables and fire grills are provided. Drinking water and flush toilets are available. Limited supplies are available in Tom's Place and at Rock Creek Lakes Resort. Leashed pets are permitted.

Reservations, fees: Reservations are accepted at 877/444-6777 or www.recreation.gov ($9 reservation fee). Sites are $20 per night, $7 per night for each additional vehicle. Open early May through October.

Directions: From Mammoth Lakes at the junction of U.S. 395 and Highway 203, drive south on U.S. 395 for 15 miles south to Tom's Place and Rock Creek Road. Turn right (toward the Sierra) at Rock Creek Road and drive five miles to the campground access road on the left.

Contact: Inyo National Forest, White Mountain Ranger District, 760/873-2500, www.fs.usda.gov/inyo.

98 PINE GROVE AND UPPER PINE GROVE

Scenic rating: 8

in Rock Creek Canyon in Inyo National Forest

Map 10.2, page 548

Pine Grove is one of the smaller camps in the series of campgrounds along Rock Creek. Of the five camps in this canyon, this one is the closest to Rock Creek Lake, just a two-mile drive away (Rock Creek Lake Campground is closer, of course). The aspens here are stunning in September, when miles of mountains turn to shimmering golds. Some of the campsites are along the creek. The elevation is 9,300 feet.

Campsites, facilities: There are 19 sites for tents or RVs up to 16 feet (no hookups). Picnic tables and fire grills are provided. Drinking water and vault toilets are available. Horseback-riding facilities are nearby. Limited supplies can be obtained in Tom's Place and at Rock Creek Lakes Resort. Leashed pets are permitted.

Reservations, fees: Reservations are not accepted. Sites are $20 per night. Open mid-May through mid-October.

Directions: From Mammoth Lakes at the junction of U.S. 395 and Highway 203, drive south on U.S. 395 for 15 miles south to Tom's Place and Rock Creek Road. Turn right (toward the Sierra) at Rock Creek Road and drive seven miles to the campground.

Contact: Inyo National Forest, White Mountain Ranger District, 760/873-2500, www.fs.usda.gov/inyo.

99 ROCK CREEK LAKE

Scenic rating: 9

in Inyo National Forest

Map 10.2, page 548

Rock Creek Lake, set at an elevation of 9,600 feet, is a small but beautiful lake that features cool, clear water, small trout, and a great trailhead for access to the adjacent John Muir Wilderness, with 50 other lakes within a two-hour hike. The setting is drop-dead beautiful, hence the high rating for scenic beauty, but note that the campsites are set closely together, side by side, in a paved parking area. This 63-acre lake has a 5-mph speed limit and swimming is allowed. The lake is stocked with Alpers trout, and they are joined by resident brown trout in the 10- to 16-pound class. At times, especially afternoons in late spring, winds out of the west can be cold and pesky at the lake. If this campground is full, the nearby Mosquito Flat walk-in campground provides an option. Note that Mosquito Flat has a limit of one night and is designed as a staging area for wilderness backpacking trips, with tent camping only. Insider's tip: Rock Creek Lakes Resort has mouth-watering homemade pie available in the café.

Campsites, facilities: There are 26 sites for tents or RVs up to 22 feet (no hookups), and

one group tent site for up to 25 people; some of the sites require a short walk in. Picnic tables and fire grills are provided. Drinking water, flush toilets, an unimproved boat launch, and boat rentals are available. Horseback-riding facilities and a café are nearby. Limited supplies can be obtained in Tom's Place and at Rock Creek Lakes Resort. Leashed pets are permitted.

Reservations, fees: Reservations are accepted for individual sites and required for group sites at 877/444-6777 or www.recreation.gov ($9 reservation fee). Sites are $20 per night, $65 per night for a group site. Open mid-May through October, weather permitting.

Directions: From the junction of U.S. 395 and Highway 203 (the Mammoth Lakes turnoff), drive 15 miles south on U.S. 395 to Tom's Place. Turn right (toward the Sierra) at Rock Creek Road and drive seven miles to the campground.

Contact: Inyo National Forest, White Mountain Ranger District, 760/873-2500, www.fs.usda.gov/inyo; Rock Creek Pack Station, 760/935-4493, www.rockcreekpackstation.com.

100 PLEASANT VALLEY
🏃 ⛵ 🎣 🐴 ♿ 🚐 ⛺

Scenic rating: 7

near Pleasant Valley Reservoir

Map 10.2, page 548

Pleasant Valley County Campground is set near long, narrow Pleasant Valley Reservoir, created by the Owens River. A 15-minute walk from camp will take you to the lake. It is east of the Sierra range in the high desert plateau country; the elevation is 4,200 feet. That makes it available for year-round fishing, and trout are stocked. The Owens River passes through the park, providing wild trout fishing, with most anglers practicing catch-and-release fly-fishing. This is also near a major jump-off point for hiking, rock-climbing, and wilderness fishing at the Bishop Pass area to the west.

Campsites, facilities: There are 200 sites for tents or RVs of any length (no hookups). Picnic tables and fire grills are provided. Drinking water (hand-pumped well water) and vault toilets are available. Groups can be accommodated. Some facilities are wheelchair-accessible. Leashed pets are permitted.

Reservations, fees: Reservations are not accepted. Sites are $10 per night per vehicle. Open year-round.

Directions: Drive on U.S. 395 to Pleasant Valley Road (seven miles north of Bishop) on the east side of the road. Turn northeast and drive one mile to the park entrance.

Contact: Inyo County Parks Department, 760/873-5577, www.inyocountycamping.com.

101 PLEASANT VALLEY PIT CAMPGROUND
🏃 🚲 🎣 🐴 🚐 ⛺

Scenic rating: 6

near Bishop off U.S. 395

Map 10.2, page 548

This camp is set in a rocky desert area just south of Pleasant Valley Reservoir. It's a good spot for kids, with boulder scrambling the primary recreation, and is also a good area to see a variety of raptors. Few travelers on U.S. 395 know about the campground, operated by the Bureau of Land Management.

Campsites, facilities: There are 75 sites for tents or RVs (no hookups). Vault toilets and a dumpster are provided. There is a campground host, as well as law enforcement patrols, and the campground sees regular maintenance. Fires, charcoal grills, and portable stoves outside developed campgrounds require a permit, when allowed. Leashed pets are permitted.

Reservations, fees: Reservations are not accepted. Sites are $2 per night. There is a 60-day limit. Open November to early May, weather permitting.

Directions: From Bishop, drive north on U.S. 395 for about five miles to Pleasant Valley Road. Turn right on Pleasant Valley Road and proceed approximately one-half mile to the gravel road on the left (west) side of the road. Turn left on the gravel road and drive to the Pleasant Valley Pit Campground.

Contact: Bureau of Land Management, Bishop Field Office, 760/872-5008, www.blm.gov/ca.

102 HIGHLANDS RV PARK

Scenic rating: 3

near Bishop

Map 10.2, page 548

This is a privately operated RV park near Bishop that is set up for U.S. 395 cruisers. There is a casino in town. A great side trip is up two-lane Highway 168 to Lake Sabrina. The elevation is 4,300 feet. Note that a few sites are occupied by long-term renters.

Campsites, facilities: There are 103 sites with full hookups (30 and 50 amps) for RVs of any length; many sites are pull-through. No tents. Picnic tables and cable TV are provided. Drinking water, restrooms with flush toilets and showers, dump station, social room with pool table, Wi-Fi, propane gas, ice, fish-cleaning station, and coin laundry are available. Supplies are available nearby. Some facilities are wheelchair-accessible. Leashed pets are permitted.

Reservations, fees: Reservations are recommended. Sites are $40 per night, $1 per person per night for more than two people. Weekly and monthly rates available. Some credit cards accepted. Open year-round.

Directions: From Bishop, drive two miles north on U.S. 395/North Sierra Highway to the campground on the right (east side of road) at 2275 North Sierra Highway.

Contact: Highlands RV Park, 760/873-7616.

SEQUOIA AND KINGS CANYON

© KLOTZ/123RF.COM

BEST CAMPGROUNDS

There is no place on earth like the high Sierra,

from Mount Whitney north through Sequoia and Kings Canyon National Parks. This is a paradise filled with deep canyons, high peaks, and fantastic natural beauty, and sprinkled with groves of the largest living things in the history of the earth − giant sequoias.

Though the area is primarily known for the national parks, the campgrounds available span a great variety of settings. The most popular spots, though, are in the vicinity of Sequoia and Kings Canyon National Parks, or on the parks' access roads.

Sooner or later, everyone will want to see the biggest tree of them all − the General Sherman Tree, estimated to be 2,300-2,700 years old and with a circumference of 102.6 feet. It is in the Giant Forest at Sequoia National Park. To stand in front of it is to know true awe. That said, I find the Grant Grove and the Muir Grove even more enchanting.

These are among the highlights of a driving tour through both parks. A must for most is taking in the view from Moro Rock − parking and then making the 300-foot walk up a succession of stairs to reach the 6,725-foot summit. Here you can scan a series of mountain rims and granite peaks, highlighted by the Great Western Divide.

The drive out of Sequoia and into Kings Canyon features rim-of-the-world-type views as you first enter the Kings River canyon. You then descend to the bottom of the canyon, right along the Kings River, gaze up at the high glacial-carved canyon walls, and drive all the way out to Cedar Grove, the end of the road. The canyon rises 8,000 feet from the river to Spanish Peak, making it the deepest canyon in the continental United States.

Crystal Cave is another point of fascination. Among the formations are adjoined crystal columns that look like the sound pipes in the giant organ at the Mormon Tabernacle. Lights are placed strategically for perfect viewing.

This is only a start. Bears, marmots, and deer are abundant and are commonly seen in Sequoia, especially at Dorst Creek Campground. If you drive up to Mineral King and take a hike, it can seem like the marmot capital of the world.

But this region also harbors many wonderful secrets having nothing to do with the national parks. One of them, for instance, is the Muir Trail Ranch near Florence Lake. The ranch is set in the John Muir Wilderness and requires a trip by foot, boat, or horse to reach it. Other unique launching points for trips into the wilderness lie nearby.

On the western slopes of the Sierra, pretty lakes with good trout fishing include Edison, Florence, and Hume Lakes. Hidden spots in Sierra National Forest provide continual fortune hunts, especially up the Dinkey Creek drainage above Courtright Reservoir. On the eastern slopes, a series of small streams offers good vehicle access; here, too, you'll encounter the beautiful Rock Creek Lake, Sabrina and South Lakes (west of Bishop), and great wilderness trailheads at the end of almost every road.

The remote Golden Trout Wilderness on the southwest flank of Mount Whitney is one of the most pristine areas in California. Yet it is lost in the shadow of giant Whitney, elevation 14,497.6 feet, the highest point in the continental United States, where hiking has become so popular that reservations are required at each trailhead for overnight use, and quotas are enforced to ensure an undisturbed experience for each visitor.

In the Kernville area, there are campgrounds along the Kern River. Most choose this canyon for one reason: the outstanding white-water rafting and kayaking.

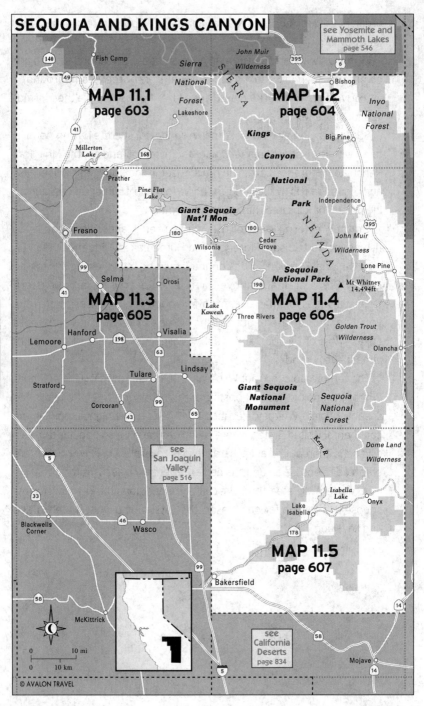

SEQUOIA AND KINGS CANYON

see Yosemite and Mammoth Lakes page 546

MAP 11.1
page 603

MAP 11.2
page 604

MAP 11.3
page 605

MAP 11.4
page 606

MAP 11.5
page 607

see San Joaquin Valley page 516

see California Deserts page 834

Sierra

National

Forest

John Muir
Wilderness

SIERRA

Kings

Canyon

National

Park

NEVADA

Inyo

National

Forest

John Muir

Wilderness

Giant Sequoia Nat'l Mon

Sequoia
National Park

Golden Trout
Wilderness

Giant Sequoia
National
Monument

Sequoia
National
Forest

Dome Land
Wilderness

Fish Camp

Lakeshore

Millerton
Lake

Prather

Pine Flat
Lake

Fresno

Selma

Orosi

Hanford

Visalia

Lemoore

Tulare

Lindsay

Stratford

Corcoran

Blackwells
Corner

Wasco

McKittrick

Bakersfield

Wilsonia

Cedar
Grove

Lake
Kaweah

Three Rivers

Kern R.

Isabella
Lake

Lake
Isabella

Onyx

Bishop

Big Pine

Independence

Lone Pine

▲ Mt Whitney
14,494ft

Olancha

Mojave

0   10 mi
0   10 km

© AVALON TRAVEL

Map 11.1

Sites 1-40
Pages 608-626

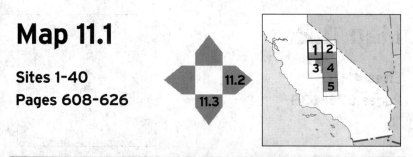

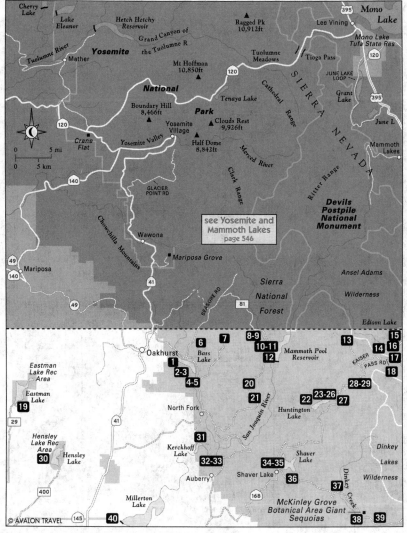

Map 11.2

Sites 41-70
Pages 626-638

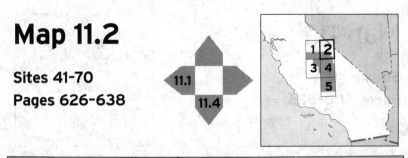

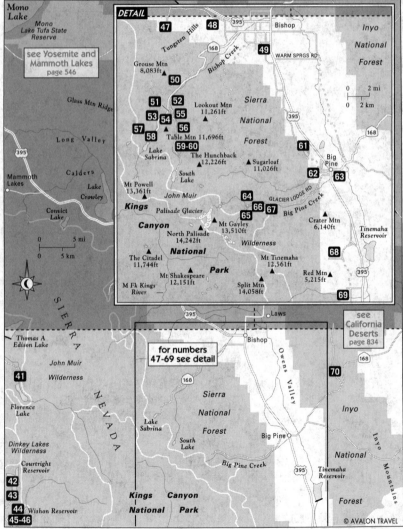

Mono Lake

Mono Lake Tufa State Reserve

see Yosemite and Mammoth Lakes page 546

Glass Mtn Ridge

Long Valley

Caldera

Mammoth Lakes

Lake Crowley

Convict Lake

Kings

Canyon

National

Park

SIERRA

NEVADA

Thomas A Edison Lake

John Muir Wilderness

41

Florence Lake

Dinkey Lakes Wilderness

Courtright Reservoir

42
43
44
45-46

Wishon Reservoir

DETAIL

47   **48**   Bishop

Tungsten Hills

Bishop Creek

Inyo

National

Forest

49   WARM SPRGS RD

Grouse Mtn 8,083ft

50

51   **52**   Lookout Mtn 11,261ft

53 **54** **55**

57 **58**   **56**   Table Mtn 11,696ft

Sierra

National

Forest

59-60

Lake Sabrina

The Hunchback 12,226ft

Sugarloaf 11,026ft

61

Big Pine

62   **63**

South Lake

Mt Powell 13,361ft

John Muir

Kings   Palisade Glacier

Canyon

National

Park

The Citadel 11,744ft

M Fk Kings River

North Palisade 14,242ft

Mt Shakespeare 12,151ft

64

65 **66** **67**   GLACIER LODGE RD   Big Pine Creek

Mt Gayley 13,510ft

Wilderness

Mt Tinemaha 12,561ft

Split Mtn 14,058ft

Crater Mtn 6,140ft

Red Mtn 5,215ft

68

69

Tinemaha Reservoir

Laws

Bishop

for numbers 47-69 see detail

Sierra

National

Forest

Lake Sabrina

South Lake

Big Pine Creek

Big Pine

Owens Valley

see California Deserts page 834

70

Inyo

National

Forest

Inyo Mountains

Tinemaha Reservoir

© AVALON TRAVEL

Map 11.3

Sites 71-80
Pages 638-642

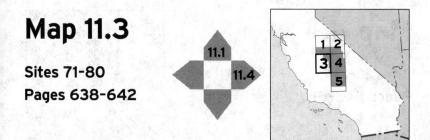

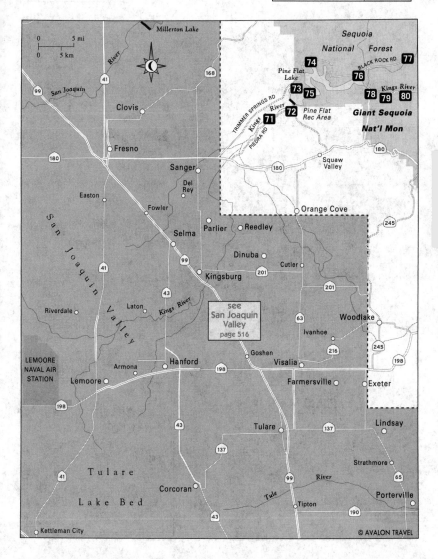

Map 11.4

Sites 81-134
Pages 643-667

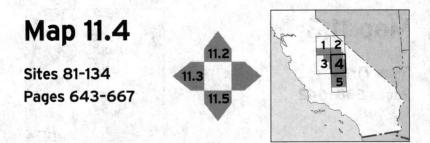

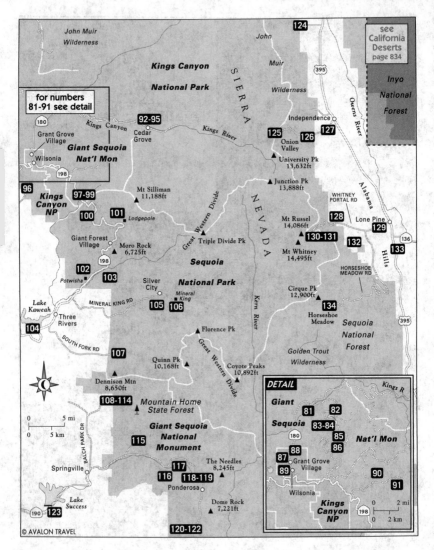

Map 11.5

Sites 135-173
Pages 668-684

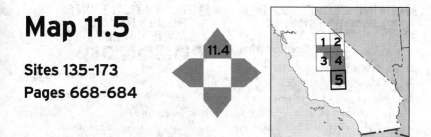

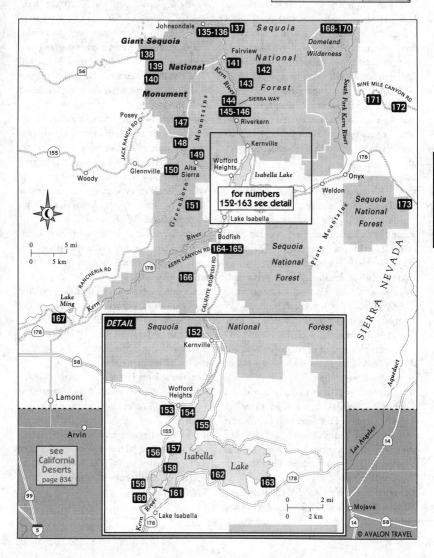

1 LUPINE-CEDAR BLUFF

Scenic rating: 8

on Bass Lake in Sierra National Forest

Map 11.1, page 603

Bass Lake is a popular vacation spot, a pretty lake, long and narrow, covering 1,200 acres when full and surrounded by national forest. The elevation is 3,500 feet. This is camping headquarters, with the only year-round individual sites at the lake. Though these camps are adjoining, the concessionaire treats them as separate camps, with Cedar Bluff reserved for RV camping only. Most of the campgrounds are filled on weekends and three-day holidays. Fishing is best in the spring for rainbow trout and largemouth bass, and by mid-June waterskiers have usually taken over. Boats must be registered at the Bass Lake observation tower after launching.

Campsites, facilities: There are 113 sites for tents or RVs up to 40 feet (no hookups); 51 sites are at Lupine and 62 sites are at Cedar Bluff. Picnic tables and fire grills are provided. Drinking water, flush toilets, and a camp host are available. Groceries, coin showers, and boat ramp are within two miles. Some facilities are wheelchair-accessible. Leashed pets are permitted.

Reservations, fees: Reservations are accepted at 877/444-6777 or www.recreation.gov ($9 reservation fee). Single sites are $23.42 per night $44.14 per night for double sites, $87.39 for quadruple sites, $5 per night for each additional vehicle. Fees increase on holiday weekends. Open year-round.

Directions: From Fresno, drive north on Highway 41 to Oakhurst and continue 2.5 miles to Yosemite Forks and Bass Lake Road/County Road 222. Turn right at Bass Lake Road and drive eight miles (staying right at two forks) to the campground (on the south shore of Bass Lake).

Contact: Sierra National Forest, Bass Lake Ranger District, 559/877-2218, www.fs.usda.gov/sierra; California Land Management, 559/642-3212.

2 RECREATION POINT GROUP AND CRANE VALLEY GROUP

Scenic rating: 8

on Bass Lake in Sierra National Forest

Map 11.1, page 603

Bass Lake is a long, narrow, mountain lake set in the Sierra foothills at 3,400 feet elevation. It's especially popular in the summer for waterskiing, personal watercraft riding, and swimming. There are two separate group camps at Bass Lake: Recreation Point and Crane Valley. Recreation Point is the better of the two because it has drinking water and flush toilets.

Campsites, facilities: At Recreation Point, there are four group sites for tents only that can accommodate 30–50 people. Picnic tables and fire grills are provided. Drinking water and flush toilets are available. At Crane Valley, there are seven group sites for tents or RVs up to 40 feet (no hookups) that can accommodate 12–30 people each. Vault toilets are available, but there is no drinking water. Picnic tables and fire grills are provided at both camps. A store is nearby. Leashed pets are permitted.

Reservations, fees: Reservations are required at 877/444-6777 or www.recreation.gov ($9 reservation fee). Sites are $130–220 per night at Recreation Point; sites are $35–95 per night at Crane Valley. All vehicles pay a $3–5 parking fee. Open year-round.

Directions: From Fresno, drive north on Highway 41 to Oakhurst and continue 2.5 miles to Yosemite Forks and Bass Lake Road/County Road 222. Turn right at Bass Lake Road and drive four miles to the campground.

Contact: Sierra National Forest, Bass Lake Ranger District, 559/877-2218, www.fs.usda.gov/sierra; California Land Management, 559/642-3212.

3 FORKS

Scenic rating: 8

on Bass Lake in Sierra National Forest

Map 11.1, page 603

Bass Lake is set in a canyon. It's a long, narrow, deep lake that is popular for fishing in the spring and waterskiing in the summer. It's a pretty spot, set at 3,500 feet elevation in the Sierra National Forest. This is one of several camps at the lake. Boats must be registered at the Bass Lake observation tower after launching.

Campsites, facilities: There are 27 sites for tents or RVs up to 40 feet (no hookups). Picnic tables and fire grills are provided. Drinking water, flush toilets, and a camp host are available. A store, dump station, and coin laundry are nearby. Some facilities are wheelchair-accessible. Leashed pets are permitted.

Reservations, fees: Reservations are accepted at 877/444-6777 or www.recreation.gov ($9 reservation fee). Single sites are $22 per night, double sites are $44 per night, $5 per night for each additional vehicle. Fees increase on holiday weekends. Open May through September.

Directions: From Fresno, drive north on Highway 41 to Oakhurst and continue 2.5 miles to Yosemite Forks and Bass Lake Road/County Road 222. Turn right at Bass Lake Road and drive six miles (staying right at two forks) to the campground (on the south shore of Bass Lake). Note: The road is narrow and curvy.

Contact: Sierra National Forest, Bass Lake Ranger District, 559/877-2218, www.fs.usda.gov/sierra; California Land Management, 559/642-3212.

4 SPRING COVE

Scenic rating: 8

on Bass Lake in Sierra National Forest

Map 11.1, page 603

This is one of several camps beside Bass Lake, a long, narrow reservoir in the Sierra foothill country. A bonus here is that the shoreline is quite sandy nearly all around the lake. That makes for good swimming and sunbathing. Expect hot weather in the summer. Boats must be registered at the Bass Lake observation tower after launching. The elevation is 3,400 feet.

Campsites, facilities: There are 62 sites for tents or RVs up to 35 feet (no hookups). Picnic tables and fire grills are provided. Drinking water, flush toilets, and camp host are available. Groceries and a boat ramp are nearby. Some facilities are wheelchair-accessible. Leashed pets are permitted.

Reservations, fees: Reservations are accepted at 877/444-6777 or www.recreation.gov ($9 reservation fee). Single sites are $22 per night, double sites are $44 per night, $5 per night for each additional vehicle. Fees increase on holiday weekends. Open May through August.

Directions: From Fresno, drive north on Highway 41 to Oakhurst and continue 2.5 miles to Yosemite Forks and Bass Lake Road/County Road 222. Turn right at Bass Lake Road and drive 8.5 miles (staying right at two forks) to the campground (on the south shore of Bass Lake).

Contact: Sierra National Forest, Bass Lake Ranger District, 559/877-2218, www.fs.usda.gov/sierra; California Land Management, 559/642-3212.

5 WISHON POINT

Scenic rating: 9

on Bass Lake in Sierra National Forest

Map 11.1, page 603

This camp on Wishon Point is the smallest, and many say the prettiest, of the camps at Bass Lake. The elevation is 3,400 feet.

Campsites, facilities: There are 47 sites for tents or RVs up to 30 feet (no hookups). Some sites are pull-through. Picnic tables and fire grills are provided. Drinking water and flush toilets are available. Groceries and a boat ramp are nearby. Some facilities are wheelchair-accessible. Leashed pets are permitted.

Reservations, fees: Reservations are accepted at 877/444-6777 or www.recreation.gov ($9 reservation fee). Single sites are $22 per night, double sites are $44, $5 per night for additional vehicle. Fees increase on holiday weekends. Open late April to early September.

Directions: From Fresno, drive north on Highway 41 to Oakhurst and continue 2.5 miles to Yosemite Forks and Bass Lake Road/County Road 222. Turn right at Bass Lake Road and drive nine miles (staying right at two forks) to the campground (on the south shore of Bass Lake).

Contact: Sierra National Forest, Bass Lake Ranger District, 559/877-2218, www.fs.usda.gov/sierra; California Land Management, 559/642-3212.

6 CHILKOOT
Scenic rating: 7

near Bass Lake in Sierra National Forest

Map 11.1, page 603

A lot of people have heard of Bass Lake, but only the faithful know about Chilcoot Creek. That's where this camp is, but it's just two miles from Bass Lake. It provides a primitive option to use either as an overflow area for Bass Lake or for folks who don't want to get jammed into one of the Bass Lake campgrounds on a popular weekend. The elevation is 4,600 feet.

Campsites, facilities: There are 11 sites for tents or RVs up to 20 feet (no hookups). Picnic tables and fire grills are provided. Vault toilets are available. No drinking water is available. Groceries and a coin laundry are available at Bass Lake. Leashed pets are permitted.

Reservations, fees: Reservations are accepted at 877/444-6777 or www.recreation.gov ($9 reservation fee). Single sites are $17 per night, double sites are $34, $5 per night for each additional vehicle. Open early May through early September.

Directions: From Fresno, drive north on Highway 41 to Oakhurst and continue 2.5 miles to Yosemite Forks and Bass Lake Road/County Road 222. Turn right at Bass Lake Road and drive six miles to the town of Bass Lake and Beasore Road. Turn left at Beasore Road and drive 4.5 miles to the campground.

Contact: Sierra National Forest, Bass Lake Ranger District, 559/877-2218, www.fs.usda.gov/sierra.

7 GAGGS CAMP
Scenic rating: 7

in Sierra National Forest

Map 11.1, page 603

The masses are not exactly beating a hot trail to this camp. It's a small, remote, and primitive spot, set along a little creek at 5,700 feet elevation, deep in the interior of Sierra National Forest. A Forest Service map is advisable. With that in hand, you can make the three-mile drive to Little Shuteye Pass, where the road is often gated in the winter (the gate is open when the look-out station is staffed); from here it is a three-mile trip to Shuteye Peak, at 8,351 feet, where there is a drop-dead gorgeous view of the surrounding landscape.

Campsites, facilities: There are 11 sites for tents or RVs up to 16 feet (no hookups). Picnic tables and fire grills are provided. Vault toilets are available. No drinking water is available. Garbage bins are located at campground entrance. Leashed pets are permitted.

Reservations, fees: Reservations are not accepted. Single sites are $17 per night, double sites are $34 per night, $5 per night for each additional vehicle. Open June through October, weather permitting.

Directions: From Fresno, drive north on Highway 41 for about 25 miles to North Fork Road/County Road 200. Turn right and drive northeast for 17.5 miles to Auberry Road/County Road 222. Turn left (north) and drive one mile to the town of North Fork and Mammoth Pool Road. Turn right and drive 0.5 mile to Malum Ridge Road/County Road 274. Turn left (north) and drive 4.5 miles to Central Camp Road/Forest Road 6S42. Turn right and drive 11.5 miles (narrow, dirt road) to the campground on the right.

Contact: Sierra National Forest, Bass Lake Ranger District, 559/877-2218, www.fs.usda. gov/sierra.

8 SODA SPRINGS

Scenic rating: 7

on the West Fork of Chiquito Creek in Sierra National Forest

Map 11.1, page 603

Soda Springs is set at 4,400 feet elevation on West Fork Chiquito Creek, about five miles from Mammoth Pool Reservoir. It is used primarily as an overflow area if the more developed camps with drinking water have filled up. As long as you remember that the camp is primitive, it is a good overflow option.

Campsites, facilities: There are 18 sites for tents or RVs up to 20 feet (no hookups). Picnic tables and fire grills are provided. Vault toilets are available. No drinking water is available. A store and boat ramp are nearby. Leashed pets are permitted.

Reservations, fees: Reservations are not accepted. Single sites are $17 per night, $34 per night for double sites, $5 per night for each additional vehicle. Open May through September, weather permitting.

Directions: From Fresno, drive north on Highway 41 for about 25 miles to North Fork Road/County Road 200. Turn right and drive northeast for 17.5 miles to Auberry Road/ County Road 222. Turn left (north) and drive one mile to the town of North Fork and Mammoth Pool Road. Turn right and drive 1.5 miles to County Road 225 (still Mammoth Pool

Road). Turn right and drive 35 miles (the road becomes Minarets Road/Forest Road 81) to the campground.

Contact: Sierra National Forest, Bass Lake Ranger District, 559/877-2218, www.fs.usda. gov/sierra.

9 LOWER CHIQUITO

Scenic rating: 7

on Chiquito Creek in Sierra National Forest

Map 11.1, page 603

Lower Chiquito is a primitive, little-known, pretty camp in Sierra National Forest, about eight miles from Mammoth Pool Reservoir. Mosquitoes can be abundant in summer. The elevation is 4,900 feet, with a very warm climate in summer. Note that Lower Chiquito is a long distance (a twisting, 30- to 40-minute drive) from Upper Chiquito, despite the similarity in names and streamside settings along the same creek.

Campsites, facilities: There are seven sites for tents or RVs up to 25 feet (no hookups). Picnic tables and fire grills are provided. Vault toilets are available. No drinking water is available. Leashed pets are permitted.

Reservations, fees: Reservations are not accepted. Single sites are $17 per night, $34 per night for double sites, $5 per night for each additional vehicle. Open June through September, weather permitting.

Directions: From the town of North Fork (south of Bass Lake), drive east on Mammoth Pool Road/County Road 225 (it becomes Minarets Road/Forest Road 4S81). Bear left (north, still Minarets Road/Forest Road 4S81) and drive to Forest Road 6S71. Turn left on Forest Road 6S71 and drive three miles to the campground. (The distance is about 40 miles from North Fork.)

Contact: Sierra National Forest, Bass Lake Ranger District, 559/877-2218, www.fs.usda. gov/sierra.

10 PLACER

Scenic rating: 7

near Mammoth Pool Reservoir on
Chiquito Creek in Sierra National Forest

Map 11.1, page 603

This little camp is just three miles from Mammoth Pool Reservoir. With Forest Road access and a pretty setting along Chiquito Creek, it is one of the better campgrounds used as an overflow area for Mammoth Pool visitors. The elevation is 4,100 feet. (For more information, see the Mammoth Pool listing in this chapter.)

Campsites, facilities: There are eight sites for tents or RVs up to 30 feet. Picnic tables and fire grills are provided. Vault toilets are available. No drinking water is available. Leashed pets are permitted.

Reservations, fees: Reservations are not accepted. Single sites are $17 per night, $34 per night for double sites, $5 per night for each additional vehicle. Open May through September.

Directions: From Fresno, drive north on Highway 41 for about 25 miles to North Fork Road/County Road 200. Turn right and drive northeast for 17.5 miles to Auberry Road/County Road 222. Turn left (north) and drive one mile to the town of North Fork and Mammoth Pool Road. Turn right and drive 1.5 miles to County Road 225 (still Mammoth Pool Road). Turn right and drive about 37 miles (the road becomes Minarets Road/Forest Road 81) to a junction. Bear right (still Mammoth Pool Road) and drive one mile to the campground on the right. The drive from North Fork takes 1.5–2 hours.

Contact: Sierra National Forest, Bass Lake Ranger District, 559/877-2218, www.fs.usda.gov/sierra.

11 SWEETWATER

Scenic rating: 6

near Mammoth Pool Reservoir on
Chiquito Creek in Sierra National Forest

Map 11.1, page 603

Sweetwater is small and primitive, but if the camp at Mammoth Pool Reservoir is filled up, this spot provides an alternative. It is set on Chiquito Creek, just a mile from the lake. The elevation is 3,800 feet. (See the Mammoth Pool listing in this chapter for more information.)

Campsites, facilities: There are seven sites for tents or RVs up to 20 feet (no hookups). Picnic tables and fire grills are provided. Vault toilets are available. No drinking water is available. A store and boat ramp are within 1.5 miles. Leashed pets are permitted.

Reservations, fees: Reservations are accepted at 877/444-6777 or www.recreation.gov ($9 reservation fee). Single sites are $17 per night, double sites are $34 per night, $5 per night per additional vehicle. Open mid-May through mid-September.

Directions: From Fresno, drive north on Highway 41 for about 25 miles to North Fork Road/County Road 200. Turn right and drive northeast for 17.5 miles to Auberry Road/County Road 222. Turn left (north) and drive one mile to the town of North Fork and Mammoth Pool Road. Turn right and drive 1.5 miles to County Road 225 (still Mammoth Pool Road). Turn right and drive about 37 miles (the road becomes Minarets Road/Forest Road 81) to a junction. Bear right (still Mammoth Pool Road) and drive 1.5 miles to the campground on the right. The drive from North Fork takes 1.5–2 hours.

Contact: Sierra National Forest, Bass Lake Ranger District, 559/877-2218, www.fs.usda.gov/sierra; California Land Management, 559/642-3212.

12 MAMMOTH POOL

Scenic rating: 7

near Mammoth Pool Reservoir in
Sierra National Forest

Map 11.1, page 603

Mammoth Pool was created by a dam in the San Joaquin River gorge, a steep canyon, resulting in a long, narrow lake with steep, high walls. The lake seems much higher than its official elevation of 3,330 feet, but that is because of the high ridges. This is the only drive-in camp at the lake, though there is a boat-in camp, China Camp, on the lake's upper reaches. Trout fishing can be good in the spring and early summer, with waterskiing dominant during warm weather. All water sports are allowed during part of the season, but get this: Water sports are restricted from May 1 to June 15 because of deer migrating across the lake—that's right, swimming—but the campgrounds here are still open. Note that the water level can drop significantly by late summer.

Campsites, facilities: There are 47 sites for tents or RVs up to 30 feet (no hookups). Picnic tables and fire grills are provided. Drinking water and vault toilets are available. A store and boat ramp are within a mile. Leashed pets are permitted.

Reservations, fees: Reservations are accepted at 877/444-6777 or www.recreation.gov ($9 reservation fee). Single sites are $18 per night, double sites are $36 per night, $5 per night per additional vehicle. Open June through October.

Directions: From Fresno, drive north on Highway 41 for about 25 miles to North Fork Road/County Road 200. Turn right and drive northeast for 17.5 miles to Auberry Road/County Road 222. Turn left (north) and drive one mile to the town of North Fork and Mammoth Pool Road. Turn right and drive 1.5 miles to County Road 225 (still Mammoth Pool Road). Turn right and drive about 37 miles (the road becomes Minarets Road/Forest Road 81) to a junction. Bear right (still Mammoth Pool Road) and drive three miles to Mammoth Pool Reservoir and the campground. The drive from North Fork takes 1.5–2 hours.

Contact: Sierra National Forest, Bass Lake Ranger District, 559/877-2218, www.fs.usda.gov/sierra; California Land Management, 559/642-3212.

13 SAMPLE MEADOW

Scenic rating: 7

on Kaiser Creek in Sierra National Forest

Map 11.1, page 603

This is a pretty, secluded spot set at 7,800 feet elevation along Kaiser Creek, with nearby trailheads available for backpackers. While there is a trail out of camp, most hikers drive a mile down Forest Road 80 to the Rattlesnake Parking Area. From here, one trail is routed three miles southwest to Kaiser Ridge and Upper and Lower Twin Lakes in the Kaiser Wilderness, a great hike. Another trail is routed north for three miles to Rattlesnake Creek, and then enters the western slopes of the Ansel Adams Wilderness, with this section featuring a series of canyons, streams, and very few people. Horse camping is permitted.

Campsites, facilities: There are 16 sites for tents or RVs up to 16 feet (no hookups). Picnic tables and fire grills are provided. Vault toilets are available. No drinking water is available. Garbage must be packed out. Leashed pets are permitted.

Reservations, fees: Reservations are not accepted. There is no fee for camping. Open June through October, weather permitting.

Directions: From Fresno, drive east on Highway 168 to Shaver Lake, and then continue 21 miles to Huntington Lake and Kaiser Pass Road/Forest Road 80. Bear right on Forest Road 80 and drive eight miles to a fork with Forest Road 7505. Turn left on Forest Road 7505 and drive 3.5 miles to a fork with the campground entrance road. Bear left at the campground entrance road and drive 0.25 mile to the campground. The road is narrow and curvy, with blind turns.

Contact: Sierra National Forest, High Sierra Ranger District, 559/855-5355, www.fs.usda. gov/sierra.

14 PORTAL FOREBAY

Scenic rating: 8

on Forebay Lake in Sierra National Forest

Map 11.1, page 603

This small, primitive camp is set along the shore of little Forebay Lake at 7,200 feet elevation. The camp is pretty and provides a good hiking option, with a trailhead near the camp that is routed up Camp 61 Creek and then to Mono Creek, with a ford of Mono Creek required about two miles in. Another side trip is visiting Mono Hot Springs about five miles to the east, just off the road to Lake Edison.

Campsites, facilities: There are 11 sites for tents or RVs up to 16 feet (no hookups). Picnic tables and fire grills are provided. Vault toilets are available. No drinking water is available. Groceries are available nearby at Mono Hot Springs. Leashed pets are permitted.

Reservations, fees: Reservations are not accepted. Single sites are $16 per night, double sites are $32 per night, $5 per night per each additional vehicle. Open June through October.

Directions: From Fresno, drive east on Highway 168 to Shaver Lake, and then continue 21 miles to Huntington Lake and Kaiser Pass Road/Forest Road 80. Bear right on Forest Road 80 and drive eight miles to a fork with Forest Road 5. Stay right at the fork on Forest Road 80 and continue five miles to the campground entrance on the left. The road is narrow and curvy, with blind turns.

Contact: Sierra National Forest, High Sierra Ranger District, 559/855-5355, www.fs.usda. gov/sierra; California Land Management, 559/893-2111.

15 VERMILLION

Scenic rating: 8

on Edison Lake in Sierra National Forest

Map 11.1, page 603   BEST (

If you don't mind the drive, Edison Lake is a premium vacation destination. It is a large, high-mountain camp set just a few miles from the border of the John Muir Wilderness. A 15-mph speed limit on the lake guarantees quiet water, and trout fishing is often quite good in early summer, with occasionally huge brown trout hooked. Swimming is allowed. A day-trip option is to hike the trail from the camp out along the north shore of Edison Lake for five miles to Quail Meadows, where it intersects with the Pacific Crest Trail in the John Muir Wilderness. A lodge at the lake provides meals and supplies, with a hikers boat shuttle available to the head of the lake. Hang out here for long and you are bound to see John Muir Trail hikers taking a break. Note that the drive in is long and extremely twisty on a narrow road. Also note that the lake level can drop dramatically here by late summer. The elevation is 7,700 feet.

Campsites, facilities: There are 31 sites for tents or RVs up to 25 feet (no hookups). Picnic tables, fire grills, and food lockers are provided. Vault toilets are available. Drinking water is on-site but boiling it is recommended. A boat ramp, boat rentals, bait and tackle, horseback-riding facilities, convenience store, and restaurant are nearby. Leashed pets are permitted.

Reservations, fees: Reservations are accepted at 877/444-6777 or www.recreation.gov ($9 reservation fee). Single sites are $19 per night, double sites are $38 per night, $5 per night for each additional vehicle. Open June through October.

Directions: From the town of Shaver Lake, drive east on Highway 168 for 21 miles to Kaiser Pass Road. Bear northeast on Kaiser Pass Road/Forest Road 80 (slow and curvy) to Mono Hot Springs (the road becomes Edison

Lake Road). Continue on Kaiser Pass/Edison Lake Road for five miles to the campground. It is about 0.25 mile from the west shore of Edison Lake. Be warned that the access road is narrow with many blind turns and may be difficult for RVs.

Contact: Sierra National Forest, High Sierra Ranger District, 559/855-5355, www.fs.usda. gov/sierra; California Land Management, 559/893-2111.

16 MONO HOT SPRINGS

Scenic rating: 8

on the San Joaquin River in
Sierra National Forest

Map 11.1, page 603

The campground is set in the Sierra at 7,400 feet elevation along the San Joaquin River directly adjacent to the Mono Hot Springs Resort. The hot springs are typically 104°F, with public pools (everybody wears swimming suits) available just above the river on one side, and the private resort (rock cabins available) with its private baths on the other. A small convenience store and excellent restaurant are available at the lodge. Many find the hot springs perfect, but for some the water is too hot. No problem; the best swimming lake in the Sierra Nevada, Dorris Lake, is a 15-minute walk past the lodge. Dorris is clear, clean, and not too cold since it too is fed by hot springs. There are walls on one side for fun jumps into deep water. The one downer: The drive in to the campground is long, slow, and hellacious, with many blind corners in narrow sections.

Campsites, facilities: There are 31 sites for tents or RVs up to 25 feet (no hookups). Picnic tables and fire grills are provided. Vault toilets are available. Drinking water is not available. You can buy supplies in Mono Hot Springs. Leashed pets are permitted.

Reservations, fees: Reservations are accepted at 877/444-6777 or www.recreation.gov ($9 reservation fee). Single sites are $19 per night,

$40 per night for double sites, $5 per night for additional vehicle. Open June through mid-September, weather permitting.

Directions: From the town of Shaver Lake, drive east on Highway 168 for 21 miles to Kaiser Pass Road. Bear northeast on Kaiser Pass Road/Forest Road 80 (slow and curvy) to Mono Hot Springs Campground Road (signed). Turn left and drive a short distance to the campground. Be warned that the access road is narrow with many blind turns and may be difficult for RVs.

Contact: Sierra National Forest, High Sierra Ranger District, 559/855-5355, www.fs.usda. gov/sierra; California Land Management, 559/893-2111.

17 MONO CREEK

Scenic rating: 7

near Lake Edison in Sierra National Forest

Map 11.1, page 603

Here's a beautiful spot in the forest near Mono Creek that makes for an overflow campground when the camps at Mono Hot Springs and Lake Edison are filled, or when you want a quieter, more remote spot. The camp is set at 7,400 feet elevation about three miles from Lake Edison, via a twisty and bumpy road. Edison has good evening trout fishing and a small restaurant. For side trips, the Mono Hot Springs Resort is three miles away (slow, curvy, and bumpy driving), and there are numerous trails nearby into the backcountry. A camp host is on-site.

Campsites, facilities: There are 14 sites for tents or RVs up to 25 feet (no hookups). Picnic tables, fire grills, and food lockers are provided. Vault toilets are available. Drinking water is not available. Limited supplies and small restaurants are at Lake Edison and Mono Hot Springs. Some facilities are wheelchair accessible. Leashed pets are permitted.

Reservations, fees: Reservations are accepted at 877/444-6777 or www.recreation.gov ($9

reservation fee). Single sites are $19 per night, $40 per night for double site, $5 per night for each additional vehicle. Open June through October, weather permitting.

Directions: From the town of Shaver Lake, drive east on Highway 168 for 21 miles to Kaiser Pass Road. Bear northeast on Kaiser Pass Road/Forest Road 80 (slow and curvy) to Mono Hot Springs (the road becomes Edison Lake Road). Continue on Kaiser Pass/Edison Lake Road for three miles to the campground on the left.

Contact: Sierra National Forest, High Sierra Ranger District, 559/855-5355, www.fs.usda. gov/sierra; California Land Management, 559/893-2111.

18 BOLSILLO
🏃🛶🏕5%⛺

Scenic rating: 4

on Bolsillo Creek in Sierra National Forest
Map 11.1, page 603

This tiny camp has many first-class bonuses. It is set at 7,400 feet elevation along Bolsillo Creek, just three miles by car to Mono Hot Springs and seven miles to Lake Edison. A trailhead out of camp provides the chance for a three-mile hike south, climbing along Bolsillo Creek and up to small, pretty Corbett Lake on the flank of nearby Mount Givens, at 10,648 feet.

Campsites, facilities: There are three tent sites. Picnic tables and fire grills are provided. Drinking water and vault toilets are available. Garbage must be packed out. You can buy supplies in Mono Hot Springs. Leashed pets are permitted.

Reservations, fees: Reservations are not accepted. There is no fee for camping. Open June through October, weather permitting.

Directions: From Fresno, drive east on Highway 168 to Shaver Lake, then continue 21 miles to Huntington Lake and Kaiser Pass Road/Forest Road 80. Bear right on Forest Road 80 and drive eight miles to a fork with

Forest Road 5. Stay right on Forest Road 80 and drive seven miles (two miles past Portal Forebay) to the campground entrance on the right. The road is narrow and curvy with blind turns, and RVs and trailers are not recommended.

Contact: Sierra National Forest, High Sierra Ranger District, 559/855-5355, www.fs.usda. gov/sierra.

19 CODORNIZ RECREATION AREA
🏃🚲🏊🛶🚤🏕🤸♿🚐⛺

Scenic rating: 6

on Eastman Lake
Map 11.1, page 603

Eastman Lake provides relief on your typical 90- and 100-degree summer day out here. It is tucked in the foothills of the San Joaquin Valley at an elevation of 650 feet and covers 1,800 surface acres. Shade shelters have been added at 12 of the more exposed campsites, a big plus. The warm water in summer makes it a good spot for a dip, thus it is a favorite for waterskiing, swimming, and, in the spring, fishing. Swimming is best at the large beach on the west side. The Department of Fish and Game has established a trophy bass program here, and fishing can be good in the appropriate season for rainbow trout, catfish, bluegill, and redear sunfish. Check fishing regulations, posted on all bulletin boards. The lake is also a designated "Watchable Wildlife" site; it is home to 163 species of birds and a nesting pair of bald eagles. A small area near the upper end of the lake is closed to boating to protect a bald eagle nest site. Some may remember the problem that Eastman Lake had with hydrilla, an invasive weed. The problem has been largely solved, and a buoy line has been placed at the mouth. No water activities are allowed upstream of this line. Mild winter temperatures are a tremendous plus at this lake.

Campsites, facilities: There are 81 sites for tents or RVs of any length (some have full hookups/50 amps and one is pull-through), three group sites for 40–160 people, three equestrian sites, and one group equestrian site. Picnic tables and fire grills are provided. Drinking water, flush toilets with showers, dump station, playground, horseshoe pits, volleyball court, Frisbee golf course, and two boat ramps are available. An equestrian staging area is available for overnight use, and there are seven miles of hiking, biking, and equestrian trails. Some facilities are wheelchair accessible. Leashed pets are permitted.

Reservations, fees: Reservations are accepted at 877/444-6777 or www.recreation.gov ($9 reservation fee). Sites are $20–30 per night, $80–100 per night for group sites, and $20–60 per night for equestrian sites. Open year-round.

Directions: Drive on Highway 99 to Chowchilla and the Avenue 26 exit. Take that exit and drive east for 17 miles to County Road 29. Turn left (north) on County Road 29 and drive eight miles to the lake.

Contact: U.S. Army Corps of Engineers, Sacramento District, Eastman Lake, 559/689-3255.

20 ROCK CREEK
🏃🐕🚐🏕

Scenic rating: 6

in Sierra National Forest

Map 11.1, page 603

Drinking water is the big bonus here. It's easier to live with than the no-water situation at Fish Creek, the other camp in the immediate area. It is also why this camp tends to fill up on weekends. A side trip is the primitive road that heads southeast out of camp. It has a series of sharp turns as it heads east and drops down the canyon near where pretty Aspen Creek feeds into Rock Creek. The elevation at camp is 4,300 feet. (For the best camp in the immediate region, see the Mammoth Pool listing in this chapter.)

Campsites, facilities: There are 18 sites for tents or RVs up to 30 feet (no hookups). Picnic tables and fire grills are provided. Drinking water and vault toilets are available. A camp host is on-site. Leashed pets are permitted.

Reservations, fees: Reservations are accepted at 877/444-6777 or www.recreation.gov ($9 reservation fee). Single sites are $18 per night, $36 per night for a double site, $5 per night per each additional vehicle. Open mid-May through September, weather permitting.

Directions: From Fresno, drive north on Highway 41 for about 25 miles to North Fork Road/County Road 200. Turn right and drive northeast for 17.5 miles to Auberry Road/County Road 222. Turn left (north) and drive one mile to the town of North Fork and Mammoth Pool Road. Turn right and drive 1.5 miles to County Road 225 (still Mammoth Pool Road). Turn right and drive about 25 miles (the road becomes Minarets Road/Forest Road 81) to the campground on the right.

Contact: Sierra National Forest, Bass Lake Ranger District, 559/877-2218, www.fs.usda.gov/sierra; California Land Management, 559/642-3212.

21 FISH CREEK
🏃🛶🐕🚐🏕

Scenic rating: 6

in Sierra National Forest

Map 11.1, page 603

This is a small, primitive camp set along Fish Creek at 4,600 feet elevation in the Sierra National Forest. It's a nearby option to Rock Creek, both set on the access road to Mammoth Pool Reservoir.

Campsites, facilities: There are seven sites for tents or RVs up to 20 feet (no hookups). Picnic tables and fire grills are provided. Vault toilets are available. No drinking water is available. Leashed pets are permitted.

Reservations, fees: Reservations are accepted at 877/444-6777 or www.recreation.gov ($9 reservation fee). Sites are $17–34 per night, $5 per night per each additional vehicle. Open June through November, weather permitting.

Directions: From Fresno, drive north on High-way 41 for about 25 miles to North Fork Road/County Road 200. Turn right and drive north-east for 17.5 miles to Auberry Road/County Road 222. Turn left (north) and drive one mile to the town of North Fork and Mammoth Pool Road. Turn right and drive 1.5 miles to County Road 225 (still Mammoth Pool Road). Turn right and drive about 21 miles (the road becomes Minarets Road/Forest Road 81) to the campground on the right.

Contact: Sierra National Forest, Bass Lake Ranger District, 559/877-2218, www.fs.usda. gov/sierra; California Land Management, 559/642-3212.

22 UPPER AND LOWER BILLY CREEK

🏃 🏊 🚣 🚐 🏕 🐕 🚼 ⛺

Scenic rating: 8

on Huntington Lake in Sierra National Forest

Map 11.1, page 603

Huntington Lake is at an elevation of 7,000 feet in the Sierra Nevada. These camps are at the west end of the lake along the north shore, where Billy Creek feeds the lake. Of these two adjacent campgrounds, Lower Billy Creek is smaller than Upper Billy and has lakeside sites available. The lake is four miles long and 0.5 mile wide, with 14 miles of shoreline, several resorts, boat rentals, and a trailhead for hiking into the Kaiser Wilderness.

Campsites, facilities: Upper Billy has 44 sites for tents or RVs up to 30 feet. Lower Billy has 15 sites for tents or RVs up to 30 feet. No hookups. Picnic tables and fire grills are provided. Drinking water and vault toilets are available at both camps; Upper Billy also has flush toilets available. A camp host is on-site. Campfire programs are often available. A small store is nearby. Leashed pets are permitted.

Reservations, fees: Reservations are accepted at 877/444-6777 or www.recreation.gov ($9 reservation fee). Single sites are $20–26 per night, double sites are $40–47, $5 per night for

each additional vehicle. Open June through October, weather permitting.

Directions: From Fresno, drive east on High-way 168 to Shaver Lake, then continue 21 miles to Huntington Lake and Huntington Lake Road. Turn left on Huntington Lake Road and drive about five miles to the camp-grounds on the left.

Contact: Sierra National Forest, High Sierra Ranger District, 559/855-5355, www.fs.usda. gov/sierra; California Land Management, 559/893-2111.

23 CATAVEE

🏃 🏊 🚣 🚐 🏕 🐕 🚼 🚗 ⛺

Scenic rating: 7

on Huntington Lake in Sierra National Forest

Map 11.1, page 603

Catavee is one of three camps in the immediate vicinity, set on the north shore at the eastern end of Huntington Lake. The camp sits near where Bear Creek enters the lake. Huntington Lake is a scenic, High Sierra Ranger District lake at 7,000 feet elevation, where visitors can enjoy fishing, hiking, and sailing. Sailboat regattas take place here regularly during the summer. All water sports are allowed. Nearby resorts offer boat rentals and guest docks, and a boat ramp is nearby. Tackle rentals and bait are also available. A trailhead near camp offers access to the Kaiser Wilderness.

Campsites, facilities: There are 23 sites for tents or RVs up to 30 feet (no hookups). Picnic tables and fire grills are provided. Drinking water and flush toilets are available. A camp host is on-site. Horseback-riding facilities and a small store are nearby. Some facilities are wheelchair-accessible. Leashed pets are permitted.

Reservations, fees: Reservations are accepted at 877/444-6777 or www.recreation.gov ($9 reservation fee). Single sites are $26 per night, double sites are $51, $5 per night for each ad-ditional vehicle. Open June through October, weather permitting.

Directions: From Fresno, drive east on Highway 168 to Shaver Lake, then continue 21 miles to Huntington Lake and Huntington Lake Road. Turn left on Huntington Lake Road and drive one mile (just past Kinnikinnick) to the campground on the right.

Contact: Sierra National Forest, High Sierra Ranger District, 559/855-5355, www.fs.usda.gov/sierra; California Land Management, 559/893-2111.

24 KINNIKINNICK

Scenic rating: 7

on Huntington Lake in Sierra National Forest

Map 11.1, page 603

Flip a coin; there are three camps in the immediate vicinity on the north shore of the east end of Huntington Lake and, with a boat ramp nearby, they are all favorites. Kinnikinnick is set between Catavee and Deer Creek Campgrounds. The elevation is 7,000 feet.

Campsites, facilities: There are 27 sites for tents or RVs up to 40 feet (no hookups). Picnic tables and fire grills are provided. Drinking water and flush toilets are available. Horseback-riding facilities and a store are nearby. Some facilities are wheelchair-accessible. Leashed pets are permitted.

Reservations, fees: Reservations are accepted at 877/444-6777 or www.recreation.gov ($9 reservation fee). Sites are $26–51 per night, $5 per night for each additional vehicle. Open June through October, weather permitting.

Directions: From Fresno, drive east on Highway 168 to Shaver Lake, then continue 21 miles to Huntington Lake and Huntington Lake Road. Turn left on Huntington Lake Road and drive one mile to the campground on the right.

Contact: Sierra National Forest, High Sierra Ranger District, 559/855-5355, www.fs.usda.gov/sierra; California Land Management, 559/893-2111.

25 DEER CREEK

Scenic rating: 8

on Huntington Lake in Sierra National Forest

Map 11.1, page 603

This is one of the best camps at Huntington Lake, set near lakeside at Bear Cove with a boat ramp nearby. It is on the north shore of the lake's eastern end. Huntington Lake is four miles long and 0.5 mile wide, with 14 miles of shoreline, several resorts, boat rentals, and a trailhead for hiking into the Kaiser Wilderness. Two other campgrounds are nearby.

Campsites, facilities: There are 28 sites for tents or RVs up to 40 feet (no hookups). Picnic tables and fire grills are provided. Drinking water and flush toilets are available. A store and propane gas are nearby. Some facilities are wheelchair-accessible. Leashed pets are permitted.

Reservations, fees: Reservations are accepted at 877/444-6777 or www.recreation.gov ($9 reservation fee). Sites are $26–51 per night, $5 per night for each additional vehicle. Open June through October, weather permitting.

Directions: From Fresno, drive east on Highway 168 to Shaver Lake, then continue 21 miles to Huntington Lake and Huntington Lake Road. Turn left on Huntington Lake Road and drive one mile to the campground entrance road on the left.

Contact: Sierra National Forest, High Sierra Ranger District, 559/855-5355, www.fs.usda.gov/sierra; California Land Management, 559/893-2111.

26 COLLEGE

Scenic rating: 7

on Huntington Lake in Sierra National Forest

Map 11.1, page 603

College is a beautiful site along the shore of the northeastern end of Huntington Lake, at 7,000 feet elevation. This camp is close to a small store in the town of Huntington Lake.

Campsites, facilities: There are 11 sites for tents or RVs up to 30 feet (no hookups). Picnic tables and fire grills are provided. Vault and flush toilets, drinking water and a camp host are available. Interpretive programs are offered. Horseback-riding facilities, store, and propane gas are nearby. Leashed pets are permitted.

Reservations, fees: Reservations are accepted at 877/444-6777 or www.recreation.gov ($9 reservation fee). Single sites are $24–26 per night, double sites are $48–52 per night, $5 per night for each additional vehicle. Open June through mid-September, weather permitting.

Directions: From Fresno, drive east on Highway 168 to Shaver Lake, then continue 21 miles to Huntington Lake and Huntington Lake Road. Turn left on Huntington Lake Road and drive 0.5 mile to the campground.

Contact: Sierra National Forest, High Sierra Ranger District, 559/855-5355, www.fs.usda.gov/sierra; California Land Management, 559/893-2111.

27 RANCHERIA

🥾 🏊 🚣 🚤 🐴 🚐 ⛺

Scenic rating: 8

on Huntington Lake in Sierra National Forest

Map 11.1, page 603

This is the granddaddy of the camps at Huntington Lake, and also the easiest to reach. It is along the shore of the lake's eastern end. A bonus here is nearby Rancheria Falls National Recreation Trail, which provides access to beautiful Rancheria Falls. Another side trip is the 15-minute drive to Bear Butte (the access road is across from the campground entrance) at 8,598 feet elevation, providing a sweeping view of the lake below. The elevation at camp is 7,000 feet.

Campsites, facilities: There are 149 sites for tents or RVs up to 40 feet (no hookups). Picnic tables and fire grills are provided. Drinking water and flush and vault toilets are available. A camp host is on-site. Interpretive programs are offered. A store and propane gas are nearby. Leashed pets are permitted.

Reservations, fees: Reservations are accepted at 877/444-6777 or www.recreation.gov ($9 reservation fee). Tent sites are $20–22 per night, RV sites are $20–45 per night, $5 per night for each additional vehicle. Open June through October, weather permitting.

Directions: From Fresno, drive east on Highway 168 to Shaver Lake, then continue 20 miles to Huntington Lake and the campground on the left.

Contact: Sierra National Forest, High Sierra Ranger District, 559/855-5355, www.fs.usda.gov/sierra; California Land Management, 559/893-2111.

28 BADGER FLAT

🥾 🐴 🚐 ⛺

Scenic rating: 7

on Rancheria Creek in Sierra National Forest

Map 11.1, page 603

This camp is a good launching pad for backpackers. It is set at 8,200 feet elevation along Rancheria Creek. The trail leading out of the camp is routed into the Kaiser Wilderness to the north and Dinkey Lakes Wilderness to the south. Horses are permitted, but there are no facilities are available.

Campsites, facilities: There are 15 sites for tents or RVs up to 25 feet (no hookups). Fire grills and picnic tables are provided. Vault toilets are available. No drinking water is available. Leashed pets are permitted.

Reservations, fees: Reservations are not accepted. Sites are $18 per night, $5 per night for each additional vehicle. Fees increase on holidays. Open June through October, weather permitting.

Directions: From Fresno, drive east on Highway 168 to Shaver Lake, then continue 21 miles to Huntington Lake and Kaiser Pass Road/Forest Road 80. Turn right and drive four miles to the campground.

Contact: Sierra National Forest, High Sierra Ranger District, 559/855-5355, www.fs.usda. gov/sierra; California Land Management, 559/893-2111.

29 BADGER FLAT GROUP AND HORSE CAMP

Scenic rating: 7

on Rancheria Creek in Sierra National Forest

Map 11.1, page 603

Badger Flat is a primitive site along Rancheria Creek at 8,200 feet elevation, about five miles east of Huntington Lake. It is a popular horse camp and a good jump-off spot for wilderness trekkers. A trail that passes through camp provides two options: Head south for three miles to enter the Dinkey Lakes Wilderness, or head north for two miles to enter the Kaiser Wilderness.

Campsites, facilities: There is one group site for tents or RVs up to 35 feet (no hookups) that can accommodate up to 100 people. Picnic tables, fire grills, and food lockers are provided. Vault toilets are available. No drinking water is available. A store is nearby. Leashed pets are permitted.

Reservations, fees: Reservations are required at 877/444-6777 or www.recreation. gov ($9 reservation fee). Sites are $124.80 per night. Open June through October, weather permitting.

Directions: From Fresno, drive east on Highway 168 to Shaver Lake, then continue 21 miles to Huntington Lake and Kaiser Pass Road/Forest Road 80. Turn right and drive five miles to the campground on the right.

Contact: Sierra National Forest, High Sierra Ranger District, 559/855-5355, www.fs.usda. gov/sierra; California Land Management, 559/893-2111.

30 HIDDEN VIEW

Scenic rating: 5

north of Fresno on Hensley Lake

Map 11.1, page 603

Hensley Lake is popular with water-skiers and personal watercraft users in spring and summer, and it has good prospects for bass fishing as well. Hensley covers 1,500 surface acres with 24 miles of shoreline and, as long as water levels are maintained, makes for a wonderful water playland. Swimming is good, with the best spot at Buck Ridge on the east side of the lake, where there are picnic tables and trees for shade. The reservoir was created by a dam on the Fresno River. A nature trail is also here. The elevation is 540 feet.

Campsites, facilities: There are 55 sites for tents or RVs of any length, some with electric hookups (30 amps), and two group sites for 50 people each. Picnic tables and fire grills are provided. Restrooms with flush toilets and showers, drinking water, dump station, playground, and boat ramp are available. Some facilities are wheelchair accessible. Leashed pets are permitted.

Reservations, fees: Reservations are accepted at 877/444-6777 or www.recreation.gov ($9 reservation fee). Sites are $20–30 per night, $100 per night for group sites, $4 per night per additional vehicle. Boat launching is free for campers. Open year-round.

Directions: From Madera, drive northeast on Highway 145 for about six miles to County Road 400. Bear left on County Road 400 and drive to County Road 603 below the dam. Turn left and drive about two miles on County Road 603 to County Road 407. Turn right on County Road 407 and drive 0.5 mile to the campground.

Contact: U.S. Army Corps of Engineers, Sacramento District, Hensley Lake, 559/673-5151.

31 SMALLEY COVE

🚶‍♀️ 🛶 ⛵ 🐕 ♿ ⛺

Scenic rating: 7

on Kerckhoff Reservoir near Madera

Map 11.1, page 603

Kerckhoff Reservoir can get so hot that it might seem you could fry an egg on the rocks. Campers should be certain to have some kind of tarp they can set up as a sun screen. The lake is small and remote, and the use of boat motors more than five horsepower is prohibited. Most campers bring rafts or canoes, and there is a good swimming beach near the picnic area and campground. Fishing is not so good here. The elevation is 1,000 feet.

Campsites, facilities: There are five sites for tents only. Picnic tables and fire grills are provided. Drinking water and vault toilets are available. Five group picnic sites are available. Supplies are available in Auberry. Some facilities are wheelchair-accessible. Leashed pets are permitted.

Reservations, fees: Reservations are not accepted. Sites are $14 per night, $3 per night for each additional vehicle, $1 per pet per night. Open year-round.

Directions: From Fresno, take Highway 41 north for three miles to the exit for Highway 168 east. Take that exit and drive east on Highway 168 for about 22 miles to Auberry Road. Turn left (north) and drive 2.8 miles to Powerhouse Road. Turn left and drive 8.5 miles to the campground.

Contact: PG&E Land Services, 916/386-5164, www.pge.com/recreation.

32 YEH-GUB-WEH-TUH CAMPGROUND

🚶‍♀️ 🛶 🐕 ♿ ⛺

Scenic rating: 8

on the San Joaquin River

Map 11.1, page 603

Not many folks know about this spot. It's a primitive setting, but it has some bonuses. For one thing, there's access to the San Joaquin River if you drive to the fishing access trailhead at the end of the road. From there, you get great views of the San Joaquin River Gorge. The camp is a trailhead for two excellent hiking and equestrian trails. Note that the terrain is steep and can be difficult to traverse. Also, this area has poison oak and rattlesnakes. And one more thing: It can get very hot here in summer. Are we having fun yet? The setting is primarily oaks, gray pine, and chaparral. Beautiful wildflower displays are highlights in the late winter and spring.

Campsites, facilities: There are six walk-in sites for tents only, including two double sites and one triple site for up to 24 people. Drinking water and vault toilets are available. A camp host is on site. Bring your own firewood. Supplies are available in Auberry. Some facilities are wheelchair-accessible. Leashed pets are permitted.

Reservations, fees: Reservations are not accepted. Single sites are $10 per night, double sites are $15 per night. Open year-round.

Directions: From Fresno, take Highway 41 north for three miles to the exit for Highway 168 east. Take that exit and drive east on Highway 168 for about 22 miles to Auberry Road. Turn left and drive 2.8 miles to Powerhouse Road. Turn left and drive two miles to Smalley Road (signed "Smalley Road and San Joaquin River Gorge Management Area"). Turn left and drive four miles to the campground on the right.

Contact: San Joaquin River Gorge Management Area, 559/855-3492; Bureau of Land Management, Bakersfield Field Office, 661/391-6000, www.blm.gov/ca.

33 AHOLUL GROUP AND EQUESTRIAN CAMP

🚶‍♀️ 🛶 🐕 ♿ ⛺

Scenic rating: 8

on the San Joaquin River

Map 11.1, page 603

Aholul is located near Yeh-gub-weh-tuh Campground, and is the group site option.

We have no idea how you pronounce Aholul or Yeh-gub-weh-tuh, and the kind fellow at BLM refused to try. Heh, heh.

Campsites, facilities: There is one group site for tents only that can accommodate up to 250 people and an equestrian camp for family camping. A large paved parking lot at Aholul can accommodate RVs and large trailers. Stock water (bring your own bucket) and vault toilets are available. Bring your own drinking water and firewood. Horse corrals are available and are very popular; call 559/855-3492 for availability. Supplies are available in Auberry. Some facilities are wheelchair-accessible. Leashed pets are permitted.

Reservations, fees: Reservations are required at 661/391-6000. The group fee is $175 per night; equestrian sites are $25 per night. Open year-round.

Directions: From Fresno, take Highway 41 north for three miles to the exit for Highway 168 east. Take that exit and drive east on Highway 168 for about 22 miles to Auberry Road. Turn left and drive 2.8 miles to Powerhouse Road. Turn left and drive two miles to Smalley Road (signed "Smalley Road and San Joaquin River Gorge Management Area"). Turn left and drive four miles to the campground on the right.

Contact: San Joaquin River Gorge Management Area, 559/855-3492; Bureau of Land Management, Bakersfield Field Office, 661/391-6000, www.blm.gov/ca.

34 CAMP EDISON

🏊 🚣 🏕 🐎 ♿ 🚐 ⛺

Scenic rating: 8

on Shaver Lake

Map 11.1, page 603

Camp Edison is the best camp at Shaver Lake, set on a peninsula along the lake's western shore, with a boat ramp and marina. The lake is at an elevation of 5,370 feet in the Sierra, a pretty area that has become popular for its calm, warm days and cool water.

Boat rentals and bait and tackle are available at the marina. Newcomers with youngsters will discover that the best area for swimming and playing in the water is on the east side of the lake. Though more distant, this part of the lake offers sandy beaches rather than rocky drop-offs.

Campsites, facilities: There are 252 sites for RVs or tents, including 27 group sites; some sites have full or partial hookups (20, 30, and 50 amps). During the summer season, six tent trailers also are available. Picnic tables, fire rings, and barbecues are provided. Restrooms with flush toilets and pay showers, drinking water, cable TV, Wi-Fi, general store, dump station, laundry, marina, boat ramp, and horseback-riding facilities are available. Some facilities are wheelchair-accessible. Leashed pets are permitted.

Reservations, fees: Reservations are required and must be made by fax or mail. Standard sites are $28 per night, preferred sites are $35 per night, paved sites are $36 per night, RV sites with full hookups are $45 per night, lakeside sites are $43 per night, premium front sites are $65 per night, $6 per night for each additional vehicle, $5 per person per night for more than two people, $6 per day for boat launching, $6 per pet per night. Winter rates are $35 per night. Group sites are $140–375 per night. Open year-round with limited winter services.

Directions: From Fresno, take the exit for Highway 41 north and drive north on Highway 41 to the exit for Highway 180 east. Take that exit and drive east on Highway 180 to Highway 168 east. Take that exit and drive east on Highway 168 to the town of Shaver Lake. Continue one mile on Highway 168 to the campground entrance road on the right. Turn right and drive to the campground on the west shore of Shaver Lake.

Contact: Camp Edison, P.O. Box 600, 42696 Tollhouse Road, Shaver Lake, CA 93664; Southern California Edison, 559/841-3134, www.sce.com/campedison.

35 DORABELLE

🚶 🏊 🛶 🎣 🐎 🚐 ⛺

Scenic rating: 7

on Shaver Lake in Sierra National Forest

Map 11.1, page 603

This is one of the few Forest Service camps in the state that is set up more for RVers than for tenters. The camp is along a long cove at the southwest corner of the lake, well protected from winds out of the northwest. Several hiking trails are available here. Shaver Lake is a popular lake for vacationers, and waterskiing and wakeboarding are extremely popular. It is well stocked with trout and kokanee salmon. Boat rentals and bait and tackle are available at the nearby marina. The elevation is 5,400 feet.

Campsites, facilities: There are 68 sites for tents or RVs up to 40 feet (no hookups). Picnic tables and fire grills are provided. Drinking water and vault toilets are available. A store is nearby. Leashed pets are permitted.

Reservations, fees: Reservations are accepted at 877/444-6777 or www.recreation.gov ($9 reservation fee). Sites are $21–23 per night, $5 per night for each additional vehicle. Open May through September, weather permitting.

Directions: From Fresno, drive east on Highway 168 to Dorabelle Road (on the right just as you enter the town of Shaver Lake). Turn right on Dorabelle Road and drive one mile to the campground at the southwest end of Shaver Lake.

Contact: Sierra National Forest, High Sierra Ranger District, 559/855-5355, www.fs.usda. gov/sierra; California Land Management, 559/893-2111.

36 SWANSON MEADOW

🐎 🚐 ⛺

Scenic rating: 4

near Shaver Lake in Sierra National Forest

Map 11.1, page 603

This is the smallest and most primitive of the camps near Shaver Lake; it is used primarily as an overflow area if lakeside camps are full. It is about two miles south of Shaver Lake at an elevation of 5,600 feet.

Campsites, facilities: There are eight sites for tents or RVs up to 25 feet (no hookups). Picnic tables and fire grills are provided. Vault toilets are available. No drinking water is available. A camp host is on site and a store is nearby. Leashed pets are permitted.

Reservations, fees: Reservations are not accepted. Single sites are $16 per night, double sites are $32 per night, $5 per night for each additional vehicle. Open May through October, weather permitting.

Directions: From Fresno, drive east on Highway 168 to Dinkey Creek Road (on the right just as you enter the town of Shaver Lake). Turn right and drive three miles to the campground entrance road on the left. Turn left and drive a short distance to the campground.

Contact: Sierra National Forest, High Sierra Ranger District, 559/855-5355, www.fs.usda. gov/sierra; California Land Management, 559/893-2111.

37 DINKEY CREEK AND GROUP CAMP

🚶 🏊 🎣 🐎 ♿ 🚐 ⛺

Scenic rating: 7

in Sierra National Forest

Map 11.1, page 603

This is a huge Forest Service camp set along Dinkey Creek at 5,700 feet elevation, well in the interior of Sierra National Forest. It is a popular camp for anglers who take the trail and hike upstream along the creek for small-trout fishing in a pristine setting. Backpackers occasionally lay over here before driving on to the Dinkey Lakes Parking Area, for hikes to Mystery Lake, Swede Lake, South Lake, and others in the nearby Dinkey Lakes Wilderness.

Campsites, facilities: There are 128 sites for tents or RVs up to 35 feet (no hookups), and

one group site for up to 50 people. Picnic tables and fire grills are provided. Drinking water, flush and vault toilets, coin showers, interpretive programs and a camp host are available. Horseback-riding facilities are nearby. You can buy supplies in Dinkey Creek. Some facilities are wheelchair-accessible. Leashed pets are permitted.

Reservations, fees: Reservations are required at 877/444-6777 or www.recreation.gov ($9 reservation fee). Single sites are $24 per night, double sites are $48 per night, $5 per night for each additional vehicle, $165–167 per night for the group site. Open May through September, weather permitting.

Directions: From Fresno, drive east on Highway 168 to Dinkey Creek Road (on the right just as you enter the town of Shaver Lake). Turn right and drive 13 miles to the campground. A map of Sierra National Forest is advised.

Contact: Sierra National Forest, High Sierra Ranger District, 559/855-5355, www.fs.usda.gov/sierra; California Land Management, 559/893-2111.

38 GIGANTEA

🚶 🏕 🚐 ⛰

Scenic rating: 7

on Dinkey Creek in Sierra National Forest

Map 11.1, page 603

This primitive campground is set along Dinkey Creek adjacent to the McKinley Grove Botanical Area, which features a little-known grove of giant sequoias. The campground is set on a short loop spur road, and day visitors are better off stopping at the McKinley Grove Picnic Area. The elevation is 6,400 feet.

Campsites, facilities: There are 10 sites for tents or RVs up to 35 feet (no hookups). Picnic tables and fire grills are provided. Vault toilets are available. No drinking water is available. Supplies are available in Dinkey Creek. Leashed pets are permitted.

Reservations, fees: Reservations are not accepted. Sites are $16 per night, $5 per night for each additional vehicle. Open May through October, weather permitting.

Directions: From Fresno, drive east on Highway 168 to Dinkey Creek Road (on the right just as you enter the town of Shaver Lake). Turn right and drive 13 miles to McKinley Grove Road/Forest Road 40. Turn right and drive 6.5 miles to the campground.

Contact: Sierra National Forest, High Sierra Ranger District, 559/855-5355, www.fs.usda.gov/sierra; California Land Management, 559/893-2111.

39 BUCK MEADOW

🚶 🏕 🐕 ♿ 🚐 ⛰

Scenic rating: 7

on Deer Creek in Sierra National Forest

Map 11.1, page 603

This is one of the three little-known, primitive camps in the area. It's set at 6,800 feet elevation along Deer Creek, about seven miles from Wishon Reservoir, a more popular destination.

Campsites, facilities: There are 10 sites for tents or RVs up to 35 feet (no hookups). Picnic tables and fire grills are provided. Vault toilets are available. No drinking water is available. Garbage must be packed out. Some facilities are wheelchair-accessible. Leashed pets are permitted.

Reservations, fees: Reservations are not accepted. Sites are $16 per night, $5 per night for each additional vehicle. Open May through October, weather permitting.

Directions: From Fresno, drive east on Highway 168 to Dinkey Creek Road (on the right just as you enter the town of Shaver Lake). Turn right and drive 13 miles to McKinley Grove Road (Forest Road 40). Turn right and drive eight miles to the campground.

Contact: Sierra National Forest, High Sierra Ranger District, 559/855-5355, www.fs.usda.gov/sierra; California Land Management, 559/893-2111.

40 MILLERTON LAKE STATE RECREATION AREA

🏃 ⛱ 🏊 🚣 🎣 🦌 ♿ 🚐 ⛺

Scenic rating: 6

near Madera

Map 11.1, page 603

As the temperature gauge goes up in the summer, the value of Millerton Lake increases at the same rate. The lake is set at 578 feet in the foothills of the San Joaquin Valley, and the water is like gold here. The campground and recreation area are set on a peninsula along the north shore of the lake; there are sandy beach areas on both sides of the lake with boat ramps available near the campgrounds. It's a big lake, with 43 miles of shoreline, from a narrow lake inlet extending to an expansive main lake body. The irony at Millerton is that when the lake is filled to the brim, the beaches are covered, so ideal conditions are actually when the lake level is down a bit, typically from early summer on. Fishing for bass can be good here in spring. Catfish are popular for shoreliners on summer evenings. Waterskiing is very popular in summer, of course. Anglers head upstream, water-skiers downstream. The lake's south side has a huge day-use area. During winter, boat tours are available to view bald eagles. A note of history: The original Millerton County Courthouse, built in 1867, is in the park.

Campsites, facilities: There are 148 sites, 26 with full hookups, for tents or RVs up to 36 feet, three boat-in sites, and two group sites for 45–75 people. Picnic tables and fire grills are provided. Drinking water, restrooms with flush toilets and coin showers, dump station, picnic areas, full-service marina, snack bar, boat rentals, and boat ramps are available. You can buy supplies in Friant. Some facilities are wheelchair-accessible. Leashed pets are permitted.

Reservations, fees: Reservations are accepted at 800/444-7275 or www.reserveamerica.com ($8 reservation fee). Drive-in sites are $30 per night, RV sites (hookups) are $40 per night, $8 per night for each additional vehicle, $11 for boat-in sites, $150–200 per night for group sites. Boat launching is $7 per day. Open year-round.

Directions: Drive on Highway 99 to Madera at the exit for Highway 145 East. Take that exit east and drive on Highway 145 for 22 miles (six miles past the intersection with Highway 41) to the park entrance on the right.

Contact: Millerton Lake State Recreation Area, 559/822-2332, www.parks.ca.gov.

41 JACKASS MEADOW

🏃 ⛱ 🏊 🚣 🎣 🦌 ♿ 🚐 ⛺

Scenic rating: 7

on Florence Lake in Sierra National Forest

Map 11.2, page 604

Jackass Meadow is a pretty spot adjacent to Florence Lake, near the Upper San Joaquin River. There are good canoeing, rafting, and float-tubing possibilities, all high-Sierra style, and swimming is allowed. The boat speed limit is 15 mph. The elevation is 7,200 feet. The lake is remote and can be reached only after a long, circuitous drive on a narrow road with many blind turns. A trailhead at the lake offers access to the wilderness and the John Muir Trail. A hikers water taxi is available.

Campsites, facilities: There are 44 sites for tents or RVs up to 25 feet (no hookups). Picnic tables and fire grills are provided. Vault toilets are available, but there is no drinking water. A boat launch, fishing boat rentals, and wheelchair-accessible fishing pier are available nearby. Leashed pets are permitted.

Reservations, fees: Reservations are accepted at 877/444-6777 or www.recreation.gov ($9 reservation fee). Single sites are $19 per night, $40 per night for a double site, $5 per night for each additional vehicle. Open June through October, weather permitting.

Directions: From the town of Shaver Lake, drive east on Highway 168 for 21 miles to Kaiser Pass Road. Bear northeast on Kaiser Pass Road/Forest Road 80 (slow and curvy) to a junction (left goes to Mono Hot Springs and Lake Edison) with Florence Lake Road. Bear right at the junction and drive seven miles to the campground.

Contact: Sierra National Forest, High Sierra Ranger District, 559/855-5355, www.fs.usda. gov/sierra; California Land Management, 559/893-2111.

42 TRAPPER SPRINGS

Scenic rating: 8

on Courtright Reservoir in
Sierra National Forest

Map 11.2, page 604

Trapper Springs is on the west shore of Courtright Reservoir, set at 8,200 feet elevation on the west slope of the Sierra. Courtright is a great destination, with excellent camping, boating, fishing, and hiking into the nearby John Muir Wilderness. A 15-mph speed limit makes the lake ideal for fishing, canoeing, and rafting. Swimming is allowed, but the water is very cold. The lake level can drop dramatically by late summer. A trailhead a mile north of camp by car heads around the north end of the lake to a fork; to the left it is routed into the Dinkey Lakes Wilderness, and to the right it is routed to the head of the lake, then follows Dusy Creek in a long climb into spectacular country in the John Muir Wilderness. There are two driving routes to this lake, one from Shaver Lake and the other from Pine Flat Reservoir; both are very long, slow, and twisty drives.

Campsites, facilities: There are 70 sites for tents or RVs up to 35 feet (no hookups). Picnic tables and fire grills are provided. Drinking water and vault toilets are available. A boat ramp is nearby. Some facilities are wheelchair-accessible. Leashed pets are permitted.

Reservations, fees: Reservations are not accepted. Sites are $24 per night, $9 per night for additional RV, $3 per night for each additional vehicle, $1 per pet per night. Open mid-June through mid-October.

Directions: From Fresno, drive east on Highway 168 to Dinkey Creek Road (on the right just as you enter the town of Shaver Lake). Turn right and drive 13 miles to McKinley Grove Road/Forest Road 40. Turn right and drive 14 miles to Courtright Road. Turn left (north) and drive 12 miles to the campground entrance road on the right.

Contact: Sierra National Forest, High Sierra Ranger District, 559/855-5355, www.fs.usda. gov/sierra; PG&E Land Services, 916/386-5164, www.pge.com/recreation.

43 MARMOT ROCK

Scenic rating: 8

on Courtright Reservoir in
Sierra National Forest

Map 11.2, page 604

Courtright Reservoir is in the high country at 8,200 feet elevation. Marmot Rock is set at the southern end of the lake, with a boat ramp nearby. This is a pretty Sierra lake that provides options for boaters and hikers. Trout fishing can also be good here. Boaters must observe a 15-mph speed limit, which makes for quiet water. There are two driving routes to this lake, one from Shaver Lake and the other from Pine Flat Reservoir; both are very long, slow, and twisty drives.

Campsites, facilities: There are 15 sites for tents or small RVs; most sites are walk-in. Picnic tables and fire grills are provided. Vault toilets are available, but there is no drinking water. A boat ramp is nearby. Leashed pets are permitted.

Reservations, fees: Reservations are not accepted. Sites are $24 per night, $3 per night for each additional vehicle, overflow parking is $18 per night, $1 per pet per night. Open mid-June through mid-October.

Directions: From Fresno, drive east on Highway 168 to Dinkey Creek Road (on the right just as you enter the town of Shaver Lake). Turn right and drive 13 miles to McKinley Grove Road/

Forest Road 40. Turn right and drive 14 miles to Courtright Road. Turn left (north) and drive 10 miles to the campground entrance road on the right (on the south shore of the lake). Park and walk a short distance to the campground.
Contact: PG&E Land Services, 916/386-5164, www.pge.com/recreation; Sierra National Forest, High Sierra Ranger District, 559/855-5355, www.fs.usda.gov/sierra.

44 WISHON VILLAGE RV RESORT
🏃 🏊 🛶 🚣 🛥 🐕 🚐 ⛺

Scenic rating: 7
near Wishon Reservoir
Map 11.2, page 604

This privately operated mountain park is set near the shore of Wishon Reservoir, about one mile from the dam. Trout stocks often make for good fishing in early summer, and anglers with boats love the 15-mph speed limit, which keeps personal watercraft off the water. Backpackers and hikers can find a great trailhead at the south end of the lake at Coolidge Meadow, where a trail awaits that is routed to the Woodchuck Creek drainage and numerous lakes in the John Muir Wilderness. The elevation is 6,772 feet.
Campsites, facilities: There are 97 sites with full hookups (50 amps) for RVs up to 45 feet, and 26 sites for tents. Two rental trailers are also available. Picnic tables and fire pits are provided. Restrooms with coin showers, drinking water, a general store, WiFi, and Sunday church services are available. Coin laundry, ice, boat ramp, motorboat rentals, bait and tackle, boat slips, volleyball, horseshoes, and propane gas are nearby. Leashed pets are permitted.
Reservations, fees: Reservations are recommended. RV sites are $37–49 per night, tent sites are $27–39 per night, $3 per person per night for more than two people, $5 per night per additional vehicle, $3 per pet per night. Weekly and monthly rates available. Open May through September.
Directions: From Fresno, drive east on

Highway 168 to Dinkey Creek Road (on the right just as you enter the town of Shaver Lake). Turn right and drive 13 miles to McKinley Grove Road (Forest Road 40). Turn right and drive 15 miles to the park (66500 McKinley Grove Road/Forest Road 40).
Contact: Wishon Village RV Resort, 559/865-5361, www.wishonvillage.com.

45 LILY PAD
🏃 🏊 🛶 🚣 🛥 🐕 ♿ 🚐 ⛺

Scenic rating: 7
near Wishon Reservoir in Sierra National Forest
Map 11.2, page 604

This is the smallest of the three camps at Wishon Reservoir. It is set along the southwest shore at 6,500 feet elevation, about a mile from both the lake and a good boat ramp. A 15-mph speed limit ensures quiet water, making this an ideal destination for families with canoes or rafts. The conditions at this lake are similar to those at Courtright Reservoir. There are two driving routes to this lake, one from Shaver Lake and the other from Pine Flat Reservoir; both are very long, slow, and twisty drives.
Campsites, facilities: There are 11 sites for tents or RVs up to 35 feet (no hookups), and four hike-in sites. Picnic tables and fire grills are provided. Vault toilets are available, but there is no drinking water. Groceries, boat rentals, boat ramp, and propane gas are nearby. Some facilities are wheelchair-accessible. Leashed pets are permitted.
Reservations, fees: Reservations are not accepted. Sites are $24 per night, $7 per night for additional RV, $3 per night for each additional vehicle, $1 per pet per night. Open late May through mid-October, weather permitting.
Directions: From Fresno, drive east on Highway 168 to Dinkey Creek Road (on the right just as you enter the town of Shaver Lake). Turn right and drive 13 miles to McKinley Grove Road (Forest Road 40). Turn right and drive 16 miles to the campground on the right.

Contact: Sierra National Forest, High Sierra Ranger District, 559/855-5355, www.fs.usda. gov/sierra; PG&E Land Services, 916/386-5164, www.pge.com/recreation.

46 UPPER KINGS RIVER GROUP CAMP

🥾 🏊 🎣 🛶 🚲 🐾 🚐 ⛺

Scenic rating: 8

on Wishon Reservoir

Map 11.2, page 604

Wishon Reservoir is a great place for a camping trip. When the lake is full, which is not often enough, the place has great natural beauty, set at 6,400 feet elevation and surrounded by national forest. The fishing is fair enough on summer evenings, and a 15-mph speed limit keeps the lake quiet. Swimming is allowed, but the water is very cold. A side-trip option is hiking from the trailhead at Woodchuck Creek, which within the span of a one-day hike takes you into the John Muir Wilderness and past three lakes—Woodchuck, Chimney, and Marsh. There are two driving routes to this lake, one from Shaver Lake and the other from Pine Flat Reservoir; both are very long, slow, and twisty drives.

Campsites, facilities: There is a group site for tents or RVs up to 40 feet (no hookups) that can accommodate up to 50 people. Picnic tables and fire grills are provided. Drinking water and vault toilets are available. Leashed pets are permitted.

Reservations, fees: Reservations are required at 916/386-5164. Sites are $200 per night, two-night minimum on weekdays, three-night minimum on holidays. Open late June through early October, weather permitting.

Directions: From Fresno, drive east on Highway 168 to Dinkey Creek Road (on the right just as you enter the town of Shaver Lake). Turn right and drive 13 miles to McKinley Grove Road/Forest Road 40. Turn right and drive to the Wishon Dam. The campground is near the base of the dam.

Contact: PG&E Land Services, 916/386-5164, www.pge.com/recreation.

47 HORTON CREEK

🥾 🐾 🚐 ⛺

Scenic rating: 7

near Bishop

Map 11.2, page 604

This is a little-known, primitive BLM camp set along Horton Creek, northwest of Bishop. It can make a good base camp for hunters in the fall, with wild, rugged country to the west. The elevation is 4,975 feet.

Campsites, facilities: There are 49 sites for tents or RVs up to 30 feet (no hookups). Picnic tables and fire grills are provided. Drinking water, lantern holders, vault toilets, and garbage containers are available. Leashed pets are permitted.

Reservations, fees: Reservations are not accepted. Sites are $5 per night; LTVA season passes are available for $300. There is a 14-day stay limit. Open early May through October, weather permitting.

Directions: Drive on U.S. 395 to Sawmill Road (eight miles north of Bishop). Turn left (northwest, toward the Sierra) and drive a very short distance to Round Valley Road. Turn right and drive approximately five miles to the campground entrance on the left.

Contact: Bureau of Land Management, Bishop Field Office, 760/872-4881, www.blm.gov/ca.

48 BROWN'S MILLPOND CAMPGROUND

🥾 🏊 🛶 🎣 🐾 ♿ 🚐 ⛺

Scenic rating: 6

near Bishop

Map 11.2, page 604

This privately operated camp is adjacent to the Millpond Recreation Area, which offers ball fields, playgrounds, and a swimming lake.

No powerboats are allowed. There are opportunities for sailing, archery, tennis, horseshoe games, and fishing.

Campsites, facilities: There are 72 sites for tents or RVs of any length; some sites have partial hookups (30 amps). Picnic tables and fire grills are provided. Restrooms with flush toilets and coin showers, drinking water, and coin laundry are available. Some facilities are wheelchair accessible. A limit of one vehicle per site is enforced. Leashed pets are permitted.

Reservations, fees: Reservations are accepted. Sites are $23–28 per vehicle per night, $5 for each additional vehicle. Open March through October.

Directions: Drive on U.S. 395 to a road signed "Millpond/County Park" (seven miles north of Bishop). Turn southwest (toward the Sierra) at that road (Ed Powers Road) and drive 0.2 mile to Sawmill Road. Turn right and drive 0.8 mile to Millpond Road. Turn left and drive a short distance to the campground.

Contact: Brown's Millpond Campground, 760/873-5342, www.brownscampgrounds. com.

49 BROWN'S TOWN

Scenic rating: 5

near Bishop

Map 11.2, page 604

This privately operated campground is one of several in the vicinity of Bishop. It's all shade and grass, and it's next to the golf course.

Campsites, facilities: There are 106 sites with no hookups for tents or RVs of any length and 44 sites with partial hookups (30 amps) for tents or RVs. Some sites are pull-through. Picnic tables are provided, and fire grills are provided at most sites. Restrooms with flush toilets and coin showers, drinking water, cable TV at 10 sites, coin laundry, dump station, museum, convenience store,

and snack bar are available. Leashed pets are permitted.

Reservations, fees: Reservations are accepted. RV sites are $28–32 per night, tent sites are $23 per night, $1 per person per night for more than four people, $10 per night per additional vehicle. One-vehicle limit per site. Fourteen-day stay limit per season. Some credit cards accepted. Open March through Thanksgiving, weather permitting.

Directions: On U.S. 395, drive to Schober Lane (one mile south of Bishop) and the campground entrance. Turn northwest (toward the Sierra) and into the campground.

Contact: Brown's Town, 760/873-8522, www. brownscampgrounds.com.

50 BITTERBRUSH

Scenic rating: 7

near Bishop in the Inyo National Forest

Map 11.2, page 604

Bitterbrush opened in 2007 and is situated along Bishop Creek with piñon pines and sagebrush providing the scenery. In the fall, the aspens are spectacular in the canyon between here and beautiful Lake Sabrina. The elevation is 7,350 feet.

Campsites, facilities: There are 30 sites for tents or RVs to 40 feet (no hookups). Picnic tables, bear-proof lockers, and fire rings are provided. Drinking water (seasonal), vault toilets, and a dump station are available. Some facilities are wheelchair-accessible. Leashed pets are permitted.

Reservations, fees: Reservations are not accepted. Sites are $21 per night; free when water becomes unavailable. There is a maximum 14-day limit. Open year-round, weather permitting.

Directions: From Bishop drive west on Highway 168 for nine miles to the campground.

Contact: Inyo National Forest, White Mountain Ranger District, 760/873-2500, www. fs.usda.gov.

51 FORKS

Scenic rating: 7

near South Lake in Inyo National Forest

Map 11.2, page 604

After a visit here, it's no mystery how the Forest Service named this camp. It is at the fork in the road, which gives you two options: You can turn south on South Lake Road and drive along the South Fork of Bishop Creek up to pretty South Lake, or you can keep driving on Highway 168 to another beautiful lake, Lake Sabrina, where hikers will find a trailhead that offers access to the John Muir Wilderness. The elevation is 7,800 feet.

Campsites, facilities: There are 31 sites for RVs up to 30 feet (no hookups). Picnic tables and fire grills are provided. Drinking water and flush toilets are available. Some facilities are wheelchair accessible. Supplies are available in Bishop. Leashed pets are permitted.

Reservations, fees: Reservations are not accepted. Single sites are $22 per night, double sites are $44 per night, $5 per night per additional vehicle. Open late April through October, weather permitting.

Directions: Drive on U.S. 395 to Bishop and Highway 168. Turn west (toward the Sierra) on Highway 168 and drive 14 miles to South Lake Road. Turn left and drive 0.25 mile to the campground entrance on the right.

Contact: Inyo National Forest, White Mountain Ranger District, 760/873-2500, www.fs.usda.gov; Rainbow Pack Outfitters, 760/873-8877.

52 BIG TREES

Scenic rating: 8

on Bishop Creek in Inyo National Forest

Map 11.2, page 604

This is a small Forest Service camp on Bishop Creek at 7,500 feet elevation. This section of the stream is stocked with small trout by the Department of Fish and Game. Both South Lake and Lake Sabrina are about 10 miles away.

Campsites, facilities: There are 16 sites for tents or RVs up to 30 feet (no hookups). Picnic tables and fire grills are provided. Drinking water and flush toilets are available. A dump station is two miles away at Four Jeffrey. Horseback-riding facilities are approximately seven miles away. Supplies are available in Bishop. Leashed pets are permitted.

Reservations, fees: Reservations are not accepted. Sites are $21 per night. Open late April through October, weather permitting.

Directions: Drive on U.S. 395 to Bishop and Highway 168. Turn west (toward the Sierra) on Highway 168 and drive 11 miles to the campground access road on the left. Turn left and drive two miles on a dirt road to the campground.

Contact: Inyo National Forest, White Mountain Ranger District, 760/873-2500, www.fs.usda.gov; Rainbow Pack Outfitters, 760/873-8877.

53 BISHOP PARK AND GROUP

Scenic rating: 6

near Lake Sabrina in Inyo National Forest

Map 11.2, page 604

Bishop Park Camp is one in a series of camps along Bishop Creek. This one is set just behind the summer community of Aspendell. It is about two miles from Lake Sabrina, an ideal day trip or jump-off spot for a backpacking expedition into the John Muir Wilderness. The elevation is 8,400 feet.

Campsites, facilities: There are 20 sites for tents or RVs up to 22 feet (no hookups), and a group tent site for up to 25 people. Picnic tables, fire grills, and food lockers are provided. Drinking water and flush toilets are available. Horseback-riding facilities are nearby. Supplies are available in Bishop. Some facilities are wheelchair-accessible. Leashed pets are permitted.

Reservations, fees: Reservations are not accepted

for the family sites, but are required for the group site at 877/444-6777 or www.recreation.gov ($9 reservation fee). Sites are $21 per night, $65 per night for group site. Open mid-May through mid-October, weather permitting.

Directions: Drive on U.S. 395 to Bishop and Highway 168. Turn west (toward the Sierra) on Highway 168 and drive 15 miles to the campground.

Contact: Inyo National Forest, White Mountain Ranger District, 760/873-2500, www.fs.usda.gov/inyo; Rainbow Pack Outfitters, 760/873-8877; campground management, 760/872-7018.

54 INTAKE AND INTAKE WALK-IN

Scenic rating: 7

on Sabrina Creek in Inyo National Forest

Map 11.2, page 604

This small camp, set at 8,200 feet elevation at a tiny reservoir on Bishop Creek, is about three miles from Lake Sabrina where a trailhead leads into the John Muir Wilderness. Nearby North Lake and South Lake provide side-trip options. All three are beautiful alpine lakes.

Campsites, facilities: There are eight sites for tents or RVs up to 40 feet (no hookups), and five walk-in tent sites. Picnic tables, food lockers, and fire grills are provided. Drinking water and flush toilets are available. A dump station is available 1.5 miles away at Four Jeffrey. Supplies are available in Bishop. Some facilities are wheelchair accessible. Leashed pets are permitted.

Reservations, fees: Reservations are not accepted. Sites are $21 per night. The walk-in sites are open year-round, weather permitting. Drive-in sites are open April through October, weather permitting.

Directions: Drive on U.S. 395 to Bishop and Highway 168. Turn west (toward the Sierra) on Highway 168 and drive 14.5 miles to the campground entrance.

Contact: Inyo National Forest, White Mountain Ranger District, 760/873-2500, www.fs.usda.gov/inyo.

55 FOUR JEFFREY

Scenic rating: 8

near South Lake in Inyo National Forest

Map 11.2, page 604

The camp is set on the South Fork of Bishop Creek at 8,100 feet elevation, about four miles from South Lake. If you can arrange a trip in the fall, make sure you visit this camp. The fall colors are spectacular, with the aspen trees exploding in yellows and oranges. It is also the last camp on South Lake Road to be closed in the fall, and though nights are cold, it is well worth the trip. This is by far the largest of the Forest Service camps in the vicinity. There are three lakes in the area: North Lake, Lake Sabrina, and South Lake. South Lake is stocked with trout and has a 5-mph speed limit.

Campsites, facilities: There are 106 sites for tents or RVs up to 30 feet (no hookups). Picnic tables, food lockers, and fire grills are provided. Drinking water, flush toilets, and a dump station are available. Horseback-riding facilities are available nearby. A café, a small store, and fishing-boat rentals are available at South Lake. Supplies are available in Bishop. Some facilities are wheelchair-accessible. Leashed pets are permitted.

Reservations, fees: Reservations are accepted at 877/444-6777 or www.recreation.gov ($9 reservation fee). Sites are $21 per night. Open mid-April through October, weather permitting.

Directions: Drive on U.S. 395 to Bishop and Highway 168. Turn west (toward the Sierra) on Highway 168 and drive 14 miles to South Lake Road. Turn left and drive 0.5 mile to the campground.

Contact: Inyo National Forest, White Mountain Ranger District, 760/873-2500, www.fs.usda.gov/inyo; Rainbow Pack Outfitters, 760/873-8877, rainbow.zb-net.com.

56 CREEKSIDE RV PARK

Scenic rating: 7

on the South Fork of Bishop Creek

Map 11.2, page 604

This privately operated park in the high country is set up primarily for RVs. A lot of folks are surprised to find it here. The South Fork of Bishop Creek runs through the park. A bonus is a fishing pond stocked with Alpers trout. North, Sabrina, and South Lakes are in the area. The elevation is 8,300 feet.

Campsites, facilities: There are 45 sites with full or partial hookups (20 and 30 amps) for RVs up to 35 feet, and four sites for tents. Fourteen rental trailers are also available. Restrooms with flush toilets and coin showers, drinking water, convenience store, propane, horseshoes, and fish-cleaning facilities are available. Leashed pets are permitted.

Reservations, fees: Reservations are accepted. RV sites are $47 per night, tent sites are $35 per night, $1 per person per night for more than two people, $5 per night for each additional vehicle, $5 per pet per night. Open May through October. Some credit cards accepted.

Directions: Drive on U.S. 395 to Bishop and Highway 168. Turn west (toward the Sierra) on Highway 168 and drive 14 miles to South Lake Road. Turn left and drive two miles to the campground entrance on the left (1949 South Lake Road).

Contact: Creekside RV Park, 760/873-4483, www.bishopcreeksidervpark.com.

57 NORTH LAKE

Scenic rating: 8

on Bishop Creek near North Lake in
Inyo National Forest

Map 11.2, page 604

North Lake is a beautiful Sierra lake set at an elevation of 9,500 feet, with good trout fishing much of the season and surrounded by beautiful aspens. No motors are allowed on this 13-acre lake. The camp is set on the North Fork of Bishop Creek near North Lake and close to a trailhead that offers access to numerous lakes in the John Muir Wilderness and eventually connects with the Pacific Crest Trail. There is also an outstanding trailhead that leads to several small alpine lakes in the nearby John Muir Wilderness for day hikes, or all the way up to Bishop Pass and Dusy Basin.

Campsites, facilities: There are 11 sites for tents only. Picnic tables and fire grills are provided. Drinking water and vault toilets are available. Horseback-riding facilities are available nearby. Supplies are available in Bishop. Leashed pets are permitted.

Reservations, fees: Reservations are not accepted. Sites are $21 per night. Open early June through mid-September, weather permitting.

Directions: Drive on U.S. 395 to Bishop and Highway 168. Turn west (toward the Sierra) on Highway 168 and drive 17 miles to Forest Road 8S02 (signed "North Lake"). Turn right (north) on Forest Road 8S02 and drive two miles to the campground.

Contact: Inyo National Forest, White Mountain Ranger District, 760/873-2500, www.fs.usda.gov/inyo; Bishop Pack Outfitters, 760/873-4785.

58 SABRINA

Scenic rating: 8

near Lake Sabrina in Inyo National Forest

Map 11.2, page 604

You get the best of both worlds at this camp. It is set at 9,000 feet elevation on Bishop Creek, just 0.5 mile from 200-acre Lake Sabrina, one of the prettiest alpine lakes in California that you can reach by car. A 10-mph boat speed limit is in effect. Sabrina is stocked with trout, including some big Alpers trout. Trails nearby are routed into the high country of the John Muir Wilderness. Take your pick. Whatever your choice, it's a good one. By the way, Sabrina is pronounced "Sa-bry-na," not "Sa-bree-na."

Campsites, facilities: There are 18 sites for tents or RVs up to 30 feet (no hookups). Picnic tables and fire grills are provided. Drinking water and pit toilets are available. A boat ramp and rentals are nearby. Supplies are available in Bishop. Some facilities are wheelchair accessible. Leashed pets are permitted.

Reservations, fees: Reservations are not accepted. Sites are $21 per night. Open mid-May through mid-September, weather permitting.

Directions: Drive on U.S. 395 to Bishop and Highway 168. Turn west (toward the Sierra) on Highway 168 and drive 17 miles (signed "Lake Sabrina" at a fork) to the campground.

Contact: Inyo National Forest, White Mountain Ranger District, 760/873-2500, www. fs.usda.gov/inyo; Bishop Pack Outfitters, 760/873-4785.

59 WILLOW

Scenic rating: 8

on Bishop Creek in Inyo National Forest

Map 11.2, page 604

This is one in a series of pretty Forest Service camps set along the south fork of Bishop Creek. Willow is located near Mountain Glen (see listing in this chapter) at an elevation of 9,000 feet. Primitive and beautiful, this is a favorite. Just up the road is the trailhead to the Chocolate Lakes and Bishop Pass, as well as low-speed boating and fishing at Lake Sabrina and South Lake. A good spot to set up shop.

Campsites, facilities: There are 10 sites for tents or RVs to 25 feet (no hookups). Picnic tables, bear-proof, lockers, and fire rings are provided. Vault toilets are available. There is no drinking water. A nearby spring has water that looks good but must be treated before use. Leashed pets are permitted.

Reservations, fees: Reservations are not accepted. Sites are $20 per night. There is a 7-day stay limit. Open late May to late September.

Directions: From Bishop drive west 13 miles on Highway 168 to South Lake Road. Turn left and drive 5.5 miles to the campground.

Contact: Inyo National Forest, White Mountain Ranger District, 760/873-2500, www. fs.usda.gov/inyo.

60 MOUNTAIN GLEN

Scenic rating: 8

on Bishop Creek in Inyo National Forest

Map 11.2, page 604

Mountain Glen rests along the south fork of Bishop Creek. Jeffrey pines, piñon pines, aspen, and sagebrush green the campground, but come in mid-September when the aspens explode in a riot of colors, bringing the canyon to life. You can often have this place to yourself then. Little Bishop Creek is nearby and is stocked with small trout. The elevation is 8,200 feet.

Campsites, facilities: There are five sites for tents or small RVs (no hookups). Picnic tables, bear-proof lockers, and fire rings are provided. Vault toilets are available, but there is no drinking water. Leashed pets are permitted.

Reservations, fees: Reservations are not accepted. Sites are $20 per night. There is a maximum 7-day limit. Open late May to late September.

Directions: From Bishop drive west 13 miles on Highway 168 to South Lake Road. Turn left and drive three miles to the campground.

Contact: Inyo National Forest, White Mountain Ranger District, 760/873-2500, www. fs.usda.gov/inyo.

61 KEOUGH'S HOT SPRINGS

Scenic rating: 5

in Owens Valley on U.S. 305

Map 11.2, page 604

This private facility is the site of the Eastern Sierra's largest natural hot springs pool. The landscape is the stark high desert, but makes for sensational sunsets with colors sometimes refracting across what seems an infinite sky. With the public springs at Hot Creek now off limits, Keough's is a very good choice.

Campsites, facilities: There are 10 tent sites and 10 sites for RVs up to 40 feet (partial 30-amp hookups), plus four furnished tent cabins. Picnic tables are provided, and campers can bring their own above-ground fire pit. Drinking water, flush toilets, coin showers, a snack bar, and a gift shop are available. Leashed pets are permitted.

Reservations, fees: Reservations are accepted. Sites are $23–28 per night, $1 per person per night for more than two people. There is a maximum 14-day limit. Open year round, weather permitting.

Directions: From Bishop drive south on Highway 395 for seven miles to Keough's Hot Springs Road. Turn right on Keough's Hot Springs Road and drive one mile to the resort.

Contact: Keough's Hot Springs, 760/872-4670, www.keoughshotsprings.com.

62 BAKER CREEK CAMPGROUND

Scenic rating: 4

near Big Pine

Map 11.2, page 604

Because this is a county-operated RV park, it is often overlooked by campers who consider only camps on reservations systems. That makes this a good option for cruisers touring the eastern Sierra on U.S. 395. It's ideal for a quick overnighter, with easy access from Big Pine. The camp is set along Baker Creek at 4,000 feet elevation in the high plateau country of the eastern Sierra. An option is fair trout fishing during the evening bite on the creek.

Campsites, facilities: There are 70 sites for tents or RVs up to 30 feet (no hookups). Picnic tables and fire grills are provided. Vault toilets and hand-pumped well water are available.

You can buy supplies about 1.5 miles away in Big Pine. Leashed pets are permitted.

Reservations, fees: Reservations are not accepted. Sites are $10 per vehicle per night. Open year-round, weather permitting.

Directions: Drive on U.S. 395 to Big Pine and Baker Creek Road. Turn west (toward the Sierra) on Baker Creek Road and drive a mile to the campground.

Contact: Inyo County Parks Department, 760/873-5577, www.inyocountycamping.com.

63 GLACIER VIEW

Scenic rating: 4

near Big Pine

Map 11.2, page 604

This is one of two county camps near the town of Big Pine, providing U.S. 395 cruisers with two options. The camp is set along the Big Pine Canal at 3,900 feet elevation. It is owned by the county but operated by a concessionaire, Brown's, which runs five small campgrounds in the area: Glacier View, Keough Hot Springs, Millpond, Brown's Owens River, and Brown's Town.

Campsites, facilities: There are 40 sites for tents or RVs of any length; some sites have partial hookups (30 amps) and/or are pull-through. Picnic tables and fire grills are provided. Restrooms with flush toilets and coin showers and drinking water are available. Supplies are available in Big Pine. Leashed pets are permitted.

Reservations, fees: Reservations are not accepted. Tent sites are $12 per night, RV sites (hookups) are $17 per night. Open year-round.

Directions: Drive on U.S. 395 to the park entrance (0.5 mile north of Big Pine) on the southeast side of the road. Turn east (away from the Sierra) and enter the park.

Contact: Inyo County Parks Department, 760/872-6911, www.inyocountycamping.com.

64 PALISADE GLACIER AND CLYDE GLACIER GROUP CAMPS

🏃 🛶 🎣 ♿ 🚐 ⛺

Scenic rating: 8

on Big Pine Creek in Inyo National Forest

Map 11.2, page 604

This is a trailhead camp set at 7,600 feet elevation, most popular for groups planning to rock-climb the Palisades. This climbing trip is for experienced mountaineers only; it's a dangerous expedition where risk of life can be included in the bargain. Safer options include exploring the surrounding John Muir Wilderness.

Campsites, facilities: Each campground has two group sites for tents or RVs up to 30 feet (no hookups) that can accommodate up to 20 and 25 people respectively. Picnic tables and fire grills are provided. Drinking water and vault toilets are available. Some facilities are wheelchair-accessible. Leashed pets are permitted.

Reservations, fees: Reservations are required at 877/444-6777 or www.recreation.gov ($9 reservation fee). Note that Recreation.gov lists both of these campgrounds under Big Pine Canyon. Sites are $65 per night. Open mid-May through mid-October.

Directions: Drive on U.S. 395 to Big Pine and Crocker Street/Glacier Lodge Road. Turn west (toward the Sierra) and drive nine miles (it becomes Glacier Lodge Road) to the campground on the left.

Contact: Inyo National Forest, White Mountain Ranger District, 760/873-2500, www.fs.usda.gov/inyo.

65 BIG PINE CREEK

🏃 🛶 🎣 ♿ 🚐 ⛺

Scenic rating: 8

in Inyo National Forest

Map 11.2, page 604

This is another good spot for backpackers to launch a multiday trip. The camp is set along Big Pine Creek at 7,700 feet elevation, with trails near the camp that are routed to the numerous lakes in the high country of the John Muir Wilderness.

Campsites, facilities: There are 29 sites for tents or RVs up to 22 feet (no hookups). Picnic tables, food lockers, and fire grills are provided. Drinking water and vault toilets are available. Some facilities are wheelchair-accessible. Leashed pets are permitted.

Reservations, fees: Reservations are accepted at 877/444-6777 or www.recreation.gov ($9 reservation fee). Sites are $20 per night. Open early May through October, weather permitting.

Directions: Drive on U.S. 395 to Big Pine and Crocker Street/Glacier Lodge Road. Turn west (toward the Sierra) and drive nine miles (it becomes Glacier Lodge Road) to the campground.

Contact: Inyo National Forest, White Mountain Ranger District, 760/873-2500, www.fs.usda.gov/inyo.

66 UPPER SAGE FLAT

🏃 🛶 🎣 ♿ 🚐 ⛺

Scenic rating: 8

on Big Pine Creek in Inyo National Forest

Map 11.2, page 604

This is one in a series of Forest Service camps in the area set up primarily for backpackers taking off on wilderness expeditions. Several trails are available nearby that lead into the John Muir Wilderness. The best of these is routed west past several lakes to the base of the Palisades, and beyond to John Muir Trail. Even starting at 7,600 feet, expect a steep climb.

Campsites, facilities: There are 20 sites for tents or RVs up to 25 feet (no hookups). Picnic tables, food lockers, and fire grills are provided. Drinking water and vault toilets are available. Some facilities are wheelchair-accessible. Leashed pets are permitted.

Reservations, fees: Reservations are accepted

at 877/444-6777 or www.recreation.gov ($9 reservation fee). Sites are $20 per night. Open late April through mid-September, weather permitting.

Directions: Drive on U.S. 395 to Big Pine and Crocker Street/Glacier Lodge Road. Turn west (toward the Sierra) and drive 8.5 miles (it becomes Glacier Lodge Road) to the campground.

Contact: Inyo National Forest, White Mountain Ranger District, 760/873-2500, www.fs.usda.gov/inyo.

67 SAGE FLAT

Scenic rating: 8

on Big Pine Creek near Big Pine in Inyo National Forest

Map 11.2, page 604

This camp, like the others in the immediate vicinity, is set up primarily for backpackers who are getting ready to head out on multiday expeditions into the nearby John Muir Wilderness. The trail is routed west past several lakes to the base of the Palisades, and beyond to John Muir Trail. Your hike from here will begin with a steep climb from the trailhead at 7,600 feet elevation. The camp is set along Big Pine Creek, which is stocked with small trout.

Campsites, facilities: There are 28 sites for tents or RVs up to 35 feet (no hookups). Picnic tables, food lockers, and fire grills are provided. Drinking water and vault toilets are available. Leashed pets are permitted.

Reservations, fees: Reservations are not accepted. Sites are $20 per night. Open late mid-April through mid-September, weather permitting.

Directions: Drive on U.S. 395 to Big Pine and Crocker Street/Glacier Lodge Road. Turn west (toward the Sierra) and drive eight miles (it becomes Glacier Lodge Road) to the campground.

Contact: Inyo National Forest, White

Mountain Ranger District, 760/873-2500, www.fs.usda.gov/inyo.

68 TINNEMAHA CAMPGROUND

Scenic rating: 6

near Big Pine

Map 11.2, page 604

This primitive, little-known (to out-of-towners) county park campground is on Tinnemaha Creek at 4,400 feet elevation. The creek is stocked with Alpers trout. Horse camping is allowed, but call ahead.

Campsites, facilities: There are 55 sites for tents or RVs of any length (no hookups). Picnic tables and fire grills are provided. Vault toilets are available. No drinking water is available so bring your own. Stream water is available and must be boiled or pump-filtered before use. Leashed pets are permitted.

Reservations, fees: Reservations are not accepted. Sites are $10 per vehicle per night. Open year-round.

Directions: Drive on U.S. 395 to Tinnemaha Creek Road (seven miles south of Big Pine and 19.5 miles north of Independence). Turn west (toward the Sierra) on Fish Springs Road and drive 0.5 mile to Tinnemaha Creek Road. Turn west (left) and drive two miles to the park on the right.

Contact: Inyo County Parks Department, 760/873-5577, www.inyocountycamping.com.

69 TABOOSE CREEK CAMPGROUND

Scenic rating: 4

near Big Pine

Map 11.2, page 604

The eastern Sierra is stark country, but this little spot provides a stream (Taboose Creek) and a few aspens near the campground. The setting is high desert, with a spectacular view to the west of the high Sierra rising up from sagebrush. There is an opportunity for trout fishing—fair, not spectacular. The easy access off U.S. 395 is a bonus. The hike up to Taboose Pass from here is one of the steepest grinds in the Sierra. Only the deranged need apply—which is why I did it, of course. The route provides one-day access to the interior of the John Muir Wilderness. The elevation is 3,900 feet.

Campsites, facilities: There are 50 sites for tents or RVs up to 40 feet (no hookups). Picnic tables and fire grills are provided. Drinking water (hand-pumped from a well) and vault toilets are available. Supplies are available in Big Pine or Independence. Leashed pets are permitted.

Reservations, fees: Reservations are not accepted. Sites are $10 per vehicle per night. Open year-round.

Directions: Drive on U.S. 395 to Taboose Creek Road (11 miles south of Big Pine and 14 miles north of Independence). Turn west (toward the Sierra) on Taboose Creek Road and drive 2.5 miles to the campground (straight in).

Contact: Inyo County Parks Department, 760/873-5577, www.inyocountycamping.com.

70 GRANDVIEW

Scenic rating: 6

near Big Pine in Inyo National Forest
Map 11.2, page 604

This is a primitive and little-known camp in the White Mountains east of Bishop at 8,600 feet elevation along White Mountain Road. The road borders the Ancient Bristlecone Pine Forest to the east and leads north to jump-off spots for hikers heading up Mount Barcroft (13,023 feet) or White Mountain (14,246 feet, the third-highest mountain in California). A trail out of the camp leads up to an old

mining site. The folks who find this area earn their solitude.

Campsites, facilities: There are 26 sites for tents or RVs up to 35 feet (no hookups). Picnic tables and fire grills are provided. Vault toilets are available. No drinking water is available. Garbage must be packed out. Some facilities are wheelchair accessible. Leashed pets are permitted.

Reservations, fees: Reservations are not accepted. There is no fee for camping, but donations are accepted. Open year-round, weather permitting.

Directions: From Big Pine on U.S. 395, turn east on Highway 168 and drive 13 miles. Turn north on White Mountain/Bristlecone Forest Road (Forest Road 4S01) and drive 5.5 miles to the campground.

Contact: Inyo National Forest, White Mountain Ranger District, 760/873-2500, www.fs.usda.gov/inyo.

71 CHOINUMNI

Scenic rating: 7

on lower Kings River
Map 11.3, page 605

This campground is set in the San Joaquin foothills on the Kings River, a pretty area. Since the campground is operated by Fresno County, it is off the radar of many visitors. Fishing, rafting, canoeing, and hiking are popular. The elevation is roughly 1,000 feet, surrounded by a landscape of oak woodlands and grassland foothills. The park is roughly 33 miles east of Fresno.

Campsites, facilities: There are 75 sites for tents or RVs of any length (no hookups), and one group site for up to 75 people. Some sites are pull-through. Picnic tables and fire rings are provided. Drinking water, flush toilets, and dump station are available. Canoe rentals are available nearby. No facilities within 10 miles. Leashed pets are permitted.

Reservations, fees: Reservations are accepted

for the group site only. Sites are $18 per night, $5 per night for each additional vehicle, $110 per night for the group site. Open year-round.

Directions: From Fresno, drive east on Highway 180 for 17.5 miles to Piedra Road. Turn left on Piedra Road and drive eight miles to Trimmer Springs Road. Turn right on Trimmer Springs Road and drive one mile to Pine Flat Road. Turn right and drive 100 yards to the camp entrance on the right.

Contact: Fresno County Parks Department, 559/488-3004, www2.co.fresno.ca.us.

72 PINE FLAT RECREATION AREA

Scenic rating: 7

near Pine Flat Lake

Map 11.3, page 605

This is a county park that is open all year, set below the dam of Pine Flat Lake, actually not on the lake at all. As a county park campground, it is often overlooked by out-of-towners.

Campsites, facilities: There are 52 pull-through sites for tents or RVs of any length (no hookups). Fire grills and picnic tables are provided. Restrooms with flush toilets, drinking water, dump station and a wheelchair-accessible fishing area are available. A store, coin laundry, and propane gas are nearby (within a mile). Leashed pets are permitted.

Reservations, fees: Reservations are not accepted. Sites are $18 per night, $5 per night for each additional vehicle. Open year-round.

Directions: From Fresno, drive east on Highway 180 for 17.5 miles to Trimmer Springs Road. Turn left and drive eight miles to the town of Piedra. Continue on Trimmer Springs Road for one mile to Pine Flat Road. Turn right and drive three miles to the campground on the right.

Contact: Fresno County Parks Department, 559/488-3004, www2.co.fresno.ca.us.

73 ISLAND PARK

Scenic rating: 7

on Pine Flat Lake

Map 11.3, page 605

This is one of three (four if you add Trimmer) Army Corps of Engineer campgrounds available at Pine Flat Lake, a popular lake set in the foothill country east of Fresno. When Pine Flat is full, or close to full, it is very pretty. The lake is 21 miles long with 67 miles of shoreline and 4,270 surface acres. Right—a big lake with unlimited potential. Because the temperatures get warm here in spring, then smoking hot in summer, the lake is like Valhalla for boating and water sports. The fishing for white bass is often excellent in late winter and early spring and, after that, conditions are ideal for water sports. The elevation is 1,000 feet.

Campsites, facilities: There are 97 sites for tents or RVs of any length (some hookups) and two group sites for tents or RVs up to 45 feet for 80 people each. Picnic tables and fire grills are provided. Restrooms with flush toilets and coin showers, drinking water, pay telephone, boat ramp, fish-cleaning station, and dump station are available. There is a seasonal store at the campground entrance. Boat rentals are available within five miles. Some facilities are wheelchair-accessible. Leashed pets are permitted.

Reservations, fees: Reservations are accepted for individual sites and required for the group sites at 877/444-6777 or www.recreation.gov ($9 reservation fee). Sites are $20–30 per night, $100 per night for group site. Boat launch is $4 per day. Open year-round.

Directions: From Fresno, drive east on Highway 180 for 17.5 miles to Trimmer Springs Road. Turn left and drive eight miles to the town of Piedra. Continue on Trimmer Springs Road for one mile to Pine Flat Road. Turn right and drive 0.25 mile to the park entrance (signed "Island Park").

Contact: U.S. Army Corps of Engineers, Sacramento District, Pine Flat Field Office, 559/787-2589.

74 TRIMMER

Scenic rating: 7

on Pine Flat Lake in Kings Canyon

Map 11.3, page 605

Trimmer is a small campground on the shore of Pine Flat Lake. The lake spans 20 miles and offers 67 miles of shoreline; recreation opportunities include fishing for trout and bass, boating, and wildlife watching for the occasional bobcat or hawk. The nearby Kings River offers whitewater rafting. When the lake level is high, this camp rates much higher for scenic beauty, but the lake level often falls by mid-summer.

Campsites, facilities: There are 10 sites for tents or RVs up to 30 feet (no hookups). Picnic tables and fire grills are provided. Drinking water and restrooms with flush toilets and free showers are available. A boat ramp (seasonal) and dock are adjacent to the campground and a marina is nearby. Some facilities are wheelchair-accessible. Leashed pets are permitted.

Reservations, fees: Reservations are accepted at 877/444-6777 or www.recreation.gov ($9 reservation fee). Sites are $20 per night, $4 per each additional vehicle. Open year-round, weather permitting.

Directions: From Fresno, drive east on Highway 180/Kings Canyon Highway to the Clovis Avenue exit. Turn right onto North Clovis Avenue and then immediately turn left on East Belmont Avenue. After about 13 miles the road veers left and becomes East Trimmer Springs Road. Continue traveling on this road for 18 miles; the entrance to Trimmer Recreation Area is on the right.

Contact: U.S. Army Corps of Engineers, Sacramento District, Pine Flat Field Office, 559/787-2589.

75 LAKERIDGE CAMPING AND BOATING RESORT

Scenic rating: 7

on Pine Flat Lake

Map 11.3, page 605

Pine Flat Lake is a 20-mile-long reservoir with seemingly unlimited recreation potential. It is an excellent lake for all water sports. It is in the foothills east of Fresno at 970 feet elevation, covering 4,912 surface acres with 67 miles of shoreline. The lake's proximity to Fresno has made it a top destination for boating and water sports. Fishing for white bass can be excellent in the spring and early summer. There are also rainbow trout, largemouth bass, smallmouth bass, bluegill, catfish, and black crappie. Note: A downer is that there are only a few sandy beaches, and the lake level can drop to as low as 20 percent full.

Campsites, facilities: There are 107 sites with full or partial hookups (50 amps) for tents or RVs up to 40 feet. Picnic tables and barbecue grills are available at some sites. Restrooms with showers, WiFi, coin laundry, dump station, ice, horseshoes, and pay phone are available. A convenience store and boat and houseboat rentals are nearby. Leashed pets are permitted.

Reservations, fees: Reservations are recommended at 877/787-2260. RV sites are $35–40 per night, tent sites are $25–30, $5 per pet per night. Weekly and monthly rates available. Some credit cards accepted. Open year-round.

Directions: From Fresno, drive east on Highway 180 for 17.5 miles to Trimmer Springs Road. Turn left and drive eight miles to the town of Piedra. Continue on Trimmer Springs Road for four miles to Sunnyslope Road. Turn right and drive one mile to the resort on the right.

Contact: Lakeridge Camping and Boating Resort, 877/787-2260, www.lakeridgecampground.com; Pine Flat Marina, 559/787-2506, www.pineflatlakemarina.com.

76 KIRCH FLAT

🏃 ≈ 🚣 🎣 🏕 ♿ 🚗 ⛰

Scenic rating: 8

on the Kings River in Sierra National Forest

Map 11.3, page 605   BEST (

Kirch Flat is on the Kings River, about five miles from the head of Pine Flat Lake. This campground is a popular take-out spot for rafters and kayakers running the Middle Kings, putting in at Garnet Dike dispersed camping area and then making the 10-mile, Class III run downstream to Kirch Flat. The camp is set in the foothill country at 1,100 feet elevation, where the temperatures are often hot and the water cold.

Campsites, facilities: There are 17 sites for tents or RVs up to 30 feet (no hookups), and one group camp for up to 50 people and RVs to 35 feet. Picnic tables and fire grills are provided. Vault toilets are available. No drinking water is available. Some facilities are wheelchair-accessible. Leashed pets are permitted.

Reservations, fees: Reservations are not accepted for individual sites, but are required for the group site at 559/855-5355. There is no fee for camping. Reservation applications are open from March through July with a lottery to select the winners. Open year-round.

Directions: From Fresno, drive east on Highway 180 for 17.5 miles to Trimmer Springs Road. Turn left and drive 28 miles to Trimmer. Continue east on Trimmer Springs Road (along the north shore of Pine Flat Lake) and drive 18 miles to the campground on the right.

Contact: Sierra National Forest, High Sierra Ranger District, 559/855-5355, www.fs.usda.gov/sierra.

77 BLACK ROCK

🚣 🏕 🚗 ⛰

Scenic rating: 7

on Black Rock Reservoir in Sierra National Forest

Map 11.3, page 605

Little Black Rock Reservoir is a little-known spot that can provide a quiet respite compared to the other big-time lakes and camps in the region. The camp is set near the outlet stream on the west end of the lake, created from a small dam on the North Fork Kings River at 4,200 feet elevation.

Campsites, facilities: There are 10 sites for tents or small RVs. Picnic tables and fire grills are provided. Vault toilets are available. There is no drinking water. Garbage must be packed out. Leashed pets are permitted.

Reservations, fees: Reservations are not accepted. Sites are $14 per night, $7 per night per additional RV, $3 per night for additional vehicle, $1 per pet per night. Open year-round, weather permitting.

Directions: From Fresno, drive east on Highway 180 for 17.5 miles to Trimmer Springs Road. Turn left and drive 28 miles to Trimmer. Continue east on Trimmer Springs Road (along the north shore of Pine Flat Lake) and drive 18 miles to Black Road. Turn left and drive 10 miles to the campground.

Contact: Sierra National Forest, High Sierra Ranger District, 559/855-5355, www.fs.usda.gov/sierra; PG&E Land Services, 916/386-5164, www.pge.com/recreation.

78 CAMP 4 1/2

🏃 🚣 🏕 ⛰

Scenic rating: 7

on the Kings River in Sequoia National Forest

Map 11.3, page 605

On my visit to this primitive camp, I found five sites here, not "four and a half." This Sequoia National Forest campground is small, primitive, and usually hot. The elevation is 1,000 feet. It is one in a series of camps just east of Pine Flat Lake along the Kings River, primarily used for rafting access. (See the Kirch Flat and Mill Flat listings in this chapter for more information.)

Campsites, facilities: There are five sites for tents only. There are no services or facilities: no drinking water, no picnic tables, no fire rings, and no toilets. Garbage must be packed out. Leashed pets are permitted.

Reservations, fees: Reservations are not accepted. There is no fee for camping. Open year-round.

Directions: From Fresno, drive east on Highway 180 for 17.5 miles to Trimmer Springs Road. Turn left and drive 28 miles to Trimmer. Continue east on Trimmer Springs Road (along the north shore of Pine Flat Lake) and drive 18 miles (it becomes Forest Road 11S12) to Forest Road 12S01 (crossing the river). Take Forest Road 12S01 for one mile (along the river) to a dirt road on the right (at the junction of the second bridge). Turn right (still Forest Road 12S01) and drive 0.7 mile to the campground. Not advised for trailers or large RVs.

Contact: Sequoia National Forest, Hume Lake Ranger District, 559/338-2251, www.fs.usda.gov/sequoia.

79 CAMP 4

🏃 🏊 🛶 🎣 🏕 ⛰

Scenic rating: 7

on the Kings River in Sequoia National Forest

Map 11.3, page 605

This is one in a series of camps set on the Kings River upstream from Pine Flat Lake, a popular access point for rafters and kayakers. The Kings River is well known for providing some of the best rafting and kayaking water in California. The weather gets so hot that many take a dunk in the river on purpose; non-rafters had better bring a cooler stocked with ice and drinks. Camp 4 is a mile from Mill Creek Flat.

Campsites, facilities: There are five sites for tents only. Picnic tables and fire grills are provided. Vault toilets are available. No drinking water is available. Garbage must be packed out. Leashed pets are permitted.

Reservations, fees: Reservations are not accepted. There is no fee for camping. Open year-round.

Directions: From Fresno, drive east on Highway 180 for 17.5 miles to Trimmer Springs Road. Turn left and drive 28 miles to Trimmer. Continue east on Trimmer Springs Road (along the north shore of Pine Flat Lake) and drive 18 miles (it becomes Forest Road 11S12) to Forest Road 12S01 (crossing the river). Take Forest Road 12S01 for one mile (along the river) to a dirt road on the right (at the junction of the second bridge). Turn right (still Forest Road 12S01) and drive 1.5 miles to the campground (on the south side of the river). Not advised for trailers and large RVs.

Contact: Sequoia National Forest, Hume Lake Ranger District, 559/338-2251, www.fs.usda.gov/sequoia.

80 MILL FLAT

🏃 🛶 🏕 ⛰

Scenic rating: 7

on the Kings River in Sequoia National Forest

Map 11.3, page 605

This camp is on the Kings River at the confluence of Mill Creek. It's a small, primitive spot that gets very hot in the summer. The elevation is 1,100 feet. Rafters sometimes use this as an access point for trips down the Kings River. This is best in spring and early summer, when melting snow from the high country fills the river with water.

Campsites, facilities: There are five sites for tents only. Picnic tables and fire grills are provided. Vault toilets are available. No drinking water is available. Garbage must be packed out. Leashed pets are permitted.

Reservations, fees: Reservations are not

accepted. There is no fee for camping. Open year-round.

Directions: From Fresno, drive east on Highway 180 for 17.5 miles to Trimmer Springs Road. Turn left and drive 28 miles to Trimmer. Continue east on Trimmer Springs Road (along the north shore of Pine Flat Lake) and drive 18 miles (it becomes Forest Road 11S12) to Forest Road 12S01 (crossing the river). Take Forest Road 12S01 for one mile (along the river) to a dirt road on the right (at the junction of the second bridge). Turn right (still Forest Road 12S01) and drive 2.5 miles to the campground (on the south side of the river). Not advised for trailers and large RVs.

Contact: Sequoia National Forest, Hume Lake Ranger District, 559/338-2251, www.fs.usda.gov/sequoia.

81 PRINCESS

Scenic rating: 7

on Princess Meadow in
Giant Sequoia National Forest

Map 11.4, page 606

This mountain camp is at 5,900 feet elevation. It is popular because of its proximity to both Hume Lake and the star attractions at Kings Canyon National Park. Hume Lake is just four miles from the camp. The Grant Grove entrance to Kings Canyon National Park is only six miles away to the south, while continuing on Highway 180 to the east will take you into the heart of Kings Canyon.

Campsites, facilities: There are 90 sites for tents or RVs up to 22 feet (no hookups). Picnic tables and fire grills are provided. Drinking water, vault toilets, amphitheater, and dump station are available. A store is four miles away at Hume Lake. Leashed pets are permitted.

Reservations, fees: Reservations are accepted at 877/444-6777 or www.recreation.gov ($9 reservation fee). Sites are $18–20 per night, $36–38 per night for a double site, $5 per night for each additional vehicle, plus $20

per vehicle national park entrance fee. Prices are higher on holiday weekends. Open May through September, weather permitting.

Directions: From Fresno, drive east on Highway 180 for 55 miles to the Big Stump Entrance Station at Sequoia and Kings Canyon National Parks. Continue 1.5 miles to a junction (signed left for Grant Grove). Turn left and drive 1.5 miles to Grant Grove Village, then continue for 4.5 miles to the campground on the right.

Contact: Sequoia National Forest, Hume Lake Ranger District, 559/338-2251, www.fs.usda.gov/sequoia; California Land Management, 559/335-2232.

82 HUME LAKE

Scenic rating: 8

in Giant Sequoia National Forest

Map 11.4, page 606

For newcomers, Hume Lake is a surprise: a pretty lake, with great summer camps for teenagers. Canoeing and kayaking are excellent, and so is the trout fishing, especially near the dam. Swimming is allowed. A 5-mph speed limit is in effect on this 85-acre lake, and only electric motors are permitted. Another surprise is the adjacent religious camp center. The nearby access to Kings Canyon National Park adds a bonus. The elevation is 5,200 feet.

Campsites, facilities: There are 60 tent sites and 14 sites for tents or RVs up to 22 feet (no hookups). Picnic tables and fire grills are provided. Drinking water and flush toilets are available. A store, café, bicycle rentals, and boat rentals are nearby. Leashed pets are permitted.

Reservations, fees: Reservations are accepted at 877/444-6777 or www.recreation.gov ($9 reservation fee). Sites are $20–42 per night, $5 per night for each additional vehicle, plus $20 per vehicle national park entrance fee. Rates are higher on holiday weekends.

Open mid-May through September, weather permitting.

Directions: From Fresno, drive east on Highway 180 for 55 miles to the Big Stump Entrance Station at Sequoia and Kings Canyon National Parks. Continue 1.5 miles to a junction (signed left for Grant Grove). Turn left and drive six miles to the Hume Lake Road junction. Turn right and drive three miles to Hume Lake and the campground entrance road. Turn right and drive 0.25 mile to the campground on the left.

Contact: Sequoia National Forest, Hume Lake Ranger District, 559/338-2251, www.fs.usda. gov/sequoia; California Land Management, 559/335-2232.

83 ASPEN HOLLOW GROUP CAMP

Scenic rating: 6

near Hume Lake in Sequoia National Forest

Map 11.4, page 606

This large group camp is set at 5,200 feet elevation about a mile south of Hume Lake near a feeder to Tenmile Creek, the inlet stream to Hume Lake. Entrances to Kings Canyon National Park are nearby.

Campsites, facilities: This is a group camp for tents or RVs of any length (no hookups) that can accommodate up to 100 people. Picnic tables, food lockers, and fire grills are provided. Drinking water and vault toilets are available. A store is nearby. Some facilities are wheelchair-accessible. Leashed pets are permitted.

Reservations, fees: Reservations are required at 877/444-6777 or www.recreation.gov ($9 reservation fee). The camp is $225 per night, plus $20 per vehicle national park entrance fee. Open mid-May through mid-September, weather permitting.

Directions: From Fresno, drive east on Highway 180 for 55 miles to the Big Stump Entrance Station at Sequoia and Kings Canyon

National Parks. Continue 1.5 miles to a junction (signed left for Grant Grove). Turn left and drive six miles to the Hume Lake Road junction. Turn right and drive three miles to Hume Lake and the campground entrance road. Turn right and drive around Hume Lake. Continue south one mile (past the lake) to the campground entrance road.

Contact: Sequoia National Forest, Hume Lake Ranger District, 559/338-2251, www.fs.usda. gov/sequoia.

84 LOGGER FLAT GROUP CAMP

Scenic rating: 7

on Tenmile Creek in Giant Sequoia National Forest

Map 11.4, page 606

This is the group-site alternative to Landslide campground. This camp is set near the confluence of Tenmile Creek and Landslide Creek at 5,300 feet elevation, about two miles upstream from Hume Lake. (For more information, see the Landslide listing in this chapter.)

Campsites, facilities: This is a group campsite for tents or RVs of any length (no hookups) that can accommodate up to 50 people. Picnic tables, food lockers, and fire ring are provided. Drinking water and vault toilets are available. A store is nearby. Some facilities are wheelchair-accessible. Leashed pets are permitted.

Reservations, fees: Reservations are required at 877/444-6777 or www.recreation.gov ($9 reservation fee). The camp is $122.50 per night, plus $20 per vehicle national park entrance fee. Open mid-May through mid-September, weather permitting.

Directions: From Fresno, drive east on Highway 180 for 55 miles to the Big Stump Entrance Station at Sequoia and Kings Canyon National Parks. Continue 1.5 miles to a junction (signed left for Grant Grove). Turn left and drive six miles to the Hume Lake Road junction. Turn right and drive three miles to Hume Lake and the campground entrance road. Turn right and drive around Hume Lake to Tenmile Road. Continue south three miles to the campground entrance on the right.

Contact: Sequoia National Forest, Hume Lake Ranger District, 559/338-2251, www.fs.usda. gov/sequoia.

85 LANDSLIDE
🏊 🛶 🚐 ⛺

Scenic rating: 7

on Landslide Creek in
Giant Sequoia National Forest

Map 11.4, page 606

If you want quiet, you got it; few folks know about this camp. If you want a stream nearby, you got it; Landslide Creek runs right beside the camp. If you want a lake nearby, you got it; Hume Lake is just to the north. If you want a national park nearby, you got it; Kings Canyon National Park is nearby. Add it up: You got it. The elevation is 5,800 feet.

Campsites, facilities: There are nine sites for tents only and one site for RVs up to 22 feet (no hookups). Picnic tables and fire grills are provided. Drinking water and vault toilets are available. A store is nearby. Leashed pets are permitted.

Reservations, fees: Reservations are not accepted. Sites are $16 per night, $32 per night for a double site, $5 per night for each additional vehicle, plus $20 per vehicle national park entrance fee. Open May through September, weather permitting.

Directions: From Fresno, drive east on Highway 180 for 55 miles to the Big Stump Entrance Station at Sequoia and Kings Canyon National Parks. Continue 1.5 miles to a junction (signed left for Grant Grove). Turn right at Generals Highway and drive three miles to Hume Lake Road/Tenmile Road (Forest Road 13S09). Turn left and drive about seven miles (past Tenmile campground) to the campground on the left.

Contact: Sequoia National Forest, Hume Lake Ranger District, 559/338-2251, www.fs.usda. gov/sequoia.

86 TENMILE
🏊 🛶 ♿ 🚐 ⛺

Scenic rating: 7

on Tenmile Creek in
Giant Sequoia National Forest

Map 11.4, page 606

This is one of three small, primitive campgrounds along Tenmile Creek south (and upstream) of Hume Lake. RV campers are advised to use the lower campsites because they are larger. This one is about four miles from the lake at 5,800 feet elevation. It provides an alternative to camping in nearby Kings Canyon National Park.

Campsites, facilities: There are 11 sites for tents or RVs up to 22 feet (no hookups). Picnic tables and fire grills are provided. Vault toilets are available. No drinking water is available. Some facilities are wheelchair-accessible. Leashed pets are permitted.

Reservations, fees: Reservations are not accepted. Sites are $16 per night, $32 per night for a double site, $5 per night for each additional vehicle, plus $20 per vehicle national park entrance fee. Camping fees are higher on holiday weekends. Open May through mid-September, weather permitting.

Directions: From Fresno, drive east on Highway 180 for 55 miles to the Big Stump Entrance Station at Sequoia and Kings Canyon National Parks. Continue 1.5 miles to a junction (signed left for Grant Grove). Turn right at Generals Highway and drive three miles to Hume Lake Road/Tenmile Road (Forest Road 13S09). Turn left and drive about five miles to the campground on the left.

Contact: Sequoia National Forest, Hume Lake Ranger District, 559/338-2251, www.fs.usda. gov/sequoia.

87 AZALEA
🚶 🐴 ♿ 🚐 ⛺

Scenic rating: 7

in Kings Canyon National Park

Map 11.4, page 606

This camp is tucked just inside the western border of Kings Canyon National Park, a mere six miles from the Big Stump entrance. The General Grant Grove of giant sequoias is only a one-mile hike away and services at Grant Grove Village are right across the highway. The spectacular Kings Canyon, one of the deepest gorges in North America, is further north Highway 180. The elevation is 6,600 feet.

Campsites, facilities: There are 110 sites for tents or RVs up to 30 feet (no hookups). Picnic tables, food lockers, and fire grills are provided. Drinking water and flush toilets are available. Evening ranger programs are often offered. Horseback-riding facilities are nearby. Supplies and showers are available in Grant Grove Village during the summer. Some facilities are wheelchair-accessible. Leashed pets are permitted, except on trails.

Reservations, fees: Reservations are not accepted. Sites are $18 per night, plus $20 per vehicle national park entrance fee. Open year-round.

Directions: From Fresno, drive east on Highway 180 for 55 miles to the Big Stump Entrance Station at Sequoia and Kings Canyon National Parks. Continue 1.5 miles to a junction (signed left for Grant Grove). Turn left and drive 1.5 miles to Grant Grove Village, then continue for 0.7 mile to the campground entrance on the left.

Contact: Sequoia and Kings Canyon National Parks, 559/565-3341, www.nps.gov/seki; Kings Canyon Visitor Center, 559/565-4307; Grant Grove Horse Stables, 559/335-9292.

88 CRYSTAL SPRINGS
🚶 🐴 ♿ 🚐 ⛺

Scenic rating: 5

in Kings Canyon National Park

Map 11.4, page 606

Crystal Springs is one of three camps in the Grant Grove area, catering primarily to groups. Directly south of the camp is Grant Grove Village and its visitor center. Across Highway 180 lies the trailhead for the Grant Grove of Giant Sequoias. Continuing north on Highway 180 provides access to the Kings Canyon, Cedar Grove Village, the Kings River. The road finally comes to a dead-end loop, taking in the drop-dead gorgeous landscape of one of the deepest gorges in North America. One of the best hikes, but also the most demanding, is the 13-mile round-trip to Lookout Peak, out of the Cedar Grove Village area. It involves a 4,000-foot climb to 8,531 feet elevation, and with it a breathtaking view of Sierra ridges, Cedar Grove far below, and Kings Canyon.

Campsites, facilities: There are 36 sites for tents or RVs up to 22 feet (no hookups) and 14 group sites for 7–15 people each. Picnic tables, food lockers, and fire grills are provided. Drinking water and flush toilets are available. Horseback-riding facilities are nearby. Evening ranger programs are often offered in the summer. Supplies and howers are available in Grant Grove Village during the summer season. Some facilities are wheelchair-accessible. Leashed pets are permitted, except on trails.

Reservations, fees: Reservations are not accepted. Sites are $18 per night, plus $20 per vehicle national park entrance fee; group sites are $35 per night. Open mid-May through mid-September, weather permitting.

Directions: From Fresno, drive east on Highway 180 for 55 miles to the Big Stump Entrance Station at Sequoia and Kings Canyon National Parks. Continue 1.5 miles to a junction (signed left for Grant Grove). Turn left and drive 1.5 miles to Grant Grove Village, then continue for 0.7 mile to the campground entrance on the right.

Contact: Sequoia and Kings Canyon National Parks, 559/565-3341; Kings Canyon Visitor Center, 559/565-4307, www.nps.gov/seki.

89 SUNSET
🏃 🐕 ♿ 🚐 ⛺

Scenic rating: 7

in Kings Canyon National Park

Map 11.4, page 606

This is the biggest of the three camps that are just inside the Kings Canyon National Park boundaries near Grant Grove Village, at 6,600 feet elevation. The nearby General Grant Grove of giant sequoias is the main attraction. There are many short, easy walks among the sequoias, each breathtakingly beautiful. They include Big Stump Trail, Sunset Trail, North Grove Loop, General Grant Tree, Manzanita and Azalea Loop, and Panoramic Point and Park Ridge Trail. Seeing the General Grant Tree is a rite of passage for newcomers; after a half-hour walk you arrive at a sequoia that is approximately 1,800 years old, 107 feet in circumference, and 267 feet tall.

Campsites, facilities: There are 157 sites for tents or RVs up to 30 feet (no hookups) and two group sites for 15–30 people each. Picnic tables, food lockers, and fire grills are provided. Drinking water and flush toilets are available. In the summer, evening ranger programs are often available. Horseback-riding facilities are nearby. Supplies and showers are available in Grant Grove Village during the summer. Some facilities are wheelchair-accessible. Leashed pets are permitted, except on trails.

Reservations, fees: Reservations are not accepted for individual sites but are required for the group sites November through April. To reserve a group site, call 559/565-4357 or 559/565-4335 for information. Reservations must be made by mail or fax to: Sunset Group Sites, P.O. Box 926, Kings Canyon National Park, CA 93633, or fax 559/565-4391. Sites are $18 per night, plus $20 per vehicle national park entrance fee. Group sites are $40 per night. Open late May through mid-September, weather permitting.

Directions: From Fresno, drive east on Highway 180 for 55 miles to the Big Stump Entrance Station at Sequoia and Kings Canyon National Parks. Continue 1.5 miles to a junction (signed left for Grant Grove). Turn left (still Highway 180) and drive one mile to the campground entrance (0.5 mile before reaching Grant Grove Village).

Contact: Sequoia and Kings Canyon National Parks, 559/565-3341; Kings Canyon Visitor Center, 559/565-4307, www.nps.gov/seki.

90 BUCK ROCK
🐕 🚐 ⛺

Scenic rating: 4

near Big Meadows Creek in
Giant Sequoia National Monument

Map 11.4, page 606

This is a remote camp that provides a little-known option to nearby Sequoia and Kings Canyon National Parks. If the national parks are full and you're stuck, this camp provides an insurance policy. The elevation is 7,500 feet.

Campsites, facilities: There are five primitive sites for tents or RVs up to 25 feet (no hookups). Picnic tables and fire grills are provided. Vault toilets are available. No drinking water is available. Leashed pets are permitted.

Reservations, fees: Reservations are not accepted. There is no fee for camping, but there is a $20 per vehicle national park entrance fee. Open May to early September, weather permitting.

Directions: From Fresno, drive east on Highway 180 for 55 miles to the Big Stump Entrance Station at Sequoia and Kings Canyon National Parks. Continue 1.5 miles to a junction (signed left for Grant Grove). Turn right at Generals Highway and drive about five miles to Big Meadows Road/Forest Road

14S11. Turn left on Big Meadows Road and drive five miles to the campground entrance road on the left. Turn left and drive a short distance to the campground.

Contact: Sequoia National Forest, Hume Lake Ranger District, 559/338-2251, www.fs.usda.gov/sequoia.

91 BIG MEADOWS

Scenic rating: 7

on Big Meadows Creek in
Giant Sequoia National Monument

Map 11.4, page 606

This primitive, high-mountain camp (7,600 feet) is beside little Big Meadows Creek. Backpackers can use this as a launching pad, with the nearby trailhead (one mile down the road to the west) leading to the Jennie Lake Wilderness. Kings Canyon National Park, only a 12-mile drive away, is a nearby side trip.

Campsites, facilities: There are 25 sites along Big Meadows Creek and Big Meadows Road for tents or RVs up to 22 feet (no hookups). Picnic tables and fire grills are provided. Vault toilets are available. No drinking water is available. Leashed pets are permitted.

Reservations, fees: Reservations are not accepted. There is no fee for camping, but there is a $20 per vehicle national park entrance fee. Open May through early October, weather permitting.

Directions: From Fresno, drive east on Highway 180 for 55 miles to the Big Stump Entrance Station at Sequoia and Kings Canyon National Parks. Continue 1.5 miles to a junction (signed left for Grant Grove). Turn right at Generals Highway and drive about five miles to Big Meadows Road/Forest Road 14S11. Turn left on Big Meadows Road and drive five miles to the camp.

Contact: Sequoia National Forest, Hume Lake Ranger District, 559/338-2251, www.fs.usda.gov/sequoia.

92 SENTINEL

Scenic rating: 8

in Kings Canyon National Park

Map 11.4, page 606

This camp provides an alternative to nearby Sheep Creek (see listing in this chapter). They both tend to fill up quickly in the summer. It's a short walk to Cedar Grove Village, the center of activity in the park. The elevation is 4,600 feet. Hiking and trout fishing are excellent in the vicinity. The entrance road provides stunning rim-of-the-world views of Kings Canyon, and then drops to right along the Kings River.

Campsites, facilities: There are 82 sites for tents or RVs up to 30 feet (no hookups). Picnic tables, food lockers, and fire grills are provided. Restrooms with flush toilets and drinking water are available. A store, coin showers, coin laundry, riding stables, and snack bar are nearby. Some facilities are wheelchair-accessible. Leashed pets are permitted.

Reservations, fees: Reservations are not accepted. Sites are $18 per night, plus $20 per vehicle national park entrance fee. Open late April through October, weather permitting.

Directions: From Fresno, drive east on Highway 180 for 55 miles to the Big Stump Entrance Station at Sequoia and Kings Canyon National Parks. Continue 1.5 miles to a junction (signed left for Grant Grove). Turn left and drive 32 miles to the campground entrance on the left (near Cedar Grove Village).

Contact: Sequoia and Kings Canyon National Parks, 559/565-3341; Cedar Grove Visitor Center, 559/565-3793, www.nps.gov/seki.

93 SHEEP CREEK

Scenic rating: 8

in Kings Canyon National Park

Map 11.4, page 606

This is one of the camps that always fills up quickly on summer weekends. It's a pretty spot and just a short walk from Cedar Grove Village. The camp is set along Sheep Creek at 4,600 feet elevation.

Campsites, facilities: There are 111 sites for tents or RVs up to 30 feet (no hookups). Picnic tables and fire grills are provided. Restrooms with flush toilets and drinking water are available. A store, coin laundry, snack bar, and coin showers are available nearby. Leashed pets are permitted.

Reservations, fees: Reservations are not accepted. Sites are $18 per night, plus $20 per vehicle national park entrance fee. Open late April through mid-November.

Directions: From Fresno, drive east on Highway 180 for 55 miles to the Big Stump Entrance Station at Sequoia and Kings Canyon National Parks. Continue 1.5 miles to a junction (signed left for Grant Grove). Turn left and drive 31.5 miles to the campground entrance on the left (near Cedar Grove Village).

Contact: Sequoia and Kings Canyon National Parks, 559/565-3341; Cedar Grove Visitor Center, 559/565-3793, www.nps.gov/seki.

94 CANYON VIEW GROUP CAMP

Scenic rating: 8

in Kings Canyon National Park

Map 11.4, page 606   **BEST (**

If it weren't for this group camp in the Cedar Grove Village area, large gatherings wishing to camp together in Kings Canyon National Park would be out of luck. The access road leads to dramatic views of the deep Kings River Canyon, one of the deepest gorges in North America. One of the best hikes here, but also one of the most demanding, is the 13-mile round-trip to Lookout Peak out of the Cedar Grove Village area. It involves a 4,000-foot climb to 8,531 feet elevation, and with it, a breathtaking view of Sierra ridges, Cedar Grove far below, and Kings Canyon. The elevation is 4,600 feet.

Campsites, facilities: There are 23 sites for tents only that accommodate up to six people per site. There are also five group sites that accommodate 7–15 people per site. Picnic tables, food lockers, and fire grills are provided. Drinking water and flush toilets are available. Coin showers, store, snack bar, and coin laundry are nearby. Leashed pets are permitted.

Reservations, fees: Reservations are not accepted for the 12 tent-only group sites, but they are required for the four sites that accommodate 20–40 people each (write to Canyon View Group Sites, P.O. Box 926, Kings Canyon National Park, CA 93633, or fax 559/565-0314 May–Oct., or 559/565-4391 Nov.–Apr.). Sites are $18 per night, the group sites are $35 per night, and there is a $20 per vehicle national park entrance fee. Open May through October (the group site is open June–Sept.), weather permitting.

Directions: From Fresno, drive east on Highway 180 for 55 miles to the Big Stump Entrance Station at Sequoia and Kings Canyon National Parks. Continue 1.5 miles to a junction (signed left for Grant Grove). Turn left and drive 32.5 miles to the campground entrance (0.5 mile past the ranger station, near Cedar Grove Village).

Contact: Sequoia and Kings Canyon National Parks, 559/565-3341; Cedar Grove Visitor Center, 559/565-3793, www.nps.gov/seki.

95 MORAINE

Scenic rating: 8

in Kings Canyon National Park

Map 11.4, page 606

This is one in a series of camps in the Cedar Grove Village area of Kings Canyon National Park. This camp is used only as an overflow area. Hikers should drive past the Cedar Grove Ranger Station to the end of the road at Copper Creek, a prime jump-off point for a spectacular hike. The elevation is 4,600 feet.

Campsites, facilities: There are 120 sites for tents or RVs up to 30 feet (no hookups). Picnic tables and fire grills are provided. Drinking water and flush toilets are available. Coin showers, store, snack bar, and coin laundry are nearby. Leashed pets are permitted.

Reservations, fees: Reservations are not accepted. Sites are $18 per night, plus $20 per vehicle national park entrance fee. Open May through October, weather permitting.

Directions: From Fresno, drive east on Highway 180 for 55 miles to the Big Stump Entrance Station at Sequoia and Kings Canyon National Parks. Continue 1.5 miles to a junction (signed left for Grant Grove). Turn left and drive 33 miles to the campground entrance (one mile past the ranger station, near Cedar Village).

Contact: Sequoia and Kings Canyon National Parks, 559/565-3341; Cedar Grove Visitor Center, 559/565-3793, www.nps.gov/seki.

96 ESHOM

Scenic rating: 7

on Eshom Creek in
Giant Sequoia National Monument

Map 11.4, page 606

The campground at Eshom Creek is just two miles outside the boundaries of Sequoia National Park. It is well hidden and a considerable distance from the crowds and sights in the park interior. It is set along Eshom Creek at an elevation of 4,800 feet. Many campers at Eshom Creek hike straight into the national park, with a trailhead at Redwood Saddle (just inside the park boundary) providing a route to see the Redwood Mountain Grove, Fallen Goliath, Hart Tree, and Hart Meadow in a sensational loop hike.

Campsites, facilities: There are 24 sites for tents or RVs up to 22 feet (no hookups), and five group sites for up to 12 people each. Picnic tables and fire grills are provided. Drinking water and vault toilets are available. Leashed pets are permitted.

Reservations, fees: Reservations are not accepted. Sites are $18 per night, $5 per night for each additional vehicle, $38 per night for group site. Camping fees are higher on holiday weekends. Open May through early October, weather permitting.

Directions: Drive on Highway 99 to Visalia and the exit for Highway 198 east. Take that exit and drive east on Highway 198 for 11 miles to Highway 245. Turn left (north) on Highway 245 and drive 18 miles to Badger and County Road 465. Turn right and drive eight miles to the campground.

Contact: Sequoia National Forest, Hume Lake Ranger District, 559/338-2251, www.fs.usda.gov/sequoia; California Land Management, 559/335-2232.

97 FIR GROUP CAMPGROUND

Scenic rating: 6

near Stony Creek in
Giant Sequoia National Monument

Map 11.4, page 606

This is one of two large group camps in the Stony Creek area.

Campsites, facilities: This group camp for tents or RVs up to 30 feet (no hookups) can accommodate up to 100 people. Picnic tables, food lockers, and fire grills are provided. Drinking water and vault toilets are available. A store and coin laundry are nearby. Leashed pets are permitted.

Reservations, fees: Reservations are required at 877/444-6777 or www.recreation.gov ($9 reservation fee). The camp is $225 per night, plus $20 per vehicle national park entrance fee. Fees are higher on holiday weekends. Open mid-May through mid-September, weather permitting.

Directions: From Fresno, drive east on Highway 180 for 55 miles to the Big Stump

Entrance Station at Sequoia and Kings Canyon National Parks. Continue 1.5 miles to a junction (signed left for Grant Grove). Turn right at Generals Highway and drive about 14 miles to the campground entrance on the left.

Contact: Sequoia National Forest, Hume Lake Ranger District, 559/338-2251, www.fs.usda. gov/sequoia.

98 STONY CREEK

Scenic rating: 6

in Giant Sequoia National Monument

Map 11.4, page 606

Stony Creek Camp provides a good option if the national park camps are filled. It is set creekside at 6,400 feet elevation. Sequoia and Kings Canyon National Parks are nearby.

Campsites, facilities: There are 48 sites for tents or RVs up to 22 feet (no hookups). Picnic tables and fire grills are provided. Drinking water, food lockers, flush toilets, and an amphitheater are available. A store and coin laundry are nearby. Leashed pets are permitted.

Reservations, fees: Reservations are accepted at 877/444-6777 or www.recreation.gov ($9 reservation fee). Sites are $20–42 per night, $5 per night for each additional vehicle, plus $20 per vehicle national park entrance fee. Fees are higher on holiday weekends. Open May through early September, weather permitting.

Directions: From Fresno, drive east on Highway 180 for 55 miles to the Big Stump Entrance Station at Sequoia and Kings Canyon National Parks. Continue 1.5 miles to a junction (signed left for Grant Grove). Turn right at Generals Highway and drive about 13 miles to the campground entrance on the right.

Contact: Sequoia National Forest, Hume Lake Ranger District, 559/338-2251, www.fs.usda. gov/sequoia.

99 COVE GROUP CAMP

Scenic rating: 6

near Stony Creek in
Giant Sequoia National Monument

Map 11.4, page 606

This large group camp is beside Stony Creek. The elevation is 6,500 feet.

Campsites, facilities: There is one group site for tents or RVs up to 25 feet (no hookups) that accommodates up to 50 people. Picnic tables and fire grills are provided. Drinking water, flush toilets, and dump station are available. A store, coin showers, and coin laundry are eight miles away. Some facilities are wheelchair-accessible. Leashed pets are permitted.

Reservations, fees: Reservations are required at 877/444-6777 or www.recreation.gov ($9 reservation fee). The camp is $112.50 per night, plus $20 per vehicle national park entrance fee. Fees are higher on holiday weekends. Open mid-May through mid-September, weather permitting.

Directions: From Fresno, drive east on Highway 180 for 55 miles to the Big Stump Entrance Station at Sequoia and Kings Canyon National Parks. Continue 1.5 miles to a junction (signed left for Grant Grove). Turn right at Generals Highway and drive about 14 miles to the campground entrance on the left (just past Fir Group Campground).

Contact: Sequoia National Forest, Hume Lake Ranger District, 559/338-2251, www.fs.usda. gov/sequoia.

100 DORST CREEK

Scenic rating: 7

on Dorst Creek in Sequoia National Park

Map 11.4, page 606   **BEST (**

This camp is set on Dorst Creek at 6,700 feet elevation, near a trail routed into the backcountry and through Muir Grove. Dorst Creek is a favorite for families because the spacious sites are set beneath a forest canopy and the campground itself is huge. There is plenty of room to run around and youngsters are apt to make friends with kids from other sites. The hike to the Muir Grove of Giant Sequoias is an easy hike, not too hard for children and their parents. It is one in a series of big, popular camps in Sequoia National Park. Bear visits are common here.

Campers must keep food in a bear-proof food locker or you will get a ticket. The reason why? Things that go bump in the night swing through Dorst Creek camp all summer long. That's right, Mr. Bear (a whole bunch of them) makes food raids like UPS drivers on pick-up routes. That's why keeping your food in a bear-proof locker is not only a must, it's the law.

Campsites, facilities: There are 202 sites for tents or RVs up to 30 feet (no hookups) and four group sites for 25–50 people each. Picnic tables and fire grills are provided. Drinking water, flush toilets, and dump station are available. A store, coin showers, and coin laundry are eight miles away. Some facilities are wheelchair-accessible. Leashed pets are permitted.

Reservations, fees: Reservations are accepted at 877/444-6777 or www.recreation.gov ($9 reservation fee). Sites are $20 per night (includes reservation fee), $40–60 per night for group sites, plus $20 per vehicle national park entrance fee. Open Memorial Day through Labor Day, weather permitting.

Directions: From Fresno, drive east on Highway 180 for 55 miles to the Big Stump Entrance Station at Sequoia and Kings Canyon National Parks. Continue 1.5 miles to a junction (signed left for Grant Grove). Turn right at Generals Highway and drive about 25.5 miles to the campground entrance on the right.

Contact: Sequoia and Kings Canyon National Parks, 559/565-3341; Lodgepole Visitor Center, 559/565-4436, www.nps.gov/seki.

101 LODGEPOLE

Scenic rating: 8

on the Marble Fork of the Kaweah River in Sequoia National Park

Map 11.4, page 606

This giant, pretty camp on the Marble Fork of the Kaweah River is typically crowded. A bonus here is an excellent trailhead nearby that leads into the backcountry of Sequoia National Park. The elevation is 6,700 feet. For information on backcountry permits, phone the Mineral King Ranger Station, 559/565-3135.

Campsites, facilities: There are 204 sites for tents or RVs up to 40 feet (no hookups). Picnic tables and fire grills are provided. Restrooms with flush toilets, drinking water, dump station, gift shop, and evening ranger programs are available. A store, deli, coin showers, and coin laundry are nearby. Leashed pets are permitted.

Reservations, fees: Reservations are accepted at 877/444-6777 or www.recreation.gov ($9 reservation fee). Sites are $20 per night (includes reservation fee), plus $20 per vehicle national park entrance fee. Open year-round, with limited winter services.

Directions: From Fresno, drive east on Highway 180 for 55 miles to the Big Stump Entrance Station at Sequoia and Kings Canyon National Parks. Continue 1.5 miles to a junction (signed left for Grant Grove). Turn right at Generals Highway and drive about 25 miles to Lodgepole Village and the turnoff for Lodgepole Campground. Turn left and drive 0.25 mile (past Lodgepole Village) to the campground.

Contact: Sequoia and Kings Canyon National Parks, 559/565-3341; Lodgepole Visitor Center, 559/565-4436, www.nps.gov/seki.

102 POTWISHA

🚶 ⛵ 🏕 🐕 ♿ 🚙 ⛺

Scenic rating: 7

on the Marble Fork of the Kaweah River in
Sequoia National Park

Map 11.4, page 606

This pretty spot on the Marble Fork of the
Kaweah River is one of Sequoia National
Park's smaller drive-to campgrounds. By
looking at maps, newcomers may think it is a
very short drive farther into the park to see the
General Sherman Tree, Giant Forest, and the
famous trailhead for the walk up Moro Rock.
Nope. It's a slow, twisty drive, but with many
pullouts for great views. A few miles east of the
camp, visitors can find Buckeye Flat and a trail
that is routed along Paradise Creek.

Campsites, facilities: There are 42 sites for
tents or RVs up to 30 feet (no hookups). Picnic
tables, food lockers, and fire grills are provided. Drinking water, flush toilets, dump
station, and evening ranger programs are available. Some facilities are wheelchair-accessible.
Leashed pets are permitted.

Reservations, fees: Reservations are not
accepted. Sites are $18 per night, plus $20
per vehicle national park entrance fee. Open
year-round.

Directions: From Visalia, drive east on Highway 198 for 36 miles to the Ash Mountain
entrance station to Sequoia and Kings Canyon National Parks. Continue into the park
(the road becomes Generals Highway) and
drive four miles to the campground on the
left. Vehicles of 22 feet or longer are not advised on Generals Highway from Potwisha to
Giant Forest Village and are advised to use
Highway 180 through the Big Stump entrance
station.

Contact: Sequoia and Kings Canyon National
Parks, 559/565-3341; Lodgepole Visitor Center, 559/565-4436, www.nps.gov/seki.

103 BUCKEYE FLAT

🚶 ⛵ 🏕 🐕 ♿ ⛺

Scenic rating: 8

on the Middle Fork of the Kaweah River in
Sequoia National Park

Map 11.4, page 606

In any big, popular national park such as Sequoia, the smaller the campground, the better.
Well, Buckeye Flat is one of the smaller ones,
set on the Middle Fork of the Kaweah River
with a trail just south of camp that runs beside
pretty Paradise Creek.

Campsites, facilities: There are 28 tent sites.
Picnic tables, food lockers, and fire grills are
provided. Drinking water and flush toilets
are available. Some facilities are wheelchair-
accessible. Leashed pets are permitted.

Reservations, fees: Reservations are not
accepted. Sites are $18 per night, plus $20
per vehicle national park entrance fee. Open
mid-April through mid-September, weather
permitting.

Directions: From Visalia, drive east on Highway 198 for 36 miles to the Ash Mountain
entrance station to Sequoia and Kings Canyon
National Parks. Continue into the park (the
road becomes Generals Highway) and drive
6.2 miles to the turnoff (across from Hospital
Rock) for Buckeye Flat Campground. Turn
right and drive 0.6 mile to the campground.
Vehicles of 22 feet or longer are not advised
on Generals Highway from Potwisha to Giant
Forest Village and are advised to use Highway 180 through the Big Stump entrance
station.

Contact: Sequoia and Kings Canyon National
Parks, 559/565-3341; Lodgepole Visitor Center, 559/565-4436, www.nps.gov/seki.

104 HORSE CREEK

Scenic rating: 6

on Lake Kaweah

Map 11.4, page 606

Lake Kaweah is a big lake, covering nearly 2,000 acres with 22 miles of shoreline. This camp is set on the southern shore of the lake. In the spring when the lake is full and the surrounding hills are green, you may even think you have found Valhalla. With such hot weather in the San Joaquin Valley, it's a boater's heaven, ideal for water-skiers. In spring, when the water is too cool for water sports, anglers can have the lake to themselves for good bass fishing. Other species include trout, catfish, and crappie. By early summer, it's crowded with personal watercraft and ski boats. The lake level fluctuates and flooding is a potential problem in some years. Another problem is that the water level drops a great deal during late summer, as thirsty farms suck up every drop they can get, killing prospects of developing beaches for swimming and wading. The elevation is 300 feet.

Campsites, facilities: There are 76 sites for tents or RVs up to 30 feet (no hookups), including four equestrian sites with horse corrals. Picnic tables and fire grills are provided. Restrooms with flush toilets and showers, drinking water, playground, and a dump station are available. Two paved boat ramps are available at Kaweah Recreation Area and Lemon Hill Recreation Area. A store, coin laundry, boat and water-ski rentals, ice, snack bar, restaurant, gas station, and propane gas are nearby. Some facilities are wheelchair-accessible. Leashed pets are permitted.

Reservations, fees: Reservations are accepted at 877/444-6777 or www.recreation.gov ($9 reservation fee). Sites are $20–25 per night, equestrian sites are $20–40 per night. Some credit cards accepted. Open year-round.

Directions: From Visalia, drive east on Highway 198 for 25 miles to Lake Kaweah's south shore and the camp on the left.

Contact: U.S. Army Corps of Engineers, Lake Kaweah, 559/597-2301.

105 ATWELL MILL

Scenic rating: 7

on Atwell Creek in Sequoia National Park

Map 11.4, page 606

This small, pretty camp in Sequoia National Park is on Atwell Creek near the East Fork of the Kaweah River, at an elevation of 6,650 feet. While the road in is paved, it is slow and twisty, with many blind turns. The terrain in this canyon is open and dry, overlooking the East Fork Kaweah River well below. A trail at camp is routed south for a mile down to the Kaweah River, then climbs out of the canyon and along Deer Creek for another two miles through the East Fork Grove, an outstanding day hike.

Campsites, facilities: There are 21 tent sites; no RVs or trailers are permitted. Picnic tables, food lockers, and fire grills are provided. Drinking water (until mid-October) and pit toilets are available. A small store is nearby. Some facilities are wheelchair-accessible. Leashed pets are permitted.

Reservations, fees: Reservations are not accepted. Sites are $12 per night, plus $20 per vehicle park entrance fee. Open late May through October, weather permitting.

Directions: From Visalia, drive east on Highway 198 for 36 miles to the town of Three Rivers. Continue east for three miles to Mineral King Road. Turn right on Mineral King Road and drive 19 miles (slow, steep, narrow, and twisty, with blind curves) to the campground. RVs and trailers are not recommended.

Contact: Sequoia and Kings Canyon National Parks, 559/565-3341; Lodgepole Visitor Center, 559/565-4436, www.nps.gov/seki.

106 COLD SPRINGS
🏊‍♂️ 🚣 🐕 🏕

Scenic rating: 9

on the East Fork of the Kaweah River in
Sequoia National Park

Map 11.4, page 606

This high-country camp at Sequoia National Park is set at 7,500 feet elevation on the East Fork of the Kaweah River. There is a stellar hiking trail from here, with the trailhead just west of the camp. The hike is routed south along Mosquito Creek, climbing over the course of about three miles to the pretty Mosquito Lakes, a series of four small, beautiful lakes set on the north flank of Hengst Peak (11,127 feet). At road's end, there are two wilderness trailheads for sensational hikes, including one routed out to the Great Western Divide. The Mineral King area is marmot central; those little guyes are everywhere.

Campsites, facilities: There are 48 tent sites. Picnic tables, food lockers, and fire grills are provided. Drinking water (until mid-October) and pit toilets are available. A store is nearby. Leashed pets are permitted.

Reservations, fees: Reservations are not accepted. Sites are $12 per night, plus $20 per vehicle national park entrance fee. Open May through October.

Directions: From Visalia, drive east on Highway 198 for 36 miles to the town of Three Rivers. Continue east for three miles to Mineral King Road. Turn right on Mineral King Road and drive 23 miles (slow, steep, narrow, and twisty, with blind curves) to the campground. RVs and trailers are not recommended.

Contact: Sequoia and Kings Canyon National Parks, 559/565-3341; Lodgepole Visitor Center, 559/565-4436, www.nps.gov/seki.

107 SOUTH FORK
🏊‍♂️ 🚣 🐕 🏕

Scenic rating: 7

on the South Fork of the Kaweah River in
Sequoia National Park

Map 11.4, page 606

The smallest developed camp in Sequoia National Park might be just what you're looking for. It is set at 3,650 feet elevation on the South Fork of the Kaweah River, just inside the southwestern border of Sequoia and Kings Canyon National Parks. While it is technically in the park, it is nothing like at the Giant Forest. Instead, the road in is twisty and slow, the landscape open and hot. A trail heads east from the camp and traverses Dennison Ridge, eventually leading to Hockett Lakes, a long, demanding overnight trip. This is black-bear habitat, so proper food storage is required.

Campsites, facilities: There are 10 sites for tents only. Picnic tables, food lockers, and fire grills are provided. Pit toilets are available. No drinking water is available. Leashed pets are permitted, except on trails.

Reservations, fees: Reservations are not accepted. Sites are $12 per night from May through October; there is no fee in other months. The national park entrance fee is $20 per vehicle. Open year-round.

Directions: From Visalia, drive east on Highway 198 for 35 miles to South Fork Road (one mile before reaching the town of Three Rivers). Turn right on South Fork Road and drive 13 miles to the campground (the road is dirt for the last four miles).

Contact: Sequoia and Kings Canyon National Parks, 559/565-3341; Lodgepole Visitor Center, 559/565-4436, www.nps.gov/seki.

108 BALCH PARK

Scenic rating: 6

near Mountain Home State Forest

Map 11.4, page 606

Balch Park is surrounded by Mountain Home State Forest and Giant Sequoia National Monument. A nearby grove of giant sequoias is a feature attraction. The elevation is 6,500 feet. Two stocked fishing ponds are also available.

Campsites, facilities: There are 71 sites for tents or RVs up to 40 feet (no hookups); some sites are pull-through. Picnic tables and fire grills are provided. Drinking water and flush toilets are available. Leashed pets are permitted.

Reservations, fees: Reservations are not accepted. Sites are $16 per night, $5 per night for each additional vehicle, $3 per pet per night. Open May through late October.

Directions: From Porterville, drive east on Highway 190 for 19 miles (a mile past the town of Springville) to Balch Park Road. Turn left (north) at Balch Park Road and drive three miles to Bear Creek Road. Turn east (right) and drive 15 miles (extremely slow and curvy) to the campground (RVs not recommended).

Alternate route for RV drivers: After turning north onto Balch Park Road, drive 40 miles (long and curvy) to the park.

Contact: Balch Park, Tulare County, 559/539-3896, www.co.tulare.ca.us.

109 HIDDEN FALLS WALK-IN

Scenic rating: 7

on the Tule River in Mountain Home State Forest

Map 11.4, page 606

This small, quiet camp, set at 5,900 feet elevation along the Tule River near Hidden Falls, is one of the prettier camps in Mountain Home State Forest. It is remote and overlooked by all but a handful of insiders who know its qualities.

Campsites, facilities: There are eight walk-in sites for tents only. Picnic tables, food lockers, and fire grills are provided. Drinking water and pit toilets are available. Leashed pets are permitted.

Reservations, fees: Reservations are not accepted. Sites are $15 per night, $5 per night for additional vehicle. No trailers are permitted. Open mid-May through early October, weather permitting.

Directions: From Porterville, drive east on Highway 190 for 19 miles (a mile past the town of Springville) to Balch Park Road. Turn left (north) at Balch Park Road and drive about 23 miles to the Mountain Home State Forest sign. Continue on Balch Park Road (the road is long and twisty) and follow the signs to the State Forest Headquarters (where free forest maps are available). From this point, the campgrounds are well signed.

Contact: Mountain Home State Forest, 559/539-2321 (summer) or 559/539-2855 (winter).

110 MOSES GULCH

Scenic rating: 7

on the Tule River in Mountain Home State Forest

Map 11.4, page 606

Obscure Moses Gulch sits on the Tule River in a canyon below Moses Mountain (9,331 feet) to the nearby north. A trailhead at the eastern end of the state forest provides access both north and south along the North Fork of the Middle Fork Tule River for a scenic hike. The elevation here is 5,400 feet. Mountain Home State Forest is surrounded by Sequoia National Forest.

Campsites, facilities: There are 10 sites for tents only. Picnic tables, food lockers, and fire grills are provided. Drinking water and vault toilets are available. Leashed pets are permitted.

Reservations, fees: Reservations are not accepted. Sites are $15 per night, $5 per night for additional vehicle. No trailers are permitted. Open mid-May through October, weather permitting.

Directions: From Porterville, drive east on Highway 190 for 19 miles (a mile past the town of Springville) to Balch Park Road. Turn left (north) at Balch Park Road and drive about 23 miles to the Mountain Home State Forest sign. Continue on Balch Park Road (the road is long and twisty) and follow the signs to the State Forest Headquarters (where free forest maps are available). The campgrounds are well signed from this point.

Contact: Mountain Home State Forest, 559/539-2321 (summer) or 559/539-2855 (winter).

111 FRAZIER MILL

Scenic rating: 8

in Mountain Home State Forest

Map 11.4, page 606

Abundant old-growth sequoias are the prime attraction at this remote camp. The Wishon Fork of the Tule River is the largest of the several streams that pass through this forest.

Campsites, facilities: There are 49 sites for tents, with a few of these sites also for RVs up to 35 feet (no hookups). Picnic tables and fire grills are provided. Drinking water, food lockers, and vault toilets are available. Some facilities are wheelchair-accessible. Leashed pets are permitted.

Reservations, fees: Reservations are not accepted, except for the site that is wheelchair-accessible. Sites are $15 per night, $5 per night for additional vehicle. Open mid-May through early October, weather permitting.

Directions: From Porterville, drive east on Highway 190 for 19 miles (a mile past the town of Springville) to Balch Park Road. Turn left (north) at Balch Park Road and drive about 23 miles to the Mountain Home State Forest sign. Continue on Balch Park Road (the road is long and twisty) and follow the signs to the State Forest Headquarters (where free forest maps are available). The campgrounds are well signed from this point.

Contact: Mountain Home State Forest, 559/539-2321 (summer) or 559/539-2855 (winter).

112 SHAKE CAMP

Scenic rating: 6

in Mountain Home State Forest

Map 11.4, page 606

This is a little-known spot for horseback riding. Horses can be rented for the day, hour, or night. The camp is set at 6,500 feet elevation and there's a trailhead here for trips into the adjoining Sequoia National Forest and beyond to the east into the Golden Trout Wilderness. Hikers should note that the Balch Park Pack Station, a commercial outfitter, is nearby, so you can expect horse traffic on the trail.

Campsites, facilities: There are 11 sites for tents or RVs up to 20 feet (no hookups). Picnic tables and fire grills are provided. Drinking water, food lockers, and vault toilets are available. A public pack station with corrals is nearby. Some facilities are wheelchair-accessible. Leashed pets are permitted.

Reservations, fees: Reservations are not accepted. Sites are $15 per night, $5 per night for additional vehicle. Open mid-May through early October, weather permitting.

Directions: From Porterville, drive east on Highway 190 for 19 miles (a mile past the town of Springville) to Balch Park Road. Turn left (north) at Balch Park Road and drive about 23 miles to the Mountain Home State Forest sign. Continue on Balch Park Road (the road is long and twisty) and follow the signs to the State Forest Headquarters (where free forest maps are available). The campgrounds are well signed from this point.

Contact: Mountain Home State Forest, 559/539-2321 (summer) or 559/539-2855 (winter); Balch Park Pack Station, 559/539-2227.

113 HEDRICK POND

Scenic rating: 6

in Mountain Home State Forest

Map 11.4, page 606

Mountain Home State Forest is highlighted by giant sequoias, and Hedrick Pond provides a fishing opportunity, as it's stocked occasionally in summer with rainbow trout. This camp is set at 6,200 feet elevation, one of five campgrounds in the immediate region. (See the Methuselah Group Camp listing in this chapter for recreation options.)

Campsites, facilities: There are 14 sites for tents or RVs up to 20 feet (no hookups). Picnic tables, food lockers, and fire grills are provided. Drinking water and vault toilets are available. Some facilities are wheelchair-accessible. Leashed pets are permitted.

Reservations, fees: Reservations are not accepted. Sites are $15 per night, $5 per night for additional vehicle. Open mid-May through October, weather permitting.

Directions: From Porterville, drive east on Highway 190 for 19 miles (a mile past the town of Springville) to Balch Park Road. Turn left (north) at Balch Park Road and drive about 23 miles to the Mountain Home State Forest sign. Continue on Balch Park Road (the road is long and twisty) and follow the signs to the State Forest Headquarters (where free forest maps are available). The campgrounds are well signed from this point.

Contact: Mountain Home State Forest, 559/539-2321 (summer) or 559/539-2855 (winter).

114 METHUSELAH GROUP CAMP

Scenic rating: 6

in Mountain Home State Forest

Map 11.4, page 606

Mountain Home State Forest is best known for its remoteness, old-growth giant sequoias (hence the name of this camp, Methuselah), trails that provide access to small streams, and horseback trips into the surrounding Sequoia National Forest. This is a primitive group camp for tents or a few self-contained RVs. Remember to bring water. The elevation is 5,900 feet.

Campsites, facilities: There is one group site for tents or 1–2 RVs up to 20 feet (no hookups) that can accommodate 20–80 people. Fire grills and picnic tables are provided. Vault toilets are available. Garbage collection and food lockers are available, but there is no drinking water. Leashed pets are permitted.

Reservations, fees: Reservations are required at 559/539-2855. The fee is $50 per night. Open mid-May through early October, weather permitting.

Directions: From Porterville, drive east on Highway 190 for 19 miles (a mile past the town of Springville) to Balch Park Road. Turn left (north) at Balch Park Road and drive about 23 miles to the Mountain Home State Forest sign. Continue on Balch Park Road (the road is long and twisty) and follow the signs to the State Forest Headquarters (where free forest maps are available). The campgrounds are well signed from this point.

Contact: Mountain Home State Forest, 559/539-2321 (summer) or 559/539-2855 (winter).

115 WISHON

Scenic rating: 8

on the Tule River in
Giant Sequoia National Monument

Map 11.4, page 606

Wishon Camp is set at 3,900 feet elevation on the Middle Fork of the North Fork Tule River, just west of the Doyle Springs Summer Home Tract. Just down the road to the east, on the left side, is a parking area for a trailhead. The hike here is routed for a mile to the Tule River and then runs along the stream for about five miles, to Mountain Home State Forest.

Campsites, facilities: There are 39 sites for tents or RVs up to 22 feet (no hookups). Picnic tables and fire grills are provided. Drinking water and vault toilets are available. Leashed pets are permitted.

Reservations, fees: Reservations are accepted at 877/444-6777 or www.recreation.gov ($9 reservation fee). Sites are $18–38 per night, $5 per night for each additional vehicle. Fees are higher on holiday weekends. Open year-round.

Directions: From Porterville, drive east on Highway 190 for 25 miles to County Road 209/Wishon Drive. Turn left at County Road 208/Wishon Drive and drive 3.5 miles (narrow, curvy—RVs not advised).

Contact: Sequoia National Forest and Giant Sequoia National Monument, Western Divide Ranger District, 559/539-2607, www.fs.usda.gov/sequoia.

116 COY FLAT

Scenic rating: 4

in Giant Sequoia National Monument

Map 11.4, page 606

Coy Flat is set between Coy Creek and Bear Creek, small forks of the Tule River, at 5,000 feet elevation. The road out of camp is routed five miles (through Rogers' Camp, which is private property) to the Black Mountain Grove of redwoods, with some giant sequoias set just inside the border of the neighboring Tule River Indian Reservation. From camp, a hiking trail (Forest Trail 31S31) is routed east for two miles through the Belknap Camp Grove of sequoias and then turns and heads south for four miles to Slate Mountain, where it intersects with Summit National Recreation Trail, a steep butt-kicker of a hike that tops out at over 9,000 feet elevation.

Campsites, facilities: There are 18 single sites and one double site for tents or RVs up to 22 feet (no hookups). Picnic tables and fire grills are provided. Drinking water and vault toilets are available. Leashed pets are permitted.

Reservations, fees: Reservations are accepted at 877/444-6777 or www.recreation.gov ($9 reservation fee). Sites are $18–38 per night, $5 per night for each additional vehicle. Camping fees are higher for holiday weekends. Open mid-April through mid-November.

Directions: From Porterville, drive east on Highway 190 for 34 miles to Camp Nelson and Coy Flat Road. Turn right on Coy Flat Road and drive one mile to the campground.

Contact: Sequoia National Forest and Giant Sequoia National Monument, Western Divide Ranger District, 559/539-2607, www.fs.usda.gov/sequoia.

117 BELKNAP

Scenic rating: 7

on the South Fork of Middle Fork Tule River in Giant Sequoia National Monument

Map 11.4, page 606

The groves of sequoias in this area are a highlight wherever you go. This camp is set on the South Fork of the Middle Fork Tule River near McIntyre Grove and Belknap Camp Grove; a trail from camp is routed east for three miles through Wheel Meadow Grove to the junction with Summit National Recreation Trail at Quaking Aspen camp. The elevation is 5,000 feet.

Campsites, facilities: There are 13 sites for tents only. Picnic tables and fire grills are provided. Drinking water and vault toilets are available. A store is nearby. Leashed pets are permitted.

Reservations, fees: Reservations are accepted at 877/444-6777 or www.recreation.gov ($9 reservation fee). Sites are $18–20 per night, $5 per night for each additional vehicle. Fees are higher on holiday weekends. Open mid-April through mid-November.

Directions: From Porterville, drive east on Highway 190 for 34 miles to Camp Nelson and Nelson Drive. Turn right on Nelson Drive and continue one mile to the camp.

Contact: Sequoia National Forest and Giant Sequoia National Monument, Western Divide Ranger District, 559/539-2607, www.fs.usda. gov/sequoia.

118 QUAKING ASPEN AND GROUP

Scenic rating: 4

in Giant Sequoia National Monument

Map 11.4, page 606

Quaking Aspen sits at a junction of Forest Service roads at 7,000 feet elevation, near the headwaters of Freeman Creek. A trailhead for Summit National Recreation Trail runs right through camp; it's a popular trip on horseback, heading deep into Sequoia National Forest. Another trailhead is 0.5 mile away on Forest Road 21S50. This hike is routed east along Freeman Creek and reaches the Freeman Grove of sequoias in four miles.

Campsites, facilities: There are 26 sites for tents or RVs up to 24 feet (no hookups) and seven group sites for 12–50 people. Picnic tables and fire grills are provided. Drinking water and vault toilets are available. An amphitheater is available. A store is nearby. Some facilities are wheelchair-accessible. Leashed pets are permitted.

Reservations, fees: Reservations are accepted at 877/444-6777 or www.recreation.gov ($9 reservation fee). Sites are $18–20, group sites are $27–112.50, $5 per night for each additional vehicle. Fees are higher on holiday weekends. Open May through mid-November, weather permitting.

Directions: From Porterville, drive east on Highway 190 for 34 miles to Camp Nelson. Continue east on Highway 190 for 11 miles to the campground on the right.

Contact: Sequoia National Forest and Giant Sequoia National Monument, Western Divide Ranger District, 559/539-2607, www.fs.usda. gov/sequoia.

119 QUAKING ASPEN GROUP CAMP

Scenic rating: 4

at the headwaters of the South Fork of the Middle Fork Tule River in Giant Sequoia National Monument

Map 11.4, page 606

For groups, here is an alternative to nearby Peppermint (see listing in this chapter for details.) The elevation is 7,000 feet. (For details recreation information, see the Quaking Aspen listing in this chapter.)

Campsites, facilities: There are seven group sites for tents or RVs up to 24 feet (no hookups) that can accommodate 12–50 people each. Picnic tables and fire grills are provided. Drinking water and vault toilets are available. A lodge with limited supplies is nearby. Some facilities are wheelchair-accessible. Leashed pets are permitted.

Reservations, fees: Reservations are required at 877/444-6777 or www.recreation.gov ($9 reservation fee). Sites are $27–112.50 per night, depending on group size. Open mid-May through mid-November.

Directions: From Porterville, drive east on Highway 190 for 34 miles to Camp Nelson. Continue east on Highway 190 for 11 miles to the campground on the right.

Contact: Sequoia National Forest and Giant Sequoia National Monument, Western Divide Ranger District, 559/539-2607, www.fs.usda. gov/sequoia.

120 HOLEY MEADOW GROUP CAMP

Scenic rating: 7

on Double Bunk Creek in Giant Sequoia National Monument

Map 11.4, page 606

Holey Meadow is set at 6,400 feet elevation on the western slopes of the Sierra, near Redwood and Long Meadow. Parker Pass is a mile to the west, and if you drive on the Forest Service road over the pass, continue southwest (four miles from camp) to Cold Springs Saddle, and then turn east on the Forest Service spur road, it will take you two miles to Starvation Creek and the Starvation Creek Grove.

Campsites, facilities: There is a group site for tents or RVs up to 20 feet (no hookups) that can accommodate up to 60 people. Fire grills and picnic tables are provided. Vault toilets are available. There is no drinking water; water is available 2.5 miles away at Redwood Meadow campground. Leashed pets are permitted.

Reservations, fees: Reservations are required at 877/444-6777 or www.recreation.gov ($9 reservation fee). The camp is $135 per night. Open June through October.

Directions: Drive on Highway 99 to Earlimart (about eight miles north of Delano) and the exit for Avenue 56/County Road J22. Take that exit east and drive 39 miles to the town of California Hot Springs and Parker Pass Road/County Road M50. Turn left on Parker Pass Road and drive 12 miles to Western Divide Highway/County Road M107. Turn left on Western Divide Highway and drive 0.5 mile to the campground entrance.

Contact: Sequoia National Forest and Giant Sequoia National Monument, Western Divide Ranger District, 559/539-2607, www.fs.usda.gov/sequoia.

121 REDWOOD MEADOW
🚶 🐕 ♿ 🚐 ⛺

Scenic rating: 7

near Parker Meadow Creek in
Giant Sequoia National Monument

Map 11.4, page 606

The highlight here is the 1.5-mile Trail of the Hundred Giants, which is routed through a grove of giant sequoias and is accessible for wheelchair hikers. This is the site where President Clinton proclaimed the Giant Sequoia National Monument in 2000. The camp is set near Parker Meadow Creek at 6,100 feet elevation. Despite its remoteness, this has become a popular place.

Campsites, facilities: There are 15 sites for tents or RVs up to 16 feet (no hookups). Picnic tables and fire grills are provided. Drinking water and vault toilets are available. Some facilities are wheelchair accessible. Leashed pets are permitted.

Reservations, fees: Reservations are accepted at 877/444-6777 or www.recreation.gov ($9 reservation fee). Sites are $18 per night, $5 per night for each additional vehicle. Camping fees are higher on holiday weekends. Open mid-May through October, weather permitting.

Directions: Drive on Highway 99 to Earlimart (about eight miles north of Delano) and the exit for Avenue 56/County Road J22. Take that exit east and drive 39 miles to the town of California Hot Springs and Parker Pass Road/County Road M50. Turn left on Parker Pass Road and drive 12 miles to Western Divide Highway/County Road M107. Turn left on Western Divide Highway and drive three miles to the campground entrance.

Contact: Sequoia National Forest and Giant Sequoia National Monument, Western Divide Ranger District, 559/539-2607, www.fs.usda.gov/sequoia.

122 LONG MEADOW GROUP CAMP
🚶 🛶 🐕 🚐 ⛺

Scenic rating: 8

in Giant Sequoia National Monument

Map 11.4, page 606

Long Meadow is set on little Long Meadow Creek at an elevation of 6,000 feet, within a mile of the remote Cunningham Grove of redwoods to the east. Note that Redwood Meadow is just one mile to the west, where the Trail of the Hundred Giants is a feature attraction.

Campsites, facilities: There is one group site for tents or RVs up to 16 feet (no hookups) that can accommodate up to 36 people. Picnic tables and fire grills are provided. Vault toilets are available. No drinking water is available. Leashed pets are permitted.

Reservations, fees: Reservations are required at 877/444-6777 or www.recreation.gov ($9 reservation fee). The camp is $81 per night. Open mid-May through mid-November.

Directions: Drive on Highway 99 to Earlimart (about eight miles north of Delano) and the exit for Avenue 56/County Road J22. Take that exit east and drive 39 miles to the town of California Hot Springs and Parker Pass Road/ County Road M50. Turn left on Parker Pass Road and drive 12 miles to Western Divide Highway/County Road M107. Turn left on Western Divide Highway and drive four miles to the campground entrance.

Contact: Sequoia National Forest and Giant Sequoia National Monument, Western Divide Ranger District, 559/539-2607, www.fs.usda. gov/sequoia.

123 TULE

Scenic rating: 7

on Lake Success

Map 11.4, page 606

Lake Success is a big lake with many arms, providing 30 miles of shoreline and making the place seem like a dreamland for boaters on hot summer days. The lake is set in the foothill country, at an elevation of 650 feet, where day after day of 100-degree summer temperatures are common. That is why boating, waterski-ing, and personal-watercraft riding are so popular—anything to get wet. In the winter and spring, fishing for trout and bass is good, including the chance for largemouth bass. No beaches are developed for swimming because of fluctuating water levels, though the day-use area has a decent sloped stretch of shore that is good for swimming. Lake Success is much shallower than most reservoirs, and the water can fluctuate from week to week, with major

drawdowns during the summer. The wildlife area along the west side of the lake is worth exploring, and there is a nature trail below the dam. The campground is the centerpiece of the Tule Recreation Area.

Campsites, facilities: There are 103 sites for tents or RVs of any length; some sites have electrical hookups (30 and 50 amps) and some are pull-through. Picnic tables and fire grills are provided. Restrooms with flush toilets and showers, dump station, picnic areas, and playground are available. A store, marina, boat ramp, houseboat, boat and water-ski rentals, bait and tackle, propane gas, restau-rant, and gas station are nearby. Some facilities are wheelchair accessible. Leashed pets are permitted.

Reservations, fees: Reservations are accepted at 877/444-6777 or www.recreation.gov ($9 reservation fee). Sites are $20–30 per night. Open year-round.

Directions: Drive on Highway 65 to Porter-ville and the junction with Highway 190. Turn east on Highway 190 and drive eight miles to Lake Success and the campground entrance on the left.

Contact: U.S. Army Corps of Engineers, Sacramento District, 559/784-0215; Success Marina, 559/781-2078.

124 GOODALE CREEK

Scenic rating: 6

near Independence

Map 11.4, page 606

This obscure BLM camp is set along little Goodale Creek at 4,000 feet elevation. It is a good layover spot for U.S. 395 cruisers head-ing north. In hot summer months, snakes are occasionally spotted near this campground.

Campsites, facilities: There are 62 sites for tents or RVs up to 30 feet (no hookups); some sites are pull-through. Picnic tables and fire rings are provided. Vault toilets are available. No drinking water is available, but a well is being drilled and a water tank has been installed; check for water availability. Leashed pets are permitted.

Reservations, fees: Reservations are not accepted. Sites are $5 per night. Maximum stay is 14 days. A LTVA Permit ($300) allows all season access to this and two other BLM campgrounds, Tuttle Creek (see listing in this chapter) and Crowley. Open early April through October, weather permitting.

Directions: Drive on U.S. 395 to Aberdeen Road (12 miles north of Independence). Turn west (toward the Sierra) on Aberdeen Road and drive two miles to the campground on the left.

Contact: Bureau of Land Management, Bishop Field Office, 760/872-4881, www.blm.gov/ca.

125 ONION VALLEY

Scenic rating: 8

in Inyo National Forest

Map 11.4, page 606   BEST (

Onion Valley is one of the best trailhead camps for backpackers in the Sierra. The camp is set at 9,200 feet elevation, and from here it's a 2,600-foot climb over the course of about three miles to awesome Kearsarge Pass (11,823 feet). From there you can camp at the Kearsarge Lakes, explore the Kearsarge Pinnacles, or join the John Muir Trail and venture to your choice of many wilderness lakes. This is also the fastest launch point over Kearsarge, then Glen Pass to Rae Lakes, in Kings Canyon National Park. A wilderness map and a wilderness permit are your passports to the high country from this camp. For backpackers, trailhead reservations are required. Note: Bears frequent this camp almost every night of summer. Do not keep your food in your vehicle. Many cars have been severely damaged by bears. Use bear-proof food lockers at the campground and parking area, or use bear-proof food canisters as required in adjacent wilderness area.

Campsites, facilities: There are 28 sites for tents or RVs up to 16 feet (no hookups). Picnic tables and fire grills are provided. Drinking water and vault toilets are available. Some facilities are wheelchair accessible. Leashed pets are permitted.

Reservations, fees: Reservations are accepted at 877/444-6777 or www.recreation.gov ($9 reservation fee). Sites are $14–16 per night, $7 per night for additional vehicle. Maximum stay is 14 days. Open late May through September, weather permitting.

Directions: Drive on U.S. 395 to Independence and Market Street. Turn west (toward the Sierra) at Market Street (becomes Onion Valley Road) and drive 15 miles to the campground at the road's end.

Contact: Inyo National Forest, Mount Whitney Ranger District, 760/876-6200, www.fs.usda.gov/inyo; Interagency Visitor Center, 760/876-6222.

126 UPPER AND LOWER GRAY'S MEADOW

Scenic rating: 6

on Independence Creek in Inyo National Forest

Map 11.4, page 606

Gray's Meadow provides two adjacent camps that are set along Independence Creek. Upper Gray's is set at an elevation of 6,200 feet; Lower Gray's is 200 feet lower down canyon. The creek is stocked with small trout by the Department of Fish and Game. The highlight in the immediate area is the trailhead at the end of the road at Onion Valley camp. For U.S. 395 cruisers looking for a spot, this is a pretty alternative to the camps in Bishop.

Campsites, facilities: Lower Gray's has 15 sites for tents or RVs up to 34 feet (no hookups). Upper Gray's has 34 sites for tents or RVs. Picnic tables, food lockers, and fire grills are provided. Drinking water and flush toilets are available. Supplies and a coin laundry are in Independence. Leashed pets are permitted.

Reservations, fees: Reservations are accepted at 877/444-6777 or www.recreation.gov ($9 reservation fee; look for Grays Meadow). Sites are $16 per night, $7 per night for additional vehicle. Open late March through mid-October, with a 14-day limit.

Directions: Drive on U.S. 395 to Independence and Market Street. Turn west (toward the Sierra) at Market Street (becomes Onion Valley Road) and drive five miles to the campground on the right.

Contact: Inyo National Forest, Mount Whitney Ranger District, 760/876-6200, www.fs.usda.gov/inyo; Interagency Visitor Center, 760/876-6222.

127 INDEPENDENCE CREEK

Scenic rating: 4

in Independence

Map 11.4, page 606

This unpublicized county park is often overlooked among U.S. 395 cruisers. It is set at 3,900 feet elevation, one mile outside the town of Independence, which is spiraling downward into something resembling a ghost town. True to form, maintenance is sometimes lacking here. Independence Creek runs through the campground and a museum is within walking distance. At the rate it's going, the whole town could be a museum.

Campsites, facilities: There are 25 sites for tents or RVs up to 30 feet (no hookups). Picnic tables and fire grills are provided. Drinking water and vault toilets are available. Some facilities are wheelchair-accessible. Supplies and a coin laundry are available in Independence. Leashed pets are permitted.

Reservations, fees: Reservations are not accepted. Sites are $10 per vehicle per night. Open year-round.

Directions: Drive on U.S. 395 to Independence and Market Street. Turn west (toward the Sierra) at Market Street and drive one mile (outside the town limits) to the campground.

Contact: Inyo County Parks Department, 760/873-5577, www.inyocountycamping.com.

128 LONE PINE AND LONE PINE GROUP

Scenic rating: 8

near Mount Whitney in Inyo National Forest

Map 11.4, page 606

This is an alternative for campers preparing to hike Mount Whitney or start the John Muir Trail. It is set at 6,000 feet elevation, 2,000 feet below Whitney Portal (the hiking jump-off spot), providing a lower-elevation location for hikers to acclimate themselves to the altitude. The camp is set on Lone Pine Creek, with decent fishing and spectacular views of Mount Whitney. Because of its exposure to the east, there are also beautiful sunrises, especially in fall.

Campsites, facilities: There are 38 sites for tents or RVs up to 35 feet (no hookups), and one tent-only group site for up to 15 people. Picnic tables and fire grills are provided; some sites have stone ovens. Drinking water and flush toilets are available. Supplies are available in Lone Pine. Some facilities are wheelchair accessible. Leashed pets are permitted.

Reservations, fees: Reservations are accepted at 877/444-6777 or www.recreation.gov ($9 reservation fee). Sites are $17 per night, $5 per night per each additional vehicle, $60 per night for the group site. Open late April through mid-October, with a 14-day limit.

Directions: From U.S. 395, drive to Lone Pine and Whitney Portal Road. Turn west (toward the Sierra) on Whitney Portal Road and drive six miles to the campground on the left.

Contact: Inyo National Forest, Mount Whitney Ranger District, 760/876-6200, www.fs.usda.gov/inyo; Interagency Visitor Center, 760/876-6222.

129 PORTAGEE JOE CAMPGROUND

Scenic rating: 4

near Lone Pine

Map 11.4, page 606

This small, little-known county park provides an option for both Mount Whitney hikers and U.S. 395 cruisers. The sparse setting is high desert sprinkled with a few aspens, with Mount Whitney and the Sierra crest looming high to the west. The camp is located about five miles from Diaz Lake, set on a small creek at 3,750 feet. Very few out-of-towners know about this spot, a nice insurance policy if you find yourself stuck for a campsite in this region.

Campsites, facilities: There are 15 sites for tents or RVs up to 30 feet (no hookups). Picnic tables and fire grills are provided. Vault toilets and well water are available. Supplies and a coin laundry are available in Lone Pine. Leashed pets are permitted.

Reservations, fees: Reservations are not accepted. Sites are $10 per vehicle per night. Open year-round.

Directions: From U.S. 395, drive to Lone Pine and Whitney Portal Road. Turn west (toward the Sierra) on Whitney Portal Road and drive one mile to Tuttle Creek Road. Turn left (south) at Tuttle Creek Road and drive 0.1 mile to the campground on the right.

Contact: Inyo County Parks Department, 760/878-0272 or 760/873-5577, www.inyo-countycamping.com.

130 WHITNEY TRAILHEAD WALK-IN

Scenic rating: 9

in Inyo National Forest

Map 11.4, page 606 **BEST (**

If Whitney Portal is full (common for this world-class trailhead), this camp at 8,300 feet elevation can be reached by hiking in 0.25 mile.

Reservations for the summit hike are required. That accomplished, this hike-in camp is an excellent spot for spending a day to become acclimated to the high altitude. The trailhead to the Mount Whitney summit (14,497 feet) is nearby. Mount Whitney is the beginning of the 211-mile John Muir Trail to Yosemite Valley. Food-raiding bears are a common problem here. Campers are required to use bear-proof food lockers or food canisters. There is a one-night stay limit. For information on backcountry permits, call the ranger district.

Campsites, facilities: There are 10 walk-in tent sites. Picnic tables and fire grills are provided. Drinking water and vault toilets are available. Garbage must be packed out. Supplies are available in Lone Pine. Some facilities are wheelchair accessible. Leashed pets are permitted.

Reservations, fees: Reservations are not accepted. Sites are $10 per night. Open mid-May through late October, with a one-night stay limit.

Directions: Drive on U.S. 395 to Lone Pine and Whitney Portal Road. Turn west (toward the Sierra) and drive 13 miles to the parking lot at Whitney Portal. Park and hike 0.25 mile to the campground.

Contact: Inyo National Forest, Mount Whitney Ranger District, 760/876-6200, www.fs.usda.gov/inyo; Interagency Visitor Center, 760/876-2222.

131 WHITNEY PORTAL AND GROUP

Scenic rating: 9

near Mount Whitney in Inyo National Forest

Map 11.4, page 606

This camp is home to a world-class trailhead. It is regarded as the number-one jump-off spot for the hike to the top of Mount Whitney, the highest spot in the continental United States, at 14,497.6 feet, as well as the start of the 211-mile John Muir Trail from Mount Whitney to Yosemite Valley. Hikers planning to scale the summit must have a wilderness permit, available by reservation at the Forest Service office in Lone Pine. The camp is at 8,000 feet elevation, and virtually everyone staying here plans to make the trek to the Whitney summit, a climb of 6,500 feet over the course of 10 miles. The trip includes an ascent over 100 switchbacks (often snow-covered in early summer) to top Wotan's Throne and reach Trail Crest (13,560 feet). Here you turn right and take Summit Trail, where the ridge is cut by huge notch windows providing a view down more than 10,000 feet to the little town of Lone Pine and the Owens Valley. When you sign the logbook on top, don't be surprised if you see my name in the registry. A plus at the campground is watching the JMT hikers arrive who are just finishing the trail from north to south—that is, from Yosemite to Whitney. There is no comparing the happy look of success when they drop their packs for the last time, head into the little store, and pick a favorite refreshment for celebration.

Campsites, facilities: There are 41 sites for tents or RVs up to 22 feet (no hookups), and three group sites for up to 15 people each. Picnic tables, food lockers, and fire grills are provided. Drinking water and flush toilets are available. Supplies are available in Lone Pine. Leashed pets are permitted.

Reservations, fees: Reservations are accepted at 877/444-6777 or www.recreation.gov ($9 reservation fee). Sites are $17–19 per night, $7 per night per each additional vehicle, $45–60 per night for a group site. One-night limit for walk-in tent sites; seven-day stay limit for group site. Open late May through mid-October.

Directions: Drive on U.S. 395 to Lone Pine and Whitney Portal Road. Turn west (toward the Sierra) on Whitney Portal Road and drive 13 miles to the campground on the left.

Contact: Inyo National Forest, Mount Whitney Ranger District, 760/876-6200; Interagency Visitor Center, 760/876-2222, www.fs.usda.gov/inyo; California Land Management, 760/937-6070.

132 TUTTLE CREEK
🏃 🐕 🚐 ⛺

Scenic rating: 4

near Mount Whitney

Map 11.4, page 606

This primitive BLM camp is set at the base of Mount Whitney along Tuttle Creek at 5,120 feet elevation and is shadowed by several impressive peaks (Mount Whitney, Lone Pine Peak, and Mount Williamson). It is often used as an overflow area if the camps farther up Whitney Portal Road are full. Note: This campground is often confused with a small county campground also on Tuttle Creek Road just off Whitney Portal Road.

Campsites, facilities: There are 85 sites for tents or RVs up to 30 feet (no hookups); some sites are pull through. A group site is available for up to 25 people. Picnic tables and fire rings are provided. Vault toilets are available. Drinking water is available seasonally; a dump station at this campground is available only when water is available. Horses are not prohibited, but not encouraged. Supplies are available in Lone Pine. Leashed pets are permitted.

Reservations, fees: Reservations are not accepted for single sites but are required for the group site at 760/872-5008. Single sites are $5 per night; the group site is $30 per night; season passes are $300. Open year-round.

Directions: Drive on U.S. 395 to Lone Pine and Whitney Portal Road. Turn west (toward the Sierra) on Whitney Portal Road and drive 3.5 miles to Horseshoe Meadow Road. Turn left and drive 1.5 miles to Tuttle Creek Road and the campground entrance (a dirt road) on the right.

Contact: Bureau of Land Management, Bishop Field Office, 760/872-4881, www.blm.gov/ca.

133 DIAZ LAKE

Scenic rating: 7

near Lone Pine

Map 11.4, page 606

Diaz Lake, set at 3,650 feet elevation in the Owens Valley, is sometimes overlooked by visitors to nearby Mount Whitney. It's a small lake, just 85 acres, and it is popular for trout fishing in the spring when a speed limit of 15 mph is enforced. The lake is stocked with Alpers trout and also has a surprise population of bass. From May through October, when hot weather takes over and the speed limit is bumped up to 35 mph, you can say *adios* to the anglers and *hola* to waterskiers. Diaz Lake is extremely popular for waterskiing and swimming and it is sunny most of the year. A 20-foot limit is enforced for boats. A nine-hole golf course is nearby. Boats must be inspected for quagga mussels prior to launching; the launch is closed on Mondays and Tuesdays.

Campsites, facilities: There are 200 sites for tents or RVs of any length; some have partial hookups. Picnic tables and fire grills are provided. Restrooms with flush and vault toilets, drinking water (from a well), playground, and boat ramp are available. Supplies and a coin laundry are in Lone Pine. Some facilities are wheelchair accessible. Leashed pets are permitted.

Reservations, fees: Reservations are accepted at 760/876-4700. Sites are $25 per night, $3 per additional person, boat launch fee is $10. Open year-round.

Directions: From U.S. 395, drive three miles south of Lone Pine to the Diaz Lake entrance on the west side of the road.

Contact: Inyo County Parks Department, 760/876-4700, www.inyocountycamping.com.

134 HORSESHOE MEADOW WALK-IN AND EQUESTRIAN

Scenic rating: 8

near the John Muir Wilderness in Inyo National Forest

Map 11.4, page 606

Horseshoe Meadow features three trailhead camps, remote and choice, for backpackers heading into the adjacent John Muir Wilderness and Golden Trout Wilderness. The three camps are Cottonwood Pass Walk-In, Cottonwood Lakes Walk-In, and Horseshoe Meadow Equestrian. The camps are set at 10,000 feet elevation near the wilderness border, one of the highest trailheads and drive-to campgrounds in the state. Several trails lead out of camp. The best heads west through Horseshoe Meadow and along a creek, then rises steeply for four miles to Cottonwood Pass, where it intersects with the Pacific Crest Trail. From here backpackers can hike north on the Pacific Crest Trail to Chicken Spring Lake to set up camp, a rewarding overnighter, or drop into Big Whitney Meadow in the Golden Trout Wilderness. Some use this camp as a starting point to climb Mount Whitney from its back side (via Guitar Lake). Trailhead reservations are required. There is a one-night stay limit. Food-raiding bears mean that campers are required to use bear-proof food lockers or bear-proof food canisters. The drive in is one of the most spectacular anywhere, with the access road following a cliff edge much of the way, with a 6,000-foot drop to the Owens Valley below. You will also pass fantastic volcanics, the site of many movie settings, including Star Trek with Captain Kirk and a lizard creature. (Can you remember the old episode? My kids, Jeremy and Kris, could, and they simulated a scene playing on the rocks.)

Campsites, facilities: Cottonwood Pass has 12 walk-in sites, Cottonwood Lakes has 12 walk-in sites, and Horseshoe Meadow Equestrian has 10 sites. No hookups. Picnic tables and fire grills are provided. Vault toilets are available; check with rangers for water availability. A pack station and horse facilities are also available at the equestrian camp; campers are encouraged to pack out all livestock waste. Leashed pets are permitted.

Reservations, fees: Reservations are not accepted. Sites are $6 per night for walk-in sites, $12 per night for equestrian sites. Open late May through mid-October, with a one-night stay limit.

Directions: Drive on U.S. 395 to Lone Pine and Whitney Portal Road. Turn west (toward the Sierra) on Whitney Portal Road and drive 3.5 miles to Horseshoe Meadows Road. Turn left on Horseshoe Meadows Road and drive 19 miles to the end of the road (a nearly 7,000-foot climb) and the parking area. Park and walk a short distance to the campground.

Contact: Inyo National Forest, Mount Whitney Ranger District, 760/876-6200, www.fs.usda.gov/inyo; Interagency Visitor Center, 760/876-2222.

135 UPPER PEPPERMINT
🚶 ⛵ 🏕 🚐 ⛰

Scenic rating: 6

on Peppermint Creek in
Giant Sequoia National Monument

Map 11.5, page 607

This is one of two primitive campgrounds at Peppermint Creek, but a road does not directly connect the two camps. Several backcountry access roads snake throughout the area, as detailed on a Forest Service map, and exploring them can make for some self-styled fortune hunts. For the ambitious, hiking the two-mile trail at the end of nearby Forest Road 21S05 leads to a fantastic lookout at The Needles (8,245 feet). The camp elevation is 7,100 feet. There is fire damage in some of the surrounding area.

Campsites, facilities: There is dispersed camping for tents or RVs up to 24 feet (no hookups). Picnic tables and fire rings are provided. Vault toilets are available. No drinking water

is available. Garbage must be packed out. A lodge with limited supplies is nearby. Leashed pets are permitted.

Reservations, fees: Reservations are not accepted. There is no fee for camping. A fire permit is required. Open June through September, weather permitting.

Directions: From Porterville, drive east on Highway 190 for 34 miles to Camp Nelson. Continue east on Highway 190 for 15 miles to the campground entrance road.

Contact: Sequoia National Forest and Giant Sequoia National Monument, Western Divide Ranger District, 559/539-2607, www.fs.usda.gov/sequoia.

136 LOWER PEPPERMINT
🚶 ⛵ 🏕 🚐 ⛰

Scenic rating: 6

in Giant Sequoia National Monument

Map 11.5, page 607

This is a little-known camp in Sequoia National Forest, set along Peppermint Creek at 5,300 feet elevation. This area has a vast network of backcountry roads, which are detailed on a Forest Service map.

Campsites, facilities: There are 17 sites for tents or RVs up to 16 feet (no hookups). Picnic tables and fire grills are provided. Drinking water and vault toilets are available. Leashed pets are permitted.

Reservations, fees: Reservations are not accepted. Sites are $17 per night. Open June through September.

Directions: From Bakersfield, drive east on Highway 178 for 40 miles to the town of Lake Isabella and Highway 155/Burlando Way. Turn left (north) and drive 10 miles to Kernville Sierra Way. Turn (north) and drive 24 miles to Johnsondale and Forest Road 22S82/Lloyd Meadow Road. Turn right and drive about 10.5 miles (paved road) to the campground.

Contact: Sequoia National Forest and Giant Sequoia National Monument, Western Divide

Ranger District, 559/539-2607, www.fs.usda.
gov/sequoia.

137 LIMESTONE
🏃 🛶 🏕 🚙 ⛺

Scenic rating: 5

on the Kern River in Sequoia National Forest

Map 11.5, page 607

Set deep in the Sequoia National Forest at
3,800 feet, Limestone is a small campground
along the Kern River, fed by snowmelt from
Mount Whitney. This stretch of the Kern is
extremely challenging and sensational for
white-water rafting, with cold water and many
of the rapids rated Class IV and Class V—for
experts with guides only. The favored put-in is
at the Johnsondale Bridge, and from here it's a
21-mile run to Kernville. The river pours into
Isabella Lake many miles later. Two sections
are unrunnable: Fairview Dam (Mile 2.5) and
Salmon Falls (Mile 8). For nonrafters, South
Creek Falls provides a side trip, one mile to
the west. There is fire damage in some of the
surrounding area.

Campsites, facilities: There are 20 sites for
tents or RVs up to 30 feet (no hookups). Picnic
tables and fire grills are provided. Vault toilets
are available. No drinking water is available.
Supplies and a coin laundry are in Kernville.
Leashed pets are permitted.

Reservations, fees: Reservations are not accepted. Sites are $16 per night, $5 per night for
each additional vehicle. Open April through
November, weather permitting.

Directions: From Bakersfield, drive east on
Highway 178 for about 40 miles to the town
of Lake Isabella and Highway 155/Burlando
Way. Turn left (north) and drive 10 miles to
Kernville and the Kern River Highway/Sierra
Way. Turn left on the Kern River Highway
and drive 19 miles (two miles past Fairview)
to the campground entrance.

Contact: Sequoia National Forest, Kern River
Ranger District, Kernville Office, 760/376-
3781, www.fs.usda.gov/sequoia.

138 LEAVIS FLAT
🛶 〰️ 🏕 🚙 ⛺

Scenic rating: 7

on Deer Creek in
Giant Sequoia National Monument

Map 11.5, page 607

Leavis Flat is just inside the western border of
Sequoia National Forest along Deer Creek, at
an elevation of 3,000 feet. The highlight here
is the adjacent California Hot Springs.

Campsites, facilities: There are nine sites for
tents or RVs up to 16 feet (no hookups). Picnic
tables and fire grills are provided. Vault toilets
are available, but there is no drinking water.
A store, coin laundry, and propane gas can be
found nearby. Leashed pets are permitted.

Reservations, fees: Reservations are not accepted. There is no fee for camping. Open
year-round.

Directions: Take Highway 99 to Earlimart
(about eight miles north of Delano) and the
exit for Avenue 56/County Road J22. Take that
exit east and drive 39 miles to the town of California Hot Springs and the campground.

Contact: Sequoia National Forest and Giant
Sequoia National Monument, Western Divide
Ranger District, 559/539-2607, www.fs.usda.
gov/sequoia.

139 WHITE RIVER
🏃 🛶 🏕 🚙 ⛺

Scenic rating: 7

in Giant Sequoia National Monument

Map 11.5, page 607

White River is set at 4,000 feet elevation, on
the White River near where little Dark Canyon Creek enters it. A trail from camp follows
downstream along the White River to the west
for three miles, dropping into Ames Hole and
Cove Canyon. The region's hot springs are
about a 10-minute drive away to the north.

Campsites, facilities: There are 12 sites for
tents or RVs up to 24 feet (no hookups). Picnic
tables and fire grills are provided. Drinking

water and vault toilets are available. Leashed pets are permitted.

Reservations, fees: Reservations are accepted at 877/444-6777 or www.recreation.gov ($9 reservation fee). Sites are $18–20 per night, $5 per night for each additional vehicle. Camping fees are higher on holiday weekends. Open mid-April through mid-October.

Directions: Drive on Highway 99 to Delano and the exit for Highway 155. Take that exit and drive east for about 40 miles to Jack Ranch Road (just west of Glennville). Turn left on Jack Ranch Road and drive about four miles to White River Road/Sugarloaf Drive. Turn right and drive 1.5 miles to Forest Road 24S05. Bear left and drive 0.75 mile to Idlewild, and continue (on this dirt road) for six miles to the campground.

Contact: Sequoia National Forest and Giant Sequoia National Monument, Western Divide Ranger District, 559/539-2607, www.fs.usda.gov/sequoia.

140 FROG MEADOW
🏃 🐕 5% 🚐 ⛺

Scenic rating: 6

near Giant Sequoia National Monument

Map 11.5, page 607

This small, primitive camp, set near Tobias Creek at 7,500 feet elevation, is in the center of a network of Forest Service roads that explore the surrounding Sequoia National Forest. The nearby feature destination is the Tobias Peak Lookout (8,284 feet), two miles directly south of the camp.

Campsites, facilities: There are 10 sites for tents or RVs up to 16 feet (no hookups). Vault toilets are available. No drinking water is available. Garbage must be packed out. Leashed pets are permitted.

Reservations, fees: Reservations are not accepted. There is no fee for camping. Open June through September, weather permitting.

Directions: Drive on Highway 99 to Delano and the exit for Highway 155. Take that exit and drive east for about 40 miles to Jack Ranch

Road (just west of Glennville). Turn left on Jack Ranch Road and drive about four miles to White River Road/Sugarloaf Drive. Turn right on Sugarloaf Drive and drive 4.5 miles to Guernsey Mill/Sugarloaf Drive. Continue on Sugarloaf Road/Forest Road 23S16 for about seven miles to Forest Road 24S50 (a dirt road). Turn left on Forest Road 24S50 and drive four miles to Frog Meadow and the campground. The route is long, slow, and circuitous. A map of Sierra National Forest is required.

Contact: Sequoia National Forest and Giant Sequoia National Monument, Western Divide Ranger District, 559/539-2607, www.fs.usda.gov/sequoia.

141 FAIRVIEW
🏃 🚣 🏊 🐕 ♿ 🚐 ⛺

Scenic rating: 4

on the Kern River in Sequoia National Forest

Map 11.5, page 607   **BEST (**

Fairview is one of six campgrounds set on the Upper Kern River above Isabella Lake and adjacent to the Kern River, one of the prime rafting and kayaking rivers in California. This camp sits at 3,500 feet elevation. Many of the rapids are rated Class IV and Class V—for experts with guides only. The favored put-in is at the Johnsondale Bridge, and from here it's a 21-mile run to Kernville. The river eventually pours into Isabella Lake. Two sections are unrunnable: Fairview Dam (Mile 2.5) and Salmon Falls (Mile 8). There is fire damage in some of the surrounding area.

Campsites, facilities: There are 55 sites for tents or RVs up to 45 feet (no hookups). Picnic tables and fire grills are provided. Drinking water, vault toilets, and a dump station are available. Supplies and a coin laundry are available in Kernville. Some facilities are wheelchair-accessible. Leashed pets are permitted.

Reservations, fees: Reservations are accepted at 877/444-6777 or www.recreation.gov ($9 reservation fee). Sites are $18–20 per night, $5 per night for each additional vehicle. Camping fees are higher on holiday weekends. Open April through October, weather permitting.

Directions: From Bakersfield, drive east on Highway 178 for about 40 miles to the town of Lake Isabella and Highway 155/Burlando Way. Turn left (north) and drive 10 miles to Kernville and the Kern River Highway/Sierra Way. Turn left on the Kern River Highway and drive 18 miles to the town of Fairview. Continue to the north end of town to the campground entrance.

Contact: Sequoia National Forest, Kern River Ranger District, Kernville Office, 760/376-3781, www.fs.usda.gov/sequoia.

142 HORSE MEADOW

Scenic rating: 8

on Salmon Creek in Sequoia National Forest

Map 11.5, page 607

This is a little-known spot set along Salmon Creek at 7,600 feet elevation. It is a region known for big meadows, forests, backcountry roads, and plenty of horses. It is just west of the Dome Land Wilderness, and there is a series of three public pastures for horses in the area, as well as trails ideal for horseback riding. From camp, one such trail follows along Salmon Creek to the west to Salmon Falls, a favorite for the few who know of it. A more popular overnight trip is to head to a trailhead about five miles east, which provides a route to Manter Meadows in the Dome Lands.

Campsites, facilities: There are 37 sites for tents or RVs up to 22 feet (no hookups). Picnic tables and fire grills are provided. Drinking water and vault toilets are available. Garbage must be packed out. Leashed pets are permitted.

Reservations, fees: Reservations are not accepted. Sites are $17 per night, $5 per night for each additional vehicle. Open June through October, weather permitting.

Directions: From Bakersfield, drive east on Highway 178 for about 40 miles to the town of Lake Isabella and Highway 155/Burlando Way. Turn left (north) and drive 10 miles to Kernville

and the Kern River Highway/Sierra Way. Turn left on the Kern River Highway for about 20 miles to Sherman Pass Road (signed "Highway 395/Black Rock Ranger Station"). Make a sharp right on Sherman Pass Road and drive about 6.5 miles to Cherry Hill Road/Forest Road 22S12 (there is a green gate with a sign that says "Horse Meadow/Big Meadow"). Turn right and drive about four miles (the road becomes dirt) and continue for another three miles (follow the signs) to the campground entrance road.

Contact: Sequoia National Forest, Kern River Ranger District, Kernville Office, 760/376-3781, www.fs.usda.gov/sequoia.

143 GOLDLEDGE

Scenic rating: 7

on the Kern River in Sequoia National Forest

Map 11.5, page 607

This is another in the series of camps on the Kern River north of Isabella Lake. This one is set at 3,200 feet elevation.

Campsites, facilities: There are 33 sites for tents or RVs up to 30 feet (no hookups). Picnic tables and fire grills are provided. Drinking water and vault toilets are available. Supplies and a coin laundry are available in Kernville. Leashed pets are permitted.

Reservations, fees: Reservations are accepted at 877/444-6777 or www.recreation.gov ($9 reservation fee). Sites are $18–20 per night, $5 per night for each additional vehicle. Camping fees are higher on holiday weekends. Open May through August.

Directions: From Bakersfield, drive east on Highway 178 for about 40 miles to the town of Lake Isabella and Highway 155/Burlando Way. Turn left (north) and drive 10 miles to Kernville and the Kern River Highway/Sierra Way. Turn left on the Kern River Highway and drive 10 miles to the campground.

Contact: Sequoia National Forest, Kern River Ranger District, Kernville Office, 760/376-3781, www.fs.usda.gov/sequoia.

144 HOSPITAL FLAT

🏊 🎣 🏕 🐎 ♿ 🚐 ⛺

Scenic rating: 8

on the North Fork of the Kern River in Sequoia National Forest

Map 11.5, page 607

It's kind of like the old shell game, trying to pick the best of the campgrounds along the North Fork of the Kern River. This one is seven miles north of Isabella Lake. The elevation is 2,800 feet. (For information on rafting on the Kern River, see the Fairview listing in this chapter.)

Campsites, facilities: There are 40 sites for tents or RVs up to 30 feet (no hookups). Picnic tables and fire grills are provided. Drinking water and vault toilets are available. Supplies and a coin laundry are available in Kernville. Some facilities are wheelchair-accessible. Leashed pets are permitted.

Reservations, fees: Reservations are accepted at 877/444-6777 or www.recreation.gov ($9 reservation fee). Sites are $18–20 per night, $5 per night for each additional vehicle. Camping fees are higher on holiday weekends. Open May through August.

Directions: From Bakersfield, drive east on Highway 178 for about 40 miles to the town of Lake Isabella and Highway 155/Burlando Way. Turn left (north) and drive 10 miles to Kernville and the Kern River Highway/Sierra Way. Turn left on the Kern River Highway and drive 6.5 miles to the campground.

Contact: Sequoia National Forest, Kern River Ranger District, Kernville Office, 760/376-3781, www.fs.usda.gov/sequoia.

145 CAMP THREE

🏊 🎣 🏕 ♿ 🚐 ⛺

Scenic rating: 9

on the North Fork of the Kern River in Sequoia National Forest

Map 11.5, page 607

This is the second in a series of camps along the North Fork Kern River north of Isabella Lake (in this case, five miles north of the lake). If you don't like this spot, Hospital Flat is just two miles upriver and Headquarters is just one mile downriver. The camp elevation is 2,800 feet. Note: In past editions, this was listed as "Camp 3." But if you are making an online reservation, you must spell it out or the camp will not be recognized.

Campsites, facilities: There are 50 sites for tents or RVs up to 30 feet (no hookups) and two group sites for up to 20 people. Picnic tables and fire grills are provided. Drinking water and vault toilets are available. A store and coin laundry are available in Kernville. Some facilities are wheelchair-accessible. Leashed pets are permitted.

Reservations, fees: Reservations are accepted for individual sites and required for the group sites at 877/444-6777 or www.recreation.gov ($9 reservation fee). Sites are $18–20 per night, $5 per night for each additional vehicle, $85 per night for the group sites. Camping fees are higher on holiday weekends. Open May through August.

Directions: From Bakersfield, drive east on Highway 178 for about 40 miles to the town of Lake Isabella and Highway 155/Burlando Way. Turn left (north) and drive 10 miles to Kernville and the Kern River Highway/Sierra Way. Turn left on the Kern River Highway and drive five miles to the campground.

Contact: Sequoia National Forest, Kern River Ranger District, Kernville Office, 760/376-3781, www.fs.usda.gov/sequoia.

146 HEADQUARTERS

🏊 🎣 🏊 🏕 ♿ 🚐 ⛺

Scenic rating: 8

on the North Fork of the Kern River in Sequoia National Forest

Map 11.5, page 607

As you head north from Isabella Lake on Sierra Way, this is the first in a series of Forest Service campgrounds from which to take your pick, all of them set along the North

Fork of the Kern River. The North Fork Kern is best known for offering prime white water for rafting and kayaking. The elevation is 2,800 feet.

Campsites, facilities: There are 37 sites for tents or RVs up to 27 feet (no hookups). Picnic tables and fire grills are provided. Drinking water and vault toilets are available. Some facilities are wheelchair-accessible. Supplies and a coin laundry are available in Kernville. Leashed pets are permitted.

Reservations, fees: Reservations are accepted at 877/444-6777 or www.recreation.gov ($9 reservation fee). Sites are $18–20 per night, $5 per night for each additional vehicle. Camping fees are higher on holiday weekends. Open year-round.

Directions: From Bakersfield, drive east on Highway 178 for about 40 miles to the town of Lake Isabella and Highway 155/Burlando Way. Turn left (north) and drive 10 miles to Kernville and the Kern River Highway/Sierra Way. Turn left on the Kern River Highway and drive three miles to the campground.

Contact: Sequoia National Forest, Kern River Ranger District, Kernville Office, 760/376-3781, www.fs.usda.gov/sequoia.

147 PANORAMA
Scenic rating: 7

in Giant Sequoia National Monument

Map 11.5, page 607

This pretty spot is set at 7,200 feet elevation in a region of Sequoia National Forest filled with a network of backcountry roads. The camp is set in an inconspicuous spot and is easy to miss. A good side trip is to drive two miles south, turn left, and continue a short distance to a trailhead on the right side of the road for Portuguese Peak (a Forest Service map is strongly advised). From here, it's a one-mile butt-kicker to the top of Portuguese Peak, at 7,914 feet elevation.

Campsites, facilities: There is dispersed camping for tents or RVs up to 16 feet (no hookups). No drinking water is available. Garbage must be packed out. Leashed pets are permitted.

Reservations, fees: Reservations are not accepted. There is no fee for camping. Open June through August.

Directions: Drive on Highway 99 to Delano and the exit for Highway 155. Take that exit and drive east for about 40 miles to Jack Ranch Road (just west of Glennville). Turn left on Jack Ranch Road and drive about four miles to White River Road/Sugarloaf Drive. Turn right on Sugarloaf Drive and drive 4.5 miles to Guernsey Mill/Sugarloaf Drive. Continue on Sugarloaf Road/Forest Road 23S16 for about six miles to the campground (paved all the way).

Contact: Sequoia National Forest and Giant Sequoia National Monument, Western Divide Ranger District, 559/539-2607, www.fs.usda.gov/sequoia.

148 CEDAR CREEK
Scenic rating: 7

in Sequoia National Forest

Map 11.5, page 607

This is a little-known, primitive Forest Service camp set at 4,800 feet elevation on the southwest flank of Sequoia National Forest, right along little Cedar Creek, with easy access off Highway 155. Greenhorn Mountain Park and Alder Creek provide nearby alternatives.

Campsites, facilities: There are 11 sites for tents only. Picnic tables and fire grills are provided. Drinking water is available (May to October). Vault toilets are available. Garbage must be packed out. Leashed pets are permitted.

Reservations, fees: Reservations are not accepted. There is no fee for camping. Open May through October.

Directions: Drive on Highway 99 to Delano and the exit for Highway 155. Take that exit and drive east on Highway 155 for 41 miles to Glennville. Continue east for nine miles to the campground.

Contact: Sequoia National Forest, Kern River Ranger District, Lake Isabella Office, 760/379-5646, www.fs.usda.gov/sequoia.

149 GREENHORN MOUNTAIN PARK
🏃 ❄ 🐕 🚐 ⛺

Scenic rating: 7

near Shirley Meadows

Map 11.5, page 607

This county campground is near the Shirley Meadows Ski Area, a small ski park open on weekends in winter when there is sufficient snow. Greenhorn Mountain Park covers 160 acres, set at 6,000 feet elevation. The region is filled with a network of Forest Service roads, detailed on a map of Sequoia National Forest. Isabella Lake is a 15-minute drive to the east.

Campsites, facilities: There are 50 sites for tents or RVs up to 24 feet (no hookups). Fourteen cabins are also available as a group rental. Picnic tables and fire pits or fire rings are provided. Drinking water, restrooms with flush toilets and showers, and a dump site are available. Leashed pets are permitted.

Reservations, fees: Reservations are accepted for groups of at least 40 people. Sites are $22 per night, $10 per night for additional vehicle, $4 per night per dog (limit 2). Fees are lower mid-October to mid-March. Open spring through fall, weather permitting.

Directions: From Bakersfield, drive east on Highway 178 for about 40 miles to the town of Lake Isabella and Highway 155/Burlando Way. Turn left (north) and drive six miles to Wofford Heights. Turn left (west) on Highway 155 and drive 10 miles to the park on the left.

Contact: Kern County Parks, 661/868-7000, www.co.kern.ca.us/parks.

150 ALDER CREEK
🏃 🏊 🐕 🚐 ⛺

Scenic rating: 7

in Sequoia National Forest

Map 11.5, page 607

This primitive camp is just inside the western border of Sequoia National Forest, an obscure spot that requires traversing a very twisty and, at times, rough road. It is set at 3,900 feet elevation, just 0.25 mile upstream from where Alder Creek meets Slick Rock Creek. There is a trail out of the camp that runs north for two miles along Slick Rock Creek.

Campsites, facilities: There is room for dispersed camping. Vault toilets are available. No drinking water is available. Garbage must be packed out. Leashed pets are permitted.

Reservations, fees: Reservations are not accepted. There is no fee for camping. Open May through October.

Directions: Take Highway 99 to Delano and the exit for Highway 155. Take that exit and drive east on Highway 155 for 41 miles to Glennville. Continue east for eight miles to Alder Creek Road. Turn right on Alder Creek Road and drive three miles to the campground.

Contact: Sequoia National Forest, Kern River Ranger District, Lake Isabella Office, 760/379-5646, www.fs.usda.gov/sequoia.

151 EVANS FLAT
🏃 🐕 🚐 ⛺

Scenic rating: 4

in Sequoia National Forest

Map 11.5, page 607

Evans Flat is an obscure campground in the southwest region of Sequoia National Forest, about 10 miles west of Isabella Lake, with no other camps in the vicinity. You have to earn this one, but if you want solitude, Evans Flat can provide it. It is set at 6,100 feet elevation, with Woodward Peak 0.5 mile to the east. A natural spring is east of camp within walking distance.

Campsites, facilities: There are 20 sites for tents or RVs up to 20 feet (no hookups). Fire grills and picnic tables are provided. A vault toilet is available. No drinking water is available. Garbage must be packed out. Leashed pets are permitted.

Reservations, fees: Reservations are not accepted. There is no fee for camping. Open May through October.

Directions: From Bakersfield, drive east on Highway 178 for about 40 miles to the town of Lake Isabella and Highway 155. Turn left (north) and drive six miles to Wofford Heights. Turn left (west) on Highway 155 and drive seven miles to Rancheria Road. Turn left and drive 8.3 miles (first paved, then dirt) to the campground.

Contact: Sequoia National Forest, Kern River Ranger District, Lake Isabella office, 760/379-5646, www.fs.usda.gov/sequoia.

152 RIVERNOOK CAMPGROUND
🏊 🛶 🏊 🐾 ♿ 🚐 ⛺

Scenic rating: 7

on the North Fork of the Kern River

Map 11.5, page 607

This is a large, privately operated park set near Isabella Lake a few miles from the head of the lake. Boat rentals are available at one of the nearby marinas. An optional side trip is to visit Keysville, the first town to become established on the Kern River during the gold rush days. The elevation is 2,665 feet.

Campsites, facilities: There are 30 pull-through sites with full hookups (30 and 50 amps) for RVs, 41 sites with partial hookups for RVs, and 59 sites for tents. Picnic tables, fire rings, and drinking water are provided. Restrooms with flush toilets and showers, three dump stations, and cable TV are available. Some facilities are wheelchair-accessible. Leashed pets are permitted.

Reservations, fees: Reservations are recommended. RV sites are $40–45 per night, tent sites are $35 per night, $5 per person per night for more than two people. Some credit cards accepted. Open year-round.

Directions: From Bakersfield, drive east on Highway 178 for about 40 miles to the town of Lake Isabella and Highway 155/Burlando Way. Turn left (north) and drive 10 miles to Kernville and the Kern River Highway/Sierra Way. Turn left on Sierra Way and drive 0.5 mile to the park entrance (14001 Sierra Way).

Contact: Rivernook Campground, 760/376-2705.

153 LIVE OAK NORTH AND SOUTH
🏊 🛶 🏊 🐾 🚐 ⛺

Scenic rating: 8

on Isabella Lake

Map 11.5, page 607

This is one of two camps set in the immediate area on Isabella Lake's northwest side; the other is Tillie Creek. Live Oak is on the west side of the road; Tillie Creek is on the eastern, lake side of the road. Note that "North" and "South" are not displayed on the campground signs. (For recreation information, see the Tillie Creek listing in this chapter.)

Campsites, facilities: There are 59 sites for tents or RVs up to 30 feet (no hookups) at Live Oak North. There is one group site for up to 150 people at Live Oak. Picnic tables and fire grills are provided. Drinking water and restrooms with coin showers and flush toilets are available. Supplies are available in nearby Wofford Heights. Leashed pets are permitted.

Reservations, fees: Reservations are accepted for individual sites (Live Oak South) and required for the group site (Live Oak) at 877/444-6777 or www.recreation.gov ($9 reservation fee). Sites are $20–22 per night, $5 per night for each additional vehicle, $300 per night for the group site. Open May through September.

Directions: From Bakersfield, drive east on Highway 178 for about 40 miles to the town of Lake Isabella and Highway 155. Turn left (north) and drive six miles to the campground entrance road on the left (0.5 mile before reaching Wofford Heights).

Contact: Sequoia National Forest, Kern River Ranger District, Lake Isabella Office, 760/379-5646, www.fs.usda.gov/sequoia.

154 TILLIE CREEK

Scenic rating: 9

on Isabella Lake

Map 11.5, page 607

This is one of two camps (the other is Live Oak) near where Tillie Creek enters Isabella Lake, set on the northwest shore of the lake near the town of Wofford Heights. Isabella Lake is a large lake, and with it comes a dynamic array of campgrounds, marinas, and facilities. It is set at 2,650 feet elevation in the foothills east of Bakersfield, fed by the Kern River, and dominated by water sports of all kinds.

Campsites, facilities: There are 155 sites for tents or RVs up to 45 feet and four group sites for tents or RVs up to 45 feet that can accommodate 80–150 people each. No hookups. Picnic tables and fire grills are provided. Drinking water and restrooms with showers and flush toilets are available. Dump station, playground, amphitheater, and a fish-cleaning station are nearby. Supplies are nearby in Wofford Heights. Some facilities are wheelchair-accessible. Leashed pets are permitted.

Reservations, fees: Reservations are accepted for individual sites and required for group sites at 877/444-6777 or www.recreation.gov ($9 reservation fee). Sites are $20–22 per night, $5 per night for each additional vehicle,

$150–300 per night for group sites. Open year-round.

Directions: From Bakersfield, drive east on Highway 178 for about 40 miles to the town of Lake Isabella and Highway 155. Turn left (north) and drive five miles to the campground (0.5 mile before reaching Wofford Heights).

Contact: Sequoia National Forest, Kern River Ranger District, Lake Isabella Office, 760/379-5646, www.fs.usda.gov/sequoia.

155 CAMP 9

Scenic rating: 8

on Isabella Lake

Map 11.5, page 607

This campground is primitive and sparsely covered, but it has several bonus features. It is set along the northeast shore of Isabella Lake, known for good boating, waterskiing in the summer, and fishing in the spring. Other options include great rafting and kayaking waters along the North Fork of the Kern River (north of the lake), a good bird-watching area at the South Fork Wildlife Area (along the east side of the lake), and an off-highway-motorcycle park across the road from this campground. The elevation is 2,650 feet.

Campsites, facilities: There are 109 primitive sites for tents or RVs of any length (no hookups), and eight group sites that can accommodate 20–35 people each. Picnic tables and fire rings are provided. Drinking water, flush and vault toilets, dump station, boat launch, and fish-cleaning station are available. Supplies and a coin laundry are nearby in Kernville. Some facilities are wheelchair-accessible. Leashed pets are permitted.

Reservations, fees: Reservations are accepted for individual sites and are required for the group site at 877/444-6777 or www.recreation.gov ($9 reservation fee). Sites are $17 per night, $5 per night for each additional vehicle, $50–160 per night for a group site. Open year-round.

Directions: From Bakersfield, drive east on Highway 178 for about 40 miles to the town of Lake Isabella and Highway 155. Turn right (south) and drive six miles to the campground entrance on the right (on the northeast shore of Isabella Lake). The campground entrance is just south of the small airport at Lake Isabella.

Contact: Sequoia National Forest, Kern River Ranger District, Lake Isabella Office, 760/379-5646, www.fs.usda.gov/sequoia.

156 HUNGRY GULCH

Scenic rating: 9

near Isabella Lake in Sequoia National Forest

Map 11.5, page 607

Hungry Gulch is on the western side of Isabella Lake, but across the road from the shore. Nearby Boulder Gulch camp, directly across the road, is an alternative. There are no boat ramps in the immediate area. (For details about Isabella Lake, see the Pioneer Point listing in this chapter.)

Campsites, facilities: There are 74 sites for tents or RVs up to 30 feet (no hookups). Picnic tables and fire grills are provided. Drinking water, restrooms with coin showers and flush toilets, and fish-cleaning station are available. A playground is nearby. Supplies and a coin laundry are available in Lake Isabella. Leashed pets are permitted.

Reservations, fees: Reservations are accepted at 877/444-6777 or www.recreation.gov ($9 reservation fee). Sites are $20–22 per night, $5 per night for each additional vehicle. Open April through September.

Directions: From Bakersfield, drive east on Highway 178 for about 40 miles to the town of Lake Isabella and Highway 155. Turn left (north) and drive four miles on Highway 155 to the campground.

Contact: Sequoia National Forest, Kern River Ranger District, Lake Isabella Office, 760/379-5646, www.fs.usda.gov/sequoia.

157 BOULDER GULCH

Scenic rating: 8

on Isabella Lake

Map 11.5, page 607

Boulder Gulch lies fairly near the western shore of Isabella Lake, across the road from Hungry Gulch. Take your pick. Isabella is one of the biggest lakes in Southern California and a prime destination point for Bakersfield area residents. Fishing for trout and bass is best in the spring. The lake is stocked with trout in winter, and other species are bluegill, catfish, and crappie. By the dog days of summer, when people are bow-wowin' at the heat, water-skiers take over, along with folks just looking to cool off. Like a lot of lakes in the valley, Isabella is subject to drawdowns. The elevation is 2,650 feet. (For more information, see the Pioneer Point listing in this chapter.)

Campsites, facilities: There are 58 sites for tents or RVs up to 45 feet (no hookups). Picnic tables and fire grills are provided. Restrooms with flush toilets and coin showers, drinking water, playground, marina, and fish-cleaning station are available. Supplies and a coin laundry are available in the town of Lake Isabella. Leashed pets are permitted.

Reservations, fees: Reservations are accepted at 877/444-6777 or www.recreation.gov ($9 reservation fee). Sites are $20–22 per night, $5 per night for each additional vehicle. Open April through September.

Directions: From Bakersfield, drive east on Highway 178 for about 40 miles to the town of Lake Isabella and Highway 155. Turn left (north) and drive four miles to the campground entrance.

Contact: Sequoia National Forest, Kern River Ranger District, Lake Isabella Office, 760/379-5646, www.fs.usda.gov/sequoia.

158 FRENCH GULCH GROUP CAMP

Scenic rating: 9

on Isabella Lake

Map 11.5, page 607

This is a large group camp on Isabella Lake at the southwest end of the lake about two miles north of Pioneer Point and the spillway. The elevation is 2,700 feet. (For recreation information, see the Pioneer Point listing in this chapter.)

Campsites, facilities: There is one large group site for tents or RVs of any length (no hookups) that can accommodate up to 100 people. Picnic tables and fire grills are provided. Drinking water and restrooms with flush toilets and solar-heated showers are available. A store, coin laundry, and propane gas are nearby. Leashed pets are permitted.

Reservations, fees: Reservations are required at 877/444-6777 or www.recreation.gov ($9 reservation fee). The camp is $300 per night. Open year-round.

Directions: From Bakersfield, drive east on Highway 178 for about 40 miles to the town of Lake Isabella and Highway 155. Turn left (north) and drive three miles to the campground entrance on the right.

Contact: Sequoia National Forest, Kern River Ranger District, Lake Isabella Office, 760/379-5646, www.fs.usda.gov/sequoia.

159 PIONEER POINT

Scenic rating: 9

on Isabella Lake in Sequoia National Forest

Map 11.5, page 607

Isabella Lake is one of the largest freshwater lakes in Southern California, and with it comes a dynamic array of campgrounds, marinas, and facilities. It is set at 2,650 feet elevation in the foothills east of Bakersfield, fed by the Kern River, and dominated by boating sports of all kinds. This camp is at the lake's southwest corner, between the spillway and the main dam, with a boat ramp available a mile to the east. Isabella is a first-class lake for waterskiing, but in the spring and early summer sailboarding is also excellent, best just east of the Auxiliary Dam. Boat rentals of all kinds are available at several marinas.

Campsites, facilities: There are 73 sites for tents or RVs up to 30 feet (no hookups). Picnic tables and fire grills are provided. Drinking water and restrooms with coin showers and flush toilets are available. A playground and fish-cleaning station are available nearby. A boat ramp is three miles from camp. Supplies and a coin laundry are available in the town of Lake Isabella. Leashed pets are permitted.

Reservations, fees: Reservations are accepted at 877/444-6777 or www.recreation.gov ($9 reservation fee). Sites are $20–22 per night, $5 per night for each additional vehicle. Open year-round.

Directions: From Bakersfield, drive east on Highway 178 for about 40 miles to the town of Lake Isabella and Highway 155. Turn left (north) and drive 2.5 miles north on Highway 155 to the campground.

Contact: Sequoia National Forest, Kern River Ranger District, Lake Isabella Office, 760/379-5646, www.fs.usda.gov/sequoia.

160 KEYESVILLE SPECIAL MANAGEMENT AREA

Scenic rating: 5

on the Kern River near Lake Isabella

Map 11.5, page 607

The Keyesville area originally was developed in the 1850s during the California gold rush; gold was first discovered in this area in 1851. Very few historical buildings remain, however, since much of the old town of Keyesville was comprised of tents and small shacks along trails. Today, this camp is used primarily by OHV enthusiasts and miners and is an alternative to the more crowded and developed campgrounds around Lake Isabella. The Kern River runs through this 7,133-acre BLM area and campsites are available near the river; dispersed camping is also allowed. The Sequoia National Forest borders this area to the north and west. Keyesville has multi-use trails and specific areas for recreational mining and OHV use. Hunting is allowed in season. Fishing for trout or bass is another option. Swimming is not recommended because of the swift water, undercurrents, and obstacles. A free permit is required for whitewater rafting and is available at the forest service office in Lake Isabella (call 760/379-5646).

Campsites, facilities: There is dispersed camping for tents or RVs up to 30 feet (no hookups). Picnic tables and fire rings are provided. Vault toilets are available. There is no drinking water. Garbage must be packed out. Leashed pets are permitted.

Reservations, fees: Reservations are not accepted. There is no fee for camping. A 14-day stay limit per year is enforced. Open year-round.

Directions: From Bakersfield, drive east on Highway 178 for approximately 40 miles to the town of Lake Isabella and Highway 155. Turn left (north) on Highway 155 and drive one mile to Keyesville Road. Turn left and drive 0.5 mile to the Special Management Area entrance.

Contact: Bureau of Land Management, Bakersfield Field Office, 661/391-6000, www.blm.gov/ca.

161 AUXILIARY DAM

Scenic rating: 8

on Isabella Lake

Map 11.5, page 607

This primitive camp was designed to be an overflow area if other camps at Isabella Lake are packed. It's the only camp directly on the shore of the lake, and many people like it. In addition, a boat ramp is just a mile east for good lake access, and the sailboarding prospects adjacent to the campground are the best of the entire lake. The winds come up and sail right over the dam, creating a steady breeze in the afternoon that is not gusty. The elevation is 2,650 feet.

Campsites, facilities: There are a number of primitive, undesignated sites for tents or RVs of any length (no hookups). Drinking water and restrooms with flush toilets and showers are available. Supplies and a coin laundry are available in the town of Lake Isabella. Some facilities are wheelchair-accessible. Leashed pets are permitted.

Reservations, fees: Reservations are not accepted. Sites are $10 per night per vehicle May through September or $50 for a season pass. There is no fee for camping October through April. Open year-round.

Directions: From Bakersfield, drive east on Highway 178 for about 40 miles to the town of Lake Isabella. Continue east on Highway 178 for one mile to the campground entrance.

Contact: Sequoia National Forest, Kern River Ranger District, Lake Isabella Office, 760/379-5646, www.fs.usda.gov/sequoia.

162 PARADISE COVE

Scenic rating: 6

on Isabella Lake

Map 11.5, page 607

Paradise Cove is on the southeast shore of Isabella Lake at 2,600 feet elevation. A boat ramp is about two miles away to the west, near the South Fork Picnic Area. While the camp is not directly at the lakeshore, it does overlook the broadest expanse of the lake. This part of the lake is relatively undeveloped compared to the areas near Wofford Heights and the dam.

Campsites, facilities: There are 46 sites for tents and a primitive area for up to 80 RVs of any length (no hookups). Picnic tables and fire grills are provided at some sites. Drinking water, restrooms with flush toilets and coin showers, dump station, and fish-cleaning station are available. A camp host is on-site. Some facilities are wheelchair-accessible. Supplies, dump station, and coin laundry are available in Mountain Mesa. Leashed pets are permitted.

Reservations, fees: Reservations are accepted at 877/444-6777 or www.recreation.gov ($9 reservation fee). Sites are $20–22 per night, $5 per night for each additional vehicle. Open year-round.

Directions: From Bakersfield, drive east on Highway 178 for about 40 miles to the town of Lake Isabella. Continue east on Highway 178 for six miles to the campground entrance.

Contact: Sequoia National Forest, Kern River Ranger District, Lake Isabella Office, 760/379-5646, www.fs.usda.gov/sequoia.

163 KOA LAKE ISABELLA/ KERN RIVER

Scenic rating: 4

on Isabella Lake

Map 11.5, page 607

This KOA camp provides a good, clean option to the Forest Service camps on the southern end of Isabella Lake, Southern California's largest lake. It is set in South Fork Valley (elevation 2,600 feet), east of the lake off Highway 178. The nearest boat ramp is at South Fork Picnic Area (about a five-minute drive to the west), where there is also a good view of the lake.

Campsites, facilities: There are 70 sites with full or partial hookups (30 amps) for tents or RVs up to 40 feet; some sites are pull-through. Picnic tables and fire rings are provided. Restrooms with flush toilets and showers, drinking water, playground, seasonal swimming pool, coin laundry, recreation room, pub, convenience store, dump station, firewood, and propane gas are available. Leashed pets are permitted with some restrictions.

Reservations, fees: Reservations are accepted at 800/562-2085. RV sites are $42–48

per night, tent sites are $29–37 per night, $5 per person per night for more than two people. Some credit cards accepted. Open year-round.

Directions: From Bakersfield, drive east on Highway 178 for about 40 miles to the town of Lake Isabella. Continue east on Highway 178 for 10 miles to the campground entrance on the left (well signed).

Contact: KOA Lake Isabella/Kern River, 760/378-2001, www.koa.com.

164 SANDY FLAT

Scenic rating: 6

on the Kern River in Sequoia National Forest

Map 11.5, page 607

This camp is opened as an overflow camp if Hobo is filled. It is about a mile from Hobo. It is a low-use campground, with less shade than Hobo; some sites are shaded, others, well, nope. It is used primarily as a boat launch area for kayakers and rafters. Fishing is fair for catfish, bass, and rainbow trout. The river is stocked with trout in the summer.

Campsites, facilities: There are 33 sites for tents or RVs up to 24 feet (no hookups), including six walk-in sites. Fire rings and picnic tables are provided. Vault toilets and drinking water are available. Some facilities are wheelchair-accessible. Leashed pets are permitted.

Reservations, fees: Reservations are accepted at 877/444-6777 or www.recreation.gov ($9 reservation fee). Sites are $18–20 per night, $5 per night for each additional vehicle. Open year-round.

Directions: From Bakersfield, drive east on Highway 178 for 35 miles to Borel Road (five miles from Lake Isabella). Turn right (south) at Borel Road and drive 0.3 mile to Old Kern Canyon Road. Turn right and drive one mile to the campground on your right.

Contact: Sequoia National Forest, Kern River Ranger District, Lake Isabella Office, 760/379-5646, www.fs.usda.gov/sequoia.

165 HOBO

⬛ 🌊 🐕 ♿ 🚐 ⛺

Scenic rating: 7

on the Kern River in Sequoia National Forest

Map 11.5, page 607   **BEST (**

The secret is out about Hobo: It is set adjacent to a mineral hot springs, that is, an open-air springs, with room for about 10 people at once. The camp is also situated along the lower Kern River, about 10 miles downstream of the dam at Isabella Lake. Rafters sometimes use this camp as a put-in spot for an 18-mile run to the takeout at Democrat Picnic Area, a challenging Class IV run. The elevation is 2,300 feet.

Campsites, facilities: There are 24 sites for tents or RVs up to 22 feet (no hookups). Fire grills and picnic tables are provided. Drinking water, vault toilets, showers, and dump station are available. Some facilities are wheelchair accessible. Leashed pets are permitted.

Reservations, fees: Reservations are not accepted. Sites are $18 per night, $5 per night for each additional vehicle. Open April through September.

Directions: From Bakersfield, drive east on Highway 178 for 35 miles to Borel Road (five miles from Lake Isabella). Turn right (south) at Borel Road and drive 0.3 mile to Old Kern Road. Turn right and drive two miles to the campground on your right.

Contact: Sequoia National Forest, Kern River Ranger District, Lake Isabella Office, 760/379-5646, www.fs.usda.gov/sequoia.

166 BRECKENRIDGE

🐕 ⛺

Scenic rating: 7

in Sequoia National Forest

Map 11.5, page 607

This is a popular spot for people to visit with sport utility vehicles. It is a tiny, primitive camp set at 6,600 feet elevation near Breckenridge Mountain (a good lookout here) in a little-traveled southwest sector of the Sequoia National Forest. From camp, it's a two-mile drive south up to the lookout, with sweeping views afforded in all directions. There are no other camps in the immediate area.

Campsites, facilities: There are eight tent sites. Picnic tables and fire grills are provided. Vault toilets are available. No drinking water is available. Garbage must be packed out. Leashed pets are permitted.

Reservations, fees: Reservations are not accepted. There is no fee for camping. Open May through September.

Directions: From Bakersfield, drive east on Highway 178 for about 40 miles to the town of Lake Isabella and Lake Isabella Boulevard. Turn right (south) on Lake Isabella Boulevard and drive two miles to a Y intersection with Kern River Canyon Road and Caliente Bodfish Road. Bear left on Caliente Bodfish Road and drive nine miles to the town of Havilah. Continue on Caliente Bodfish Road for two miles to Forest Road 28S06. Turn right and drive about 10 miles to the campground.

Contact: Sequoia National Forest, Kern River Ranger District, Lake Isabella Office, 760/379-5646, www.fs.usda.gov/sequoia.

167 KERN RIVER CAMPGROUND

⬛ 🚤 🐕 🎣 ♿ 🚐 ⛺

Scenic rating: 6

at Lake Ming

Map 11.5, page 607

The campground is set at Lake Ming, a small but exciting place. The lake covers just 205 surface acres, and with the weather so hot, the hot jet boats can make it a wild affair here. It's become a popular spot for southern valley residents, only a 15-minute drive from Bakersfield. It is so popular for water sports that every year, beginning in March, the lake is closed to the public one weekend per month for private boat races and waterskiing competitions. The lake is restricted to sailing and sailboarding on the second weekend of every month and on

Tuesday and Thursday afternoons. All other boating, including waterskiing, is permitted on the remaining days. All boats are required to have a permit; boaters may buy one at the park. Swimming is not allowed because there is a parasite in the water that has been known to cause swimmer's itch. Yikes. The lake is stocked with rainbow trout in the winter months, and they join a sprinkling of bluegill, catfish, crappie, and bass. The elevation is 450 feet. Maximum stay is 10 days.

Campsites, facilities: There are 50 sites for tents or RVs up to 28 feet. Picnic tables and fire rings are provided. Restrooms with flush toilets and coin showers, drinking water, dump station, playground, concession stand, picnic area, and boat ramp are available. Some facilities are wheelchair-accessible. A store is nearby. Leashed pets are permitted.

Reservations, fees: Reservations are not accepted. Sites are $22 per night, $10 per night for a second vehicle, $5 per night for a towed vehicle, $4 per night per pet. Discounted prices in winter. Open year-round.

Directions: From Bakersfield, drive east on Highway 178 for 11 miles to Alfred Harrell Highway. Turn left (north) on Alfred Harrell Highway and drive four miles to Lake Ming Road. Turn right on Lake Ming Road and follow the signs to the campground on the right, 0.25 mile west of the lake.

Contact: Kern County Parks and Recreation Department, 661/868-7000, www.co.kern.ca.us/parks.

168 TROY MEADOWS

🏃 🏊 🐕 ♿ 🚐 ⛺

Scenic rating: 7

on Fish Creek in Sequoia National Forest

Map 11.5, page 607

Obscure? Yes, but what the heck, it gives you an idea of what is possible out in the boondocks. The camp is set at 7,800 feet elevation right along Fish Creek. Black Rock Ranger Station is available two miles northwest. You are advised to stop there before any backcountry trips. Note that off-highway vehicles (OHVs) are allowed in this area. Also note that Jackass National Recreation Trail is a short drive to the east; it runs north aside Jackass Creek to its headwaters just below Jackass Peak (9,245 feet).

Campsites, facilities: There are 70 sites for tents or RVs up to 20 feet (no hookups). Picnic tables and fire grills are provided. Drinking water and vault toilets are available. Garbage must be packed out. Some facilities are wheelchair-accessible. Leashed pets are permitted.

Reservations, fees: Reservations are not accepted. Sites are $17 per night, $5 per night per each additional vehicle. Open June through October, weather permitting.

Directions: Drive on U.S. 395 to Ninemile Canyon Road (four miles north of the town of Pearsonville, 48 miles south of Lone Pine). Turn west on Ninemile Canyon Road and drive 31 miles (the road becomes Sherman Pass Road) to the campground.

Contact: Sequoia National Forest, Kern River Ranger District, Kernville Office, 760/376-3781, www.fs.usda.gov/sequoia.

169 FISH CREEK

🏃 🏊 🐕 🚐 ⛺

Scenic rating: 8

in Sequoia National Forest

Map 11.5, page 607

This is a pretty spot set at the confluence of Fish Creek and Jackass Creek. The elevation is 7,500 feet. The nearby trails are used by off-highway vehicles, which can make this a noisy campground during the day.

Campsites, facilities: There are 37 sites for tents or RVs up to 27 feet (no hookups). Picnic tables and fire grills are provided. Drinking water and vault toilets are available. Garbage must be packed out. Leashed pets are permitted.

Reservations, fees: Reservations are not accepted. Sites are $17 per night, $5 per night per each additional vehicle. Open June through October, weather permitting.

Directions: Take U.S. 395 to Ninemile Canyon Road (four miles north of the town of Pearsonville, 48 miles south of Lone Pine). Turn west on Ninemile Canyon Road and drive 28 miles (the road becomes Sherman Pass Road) to the campground.

Contact: Sequoia National Forest, Kern River Ranger District, Kernville Office, 760/376-3781, www.fs.usda.gov/sequoia.

170 KENNEDY MEADOWS
🏃🏊🎣🐕🚐🏕️

Scenic rating: 8

on the South Fork of the Kern River in Sequoia National Forest

Map 11.5, page 607

This is a pretty Forest Service campground set amid piñon pine and sage country, with the Pacific Crest Trail running by the camp. That makes it a great trailhead camp, as well as a refreshing stopover for PCT through-hikers. A highlight is the nearby South Fork Kern River, which provides fishing for rainbow trout. The camp receives moderate use and is a lifesaver for PCT through-hikers.

Campsites, facilities: There are 37 sites for tents or RVs up to 30 feet (no hookups) and three sites for RVs of any length. Picnic tables and fire rings are provided. Drinking water (seasonal) and vault toilets are available. Garbage must be packed out. Leashed pets are permitted.

Reservations, fees: Reservations are not accepted. Sites are $17 per night, $5 per night per each additional vehicle. Open year-round, weather permitting.

Directions: Drive on U.S. 395 to Ninemile Canyon Road (four miles north of the town of Pearsonville, 48 miles south of Lone Pine). Turn west on Ninemile Canyon Road and drive 21 miles to a small store. Bear right at the store (still Ninemile Canyon Road) and continue for three miles to the campground.

Contact: Sequoia National Forest, Kern River Ranger District, Kernville Office, 760/376-3781, www.fs.usda.gov/sequoia.

171 LONG VALLEY
🏃🐕5%🏕️

Scenic rating: 5

near the Dome Land Wilderness

Map 11.5, page 607

This one is way out there. It's set at road's end in Long Valley, a mile from the border of the Dome Land Wilderness to the east, and the camp is used primarily as a jump-off spot for hikers. A trail from camp leads 2.5 miles west, climbing along a small stream and reaching the South Fork of the Kern River, in rugged and remote country. The elevation is 5,200 feet.

Campsites, facilities: There are 13 tent sites. Picnic tables and fire grills are provided. Vault toilets are available. No drinking water is available. Garbage must be packed out. Leashed pets are permitted.

Reservations, fees: Reservations are not accepted. There is no fee for camping, but donations are encouraged. Open year-round.

Directions: Drive on U.S. 395 to Ninemile Canyon Road (four miles north of the town of Pearsonville, 48 miles south of Lone Pine). Turn west on Ninemile Canyon Road and drive 11 miles to the BLM Work Station and Cane Brake Road. Turn left on Cane Brake Road (the dirt road opposite the BLM station) and drive six miles to Long Valley Road. Turn right and drive eight miles to the campground entrance road on the left. Turn left and drive one mile to the campground.

Contact: Bureau of Land Management, Bakersfield Field Office, 661/391-6000, www.blm.gov/ca.

172 CHIMNEY CREEK
🏃🐕5%🚐🏕️

Scenic rating: 5

on the Pacific Crest Trail

Map 11.5, page 607

This BLM camp is set at 5,900 feet elevation along the headwaters of Chimney Creek, on the southern flank of Chimney Peak (7,990 feet) two miles to the north. This is a trailhead camp for the Pacific Crest Trail, one of its relatively obscure sections. The PCT heads north from camp and in 10 miles skirts the eastern border of Dome Land Wilderness.

Campsites, facilities: There are 32 sites for tents or RVs up to 25 feet (no hookups). Picnic tables and fire grills are provided. Vault toilets are available. Drinking water is seasonally available at the campground. Garbage must be packed out. Horses and leashed pets are permitted.

Reservations, fees: Reservations are not accepted. There is no fee for camping, but donations are encouraged. Open year-round.

Directions: Drive on U.S. 395 to Ninemile Canyon Road (four miles north of the town of Pearsonville, 48 miles south of Lone Pine). Turn west on Ninemile Canyon Road and drive 11 miles to the BLM Work Station and Cane Brake Road. Turn left on Cane Brake Road (the dirt road opposite the BLM station) and drive three miles to the camp on the left.

Contact: Bureau of Land Management, Bakersfield Field Office, 661/391-6000, www.blm.gov/ca.

173 WALKER PASS WALK-IN

Scenic rating: 6

on the Pacific Crest Trail southwest of Death Valley National Park

Map 11.5, page 607

Long-distance hikers on the Pacific Crest Trail treat this camp as if they were arriving at Valhalla. That's because it is set right on the trail. The camp is set at 5,200 feet elevation, southwest of Death Valley National Park. And if you guessed it was named for Joe Walker, the West's greatest trailblazer and one of my heroes, well, right you are. If you arrive by car instead of on the PCT, use this spot as a base camp. Because of its desert remoteness, very few hikers start trips from this location.

Campsites, facilities: There are two sites for tents or RVs up to 20 feet (no hookups) with limited parking and 11 walk-in sites for tents only. Picnic tables and fire rings are provided. No drinking water is available at the campground, but a spring development is located 0.1 mile west on Highway 178, in the bottom of the drainage by the 30-mph sign. Pit toilets are available. Hitching racks and corrals are available. Garbage must be packed out. Leashed pets are permitted.

Reservations, fees: Reservations are not accepted. There is no fee for camping, but donations are encouraged. A 14-day stay limit is enforced. Open year-round.

Directions: From Bakersfield, drive east on Highway 178 for about 40 miles to the town of Lake Isabella. Continue east on Highway 178 to Onyx and continue 14 miles to Walker Pass and the right side of the road (where a sign is posted for the Pacific Crest Trail). Park and walk 0.25 mile to the campground.

Contact: Bureau of Land Management, Bakersfield Field Office, 661/391-6000, www.blm.gov/ca.

SANTA BARBARA AND VICINITY

© CHEE-ONN LEONG/123RF.COM

BEST CAMPGROUNDS

For many, this region of the California coast is like

a dream, the best place to live on earth. Visitors, picking one or several of the dozens of campgrounds in the region, can get a taste of why it is so special. What you will likely find, however, is that a taste will only whet your appetite. That's how it is here. Many keep coming back for more. Some eventually even move here.

The region is a unique mix of sun-swept sand beaches that stretch 200 miles and surprise inland coastal forests. The coast offers a series of stunning state beaches, where getting a campsite reservation can feel like winning the lottery. If you have a dream trip in mind in which you cruise the coast highway the entire length, you'd better have the reservation system wired from the start. These campsites go fast and are filled every night of the vacation season. There are many highlights on the coast: San Simeon, Hearst Castle, all the state beaches, the stunning towns of Cambria, Goleta, and Cayucos, and the Coast Highway that provides a route through all of it.

Yet as popular as the coast is, just inland lie many remote, hidden campsites and destinations. Los Padres National Forest spans a matrix of canyons with small streams, mountaintop lookouts, and wilderness trailheads. In fact, rangers reviewing the text for this book requested that I remove one of the trails highlighted from a campground because it was too primitive and difficult for most visitors to successfully follow to its end at a mountaintop. The landscape is a mix of pine, deep canyons, chaparral, and foothills.

Two of California's best recreation lakes also provide major destinations – Lake Nacimiento and San Antonio Reservoir. Nacimiento is one of the top family-oriented lakes for water sports, and it also provides sensational fishing for white bass and largemouth bass in the spring. San Antonio is a great lake for bass, at times even rating as one of the best in America, and tours to see bald eagles are also popular in the winter. Cachuma Lake and Lake Casitas near Santa Barbara have produced some of the largest bass caught in history.

The ocean is dramatic here, the backdrop for every trip on the Coast Highway, and it seems to stretch to forever. Maybe it does. For many visiting here, forever is how long they wish to stay.

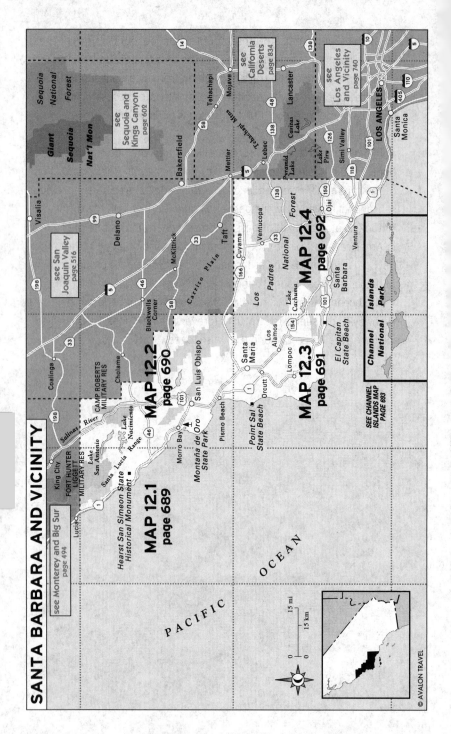

SANTA BARBARA AND VICINITY

Map 12.1

Sites 1-3
Pages 694-695

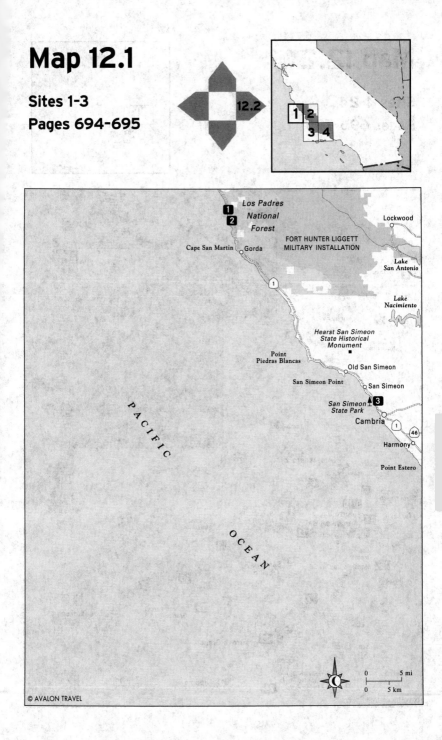

© AVALON TRAVEL

Map 12.2

Sites 4-24
Pages 695-705

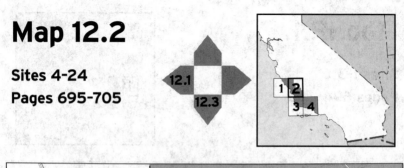

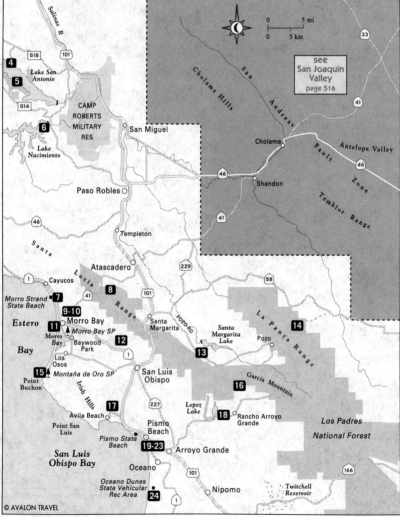

Map 12.3

Sites 25-35
Pages 706-711

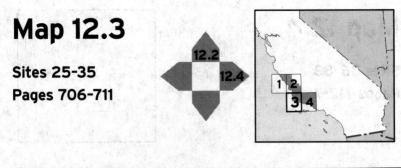

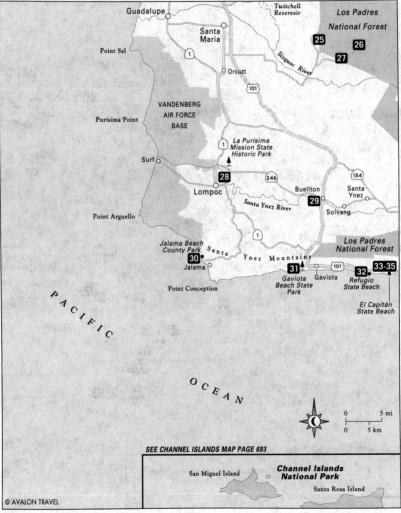

SEE CHANNEL ISLANDS MAP PAGE 693

© AVALON TRAVEL

Map 12.4

Sites 36-83
Pages 712-733

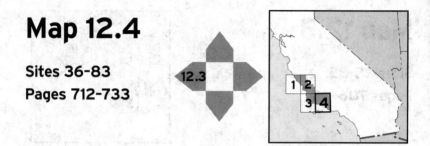

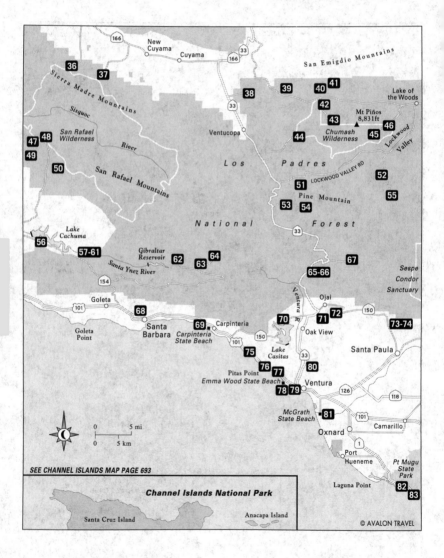

SEE CHANNEL ISLANDS MAP PAGE 693

Channel Islands National Park

Santa Cruz Island   Anacapa Island

© AVALON TRAVEL

CHANNEL ISLANDS DETAIL
Sites 84-88 Pages 733-736

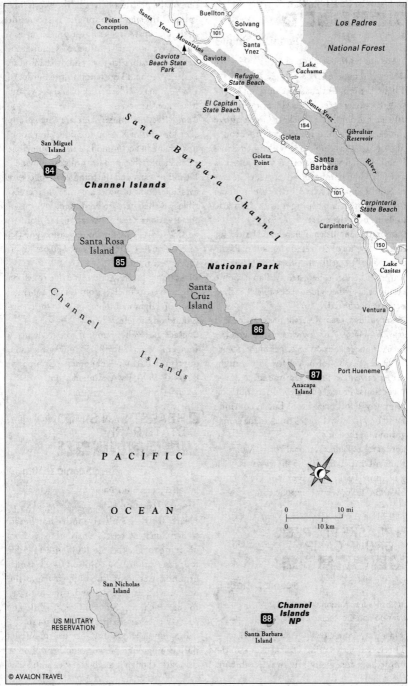

Point Conception

Buellton

Solvang

Santa Ynez

Los Padres

National Forest

Santa Ynez Mountains

Gaviota Beach State Park

Gaviota

Lake Cachuma

Refugio State Beach

El Capitán State Beach

Santa Ynez River

Goleta

Gibraltar Reservoir

San Miguel Island

84

Santa Barbara Channel

Channel Islands

Goleta Point

Santa Barbara

Carpinteria State Beach

Santa Rosa Island

85

National Park

Santa Cruz Island

Carpinteria

Lake Casitas

86

Ventura

Channel

Islands

87

Anacapa Island

Port Hueneme

P A C I F I C

O C E A N

0   10 mi

0   10 km

San Nicholas Island

US MILITARY RESERVATION

Channel Islands NP

88

Santa Barbara Island

© AVALON TRAVEL

1 PLASKETT CREEK

🚶 ⛱ 🚣 🐕 ♿ 🚐 ⛺

Scenic rating: 8

in Los Padres National Forest

Map 12.1, page 689

This is a premium coastal camp for Highway 1 cruisers, set at an elevation of just 100 feet along little Plaskett Creek above the Pacific Ocean. It is slightly farther south of Big Sur than most are willing to drive from Monterey, and is often overlooked as a result. The campground provides access to Sand Dollar Beach. A little café in Lucia provides open-air dining with a dramatic lookout over the coast.

Campsites, facilities: There are 41 sites for tents or RVs up to 30 feet (no hookups). Picnic tables and fire grills are provided. Drinking water and flush toilets are available. Some facilities are wheelchair accessible. Leashed pets are permitted.

Reservations, fees: Reservations are accepted at 877/444-6777 or www.recreation.gov ($9 reservation fee). Sites are $22 per night, $5 per night per person for bicyclists, $5 per night per extra vehicle. Open year-round.

Directions: From Monterey, drive south on Highway 1 to Lucia. From Lucia, continue south on Highway 1 for 9.5 miles to the campground on the left.

Contact: Los Padres National Forest, Monterey Ranger District, 831/385-5434, www.fs.usda.gov/lpnf; Parks Management Company, 805/434-1996, www.campone.com.

2 PLASKETT CREEK GROUP CAMP

🚶 ⛱ 🚣 🐕 ♿ 🚐 ⛺

Scenic rating: 8

in Los Padres National Forest overlooking the Pacific Ocean

Map 12.1, page 689

This is one of two prime coastal camps in the immediate area along Highway 1, which is one of the prettiest drives in the West. The camp is for small groups and is set beside little Plaskett Creek. For a premium day trip, drive north five miles to Nacimiento-Ferguson Road, turn east, and drive into Los Padres National Forest and to the border of the Ventana Wilderness. Coastal views and hikes are first-class.

Campsites, facilities: There are three group sites for tents or RVs up to 30 feet (no hookups) that can accommodate up to 40 people each. Picnic tables and fire grills are provided. Drinking water and flush and vault toilets are available. Some facilities are wheelchair accessible. Leashed pets are permitted.

Reservations, fees: Reservations are required at 877/444-6777 or www.recreation.gov ($9 reservation fee). Group sites are $80 per night. Open year-round.

Directions: From Monterey, drive south on Highway 1 to Lucia. From Lucia, continue south on Highway 1 for 9.5 miles to the campground on the left.

Contact: Los Padres National Forest, Monterey Ranger District, 831/385-5434, www.fs.usda.gov/lpnf; Parks Management Company, 805/434-1996, www.campone.com.

3 HEARST SAN SIMEON STATE PARK

🚶 🚲 ⛱ 🚣 🐕 ♿ 🚐 ⛺

Scenic rating: 9

in San Simeon State Park

Map 12.1, page 689

Hearst Castle is only five miles northeast, so San Simeon Creek is a natural for visitors planning to take the tour (800/444-4445 for tour reservations). San Simeon Creek campground is set across the highway from the ocean, with easy access under the highway to the beach. San Simeon Creek, while not exactly the Mississippi, runs through the campground and adds a nice touch. Washburn campground provides another option at this park; though it has better views, the sites are exposed and can be windy. It is one mile inland on a plateau overlooking the Pacific Ocean and Santa Lucia Mountains. The best hike in the area is from Leffingwell Landing to Moonstone Beach, featuring sweeping views of the coast from ocean bluffs and a good chance to see passing whales. There are three preserves in the park, including a wintering site for monarch butterfly populations, and it has an archaeological site dating from more than 5,800 years ago. In the summer, junior ranger programs and interpretive programs are offered.

Campsites, facilities: At San Simeon Creek camp, there are 115 sites for tents or RVs up to 35 feet (no hookups), 10 sites for tents only, and two hike-in/bike-in sites. Picnic tables and fire grills are provided. Drinking water, dump station, and restrooms with flush toilets and coin showers are available. At Washburn camp, there are 70 sites for tents or RVs up to 31 feet (no hookups). Picnic tables and fire grills are provided. Drinking water, pit and flush toilets, and firewood are available. A grocery store, coin laundry, gas station, restaurants, and propane gas are two miles away in Cambria. Some facilities are wheelchair-accessible. Leashed pets are permitted in the campgrounds only.

Reservations, fees: Reservations are accepted March 30 through September 30 at 800/444-7275 (800/444-PARK) or www.reserveamerica.com ($8 reservation fee). Sites are $35 per night at San Simeon Creek, $20 per night at Washburn, $8 per night for each additional vehicle, $5 per person per night for hike-in/bike-in sites. Open year-round.

Directions: From Cambria, drive two miles north on Highway 1 to San Simeon Creek Road. Turn east and drive 0.2 mile to the park entrance on the right.

Contact: San Simeon State Park, 805/927-2035, www.parks.ca.gov.

4 NORTH SHORE SAN ANTONIO

🏃 🚴 🏊 🛶 🎣 🐕 ♿ 🚐 ⛺

Scenic rating: 7

on Lake San Antonio

Map 12.2, page 690   **BEST (**

Lake San Antonio makes a great year-round destination for adventure. It is a big, warm-water lake, long and narrow, set at an elevation of 780 feet in the foothills north of Paso Robles. The camp features four miles of shoreline camping, with the bonus of primitive sites along Pleyto Points. The lake is 16 miles long, covers 5,500 surface acres, and has 60 miles of shoreline and average summer water temperatures in the 70s, making it an ideal place for fun in the sun. It is one of the top lakes in California for bass fishing, best in spring and early summer. It is also good for striped bass, catfish, crappie, sunfish, and bluegill. It provides the best wintering habitat in the region for bald eagles, and eagle-watching tours are available from the south shore of the lake. Of course, the size of the lake, along with hot temperatures all summer, make waterskiing and water sports absolutely first-class. Note that boat rentals are not available here, but are at South Shore. Equestrian trails are also available.

Campsites, facilities: There are 200 sites for tents or RVs of any length (no hookups), 24 sites with full or partial hookups (30 amps) for tents or RVs of any length, and up to 1,800 primitive dispersed sites near the shoreline. The Los Robles HorseWorld is open to equestrian camping only. Mobile home rentals are also available. Fire grills and picnic tables are provided. Restrooms with showers, drinking water, dump station, boat ramp, hitching posts and corrals, general store, and volleyball are available. Some facilities are wheelchair accessible. Leashed pets are permitted.

Reservations, fees: Reservations are accepted up to one week in advance at 805/472-2456 or 888/588-2267 ($5 reservation fee). Sites are $28–30 per night, $15 per night for each additional vehicle, $2 per pet per night. Boat launch is $6 per day. Off-season discounts available. Some credit cards accepted. Open year-round.

Directions: On U.S. 101, drive to the Jolon Road/G14 exit (just north of King City). Take that exit and turn south on Jolon Road and drive 27 miles to Pleyto Road (curvy road). Turn right and drive three miles to the North Shore entrance of the lake. Note: When arriving from the south or east on U.S. 101 near Paso Robles, it is faster to take the G18/Jolon Road exit.

Contact: North Shore, 805/472-2456, www.co.monterey.ca.us/parks.

5 SOUTH SHORE SAN ANTONIO

🚶 🚴 🏊 🛶 🎣 🐾 🐎 🚐 ⛺

Scenic rating: 7

on Lake San Antonio

Map 12.2, page 690   BEST (

Harris Creek, Redondo Vista, and Lynch are the three campgrounds set near each other along the south shore of Lake San Antonio, a 16-mile reservoir that provides good bass fishing in the spring and waterskiing in the summer. There are also 26 miles of good biking and hiking trails in the park. A museum and a visitors center are available at the park's administration building. In the winter, the Monterey County Department of Parks offers a unique eagle-watching program here, which includes boat tours. (See the North Shore listing for more details about the lake.)

Campsites, facilities: Redondo Vista has 173 sites for tents or RVs (no hookups) and 86 sites with full hookups (30 amps) for tents or RVs; Lynch has 52 sites for tents and 54 sites with partial hookups for tents or RVs; Harris Creek has 88 sites for tents and 26 sites with partial hookups for tents or RVs. Group camping is available for groups reserving 10 or more sites. Mobile-home rentals are also available. Picnic tables and fire grills are provided. Drinking water and flush toilets are available. Restrooms with showers, dump station, marina, boat ramp, boat rentals, boat slips, bait and tackle, playground, recreation room, coin laundry, general store, and fishing licenses are available nearby. Leashed pets are permitted.

Reservations, fees: Reservations are accepted for Redondo Vista group sites at 888/588-2267. Other group reservations are available at 805/472-2311 ($15 reservation fee). All other sites are first come, first served. Tent sites are $28–30 per night, RV sites (hookups) are $38–40 per night, $15 per night for each additional vehicle, $2 per pet per night. Boat launch is $6 per day. Some credit cards accepted. Off-season discounts available. Open year-round.

Directions: From the north, on U.S. 101 (just north of King City), take the Jolon Road/G14 exit. Turn south on Jolon Road and drive 21 miles to Lockwood and Interlake Road (G14). Turn right and drive 18 miles to San Antonio Lake Road. Turn left and drive three miles to the South Shore entrance of the lake.

From the south, drive on U.S. 101 to Paso Robles and the 24th Street exit (G14 west). Take that exit and drive 14 miles to Lake Nacimiento Drive. Turn right and drive across Lake Nacimiento Dam to Interlake Road. Turn left and drive seven miles to Lake San Antonio Road. Turn right and drive three miles to the South Shore entrance.

Contact: South Shore, 805/472-2311, www.co.monterey.ca.us/parks.

6 LAKE NACIMIENTO RESORT

🏊 🛶 🚤 🏕 🐾 ♿ 🚐 ⛺

Scenic rating: 8

at Lake Nacimiento

Map 12.2, page 690   BEST (

This is the only game in town at Nacimiento, and the management plays it well. It's an outstanding operation, with headquarters for a great fishing or water-sports trip. The fishing for white bass and largemouth bass can be incredible. And the water play is also great, with such a big lake, 70-degree temperatures, and some of the best waterskiing in California. The lake has 165 miles of shoreline with an incredible number of arms, many ideal for bass fishing. Nacimiento hosts about 25 fishing tournaments per year. Not only is bass fishing good, but there are also opportunities for trout (in cool months) and bluegill and catfish (in warm months). The resort has a lake-view restaurant open during the summer, and the campsites provide limited tree cover with pines and oaks. Two camps are on the lake's shore, and the rest are set back about 0.75 mile from the lake. Lakeview lodging is also available.

Campsites, facilities: There are a series of campgrounds with 297 sites with no hookups for tents or RVs of any length, 40 sites with full hookups for RVs up to 35 feet, and 12 group sites for 15–40 people each. Nineteen lodges, eight trailers, and two mobile homes are also available for rent. Picnic tables and fire grills are provided. Drinking water, restrooms with showers and flush toilets, dump station, boat ramp, boat docks, boat rentals, seasonal swimming pool, seasonal restaurant, coin laundry, general store, fishing licenses, swimming beaches, basketball and volleyball courts, and horseshoe pits are available. Some facilities are wheelchair accessible. Leashed pets are permitted.

Reservations, fees: Reservations are accepted for tent sites and are required for RV sites with full hookups. Tent sites are $30 per night, RV sites (hookups) are $40 per night, $30–40 per extra vehicle, $2 per pet per night. Some credit cards accepted. Open year-round.

Directions: From U.S. 101 north, drive to Paso Robles and the 46E exit; from U.S. 101 south, drive to Paso Robles and the 24th Street exit (same exit, different names depending on which direction you're coming from). Turn west on 24th Street (becomes Lake Nacimiento Drive/G14) and drive for nine miles. Bear right on Lake Nacimiento Drive and continue for seven miles to the resort entrance on the left. Note: If you cross the Lake Nacimiento dam, you've gone too far.

Contact: Lake Nacimiento Resort, 805/238-3256 or 800/323-3839, www.nacimientoresort.com.

7 MORRO STRAND STATE BEACH

⚂ 🏖 🐾 📷 ⛺

Scenic rating: 7

near Morro Bay

Map 12.2, page 690

A ton of Highway 1 cruisers plan to stay overnight at this state park. It is set along the ocean near Morro Bay, right on the beach, a pretty spot year-round. The park features a three-mile stretch of beach that connects the southern and northern entrances to the state beach. Fishing, jogging, sailboarding, and kite flying are popular.

Note: This park is on the closure list developed by the California Department of Parks, pending final state budget decisions or the possible transfer of park management to other park agencies or volunteer groups. Three nonprofit groups have submitting partnership proposals; check online for current status.

Campsites, facilities: There are 76 sites for tents or RVs up to 24 feet (no hookups). Picnic tables and fire grills are provided. Drinking water and flush toilets are available. Cold, outdoor showers are also available. Supplies and a coin laundry are in Morro Bay. Leashed pets are permitted, but not on the beach.

Reservations, fees: Reservations are not accepted at this time. Sites may still be available on a first-come, first served basis. Sites are $35 per night, $8 per night for each additional vehicle. Open year-round.

Directions: On Highway 1, drive to Morro Bay. Take the Yerba Buena Street/Morro Strand State Beach exit. Turn west on Yerba Buena Street and drive one block to the campground.

Contact: Morro Strand State Beach, 805/772-8812; San Luis Obispo Coast District, 805/927-2065, www.parks.ca.gov.

8 CERRO ALTO

Scenic rating: 7

near San Luis Obispo

Map 12.2, page 690

This camp is set near Morro Creek, which runs most of the year but can disappear in late summer in dry years. Some sites are along the creek, nicely spaced, with sycamore and bay trees peppering the hillside. There are numerous hiking and mountain-biking trails. The best of these is Cerro Alto Trail, which is accessible from camp and then is routed four miles up to Cuesta Ridge for sweeping views of Morro Bay.

Campsites, facilities: There are 22 sites for tents or RVs up to 30 feet (no hookups). Picnic tables and fire grills are provided. Drinking water and vault toilets are available. A camp host and pay phone are nearby. Some facilities are wheelchair-accessible. Leashed pets permitted.

Reservations, fees: Reservations are accepted at 877/444-6777 or www.recreation.gov ($9 reservation fee). Sites are $18 per night, $5 per night per additional vehicle. Open year-round, weather permitting.

Directions: From U.S. 101 at Atascadero, take the Highway 41 west exit. Drive west on Highway 41 for eight miles to the campground on the left.

Contact: Los Padres National Forest, Santa Lucia Ranger District, 805/925-9538, www.fs.usda.gov/lpnf; Parks Management Co., 805/434-1996.

9 RANCHO COLINA RV PARK

Scenic rating: 6

in Morro Bay

Map 12.2, page 690

This privately operated RV park is one of several camping options in the Morro Bay area. Folks who park here typically stroll the boardwalk, exploring the little shops. (For recreation, see the Morro Bay State Park listing in this chapter.) About 20 percent of the sites here are long-term rentals.

Campsites, facilities: There are 57 sites with full hookups (30 amps) for RVs up to 40 feet. No tents. Picnic tables are provided. Restrooms with showers, laundry facilities, and a recreation room are available. Some facilities are wheelchair accessible. Leashed pets are permitted.

Reservations, fees: Reservations are accepted. Sites are $35 per night. Monthly rates available. Some credit cards accepted. Open year-round.

Directions: From Morro Bay on Highway 1, drive one mile east on Atascadero Road/Highway 41 to the park at 1045 Atascadero Road.

Contact: Rancho Colina RV Park, 805/772-8420.

10 MORRO DUNES RV PARK

Scenic rating: 6

in Morro Bay

Map 12.2, page 690

A wide array of side-trip possibilities and great natural beauty make Morro Bay an attractive destination. Most visitors will walk the boardwalk, try at least one of the coastal restaurants, and then head to Morro Bay State Park for hiking or sea kayaking. Other folks will head straight to the port for fishing, or just explore the area before heading north to San Simeon for the Hearst Castle tour. (See the Morro Bay State Park listing for more information.)

Campsites, facilities: There are 152 sites with full or partial hookups (30 amps) for RVs of any length and 18 sites for tents. Some sites are pull-through. Picnic tables and fire grills are provided. Restrooms with showers, drinking water, cable TV, Wi-Fi, modem access, coin laundry, general store, clubhouse, RV storage, RV supplies and repair, recreation hall, group facilities, horseshoes, basketball, firewood, ice, and dump station are available. Propane gas, golf course, playground, and boat rentals are nearby. Some facilities are wheelchair-accessible. Leashed pets are permitted.

Reservations, fees: Reservations are accepted. RV sites are $37.40–44.00 per night, tent sites are $27.50 per night, $1 per person per night for more than two people, $1 per pet per night. Weekly and monthly rates are available during the winter. Some credit cards accepted. Open year-round.

Directions: Drive on Highway 1 to Morro Bay and the exit for Highway 41. Take that exit and turn west on Atascadero Road/Highway 41 and drive 0.5 mile to 1700 Embarcadero/Atascadero Road.

Contact: Morro Dunes RV Park, 805/772-2722, www.morrodunes.com.

11 MORRO BAY STATE PARK

🏃 🚴 🏊 🛶 🚤 ⛵ 🐾 ♿ 🚐 ⛺

Scenic rating: 9

in Morro Bay

Map 12.2, page 690

Reservations are strongly advised at this popular campground. This is one of the premium stopover spots for folks cruising on Highway 1. The park offers a wide range of activities and exhibits covering the natural and cultural history of the area. The park features lagoon and natural bay habitat. The most prominent feature is Morro Rock. A "morro" is a small volcanic peak, and there are nine of them along the local coast. The top hike at the park climbs one of them, Black Hill, and rewards hikers with sensational coastal views. The park has a marina and golf course, with opportunities for sailing, fishing, and bird-watching. Activities include beach walks, kayaking in Morro Bay, ocean fishing on a party boat, and touring Hearst Castle.

Campsites, facilities: There are 94 sites for tents or RVs up to 35 feet (no hookups), 30 sites with partial hookups (15 and 30 amps) for RVs up to 35 feet, five hike-in/bike-in sites, and two group sites for 25–35 people. Picnic tables, food lockers, and fire rings are provided. Restrooms with flush toilets and coin showers, drinking water, dump station, Wi-Fi, museum exhibits, nature walks, and interpretive programs are available. A coin laundry, grocery store, propane gas, boat ramp, mooring, boat rentals, gas stations, and food service are available in Morro Bay. Some facilities are wheelchair-accessible. Leashed pets are permitted, but not on the beach.

Reservations, fees: Reservations are accepted at 800/444-7275 (800/444-PARK) or www.reserveamerica.com ($8 reservation fee). Tent sites are $35 per night, RV sites (hookups) are $50 per night, $8 per night for each additional vehicle, $5 per person per night for hike-in/bike-in sites. Chorro Group Site is $165 per night, Osos Group Camp is $100 per night. Open year-round.

Directions: On Highway 1, drive to Morro Bay and take the exit for Los Osos–Baywood Park/Morro Bay State Park. Turn south and drive one mile to State Park Road. Turn right and drive one mile to the park entrance on the right.

Contact: Morro Bay State Park, 805/772-7434; San Luis Obispo Coast District, 805/927-2065, www.parks.ca.gov.

12 EL CHORRO REGIONAL PARK

🏃 🏕 🏀 🚐 ⛺

Scenic rating: 6

near San Luis Obispo

Map 12.2, page 690

North of Morro Bay on the way to San Simeon and Hearst Castle, this can be a prime spot for RV travelers. Note that the campground isn't in the state park reservation system, which means there are times when coastal state parks can be jammed full and this regional park may still have space. Morro Bay, six miles away, provides many possible side trips. The park has full recreational facilities, including a golf course, volleyball, horseshoe pits, softball fields, hiking trails, and botanical gardens. Note that there's a men's prison about four miles away. For some people, this can be a real turnoff.

Campsites, facilities: There are 63 sites for tents or RVs up to 40 feet and some undesignated overflow sites; 45 sites have full hookups and the remaining sites have no hookups. Some primitive sites are pull-through. Fire grills and picnic tables are provided. Restrooms with flush toilets and showers, drinking water, playground, picnic area, off-leash dog area, and recreational facilities are available. Supplies and a coin laundry are nearby in San Luis Obispo. Leashed pets are permitted.

Reservations, fees: Reservations are accepted for groups only (minimum of three campsites, $9 reservation fee). Primitive tent sites are $25 per night, RV sites are $29 (partial hookups) and $33 (full hookups) per night, $13 per night for each additional vehicle, $3 per pet per night. Coastal Dunes camping is $49 per night. Group camping is $21 per unit for primitive camping, $80 for the backcountry group area. Campsites discounted on weekdays and in off-season. Two-week maximum stay. Some credit cards accepted. Open year-round.

Directions: From San Luis Obispo, drive 4.5 miles north on Highway 1 to the park entrance on the right side of the highway.

Contact: El Chorro Regional Park, 805/781-5930, www.slocountyparks.org.

13 SANTA MARGARITA KOA
🏊 🐕 ⛵ ♿ 🚐 ⛺

Scenic rating: 6

near Santa Margarita Lake

Map 12.2, page 690

Santa Margarita Lake should have a sign at its entrance that proclaims, "Fishing Only!" That's because the rules here do not allow waterskiing or any water contact, including swimming, wading, using float tubes, or sailboarding. The excellent prospects for bass fishing, along with the prohibitive rules, make this lake a favorite among anglers. Santa Margarita Lake covers nearly 800 acres, most of it long

and narrow and set in a dammed-up valley in the foothill country at an elevation of 1,300 feet, just below the Santa Lucia Mountains. Horseback riding is available nearby.

Campsites, facilities: There are 65 sites for tents or RVs up to 40 feet; most have full or partial hookups (30 and 50 amps) and one site is pull-through. There are also 11 cabins, four lodges, and two yurts. Picnic tables and fire grills are provided. Restrooms with flush toilets and showers, drinking water, Wi-Fi, seasonal swimming pool, playground, coin laundry, convenience store, dump station, and propane gas are available. Some facilities are wheelchair accessible. Leashed pets are permitted.

Reservations, fees: Reservations are accepted at 800/562-5619. RV sites are $40–60 per night, tent sites are $30–50 per night, $5 per person per night for more than two people over age six. Cabins are $65–95 per night, lodges are $115–195 per night, yurts are $85–105 per night. Some credit cards accepted. Open year-round.

Directions: From San Luis Obispo, drive north on U.S. 101 for eight miles to the Highway 58/Santa Margarita Lake exit. Take that exit and drive through the town of Santa Margarita to Estrada. Turn right on Estrada and drive eight miles (Estrada becomes Pozo Road) to Santa Margarita Lake Road. Turn left and drive 0.5 mile to the campground on the right.

Contact: Santa Margarita KOA, 805/438-5618, www.koa.com.

14 LA PANZA
🥾 🐕 🚐 ⛺

Scenic rating: 3

in Los Padres National Forest

Map 12.2, page 690

This primitive spot sits at 2,200 feet elevation in the La Panza Range, an oak woodland area that is crisscrossed by numerous off-highway-vehicle and hiking trails and small streams. Some of the trails are not maintained. The Machesna Mountain Wilderness is to the south. Water is scarce.

Campsites, facilities: There are 12 sites for tents or RVs up to 16 feet (no hookups). Picnic tables and fire grills are provided. Vault toilets are available. There is no drinking water. Garbage must be packed out. Leashed pets are permitted.

Reservations, fees: Reservations are not accepted. There is no fee for camping. An Adventure Pass ($30 annual fee or a $5 daily fee) per parked vehicle is required. Open year-round.

Directions: From San Luis Obispo, drive eight miles north on U.S. 101. Turn east on Highway 58 and drive four miles (two miles past Santa Margarita). Turn southeast on Pozo Road and drive for 16 miles to the town of Pozo and Pozo Grade Road. Turn right and drive five miles to Red Hill Road. Turn right and drive one mile to the camp on the left.

Contact: Los Padres National Forest, Santa Lucia Ranger District, 805/925-9538, www.fs.usda.gov/lpnf.

15 MONTANA DE ORO STATE PARK
🚶 🚴 🛶 🐾 � ⛺

Scenic rating: 9

near Morro Bay

Map 12.2, page 690

This sprawling chunk of primitive land includes coastline, 8,500 acres of foothills, and 1,373-foot Valencia Peak. The name means "Mountain of Gold," named for the golden wildflowers that bloom here in the spring. The camp is perched near a bluff, and while there are no sweeping views from campsites, they await nearby. Bluffs Trail is one of the best easy coastal walks anywhere, offering stunning views of the ocean and cliffs and, in the spring, tons of wildflowers over the course of just 1.5 miles. Another hiking option at the park is to climb Valencia Peak, a little butt-kicker of an ascent that tops out at 1,373 feet, providing more panoramic coastal views. These are the two best hikes among 50 miles of trails for horses, mountain bikers, and hikers, with trails accessible right out of the campground.

Campsites, facilities: There are 48 sites for tents or RVs up to 27 feet (no hookups), four walk-in (50- to 150-yard walk) environmental sites, four equestrian sites, and two group equestrian sites for up to 50 people and 25 horses. Picnic tables and fire grills are provided, but fires are not allowed at the environmental sites. Vault toilets are available. Drinking water is available only at the main campground; stock water is available at the equestrian campground. There is limited corral space and single-site equestrian camps with two stalls each. Garbage from equestrian and environmental sites must be packed out. Supplies and a coin laundry are available five miles away in the town of Los Osos. Leashed pets are permitted, except at the environmental sites and on trails.

Reservations, fees: Reservations are accepted May through mid-September at 800/444-7275 (800/444-PARK) or www.reserveamerica.com ($8 reservation fee). Sites are first-come, first-served October through April. Sites are $35 per night, $8 per night for each additional vehicle, $25 per night for environmental sites, $5 per night for hike-in/bike-in sites, $50 for equestrian sites, $100–165 per night for the group sites. Open year-round.

Directions: From Morro Bay, drive two miles south on Highway 1. Turn on South Bay Boulevard and drive four miles to Los Osos. Turn right on Los Osos Valley Road and drive five miles (it becomes Pecho Valley Road) to the park.

Contact: Montana de Oro State Park, 805/528-0513; San Luis Obispo Coast District, 805/927-2065, www.parks.ca.gov.

16 HI MOUNTAIN
🚶 🐾 ♿ � ⛺

Scenic rating: 4

in Los Padres National Forest

Map 12.2, page 690

At an elevation of 2,800 feet, this camp is on the edge of the Santa Lucia Wilderness.

You can reach the Hi Mountain Lookout if you continue driving 1.5 miles past the campground. The Lookout has awesome 360-degree views from the 3,180-foot summit.

Campsites, facilities: There are 11 sites for tents or RVs up to 16 feet (no hookups). Note that trailers are not recommended. Picnic tables and fire grills are provided. Vault toilets are available. There is no drinking water. Garbage must be packed out. Some facilities are wheelchair accessible. Leashed pets are permitted.

Reservations, fees: Reservations are not accepted. There is no fee for camping. An Adventure Pass ($30 annual fee or a $5 daily fee) per parked vehicle is required. Open year-round, weather permitting (road may be closed during heavy rains).

Directions: From San Luis Obispo, drive eight miles north on U.S. 101. Turn east on Highway 58 and drive four miles (four miles past Santa Margarita) to Pozo Road/Santa Margarita Lake. Turn right (southeast) and drive 16 miles to the town of Pozo and Hi Mountain Road. Turn right on Hi Mountain Road (next to the Pozo fire station) and drive four miles to the campground. Four-wheel-drive vehicles are recommended.

Contact: Los Padres National Forest, Santa Lucia Ranger District, 805/925-9538, www.fs.usda.gov/lpnf.

17 AVILA HOT SPRINGS RESORT

🏊 ♨ 🏠 👥 ♿ 🚐 🏕

Scenic rating: 6

on San Luis Obispo Bay

Map 12.2, page 690

The hot mineral pool here is a featured attraction. This is a natural mineral hot springs with an artesian well that produces water directly into the spas at 104°F. A pizza kitchen and snack bar are available as well. Nearby recreation options include Avila State Beach and Pismo State Beach.

Campsites, facilities: There are 13 RV sites with full hookups, seven RV sites with no hookups, 13 tent sites in three areas, and 28 cabins (26 are rented monthly, two are rented nightly). Picnic tables and fire grills (at some sites) are provided. Restrooms with showers, laundry, heated swimming pool, hot mineral pool, spa, dump station, recreation room, arcade, restaurant, playground, and group barbecue pits are available. An 18-hole golf course is nearby. Leashed pets are permitted. Some facilities are wheelchair-accessible.

Reservations, fees: Reservations are accepted at 805/595-2359. RV sites are $35–45 per night, tent sites are $30 per night, $5 per night for each additional vehicle, $5 per night per pet. Some credit cards accepted. Open year-round.

Directions: From San Luis Obispo, drive south on U.S. 101 for nine miles to the Avila Beach Drive exit. Take that exit and drive a short distance to the park at 250 Avila Beach Drive.

Contact: Avila Hot Springs Resort, 805/595-2359, www.avilahotsprings.com.

18 LOPEZ LAKE RECREATION AREA

🚶 🚴 🏊 🚣 🛥 🏕 🐕 👥 ♿ 🚗 🏕

Scenic rating: 7

near Arroyo Grande

Map 12.2, page 690

Lopez Lake has become an example of how to do something right, with specially marked areas set aside exclusively for waterskiing, personal watercraft, and sailboarding, and the rest of the lake designated for fishing and low-speed boating. There are also full facilities for swimming, with a big swimming beach and two giant water slides, a children's wading pool, and a nice beach area. Another bonus is the scenic boat tours available on Saturdays, which get plenty of takers. A 25-mile trail system provides opportunities for biking, hiking, and horseback riding. That makes it perfect for just about everyone and, with good bass fishing, the lake has become very popular, especially on spring weekends when the bite is on. Other species include trout, bluegill, crappie, and catfish. Lopez Lake is set amid oak woodlands southeast of San Luis Obispo. The lake is shaped something like a horseshoe, has 940 surface acres with 22 miles of shoreline when full, and gets excellent weather most of the year. Features of the park in summer are ranger-led hikes and campfire shows. Many campsites overlook the lake or are nestled among oaks. Note: All boats must be certified mussel-free before launching.

Campsites, facilities: There are 143 sites with full hookups (20 and 30 amps) for tents or RVs, 211 sites for tents, and six group sites for 30–100 people each. An equestrian camp with 18 corrals will accommodate up to 10 vehicles. Picnic tables and fire rings are provided. Restrooms with showers, playground, children's wading pool, coin laundry, convenience store, ice, snack bar, marina, boat ramp, mooring, boat fuel (dry land fueling only), tackle, boat rentals, and water slides are available. Some facilities are wheelchair-accessible. Leashed pets are permitted.

Reservations, fees: Reservations are required by phone or online ($9 reservation fee). Tent sites are $25 per night, RV sites are $29 (water and electricity) and $33 (full hookups) per night, $13 per night for each additional vehicle, $3 per pet per night, boat launching is $10 per day. Group sites are $21 per unit ($27 reservation fee), coastal dunes camping is $49 per night. Site fees discounted on weekdays and in off-season. Two-week maximum stay in summer. Some credit cards accepted. Open year-round.

Directions: From Arroyo Grande on U.S. 101, take the Grand Avenue exit. Turn east and drive through Arroyo Grande to Lopez Drive. Turn left (northeast) on Lopez Drive and drive 10 miles to the park.

Contact: Lopez Lake Recreation Area, 805/788-2381; Lopez Lake Marina, 805/489-1006, www.slocountyparks.org.

19 NORTH BEACH

Scenic rating: 7

in Pismo State Beach

Map 12.2, page 690

Pismo State Beach is nationally renowned for its beaches, dunes, and, in the good old days, clamming. The adjacent tree-lined dunes make for great walks or, for kids, great rolls. The beach is popular with birdwatchers, and the habitat supports the largest wintering colony of monarch butterflies in the United States. Plan on a reservation and having plenty of company in summer. This is an exceptionally popular state beach, either as an ultimate destination or as a stopover for folks cruising Highway 1. There are four restaurants and ATV rentals within two blocks. A trolley service provides a shuttle to the surrounding community. The clamming on minus low tides was legendary. Poaching has devastated the clamming here, with no legal clams taken for years.

Campsites, facilities: There are 103 sites for tents or RVs up to 36 feet. Fire grills and picnic tables are provided. Restrooms with showers and flush toilets, drinking water, Wi-Fi, and a dump station are available. Horseback-riding facilities, grocery store, ATV rentals, restaurants, coin laundry, and propane gas are nearby. Some facilities are wheelchair-accessible. Leashed pets are permitted at the campground and on the beach.

Reservations, fees: Reservations are accepted at 800/444-7275 (800/444-PARK) or www.reserveamerica.com ($8 reservation fee). Sites are $35 per night, RV sites (hookups) are $50 per night, $8 per night for each additional vehicle. Sites discounted in off-season. Open year-round.

Directions: On Highway 1 in Pismo Beach, take the North Beach/State Campground exit (well signed) and drive to the park entrance.

Contact: Pismo State Beach, 805/473-7220, www.parks.ca.gov.

20 OCEANO

🚶 🚲 🏊 ⛵ 🐕 ♿ 🚐 ⛺

Scenic rating: 6

in Pismo State Beach

Map 12.2, page 690

This is a prized state beach campground, with Pismo Beach and its sand dunes and coastal frontage a centerpiece for the state park system. Its location on the central coast on Highway 1, as well as its beauty and recreational opportunities, make it extremely popular. It fills to capacity most nights, and reservations are usually a necessity. (For more information on Pismo State Beach, see the Pismo State Beach: North Beach listing in this chapter.)

Campsites, facilities: There are 40 sites for tents or RVs up to 31 feet (no hookups), 42 sites with partial hookups for trailers and RVs up to 36 feet. Picnic tables and fire grills are provided. Drinking water and restrooms with flush toilets and coin showers are available. Horseback-riding facilities, grocery store, coin laundry, dump station, restaurants, and gas stations are nearby. Some facilities are wheelchair accessible, including a fishing overlook at Oceano Lagoon. Leashed pets are permitted at the campground and beach.

Reservations, fees: Reservations are accepted at 800/444-7275 (800/444-PARK) or www.reserveamerica.com ($8 reservation fee). Sites are $35 per night, RV sites (hookups) are $50 per night, $8 per night for additional vehicle. Discounts in off-season. Open year-round.

Directions: From Pismo Beach, drive two miles south on Highway 1 to Pier Avenue. Turn right and drive 0.2 mile to the campground entrance.

Contact: Pismo State Beach, 805/473-7220, www.parks.ca.gov.

21 PISMO COAST VILLAGE RV RESORT

🚶 🚲 🏊 ⛵ 🐕 🎣 ♿ 🚐

Scenic rating: 7

in Pismo Beach

Map 12.2, page 690

This big-time RV park gets a lot of use by Highway 1 cruisers. Set near the ocean, its location is a plus. Pismo Beach is well known for its sand dunes and beautiful coastal frontage.

Campsites, facilities: There are 400 sites with full hookups (30 and 50 amps) for RVs up to 40 feet. No tents. Picnic tables, fire rings, and satellite TV are provided. Restrooms with showers, free Wi-Fi, playgrounds, heated swimming pool, coin laundry, convenience store, firewood, ice, recreation room, propane gas, seasonal recreation programs, restaurant, RV supplies and repair, bicycle rentals, and a nine-hole miniature golf course are available. Some facilities are wheelchair-accessible. Leashed pets are permitted, with restrictions on certain breeds.

Reservations, fees: Reservations are accepted at 888/RV-BEACH (888/782-3224). Sites are $44–60 per night, $2 per night for additional person. Group discounts available in the off-season. There is a 29-day maximum stay. Some credit cards accepted. Open year-round.

Directions: In Pismo Beach, drive on Highway 1/Pacific Coast Highway to the park at 165 South Dolliver Street/Highway 1.

Contact: Pismo Coast RV Resort, 805/773-1811, www.pismocoastvillage.com.

22 LE SAGE RIVIERA

🚶 🏊 ⛵ 🐕 ♿ 🚐

Scenic rating: 6

near Pismo State Beach

Map 12.2, page 690

This is a year-round RV park that can serve as headquarters for folks who are interested in visiting several nearby attractions, including neighboring Pismo State Beach and Lopez Lake, 10 miles to the east. The park is set on the ocean side of Highway 1, 250 yards from the beach. Note that many sites are filled with seasonal renters.

Campsites, facilities: There are 60 sites with full hookups (30 and 50 amps) for self-contained RVs up to 55 feet; many are pull-through. No tents. Picnic tables are provided. Restrooms with showers, drinking water, and coin laundry are available. Stores, restaurants, and golf courses are nearby. Some facilities are wheelchair-accessible. Leashed pets are permitted with certain restrictions.

Reservations, fees: Reservations are accepted at 866/489-5506. Sites are $38–51 per night from May through Labor Day weekend, $32–44 mid-September through April, $3 per night for each additional person, $3 per night for each additional vehicle. Holiday rates are higher. Some credit cards accepted. Open year-round.

Directions: In Pismo Beach on Highway 1, drive south on Highway 1 for 0.5 mile to the park on the right (west side) to 319 North Highway 1 (in Grover Beach).

Contact: Le Sage Riviera, 805/489-5506, www.lesageriviera.com.

23 OCEANO MEMORIAL PARK AND CAMPGROUND

🏊 🚴 📷 🚶 🚐 ⛺

Scenic rating: 7

in Oceano

Map 12.2, page 690

This San Luis Obispo county park is extremely busy during the summer and busy the rest of the year. The location is a bonus; it's set within a quarter mile of the Pismo State Beach entrance, the site of great sand dunes and wide-open ocean frontage. Oceano has a fishing lagoon.

Campsites, facilities: There are 22 sites for tents or RVs up to 40 feet (full hookups). No pull-through sites. Picnic tables and fire grills are provided. Drinking water, restrooms with coin showers and flush toilets, basketball court, horseshoes, athletic field, and picnic

area are available. A playground, coin laundry, grocery store, and propane gas are available nearby. Leashed pets are permitted.

Reservations, fees: Reservations are required by phone or online ($9 reservation fee). Tent sites are $25 per night, RV sites are $29 (water and electricity) and $33 (full hookups) per night, $13 per night for each additional vehicle, $3.50 per pet per night, boat launching is $10 per day. Group sites are $21 per unit ($27 reservation fee), coastal dunes camping is $49 per night. Site fees discounted on weekdays and in off-season. Four-week maximum stay in summer. Some credit cards accepted. Open year-round.

Directions: From Pismo Beach, drive south on U.S. 101 to the Pismo Beach/Grand Avenue exit west to Highway 1. Take that exit and turn south on Highway 1 and drive 1.5 miles to Pier Avenue. Turn right on Pier Avenue and drive a short distance to Norswing. Turn left and drive to the end of the street and Mendel Avenue. Turn right and drive to Air Park Drive. Turn right and drive to the park on the right.

Contact: Oceano Memorial Park and Campground, 805/781-5930, www.slocountyparks.org.

24 OCEANO DUNES STATE VEHICULAR RECREATION AREA

🚶 🏊 🚴 📷 🚐 ⛺

Scenic rating: 6

south of Pismo Beach

Map 12.2, page 690

This is "national headquarters" for all-terrain vehicles (ATVs)—you know, those three- and four-wheeled motorcycles that turn otherwise normal people into lunatics. The camps are along one to three miles of beach and 1,500 acres of open sand dunes, and since not many make the walk to the campsites, four-wheel drives or ATVs are needed for access. The area covers 3,600 acres, including 5.5 miles of beach open for vehicles and 1,500 acres of sand dunes available for OHVs. They roam wild on the dunes here; that's the law, so don't go planning a quiet stroll. If you don't like 'em, you are strongly advised to go elsewhere. If this is your game, have fun and try to keep from killing yourself. Each fall, the "National Sand Drags" are held here. More than one million people visit each year. High tides can limit access. A beach towing service for RVs and trailers is available. Activities include swimming, surfing, surf fishing, horseback riding, and bird- and nutcase-watching.

Campsites, facilities: There are 1,000 sites for tents or RVs of any length (no hookups). Chemical and vault toilets are provided. There is no drinking water. Drinking water, horseback-riding facilities, grocery store, coin laundry, restaurants, gas stations, Wi-Fi, and dump station are available nearby. Leashed pets are permitted at the campground and beach.

Reservations, fees: Reservations are accepted at 800/444-7275 (800/444-PARK) or www.reserveamerica.com ($8 reservation fee). Sites are $10 per night per vehicle. Open year-round.

Directions: Drive on U.S. 101 to Arroyo Grande and take the Grand Avenue exit. Turn left (toward the beach) on Grand Avenue and drive four miles until the road ends at the North Entrance beach camping area. The South Entrance is one mile south. To get there from Highway 1, take Pier Avenue.

Contact: Oceano Dunes, 805/473-7220 or 805/773-7170, www.ohv.parks.ca.gov or www.parks.ca.gov.

25 COLSON CANYON
🏃🏿 🐕 5% ⛺

Scenic rating: 6

in Los Padres National Forest

Map 12.3, page 691

Colson is set just a mile from the western border of Los Padres National Forest, making it far easier to reach than other Forest Service camps in this region. The camp is named after the canyon in which it sits, Colson Canyon. This area really has just two seasons when you should visit, spring and fall. In the summer, it's hot and dry, with no water available, and is scarcely fit for habitation. The elevation is 2,100 feet.

Campsites, facilities: There are five tent sites. Picnic tables and fire grills are provided. Vault toilets are available. There is no drinking water. Garbage must be packed out. Leashed pets are permitted.

Reservations, fees: Reservations are not accepted. There is no fee for camping. An Adventure Pass ($30 annual fee or a $5 daily fee) per parked vehicle is required. Open year-round.

Directions: From U.S. 101 in Santa Maria, take the Betteravia Road exit east and drive eight miles to a fork with Santa Maria Mesa Road. Bear left at the fork and drive southeast on Santa Maria Mesa Road to Tepusquet Road. Turn left on Tepusquet Road and drive 6.5 miles to Colson Canyon Road. Turn right on Colson Canyon Road/Forest Road 11N04 and drive four miles to the campground on the left. Colson Canyon Road can be impassable when wet.

Contact: Los Padres National Forest, Santa Lucia Ranger District, 805/925-9538, www.fs.usda.gov/lpnf.

26 WAGON FLAT
🏃🏿 🐕 5% ⛺

Scenic rating: 6

on the North Fork of La Brea Creek in Los Padres National Forest

Map 12.3, page 691

Not many folks know about this obscure spot, and if it's a hot, late-summer day, they're probably better off for it. The camp is set at an elevation of 1,400 feet, pretty in spring, but in summer often a hot, dry region of Los Padres National Forest. The bright spot is little La Brea Creek, which runs by the camp.

Campsites, facilities: There are three tent sites. Picnic tables and fire grills are provided. Pit toilets are available. Drinking water is not available. Garbage must be packed out. Leashed pets are permitted.

Reservations, fees: Reservations are not accepted. There is no fee for camping. An Adventure Pass ($30 annual fee or $5 daily pass) per parked vehicle is required. Open seasonally, road conditions permitting (call ahead during wet weather).

Directions: From U.S. 101 in Santa Maria, take the Betteravia Road exit east and drive eight miles to a fork with Santa Maria Mesa Road. Bear left at the fork and drive southeast on Santa Maria Mesa Road to Tepusquet Road. Turn left on Tepusquet Road and drive 6.5 miles to Colson Canyon Road. Turn right on Colson Canyon Road/Forest Road 11N04 and drive seven miles to La Brea Canyon Road. Turn left and drive four miles to the campground. Note: In the winter and spring, multiple stream crossings are required and a high-clearance vehicle may be necessary; Colson Canyon Road can become impassable.

Contact: Los Padres National Forest, Santa Lucia Ranger District, 805/925-9538, www.fs.usda.gov/lpnf.

27 BARREL SPRINGS
🥾 🐕 5% 🔼

Scenic rating: 7

in Los Padres National Forest

Map 12.3, page 691

This small, primitive camp sits at 1,000 feet elevation along La Brea Creek and is shaded by the oaks in La Brea Canyon. It is named after nearby Barrel Springs, which forms a small creek and feeds into La Brea Creek.

Campsites, facilities: There are six tent sites. Picnic tables and fire grills are provided. Vault toilets are available. There is no drinking water. Garbage must be packed out. Leashed pets are permitted.

Reservations, fees: Reservations are not accepted. There is no fee for camping. An Adventure Pass ($30 annual fee or $5 daily pass) per parked vehicle is required. Open seasonally. Access roads may be closed in wet weather.

Directions: From U.S. 101 in Santa Maria,

take the Betteravia Road exit east and drive eight miles to a fork with Santa Maria Mesa Road. Bear left at the fork and drive southeast on Santa Maria Mesa Road to Tepusquet Road. Turn left on Tepusquet Road and drive 6.5 miles to Colson Canyon Road. Turn right on Colson Canyon Road/Forest Road 11N04 and drive eight miles to the campground. Note: In the winter and spring, multiple stream crossings are required and a high-clearance vehicle may be necessary; Colson Canyon Road can become impassable.

Contact: Los Padres National Forest, Santa Lucia Ranger District, 805/925-9538, www.fs.usda.gov/lpnf.

28 RIVER PARK
🥾 🚲 🛶 🎣 🐎 🚐 🔼

Scenic rating: 4

in Lompoc

Map 12.3, page 691

River Park is set next to the lower Santa Ynez River, which looks quite a bit different than it does up in Los Padres National Forest. A small fishing lake within the 45-acre park is stocked with trout and catfish. A camp host and resident ranger are on-site. Side-trip possibilities include the nearby La Purisima Mission State Historic Park and Jalama Beach. Before checking in here you'd better get a lesson in how to pronounce Lompoc. It's "Lom-Poke." If you arrive and say, "Hey, it's great to be in Lom-Pock," they might just tell ya to get on back to the other cowpokes.

Campsites, facilities: There are 33 sites for RVs up to 40 feet (full hookups) and a group camping area for tents or RVs. No pull-through sites. Picnic tables and barbecues are provided. Restrooms with flush toilets and coin showers, drinking water, dump station, fishing pond, trail, sand volleyball, horseshoes, group facilities, and playground are available. Supplies and a coin laundry are nearby. Leashed pets are permitted with certain restrictions.

Reservations, fees: Reservations are not

accepted for family sites but are required for groups at 805/875-8036. Sites are $5 per night plus $10 per vehicle, RV sites (full hookups) are $20 per night or $130 per week, hike-in/bike-in sites are $5 per night, pets are $1 per pet per night. Group fees are $5 per night per tent, $10 per night per RV, with a $25 minimum. Weekly rates available. Some credit cards accepted. Open year-round.

Directions: In Lompoc, drive to the junction of Highway 246 and Sweeney Road at the southwest edge of town and continue to the park at 401 East Highway 246.

Contact: Lompoc Parks and Recreation Department, 805/875-8100, www.cityoflompoc.com/parks_rec/river.

29 FLYING FLAGS RV RESORT AND CAMPGROUND

Scenic rating: 3

near Solvang

Map 12.3, page 691

This is one of the few privately operated parks in the area that welcomes tenters as well as RVers. Nearby side trips include the Santa Ynez Mission, just east of Solvang. The town of Solvang is of interest. It was originally a small Danish settlement that has expanded since the 1920s yet managed to keep its cultural heritage intact through the years. The town is exceptionally clean, an example of how to do something right. Wineries are nearby.

Campsites, facilities: There are 228 sites with full or partial hookups (30 and 50 amps) for RVs of any length and 125 sites for tents. Most sites are pull-through. Cabins and cottages are also available. Picnic tables are provided. Restrooms with showers, cable TV, playground, heated swimming pool, spa, coin laundry, convenience store, dump station, ice, recreation room, free Wi-Fi, internet workstations, dog park, arcade, five clubhouses, group facilities, and propane gas are available. A nine-hole golf course, boat launch, and boat rentals are nearby. Some

facilities are wheelchair-accessible. Leashed pets are permitted with certain restrictions.

Reservations, fees: Reservations are accepted by phone or online. Sites are $25–88 in summer, $28–98 on holidays, $22–68 in winter, $3 per person per night for more than two people, $5 per night for each additional vehicle, $1 per pet per night for more than two dogs. Holiday rates are higher. Weekly and monthly rates available. Open year-round. Some credit cards accepted.

Directions: From Santa Barbara, drive 45 miles north on U.S. 101 to Highway 246. Turn west (left) on Highway 246 and drive about 0.5 mile to Avenue of the Flags (a four-way stop). Turn left on Avenue of the Flags and drive about one block to the campground entrance on the left at 180 Avenue of the Flags.

Contact: Flying Flags RV Resort and Campground, 805/688-3716, www.flyingflags.com.

30 JALAMA BEACH COUNTY PARK

Scenic rating: 8

near Lompoc

Map 12.3, page 691

This is a pretty spot set where Jalama Creek empties into the ocean, about five miles north of Point Conception and just south of Vandenberg Air Force Base. The area is known for its sunsets and beachcombing. The camp is so popular that a waiting list is common in summer. Activities include surfing, sailboarding, and fishing for perch, cabezon, kelp bass, and halibut.

Campsites, facilities: There are 98 sites for tents or RVs up to 40 feet and two group sites for eight vehicles and up to 20–40 people each. Some sites have electrical (30 amps) hookups. Picnic tables and fire pits are provided. Restrooms with flush toilets and showers, drinking water, dump station, general store, snack bar, bait and tackle, picnic area, firewood, and ice are available. Note that the nearest gas station is 20 miles away. Some facilities are wheelchair-accessible. Leashed pets are permitted, but a vaccination certificate is required.

Reservations, fees: Reservations are not accepted for individual sites; a waiting list (first-come, first-served) is available when the camp fills. Group reservations are required at 805/934-6211 or online at www.reservations.sbparks.org ($25 reservation fee). Tent sites are $25 per night, RV sites (water and electricity) are $35 per night, $10 per night for each additional vehicle, $200 per night for a group site, $3 per pet per night. Weekly rates available in the off-season. Some credit cards accepted. Open year-round.

Directions: From Lompoc, drive about five miles south on Highway 1. Turn southwest on Jalama Road and drive 14 miles to the park.

Contact: Jalama Beach County Park, 805/736-6316 or 805/736-3504, www.countyofsb.org/parks.

31 GAVIOTA STATE PARK

🏃 🚲 🏊 🚣 🛶 〰️ 🐴 ♿ 🚐 ⛺

Scenic rating: 10

near Santa Barbara

Map 12.3, page 691   **BEST (**

This is the granddaddy, the biggest of the three state beaches along U.S. 101 northwest of Santa Barbara. Spectacular and beautiful, the park covers 2,700 acres, providing trails for hiking and horseback riding, as well as a mile-long stretch of stunning beach frontage. Gaviota means "seagull" and was first named by the soldiers of the Portola Expedition in 1769, who learned why you always wear a hat (or a helmet) when they are passing overhead. The ambitious can hike the beach to get more seclusion. Trails to Gaviota Overlook (1.5 miles) and Gaviota Peak (3.2 miles one-way) provide lookouts with drop-dead gorgeous views of the coast and Channel Islands. Want more? There is also a 0.5-mile trail to the hot springs. This park is known for being windy and for shade being hard to find. Unfortunately, a railroad trestle crosses above the day-use parking lot.

You know what that means? Of course you do. It means trains run through here day and night, and with them, noise. This is a popular beach for swimming and surf fishing, as well as boat launching and fishing from the pier.

Campsites, facilities: There are 38 sites for tents or RVs up to 30 feet (no hookups) and an area for hike-in/bike-in sites. Picnic tables and fire grills are provided. Restrooms with flush toilets and coin showers, drinking water, summer lifeguard service, and boat hoist (two-ton maximum weight) are available. A convenience store (open summer only) is nearby. Some facilities are wheelchair-accessible. Leashed pets are permitted at campsites.

Reservations, fees: Reservations are accepted for about half the sites from Memorial Day weekend through Labor Day weekend at 800/444-7275 (800/444-PARK) or www.reserveamerica.com ($8 reservation fee). Sites are $35 per night, $10 per night for each additional vehicle, $10 per person per night for hike-in/bike-in sites. Boat launching is $8 per day. One-week maximum stay in summer; two-week maximum stay in winter. Open year-round.

Directions: From Santa Barbara, drive north on U.S. 101 for 30 miles to the Gaviota State Beach exit. Take that exit and turn west and drive a short distance to the park entrance.

Contact: Gaviota State Park, Channel Coast District, 805/968-1033 or 805/585-1850, www.parks.ca.gov.

32 REFUGIO STATE BEACH

🏃 🚲 🏊 🚣 🐴 ♿ 🚐 ⛺

Scenic rating: 9

near Santa Barbara

Map 12.3, page 691

Refugio State Beach is the smallest of the three beautiful state beaches along U.S. 101 north of Santa Barbara. The others are Gaviota and El Capitán, which also have campgrounds. Palm trees planted close to Refugio Creek provide a unique look to this beach and campground. This is a great spot for family campers with bikes, with a paved two-mile bike trail connecting Refugio campground with El Capitán. Fishing is often good in this area of the coast. Reservations are strongly advised and are often a necessity throughout the vacation season, as with all state beaches and private camps on the Coast Highway.

Campsites, facilities: There are 66 sites for tents or RVs up to 30 feet (no hookups), one hike-in/bike-in site, and three group sites for tents or RVs that can accommodate up to 80 people and 25 vehicles. Picnic tables and fire grills are provided. Restrooms with flush toilets and coin showers, drinking water, summer lifeguard service, summer convenience store, and food services are available. Some facilities are wheelchair-accessible. Leashed pets are permitted at campsites.

Reservations, fees: Reservations are accepted at 800/444-7275 (800/444-PARK) or www.reserveamerica.com ($8 reservation fee). Standard sites are $45 per night, premium sites are $55 per night, $10 per night for each additional vehicle, hike-in/bike-in sites are $10 per night, Anapamu and Yanonali group sites are $235 per night, Bouchard Group Site is $350 per night. One-week maximum stay in summer; two-week maximum stay in winter. Open year-round, weather permitting.

Directions: From Santa Barbara, drive northwest on U.S. 101 for 23 miles to the Refugio State Beach exit. Take that exit and turn west (left) and drive a short distance to the campground entrance.

Contact: Refugio State Beach, Channel Coast District, 805/968-1033 or 805/585-1850, www.parks.ca.gov.

33 EL CAPITAN CANYON

Scenic rating: 8

near Goleta

Map 12.3, page 691　　　**BEST**

El Capitan Canyon is a unique campground where you do not bring your own tent, but rather rent permanent safari tents or cabins on-site. The tent cabins are situated on 12-by-14-foot wood platforms, and they come fully furnished with beds and linens. The safari tents are heated and have electricity. The park covers 65 acres in the coastal foothills north of Santa Barbara and offers visitors the best of both worlds: There are 2,200 acres of public land near the camp with backcountry hiking and mountain-biking trails, or for those who prefer the sand and surf, beach access is within walking distance and ocean kayaking and deep-sea fishing trips can be booked at the resort. In the summer live entertainment is available, including a concert series and the "Blues and Barbecue" event every Saturday night. Dogs are strictly prohibited in a mission here to stop the spread of nonnative plants; this in turn has inspired a return of native habitat and the birds and wildlife that rely on it.

Campsites, facilities: There are 26 tent cabins, 108 cabins, and three yurts. Picnic tables and fire pits are provided. Restrooms with flush toilets and showers, drinking water, heated swimming pool, outdoor hot tub, children's playground, live music (Saturday nights, May–Oct.), WiFi, convenience store, massage service, free use of bicycles, and firewood are available. Horseback-riding facilities are nearby. Some facilities are wheelchair-accessible.

Reservations, fees: Reservations are recommended at 866/352-2729. Tent cabins are $135–155 per night, cabins are $185–355 per night, and yurts are $175–205. Discounts are available Monday through Thursday and in the off-season. Some credit cards accepted. Open year-round.

Directions: From Santa Barbara, drive about 20 miles northwest on U.S. 101 to the El Capitán State Beach exit. Go straight on the frontage road paralleling the freeway for about 100 yards. Turn right at the sign for El Capitan Canyon on the mountain side of the freeway.

Contact: El Capitan Canyon, 805/685-3887, www.elcapitancanyon.com.

34 OCEAN MESA

🚶 🏊 🏕 ⛺ 🚐

Scenic rating: 8

near Goleta

Map 12.3, page 691

Ocean Mesa Campground sits on an inland bluff surrounded by Los Padres National Forest and overlooking the Pacific Ocean. Sites are paved and shaded, some with ocean views, while tenters can soak in the rolling hills. Plenty of amenities will keep you grounded, or it's just a 20-minute drive to downtown Santa Barbara for dining or tidepooling at El CapitaÁn State Beach. On Saturday evenings there's live music at El Capitan Canyon.

Campsites, facilities: There are 20 sites for tents and 80 sites with full hookups for RVs up to 50 feet (some pull-through). Picnic tables and fire rings are provided. Drinking water, flush toilets, heated pool and spa, WiFi, cable TV, convenience store and snack bar, and horseback riding facilities are available. Leashed pets are permitted, but not on the hiking trails.

Reservations, fees: Reservations are accepted at 866/410-5783 or online at www. oceanmesa.com. Tent sites are $40–50 per night and RV sites are $70–90 per night. Open year-round; two-night minimum stay on weekends.

Directions: From Santa Barbara, drive about 20 miles northwest on U.S. 101 to the El Capitán State Beach exit. Drive past the entrance to El Capitan Canyon to Calle Real. Turn right on Calle Real and drive to El Capitan Terrace Lane. Turn right on El Capitan Terrace Lane and drive to the office/store.

Contact: Ocean Mesa Campground, 866/410-5783, www.oceanmesa.com.

35 EL CAPITÁN STATE BEACH

🚶 🚲 🏊 🛶 🏕 ♿ 🚐 ⛺

Scenic rating: 10

near Santa Barbara

Map 12.3, page 691

This is one in a series of beautiful state beaches along the Santa Barbara coast. El Capitán has a sandy beach and rocky tidepools. The water is warm, the swimming good. A stairway descends from the bluffs to the beach, a beautiful setting, and sycamores and oaks line El Capitán Creek. A paved, two-mile bicycle trail is routed to Refugio State Beach, a great family trip. This is a perfect layover for Coast Highway vacationers, and reservations are usually required to assure a spot. Refugio State Beach to the north is another camping option.

Campsites, facilities: There are 130 sites for tents or RVs up to 40 feet, one hike-in/bike-in site, two group sites for tents or RVs that can accommodate 50–125 people each, and five group sites for tents only that can accommodate 50–125 people each. No hookups. Picnic tables and fire grills are provided. Restrooms with flush toilets and coin showers, drinking water, summer lifeguard service, and a summer convenience store are available. Some facilities are wheelchair-accessible. Leashed pets are permitted in the campgrounds, but not on the beach.

Reservations, fees: Reservations are accepted at 800/444-7275 (800/444-PARK) or www. reserveamerica.com ($8 reservation fee). Sites are $35 per night, $10 per night for each additional vehicle, $10 per person per night for hike-in/bike-in sites. Group sites are $165, $185, $225, $250, and $420 per night depending on size. One-week maximum stay in summer and two-week maximum in winter. Open year-round, weather permitting.

Directions: From Santa Barbara, drive north on U.S. 101 for 20 miles to the Capitán State Beach exit. Turn west (left) and drive a short distance to the campground entrance.

Contact: El Capitán State Beach, Channel Coast District, 805/968-1033 or 805/585-1850, www.parks.ca.gov.

36 BATES CANYON

Scenic rating: 7

in Los Padres National Forest

Map 12.4, page 692

This camp is on the northeast flank of the Sierra Madre, along a small stream in Bates Canyon, at 2,900 feet elevation. Note that the primitive access road out of camp to the south is often gated; it leads to the Sierra Madre Ridge, where a road contours right along the ridge on the border of the San Rafael Wilderness, passing from peak to peak.

Campsites, facilities: There are six tent sites. Picnic tables and fire grills are provided. Vault toilets are available. There is no drinking water. Garbage must be packed out. Some facilities are wheelchair accessible. Leashed pets are permitted.

Reservations, fees: Reservations are not accepted. There is no fee for camping. An Adventure Pass ($30 annual fee or $5 daily pass) per parked vehicle is required. Open year-round. Note that access roads can be closed during and after heavy rains.

Directions: From Santa Maria, drive east on Highway 166 for 50 miles to Cottonwood Canyon Road. Turn right on Cottonwood Canyon Road and drive southwest for 7.5 miles to the campground.

Contact: Los Padres National Forest, Santa Lucia Ranger District, 805/925-9538, www.fs.usda.gov/lpnf.

37 ALISO PARK

Scenic rating: 6

in Los Padres National Forest

Map 12.4, page 692

This primitive, quiet camp is set at the foot of the Sierra Madre at 3,200 feet, directly below McPherson Peak (5,749 feet). It is just inside the northeast boundary of Los Padres National Forest, making it easily accessible from Highway 166.

Campsites, facilities: There are 10 sites for tents or RVs up to 28 feet (no hookups). Picnic tables and fire grills are provided. Pit toilets are available. Drinking water is not available. Garbage must be packed out. Some facilities are wheelchair-accessible. Leashed pets are permitted.

Reservations, fees: Reservations are not accepted. There is no fee for camping. An Adventure Pass ($30 annual fee or $5 daily pass) per parked vehicle is required. Open year-round.

Directions: From Santa Maria, drive east on Highway 166 for 59 miles to Aliso Canyon Road/Forest Road 10N04. Turn right on Aliso Canyon Road/Forest Road 10N04 and drive south about six miles to the campground at the end of the road.

Contact: Los Padres National Forest, Mount Piños Ranger District, 661/245-3731, www.fs.usda.gov/lpnf.

38 BALLINGER

Scenic rating: 3

in Los Padres National Forest

Map 12.4, page 692

Ballinger Camp is right inside the boundary of Los Padres National Forest in the Mount Piños Ranger District, just six miles east of Highway 33. During the week, this camp receives very little use. On weekends, it gets moderate, even heavy use at times, from OHV owners. Note that the California "green sticker" or "red sticker" is required to ride OHVs here. The camp is set at an elevation of 3,000 feet.

Campsites, facilities: There are 20 sites for tents or RVs up to 32 feet (no hookups). Picnic tables and fire grills are provided. Vault toilets are available. No drinking water is available. Garbage must be packed out. Leashed pets are permitted.

Reservations, fees: Reservations are not

accepted. There is no fee for camping. An Adventure Pass ($30 annual fee or $5 daily pass) per parked vehicle is required. Open year-round.

Directions: From Maricopa, drive southwest on Highway 166 about 14 miles to Highway 33. Turn south on Highway 33 and drive about 3.5 miles to Ballinger Canyon Road/ Forest Road 9N10. Turn left (east) and drive three miles to the campground.

Contact: Los Padres National Forest, Mount Piños Ranger District, 661/245-3731, www. fs.usda.gov/lpnf.

39 VALLE VISTA

Scenic rating: 8

in Los Padres National Forest

Map 12.4, page 692

The view of the southern San Joaquin Valley and the snow-capped Sierra is the highlight of this primitive camp. It is set at 4,800 feet elevation, near the boundary of Los Padres National Forest. Visitors have an opportunity to view condors here, and you can usually spot a few buzzards, er, turkey vultures, circling around. If you don't bring your own water, they might just start circling you. Little-known fact: This camp sits exactly on the border of Kern County and Ventura County.

Campsites, facilities: There are seven sites for tents or RVs up to 22 feet (no hookups). Picnic tables and fire grills are provided. Pit toilets are available. No drinking water is available. Garbage must be packed out. Leashed pets are permitted.

Reservations, fees: Reservations are not accepted. There is no fee for camping. An Adventure Pass ($30 annual fee or $5 daily pass) per parked vehicle is required. Open year-round.

Directions: From Maricopa, drive south on Highway 166 about nine miles to Cerro Noroeste Road. Turn left and drive 12 miles to the campground on the left.

Contact: Los Padres National Forest, Mount Piños Ranger District, 661/245-3731, www. fs.usda.gov/lpnf.

40 CABALLO

Scenic rating: 4

in Los Padres National Forest

Map 12.4, page 692

Caballo is set at 5,850 feet elevation on a small creek that is the headwaters for Santiago Creek, on the northern flank of Mount Abel. The creek flows only about 10 days a year, usually before the opening of the campground, so do not count on it for water. It is one of several primitive camps in the immediate area—a take-your-pick offer. But it's an offer not many folks even know about.

Campsites, facilities: There are five sites for tents or RVs up to 16 feet (no hookups). Picnic tables and fire grills are provided. Pit toilets are available. No drinking water is available. Garbage must be packed out. Leashed pets are permitted.

Reservations, fees: Reservations are not accepted. There is no fee for camping. An Adventure Pass ($30 annual fee or $5 daily pass) per parked vehicle is required. Open early May through October, weather permitting.

Directions: Drive on I-5 to just south of Lebec to the Frazier Park exit. Take that exit and drive west on Frazier Mountain Road to the town of Lake of the Woods and Cuddy Valley Road. Continue straight on Cuddy Valley Road for six miles to Mil Potrero Highway (signed "Pine Mountain Club"). Turn right and drive 10 miles to Forest Road 9N27. Turn right and drive a short distance to the campground. Note: To reach Marian campground, continue for another mile. High-clearance vehicles are recommended for the dirt access road.

Contact: Los Padres National Forest, Mount Piños Ranger District, 661/245-3731, www. fs.usda.gov/lpnf.

41 MARIAN

Scenic rating: 4

in Los Padres National Forest

Map 12.4, page 692

Marian is extremely primitive, set on the outskirts of Los Padres National Forest at 6,600 feet elevation, between Brush Mountain to the immediate northwest and San Emigdio Mountain to the immediate southeast. The road in is rough, as is the route out of camp that leads three miles to the San Emigdio summit, at 7,495 feet. A network of Forest Service roads provides access to a number of other camps in the area, as well as to Mount Abel (8,286 feet) and Mount Piños (8,831 feet). The access gate is usually locked in winter, when reaching this camp requires a two-mile hike. Nearby Toad Springs and Caballo are smaller but more easily accessible. Note that there is no drinking water available and no toilets either.

Campsites, facilities: There are five sites for tents or RVs up to 16 feet (no hookups). Picnic tables and fire grills are provided. No drinking water or toilets are available, so bring your own. Garbage must be packed out. Leashed pets are permitted.

Reservations, fees: Reservations are not accepted. There is no fee for camping. Open early May through October, weather permitting.

Directions: Drive on I-5 to just south of Lebec to the Frazier Park exit. Take that exit and drive west on Frazier Mountain Road to the town of Lake of the Woods and Cuddy Valley Road. Continue straight on Cuddy Valley Road for six miles to Mil Potrero Highway (signed "Pine Mountain Club"). Turn right and drive 10 miles to Forest Road 9N27. Turn right and drive one mile (passing Caballo campground) to the camp. Note: Four-wheel-drive or high-clearance vehicles are recommended.

Contact: Los Padres National Forest, Mount Piños Ranger District, 661/245-3731, www.fs.usda.gov/lpnf/lospadres.

42 TOAD SPRINGS

Scenic rating: 8

in Los Padres National Forest

Map 12.4, page 692

Toad Springs is set at 5,700 feet elevation near Apache Saddle, on the northwest flank of Mount Abel (8,286 feet). It is at the head of Quatal Canyon with a spectacular badlands landscape. No water or toilets are available, so forget this one for your honeymoon. Note that a landslide destroyed a primitive trail (about a mile out of camp) that once was routed south out of camp for six miles to Mesa Springs and a trail camp. It is considered too dangerous for use.

Campsites, facilities: There are three sites for tents or RVs up to 16 feet (no hookups). Picnic tables and fire grills are provided. There are no toilets and no drinking water. Garbage must be packed out. Leashed pets are permitted.

Reservations, fees: Reservations are not accepted. There is no fee for camping. An Adventure Pass ($30 annual fee or $5 daily pass) per parked vehicle is required. Open early May through October, weather permitting.

Directions: Drive on I-5 to just south of Lebec to the Frazier Park exit. Take that exit and drive west on Frazier Mountain Road to the town of Lake of the Woods and Cuddy Valley Road. Continue straight on Cuddy Valley Road for six miles to Mil Potrero Highway (signed "Pine Mountain Club"). Turn right and drive 10 miles to the campground on the left.

Contact: Los Padres National Forest, Mount Piños Ranger District, 661/245-3731, www.fs.usda.gov/lpnf.

43 CAMPO ALTO

Scenic rating: 6

in Los Padres National Forest

Map 12.4, page 692

Campo Alto means "High Camp," and you'll find when you visit that the name fits. The camp is set high (8,250 feet) on Cerro Noroeste/Mount Abel in Los Padres National Forest. Don't show up thirsty, as there's no drinking water. About half a mile from camp there is a trailhead on the southeast side of the road. From here, you can hike two miles to Grouse Mountain, and in another mile, reach remote, hike-in Sheep Camp.

Campsites, facilities: There are 12 sites for tents or RVs up to 30 feet (no hookups) and one group site. Picnic tables and fire grills (stoves) are provided. Vault toilets are available. No drinking water is available. Garbage must be packed out. Leashed pets are permitted.

Reservations, fees: Reservations are not accepted. There is no fee for camping. An Adventure Pass ($30 annual fee or $5 daily pass) per parked vehicle is required. Open May through October, weather permitting.

Directions: Drive on I-5 to just south of Lebec to the Frazier Park exit. Take that exit and drive west on Frazier Mountain Road to the town of Lake of the Woods and Cuddy Valley Road. Continue straight on Cuddy Valley Road and drive six miles to Mil Potrero Highway (signed "Pine Mountain Club"). Turn right and drive nine miles to Cerro Noroeste Road (Forest Road 9N07). Turn left and drive nine miles to the campground.

Contact: Los Padres National Forest, Mount Piños Ranger District, 661/245-3731, www.fs.usda.gov/lpnf.

44 NETTLE SPRINGS

Scenic rating: 4

in Los Padres National Forest

Map 12.4, page 692

This remote camp borders the Chumash Wilderness, set near the end of a Forest Service road in Apache Canyon. A mile east of camp, via the access road, is a primitive trailhead on the left side. This trail is routed four miles to Mesa Springs and a trail camp. The elevation is 4,400 feet.

Campsites, facilities: There are nine sites for

tents or RVs up to 22 feet (no hookups). Picnic tables and fire grills are provided. Vault toilets are available, but there is no drinking water. Garbage must be packed out. Leashed pets are permitted.

Reservations, fees: Reservations are not accepted. There is no fee for camping. An Adventure Pass ($30 annual fee or $5 daily pass) per parked vehicle is required. Open year-round.

Directions: From Maricopa, drive 14 miles south on Highway 166 to the Highway 33 exit. Turn south on Highway 33 and drive about 13 miles to Apache Canyon Road (Forest Road 8N06). Turn left and drive about 11 miles to the campground. Note: The last 10 miles are rough; high-clearance vehicles are advised.

Contact: Los Padres National Forest, Mount Piños Ranger District, 661/245-3731, www.fs.usda.gov/lpnf.

45 MOUNT PIÑOS

Scenic rating: 7

in Los Padres National Forest

Map 12.4, page 692

This camp is set at 7,800 feet elevation, one of three camps on the eastern flank of Mount Piños (8,831 feet). This is one of the few places on earth where it is possible to see flying California condors, the largest bird in North America. Note that a once-popular drive to the top of Mount Piños for beautiful and sweeping views is now closed after being recognized as a Chumash holy site. There's access to the Mount Piños summit trail 2.5 miles away on Mil Potrero Highway at the Chula Vista parking area. From there it's about two miles to the summit, which is a designated botanical area. July and August usually are the best months for wildflower displays. McGill (see listing in this chapter) provides a nearby camping alternative.

Campsites, facilities: There are 19 sites for tents or RVs up to 16 feet (no hookups). Picnic tables and fire rings are provided. Vault toilets are available, but there is no drinking water. Leashed pets are permitted.

Reservations, fees: Reservations are not accepted. Sites are $20 per night. Open late May through October, weather permitting.

Directions: Drive on I-5 to just south of Lebec to the Frazier Park exit. Take that exit and drive west on Frazier Mountain Road to the town of Lake of the Woods and Cuddy Valley Road. Continue straight on Cuddy Valley Road and drive about six miles to Mount Piños Highway. Bear left and drive five miles (the road name changes several times, but stay on the main road) to the campground.

Contact: Los Padres National Forest, Mount Piños Ranger District, 661/245-3731, www.fs.usda.gov/lpnf; Rocky Mountain Recreation Co., 805/967-8766.

46 McGILL

Scenic rating: 6

near Mount Piños in
Los Padres National Forest

Map 12.4, page 692

The camp is set at 7,400 feet elevation, about four miles from the top of nearby Mount Piños. Although the road is closed to the top of Mount Piños, there are numerous hiking and biking trails in the area that provide spectacular views. On clear days, there are vantage points to the high Sierra, the San Joaquin Valley, and Antelope Valley.

Campsites, facilities: There are 78 sites for tents or RVs up to 16 feet (no hookups), and two group sites for 60 and 80 people. Picnic tables and fire grills are provided. Pit toilets are available. There is no drinking water. Some facilities are wheelchair-accessible. Leashed pets are permitted.

Reservations, fees: Reservations are required for group sites at 877/444-6777 or www.recreation.gov ($9 reservation fee). Sites are $20 per night, $85 per night for a group site. Open late May through October.

Directions: Drive on I-5 to just south of Lebec to the Frazier Park exit. Take that exit and drive west on Frazier Mountain Road to the town of Lake of the Woods and Cuddy Valley Road. Continue straight on Cuddy Valley Road and drive about six miles to Mount Piños Highway. Bear left and drive about five miles to the campground on the right.

Contact: Los Padres National Forest, Mount Piños Ranger District, 661/245-3731, www.fs.usda.gov/lpnf; Rocky Mountain Recreation Co., 805/967-8766.

47 DAVY BROWN

Scenic rating: 7

on Davy Brown Creek in
Los Padres National Forest

Map 12.4, page 692

This is a pretty spot, set along little Davy Brown Creek at 2,100 feet elevation, deep in Los Padres National Forest. The border of the San Rafael Wilderness and an excellent trailhead are just two miles down the road (along Davy Brown Creek) to the northeast at Nira (see the Nira listing in this chapter for hiking options).

Campsites, facilities: There are 13 sites for tents or RVs up to 25 feet (no hookups). Picnic tables and fire grills are provided. Vault toilets are available. No drinking water is available. Garbage must be packed out. Leashed pets are permitted.

Reservations, fees: Reservations are not accepted. There is no fee for camping. An Adventure Pass ($30 annual fee or $5 daily pass) per parked vehicle is required. Open year-round.

Directions: From U.S. 101 in Santa Barbara, take Highway 154 and drive northeast for 22 miles to Armour Ranch Road. Turn right on Armour Ranch Road and drive 1.5 miles to Happy Canyon Road. Turn right on Happy Canyon Road/County Route 3350 and drive 11 miles to Cachuma Saddle. Continue straight (north) on Sunset Valley/Cachuma

Road/Forest Road 8N09 for four miles to the campground.

Contact: Los Padres National Forest, Santa Lucia Ranger District, 805/925-9538, www. fs.usda.gov/lpnf.

48 NIRA

Scenic rating: 8

on Manzana Creek in
Los Padres National Forest

Map 12.4, page 692

Nira is a premium jump-off spot for backpackers, set at 1,000 feet elevation along Manzana Creek, on the border of the San Rafael Wilderness. A primary wilderness trailhead is available, routed east into the San Rafael Wilderness through Lost Valley, along Fish Creek, and to Manzana Creek (and beyond), all in just six miles, with a series of hike-in camps available as the trail enters the wilderness interior. Today's history lesson? This camp was originally an NRA (National Recovery Act) camp during the Depression, hence the name Nira.

Campsites, facilities: There are 11 sites for tents or RVs up to 16 feet (no hookups). Picnic tables and fire grills are provided. Vault toilets, hitching posts, and horse trailer parking are available. No drinking water is available. Garbage must be packed out. Some facilities are wheelchair-accessible. Leashed pets are permitted.

Reservations, fees: Reservations are not accepted. There is no fee for camping. An Adventure Pass ($30 annual fee or $5 daily pass) per parked vehicle is required. Open year-round, but access roads may be closed during and after heavy rains.

Directions: From U.S. 101 in Santa Barbara, take Highway 154 northeast and drive 22 miles to Armour Ranch Road. Turn right on Armour Ranch Road and drive 1.5 miles to Happy Canyon Road. Turn right on Happy Canyon Road and drive 11 miles to Cachuma Saddle. Continue straight (north) on Sunset Valley/Cachuma Road/Forest Road 8N09 for six miles to the campground.

Contact: Los Padres National Forest, Santa Lucia Ranger District, 805/925-9538, www. fs.usda.gov/lpnf.

49 FIGUEROA

Scenic rating: 7

in Los Padres National Forest

Map 12.4, page 692

This is one of the more attractive camps in Los Padres National Forest. It is set at 3,500 feet elevation beneath an unusual stand of oak and huge manzanita trees and offers a view of the Santa Ynez Valley. Nearby attractions include the Piño Alto Picnic Area, 2.5 miles away, offering a panoramic view of the adjacent wildlands with a 0.5-mile, wheelchair-accessible nature trail. An exceptional view is also available from the nearby Figueroa fire lookout. Though it requires a circuitous 10-mile ride around Figueroa Mountain to get there, Nira to the east provides the best trailhead in this area for the San Rafael Wilderness.

Campsites, facilities: There are 33 sites for tents or RVs up to 25 feet (no hookups). Picnic tables and fire grills are provided. Vault toilets are available. No drinking water is available. Garbage must be packed out. Leashed pets are permitted.

Reservations, fees: Reservations are not accepted. There is no fee for camping. An Adventure Pass ($30 annual fee or $5 daily pass) per parked vehicle is required. Open year-round.

Directions: Drive on Highway 154 to Los Olivos and Figueroa Mountain Road. Turn northeast on Figueroa Mountain Road and drive 12.5 miles to the campground. Note that the last 6.6 miles of Figueroa Mountain Road are not RV friendly.

Contact: Los Padres National Forest, Santa Lucia Ranger District, 805/925-9538, www. fs.usda.gov/lpnf.

50 CACHUMA

🏕 🐕 ⛺

Scenic rating: 6

near Cachuma Creek in
Los Padres National Forest

Map 12.4, page 692

This camp is set at 2,200 feet elevation along one of the major streams that feeds Cachuma Lake, just 10 miles downstream. A dirt road south of the camp follows the creek to the lake.

Campsites, facilities: There are six tent sites. Picnic tables and fire grills are provided. Vault toilets are available, but there is no drinking water. Drinking water is available at Figueroa Campground eight miles away. Garbage must be packed out. Leashed pets are permitted.

Reservations, fees: Reservations are not accepted. There is no fee for camping. An Adventure Pass ($30 annual fee or $5 daily pass) per parked vehicle is required. Open year-round.

Directions: From U.S. 101 in Santa Barbara, take Highway 154 and drive northeast for 22 miles to Armour Ranch Road. Turn right on Armour Ranch Road and drive 1.5 miles to Happy Canyon Road. Turn right on Happy Canyon Road/County Route 3350 and drive 9.5 miles to the campground.

Contact: Los Padres National Forest, Santa Barbara Ranger District, 805/967-3481, www. fs.usda.gov/lpnf.

51 REYES CREEK FAMILY AND EQUESTRIAN CAMP

🏕 🏊 🛶 🐕 ♿ �car ⛺

Scenic rating: 7

in Los Padres National Forest

Map 12.4, page 692

This developed Forest Service camp sits at the end of an old spur, Forest Road 7N11. The camp is set at 3,960 feet elevation along Reyes Creek, which is stocked with trout in early summer. The Piedra Blanca/Gene Marshall Trail is routed out of camp to the south and climbs three miles to Upper Reyes backpack camp, and beyond, up a ridge and down to Bear-trap Creek and several trail camps along that creek. In all, the trail covers approximately 20 miles.

Campsites, facilities: There are 30 sites for tents or RVs up to 22 feet (no hookups). Picnic tables and fire grills are provided. Pit toilets and a corral are available, but there is no drinking water. Garbage must be packed out. A small store, bar, and café are nearby. Some facilities are wheelchair-accessible. Leashed pets are permitted.

Reservations, fees: Reservations are not accepted. There is no fee for camping. An Adventure Pass ($30 annual fee or $5 daily pass) per parked vehicle is required. Open year-round.

Directions: From Ojai, drive north on Highway 33 for 36 miles to Lockwood Valley Road. Turn right on Lockwood Valley Road (Ozena Road) and drive about 3.5 miles to Forest Road 7N11. Turn right and drive about 1.5 miles to the village of Camp Scheideck and a T intersection. Bear left at the T intersection and drive 0.25 mile to the campground.

Contact: Los Padres National Forest, Mount Piños Ranger District, 661/245-3731, www. fs.usda.gov/lpnf.

52 PINE SPRINGS

🏊 🏕 �car ⛺

Scenic rating: 6

near San Guillermo Mountain in
Los Padres National Forest

Map 12.4, page 692

This primitive camp is set at 5,800 feet elevation on a short spur road that dead-ends on the east flank of San Guillermo Mountain (6,569 feet). Pine Springs feeds the tiny headwaters of Guillermo Creek at this spot. This is a quiet spot. It gets little use, primarily in the fall by hunters.

Campsites, facilities: There are 12 sites for

tents or RVs up to 22 feet (no hookups). Picnic tables and fire grills are provided. Vault toilets are available, but there is no drinking water. Garbage must be packed out. Leashed pets are permitted.

Reservations, fees: Reservations are not accepted. There is no fee for camping. An Adventure Pass ($30 annual fee or $5 daily pass) per parked vehicle is required. Open early May through October, weather permitting.

Directions: Drive on I-5 to just south of Lebec to the Frazier Park exit. Take that exit and drive west on Frazier Mountain Road to the town of Lake of the Woods and Lockwood Valley Road. Turn left on Lockwood Valley Road (take the left fork) and drive about 12 miles to Grade Valley Road (Forest Road 7N03). Turn left and drive 3.5 miles to Forest Road 7N03A. Turn right and drive one mile to the campground.

Contact: Los Padres National Forest, Mount Piños Ranger District, 661/245-3731, www. fs.usda.gov/lpnf.

53 PINE MOUNTAIN
🏃 🐕 ⛰

Scenic rating: 6

in Los Padres National Forest

Map 12.4, page 692

Pine Mountain, along with nearby Reyes Peak campground (0.25 mile to the east; see listing in this chapter), is a tiny, primitive campground in a pretty setting with a few trailheads close at hand. The two best nearby hikes lead to springs. A trail is routed out of camp and into Boulder Canyon for a mile down the mountain, where it meets another trail that turns left and heads 0.25 mile to McGuire Spring Trail camp (piped spring water is available there). It's advisable to obtain a Forest Service map. A popular launch area for hang gliders is 1.5 miles west of the campground. The elevation is 6,700 feet.

Campsites, facilities: There are six tent sites. Picnic tables and fire grills are provided. A pit

toilet is available. There is no drinking water. Garbage must be packed out. Leashed pets are permitted.

Reservations, fees: Reservations are not accepted. There is no fee for camping. An Adventure Pass ($30 annual fee or $5 daily pass) per parked vehicle is required. Open April through early November, weather permitting.

Directions: From Ojai, drive north on Highway 33 for 33 miles to Reyes Peak Road. Turn right on Pine Mountain/Reyes Peak Road and drive five miles to the campground on the left.

Contact: Los Padres National Forest, Ojai Ranger District, 805/646-4348, www.fs.usda. gov/lpnf.

54 REYES PEAK
🏃 🐕 ⛰

Scenic rating: 6

in Los Padres National Forest

Map 12.4, page 692

Reyes Peak is a primitive camp set at 6,800 feet elevation. Three short hikes in the immediate vicinity lead to trail camps. The closest is from a trailhead just to the west of camp, which provides an easy, 0.5-mile hike north to Raspberry Spring (a backcountry camp is available there). A popular launch area for hang gliders is 0.5 mile from camp. Nearby Pine Mountain campground (see listing in this chapter) provides an alternative for camping.

Campsites, facilities: There are six tent sites. Picnic tables and fire grills are provided. A pit toilet is available. There is no drinking water. Garbage must be packed out. Leashed pets are permitted.

Reservations, fees: Reservations are not accepted. There is no fee for camping. An Adventure Pass ($30 annual fee or $5 daily pass) per parked vehicle is required. Open April through early November, weather permitting.

Directions: From Ojai, drive north on

Highway 33 for 33 miles to Reyes Peak Road. Turn right on Reyes Peak Road and drive 5.5 miles to the campground.

Contact: Los Padres National Forest, Ojai Ranger District, 805/646-4348, www.fs.usda. gov/lpnf.

55 THORN MEADOWS FAMILY AND EQUESTRIAN CAMP

Scenic rating: 7

on Piru Creek in Los Padres National Forest

Map 12.4, page 692

The reward at Thorn Meadows is a small, quiet spot along Piru Creek at 5,000 feet elevation, deep in Los Padres National Forest. A trail out of camp leads three miles up to Thorn Point, a magnificent 6,935-foot lookout. It is by far the best view in the area, worth the 2,000-foot climb, and on a clear day you can see the Channel Islands.

Campsites, facilities: There are five sites for tents or RVs up to 16 feet (no hookups). Picnic tables and fire grills are provided. A toilet and a pipe corral are available. There is no drinking water. Garbage must be packed out. Leashed pets are permitted.

Reservations, fees: Reservations are not accepted. There is no fee for camping. An Adventure Pass ($30 annual fee or $5 daily pass) per parked vehicle is required. Open early May through October, weather permitting.

Directions: Drive on I-5 to just south of Lebec and the Frazier Park exit. Take that exit and drive west on Frazier Mountain Road to the town of Lake of the Woods and Lockwood Valley Road. Turn left on Lockwood Valley Road and drive about 12 miles to Mutau Flat Road (Forest Road 7N03/Grade Valley Road). Turn left and drive seven miles to Forest Road 7N03B. Turn right and drive one mile to the campground. A high-clearance vehicles is recommended.

Contact: Los Padres National Forest, Mount Piños Ranger District, 661/245-3731, www. fs.usda.gov/lpnf.

56 CACHUMA LAKE RECREATION AREA

Scenic rating: 7

near Santa Barbara

Map 12.4, page 692   **BEST (**

Cachuma has become one of the best lakes in America for fishing big bass, and the ideal climate makes it a winner for camping as well. Cachuma is set at 750 feet elevation in the foothills northwest of Santa Barbara, a big, beautiful lake covering 3,200 acres. In low-rain years the drawdowns are so significant that you'd hardly recognize the place. The rules are perfect for fishing: No waterskiing, personal watercraft riding, swimming, canoeing, kayaking, or sailboarding is permitted; for fishing boats there is a 5-mph speed limit in the coves and a 40-mph limit elsewhere. After fishing, picnicking and camping come in a distant second and third in popularity, respectively. Note: All boats must be certified mussel-free before launching.

Campsites, facilities: There are 420 sites for tents or RVs of any length, and nine group areas for 8–30 vehicles (32–100 people). Some sites have full or partial hookups (30 amps) and/or are pull-through. Yurts and cabins are also available. Picnic tables and fire pits are provided. Drinking water, restrooms with flush toilets and coin showers, and coin laundry are available. Playground, general store, propane gas, seasonal swimming pool, full-service marina, fishing piers, bait and tackle, boat ramp, mooring, boat fuel, boat and water bike rentals, bicycle rentals, nature cruises, miniature golf, dump station, group facilities, RV storage, gas station, ice, and snack bar are nearby. Watercraft under 10 feet and inflatables under 12 feet are prohibited on the lake. Leashed pets are permitted, but they must be kept at least 50 feet from the lake.

Reservations, fees: Reservations are accepted only for groups and yurts at 805/686-5050 ($30 reservation fee). Tent sites are $20–25 per night, RV sites (water and electricity) are $35–45 per night, $10 per night for each additional vehicle, yurts are $60–85 per night, cabins $80–125, the group sites are $200–750 per night, $3 per pet per night. Some credit cards accepted. Open year-round.

Directions: From Santa Barbara, drive 18 miles north on Highway 154 to the campground entrance on the right.

Contact: Cachuma Lake Recreation Area, 805/686-5054, www.countyofsb.org/parks; Cachuma Marina and Boat Rentals, 805/688-4040; Cachuma Boat Tours, 805/686-5050 or 805/688-4515.

57 FREMONT

Scenic rating: 7

near the Santa Ynez River in
Los Padres National Forest

Map 12.4, page 692

As you travel west to east, Fremont is the first in a series of Forest Service campgrounds near the Santa Ynez River. This one is just inside the boundary of Los Padres National Forest at 900 feet elevation, nine miles east of Cachuma Lake to the west.

Campsites, facilities: There are 15 sites for tents or RVs up to 22 feet (no hookups). Picnic tables and fire grills are provided. Drinking water and flush toilets are available. Some facilities are wheelchair-accessible. Groceries are available within two miles and propane gas is available at Cachuma Lake nine miles away. Leashed pets are permitted.

Reservations, fees: Reservations are accepted at 877/444-6777 or www.recreation.gov ($9 reservation fee). Sites are $20 per night, $5 per night for each additional vehicle. Open early April through late October.

Directions: From Santa Barbara, drive northwest on Highway 154 for about 10 miles to Paradise Road/Forest Road 5N18. Turn right on Paradise Road/Forest Road 5N18 and drive 2.5 miles to the campground on the right.

Contact: Los Padres National Forest, Santa Barbara Ranger District, 805/967-3481, www.fs.usda.gov/lpnf; Rocky Mountain Recreation Company, 805/521-1319.

58 LOS PRIETOS

Scenic rating: 7

near the Santa Ynez River in
Los Padres National Forest

Map 12.4, page 692

Los Prietos is set across from the Santa Ynez River at an elevation of 1,000 feet, just upstream from nearby Fremont campground to the west. There are several nice hiking trails nearby; the best starts near the Los Prietos Ranger Station, heading south for two miles to Wellhouse Falls (get specific directions and a map at the ranger station). River access is available 0.25 mile away at the White Rock day-use area.

Campsites, facilities: There are 38 sites for tents or RVs up to 22 feet (no hookups). Picnic tables and fire grills are provided. Drinking water and flush toilets are available. Leashed pets are permitted.

Reservations, fees: Reservations are accepted at 877/444-6777 or www.recreation.gov ($9 reservation fee). Sites are $20 per night, $5 per night for each additional vehicle. Open early April through late October.

Directions: From Santa Barbara, take Highway 154 and drive 10 miles northeast to Paradise Road/Forest Road 5N18. Turn right on Paradise Road/Forest Road 5N18 and drive 3.8 miles to the campground.

Contact: Los Padres National Forest, Santa Barbara Ranger District, 805/967-3481, www.fs.usda.gov/lpnf; Rocky Mountain Recreation, 805/521-1319.

59 UPPER OSO FAMILY AND EQUESTRIAN CAMP

🏃 🐎 ♿ 🚐 ⛺

Scenic rating: 7

near the Santa Ynez River in
Los Padres National Forest

Map 12.4, page 692

This is one of the Forest Service campgrounds in the Santa Ynez Recreation Area. It is set in Oso Canyon at 1,100 feet elevation, one mile from the Santa Ynez River. This is a prime spot for equestrians, with horse corrals available at adjacent campsites. Note that at high water this campground can become inaccessible. A mile north of camp is the Santa Cruz trailhead for a hike that is routed north up Oso Canyon for a mile, then three miles up to Happy Hollow, and beyond that to a trail camp just west of Little Pine Mountain, elevation 4,508 feet. A trailhead into the San Rafael Wilderness is nearby, and once on the trail, you'll find many primitive sites in the backcountry.

Campsites, facilities: There are 23 sites for tents or RVs up to 22 feet (no hookups). Picnic tables and fire grills are provided. Drinking water and flush toilets are available. Some facilities are wheelchair-accessible. Many sites have horse corrals and there is a horse-watering station. Leashed pets are permitted.

Reservations, fees: Reservations are accepted at 877/444-6777 or www.recreation.gov ($9 reservation fee). Sites are $19 per night, $24 per night for equestrian sites, $5 per night for each additional vehicle. Open year-round, weather permitting.

Directions: From Santa Barbara, take Highway 154 and drive 10 miles northeast to Paradise Road/Forest Road 5N18. Turn right on Paradise Road/Forest Road 5N18 and drive six miles to Upper Oso Road. Turn left on Upper Oso Road and drive one mile to the campground at the end of the road.

Contact: Los Padres National Forest, Santa Barbara Ranger District, 805/967-3481, www.fs.usda.gov/lpnf; Rocky Mountain Recreation, 805/521-1319.

60 PARADISE

🏊 🐎 ♿ 🚐 ⛺

Scenic rating: 7

near the Santa Ynez River in
Los Padres National Forest

Map 12.4, page 692

Here is yet another option among the camps along the Santa Ynez River. As you drive east it is the second camp you will come to, just after Fremont. Trout are usually planted upriver of the campground during the spring. The best hiking trailheads nearby are at Upper Oso Camp and the Sage Hill Group Campground. Cachuma Lake is six miles to the west.

Campsites, facilities: There are 15 sites for tents or RVs up to 22 feet. Picnic tables and fire grills are provided. Drinking water and flush toilets are available. Groceries are available nearby. Some facilities are wheelchair-accessible. Leashed pets are permitted.

Reservations, fees: Reservations are accepted at 877/444-6777 or www.recreation.gov ($9 reservation fee). Single sites are $20 per night, double sites are $35 per night, $5 per night for each additional vehicle. Open year-round.

Directions: From Santa Barbara, take Highway 154 and drive 10 miles northeast to Paradise Road/Forest Road 5N18. Turn right on Paradise Road/Forest Road 5N18 and drive three miles to the campground on the right.

Contact: Los Padres National Forest, Santa Barbara Ranger District, 805/967-3481, www.fs.usda.gov/lpnf; Rocky Mountain Recreation, 805/521-1319.

61 SAGE HILL GROUP AND EQUESTRIAN CAMP

🏃 🏊 🛶 🐎 ♿ 🚐 ⛺

Scenic rating: 7

on the Santa Ynez River in
Los Padres National Forest

Map 12.4, page 692

This is one in a series of camps along the Santa Ynez River in Los Padres National Forest. Sage

Hill is set at 2,000 feet elevation and was designed for large groups as well as equestrians, with horse corrals available next to one group site. A 3.5-mile loop trail starts at the back end of Sage Hill Group Camp. The first mile is a self-guided interpretive trail.

Campsites, facilities: There are five group areas for tents or RVs up to 32 feet (no hookups) that can accommodate 50–60 people each. Picnic tables and fire grills are provided. Drinking water and flush toilets are available. Horse corrals and hitching posts are in the Caballo group site. Some facilities are wheelchair-accessible. Leashed pets are permitted.

Reservations, fees: Reservations are required at 877/444-6777 or www.recreation.gov ($9 reservation fee). Sites are $91–116 per night. Open year-round, weather permitting.

Directions: From Santa Barbara, take Highway 154 and drive 10 miles northeast to Paradise Road/Forest Road 5N18. Turn right on Paradise Road/Forest Road 5N18 and drive five miles to the ranger station and the campground entrance road. Turn left and drive 0.5 mile to the campground.

Contact: Los Padres National Forest, Santa Barbara Ranger District, 805/967-3481, www. fs.usda.gov/lpnf; Rocky Mountain Recreation, 805/521-1319, www.rockymountain-rec.com.

62 MONO HIKE-IN

🚶 🏊 🐕 5% 🏕

Scenic rating: 7

on Mono Creek in Los Padres National Forest

Map 12.4, page 692

Not many folks know about this spot. The camp is small and primitive, at 1,500 feet elevation on little Mono Creek. Also note that Little Caliente Hot Springs is one mile northeast of the campground. Mono Creek is a feeder to Gibraltar Reservoir, a long, narrow lake with no direct access available.

Campsites, facilities: There are three tent sites. Picnic tables and fire grills are provided. Vault toilets are available. No drinking water is available. Garbage must be packed out. Leashed pets are permitted.

Reservations, fees: Reservations are not accepted. There is no fee for camping. An Adventure Pass ($30 annual fee or $5 daily pass) per parked vehicle is required. Open year-round, weather permitting.

Directions: From U.S. 101 in Santa Barbara, take Highway 154 and drive northeast for eight miles to East Camino Cielo/Forest Road 5N12. Turn right on East Camino Cielo/Forest Road 5N12 and drive 18 miles to the end of the paved road at Camuesa Road/Forest Road 5N15 (a dirt road). Continue on Camuesa Road for five miles to the old Juncal Campground (closed). Turn left (still on Forest Road 5N15) and drive seven miles to the parking area for Mono Hike-In. Park and hike approximately 100 yards to the campground.

Contact: Los Padres National Forest, Santa Barbara Ranger District, 805/967-3481, www. fs.usda.gov/lpnf.

63 P-BAR FLAT

🚶 🏊 🐕 🏕

Scenic rating: 7

on the Santa Ynez River in Los Padres National Forest

Map 12.4, page 692

The best thing—or the worst thing, depending on how you look at it—about P-Bar Flat is a trailhead that is routed north into the remote wildlands of Los Padres National Forest. The camp is very small and primitive, set at 1,800 feet elevation along the Santa Ynez River. The trail starts by heading up Horse Canyon along a creek, but eventually it is routed 10 miles to Hildreth Peak, at 8,066 feet, a 6,000-foot butt-kicker of a climb. A lot of guys in prison get less punishment.

Campsites, facilities: There are four tent sites. Picnic tables and fire grills are provided. Vault toilets are available. No drinking water is available. Garbage must be packed out. Leashed pets are permitted.

Reservations, fees: Reservations are not accepted. There is no fee for camping. An Adventure Pass ($30 annual fee or $5 daily pass) per parked vehicle is required. Open year-round, weather permitting.

Directions: From U.S. 101 in Santa Barbara, take Highway 154 and drive northeast for eight miles to East Camino Cielo/Forest Road 5N12. Turn right on East Camino Cielo/Forest Road 5N12 and drive 18 miles to the end of the paved road at Camuesa Road/Forest Road 5N15 (a dirt road). Continue on Camuesa Road for five miles to the old Juncal Campground (closed). Turn left (still on Forest Road 5N15) and drive four miles to the campground.

Contact: Los Padres National Forest, Santa Barbara Ranger District, 805/967-3481, www.fs.usda.gov/lpnf.

64 MIDDLE SANTA YNEZ

Scenic rating: 7

on the Santa Ynez River in
Los Padres National Forest

Map 12.4, page 692

There are four camps bordering the Santa Ynez River between Gibraltar Reservoir to the west and little Jameson Lake to the east. Look them over and pick the one you like best. This one is set at an elevation of 1,500 feet, about 0.5 mile east of P-Bar Flat (see the P-Bar Flat listing in this chapter for information about a trailhead there).

Campsites, facilities: There are 13 tent sites. Picnic tables and fire grills are provided. Vault toilets are available. No drinking water is available. Garbage must be packed out. Leashed pets are permitted.

Reservations, fees: Reservations are not accepted. There is no fee for camping. An Adventure Pass ($30 annual fee or $5 daily pass) per parked vehicle is required. Senior

discount available. Open year-round, weather permitting.

Directions: From U.S. 101 in Santa Barbara, take Highway 154 and drive northeast for eight miles to East Camino Cielo/Forest Road 5N12. Turn right on East Camino Cielo/Forest Road 5N12 and drive 18 miles to the end of the paved road at Camuesa Road/Forest Road 5N15 (a dirt road). Continue on Camuesa Road for five miles to the old Juncal Campground (closed). Turn left (still on Forest Road 5N15) and drive three miles to the campground.

Contact: Los Padres National Forest, Santa Barbara Ranger District, 805/967-3481, www.fs.usda.gov/lpnf.

65 HOLIDAY GROUP CAMP

Scenic rating: 7

on Matilija Creek in Los Padres National Forest

Map 12.4, page 692

This group site, set at 2,000 feet elevation, is near the North Fork of the Matilija. It's only three miles uphill from Matilija Reservoir.

Campsites, facilities: There is one group site for tents or RVs up to 22 feet (no hookups) that can accommodate up to 75 people. An adjacent parking lot has room for 10 vehicles. Picnic tables and fire grills are provided. Vault toilets are available, but there is no drinking water. Garbage must be packed out. Leashed pets are permitted.

Reservations, fees: Reservations are required at 877/444-6777 or www.recreation.gov ($9 reservation fee). The camp is $75–100 per night, $10 per night per each additional vehicle. Open year-round.

Directions: From Ojai, drive northwest on Highway 33 for nine miles to the campground entrance on the right.

Contact: Los Padres National Forest, Ojai Ranger District, 805/646-4348, www.fs.usda.gov/lpnf; Rocky Mountain Recreation, 805/968-6640 or 661/702-1420.

66 WHEELER GORGE

Scenic rating: 7

on Matilija Creek in Los Padres National Forest

Map 12.4, page 692

This developed Forest Service camp is set at 2,000 feet elevation and is one of the more popular spots in the area. The North Fork of the Matilija runs beside the camp and provides some fair trout fishing in the spring and good swimming holes in early summer. Interpretive programs are also available, a nice plus, and a nature trail is adjacent to the campground.

Campsites, facilities: There are 67 sites for tents or RVs up to 35 feet (no hookups), including six double sites. Picnic tables and fire grills are provided. Vault toilets are available, but there is no drinking water. Garbage must be packed out. Some facilities are wheelchair-accessible. Leashed pets are permitted.

Reservations, fees: Reservations are accepted at 877/444-6777 or www.recreation.gov ($9 reservation fee). Single sites are $23 per night, double sites are $46 per night, $10 per night for each additional vehicle. Winter rates are lower. Open year-round.

Directions: From Ojai, drive northwest on Highway 33 for 8.5 miles to the campground entrance on the left.

Contact: Los Padres National Forest, Ojai Ranger District, 805/646-4348, www. fs.usda.gov/lpnf; Rocky Mountain Recreation, 805/640-1977 or 661/702-1420.

67 ROSE VALLEY

Scenic rating: 8

in Los Padres National Forest

Map 12.4, page 692

The short walk to Rose Valley Falls, a 300-foot waterfall that provides a happy surprise, makes this camp a sure winner in late winter and spring. The walk to the waterfall is just 0.5-mile round-trip. Note that there are two views of it: a long-distance view of the entire waterfall, and at the base a view of just the lower tier. It is one of the scenic highlights in this section of Los Padres National Forest. The camp is set at 3,400 feet elevation next to Rose Valley Creek, about two miles from Sespe Creek. If this campground is full, there is another campground, Middle Lion, two miles beyond Rose Valley camp.

Campsites, facilities: There are nine sites for tents or RVs up to 30 feet (no hookups). Picnic tables and fire grills are provided. Vault toilets are available. There is no drinking water. Horseback-riding facilities are nearby. Garbage must be packed out. Some facilities are wheelchair-accessible. Leashed pets are permitted.

Reservations, fees: Reservations are not accepted. There is no fee for camping. An Adventure Pass ($30 annual fee or $5 daily pass) per parked vehicle is required. Open year-round, weather permitting.

Directions: From Ojai, drive north on Highway 33 for 15 miles to Sespe River Road/Rose Valley Road. Turn right on Sespe River Road/Rose Valley Road and drive 5.5 miles to the campground entrance.

Contact: Los Padres National Forest, Ojai Ranger District, 805/646-4348, www.fs.usda.gov/lpnf.

68 SANTA BARBARA SUNRISE RV PARK

Scenic rating: 3

in Santa Barbara

Map 12.4, page 692

RV cruisers get a little of two worlds here. For one thing, the park is close to the beach; for another, the downtown shopping area isn't too far away, either. This is the only RV park in Santa Barbara. It is close to the highway, so noise can be a problem for RVs that are less than soundproof. In addition, access is difficult for RVs over 30 feet.

Campsites, facilities: There are 33 sites with full hookups (20, 30 and 50 amps) for RVs up to 45 feet, including 10 pull-through sites. No tents. Picnic tables, restrooms with free showers, cable TV, free Wi-Fi, and coin laundry are available. A grocery store, golf course, tennis courts, and propane gas are nearby. Leashed pets are permitted.

Reservations, fees: Reservations are accepted up to 45 days in advance. Sites start at $50 per night, $5 per person per night for more than two people, $5 per night for each additional vehicle, $5 per pet per night. Some credit cards accepted. Open year-round.

Directions: In Santa Barbara on U.S. 101 northbound, drive to the Salinas Street exit. Take that exit and drive to the park (well signed) at 516 South Salinas Street, near the highway exit.

In Santa Barbara on U.S. 101 southbound, drive to the Milpas Street exit. Take that exit and turn left on Milpas Street. Drive under the freeway to Carpinteria Street. Turn right and drive 0.5 mile to Salinas Street. Turn right and drive 0.5 mile to the park on the right.

Contact: Santa Barbara Sunrise RV Park, 805/966-9954 or 800/345-5018.

69 CARPINTERIA STATE BEACH

🚶 🚴 ♒ 🛶 🎣 ♿ 🚐 ⛺

Scenic rating: 8

near Santa Barbara

Map 12.4, page 692

First, plan on reservations, and then, plan on plenty of neighbors. This state beach is one pretty spot, and a lot of folks cruising up the coast like the idea of taking off their boots here for a while. This is an urban park; that is, it is within walking distance of downtown, restaurants, and shopping. You can love it or hate it, but this camp is almost always full. It features one mile of beach and 21 campgrounds,

including seven group sites. Harbor seals can be seen December through May, along with an occasional passing gray whale. Tidepools here are protected and contain starfish, sea anemones, crabs, snails, octopus, and sea urchins. In the summer, the visitors center features a living tidepool exhibit. Other state beaches to the nearby north are El Capitán State Beach and Refugio State Beach, both with campgrounds.

Campsites, facilities: There are 65 sites with no hookups for tents, 79 sites with full or partial hookups (30 amps) for RVs up to 30 feet, 29 sites with partial hookups for RVs up to 35 feet, 38 sites with no hookups for RVs up to 21 feet, one hike-in/bike-in site, and seven group sites that can accommodate 25–65 people each. Picnic tables and fire rings are provided. Drinking water, restrooms with flush toilets and coin showers, and a picnic area are available. A convenience store, coin laundry, restaurants, and propane gas are nearby in the town of Carpinteria. Some facilities are wheelchair-accessible. Leashed pets are permitted, except on the beach.

Reservations, fees: Reservations are accepted at 800/444-7275 (800/444-PARK) or www.reserveamerica.com ($8 reservation fee). Tent sites are $35–45 per night, premium tent sites are $50–60 per night; RV sites (hookups) are $50–80 per night; premium RV sites (hookups) are $60–80 per night; $10 per night for each additional vehicle, $10 per person per night for hike-in/bike-in site; group sites are $180–430 per night. Open year-round, except for group sites.

Directions: From Santa Barbara, drive south on U.S. 101 for 12 miles to Carpinteria and the Casitas Pass Road exit. Take that exit and turn right on Casitas Pass Road and drive about a block to Carpinteria Avenue. Turn right and drive a short distance to Palm Avenue. Turn left and drive about six blocks to the campground at the end of Palm Avenue.

Contact: Carpinteria State Beach, 805/684-2811; Channel Coast District, 805/968-1033, www.parks.ca.gov.

70 LAKE CASITAS RECREATION AREA

🚴 🛶 🗨 🏕 🎣 ♿ 🚐 ⛰️

Scenic rating: 7

north of Ventura

Map 12.4, page 692

Lake Casitas is known as one of Southern California's world-class fish factories, with more 10-pound bass produced here than anywhere and including the former state record, a bass that weighed 21 pounds, 3 ounces. Other fish species include catfish, crappie, and sunfish. Fishing at night is permitted on select weekends. The ideal climate in the foothill country gives the fish a nine-month growing season and provides excellent weather for camping. Casitas is north of Ventura at an elevation of 567 feet in the foothills bordering Los Padres National Forest. The lake has 32 miles of shoreline with a huge number of sheltered coves, covering 2,710 acres. The lake is managed primarily for anglers. Waterskiing, personal watercraft, and swimming are not permitted. The park holds many special events, including the Ojai Wine Festival and the Ojai Renaissance Festival. Note: All boats must be certified mussel-free before launching (call 805/649-2233 for an appointment).

Campsites, facilities: There are 400 sites for tents or RVs of any length and three group sites for a maximum of 10 vehicles each; some sites have full or partial hookups (30 and 50 amps) and/or are pull-through. Picnic tables and fire rings are provided. Restrooms with flush toilets and showers, drinking water, two dump stations, playgrounds, general store, picnic areas, propane, ice, snack bar, water playground, and full-service marina (including boat ramps, boat rentals, slips, fuel, tackle, and bait) are available. Some facilities are wheelchair-accessible. Leashed pets are permitted, except on the lake.

Reservations, fees: Reservations are accepted at 805/649-1122 ($7.50 reservation fee, $75 reservation fee for group sites) or online at www.casitaswater.org or www.lakecasitas.info. Tent sites are $25–30 per night, RV sites are $35–40 (water and electricity) and $55–60 (full hookups) per night, $17 per night for each additional vehicle, $3 per pet per night. The group sites are $250 per night with a two-night, 10-vehicle maximum. Some credit cards accepted. Open year-round.

Directions: From Ventura, drive north on Highway 33 for 10.5 miles to Highway 150/Baldwin Road. Turn left (west) on Highway 150 and drive three miles to Santa Ana Road. Turn left and drive to the lake and campground entrance at 11311 Santa Ana Road.

Contact: Lake Casitas Recreation Area, 805/649-2233; Lake Casitas Marina, 805/649-2043; Nature Cruises, 805/640-6844, ext. 654, www.lakecasitas.info.

71 CAMP COMFORT PARK OJAI

🏕 🎣 🚐 ⛰️

Scenic rating: 4

on San Antonio Creek north of Ventura

Map 12.4, page 692

This Ventura County park gets missed by many. It's set in a residential area in the Ojai Valley foothill country at 1,000 feet elevation. San Antonio Creek runs through the park and there are shade trees. Lake Casitas Recreation Area is 10 miles away.

Campsites, facilities: There are 15 sites with full hookups (30 and 50 amps) for tents or RVs up to 34 feet. Picnic tables and fire pits are provided. Restrooms with flush toilets and showers, drinking water, coin laundry, cable TV, picnic areas, group facilities, clubhouse, and playground are available. Supplies are nearby. Leashed pets are permitted in the campground only.

Reservations, fees: Reservations are accepted with a non-refundable reservation fee ($10). Sites are $40 per night per vehicle, $1 per pet per night. Open year-round.

Directions: From Ventura, take Highway 33 north to North Creek Road. Turn right and drive 4.5 miles to the park at 11969 North Creek Road.

Contact: Camp Comfort Park Ojai, 805/654-3951, www.venturaparks.org.

72 DENNISON CAMPGROUND
🏕️ 🎣 🚐 ⛺

Scenic rating: 8

in Ojai

Map 12.4, page 692

Dennison Campground is located in the foothills of Ojai. This is a nice, calm place to relax, with shade trees and an outstanding view of the Ojai Valley. As a county park, it is often overlooked by out-of-towners. Lake Casitas, known for huge but hard-to-catch bass, is located to the west.

Campsite, facilities: There are 46 sites for tents or RVs up to 35 feet (no hookups). Picnic tables and fire pits are provided. Drinking water, restrooms with flush toilets and coin showers, horseshoe pits, a playground, and a camp host are available.

Reservations, fees: Reservations are accepted at www.venturaparks.org ($10 reservation fee, $20 for groups). Sites are $20 per night (one RV, one tent maximum), $1 per pet per night. Open year-round.

Directions: From Ventura, drive north on Highway 33 for 13 miles to E. Ojai Ave. Continue on E. Ojai Ave. for 3.5 miles to a slight right on Ojai Santa Paula Rd (Highway 150). Continue 1.5 miles to Dennison Park.

Contact: Ventura County Parks Department, 805/654-3951, www.venturaparks.org.

73 VENTURA RANCH KOA
🏕️ 🐴 🚐 ⛺

Scenic rating: 7

on Santa Paula Creek east of Ventura

Map 12.4, page 692

Ventura Ranch KOA is set near little Santa Paula Creek in the foothill country adjacent to Steckel County Park. For those who want a well-developed park with a lot of amenities, the shoe fits.

Note that at one time the two campgrounds, Ventura Ranch KOA and Steckel County Park, were linked. No more, and for good reason. Ventura Ranch KOA is a tight ship where the gates close at 10 P.M. and quiet time assures campers of a good night's sleep. It is a good place to bring a family. Steckel County Park, on the other hand, has a problematic campground—loud noise, partying, and fights. So what do you do? Go next door to Ventura Ranch KOA where the inmates aren't running the asylum, and the days are fun and nights are peaceful.

Campsites, facilities: There are 72 sites with full or partial hookups (20, 30, and 50 amps) for RVs up to 70 feet, and a tent area for up to 400 people. Picnic tables and fire rings are provided. Restrooms with flush toilets and showers, drinking water, coin laundry, Wi-Fi for RVs, dump station, zip line, clubhouse, video room, RV storage, guided hikes, rock-climbing wall, and horseshoes are available. Supplies are nearby. Leashed pets are permitted.

Reservations, fees: Reservations are accepted for RV sites and are required for the tent area. RV sites are $39–62 per night, $10 per night for each additional vehicle. Tent sites are $32–36 per night. Group rates available (eight RV minimum). Weekly and monthly rates available. Some credit cards accepted. Open year-round.

Directions: From Ventura, drive east on Highway 126 for 14 miles to Highway 150. Turn northwest on Highway 150 and drive five miles to the resort entrance on the right.

Contact: Ventura Ranch KOA, 805/933-3200 or 800/562-1899, www.koa.com.

74 RIVER VIEW CAMPGROUND
🚶 🏕️ 🎣 🚐 ⛺

Scenic rating: 7

in Steckel Park

Map 12.4, page 692

Santa Paula Creek flows through Steckel Park, a pretty county park that has put some work into their campground. It offers enough shade trees so that you don't feel jammed in, an aviary, fishing, and hiking. To the near north is the Sespe Wilderness, fronted by Santa Paula Ridge and the Topatopa Mountains. This area is also a refuge for the California condor.

Campsites, facilities: There are 48 sites for tents and RVs; 10 sites have full 20-, 30-, and 50-amp hookups. Picnic tables and fire pits are provided. Drinking water, restrooms with flush toilets and coin showers, horseshoe pits, a playground, a softball field, and a camp host are available.

Reservations, fees: Reservations are accepted at www.venturaparks.org ($10 individual, $20 group reservation fee). Tent sites are $22 per night, RV sites are $36 per night (one RV, one tent maximum), pets are $1 per day (allowed only in campground). Open year-round.

Directions: From Ventura, drive east on Highway 126 for 14 miles to Highway 150. Turn left (northwest) on Highway 150 and drive five miles to the campground entrance on right.

Contact: Ventura County Parks Department, 805/654-3951, www.venturaparks.org.

7.5 HOBSON COUNTY PARK

Scenic rating: 6

north of Ventura

Map 12.4, page 692

This county park is at the end of Rincon Parkway, kind of like a crowded cul-de-sac, with easy access to the beach and many side-trip possibilities. There is a great reef here for exploring at low tides. Emma Wood State Beach, San Buenaventura State Beach, and McGrath State Beach are all within 11 miles of the park.

Campsites, facilities: There are 31 sites for tents or RVs up to 34 feet; 15 sites have full hookups, including cable TV. Picnic tables and fire pits are provided. Restrooms with flush toilets and coin showers, drinking water, and snack bar are available. Leashed pets are permitted, but not on the beach.

Reservations, fees: Reservations are accepted November through March at www.venturaparks.org ($10 individual, $20 group reservation fee). Tent sites are $32 per night, RV sites are $47 per night (one RV, one tent maximum), pets are $1 per day (allowed only in campground). Open year-round.

Directions: From Ventura, drive northwest on U.S. 101 for three miles to the State Beaches exit. Take that exit and turn north on West Pacific Highway and drive five miles to the campground on the left.

Contact: Ventura County Parks Department, 805/654-3951, www.venturaparks.org.

7.6 FARIA COUNTY PARK

Scenic rating: 7

north of Ventura

Map 12.4, page 692

This county park provides a possible base of operations for beach adventures, including surf fishing. It is set along the ocean, with Emma Wood State Beach, San Buenaventura State Beach, and McGrath State Beach all within 10 miles of the park.

Campsites, facilities: There are 42 sites for tents or RVs up to 34 feet; 10 sites have full hookups (30 amps), including cable TV. Picnic tables and fire pits are provided. Restrooms with flush toilets and coin showers, drinking water, playground, and snack bar are available. Leashed pets are permitted.

Reservations, fees: Reservations are not accepted. RV sites are $32 (no hookups) and $47–50 (hookups) per night, $1 per pet per night. Open year-round.

Directions: From Ventura, drive north on U.S. 101 for three miles to the State Beaches exit. Take that exit and turn north on West Pacific Highway and drive four miles to the campground.

Contact: Ventura County Parks Department, 805/654-3951, www.venturaparks.org.

77 RINCON PARKWAY

Scenic rating: 5

north of Ventura

Map 12.4, page 692

This is basically an RV park near the ocean, where the sites are created by parking end-to-end along old Highway 1. It is not quiet. Passing trains across the highway vie for noise honors with the surf. Emma Wood State Beach, San Buenaventura State Beach, and McGrath State Beach are all within 10 miles. Two activities you can do here are surf fish and watch great sunsets.

Campsites, facilities: There are 127 sites for self-contained RVs up to 40 feet (no hookups). Supplies are available nearby. Leashed pets are allowed, but not on the beach.

Reservations, fees: Reservations are not accepted. RV sites are $27 per night per vehicle, $1 per pet per night. Open year-round.

Directions: From Ventura, drive northwest on U.S. 101 for three miles to the State Beaches exit. Take that exit and turn north on West Pacific Highway and drive 4.5 miles to the campground on the left.

Contact: Ventura County Parks Department, 805/654-3951, www.venturaparks.org.

78 EMMA WOOD STATE BEACH

Scenic rating: 8

north of Ventura

Map 12.4, page 692

This is more of a parking lot than a campground with individual sites. And oh, what a place to camp: It is set along the ocean, a pretty spot with tidepools full of all kinds of little marine critters waiting to be discovered. It is also just a short drive from the town of Ventura and the Mission San Buenaventura. One downer, a big one for many: noise from passing trains. Another downer: no toilets at

night, so you must have a self-contained vehicle. The gate closes at 10 P.M. and reopens at 6 A.M.

Campsites, facilities: There are 86 sites for RVs up to 40 feet (no hookups). No tents. Chemical toilets are available for day use only. No drinking water is available. Supplies and a coin laundry are three miles away. Leashed pets are permitted, but not on the beach.

Reservations, fees: Reservations are required mid-May through Labor Day weekend at 800/444-7275 or www.reserveamerica.com ($8 reservation fee). Sites are $30–40 per night, $10 per night for each additional vehicle. Open year-round, weather and tides permitting.

Directions: From Ventura drive north on U.S. 101 for three miles to the State Beaches exit. Take that exit, drive under the freeway, and continue less than a mile to the park entrance on the left.

Contact: Emma Wood State Beach, Channel Coast District, 805/585-1850, www.parks.ca.gov.

79 VENTURA RIVER GROUP CAMP

Scenic rating: 1

at Emma Wood State Beach near Ventura

Map 12.4, page 692

This is an extremely noisy area and the campsites are also downright ugly. It is set near the freeway and railroad tracks, and you get a lot of noise from both. It's not popular either. What you have here is mainly a dry riverbed. It is saved somewhat by a freshwater marsh at the southwest end of the beach that attracts red-tailed hawks, songbirds, and raccoons.

Campsites, facilities: There are four group tent sites for up to 30 people each, one group site for RVs of up to 45 feet that can accommodate up to 50 people, and 15 hike-in/bike-in sites. Picnic tables and fire rings are provided. Drinking water, chemical toilets, and cold showers are available. Leashed pets are permitted in the campground, but not on the beach. Supplies are within one mile.

Reservations, fees: Reservations are required for the group sites at 800/444-7275 (800/444-PARK) or www.reserveamerica.com ($8 reservation fee). The tent group camps are $150 per night, the RV group camp is $300 per night, $10 per person per night for hike-in/bike-in sites. Lower rates October through April. Open year-round.

Directions: On U.S. 101 in Ventura, take the Main Street exit and turn west. Drive one mile on Main Street to the campground on the left.

Contact: Emma Wood State Beach, Channel Coast District, 805/585-1850, www.parks.ca.gov.

80 RESIDENCE CAMPGROUND

Scenic rating: 6

in Foster Park in Ventura

Map 12.4, page 692

The Ventura River meanders through this park and its campground. The park has shade trees, a small amphitheater, an equestrian area, and is close to the trailhead for the Ojai Valley trail. Fishing and hiking round out the recreation options, however, there have been complaints of traffic noise.

Campsites, facilities: There are 16 sites for tents and RVs; 10 sites have 20, 30, and 50-amp hookups. Picnic tables and fire pits are provided, and there is an area for group barbecues. Drinking water, restrooms with flush toilets, a playground, horseshoe pits, and a camp host are available. Leashed pets are permitted in the campground only.

Reservations, fees: Reservations are accepted ($10 individual, $20 group reservation fee). Tent sites are $20 per night, RV sites (hookups) are $34 per night, one RV and one tent

maximum per site. Pets are $1 per night. Open year-round.

Directions: From Ventura, drive north on Highway 33 for 4.5 miles to the N. Ventura Ave exit (immediately before the freeway ends). Turn right on N. Ventura and then right again almost immediately onto Casitas Vista. The park entrance is at 438 Casitas Vista Road.

Contact: Ventura County Parks Department, 805/654-3951, www.venturaparks.org.

81 McGRATH STATE BEACH

Scenic rating: 9

south of Ventura

Map 12.4, page 692

This is a pretty spot just south of Ventura Harbor. Campsites are about 400 yards from the beach. This park features two miles of beach frontage, as well as lush riverbanks and sand dunes along the ocean shore. That gives rise to some of the best bird-watching in California. The north tip of the park borders the Santa Clara River Estuary Natural Preserve, where the McGrath State Beach Nature Trail provides an easy walk (wheelchair-accessible) along the Santa Clara River as it feeds into the estuary and then into the ocean. Rangers caution all considering swimming here to beware of strong currents and rip tides; they can be deadly. Beach access from the campground is limited due to flooding and nesting habitat protection. Campers must walk approximately 0.5 mile or more to get around the inland lagoon.

Note: This park is on the closure list developed by the California Department of Parks, pending final state budget decisions or the possible transfer of park management to other park agencies or volunteer groups.

Campsites, facilities: There are 174 sites for tents or RVs up to 30 feet (no hookups); 29 of the sites can be used as group sites. There is also a hike-in/bike-in site. Picnic tables and fire grills are provided. Restrooms with flush toilets and coin showers, drinking water, and a dump station are available. Supplies and a coin laundry are nearby. Some facilities are wheelchair-accessible. Leashed pets are permitted in campsites only.

Reservations, fees: Reservations are not accepted at this time; all sites are first-come, first-served through at least April 2013. Sites are $45 per night, $10 per night for each additional vehicle, $10 per person per night for hike-in/bike-in site. For group prices and reservations, phone 805/648-3918. Open year-round, weather and river conditions permitting.

Directions: Drive on U.S. 101 to south of Ventura and the Seaward exit. Take that exit and drive to the stoplight and Harbor Boulevard. Turn west on Harbor Boulevard and drive four miles to the park (signed).

Contact: McGrath State Beach or Emma Wood State Beach, Channel Coast District, 805/585-1850, www.parks.ca.gov.

82 THORNHILL BROOME AND LA JOLLA GROUP

🚶 🏊 🛶 ♿ 🚐 ⛺

Scenic rating: 7

in Point Mugu State Park

Map 12.4, page 692

Point Mugu State Park is known for its rocky bluffs, sandy beaches, rugged hills, and uplands. There are two major river canyons and wide grassy valleys sprinkled with sycamores, oaks, and a few native walnut trees. Of the campgrounds at Point Mugu, Thornhill Broome is more attractive than Sycamore Canyon (see listing in this chapter) for many visitors because it is on the ocean side of the highway (Sycamore Canyon is on the north side of the highway). It is a 2.5-mile walk to reach La Jolla Valley. While the beachfront is pretty and you can always just lie there in the sun and pretend you're a beached whale, the park's expanse on the east side of the highway in the Santa Monica Mountains provides more recreation. That includes two stellar hikes, the 9.5-mile Sycamore Canyon Loop and the seven-mile La Jolla Valley Loop. In all, the park covers 14,980 acres, far more than the obvious strip of beachfront. The park has more than 70 miles of hiking trails and five miles of ocean shoreline. Swimming, body surfing, and surf fishing are available on the beach. Note: The front gate for Thornhill Broome closes at 10 P.M. and reopens at 8 A.M.

Campsites, facilities: Thornhill Broome has 65 primitive sites for tents or RVs up to 31 feet (no hookups); La Jolla Group has a group camping area for tents only accommodating 9–50 people. There are also 10 environmental walk-in sites. Picnic tables and fire rings are provided at some sites; no open fires are allowed at the environmental walk-in sites. Drinking water and chemical toilets are available at Thornhill Broome; drinking water and flush toilets are available at La Jolla Group. Supplies can be obtained nearby. Note that nearby Sycamore Canyon has a dump station and nature center. Some facilities are wheelchair-accessible.

Reservations, fees: Reservations are accepted at 800/444-7275 (800/444-PARK) or www.reserveamerica.com ($8 reservation fee). Environmental sites are first-come, first-served. Thornhill Broome sites are $35 per night, $12 per night for each additional vehicle; hike-in/bike-in sites are $7 per person per night; La Jolla Group Camp is $225 per night. Open year-round, but subject to closure during fire season.

Directions: From Oxnard, drive 15 miles south on Highway 1 to the camp entrance. Thornhill Broome is on the right, La Jolla Group is on the left.

Contact: California State Parks, Angeles District, 818/880-0363 or 805/488-5223, www.parks.ca.gov.

83 SYCAMORE CANYON

🚶 🚴 🏊 🛶 ♿ 🚐 ⛺

Scenic rating: 6

in Point Mugu State Park

Map 12.4, page 692

While this camp is across the highway from the ocean, it is also part of Point Mugu State Park, which covers 14,980 acres. That gives you plenty of options. One of the best is taking the Sycamore Canyon Loop, a long hiking route with great views that starts right at the camp. In all, it's a 9.5-mile loop that climbs to a ridge top and offers beautiful views of nearby canyons and long-distance vistas of the coast. Note: The front gate closes at 10 P.M. and reopens at 8 A.M.

Campsites, facilities: There are 55 sites for tents or RVs up to 31 feet (no hookups) and one hike-in/bike-in site. Picnic tables and fire grills are provided. Restrooms with flush toilets and showers (token required; bring $1 bills), drinking water, and a dump station are available. A weekend nature center is within walking distance. Supplies can be obtained nearby. Some facilities are wheelchair-accessible.

Reservations, fees: Reservations are accepted at 800/444-7275 (800/444-PARK) or www. reserveamerica.com ($8 reservation fee). Sites are $45 per night, $12 per night for each additional vehicle, $7 per person per night for hike-in/bike-in site. Open year-round.

Directions: From Oxnard, drive south on Highway 1 for 16 miles to the camp entrance on the left.

Contact: California State Parks, Angeles District, 818/880-0363, www.parks.ca.gov.

84 SAN MIGUEL ISLAND

🚶 🏊 🛶 5% ⛺

Scenic rating: 10

in Channel Islands National Park

Channel Islands map, page 693 BEST (

There is no camping trip like this one anywhere in America. It starts with a three-hour boat ride, after which you arrive at San Miguel Island, the most unusual of the five Channel Islands. It is distant, extremely rugged, and is home to unique birds and much wildlife, including elephant seals and one of the largest seal and sea lion rookeries in the world (best on the south side of the island). Only rarely do people take advantage of this island paradise, limited to no more than 75 people at any one time on the entire island. To reach the campground start from Cuyler Harbor, where you will be dropped off, and then hike up Nidever Canyon and take the left fork. Bring plenty of water, warm clothes, and be prepared for the chance of fog and wind; the boat typically will not return to pick you up for several days. That's why camping here is like staking out your own personal island wilderness.

Campsites, facilities: There are nine primitive tent sites. Picnic tables and food lockers are provided. Pit toilets and windbreaks are available. No drinking water is available, and garbage must be packed out. No open fires are allowed; bring a camp stove for cooking. No pets are permitted.

Reservations, fees: Reserve transportation by calling Island Packers at 805/642-1393. After arranging transportation, you must obtain a camping reservation at 877/444-6777 or www.recreation.gov ($9 reservation fee). Sites are $15 per night. There is a fee for round-trip boat transportation. Open year-round, weather permitting.

Directions: To reach Island Packers in Ventura, take U.S. 101 south to Ventura and the Seaward exit. Take that exit and turn west on Seaward Avenue and drive to Harbor Boulevard. Turn left on Harbor Boulevard and drive about two miles to Spinnaker Drive. Turn right and drive a short distance to the harbor. The boat ride is at least three hours each way.

Contact: Channel Islands National Park Visitor Center, 805/658-5730, www.nps.gov/chis.

85 SANTA ROSA ISLAND

🚶 ≈ 🛶 5% ⛺

Scenic rating: 10

in Channel Islands National Park

Channel Islands map, page 693 BEST (

Santa Rosa, the second-largest of the Channel Islands (the largest is Santa Cruz), is 10 miles wide and 15 miles long, and it holds many mysteries and adventures. A camping trip to Santa Rosa Island, available Friday through Sunday, will be an unforgettable experience even for those who think they've seen it all. The island is beautiful in the spring, when its grasslands turn emerald green and are sprinkled with wildflowers. There are many good hikes; the best are the Cherry Canyon Trail into the island's interior. Another great one is the five-mile Torrey Pines Trail. The Lobo Canyon Trail is a personal favorite. Because the boat ride to Santa Rosa is approximately 2.5 hours, longer than the trip to Santa Cruz, this island often receives fewer visitors than its nearby neighbor, which makes it even more special. Bring warm clothes because of the chance of fog and wind. A huge bonus is drinking water and showers at the camp.

Campsites, facilities: There are 15 primitive tent sites. Picnic tables and windbreaks are provided. Drinking water and pit toilets are available. No open fires are allowed; bring a camp stove for cooking. Garbage must be packed out. No pets are permitted.

Reservations, fees: Reserve transportation by calling Island Packers at 805/642-1393. Channel Islands Aviation (805/987-1301) will fly campers to Santa Rosa Island. After arranging transportation, you must obtain a camping reservation at 877/444-6777 or www.recreation.gov ($9 reservation fee). Sites are $15 per night. There is a fee for round-trip transportation. Open year-round, weather permitting.

Directions: To reach Island Packers in Ventura: Drive on U.S. 101 to Ventura and the Seaward exit. Take that exit and turn west on Seaward Avenue and drive to Harbor Boulevard. Turn left on Harbor Boulevard and drive about two miles to Spinnaker Drive. Turn right and drive a short distance to the harbor. The boat ride is at least 2.5 hours each way.

To reach Channel Islands Aviation in Camarillo: Drive on U.S. 101 to Camarillo to the exit for Los Posas West. Take that exit to Los Posas West and drive to Pleasant Valley. Turn right on Pleasant Valley and drive to Airport Way. Turn right on Airport Way and drive to Durley Avenue. Drive past the hangar and turn into the parking lot on the right. The office for Channel Islands Aviation is at 305 Durley Avenue, located next to the Wave Point Café.

Contact: Channel Islands National Park Visitor Center, 805/658-5730, www.nps.gov/chis.

86 SANTA CRUZ ISLAND

🚶 ≈ 🛶 🚤 5% ⛺

Scenic rating: 10

in Channel Islands National Park

Channel Islands map, page 693 BEST (

Santa Cruz is the largest of the Channel Islands, perfect for camping and multi-day visits. It covers 96 square miles, features a 2,450-foot mountain (Devil's Peak), and boasts an incredible array of flora and fauna, sheltered canyons, and sweeping ocean views. Kayaking through sea caves is outstanding, but can be dangerous, so use caution. The Scorpion campground is set in a eucalyptus grove in a valley, with trailheads near camp that hikers can take to the surrounding ridgeline. A great three-mile hike from Prisoner's Harbor to Pelican Bay is a routed along the coast to a beautiful beach. The hike is on Nature Conservancy property and requires a guide from Island Packers; the hike can be arranged at the same time as the transportation.

Campsites, facilities: Scorpion campground has 40 hike-in sites. There are four primitive backcountry sites at Del Norte. Picnic tables are provided. Pit toilets are available. Drinking water is available at Scorpion, but not at Del Norte. No open fires are allowed; bring a camp stove for cooking. Garbage must be packed out. No pets are permitted.

Reservations, fees: Reserve transportation by calling Island Packers at 805/642-1393. After arranging transportation, you must obtain a camping reservation at 877/444-6777 or www.recreation.gov ($9 reservation fee). Sites are $15 per night. There is a fee for round-trip boat transportation. Open year-round, weather permitting.

Directions: To reach Island Packers in Ventura, drive on U.S. 101 to Ventura and the Seaward exit. Take that exit and turn west on Seaward Avenue and drive to Harbor Boulevard. Turn left on Harbor Boulevard and drive about two miles to Spinnaker Drive. Turn right and drive a short distance to the harbor. The boat ride is at least one hour each way.

Contact: Channel Islands National Park Visitor Center, 805/658-5730, www.nps.gov/chis.

87 ANACAPA ISLAND
🚶 🏕 🛶 🏊 5% ⛰

Scenic rating: 10

in Channel Islands National Park

Channel Islands map, page 693 BEST (

Little Anacapa, long and narrow, is known for its awesome caves, cliffs, and sea lion rookeries that range near huge kelp beds. After landing on the island, you face a 154-step staircase trail that leaves you perched on an ocean bluff. From there, it is a 0.5-mile hike to the camp. Other trails venture past Inspiration Point and Cathedral Cove and provide vast views of the channel. The inshore waters are a marine preserve loaded with marine life and seabirds, and, with the remarkably clear water, this island makes a great destination for snorkeling and sea kayaking. At only 50

minutes, the boat ride here is the shortest one to the Channel Islands.

Campsites, facilities: There are seven primitive tent sites. Picnic tables are provided. Pit toilets are available. No drinking water is available. Garbage must be packed out. No open fires are allowed; bring a camp stove for cooking. Garbage must be packed out. No pets are permitted.

Reservations, fees: Reserve transportation by calling Island Packers at 805/642-1393. After arranging transportation, you must obtain a camping reservation at 877/444-6777 or www.recreation.gov ($9 reservation fee). Sites are $15 per night. There is a fee for round-trip boat transportation. Open year-round, weather permitting.

Directions: To reach Island Packers in Ventura, drive on U.S. 101 to Ventura and the Seaward exit. Take that exit and turn west on Seaward Avenue and drive to Harbor Boulevard. Turn left on Harbor Boulevard and drive about two miles to Spinnaker Drive. Turn right and drive a short distance to the harbor. The boat ride is approximately one hour each way.

Contact: Channel Islands National Park Visitor Center, 805/658-5730, www.nps.gov/chis.

88 SANTA BARBARA ISLAND
🚶 🏕 🛶 5% ⛰

Scenic rating: 10

in Channel Islands National Park

Channel Islands map, page 693

This is a veritable dot of an island, well to the south of the four others that make up the Channel Islands. It is best known for its five miles of hiking trails, solitude, snorkeling, swimming, and excellent viewing of marine mammals. It is a breeding ground for elephant seals, with dolphins, sea lions, and whales (in the winter) all common in the area. The snorkeling can be wonderful, as you dive amid playful seals. The only negative is the long boat ride, three hours from the mainland. After landing, it is a steep hike to the campground (no stairs up the bluff), covering about 0.5 mile. Most campers treat this as a wilderness backpacking experience with a long boat ride instead of a long hike.

Campsites, facilities: There are 10 primitive tent sites. Picnic tables are provided. Pit toilets are available. No drinking water is available. Garbage must be packed out. No open fires are allowed; bring a camp stove for cooking. No pets are permitted.

Reservations, fees: Reserve transportation by calling Island Packers at 805/642-1393. After arranging transportation, you must obtain a camping reservation at 877/444-6777 or www.recreation.gov ($9 reservation fee). Sites are $15 per night. There is a fee for round-trip boat transportation. Open year-round, weather permitting.

Directions: To reach Island Packers in Ventura, drive on U.S. 101 to Ventura and the Seaward exit. Take that exit and turn west on Seaward Avenue and drive to Harbor Boulevard. Turn left on Harbor Boulevard and drive about two miles to Spinnaker Drive. Turn right and drive a short distance to the harbor. The boat ride is at least three hours each way.

Contact: Channel Islands National Park Visitor Center, 805/658-5730, www.nps.gov/chis.

LOS ANGELES AND VICINITY

© KLOTZ/123RF.COM

BEST CAMPGROUNDS

The stereotypical image of the region you see on TV – the blonde in a convertible, the surfer with the movie-star jaw-line – is so flawed as to be ridiculous, pathetic, and laughable. And while there are some classic beaches, lifeguards and all, the surrounding area offers some of the best recreation opportunities in California.

In fact, there are more campgrounds in this region than any other in California's 16 geographic regions except for three: Tahoe and the Northern Sierra, Sequoia and Kings Canyon, and Shasta and Trinity. It stuns some to learn that Los Angeles and its nearby forests provide more campgrounds than even the Yosemite area, and three times as many as the San Francisco Bay Area and its 1.2 million acres of greenbelt.

But for those of us who know this landscape, it does not come as a surprise. The area has a tremendous range of national forests, canyons, mountains, lakes, coast, and islands. In fact, there are so many hidden gems that it is like a giant treasure hunt for those who love the outdoors.

While most people first think of the coast, highways, and beaches when envisioning this region, it is the opportunities for camping and hiking in the national forests that surprise most. Angeles National Forest and San Bernardino National Forest provide more than one million acres, 1,000 miles of trails, and dozens of hidden campgrounds, including remote sites along the Pacific Crest Trail, that make perfect launching points for weekend trips.

The mountaintop views are incredible, probably best from Mount Baldy (10,064 feet), Mount San Jacinto (10,834 feet), and Mount San Gorgonio (11,490 feet). A series of great campgrounds are nestled on the flanks of all three of these destinations. It is only a start.

Even more famous is the region's top recreation lake, Big Bear, for fishing and boating. Though the region is known for its population density – and Big Bear is no exception on weekends – the relatively few people on weekdays, especially Monday to Thursday mornings, can be stunning to discover. Other top lakes include Arrowhead, Castaic, and several smaller reservoirs.

Yet this is not even the best of it. Look over the opportunities and take your pick. People? What people?

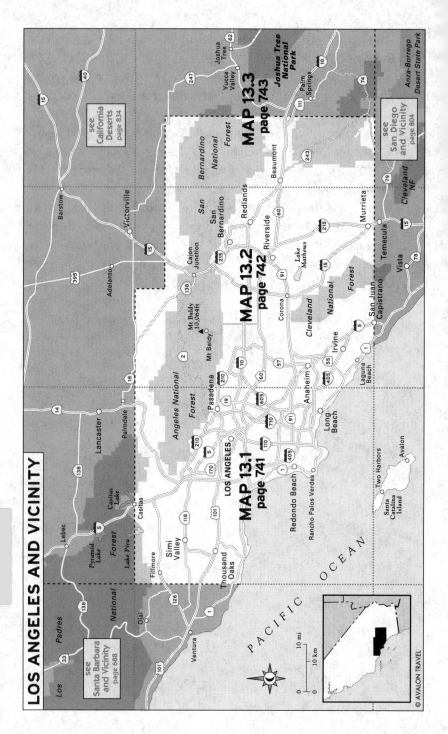

LOS ANGELES AND VICINITY

MAP 13.3
page 743

MAP 13.2
page 742

MAP 13.1
page 741

see
California
Deserts
page 834

see
San Diego
and Vicinity
page 804

see
Santa Barbara
and Vicinity
page 688

Joshua Tree
National
Park

Anza-Borrego
Desert State Park

Cleveland
NF

San Bernardino National Forest

Cleveland National Forest

Angeles National Forest

Los Padres National Forest

Joshua Tree
Yucca Valley
Palm Springs
Beaumont
Redlands
San Bernardino
Riverside
Lake Mathews
Corona
Murrieta
Temecula
Vista
Anaheim
Irvine
Laguna Beach
San Juan Capistrano
Long Beach
Rancho Palos Verdes
Redondo Beach
LOS ANGELES
Pasadena
Mt Baldy 10,064ft
Mt Baldy
Cajon Junction
Adelanto
Victorville
Barstow
Lancaster
Palmdale
Pyramid Lake
Lebec
Lake Piru
Casitas
Casitas Lake
Fillmore
Ojai
Ventura
Simi Valley
Thousand Oaks
Avalon
Two Harbors
Santa Catalina Island

PACIFIC OCEAN

10 mi
10 km

© AVALON TRAVEL

Map 13.1

Sites 1-26
Pages 744-757

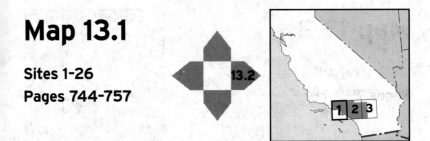

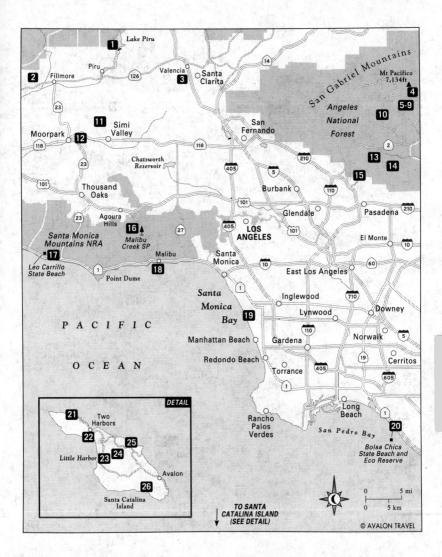

Map 13.2

Sites 27-74
Pages 758-781

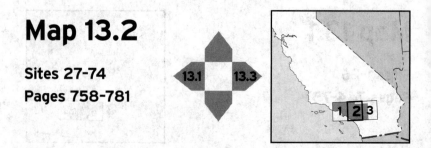

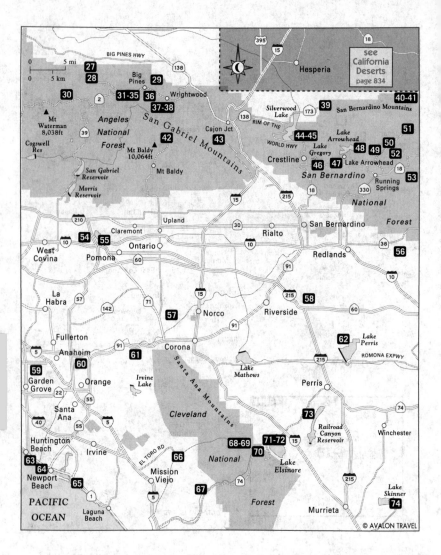

© AVALON TRAVEL

Map 13.3

Sites 75-109
Pages 782-799

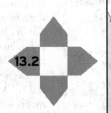

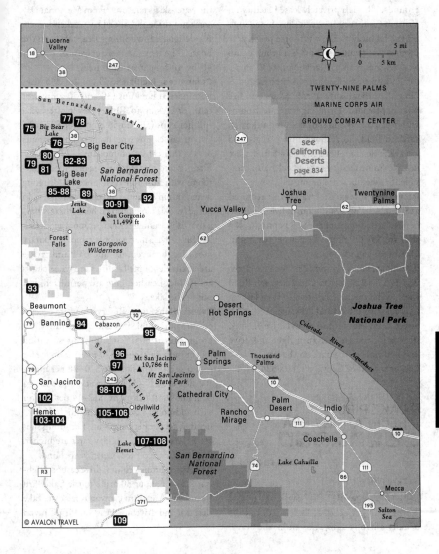

1 KENNEY GROVE PARK AND GROUP CAMPGROUND

Scenic rating: 4

near Fillmore

Map 13.1, page 741

A lot of folks miss this spot, a park tucked away among orchards, coast live oaks, and eucalyptus groves, with several group campgrounds. This is a privately leased facility on Ventura County property. It's just far enough off the highway to allow for some privacy.

Campsites, facilities: This is a group camp with 33 sites with partial hookups (30 amps) for RVs up to 40 feet and 18 sites for tents. No pull-through sites. Picnic tables and fire pits are provided. Drinking water, restrooms with flush toilets and showers, amphitheater, softball field, horseshoes, and playground are available. Supplies and a coin laundry are nearby. Some facilities are wheelchair accessible. Leashed pets are permitted.

Reservations, fees: Reservations are required at 805/524-0750; a minimum of five sites must be reserved. Tent sites are $28 per night, RV sites are $31 per night, $1 per pet per night. Open year-round.

Directions: From Ventura, drive east on Highway 126 for 22 miles to Old Telegraph Road (before the town of Fillmore). Turn left on Old Telegraph Road and drive 0.6 mile to 7th Street. Turn left (northwest) and drive 0.3 mile to North Oak Avenue. Turn right and drive one-half mile to the park on the left.

Contact: Kenney Grove, tel. 805/524-0750.

2 LAKE PIRU RECREATION AREA

Scenic rating: 7

on Lake Piru

Map 13.1, page 741   **BEST (**

Things can get crazy at Lake Piru, but it's usually a happy crazy, not an insane crazy.

Lake Piru (1,055 feet elevation) is shaped like a teardrop and covers 1,200 acres when full. This is a lake set up for waterskiing, with lots of fast boats. All others be forewarned: The rules prohibit boats under 12 feet or over 26 feet, as well as personal watercraft. Canoes and kayaks over eight feet are permitted in a special-use area. (All boats must be certified mussel-free before launching.) Bass and trout fishing can be quite good in the spring before the water-skiers take over. From Memorial Day weekend through Labor Day weekend, there is a designated swimming area, safe from the boats. The tent sites here consist of roughly 40-by-40-foot areas amid trees.

Campsites, facilities: There are 235 sites with partial hookups (30 and 50 amps) for tents or RVs up to 40 feet, seven sites with full hookups (30 and 50 amps) for RVs, and two group camps with no hookups for tents or RVs that can accommodate 4–12 vehicles. Fire pits and picnic tables are provided. Restrooms with flush toilets and showers, drinking water, dump station, convenience store, coin laundry, WiFi, picnic area, boat storage, propane, fish-cleaning station, seasonal snack bar, ice, full-service marina, boat ramp, temporary mooring, boat rentals, and bait and tackle are available. Some facilities are wheelchair-accessible. Leashed pets are permitted, but not in the lake.

Reservations, fees: Reservations are accepted for individual sites and are required for group sites at 805/521-1500 ($8 reservation fee for individual sites; $20 reservation fee for group sites). Tent sites are $20–28 per night, RV sites are $22–32 (electricity) and $32–44 (full hookups) per night, $12–14 per day for each additional vehicle, boat permit is $10–13 per day, $2 per pet per night. The group sites are $112 per night. Holiday rates are higher. Credit cards accepted. Open year-round.

Directions: From Ventura, drive east on Highway 126 for about 30 miles to the Lake Piru Recreation Area/Piru Canyon Road exit. Take that exit and drive northeast on Piru Canyon

Road for about six miles to the campground at the end of the road.

Contact: Lake Piru Recreation Area, 805/521-1500, www.camplakepiru.com.

🛈 VALENCIA TRAVEL VILLAGE
🏊 🐕 ♿ 🚐

Scenic rating: 5

in Valencia

Map 13.1, page 741

This huge RV park is in the scenic San Fernando foothills, just five minutes from Six Flags Magic Mountain. Lake Piru and Lake Castaic are only 15 minutes away. The camp was built on a 65-acre horse ranch. Note: There are roughly 300 long-term residents here, so temporary camping space may be limited.

Campsites, facilities: There are 381 sites, including about 300 with permanent residents, with full or partial hookups (30 and 50 amps) for RVs; most are pull-through. No tents. Picnic tables and fire pits (some sites) are provided. A market, two heated swimming pools, spa, lounge, video and games arcade, playground, shuffleboard, horseshoes, volleyball courts, ping pong, coin laundry, Wi-Fi, propane, and dump station are available. Some facilities are wheelchair-accessible. Leashed pets are permitted.

Reservations, fees: Reservations are recommended at 888/LUV-TORV (888/588-8678). RV sites (hookups) are $50 per night, $2 per person per night for more than two people. Weekly and monthly rates are available. Some credit cards accepted. Some discounts available. Open year-round.

Directions: Drive on I-5 to Santa Clarita and Highway 126 west/Henry Mayo Road. Take that exit and drive west on Highway 126 for one mile to the camp on the left.

Contact: Valencia Travel Village, 661/257-3333, www.valenciatravelvillagellc.com.

🛈 MOUNT PACIFICO
🚶 🐕 ⛺

Scenic rating: 7

on the Pacific Crest Trail in
Angeles National Forest

Map 13.1, page 741

Note: As this book went to press, Mount Pacific campround remained closed. Please call before planning a trip here.

This is one of the great primitive camps in Angeles National Forest. It is set near the top of Mount Pacifico at an elevation of 7,134 feet, with the Pacific Crest Trail located 0.5 mile from camp. The views are outstanding, especially to the north of the sparse Antelope Valley and beyond. From here, the PCT is routed through a series of ravines and draws and up short ridges, pleasant but not inspiring.

Campsites, facilities: There are eight tent sites. Picnic tables and fire grills are provided. Vault toilets are available. No drinking water is available. Garbage must be packed out. Leashed pets are permitted.

Reservations, fees: Reservations are not accepted. An Adventure Pass ($30 annual fee or $5 daily pass per vehicle) is required. Open mid-May through mid-November, weather permitting.

Directions: From Pasadena, drive north on I-210 for four miles to the exit for Highway 2/Angeles Crest Highway. Take that exit and drive north on Highway 2 for nine miles to Angeles Forest Highway/County Road N3. Turn left on Angeles Forest Highway and drive about 12 miles to the intersection with Santa Clara Divide Road/Forest Road 3N17 (look for the Mill Creek Summit sign). Turn right (east) and drive about six miles to Mount Pacifico Road. Turn left on the dirt road and drive four miles to the campground. High-clearance vehicles are recommended.

Note that at Mill Creek Summit, the gate is locked from November 15 to May 15 and it will be necessary to hike from the gate. When

Santa Clara Divide Road is impassable because of weather conditions, it will be necessary to hike from Alder Saddle.

Contact: Angeles National Forest, Los Angeles River Ranger District, 818/899-1900, www. fs.usda.gov/angeles.

5 HORSE FLATS
🏃 🐴 🚌 ⛺

Scenic rating: 7

near the San Gabriel Wilderness in
Angeles National Forest

Map 13.1, page 741

This is one of several options in the immediate area: Chilao, Bandido Group Camp, and Coulter Group Camp are the other three. Horse Flats is set at 5,700 feet elevation along a national recreation trail (Silver Moccasin Trail). Two trails into the San Gabriel Wilderness are nearby.

Campsites, facilities: There are 25 sites for tents or RVs up to 22 feet (no hookups). Picnic tables and fire pits are provided. Vault toilets, hitching rails, and horse corrals are available. No drinking water is available. Leashed pets are permitted.

Reservations, fees: Reservations are not accepted. Sites are $12 per night. Open April through mid-November, weather permitting.

Directions: From Pasadena, drive north on I-210 for four miles to the exit for Highway 2/Angeles Crest Highway. Take that exit and drive northeast on Highway 2 for 30 miles to Santa Clara Divide Road/Forest Road 3N17 at Three Points (signed). Turn left and drive three miles to Horse Flats Road. Turn left and drive one mile to the campground.

Contact: Angeles National Forest, Los Angeles River Ranger District, 818/899-1900, www. fs.usda.gov/angeles.

6 BANDIDO GROUP CAMP
🏃 🐴 🚌 ⛺

Scenic rating: 6

near the Pacific Crest Trail in
Angeles National Forest

Map 13.1, page 741

This is a base camp for groups preparing to hike into the surrounding wilderness. A trail out of the camp heads east and intersects with the Pacific Crest Trail a little over two miles away at Three Points, a significant PCT junction. Before heading out visitors must check in and register with the rangers at the Los Angeles River Ranger District office, two miles west of Three Points on Highway 2. The elevation is 5,840 feet.

Campsites, facilities: There are five group camps for tents or RVs up to 40 feet (no hookups) that accommodate 12–60 people. Picnic tables and fire rings are provided. Pit toilets, corrals, and water troughs are available. There is no drinking water. Leashed pets are permitted.

Reservations, fees: Reservations are required at 877/444-6777 or www.recreation.gov ($9 reservation fee). The camp is $24–120 per night. Open April through mid-November, weather permitting.

Directions: From Pasadena, drive north on I-210 for four miles to the exit for Highway 2/Angeles Crest Highway. Take that exit and drive northeast on Highway 2 for 30 miles to Santa Clara Divide Road/Forest Road 3N17 at Three Points (signed). Turn left and drive two miles to the campground on the left.

Contact: Angeles National Forest, Los Angeles River Ranger District, 818/899-1900, www. fs.usda.gov/angeles.

7 CHILAO CAMPGROUND

🚶 🐕 ♿ 🚐 ⛺

Scenic rating: 6

near the San Gabriel Wilderness in
Angeles National Forest

Map 13.1, page 741

A national recreation trail runs right by here and as such this popular trailhead camp gets a lot of use. Access to the Pacific Crest Trail is three miles north at Three Points (five miles if hiking the Silver Moccasin Trail) and parking is available there. An Adventure Pass is required to park at all trailheads. The elevation is 5,300 feet. Note: There is frequent bear activity, so use precautions.

Campsites, facilities: There are 83 sites for tents or RVs up to 40 feet (no hookups). Picnic tables and fire rings are provided. Drinking water and vault toilets are available. Some facilities are wheelchair-accessible. Leashed pets are permitted.

Reservations, fees: Reservations are not accepted. Sites are $12 per night. Open April through mid-November, weather permitting.

Directions: From Pasadena, drive north on I-210 for four miles to the exit for Highway 2/Angeles Crest Highway. Take that exit and drive northeast on Highway 2 for 27 miles to the campground entrance road (signed) on the left.

Contact: Angeles National Forest, Los Angeles River Ranger District, 818/899-1900, www.fs.usda.gov/angeles.

8 COULTER GROUP CAMP

🚶 🐕 🚐 ⛺

Scenic rating: 6

near the San Gabriel Wilderness in
Angeles National Forest

Map 13.1, page 741

This is a popular group camp set near both a visitors center and a trailhead for the Pacific Crest Trail. Access to the PCT is 3.5 miles

north at Three Points (5.5 miles if hiking the Silver Moccasin Trail), and parking is available. An Adventure Pass is required to park at the trailheads. The elevation is 5,300 feet. It is close to Chilao Campground.

Campsites, facilities: There is one group site for up to 50 people (no hookups) and RVs up to 40 feet. Four picnic tables, a barbecue pit, fire ring, vault toilet, and drinking water are available. Leashed pets are permitted.

Reservations, fees: Reservations are required at 877/444-6777 or www.recreation.gov ($9 reservation fee). The camp is $100 per night. Open April through mid-November, weather permitting.

Directions: From Pasadena, drive north on I-210 for four miles to the exit for Highway 2/Angeles Crest Highway. Take that exit and drive northeast on Highway 2 for 27 miles to the campground entrance road on the left (enter through the Litle Pines Loop at Chilao Campground).

Contact: Angeles National Forest, Los Angeles River Ranger District, 818/899-1900, www.fs.usda.gov/angeles.

9 SULPHUR SPRINGS WALK-IN

🚶 🐕 ⛺

Scenic rating: 6

near the Pacific Crest Trail in
Angeles National Forest

Map 13.1, page 741

This walk-in camp is on the South Fork of Little Rock Creek, a short distance from a trailhead for the Pacific Crest Trail. It is set at 5,300 feet elevation amid pines and is a popular jump-off point for hikes. It was formerly a drive-in camp, but the road washed out and the Forest Service has since made it a permanent walk-in site. Some familiar with this area may remember that campers with horses once used this site. No more—the equestrian facilities have been removed.

Campsites, facilities: There are six sites for

tents only. Picnic tables and stoves are provided. Pit toilets are available. There is no drinking water. Leashed pets are permitted.

Reservations, fees: Reservations are not accepted. There is no fee for camping. An Adventure Pass ($30 per year or $5 per day) is required. Open April through mid-November, weather permitting.

Directions: From Pasadena, drive north on I-210 for four miles to the exit for Highway 2/Angeles Crest Highway. Take that exit and drive northeast on Highway 2 for 30 miles to Santa Clara Divide Road/Forest Road 3N17 at Three Points. Turn left on Santa Clara Divide Road/Forest Road 3N17 and drive 4.5 miles to Alder Saddle. Bear right (north), onto the pavement, and drive one mile to the Pacific Crest Trail (100 yards before the road closure gate). Park your vehicle and walk east (downhill) on the Pacific Crest Trail for 0.75 mile to the camp.

Contact: Angeles National Forest, Los Angeles River Ranger District, 818/899-1900, www.fs.usda.gov/angeles.

10 MONTE CRISTO

Scenic rating: 7

on Mill Creek in Angeles National Forest

Map 13.1, page 741

This is a Forest Service camp on Mill Creek at 3,600 feet elevation, just west of Iron Mountain. The camp is situated under sycamore trees, which provide great color in the fall. In most years Mill Creek flows six months out of the year.

Campsites, facilities: There are 22 sites for tents or RVs up to 30 feet (no hookups). Picnic tables and fire grills are provided. Drinking water and vault toilets are available. Some facilities are wheelchair-accessible. Leashed pets are permitted.

Reservations, fees: Reservations are not accepted. Sites are $12 per night. Open year-round.

Directions: From Pasadena, drive north on I-210 for four miles to the exit for Highway 2/Angeles Crest Highway. Take that exit and drive northeast on Highway 2 for nine miles to Angeles Forest Highway/County Road N3. Turn left on Angeles Forest Highway and drive about ten miles to the campground on the right.

Contact: Angeles National Forest, Los Angeles River Ranger District, 818/899-1900, www.fs.usda.gov/angeles.

11 TAPO CANYON COUNTY PARK

Scenic rating: 7

off Tapo Canyon Road in Simi Valley

Map 13.1, page 741

The campground features a large undeveloped area for tents, and slots with hookups for RVs. Highlights are a grassy picnic area and an arena for horseback riding; a camp host is a plus. This county park has quickly become a favorite site for youth groups.

Campsites, facilities: There are 16 sites with hookups (20-, 30-, and 50-amps) for RVs of any length. Picnic tables and fire rings are provided. Drinking water, restrooms with flush toilets, and coin showers are available. A dump station, equestrian arena, horse watering station, and hitching posts are also available. A camp host is on site.

Reservations, fees: Reservations are accepted for the individual sites and required for the group sites at 805/654-3951, www.ventura-parks.org ($10 reservation fee). Sites are $37 per night, $32 per night in winter. Call for group rates.

Directions: From Highway 101 north of Thousand Oaks, turn north on Highway 23 and drive eight miles to Highway 118. Merge onto Highway 118 East and drive 4.1 miles to Tapo Canyon Road, Exit 27. Take that exit and turn left onto Tapo Canyon Road. Drive three miles to the campground.

Contact: Tapo Canyon Park, Ventura, 805/654-3951, www.portal.countyofventura.org.

12 OAK PARK
🏃 🐕 🛶 🚐 ⛺

Scenic rating: 3

in Simi Valley near Moorpark

Map 13.1, page 741

One of the frustrations at many state and national park campgrounds is that they are full from reservations, especially at the state beaches. The county parks often provide a safety valve, and Oak Park certainly applies—but not always. This is oft overlooked county park is set in the foothill country of Simi Valley and has many trails offering good hiking possibilities. The camp is somewhat secluded, more so than many expect. The catch? Sometimes the entire campground is rented to a single group. Note: Gates close at dusk and reopen at 8 A.M.

Campsites, facilities: There are 16 sites with partial hookups (20 and 30 amps) for RVs. Picnic tables and fire pits are provided. Drinking water, restrooms with flush toilets, and a dump station are available. Group facilities are available by reservation only. Horseshoe pits, a playground, and basketball and volleyball courts are available nearby. Supplies and a coin laundry are within two miles. Leashed pets are permitted.

Reservations, fees: Reservations are accepted. Sites are $30 per night and include one RV, one vehicle, and one tent maximum with no more than six people per site, $1 per pet per night. There is a 14-day stay limit. Off-season discounts available. Open year-round, except Christmas Day.

Directions: From Ventura, drive south on U.S. 101 to Highway 23. Turn north on Highway 23 (which becomes Highway 123 East) and drive about three miles to the Collins Street exit. Continue straight through the intersection (it becomes Old Los Angeles Avenue)

and drive 1.5 miles to the park entrance on the left.

Contact: Oak Park, 805/654-3951, www.countyofventura.org.

13 VALLEY FORGE HIKE-IN
🏃 🏊 🏠 5% ⛺

Scenic rating: 8

on the San Gabriel River in Angeles National Forest

Map 13.1, page 741

Valley Forge is a good camp for anglers or hikers who are looking for a short backpacking trip. A 2.5-mile hike is required to reach this campground. For hikers, a national recreation trail passes close to the camp. For anglers, there are small but feisty native trout. The elevation is 3,500 feet.

Campsites, facilities: There are six tent sites. Picnic tables and fire rings are provided. Pit toilets are available. No drinking water is available. Stream water can be used if it is boiled or pump-filtered. Garbage must be packed out. Leashed pets are permitted.

Reservations, fees: Reservations are not accepted. There is no fee for camping. An Adventure Pass ($30 annual fee or $5 daily fee per vehicle) is required. Open year-round, weather permitting.

Directions: From Pasadena, drive north on I-210 for four miles to the exit for Highway 2/Angeles Crest Highway. Take that exit and drive north on Highway 2 for 14 miles to Mount Wilson Road. Turn right on Mount Wilson Road, then immediately turn left into the parking lot. Access the Gabrielino National Recreation Trail, which is located behind the restrooms, and hike 2.5 miles to the campground.

Contact: Angeles National Forest, Los Angeles River Ranger District, 818/899-1900, www.fs.usda.gov/angeles.

14 WEST FORK HIKE-IN
🏃 🛶 🏕 5% ⛺

Scenic rating: 8

on the West Fork of the San Gabriel River in
Angeles National Forest

Map 13.1, page 741

It takes a circuitous drive and a four- to five-
mile hike to reach this camp, but for backpackers it is worth it. The camp is on the West Fork
of the San Gabriel River amid pine woodlands,
with two national recreation trails intersecting
at the campground. The canyon is deep and the
river is beautiful. The elevation is 3,100 feet.

Campsites, facilities: There are seven tent
sites. Picnic tables and fire rings are provided.
Pit toilets are available. No drinking water
is available. Stream water can be used if it
is boiled or pump-filtered. Garbage must be
packed out. Leashed pets are permitted.

Reservations, fees: Reservations are not accepted. There is no fee for camping. An Adventure
Pass ($30 annual fee or $5 daily fee per parked
vehicle) is required. Open year-round.

Directions: From Pasadena, drive north on
I-210 for four miles to the exit for Highway
2/Angeles Crest Highway. Take that exit and
drive north on Highway 2 for 14 miles to
Mount Wilson Road. Turn right on Mount
Wilson Road, then immediately turn left
into the parking lot. Access the Gabrielino
National Recreation Trail, which is located
behind the restrooms, and hike five miles to
the campground.

Contact: Angeles National Forest, Los Angeles
River Ranger District, 818/899-1900, www.
fs.usda.gov/angeles.

15 MILLARD
🏃 🐴 ⛺

Scenic rating: 8

near Millard Falls in Angeles National Forest

Map 13.1, page 741

This tiny, pretty camp, set near a creek amid
oak and alder woodlands, is best known as the

launching point for some excellent hikes. The
best is the 0.5-mile hike to Millard Falls, where
you actually rock-hop your way upstream to
the 60-foot waterfall, a drop-dead beautiful
sight. On weekends, there can be lots of foot
traffic through the campground with hikers
on their way to the falls. Another trail out of
camp leads to Inspiration Point and continues
to San Gabriel Peak. It's a short walk to the
campsites.

Campsites, facilities: There are six tent sites.
Picnic tables and fire pits are provided. Vault
toilets are available. No drinking water is
available, but stream water may be boiled or
filtered. Garbage must be packed out. Leashed
pets are permitted.

Reservations, fees: Reservations are not accepted. There is no fee for camping. An Adventure
Pass ($30 annual fee or $5 daily fee per parked
vehicle) is required. Open year-round.

Directions: From Pasadena, drive north on
I-10 to the exit for Lake Avenue. Take that
exit north and drive 3.5 miles to Loma Alta
Drive. Turn left (west) at Loma Alta Drive
and drive one mile to Chaney Trail Road
(at the flashing yellow light). Turn right at
Chaney Trail and drive 1.5 miles (keep left
at the fork) to the parking lot for the campground. It is a short walk on a fire road to
the campground. Note: A gate is locked at
Chaney Trail from 8 P.M. to 6 A.M., preventing drive-in access approximately 1.5 miles
from the campground.

Contact: Angeles National Forest, Los Angeles
River Ranger District, 818/899-1900, www.
fs.usda.gov/angeles.

16 MALIBU CREEK STATE PARK
🏃 🚴 🏊 🛶 🐴 ♿ 🚐 ⛺

Scenic rating: 9

near Malibu

Map 13.1, page 741

If you plan on staying here, be sure to get
your reservation in early. This 6,600-acre

state park is just a few miles out of Malibu between Highway 1 and U.S. 101, two major thoroughfares for vacationers. Despite its popularity, the park manages to retain a natural setting, with miles of trails for hiking, biking, and horseback riding, and inspiring scenic views. The park offers 15 miles of streamside trail through oak and sycamore woodlands and also some chaparral-covered slopes. It is an ideal spot for a break on a coastal road trip. This park was once used as a setting for the filming of some movies and TV shows, including Planet of the Apes and M*A*S*H.

Campsites, facilities: There are 57 sites for tents or RVs up to 30 feet (no hookups) and a group tent site for up to 60 people. Picnic tables are provided. No wood fires are permitted in the summer, but propane and charcoal barbecues are allowed. Drinking water, restrooms with flush toilets and coin showers, and a dump station are available. Some facilities are wheelchair-accessible. Leashed pets are permitted, but only in the campground area.

Reservations, fees: Reservations are accepted at 800/444-7275 (800/444-PARK) or www.reserveamerica.com ($8 reservation fee). Sites are $45 per night, $8 per night for each additional vehicle, $225 per night for group site. Open year-round.

Directions: From U.S. 101: Drive on U.S. 101 to the exit for Las Virgenes Canyon Road (on the western border of Calabasas). Take that exit south and drive on Las Virgenes Canyon Road/County Road N1 for four miles to the park entrance on the right.

From Highway 1: Drive on Highway 1 to Malibu and Malibu Canyon Road. Turn north on Malibu Canyon Road and drive north for 5.5 miles (the road becomes Las Virgenes Canyon Road/County Road N1) to the park entrance on the left.

Contact: Malibu Creek State Park, 818/880-0367, www.parks.ca.gov.

17 LEO CARRILLO STATE PARK
🥾 🚴 ♒ 🛶 🐴 ♿ 🚙 ⛺

Scenic rating: 8

north of Malibu

Map 13.1, page 741

The camping area at this state park is set in a canyon, and reservations are essential during the summer and on weekends the remainder of the year. Large sycamore trees shade the campsites. The Nicholas Flat Trail provides an excellent hike to the Willow Creek Overlook for beautiful views of the beach. In addition, a pedestrian tunnel provides access to a wonderful coastal spot with sea caves, tunnels, tidepools, and patches of beach. This park features 1.5 miles of beach for swimming, surfing, and surf fishing. In the summer, lifeguards are posted at the beach. Many will remember a beach camp that was once popular here. Well, that sucker is gone, wiped out by a storm.

Campsites, facilities: There are 127 sites for tents or RVs up to 31 feet (no hookups), one hike-in/bike-in area for up to 24 people, and one group tent site for 9–50 people. Picnic tables and fire rings are provided. Restrooms with flush toilets and coin showers, drinking water, a dump station, a seasonal visitors center, Wi-Fi, summer programs, and a summer convenience store are available. Some facilities are wheelchair-accessible. Leashed pets are permitted. Front gates close at 10 P.M. and reopen at 7 A.M.

Reservations, fees: Reservations are recommended at 800/444-7275 (800/444-PARK) or www.reserveamerica.com ($8 reservation fee). Sites are $45 per night, $10 per night for each additional vehicle, $10 per person per night for hike-in/bike-in site, $225 per night for group tent site. Open year-round.

Directions: From Santa Monica, drive north on Highway 1 for 28 miles to the park entrance (signed) on the right.

From Oxnard, drive south on Highway 1 for 20 miles to the park entrance (signed) on the left.

Contact: California State Parks, Angeles District, 818/880-0350, www.parks.ca.gov.

18 MALIBU BEACH RV PARK

🏊 🛶 🏕 🎣 ♿ 🚐 ⛺

Scenic rating: 7

in Malibu

Map 13.1, page 741

This is one of the few privately developed RV parks in the region that provides some sites for tent campers as well. It's one of the nicer spots in the area, set on a bluff overlooking the Pacific Ocean, near both Malibu Pier (for fishing) and Paradise Cove. Each RV site and many of the tent sites have views of either the ocean or adjacent mountains. Sites with ocean views are charged a small premium. Whale-watching is best in March and April, and then again in October and November. Dolphin-watching is popular year-round.

Campsites, facilities: There are 35 sites for tents (four-person maximum per site) and 140 sites with full or partial hookups (30 and 50 amps) for RVs; some sites are pull-through. Picnic tables and barbecue grills are provided. Restrooms with showers, spa, recreation room, playground, coin laundry, Wi-Fi, dog walk area, propane gas, ice, cable TV, dump station, and convenience store are available. Some facilities are wheelchair-accessible. Leashed pets are permitted, except in the tent area, and certain breeds are prohibited.

Reservations, fees: Reservations are recommended at 800/622-6052. Ocean-view RV sites (full hookups) are $80–115 per night, mountain-view RV sites (full hookups) are $66–95 per night, RV sites with partial hookups are $53–90 per night, tent sites are $42–60 per night, $10 per night for each additional vehicle, $5 per person per night for more than two people, $3 per pet per night. Discounts available weekdays and off-season. Credit cards accepted. Open year-round.

Directions: Drive on Pacific Coast Highway/

Highway 1 to the Malibu area. The park is two miles north of the intersection of Highway 1 and Malibu Canyon Road on the east side of the road.

Contact: Malibu Beach RV Park, 310/456-6052, www.maliburv.com.

19 DOCKWEILER BEACH RV PARK

🚴 🏊 🏕 ♿ 🚐

Scenic rating: 8

near Manhattan Beach

Map 13.1, page 741

Dockweiler is L.A. County's only RV campground on the beach. This layover spot for coast cruisers is just a hop from the beach and the Pacific Ocean. There is access to a 26-mile-long coastal bike path.

Campsites, facilities: There are 117 sites with full hookups (20, 30, and 50 amps) for RVs up to 37 feet. No tents. Picnic tables and barbecue grills are provided. Restrooms with flush toilets and showers, dump station, and coin laundry are available. Some facilities are wheelchair-accessible. You can buy supplies nearby. Leashed pets are permitted, with a two-dog limit.

Reservations, fees: Reservations are accepted at 310/322-4951 or 800/950-7275 ($10 reservation fee). RV sites (full hookups) are $55–65 per night (depending on location and view), $3 per person per night for more than four people, $3 per pet per night. Holiday rates are an additional $4 per night. Open year-round, except in January. Some credit cards accepted.

Directions: From Santa Monica, take I-405 south to the 105/Imperial Highway. Take the 105 and continue as it becomes Imperial Highway. When road name changes to Imperial Highway, drive west for four miles to the park (signed) on the left.

Contact: Dockweiler Beach RV Park, Los Angeles County, 310/322-7036, www.beaches.lacounty.gov.

20 BOLSA CHICA STATE BEACH

🏃 🚴 🏊 🛶 🐕 ♿ 🚐

Scenic rating: 7

near Huntington Beach

Map 13.1, page 741

This state beach extends three miles from Seal Beach to Huntington Beach City Pier. A bikeway connects it with Huntington State Beach, seven miles to the south. Across the road from Bolsa Chica is the 1,000-acre Bolsa Chica Ecological Preserve, managed by the Department of Fish and Game. The campground consists of basically a beachfront parking lot, but a popular one at that. A great little walk is available at the adjacent Bolsa Chica State Reserve, a 1.5-mile loop that provides an escape from the parking lot and entry into the 530-acre nature reserve, complete with egrets, pelicans, and many shorebirds. Lifeguard service is available during the summer. This camp has a seven-day maximum stay during the summer and a 14-day maximum stay during the winter. Surf fishing is popular here for perch, cabezon, small sharks, and croaker. There are also occasional runs of grunion, a small fish that spawns in hordes on the sandy beaches of Southern California.

Campsites, facilities: There are 55 sites with full hookups (30 and 50 amps) available in a parking lot configuration for RVs up to 48 feet. Fire rings are provided. Restrooms with flush toilets and coin showers, drinking water, Wi-Fi, dump station, picnic areas, bicycle trail, volleyball, basketball, and food service (seasonal) are available. Some facilities are wheelchair-accessible, including a paved ramp for wheelchair access to the beach. Leashed pets are permitted at campsites.

Reservations, fees: Reservations are accepted at 800/444-7275 (800/444-PARK) or www.reserveamerica.com ($8 reservation fee). Tent and RV sites (hookups) are $50 per night, premium beachfront sites are $65 per night, $10 per night for each additional vehicle. Open year-round.

Directions: Drive on Highway 1 to the park entrance (1.5 miles north of Huntington Beach).

Contact: Bolsa Chica State Beach, 714/846-3460, www.parks.ca.gov.

21 PARSON'S LANDING HIKE-IN

🏃 🏊 🛶 5% ⛰

Scenic rating: 10

on Catalina Island

Map 13.1, page 741　　　　　　**BEST (**

This primitive campground is one of five on Catalina Island. It is set on the island's northern end, seven miles from the island's isthmus and the village of Two Harbors. If you want to try to avoid the crowds, this is the area to visit; forget Avalon and head instead to Two Harbors.

Note: The ferry to Avalon is available from Long Beach, Dana Point, or San Pedro. The ferry to Two Harbors is available only from San Pedro. Once at Avalon, there is a Safari Bus (310/510-2800) to Two Harbors that runs once a day, departing at noon, for $26–32 one-way.

Campsites, facilities: There are eight tent sites, each for up to six campers. Picnic tables, barbecue and fire rings, and a locker with firewood and 2.5 gallons of drinking water are provided. Chemical toilets are available. There are no sun shades, so bring your own. Firewood, charcoal, and propane sold only at ranger station (May through Labor Day). No radios permitted.

Campers must first check-in at Two Harbors Visitor Services to get a key for a lock box containing wood and water. A concessionaire rents a full array of camping equipment, including tents, sleeping bags, pads, stoves and lanterns.

Reservations, fees: Reservations are required at 310/510-8368 ($25 reservation fee) or www.visitcatalinaisland.com; make group reservations for 20 or more at 310/510-8368, ext.

1414 or www.visitcatalinaisland.com (no reservation fee for reservations made online). Sites are $16–18 per person per night, $8–9 per person per night for ages 11 and under, plus $14 first night for wood and water. A fee is charged for the ferry ride to Avalon at Catalina Island from Dana Point, Long Beach, or San Pedro. Discounts available weekdays and off-season. Open year-round, weather permitting, with a 10-day maximum stay.

Directions: Take ferry boat ride to Avalon. From Avalon, take shuttle bus to Two Harbors. At Two Harbors, check in at the visitor information booth to validate your camping permit and obtain locker key for water and wood. From Two Harbors, hike seven miles to campsites. Note: A shuttle boat is sometimes available from Two Harbors to Emerald Bay; from Emerald Bay, it is a 1.5-mile hike to the campground.

Contact: For ferry information, camp reservations, or general information: Avalon, 310/510-2800; Two Harbors Visitor Services, 310/510-4205; concessionaire 310/510-8368; www.visitcatalinaisland.com or www.visit-twoharbors.com.

22 TWO HARBORS

Scenic rating: 10

on Catalina Island

Map 13.1, page 741   **BEST (**

This campground is only 0.25 mile away from the village of Two Harbors. Nearby attractions include the Two Harbors Dive Station with snorkeling equipment, paddleboard rentals, and scuba tank fills to 3,000 psi. There are guided tours of the island and a scheduled bus service between Two Harbors and Avalon; the bus stops at all the interior campgrounds. An excellent hike is the nine-mile round-trip from Two Harbors to Emerald Bay, featuring a gorgeous coast and pretty valleys. A 0.25-mile hike is required to reach this campground.

Note: The ferry to Avalon is available from Long Beach, Dana Point, or San Pedro. The ferry to Two Harbors is available only from San Pedro. Once at Avalon, there is a Safari Bus (310/510-2800) to Two Harbors that runs once a day, departing at noon, for $26–32 one-way.

Campsites, facilities: There are 42 sites for tents, three group sites for up to 25 people each, and 13 tent cabins for up to six people each. Picnic tables and fire grills are provided. Drinking water, sun shades (at most sites), cold showers, and chemical toilets are available. Tent cabin sites also include cots, camp stove, and lantern. No radios permitted. Firewood, charcoal, and propane are sold at the ranger station (May through Labor Day) and can also be ordered in advance. A general store, restaurant and saloon, snack bar, tennis courts, volleyball, coin laundry, and hot showers are available in the town of Two Harbors.

Campers must first check-in at Two Harbors Visitor Services to get a key for a lock box containing wood and water. A concessionaire rents a full array of camping equipment, including tents, sleeping bags, pads, stoves and lanterns.

Reservations, fees: Reservations are required at 310/510-8368 ($25 reservation fee) or online at www.visitcatalinaisland.com; make group reservations for 20 or more at 310/510-8368, ext. 1412 (no reservation fee for reservations made online). Sites are $21 per person per night, $12 per night for ages 11 and under. A fee is charged for the round-trip ferry ride to Avalon at Catalina Island from Dana Point, Long Beach, or San Pedro. Discounts midweek and in winter. Open year-round, weather permitting, except for tent cabins, which are open April through October. Maximum stay is 10 days.

Directions: Take ferry boat ride to Avalon. From Avalon, take shuttle bus to Two Harbors. At Two Harbors, check in at the visitor information booth to validate your camping permit and obtain locker key for water and wood. From Two Harbors, hike 0.25 mile to campground.

Contact: For ferry information, camp reservations, or general information: Avalon, 310/510-2800; Two Harbors Visitor Services, 310/510-4205; concessionaire 310/510-8368; www.visitcatalinaisland.com or www.visittwoharbors.com.

23 LITTLE HARBOR HIKE-IN
🏃🏊🚣5%⛺

Scenic rating: 10

on Catalina Island

Map 13.1, page 741   **BEST (**

There is plenty to do here: You can swim, dive, fish, or go for day hikes. There are two sandy beaches near this camp. One is great for swimming and snorkeling, and the other has surf for boogie boarding. A Native American historic site is nearby. Two Harbors has several excellent hikes, including the nine-mile excursion to Emerald Bay. Of course, you could always take the shuttle bus. Many folks consider this to be the pick of the campgrounds on the island. It is a gorgeous place—small wonder that some big Hollywood flicks have been shot here.

Note: The ferry to Avalon is available from Long Beach, Dana Point or San Pedro. The ferry to Two Harbors is available only from San Pedro. Once at Avalon, there is a Safari Bus (310/510-2800) to Two Harbors that runs once a day, departing at noon, for $26–32 one-way (depending on destination).

Campsites, facilities: There are 21 tent sites, including eight group sites. Picnic tables and fire rings are provided. Drinking water, cold showers, sun shades (at most sites), pay telephone, shuttle bus service, and chemical toilets are available. No radios permitted. Wood, charcoal, and propane are available from the ranger station (May through Labor Day), and it is recommended that you order in advance. Kayak and snorkel gear rentals are available in Two Harbors.

Campers must first check-in at Two Harbors Visitor Services to get a key for a lock box containing wood and water. A concessionaire rents a full array of camping equipment, including tents, sleeping bags, pads, stoves and lanterns.

Reservations, fees: Reservations are required at 310/510-8368 ($25 reservation fee) or online at www.visitcatalinaisland.com; make group reservations for 20 or more at 310/510-8368, ext. 1414 (no reservation fee for reservations made online). Sites are $16–18 per person per night, $8–9 per person per night for ages 11 and under. Tent cabins are $50 per night. A fee is charged for the round-trip ferry ride to Avalon at Catalina Island from Dana Point, Long Beach, or San Pedro. Discounts mid-week and in winter. Open year-round, weather permitting, with a maximum stay of 10 days.

Directions: Take ferry boat ride to Avalon. From Avalon, take shuttle bus (or hike or bike) to Little Harbor. Check in at the visitor information booth to validate your camping permit and obtain locker key for water and wood. From Little Harbor, hike 6.8 miles to the campground. The campground is about 16 miles from Avalon.

Contact: For ferry information, camp reservations, or general information: Avalon, 310/510-2800; Two Harbors Visitor Services, 310/510-4205; concessionaire 310/510-8368; Wet Spot Rentals, 310/510-2229; www.visitcatalinaisland.com or www.visittwoharbors.com.

24 BLACK JACK HIKE-IN
🏃🏊🚣5%⛺

Scenic rating: 7

on Catalina Island

Map 13.1, page 741

This camp is named after Mount Black Jack (2,008 feet), the island's highest point, and it is a great place to hunker down for a spell. It's also the site of the old Black Jack Mine. This is the least-popular campground on the island, viewed by most as a stopover site, not a base camp. From Black Jack Junction (accessible by shuttle bus), it is a 1.5-mile hike to the camp. Note that shuttle bus service is limited October through mid-June. The camp is set at 1,500 feet elevation. The camp is nine miles from Avalon and 11.8 miles from Two Harbors. If you stand in just the right spot, you can see the mainland, but Los Angeles will seem like a million miles away.

Note: The ferry to Avalon is available from Long Beach, Dana Point, or San Pedro. The ferry to Two Harbors is available only from San Pedro. Once at Avalon, there is a Safari Bus (310/510-2800) to Two Harbors that runs once a day, departing at noon, for $26–32 one-way (depending on destination).

Campsites, facilities: There are 11 tent sites with a maximum of six campers per site. Drinking water, picnic tables, fire rings, cold showers, and a locker with firewood are provided. No radios permitted. Chemical toilets are available. A pay phone is nearby. Firewood, charcoal, and propane sold only at ranger station (May through Labor Day). Kayak and snorkel gear at Two Harbors is available at West End Diver Center.

Campers must first check-in at Two Harbors Visitor Services to get a key for a lock box containing wood and water. A concessionaire rents a full array of camping equipment, including tents, sleeping bags, pads, stoves and lanterns.

Reservations, fees: Reservations are required at 310/510-8368 ($25 reservation fee) or online at www.visitcatalinaisland.com; make group reservations for 20 or more at 310/510-8368, ext. 1414 ($15 reservation fee). There is no reservation fee for reservations made online. Sites are $16–18 per person per night, $8–9 per person per night for ages 11 and under. A fee is charged for the round-trip ferry ride to Avalon at Catalina Island from Dana Point, Long Beach, or San Pedro. Discounts mid-week and in winter. Open year-round, weather permitting, with a maximum stay of 10 days.

Directions: Take ferry boat ride to Avalon.

From Avalon, take the shuttle bus to Black Jack Junction. Check in at the visitor information booth to validate your camping permit and obtain locker key for water and wood. From Black Jack Junction hike 1.3 miles to the campground.

Contact: For ferry information and reservations: Avalon, 310/510-2800; Two Harbors Visitor Services, 310/510-4205; concessionaire 310/510-8368; www.visitcatalinaisland.com or www.visittwoharbors.com. For boat-in camping: www.campingcatalinaisland.com.

25 CATALINA ISLAND BOAT-IN

🚶 🏊 🛶 🎣 🏕 🐴 5% ⛺

Scenic rating: 10

on Catalina Island

Map 13.1, page 741   **BEST (**

Here is one of the most unusual and best camping experiences in California: the 17 boat-in sites at nine locations on Catalina Island. These primitive camps are on the north shore of the island, between Avalon and Two Harbors. You reach them by private boat or by paddling there (kayak rentals available). There are no overnight powerboat rentals on the island. A ranger checks each boat-in site daily and collects any fees. There are no moorings, so you must anchor your boat and use a dinghy to reach shore. Since these sites are primitive, they have no toilets, no drinking water, no fire rings, and no sun shade. That means you must plan your trip carefully.

Note: The ferry to Avalon is available from Long Beach, Dana Point or San Pedro. The ferry to Two Harbors is only available from San Pedro. Once at Avalon, there is a Safari Bus (310/510-2800) to Two Harbors that runs once a day, departing at noon, for $26–32 one-way.

Campsites, facilities: There are 17 primitive boat-in sites for tents. Picnic tables are provided. There are no toilets; bring your own portable chemical toilet or buy waste-disposal bags from the ranger. There is no drinking water or shade. No campfires or beach fires are allowed. Charcoal and propane stoves are permitted; firewood, charcoal, and propane sold only at ranger station (May through Labor Day). No radios permitted. Garbage must be packed out. Kayak and snorkel gear at Two Harbors is available at West End Diver Center. No moorings. Leashed pets are permitted.

Reservations, fees: Reservations are accepted at 310/510-8368 ($15 reservation fee) or online at www.visitcatalinaisland.com (there is no reservation fee for reservations made online). With reservations, sites are $16 per adult per night, $8 per child (age 11 and younger) per night. Without reservations, sites are $20 per adult per night, $10 per child per night. Fishing permitted with license. Open year-round, weather permitting, with a maximum stay of 10 days.

Directions: Boat-in or take ferry boat ride to Avalon. From Avalon or Two Harbors, rent kayak and paddle to campsite or reach the camp by private boat.

Contact: For ferry information, camp reservations, or general information: Avalon, 310/510-2800; Two Harbors Visitor Services, 310/510-4205, www.campingcatalinaisland. com.

26 HERMIT GULCH
🏃 🚴 ⛵ 🛶 🏕 5% ⛰

Scenic rating: 10

on Catalina Island

Map 13.1, page 741

This is the closest campground to the town of Avalon, the gateway to Catalina. Reaching the camp requires a 1.5-mile hike up Avalon Canyon. If you're making a tourist trip, there are a ton of things to do here: Visit Avalon's underwater city park, play the nine-hole golf course, rent a bicycle, or visit the famous casino. Scenic tours, glass-bottomed boat tours, and Wrigley Memorial and Botanical Gardens are available. Fishing can be excellent,

including angling for white seabass, yellowtail, and, in the fall, even marlin. The best hiking experience in the Avalon area is found by taking the shuttle bus to the Airport in the Sky and from there hiking along Empire Landing Road. The route traces the island's curving, hilly northern shore, providing great views of secluded beaches, coves, and rock formations, and a chance to see wildlife, at times even buffalo. Note that free hiking permits are required. Also, if cycling outside of Avalon, a $50 permit is required! Taxi service is available in Avalon, but it is expensive.

Note: The ferry to Avalon is available from Long Beach, Dana Point, or San Pedro. The ferry to Two Harbors is available only from San Pedro. Once at Avalon, there is a Safari Bus (310/510-2800) to Two Harbors that runs once a day, departing at noon, for $26–32 one-way (depending on destination).

Campsites, facilities: There are 40 sites for tents, nine tent cabins, and one group site for up to 35 people. Picnic tables and barbecue pits are provided. Restrooms with flush toilets and coin showers, drinking water, ice, lockers, playground, coin microwave, vending machines, and pay phone are available. No radios permitted. Fires are not allowed; any fires will result in a severe fine. Charcoal and propane sold only at ranger station (May through Labor Day). Some camping equipment is available for rent. Kayak and snorkel gear is available at West End Diver Center at Two Harbors.

Campers must first check-in at Two Harbors Visitor Services to get a key for a lock box containing wood and water. A concessionaire rents a full array of camping equipment, including tents, sleeping bags, pads, stoves and lanterns.

Reservations, fees: Reservations are required at 310/510-8368 ($25 reservation fee) or www. visitcatalinaisland.com (no reservation fee for reservations made online). Sites are $21 per night, $12 per person per night for ages 11 and under. Tent cabins are $50 per night. A fee is charged for the round-trip ferry ride to Avalon at Catalina Island from Dana Point, Long

Beach, or San Pedro. Discounts mid-week or in winter. Open year-round, weather permitting, with a maximum stay of 10 days.

Directions: Take ferry boat ride to Avalon. Check in at the visitor information booth to validate your camping permit and obtain locker key for water and wood. In Avalon at Sumner Avenue, walk up Avalon Canyon (follow the "Avalon Canyon Road" sign) for 1.5 miles to the campground. The camp is across from the picnic area.

Contact: For ferry information, camp reservations, or general information: Avalon, 310/510-2800; Two Harbors Visitor Services, 310/510-4205; concessionaire 310/510-8368; www.visitcatalinaisland.com or www.visit-twoharbors.com.

27 SYCAMORE FLATS
🐕 🚐 ⛰️

Scenic rating: 7

on Big Rock Creek in Angeles National Forest
Map 13.2, page 742

Sycamore Flats is a developed camp just inside the northern boundary of Angeles National Forest, set at 4,200 feet on the southwest flank of Pinyon Ridge. While there are no trails leading out from this camp, a trailhead is at South Fork, which is two miles to the south.

Campsites, facilities: There are 12 sites for tents or RVs up to 18 feet (no hookups). Picnic tables and fire grills are provided. Drinking water and vault toilets are available seasonally; there is no drinking water in winter or in dry years. Garbage must be packed out. Leashed pets are permitted.

Reservations, fees: Reservations are not accepted. There is no fee for camping. An Adventure Pass ($30 annual fee or a $5 daily pass) is required. Open year-round, weather permitting.

Directions: From Palmdale (at the junction of Highway 14 and Highway 138), take Highway 138 southeast and drive about 10 miles to Pearblossom and Longview Road. Turn south (right) and drive a short distance to Avenue W/Valyermo Road. Turn left on Avenue W/Valyermo Road and drive about 20 miles into the national forest (past the ranger station) to Big Rock Road. Turn right on Big Rock Road and drive about two miles to the campground entrance.

Contact: Angeles National Forest, Santa Clara/Mojave Rivers Ranger District, 661/269-2808, www.fs.usda.gov/angeles.

28 SOUTH FORK
🥾 🏊 🐕 🚐 ⛰️

Scenic rating: 7

on Big Rock Creek in Angeles National Forest
Map 13.2, page 742

This is an excellent trailhead camp set at 4,500 feet elevation along South Fork Creek. One trail climbs 2.2 miles to the west to Devils Punchbowl County Park, topping out at Devils Chair (the trail includes a steep descent and climb). There are two other options: One is routed south along Big Rock Creek, and the other heads east on High Desert National Recreation Trail (also called Manzanita Trail).

Campsites, facilities: There are 21 sites for tents or RVs up to 16 feet (no hookups). Picnic tables and fire rings are provided. Vault toilets are available. No drinking water is available. Garbage must be packed out. Leashed pets are permitted.

Reservations, fees: Reservations are not accepted. There is no fee for camping. An Adventure Pass ($30 annual fee or a $5 daily pass) is required. Open year-round, weather permitting.

Directions: From Palmdale (at the junction of Highway 14 and Highway 138), take Highway 138 southeast and drive about 10 miles to Pearblossom and Longview Road. Turn south (right) and drive a short distance to Avenue W/Valyermo Road. Turn left on Avenue W/Valyermo Road and drive about 20 miles into the national forest (past the ranger station) to Big Rock Road. Turn right on Big Rock Road and drive about two miles up the canyon (past

the Sycamore Flat campground entrance) to the South Fork campground entrance.
Contact: Angeles National Forest, Santa Clara/Mojave Rivers Ranger District, 661/269-2808, www.fs.usda.gov/angeles.

29 TABLE MOUNTAIN

Scenic rating: 6

in Angeles National Forest

Map 13.2, page 742

This is a family campground that accommodates both tents and RVs. The road leading in is a paved two-lane county road, easily accessible by any vehicle. The nearby Big Pines Visitor Information Center, one mile to the south, can provide maps and information on road conditions. The camp elevation is 7,200 feet. A rough road for four-wheel-drive rigs is available out of camp that leads north along the Table Mountain Ridge.

Campsites, facilities: There are 115 sites for tents or RVs up to 32 feet (no hookups) and a group site for up to 32 people. Picnic tables and fire pits are provided. Drinking water, vault toilets, and an amphitheater (available for groups by reservation) are available. Some facilities are wheelchair accessible. Leashed pets are permitted.

Reservations, fees: Reservations are accepted at 877/444-6777 or www.recreation.gov ($9 reservation fee). Single sites are $20 per night, double sites $40 per night, and the group site is $80 per night. Open May to November, weather permitting.

Directions: Drive on I-15 to Cajon Junction (north of San Bernardino) and the exit for Highway 138 west. Take that exit and drive west on Highway 138 to Angeles Crest Highway/Highway 2. Turn west on Angeles Crest Highway and drive five miles to Wrightwood, then continue for three miles to Big Pines and Table Mountain Road. Turn right on Table Mountain Road and drive one mile to the campground.

Contact: Angeles National Forest, Santa Clara/Mojave Rivers Ranger District, 661/269-2808, www.fs.usda.gov/angeles; Big Pines Information Station, 760/249-3504.

30 BUCKHORN

Scenic rating: 9

near Snowcrest Ridge in Angeles National Forest

Map 13.2, page 742   **BEST (**

This is a prime jump-off spot for backpackers in Angeles National Forest. The camp is set at 6,300 feet elevation among huge pine and cedar trees, along a small creek near Mount Waterman (8,038 feet). A great day hike begins here, a tromp down to Cooper Canyon and the PCT; hikers will be rewarded by beautiful Cooper Falls on this three-hour round-trip. Want a weekend trip? You got it: The Burkhart National Recreational Trail descends into Caruthers Canyon where hikers can access the High Desert National Recreational Trail. From here, you can head east to Devil's Punchbowl County Park to Vincent's Gap and the Pacific Crest Trail.

Campsites, facilities: There are 38 sites for tents or RVs up to 18 feet (no hookups). Picnic tables and fire pits are provided. Drinking water and vault toilets are available. Some facilities are wheelchair accessible. Leashed pets are permitted.

Reservations, fees: Reservations are not accepted. Sites are $12 per night. An Adventure Pass ($30 annual fee or $5 daily fee per parked vehicle) is required. Open April through mid-November, weather permitting.

Directions: From Pasadena, drive north on I-210 for four miles to the exit for Highway 2/Angeles Crest Highway. Take that exit and drive northeast on Highway 2 for 35 miles to the signed campground entrance.

Contact: Angeles National Forest, Los Angeles River Ranger District, 818/899-1900, www.fs.usda.gov/angeles.

31 JACKSON FLATS GROUP CAMP WALK-IN

Scenic rating: 4

near the Pacific Crest Trail in
Angeles National Forest

Map 13.2, page 742

This is a good spot for a group to overnight, assess themselves, and get information before heading out into the surrounding wildlands. The camp is set in the Angeles National Forest high country at 7,500 feet elevation, near the end of a short spur road. It takes a 200-yard walk to reach this campground from the parking area. There are two nature trails and an observation deck on site. The Pacific Crest Trail passes just north of camp and can be reached by a short connecting link trail.

Campsites, facilities: There are five group tent sites for 30–40 people each. Picnic tables, food lockers, and fire pits are provided. Drinking water and flush toilets are available. Leashed pets are permitted.

Reservations, fees: Reservations are required at 877/444-6777 or www.recreation. gov ($9 reservation fee, search for Jackson Flat not Flats). Sites are $130–150 per night. Open early May through October, weather permitting.

Directions: Drive on I-15 to Cajon Junction (north of San Bernardino) and the exit for Highway 138 west. Take that exit and drive west on Highway 138 to Angeles Crest Highway/Highway 2. Turn west on Angeles Crest Highway and drive five miles to Wrightwood, then continue for three miles to Big Pines. Bear left (still on Angeles Crest Highway) and drive two miles to a Forest Service road (opposite the sign for Grassy Hollow Campground). Turn right and drive one mile to the campground parking lot. Walk 200 yards to the campground.

Contact: Angeles National Forest, Santa Clara/ Mojave Rivers Ranger District, 661/269-2808 or 760/249-3526 for information, www. fs.usda.gov/angeles.

32 APPLETREE

Scenic rating: 6

near Jackson Lake in Angeles National Forest

Map 13.2, page 742

This is one of four camps set on Big Pines "Highway" near Jackson Lake. This "lake" is more of a pond and is about 0.5 mile to the west, just up the road. Lake and Peavine Camps are between Appletree and Jackson Lake, while Mountain Oak is just beyond the lake. Any questions? Rangers can answer them at the nearby Big Pines Information Station and ski complex. The elevation is 6,200 feet.

Campsites, facilities: There are eight tent sites. Picnic tables and fire rings are provided. Vault toilets are available. There is no drinking water. Garbage must be packed out. Some facilities are wheelchair accessible. Leashed pets are permitted.

Reservations, fees: Reservations are not accepted. There is no fee for camping. An Adventure Pass ($30 annual fee or a $5 daily pass) is required. Open year-round, weather permitting.

Directions: Drive on I-15 to Cajon Junction (north of San Bernardino) and the exit for Highway 138 west. Take that exit and drive west on Highway 138 to Angeles Crest Highway/Highway 2. Turn west on Angeles Crest Highway and drive five miles to Wrightwood, and then continue for three miles to Big Pines and Big Pines Highway/ County Road N4. Bear right on Big Pines Highway and drive two miles to the campground.

Contact: Angeles National Forest, Santa Clara/ Mojave Rivers Ranger District, 661/269-2808, www.fs.usda.gov/angeles.

33 MOUNTAIN OAK

Scenic rating: 4

near Jackson Lake in Angeles National Forest

Map 13.2, page 742

This is one of four camps within a mile of little Jackson Lake on Big Pines Highway. The others are Lake, Peavine, and Appletree. This camp is about 0.25 mile northwest of the lake. The elevation is 6,200 feet.

Campsites, facilities: There are 17 sites for tents or RVs up to 18 feet (no hookups). Picnic tables and fire pits are provided. Drinking water and flush toilets are available. Groceries and propane gas are nearby. Leashed pets are permitted.

Reservations, fees: Reservations are accepted at 877/444-6777 or www.recreation.gov ($9 reservation fee). Sites are $20 per night. Open May through November, weather permitting.

Directions: Drive on I-15 to Cajon Junction (north of San Bernardino) and the exit for Highway 138 west. Take that exit and drive west on Highway 138 to Angeles Crest Highway/Highway 2. Turn west on Angeles Crest Highway and drive five miles to Wrightwood, and then continue for three miles to Big Pines and Big Pines Highway/County Road N4. Bear right on Big Pines Highway and drive three miles to the campground.

Contact: Angeles National Forest, Santa Clara/Mojave Rivers Ranger District, 661/269-2808, www.fs.usda.gov/angeles.

34 LAKE CAMPGROUND

Scenic rating: 8

on Jackson Lake in Angeles National Forest

Map 13.2, page 742

This is a pretty setting on the southeast shore of little Jackson Lake. Of the four camps within a mile, this is the only one right beside the lake. The elevation is 6,100 feet.

Campsites, facilities: There are eight sites for tents or RVs up to 18 feet (no hookups). Picnic tables, food lockers, and fire pits are provided. Drinking water and vault toilets are available. Leashed pets are permitted.

Reservations, fees: Reservations are accepted at 877/444-6777 or www.recreation.gov ($9 reservation fee). Sites are $20 per night.

Open May through November, weather permitting.

Directions: Drive on I-15 to Cajon Junction (north of San Bernardino) and the exit for Highway 138 west. Take that exit and drive west on Highway 138 to Angeles Crest Highway/Highway 2. Turn west on Angeles Crest Highway and drive five miles to Wrightwood, and then continue for three miles to Big Pines and Big Pines Highway/County Road N4. Bear right on Big Pines Highway and drive 2.5 miles to the campground.

Contact: Angeles National Forest, Santa Clara/Mojave Rivers Ranger District, 661/269-2808, www.fs.usda.gov/angeles.

35 PEAVINE

Scenic rating: 4

near Jackson Lake in Angeles National Forest

Map 13.2, page 742

This tiny camp is one of four in the immediate area, just 0.5 mile east of little eight-acre Jackson Lake. This area is popular for snow play in the winter. The elevation is 6,100 feet.

Campsites, facilities: There are four tent sites. Picnic tables and fire pits are provided. Vault toilets are available. There is no drinking water. Garbage must be packed out. A store and propane gas are nearby. Some facilities are wheelchair accessible. Leashed pets are permitted.

Reservations, fees: Reservations are not accepted. There is no fee for camping. An Adventure Pass ($30 annual fee or a $5 daily pass) is required. Open year-round, weather permitting.

Directions: Drive on I-15 to Cajon Junction (north of San Bernardino) and the exit for Highway 138 west. Take that exit and drive west on Highway 138 to Angeles Crest Highway/Highway 2. Turn west on Angeles Crest Highway and drive five miles to Wrightwood, and then continue for three miles to Big Pines and Big Pines Highway/County Road N4.

Bear right on Big Pines Highway and drive and drive 2.7 miles to the campground.

Contact: Angeles National Forest, Santa Clara/Mojave Rivers Ranger District, 661/269-2808, www.fs.usda.gov/angeles.

36 BLUE RIDGE
🏃 🎿 🏠 🚗 ⛺

Scenic rating: 8

on the Pacific Crest Trail in
Angeles National Forest

Map 13.2, page 742

Blue Ridge is set high in Angeles National Forest at 8,000 feet elevation and makes a jump-off spot for a multiday backpacking trip. The Pacific Crest Trail runs right alongside the camp. Guffy, also aside the PCT, provides an option two miles to the southeast. Note that some of the surrounding area is closed to vehicles to protect the yellow-legged frog.

Campsites, facilities: There are eight sites for tents or RVs up to 20 feet. Picnic tables and fire rings are provided. Vault toilets are available. No drinking water is available. Garbage must be packed out. Leashed pets are permitted.

Reservations, fees: Reservations are not accepted. There is no fee for camping. An Adventure Pass ($30 annual fee or a $5 daily pass) is required. Open May through November, weather permitting.

Directions: Drive on I-15 to Cajon Junction (north of San Bernardino) and the exit for Highway 138 west. Take that exit and drive west on Highway 138 to Angeles Crest Highway/Highway 2. Turn west on Angeles Crest Highway and drive five miles to Wrightwood, and then continue for three miles to Big Pines. Bear left (still on Angeles Crest Highway) and drive 1.5 miles to Blue Ridge Road (adjacent to Inspiration Point). Turn left on Blue Ridge Road and drive three miles to the campground.

Contact: Angeles National Forest, Santa Clara/Mojave Rivers Ranger District, 661/269-2808

or 661/269-2808 for information, www.fs.usda.gov/angeles.

37 LUPINE WALK-IN
🏃 🎿 🏠 5% ⛺

Scenic rating: 7

on Prairie Fork Creek in
Angeles National Forest

Map 13.2, page 742

This little-known, hard-to-reach camp, set at 6,500 feet elevation along Prairie Fork Creek, is now a walk-in camp. It is closed to vehicles in order to protect the yellow-legged frog. A challenging butt-kicker hike on a primitive trail starts here. The trail leads from the camp over Pine Mountain Ridge, down into a canyon, and then winds to the east up Dawson Peak—long, difficult, and completed by few.

Campsites, facilities: There are 11 sites for tents only. Picnic tables and fire pits are provided. Vault toilets are available. No drinking water is available. Garbage must be packed out. Leashed pets are permitted.

Reservations, fees: Reservations are not accepted. There is no fee for camping. An Adventure Pass ($30 annual fee or a $5 daily pass) is required. Open May through November, weather permitting.

Directions: Drive on I-15 to Cajon Junction (north of San Bernardino) and the exit for Highway 138 west. Take that exit and drive west on Highway 138 to Angeles Crest Highway/Highway 2. Turn west on Angeles Crest Highway and drive five miles to Wrightwood, and then continue for three miles to Big Pines. Bear left (still on Angeles Crest Highway) and drive 1.5 miles to Blue Ridge Road (adjacent to Inspiration Point). Turn left on Blue Ridge Road and drive five miles to the locked gate. From here, you can hike, bike, or ride a horse for three miles to the campground.

Contact: Angeles National Forest, Santa Clara/Mojave Rivers Ranger District, 661/269-2808, www.fs.usda.gov/angeles.

38 GUFFY HIKE-IN
🏃 🐕 5% ⛺

Scenic rating: 7

on the Pacific Crest Trail in
Angeles National Forest

Map 13.2, page 742

A short trail right out of this camp connects with the Pacific Crest Trail, making Guffy a backpacker's special. The camp and access road are closed to vehicles in order to protect the yellow-legged frog. The elevation is 8,300 feet.

Campsites, facilities: There are six tent sites. Picnic tables and fire rings are provided. Vault toilets are available. No drinking water is available. Garbage must be packed out. Leashed pets are permitted.

Reservations, fees: Reservations are not accepted. An Adventure Pass ($30 annual fee or a $5 daily pass) is required. Open May through November, weather permitting.

Directions: From I-15 near Cajon, take Highway 138 west. Turn west on Angeles Crest Highway/Highway 2 and drive five miles to Wrightwood. Continue for three miles to Big Pines. Bear left and continue on Angeles Crest Highway for 1.5 miles to Blue Ridge Road. Turn left (opposite Inspiration Point) on Blue Ridge Road and park. From here, you can hike, bike, or ride a horse six miles to the campground.

Contact: Angeles National Forest, Santa Clara/Mojave Rivers Ranger District, 661/269-2808, www.fs.usda.gov/angeles.

39 MOJAVE RIVER FORKS REGIONAL PARK
🏃 🐕 🚐 ⛺

Scenic rating: 7

near Silverwood Lake

Map 13.2, page 742

You can usually find a spot here—it's quiet and enjoyable. Full hookups are a bonus for RV drivers, as is the park's proximity to Silverwood Lake—which is only nine miles away but does not have any sites with hookups. The sites here are well spaced, but the nearby "river" is usually dry. The elevation at this 840-acre park is 3,200 feet.

Campsites, facilities: There are 25 sites with full hookups (20 and 30 amps) for RVs up to 40 feet, 25 sites with no hookups for RVs, 20 walk-in tent sites, and four group sites for 200–300 people each. Several sites are pull-through. Picnic tables and fire grills are provided. Restrooms with showers and flush toilets, drinking water, and a dump station are available. Leashed pets are permitted.

Reservations, fees: Reservations are accepted online for walk-in sites and are required for group sites ($5 reservation fee). Sites with hookups are $30 per night, sites without hookups are $25 per night, walk-in tent sites are $20 per night, $1 per pet per night. Call for group rates. Some credit cards accepted. Campers must show proof of current vehicle registration and insurance. Open year-round.

Directions: From I-15, drive to Cajon Junction (north of San Bernardino) and the exit for Highway 138/Silverwood. Take that exit east and drive nine miles to a fork with Highway 173. Bear left at the fork on Highway 173 and drive six miles to the park on the right.

Contact: Mojave River Forks Regional Park, 760/389-2322, www.sbcountyparks.com.

40 BIG PINE FLATS
🐕 ♿ 🚐 ⛺

Scenic rating: 6

in San Bernardino National Forest

Map 13.2, page 742

This is a favorite staging area for OHV users, with many OHV trails nearby. It is a pretty spot set at 6,800 feet elevation in San Bernardino National Forest and provides a little of both worlds: You are surrounded by wildlands near Redondo Ridge, yet you're not a long drive (about 45 minutes) from Big Bear Lake to the south. Any questions? The firefighters at Big Pine Flats Fire Station, just across the road, can answer them.

Campsites, facilities: There are 19 sites for tents or RVs up to 30 feet (no hookups). Picnic tables and fire grills are provided. Drinking water is available but limited; owners of trailers and RVs should fill up their water tanks prior. Vault toilets are available. Some facilities are wheelchair-accessible. Leashed pets are permitted.

Reservations, fees: Reservations are not accepted. Sites are $20 per night, $5 per night per extra vehicle. Open mid-May through mid-October.

Directions: Drive on Highway 30 to the junction with Highway 330 (east of San Bernardino near Highland). Take Highway 330 north (signed "Mountain Resorts") and drive 35 miles to the dam on Big Bear Lake and a fork with Highway 38. Continue straight on Highway 38 and drive about four miles to the town of Fawnskin and Rim of the World Highway. Turn left and drive seven miles (after 0.5 mile it becomes Forest Road 3N14, a dirt road) to Big Pine Flats Fire Station and the campground on the right.

Contact: San Bernardino National Forest, Mountaintop Ranger District, Big Bear Ranger Station/Discovery Center, 909/382-2790, www.fs.usda.gov/sbnf.

41 BIG PINE GROUP AND EQUESTRIAN
🏃 🐴 ♿ 🚐 ⛺

Scenic rating: 3

in San Bernardino National Forest

Map 13.2, page 742

This camp is adjacent to the Big Pine Flats Fire Station and is used by equestrians and OHV riders. A trailhead for the Pacific Crest Trail is about two miles to the southeast of the camp via Forest Road 3N14. The elevation is 6,700 feet.

Campsites, facilities: There is one group camp for tents or RVs up to 32 feet (no hookups) that can accommodate up to 25 people. Picnic tables and fire grills are provided. Vault toilets and

drinking water are available. Horse facilities include corrals, hitching racks, a staging area, and water troughs. Some facilities are wheelchair-accessible. Leashed pets are permitted.

Reservations, fees: Reservations are required at 877/444-6777 or www.recreation.gov ($9 reservation fee). The camp is $85 per night. Open mid-May through mid-November.

Directions: Drive on Highway 30 to the junction with Highway 330 (east of San Bernardino near Highland). Take Highway 330 north (signed "Mountain Resorts") and drive 35 miles to the dam on Big Bear Lake and a fork with Highway 38. Continue straight on Highway 38 and drive about four miles to the town of Fawnskin and Rim of the World Highway. Turn left and drive seven miles (after 0.5 mile it becomes Forest Road 3N14, a dirt road) to Forest Road 3N16. Turn left and drive 0.25 mile to the campground on the right.

Contact: San Bernardino National Forest, Mountaintop Ranger District, Big Bear Ranger Station/Discovery Center, 909/382-2790, www.fs.usda.gov/sbnf.

42 MANKER FLATS
🏃 🐴 🚐 ⛺

Scenic rating: 7

near Mount Baldy in Angeles National Forest

Map 13.2, page 742　　　　　BEST (

This camp is best known for its proximity to Mount Baldy and the nearby trailhead to reach San Antonio Falls. The trail to San Antonio Falls starts at an elevation of 6,160 feet, 0.3 mile up the road on the left. From here, it's a 1.5-mile saunter on a ski park maintenance road to the waterfall, a pretty 80-footer. The wild and ambitious can continue six more miles and climb to the top of Mount Baldy (10,064 feet) for breathtaking 360-degree views. Making this all-day butt-kicker is like a baptism for Southern California hikers.

Campsites, facilities: There are 21 sites for tents or RVs up to 16 feet (no hookups). Picnic tables and fire grills are provided. Drinking water and flush toilets are available. Leashed pets are permitted. There is no drinking water in dry years.

Reservations, fees: Reservations are not accepted. Sites are $12 per night, $5 per night for each additional vehicle. Open May through September.

Directions: Drive on I-10 to Ontario and the exit for Highway 83. Take that exit and drive north on Highway 83 to Mount Baldy Road. Continue north on Mount Baldy Road for nine miles to the campground.

Contact: Angeles National Forest, San Gabriel River Ranger District, 626/335-1251 or 909/982-2829, www.fs.usda.gov/angeles.

43 APPLEWHITE

Scenic rating: 5

near Lytle Creek in
San Bernardino National Forest

Map 13.2, page 742

Nothing like a little insiders' know-how, especially at this camp, set at 3,300 feet elevation near Lytle Creek. You can reach the Middle Fork of Lytle Creek by driving north from Fontana via Serra Avenue to the Lytle Creek area. To get to the stretch of water that is stocked with trout by the Department of Fish and Game, turn west on Middle Fork Road, which is 1.5 miles before the campground at Apple White. The first mile upstream is stocked every other week in spring and early summer.

Campsites, facilities: There are 44 sites for tents or RVs up to 30 feet (no hookups). Picnic tables and fire grills are provided. Restrooms with flush toilets and drinking water are available. A store is nearby. Some facilities are wheelchair-accessible. Leashed pets are permitted.

Reservations, fees: Reservations are not accepted. Single sites are $10 per night, double sites are $15 per night, $3 per night for each additional vehicle. Open year-round; closed Wednesdays and Thursdays.

Directions: Drive to Ontario and the junction of I-10 and I-15. Take I-15 north and drive 11 miles to the Sierra Avenue exit. Take that exit and turn left, go under the freeway, and continue north (into the national forest) for about nine miles to the campground on the right.

Contact: San Bernardino National Forest, Front Country Ranger District, Lytle Creek Ranger Station, 909/382-2851, www.fs.usda.gov/sbnf.

44 MESA

Scenic rating: 8

on Silverwood Lake in
Silverwood Lake State Recreation Area

Map 13.2, page 742   **BEST (**

This state park campground is on the west side of Silverwood Lake at 3,355 feet elevation, bordered by San Bernardino National Forest to the south and high desert to the north. The hot weather and proximity to San Bernardino make it a winner with boaters, who have 1,000 surface acres of water and 13 miles of shoreline to explore. All water sports are allowed. It's a great lake for waterskiing (35-mph speed limit), water sports (5-mph speed limit in major coves), and sailboarding, with afternoon winds usually strong in the spring and early summer. Note that the quota on boats is enforced, with a maximum of 166 boats per day, and that boat-launch reservations are required on summer weekends and holidays. There are also designated areas for boating, waterskiing, and fishing to reduce conflicts. Fishing varies dramatically according to season, with trout planted in the cool months, and largemouth bass, bluegill, striped bass, catfish, and crappie caught the rest of the year. (Note: All boats must be certified mussel-free before launching.) A large sandy swimming beach is available on the lake's southeast side at the Sawpit Recreation Area. The park also has a modest trail system with both nature and bike trails. Miller Canyon is off-limits during bald eagle nesting season.

Sites 1–13 were burned in the Old Fire of 2003 and there is no shade, so bring your own. A bonus is that there are also some hike-in/bike-in campsites.

Campsites, facilities: There are 134 sites for tents or RVs up to 22 feet (no hookups), with a few for RVs of any length, and four hike-in/bike-in sites. Some sites are pull-through. Picnic tables and fire rings (fire restriction may be in effect) are provided. Restrooms with flush toilets and coin showers, drinking water, Wi-Fi, dump station, boat ramp, marina, boat rentals, and small store are available. Some facilities are wheelchair-accessible. Leashed pets are permitted.

Reservations, fees: Reservations are accepted at 800/444-7275 (800/444-PARK) or www.reserveamerica.com ($8 reservation fee). Sites are $45–50 per night, $8 per night for each additional vehicle, $5 per night per person for hike-in/bike-in sites. Open year-round.

Directions: Drive on I-15 to Cajon Junction (north of San Bernardino) and the exit for Highway 138 east. Take that exit and drive east on Highway 138 for 12 miles to the park entrance on the right.

Contact: Silverwood Lake State Recreation Area, 760/389-2303 or 760/389-2281; Silverwood Lake Marina, 760/389-2299, www.parks.ca.gov.

45 WEST FORK GROUP CAMPS

Scenic rating: 4

at Silverwood Lake in
Silverwood Lake State Recreation Area

Map 13.2, page 742

This is a large camping complex for groups at Silverwood Lake. For more information on Silverwood Lake, see the Mesa listing in this chapter.

Campsites, facilities: There are six group

camps for tents or RVs of any length (no hookups): three group camps for up to 40 people and three group camps for up to 100 people. Picnic tables and fire rings (fire restriction may be in effect) are provided. Restrooms with flush toilets and coin showers and drinking water are available. Some facilities are wheelchair-accessible. Shaded picnic areas, fishing, hiking, swimming, boating, food service, and a store are available nearby. A dump station is available at Mesa campground. Leashed pets are permitted.

Reservations, fees: Reservations are required at 800/444-7275 (800/444-PARK) or www.reserveamerica.com ($8 reservation fee). Site are $150–325 per night. Open April through October.

Directions: Take I-15 to Cajon Junction (north of San Bernardino) and the exit for Highway 138 east. Take that exit and drive east on Highway 138 for 12 miles to the park entrance on the right.

Contact: Silverwood Lake State Recreation Area, 760/389-2303 or 760/389-2281, www.parks.ca.gov.

46 CAMP SWITZERLAND

Scenic rating: 7

near Lake Gregory

Map 13.2, page 742

This camp is set in a wooded canyon at 4,500 feet elevation below the dam at little Lake Gregory. On my visit here, I noticed that it really doesn't look much like Switzerland. Since the camp is well below the dam, there are no lake views or even much of a sense that the lake is nearby. Yet it is only a short distance away. Lake Gregory covers just 120 acres, and while no privately owned boats are permitted here, boats can be rented at the marina. No gas motors are permitted at the lake, but electric motors are allowed. Trout and steelhead are stocked. It is surrounded by the San Bernardino National Forest. A large swimming beach is available on the south shore (about 0.75 mile away) with a water slide and dressing rooms. There is some road noise, but the quiet time rule at night is strictly enforced—a plus. (Note: The owner rarely answers the phone, as best I could tell.)

Campsites, facilities: There are 40 sites with full or partial hookups (30 amps) for tents or RVs up to 27 feet. Two cabins are also available. Picnic tables are provided. Restrooms with flush toilets, coin showers, drinking water, and a dump station are available. A store and propane gas are nearby. Leashed pets are permitted, but dogs over 25 pounds are not allowed.

Reservations, fees: Reservations are accepted ($10 reservation fee). RV sites (hookups) start at $40 per night, tent sites start at $35 per night, both rates are for a family of four, $8 per adult for more than two people, $10 per night for each additional vehicle, $10 per pet per night. Cabins start at $85 per night. Open year-round, weather permitting.

Directions: Drive on Highway 210 to San Bernardino and the Waterman Avenue exit. Take that exit and drive north on Waterman Avenue until it becomes Highway 18. Continue on Highway 18 to Crestline/Highway 138. Turn north (left) on Highway 138 and drive two miles to Lake Drive. Continue straight and drive three miles to the campground entrance (signed, just past the fire station, below the dam at the north end of Lake Gregory).

Contact: Camp Switzerland, 909/338-2731, www.campswitzerland.net.

47 DOGWOOD
♨ 🏕 🐕 ♿ 🚐 ⛺

Scenic rating: 6

near Lake Arrowhead in
San Bernardino National Forest

Map 13.2, page 742

So close, yet so far—that's the paradox between Lake Arrowhead and Dogwood. The lake is just a mile away, but there is no public

access. The lake is ringed by gated trophy homes. The elevation is 5,600 feet. Any questions? The rangers at the Arrowhead Ranger Station, about 1.5 miles down the road to the east, can answer them.

Campsites, facilities: There are 94 sites for tents or RVs up to 40 feet (no hookups); some sites have partial hookups (30 amps). Picnic tables and fire grills are provided. Drinking water, restrooms with flush toilets and coin showers, and a dump station are available. An amphitheater and campfire programs are available. A store is nearby. Some facilities are wheelchair-accessible. Leashed pets are permitted.

Reservations, fees: Reservations are accepted at 877/444-6777 or www.recreation.gov ($9 reservation fee). Single sites are $28–30 per night, $56–58 per night for double sites, and it's $5 per night for each additional vehicle. Open mid-May through October.

Directions: Drive on Highway 30 to San Bernardino and Highway 18 (two miles east of the junction of Highway 30 and Highway 215). Turn north on Highway 18 and drive 15 miles to Rim of the World Highway. Continue on Highway 18 for 0.3 mile to the road immediately after Daley Canyon Road. Turn left and make an immediate right on the Daley Canyon access road. Drive a short distance to the campground entrance on the left.

Contact: San Bernardino National Forest, Mountaintop Ranger District, Arrowhead Ranger Station, 909/382-2782, www.fs.usda.gov/sbnf.

48 NORTH SHORE
🧍 ♨ 🏕 ♿ 🚐 ⛺

Scenic rating: 8

on Lake Arrowhead in
San Bernardino National Forest

Map 13.2, page 742

Of the two camps at Lake Arrowhead, this one is preferable. It is set at 5,300 feet elevation near the northeastern shore of the lake, which provides decent trout fishing in the spring and early summer from a boat. Note that this is a private lake, and there is no shore access. To the nearby north, Deep Creek in San Bernardino National Forest is well worth exploring; a hike along the stream to fish for small trout (catch-and-release only) or see a unique set of small waterfalls is highly recommended.

Campsites, facilities: There are 27 sites for tents or RVs up to 22 feet (no hookups). Picnic tables and fire rings are provided. Drinking water and flush toilets are available. A store is nearby. Some facilities are wheelchair-accessible. Leashed pets are permitted.

Reservations, fees: Reservations are accepted at 877/444-6777 or www.recreation.gov ($9 reservation fee). Single sites are $19–21 per night, double sites are $38–40 per night, $5 per night for each additional vehicle. Open May through September.

Directions: Drive on Highway 30 to San Bernardino and the Waterman exit. Take that exit and drive north on Waterman Avenue until it becomes Highway 18. Continue on Highway 18/Rim of the World Highway and drive 17 miles to Highway 173. Turn left on Highway 173 and drive north for 1.6 miles to the stop sign. Turn right (still on Highway 173) and drive 2.9 miles to Hospital Road. Turn right and continue 0.1 mile to the top of the small hill. Turn left just past the hospital entrance and continue a short distance to the campground.

Contact: San Bernardino National Forest, Mountaintop Ranger District, Big Bear Ranger Station/Discovery Center, 909/382-2790, www.fs.usda.gov/sbnf.

49 TENT PEG GROUP
🏃 🚣 🐕 ♿ 5% ⛺

Scenic rating: 5

near the Pacific Crest Trail in
San Bernardino National Forest

Map 13.2, page 742

This camp would be a lot easier to reach with a helicopter than a vehicle. But that's why

Tent Peg is a well-loved camp for the few who book it: It's a primitive camp for groups at 5,400 feet elevation, complete with trailhead. A rough jeep road heads out of camp to the west and down into Deep Creek. In addition, there is a trailhead for a three-mile hike down the canyon to the south to Fisherman's Hike-In campground, set along Deep Creek. The trout are small but willing (catch-and-release only).

Note: Tent Peg, Crab Flats, and Green Valley were damaged in the 2008 Glide Fire, but the site is still open for camping.

Campsites, facilities: There is one group camp that will accommodate 10–40 people and five vehicles. Picnic tables and fire grills are provided. Vault toilets are available. No drinking water is available. A store is approximately five miles away. Some facilities are wheelchair-accessible. Leashed pets are permitted.

Reservations, fees: Reservations are required at 877/444-6777 or www.recreation.gov ($9 reservation fee). The camp is $70 per night. Open mid-May through October.

Directions: From San Bernardino, drive east on Highway 30 to the junction with Highway 330 (east of San Bernardino near Highland). Take Highway 330 north (signed "Mountain Resorts") and drive to Running Springs and the junction with Highway 18. Turn east on Highway 18 and drive to Green Valley Road. Turn left on Green Valley Road and drive three miles to Forest Road 3N16 (a dirt road). Turn left and drive four miles (you will cross two creeks that vary in depth depending on season; high clearance is recommended but is typically not necessary) to the campground (one mile past the town of Green Valley Lake) to an intersection with Forest Road 3N34. Bear left on Forest Road 3N34 and drive one mile to the campground on the left.

Contact: San Bernardino National Forest, Mountaintop Ranger District, Arrowhead Ranger Station, 909/382-2782, www.fs.usda.gov/sbnf.

50 CRAB FLATS
🐾 🚐 ⛰️

Scenic rating: 4

near Crab Creek in
San Bernardino National Forest

Map 13.2, page 742

Four-wheel-drive cowboys and dirt-bike enthusiasts often make this a base camp, known as a staging area for off-highway vehicles. It is a developed Forest Service camp set at a fork in the road at 6,200 feet elevation. A challenging jeep road and motorcycle trail is available from here, heading west into Deep Creek Canyon. Note that Tent Peg Group camp (see listing in this chapter) is just 0.5 mile to the west on Forest Road 3N34 (hiking trails are available there).

Campsites, facilities: There are 27 sites for tents or RVs up to 28 feet (no hookups). Picnic tables and fire rings are provided. Drinking water and vault toilets are available. Leashed pets are permitted.

Reservations, fees: Reservations are accepted at 877/444-6777 or www.recreation.gov ($9 reservation fee). Sites are $18–20 per night. Open mid-May through October.

Directions: From San Bernardino, drive east on Highway 30 to the junction with Highway 330 (east of San Bernardino near Highland). Take Highway 330 north (signed "Mountain Resorts") and drive to Running Springs and the junction with Highway 18. Turn east on Highway 18 and drive to Green Valley Road. Turn left on Green Valley Road and drive three miles to Forest Road 3N16 (a dirt road). Turn left and drive four miles (you will cross two creeks that vary in depth depending on season; high clearance is recommended but is typically not necessary) to an intersection. Bear left at the intersection and drive a very short distance to the campground entrance on the right.

Contact: San Bernardino National Forest, Mountaintop Ranger District, Arrowhead Ranger Station, 909/382-2782, www.fs.usda.gov/sbnf.

51 FISHERMAN'S HIKE-IN
🥾 🏊 🐾 5% ⛰️

Scenic rating: 8

on Deep Creek in
San Bernardino National Forest

Map 13.2, page 742

Get here and you join the 5 Percent Club. Fisherman's Hike-In is a secluded, wooded campground set deep in San Bernardino National Forest at 5,400 feet elevation. Deep Creek, a designated Wild and Scenic River, runs alongside, providing stream trout fishing and a beautiful setting. It's worth the significant effort required to get here. Once here, you will find a primitive route along the creek (which looks more like a deer trail than a hiking trail) that anglers use to tromp along the stream. The trout are small but well colored, and the first cast into the head of a pool often results in a strike. Remember, it is catch-and-release fishing only in this area. Note that a forest fire once burned through part of the Deep Creek Canyon area, but it looks great again.

Campsites, facilities: There are four tent sites for groups of up to eight people per site. Picnic tables and fire grills are provided. Vault toilets are available. No drinking water is available. Garbage must be packed out. Horses and leashed pets are permitted, but corrals and water troughs are not available.

Reservations, fees: Reservations are required at 877/444-6777 or www.recreation.gov ($9 reservation fee). Sites are $10 per night. Open year-round, weather permitting.

Directions: From San Bernardino, drive east on Highway 30 to the junction with Highway 330 (east of San Bernardino near Highland). Take Highway 330 north (signed "Mountain Resorts") and drive to Running Springs and the junction with Highway 18. Turn east on Highway 18 and drive to Green Valley Road. Turn left on Green Valley Road and drive three miles to Forest Road 3N16 (a dirt road). Turn left and drive four miles (you will cross two creeks that vary in depth depending on season; high clearance is recommended but is typically not necessary) to the campground (one mile past the town of Green Valley Lake) to an intersection with Forest Road 3N34. Bear left on Forest Road 3N34 and drive west for 1.3 miles to Forest Service Trail 2W07 on your left. Park and take this hiking trail for 2.5 miles southwest to Deep Creek. The campground is on the other side of the creek.

Contact: San Bernardino National Forest, Mountaintop Ranger District, Arrowhead Ranger Station, 909/382-2782, www.fs.usda.gov/sbnf. For fire information, call Big Bear Discovery Center, 909/866-3437; Arrowhead Ranger Station, 909/382-2782.

52 GREEN VALLEY

Scenic rating: 4

near Green Valley Lake in San Bernardino National Forest

Map 13.2, page 742

This camp sits along Green Valley Creek at an elevation of 7,000 feet. Little Green Valley Lake is a mile to the west; it is privately owned, but public access is allowed. It's quiet and intimate at this lake, and kayaks and rowboats can be rented. The lake is stocked with trout by the Department of Fish and Game and it is also a good spot to take a flying leap and belly flop when water levels are high enough.

Note: Tent Peg, Crab Flats, and Green Valley were damaged in the 2008 Glide Fire, but the site is still open for camping.

Campsites, facilities: There are 36 sites for tents or RVs up to 22 feet (no hookups). Picnic tables and fire grills are provided. Drinking water and flush toilets are available. A store and coin laundry are nearby. Leashed pets are permitted.

Reservations, fees: Reservations are accepted at 877/444-6777 or www.recreation.gov ($9 reservation fee). Single sites are $20 per night, double sites are $40–42 per night, $5

per night for each additional vehicle. Open May through October.

Directions: From San Bernardino, take Highway 30 east to the junction with Highway 330 (east of San Bernardino near Highland). Take Highway 330 north (signed "Mountain Resorts") and drive to Running Springs and the junction with Highway 18. Turn east on Highway 18 and drive to Green Valley Lake Road. Turn left on Green Valley Lake Road and drive five miles to the campground (one mile past the town of Green Valley Lake).

Contact: San Bernardino National Forest, Mountaintop Ranger District, Arrowhead Ranger Station, 909/382-2782, www.fs.usda.gov/sbnf.

53 SHADY COVE GROUP AND WALK-IN

Scenic rating: 7

near the Children's Forest in San Bernardino National Forest

Map 13.2, page 742

The highlight here is the adjacent short looped trail that is routed through the Children's Forest. The camp is excellent for Boy Scout and Girl Scout troops. The walk to the camp is about 100 yards. The elevation is 7,500 feet.

Campsites, facilities: There are three group sites for up to 30 people each. Picnic tables and fire grills are provided. Drinking water and vault toilets are available. Some facilities are wheelchair-accessible. Leashed pets are permitted.

Reservations, fees: Reservations are required at 877/444-6777 or www.recreation.gov ($9 reservation fee). The group sites are $60 per night. Note: The camp is gated for safety; groups are given a combination. Open May through mid-October, weather permitting.

Directions: From San Bernardino and Highway 330, drive north on Highway 330 to the town of Running Springs. Continue just past Running Springs to Keller Peak Road (just past Deer Lick Fire Station). Turn right (south) on Keller Peak Road and drive four miles to the Children's Forest. Bear left to the parking area. The walk-in sites are 100 yards from the parking area.

Contact: San Bernardino National Forest, Mountaintop Ranger District, Arrowhead Ranger Station, 909/382-2782, www.fs.usda. gov/sbnf.

54 LOS ANGELES/POMONA/ FAIRPLEX KOA

🏊 🏕 ♿ 🚐 ⛺

Scenic rating: 4

in Pomona

Map 13.2, page 742

This is what you might call an urban RV park. Then again, the L.A. County Fairgrounds are right across the street, and there's something going on there every weekend. Frank G. Bonnelli Regional Park, which includes Puddingstone Lake, is only 15 minutes away. Note that about 100 of the sites are occupied by permanent residents.

Campsites, facilities: There are 182 pull-through sites with full hookups (50 amps) for RVs and 11 tent sites. Two cabins are also available. Restrooms with showers, pool and spa, convenience store, dump station, dog walk, and coin laundry are available. Some facilities are wheelchair-accessible. Leashed pets are permitted, with certain restrictions.

Reservations, fees: Reservations are accepted. RV sites (full hookups) are $44–67 per night, tent sites are $29 per night, $10 per night for each additional vehicle, $5.50 per person per night for more than two people. Camping cabins are $54–64 per night. Some credit cards accepted. Open year-round.

Directions: Drive on I-10 to the exit for Fairplex Drive (five miles west of Pomona). Take that exit north (toward the mountain) and drive two miles to McKinley Avenue. Turn right on McKinley Avenue and drive one mile to White Avenue. Turn left and drive about 0.5 mile (0.2 mile south of Arrow Street) to the park on the right (2200 North White Avenue).

Contact: Los Angeles/Pomona/Fairplex KOA, 909/593-8915, www.koa.com.

55 EAST SHORE RV PARK

🏊 🛶 🚐 🏕 🏃 ♿ 🚐 ⛺

Scenic rating: 7

at Puddingstone Lake

Map 13.2, page 742

Considering how close Puddingstone Lake is to so many people, the quality of fishing and waterskiing might be a surprise to newcomers. The lake covers 250 acres and is an excellent recreation facility. For the most part, rules permit waterskiing and personal watercraft between 10 A.M. and sunset, making it an excellent lake for fishing for bass and trout (in season) during the morning and evening. All water sports are allowed here, with specific days and hours for powerboating and personal watercraft. A ski beach is available on the north shore, and there is a large, sandy swimming beach on the southwest shore about a mile away. The lake is just south of Raging Waters in San Dimas and is bordered to the south by Bonnelli Regional Park; there are also a golf course and equestrian facilities adjacent. The park has roughly 50 monthly residents. Insider's tip: There is a nice tent site available on a hilltop with trees that provides more privacy.

Campsites, facilities: There are 518 sites with full hookups (20, 30, and 50 amps) for RVs of any length, 25 walk-in sites for tents, and three group tent sites. Some sites are pull-through. Restrooms with showers, cable TV, Wi-Fi, recreation room, swimming pools, general store, playground, basketball, volleyball, horseshoes, propane gas delivery, 24-hour ranger service, and coin laundry are available. A hot-tub facility is nearby. Some facilities are wheelchair-accessible. Leashed pets are permitted at RV sites, but not at tent sites.

Reservations, fees: Reservations are accepted at 800/809-3778. RV sites are $42–51 per night for up to two people, tent sites are $27 per night for up to three people, $3 per night for each additional person, $3 per pet per night. Group, monthly, and seasonal rates available. Some credit cards accepted. Open year-round.

Directions: Drive on I-10 to the exit for Fairplex Drive (five miles west of Pomona). Take that exit north to Via Verde (the first traffic light). Turn left on Via Verde and drive to the first stop sign at Campers View. Turn right on Campers View and drive into the park.

Contact: East Shore RV Park, 909/599-8355 or 800/809-3778, www.eastshorervpark.com.

56 YUCAIPA REGIONAL PARK

Scenic rating: 7

near Redlands

Map 13.2, page 742

This is a great family-oriented county park, complete with water slides and paddleboats for the kids and fishing access and hiking trails for adults. Three lakes are stocked weekly with catfish in the summer and trout in the winter, the closest thing around to an insurance policy for anglers. Spectacular scenic views of the Yucaipa Valley, the San Bernardino Mountains, and Mount San Gorgonio are possible from the park. The park covers 885 acres in the foothills of the San Bernardino Mountains. A one-acre swimming lagoon and two water slides make this a favorite for youngsters. The Yucaipa Adobe and Mousley Museum of Natural History is nearby.

Campsites, facilities: There are 42 sites for RVs of any length and nine sites for tents. All RV sites have full hookups (20, 30, and 50 amps) and/or are pull-through. Picnic tables and fire rings are provided at most sites. Drinking water and restrooms with flush toilets and showers are available, and shade ramadas are available at tent sites. A seasonal swimming lagoon and water slides, fishing ponds, seasonal paddleboat

and aquacycle rentals, pay phone, seasonal snack bar, picnic shelters, playground, volleyball (bring net), horseshoes, group facilities, bait shop, and dump station are nearby. The water slide is open Memorial Day weekend through Labor Day weekend. Some facilities are wheelchair-accessible. Leashed pets are permitted.

Reservations, fees: Reservations are accepted at www.sbcountyparks.com ($10 reservation fee). Tent sites are $25 per tent per night, RV sites (full hookups) are $35 per night, $1 per pet per night. Weekly, senior, and youth group rates available. Some credit cards accepted. Additional charges apply for fishing, swimming, and use of the water slide. Proof of vehicle registration required for campers. Maximum 14-day stay in any 30-day period. Open year-round.

Directions: Drive on I-10 to Redlands and the exit for Yucaipa Boulevard. Take that exit and drive east on Yucaipa Boulevard to Oak Glen Road. Turn left and continue two miles to the park on the left.

Contact: Yucaipa Regional Park, 909/790-3127, www.sbcountyparks.com.

57 PRADO REGIONAL PARK

Scenic rating: 6

on Prado Park Lake near Corona

Map 13.2, page 742

Prado Park Lake is the centerpiece of a 2,280-acre recreation-oriented park that features hiking trails, an equestrian center, athletic fields, shooting range, dog-training facility, and 36-hole golf course. The lake is small and used primarily for paddling small boats and fishing, which is best in the winter and early spring when trout are planted, and then in early summer for catfish and bass. Gas motors, inflatables, sailboarding, swimming, and water/body contact are not permitted. The shooting facility, the site of the 1984 Olympic shooting venue, is outstanding.

Campsites, facilities: There are 75 sites with full hookups (30 and 50 amps) for RVs of any length, 15 tent sites, and nine group sites. Most sites are pull-through. Picnic tables and fire rings are provided. Restrooms with showers, coin laundry, pay phone, snack bar, picnic area, playground, group facilities, boat ramp, and bait shop are available. A playing field with softball, soccer, and horseshoes is on-site. Some facilities are wheelchair-accessible. Leashed pets are permitted.

Reservations, fees: Reservations accepted at 909/597-4260 or at www.sbcountyparks.com ($5 reservation fee, $10 for group sites). Sites are $30 per night, good for four people and two vehicles, $1 per pet per night. Group sites are $3 per person per night with a 20-person minimum. Weekly rates available. A fee is charged for fishing. Campers must show proof of vehicle registration and insurance. Some credit cards accepted. Open year-round, with a maximum 14-day stay in a 30-day period.

Directions: Drive on Highway 91 to Highway 71 (west of Norco and Riverside). Take Highway 71 north and drive four miles to Highway 83/Euclid Avenue. Turn right on Euclid Avenue and drive one mile to the park entrance on the right.

Contact: Prado Regional Park, 909/597-4260, www.sbcountyparks.com.

58 RANCHO JURUPA PARK
🚶 🚴 🏊 🐕 ♿ 🚐 ⛺

Scenic rating: 4

near Riverside

Map 13.2, page 742

Lord, it gets hot in the summertime, but there is shade and grass here at this 200-acre park. The setting is along the Santa Ana River, amid cottonwood trees and meadows. This Riverside County park stocks trout and catfish in a three-acre fishing lake. Hiking, cycling, and equestrian trails are also available in the park. Shaded picnic sites are a plus. Summer visitors will find that the nearest lake for swimming and water sports is Lake Perris, about a 20-minute drive away. The elevation is 780 feet.

Campsites, facilities: There are 67 sites: 12 sites with full hookups and 55 sites with partial hookups (30 and 50 amps) for tents or RVs of any length. Picnic tables and fire grills are provided. Drinking water, flush toilets with showers, and a dump station are available. Some facilities are wheelchair-accessible. Leashed pets are permitted.

Reservations, fees: Reservations are accepted for the individual sites and required for the group camp at 800/234-7275 ($8 reservation fee, $15 for group camp). Tent sites are $15 per night, RV sites (partial hookups) are $25–35 per night, $1 per pet per night, and $1 per horse per night. Group sites are $150 per night for primitive tent camping, $225 per night for a developed site; youth group camping is available. A fishing fee is charged. Some credit cards accepted. Open year-round, with a maximum 14-day stay in a 28-day period.

Directions: Drive on I-215 to Riverside and Highway 60. Take Highway 60 east and drive seven miles to Rubidoux Boulevard. Turn left on Rubidoux Boulevard and drive 0.5 mile to Mission Boulevard. Turn left on Mission Boulevard and drive about one mile to Crestmore Road. Turn right and drive 1.5 miles to the park gate on the left (4800 Crestmore Road).

Contact: Rancho Jurupa Park, 951/684-7032, www.rivcoparks.org.

59 ANAHEIM RV VILLAGE
🏊 🏕 🚴 ♿ 🚐 ⛺

Scenic rating: 1

near Disneyland

Map 13.2, page 742

This is the newest RV park in Anaheim and it is one of the most popular RV parks for visitors to Disneyland and other nearby attractions. It is easy to see why, with the park just 0.5 mile from Disneyland. A shuttle service is available to Disneyland for a fee.

Campsites, facilities: There are 293 sites with full hookups (20, 30, and 50 amps) for tents or

RVs up to 45 feet, with 23 65–70-foot concrete pads for RVs with trailers; some sites are pull-through. Picnic tables are provided. Restrooms with showers, Wi-Fi, playground, game room, heated swimming pool, coin laundry, convenience store, dump station, ice, recreation room, RV wash rack, and propane gas are available. Some facilities are wheelchair-accessible. Leashed pets are permitted, with breed restrictions.

Reservations, fees: Reservations are recommended. Premium pull-through RV sites (full hookups) are $78 per night, pull-through RV sites (hookups) are $68 per night, standard back-in RV sites (hookups) are $53 per night, tent sites are $35 per night, $2 per person per night for more than two people, $5 per night for each additional vehicle. Pets are free. Discounts available, including off-season rates. Some credit cards accepted. Open year-round.

Directions: Take I-5 to Anaheim and the exit for Ball Road. Take that exit and drive on Ball Road for about one block to the park on the left.

Directions for RVs from I-5 South: Drive on I-5 south to Disney Way/Anaheim Boulevard (Exit 109B). Turn left (east) on Disney Way and drive to Anaheim Boulevard. Turn left on Anaheim Boulevard. and drive to Ball. Turn left on Ball and drive to park.

Directions for RVs from I-5 North: Drive on I-5 north to Katella Avenue/Disney Way (Exit 109). Take that exit and drive across Katella to Anaheim Boulevard. Turn right on Anaheim Boulevard and drive to Ball. Turn left on Ball and drive to park.

Contact: Anaheim RV Village, 714/991-0100, www.anaheimrvvillage.com.

60 ORANGELAND RV PARK

Scenic rating: 1

near Disneyland

Map 13.2, page 742

This park is about three miles east of Disneyland. If the other RV parks near Disneyland are filled, this is a useful alternative. Note that about half of the sites are filled with long-term renters.

Campsites, facilities: There are 195 sites for RVs of any length (full hookups); some sites are pull-through. Picnic tables are provided. Restrooms with showers, two fire grills, playground, heated swimming pool, spa, exercise room, coin laundry, convenience store, Wi-Fi, cable TV, car wash, shuffleboard court, billiards, dump station, ice, and recreation room are available. Some facilities are wheelchair-accessible. Leashed pets are permitted, with certain restrictions.

Reservations, fees: Reservations are recommended. Deluxe RV sites (full hookups) are $80 per night, preferred sites are $75 per night, premium sites are $70 per night, regular sites are $65, $2 per person for more than eight, $1 per pet per night. Weekly and monthly rates available. Some credit cards accepted. Open year-round.

Directions: Drive on I-5 to Anaheim and the exit for Katella Avenue. Take that exit east for Katella Avenue and drive two miles (passing Anaheim Stadium and the Santa Ana River) to Struck Avenue. Turn right and drive 200 yards to the park on the right (1600 West Struck Avenue).

Contact: Orangeland RV Park, 714/633-0414, www.orangeland.com.

61 CANYON RV PARK GROUP CAMPGROUND

Scenic rating: 6

near Yorba Linda

Map 13.2, page 742

The group campground is set in a mature grove of cottonwood and sycamore trees, with natural riparian wildland areas and open spaces nearby. It is near the Santa Ana River (swimming or wading at the lake or creek is prohibited). The Santa Ana River Bicycle Trail runs through this park, which runs from Orange in Riverside County to Huntington Beach and the Pacific Ocean. Side-trip possibilities include Chino

Hills State Park to the north, Cleveland National Forest to the south, and Lake Matthews to the southeast. The park is also close to Disneyland and Knott's Berry Farm. Canyon RV Park is a private group campground operating under a long-term lease from Orange County. It is at Featherly Regional Park.

Campsites, facilities: There are 140 sites with full hookups (30 and 50 amps) for RVs up to 45 feet and 10 cabins. Picnic tables and fire pits are provided. Restrooms with flush toilets and showers, two dump stations, seasonal swimming pool, horseshoes, firewood, ice, and two playgrounds are available. A visitors center and two amphitheaters are on-site. A convenience store, coin laundry, and propane are also available. Restaurants are nearby. Some facilities are wheelchair-accessible. Leashed pets are permitted, with some restrictions.

Reservations, fees: Reservations are accepted by phone, or website. RV sites (full hookups, 50 amp) are $45 per night, $10 per night for tents allowed within RV sites, $5 per night for each additional vehicle, $2 per person per night for more than two people, $1 per dog per night. Cabins are $60 per night. Weekly rates available. Call for youth-group rates. Some credit cards accepted. Open year-round.

Directions: Drive on I-5 to Highway 91 in Anaheim. Take Highway 91 east and drive 13 miles to the exit for Gypsum Canyon Road. Take that exit to Gypsum Canyon Road. Turn left, drive under the freeway, and drive about one block to the park entrance on the left.

Contact: Canyon RV Park, 714/637-0210, www.canyonrvpark.com.

62 LAKE PERRIS STATE RECREATION AREA

🚶 🚴 🏊 🛶 🚤 🏕 🐴 ♿ 🚗 ⛰

Scenic rating: 7

on Lake Perris

Map 13.2, page 742   **BEST (**

Lake Perris is a great recreation lake with first-class fishing for spotted bass, and many fishing records have been set here. In the summer, it's an excellent destination for boating and water sports. It is set at 1,500 feet elevation in Moreno Valley, just southwest of the Badlands foothills. The lake has a roundish shape, covering 2,200 acres, with an island that provides a unique boat-in picnic site. There are large ski beaches on the northeast and southeast shores and a designated sailing cove on the northwest side, an ideal spot for various water sports; inflatables are not permitted. Swimming is also excellent, but it's allowed only at the developed beaches a short distance from the campground. The recreation area covers 8,300 acres and includes 10 miles of paved bike trails, including a great route that circles the lake, 15 miles of equestrian trails, and five miles of hiking trails. Summer campfire and junior ranger programs are offered. There is also a special area for scuba diving, and a rock-climbing area is just south of the dam. Note: All boats must be certified mussel-free before launching.

Campsites, facilities: There are 177 sites for tents only, 254 sites with partial hookups (30 amps) for tents or RVs up to 31 feet, seven primitive horse camps with corrals and water troughs, and six group sites with no hookups for 25–100 people each. Picnic tables and fire grills are available. Restrooms with flush toilets and coin showers, drinking water, Wi-Fi, dump station, playground, convenience store, two swimming beaches, boat launch, and fishing boat rentals are available. Some facilities are wheelchair-accessible. Leashed pets are permitted, with certain restrictions, except at the beach or in the water.

Reservations, fees: Reservations are accepted for individual sites at 800/444-7275 (800/444-PARK) or www.reserveamerica.com ($8 reservation fee). Tent sites are $30 per night, RV sites are $45 per night, equestrian sites are $21 per night, $10 per night for each additional vehicle, $225 per night for group sites plus $8 per vehicle. Reserve group and equestrian sites at 951/940-5603. Open year-round.

Directions: From Riverside, drive southeast on Highway 215/60 for about five miles to the 215/60 split. Bear south on 215 at the split and drive six miles to Ramona Expressway. Turn left (east) and drive 3.5 miles to Lake Perris Drive. Turn left and drive 0.75 mile to the park entrance.

Contact: Lake Perris State Recreation Area, 951/940-5600, or Lake Perris Marina, 951/657-2179, www.parks.ca.gov.

63 SUNSET VISTA RV PARK
🏃 🏊 🎣 🏠 ♿ 🚐 📷

Scenic rating: 7

in Huntington Beach

Map 13.2, page 742

This RV park is operated by the city of Huntington Beach, and is a helpful layover for Highway 1 cruisers. Bolsa Chica State Beach provides an alternative spot to park an RV. The best nearby adventure is the short loop walk at Bolsa Chica State Reserve (see the Bolsa Chica State Beach listing in this chapter for more information).

Campsites, facilities: There are 46 sites with partial hookups (30 and 50 amps) for RVs up to 45 feet. Fire rings are provided. Drinking water, outdoor cold showers, flush toilets, and dump station are available. Supplies are available within a mile. Some facilities are wheelchair accessible. Leashed pets are permitted.

Reservations, fees: Reservations are accepted online or by mail (print out the online reservation form and mail it). Sites are $60 per night, with a one-time processing fee of $10. Discounts available for seniors and disabled. Open October through May.

Directions: Drive on I-405 to Huntington Beach and the exit for Beach Boulevard. Take that exit west and drive on Beach Boulevard to Highway 1/Pacific Coast Highway. Turn right (north) and drive approximately one mile to 1st Street. Turn left and drive a short distance to the park entrance.

Contact: Huntington Beach, Parks Department, 103 Pacific Coast Highway, Huntington Beach, CA 92648, 714/536-5280, www.sunsetvistacamping.huntingtonbeachca.gov.

64 NEWPORT DUNES WATERFRONT RESORT
🚴 🏊 🎣 🍴 🚐 🐕 🏃 ♿ 🚐 ⛰

Scenic rating: 9

in Newport Beach

Map 13.2, page 742

This five-star resort is set in a pretty spot on the bay, with a beach, boat ramp, and storage area providing bonuses. The resort received the "Mega Park of the Year Award 2003" from the California Travel Parks Association. It is situated on 100 acres of Newport Bay beach, beautiful and private, without public access. It features one mile of beach and a swimming lagoon, beachfront sites, and 24-hour security. A one-mile promenade circles the resort and is popular for cycling and inline skating. Nearby to the west is Corona del Mar State Beach, and to the south, Crystal Cove State Park. The park is five minutes' walking distance from Balboa Island and is next to the largest estuary in California, the Upper Newport Bay Ecological Reserve.

Campsites, facilities: There are 382 sites with full hookups (30 and 50 amps) for tents or RVs up to 50 feet and 24 cottages. Picnic tables are provided. Restrooms with showers, heated swimming pool and spa, waveless saltwater lagoon, 440-slip marina, satellite TV, Wi-Fi, organized activities, beach volleyball, coin laundry, market, waterfront restaurant, café, fitness center, game room/video arcade, group facilities, dog run, playground, RV and boat storage, RV and boat wash, and marina with boat launch ramp are available. Boat, kayak, sailboard, golf cart, and bicycle rentals are available, along with lessons for various water sports. Some facilities are wheelchair-accessible. Leashed pets are permitted, with some restrictions, including a maximum of two leashed pets; no pit bulls or rottweilers, and no pets in the cottages. No smoking in cottages.

Reservations, fees: Reservations are accepted up to two years in advance (up to one year in advance for the week of July 4) at 800/765-7661. Rates for RV sites (full hookups) vary widely: standard RV sites are $73–158 per night; select, partial-view RV sites start at $215 per night; beachfront RV sites at $276 per night; $8 per night for each additional vehicle, $2 per pet per night. Nightly rates are roughly half in winter. Monthly and weekly rates available. Group rates are available. Note that long-term stays are limited to five-and-a-half months. Some credit cards accepted. Open year-round.

Directions: Drive on I-405 to the exit for Highway 55. Take that exit south and drive on Highway 55 to Highway 73. Turn south on Highway 73 and drive three miles to the Jamboree Road exit. Take that exit, turn right, and drive south on Jamboree Road for five miles to Back Bay Drive. Turn right and drive a short distance to the resort on the left.

Contact: Newport Dunes Waterfront Resort, 949/729-3863, www.newportdunes.com.

65 CRYSTAL COVE STATE PARK

🚶 🚴 🏊 ⛵ ⛺

Scenic rating: 9

south of Corona del Mar

Map 13.2, page 742

First, get this straight: This park does not provide beach camping. The campsites require hikes of 3.5–4.5 miles. That known, this place is very special. This is a gorgeous park that covers 2,200 acres, featuring 3.5 miles of coast and a 1,140-acre underwater park that is popular with scuba divers and snorkelers. The inland acreage is popular with mountain bikers and hikers, and the beach is popular with swimmers and surfers. The two Moro camps have a ridge-top vantage point and beautiful views of the ocean. Deer Canyon camp is sheltered by a grove of oaks and offers privacy, but no views. El Moro Canyon is shady and tree-lined. Note that El Moro Creek flows only in the wet season. The camps are rarely full. Most of the park's backcountry is grass hills and some foothill woodlands. Guided nature hikes are offered.

Campsites, facilities: There are 32 hike-in/ bike-in and equestrian sites at three environmental campgrounds: Lower Moro, Upper Moro, and Deer Canyon (horses are not allowed at Lower Moro). A permit is required for these campsites and is available online or at the Moro Campground kiosk. Picnic tables are provided. Pit toilets are available. No drinking water is available. No fires are permitted; bring a backpacking stove for cooking.

Moro Campground has 28 RV sites with partial hookups and 30 tent sites. Picnic tables are provided. Showers and flush toilets are available. Some facilities are wheelchair accessible. Leashed pets are permitted but are not allowed on the beach or in the backcountry.

Reservations, fees: Reservations are accepted at 800/444-7275 (800/444-PARK) or www. reserveamerica.com ($8 reservation fee). Tent sites are $50 per night, RV sites are $75 per night, environmental sites are $25 per night, $10 per night for each additional vehicle. Registration at the visitors center is required. Open year-round.

Directions: Drive on Highway 1 to the park entrance (three miles south of Corona del Mar) on the east side of the highway. Register at the visitors center. The Moro camps require a 3.5- to four-mile walk. The Deer Canyon camp requires a 4.5-mile walk.

Contact: Crystal Cove State Park, 949/494-3539; Orange Coast District, Central Sector, 949/492-0802, www.crystalcovestatepark.com or www.parks.ca.gov.

66 O'NEILL REGIONAL PARK AND EQUESTRIAN CAMP

🚶 🚴 🏠 🐕 👪 ♿ 🚐 ⛺

Scenic rating: 6

near Cleveland National Forest

Map 13.2, page 742

This Orange County park is just far enough off the main drag to get missed by most of the RV cruisers on I-5. It is set near Trabuco Canyon, adjacent to Cleveland National Forest to the east. About 70 percent of the campsites are set under a canopy of sycamore and oak, and, in general, the park is heavily wooded. The park covers 3,800 acres and features 18 miles of trails, including those accessible by equestrians. Several roads near this park lead to trailheads into Cleveland National Forest. Rangers occasionally post mountain lion warnings at this park. The elevation is 1,000 feet.

Campsites, facilities: There are 79 sites for tents and RVs of any length (no hookups), five equestrian sites for up to six horses per site, and two group camping areas for 20–80 people each. A few sites are pull-through. Picnic tables and fire rings are provided. Restrooms with flush toilets and showers, drinking water, playground, picnic area, amphitheater, horseshoes, firewood, and a dump station are available. Horse corral, water faucets, small corrals, and an arena are available at equestrian sites. An interpretive center is open on weekends. A store is nearby. Some facilities are wheelchair-accessible. Leashed pets are permitted but not in wilderness areas.

Reservations, fees: Reservations are recommended for individual sites and are required for group sites. Sites are $20 per night, $3 per horse per night. Call for group rates. Some credit cards accepted. Open year-round.

Directions: From I-5 in Laguna Hills, take the County Road S18/El Toro Road exit and drive east (past El Toro) for 7.5 miles. Turn right onto Live Oak Canyon Road/County Road S19 and drive about three miles to the park on the right.

Contact: O'Neill Regional Park, 949/923-2260 or 949/923-2256, www.ocparks.com.

live oak and magnificent stands of California sycamore. Highway 74 provides access to this regional park. It is a popular spot for picnics, day hikes, horseback riding, and cycling. A highlight is 30 miles of trails. Much of the land is pristine and protected in its native state. It is bordered to the south by the San Juan Creek and to the east by the Cleveland National Forest and the San Mateo Canyon Wilderness, adding to its protection.

Campsites, facilities: There are 42 sites (no hookups) and 13 sites (electric only) for tents or RVs of any length, 22 equestrian sites, and five sites for groups of up to 60 people. Picnic tables, fire pits, and barbecues are provided. Drinking water, restrooms with flush toilets and showers, dump station, corrals, amphitheater, museum with interpretive programs, and a playground are available. Some facilities are wheelchair-accessible. Pets are not allowed.

Reservations, fees: Reservations are required at 800/600-1600 or online at www.reserveamerica.com; group reservations are required at 949/923-2210. Single sites are $20 per night, $5 per night per additional vehicle, $3 per horse per night. Group sites are $240–360 per night. Youth group discounts are available. Some credit cards accepted. Open year-round.

Directions: Drive on I-5 to San Juan Capistrano and Highway 74/Ortega Highway. Turn east on Ortega Highway and drive 7.5 miles northeast to the signed park entrance on the left.

Contact: Caspers Wilderness Park, Orange County, 949/923-2210, www.ocparks.com.

67 CASPERS WILDERNESS PARK

🚶 🚴 🐴 ♿ 🚐 ⛺

Scenic rating: 6

on San Juan Creek

Map 13.2, page 742

This is an 8,500-acre protected wilderness preserve that is best known for coastal stands of

68 FALCON GROUP CAMPS

🚶 🐴 🚐 ⛺

Scenic rating: 4

in the Santa Ana Mountains in Cleveland National Forest

Map 13.2, page 742

At an elevation of 3,300 feet, Falcon is near the trailheads for the San Juan and Chiquito

Trails, which both lead into the backcountry and the Santa Ana Mountains. There are three group campgrounds here, with limited parking at Lupine and Yarrow Campgrounds.

Campsites, facilities: There are three group sites for tents or RVs (no hookups). Sage Camp accommodates 30 people and six RVs up to 40 feet; Lupine Camp accommodates 40 people and eight RVs up to 20 feet; and Yarrow Camp accommodates 70 people and 10 RVs up to 30 feet. Picnic tables and fire rings are provided. Drinking water and vault toilets are available. A store is within five miles. Leashed pets are permitted.

Reservations, fees: Reservations are required at 877/444-6777 or www.recreation.gov ($9 reservation fee). Sites are $60–120 per night. Open year-round, weather permitting.

Directions: Drive on I-15 to Lake Elsinore and the Central exit to Highway 74 west. Take that exit and drive west on Highway 74 for 12 miles (the road becomes Grand Avenue for a couple of miles in Lake Elsinore, then bears right) to Forest Road 6S05 (Long Canyon Road). Turn right and drive approximately 4.5 miles to the campground entrance on the left.

Contact: Cleveland National Forest, Trabuco Ranger District, 951/736-1811, www.fs.usda.gov/cleveland.

69 BLUE JAY

Scenic rating: 4

in the Santa Ana Mountains in
Cleveland National Forest

Map 13.2, page 742

The few hikers who know of this spot like it and keep coming back, provided they time their hikes when temperatures are cool. The trailheads to San Juan Trail and Chiquito Trail (which is accessed from the San Juan Trail), both of which lead into the backcountry and the Santa Ana Mountains, are adjacent to the camp. A Forest Service map is strongly advised. The elevation is 3,400 feet.

Campsites, facilities: There are 50 sites for tents or RVs up to 20 feet (no hookups). Picnic tables and fire rings are provided. Drinking water and vault toilets are available. A store is within five miles. Leashed pets are permitted.

Reservations, fees: Reservations are not accepted. Sites are $20–28 per night, $5 per night per additional vehicle. Open year-round, weather permitting.

Directions: From Lake Elsinore, take Route 74 south for 5.7 miles to the sign for Blue Jay campground. Turn right and proceed 5.1 miles to the campground on the right.

Contact: Cleveland National Forest, Trabuco Ranger District, 951/736-1811, www.fs.usda.gov/cleveland.

70 EL CARISO NORTH CAMPGROUND

Scenic rating: 5

near Lake Elsinore in
Cleveland National Forest

Map 13.2, page 742

This pretty, shaded spot at 2,600 feet elevation is just inside the border of Cleveland National Forest, with Lake Elsinore to the east. On the drive in there are great views to the east, looking down at Lake Elsinore and across the desert country. Hikers should head west to the Upper San Juan Campground.

Campsites, facilities: There are 24 sites for tents or RVs up to 22 feet (no hookups). Picnic tables and fire rings are provided. Drinking water and vault toilets are available. Leashed pets are permitted.

Reservations, fees: Reservations are not accepted. Sites are $15 per night. Open year-round, weather permitting.

Directions: Drive on I-15 to Lake Elsinore and the Central exit to Highway 74 west. Take that exit and drive west on Highway 74 for 12 miles (the road becomes Grand Avenue for a couple of miles in Lake Elsinore, then bears right) to the campground on the right.

Drive on I-5 to San Juan Capistrano and Highway 74/Ortega Highway. Turn east on the Ortega Highway and drive 24 miles northeast (into national forest) to the campground.

Contact: Cleveland National Forest, Trabuco Ranger District, 951/736-1811, www.fs.usda.gov/cleveland.

71 LAKE ELSINORE WEST MARINA AND RV RESORT

Scenic rating: 7

on Lake Elsinore

Map 13.2, page 742

This privately operated RV park has 1,000 feet of lake frontage, and boat rentals are nearby. Note that about a third of the sites are occupied by long-term renters. (For information about Lake Elsinore, see the La Laguna Resort listing in this chapter.)

Campsites, facilities: There are 184 sites with full hookups (50 amps) for RVs up to 40 feet and 60 lakeshore tent sites. Picnic tables and cable TV are provided. Restrooms with showers, dump station, horseshoe pit, clubhouse, WiFi, convenience store, group facilities, propane, and boat ramp are available. Some facilities are wheelchair-accessible. Leashed pets are permitted, with some restrictions.

Reservations, fees: Reservations are accepted at 800/328-6844 or at www.lakeelsinoremarina.com. RV sites (full hookups) are $45 per night, tent sites are $25 per night, $3 per person per night for more than two people, $1 per pet per night. Monthly and weekly rates available. Some credit cards accepted. Open year-round.

Directions: Drive to the junction of I-15 and Highway 74. At that junction, take Highway 74 west/Central Avenue and drive west for four miles to the entrance to the park on the left (32700 Riverside Drive).

Contact: Lake Elsinore West Marina, 951/678-1300 or 800/328-6844, www.lakeelsinoremarina.com.

72 LA LAGUNA RESORT

Scenic rating: 7

on Lake Elsinore

Map 13.2, page 742   BEST (

The weather is hot and dry enough in this region to make the water in Lake Elsinore more valuable than gold. Elsinore is a huge, wide lake—the largest natural freshwater lake in Southern California—where water-skiers, personal-watercraft riders, and sailboarders can find a slice of heaven. This camp is set along the north shore, where there are also several trails for hiking, biking, and horseback riding. There is a designated area near the campground for swimming and water play; a gently sloping lake bottom is a big plus here. Fishing has improved greatly in recent years and the lake is stocked with trout and striped bass. Other fish species include channel catfish, crappie, and bluegill. Night fishing is available. Anglers have a chance to fish for Whiskers, a very special catfish. It is a hybrid channel catfish that was stocked in 2000. It is a genetic cross between a blue and channel catfish, meaning that Whiskers could grow to more than 100 pounds. If you like thrill sports, hang gliding and parachuting are also available at the lake and, as you scan across the water, you can often look up and see these daredevils soaring overhead. The recreation area covers 3,300 acres and has 15 miles of shoreline. The elevation is 1,239 feet. While the lake is huge when full, in low-rain years Elsinore's water level can be subject to extreme and erratic fluctuations. Boaters planning to visit this lake should call first to get the latest on water levels and quality. Those familiar with this area will remember it was once named Lake Elsinore Campground and Recreation Area.

Campsites, facilities: There are 120 sites with partial hookups for tents or RVs up to 40 feet, 10 sites for RVs only with full hookups (30 amps), 51 tent sites, and 10 group sites for groups of 30–150 people. Picnic tables and fire pits are provided at some sites. Restrooms with flush toilets and showers, drinking water, picnic area, and dump station are available. Supplies and coin laundry are nearby. Some facilities are wheelchair-accessible. Leashed pets are permitted.

Reservations, fees: Reservations are accepted at 800/416-6992 ($8 reservation fee). Tent sites are $25–30 per night, RV sites (electricity, sewer and water) are $35 per night, $5 per night per additional person, $10 per night per additional vehicle, $5 per pet per night; group sites are $75 per night. Some credit cards accepted. Open year-round.

Directions: Drive to the junction of I-15 and Highway 74. At that junction, take Highway 74 west/Central Avenue. Drive a short distance on Central Avenue to Collier. Turn right on Collier and drive 0.25 mile to Riverside Drive. Turn left and drive approximately 1.5 miles to the campground on the left.

Contact: La Laguna Resort, 951/471-1212, www.rockymountainrec.com; City of Lake Elsinore, 951/674-3124, ex 265.

73 PALM VIEW RV PARK
🏊 🐕 🚴 ♿ 🚐 ⛺

Scenic rating: 5

near Lake Elsinore

Map 13.2, page 742

This privately operated RV park is in a quiet valley at 700 feet elevation and has a duck pond. The sites are fairly rustic, with some shade trees. The park's recreation area offers basketball, volleyball, horseshoes, tetherball, and a playground. For you wonderful

goofballs, bungee jumping and parachuting are available in the town of Perris. Note that 50 percent of the sites are occupied by long-term renters.

Campsites, facilities: There are 41 sites with full hookups (30 amps) for RVs, nine tent sites, and a group tent area that can accommodate up to 200 people. Some sites are pull-through. Picnic tables and fire rings are provided. Restrooms, dump station, recreation area, seasonal swimming pool, coin laundry, playground, convenience store, ice, and firewood are available. Some facilities are wheelchair accessible. Leashed pets are permitted.

Reservations, fees: Reservations are not accepted. RV sites (full hookups) are $32 per night, tent sites are $25 per night, $3 per person per night for more than four people. Monthly and weekly rates available. Open year-round.

Directions: Drive to the junction of I-15 and Highway 74. At that junction, take Highway 74/Central Avenue and drive east on Highway 74 for 4.5 miles to River Road. Turn right (south) and drive one mile to the park on the left (22200 River Road).

Contact: Palm View RV Park, 951/657-7791.

74 LAKE SKINNER RECREATION AREA
🏊 🚣 🏄 🚤 🐕 🚴 ♿ 🚐 ⛺

Scenic rating: 7

on Lake Skinner

Map 13.2, page 742

Lake Skinner is set within a Riverside County park at an elevation of 1,470 feet in sparse foothill country, where the water can sparkle, and it covers 1,200 surface acres. There is a speed limit of 10 mph and only four-stroke engines are allowed. Unlike nearby Lake Elsinore, which is dominated by fast boats and water-skiers, no water-contact sports are permitted here; hence no waterskiing, no swimming, no sailboarding. However, a half-acre swimming pool is available in the summer. Afternoon winds make for great sailing, and you can count on consistent midday breezes. The fishing can be good. Many fish are stocked at this lake, including trophy-sized bass and trout, along with catfish and bluegill. The fishing records here include a 39.5-pound striped bass, 33-pound catfish, and 14-pound, 8-ounce largemouth bass. The recreation area also provides hiking trails. Note: All boats must be certified mussel-free before launching.

Campsites, facilities: There are 241 sites for tents or RVs of any length, an overflow area, and two group camping areas; 184 sites have full hookups, 16 sites have electricity (50 amps) and water, 41 sites have water only. Many sites are pull-through. Picnic tables and fire grills are provided. Restrooms with flush toilets and coin showers, drinking water, playground, convenience store, picnic area, group facilities, ice, bait, dump station, swimming pool (in the summer), boat ramp, marina, mooring, boat rentals, and propane gas are available. Some facilities are wheelchair-accessible. Leashed pets are permitted.

Reservations, fees: Reservations are accepted at 800/234-7275 ($7 reservation fee). Tent sites are $13 per night, RV sites are $26 (full hookups), $21 (water and electricity), or $20 per night (no hookups) per night; the overflow area is $13 per night, $5 per night per additional vehicle, $150–280 per night for group sites (with special rates for youth groups), $1 per pet per night. Weekly and monthly rates are available. Some credit cards accepted. Open year-round.

Directions: Drive on I-15 to Temecula and the exit for Rancho California. Take that exit and drive northeast 9.5 miles to the park entrance on the right.

Contact: Lake Skinner Recreation Area, 951/926-1541, www.rivcoparks.org.

75 HANNA FLAT

🏃 🐕 ♿ 🚐 ⛺

Scenic rating: 8

near Big Bear Lake in
San Bernardino National Forest

Map 13.3, page 743

Over the years, Hanna Flat has been one of the largest, best maintained, and most popular of the Forest Service camps in the Big Bear Lake District (Serrano Campground is the most popular). The camp is set at 7,000 feet elevation on the slopes on the north side of Big Bear Lake, just under three miles from the lake. Big Bear is a beautiful mountain lake covering more than 3,000 acres, with 22 miles of shoreline and often excellent trout fishing and waterskiing. A trailhead for the Pacific Crest Trail is a mile by road north of the camp. Hanna Flat reopened in 2010 after closing for renovation from the 2007 Butler Fire. The repair work was excellent and the campground is very popular again.

Campsites, facilities: There are 88 sites for tents or RVs up to 26 feet (no hookups). Picnic tables and fire grills are provided. Drinking water and vault toilets are available. Some facilities are wheelchair-accessible. Leashed pets are permitted.

Reservations, fees: Reservations are accepted at 877/444-6777 or www.recreation.gov ($9 reservation fee). Single sites are $24–26 per night, double sites are $48–50 per night, $5 per night for each additional vehicle. Open May through September.

Directions: Drive on Highway 30 to the junction with Highway 330 (east of San Bernardino near Highland). Take Highway 330 north (signed "Mountain Resorts") and drive 28 miles (Highway 330 becomes Highway 18/Rim of the World Highway) to the Big Bear Lake Dam and a fork with Highway 38 and Highway 18. Continue straight on Highway 38 and drive approximately four miles to the town of Fawnskin and Rim of the World Highway. Turn left and drive three miles (after

0.5 mile, it becomes Forest Road 3N14, a dirt road) to the campground on the left.

Contact: San Bernardino National Forest, Mountaintop Ranger District, Big Bear Ranger Station/Discovery Center, 909/382-2790, www.fs.usda.gov/sbnf.

76 SERRANO

Scenic rating: 8

on Big Bear Lake in
San Bernardino National Forest

Map 13.3, page 743   **BEST**

This campground opened in the 1990s and became the first National Forest campground to offer state-of-the-art restrooms and hot showers. That is why it costs more to camp here. Regardless, it has since become the most popular campground in the region. Location is also a big plus, as this is one of the few camps at Big Bear within walking distance of the lakeshore. It covers 60 acres, another big plus. Another bonus is a paved trail that is wheelchair-accessible. Want more? Big Bear is the jewel of Southern California lakes, the Lake Tahoe of the South, with outstanding trout fishing and waterskiing. All water sports are allowed. The lake is stocked with trout and catfish, and it also has large- and smallmouth bass, crappie, bluegill, and sunfish. Swimming is excellent at this lake, with large, sandy beaches around the shoreline. However, the water is cold. A trailhead for the Pacific Crest Trail is nearby, and Canada is only 2,200 miles away. The elevation is 6,800 feet.

Campsites, facilities: There are 132 sites for tents or RVs up to 35 feet; some sites have full hookups (30 amps). Picnic tables and fire rings are provided. Restrooms with flush toilets and coin showers, drinking water, camp host, interpretive trails and programs, and a dump station are available. A store is nearby. Some facilities are wheelchair-accessible. Leashed pets are permitted.

Reservations, fees: Reservations are accepted at 877/444-6777 or www.recreation.gov ($9 reservation fee). Single sites are $28–30 per night, $56–58 per night for double sites, $5 per night per each additional vehicle. Open April through November.

Directions: Drive on Highway 30 to the junction with Highway 330 (east of San Bernardino near Highland). Take Highway 330 north (signed "Mountain Resorts") and drive 28 miles (Highway 330 becomes Highway 18/Rim of the World Highway) to the Big Bear Lake Dam and a fork with Highway 38 and Highway 18. Continue straight on Highway 38 and drive about 2.5 miles to Fawnskin and North Shore Lane (signed "Serrano Campground"). Turn right on North Shore Lane and drive to the campground entrance.

Contact: San Bernardino National Forest, Mountaintop Ranger District, Big Bear Ranger Station/Discovery Center, 909/382-2790, www.fs.usda.gov/sbnf; California Land Management, 909/866-8021.

77 HOLCOMB VALLEY

Scenic rating: 7

near the Pacific Crest Trail in
San Bernardino National Forest

Map 13.3, page 743

This camp is set near the Holcomb Valley Historic Area, at 7,400 feet elevation in the mountains about four miles north of Big Bear Lake. On the way in on Van Dusen Canyon Road you will pass a trailhead for the Pacific Crest Trail (two miles southeast of the camp). From here you can make the two-mile climb southwest to Bertha Peak, at 8,198 feet, overlooking Big Bear to the south.

Campsites, facilities: There are 19 sites for tents or RVs up to 32 feet (no hookups). Picnic tables and fire grills are provided. Vault toilets are available. No drinking water is available. Leashed pets are permitted.

Reservations, fees: Reservations are not accepted. Sites are $12–16 per night. Open year-round, but access is based on road conditions.

Directions: Drive on Highway 30 to the junction with Highway 330 (east of San Bernardino near Highland). Take Highway 330 north (signed "Mountain Resorts") and drive 28 miles (Highway 330 becomes Highway 18/Rim of the World Highway) to the Big Bear Lake Dam and a fork with Highway 38 and Highway 18. Continue straight on Highway 38 and drive about 10 miles to Van Dusen Canyon Road/Forest Road 3N09. Turn left and drive three miles (a dirt road) to Forest Road 3N16. Turn left and drive to the campground on the right.

Contact: San Bernardino National Forest, Mountaintop Ranger District, Big Bear Ranger Station/Discovery Center, 909/382-2790, www.fs.usda.gov/sbnf.

78 TANGLEWOOD GROUP CAMP

🚶 🐕 ♿ 🚐 ⛺

Scenic rating: 4

on the Pacific Crest Trail in
San Bernardino National Forest

Map 13.3, page 743

This primitive group camp is off an old spur road with the trailhead for the Pacific Crest Trail—the primary highlight. It is set at 7,400 feet elevation in a flat but wooded area northeast of Big Bear Lake. It is about a 10- to 15-minute drive from Big Bear City.

Campsites, facilities: There is one group campsite for tents or RVs up to 32 feet (no hookups) that can accommodate up to 40 people. Picnic tables and fire grills are provided. Vault toilets are available. No drinking water is available. Leashed pets are permitted.

Reservations, fees: Reservations are required at 877/444-6777 or www.recreation.gov ($9 reservation fee). The camp is $85 per night. Open mid-May through September.

Directions: Drive on Highway 30 to the junction with Highway 330 (east of San Bernardino near Highland). Take Highway 330 north (signed "Mountain Resorts") and drive 28 miles (Highway 330 becomes Highway 18/Rim of the World Highway) to the Big Bear Lake Dam and a fork with Highway 38 and Highway 18. Continue straight on Highway 38 and drive about 10 miles to Van Dusen Canyon Road/Forest Road 3N09. Turn left (dirt road) and drive four miles to Forest Road 3N16. Turn right and drive 1.7 miles to Forest Road 3N79. Turn right and drive 0.5 mile to the campground. Trailers are not recommended.

Contact: San Bernardino National Forest, Mountaintop Ranger District, Big Bear Ranger Station/Discovery Center, 909/382-2790, www.fs.usda.gov/sbnf.

79 BLUFF MESA GROUP CAMP

🚶 🐕 ♿ 🚐 ⛺

Scenic rating: 7

near Big Bear Lake in
San Bernardino National Forest

Map 13.3, page 743

Bluff Mesa Group Camp is one of several camps south of Big Bear Lake. A highlight here is the trailhead (signed on the access road on the way in) for the 0.5-mile walk to the Champion Lodgepole Pine, the largest lodgepole pine in the world: 400 years old, 112 feet tall, with a circumference of 20 feet. Many Forest Service roads are available nearby for self-planned side trips. The elevation is 7,600 feet.

Campsites, facilities: There is one group campsite for tents or RVs up to 20 feet (no hookups) that can accommodate up to 40 people. Picnic tables and fire grills are provided. Vault toilets are available. No drinking water is available. Garbage must be packed out. Some facilities are wheelchair accessible. Leashed pets are permitted.

Reservations, fees: Reservations are required at 877/444-6777 or www.recreation.gov ($9 reservation fee). The camp is $70 per night. Open mid-May through mid-October.

Directions: Drive on Highway 30 to the junction with Highway 330 (east of San Bernardino near Highland). Take Highway 330 north (signed "Mountain Resorts") and drive 28 miles (Highway 330 becomes Highway 18/Rim of the World Highway) to the Big Bear Lake Dam and a fork with Highway 38 and Highway 18. Turn right at Highway 18 and drive about four miles to Mill Creek Road. Turn right on Mill Creek Road and drive about 1.5 miles to the sign at the top of the hill and Forest Road 2N10. Turn right on Forest Road 2N10 and drive three miles (dirt road) to Forest Road 2N86. Turn right on Forest Road 2N86 and drive 0.25 mile to the campground.

Contact: San Bernardino National Forest, Mountaintop Ranger District, Big Bear Ranger Station/Discovery Center, 909/382-2790, www.fs.usda.gov/sbnf; fire regulations: Discovery Center, 909/866-3437.

80 HOLLOWAY'S MARINA AND RV PARK
🏊 ⛴ 🚐 🏕 ♿ 🚗

Scenic rating: 6

on Big Bear Lake

Map 13.3, page 743

This privately operated RV park (no tent sites) is a good choice at Big Bear Lake with boat rentals, ramp, and full marina available. Big Bear is the jewel of Southern California's lakes, covering more than 3,000 surface acres with 22 miles of shoreline. Its cool waters make for excellent trout fishing, and yet, by summer, it has heated up enough to make for superb waterskiing. A bonus in the summer is that a breeze off the lake keeps the temperature in the mid-80s. Note that about one-third of the sites are occupied by long-term renters. (For details about the lake, see the Serrano listing in this chapter.)

Campsites, facilities: There are 116 sites with full hookups (30 and 50 amps) for RVs up to 40 feet. Limited group camping is available. Picnic tables and fire grills are provided. Restrooms with flush toilets and showers, drinking water, dump station, cable TV, convenience store, ice, propane gas, coin laundry, playground, basketball court, horseshoe pits, and full marina with boat rentals are on the premises. A pirate ship tour is available. Leashed pets are permitted, including on rental boats.

Reservations, fees: Reservations are accepted at 800/448-5335. RV sites (full hookups) are $50–60 per night, $10 per night for each additional vehicle. Monthly rates available. Some credit cards accepted. Open year-round, weather permitting.

Directions: Drive on Highway 30 to the junction with Highway 330 (east of San Bernardino near Highland). Take Highway 330 north (signed "Mountain Resorts") and drive 28 miles (Highway 330 becomes Highway 18/Rim of the World Highway) to the Big Bear Lake Dam and a fork with Highway 38 and Highway 18. Turn left on Highway 18 and drive three miles to Edgemoor Road. Turn left at Edgemoor Road and drive 0.25 mile to the park entrance on the left.

Contact: Holloway's Marina and RV Park, 909/866-5706 or 800/448-5335, www.bigbearboating.com/rvpark.php.

81 BOULDER GROUP CAMP
🏕 🚐 🅰

Scenic rating: 6

near Big Bear Lake in
San Bernardino National Forest

Map 13.3, page 743

This is a primitive camp at 7,500 feet elevation, just far enough away from some prime attractions to make you wish you could move the camp to a slightly different spot. The headwaters of Metcalf Creek are hidden in the forest on the other side of the road, tiny Cedar Lake is about a half-mile drive north, and Big Bear Lake is about two miles north. You get the idea.

Campsites, facilities: There is one group campsite for tents and RVs up to 20 feet (no hookups) that can accommodate up to 40 people. Picnic tables and fire grills are provided. Vault toilets are available. No drinking water is available. Garbage must be packed out. A store and coin laundry are nearby. Leashed pets are permitted.

Reservations, fees: Reservations are required at 877/444-6777 or www.recreation.gov ($9 reservation fee). The camp is $70 per night. Open mid-May through mid-October.

Directions: Drive on Highway 30 to the junction with Highway 330 (east of San Bernardino near Highland). Take Highway 330 north (signed "Mountain Resorts") and drive 28 miles (Highway 330 becomes Highway 18/Rim of the World Highway) to the Big Bear Lake Dam and a fork with Highway 38 and Highway 18. Turn right at Highway 18 and drive about four miles to Mill Creek Road. Turn right on Mill Creek Road and drive about 1.5 miles to the sign at the top of the hill and Forest Road 2N10. Turn right on Forest Road 2N10 and drive about two miles to the campground entrance road (Forest Road 2M10B). Turn right and drive to the camp.

Contact: San Bernardino National Forest, Mountaintop Ranger District, Big Bear Ranger Station/Discovery Center, 909/382-2790, www.fs.usda.gov/sbnf; fire regulations: Discovery Center, 909/866-3437.

82 PINEKNOT

Scenic rating: 6

near Big Bear Lake in San Bernardino National Forest

Map 13.3, page 743

This popular, developed Forest Service camp is set just east of Big Bear Lake Village (on the southern shore of the lake) about two miles from the lake. It is a popular spot for mountain biking, with several ideal routes available. Of the camps at Big Bear, this is the closest to supplies. The elevation is 7,000 feet. (For details about the lake, see the Serrano listing in this chapter.)

Campsites, facilities: There are 52 sites for tents or RVs up to 35 feet (no hookups). Picnic tables and fire grills are provided. Drinking water and flush toilets are available. A store and coin laundry are nearby. Leashed pets are permitted.

Reservations, fees: Reservations are accepted at 877/444-6777 or www.recreation.gov ($9 reservation fee). Sites are $22–24 per night, $5 per night per each additional vehicle. Open May through mid-October.

Directions: Drive on Highway 30 to the junction with Highway 330 (east of San Bernardino near Highland). Take Highway 330 north (signed "Mountain Resorts") and drive 28 miles (Highway 330 becomes Highway 18/Rim of the World Highway) to the Big Bear Lake Dam and a fork with Highway 38 and Highway 18. Turn right at Highway 18 and drive about six miles to Summit Boulevard. Turn right and drive through the parking area to the road on the left (just before the gate to the ski area). Turn left and drive 0.25 mile to the campground on the right.

Contact: San Bernardino National Forest, Mountaintop Ranger District, Big Bear Ranger Station/Discovery Center, 909/382-2790, www.fs.usda.gov/sbnf.

83 BUTTERCUP GROUP CAMP

Scenic rating: 5

near the town of Big Bear Lake in San Bernardino National Forest

Map 13.3, page 743

This is a forested camp designed for large groups looking for a developed site near Big Bear Lake. It is about four miles from the southeast side of the lake, just outside the Snow Summit Ski Area. The elevation is 7,000 feet.

Campsites, facilities: There is one group campsite for tents or RVs up to 25 feet (no hookups) that can accommodate up to 40 people. Picnic tables and fire rings are provided. Drinking water and vault toilets are available. A store and coin laundry are nearby. Garbage must be packed out. Some facilities are wheelchair-accessible. Leashed pets are permitted.

Reservations, fees: Reservations are required at 877/444-6777 or www.recreation.gov ($9 reservation fee). The camp is $100 per night. Open mid-May through mid-October.

Directions: Drive on Highway 30 to the junction with Highway 330 (east of San Bernardino near Highland). Take Highway 330 north (signed "Mountain Resorts") and drive 28 miles (Highway 330 becomes Highway 18/Rim of the World Highway) to the Big Bear Lake Dam and a fork with Highway 38 and Highway 18. Turn right at Highway 18 and drive about six miles to Summit Boulevard. Turn right and drive through the parking area to the road on the left (just before the gate to the ski area). Turn left and drive 0.5 mile (past Pineknot Camp) to the campground on the right.

Contact: San Bernardino National Forest, Mountaintop Ranger District, Big Bear Ranger Station/Discovery Center, 909/382-2790, www.fs.usda.gov/sbnf; fire regulations: Discovery Center, 909/866-3437.

84 JUNIPER SPRINGS GROUP CAMP

Scenic rating: 3

in San Bernardino National Forest

Map 13.3, page 743

This is a little-known group camp, set at 7,700 feet elevation in a desertlike area about 10 miles east of Big Bear Lake. It is little known because there are not a lot of reasons to camp here. You need to be creative. Got a Scrabble game? Want to watch the junipers grow? Or maybe watch the features of the land change colors as the day passes? You get the idea.

Campsites, facilities: There is one group camp for tents and RVs up to 20 feet (no hookups) that can accommodate up to 40 people. Picnic tables and fire grills are provided. Vault toilets are available. No drinking water is available. Garbage must be packed out. Leashed pets are permitted.

Reservations, fees: Reservations are required at 877/444-6777 or www.recreation.gov ($9 reservation fee). The camp is $70–77 per night. Open year-round.

Directions: Drive on I-10 to Redlands and Highway 38. Take Highway 38 northeast and drive about 40 miles (1.5 miles past Onyx Summit) to Forest Road 2N01 on the right. Turn right (dirt road) and drive three miles to a Forest Service road (opposite the sign on the left posted Forest Road 2N04). Turn right and drive into the campground.

Contact: San Bernardino National Forest, Mountaintop Ranger District, Big Bear Ranger Station/Discovery Center, 909/382-2790, www.fs.usda.gov/sbnf; fire regulations: Discovery Center, 909/866-3437.

85 COUNCIL GROUP CAMP

Scenic rating: 5

near Jenks Lake and the San Gorgonio Wilderness in San Bernardino National Forest

Map 13.3, page 743

This is a group camp in a pretty wooded area 0.5 mile from little Jenks Lake (there is a nice, easy walk around the lake) and a few miles north of the northern border of the San Gorgonio Wilderness. There are several other camps in the area.

Campsites, facilities: There is one group campsite for tents or RVs up to 22 feet (no hookups) that can accommodate up to 50 people. Picnic tables and fire rings are provided. Drinking water and vault toilets are available. Some facilities are wheelchair-accessible. Leashed pets are permitted.

Reservations, fees: Reservations are required

at 877/444-6777 or www.recreation.gov ($9 reservation fee). The camp is $130 per night, $143 per night on holidays. Open May through mid-November.

Directions: Drive on I-10 to Redlands and Highway 38. Take Highway 38 northeast and drive 26 miles to the campground on the left, just past the Barton Flats Visitor Center.

Contact: San Bernardino National Forest, Mountaintop Ranger District, Big Bear Ranger Station/Discovery Center, 909/382-2790, www.fs.usda.gov/sbnf; fire regulations: Discovery Center, 909/866-3437.

86 BARTON FLATS

Scenic rating: 7

near Jenks Lake in
San Bernardino National Forest

Map 13.3, page 743

This is one of the more developed Forest Service camps in San Bernardino National Forest. The camp is set at 6,500 feet elevation, about two miles from Jenks Lake, a small, pretty lake with good hiking and a picnic area. Barton Creek, a small stream, runs nearby, although it may be waterless in late summer. The San Gorgonio Wilderness, one mile to the south, is accessible via Forest Service roads to the wilderness area trailhead. Permits are required for overnight camping within the wilderness boundaries and are available at Forest Service ranger stations. For those driving in on Highway 38, stop at the Mill Creek Ranger Station in Redlands.

Campsites, facilities: There are 52 sites for tents or RVs of any length (no hookups). Picnic tables and fire grills are provided. Drinking water, a dump station, and restrooms with coin showers and flush toilets are available. Some facilities are wheelchair-accessible. Leashed pets are permitted.

Reservations, fees: Reservations are accepted at 877/444-6777 or www.recreation.gov ($9 reservation fee). Sites are $25 per night, $50

per night for multifamily sites, $10 per night for each additional vehicle. Open May through mid-November.

Directions: Drive on I-10 to Redlands and Highway 38. Take Highway 38 northeast and drive 27.5 miles to the campground on the left.

Contact: San Bernardino National Forest, Mountaintop Ranger District, Big Bear Ranger Station/Discovery Center, 909/382-2790, www.fs.usda.gov/sbnf; campground, 909/389-4517.

87 SAN GORGONIO

Scenic rating: 7

near the San Gorgonio Wilderness in
San Bernardino National Forest

Map 13.3, page 743

San Gorgonio is one in a series of Forest Service camps along Highway 38 and about 2.5 miles from Jenks Lake. (See the Barton Flats listing in this chapter for details.) The elevation is 6,500 feet.

Campsites, facilities: There are 54 sites for tents or RVs of any length (no hookups). Picnic tables and fire grills are provided. Drinking water and restrooms with flush toilets and coin showers are available. Some facilities are wheelchair-accessible. Leashed pets are permitted.

Reservations, fees: Reservations are accepted at 877/444-6777 or www.recreation.gov ($9 reservation fee). Sites are $25 per night, $27 per night holiday weekends, $50 per night for multifamily sites, $10 per night for each additional vehicle. Open mid-May through mid-October.

Directions: Drive on I-10 to Redlands and Highway 38. Take Highway 38 northeast and drive 28 miles to the campground.

Contact: San Bernardino National Forest, Mountaintop Ranger District, Big Bear Ranger Station/Discovery Center, 909/382-2790, www.fs.usda.gov/sbnf.

88 OSO AND LOBO GROUP
🏇 🚗 ⛺

Scenic rating: 6

near the San Gorgonio Wilderness in
San Bernardino National Forest

Map 13.3, page 743

Oso and Lobo Group Camps are set directly adjacent to each other at 6,600 feet elevation. The camps are about three-quarters of a mile from the Santa Ana River. Little Jenks Lake is two miles away to the west, and the northern border of the San Gorgonio Wilderness is just a few miles to the south.

Campsites, facilities: There are two group sites for tents or RVs of any length (no hookups) that can accommodate 75–100 people each. Picnic tables and fire grills are provided. Drinking water and vault toilets are available. Leashed pets are permitted.

Reservations, fees: Reservations are required at 877/444-6777 or www.recreation.gov ($9 reservation fee). Sites are $190–250 per night. Open May through mid-October, weather permitting.

Directions: From I-10 in Redlands, drive 29 miles east on Highway 38 to the campground entrance road on the left.

Contact: San Bernardino National Forest, Mountaintop Ranger District, Big Bear Ranger Station/Discovery Center, 909/382-2790, www.fs.usda.gov/sbnf; fire regulations: Discovery Center, 909/866-3437.

89 SOUTH FORK
🛶 🏇 🚗 ⛺

Scenic rating: 7

near the Santa Ana River in
San Bernardino National Forest

Map 13.3, page 743

This is an easy-access Forest Service camp just off Highway 38, set at 6,400 feet elevation near the headwaters of two rivers, the South Fork River and the Santa Ana River. It is part of the series of camps in the immediate area, just north of the San Gorgonio Wilderness. This one is a four-mile drive from little Jenks Lake. (See the Barton Flats listing in this chapter for more details.)

Campsites, facilities: There are 24 sites for tents or RVs up to 30 feet (no hookups). Picnic tables and fire rings are provided. Drinking water and vault toilets are available. Leashed pets are permitted.

Reservations, fees: Reservations are not accepted. Sites are $20–22 per night, $10 per night for each additional vehicle. Open mid-May through September.

Directions: Drive on I-10 to Redlands and Highway 38. Take Highway 38 northeast and drive 29.5 miles to the campground entrance road.

Contact: San Bernardino National Forest, Mountaintop Ranger District, Big Bear Ranger Station/Discovery Center, 909/382-2790, www.fs.usda.gov/sbnf.

90 HEART BAR FAMILY AND SKYLINE GROUP CAMPS
🏃 🏇 ♿ 🚗 ⛺

Scenic rating: 4

in San Bernardino National Forest

Map 13.3, page 743

It's a good thing there is drinking water at this camp. Why? Because Heart Bar Creek often isn't much more than a trickle and can't be relied on for water. The camp is set at 6,900 feet elevation near Big Meadows and Aspen Grove. A challenging butt-kicker of a hike has a trailhead about 0.5-mile away to the north off a spur road, midway between the camp and the fire station. The trail here is routed along Wildhorse Creek to Sugarloaf Mountain (9,952 feet, about 8–9 miles one-way to the top). Insider's note: Just past the midway point on the trail to Sugarloaf Mountain is a trail camp on Wildhorse Creek.

Campsites, facilities: There are 66 sites for tents or RVs up to 40 feet (no hookups), and one group tent site for up to 25 people. Picnic tables and fire grills are provided. Drinking water and vault toilets are available. Some facilities are wheelchair-accessible. Leashed pets are permitted.

Reservations, fees: Reservations are accepted for individual sites and required for the group site at 877/444-6777 or www.recreation.gov ($9 reservation fee). Sites are $20–22 per night, $40–42 per night for multifamily sites, $70–77 per night for the group site, $10 per night for each additional vehicle. Open mid-May through early October.

Directions: Drive on I-10 to Redlands and Highway 38. Take Highway 38 northeast and drive 33.5 miles to Forest Road 1N02. Turn right and drive one mile to the campground.

Contact: San Bernardino National Forest, Mountaintop Ranger District, Big Bear Ranger Station/Discovery Center, 909/382-2790, www.fs.usda.gov/sbnf; fire regulations: Discovery Center, 909/866-3437

91 HEART BAR EQUESTRIAN GROUP AND WILD HORSE EQUESTRIAN

🏃 🐎 ♿ 🚐 ⛺

Scenic rating: 5

in San Bernardino National Forest

Map 13.3, page 743

You might not meet Mr. Ed here, but bring an apple anyway. Heart Bar is a horse camp on Heart Bar Creek, less than a mile east of Heart Bar Family Camp. Wild Horse is just 0.1 mile before Heart Bar Family Camp. A good trail that leads into the San Gorgonio Wilderness starts four miles down the road at Fish Creek Meadows. It is routed west for three miles to Fish Creek and then up Grinnell Mountain to the north peak of the Ten Thousand Foot Ridge. A wilderness permit is required. The elevation is 7,000 feet.

Campsites, facilities: Heart Bar has 46 corrals and one group campsite for tents or RVs up to 22 feet (no hookups) that can accommodate up to 65 people. Campers without horses are not permitted. Wild Horse has 11 equestrian sites, including three double sites, and 24 corrals. Picnic tables and fire grills are provided. Drinking water, coin showers,

and flush toilets are available. Water is available for horses. Some facilities are wheelchair-accessible. Leashed pets are permitted.

Reservations, fees: Reservations are required at 877/444-6777 or www.recreation.gov ($9 reservation fee). Sites are $25–52 per night for equestrian sites at Wild Horse and $250–275 per night for the group camp at Heart Bar. Open May through early October.

Directions: From San Bernardino, take I-10 east to Redlands and Highway 38. Take Highway 38 northeast and drive 33.5 miles to Forest Road 1N02. Turn right and drive a mile to the Heart Bar Group Campground on the right. Continue for 0.1 mile to the Wild Horse camp on the left. To reach Heart Bar Group Equestrian Campground, continue another 0.1 mile.

Contact: San Bernardino National Forest, Mountaintop Ranger District, Big Bear Ranger Station/Discovery Center, 909/382-2790, www.fs.usda.gov/sbnf; fire regulations: Discovery Center, 909/866-3437.

92 COON CREEK CABIN GROUP CAMP

🏃 🚻 ⛺

Scenic rating: 4

on the Pacific Crest Trail in San Bernardino National Forest

Map 13.3, page 743

Backpackers call this the "Coon Creek jump-off" because it is set on the Pacific Crest Trail at 8,200 feet elevation and provides a "jump-off" for a trek on the Pacific Crest Trail. The camp is set on Coon Creek, but the creek often runs dry by summer. Note that in the off-season the access road, Forest Road 1N02, can be gated; campers must hike or cross-country ski to the camp.

Campsites, facilities: There is one group camp for tents only for up to 25 people and 10 vehicles (no trailers or RVs). Picnic tables and fire grills are provided. Vault toilets are available. No drinking water is available. Leashed pets are permitted.

Reservations, fees: Reservations are required

at 877/444-6777 or www.recreation.gov ($9 reservation fee). The camp is $70–77 per night. Open year-round.

Directions: From San Bernardino, take I-10 east to Redlands and Highway 38. Take Highway 38 northeast and drive 33.5 miles to Forest Road 1N02. Turn right and drive five miles to the campground entrance (dirt road).

Contact: San Bernardino National Forest, Mountaintop Ranger District, Big Bear Ranger Station/Discovery Center, 909/382-2790, www.fs.usda.gov/sbnf; fire regulations: Discovery Center, 909/866-3437.

93 BOGART PARK/FAMILY, GROUP, AND EQUESTRIAN

🏃 🏠 ♿ �car 🛖

Scenic rating: 4

in Cherry Valley

Map 13.3, page 743

This county park is overlooked by many vacationers on I-10, and it is as pretty as it gets for this area. There are two miles of horse trails and some hiking trails for a recreation option during the cooler months. It covers 414 acres of Riverside County foothills set at the north end of Cherry Valley. The elevation is 2,800 feet. Bears frequent this area, so store your food properly and avoid scented products.

Campsites, facilities: There are 26 sites for tents or RVs up to 40 feet (no hookups), a group campground for tents that can accommodate up to 100 people, and a group equestrian campground. Fire grills and picnic tables are provided. Drinking water and flush toilets are available. The equestrian camp has corrals, stalls, and water troughs. Supplies are available in Beaumont. Some facilities are wheelchair-accessible. Leashed pets are permitted.

Reservations, fees: Reservations are accepted for individual sites and are required for the group camp at 800/234-7275 ($7 reservation fee). Developed sites are $12 per night, primitive sites are $10 per night. The group site is $144 per night, the group equestrian camp is $120

per night, $1 per night per pet or horse. Youth group rates are available. Open year-round, but closed on Tuesday and Wednesday.

Directions: From San Bernardino, take I-10 east to Beaumont and the exit for Beaumont Avenue. Take that exit north and drive four miles to Brookside. Turn right and drive 0.5 mile to Cherry Avenue. Turn left at Cherry Avenue and drive to the park on the right (9600 Cherry Avenue).

Contact: Bogart Park, 951/845-3818; Riverside County Parks, 800/234-7275, www.rivcoparks.org.

94 BANNING STAGECOACH KOA

🏊 🏠 🚴 🚐 🛖

Scenic rating: 2

in Banning

Map 13.3, page 743

Banning Stagecoach KOA (formerly Pine Ranch RV Park) is considered the gateway to mile-high Idylwild. Banning may not seem like a hotbed of civilization at first glance, but this clean, comfortable park is a decent spot to make camp while exploring some of the area's hidden attractions, including Agua Caliente Indian Canyons and the Lincoln Shrine. It is set at 2,400 feet elevation, 22 miles from Palm Springs. A good side trip is to head south on curving "Highway" 240 up to Vista Point in the San Bernardino National Forest.

Campsites, facilities: There are 91 RV sites with full hookups (30 and 50 amps); many sites are pull-through. There are also four tent sites and eight park models. Picnic tables and fire grills are provided. Restrooms with showers, cable TV, playground, swimming pool, clubhouse, coin laundry, Wi-Fi, dump station, ice, horseshoes, and propane gas are available. Leashed pets are permitted, with certain restrictions.

Reservations, fees: Reservations are recommended at 800/562-4110. RV sites are $40–43 per night, tent sites are $25 per night, park models are $80 per night, $2 per additional person per night, $1 per night for each additional vehicle. Some credit cards accepted. Open year-round.

Directions: From San Bernardino, take I-10 east to Banning and the exit for Highway 243. Take that exit south and take 8th Street south for one block to Lincoln. Turn left on Lincoln and drive two blocks to San Gorgonio. Turn right and drive one mile to the park.

Contact: Banning Stagecoach KOA, 951/849-7513, www.koa.com.

95 WILDERNESS WALK-IN CAMPS

Scenic rating: 10

in Mount San Jacinto State Park

Map 13.3, page 743   BEST (

This is one of the most spectacular getaways in the western United States. It includes a tram ride that will take you from 2,643 feet to 8,516 feet elevation, with stunning views across the desert and especially heart-breaking sunsets. On clear days, you can see the Salton Sea 50 miles to the south. From the tram, you then hike up to 2.75 miles to the camps, set at 9,100 feet, an ideal launch point for the hike to the Mount San Jacinto summit, at 10,834 feet the second-highest peak in Southern California. From Round Valley Camp, it is a 7.5-mile round-trip (just add another mile round-trip from Tamarack Valley Camp). On clear days from the summit, you can see 100 miles, including the Channel Islands, Mexico, and Nevada. On summer weekends, these campgrounds are often filled for dates more than a month in advance. Insider's tip: Be prepared for all types of weather conditions; weather can turn cold/rainy/snowy/windy quickly here. Snow camping is allowed.

Campsites, facilities: There are 25 tent sites at Round Valley, 12 tent sites at Tamarack Valley, and six sites at Little Round Valley. Groups are limited to 15 people. Pit toilets

are available. No drinking water is available. There is seasonal stream water that must be boiled or pump-filtered before use. No campfires are permitted. Bring a camp stove (propane or gas) for cooking. Smoking is not allowed. Garbage must be packed out. No firearms or wheels are permitted. Horses are allowed, but bring weed-free feed and water for the horses. Cell phone reception is virtually nonexistent.

Reservations, fees: Reservations are accepted online Sunday–Thursday and are highly recommended for Friday and Saturday nights in peak season. Sites are $5 per person. A camping permit is required and can be obtained at the park office or by mail to Mount San Jacinto State Park (include a stamped, self-addressed envelope); or apply online up to eight weeks in advance. A fee is charged for the tram ride. Open year-round, except when the tram is closed for maintenance.

Directions: From Banning, drive east on I-10 for 12 miles to the Highway 111/Palm Springs exit. Take that exit to Highway 111 and drive south nine miles to Tramway Road. Turn right and drive three miles to the parking area for Palm Springs Aerial Tramway. Ride the tram to Mountain Station. Hike 2.25 miles to Round Valley Camp, or continue from Round Valley Camp for another 0.5 mile to Tamarack Valley Camp.

Contact: Mount San Jacinto State Park, P.O. Box 308, Idyllwild, CA 92549, 951/659-2607, www.parks.ca.gov; Palm Springs Aerial Tramway, 888/515-8726, www.pstramway.com.

96 BLACK MOUNTAIN GROUP CAMP

Scenic rating: 6

near Mount San Jacinto in San Bernardino National Forest

Map 13.3, page 743

This is a beautiful scenic area, particularly to the north on the edge of the San Jacinto

Wilderness and to the east of Mount San Jacinto State Park. The camp is set at 7,500 feet elevation and is within a mile of a trailhead for the Pacific Crest Trail. Here you can turn southeast and hike along Fuller Ridge for another mile to the border of Mount San Jacinto State Park. Note that Black Mountain Lookout is just a two-mile drive, close to Boulder Basin Camp.

Campsites, facilities: There is one group camp for tents and RVs up to 16 feet (no hookups) that can accommodate up to 100 people. Picnic tables and fire rings are provided. Vault toilets are available. Drinking water is available at Cinca Posa Spring, about two miles away. Leashed pets are permitted.

Reservations, fees: Reservations are required at 877/444-6777 or www.recreation.gov ($9 reservation fee). The camp is $60–120 per night. Open May through mid-October.

Directions: Drive on I-10 to Banning and Highway 243/Pines to Palms Scenic Highway. Turn south on Pines to Palms Scenic Highway and drive about 15 miles to Forest Road 4S01. Turn left on Forest Road 4S01 and drive eight miles (a narrow dirt road) to the campground on the right. Trailers are not advised.

Contact: San Bernardino National Forest, San Jacinto Ranger District, 909/382-2922, www.fs.usda.gov/sbnf.

97 BOULDER BASIN

Scenic rating: 8

near the San Jacinto Wilderness in
San Bernardino National Forest

Map 13.3, page 743

This camp is on the top of the world for these parts: 7,300 feet elevation, adjacent to the Black Mountain Fire Lookout with great views in all directions and highlighted by Tahquitz Peak (8,828 feet) 10 miles to the southeast. Boulder Basin is also near the San Jacinto Wilderness (to the northeast) and makes a

good trailhead camp for hikers. A trail starting at Black Mountain Lookout leads west, dropping steeply into a canyon and also into a designated scenic area.

Campsites, facilities: There are 34 sites for tents or RVs up to 15 feet (no hookups). Note that trailers and RVs are not recommended. Picnic tables and fire rings are provided. Vault toilets are available, but there is no drinking water. Leashed pets are permitted.

Reservations, fees: Reservations are accepted at 877/444-6777 or www.recreation.gov ($9 reservation fee). Sites are $10 per night, $5 per night per additional vehicle. Open May through mid-October.

Directions: Drive on I-10 to Banning and Highway 243/Pines to Palms Scenic Highway. Turn south on Pines to Palms Scenic Highway and drive about 15 miles to Forest Road 4S01/Black Mountain Road. Turn left and drive six miles (a narrow dirt road) to the campground on the right. RVs not advised.

Contact: San Bernardino National Forest, San Jacinto Ranger District, 909/382-2922, www.fs.usda.gov/sbnf.

98 DARK CANYON

Scenic rating: 7

in the San Jacinto Mountains in
San Bernardino National Forest

Map 13.3, page 743

This pretty setting is on the slopes of the San Jacinto Mountains at 5,800 feet elevation. Hikers can drive to the Seven Pines Trailhead less than a mile north of camp at the end of Forest Road 4S02. The trail leads east for three miles into Mount San Jacinto State Park to Deer Springs, where there is a trail camp and a junction with the Pacific Crest Trail. A wilderness permit is required. While the North Fork of the San Jacinto River runs near the campground, access is closed to protect the mountain yellow-legged frog.

Campsites, facilities: There are 17 sites for tents or RVs up to 17 feet (no hookups). Picnic tables and fire grills are provided. Drinking water and vault toilets are available. Leashed pets are permitted.

Reservations, fees: Reservations are accepted at 877/444-6677 or www.recreation.gov ($9 reservation fee). Sites are $12 per night, $5 per night per additional vehicle. Open mid-May through mid-September.

Directions: Drive on I-10 to Banning and Highway 243/Pines to Palms Scenic Highway. Turn south on Pines to Palms Scenic Highway and drive about 13 miles to Forest Road 4S02. Turn left on Forest Road 4S02 and drive three miles (narrow paved road) to the campground.

Contact: San Bernardino National Forest, San Jacinto Ranger District, 909/382-2922, www. fs.usda.gov/sbnf.

99 MARION MOUNTAIN
🚶 🚐 ⛺

Scenic rating: 7

in San Bernardino National Forest

Map 13.3, page 743

You get good lookouts and a developed campground at this spot. Nearby Black Mountain is a good side trip that includes a drive-to scenic lookout point. In addition, there are several trailheads in the area. The best one starts near this camp and heads up the slopes to Marion Mountain and east into adjacent Mount San Jacinto State Park. The elevation is 6,400 feet.

Campsites, facilities: There are 24 sites for tents or RVs up to 15 feet (no hookups). Picnic tables and fire grills are provided. Drinking water and vault toilets are available. Leashed pets are permitted.

Reservations, fees: Reservations are accepted

at 877/444-6677 or www.recreation.gov ($9 reservation fee). Sites are $10 per night, $5 per night per additional vehicle. Open mid-May through mid-October.

Directions: Drive on I-10 to Banning and Highway 243/Pines to Palms Scenic Highway. Turn south on Pines to Palms Scenic Highway and drive about 13 miles south to Forest Road 4S02. Turn left on Forest Road 4S02 and drive two miles (narrow paved road) to the campground.

Contact: San Bernardino National Forest, San Jacinto Ranger District, 909/382-2922, www. fs.usda.gov/sbnf.

100 FERN BASIN
🚶 🐴 🚐 ⛺

Scenic rating: 7

near Mount San Jacinto State Park in San Bernardino National Forest

Map 13.3, page 743

This is a nearby alternative to Stone Creek (you'll pass it on the way in) and Dark Canyon (another three miles in). Marion Mountain Trailhead is accessible within 0.5 mile of the campground by driving east on Forest Road 4S02.

Campsites, facilities: There are 22 sites for tents or RVs up to 15 feet (no hookups). Picnic tables and fire rings are provided. Drinking water and vault toilets are available. Leashed pets are permitted.

Reservations, fees: Reservations are accepted at 877/444-6677 or www.recreation.gov ($9 reservation fee). Sites are $10 per night, $5 per night per additional vehicle. Open mid-May through mid-October.

Directions: Drive on I-10 to Banning and Highway 243/Pines to Palms Scenic Highway. Turn south on Pines to Palms Scenic Highway and drive about 13 miles south to Forest Road 4S02. Turn left on Forest Road

4S02 and drive one mile (narrow paved road) to the campground on the left.

Contact: San Bernardino National Forest, San Jacinto Ranger District, 909/382-2922, www. fs.usda.gov/sbnf.

101 STONE CREEK
🥾 🚐 ♿ 🚗 ⛺

Scenic rating: 7

in Mount San Jacinto State Park

Map 13.3, page 743

This is a wooded camp set in Mount San Jacinto State Park. The elevation is 5,900 feet, 0.25 mile off the main road along Stone Creek, just outside the national forest boundary. It is less than a mile from Fern Basin and less than three miles from Dark Canyon. The best trailhead in the immediate area is Seven Pines Trail out of Marion Mountain Camp, one-half mile from this camp.

Campsites, facilities: There are 50 sites for tents or RVs up to 24 feet (no hookups). Picnic tables and fire rings are provided. Drinking water and vault toilets are available. Supplies and coin laundry are three miles away in Pine Cove. Some facilities are wheelchair-accessible. Leashed pets are permitted.

Reservations, fees: Reservations are accepted at 800/444-7275 (800/444-PARK) or www. reserveamerica.com ($8 reservation fee). Sites are $20 per night, $8 per night for each additional vehicle. Discounts in winter. Open year-round.

Directions: Drive on I-10 to Banning and Highway 243/Idyllwild Panoramic Highway. Turn south on Idyllwild Panoramic Highway and drive about 13 miles south to the park entrance on the left.

Contact: Mount San Jacinto State Park, 951/659-2607; Inland Empire District, 951/443-2423, www.parks.ca.gov.

102 GOLDEN VILLAGE PALMS RV RESORT
🏊 🐕 ♿ 🚗

Scenic rating: 5

in Hemet

Map 13.3, page 743

This RV resort is for those ages 55 and over. It is the biggest RV park in Southern California. The grounds are lush, with gravel pads for RVs. It is set near Diamond Valley Lake, about 10 miles south, a new lake that is the largest reservoir in Southern California. A golf course is nearby, Lake Hemet is 20 miles east, and winery tours are available in Temecula, a 30-minute drive. About 250 of the 1,019 sites are rented on a year-round basis.

Campsites, facilities: There are 1,019 sites with full hookups (20, 30, and 50 amps) for RVs up to 45 feet; some sites are pull-through. No tent sites. Restrooms with flush toilets and showers, drinking water, cable TV, Wi-Fi, business services, three heated swimming pools, three spas, recreation room, fitness center, billiard room, coin laundry, large clubhouse, banquet and meeting rooms, organized activities, pavilion, church services, library, ballroom, shuffleboard, nine-hole putting green, volleyball courts, and horseshoe pits are available. A day-use area with propane barbecues is also available. Some facilities are wheelchair accessible. Leashed pets are permitted.

Reservations, fees: Reservations are accepted at 866/477-6154. RV sites (hookups) are $40–70 per night, $10 per person per night for more than two people. Group rates available. Weekly, monthly, and annual rates available. Open year-round.

Directions: Drive to the junction of I-215 and Highway 74 (near Perris). At that junction, take Highway 74 east and drive 14 miles to Hemet (the highway becomes Florida Avenue in Hemet) and continue to the resort on the left.

Contact: Golden Village Palms RV Resort, 951/925-2518, www.goldenvillagepalms.com.

103 CASA DEL SOL RV PARK RESORT

Scenic rating: 3

in Hemet

Map 13.3, page 743

Hemet is a retirement town, so if you want excitement, the four lakes in the area are the best place to look for it: Lake Perris to the northwest, Diamond Valley Lake and Lake Skinner to the south, and Lake Hemet to the east. The elevation at this 20-acre resort is 1,575 feet. Note that many of the sites are taken by year-round or long-term rentals.

Campsites, facilities: There are 358 sites with full hookups (30 and 50 amps) for RVs up to 45 feet. Restrooms with flush toilets and showers, drinking water, cable TV, WiFi, ice, library, heated swimming pool, spa, recreation room, exercise room, billiard room, shuffleboard courts, golf driving cage, dog runs, and coin laundry are available. Some facilities are wheelchair accessible. Leashed pets are permitted.

Reservations, fees: Reservations are accepted at 888/925-2516. RV sites (hookups) are $39 per night, $5 per person per night for more than two people. Weekly and monthly rates available; discounts available. Some credit cards accepted. Open year-round.

Directions: Drive to the junction of I-215 and Highway 74 (near Perris). At that junction, take Highway 74 east and drive 15 miles to Hemet (the highway becomes Florida Avenue in Hemet) and drive to Kirby Avenue. Turn right (south) on Kirby Avenue and drive a half block to the resort (2750 West Acacia Avenue).

Contact: Casa del Sol RV Park Resort, 951/925-2515, www.casadelsolrvpark.com.

104 MOUNTAIN VALLEY RV RESORT

Scenic rating: 3

in Hemet

Map 13.3, page 743

This is one of three RV parks in the Hemet area. Four lakes in the area provide side-trip possibilities: Lake Perris to the northwest, Lake Skinner and Diamond Valley Lake to the south, and Lake Hemet to the east. Golf courses are nearby.

Campsites, facilities: There are 170 sites with full hookups (30 and 50 amps) for RVs up to 40 feet. Restrooms with flush toilets and showers, cable TV, drinking water, a fireside room, heated swimming pool, enclosed spa, fitness center, golf driving cage, card-access laundry, billiards room, meeting room, group facilities, Wi-Fi, and telephone hookups are available. A store and propane gas are nearby. Some facilities are wheelchair-accessible. Leashed pets are permitted, with some breeds prohibited.

Reservations, fees: Reservations are accepted at 800/926-5593. RV sites (hookups) are $37 per night, $5 per person per night for more than two people, $2 per pet per night. Weekly, monthly, and annual rates available. Some credit cards accepted. Open year-round.

Directions: Drive to the junction of I-215 and Highway 74 (near Perris). At that junction, take Highway 74 east and drive 15 miles to Hemet (the highway becomes Florida Avenue in Hemet) and continue to South Lyon Avenue. Turn right on South Lyon Avenue and drive to the park at the corner of Lyon and South Acacia (235 South Lyon).

Contact: Mountain Valley RV Resort, 951/925-5812, www.mountainvalleyrvp. com.

105 IDYLLWILD COUNTY PARK

🚶 🐕 ⛺ 👤 🏕

Scenic rating: 6

near San Bernardino National Forest

Map 13.3, page 743

This Riverside County park covers 202 acres, set at 5,300 feet elevation and surrounded by Mount San Jacinto State Park, San Jacinto Wilderness, and the San Bernardino National Forest lands. That provides plenty of options for visitors. The park has equestrian trails and an interpretive trail. The top hike in the region is the ambitious climb up the western slopes to the top of Mount San Jacinto (10,804 feet), a terrible challenge of a butt-kicker that provides one of the most astounding views in all the land. (The best route, however, is out of Palm Springs, taking the aerial tramway, which will get you to 8,516 feet elevation before you hike out the rest.)

Campsites, facilities: There are 88 sites for tents or RVs up to 40 feet (no hookups). Fire grills and picnic tables are provided. Drinking water and restrooms with flush toilets and coin showers are available. A store, coin laundry, and propane gas are nearby. There is no drinking water in dry years. Some facilities are wheelchair-accessible. Leashed pets are permitted.

Reservations, fees: Reservations are accepted at 800/234-PARK 800/234-7275 ($6.50 reservation fee). Sites are $20 per night, $1 per pet per night. Some credit cards accepted. Open year-round.

Directions: Drive on I-10 to Banning and Highway 243/Idyllwild Panoramic Highway. Turn south on Idyllwild Panoramic Highway and drive to Idyllwild and Riverside County Playground Road. Turn west on Riverside County Playground Road and drive 0.5 mile (follow the signs) to the park entrance on the right.

Contact: Idyllwild County Park, 951/659-2656, www.rivcoparks.org.

106 IDYLLWILD

🚶 🚴 ⛺ ♿ 🚐 🏕

Scenic rating: 8

in Mount San Jacinto State Park

Map 13.3, page 743

This is a prime spot for hikers and one of the better jump-off points for trekking in the area, set at 5,400 feet elevation. There are no trails from this campground. But 0.5 mile north is Deer Spring Trail, which is connected with the Pacific Crest Trail and then climbs on to Mount San Jacinto (10,834 feet) and its astounding lookout.

Campsites, facilities: There are 24 sites for tents only, nine sites for tents or RVs up to 24 feet (three with full hookups, six with partial), and one hike-in/bike-in site. Fire grills and picnic tables are provided. Drinking water, restrooms with flush toilets and coin showers, and Wi-Fi are available. Supplies and coin laundry (100 yards) are nearby. Some facilities are wheelchair-accessible. Leashed pets are permitted.

Reservations, fees: Reservations are accepted at 800/444-7275 (800/444-PARK) or www.reserveamerica.com ($8 reservation fee). Sites are $25 per night, $8 per night for each additional vehicle, $3 per person per night for hike-in/bike-in site. Open year-round.

Directions: In Idyllwild, drive to the north end of town on Highway 243 to the park entrance on the left (next to the fire station). Note: From I-10 in Banning, take the A Street exit onto Highway 243. Drive south for 23.8 miles to the campground on the right, just before Idyllwild.

From I-10 in Banning, take the A Street exit onto Highway 243. Drive south on Highway 243 for 23.8 miles to the campground on the right, just before the town of Idyllwild.

Contact: Mount San Jacinto State Park, 951/659-2607; Inland Empire District, 951/443-2423, www.parks.ca.gov.

107 LAKE HEMET

Scenic rating: 7

near Hemet

Map 13.3, page 743

Lake Hemet covers 420 acres, is set at 4,340 feet elevation, and sits near San Bernardino National Forest just west of Garner Valley. Many campsites have lake views. It provides a good camping/fishing destination, with large stocks of trout each year, and yep, catch rates are good. The lake also has bass, bluegill, and catfish. Boating rules prohibit boats under 10 feet, canoes, sailboats, inflatables, and swimming—no swimming or wading at Lake Hemet. The boat speed limit is 10 mph.

Campsites, facilities: There are 275 sites for RVs up to 40 feet, 250 dry sites for tents, and four group sites a minimum of 25 people, including equestrian groups. Park model cabins are also available. All sites have full hookups (20 amps). Picnic tables and fire rings are provided. Restrooms with flush toilets and coin showers, drinking water, dump station, playground, basketball and volleyball courts, horseshoes, boat ramp, boat rentals, convenience store, coin laundry, and propane gas are available. No generators permitted at campsites. Some facilities are wheelchair-accessible. Leashed pets are permitted.

Reservations, fees: Reservations are accepted and are required for the group sites at 951/659-2680 ($9 reservation fee). Tent sites are $21–25 per night, double and triple sites are $35–49 per night, RV sites are $27–35 per night, $4 per person per night for more than two people, $12 per night for additional vehicle, $3 per pet per night. Some credit cards accepted. Open year-round.

Directions: From Palm Desert, drive southwest on Highway 74 for 33 miles (near Lake Hemet) to the campground entrance on the left. For directions if arriving from the west (several options), phone 951/659-2680, ext. 2.

Contact: Lake Hemet, 951/659-2680, www.lakehemet.org.

108 HURKEY CREEK PARK

Scenic rating: 5

near Lake Hemet

Map 13.3, page 743

This large Riverside County park is just east (across the road) of Lake Hemet, beside Hurkey Creek (which runs in winter and spring). The highlight, of course, is the nearby lake, known for good fishing in the spring. No swimming is permitted. The camp elevation is 4,800 feet. The park covers 59 acres.

Campsites, facilities: There are 130 sites and five group sites for tents or RVs up to 40 feet (no hookups) that can accommodate up to 100 people each. Fire grills and picnic tables are provided. Drinking water, restrooms with flush toilets and coin showers, a playground, and picnic areas are available. Some facilities are wheelchair-accessible. A small general store is nearby and a dump station is available at nearby Lake Hemet. Leashed pets are permitted.

Reservations, fees: Reservations are accepted for individual sites and required for the group sites at 800/234-7275 ($7 reservation fee). Sites are $20 per night, $1 per pet per night. Group sites are $4 per person with a minimum of 40 people. Some credit cards accepted. Open year-round.

Directions: From Palm Desert, drive southwest on Highway 74 for 32 miles (near Lake Hemet) to the campground entrance on the right.

Contact: Hurkey Creek Park, 951/659-2050, www.rivcoparks.org.

109 ANZA RV RESORT

Scenic rating: 4

near Anza

Map 13.3, page 743

This is a year-round RV park set at 4,100 feet elevation, with many nearby recreation options. Lake Hemet is 16 miles away, with hiking, motorbiking, and jeep trails nearby in San Bernardino National Forest. Pacific Crest Trail hikers are welcome to clean up and to arrange for food and mail pick-up. Note that most sites are filled with long-term renters.

Campsites, facilities: There are 116 sites for tents and RVs; many have full hookups (30 and 50 amps) and some sites are pull-through. Picnic tables are provided. Restrooms with showers, catch-and-release fishing pond, horseshoe pits, coin laundry, convenience store, dump station, ice, recreation room, and propane gas are available. Leashed pets are permitted, with certain restrictions.

Reservations, fees: Reservations are accepted at 888/763-4819. RV sites (hookups) are $20 per night, tent sites are $15 per night, $1 per person per night for more than two people. Discounts weekdays. Credit cards accepted online only. Open year-round.

Directions: From Palm Desert, drive west on Highway 74 for 24 miles to Highway 371. Turn left on Highway 371 and drive west to the town of Anza and Kirby Road. Turn left on Kirby Road and drive 3.5 miles to the campground on the left at Terwilliger Road (look for the covered wagon out front).

Contact: Anza RV Resort, 951/763-4819 or 888/763-4819, www.anzarvresort.com.

SAN DIEGO AND VICINITY

BEST CAMPGROUNDS

◖ **Fishing**
Campland on the Bay, **page 812.**

◖ **State Parks**
Palomar Mountain State Park, **page 815.**

San Diego was picked as one of the best regions

to live in America in an unofficial vote at a national conference for the Outdoors Writers Association of America.

It is easy to understand why: the weather, the ocean and beaches, the lakes and fishing, Cleveland National Forest, the state parks, the mountains, the hiking, the biking, and the water sports. What more could anyone ask for? For many, the answer is you don't ask for more, because it does not get any better than this.

The weather is near perfect. It fits a warm coastal environment with an azure-tinted sea that borders foothills and mountains. In a relatively small geographic spread, you get it all.

The ocean here is warm and beautiful, with 70 miles of beaches and often sensational fishing offshore for albacore, yellowtail, and marlin. The foothills provide canyon settings for many lakes, including Lower Otay, Morena, Barrett, El Capitan, Cuyamaca, San Vicente, Hodges, Henshaw, and several more − with some of the biggest lake-record bass ever caught in the world.

Cleveland National Forest provides a surprise for many − remote mountains with canyons, hidden streams, small campgrounds, and a terrain with a forest of fir, cedar, and hardwoods such as oak. A landmark is Palomar Mountain, with several campgrounds at Palomar State Park and nearby in the national forest. This is a great family destination. Long-distance views, stargazing, and watching meteor showers from the 5,000-foot ridges and lookouts set on the edge of Anza-Borrego Desert to the nearby east are all among the best anywhere in the state.

For more urban pursuits, San Diego's Mission Bay Park offers a fantastic network of recreation opportunities, with trails for biking and inline skating, and beaches and boating access.

Everywhere you go, you will find campgrounds and parks, from primitive to deluxe. Some of the more remote sections of Cleveland National Forest, as well as Cuyamaca Rancho State Park, provide access to wildlands and primitive campsites. There are developed RV parks in the San Diego area that cost as much as fine hotel rooms in other parts of the state, and they're worth it, like silver dollars in a sea of pennies.

The region is one of the few that provides year-round recreation at a stellar level.

If you could live anywhere in America, where would it be? Well, that's what makes it so special to explore and visit, camping along the way.

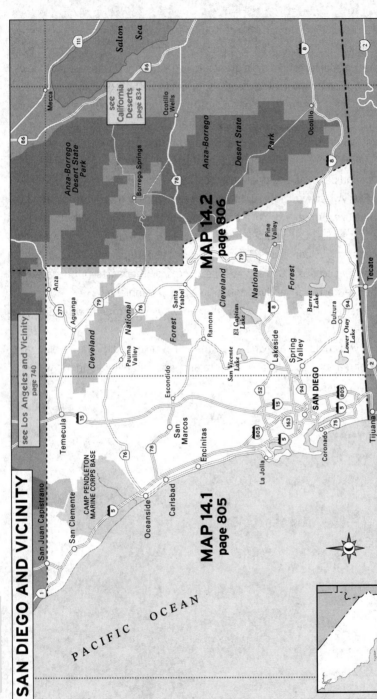

SAN DIEGO AND VICINITY

see Los Angeles and Vicinity
page 740

see California Deserts page 834

MAP 14.2
page 806

MAP 14.1
page 805

© AVALON TRAVEL

Salton Sea

Mecca

Ocotillo Wells

Borrego Springs

Anza-Borrego Desert State Park

Anza-Borrego Desert State Park

Ocotillo

Tecate

MEXICO

Anza

Aguanga

Santa Ysabel

Pine Valley

Cleveland National Forest

Pauma Valley

Ramona

El Capitan Lake

Barrett Lake

Dulzura

Cleveland National Forest

San Vicente Lake

Lakeside

Spring Valley

Lower Otay Lake

Escondido

Temecula

San Marcos

Encinitas

SAN DIEGO

Coronado

Tijuana

Camp Pendleton Marine Corps Base

Oceanside

Carlsbad

La Jolla

Pauma Valley

PACIFIC OCEAN

0   10 mi
0   10 km

Map 14.1

Sites 1-15
Pages 807-814

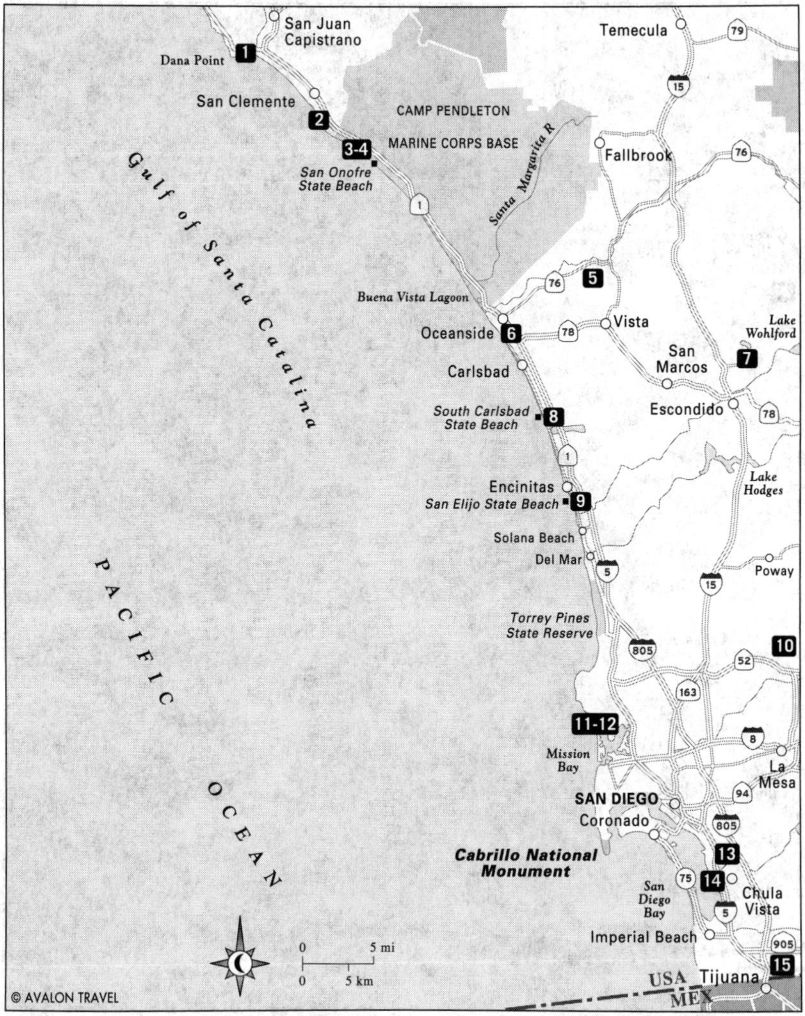

14.2

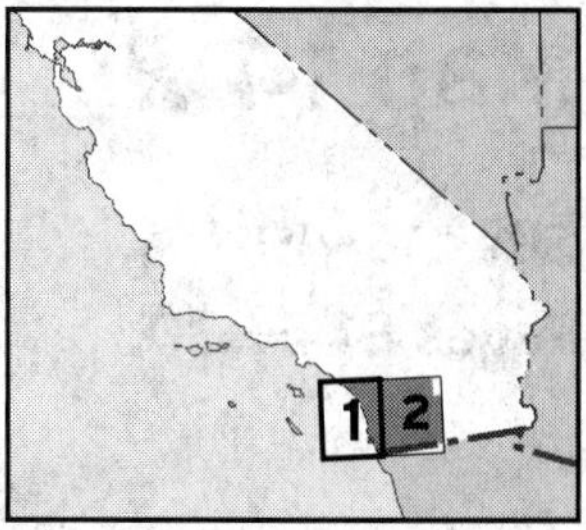

San Juan
Capistrano
Dana Point **1**
Temecula (79)

San Clemente
2 (15)
CAMP PENDLETON
3-4 MARINE CORPS BASE
San Onofre
State Beach
Fallbrook (76)

(1)

Santa Margarita R.

(76) **5**

Buena Vista Lagoon
(78) Vista
Oceanside **6**
San
Marcos
Lake
Wohlford

7
Carlsbad

South Carlsbad
State Beach **8**
Escondido (78)

(1)

Lake
Hodges

Encinitas
San Elijo State Beach **9**

Solana Beach
Del Mar (5)
Poway (15)

Torrey Pines
State Reserve
(805)
(52) **10**

(163)
(8)

11-12
Mission
Bay
La
Mesa

SAN DIEGO
Coronado
(94)
(805)

Cabrillo National
Monument
13

San
Diego
Bay **14**
Chula
Vista
(75)
(5)

Imperial Beach
(905)

USA
Tijuana **15**
MEX

Gulf of Santa Catalina

PACIFIC OCEAN

0   5 mi
0   5 km

© AVALON TRAVEL

Map 14.2

Sites 16-49
Pages 814-830

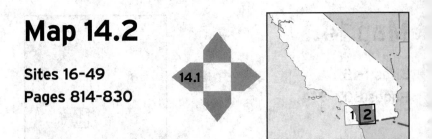

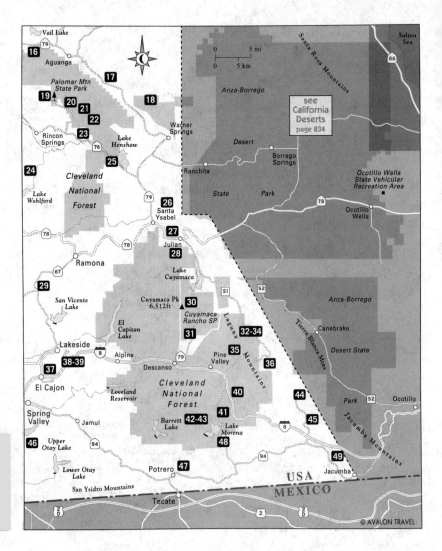

❶ DOHENY STATE BEACH

🏃 🚵 🏊 🛶 🐕 ♿ 🚐 ⛺

Scenic rating: 10

on Dana Point Harbor

Map 14.1, page 805

Doheny is a gorgeous park with a campground that requires working the reservation system the first morning campsites become available. Some campsites are within steps of the beach, yet this state beach is right in town, set at the entrance to Dana Point Harbor. It is a pretty spot with easy access off the highway. A lifeguard service is available in the summer, and campfire and junior ranger programs are also offered. A day-use area has a lawn with picnic area and volleyball courts. Bonfire rings are set up on the beach. Surfing is popular, but note that it is permitted at the north end of the beach only. San Juan Capistrano provides a nearby side trip, just three miles away.

Campsites, facilities: There are 115 sites for tents or RVs up to 35 feet (no hookups), one hike-in/bike-in site, and a group site for up to 40 people. Picnic tables and fire grills are provided. Drinking water, restrooms with flush toilets and coin showers, dump station, Wi-Fi, aquarium, and seasonal snack bar are available. Propane gas and gasoline are nearby. Some facilities are wheelchair-accessible. Leashed pets are permitted in campground only, not on the beach.

Reservations, fees: Reservations are accepted at www.reserveamerica.com ($8 reservation fee). Inland sites are $35 per night, premium beachfront sites are $60 per night, $10 per night for each additional vehicle, $5 per person per night for hike-in/bike-in site (photo ID required). The group site is $300 per night. Open year-round.

Directions: Drive on I-5 to the exit for Pacific Coast Highway/Camino de las Ramblas (three miles south of San Juan Capistrano). Take that exit and drive to Dana Point/Harbor Drive (second light). Turn left and drive one block to the park entrance. Doheny State Beach is about one mile from I-5.

Contact: Doheny State Beach, 949/496-6172; Orange Coast District, San Clemente Sector, 949/492-0802, www.parks.ca.gov.

❷ SAN CLEMENTE STATE BEACH

🏃 🚵 🏊 🛶 🐕 ♿ 🚐 ⛺

Scenic rating: 8

near San Clemente

Map 14.1, page 805

The campground at San Clemente State Beach is set on a bluff, not on a beach. A few campsites here have ocean views. Surfing is popular on the north end of a one-mile beach. The beach is popular for swimming, body surfing, and skin diving. Of the three local state beaches that provide easy access and beachfront camping, this one offers full hookups. The others are Doheny State Beach to the north and San Onofre State Beach to the south. A feature at this park is a two-mile long interpretive trail, along with hike-in/bike-in campsites. Surfing camp is held here during the summer.

Campsites, facilities: There are 160 sites, 72 sites have full hookups (30 amps) for tents or RVs up to 40 feet. There is also a hike-in/bike-in site and two group sites (one with hookups) for tents or RVs for up to 50 people and 20 vehicles. Picnic tables and fire grills are provided. Restrooms with flush toilets and coin showers, dump station, Wi-Fi, summer lifeguard service, and summer programs are available. A store, coin laundry, and propane gas are nearby. Some facilities are wheelchair-accessible. Leashed pets are permitted in the campground only.

Reservations, fees: Reservations are accepted at www.reserveamerica.com ($8 reservation fee). Tent sites are $35 per night, RV sites (with hookups) are $60 per night, $10 per night for each additional vehicle, the group sites are $280 per night, $5 per person per night for hike-in/bike-in sites. Open year-round.

Directions: From I-5 in San Clemente, take the Avenida Calafia exit. Drive west for a short distance to the park entrance on the left.

Contact: San Clemente State Beach, 949/492-3156; Orange Coast District, 949/492-0802, www.parks.ca.gov.

❸ BLUFF AREA
🏃 🚴 🏊 🎣 🐕 ♿ 🚐 ⛺

Scenic rating: 7

in San Onofre State Beach near San Clemente

Map 14.1, page 805

This camp may appear perfect at first glance, but nope, it is very noisy. Both the highway and train tracks are within very close range. You can practically feel the ground rumble, and that's not all: With Camp Pendleton just on the other side of the freeway, there is considerable noise from helicopters and other operations. Too bad. This is one of three parks set along the beach near San Clemente, just off the busy Coast Highway. The campground is set on top of a 90-foot bluff. This state beach covers more than 3,000 acres, featuring 3.5 miles of sandy beaches and access trails on the neighboring bluffs. This area is one of the most popular in California for surfing, and is also good for swimming. The shadow of the San Onofre Nuclear Power Plant is nearby. Other state beaches in the area are San Clemente State Beach and Doheny State Beach, both situated to the north.

Campsites, facilities: There are 175 sites for tents or RVs up to 38 feet (no hookups) and one group site for up to 50 people. Picnic tables and fire rings are provided. Drinking water, flush toilets, cold outdoor showers, and a dump station are available. A store, coin laundry, and propane gas are available within about five miles. Some facilities are wheelchair-accessible. Leashed pets are permitted at the campground and beach, but must stay on designated trails to access the beach.

Reservations, fees: Reservations are accepted at www.reserveamerica.com ($8 reservation fee). Sites are $35 per night, $10 per night for each additional vehicle, $225 per night for the group site. Open mid-May through October, weather permitting.

Directions: From San Clemente, drive south on I-5 for three miles to the Basilone Road exit. Take that exit and drive south on Basilone Road for two miles to the park.

Contact: San Onofre State Beach, 949/492-4872; Orange Coast District Office, 949/492-0802 or 949/366-8500, www.parks.ca.gov.

❹ SAN MATEO
🏃 🐕 ♿ 🚐 ⛺

Scenic rating: 9

in San Onofre State Beach near San Clemente

Map 14.1, page 805

This state beach is considered one of the best surf breaks in the United States—it's well known as the outstanding Trestles Surfing Area. The camp is set inland and includes a nature trail, featuring a marshy area where San Mateo Creek meets the shoreline. Although this is a state beach, the camp is relatively far from the ocean; it is a 1.5-mile walk to the beach. But it sure is a lot quieter than the nearby option, Bluff Area campground.

Campsites, facilities: There are 157 sites for tents or RVs up to 35 feet; 67 sites have partial hookups (30 amps). Picnic tables and fire grills are provided. A dump station and restrooms with coin showers and flush toilets are available. A store, propane gas, and coin laundry are nearby. Some facilities are wheelchair-accessible. Leashed pets are permitted.

Reservations, fees: Reservations are accepted at www.reserveamerica.com ($8 reservation fee). Sites are $35 per night, $10 per night for each additional vehicle, RV sites (hookups) are $60 per night. Open year-round.

Directions: Drive on I-5 to the southern end of San Clemente and the Cristianitos Road exit. Take that exit and drive east on Cristianitos Road for 1.5 miles to the park entrance on the right.

Contact: San Onofre State Beach, 949/492-4872; Orange Coast District Office, 949/492-0802 or 949/366-8500, www.parks.ca.gov.

5 GUAJOME COUNTY PARK

Scenic rating: 5

in Oceanside

Map 14.1, page 805

Guajome means "home of the frog" and, yep, so it is with little Guajome Lake and the adjacent marsh, both of which can be explored on a delightful two-mile hike. The lake provides a bit of fishing for warm-water species, mainly sunfish and catfish. Swimming is prohibited. Because of the wetlands, a huge variety of birds stop here on their migratory journeys, making this a favorite area for bird-watching. A historic adobe house in the park is a must-see. The park covers 557 acres and features several miles of trails for hiking and horseback riding, and a nearby museum with antique gas and steam engines and farm engines.

Campsites, facilities: There are 32 sites with full hookups (30 amps) for tents or RVs up to 45 feet; a few sites are pull-through. Group camping (at least 10 sites) is available by reservation. A camping cabin is also available. Picnic tables and fire grills are provided. Drinking water, restrooms with flush toilets and showers, dump station, basketball court, and playground are available. An enclosed pavilion and gazebo can be reserved for groups. A store and propane gas are nearby. Leashed pets are permitted.

Reservations, fees: Reservations are accepted at 858/565-3600 or 877/565-3600 or online at www.sdparks.org ($5 reservation fee). Sites are $24 per night, $4 per night per each additional vehicle, $1 per pet per night. Some credit cards accepted. Open year-round.

Directions: From Oceanside, drive east on Highway 76/Mission Avenue for seven miles to Guajome Lakes Road. Turn right (south) on Guajome Lakes Road and drive to the entrance.

Contact: San Diego County Parks Department, Guajome County Park, 760/724-4489, www.sdparks.org.

6 PARADISE BY THE SEA RV RESORT

Scenic rating: 7

in Oceanside

Map 14.1, page 805

This is a classic oceanfront RV resort, but no tenters need apply. It's an easy walk to the beach. The main coastal rail line runs adjacent to the resort, so expect some noise. For boaters, Oceanside Marina to the immediate north is the place to go. Oceanside is an excellent headquarters for deep-sea fishing, with charter trips available; contact Helgren's Sportfishing (760/722-2133) to arrange charters. Legoland is six miles from the resort, and the Wave Waterpark and Mission San Luis Rey are seven miles away. Camp Pendleton, a huge Marine Corps training complex, is to the north.

Campsites, facilities: There are 102 sites with full hookups (30 amps) for RVs up to 40 feet; a few sites are pull-through. Picnic tables are provided. Showers, flush toilets, cable TV, Wi-Fi, heated swimming pool, spa, clubhouse, banquet room, coin laundry, RV supplies, and convenience store are available. Boat rentals are nearby. Leashed pets are permitted, with certain breeds prohibited.

Reservations, fees: Reservations are recommended. Sites are $79–109 in summer, $54–69 in off-season, $5 per person ($3 in off-season) per night for more than two people, $15 per night ($5 in off-season) for each additional vehicle, $2–3 per pet per night. There is a 90-day limit per stay. Weekly and monthly rates available. Credit cards accepted. Open year-round.

Directions: Drive on I-5 to Oceanside and the Oceanside Boulevard exit. Take that exit and drive west on Oceanside Boulevard for 0.5 mile to South Coast Highway. Turn left on South Coast Highway and drive to the park on the right (1537 South Coast Highway).

Contact: Paradise by the Sea RV Resort, 760/439-1376, www.paradisebythesearvresort.com.

7 DIXON LAKE RECREATION AREA

🚶 🚣 🏊 ⛵ ♿ 🚐 ⛺

Scenic rating: 7

near Escondido

Map 14.1, page 805

Little Dixon Lake is the centerpiece of a regional park in the Escondido foothills. The camp is set at an elevation of 1,405 feet, about 400 feet above the lake's shoreline. No private boats or swimming are permitted, and a 5-mph speed limit for rental boats keeps things quiet. The water is clear, with fair bass fishing (a few huge lunkers). "Dottie," a 25 lb. 1 oz. bass—the biggest bass documented in the world—was snagged and released in 2006, then floated up dead from old age in 2008. The best success for bass is in the spring, with trout fishing best in the winter and early spring. Catfish are stocked in the summer, trout in winter and spring. In the summer, the lake is open at night for fishing for catfish. A pretty and easy hike is Jack Creek Nature Trail, a one-mile walk to a seasonal 20-foot waterfall. that no wood fires are permitted, but charcoal and gas are allowed.

Campsites, facilities: There are 45 sites for tents or RVs up to 35 feet; 11 sites have full hookups (30 amps). A cabin is also available. Picnic tables, fire grills, and food lockers are provided. Drinking water, restrooms with flush toilets and showers, picnic shelters, boat rentals, bait, ice, snack bar, and playground are available. Some facilities are wheelchair-accessible. No pets are allowed.

Reservations, fees: Reservations are accepted at 760/741-3328 ($5 reservation fee). Standard sites are $18–25 per night, deluxe sites (with full hookups) are $28–35 per night. Groups can be accommodated. Some credit cards accepted. Discounts in off-season. Open year-round.

Directions: Drive on I-15 to the exit for El Norte Parkway (four miles north of Escondido). Take that exit northeast and drive four miles to La Honda Drive. Turn left and drive about one mile to Dixon Lake.

Contact: Dixon Lake Recreation Area, City of Escondido, 760/839-4680, www.lakedixon.com.

8 SOUTH CARLSBAD STATE BEACH

🚶 🚴 🏊 🚣 🐕 ♿ 🚐 ⛺

Scenic rating: 9

near Carlsbad

Map 14.1, page 805

No reservation? Then likely you can forget about staying here. This is a beautiful state beach and, as big as it is, the sites go fast to the coastal cruisers who reserved a spot. The campground is set on a bluff, with half the sites overlooking the ocean. The nearby beach is accessible by a series of stairs. This is a phenomenal place for scuba diving and snorkeling, with a nearby reef available. This is also a popular spot for surfing and body surfing. Legoland is one mile away.

Campsites, facilities: There are 220 sites for tents or RVs up to 35 feet; some sites have full or partial hookups. Picnic tables and fire rings are provided. Drinking water, restrooms with flush toilets and showers, Wi-Fi, and dump station are available. Lifeguard service is not provided. Garbage must be packed out. Supplies and a coin laundry are available in Carlsbad. Some facilities are wheelchair-accessible. Leashed pets are permitted, but not on the beach.

Reservations, fees: Reservations are accepted at www.reserveamerica.com ($8 reservation fee). Developed sites are $35 per night, premium sites are $50 per night, $10 per night for each additional vehicle. Open year-round, with limited facilities in the winter.

Directions: Drive on I-5 to Carlsbad and the exit for Palomar Airport Road. Take that exit and drive west for 0.3 mile to Carlsbad Boulevard South. Turn south on Carlsbad Boulevard South and drive three miles to Poinsettia Avenue and the park entrance on the right.

Contact: South Carlsbad State Beach, 760/438-3143; San Diego Coast District, 619/688-3260, www.parks.ca.gov.

9 SAN ELIJO STATE BEACH

🚶 🚵 🏊 ⛵ 🎣 ♿ 🚐 ⛺

Scenic rating: 9

in Cardiff by the Sea

Map 14.1, page 805

As with South Carlsbad State Beach, about half the sites here overlook the ocean—that is, these are bluff-top campgrounds. The swimming and surfing are good, with a reef nearby for snorkeling and diving. What more could you ask for? Well, for one thing, how about not so many trains? Yep, train tracks run nearby and the trains roll by several times a day. So much for tranquility. Regardless, it is a beautiful beach just north of the small town of Cardiff by the Sea. As at all state beaches, reservations are usually required to get a spot between Memorial Day weekend and Labor Day weekend. Nearby San Elijo Lagoon at Solana Beach is an ecological preserve. Though this is near a developed area, there are numerous white egrets, as well as occasional herons and other marine birds.

Campsites, facilities: There are 144 sites for tents or RVs up to 22 feet (no hookups) and 28 sites for tents or RVs up to 35 feet (full hookups). Picnic tables and fire rings are provided. Drinking water, restrooms with flush toilets and coin showers, Wi-Fi, coin laundry, dump station, and small store are available. Lifeguard service is not provided. Garbage must be packed out. Some facilities are wheelchair-accessible. Leashed pets are permitted, but not on the beach.

Reservations, fees: Reservations are accepted at www.reserveamerica.com ($8 reservation fee). Inland sites are $35 per night, inland RV sites (hookups) are $55 per night. Ocean sites are $50 per night, ocean RV sites (hookups) are $60 per night, $10 per night for each additional vehicle. Open year-round.

Directions: Drive on I-5 to Encinitas and the Encinitas Boulevard exit. Take that exit and drive west on Encinitas Boulevard for one mile to U.S. 101 (South Coast Highway). Turn south (left) on U.S. 101 and drive two miles to the park on the right.

Contact: San Elijo State Beach, 760/753-5091; San Diego Coast District, 619/688-3260 or 760/720-7001, www.parks.ca.gov.

10 SANTEE LAKES RECREATION PRESERVE

🏊 ⛵ 🎣 🎣 🏕 ♿ 🚐

Scenic rating: 8

near Santee

Map 14.1, page 805

This is a 190-acre park built around a complex of seven lakes. Some campsites are lakefront. The park is best known for its fishing. The lakes are stocked with large numbers of trout and catfish, with fantastic lake records including a 39-pound catfish, 13-pound rainbow trout, 13.9-pound largemouth bass, and 2.5-pound bluegill. Rowboats, pedal boats, kayaks, and canoes are available for rent. So how many lakes can you boat on? Answer: Only one, Lake 5. Fishing is now allowed on all lakes, and float tubing is permitted on four lakes for campers only. No swimming or water/body contact is allowed here, and no private motorized boats are permitted. This small regional park is 20 miles east of San Diego. It receives more than 100,000 visitors per year. The camp is set at 400 feet elevation. The Carlton Oaks Country Club is 0.5-mile away and open to the public.

Campsites, facilities: There are 300 sites with full hookups (50 amps) for RVs of any length and nine tent sites. Some sites are pull-through. Ten cabins are also available. Picnic tables are provided and some sites have barbecue grills. Restrooms with flush toilets and showers, drinking water, dump station, boat rentals, playground, seasonal swimming pool, general store, picnic area, amphitheater, RV storage, recreation center, Wi-Fi, pay phone, propane, and coin laundry are available. Some facilities are wheelchair-accessible. Leashed pets are permitted in the campground.

Reservations, fees: Reservations are accepted online and at 619/596-3141. Pull-through RV sites are $41–43 per night, deluxe RV sites (pull-through and back-in) are $47–49 per night, lakefront sites are $44–47 per night, back-in sites are $39–41 per night, lakefront cabins are $101–126 per night, floating cabins are 121–146 per night, a camping club site is $35 per night, $2 per night for each additional vehicle, $1 per pet per night. Discounts Sunday through Thursday. Weekly and monthly rates available. Some credit cards accepted. Open year-round.

Directions: Drive on I-8 to El Cajon and Highway 67. Take the Highway 67 exit north (toward Santee) and drive one mile to Bradley Avenue. Take that exit and drive a short distance to Bradley Avenue. Turn left and drive one mile to Cuyamaca Street. Turn right and drive 1.6 miles to Mission Gorge Road. Turn left (west) and drive 0.3 mile to Fanita Parkway. Turn right and drive a short distance to the campground entrance on the left at 9310 Fanita Parkway.

Contact: Santee Lakes Recreation Preserve, Padre Dam Municipal Water District, 619/596-3141, www.santeelakes.com.

11 CAMPLAND ON THE BAY

Scenic rating: 8

on Mission Bay

Map 14.1, page 805   BEST (

In 2010, Campland on the Bay was voted San Diego's "Best Campground" by the San Diego Union–Tribune. No kidding, this is one of the biggest campgrounds on this side of the galaxy. The place has a prime location: The park overlooks Kendall Frost Wildlife Preserve and is set on Mission Bay, a beautiful spot and a boater's paradise; it includes a private beach. Waterskiing, sailboarding, and ocean access for deep-sea fishing are preeminent. SeaWorld, just north of San Diego, offers a premium side trip.

Campsites, facilities: There are more than 558 sites, most with full or partial hookups (30 and 50 amps) for tents or RVs up to 45 feet. Picnic tables and fire pits are provided. Restrooms with flush toilets and showers, drinking water, cable TV, phone, Wi-Fi, swimming pools, spa,

recreation hall, arcade, playground, café, dump station, coin laundry, grocery store, amphitheater, RV and boat storage, RV supplies, propane gas, boat ramp, marina, boat docks, water toy rentals, boat and bike rentals, and organized activities and events are available. Leashed pets are permitted, with certain restrictions.

Reservations, fees: Reservations are accepted up to two years in advance at 800/422-9386 ($25 site guarantee fee) or by fax to 858/581-4206. RV sites are $50–393.65 per night, tent sites are $45–84 per night, $10 per night for each additional vehicle or boats and trailers, $5 per person per night for additional people, $3 per night per pet. Winter rates are discounted. Weekly rates are available during the winter. Some credit cards accepted. Open year-round.

Directions: Drive on I-5 south to San Diego and the Balboa-Garnet exit. Take that exit to Mission Bay Drive and drive to Grand Avenue. Turn right and drive one mile to Olney Street. Turn left on Olney Street and drive to Pacific Beach Drive. Turn left and drive a short distance to the campground entrance.

From northbound I-5 in San Diego, take the Grand-Garnet exit. Stay in the left lane to Grand Avenue. Turn left on Grand Avenue and drive to Olney Street. Turn left on Olney Street and continue as above.

Contact: Campland on the Bay, 800/422-9386, administration office, 858/581-4200, fax 858/581-4206, www.campland.com.

12 SANTA FE PARK RV RESORT

Scenic rating: 5

in San Diego

Map 14.1, page 805

This resort is a short drive from a variety of side trips, including the San Diego Zoo, SeaWorld, the historic San Diego Mission and Presidio Park, golf courses, beaches, sportfishing, and Tijuana.

Campsites, facilities: There are 129 sites with

full hookups (20, 30, and 50 amps) for RVs up to 40 feet (at three pull-through sites). Picnic tables and barbecues are provided. Restrooms with flush toilets and showers, drinking water, playground, heated swimming pool, spa, dump station, satellite TV, Wi-Fi, recreation room, mini theater, fitness center, and coin laundry are available. Some facilities are wheelchair-accessible. Leashed pets under 25 pounds are permitted, with some restrictions.

Reservations, fees: Reservations are accepted online or at 800/959-3787. RV sites (hookups) are $69–79 per night, pull-through RV sites (hookups) are $74–85 per night, $3.50 per person per night for more than three people, $3 per pet per night. Discounts weekdays and in off-season. Monthly rates available. Some credit cards accepted. Open year-round.

Directions: Drive on I-5 south to San Diego and Exit 23 for Balboa-Garnet. Take that exit, get in the left lane, and drive a short distance to the second stoplight and Damon Street. Turn left and drive 0.25 mile to Santa Fe Street. Turn left and drive 1.4 miles to the resort on the right (5707 Santa Fe Street).

On northbound I-5, drive to Exit 23 for Grand-Garnet. Take that exit and continue as it feeds to East Mission Bay Drive. Continue through four traffic signals to Damon Street. Turn right and drive 0.25 mile to Santa Fe Street. Turn left and drive 1.4 miles to the resort on the right. Note: On Santa Fe Street, disregard the sign for "Not a through street."

Contact: Santa Fe Park RV Resort, 5707 Santa Fe St., 858/272-4051 or 800/959-3787, www.santafepark.com.

13 SAN DIEGO METROPOLITAN KOA
🚲 🏊 🎣 🐕 ♿ 🚐 ⛺

Scenic rating: 6

in Chula Vista

Map 14.1, page 805

This is one in a series of parks set up primarily for RVs cruising I-5. Chula Vista is between Mexico and San Diego, allowing visitors to make side trips east to Lower Otay Lake, north to the San Diego attractions, south to Tijuana, or "around the corner" on Highway 75 to Silver Strand State Beach. Nearby San Diego Bay is beautiful, with excellent waterskiing (in designated areas), sailboarding, and a great swimming beach.

Campsites, facilities: There are 200 sites for RVs of any length (full hookups), 63 sites for tents, 27 cabins, and eight lodges. Many sites are pull-through. Picnic tables and barbecue grills are provided. Restrooms with flush toilets and showers, drinking water, modem access, Wi-Fi, playground, dump station, coin laundry, heated swimming pool, spa, bike rentals, propane gas, seasonal organized activities, and convenience store are available. Some facilities are wheelchair-accessible. Leashed pets are permitted.

Reservations, fees: Reservations are accepted at 800/562-9877. RV sites (hookups) are $62–82 per night, tent sites are $47–57 per night, $5 per night for each additional vehicle. Camping cabins are $93–105 per night, lodges are $165–235 per night. Discounts in off-season. Some credit cards accepted. Open year-round.

Directions: From I-5 in Chula Vista, take the exit for E Street and drive east on E Street for three miles to 2nd Avenue. Turn left (north) on 2nd Avenue and drive 0.75 mile to the park on the right (111 North 2nd Avenue).

Contact: San Diego Metropolitan KOA, 619/427-3601, www.sandiegokoa.com.

14 CHULA VISTA RV RESORT
🚲 🏊 🚣 🎣 🚐 🐕 🐾 ♿ 🚐

Scenic rating: 8

in Chula Vista

Map 14.1, page 805

This RV park is about 50 yards from San Diego Bay, a beautiful, calm piece of water where waterskiing is permitted in designated areas. Each site is landscaped to provide some privacy.

The park has its own marina with 552 slips. An excellent swimming beach is available, and conditions in the afternoon for sailboarding are also excellent. Bike paths are nearby.

Campsites, facilities: There are 237 sites with full hookups (30 and 50 amps) for RVs. Some sites are pull-through. No tents. Picnic tables and cable TV are provided. Restrooms with flush toilets and showers, drinking water, Wi-Fi, modem access, fitness center, playgrounds, heated swimming pool and spa, game room, two waterfront restaurants, marina, fishing pier, free boat launch, coin laundry, propane gas, bicycle rentals, car rentals, picnic area, meeting rooms, and general store are available. Some facilities are wheelchair-accessible. Leashed pets up to 20 pounds are permitted, with certain restrictions.

Reservations, fees: Reservations are accepted at 800/770-2878 or www.chulavistarv.com (deposit required). RV sites are $58–77, $3 per night per additional person for more than four people, $3 per night for each additional vehicle, $1 per pet per night, boat slips are $36–45 per night. Weekly and monthly rates are available. Discounts in off-season. Some credit cards accepted. Open year-round.

Directions: Drive on I-5 to Chula Vista and the exit for J Street/Marina Parkway. Take that exit, turn left, and drive 0.5 mile west to Sandpiper Way. Turn left and drive a short distance to the park on the left (460 Sandpiper Way).

Contact: Chula Vista RV Resort, 619/422-0111, www.chulavistarv.com.

15 LA PACIFICA RV RESORT
🏊 🐕 ♿ 🚐

Scenic rating: 6

in San Ysidro

Map 14.1, page 805

This RV park is less than two miles from the Mexican border. Note that many sites are filled with long-term renters, but some sites are available for overnight use.

Campsites, facilities: There are 179 sites with full hookups (20, 30 and 50 amps) for RVs up to 40 feet. Many sites are pull-through. Picnic tables are provided at most sites. Restrooms with flush toilets and showers, heated swimming pool, whirlpool, clubhouse, video and book library, cable TV, phone and modem hookups, Wi-Fi, recreation room, dump station, coin laundry, and propane gas are available. All facilities are wheelchair-accessible. Leashed pets are permitted with restrictions.

Reservations, fees: Reservations are accepted at 888/786-6997 or online; group reservations must be made by phone. RV sites are $39–49 per night, $5 per person for more than four people, $1 per pet. Weekly and monthly rates available. Credit cards accepted. Open year-round.

Directions: From the San Diego area, drive south on I-5 to San Ysidro and the exit for Dairymart Road. Take that exit east to Dairymart Road and drive a short distance to San Ysidro Boulevard. Turn left and drive to the park on the left (1010 San Ysidro Boulevard).

Contact: La Pacifica RV Resort, 619/428-4411, www.lapacificarvresortpark.com.

16 DRIPPING SPRINGS
🏕 🐕 🚐 ⛺

Scenic rating: 7

near the Agua Tibia Wilderness in Cleveland National Forest

Map 14.2, page 806

This is one of the premium Forest Service camps available, set just inside the national forest border near Vail Lake and adjacent to the Agua Tibia Wilderness. Dripping Springs Trail is routed south out of camp, starting at 1,600 feet elevation and climbing near the peak of Agua Tibia Mountain, at 4,779 feet.

Campsites, facilities: There are 34 sites for tents or RVs up to 22 feet (no hookups), including several double sites and five equestrian sites. Picnic tables and fire rings are provided. Drinking water and vault toilets are available. Supplies are nearby in Temecula. Leashed pets are permitted.

Reservations, fees: Reservations are not accepted. Sites are $15–30 per night, $5 per night per additional vehicle. Open June through February. Closed March through May for protection of an endangered species, the arroyo southwestern toad.

Directions: From I-15 in Temecula, drive 11 miles southeast on Highway 79 to the campground.

Contact: Cleveland National Forest, Palomar Ranger District, 760/788-0250, www.fs.usda.gov/cleveland.

17 OAK GROVE

Scenic rating: 4

near Temecula Creek in
Cleveland National Forest

Map 14.2, page 806

Oak Grove campground is on the northeastern fringe of Cleveland National Forest at 2,800 feet elevation. Easy access from Highway 79 makes this a popular camp. The Palomar Observatory is five miles up the mountain to the west, but there is no direct way to reach it from the campground and it cannot be viewed from camp. Lake Henshaw is about a half-hour drive to the south. A boat ramp and boat rentals are available there.

Campsites, facilities: There are 81 sites for tents, including 12 double sites, or RVs up to 27 feet (no hookups). Picnic tables and fire grills are provided. Drinking water and flush toilets are available. Propane gas and groceries are nearby. Leashed pets are permitted.

Reservations, fees: Reservations are not accepted. Sites are $15–30 per night, $5 per night per additional vehicle. Open year-round.

Directions: Drive on I-15 to the Highway 79 exit. Take that exit and drive south on Highway 79 to Aguanga. Continue southeast on Highway 79 for 6.5 miles to the camp entrance.

Contact: Cleveland National Forest, Palomar Ranger District, 760/788-0250, www.fs.usda.gov/cleveland.

18 INDIAN FLATS

Scenic rating: 5

near the Pacific Crest Trail in
Cleveland National Forest

Map 14.2, page 806

Indian Flats is a remote campground, set at 3,600 feet elevation just north of Pine Mountain. The Pacific Crest Trail passes only two miles down the road to the south. A two-mile hike south on the PCT will take you down into a canyon and the home of Agua Caliente Creek.

Campsites, facilities: There are 17 sites for tents or RVs up to 15 feet and a group site for 20–50 people. Picnic tables and fire grills are provided. Vault toilets are available. There is no drinking water. Leashed pets are permitted.

Reservations, fees: Reservations are not accepted. Sites are $12 per night, $5 per night per additional vehicle. Open June through February, closed March through May for protection of an endangered species, the arroyo southwestern toad.

Directions: From El Cajon, drive east on I-8 to Highway 79 (near Descanso Junction). Turn north on Highway 79 and drive to the town of Warner Springs. Continue two miles on Highway 79 to Forest Road 9S05. Turn right on Forest Road 9S05 and drive six miles to the campground.

Contact: Cleveland National Forest, Palomar Ranger District, 760/788-0250, www.fs.usda.gov/cleveland.

19 PALOMAR MOUNTAIN STATE PARK

Scenic rating: 5

near the Palomar Observatory

Map 14.2, page 806   BEST (

The long-distance views from Palomar Mountain State Park are spectacular. The park features 14 miles of trails, including several loop trails, often featuring long-distance views. This camp offers some fishing in Doane Pond (state fishing laws are in effect here—great for youngsters learning to fish). There are numerous hikes, including Boucher Trail (4 miles) and Lower Doane Valley Trail (3 miles). The view from Boucher Lookout is stunning, at 5,438 feet elevation looking out over the valley below. This developed state park is a short drive from the Palomar Observatory (not part of the park). There are four other campgrounds in the immediate area that are a short distance from the observatory. At the Palomar Observatory you'll find the 200-inch Hale Telescope, America's largest telescope. This is a private, working telescope, run by the California Institute of Technology. Observatory tours are available, and the telescope can be viewed (but not used) by the public. The campground elevation is 4,700 feet.

Note: This park was on the closure list developed by the California Department of Parks, pending final state budget decisions or the possible transfer of park management to other park agencies or volunteer groups. It is currently open via a donor agreement with Friends of Palomar Mountain State Park.

Campsites, facilities: There are 32 sites for tents or RVs up to 27 feet (no hookups) and trailers up to 24 feet, three group sites for 15–25 people, and one hike-in/bike-in site. Picnic tables, fire grills, and food lockers are provided. Drinking water and restrooms with flush toilets and coin showers are available. Some facilities are wheelchair-accessible. Leashed pets are permitted in the campground, but not on trails.

Reservations, fees: Reservations are recommended for Cedar Grove Group (Apr.–Nov.) and for Doane Valley (Apr.–Oct.) at www.reserveamerica.com ($8 reservation fee). Sites are $30 per night, $8 per night for each additional vehicle, $5 per night for the hike-in site, $90–145 per night for group sites. Fishing license required for fishing pond; buy before arrival. Open year-round.

Directions: Drive on I-15 to the Highway 76 exit (east of Oceanside). Take that exit and drive east on Highway 76 for approximately 25 miles to County Road S6 (which brings you to the top of Palomar Mountain). At the top of the mountain, turn left, drive about 50 feet to State Park Road/County Road S7. Turn left on State Park Road/County Road S7 and drive about 3.5 miles to the park entrance.

Contact: Palomar Mountain State Park, 760/742-3462, Colorado Desert District, 760/767-4087; Palomar Observatory, 760/742-2119, www.parks.ca.gov; Friends of Palomar Mountain State Park, www.friendsofpalomarsp.org.

20 FRY CREEK

Scenic rating: 6

near the Palomar Observatory in Cleveland National Forest

Map 14.2, page 806

A small, seasonal stream, Fry Creek, runs near this camp at 5,200 feet elevation. On a clear night, you can see forever from Palomar Mountain. Literally. That's because the Palomar Observatory, just a short distance from this forested camp, houses America's largest telescope. With the 200-inch Hale Telescope, it is possible for scientists to see 100 billion galaxies. It is open to public touring (check for current hours), but you cannot touch the telescope.

Campsites, facilities: There are 20 sites for tents or RVs up to 15 feet. No trailers are allowed. Picnic tables and fire rings are provided. Drinking water and vault toilets are available. A store and coin showers are nearby. Leashed pets are permitted.

Reservations, fees: Reservations are accepted at 877/444-6777 or www.recreation.gov ($9 reservation fee). Sites are $15 per night, $5 per night per additional vehicle. Open April through November, weather permitting.

Directions: Drive on I-15 to the Highway 76 exit (east of Oceanside). Take that exit and drive east on Highway 76 for 25 miles to County Road S6 (which brings you to the top of Palomar Mountain). Turn left on County Road S6 and drive about nine miles to the campground entrance on the left. The road is not recommended for trailers.

Contact: Cleveland National Forest, Palomar Ranger District, 760/788-0250, www.fs.usda.gov/cleveland.

21 OBSERVATORY

Scenic rating: 6

near the Palomar Observatory in Cleveland National Forest

Map 14.2, page 806

This Forest Service camp is a popular spot for campers visiting the nearby Palomar Observatory, housing the largest telescope in America. There are four other camps in the immediate area. The elevation is 4,800 feet. The trailhead for Observatory Trail starts at this camp. This two-hour hike from the campground to the observatory includes one short, steep climb, highlighted by a vista deck with a sweeping view of Mendenhall Valley, and then onward to the top and to the viewing area to catch a glimpse of the telescope. Tours are available, but the telescope itself is not available to the public for use.

Campsites, facilities: There are 42 sites for tents or RVs up to 27 feet (no hookups). Picnic tables and fire grills are provided. Drinking water and restrooms with flush toilets and coin showers are available. Some facilities are wheelchair-accessible. Leashed pets are permitted.

Reservations, fees: Reservations are accepted at 877/444-6777 or www.recreation.gov ($9 reservation fee). Single sites are $15 per night, double sites are $30 per night. Open May through November.

Directions: Drive on I-15 to the Highway 76

exit (east of Oceanside). Take that exit and drive east on Highway 76 for 25 miles to County Road S6 (which brings you to the top of Palomar Mountain). Turn left on County Road S6 and drive about 8.5 miles to the campground entrance on the right. The road is not recommended for large trailers.

Contact: Cleveland National Forest, Palomar Ranger District, 760/788-0250, www.fs.usda.gov/cleveland.

22 CRESTLINE GROUP CAMP

Scenic rating: 6

near the Palomar Observatory in Cleveland National Forest

Map 14.2, page 806

This Forest Service camp is designed expressly for large groups. (For adventure information, see the Palomar Mountain State Park listing in this chapter.) The elevation is 4,800 feet.

Campsites, facilities: There is one group site for tents or RVs up to 27 feet that accommodates up to 50 people. Picnic tables and fire grills are provided. Drinking water and vault toilets are available. Some facilities are wheelchair-accessible. A store is nearby. Leashed pets are permitted.

Reservations, fees: Reservations are required at 877/444-6777 or www.recreation.gov ($9 reservation fee). The site is $75 per night. Open May through November.

Directions: Drive on I-15 to the Highway 76 exit (east of Oceanside). Take that exit and drive east on Highway 76 for 25 miles to County Road S6 (which brings you to the top of Palomar Mountain). Turn left on County Road S6 and drive about 6.5 miles to the campground at the junction of County Roads S6 and S7. The road is not recommended for trailers.

Contact: Cleveland National Forest, Palomar Ranger District, 760/788-0250, www.fs.usda.gov/cleveland.

23 OAK KNOLL

🏕️ 🏊 🐕 🚶 🚙 ⛺

Scenic rating: 6

near the Palomar Observatory

Map 14.2, page 806

Oak Knoll campground is set at 3,000 feet elevation in San Diego County foothill country among giant old California oaks. It is at the western base of Palomar Mountain, and to visit the Palomar Observatory and its awesome 200-inch telescope requires a remarkably twisty 10-mile drive up the mountain (the telescope is not open to the public, but the observatory is open). The campground management suggests you bring your telescope or borrow one of theirs for nighttime stargazing. A good side trip is the Boucher Lookout in Palomar Mountain State Park. Trailheads for hikes on Palomar Mountain include Observatory Trail (starting at Observatory) and Doane Valley Loop (starting in Palomar Mountain State Park).

Campsites, facilities: There are 46 sites for tents or RVs up to 35 feet; many sites have full or partial hookups (30 amps). Picnic tables and fire barrels are provided. Drinking water, restrooms with flush toilets and coin showers, library, video arcade, Wi-Fi, recreation hall, pavilion, seasonal activities, playground, swimming pool, baseball diamond, horseshoes, basketball court, coin laundry, propane gas, and camp store are available. Leashed pets are permitted, with certain restrictions.

Reservations, fees: Reservations are accepted. Sites are $25–40 per night, $5 per person per night for more than two people, $5 per night for each additional vehicle, $3 per pet per night. Monthly rates available. Open year-round.

Directions: Drive on I-15 to the Highway 76 exit (east of Oceanside). Take that exit and drive east on Highway 76 for 21 miles to South Grade Road/County Road S6. Turn left and drive a short distance to the campground on the left.

Contact: Oak Knoll Campground, 760/742-3437, www.oakknoll.net.

24 WOODS VALLEY KAMPGROUND

🏊 🐕 🚶 🚙 ⛺

Scenic rating: 5

near Lake Wohlford

Map 14.2, page 806

This privately operated park is situated on 20 acres and is popular with families. Lake Wohlford is about 10 miles to the south and has a lake speed limit of 5 mph. The lake is stocked with rainbow trout, brown trout, steelhead, channel catfish, and blue catfish. Insider's tip: A bald eagle winters at Lake Wohlford.

Campsites, facilities: There are 59 sites for RVs of any length, and 30 sites for tents. There are also three group sites that accommodate 10–18 people each. Many of the RV sites have partial hookups and some have full hookups (30 amps). Picnic tables and fire barrels are provided. Drinking water, restrooms with flush toilets and showers, dump station, coin laundry, swimming pool, catch-and-release fishing pond, small animal farm, playground, volleyball, horseshoes, recreation hall, group facilities, and supplies are available. Leashed pets are permitted, with some dogs prohibited.

Reservations, fees: Reservations are accepted. Sites are $31–45 per night, $3 for each additional person, $3 per night for each additional vehicle, $3 per pet per night. The group sites are 290–522 per night. Weekly and monthly rates available. Open year-round.

Directions: From San Diego, drive north on I-15 to the Escondido area and take the Via Rancho Parkway exit and continue to Via Rancho Parkway. Turn right (name changes to Bear Valley Parkway) and drive approximately nine miles to a T intersection and Valley Parkway. Turn right on Valley Parkway and drive approximately six miles (name changes to Valley Center Road) to Woods Valley Road. Turn right and drive 2.2 miles to the park on the left.

Contact: Woods Valley Kampground, 760/749-2905, www.woodsvalley.com.

25 LAKE HENSHAW RESORT

Scenic rating: 7

near Santa Ysabel

Map 14.2, page 806

Lake Henshaw is the biggest lake in San Diego County, with 25 miles of shoreline, yet it has only one camp. It's a good one, with the cabin rentals a big plus. The camp is on the southern corner of the lake, at 2,727 feet elevation near Cleveland National Forest. Swimming, water/body contact, canoes, and rafts are not permitted and a 10-mph speed limit is in effect. The fishing is best for catfish, especially in the summer, and at times decent for bass, with the lake-record bass weighing 14 pounds, four ounces. Other fish species are trout, bluegill, and crappie. Like many reservoirs, Lake Henshaw is sometimes plagued by low water levels. A mobile home park is also on the premises.

Campsites, facilities: There are four acres of open sites for tents or RVs of any length (no hookups), and 16 sites with full hookups (20 amps) for tents or RVs up to 28 feet. Cabins are also available. Picnic tables and fire pits are provided. Restrooms with flush toilets and showers, cabins, swimming pool, spa, picnic area, clubhouse, playground, dump station, coin laundry, propane gas, boat and motor rentals, boat launch, bait and tackle, café, and convenience store are available. Some facilities are wheelchair-accessible. A golf course is 10 miles away. Leashed pets are permitted.

Reservations, fees: Reservations are not accepted. RV sites are $25 per night, tent sites are $20 per night, $1 per additional person per night, $2 per pet per night, and $7.50 per person per day for lake use. Weekly rates available. Boat launching is $5 per day. Cabins are $65–87 per night. Some credit cards accepted. Open year-round.

Directions: From Santa Ysabel, drive seven miles north on Highway 79 to Highway 76. Turn east on Highway 76 and drive four miles to the campground on the left.

Contact: Lake Henshaw Resort, 760/782-3501, www.lakehenshawresort.com.

26 STAGECOACH TRAILS

Scenic rating: 6

near Julian

Map 14.2, page 806

You want space? You got space. That includes 600,000 acres of public lands bordering this RV campground, making Stagecoach Trails Resort ideal for those who love horseback riding and hiking. Forty corrals and two round pens at the campground let you know right away that this camp is very horse-friendly. It is more than a horse camp, however, with amenities for various types of campers. The resort provides the perfect jumping-off place for trips into neighboring Anza-Borrego Desert State Park and onto the Pacific Crest Trail, which is 2.5 miles away. The resort's name comes from its proximity to the old Wells Fargo Butterfield Stage Route. While the scenic rating merits a 6, if the rating were based purely on cleanliness, professionalism, and friendliness, this resort would rate a 10.

Campsites, facilities: There are 250 sites with full hookups (30 amps) for RVs of any length, and a large dispersed camping area for tents. Most RV sites are pull-through. Picnic tables and fire rings are provided. Drinking water, restrooms with flush toilets and showers, a heated pool, 40 horse corrals, a roping area, guided horseback riding, convenience store, ATM, coin laundry, WiFi, group facilities, horseshoe pits, shuffleboard, 24-hour security, and propane gas are available. Some facilities are wheelchair-accessible. Leashed pets are permitted.

Reservations, fees: Reservations are accepted. RV sites are $32–35 per night ($7 per night for electricity), tent sites are $24 per night, $3–5 per person per night for more than two people, $6 per night per horse. Some credit cards accepted. Open year-round.

Directions: From Santa Ysabel, turn north on Highway 79 and drive 14 miles to County Road S2/San Felipe Road. Turn right and drive 17 miles to Highway 78. Turn right (west, toward

Julian) and drive 0.3 mile to County Road S2 (Great Southern Overland Stage Route). Turn left and drive four miles to the resort on the right (at Mile Marker 21 on Road S2). Note: There are various ways to get here. Since equestrian campers towing horse trailers and other campers may need alternate directions, and those not towing rigs might want shortcut directions, call the resort for driving details.

Contact: Stagecoach Trails Park, 760/765-3765, www.stagecoachtrails.com.

27 PINEZANITA RV PARK AND CAMPGROUNDS

Scenic rating: 6

near Julian

Map 14.2, page 806

Set at an elevation of 4,680 feet in dense pine and oak, this camp has had the same owners, the Stanley family, for more than 30 years. The fishing pond is a great attraction for kids (no license is required); no swimming allowed. The pond is stocked with bluegill and catfish, some of which are 12 inches or longer. Two possible side trips include Lake Cuyamaca, five miles to the south, and William Heise County Park, about 10 miles to the north as the crow flies.

Campsites, facilities: There are 210 sites with full or partial hookups (30 and 50 amps) for RVs, 32 sites for tents, and three cottages. Picnic tables and fire rings are provided. Restrooms with flush toilets and showers, drinking water, a general store, ice, propane, bait and tackle, fishing pond, and dump station are available. Leashed pets are permitted, but not in the cottages.

Reservations, fees: Reservations are accepted. Sites are $26 per night per vehicle, $5 per night for electricity, $2 for sewer hookup, $3 per night per person for more than two people, and $3 per night per pet, with a maximum of three pets. Some credit cards accepted. Open year-round.

Directions: From El Cajon, drive east on I-8 to Highway 79 (near Descanso Junction). Turn north on Highway 79 and drive 20 miles to Julian and the campground on the left.

Contact: Pinezanita RV Park and Campgrounds, 760/765-0429, www.pinezanita.com.

28 WILLIAM HEISE COUNTY PARK

Scenic rating: 6

near Julian

Map 14.2, page 806

This is a beautiful county park, set at 4,200 feet elevation, that offers hiking trails and a playground, all amid woodlands with a mix of oak and pine. Cabins provide a bonus opportunity for those who do not want to tent camp. A great hike starts right at camp (at the tent camping area), signed "Nature Trail." It joins Canyon Oak Trail and, after little more than a mile, links with Desert View Trail. Here you will reach an overlook with a view of the Anza-Borrego Desert and the Salton Sea. The park features more than 900 acres of mountain forests of oak, pine, and cedar. A popular equestrian trail is Kelly Ditch Trail, which is linked to Cuyamaca Rancho State Park and Lake Cuyamaca. The vast Anza-Borrego Desert State Park lies to the east, and the historic mining town of Julian is five miles away. Julian is known for its Apple Day Festival each fall.

Campsites, facilities: There are 21 sites with partial hookups (30 amps) for tents or RVs up to 40 feet, 40 sites for tents or RVs up to 40 feet (no hookups), 41 sites for tents only, two youth group sites for up to 30 people each, and six cabins. Group camping (at least 10 sites) is available by reservation. Picnic tables and fire grills are provided. Restrooms with flush toilets and showers, drinking water, coin laundry, dump station, picnic areas, and a playground are available. Supplies are available five miles away in Julian. Leashed pets are permitted.

Reservations, fees: Reservations are accepted and are required for group sites at 877/565-3600 ($5 reservation fee). RV sites (partial hookups) are $24 per night, tent and RV sites (without hookups) are $19 per night, the youth group sites is $40 per night, group camping is $75 per night, cabins are $60 per night, $1 per pet per night. Senior and disabled discounts are available. Some credit cards accepted. Open year-round.

Directions: From El Cajon, drive east on I-8 to Highway 79 (near Descanso Junction). Turn north on Highway 79 and drive to Julian and Highway 78. Turn west (left) on Highway 78 and drive to Pine Hills Road. Turn left (south) on Pine Hills Road and drive two miles to Frisius Drive. Turn left (south) on Frisius Drive and drive two miles to the park.

Contact: San Diego County Parks Department, 760/765-0650, www.sdcounty.ca.gov.

29 DOS PICOS COUNTY PARK

🏌️ 🚴 ⛴ 🐕 🛶 🚐 ⛺

Scenic rating: 5

near Ramona

Map 14.2, page 806

Dos Picos means "two peaks" and is the highlight of a landscape featuring old groves of oaks and steep, boulder-strewn mountain slopes. Some of the oaks are 300 years old. The park covers 78 acres and has a nature trail. As a county park, this camp is often missed. The park is quite picturesque, with plenty of shade trees and a small pond. Fishing is allowed in the pond, but swimming is prohibited. Several nearby recreation options are in the area, including Lake Poway and Lake Sutherland. The elevation is 1,500 feet.

Campsites, facilities: There are 57 sites (partial hookups) for RVs to 40 feet, 11 sites for tents or RVs up to 40 feet (no hookups), one youth group area for up to 25 people, and two cabins. Group camping (at least 10 sites is available by reservation). Picnic tables and fire grills are provided. Restrooms with flush toilets and showers, drinking water, dump station, playground,

horseshoes, and soccer field are available. Supplies and a coin laundry are one mile away in Ramona. Leashed pets are permitted.

Reservations, fees: Reservations are accepted and are required for group sites at 877/565-3600 ($5 reservation fee). RV sites with partial hookups are $24 per night, tent sites and RV sites (without hookups) are $19 per night, the youth group is $40 per night, group camping is $75 per night, cabins are $65 per night, $1 per pet per night. Senior/disabled discounts are available. Some credit cards accepted. Open year-round.

Directions: From I-8 in El Cajon, take the exit for Highway 67 and drive north for 22 miles to Mussey Grade Road. Turn right (a sharp turn) on Mussey Grade Road and drive two miles to the park.

Contact: San Diego County Parks Department, Dos Picos County Park, 760/789-2220, www.sdcounty.ca.gov.

30 PASO PICACHO

🏌️ 🚴 ⛴ 🐕 🚐 ⛺

Scenic rating: 6

in Cuyamaca Rancho State Park

Map 14.2, page 806

This camp is set at 5,000 feet elevation in Cuyamaca Rancho State Park, best known for Cuyamaca Peak, at 6,512 feet. Stonewall Peak Trail is accessible from across the street. This is a five-mile (sun-exposed) round-trip, featuring the climb to the summit at 5,700 feet. There are long-distance views from here, highlighted by the Salton Sea and the Anza-Borrego State Desert. It's the most popular hike in the park, a fair to moderate grade, and completed by a lot of families. Another, more ambitious, hike is the trail up to Cuyamaca Peak, starting at the southern end of the campground, a 6.5-mile round-trip tromp (alas, on a paved road; at least it's closed to traffic) with a climb of 1,600 feet in the process. The view from the top is breathtaking, with the Pacific Ocean and Mexico visible to the west and south, respectively. Cuyamaca means "The Rain Beyond."

Campsites, facilities: There are 85 sites for tents or RVs up to 30 feet long and 10 feet tall (no hookups), five cabins, a nature den cabin, four wood cabins. Fire grills and picnic tables are provided. Restrooms with flush toilets and coin showers, drinking water, Wi-Fi, and dump station are available. Supplies are nearby in Cuyamaca. Leashed pets are permitted.

Reservations, fees: Reservations are accepted April through November at www.reserveamerica.com ($8 reservation fee); sites are first-come first-served December through March. Sites are $30 per night. Open year-round.

Directions: From El Cajon, drive east on I-8 to Highway 79 (near Descanso Junction). Turn north (left) and drive 13.5 miles to the park entrance on the left.

Contact: Cuyamaca Rancho State Park, 760/765-3020, www.parks.ca.gov or www.crspia.org.

31 GREEN VALLEY

Scenic rating: 6

in Cuyamaca Rancho State Park

Map 14.2, page 806

The camp is set at 4,000 feet elevation, with Cuyamaca Peak (6,512 feet) looming overhead to the northwest. A trailhead is available (look for the picnic area) at the camp for an easy five-minute walk to Green Valley Falls, and it can be continued out to the Sweetwater River in a 1.5-mile round-trip. The park covers 25,000 acres with trails for hiking, mountain biking, and horseback riding. Green Valley is the southernmost camp in Cuyamaca Rancho State Park. The park is recovering from the 2003 Cedar Fire; both campgrounds were minimally affected and most of the big trees survived.

Campsites, facilities: There are 81 sites for tents or RVs up to 30 feet long and 10 feet tall (no hookups), 15 equestrian sites, four cabins, and one hike-in/bike-in site. Picnic tables and fire grills are provided. Restrooms with flush toilets and coin showers, drinking water, Wi-Fi, and dump station are available. A store and propane gas are nearby. Some facilities are wheelchair-accessible. Leashed pets are permitted.

Reservations, fees: Reservations are accepted at 800/444-7275 (800/444-PARK) or www.reserveamerica.com ($8 reservation fee). Sites are $30 per night, equestrian sites are $35 per night, $8 per night for each additional vehicle, $5 per person per night for hike-in/bike-in site. Open April through November.

Directions: From El Cajon, drive east on I-8 to Highway 79 (near Descanso Junction). Turn north (left) on Highway 79 and drive seven miles to the campground entrance on the left (near Mile Marker 4).

Contact: Cuyamaca Rancho State Park, 760/765-3020, www.parks.ca.gov or www.crspia.org.

32 LAGUNA

Scenic rating: 6

near Little Laguna Lake in Cleveland National Forest

Map 14.2, page 806

Laguna is set on Little Laguna Lake, one of the few lakes in America where "Little" is part of its official name. That's because for years everybody always referred to it as "Little Laguna Lake," and it became official. Yep, it's a "little" lake all right, a relative speck, and the lake can occasionally dry up. The camp is on its eastern side at an elevation of 5,550 feet. A trailhead for the Pacific Crest Trail is a mile north on the Sunrise Highway. Big Laguna Lake, which is actually a pretty small lake, is one mile to the west.

Campsites, facilities: There are 104 sites for tents or RVs up to 40 feet (no hookups). Eight sites are limited to two people each to protect the endangered Laguna Skipper butterfly. Picnic tables and fire grills are provided. Drinking water and restrooms with flush and pit toilets and coin showers are available. A store and propane gas are nearby. Some facilities are wheelchair-accessible. Leashed pets are permitted.

Reservations, fees: Reservations are accepted at 877/444-6777 or www.recreation.gov ($9 reservation fee). Sites are $20 per night, $6 per night per additional vehicle, $2 per pet (for more than one). Open year-round.

Directions: From San Diego, drive east on I-8 about 50 miles to the Laguna Junction exit for the Sunrise Highway. Turn north on the Sunrise Highway and drive 11 miles to the town of Mount Laguna. Continue north on Sunrise Highway for 2.5 miles to the campground entrance road on the left.

Contact: Cleveland National Forest, Descanso Ranger District, 619/445-6235, www.fs.usda. gov/cleveland; Laguna Mountain Visitor Center, 619/473-8547.

33 EL PRADO GROUP CAMP

🥾 🐕 ♿ 🚐 ⛺

Scenic rating: 3

in Cleveland National Forest

Map 14.2, page 806

El Prado Group Camp is directly adjacent to Laguna and is an alternative to nearby Horse Heaven Group Camp. Five separate group sites are available. Certain areas here are fenced off to protect habitat for the endangered Laguna Skipper butterfly. The elevation is 5,500 feet.

Campsites, facilities: There are five group sites for tents or RVs up to 40 feet (no hookups) that can accommodate 30–50 people each. Picnic tables and fire grills are provided. Drinking water and vault toilets are available. At Yerba Santa campground, flush toilets are available and some facilities are wheelchair-accessible. Supplies are available in Mount Laguna. Leashed pets are permitted.

Reservations, fees: Reservations are required at 877/444-6777 or www.recreation.gov ($8 reservation fee). Sites are $45–75 per night. Open Memorial Day weekend through mid-October, weather permitting.

Directions: From San Diego, drive east on I-8 about 50 miles to the Laguna Junction exit for the Sunrise Highway. Turn north on the

Sunrise Highway and drive 11 miles to the town of Mount Laguna. Continue north on Sunrise Highway for 2.5 miles to the campground entrance road on the left.

Contact: Cleveland National Forest, Descanso Ranger District, 619/445-6235, www.fs.usda. gov/cleveland.

34 HORSE HEAVEN GROUP CAMP

🥾 🐕 🚐 ⛺

Scenic rating: 3

near the Pacific Crest Trail in Cleveland National Forest

Map 14.2, page 806

Horse Heaven is set on the northeastern border of Cleveland National Forest at 5,500 feet elevation, near Mount Laguna in the Laguna Recreation Area. The Pacific Crest Trail passes near the camp. Laguna and El Prado Group Camp provide nearby options. Side-trip possibilities include visiting Little Laguna Lake to the immediate west and Desert View Picnic Area to the south at Mount Laguna. Despite its name, the campground has no equestrian sites.

Campsites, facilities: There are three group sites for tents or RVs up to 27 feet (no hookups) that can accommodate 40–100 people each. Picnic tables and fire grills are provided. Drinking water and vault toilets are available. You can buy supplies in Mount Laguna. Leashed pets are permitted.

Reservations, fees: Reservations are required at 877/444-6777 or www.recreation.gov ($8 reservation fee). Sites are $60–150 per night. Open Memorial Day weekend through Labor Day weekend.

Directions: From San Diego, drive east on I-8 about 50 miles to the Laguna Junction exit for the Sunrise Highway. Turn north on the Sunrise Highway and drive 11 miles to the town of Mount Laguna. Continue north on Sunrise Highway for two miles to the campground entrance road on the left.

Contact: Cleveland National Forest, Descanso

Ranger District, 619/445-6235, www.fs.usda. gov/cleveland.

35 WOODED HILL GROUP

Scenic rating: 5

near the Pacific Crest Trail in
Cleveland National Forest

Map 14.2, page 806

This camp is set on the southern flank of Mount Laguna. The Pacific Crest Trail is within one mile of Burnt Rancheria Campground, a mile up the road to the northwest. The elevation is 6,000 feet.

Campsites, facilities: There is one group site for tents or RVs up to 40 feet (no hookups) that can accommodate up to 110 people. Picnic tables and fire grills are provided. Drinking water and vault toilets are available. A store is nearby. Leashed pets are permitted.

Reservations, fees: Reservations are required at 877/444-6777 or www.recreation.gov ($9 reservation fee). Sites are $110 per night. Open Memorial Day weekend through Labor Day weekend.

Directions: From San Diego, drive east on I-8 about 50 miles to the Laguna Junction exit for the Sunrise Highway. Turn north on the Sunrise Highway and drive about eight miles to the campground entrance road on the left.

Contact: Cleveland National Forest, Descanso Ranger District, 619/445-6235, www.fs.usda. gov/cleveland.

36 BURNT RANCHERIA

Scenic rating: 6

near the Pacific Crest Trail in
Cleveland National Forest

Map 14.2, page 806

Burnt Rancheria is set high on the slopes of Mount Laguna in Cleveland National Forest, at an elevation of 6,000 feet. Remodeled in 2005, it is quiet and private with large, roomy sites. The Pacific Crest Trail is approximately one mile from camp. Desert View Picnic Area, a mile to the north, provides a good side trip. Wooded Hill Group Campground is one mile away.

Campsites, facilities: There are 104 sites for tents or RVs up to 40 feet (no hookups). Picnic tables and fire grills are provided. Drinking water, vault toilets, and coin showers are available. Supplies are nearby in Mount Laguna. Some facilities are wheelchair-accessible. Leashed pets are permitted.

Reservations, fees: Reservations are accepted at 877/444-6777 or www.recreation.gov ($9 reservation fee). Sites are $20 per night, $6 per night per additional vehicle, $2 per pet (for more than one). Open mid-April through October, weather permitting.

Directions: From San Diego, drive east on I-8 about 50 miles to the Laguna Junction exit for the Sunrise Highway. Turn north on the Sunrise Highway and drive about 10 miles north to the campground entrance road on the right.

Contact: Cleveland National Forest, Descanso Ranger District, 619/445-6235, www.fs.usda. gov/cleveland.

37 VACATIONER RV RESORT

Scenic rating: 3

near El Cajon

Map 14.2, page 806

This well-maintained resort is 25 minutes from San Diego, 40 minutes from Mexico. Discount tickets to area attractions such as the San Diego Zoo, SeaWorld, and the Wild Animal Park are available. There is the very real chance of getting highway noise if you have a site at the back of the park. The RV sites are on asphalt and gravel, and there are many shade trees. The elevation is 260 feet.

Campsites, facilities: There are 147 sites with full hookups (30 and 50 amps) for RVs up to 40 feet, including 13 pull-through sites. A group campground is available. Restrooms with flush toilets and showers, drinking water, coin laundry, recreation room, horseshoe pits, phone access, Wi-Fi, heated swimming pool, spa, cable TV, free video library, RV storage, and picnic area with barbecues are available. A store is nearby. Some facilities are wheelchair-accessible. Leashed pets up to 20 pounds are permitted, with certain restrictions.

Reservations, fees: Reservations are accepted at 877/626-4409. Standard RV sites are $37 per night; premium RV sites are $41–43; deluxe, luxury and elite RV sites are $46–50 per night; $2 per person per night for more than two people; $2 per night for each additional vehicle; $2 per pet per night. Some credit cards accepted. Open year-round.

Directions: From El Cajon, drive east on I-8 for three miles to the Greenfield Drive exit. Take that exit, turn north and drive 100 feet to East Main Street. Turn left (west) and drive 0.5 mile to the park on the left.

Contact: Vacationer RV Resort, 619/442-0904 or 877/626-4409, www.vacationerrv.com.

38 RANCHO LOS COCHES RV PARK

🏊 🐕 🚐 ⛺

Scenic rating: 5

near Lake Jennings

Map 14.2, page 806

This is not your typical RV park. This place has plenty of charm and a private setting. There is an abundance of history here, too. The park land was once the smallest Mexican land grant of the 19th century. The former ranch was also once a station for the Jackass Mail and Butterfield Stage routes. Windmill House, built in 1925, is featured prominently on the property and is a local historic landmark. Nearby Lake Jennings provides an option for boaters and anglers and also has a less developed camp on its northeast shore. Vista Point on the southeastern side of the lake provides a side trip. (For more information, see the Lake Jennings County Park listing in this chapter.) Casinos are nearby.

Campsites, facilities: There are 142 sites with full hookups (30 and 50 amps) for RVs up to 50 feet and four tent areas. Restrooms with flush toilets and showers, drinking water, cable TV, dump station, heated swimming pool, spa, recreation hall, fitness room, horseshoes, table tennis, Wi-Fi, and coin laundry are available. A store and gas station are one mile away. Leashed pets are permitted, with certain restrictions.

Reservations, fees: Reservations are accepted online or at 800/630-0448. RV sites (full hookups) are $36–48 per night (depending on size), tent sites are $25 per night, $3 per person per night for more than two people. Weekly and monthly rates available. Open year-round.

Directions: From El Cajon, drive east on I-8 to the Los Coches Road exit. Take that exit, and drive under the freeway to Highway 8 Business Route. Turn right on Highway 8 Business Route and drive 0.25 mile to the park entrance on the left (13468 Highway 8 Business).

Contact: Rancho Los Coches RV Park, 619/443-2025, www.rancholoscochesrv.com.

39 LAKE JENNINGS COUNTY PARK

🚶 🏊 🚐 🐕 ♿ 🚐 ⛺

Scenic rating: 6

on Lake Jennings

Map 14.2, page 806

Lake Jennings, at 108 acres, is a nice little backyard fishing hole and recreation area set at 700 feet elevation, with easy access from I-8. Most people come here for the fishing; the lake is stocked with trout and catfish. It has quality prospects for giant catfish, as well as largemouth bass, bluegill, and, in cool months, rainbow trout. The lake-record blue catfish is 60 pounds. Note that while shore fishing is available on a daily basis, boats are permitted on the lake November through August, Friday through Sunday. Night fishing is allowed on weekends during the summer. A fishing permit is required. The highlights here are evening picnics, summer catfishing, and a boat ramp and rentals. Swimming and water/body contact are prohibited. Miles of hiking trails are routed through chaparral-covered hills. Only one camp is available right at the lake, and this is it.

Campsites, facilities: There are 35 sites with full hookups (30 amps) for RVs up to 35 feet, 37 sites with partial hookups (20 amps) for RVs up to 25 feet, 26 tent sites, and a youth group area for up to 35 people. Some sites are pull-through. Picnic tables and fire grills are provided. Restrooms with flush toilets and showers, drinking water, nature trail, clubhouse, WiFi, pavilion, horseshoes, and dump station are available. A store is nearby. Some facilities are wheelchair accessible. Leashed pets are permitted.

Reservations, fees: Reservations are accepted online at www.lakejennings.org ($8 reservation fee). Tent sites are $25 per night, RV sites are $28 (partial hookups) and $32 (full hookups) per night, $1 per pet per night, youth group area is $50 per night, adult and family group area is $75 per night, $2 per night for additional person, $2 per night per additional vehicle, $1 per night per pet. Per person fees are charged for fishing. Open year-round.

Directions: From San Diego, drive east on I-8 for 21 miles to Lake Jennings Park Road. Turn north (left) on Lake Jennings Park Road and drive one mile to the park entrance.

Contact: Helix Water District, campground information 619/390-1623, www.lakejennings.org.

40 CIBBETS FLATS
🕭 🐕 🚐 ⛺

Scenic rating: 5

on Troy Canyon Creek in
Cleveland National Forest

Map 14.2, page 806

Cibbets Flat is at the southern flank of the Laguna Mountains near Troy Canyon Creek, and Kitchen Creek runs adjacent to the camp. It is an obscure, fairly remote camp and staging area for the Pacific Crest Trail. A trailhead for the PCT is a mile southeast of camp, used mostly by hikers heading north across the Laguna Mountains. The elevation is 4,200 feet.

Campsites, facilities: There are 25 sites for tents or RVs up to 27 feet (no hookups). Picnic tables and fire grills are provided. Drinking water and vault toilets are available. Leashed pets are permitted.

Reservations, fees: Reservations are not accepted. Sites are $14–28 per night. Open year-round.

Directions: From El Cajon, drive east on I-8 for about 50 miles to Boulder Oaks, then continue a short distance to the exit for Kitchen Creek/Cameron Station. Turn north on Kitchen Creek Road and drive 4.5 miles to the campground entrance on the right.

Contact: Cleveland National Forest, Descanso Ranger District, 619/445-6235, www.fs.usda.gov/cleveland.

41 BOULDER OAKS EQUESTRIAN
🕭 🐕 🚐 ⛺

Scenic rating: 4

near Lake Morena in Cleveland National Forest

Map 14.2, page 806

Boulder Oaks is easy to reach, just off I-8, yet it is a very small camp with an important trailhead for the Pacific Crest Trail running right by it. This camp also is designed as a trailhead camp for equestrians. The elevation is 3,300 feet, set in the southern end of Cleveland National Forest and the Laguna Mountains. This campground is closed March 1 through May to protect the breeding activity of the arroyo southwestern toad, an endangered species.

Campsites, facilities: There are 30 sites, including six double sites, for tents or RVs up to 27 feet (no hookups) and 17 equestrian sites. Picnic tables and fire grills are provided. Vault toilets are available, but there is no drinking water. Leashed pets are permitted.

Reservations, fees: Reservations are not accepted for individual sites. Reservations are required for equestrian sites at 877/444-6777 or www.recreation.gov ($9 reservation fee). Single sites are $14 per night, double sites are $20 per night, equestrian sites are $12–24 per night, $5 per night for additional vehicle. Open mid-June through February.

Directions: From El Cajon, drive east on I-8 to Pine Valley, then continue east for four miles to Buckman Springs Road. Take the Buckman Springs off-ramp, turn right (south) on Buckman Springs Road, and drive a short distance to a four-way stop sign at Old Highway 80. Turn left and drive 2.5 miles to the campground.

Contact: Cleveland National Forest, Descanso Ranger District, 619/445-6235, www.fs.usda.gov/cleveland.

42 BOBCAT MEADOW
🥾 🐕 🚙 ⛺

Scenic rating: 6

in Cleveland National Forest

Map 14.2, page 806

This camp, along with nearby Corral Canyon, caters primarily to OHV users. The camp is shaded with live oaks and is a 10-minute drive from Corral Canyon camp. This camp is similar, but it has no water. The more spacious sites and privacy can make up for that. Off-highway vehicles are allowed here. The elevation is 3,800 feet.

Campsites, facilities: There are 20 sites for tents or RVs up to 27 feet (no hookups). Fire pits are provided. Vault toilets are available. No drinking water is available. Garbage must be packed out. Leashed pets are permitted.

Reservations, fees: Reservations are not accepted. There is no fee for camping. An Adventure Pass ($30 annual fee or $5 daily fee per parked vehicle) is required. Open year-round.

Directions: From El Cajon, drive east on I-8 to Pine Valley, then continue east for four miles to Buckman Springs Road. Take the Buckman Springs off-ramp, turn right (south) on Buckman Springs Road, and drive 3.6 miles to Corral Canyon Road, signed "Camp Morena." Turn right and drive 6.2 miles (the road becomes Forest Service Road 17S04) to Four Corners Trailhead. Bear left (Forest Service Road 17S04) and drive a mile to the campground on the left.

Contact: Cleveland National Forest, Descanso Ranger District, 619/445-6235, www.fs.usda.gov/cleveland.

43 CORRAL CANYON
🥾 🐕 🚙 ⛺

Scenic rating: 6

in Cleveland National Forest

Map 14.2, page 806

This is a primitive camp set adjacent to a network of OHV trails leading 24 miles into the Corral Canyon area, hence the name. Most of the routes lead into a chaparral landscape. The camp is set at 3,500 feet elevation and is used primarily by the OHV crowd. The availability of drinking water at this campground is a big plus.

Campsites, facilities: There are 20 sites for tents or RVs up to 27 feet (no hookups). Fire rings are provided. Drinking water and vault toilets are available. Garbage must be packed out. Leashed pets are permitted.

Reservations, fees: Reservations are not accepted. There is no fee for camping. An Adventure Pass ($30 annual fee or $5 daily fee per parked vehicle) is required. Open year-round.

Directions: From El Cajon, drive east on I-8 to Pine Valley, then continue east for four miles to Buckman Springs Road. Take the Buckman Springs off-ramp, turn right (south) on Buckman Springs Road, and drive 3.6 miles to Corral Canyon Road, signed "Camp Morena." Turn right and drive 6.2 miles (the road becomes Forest Service Road 17S04) to the Four Corners Trailhead. Continue straight on Corral Canyon Road for one mile to the campground on the right.

Contact: Cleveland National Forest, Descanso Ranger District, 619/445-6235, www.fs.usda.gov/cleveland.

44 COTTONWOOD

Scenic rating: 4

in the McCain Valley Recreation Area

Map 14.2, page 806

This camp is set on the western edge of the McCain Valley Recreation Area. Like most Bureau of Land Management camps, it is little known and little used, but is occasionally frequented by backcountry horseback riders. Off-highway vehicles are not allowed here. The elevation is 4,000 feet.

Campsites, facilities: There are 25 sites for tents or RVs up to 35 feet (no hookups). Picnic tables and fire grills are provided. Drinking water and vault toilets are available. Two group horse corrals are also available. Leashed pets are permitted.

Reservations, fees: Reservations are not accepted. Sites are $6 per night. Open year-round.

Directions: From El Cajon, drive east on I-8 for 70 miles to the Boulevard/Campo exit. Take that exit right, then at the frontage road, turn left immediately and drive east (just south of the interstate) for two miles to McCain Valley Road. Turn left on McCain Valley Road and drive about 13 miles to the campground.

Contact: Bureau of Land Management, El Centro Field Office, 760/337-4400, www.blm.gov/ca.

45 LARK CANYON OHV

Scenic rating: 5

in the McCain Valley Recreation Area

Map 14.2, page 806

This is a small camp that few know of, set at 4,000 feet elevation in the McCain Valley National Cooperative and Recreation Area. It is near a popular off-highway-vehicle area. Many dirt bikers use it as their base camp.

Campsites, facilities: There are 15 sites for tents or RVs up to 35 feet (no hookups) and group campsites are available. Picnic tables, fire rings, and trash service are provided. Vault toilets are available, but there is no drinking water. Firewood is scarce so bring it with you. Leashed pets are permitted.

Reservations, fees: Reservations are not accepted. Sites are $6 per night. Open year-round.

Directions: From El Cajon, drive east on I-8 for 70 miles to the Boulevard/Campo exit. Take that exit right, then at the frontage road, turn left immediately and drive east (just south of the interstate) for two miles to McCain Valley Road. Turn left at McCain Valley Road and drive three miles to the campground.

Contact: Bureau of Land Management, El Centro Field Office, 760/337-4400, www.blm.gov/ca.

46 SWEETWATER SUMMIT REGIONAL PARK

Scenic rating: 7

near Sweetwater Reservoir in Bonita

Map 14.2, page 806

This regional park overlooks the Sweetwater Reservoir in Bonita. The campground is set right on the summit, overlooking the Sweetwater Valley. This camp has equestrian sites with corrals for the horses. There are 15 miles of trails in the park for hiking, mountain biking, and horseback riding. There are several golf courses nearby and it is 15 minutes from Tijuana. The Chula Vista Nature Center is nearby on the shore of south San Diego Bay.

Campsites, facilities: There are 113 sites: 56 sites (full hookups) for RVs to 45 feet, 46 sites (partial hookups, 20 amps) for tents or RVs up to 45 feet, and 11 equestrian sites with corrals. Picnic tables and fire grills are provided.

Restrooms with flush toilets and showers, drinking water, covered pavilion, exercise course, playground, and dump station are available. Some facilities are wheelchair accessible. Leashed pets are permitted.

Reservations, fees: Reservations are accepted at 858/565-3600 or 877/565-3600 ($5 reservation fee). Sites are $24–28 per night, $2 per horse per night, $1 per pet per night. Open year-round.

Directions: From San Diego, drive south on I-805 for 10 miles to Bonita Road. Turn east on Bonita Road and drive to San Miguel Road. Bear right on San Miguel Road and drive two miles to the park entrance on the left.

Contact: San Diego County Parks Department, Sweetwater Summit Regional Park, 619/472-7572, www.sdparks.org.

47 POTRERO COUNTY PARK
🐕 🚶 🚐 ⛺

Scenic rating: 4

near the Mexican border

Map 14.2, page 806

If you are looking for a spot to hole up for the night before getting through customs, this is the place. This park covers 115 acres, set at an elevation of 2,300 feet. It is a broad valley peppered with coastal live oaks amid grassy meadows and rocky foothills. The average summer high temperature is in the 90° F range, and the average winter low is 34° F. There is occasional light snowfall in the winter. Potrero means "pasturing place." Some of the summer grazers are rattlesnakes, occasionally spotted here. Side trips include the railroad museum and century-old historic stone store in Campo, and the Mexican community of Tecate. In fact, it is just a heartbeat away from the customs inspection station in Tecate. A good side trip is to the nearby Tecate Mission Chapel, where you can pray that the guards do not rip your vehicle up in the search for contraband. Insider's tip: In the spring you may hear the evening call of the Pacific tree frog.

Campsites, facilities: There are 39 sites with partial hookups (20, 30, and 50 amps) for RVs up to 45 feet, seven tent sites, and a youth group site for up to 45 people. Group camping (at least 10 sites) is available by reservation. Picnic tables and fire grills are provided. Restrooms with flush toilets and showers, drinking water, playground, ball fields, and dump station are available. Picnic areas, ball fields, and a dance pavilion are available. You can buy supplies in Potrero. Leashed pets are permitted.

Reservations, fees: Reservations are accepted at 858/565-3600 or 877/565-3600 or online at www.sdparks.org ($5 reservation fee). Tent sites are $19 per night, RV sites (partial hookups) are $24 per night, $1 per pet per night, group sites are $75 per night, and the youth group site is $40 per night. Open year-round.

Directions: From El Cajon, drive east on Highway 94 for 42 miles (near the junction of Highway 188) to Potrero Valley Road. Turn north on Potrero Valley Road and drive one mile to Potrero Park Road. Turn right (east) on Potrero Park Road and drive one mile to the park entrance.

Contact: San Diego County Parks Department, 619/478-5212, www.sdparks.org.

48 LAKE MORENA RV PARK
🏊 🎣 🐕 ♿ 🚐

Scenic rating: 6

near Campo

Map 14.2, page 806

This camp is near the southern side of Lake Morena, a great lake for fishing and off-season vacations. It is one of three camps near the lake and the best for RVs. Lake Morena, at 3,200 feet elevation, is a large reservoir in the San Diego County foothills and is known for big bass. It is also known for fluctuating water levels. Swimming is prohibited at this lake.

Campsites, facilities: There are 41 sites with full or partial hookups (30 and 50 amps) for

RVs up to 40 feet. Some picnic tables and fire rings are provided. Restrooms with flush toilets and showers, dump station, propane gas, and coin laundry are available. Some facilities are wheelchair-accessible. Leashed pets are permitted, with certain restrictions.

Reservations, fees: Reservations are recommended. RV sites are $33 per night. Some credit cards accepted. Open year-round.

Directions: From El Cajon, drive east on I-8 to Buckman Springs Road. Take the Buckman Springs off-ramp, turn right (south) on Buckman Springs Road, and drive 5.5 miles to Oak Drive. Turn right on Oak Drive and drive 1.5 miles to Lake Morena Drive. Turn left on Lake Morena Drive and drive a short distance to the park on the right (2330 Lake Morena Drive).

Contact: Lake Morena RV Park, 619/478-5677, www.lakemorenarvcamp.com.

49 SACRED ROCKS RV PARK

🏃 🏊 🎣 ♿ 🚐 ⛺

Scenic rating: 5

in Boulevard

Map 14.2, page 806

Sacred Rocks (formerly Outdoor World Retreat) sits on 163 acres and has hiking trails. The elevation is 3,800 feet. The town of Boulevard is centrally situated for a wide variety of recreation possibilities. About 10 miles to the north is Mount Laguna, with hiking trails available. About 30 minutes to the south is the nearest point of entry to Mexico at Tecate.

Fishing at Lake Morena or Lake Cuyamaca is also a possibility, as is soaking in nearby hot springs. A casino is four miles away. A train museum is available in Campo, about 16 miles away.

Campsites, facilities: There are 151 RV sites with full hookups (20, 30, and 50 amps) for RVs up to 45 feet, a primitive tent camping area, and a group camping area for up to 1,000 people. Picnic tables and fire rings are provided at some sites. A clubhouse, restrooms with showers, horseshoes, volleyball court, coin laundry, gift shop, general store, Wi-Fi, group campfire area, and organized activities and classes are available. A swimming pool and hot tub are available (May–Oct.). Golf carts are allowed. Some facilities are wheelchair-accessible. Leashed pets are permitted, with some breeds prohibited.

Reservations, fees: Reservations are accepted online (www.sacredrocksreserve.com) or at 888/703-0009. RV sites are $45 per night, $5 per person per night for more than two people, tent camping is $10 per person per night, $5 per night for each additional vehicle. Weekly, monthly, and group rates available. Credit cards accepted. Open year-round.

Directions: From El Cajon, drive east on I-8 for approximately 50 miles (past Alpine) to the Crestwood/Live Oak Springs Road exit. Take that exit and turn east and drive 0.5 mile to Church Street. Turn right and drive 4.2 miles to Highway 94. Turn left (east) and drive 1.1 miles to the resort on the right.

Contact: Sacred Rocks Reserve, 619/766-4480, www.sacredrocksreserve.com.

CALIFORNIA DESERTS

© WILLIAM PERRY/123RF.COM

BEST CAMPGROUNDS

《 State Parks
Red Rock Canyon State Park, **page 842.**
Borrego Palm Canyon, **page 872.**

《 Waterskiing
Moabi Regional Park, **page 849.**
Los Alamos, **page 850.**
Havasu Landing Resort and Casino, **page 855.**

There is no region so vast in California — yet with fewer people — than the broad expanse of the California deserts. Joshua Tree National Park, Death Valley, Mojave National Preserve, Anza-Borrego Desert State Park — each of these respective areas has distinct qualities, separate and special, yet they are also joined at the edges.

On a fall evening, you can take a seat on a ridge, overlooking hundreds of square miles of landscape, and just look. Every few minutes, you'll find, the view changes. It is like watching the face of someone you care for, one minute joyous, the next pensive, then wondrous, then mysterious.

The desert is like this, always changing the way it looks, just as the sunlight changes. The reason is that as the sun passes through the sky, its azimuth is continuously changing. In turn, that causes a continuous transformation in the way sunlight is refracted through the atmosphere and across the vast landscape. So, especially at dawn and dusk in spring and fall, the desert looks different from minute to minute. For those who appreciate this subtlety, the desert calls to them in a way that many others do not understand.

Joshua Tree National Park features a sweeping desert landscape edged by mountains and peppered with the peculiar Joshua tree. It is best known by most as the place where the high desert (Mojave Desert, 4,000 feet elevation) meets the low desert (Colorado Desert). This transition creates a setting for diversity in vegetation and habitat. The strange piles of rocks often appear to have been left there by an ancient prehistoric giant, as if chipped, chiseled, and then left in rows and piles.

The national park is far different than Mojave National Preserve. The highlights here are the Kelso Dunes, a series of volcanic cliffs and a forest of Joshua trees. It is remote and explored by relatively few visitors. The Mojave is a point of national significance because it is where three major landscapes join: the Sonoran Desert, the Colorado Desert, and the Mojave Desert.

Death Valley is the largest national park in the lower 48 states, yet there are only nine campgrounds. Because of the sparse nature of the land, campers should arrive self-contained; that is, equipped with everything they need. Some of the highlights include Badwater, at 282 feet below sea level the lowest point in the United States. Yet also in the park is Telescope Peak, towering at 11,049 feet. Crazy? Oh yeah.

When viewed from a distance, in between is a vast terrain that seems devoid of vegetation. The sub-sea-level salt flats indeed can seem like a bunch of nothing. But they are linked to barren, rising mountains, Eureka Dunes, and surrounding vastness everywhere.

Anza-Borrego Desert State Park is so big that it seems to stretch forever — and that is because it does. The park covers 600,000 acres, the largest state park in California. The landscape features virtually every type of desert terrain, but most obvious are canyons, badlands, and barren ridges. In spring, the blooming cholla can be impressive. This is habitat for the endangered desert bighorn, and seeing one can be the highlight of a lifetime of wildlife-viewing. The nearby Salton Sea, created in an accident from a broken dike, provides one of the most distinct (and strange) lakes on earth and is one of the largest inland seas in the world.

Throughout this country, campgrounds are sprinkled in most of the best spots. Some are extremely remote. Some consist of nothing but flat parking areas. Some are simple staging areas for OHV riders, and some serve as base camps for weekend parties. Somewhere amid all this, a place like no other, you will likely be able to find a match for your desires.

So if you see somebody sitting on an overlooking ridge at dusk, watching the changing colors of the landscape as if it were created from the palette of an artist, well, don't be surprised. When it comes to beautiful views, the changing colors of the emotion of the land, it doesn't get any better than this.

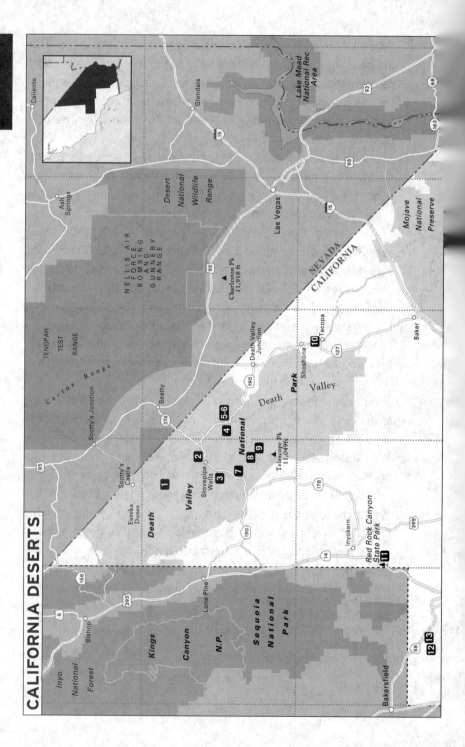

CALIFORNIA DESERTS

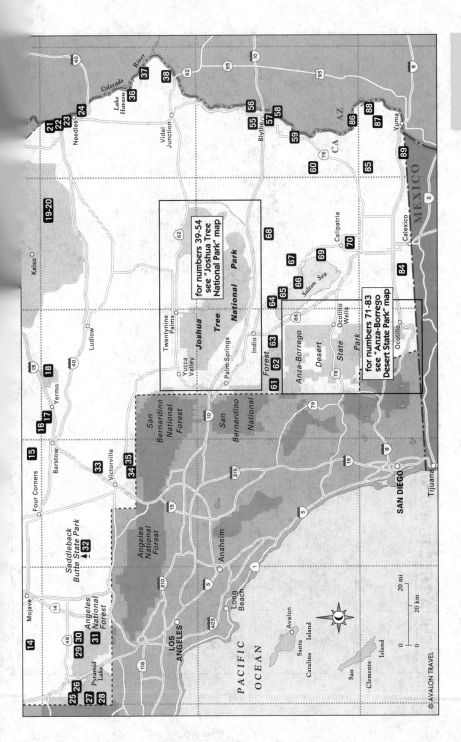

for numbers 39-54 see "Joshua Tree National Park" map

for numbers 71-83 see "Anza-Borrego Desert State Park" map

Joshua Tree National Park

Anza-Borrego Desert State Park

San Bernardino National Forest

San Bernardino National Forest

Angeles National Forest

Angeles National Forest

Saddleback Butte State Park

Salton Sea

Colorado River

Lake Havasu

PACIFIC OCEAN

MEXICO

CA / AZ

Santa Catalina Island

San Clemente Island

Pyramid Lake

Needles
Vidal Junction
Kelso
Ludlow
Yermo
Barstow
Four Corners
Victorville
Mojave
Blythe
Calipatria
Ocotillo Wells
Ocotillo
Calexico
Yuma
Twentynine Palms
Yucca Valley
Palm Springs
Indio
Anaheim
Long Beach
Avalon
LOS ANGELES
SAN DIEGO
Tijuana

20 mi
20 km

©AVALON TRAVEL

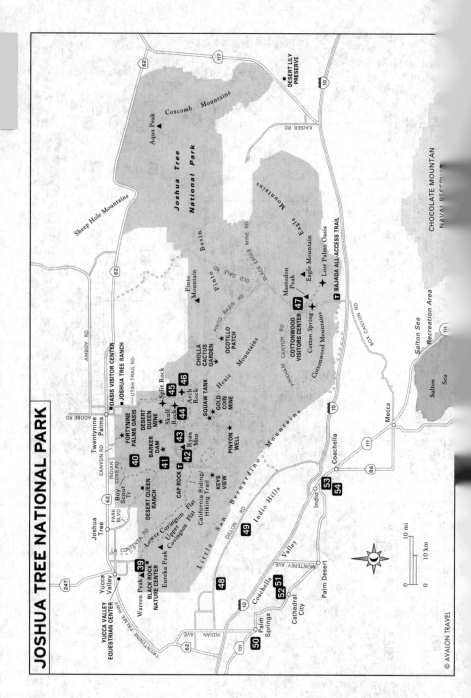

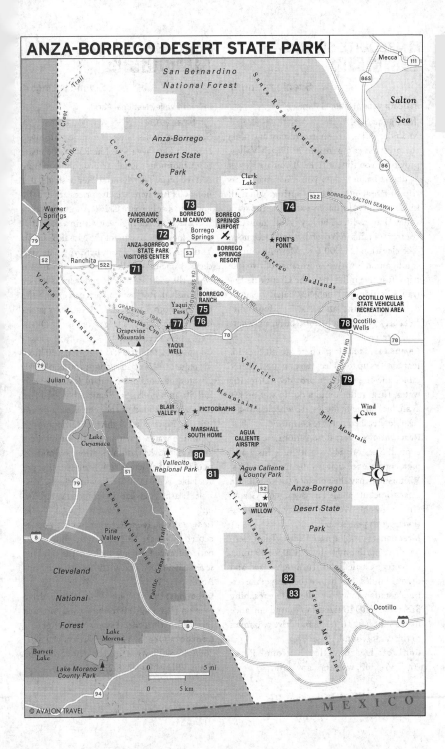

ANZA-BORREGO DESERT STATE PARK

Mecca

Salton Sea

San Bernardino National Forest

Santa Rosa Mountains

Anza-Borrego Desert State Park

Clark Lake

BORREGO-SALTON SEAWAY

73 PANORAMIC OVERLOOK
BORREGO PALM CANYON
BORREGO SPRINGS AIRPORT
74
72
Borrego Springs
ANZA-BORREGO STATE PARK VISITORS CENTER
★ FONT'S POINT
BORREGO SPRINGS RESORT

Warner Springs

Ranchita
71

Borrego Badlands

OCOTILLO WELLS STATE VEHICULAR RECREATION AREA

BORREGO RANCH
75
Yaqui Pass
77 **76**
YAQUI WELL
78 Ocotillo Wells
79

Volcan Mountains

Grapevine Mountain
Grapevine Cyn
GRAPEVINE TRAIL

Julian

Vallecito Mountains

Wind Caves

BLAIR VALLEY ★ PICTOGRAPHS
★ MARSHALL SOUTH HOME
AGUA CALIENTE AIRSTRIP

Split Mountain

Lake Cuyamaca

Vallecito Regional Park
80
81
Agua Caliente County Park

Anza-Borrego Desert State Park

BOW WILLOW

Pine Valley

Cleveland National Forest

Laguna Mountains
Pacific Crest Trail

Tierra Blanca Mtns

Lake Morena

Barrett Lake

Lake Moreno County Park

82
83

IMPERIAL HWY

Ocotillo

Jacumba Mountains

0   5 mi
0   5 km

© AVALON TRAVEL

MEXICO

❶ MESQUITE SPRING

🏃 🏕 🐕 ♿ 🚐 ⛺

Scenic rating: 7

in Death Valley National Park

Map page 834

Mesquite Spring is the northernmost and often the prettiest campground in Death Valley, providing you time it right. If you are a lover of desert beauty, then you must make this trip in late winter or early spring, when all kinds of tiny wildflowers can bring the stark valley floor to life. The key is soil moisture, courtesy of rains in November and December. The elevation is 1,800 feet. Mesquite Spring campground is within short range of two side trips. It is five miles (past the Grapevine Entrance Station) to Ubehebe Crater, a pay-off destination in the landscape, and four miles to Scotty's Castle, a historic building where tours are available.

Campsites, facilities: There are 30 sites for tents or RVs up to 30 feet (no hookups). Picnic tables and fire grills are provided. Drinking water, flush toilets, and a dump station are available. Some facilities are wheelchair-accessible. Leashed pets are permitted.

Reservations, fees: Reservations are not accepted. Sites are $12 per night, plus a $20 park entrance fee that is valid for seven days. Visitors may pay the entrance fee and obtain a park brochure at the Furnace Creek, Grapevine, Stovepipe Wells, or Beatty Ranger Stations. Open year-round.

Directions: From Furnace Creek Visitor Center, drive north on Highway 190 for 19 miles to Scotty's Castle Road. Turn right (east) and drive 33 miles (just before the Grapevine entrance station and three miles before reaching Scotty's Castle) to the campground entrance road on the left. Turn left and drive two miles to the campground.

Contact: Death Valley National Park, 760/786-3200, www.nps.gov/deva.

❷ STOVEPIPE WELLS

🏃 🏊 🏕 🐕 ♿ 🚐 ⛺

Scenic rating: 4

in Death Valley National Park

Map page 834

Stovepipe Wells is on the major highway through Death Valley. The RV sites consist of an enormous asphalt area with sites simply marked on it. There is no shelter or shade. But note: Get fuel here because prices are usually lower than at Furnace Creek. An unusual trail is available off the highway within a short distance; look for the sign for the Mosaic Canyon Trail parking area. From here you can take the easy one-mile walk up a beautiful canyon, where the walls are marble and seem as if they are polished. Rock scramblers can extend the trip for another mile. The elevation is at sea level on the edge of a large expanse of Death Valley below sea level.

Campsites, facilities: There are 190 sites for tents or RVs of any length (no hookups), 28 sites for tents only, and 14 RV sites with full 50-amp hookups. Picnic tables and fire rings are provided at the tent sites; a group fire ring is provided at the tent campground. Drinking water, restrooms with flush toilets and coin showers, dump station, swimming pool (extra fee), camp store, and gasoline are available. Some facilities are wheelchair-accessible. Leashed pets are permitted at campsites only.

Reservations, fees: Reservations are not accepted. Sites are $12 per night, plus a $20 park entrance fee per vehicle that is valid for seven days. Open mid-October through mid-April.

Directions: In Stovepipe Wells Village, drive west on Highway 190 to the signed entrance (just before the general store) on the right.

Contact: Death Valley National Park, 760/786-3200, www.nps.gov/deva; Stovepipe Wells Village, 760/786-2387.

3 EMIGRANT
🏃 🏠 ⛺

Scenic rating: 4

in Death Valley National Park

Map page 834

The key here is the elevation, and Emigrant, at 2,100 feet, is out of the forbidding subzero elevations of Death Valley. That makes it one of the more habitable camps. From the camp a good side trip is to drive south 21 miles on Emigrant Canyon Road, then turn east on Upper Wildrose Canyon Road for seven miles, the last two miles a rough dirt road. That done, you come to the trailhead for Wildrose Peak, on the left side of the road at the parking area for the Charcoal Kilns. The trail here climbs 4.2 miles to the peak, with awesome views in the last two miles; the last mile is a butt-kicker.

Campsites, facilities: There are 10 sites for tents only. Picnic tables are provided. Drinking water and flush toilets are available. Campfires are not permitted during the summer. Leashed pets are permitted at campsites only.

Reservations, fees: Reservations are not accepted. There is no fee for camping. There is is a $20 park entrance fee per vehicle that is valid for seven days. Open year-round.

Directions: In Stovepipe Wells Village, drive eight miles southwest on Highway 190 to the campground on the right.

Contact: Death Valley National Park, 760/786-3200, www.nps.gov/deva.

4 FURNACE CREEK
🏃 🏠 ♿ 🚐 ⛺

Scenic rating: 5

in Death Valley National Park

Map page 834

This is a well-developed national park site that provides a good base camp for exploring Death Valley, especially for newcomers. The nearby visitors center includes Death Valley Museum and offers maps and suggestions for hikes and drives in this unique wildland. The elevation is 190 feet below sea level. This camp offers shady sites, a rarity in Death Valley, but they are packed close together with noisy neighbors and RV generators a factor when the campground is full. It's open all year, but keep in mind that the daytime summer temperatures commonly exceed 120°F, making this area virtually uninhabitable in the summer.

Campsites, facilities: There are 130 sites for tents or RVs up to 35 feet (no hookups), and two group sites for up to 10 vehicles and 40 people each. Picnic tables and fire rings are provided. Drinking water, flush toilets, dump station, and evening ranger programs are available. Campfires are not permitted during the summer. Some facilities are wheelchair-accessible. Leashed pets are permitted at campsites only.

Reservations, fees: Reservations are recommended mid-October through mid-April at 877/444-6777 or www.recreation.gov ($9 reservation fee). Sites are first-come, first-served the rest of the year. Sites are $18 per night mid-October through mid-April, $12 per night off-season, plus a $20 park entrance fee per vehicle that is valid for seven days. Group sites are $52 per night. Open year-round.

Directions: From Stovepipe Wells, drive east on Highway 190, turning right at the intersection with Scotty's Castle Road. Furnace Creek Campground will be on the left shortly before Furnace Creek Ranch and the visitors center.

Contact: Death Valley National Park, 760/786-3200, www.nps.gov/deva.

5 TEXAS SPRING
🏃 🏠 ♿ 🚐 ⛺

Scenic rating: 2

in Death Valley National Park

Map page 834

Although this camp is slightly more protected than Sunset camp, there's limited shade and no shelter. The lower half of the campground is for tents only. It is open only in winter. The upper end of the camp has trails that provide access to the historic springs and a viewing area. The nearby visitors center, which features the Death Valley Museum, offers maps and suggestions for hikes and drives. The lowest point in the United States, Badwater, set 282 feet below sea level, is to the southwest. This camp has one truly unique feature: bathrooms that are listed on the National Historic Register.

Campsites, facilities: There are 92 sites for tents or RVs of any length (no hookups). Picnic tables and fire rings are provided. Drinking water, flush toilets, and a dump station are available. Campfires are not permitted in the summer. Some facilities are wheelchair-accessible. Leashed pets are permitted.

Reservations, fees: Reservations are not accepted. Sites are $14 per night, plus a $20 park entrance fee per vehicle that is valid for seven days. Open mid-October through mid-April.

Directions: From Furnace Creek Ranch, drive south on Highway 190 for 0.25 mile to the signed campground entrance on the left.

Contact: Death Valley National Park, 760/786-3200, www.nps.gov/deva.

6 SUNSET
🏃 🐕 ♿ 🚐

Scenic rating: 4

in Death Valley National Park

Map page 834

This camp is another enormous section of asphalt where the campsites consist of white lines for borders. Sunset is one of several options for campers in the Furnace Creek area of Death Valley, with an elevation of 190 feet below sea level. It is advisable to make your first stop at the nearby visitors center for maps and suggested hikes (according to your level of fitness) and drives.

Campsites, facilities: There are 270 sites for RVs of any length (no hookups). Drinking water, flush toilets, and a dump station are available. Campfires are not permitted in the summer. Some facilities are wheelchair-

accessible. Leashed pets are permitted at campsites.

Reservations, fees: Reservations are not accepted. Sites are $12 per night, plus a $20 park entrance fee per vehicle that is valid for seven days. Open mid-October through mid-April.

Directions: From Furnace Creek Ranch, turn south on Highway 190 and drive 0.25 mile to the signed campground entrance and turn left into the campground.

Contact: Death Valley National Park, 760/786-3200, www.nps.gov/deva.

7 WILDROSE
🏃 🐕 🚐 ⛺

Scenic rating: 4

in Death Valley National Park

Map page 834

Wildrose is set on the road that heads out to the primitive country of the awesome Panamint Range, eventually coming within range of Telescope Peak, the highest point in Death Valley National Park (11,049 feet). The elevation at the camp is 4,100 feet.

Campsites, facilities: There are 23 sites for tents or RVs up to 25 feet (no hookups). Picnic tables and fire rings are provided. Drinking water (April through November only) and pit toilets are available. Campfires are not permitted during the summer. Leashed pets are permitted at campsites only.

Reservations, fees: Reservations are not accepted. There is no fee for camping; there is a $20 park entrance fee per vehicle that is valid for seven days. Open year-round.

Directions: From Stovepipe Wells Village, drive south on Highway 190 for eight miles to Emigrant Canyon Road (just past the Emigrant rest area). Turn left (east) on Emigrant Canyon Road and drive 22 miles to the campground entrance on the left.

Contact: Death Valley National Park, 760/786-3200, www.nps.gov/deva.

8 THORNDIKE
🏃 🐕 ⛰

Scenic rating: 4

in Death Valley National Park

Map page 834

This is one of Death Valley National Park's little-known camps. It is set in the high country at 7,400 feet elevation. It's free, of course. Otherwise the park service would have to actually send somebody out to tend to the place. Nearby are century-old charcoal kilns that were built by Chinese laborers and tended by Shoshone workers. The trailhead that serves Telescope Peak (11,049 feet), the highest point in Death Valley, can be found in nearby Mahogany Flat.

Campsites, facilities: This backcountry campground is accessible only by foot or high-clearance vehicle; it has six sites for tents. Picnic tables and fire rings are provided. Pit toilets are available. No drinking water is available. Campfires are not permitted in the summer. Garbage must be packed out. Leashed pets are permitted at campsites only.

Reservations, fees: Reservations are not accepted. There is no fee for camping. There is a $20 park entrance fee per vehicle that is valid for seven days. Open March through November.

Directions: In Death Valley at Stovepipe Wells Village, drive south on Highway 190 for eight miles to Emigrant Canyon Road (just past the Emigrant rest area). Turn left (east) on Emigrant Canyon Road and drive 21 miles to Wildrose Canyon Road. Turn left and drive nine miles to the camp. (The road becomes extremely rough; high-clearance vehicle is required.)

Contact: Death Valley National Park, 760/786-3200, www.nps.gov/deva.

9 MAHOGANY FLAT FOUR-WHEEL DRIVE
🏃 🐕 ⛰

Scenic rating: 5

in Death Valley National Park

Map page 834

This is one of two primitive, hard-to-reach camps (the other is Thorndike) set in the Panamint Range high country. It is one of the few shaded camps, offering beautiful piñon pines and junipers. What makes it popular, however, is the trail to Telescope Peak leading out from camp. Only the ambitious and well conditioned should attempt the climb, a seven-mile trip one-way with breathtaking (literally) views of both Panamint Valley and Death Valley. The elevation at the campground is 8,200 feet and Telescope Peak tops out at 11,049 feet, which translates to a climb of 2,849 feet.

Campsites, facilities: There are 10 sites for tents only. Picnic tables and fire rings are provided. Pit toilets are available. No drinking water is available. Campfires are not permitted during the summer. Garbage must be packed out. The campground is accessible only by foot or high-clearance four-wheel-drive vehicle. Leashed pets are permitted at campsites only.

Reservations, fees: Reservations are not accepted. There is no fee for camping. There is a $20 park entrance fee per vehicle that is valid for seven days. Open March through November, weather permitting.

Directions: From Stovepipe Wells Village, drive south on Highway 190 for eight miles to Emigrant Canyon Road (just past the Emigrant rest area). Turn left (east) on Emigrant Canyon Road and drive 21 miles to Wildrose Canyon Road. Turn left and drive nine miles (passing Thorndike campground) to the end of the road and the camp.

Contact: Death Valley National Park, 760/786-3200, www.nps.gov/deva.

10 TECOPA HOT SPRINGS PARK

Scenic rating: 3

north of Tecopa

Map page 834

Nobody gets here by accident. This Inyo County campground is out there in no-man's land, and if it weren't for the hot springs and the good rockhounding, all you'd see around here would be a few skeletons. Regardless, it's quite an attraction in the winter, when the warm climate is a plus and the nearby mineral baths are worth taking a dunk in. Rockhounds will enjoy looking for amethysts, opals, and petrified wood in the nearby areas. The elevation is 1,325 feet.

Campsites, facilities: There are 250 sites for tents or RVs of any length (with partial hookups of 30 amps). Some sites are pull-through. Picnic tables and fire grills are provided. Restrooms with flush toilets and showers, a dump station, mineral pools, and play equipment are available. There is no drinking water. Groceries and propane gas are available within 10 miles. Leashed pets are permitted.

Reservations, fees: Reservations are accepted. Sites for tents or self-contained RVs are $16 per night, RV sites (with hookups) are $19 per night, $2 per person per night for more than two people, $5 per night for each additional vehicle. Weekly and monthly rates are available. Open year-round.

Directions: From Baker, drive north on Highway 127 for 58 miles to a county road signed "Tecopa Hot Springs" (south of the junction of Highway 178 and Highway 127). Turn right (east) and drive five miles to the park and campground entrance.

Contact: Tecopa Hot Springs Park, 760/852-4481, www.inyocountycamping.com.

11 RED ROCK CANYON STATE PARK

Scenic rating: 8

near Mojave

Map page 834   BEST (

This unique state park is one of the prettiest spots in the region year-round. A gorgeous series of geologic formations, most of them tinted red, makes it a worthwhile visit in any season. The park also has paleontology sites, as well as remnants of some 1890s-era mining operations. A great, easy hike is the two-mile walk to Red Cliffs Natural Preserve, where there are awesome 300-foot cliffs and columns, painted red by the iron in the soil. Part of this area is closed February through June to protect nesting raptors. For those who don't hike, a must is driving up Jawbone Canyon Road to see Jawbone and Last Chance Canyons. Hikers have it better. The park also has excellent wildflower blooms March through May. A primitive OHV trail also is available; check regulations. The elevation is 2,600 feet.

Campsites, facilities: There are 50 sites for tents or RVs up to 30 feet (no hookups). Picnic tables and fire grills are provided. Drinking water, pit toilets, dump station, picnic area, and seasonal visitor center and campfire programs are available. In spring and fall, volunteers lead nature walks. Some facilities are wheelchair-accessible. Leashed pets are permitted in the campground only.

Reservations, fees: Reservations are not accepted. Sites are $25 per night, and $6 for each additional vehicle. Open year-round.

Directions: Drive on Highway 14 to the town of Mojave (50 miles east of the Los Angeles Basin area). Continue northeast on Highway 14 for 25 miles to the park entrance on the left.

Contact: Red Rock Canyon State Park, 661/946-6092, www.parks.ca.gov.

12 BRITE VALLEY AQUATIC RECREATION AREA

🏔️🏊�🚣🦌👨‍👩‍👧🚙⛺

Scenic rating: 7

at Brite Lake

Map page 834

Brite Valley Lake is a speck of a water hole (90 acres) on the northern flank of the Tehachapi Mountains in Kern County, at an elevation of 4,000 feet. No gas motors are permitted on the lake, so it's perfect for canoes, kayaks, or inflatables. No swimming is permitted. Use is moderate, primarily by picnickers and anglers. The lake is stocked with trout in the spring; other species include catfish and bluegill. A golf course is nearby.

Campsites, facilities: There are six sites with full hookups and 12 sites with partial hookups (20 amps) for RVs of any length and a tent camping area. Group camping is also available. Picnic tables and fire grills are provided. Drinking water, restroom with flush toilets and showers, dump station, playground, picnic pavilions (available by reservation), and fish-cleaning station are available. Supplies are available about eight miles away in Tehachapi. Leashed pets are permitted.

Reservations, fees: Reservations are not accepted for individuals, but large RV clubs may reserve sites at 661/822-3228, ex. 10. Tent sites are $20 per night, RV sites are $20 (partial hookups) and $30 (full hookups) per night. Fishing fees are $5 per person and each angler over age 16 must have California fishing license. Open year-round.

Directions: From Bakersfield, drive east on Highway 58 for 40 miles toward the town of Tehachapi. Take the Highway 202 exit and drive three miles west to Banducci Road. Turn left and drive for about one mile to the park on the right.

Contact: Tehachapi Valley Recreation and Parks District, 661/822-3228, www.tvrpd.org; Brite Lake Campground, 661/822-8047.

13 INDIAN HILL RANCH AND RV PARK

🏔️🏊🐕🚙

Scenic rating: 7

near Tehachapi

Map page 834

This is a unique park with two seasonal ponds stocked with largemouth bass and catfish. Crappie and bluegill are other fish species. The campground is open year-round and offers spacious, private sites with oak trees and a view of Brite Valley. Some sites have lake views, while others have hill views. A bonus is the hiking trails in the park. The elevation is 5,000 feet. Although this area is known for being windy, this campground is somewhat sheltered from the wind.

Campsites, facilities: There are 37 sites with full or partial hookups for RVs; nearly half of the sites are pull-through. A group site accommodates up to 40 people. Picnic tables and fire pits are provided. Restroom with flush toilets and showers (seasonal), dump station, coin laundry, Wi-Fi, horseshoes, firewood, propane, and two stocked fishing ponds are available. Small leashed pets are permitted, with certain restrictions.

Reservations, fees: Reservations are accepted. Lakeside sites (partial and full hookups) are $30–40 per night, lakeview sites (water and 30-amp) are $25 per night, A section sites (full hookups) are $20 per night, $6 per night per extra vehicle, $6 per night per extra person. The group site is $400 per night. Monthly rates available. No credit cards accepted. Open year-round, with some sites closed November through mid-May.

Directions: Drive on Highway 58 to Tehachapi and Exit 148 for Tehachapi/Highway 202. Take that exit to Tucker Road. Turn right and drive south one mile to Highway 202/Valley Boulevard. Turn right (west) and drive four miles to Banducci Road. Turn left and drive 0.75 mile to Arosa Road. Turn left and drive 1.7 miles to the park at 18061 Arosa Road.

Contact: Indian Hill Ranch and RV Park, 661/822-6613, www.indianhillranch.com.

14 TEHACHAPI MOUNTAIN PARK

🏃 🎣 🐎 ♿ 🚗 ⛺

Scenic rating: 7

southwest of Tehachapi

Map page 835

This county park is overlooked by most out-of-towners. It is a pretty spot covering 5,000 acres, set on the slopes of the Tehachapi Mountains, with elevations in the park ranging from 5,500 to 7,000 feet. The roads to the campgrounds are steep, but the sites are flat. Trails for hikers and equestrians are available, but no horses are allowed at the campground. (A 10-horse corral is available adjacent to the Horseshoe Campground.) An interpretive trail, Nuooah Nature Trail, is available. This park is popular not only in spring, but also in winter, with the elevations sometimes high enough to get snow (chains often required for access). The park lies eight miles southwest of the town of Tehachapi on the southern side of Highway 58 between Mojave and Bakersfield. Woody's Peak, at almost 8,000 feet, overlooks the park from its dominion in the Tehachapi Mountains, the dividing line between the San Joaquin Valley and the Los Angeles Basin.

Campsites, facilities: There are 61 sites for tents or RVs of any length (no hookups), a group campsite for up to 40 people, a group campsite for up to 150 people, and group lodging with 10 cabins for a minimum of 40 people. Picnic tables and fire grills are provided. Drinking water (natural spring) and pit toilets are available. Some facilities are wheelchair-accessible. Leashed pets are permitted.

Reservations, fees: Reservations are not accepted for individual sites, but are required for the group sites and group cabins at 661/868-7000. Sites are $14 per night per vehicle, and $4 per pet per night. Sierra Flats Group Site is $60 per night, Tehachapi Group Site (includes 10 cabins) is $275 per night. Open year-round, weather permitting.

Directions: In Tehachapi, take Tehachapi Boulevard to the Cury Street exit. Take that exit south and drive about three miles to Highline Road. Turn right on Highline Road and drive two miles to Water Canyon Road. Turn left on Water Canyon Road and drive three miles to the park.

Contact: Kern County Parks Department info line, 661/868-7000, www.co.kern.ca.us/parks/index.htm.

15 OWL CANYON

🏃 🐎 ♿ 🚗 ⛺

Scenic rating: 3

near Barstow

Map page 835

The primary attraction of Owl Canyon camp is that the surrounding desert is sprinkled with exposed fossils of ancient animals. Guess they couldn't find any water. Well, if people try hiking here without a full canteen, there may soon be some human skeletons out here, too. Actually, rangers say that the general public is unlikely to spot fossils here because it takes some basic scientific knowledge to identify them. The sparse BLM land out here is kind of like an ugly dog you learn to love: After a while, when you look closely, you learn it has a heart of gold. This region is best visited in the spring and fall, of course, when hiking allows a fresh, new look at what may appear to some as a wasteland. The beauty is in the detail of it—tiny critters and tiny flowers seen against the unfenced vastness, with occasional fossils yet to be discovered. The elevation is 2,600 feet.

Campsites, facilities: There are 30 sites for tents or RVs of any length (no hookups). Two horse corrals are available at a separate group site. Picnic tables, shade ramadas, and fire grills are provided. Drinking water and vault toilets are available. A campground host is on site fall through spring. Some trash service may be offered, but prepare to pack out all garbage. Some facilities are wheelchair accessible. Leashed pets are permitted.

Reservations, fees: Reservations are not accepted. Sites are $6 per night. Open year-round.

Directions: Drive on I-15 to Barstow to the exit for 1st Street. Take that exit and drive north on 1st Street (crossing the Mojave River Bridge) for 0.75 mile to Irwin Road. Turn left and drive eight miles to Fossil Bed Road. Turn left and drive two miles to the campground on the right.

Contact: Bureau of Land Management, Barstow Field Office, 760/252-6000, www.blm.gov/ca.

16 CALICO GHOST TOWN REGIONAL PARK
🏃 🛶 ♿ 🚐 ⛺

Scenic rating: 4

near Barstow

Map page 835

Let me tell you about this ghost town: There are probably more people here now than there have ever been. In the 1880s and 1890s it was a booming silver mine town, and there are still remnants of that. Alas, it now has lots of restaurants and shops. Recreation options include riding on a narrow-gauge railroad, touring what was once the largest silver mine in California, and watching an old-style melodrama with villains and heroes. This is a 480-acre park with self-guided tours, hiking trails, gold panning, summer entertainment, and museum, with festivals held throughout the year. Whatever you do, don't take any artifacts you may come across, such as an old nail, a jar, or anything; you will be doomed with years of bad luck. No foolin'. A park representative told the story of a man from the East Coast who nabbed a beautiful rock on his visit. He then was plagued with years of bad luck, including broken bones, disappointment in his love life, and several family deaths. In desperation, he flew back to California and returned the rock to its rightful place.

Campsites, facilities: There are 265 sites for tents and RVs up to 45 feet; 104 sites have full or partial hookups (20, 30, and 50 amps) and some sites are pull-through. There are also three group camping areas, six cabins, and a bunkhouse. Fire pits are provided. Restrooms with flush toilets and showers, drinking water, and three dump stations are available. Pay phone, restaurants, and shops are on-site. Groceries, propane gas, and laundry facilities are 10 miles away. Some facilities are wheelchair-accessible. Leashed pets are permitted.

Reservations, fees: Reservations are accepted at 800/TO-CALICO (800/862-2542) ($2 reservation fee). Tent sites are $30 per night, RV sites are $34 (partial hookups) and $35 (full hookups) per night, $1 per pet per night. Cabins are $40 per night ($25 deposit), the bunkhouse is $5 per night per person for 12–20 people. Some credit cards accepted. Open year-round.

Directions: From Barstow, drive northeast on I-15 for seven miles to the exit for Ghost Town Road. Take that exit and drive north on Ghost Town Road for three miles to the park on the left.

Contact: Calico Ghost Town Regional Park, San Bernardino County, 760/254-2122, http://cms.sbcounty.gov/parks.

17 BARSTOW CALICO KOA
🏃 🏊 🛶 🐕 🚵 ♿ 🚐 ⛺

Scenic rating: 3

near Barstow

Map page 835

Don't blame me if you end up way out here. Actually, for vacationers making the long-distance grind of a drive on I-15, this KOA can seem like the promised land. It has received awards for its cleanliness, and a nightly quiet time ensures that you have a chance to get rested. Vegetation screening between sites enhance privacy. But hey, as long as you're here, you might as well take a side trip to Calico Ghost Town, about three miles to the northeast at the foot of the Calico Mountains. A unique side trip is the Calico Early Man Site, about five miles to the north; tours are available. Primitive stone tools are believed to have been discovered here in 1942. Rockhounding, hiking, and an outlet mall are other nearby options. The elevation is 1,900 feet.

Campsites, facilities: There are 15 tent sites and 66 sites with full or partial hookups (30 and 50 amps) for RVs of any length; many sites are pull-through. Lodges and a tepee are also available. Picnic tables and fire grills are provided. Drinking water, restrooms with flush toilets and showers, dump station, playground with climbing wall, heated swimming pool (seasonal), recreation room, Wi-Fi, archery range, convenience store, propane gas, ice, and coin laundry are available. Some facilities are wheelchair-accessible. Leashed pets are permitted.

Reservations, fees: Reservations are accepted at 800/KOA-0059 (800/562-0059). RV sites are $35–50 per night, tent sites are $26–33.25, $3.50 per person per night for more than two people. Lodges are $69–100 per night, the tepee is $43–52 per night. Some credit cards accepted. Open year-round.

Directions: From Barstow, drive northeast on I-15 for seven miles to the exit for Ghost Town Road. Take that exit and drive left under the freeway to a frontage road at the Shell gas station. Turn left at the frontage road and drive 0.25 mile to the campground on the right.

Contact: Barstow Calico KOA, 760/254-2311, www.barstowcalicokoa.com.

18 AFTON CANYON

Scenic rating: 6

near Barstow in
the East Mojave National Scenic Area

Map page 835

This camp is set at 1,400 feet elevation in a desert riparian habitat along the Mojave River. This is one of several Bureau of Land Management tracts near the Mojave National Preserve.

Side-trip options include the Rainbow Basin Natural Area (about an hour's drive), Soda Springs, and the Calico Early Man Site. Remember, rivers in the desert are not like rivers in cooler climates. There are no fish worth eating.

Campsites, facilities: There are 22 sites for tents or RVs up to 30 feet (no hookups). Picnic tables, shade ramadas, and fire rings are provided. Vault toilets are available. Drinking water is available intermittently, so bring your own water. Some trash service is offered but be prepared to pack out all garbage. Leashed pets are permitted.

Reservations, fees: Reservations are not accepted. Sites are $6 per night. Open year-round.

Directions: From Barstow, drive east on I-15 for 37 miles to Afton Road. Turn right (south) and drive three miles to the campground. Note: Four-wheel-drive or high-clearance vehicles are recommended since the access road can be rough and have washouts.

Contact: Bureau of Land Management, Barstow Field Office, 760/252-6000, www.blm.gov/ca.

19 MID HILLS

Scenic rating: 4

in the Mojave National Preserve

Map page 835

This is a primitive campground set among the junipers and piñon trees in a mountainous area at 5,600 feet elevation. It is one of two little-known camps in the vast desert that is managed by the National Park Service. About half of the campsites were burned in the 2005 Hackberry Fire; most of the piñon and juniper trees burned as well. There is an eight-mile one-way trail that starts across from the entrance to Mid Hills and is routed down to the Hole-in-the-Wall Campground. It a pleasant walk in spring and fall.

Campsites, facilities: There are 26 sites for

tents or RVs up to 22 feet (no hookups). Picnic tables and fire grills are provided. Drinking water, trash service, and pit toilets are available. Leashed pets are permitted.

Reservations, fees: Reservations are not accepted. Sites are $12 per night. Open year-round.

Directions: Drive on I-40 to Essex Road (near Essex, 116 miles east of Barstow). Take that exit and drive north on Essex Road for 10 miles to Black Canyon Road. Turn north and drive nine miles (at Hole-in-the-Wall campground, the road becomes dirt) and continue seven miles to Wild Horse Canyon Road. Turn left and drive two miles (rough, dirt road) to the campground on the right.

Contact: Mojave National Preserve, 760/252-6100, www.nps.gov/moja.

20 HOLE-IN-THE-WALL AND BLACK CANYON

Scenic rating: 6

in the Mojave National Preserve

Map page 835

This is the largest and best-known of the camps in the vast Mojave National Preserve. There are three camps in this area: Hole-in-the-Wall, Black Canyon Group, and Black Canyon Equestrian. All are set at 4,400 feet elevation. An interesting side trip is to the Mitchell Caverns in the nearby Providence Mountains State Recreation Area.

Campsites, facilities: There are 35 sites for tents or RVs of any length (no hookups), two walk-in sites, one group site for up to 50 people, and an equestrian camp for up to 30 people. Picnic tables and fire grills are provided. Drinking water, pit and vault toilets, trash service, and a dump station are available. The group site has a picnic shelter and corrals are provided at the equestrian site. Leashed pets are permitted.

Reservations, fees: Reservations are not accepted at Hole-in-the-Wall, but they are required at Black Canyon for groups of at least 15 people, seven vehicles, or seven horses (call 760/928-2572 or 760/252-6104). Sites at Hole-in-the-Wall are $12 per night. Sites at Black Canyon are $25 per night. Open year-round.

Directions: From I-40, take Essex Road (near Essex, 116 miles east of Barstow) north for 10 miles to Black Canyon Road. Turn north and drive nine miles to the campgrounds.

Contact: Mojave National Preserve, 760/252-6100, www.nps.gov/moja.

21 RAINBO BEACH RESORT

Scenic rating: 6

on the Colorado River

Map page 835

The big bonus here is the full marina, making this resort on the Colorado River the headquarters for boaters and water-skiers. And headquarters it is, with tons of happy folks who are extremely well lubed, both inside and out. This resort boasts 800 feet of river frontage. A 60-site mobile home park is adjacent to the RV park. (For boating details, see the Needles Marina Park listing in this chapter.)

Campsites, facilities: There are 60 sites with full hookups (30 and 50 amps) for RVs. Some sites are pull-through. Picnic tables are provided. Restrooms with showers, coin laundry, heated swimming pool, spa, recreation room, launch ramp, and a restaurant and full-service bar are available. A boat dock is nearby. Leashed pets are permitted.

Reservations, fees: Reservations are accepted. Sites are $35 per night. Seasonal rates available. Some credit cards accepted. Open year-round.

Directions: Take I-40 to Needles and River Road. Turn north on River Road and drive 1.5 miles to the resort on the right.

Contact: Rainbo Beach Resort, 3520 Needles Hwy., 760/326-3101, www.rainbobeach.com.

22 NEEDLES MARINA PARK

🏊 ⛵ 🚐 🛶 🐕 ♿ 🏕 🚗 ⛺

Scenic rating: 6

on the Colorado River

Map page 835

Bring your suntan lotion and a beach towel. This section of the Colorado River is a big tourist spot where the body oil and beer can flow faster than the river. There are a ton of hot bodies and hot boats, and waterskiing dominates the adjacent calm-water section of the Colorado River. However, note that upstream of the Needles-area put-in is the prime area for waterskiing. Downstream is the chance for canoeing or kayaking. Meanwhile, there's also an 18-hole golf course adjacent to the camp, but most folks head for the river. Compared to the surrounding desert, this park is almost a golden paradise. A mobile home park is adjacent to the RV park.

Campsites, facilities: There are 158 sites with full hookups (30 and 50 amps) for tents or RVs, and six cabins. Some sites are pull-through. Picnic tables are provided. Restrooms with flush toilets and showers, drinking water, heated pool, spa, recreation room, Wi-Fi, picnic area, boat ramp, boat slips, store, gas, and laundry facilities are available. Some facilities are wheelchair accessible. Leashed pets are permitted.

Reservations, fees: Reservations are accepted. Waterfront sites are $38 per night, non-waterfront sites are $36 per night, $5 per night for air conditioning, $9–9.50 per night per person for more than four people, $5 per pet per night. Cabins are $75 per night ($100 deposit, two-night min.). Some credit cards accepted. Open year-round.

Directions: Take I-40 to Needles and the exit for J Street. Take that exit and drive to Broadway. Turn left on Broadway and drive 0.75 mile to Needles Highway. Turn right (north) on Needles Highway and drive 0.5 mile to the park on the left.

Contact: Needles Marina Park, 760/326-2197, www.needlesmarinapark.com.

23 NEEDLES KOA

🏊 🐕 ♿ 🚗 ⛺

Scenic rating: 2

near the Colorado River

Map page 835

At least you've got the Needles KOA out here—winner of the 2012 KOA PresidentÖs Award. The swimming pool will help you get a new start, while side trips include venturing to the nearby Colorado River or heading north to Lake Mead. Of course, you could always go to Las Vegas. Nah.

Campsites, facilities: There are 93 pull-through sites with full hookups (30 and 50 amps), and 18 pull-through sites with partial hookups (30 and 50 amps) for tents or RVs of any length. Five cabins are also available. Restrooms with flush toilets and showers, drinking water, recreation room, swimming pool, playground, WiFi, store, snack bar, propane gas, and coin laundry are available. Some facilities are wheelchair-accessible. Leashed pets are permitted.

Reservations, fees: Reservations are accepted at 800/562-3407 or www.koa.com. RV sites are $27–33 per night, tent sites are $22 per night, $2 per person per night for more than two people. Cabins are $44–64 per night. Credit cards accepted. Discounts available. Open year-round.

Directions: Take I-40 to Needles and the exit for West Broadway. Take that exit to Needles Highway. Turn northwest on Needles Highway and drive 0.75 mile to National Old Trails Highway. Turn left and drive one mile to the park on the right (5400 National Old Trails Highway).

Contact: Needles KOA, 760/326-4207, www.koa.com.

24 MOABI REGIONAL PARK

Scenic rating: 7

on the Colorado River

Map page 835   **BEST (**

Campsites are situated in the main area of the park along 2.5 miles of shoreline peninsula. The park features 24 group areas. The adjacent Colorado River provides the main attraction, the only thing liquid around these parts that isn't contained in a can or bottle. The natural response when you see it is to jump in the water, and everybody does so, with or without a boat. You'll see lots of wild and crazy types having the times of their lives on the water. The boating season is a long one here, courtesy of that desert climate. Fishing is good for catfish, smallmouth bass, bluegill, striped bass, and sometimes crappie.

Campsites, facilities: There is a large grassy area for tents and more than 600 sites for RVs or tents; 157 sites have full or partial hookups (20, 30, and 50 amps) and a few are pull-through. There are also 24 group camping areas. Picnic tables and fire grills are provided at most sites. Restrooms with flush toilets and showers, coin laundry, store, ice, two dump stations, covered picnic area, marina, bait, and boat ramp are available. Volleyball, basketball, horseshoes, and putting green are also available. An 18-hole golf course is nearby. Some facilities are wheelchair-accessible. Leashed pets are permitted, with restrictions.

Reservations, fees: Reservations are accepted at 760/326-9000 or http://reservations. piratecoveresort.com ($10 reservation fee). Tent sites are $20 per night, RV sites are $30 (partial hookups) and $40 (full hookups) per night; Peninsula sites have full hookups and are $50 per night; $3 per person per night for additional person, $2 per pet per night. Long-term rates available in the winter, with limit of five months. Some credit cards accepted. Open year-round.

Directions: From Needles, drive east on I-40 for 11 miles to Park Moabi Road. Turn left on Park Moabi Road and continue 0.5 mile to the park entrance at the end of the road.

Contact: Moabi Regional Park Marina, 760/326-9000.

25 KINGS

Scenic rating: 5

near Piru Creek in Los Padres National Forest

Map page 835

The Hungry Valley State Vehicular Recreation Area is just five miles to the east. Figure it out: Right, this is a primitive but well-placed camp for four-wheel-drive and off-highway vehicles. The camp is near Piru Creek, off a short spur road, so it feels remote yet is close to one of California's top off-road areas.

Campsites, facilities: There are seven sites for tents or RVs up to 16 feet (no hookups). Picnic tables and fire grills are provided. Vault toilets are available. No drinking water is available. Garbage must be packed out. Leashed pets are permitted.

Reservations, fees: Reservations are not accepted. There is no fee for camping. An Adventure Pass ($30 annual fee or $5 daily fee) per parked vehicle is required. Open year-round.

Directions: Drive on I-5 to south of Gorman and the Gorman–Hungry Valley Road exit (the northern exit for the Hungry Valley Recreation Area). Take that exit and turn south on Hungry Valley Road (Forest Road 8N01) and drive six miles to Gold Hill Road (Forest Road 8N01). Turn right and drive six miles to Forest Road 18N01A. Turn left and drive 0.75 mile to the campground.

Contact: Los Padres National Forest, Mount Piños Ranger District, 661/245-3731, www. fs.usda.gov/lpnf.

26 LOS ALAMOS

🏃 🏊 🛶 🚣 🐕 ♿ 🚐 ⛺

Scenic rating: 4

near Pyramid Lake in Angeles National Forest

Map page 835   **BEST (**

Los Alamos is set at an elevation of 2,600 feet near the southern border of the Hungry Valley State Vehicular Recreation Area, and about 2.5 miles north of Pyramid Lake. Pyramid Lake is a big lake, covering 1,300 acres with 20 miles of shoreline, and is extremely popular for waterskiing and fast boating (35 mph speed limit), as well as for sailboarding (best at the northern launch point), fishing (best in the spring and early summer and in the fall for striped bass), and swimming. A lifeguard is on duty at the boat launch area during the summer season. Note: All boats must be certified mussel-free before launching.

Campsites, facilities: There are 93 sites and three group sites for tents or RVs up to 26 feet (no hookups) that can accommodate up to 40 people each. Picnic tables and fire pits are provided. Drinking water, flush toilets, dump station, volleyball courts, fish-cleaning stations, and a camp store are available. A boat ramp is at the Emigrant Landing Picnic Area. Some facilities are wheelchair-accessible. Leashed pets are permitted.

Reservations, fees: Reservations are accepted and are required for the group site at 877/444-6777 or www.recreation.gov ($9 reservation fee). Sites are $20–25 per night, $10 per night per each additional vehicle, $5 per night for additional person. Group sites are $85–125 per night. Open year-round.

Directions: Drive on I-5 to eight miles south of Gorman and the Smokey Bear Road exit. Take the Smokey Bear Road exit and drive west about three-quarters of a mile and follow the signs to the campground.

Contact: Parks Management Company, 805/434-1996; Angeles National Forest, Santa Clara/Mojave Rivers Ranger District, 661/269-2808, www.fs.usda.gov/angeles.

27 DUTCHMAN

🏃 🐕 ⛺

Scenic rating: 6

on Alamo Mountain in
Los Padres National Forest

Map page 835

These spots at Dutchman are best known by four-wheel-drive enthusiasts rumbling around the area. The big attraction here is access to Miller Jeep Trail, a gnarly black-diamond route that can bend metal and alter minds. This camp also provides an alternative to the Hungry Valley State Vehicular Recreation Area to the nearby northeast. (Note: The place is called Dutchman Flat, but the camp itself is just Dutchman). The elevation is 6,800 feet.

Campsites, facilities: There are eight primitive sites. Picnic tables and fire grills are provided. Pit toilets are available. No drinking water is available. Garbage must be packed out. Leashed pets are permitted.

Reservations, fees: Reservations are not accepted. There is no fee for camping. An Adventure Pass ($30 annual fee or $5 daily pass) per parked vehicle is required. Open early May through October, weather permitting.

Directions: Drive on I-5 to south of Gorman and the Gorman–Hungry Valley Road exit (the northern exit for the Hungry Valley Recreation Area). Take that exit and turn south on Hungry Valley Road (Forest Road 8N01) and drive six miles to Gold Hill Road (Forest Road 8N01). Turn right and drive 13 miles to Twin Pines campground. To reach Dutchman, at Twin Pines campground, turn right at Forest Road 7N01 and drive three miles to the campground.

Contact: Los Padres National Forest, Mount Piños Ranger District, 661/245-3731, www.fs.usda.gov/lpnf.

28 HALF MOON
🚶 🐕 �car 🔺

Scenic rating: 7

near Piru Creek in Los Padres National Forest

Map page 835

Half Moon is a primitive camp set along Piru Creek at 4,700 feet elevation. Adjacent to camp, Forest Road 7N13 follows the creek for a few miles, then dead-ends at a trailhead that continues along more remote stretches of this little stream. Hikers should also consider the trail to nearby Thorn Point for a beautiful lookout.

Campsites, facilities: There are 10 sites for tents or RVs up to 22 feet (no hookups). Picnic tables and fire grills are provided. Vault toilets are available. No drinking water is available. Garbage must be packed out. Leashed pets are permitted.

Reservations, fees: Reservations are not accepted. There is no fee for camping. An Adventure Pass ($30 annual fee or $5 daily pas) per parked vehicle is required. Open mid-May to mid-November, weather permitting.

Directions: Drive on I-5 to just south of Lebec and the Frazier Park exit. Take that exit and drive west on Frazier Mountain Road to the town of Lake of the Woods and Lockwood Valley Road. Turn left on Lockwood Valley Road and drive about 12 miles to Grade Valley Road (Forest Road 7N03). Turn left and drive 11 miles to the campground on the left. High-clearance or four-wheel-drive vehicles are recommended; access requires crossing a creek in which the current can be fairly fast and high, especially in the spring.

Contact: Los Padres National Forest, Mount Piños Ranger District, 661/245-3731, www.fs.usda.gov/lpnf.

29 SAWMILL
🚶 🐕 �car 🔺

Scenic rating: 7

on the Pacific Crest Trail in Angeles National Forest

Map page 835

This is a classic hikers trailhead camp. It is set at 5,200 feet elevation, right on the Pacific Crest Trail and just one mile from the junction with Burnt Peak Canyon Trail. For a good day hike, head southeast on the Pacific Crest Trail for one mile to Burnt Peak Canyon Trail, turn right (southwest), and hike just over a mile to Burnt Peak, at 5,788 feet elevation. Note that this camp is inaccessible after the first snow. Nearby Upper Shake provides an alternative.

Campsites, facilities: There are eight sites for tents or RVs up to 16 feet (no hookups). Note that RVs are not recommended. Picnic tables and fire pits are provided. Vault toilets are available. No drinking water is available. Garbage must be packed out. Leashed pets are permitted.

Reservations, fees: Reservations are not accepted. There is no fee for camping. An Adventure Pass ($30 annual fee or $5 daily pass) per parked vehicle is required. Open year-round, weather permitting.

Directions: Drive on I-5 to the Tehachapis near the small town of Castaic and Lake Hughes Road. Turn northeast on Lake Hughes Road and drive 27 miles to the town of Lake Hughes and Pine Canyon Road/County Road N2. Turn left on Pine Canyon Road and drive 10 miles to Bushnell Summit Road. Turn left and drive two miles to the campground on the left.

Contact: Angeles National Forest, Santa Clara/Mojave Rivers Ranger District, 661/269-2808, www.fs.usda.gov/angeles.

30 UPPER SHAKE

Scenic rating: 7

on the Pacific Crest Trail in
Angeles National Forest

Map page 835

Upper Shake, like nearby Sawmill, is right on the Pacific Crest Trail. The elevation is 4,400 feet. Hikers who plan on heading to Burnt Peak are better off departing from Sawmill (less than two miles to the west). This camp is used primarily as a jump-off point for those heading east on the PCT; Lake Hughes is the nearest destination, less than four miles away, and a mile after that is Lake Elizabeth. The camp is inaccessible after the first snow.

Campsites, facilities: There are 17 sites for tents or RVs up to 22 feet (no hookups). Picnic tables and fire pits are provided. Vault toilets are available. No drinking water is available. Garbage must be packed out. Leashed pets are permitted.

Reservations, fees: Reservations are not accepted. There is no fee for camping. An Adventure Pass ($30 annual fee or $5 daily pass) per parked vehicle is required. Open May through October, weather permitting.

Directions: Drive on I-5 to the Tehachapis near the small town of Castaic and Lake Hughes Road. Turn northeast on Lake Hughes Road and drive 27 miles to the town of Lake Hughes and Pine Canyon Road/County Road N2. Turn left on Pine Canyon Road and drive about 5.5 miles to the entrance road on the left.

Contact: Angeles National Forest, Santa Clara/ Mojave Rivers Ranger District, 661/269-2808, www.fs.usda.gov/angeles.

31 COTTONWOOD

Scenic rating: 5

near the Warm Springs Mountain Lookout in
Angeles National Forest

Map page 835

Cottonwood Camp is set at 2,680 feet elevation in remote Angeles National Forest along a small stream. The camp is on the north flank of Warm Springs Mountain. A great side trip is to the Warm Springs Mountain Lookout (4,023 feet), about a five-mile drive. Drive south on Forest Road 7N09 for three miles, turn right (west) on Forest Road 6N32, and drive for 1.5 miles to Forest Road 7N13. Turn left (south) and drive a mile to the summit.

Campsites, facilities: There are 22 sites for tents or RVs up to 22 feet (no hookups). Picnic tables and fire pits are provided. Vault toilets are available. No drinking water is available; stream water should be treated before use. Garbage must be packed out. Supplies are less than four miles away in the town of Lake Hughes. Leashed pets are permitted.

Reservations, fees: Reservations are not accepted. There is no fee for camping. An Adventure Pass ($30 annual fee or $5 daily pass) per parked vehicle is required. Open year-round, weather permitting.

Directions: Drive on I-5 to the Tehachapis near the small town of Castaic and Lake Hughes Road. Turn northeast on Lake Hughes Road and drive 27 miles to the campground on the right.

Contact: Angeles National Forest, Santa Clara/ Mojave Rivers Ranger District, 661/269-2808, www.fs.usda.gov/angeles.

32 SADDLEBACK BUTTE STATE PARK

🚶 🐕 ♿ �-road 🏕️

Scenic rating: 8

near Lancaster

Map page 835

This 3,000-acre park was originally established to preserve ancient Joshua trees. In fact, it used to be called Joshua Tree State Park, but folks kept getting it confused with Joshua Tree National Park, so it was renamed. The terrain is sparsely vegetated and desertlike, with excellent hiking trails up the nearby buttes. The best hike is Saddleback Loop, a five-mile trip that features a 1,000-foot climb to Saddleback Summit at 3,651 feet. On rare clear days, there are fantastic views in all directions, including the Antelope Valley California Poppy Preserve, the surrounding mountains, and the Mojave Desert. On the typical hazy day, the poppy preserve might as well be on the moon; you can't even come close to seeing it. The elevation is 2,700 feet.

Note: This park is on the closure list developed by the California Department of Parks, pending final state budget decisions or the possible transfer of park management to other park agencies or volunteer groups. As this book went to press, the park was open weekends only (2 P.M.–sunset) Oct. 1–Mar. 30, 2013. Check online for current park status.

Campsites, facilities: There are 50 sites for tents or RVs up to 30 feet (no hookups). A group camp is available for up to 30 people and 12 vehicles. Picnic tables, shade ramadas, and fire grills are provided. Drinking water, flush toilets, and dump station are available. A visitors center is nearby. Some facilities are wheelchair-accessible. Leashed pets are permitted in the campground only.

Reservations, fees: Reservations are not accepted; call 661/946-6092 for group camping. Sites are $20 per night, $5 per night for each additional vehicle, $100 per night for the group site. Open year-round.

Directions: Take Highway 14 north to Lancaster and the exit for Avenue J. Take that exit and drive east on Avenue J for 17 miles to the park entrance on the right. Or drive south on Highway 14 to Lancaster to the exit for 20th Street west. Take that exit, turn left, and drive to Avenue J. Turn east on Avenue J and drive 17 miles to the park entrance on the right.

Contact: Saddleback Butte State Park, Mojave Desert Information Center, 661/942-0662, www.parks.ca.gov.

33 SHADY OASIS VICTORVILLE

🏊 🐕 🚣 ♿ �-road 🏕️

Scenic rating: 3

near Victorville

Map page 835

Most long-distance trips on I-15 are grueling endurance tests with drivers making the mistake of trying to get a decent night's sleep at a roadside rest stop. Why endure the torture, especially with Shady Oasis way out here, in Victorville of all places? Where the heck is Victorville? If you are exhausted and lucky enough to find the place, you won't be making any jokes about it. Note: There are some permanent residents at this former KOA.

Campsites, facilities: There are 136 sites for tents or RVs up to 53 feet, many with full or partial hookups (50 amps) and some pull-through. There are also eight cabins. Picnic tables and fire grills are provided. Drinking water, restrooms with flush toilets and showers, recreation room, seasonal heated swimming pool, playground, Wi-Fi, convenience store, propane gas, and coin laundry are available. Some facilities are wheelchair-accessible. Leashed pets are permitted.

Reservations, fees: Reservations are accepted at 760/245-6867. Tent sites are $26–28 per night, RV sites are $28 per night (no hookups), $30 per night for partial hookups (water and electricity), and $32 per night (full hookups), $3 per person for more than two people, $1 per night for each additional vehicle. Camping cabins are $48 per night. Some credit cards accepted. Open year-round.

Directions: Drive on I-15 to Victorville and Stoddard Wells Road (north of Victorville). Turn south on Stoddard Wells Road and drive a short distance to the campground (16530 Stoddard Wells Road).

Contact: Shady Oasis Victorville, 760/245-6867, shadyoasis.tripod.com.

34 HESPERIA LAKE CAMPGROUND

Scenic rating: 5

in Hesperia

Map page 835

This is a slightly more rustic alternative than the usual Hesperia campgrounds. There is a small lake/pond for recreational fishing and there is a small fishing fee, but no fishing license is required. Boating and swimming are not allowed, but youngsters usually get a kick out of feeding the ducks and geese that live at the pond. A lake-record 268-pound sturgeon was caught and released back into the lake.

Campsites, facilities: There are 52 sites, some with partial hookups (30 and 50 amps), for tents or RVs up to 40 feet. Picnic tables and fire pits are provided. Drinking water, restrooms with flush toilets and showers, a playground, and a fishing pond are available. Some facilities are wheelchair-accessible. Leashed pets are permitted.

Reservations, fees: Reservations are accepted at 800/521-6332. Sites are $35 per night (two-night minimum), $2 per night per pet, $15 to fish at the pond. Some credit cards accepted. Open year-round.

Directions: Drive on I-15 to Hesperia and the exit for Main Street. Take that exit and drive east on Main Street for 9.5 miles (the road curves and becomes Arrowhead Lake Road) to the park on the left.

Contact: Hesperia Lake Campground, 760/244-5951 or 800/521-6332, www.hesperiaparks.com.

35 MOJAVE NARROWS REGIONAL PARK

Scenic rating: 7

on the Mojave River

Map page 835

Almost no one except the locals knows about this little county park. It is like an oasis in the Mojave Desert. There are actually two small lakes here: the larger Horseshoe Lake and Pelican Lake. No private boats are allowed and rental rowboats and pedal boats are available on weekends. Swimming and water/body contact are prohibited. It is set at 2,000 feet elevation and provides a few recreation options, including a pond stocked in season with trout and catfish, horseback-riding facilities, and equestrian trails. Hiking includes a wheelchair-accessible trail. The Mojave River level fluctuates here, almost disappearing in some years in summer and early fall. One of the big events of the year here, the Huck Finn Jubilee, is on Father's Day in June. Note: The gate closes each evening.

Campsites, facilities: There are 68 sites for tents or RVs of any length, including seven pull-through sites and 37 sites with full hookups (15 and 30 amps). Nine group areas for up to 150 people are also available. Picnic tables and barbecue grills are provided. Drinking water, restrooms with flush toilets and showers, dump station, playground, picnic shelters, bait, horse rentals, and horseback-riding facilities are available. A store is available three miles from the campground. Some facilities are wheelchair-accessible. Leashed pets are permitted.

Reservations, fees: Reservations accepted for RV and group sites ($7 reservation fee for RV sites, $20 for groups). Tent sites are $25 per night, RV sites (hookups) are $35 per night, group areas are $20 per unit per night, $3 per night per additional person, $1 per night per pet, $8 per day fishing fee. Rates increase holidays and during special events. Weekly rates available. Discounts for seniors. Some credit cards accepted. Open year-round.

Directions: Take I-15 to Victorville and the exit for Bear Valley Road. Take that exit and drive east on Bear Valley Road for six miles to Ridgecrest. Turn left on Ridgecrest, drive three miles, and make a left into the park.

Contact: Mojave Narrows Regional Park, 760/245-2226, www.cms.sbcounty.gov/parks.

36 HAVASU LANDING RESORT AND CASINO

Scenic rating: 7

on the western shore of Lake Havasu

Map page 835   **BEST (**

Situated on the western shore of Lake Havasu, this full-service resort is run by the Chemehuevi Indian Tribe. It even includes a casino with slot machines and a card room. The resort is situated in a desert landscape in the Chemehuevi Valley. A boat shuttle operates from the resort to the London Bridge and Havasu City, Arizona. A mobile-home park is within the resort and an airstrip is nearby. Some RV sites are waterfront and some are rented for the entire winter. Permits are required for off-road vehicles and can be obtained at the resort. This is one of the most popular boating areas in the southwestern United States. The lake is 45 miles long, covers 19,300 acres, and is at the low elevation of 482 feet. Havasu was created when the Parker Dam was built across the Colorado River.

Campsites, facilities: There are 180 sites with full hookups (30 and 50 amps) for RVs up to 40 feet, three large tent camping areas, and mobile home rentals. Picnic tables, restrooms with flush toilets and showers, a dump station, coin laundry, picnic areas, restaurant and lounge, casino, 24-hour security, 24-hour marina with gas dock, bait and tackle, general store and deli, boat launches, boat slips, fish-cleaning room, dry storage, boat shuttle, and boat launch and retrieval service are available. Activities include movie nights and potluck socials. An ATM is on-site. An airport is nearby. Some facilities are wheelchair-accessible. Leashed pets are permitted.

Reservations, fees: Reservations are accepted at 800/307-3610 or online at www.havasulanding.com. Sites for tents and self-contained RVs are $20 per night, RV sites are $27–32 per night, tent-only sites are $17 per night, $2 per person per night for more than two people, and $6 per night for each additional vehicle. Holiday rates are higher. Weekly and monthly rates are available. A boat-launch fee is charged. Some credit cards accepted. Open year-round.

Directions: From Needles, drive south on Highway 95 for 19 miles to Havasu Lake Road. Turn left and drive 17.5 miles to the resort on the right.

From Blythe, drive north on Highway 95 for 79 miles to Havasu Lake Road. Turn right and drive 17.5 miles to the resort on the right.

Contact: Havasu Landing Resort and Casino, 760/858-4593 or 800/307-3610, www.havasulanding.com; Lake Havasu Tourism Bureau, 928/453-3444 or 800/2-HAVASU (800/242-8278), www.golakehavasu.com; Lake Havasu Area Chamber of Commerce, 928/855-4115, www.havasuchamber.com.

37 BLACK MEADOW LANDING

Scenic rating: 7

south of Lake Havasu on the Colorado River

Map page 835

This area of the Colorado River attracts a lot of people, so reservations are highly recommended. Hot weather, warm water, and proximity to Las Vegas make this one of the top camping and boating hot spots in the West. Vacationers are here year-round, although fewer people use it in the late winter. Black Meadow Landing is a large resort with hundreds of RV sites, lodging, and a long list of amenities. Some sites—A Row—have water views. Once you arrive, everything you need for a stay should be available within the resort.

Campsites, facilities: There are 350 sites with full hookups (30 amps) for RVs up to 53 feet and tent camping is available. Park-model cabins, kitchen cabins, and a motel are also available. Restrooms with flush toilets and showers, drinking water, picnic tables, picnic areas, horseshoe pit, restaurant, convenience store, recreation room (winter only), bait and tackle, propane, full-service marina, boat launch, boat slips, boat and RV storage, a swimming lagoon, and a five-hole golf course are available. Leashed pets are permitted.

Reservations, fees: Reservations are accepted at 877/642-8278. Waterfront RV sites (A and Z Rows, full hookups) are $55–60 per night, B and C Rows are $45–50 per night, D and E Rows (water only) are $35 per night. RV Park sites (1–168) are $35–40 per night, golf course RV sites (169–209) are $35–40 per night, $6 per person per night for more than two people, $6 per night for each additional vehicle. Weekly and monthly rates are available. Some credit cards accepted. Open year-round.

Directions: From Southern California: Take I-10 east to Blythe and turn north on U.S. 95. Continue to Vidal Junction at the intersection of U.S. 95 and Highway 62. Turn east on Highway 62 and drive to Earp and Parker Dam Road. Continue straight on Parker Dam Road and drive to a Y intersection and Black Meadow Landing Road (near Parker Dam). Bear left on Black Meadow Landing Road and drive approximately nine miles to the resort at the end of the road.

From Northern California: From Barstow, take I-40 east and drive to Needles. Continue east on I-40 to Arizona Highway 95. Drive south on Arizona Highway 95 to Lake Havasu City. Continue south to the Parker Dam turnoff. Turn west and drive across the dam to a Y intersection and Black Meadow Landing Road. Bear right on Black Meadow Landing Road and drive approximately nine miles to

the resort at the end of the road. Note: Towed vehicles are not allowed to cross the dam.

Contact: Black Meadow Landing, 760/663-4901, www.blackmeadowlanding.com; Lake Havasu Tourism Bureau, 928/453-3444 or 877/2-HAVASU (877/242-8278), www.go-lakehavasu.com; Lake Havasu Area Chamber of Commerce, 928/855-4115, www.havasu-chamber.com.

38 RIVERLAND RV PARK

🏊 ⛵ 🛶 🐕 ♿ 🚐

Scenic rating: 6

on the Colorado River near Parker Dam

Map page 835

This resort is in the middle of a very popular boating area, particularly for waterskiing. Check out the park's live webcam for an on-the-spot feel for the place and the weather. Summer is the busiest time because of the sunshine and warm water. In the winter, although temperatures can get pretty cold, around 40°F at night, the campground fills with retirees from the snow and rain country. Even though the resort is way out there on the Colorado River, there are plenty of services, including a convenience store, swimming beach, and full-service marina. Insider's tip: One of the best spots for catfish is a few miles down the road below Parker Dam.

Campsites, facilities: There are 85 sites with full hookups (50 amps) for RVs up to 42 feet. There are also six bungalows and seven RV rentals. Picnic tables are provided. Restrooms with flush toilets and showers, drinking water, cable television, Wi-Fi, convenience store, coin laundry, full-service marina with gas dock, boat launch, boat slips, boat and RV storage, swimming beach, fishing pier, bait, recreation room (winter only), volleyball court, and horseshoe pits are available. An ATM is onsite and an 18-hole golf course is about 20 minutes away in Arizona. Some facilities are wheelchair-accessible. Leashed pets are permitted with restrictions.

Reservations, fees: Reservations are accepted at 760/663-3733. Sites are $52–72 per night. Weekly rates are available; monthly rates are available November through May. Some credit cards accepted. Open year-round.

Directions: From Southern California, take I-10 east to Blythe and turn north on U.S. 95. Continue to Vidal Junction at the intersection of U.S. 95 and Highway 62. Turn east on Highway 62 and drive to Earp and Parker Dam Road. Continue straight on Parker Dam Road and drive five miles to the resort on the right.

Contact: Riverland RV Park, 760/663-3733, www.riverlandresort.net.

39 BLACK ROCK CAMP AND HORSE CAMP
🚶 🐕 ♿ 🚐 ⛺

Scenic rating: 4

in Joshua Tree National Park

Joshua Tree map, page 836

This is the fanciest darn public campground this side of the desert. Why, it actually has drinking water. The camp is set at the mouth of Black Rock Canyon, at 4,000 feet elevation, which provides good winter hiking possibilities amid unique (in other words, weird) rock formations, about a half-hour drive from the campground. Show up in summer and you'll trade your gold for a sip of water. The camp is set near the excellent Black Rock Canyon Visitor Center and a trailhead for a four-mile round-trip hike to a rock wash. If you scramble onward, the route continues all the way to the top of Eureka Peak, at 5,518 feet, an 11-mile round-trip. But hey, why not just drive there?

Campsites, facilities: There are 100 sites for tents or RVs up to 35 feet (no hookups), and 15 equestrian sites for up to six people and four horses per site. Picnic tables and fire grills are provided. Drinking water, flush toilets, and dump station are available. The horse camp has hitching posts and a water faucet. Some facilities are wheelchair-accessible. Leashed pets are permitted, but not on trails.

Reservations, fees: Reservations are accepted October through May at 877/444-6777 or www.recreation.gov ($9 reservation fee). Sites are $15 per night, plus $15 park entrance fee per vehicle. Open year-round, weather permitting.

Directions: From the junction of I-10 and Highway 62 near Palm Springs, drive northeast on Highway 62 for 22.5 miles to Yucca Valley and Joshua Lane. Turn right (south) on Joshua Lane and drive about five miles to the campground.

Contact: Joshua Tree National Park, 760/367-5500 or 760/362-4367; Black Rock Nature Center, 760/367-3001, www.nps.gov/jotr.

40 INDIAN COVE CAMPGROUND
🚶 🐕 🚐 ⛺

Scenic rating: 4

in Joshua Tree National Park

Joshua Tree map, page 836

This is one of the campgrounds near the northern border of Joshua Tree National Park. The vast desert park, covering 1,238 square miles, is best known for its unique granite formations and scraggly-looking trees. If you had to withstand the summer heat here, you'd look scraggly too. Drinking water is available at the Indian Cove Ranger Station, two miles from the campground.

Campsites, facilities: There are 101 sites for tents or RVs up to 35 feet (no hookups), and 13 group sites for tents only for up to 60 people. Picnic tables and fire grills are provided. Drinking water and vault toilets are available. Gas, groceries, and laundry services are available in Twentynine Palms (seven miles) or Joshua Tree (12 miles). Leashed pets are permitted, but not on trails.

Reservations, fees: Reservations are accepted October through May at 877/444-6777 or www.recreation.gov ($9 reservation fee). Sites are $15 per night, $25–40 per night for group sites, plus $15 per vehicle park entrance fee. Open year-round.

Directions: From the junction of I-10 and Highway 62 near Palm Springs, drive northeast on Highway 62 for 22 miles to Yucca Valley, continue to the small town of Joshua Tree, and then continue nine miles to Indian Cove Road. Turn right and drive three miles to the campground.

Contact: Joshua Tree National Park, 760/367-5500 or 760/362-4367, www.nps.gov/jotr.

41 HIDDEN VALLEY

Scenic rating: 7

in Joshua Tree National Park

Joshua Tree map, page 836

This is one of California's top campgrounds for rock-climbers. Set at 4,200 feet elevation in the high desert country, this is one of several camping options in the area. A trailhead is available two miles from camp at Barker Dam, an easy one-mile loop that features the Wonderland of Rocks. The hike takes you next to a small lake with magical reflections of rock formations off its surface. The RV sites here are snatched up quickly and this campground fills almost daily with rock-climbers.

Campsites, facilities: There are 39 sites for tents or RVs up to 25 feet (no hookups). Picnic tables and fire grills are provided. Vault toilets are available. No drinking water is available. Leashed pets are permitted.

Reservations, fees: Reservations are not accepted. Sites are $10 per night, and $15 park entrance fee per vehicle. Open year-round.

Directions: From the junction of I-10 and Highway 62 near Palm Springs, drive northeast on Highway 62 for 22 miles to Yucca Valley, then continue to the small town of Joshua Tree and Park Boulevard. Turn south on Park Boulevard and drive 14 miles to the campground on the left.

Contact: Joshua Tree National Park, 760/367-5500 or 760/362-4367, www.nps.gov/jotr.

42 RYAN

Scenic rating: 4

in Joshua Tree National Park

Joshua Tree map, page 836

This is one of the high desert camps in the immediate area (see also the Jumbo Rocks listing in this chapter). Joshua Tree National Park is a forbidding paradise: huge, hot, and waterless (most of the time). The unique rock formations look as if some great artist made them with a chisel. The elevation is 4,300 feet. The best hike in the park starts here—a three-mile round-trip to Ryan Mountain is a 1,000-foot climb to the top at 5,470 feet elevation. The view is simply drop-dead gorgeous, not only of San Jacinto, Tahquitz, and San Gorgonio peaks, but of several beautiful rock-studded valleys as well as the Wonderland of Rocks.

Campsites, facilities: There are 31 sites for tents or RVs up to 25 feet (no hookups). Picnic tables and fire grills are provided. Vault toilets are available. No drinking water is available. Leashed pets are permitted.

Reservations, fees: Sites are $10 per night, and there is a $15 park entrance fee per vehicle. Open year-round.

Directions: From the junction of I-10 and Highway 62 near Palm Springs, drive northeast on Highway 62 to Twentynine Palms and Utah Trail. Turn right (south) on Utah Trail and drive about 20 miles to the campground entrance on the left.

Contact: Joshua Tree National Park, 760/367-5500 or 760/362-4367, www.nps.gov/jotr.

43 SHEEP PASS GROUP CAMP

Scenic rating: 4

in Joshua Tree National Park

Joshua Tree map, page 836

Several campgrounds are in this stretch of high desert. Ryan campground (see listing in this chapter), just a couple of miles down the road, has an excellent trailhead for a trek to Ryan Mountain, the best hike in the park. Temperatures are routinely over 100°F here in the summer. (For details on this area, see the White Tank listing in this chapter.)

Campsites, facilities: There are six group camps for tents or RVs up to 25 feet (no hookups) that can accommodate 20–50 people. Picnic tables and fire grills are provided. Vault toilets are available. No drinking water is available. Leashed pets are permitted.

Reservations, fees: Reservations are accepted at 877/444-6777 or at www.recreation.gov ($9 reservation fee). Sites are $25–40 per night, plus $15 park entrance fee per vehicle. Open year-round.

Directions: From the junction of I-10 and Highway 62 near Palm Springs, drive northeast on Highway 62 to Twentynine Palms and Utah Trail. Turn right (south) on Utah Trail and drive about 16 miles to the campground on the left.

Contact: Joshua Tree National Park, 760/367-5500 or 760/362-4367, www.nps.gov/jotr.

44 JUMBO ROCKS

Scenic rating: 4

in Joshua Tree National Park

Joshua Tree map, page 836

Joshua Tree National Park covers more than 1,238 square miles. It is striking high-desert country with unique granite formations that seem to change color at different times of the day. At 4,400 feet, this camp is one of the higher ones in the park, with adjacent boulders and rock formations that look as if they have been strewn about by an angry giant. It is a popular site for rock-climbing.

Campsites, facilities: There are 124 sites for tents and a limited number of RVs up to 35 feet (no hookups). Picnic tables and fire grills

are provided. Vault toilets are available. No drinking water is available. Leashed pets are permitted.

Reservations, fees: Reservations are not accepted. Sites are $10, and there is a $15 park entrance fee per vehicle. Open year-round.

Directions: From the junction of I-10 and Highway 62 near Palm Springs, drive northeast on Highway 62 to Twentynine Palms and Utah Trail. Turn right (south) on Utah Trail and drive about nine miles to the campground on the left side of the road.

Contact: Joshua Tree National Park, 760/367-5500 or 760/362-4367, www.nps.gov/jotr.

45 BELLE

Scenic rating: 4

in Joshua Tree National Park

Joshua Tree map, page 836

This camp is at 3,800 feet elevation in rocky high country. It is one of six camps in the immediate area. (For more details, see the White Tank listing in this chapter.)

Campsites, facilities: There are 18 sites for tents or RVs up to 25 feet (no hookups). Picnic tables and fire grills are provided. Vault toilets are available. No drinking water is available. Leashed pets are permitted.

Reservations, fees: Reservations are not accepted. Sites are $10 per night, and there is a $15 park entrance fee per vehicle. Open year-round.

Directions: From the junction of I-10 and Highway 62 near Palm Springs, drive northeast on Highway 62 to Twentynine Palms and Utah Trail. Turn right (south) on Utah Trail and drive eight miles to Pinto Basin Road. Turn left (heading toward I-10) and drive about 1.5 miles to the campground on the left.

Contact: Joshua Tree National Park, 760/367-5500 or 760/362-4367, www.nps.gov/jotr.

46 WHITE TANK

Scenic rating: 4

in Joshua Tree National Park

Joshua Tree map, page 836

Joshua Tree National Park is a unique area where the high and low desert meet. Winter is a good time to explore the beautiful boulder piles and rock formations amid scraggly Joshua trees. There are several trails in the area, with the best near Black Rock Campground, Hidden Valley, and Cottonwood. The elevation is 3,800 feet.

Campsites, facilities: There are 15 sites for tents and a limited number of RVs up to 25 feet (no hookups). Picnic tables and fire grills are provided. Vault toilets are available. No drinking water is available. Leashed pets are permitted.

Reservations, fees: Reservations are not accepted. Sites are $10 per night, and there is $15 park entrance fee per vehicle. Open year-round.

Directions: From the junction of I-10 and Highway 62 near Palm Springs, drive northeast on Highway 62 to Twentynine Palms and Utah Trail. Turn right (south) on Utah Trail and drive eight miles to Pinto Basin Road. Turn left (heading toward I-10) and drive three miles to the campground on the left.

Contact: Joshua Tree National Park, 760/367-5500 or 760/362-4367, www.nps.gov/jotr.

47 COTTONWOOD

Scenic rating: 4

in Joshua Tree National Park

Joshua Tree map, page 836

If you enter Joshua Tree National Park at its southern access point, this is the first camp you will reach. The park visitors center, where maps are available, is a mandatory stop. This park is vast, high-desert country, highlighted by unique rock formations, occasional scraggly trees, and vegetation that manages to survive the bleak, roasting summers. This camp is set at 3,000 feet elevation. A trailhead is available here for an easy one-mile nature trail, where small signs have been posted to identify different types of vegetation. You'll notice, however, that they all look like cacti (the plants, not the signs, heh, heh).

Campsites, facilities: There are 62 sites for tents or RVs up to 35 feet (no hookups), and three tent-only group sites for 15–25 people. Picnic tables and fire grills are provided. Drinking water, flush toilets, and a dump station are available. Some facilities are wheelchair-accessible. Leashed pets are permitted.

Reservations, fees: Reservations are accepted for group sites only at 877/444-6777 or www.recreation.gov ($9 reservation fee). Sites are $15 per night, group sites are $30 per night, park entrance is $15 per vehicle. Open year-round.

Directions: From Indio, drive east on I-10 for 35 miles to the exit for Pinto Basin Road/Twentynine Palms (near Chiriaco Summit). Take that exit and drive north for seven miles (entering the park) to the campground on the right.

Contact: Joshua Tree National Park, 760/367-5500 or 760/362-4367, www.nps.gov/jotr.

48 SAM'S FAMILY SPA

Scenic rating: 5

near Palm Springs

Joshua Tree map, page 836

Hot mineral pools attract swarms of winter vacationers to the Palm Springs area. The therapeutic pools are partially enclosed. This 50-acre park, set 13 miles outside of Palm Springs, provides an alternative to the more crowded spots. And this is one of the few parks in the area that allows tent campers. A mobile-home park is adjacent to the RV park. The elevation of Sam's Family Spa is 1,000 feet. (For information on the tramway ride to Desert View west of Palm Springs, or the hike to Mount San Jacinto, see the Sky Valley Resort listing in this chapter.)

Campsites, facilities: There are 170 sites for tents and RVs up to 42 feet (with full hookups of 30 and 50 amps). Six mobile-home rentals and a motel are also available. Picnic tables are provided. There is a separate area with barbecues. Restrooms with showers, playground, heated swimming pool, heated wading pool, four hot mineral pools, dry sauna and steam rooms, Wi-Fi, coin laundry, and convenience store are available. Some facilities are wheelchair-accessible. Leashed pets are permitted in the campground only.

Reservations, fees: Reservations are accepted online only; no telephone reservations. Sites are $44 per night, $8 per night per person for more than four people. Weekly and monthly rates available. Some credit cards accepted. Open year-round.

Directions: Drive on I-10 to the Palm Springs Area and the Palm Drive exit (to Desert Hot Springs). Take that exit and drive north on Palm Drive for about two miles to Dillon Road. Turn right (east) on Dillon Road and drive 4.5 miles to the park on the right (70–875 Dillon Road).

Contact: Sam's Family Spa, 760/329-6457, www.samsfamilyspa.com.

49 SKY VALLEY RESORT

Scenic rating: 5

near Palm Springs

Joshua Tree map, page 836

This 140-acre park is much like a small town, complete with RV homes, an RV park, and park-model rentals and seasonal restaurants. But itÓs the nine hot spring pools that bring people in. One of the best adventures in California is just west of Palm Springs, taking the aerial tram up from Chino Canyon to Desert View, a ride/climb of 2,600 feet for remarkable views to the east across the desert below. An option from there is hiking the flank of Mount San Jacinto, including making the ascent to the summit (10,804 feet), a round-trip buttkicker of nearly 12 miles. Golf courses are nearby. Note that there are 260 permanent residents.

Campsites, facilities: There are 618 sites with full hookups (30 and 50 amps) for RVs up to 42 feet. Restrooms with showers, cable TV, four swimming pools, nine natural hot mineral whirlpools, two laundry rooms, two large recreation rooms, fitness centers, children's playroom, seasonal grocery store, chapel program, seasonal tennis and golf lessons, pickleball court, Wi-Fi, activities director, shuffleboard, tennis, horseshoes, crafts room, and walking paths are available. Propane gas is nearby. Some facilities are wheelchair-accessible. Leashed pets are permitted.

Reservations, fees: Reservations are recommended, especially in winter, at 888/894-7727 or online. Sites are $47 per night, $5 per person per night for more than two people. Discounts off-season. Monthly rates available. Some credit cards accepted. Open year-round.

Directions: Drive on I-10 to the Palm Springs area and the Palm Drive exit (to Desert Hot Springs). Take that exit and drive north on Palm Drive for three miles to Dillon Road. Turn right on Dillon Road and drive 8.5 miles to the park on the right (74–711 Dillon Road).

Contact: Sky Valley Resort, 760/329-2909, www.skyvalleyresort.com.

50 HAPPY TRAVELER RV PARK

Scenic rating: 1

in Palm Springs

Joshua Tree map, page 836

Are we having fun yet? They are at Happy Traveler, which is within walking distance of Palm Springs shopping areas and restaurants. The Palm Springs Air Museum has a collection of World War II aircraft. A casino is one mile away.

Campsites, facilities: There are 130 sites with full hookups (30 and 50 amps) for RVs up to 40 feet. No tents or tent trailers. Picnic tables are provided. Restrooms with showers, cable TV, Wi-Fi, swimming pool, spa, clubhouse, shuffleboard, propane, seasonal activities, and coin laundry are available. Leashed pets are permitted with restrictions, including a maximum of two pets.

Reservations, fees: Reservations are accepted. Sites are $48 per night. Weekly and monthly rates available. Credit cards are not accepted. Open year-round.

Directions: Drive on I-10 to Palm Springs and Highway 111/Palm Canyon Drive. Take Palm Canyon Drive and drive 12 miles south to Mesquite Avenue. Turn right on Mesquite Avenue and drive to the park on the left (211 West Mesquite).

Contact: Happy Traveler RV Park, 760/325-8518, www.happytravelerrv.com.

51 OUTDOOR RESORT OF PALM SPRINGS
♨ 🐕 ♿ 🚐

Scenic rating: 6

near Cathedral City

Joshua Tree map, page 836

This is considered a five-star resort, beautifully landscaped, huge, and offering many activities: swimming pools galore, 27-hole golf course, tons of tennis courts, spas, and on and on. The 137-acre park is four miles from Palm Springs. Note that this is a lot-ownership park with lots for sale. About a quarter of the sites are available for rent to vacationers. One of the best adventures in California is just west of Palm Springs: taking the aerial tram up from Chino Canyon to Desert View, a ride/climb of 2,600 feet for remarkable views to the east across the desert below.

Campsites, facilities: There are 1,213 sites with full hookups (30 and 50 amps) for RVs

up to 45 feet. No tent camping. RV rentals are also available. Restrooms with showers, eight swimming pools, spas, 14 lighted tennis courts, 27-hole golf course, two clubhouses, snack bar, café, beauty salon, coin laundry, Wi-Fi, convenience store, fitness center, and planned activities are available. Some facilities are wheelchair-accessible. Leashed pets are permitted.

Reservations, fees: Reservations are accepted at 800/843-3131 (California only). Sites start at $70 per night, $1 per pet per night with a two-pet maximum. RV rentals are $32–75 per night. Monthly rates available. Some credit cards accepted. Open year-round.

Directions: Drive on I-10 to the Palm Springs area and continue to Cathedral City and the exit for Date Palm Drive. Take that exit and drive south on Date Palm Drive for two miles to Ramon Road. Turn left and drive to the resort on the right (69–411 Ramon Road).

Contact: Outdoor Resort, 760/324-4005, www.outdoorresort.com.

52 PALM SPRINGS OASIS RV PARK
♨ 🐕 ♿ 🚐

Scenic rating: 2

in Cathedral City

Joshua Tree map, page 836

This popular wintering spot is for RV cruisers looking to hole up in the Palm Springs area for awhile. Palm Springs is only six miles away. This is a seniors-only park: Children are not allowed and one person must be at least 55 years of age to check in; anyone else must be at least 40 years of age.

Campsites, facilities: There are 140 sites with full hookups (30 and 50 amps) for RVs up to 45 feet. No tents. Restrooms with showers, cable TV, Wi-Fi, two swimming pools, spa, tennis and shuffleboard courts, coin laundry, dump station, dog run, game room, and propane gas are available. An 18-hole golf course is adjacent to the park. Some facilities are wheelchair-accessible. Leashed pets are permitted, with a two-pet maximum.

Reservations, fees: Reservations are accepted. Sites are $47–52 per night, $2 per person per night for more than two people, $3 per night resort fee. Weekly, monthly, and off-season rates available. Some credit cards accepted. Open year-round.

Directions: Drive on I-10 to the Palm Springs area and continue to Cathedral City and the exit for Date Palm Drive. Take that exit and drive south on Date Palm Drive for four miles to Gerald Ford Drive and the park on the left corner (36–100 Date Palm Drive).

Contact: Palm Springs Oasis RV Park, 760/328-4813 or 800/680-0144.

53 INDIAN WELLS CAREFREE RV RESORT

🏊 🐕 ♿ 🚐

Scenic rating: 2

in Indio

Joshua Tree map, page 836

Indio is a good-sized town midway between the Salton Sea to the south and Palm Springs to the north, which is about 20 miles away. In the summer, it is one of the hottest places in America. In the winter, it is a favorite for "snowbirds," that is, RV and trailer owners from the snow country who migrate south for the winter. About half of the sites are filled with long-term renters.

Campsites, facilities: There are 306 sites with full hookups (50 amps) for RVs up to 45 feet; some are pull-through. No tents. Restrooms with showers, cable TV, Wi-Fi, three swimming pools, two therapy pools, horseshoes, basketball, volleyball, shuffleboard courts, driving net and putting green, recreation room, planned activities, ice, mini-dog run, picnic area, RV storage, and coin laundry are available. Some facilities are wheelchair-accessible. Leashed pets are permitted.

Reservations, fees: Reservations are accepted at 800/789-0895 and online. Sites are $58

per night. Weekly and monthly rates available. Some credit cards accepted. Open year-round.

Directions: Drive on I-10 to Indio and the exit for Jefferson Street. Take that exit, stay in the right lane, and drive to the light at Jefferson. Turn right at Jefferson and drive south for three miles to the park on the left (47–340 Jefferson Street).

Contact: Indian Wells RV Resort, 760/347-0895, www.carefreervresorts.com.

54 OUTDOOR RESORTS INDIO

🏊 🐕 ♿ 🚐

Scenic rating: 7

in Indio

Joshua Tree map, page 836

For owners of tour buses, motor coaches, and lavish RVs, it doesn't get any better than this in Southern California. Only RVers in Class A motor homes are allowed here. This resort bills itself as the "ultimate RV resort" and has been featured on the Travel Channel and in the Wall Street Journal. About 25 percent of the sites are available for rent; all sites are owned by RVers. This park is set close to golf, shopping, and restaurants. Jeep tours of the surrounding desert canyons and organized recreation events are offered.

Campsites, facilities: There are 419 sites with full hookups (50 amps) for Class A motor homes with a minimum length of 34 feet; no trailers or pickup-truck campers. Restrooms with showers, cable TV, Wi-Fi, swimming pools, pickleball courts, tennis courts, sauna, spas, café, fitness center, clubhouse, coin laundry, and 18-hole golf course are available. Some facilities are wheelchair-accessible. Leashed pets are permitted, with a two-pet maximum.

Reservations, fees: Reservations are accepted. Winter rates are $87–103.50 per night, $5 per night per additional person. Discounts in summer. Some credit cards accepted. Open year-round.

Directions: Drive on I-10 to Indio and the exit for Indio Boulevard/Jefferson Street. Take that exit, stay in the right lane, and drive to the light at Jefferson. Turn right at Jefferson and drive south for three miles to Avenue 48. Turn left and drive 0.25 mile to the park on the left side of the road (80–394 Avenue 48).

Contact: Outdoor Resorts Indio, 760/775-7255 or 800/892-2992 (outside California), www.orindio.com.

55 MIDLAND LONG TERM VISITOR AREA

Scenic rating: 4

west of Blythe

Map page 835

Like its neighbor to the south (Mule Mountain), this camp is attractive to snowbirds, rockhounds (geodes and agates can be collected), and stargazers. The campground is on the southwest slope of the Big Maria Mountains, a designated wilderness, set at an elevation of 250 feet. The campsites are situated on flattened desert pavements consisting of alluvium. The desert landscape is extremely stark.

Campsites, facilities: There are numerous dispersed sites for tents or RVs of any length (no hookups). No drinking water or toilets are available. A dump station and trash service are provided. Leashed pets are permitted.

Reservations, fees: Reservations are not accepted. Sites are $40 for up to 14 nights, $180 per season. Fees charged September 15 through April 15. Summer is free, with a 14-day limit. Open year-round.

Directions: From Blythe, drive east on I-10 a short distance to Lovekin Boulevard. Turn left and drive about eight miles to the campground on the right.

Contact: Bureau of Land Management, Palm Springs Field Office, 760/833-7100, www.blm.gov/ca.

56 MAYFLOWER COUNTY PARK

Scenic rating: 6

on the Colorado River

Map page 835

The Colorado River is the fountain of life around these parts and, for campers, the main attraction of this county park. It is a popular spot for waterskiing. There is river access here in the Blythe area. Fishing is good for channel and flathead catfish, striped bass, large- and smallmouth bass, bluegill, and crappie. This span of water is flanked by agricultural lands, although there are several developed recreation areas on the California side of the river south of Blythe near Palo Verde.

Campsites, facilities: There are 27 tent sites and 152 sites for RVs of any length (with partial hookups of 30 and 50 amps). Youth group camping (20 person-minimum) is available. Picnic tables and fire grills are provided. Drinking water, restrooms with flush toilets and free showers, dump station, shuffleboard, lawn bowling, horseshoes, and boat ramp are available. Some facilities are wheelchair-accessible. Leashed pets are permitted.

Reservations, fees: Reservations are not accepted. Tent sites are $20 per night, RV sites are $25 (partial hookups) and $30 (full hookups) per night, $2 boat launch fee, $1 per pet per night. Weekly and monthly rates available. Some credit cards accepted. Open year-round.

Directions: Drive on I-10 to Blythe and Highway 95. Take Highway 95 north (it becomes Intake Boulevard) and drive 3.5 miles to 6th Avenue. Turn right at 6th Avenue and drive 2.5 miles to Colorado River Road. Bear left and drive 0.5 mile to the park entrance.

Contact: Mayflower County Park, 760/922-4665, www.rivcoparks.org.

57 RIVIERA KOA

🏊 🚣 ⛽ 🐕 ♿ 🚙 ⛺

Scenic rating: 6

near the Colorado River

Map page 835

This RV park is set up for camper-boaters who want to hunker down for awhile along the Colorado River and cool off. Access to the park is easy off I-10, and a marina is available, both big pluses for those showing up with trailered boats. Swimming lagoons are another bonus. A golf course is within 10 miles. Note that about half of the sites are rented year-round.

Campsites, facilities: There are 287 sites for RVs of any length (with full hookups of 30 and 50 amps); some sites are pull-through. Tents are allowed, and seven park-model cabins are available. Picnic tables are provided. Restrooms with showers, heated swimming pool, spa, cable TV, Wi-Fi, coin laundry, convenience store, card room, 24-hour security, RV and boat storage, arcade, recreation center, boat ramps, boat fuel, bike and boat rentals, and propane gas are available. Some facilities are wheelchair-accessible. Leashed pets are permitted, with certain restrictions.

Reservations, fees: Reservations are accepted at 800/562-3948. RV sites are $45 per night, tent sites are $29 per night, $3 per person for more than four adults, $10 per night for each additional vehicle. Holiday rates are higher. Monthly rates available. Credit cards accepted. Open year-round.

Directions: Drive on I-10 to Blythe and continue east for two miles to the exit for Riviera Drive. Take that exit east and drive two miles to the park on the right (14100 Riviera Drive).

Contact: Riviera KOA, 14100 Riviera Dr., 760/922-5350, www.koa.com.

58 DESTINY McINTYRE RV RESORT

🏊 🚣 ⛽ 🐕 ♿ 🚙 ⛺

Scenic rating: 3

on the Colorado River

Map page 835

This RV park sits on the outskirts of Blythe on the Colorado River, with this stretch of river providing good conditions for boating, waterskiing, and other water sports. A swimming lagoon is a big plus, along with riverfront beach access. Fishing is an option, with a variety of fish, including striped bass, largemouth bass, and catfish, providing fair results.

Campsites, facilities: There are 40 tent sites and 30 RV sites with full hookups (30 and 50 amps), including 11 pull-through sites. Picnic tables and fire rings are provided. Drinking water, restrooms with flush toilets and showers, dump station, propane gas, store, bait, ice, and boat ramp and boat fuel are available. Some facilities are wheelchair-accessible. Leashed pets are permitted.

Reservations, fees: Reservations are accepted at 760/922-8205. Premium sites are $19–37 per night, deluxe and standard sites are $35 per night, $4 per person per night for more than two people, $10 per night for each additional vehicle. Monthly rates available. Some credit cards accepted. Open year-round.

Directions: Drive on I-10 to Blythe to the exit for Intake Boulevard south. Take that exit and drive south on Intake Boulevard for 6.5 miles to the junction with 26th Avenue (it takes off to the right) and the park entrance on the left. Turn left and enter the park.

Contact: Destiny McIntyre RV Resort, 760/922-8205, www.destinyrv.com/mcintyrervresort.htm.

59 PALO VERDE COUNTY PARK

Scenic rating: 5

near the Colorado River

Map page 835

This is the only game in town, with no other camp around for many miles. It is set near a bend in the Colorado River, not far from the Cibola National Wildlife Refuge. A boat ramp is available at the park, making it a launch point for adventure. This stretch of river is a good one for powerboating and waterskiing. The best facilities for visitors are available here and on the west side of the river between Palo Verde and Blythe, with nothing available on the east side of the river.

Campsites, facilities: There are 20 sites for tents or RVs of any length (no hookups). Picnic tables, fire rings, restrooms with flush toilets, and shade ramadas are available. No drinking water is available. A boat ramp is available. A store, coin laundry, and propane gas are available in Palo Verde. Some facilities are wheelchair accessible. Leashed pets are permitted.

Reservations, fees: Reservations are not accepted. Sites are $15 per night. A three-day limit is enforced. Open year-round.

Directions: Drive on I-10 to Highway 78 (two miles west of Blythe). Take Highway 78 south and drive about 20 miles (three miles past Palo Verde) to the park entrance road on the east side.

Contact: Palo Verde County Park, Imperial County, 760/482-4236, www.icpds.com.

60 MULE MOUNTAIN LONG TERM VISITOR AREA

Scenic rating: 4

west of Blythe

Map page 835

Mule Mountain is out in the middle of nowhere, but rockhounds and stargazers have found it anyway; it's ideal for both activities. There are two campgrounds, Coon Hollow and Wiley's Well, along with dispersed camping. Rockhounding, in particular, can be outstanding, with several geode and agate beds nearby. Hobby rock-collecting is permitted. Commercial rock-poaching is not. The site, ideal for winter camping, attracts snowbirds and is set in a desert landscape at an elevation of 150 feet. Bradshaw Trail runs east to west through the visitors area.

Campsites, facilities: There are 29 sites at Coon Hollow and 14 sites at Wiley's Well for tents or RVs up to 35 feet (no hookups). Picnic tables, shade ramadas, and fire grills are provided. Vault toilets and trash service are available. No drinking water is available. A dump station is nearby, halfway between the two campgrounds, and is available mid-September through mid-April. Some facilities are wheelchair-accessible. Leashed pets are permitted.

Reservations, fees: Reservations are not accepted. Sites are $40 for up to 14 nights, $180 per season, with a 14-day stay limit every 28 days. Open year-round.

Directions: From Blythe, drive west on I-10 about 15 miles to Wiley's Well Road. Turn left (south) and drive about nine miles (the road turns to dirt) to Wiley's Well. Continue another three miles to reach Coon Hollow. Dispersed camping is allowed once you pass the sign that indicates you're in the visitors center.

Contact: Bureau of Land Management, Palm Springs Field Office, 760/833-7100, www.blm.gov/ca.

61 TOOL BOX SPRINGS

Scenic rating: 5

in San Bernardino National Forest

Map page 835

This is a lightly used campground well off the beaten track. More like off the beaten universe. That makes it perfect for people who want to be by themselves when they go camping. Ramona Trail begins at the campground, heads out to the north, and provides a 3.5-mile one-way hike, with a 1,500-foot loss and then gain in elevation. In the winter, call for road conditions to determine accessibility. The elevation is 6,500 feet.

Campsites, facilities: There are six tent sites as well as dispersed camping. Picnic tables and fire grills are provided. Vault toilets are available, but there is no drinking water. Garbage must be packed out. Leashed pets are permitted.

Reservations, fees: Reservations are not accepted. There is no fee for camping. An Adventure Pass ($30 annual fee or $5 daily pass) per parked vehicle is required. Open year-round, but subject to closure during fire season.

Directions: From Hemet, drive east on Highway 74 into San Bernardino National Forest and continue just past Lake Hemet to Forest Road 6S13. Turn right on Forest Road 6S13 (paved, then dirt) and drive four miles to a fork. Bear left at the fork and continue on Forest Road 6S13 for 4.5 miles to the camp on the left.

Contact: San Bernardino National Forest, San Jacinto Ranger District, 909/382-2921; www.fs.usda.gov/sbnf.

62 PINYON FLAT
🏃 🛏 🚹 ♿ 🚗 ⛺

Scenic rating: 6

near Cahuilla Tewanet Vista Point in San Bernardino National Forest

Map page 835

The Cahuilla Tewanet Vista Point is just two miles east of the camp and provides a good, easy side trip, along with a sweeping view to the east of the desert on clear days. A primitive trail is available two miles away to the southeast via Forest Road 7S01 off a short spur road (look for it on the left side of the road). This hike crosses a mix of sparse forest and high-desert terrain for 10 miles, passing Cactus Spring five miles in. Desert bighorn sheep are sometimes spotted in this area. The elevation is 4,000 feet.

Campsites, facilities: There are 18 sites for tents or RVs up to 15 feet (no hookups). Picnic tables and fire rings are provided. Drinking water and vault toilets are available. Some facilities are wheelchair-accessible. Leashed pets are permitted.

Reservations, fees: Reservations are not accepted. Sites are $8 per night. Open year-round.

Directions: Drive on I-10 to Palm Springs and Highway 111. Turn south on Highway 111 and drive to Rancho Mirage and Highway 74. Turn right (south) on Highway 74 and drive 14 miles (a slow, twisty road) to the campground on the right.

Contact: San Bernardino National Forest, San Jacinto Ranger District, 909/382-2921, www.fs.usda.gov/sbnf.

63 LAKE CAHUILLA COUNTY PARK
🏃 🚣 🛏 ♿ 🚗 ⛺

Scenic rating: 7

near Indio

Map page 835

Lake Cahuilla covers just 135 acres, but those are the most loved 135 acres for miles in all directions. After all, water out here is as scarce as polar bears. This 710-acre Riverside County park provides large palm trees and a 10-acre beach and water-play area (no swimming or boating is allowed). In the winter, the lake is stocked with trout, and in the summer with catfish; other species include largemouth and striped bass, crappie, and carp up to 30 pounds. An equestrian camp is also available, complete with corrals, and equestrian and hiking trails are available on nearby public land. Morrow Trail is popular, and the trailhead is near the park's ranger station. A warning: The wind can really howl through here and temperatures well over 100°F are typical in the summer.

Campsites, facilities: There are 55 RV sites with partial hookups (30 and 50 amps), 10 RV sites (water only), a primitive camping area with 30 sites for tents or RVs (no hookups), a large group area, and an equestrian area with 20 sites (partial hookups) and horse corrals. Maximum RV length is 45 feet, except in the equestrian area where any length can be accommodated. Fire grills and picnic tables are provided. Restrooms with showers, dump station, seasonal swimming pool are available. Some facilities are wheelchair-accessible. Leashed pets are permitted.

Reservations, fees: Reservations are accepted at 800/234-7275 ($7 reservation fee). Tent sites are $15 per night, RV sites are $22–35 per night, group camping is $150–210, $1 per pet per night. Weekly rates are available during the winter. Maximum stay is two weeks. Some credit cards accepted. Open year-round; closed Tuesday–Thursday May through October.

Directions: Drive on I-10 to Indio and the exit for Monroe Street. Take that exit and drive south on Monroe Street to Avenue 58. Turn right (west) and drive two miles to the park at the end of the road.

Contact: Lake Cahuilla County Park, 760/564-4712, www.rivcoparks.org.

64 HEADQUARTERS

Scenic rating: 5

in the Salton Sea State Recreation Area

Map page 835

The giant Salton Sea is a vast, shallow, and unique lake—the center of a 360-square-mile basin and one of the world's inland seas. Salton Sea was created in 1905 when a dike broke, and in turn, the basin was flooded with saltwater. The lake is 35 miles long, but it has an average depth of just 15 feet. This is the northernmost campground, set at the recreation area headquarters just south of the town of Desert Beach at an elevation of 227 feet below sea level. Fishing for tilapia is popular, and this is also one of Southern California's most popular boating areas. Because of the low altitude, atmospheric pressure allows high performance for many ski boats. If winds are hazardous, a red beacon on the northeast shore of the lake will flash. If you see it, get to the nearest shore. Camp use is moderate year-round, but is lowest in the summer thanks to temperatures that can hover in the 110°F range for days.

Note: This park is on the closure list developed by the California Department of Parks, pending final state budget decisions or the possible transfer of park management to other park agencies or volunteer groups. At time of publication, Headquarter remained open and was the only reservable campground in Salton Sea State Recreation Area.

Campsites, facilities: There are 15 sites with full hookups (30 amps) for RVs up to 40 feet, 30–40 sites for tents or RVs with no hookups, and several hike-in/bike-in sites. Picnic tables, fire grills, and shade ramadas are provided. Drinking water, restrooms with flush toilets and coin showers, dump station, fish cleaning station, and visitors center with Wi-Fi access are available. A store is within two miles. Some facilities are wheelchair-accessible. Leashed pets are permitted in the campgrounds and on roadways only.

Reservations, fees: Reservations are accepted October through May at 800/444-7275 (800/444-PARK) or www.reserveamerica.com ($8 reservation fee). Sites (no hookups) are $15–20 per night, RV sites (full hookups) are $30 per night, hike-in/bike-in sites are $10 per person per night. Boat launching is $3 per day. Open year-round.

Directions: From Los Angeles, take I-10 east to Indio and the exit for the Highway 86 Expressway. Take that exit and drive south for 12 miles to 66th Avenue. Turn left and drive less than one mile to Mecca and Highway 111. Turn right (south) on Highway 111 and drive 12 miles to the entrance on the right.

Contact: Salton Sea State Recreation Area, 760/393-3052 or 760/393-3059, www.parks.ca.gov.

65 MECCA BEACH

🚶 🚴 🏊 🛶 🚤 🐕 ♿ 🚐 ⛺

Scenic rating: 4

in the Salton Sea State Recreation Area

Map page 835

This is one of the camps set in the Salton Sea State Recreation Area on the northeastern shore of the lake. The big attractions here are the waterfront sites, which are not available at nearby Headquarters campground (see listing in this chapter). Note that the upper loop closed in 2010.

Note: This park is on the closure list developed by the California Department of Parks, pending final state budget decisions or the possible transfer of park management to other park agencies or volunteer groups. At time of publication, the lower loop remained open on a first-come, first-served basis.

Campsites, facilities: There are 50 sites (no hookups) for tents or RVs of any length, four sites with full hookups (30 amps), and several hike-in/bike-in sites. Picnic tables and fire grills are provided. Drinking water, restrooms with flush toilets and showers, amphitheater, and a fish cleaning station are available. A dump station is one mile north of Headquarters campground and a store is within 3.5 miles. Some facilities are wheelchair-accessible. Leashed pets are permitted in the campgrounds and roadways only.

Reservations, fees: Reservations are not accepted. Sites are $15–20 per night, RV sites (hookups) are $30 per night, $10 per person per night for hike-in/bike-in sites. Boat launching is $3 per day. Open year-round.

Directions: From the Los Angeles area, take I-10 east to Indio and the exit for the Highway 86 Expressway. Take that exit and drive south for 12 miles to 66th Avenue. Turn left and drive less than one mile to Mecca and Highway 111. Turn right (south) on Highway 111 and drive 12.5 miles to the entrance on the right.

Contact: Salton Sea State Recreation Area, 760/393-3052 or 760/393-3059, www.parks.ca.gov.

66 SALT CREEK PRIMITIVE AREA

🚶 🚴 🏊 🛶 🚤 🐕 ♿ 🚐 ⛺

Scenic rating: 4

in the Salton Sea State Recreation Area

Map page 835

Waterfront campsites are a bonus at this campground, even though the campground consists of just an open area on hard-packed dirt. Birding hikes are available during winter months. Several trails leave from camp, or nearby the camp, and head 1–2 miles to the Bat Cave Buttes, which are in the Durmid Hills on Bureau of Land Management property. There are bats in the numerous caves to explore, although the nearby OHV traffic has reduced their numbers. From the buttes, which are up to 100 feet above sea level, hikers can see both the north and south ends of the Salton Sea simultaneously. This is the only easily accessible place to view both shores of the Salton Sea. Many people believe the buttes are the southernmost point of the San Andreas Fault; the fault does not exist above ground south of here. (For details on the Salton Sea State Recreation Area, see the Headquarters listing in this chapter.)

Note: This park is on the closure list developed by the California Department of Parks, pending final state budget decisions or the possible transfer of park management to other park agencies or volunteer groups. At time of publication, Salt Creek remained open on a first-come, first-served basis.

Campsites, facilities: There are 200 primitive sites for tents or RVs of any length (no hookups) and several hike-in/bike-in sites. Drinking water and vault toilets are available. Fires are permitted in metal containers only. Leashed pets are permitted in the campgrounds and on roadways only.

Reservations, fees: Reservations are not accepted. Sites are $15 per night, $10 per person per night for hike-in/bike-in sites. Open year-round.

Directions: From the Los Angeles area, take I-10 east to Indio and the exit for the Highway

86 Expressway. Take that exit and drive south for 12 miles to 66th Avenue. Turn left and drive less than one mile to Mecca and Highway 111. Turn right (south) on Highway 111 and drive 17.5 miles to the entrance on the right.

Contact: Salton Sea State Recreation Area, 760/393-3052 or 760/393-3059, www.parks. ca.gov.

67 FOUNTAIN OF YOUTH SPA

Scenic rating: 4

near the Salton Sea

Map page 835

Natural artesian steam rooms are the highlight here, but close inspection reveals that nobody seems to be getting any younger. This is a vast private park on 90 acres, set near the Salton Sea. Though this park has 1,000 sites for RVs, almost half of the sites have seasonal renters. This park is popular with snowbird campers and about 2,000 people live here during the winter. (See the Red Hill Marina County Park listing in this chapter for side-trip options.)

Campsites, facilities: There are 835 sites with full hookups (30 and 50 amps) and 165 "dry camp" sites with no hookups for tents or RVs. Park home rentals are available. Restrooms with flush toilets and showers, cable TV, natural artesian steam rooms, swimming pools, artesian mineral water spa, three freshwater spas, recreation halls, dump stations, fitness room, library, picnic areas, nine-hole desert-style golf course, horseshoes, organized activities, craft and sewing room, Wi-Fi, coin laundry, beauty parlor, masseur, church services, propane gas, and groceries are available. Some facilities are wheelchair-accessible. Leashed pets are permitted.

Reservations, fees: Reservations are not accepted. RV sites are $42–49 per night, "dry camp" sites are $23 per night, $10 per person per night for more than two people. Park home rentals are $665 per week. Discounts off-season. Weekly and monthly rates available. Some credit cards accepted. Open year-round.

Directions: From Los Angeles: Take I-10 east to Indio and the exit for the Highway 86 Expressway. Take that exit and drive south for 12 miles to Avenue 62. Turn right and drive less than one mile to Highway 111. Turn left (south) on Highway 111 and drive 44 miles to Hot Mineral Spa Road. Turn left (north) on Hot Mineral Spa Road and drive approximately four miles to Spa Road. Turn right and drive approximately 1.5 miles to the park on the left.

From Calipatria: Take Highway 111 north to Niland, and then continue north for 15 miles to Hot Mineral Spa Road. Turn right (north) on Hot Mineral Spa Road and drive approximately four miles to Spa Road. Turn right and drive about 1.5 miles to the park on the left.

Contact: Fountain of Youth Spa, 888/8000-SPA (888/800-0772) or 760/354-1340, www. foyspa.com.

68 CORN SPRINGS

Scenic rating: 4

in BLM desert

Map page 835

Just think: If you spend a night here, you can say to darn near anybody, "I've camped someplace you haven't." I don't know whether to offer my condolences or congratulations, but Corn Springs offers a primitive spot in the middle of nowhere in desert country. A 0.5-mile interpretive trail can easily be walked in athletic shoes. It is divided into 11 stops with different vegetation, wildlife habitat, and cultural notes at each stop. The side trip to Joshua Tree National Park to the north (40-minute drive to closest entrance) is also well worth the adventure. So is the aerial tram ride available west of Palm Springs (one-hour drive) for an incredible view of the desert. On the other hand, if it's a summer afternoon, tell me, just how do you spend the day here when it's 115°F?

Campsites, facilities: There are eight sites for tents or RVs up to 22 feet (no hookups) and one group site for tents or RVs (one or two only) up to 22 feet that can accommodate up to 25 people. Picnic tables and fire grills are provided. Drinking water, shade ramadas and vault toilets are available. Some facilities are wheelchair-accessible. Leashed pets are permitted.

Reservations, fees: Reservations are not accepted. Sites are $6 per night. Open year-round.

Directions: From Indio, drive east on I-10 for 60 miles to the Corn Springs Road exit. Take that exit to Old Chuckwalla Valley Road. Turn right (south) onto Old Chuckwalla Valley Road and drive 0.5 mile to Corn Springs Road. Turn right and drive 10 miles on a dirt road to the campground on the left.

Contact: Bureau of Land Management, Palm Springs Field Office, 760/833-7100, www.blm.gov/ca.

69 RED HILL MARINA COUNTY PARK

Scenic rating: 3

near the Salton Sea

Map page 835

It's called Red Hill Marina, but you won't find a marina here; it washed away in the mid-1970s. This county park is near the south end of the Salton Sea, one of the weirdest places on earth. Set 228 feet below sea level, it's a vast body of water covering 360 square miles, 35 miles long, but with an average depth of just 15 feet. It's an extremely odd place to swim, as you bob around effortlessly in the highly saline water. Note that swimming is not recommended in this park because of the muddy shore. Fishing is often good for corvina in spring and early summer. Hundreds of species of birds stop by this area as they travel along the Pacific Flyway. Several wildlife refuges are in the immediate area, including two separate chunks of the Imperial Wildfowl Management Area, to the west and south, and the huge Wister Waterfowl Management Area, northwest of Niland.

Campsites, facilities: There are 37 seasonal sites for RVs or tents. There are also nine overnight spaces, some with full or partial hookups, plus eight "dry camping" spaces. Picnic tables, cabanas, and barbecue pits are provided. Drinking water and restrooms with flush toilets and showers are available. Leashed pets are permitted.

Reservations, fees: Reservations are not accepted, but filling out an online check-in form is recommended. Sites are $10 per night, RV sites (partial hookups) are $25 per night, $2 per night for each additional vehicle. Monthly rates available. Open year-round.

Directions: From Mecca, drive south on Highway 111 to Niland, and continue to Sinclair Road. Turn right and drive 3.5 miles to Garst Road. Turn right and drive 1.5 miles to the end of Garst Road at Red Hill Road. Turn left on Red Hill Road and drive to the park at the end of the road.

From El Centro, drive north on Highway 111 to Brawley and Highway 78/Main Street. Turn west (left) on Highway 78/Main Street and drive a short distance to Highway 111. Turn right (north) and drive to Calipatria. Continue north on Highway 111 just outside of Calipatria to Sinclair Road. Turn left on Sinclair Road and drive to Garst Road. Turn right and drive 1.5 miles to where it ends at Red Hill Road. Turn left at Red Hill Road and drive to the end of the road and the marina and the campground.

Contact: Red Hill Marina, 760/482-4236, www.icpds.com.

70 WIEST LAKE COUNTY PARK

Scenic rating: 4

on Wiest Lake

Map page 835

This is a developed county park along the southern shore of Wiest Lake, which adjoins the Imperial Wildfowl Management Area to the north. Wiest Lake is just 50 acres, set 110 feet below sea level, and a prized area with such desolate country in the surrounding region.

Waterskiing and sailboarding can be excellent, although few take advantage of the latter. Swimming is allowed when lifeguards are on duty. The lake is most popular for fishing, with trout planted in winter and catfish in summer. The lake also has bass and bluegill. The Salton Sea, about a 20-minute drive to the northwest, is a worthy side trip.

Campsites, facilities: There are 30 sites with full hookups (50 amps) for RVs up to 45 feet and 10 tent sites. Picnic tables, shade ramadas, and fire grills are provided. Drinking water and restrooms with flush toilets and showers, a boat ramp, and a dump station are available. A store, coin laundry, and propane gas are available within five miles. Some facilities are wheelchair accessible. Leashed pets are permitted.

Reservations, fees: Reservations are not accepted. RV sites with full hookups are $35 per night, RV sites with partial hookups are $25 per night, and "dry" RV sites are $15 per night, tent sites are $5 per night, $2 per night for each additional vehicle. Monthly rates available. Open year-round.

Directions: From El Centro, drive north on Highway 111 to Brawley and Highway 78/Main Street. Turn west (left) on Highway 78/Main Street and drive a short distance to Highway 111. Turn right (north) on Highway 111 and drive four miles to Rutherford Road (well signed). Turn right (east) and drive two miles to the park entrance on the right.

Contact: Wiest Lake County Park, 760/482-4236, www.icpds.com.

71 CULP VALLEY PRIMITIVE CAMP AREA

Scenic rating: 4

near Peña Springs in
Anza-Borrego Desert State Park

Anza-Borrego map, page 837

Culp Valley is set near Peña Springs, which is more of a mudhole than a spring. A 600-yard hike takes you to an overlook of Hellhole Canyon and an eastern view of the Borrego Valley. The elevation at this campground is 3,400 feet.

Campsites, facilities: This is a primitive, open camping area for tents or RVs of any length (no hookups). Vault toilets are available. No drinking water is available. Fires are permitted in metal containers only. Garbage and ashes must be packed out. Leashed pets are permitted in the campground, but not on trails.

Reservations, fees: Reservations are not accepted. There is no fee for camping. Open year-round.

Directions: From Julian, at the junction of Highway 78 and Highway 79, drive east on Highway 78 (steep and curvy) for 10 miles to Highway S2. Turn left (north) and drive 16 miles to Highway S22/Borrego Salton Seaway. Turn right (east) and drive 10 miles to the campground entrance road on the left.

Contact: Anza-Borrego Desert State Park, Visitor Center, 760/767-4205; Colorado Desert District, 760/767-5311, www.parks.ca.gov.

72 BORREGO PALM CANYON

Scenic rating: 6

in Anza-Borrego Desert State Park

Anza-Borrego map, page 837   BEST (

This is one of the best camps in Anza-Borrego Desert State Park, with two excellent hikes available. The short hike into Borrego Palm Canyon is like being transported to another world, from the desert to the tropics, complete with a small waterfall, a rare sight in these parts. Panorama Overlook Trail also starts here. An excellent visitors center is available, offering an array of exhibits and a slide show. The elevation is 775 feet. Anza-Borrego Desert State Park is one of the largest state parks in the continental United States, covering more than 600,000 acres and with 500 miles of dirt roads. The park is appropriately named for the desert bighorn sheep (borrego in Spanish) that live in the mountains.

Campsites, facilities: There are 65 sites for tents or RVs up to 25 feet (no hookups), 51 sites with full hookups (30 amps) for RVs up to 35 feet, and five group tent sites for 9–25 people each. Picnic tables, shade ramadas, and fire grills are provided. Drinking water, restrooms with flush toilets and showers, and dump station are available. A store, coin laundry, and propane gas are nearby. Some facilities are wheelchair-accessible. Leashed pets are permitted.

Reservations, fees: Reservations are accepted at 800/444-7275 (800/444-PARK) or www.reserveamerica.com ($8 reservation fee). Sites are $25 per night, RV sites (full hookups) are $35 per night, additional vehicles are $8 per night, and group sites are $80 per night. Senior discounts available. Open year-round.

Directions: From Julian, at the junction of Highway 78 and Highway 79, drive east on Highway 78 (steep and curvy) for 19.5 miles to Yaqui Pass Road/County Road S3. Turn left (north) and drive eight miles to Borrego Springs and Palm Canyon Drive. Turn left (west) and drive 4.5 miles to the campground entrance road on the right.

Contact: Anza-Borrego Desert State Park, Visitor Center, 760/767-4205; Colorado Desert District, 760/767-5311, www.parks.ca.gov.

73 VERN WHITAKER HORSE CAMP
🚶 🐎 ♿ 🚐 ⛰️

Scenic rating: 5

in Anza-Borrego Desert State Park

Anza-Borrego map, page 837

This camp is popular during spring and fall, with lighter use during the winter. The 30 miles of horse trails attract equestrian campers. Campers are expected to clean up after their horses, and garbage bins are available for manure.

Campsites, facilities: There are 10 equestrian sites for tents or RVs up to 24 feet (no hookups). Picnic tables and fire grills are provided.

Restrooms with flush toilets and coin showers, drinking water, picnic areas, group gathering area, horse-washing station, and horse corrals are available. Some facilities are wheelchair accessible. Leashed pets are permitted in the campground, but not on trails or in wilderness.

Reservations, fees: Reservations are accepted at 800/444-7275 (800/444-PARK) or www.reserveamerica.com ($8 reservation fee). Sites are $25 per night, which includes two horses; $2 per additional horse per night. Open October through April.

Directions: From Julian, at the junction of Highway 78 and Highway 79, drive east on Highway 78 (steep and curvy) for 19.5 miles to Yaqui Pass Road/County Road S3. Turn left (north) and drive eight miles to Palm Canyon Drive. Turn left and drive to Borrego Springs and bear right (at the traffic circle) onto northbound Borrego Springs Road. Drive four miles on Borrego Springs Road to Henderson Canyon Road. Bear right and drive a short distance to the campground entrance road (look for the metal sign). Turn left and continue four miles to the camp. Note: Part of the last four miles are on a private road; please respect the property owner's rights.

Contact: Anza-Borrego Desert State Park, Visitor Center, 760/767-4205; Colorado Desert District, 760/767-5311, www.parks.ca.gov.

74 ARROYO SALADO PRIMITIVE CAMP AREA
🚶 🐎 🚐 ⛰️

Scenic rating: 5

in Anza-Borrego Desert State Park

Anza-Borrego map, page 837

This camp is a primitive spot set along (and named after) an ephemeral stream, the Arroyo Salado. About eight miles to the west is the trailhead for Thimble Trail, which is routed south into a wash in the Borrego Badlands. The elevation is 880 feet.

Campsites, facilities: This is a primitive, open

camping area for tents or self-contained RVs (no hookups). Vault toilets are available. No drinking water is available. Fires are allowed in metal containers only; open fires are not allowed. Garbage and ashes must be packed out. Leashed pets are permitted in the campground, but not on trails or in wilderness.

Reservations, fees: Reservations are not accepted. There is no fee for camping. Open year-round.

Directions: From Julian, at the junction of Highway 78 (steep and curvy) and Highway 79, drive east on Highway 78 for 19.5 miles to Yaqui Pass Road/County Road S3. Turn left (north) and drive eight miles to Borrego Springs and Palm Canyon Drive. Turn right on Palm Canyon Drive (becomes Highway 522) and drive 20 miles (past Fonts Point) to the campground entrance on the right.

Contact: Anza-Borrego Desert State Park, Visitor Center, 760/767-4205; Colorado Desert District, 760/767-5311, www.parks.ca.gov.

75 YAQUI PASS PRIMITIVE CAMP AREA

Scenic rating: 1

in Anza-Borrego Desert State Park

Anza-Borrego map, page 837

This extremely primitive area is set beside rough Yaqui Pass Road at an elevation of 1,730 feet. The camping area is a large, open, sloping area of asphalt, where it is darn near impossible to get an RV level. The trailhead for Kenyon Loop Trail is to the immediate south. This spot is often overlooked because the Tamarisk Grove camp nearby provides shade, drinking water, and a feature trail.

Campsites, facilities: This is a primitive, open camping area for tents or self-contained RVs of any length (no hookups). No drinking water or toilets are available. No open fires are allowed. Garbage must be packed out. Leashed pets are permitted, but not on trails or in wilderness.

Reservations, fees: Reservations are not

accepted. There is no fee for camping. Open year-round.

Directions: From Julian, at the junction of Highway 78 and Highway 79, drive east on Highway 78 (steep and curvy) for 19.5 miles to Yaqui Pass Road/County Road S3. Turn left (north) and drive 2.5 miles to the campground entrance on the right. The access road is rough and the camping area has few level areas for large RVs, so only small RVs are recommended.

Contact: Anza-Borrego Desert State Park, Visitor Center, 760/767-4205; Colorado Desert District, 760/767-5311, www.parks.ca.gov.

76 YAQUI WELL PRIMITIVE CAMP AREA

Scenic rating: 2

in Anza-Borrego Desert State Park

Anza-Borrego map, page 837

This camp is used primarily as an overflow area if the more developed Tamarisk Grove camp is full. Cactus Loop Trail, a 2.5-mile loop hike that passes seven varieties of cacti, starts at Tamarisk Grove. The elevation is 1,400 feet.

Campsites, facilities: This is a primitive, open camping area for tents or self-contained RVs (no hookups). Vault toilets are available. No drinking water is available. Fires are permitted in metal containers only. Garbage and ashes must be packed out. Open fires are not permitted. Leashed pets are permitted, but not on trails or in wilderness.

Reservations, fees: Reservations are not accepted. There is no fee for camping. Open year-round.

Directions: From Julian, at the junction of Highway 78 and Highway 79, drive east on Highway 78 (steep and curvy) for 19.5 miles to Yaqui Pass Road/County Road S3. Turn left (north) and drive a short distance to the campground entrance road on the left. The access road is rough and the camping area has few level areas for large RVs, so only small RVs are recommended.

Contact: Anza-Borrego Desert State Park, Visitor Center, 760/767-4205; Colorado Desert District, 760/767-5311, www.parks.ca.gov.

77 TAMARISK GROVE

Scenic rating: 7

in Anza-Borrego Desert State Park

Anza-Borrego map, page 837   BEST (

Tamarisk is one of three camps in the immediate area, so if this camp is full, primitive Yaqui Well to the immediate west and Yaqui Pass to the north on Yaqui Pass Road provide alternatives. Cactus Loop Trail, with the trailhead just north of camp, provides a hiking option. This is a 1.5-mile loop that passes seven varieties of cacti, some as tall as people. Side trips to Julian and Borrego Springs are just 30–45 minutes away. The elevation is 1,400 feet at this campground.

Campsites, facilities: There are 27 sites for tents or RVs up to 21 feet (no hookups). (In winter 2012, 10 small cabins were being added.) Picnic tables, shade ramadas, and fire grills are provided. Restrooms with flush toilets and coin showers and drinking water are available. Some facilities are wheelchair-accessible. Leashed pets are permitted in the campground, but not on trails or in wilderness.

Reservations, fees: Reservations are accepted at 800/444-7275 (800/444-PARK) or www.reserveamerica.com ($8 reservation fee). Sites are $25 per night, $60 cabins, $8 per night for each additional vehicle. Open October through May.

Directions: From Julian, at the junction of Highway 78 and Highway 79, drive east on Highway 78 (steep and curvy) for 19.5 miles to Yaqui Pass Road/County Road S3. Turn left (north) and drive 0.5 mile to the campground on the right.

Contact: Anza-Borrego Desert State Park, Visitor Center, 760/767-4205; Colorado Desert District, 760/767-5311, www.parks.ca.gov.

78 OCOTILLO WELLS STATE VEHICLE RECREATION AREA

Scenic rating: 4

in Ocotillo Wells

Anza-Borrego map, page 837

This can be a wild place, a giant OHV camp where the population of Ocotillo Wells can go from 10 to 5,000 overnight, no kidding. Yet if you arrive when there is no off-road event, it can also be a lonely, extremely remote destination. Some locals call the OHV crowd "escapees" and watch stunned as they arrive every February for two or three weeks. OHV events are held here occasionally as well. Mountain bikers also use these trails. One great side note is that annually there is "Desert Cleanup Day," when OHV users will clean up the place; date changes every year. The non-OHV crowd can still use this camp, but most come in the winter on weekdays, when activity is lower. The landscape is barren desert, dry as an iguana's back. A few shade ramadas are provided. The area covers 72,000 acres, ranging from below sea level to an elevation of 400 feet. It is adjacent to Anza-Borrego Desert State Park, another 600,000 acres of wildlands. The wash-and-ridge terrain includes a butte with dunes, a sand bowl, a blow sand dune, and springs. After wet winters, the blooms of wildflowers can be excellent. While this area is well known as a wild play area for the OHV crowd, it is also a place where on most days you can literally disappear and see no one. All drivers should watch for soft ground. Many vehicles get stuck here and have to be towed out. Also, dispersed camping is allowed in most of these state park lands.

Campsites, facilities: There are more than 100 dispersed primitive sites for tents or RVs of any length (no hookups). Camping is not allowed in the Shell, Reef, Devils Slide, and Blow Sand areas. Picnic tables and fire rings are provided. Vault toilets and shade ramadas are available in the Pumpkin Patch, Quarry, Cove, Main Street, Holly Road, and Hidden Valley areas. There is no drinking water. A coin-shower building is available near the ranger station, and another is 3.5 miles east at Holmes Camp. A visitor center across from the ranger station offers telescope viewing and an amphitheater with interpretive programs from October through April. A store, restaurants, propane, and auto supplies are available four miles away in Ocotillo Wells. A gas station is at the corner of S-22 and Highway 86-S in Salton City. Leashed pets are permitted.

Reservations, fees: Reservations are not accepted. There is no fee for camping. There is a 30-day maximum stay per year. Open year-round.

Directions: From Julian, at the junction of Highway 78 and Highway 79, drive east on Highway 78 for 31.5 miles to Ranger Station Road. Turn left and drive 0.25 mile to the ranger station. (Note: For an alternate route, advisable for big rigs, that avoids curvy sections of Highway 78, see the detour route detailed in the Stagecoach Trails listing in the San Diego chapter.)

Contact: Ocotillo Wells SVRA, 760/767-5391, www.parks.ca.gov or www.ohv.parks.ca.gov.

79 FISH CREEK

Scenic rating: 3

in Anza-Borrego Desert State Park

Anza-Borrego map, page 837

This primitive camp is set just inside the eastern border of Anza-Borrego Desert State Park at the foot of the Vallecito Mountains to the west. This is the closest camp to the Ocotillo Wells State Vehicular Recreation Area, which is 12 miles to the north. RVs are not recommended because of the steep access road. Note that the Elephant Tree Discovery Trail is a few miles north of camp.

Campsites, facilities: There are six sites for tents. Vault toilets are available and some sites have fire rings. No drinking water is available. Garbage must be packed out. Leashed pets are permitted.

Reservations, fees: Reservations are not accepted. There is no fee for camping. Open year-round.

Directions: From Julian, at the junction of Highway 78 and Highway 79, drive east on Highway 78 (steep and curvy) for 34 miles to Ocotillo Wells and Split Mountain Road. Turn right (south) and drive seven miles to the campground access road. Drive two miles to the campground entrance on the left.

Contact: Anza-Borrego Desert State Park, Visitor Center, 760/767-4205; Colorado Desert District, 760/767-5311, www.parks.ca.gov.

80 VALLECITO COUNTY PARK

Scenic rating: 3

near Anza-Borrego Desert State Park

Anza-Borrego map, page 837

This county park in the desert gets little attention in the face of the other nearby attractions. This is a 71-acre park built around a sod reconstruction of the historic Vallecito Stage Station. It was part of the Butterfield Overland Stage from 1858 to 1861. The route carried mail and passengers from Missouri to San Francisco in 25 days, covering 2,800 miles. Vallecito means "little valley." It provides a quiet alternative to some of the busier campgrounds in the desert. One bonus is that it is usually 10 degrees cooler here than at Agua Caliente. A covered picnic area is a big plus. Other nearby destinations include Agua Caliente Hot Springs, Anza-Borrego Desert State Park to the east, and Lake Cuyamaca and Cuyamaca Rancho State Park about 35 miles away. The elevation is 1,500 feet.

Campsites, facilities: There are 44 sites for tents or RVs up to 40 feet (no hookups), one group area for up to 15 RVs, one equestrian area with eight sites and two corrals, and one youth camping area for up to 50 people. Picnic tables and fire rings are provided. Drinking water, flush toilets, and a playground are available. Some facilities are wheelchair accessible. Leashed pets are permitted.

Reservations, fees: Reservations are accepted at 877/565-3600 ($5 reservation fee). Sites are $22 per night, the youth group area is $50–75 per night, $1 per pet per night, $2 per horse per night, $4 per night per additional vehicle. Some credit cards accepted. Open Labor Day weekend through Memorial Day weekend; closed June, July, and August.

Directions: From El Cajon, drive east on I-8 for about 75 miles to the town of Ocotillo (the first town after crossing from San Diego County to Imperial County) and County Road S2/Imperial Highway. Turn north (left) on County Road S2/Imperial Highway and drive 30 miles to the park entrance.

Contact: San Diego County Parks Department, 858/694-3049, www.sdparks.org; campground, 760/765-1188.

81 AGUA CALIENTE REGIONAL PARK

🏃 🏊 🎿 🚶 ♿ 🚐 ⛺

Scenic rating: 3

near Anza-Borrego Desert State Park

Anza-Borrego map, page 837

This is a popular park in winter. It has two naturally fed pools: A large outdoor thermal pool is kept at its natural 90°F, and an indoor pool is heated to 102°F and outfitted with jets. Everything is hot here. The weather is hot, the coffee is hot, and the water is hot. And hey, that's what "Agua Caliente" means—hot water, named after the nearby hot springs. Anza-Borrego Desert State Park is also nearby. If you would like to see some cold water, Lake Cuyamaca and Cuyamaca Rancho State Park are about 35 miles away. The elevation is 1,350 feet. The park covers 910 acres with several miles of hiking trails.

Campsites, facilities: There are 106 sites with full or partial hookups (30 amps) for RVs up to 40 feet, 35 sites with no hookups for tents or RVs, and a group area for up to 100 people. Seven camping cabins are also available. Picnic tables and fire grills are provided. Restrooms with flush toilets and showers, drinking water, outdoor and indoor pools, picnic area, and a playground with horseshoes and shuffleboard are available. Groceries and propane gas are nearby. Some facilities are wheelchair-accessible. Leashed pets are permitted, but not on trails.

Reservations, fees: Reservations are accepted at 877/565-3600 ($5 reservation fee). Tent sites are $24 per night, RV sites are $33 (full hookups) and $29 (partial hookups) per night, the group area is $100 per night. Some credit cards accepted. Open Labor Day weekend through Memorial Day weekend; closed June, July, and August.

Directions: From El Cajon, drive east on I-8 about 75 miles to the town of Ocotillo (the first town after crossing from San Diego County to Imperial County) and County Road S2/Imperial Highway. Turn north (left) on County Road S2/Imperial Highway and drive 25 miles to the park entrance.

From Julian, take Highway 78 east and drive 12 miles to County Road S2/San Felipe Road. Turn right on County Road S2/San Felipe Road and drive 21 miles south to the park entrance.

Contact: San Diego County Parks Department, 858/694-3049, www.sdparks.org, campground, 760/765-1188.

82 MOUNTAIN PALM SPRINGS PRIMITIVE CAMP AREA

🏃 🚶 🚐 ⛺

Scenic rating: 4

in Anza-Borrego Desert State Park

Anza-Borrego map, page 837

A plus for this camping area is easy access from County Road S2, but no water is a giant minus. Regardless of pros and cons, only hikers will get the full benefit of the area. A trail leads south to Bow Willow Creek (and Bow Willow) and onward into Bow Willow Canyon. The Carrizo Badlands Overlook is on the southeast side of Sweeney Pass, about a 10-minute drive south on County Road S2. The elevation is 760 feet.

Campsites, facilities: This is a primitive, open camping area for tents or RVs of any length (no hookups). Vault toilets are available. No drinking water is available. Fires are permitted in metal containers only. Garbage and ashes must be packed out. Leashed pets are permitted, but not on trails or in wilderness.

Reservations, fees: Reservations are not accepted. There is no fee for camping. Open year-round.

Directions: From El Cajon, drive east on I-8 for about 75 miles to the town of Ocotillo (the first town after crossing from San Diego County to Imperial County) and County Road S2/Imperial Highway. Turn north (left) on County Road S2/Imperial Highway and drive 27.5 miles to the campground entrance road on the left (about 0.5 mile past the Bow Willow campground turnoff). Turn left and continue 0.75 mile to the camp.

Contact: Anza-Borrego Desert State Park, Visitor Center, 760/767-4205; Colorado Desert District, 760/767-5311, www.parks.ca.gov.

83 BOW WILLOW

Scenic rating: 4

near Bow Willow Canyon in
Anza-Borrego Desert State Park

Anza-Borrego map, page 837

Bow Willow Canyon is a rugged setting that can be explored by hiking the trail that starts at this camp. A short distance east of the camp, the trail forks to the south to Rockhouse Canyon. For a good side trip, drive back to County

Road S2 and head south over Sweeney Pass for the view at the Carrizo Badlands Overlook.

Campsites, facilities: There are 16 sites for tents or RVs up to 24 feet (no hookups). Picnic tables, fire rings, and shade ramadas are provided. Limited drinking water and vault toilets are available. Leashed pets are permitted in the campground, but not on trails.

Reservations, fees: Reservations are not accepted. Sites are $15 per night, $5 per night per additional vehicle. Open year-round.

Directions: From El Cajon, drive east on I-8 about 75 miles to the town of Ocotillo (the first town after crossing from San Diego County to Imperial County) and County Road S2/Imperial Highway. Turn north (left) on County Road S2/Imperial Highway and drive 27 miles to the gravel campground entrance road on the left.

Contact: Anza-Borrego Desert State Park, Visitor Center, 760/767-4205; Colorado Desert District, 760/767-5311, www.parks.ca.gov.

84 RIO BEND RV AND GOLF RESORT

Scenic rating: 5

near El Centro

Map page 835

This resort is set at 50 feet below sea level near Mount Signal, about a 20-minute drive south of the Salton Sea. For some, this region is a godforsaken wasteland, but hey, that makes arriving at this park all the more like coming to a mirage in the desert. This resort is a combination RV park and year-round community with park models for sale. Management does what it can to offer visitors recreational options, including a nine-hole golf course. It's hot out here, sizzling most of the year, but dry and cool in the winter, the best time to visit.

Campsites, facilities: There are 500 sites for RVs to 40 feet, including 460 sites with full hookups (30 and 50 amps). Group sites have partial hookups. Picnic tables are provided. Cable TV and restrooms with showers are available. Two small, stocked lakes for catch-and-release fishing, café, heated swimming pool, spa, shuffleboard, pickle ball, volleyball, horseshoes, bocce ball, pet park, nine-hole golf course and pro shop, library, pool table, club room, organized activities, coin laundry, and WiFi are available on a seasonal basis. Some facilities are wheelchair-accessible. A small store is nearby. Leashed pets are permitted.

Reservations, fees: Reservations are accepted. Sites are $50 per night, pull-through sites (full hookups) are $70 per night, $3 per person for more than two people. Discounts off-season. Weekly, monthly, and annual rates available. Some credit cards accepted. Open year-round.

Directions: From El Centro, drive west on I-8 for seven miles to the Drew Road exit. Take that exit and drive south on Drew Road for 0.25 mile to the park on the right (1589 Drew Road).

Contact: Rio Bend RV and Golf Resort, 760/352-7061 or 800/545-6481, www.riobendrvgolfresort.com.

85 IMPERIAL SAND DUNES RECREATION AREA

🥾 🐕 🚙 ⛺

Scenic rating: 1

east of Brawley

Map page 835

Gecko, Roadrunner, and Midway campgrounds are three of the many camping options at Imperial Sand Dunes Recreation Area. There isn't a tree within a million miles of this camp. People who wind up here all have the same thing in common: They're ready to ride across the dunes in their dune buggies or off-highway vehicles. The dune season is on a weather-permitting basis. Note that several areas are off-limits to motorized vehicles and camping because of plant and habitat protection; hiking in these areas is allowed. There are opportunities for hiking on this incredible moonscape. Other recreation options include watching the sky and waiting for a cloud to show up. A gecko, by the way, is a harmless little lizard. I've had them crawl on the sides of my tent. Nice little fellows.

Campsites, facilities: There are numerous dispersed sites for tents or RVs of any length (no hookups) in the North and South Dunes campgrounds. Vault toilets and trash bins are available. No drinking water is available. A few sites have camping pads. Leashed pets are permitted.

Reservations, fees: Reservations are not accepted. Sites are $25 per week, $90 per season, if purchased from the vendor. Permits purchased onsite cost $40 per week, $120 per season, with a 14-day stay limit every 28 days. Open year-round.

Directions: From Brawley, drive east on Highway 78 for 27 miles to Gecko Road. Turn south on Gecko Road and drive three miles to the campground entrance on the left. To reach Roadrunner Camp in the North Dunes campground, continue for two miles to the campground at the end of the road.

Contact: Bureau of Land Management, El Centro Field Office, 760/337-4400, www.blm.gov/ca. For more information on closed areas, contact the Imperial Sand Dunes ranger station at 760/337-4400.

86 PICACHO STATE RECREATION AREA

🥾 🏊 🛶 🚣 🐕 🎣 ♿ 🚙 ⛺

Scenic rating: 6

near Taylor Lake on the Colorado River

Map page 835

To get here, you really have to want it. Picacho State Recreation Area is way out there, requiring a long drive north out of Winterhaven on a spindly little road. The camp is on the southern side of Taylor Lake on the

Colorado River. The park is the best deal around for many miles, though, with boat ramps, waterskiing, good bass fishing, and, occasionally, crazy folks having the time of their lives. The sun and water make a good combination. This recreation area includes eight miles of the lower Colorado River. Park wildlife includes wild burros and bighorn sheep, with thousands of migratory waterfowl on the Pacific Flyway occasionally taking up residence. More than 100 years ago, Picacho was a gold-mining town with a population of 2,500 people. Visitors should always carry extra water and essential supplies.

Note: This park is on the closure list developed by the California Department of Parks, pending final state budget decisions or the possible transfer of park management to other park agencies or volunteer groups. At time of publication, a donor agreement was in process.

Campsites, facilities: There are 54 sites for tents or RVs up to 35 feet (no hookups), two group sites for up to 50 people each, two group boat-in campsites for groups of up to 100 people, and five up-river sites (no hookups). Picnic tables and fire grills are provided. Drinking water, vault and chemical toilets, dump station, solar showers, and two boat launches are available. Some facilities are wheelchair-accessible. Leashed pets are permitted.

Reservations, fees: Reservations are accepted for group and boat-in sites only at 760/996-2963. Individual sites are $20–25 per night, group sites are $75 per night for up to 12 vehicles, group boat-in sites are $75 per night for a minimum of 15 people, $5 per person per night for additional people. Open year-round.

Directions: From El Centro, drive east on I-8 to Winterhaven and the exit for Winterhaven/4th Avenue. Take that exit to Winterhaven Drive. Turn left on Winterhaven Drive and drive 0.5 mile to County Road S24/Picacho Road. Turn right and drive 24 miles (crossing rail tracks, driving under a railroad bridge, and over the American Canal, the road becoming dirt for the last 18 miles) to the campground. The road is not suitable for large RVs. The drive takes 1–2 hours from Winterhaven. In summer, thunderstorms can cause flash flooding, making short sections of the road impassable.

Contact: Picacho State Recreation Area, Salton Sea State Recreation Area, 760/996-2963, www.parks.ca.gov.

87 SENATOR WASH RECREATION AREA

Scenic rating: 6

near Senator Wash Reservoir

Map page 835

Senator Wash Reservoir Recreation Area features two campgrounds, named (surprise) Senator Wash South Shore and Senator Wash North Shore. This recreation area is approximately 50 acres, with many trees of various types and several secluded camping areas. At Senator Wash North Shore (where there are fewer facilities than at South Shore), campsites are both on the water as well as further inland. Gravel beaches provide access to the reservoir. Boat ramps are nearby. This spot provides boating, fishing, OHV riding, wildlife-viewing, and opportunities for solitude and sightseeing.

Campsites, facilities: There are numerous dispersed sites for tents or RVs of any length (no hookups). South Shore has restrooms with flush toilets, outdoor showers, trash cans, a dump station, and drinking water. Some facilities are wheelchair-accessible. North Shore has two vault toilets and no drinking water; a boat ramp is approximately 0.25-mile away (there is no camping at the boat ramp). A buoyed swimming area and boat ramp are available providing boat-in access to campsites. Leashed pets are permitted.

Reservations, fees: Reservations are not

accepted. Sites are $15 per night. There is a year-round maximum 14-day limit for every 28 days. Open year-round.

Directions: Take I-8 to Yuma, Arizona, and the exit for 4th Avenue. Take that exit and drive to Imperial Highway/County Road S24. Turn north and drive 22 miles to Senator Wash Road. Turn left and drive about three miles south to Mesa Campground. Turn left and drive 200 yards to the South Shore Campground access road on the right. Turn right and drive to the reservoir and campground.

Contact: Bureau of Land Management, Yuma Field Office, 928/317-3200, www.blm.gov/az.

88 SQUAW LAKE

Scenic rating: 6

near the Colorado River

Map page 835

Take your pick. There are two camps near the Colorado River in this area (the other is Senator Wash). This one is near Squaw Lake, created by the nearby Imperial Dam on the Colorado River. These sites provides opportunities for swimming, fishing, boating, and hiking, featuring direct boat access to the Colorado River. Wildlife includes numerous waterfowl, as well as quail, coyotes, and reptiles. A speed limit of 5 mph is enforced on the lake; no wakes permitted. The no-wake zone ends at the Colorado River.

Campsites, facilities: There are 125 sites for RVs of any length (no hookups) and dispersed sites for tents. Picnic tables and barbecue grills are provided. Four restrooms with flush toilets and coin showers are available. Drinking water is available at a central location. Trash and gray water disposal are available. Two boat ramps and a dump station are nearby. Two buoyed swimming areas are available. Some facilities are wheelchair-accessible. Leashed pets are permitted.

Reservations, fees: Reservations are not accepted. Sites are $15 per night. There is a year-round maximum 14-day limit for every 28 days. Open year-round.

Directions: Drive on I-8 to Yuma, Arizona, and the exit for 4th Avenue. Take that exit and drive to Imperial Highway/County Road S24. Turn north and drive 22 miles to Senator Wash Road. Turn left and drive about four miles (well signed) to the lake and campground on the right.

Contact: Bureau of Land Management, Yuma Field Office, 928/317-3200, www.blm.gov/az.

89 MIDWAY

Scenic rating: 6

in the Imperial Sand Dunes Recreation Area

Map page 835

This is off-highway-vehicle headquarters, a place where people bring their three-wheelers, four-wheelers, and motorcycles. That's because a large area has been set aside just for this type of recreation. Good news is that this area has become more family-oriented because of increased enforcement, eliminating much of the lawlessness and lunatic behavior of the past. As you drive in, you will enter the Buttercup Recreation Area, which is part of the Imperial Sand Dunes Recreation Area. You camp almost anywhere you like, and nobody beefs. Note that several areas are off-limits to motorized vehicles and camping because of plant and habitat protection; hiking in these areas is allowed. (See the Imperial Sand Dunes Recreation Area listing in this chapter for more options.)

Campsites, facilities: There are several primitive sites for tents or RVs of any length (no hookups). Vault toilets are available. No drinking water is available. Leashed pets are permitted.

Reservations, fees: Reservations are not

accepted. Sites are $25 per week, $90 per season if purchased from the vendor. Permits purchased onsite cost $40 per week, $120 per season with a 14-day stay limit every 28 days. Open year-round, weather permitting.

Directions: From El Centro, drive east on I-8 for about 40 miles to Gray's Wells Road (signed Sand Dunes). Take that exit and drive (it bears to the right) to a stop sign. Continue straight on Gray's Wells Road and drive three miles to another stop sign. To reach Buttercup Recreation Area, turn left and drive a short distance. To reach Midway, continue straight on Gray's Wells Road for 1.5 miles (the road turns from pavement to dirt and then dead-ends); camping is permitted anywhere in this region.

Contact: Bureau of Land Management, El Centro Field Office, 760/337-4400, www. blm.gov/ca. For more information on closed areas, contact the Imperial Sand Dunes ranger station at 760/337-4400.

RESOURCES

NATIONAL FORESTS

The most popular National Forest campgrounds are at lakes in the Sierra Nevada, where reservations are advised on summer weekends. Many of these campgrounds often have plenty of space on summer weekdays, Sunday night through Thursday, and in the shoulder seasons.

The Forest Service also provides many secluded camps and allows camping anywhere except where it is specifically prohibited. If you ever want to clear the cobwebs from your head and get away from it all, this is the way to go. I've salvaged many a trip by camping self-contained at the end of a logging spur instead of at crowded campgrounds.

Some Forest Service campgrounds are quite remote and have no drinking water. At these, you usually don't need to check in or make reservations; sometimes there is no fee or the cost is low, with payment made on the honor system.

Before your trip, be clear on what level of infrastructure is available at the campground you plan to visit. If you want numbered sites, drinking water, showers, a camp host on site, and a boat ramp nearby, plan on making reservations in advance on weekends and popular summer dates. If a site is very remote or primitive with no water, it is not usually the kind of place to bring a family. Often the presence of a camp host can help minimize coarse behavior at night and can be an important element in your plans.

Dogs are permitted in national forests with no extra charge and no hassle. Leashes are required for dogs in some places. Always carry documentation of current vaccinations.

Most Forest Service camps are in mountain areas and are subject to winter closure due to snow or mud.

National Forest Adventure Pass

The ongoing debacle of the National Forest Adventure Pass in Southern California is expected to come to a head in 2013. In the past, the Angeles, Cleveland, Los Padres, and San Bernardino National Forests have required an Adventure Pass for each vehicle parked in 34 recreation areas managed by the Forest Service in Southern California. After the loss of a Forest Service court case (the judge said the public shouldn't have to pay a single dime to recreate on public land managed by the Forest Service), the entire program was under review. The basic conflict is this: The Forest Service believes it can charge you to park when you go for a hike; the attorneys representing hikers believe the opposite is true, and say that is exactly what the judge meant At time of publication, it appeared that the number of sites requiring an Adventure Pass will be reduced from 34 to 12 in Southern California. (And those 12 sites might be contested if somebody gets a ticket, refuses to pay, and then challenges the entire program.)

Daily forest passes cost $5 and annual passes are available for $30. You can buy Adventure Passes at national forest offices in Southern California and dozens of retail outlets and online vendors. The new charges are use fees, not entrance fees. Golden Age and Golden Access Passes are honored in lieu of an Adventure Pass. When you buy an annual Adventure Pass, you can also buy an annual second-vehicle Adventure Pass for $5. Major credit cards are accepted at most retail and online outlets and at some forest service offices. For a recording with updated information, call 909/382-2622. To purchase a pass over the phone with a credit card, call 909/382-2623.

You will not need an Adventure Pass while traveling through national forests, nor when you've paid other types of fees such as camping or ski pass fees. However, if you are camping in national forests and you leave the campground in your vehicle and park outside the campground for recreation (such as at a trailhead, day-use area, near a fishing stream, etc.), you will need an Adventure Pass for your vehicle. You also need an Adventure Pass if camping at a no-fee campground. More information about the Adventure Pass program, including a listing of retail and online vendors, can be obtained online at www.fs.fed.us/passespermits.

An America the Beautiful Pass (Interagency Pass) is available annually in lieu of an Adventure Pass. The America the Beautiful Pass is honored nationwide at all Forest Service, National Park Service, Bureau of Land Management, Bureau of Reclamation, and U.S. Fish and Wildlife Service sites charging entrance or standard amenity fees. Valid for 12 months from the month of purchase, the America the Beautiful Pass is available at most national forest or grassland offices or online at http://store.usgs.gov.

National Forest Reservations

Some of the more popular camps, and most of the group camps, are on a reservation system. Reservations can be made up to 240 days in advance, and up to 360 days in advance for groups. To reserve a site call 877/444-6777 or visit the website www.recreation.gov. The reservation fee is usually $9 for a campsite in a national forest, and major credit cards are accepted. Holders of America the Beautiful (Interagency Pass), Golden Age, or Golden Access Passes receive a 50 percent discount for campground fees, except for group sites.

National Forest Maps

National Forest maps are among the best you can get for the price; they detail all backcountry streams, lakes, hiking trails, and logging roads for access. Most maps cost $8–10, plus a $1 service charge, and they can be obtained in person at forest service offices or by contacting National Forest Store. Major credit cards are accepted if ordering by telephone.

National Forest Store
Attn: Map Sales
P.O. Box 8268
Missoula, MT 59807
406/329-3024
www.nationalforeststore.com.

Forest Service Information

Forest Service personnel are most helpful for obtaining camping or hiking trail information. Unless you are buying a map or Adventure Pass, it is advisable to phone in advance to get the best service. For specific information on a national forest, contact the following offices:

USDA Forest Service
Pacific Southwest Region
1323 Club Drive
Vallejo, CA 94592
707/562-USFS (707/562-8737)
www.fs.usda.gov/r5

Angeles National Forest
701 North Santa Anita Avenue
Arcadia, CA 91006
626/574-1613
www.fs.usda.gov/angeles

Cleveland National Forest
10845 Rancho Bernardo Road, No. 200
San Diego, CA 92127-2107
858/673-6180
www.fs.usda.gov/cleveland

Eldorado National Forest
100 Forni Road
Placerville, CA 95667
530/622-5061
www.fs.usda.gov/eldorado

Humboldt-Toiyabe National Forest
1200 Franklin Way
Sparks, NV 89431
775/331-6444
www.fs.usda.gov/htnf

Inyo National Forest
351 Pacu Lane, Suite 200
Bishop, CA 93514
760/873-2400
www.fs.usda.gov/inyo

Klamath National Forest
1312 Fairlane Road
Yreka, CA 96097-9549
530/842-6131
www.fs.usda.gov/klamath

Lake Tahoe Basin Management Unit
35 College Drive
South Lake Tahoe, CA 96150
530/543-2600
fax 530/543-2693
www.fs.fed.us/r5/ltbmu

Lassen National Forest
2550 Riverside Drive
Susanville, CA 96130
530/257-2151
www.fs.usda.gov/lassen

Los Padres National Forest
6755 Hollister Avenue, Suite 150
Goleta, CA 93117
805/968-6640
www.fs.usda.gov/lpnf

Mendocino National Forest
825 North Humboldt Avenue
Willows, CA 95988
530/934-3316
www.fs.usda.gov/mendocino

Modoc National Forest
800 West 12th Street
Alturas, CA 96101
530/233-5811
www.fs.usda.gov/modoc

Plumas National Forest
P.O. Box 11500
159 Lawrence Street
Quincy, CA 95971
530/283-2050
www.fs.usda.gov/plumas

San Bernardino National Forest
602 South Tippecanoe Avenue
San Bernardino, CA 92408-2607

909/382-2600
www.fs.usda.gov/sbnf

Sequoia National Forest
Giant Sequoia National Monument
1839 South Newcomb Street
Porterville, CA 93257
559/784-1500
www.fs.usda.gov/sequoia

Shasta-Trinity National Forest
3644 Avtech Parkway
Redding, CA 96002
530/226-2500
www.fs.usda.gov/stnf

Sierra National Forest
1600 Tollhouse Road
Clovis, CA 93611
559/297-0706
www.fs.usda.gov/sierra

Six Rivers National Forest
1330 Bayshore Way
Eureka, CA 95501
707/442-1721
www.fs.usda.gov/srnf

Stanislaus National Forest
19777 Greenley Road
Sonora, CA 95370
209/532-3671
www.fs.usda.gov/stanislaus

Tahoe National Forest
631 Coyote Street
Nevada City, CA 95959
530/265-4531
www.fs.usda.gov/tahoe

STATE PARKS

California's state parks provide some of the best and most popular campgrounds in America. The California State Parks system provides many popular camping spots in spectacular settings. These campgrounds include drive-in numbered sites, tent spaces, and picnic tables, with showers and bathrooms provided nearby. Although many parks are well known, there are still some little-known gems in the state parks system where campers can enjoy seclusion, even in the summer. There are also a good number of first-come, first-served sites that can provide surprise openings.

For peak weekend dates, campsites at the most popular parks—Doheny in Southern California, Steve Ravine Environmental Cabins in the Bay Area—can sell out in less than 15 minutes. Coastal sites along Highway 1 can also go quickly. With the ongoing budget crisis in California, the price of campsites has soared to roughly $35 a night in most parks. The low-cost alternative—Forest Service campgrounds—usually don't have amenities such as showers, as at the state park campgrounds.

State Park Reservations

Most state park campgrounds are on a reservation system and campsites can be booked up to seven months in advance at many state parks. There are also hike-in/bike-in sites available on a first-come, first-served basis. Reservations can be made by phone at 800/444-7275 (800/444-PARK) or online at www.reserveamerica.com. The reservation fee is usually $8 for per campsite. Major credit cards are accepted online and over the phone, but are usually not accepted at the parks.

Camping discounts of 50 percent are available for holders of the Disabled Discount Pass, and free camping is allowed for holders of the Disabled Veteran/Prisoner of War Pass.

For general information about California State Parks, contact:

California Department of Parks and Recreation
Public Information Office
P.O. Box 942896
1416 9th Street
Sacramento, CA 94296
916/653-6995,
Pass sales, 800/777-0369
www.parks.ca.gov

NATIONAL PARKS

California's national parks are natural wonders, varying from the spectacular yet crowded Yosemite Valley to the remote and rugged Lava Beds National Monument. Reservations for campsites are available five months in advance for many of the national parks in California. In addition to campground fees, expect to pay a park entrance fee of $20 per vehicle, or as low as $5 per person for hike-in/bike-in (you can buy an annual National Parks Pass that waives entrance fees). This entrance fee is valid for seven days. For an additional fee, an America the Beautiful sticker can be added to the National Parks Pass, thereby eliminating entrance fees at sites managed by the U.S. Fish and Wildlife Service, the U.S. Forest Service, and the Bureau of Land Management. Various discounts are available for holders of Golden Age and Golden Access passports, including a 50 percent reduction of camping fees (group camps not included) and a waiver of park entrance fees.

For reservations, call 877/444-6777 or visit www.recreation.gov ($9 reservation fee). Major credit cards accepted.

National Park Service
Pacific West Region
One Jackson Center
1111 Jackson Street, Suite 700
Oakland, CA 94607
510/817-1304
www.nps.gov

Cabrillo National Monument
1800 Cabrillo Memorial Drive
San Diego, CA 92106-3601
619/557-5450
www.nps.gov/cabr

Channel Islands National Park
1901 Spinnaker Drive
Ventura, CA 93001
805/658-5730
www.nps.gov/chis

Death Valley National Park
P.O. Box 579
Death Valley, CA 92328-0579
760/786-3200
www.nps.gov/deva

Devils Postpile National Monument
P.O. Box 3999
Mammoth Lakes, CA 93546
760/934-2289 (summer only)
www.nps.gov/depo
For year-round information, contact Sequoia and Kings Canyon National Parks (see listing in this section).

Golden Gate National Recreation Area
Fort Mason, Building 201
San Francisco, CA 94123-0022
415/561-4700
www.nps.gov/goga

Joshua Tree National Park
74485 National Park Drive
Twentynine Palms, CA 92277-3597
760/367-5500
www.nps.gov/jotr

Lassen Volcanic National Park
P.O. Box 100
Mineral, CA 96063-0100
530/595-4444
www.nps.gov/lavo

Lava Beds National Monument
1 Indian Well Headquarters
Tulelake, CA 96134
530/667-2282
www.nps.gov/labe

Mojave National Preserve
2701 Barstow Road
Barstow, CA 92311
760/252-6100
www.nps.gov/moja

Pinnacles National Monument
5000 Highway 146

Paicines, CA 95043
831/389-4485
www.nps.gov/pinn

Point Reyes National Seashore
Point Reyes Station, CA 94956-9799
415/464-5100
www.nps.gov/pore

Redwood National and State Parks
1111 2nd Street
Crescent City, CA 95531
707/464-6101
www.nps.gov/redw

Santa Monica Mountains National Recreation Area
401 West Hillcrest Drive
Thousand Oaks, CA 91360
805/370-2301
www.nps.gov/samo

Sequoia and Kings Canyon National Parks
47050 Generals Highway
Three Rivers, CA 93271-9700
559/565-3341
fax 559/565-3730
www.nps.gov/seki

Smith River National Recreation Area
P.O. Box 228
Gasquet, CA 95543
707/457-3131
www.fs.usda.gov/srnf

Whiskeytown National Recreation Area
P.O. Box 188
Whiskeytown, CA 96095
530/246-1225 or 530/242-3400
www.nps.gov/whis

Yosemite National Park
P.O. Box 577
Yosemite National Park, CA 95389
209/372-0200
www.nps.gov/yose

BUREAU OF LAND MANAGEMENT (BLM)

Most BLM campgrounds are primitive and are located in remote areas. Vast areas of desert in the Barstow/Needles area are included in BLM land, as well a remote tracts in northeastern California and areas near Clear Lake. The crown jewel is the King Range Natural Conservation Area on the "Lost Coast" of Humboldt County. Often, there is no fee charged for camping. Holders of Golden Age or Golden Access passports receive a 50 percent discount, except for group camps, at BLM fee campgrounds.

Bureau of Land Management
California State Office
2800 Cottage Way, Suite W-1623
Sacramento, CA 95825-1886
916/978-4400
www.blm.gov/ca

California Desert District Office
22835 Calle San Juan de los Lagos
Moreno Valley, CA 92553
951/697-5200
www.blm.gov/ca/cdd

Alturas Field Office
708 West 12th Street
Alturas, CA 96101
530/233-4666
www.blm.gov/ca/alturas

Arcata Field Office
1695 Heindon Road
Arcata, CA 95521-4573
707/825-2300
www.blm.gov/ca/arcata

Bakersfield Field Office
3801 Pegasus Drive
Bakersfield, CA 93308
661/391-6000
www.blm.gov/ca/bakersfield

Barstow Field Office
2601 Barstow Road
Barstow, CA 92311
760/252-6000
www.blm.gov/ca/barstow

Bishop Field Office
351 Pacu Lane, Suite 100
Bishop, CA 93514
760/872-5000
www.blm.gov/ca/bishop

Eagle Lake Field Office
2950 Riverside Drive
Susanville, CA 96130
530/257-0456
www.blm.gov/ca/eaglelake

El Centro Field Office
1661 South 4th Street
El Centro, CA 92243
760/337-4400
www.blm.gov/ca/elcentro

Folsom Field Office
63 Natoma Street
Folsom, CA 95630
916/985-4474
www.blm.gov/ca/folsom

Hollister Field Office
20 Hamilton Court
Hollister, CA 95023
831/630-5000
www.blm.gov/ca/hollister

Palm Springs/South Coast Field Office
P.O. Box 581260
North Palm Springs, CA 92258-1260
760/251-4800
www.blm.gov/ca/palmsprings

Redding Field Office
355 Hemsted Drive
Redding, CA 96002
530/224-2100
www.blm.gov/ca/redding

Ridgecrest Field Office
300 South Richmond Road
Ridgecrest, CA 93555
760/384-5400
www.blm.gov/ca/ridgecrest

Ukiah Field Office
2550 North State Street
Ukiah, CA 95482
707/468-4000
www.blm.gov/ca/ukiah

U.S. ARMY CORPS OF ENGINEERS

Sites operated by the U.S. Army Corps of Engineers often get overlooked. Few are at stellar settings. The best are at Lake Sonoma, Lake Mendocino and other reservoirs. Some of the family camps and most of the group camps operated by the U.S. Army Corps of Engineers are on a reservation system. Reservations can be made up to 240 days in advance, and up to 360 days in advance for groups. To reserve a site, call 877/444-6777 or visit www.recreation.gov. The reservation fee is usually $10, and major credit cards are accepted. Holders of Golden Age or Golden Access passports receive a 50 percent discount for campground fees, except for group sites.

South Pacific Division
333 Market Street
San Francisco, CA 94105
415/503-6804
www.spn.usace.army.mil

Sacramento District
1325 J Street
Sacramento, CA 95814
916/557-5100
www.spk.usace.army.mil

Los Angeles District
915 Wilshire Boulevard, Suite 980
Los Angeles, CA 90017-3401
213/452-3908
www.spl.usace.army.mil

OTHER VALUABLE RESOURCES

State Forests
Jackson Demonstration State Forest
802 North Main Street
Fort Bragg, CA 95437
707/964-5674
www.fire.ca.gov

Mountain Home Demonstration State Forest
P.O. Box 517
Springville, CA 93265
559/539-2321 (summer)
559/539-2855 (winter)
www.fire.ca.gov

County/Regional Park Departments
Del Norte County Parks
840 9th Street, Suite 11
Crescent City, CA 95531
707/464-7230
www.co.del-norte.ca.us

East Bay Regional Park District
P.O. Box 5381
Oakland, CA 94605-0381
888/327-2757
www.ebparks.org

Humboldt County Parks
1106 2nd Street
Eureka, CA 95501
707/445-7651
www.co.humboldt.ca.us

Marin Municipal Water District
220 Nellen Avenue
Corte Madera, CA 94925
415/945-1455
www.marinwater.org

Midpeninsula Regional Open Space District
330 Distel Circle
Los Altos, CA 94022-1404

650/691-1200
www.openspace.org

Pacific Gas and Electric Company
Corporate Real Estate/Recreation
5555 Florin-Perkins Road, Room 100
Sacramento, CA 95826
916/386-5164
www.pge.com/recreation

Sacramento County Regional Parks
3711 Branch Center Road
Sacramento, CA 95827
916/875-6961
www.msa2.saccounty.net/parks

San Diego County Parks and Recreation Department
2454 Heritage Park Row
San Diego, CA 92110
858/694-3049
www.co.san-diego.ca.us/parks

San Luis Obispo County Parks Department
1087 Santa Rosa Street
San Luis Obispo, CA 93408
805/781-5930
www.slocountyparks.org

San Mateo County Parks and Recreation Department
455 County Center, 4th floor
Redwood City, CA 94063-1646
650/363-4020
www.eparks.net

Santa Barbara County Parks and Recreation Department
610 Mission Canyon Road
Santa Barbara, CA 93105
805/568-2461
www.santabarbaraca.gov

Santa Clara County Parks Department
298 Garden Hill Drive
Los Gatos, CA 95032-7669

408/355-2200
www.parkhere.org

Sonoma County Regional Parks
2300 County Center Drive, Suite 120-A
Santa Rosa, CA 95403
707/565-2041
www.sonoma-county.org/parks

State and Federal Offices
U.S. Fish and Wildlife Service
1849 C Street NW
Washington, DC 20240
www.fws.gov

U.S. Geological Survey
Branch of Information Services
P.O. Box 25286, Bldg. 810, MS 306,
Federal Center
Denver, CO 80225
888/ASK-USGS (888/275-8747) or
303/202-4700
www.usgs.gov

California Department of Fish and Game
1416 9th Street, 12th floor
Sacramento, CA 95814
916/445-0411
www.dfg.ca.gov

Information Services
Lake County Visitor Information Center
P.O. Box 1025
6110 East Highway 20
Lucerne, CA 95458
707/274-5652 or 800/525-3743
www.lakecounty.com

Mammoth Lakes Visitors Bureau
P.O. Box 48
2520 Main St.
Mammoth Lakes, CA 93546
888/GO-MAMMOTH (888/466-2666) or
760/934-2712
www.visitmammoth.com

Mount Shasta Visitors Bureau
300 Pine Street
Mount Shasta, CA 96067
530/926-4865 or 800/926-4865
www.mtshastachamber.com

The Nature Conservancy of California
201 Mission Street, 4th floor
San Francisco, CA 94105-1832
415/777-0487
fax 415/777-0244
www.nature.org

Plumas County Visitors Bureau
550 Crescent Street
P.O. Box 4120
Quincy, CA 95971
530/283-6345 or 800/326-2247
fax 530/283-5465
www.plumascounty.org

**Shasta Cascade Wonderland
Association**
1699 Highway 273
Anderson, CA 96007
530/365-7500 or 800/474-2782
fax 530/365-1258
www.shastacascade.com

Map Companies
Map Link/Trek Tools
www.trektools.com

Tom Harrison Maps
2 Falmouth Cove
San Rafael, CA 94901-4465
415/456-7940
www.tomharrisonmaps.com

U.S. Forest Service
National Forest Store
Attn: Map Sales
P.O. Box 7669
Missoula, MT 59807
406/329-3024
www.nationalforeststore.com

U.S. Geological Survey
345 Middlefield Road
Menlo Park, CA 94025
650/853-8300
www.usgs.gov

Index

Acknowledgments

U.S. Forest Service

Jerry Reponen, Los Angeles River Ranger District, Angeles National Forest

Charlotte Whelan, San Gabriel River Ranger District, Angeles National Forest

Daniel Walsh, Descanso Ranger District, Cleveland National Forest

Debbie Hobbs, Palomar Ranger District, Cleveland National Forest

Pam Robinson, Georgetown Ranger District, Eldorado National Forest

Adrianne Thatcher, Bridgeport Ranger District, Humboldt-Toiyabe National Forest

Lindsay Pulliam, Carson Ranger District, Humboldt-Toiyabe National Forest

Shawn Biessel, Mono Basin Scenic Area and Visitor Center, Inyo National Forest

Phoebe Prather, Mount Whitney Ranger District, Inyo National Forest

John Rosenthal and Hern Crane, White Mountain Ranger District, Inyo National Forest

Tara Ware, Happy Camp and Oak Knoll Ranger Districts, Klamath National Forest

Jim Lasell, Lower Trinity Ranger District, Klamath National Forest

Jackie Hurlimann, Scott River and Salmon River Ranger Districts, Klamath National Forest

Katrena Smith, Almanor Ranger District, Lassen National Forest

Solomon Everta, Eagle Lake Ranger District, Lassen National Forest

Mike Jones, Hat Creek Ranger District, Lassen National Forest

Joan Van Pelt, Monterey Ranger District, Los Padres National Forest

Carol Lester, Mount Pinos Ranger District, Los Padres National Forest

Reynaldo Rivera, Ojai Ranger District, Los Padres National Forest

Susan Tuttle, Santa Lucia Ranger District, Los Padres National Forest

Laura Saylor, Covelo Ranger District, Mendocino National Forest

Dalles Meeks, Grindstone Ranger District, Paskenta Work Center, Mendocino National Forest

Diane Evans, Grindstone Ranger District, Stonyford Work Center, Mendocino National Forest

Ron Gregory, Red Bluff Recreation Area, Mendocino National Forest

Jessie Berner, Headquarters, Modoc National Forest

Lenni Edgerton, Big Valley Ranger District, Modoc National Forest

Allison Houser, Doublehead Ranger District, Modoc National Forest

Bill Benson, Beckwourth Ranger District, Plumas National Forest

Elizabeth Carpenter, Feather River Ranger District, Plumas National Forest

Jeanie McCoshum, Mount Hough Ranger District, Plumas National Forest

Gary Bindrup, Mountaintop Ranger Station, San Bernardino National Forest

John Ladley, San Jacinto Ranger District, San Bernardino National Forest

Carol Hallacy, Hume Lake Ranger District, Sequoia National Forest

Norma Salazar, Great Divide Ranger District, Sequoia National Forest and Giant Sequoia National Monument

Alex Specht, Kern River Ranger District, Kern River, Sequoia National Forest

Yvonne Stockwell, Kern River Ranger District, Lake Isabella, Sequoia National Forest

Barbara Paolinitti and Jan Sorochtey, McCloud Ranger District, Shasta-Trinity National Forest

Don Lee, Mount Shasta Ranger District, Shasta-Trinity National Forest

Cheryl Kochenderfer, Weaverville Ranger District, Shasta-Trinity National Forest

Jamie Schlumbohm, Bass Lake Ranger District, Sierra National Forest

Patty Richards, High Sierra Ranger District, Sierra National Forest

David Rea, Mad River Ranger District, Six Rivers National Forest

Don Pass, Six Rivers National Forest, Smith River National Recreation Area

Jerry Snyder, Stanislaus National Forest

Pat Kaunert, Calaveras Ranger District, Stanislaus National Forest

Gail Lewis, Groveland Ranger District, Stanislaus National Forest

Amanda Grogan, American River Ranger District, Foresthill Ranger Station, Tahoe National Forest

Susanne Johnson, Lake Tahoe Basin Management Unit, Tahoe National Forest

Jeff Wiley and Mary Westmoreland, Sierraville Ranger District, Tahoe National Forest

Charlotte Wehmeyer, Yuba River Ranger District, North, Tahoe National Forest

Rachel Schoeppner, Emerald Cove Marina, Yuba River Ranger District, Tahoe National Forest

U.S. Army Corps of Engineers

Michael Carroll, Lake Sonoma Recreation Area, San Francisco District

Kathy Fuente, Sacramento District

Skip Sivertsen, Englebright Lake, Sacramento District

Jacqui Zink, Martis Creek Lake, Sacramento District

Lucy Vang, Pine Flat Field Office, Sacramento District

Erik Doss, Black Butte Lake, Sacramento District

Anna McCall, Lake Mendocino, San Francisco District

Bureau of Land Management

Alex McNeill, Arcata Field Office

Peter DeWitt and Kenneth Hock, Bakersfield Field Office

Arthur Callan, Carson City Field Office

Jim Hunt, Eagle Lake Field Office

Dallas Meeks, El Centro Field Office

Sheryl Patton, Mother Lode Field Office

Donna Chirello, Palm Springs Field Office

Caroline Crowley, Ukiah Field Office

Joe Raffaele, Yuma Field Office

National Parks

Skaidra Kempkowski, Death Valley National Park

Brian Powers, Lassen Volcanic National Park

Phyllis Wilson, Sequoia and Kings Canyon National Parks

Robert Fonda, Durst Creek Campground, Sequoia and Kings Canyon National Parks

Pat Pilcher, Joshua Tree National Monument

State Parks

Ruth Coleman, director, and Roy Stearns, deputy director, Sacramento Headquarters

Ellen Absher, Mount San Jacinto State Park

John Arnold, Half Moon Bay State Beach

Ryan Banovitz, Bolsa Chica State Beach

Jill Bazemore, Emma Wood State Beach

Steven Bier, Salton Sea State Recreation Area

Avis Boutell and Star Sandoval, Bay Area Sector

Lynda Burman, Indian Grinding Rock State Historic Park

Joshua Bynum, Crystal Cove State Park

Kathy Dolinar and Kent Miller, Ocotillo Wells State Vehicular Recreation Area

Gary Brennan, Henry Cowell Redwoods State Park

Kevin Williams, Brandon Carroll, Big Basin Redwoods State Park

Eric Carter, Prairie Creek Redwoods State Park

Taya Chase, Jeanette Fenske, and Liz Hamman, Humboldt Redwoods State Park

Joni Coombe, Pfeiffer Big Sur State Park

Suzanne Downing, San Juan Bautista Section

Donna Galyean, Humboldt Lagoons State Park

Dave Garcia, Limekiln State Park

Michael Grant, Butano State Park

Greg Hall, Tolowa Dunes State Park

Ted Hannibal, Hollister Hills State Vehicular Recreation Area

John Hardcastle, Benbow Lake State Recreation Area

Kathy Hernandez, Folsom Lake State Recreation Area

Jacque Hoffman, Fort Ross State Historic Park

Laura Itogawa, Cuyamaca Rancho State Park

Travis Johnson, Palomar Mountain State Park

Gary Kinney, Seacliff State Beach

Nathan Kogen and Mike Selbo, Sunset State Beach

Lawani Kolley, Sierra District

John Kolsrud, Austin Creek State Recreation Area

Mike Lair, China Camp State Park

Sheri Larue, Malakoff Diggins State Historic Park

William Lutton, Turlock Lake State Recreation Area

Valerie Marshall, Mendocino District

Dan Martin, Woodson Bridge State Recreation Area

Melissa McGee, Standish-Hickey State Recreation Area

Maria Mendez, Colusa-Sacramento River State Recreation Area

Bill Mentzer, Marin Sector

Lynn Mochizuki, Point Mugu State Park

Javier Morales, Patrick's Point State Park

Cecelia Moreno, Auburn State Recreation Area

Dan Murray and Alison Strachan, Channel Coast District

Sean Nichols and Mark Pupich, Grover Hot Springs State Park

Jerelyn Oliveira, Colonel Allensworth State Historic Park

Denise Peterson, Brannan Island State Recreation Area

Shirley Plumhuf, McArthur-Burney Falls State Park

Christa Quick, Angeles District

Mary Rafuse, Castle Crags State Park

Kellen Riley, San Simeon State Park

Carol Schmal, South Carlsbad State Beach

Rachel Shaw, San Elijo State Beach

Dan Smith, Samuel P. Taylor State Park

Jason Smith, Sonoma Coast State Beach

Shannon Stalder, Grizzly Creek Redwoods State Park

Mike Stanley, Portola Redwoods State Park

Erin Steinart, Bothe-Napa Valley State Park

Veneta Stewart, Donner Memorial State Park

Sarah Straws and Bob Young, Calaveras Big Trees State Park

Katie Sundvall, Richardson Grove State Park

Debborah Tanner, Four Rivers Sector

Theresa Tate, New Brighton State Beach

Charlie Thompson, Sinkyone WildernessState Park

Bob Thornton, Andrea Molera State Park

Jennifer Tustison, Orange Coast District

Mckeena Vanrillaer, Salt Point State Park

John Verhoeven, Fremont Peak State Park

Tony Villareal, Pismo State Beach/Oceano Dunes State Vehicular Recreation Area

Karen Vreeland, Millerton Lake State Recreation Area

Shelley Waltman-Derr, Clear Lake State Park

Melissa Weaver, San Luis Reservoir State Recreation Area

Kathy Williams, Silverwood Lake State Recreation Area

Bob Williamson, Carnegie State Vehicular Recreation Area

Susan Wilson, Morro Bay State Park

Adam Wollter, Sugarloaf Ridge State Park

Tyson Young, Caswell Memorial State Park

State Forests

Wayne Connor, Boggs Mountain Demonstration State Forest

Lois Kauffman, LaTour Demonstration State Forest

Alan Frame, Mountain Home Demonstration State Forest

Other

Randy Akana, Siskiyou County Public Works

Doug Allen, Edward Ancheta, Mike Ekdao, John Heenan, Theresa Nance, Fred Griggs, and Reggie Zapata, Santa Clara County Parks

Joe Anderson, Napa Valley Exposition

Marian Ardohain and Amy Tischman, Merced Irrigation District

Steve Benson, Huntington Beach City Parks

Tim Bolla, Richard Chandler, and Marilea Linne, Solano County Parks

Christopher Burdette, The Presidio Trust

Cheryl Bynum and Martha Martinez, Imperial County Parks

Dolores Canali, Cindy Donald, Duane Forest, Randal Higgins, Ruben Rodriguez, and Susan Storey, Riverside County Parks

Julie Cloherty, San Diego County Parks

Peggy Davidson, Nevada Irrigation District

Anna Diaz and Ann Springer, San Luis Obispo County Parks

Brent Doan, Lake Casitas Municipal Water District

Joy Feller, Nevada County Fairgrounds

Irene Flores, Karen Montanye, Juisa Powell, and Mary Sheehan, San Bernardino Regional Parks

Pam Gallo, Ventura County Parks

Clay Garland, Santa Barbara County Parks

Colleen Ghiglia, Lompoc Parks and Recreation

Patty Guida, New Melones Visitors Center, U.S. Bureau of Reclamation

Michelle Gilroy and Dennis Redfern, California Department of Fish & Game

Sherie Harral, Shasta Dam, U.S. Bureau of Reclamation

José Gutierrez, Sacramento Municipal Utility District

Heidi Gutnecht, City of San Diego

Chuck Hamilton and Ychelle Tillemans, Inyo County Parks

David Haverty and Donna LaGraffe, Sonoma County Regional Parks

Darlene Hennings, Placer County Facilities Services

Connie Jackson, Marty Johnson, and Danae Schmidt, Stanislaus County Parks and Recreation

Sara Johnston and Karen White, United Water Conservation District

Tracy Kves, Northern California Power Agency

Cynthia McDonald, Joy Vandell, Ross Jackson, and Mike Drury, Pacific Gas and Electric

Kathy McGadden, Greg Smith, and Jim Spreng, Monterey County Parks

Bill Minor, Humboldt County Public Works

Janet Morrison, Fresno County Parks

Dave Moore, San Mateo County Parks

Julie Ola, Alpine County Public Works Department

John Parsons, Stancy Perich, and John Wilbanks, Kern County Parks and Recreation

Don Pearson, Eldorado Irrigation District

Pam Phelps, City of Escondido

Christina Phillips, Hoopa Valley Tribal Council

Neil Pilegard, Tulare County Parks and Recreation

Patty Sereni, Napa County Fairgrounds

Ron Slimm, Orange County Parks

Alicia Smolke, San Joaquin County Parks

Pat Sotelo, Livermore Area Recreation and Park District

Laurie Swanson, Tahoe City Public Utilities District

Sue Vanderschans, Turlock Irrigation District

Roberta Warden, El Dorado Irrigation District

Amy Welch, Mono County Public Works

Jerry Wright, Yolo County Parks

Others of Note

Larry Farquhar, California Land Management

Silvana Friedman, California Land Management, High Sierra District

Shawnna Heggie, Shasta Recreation Company

Lisa Walker, Inyo Recreation

And all of the owners of RV parks in California

Fieldscouts

Rambob Stienstra, Susan and Tom Vance, Michael Furniss, Bob Simms, Tom Hedtke, Doug Laughlin, Jack Trout, John Lescroart, Bill Karr, Sabrina Young, Clancy Enlow, Larry Yant

Appreciation

To the late Jeffrey "Foonsky" Patty, who inspired many of the adventures, outdoor skills, and stories detailed in the front matter of this book.

www.moon.com

DESTINATIONS | ACTIVITIES | BLOGS | MAPS | BOOKS

MOON.COM is ready to help plan your next trip! Filled with fresh trip ideas and strategies, author interviews, informative travel blogs, a detailed map library, and descriptions of all the Moon guidebooks, Moon.com is all you need to get out and explore the world—or even places in your own backyard. While at Moon.com, sign up for our monthly e-newsletter for updates on new releases, travel tips, and expert advice from our on-the-go Moon authors. As always, when you travel with Moon, expect an experience that is uncommon and truly unique.

KEEP UP WITH MOON ON FACEBOOK AND TWITTER
JOIN THE MOON PHOTO GROUP ON FLICKR

MOON CALIFORNIA CAMPING

Avalon Travel
a member of the Perseus Books Group
1700 Fourth Street
Berkeley, CA 94710, USA
www.moon.com

Editor and Series Manager: Sabrina Young
Senior Research Editor: Kathie Morgan
Research Editor: Stephani Cruickshank
Production and Graphics Coordinator:
    Elizabeth Jang
Cover Designer: Elizabeth Jang
Interior Designer: Darren Alessi
Map Editor and Cartographer: Mike Morgenfeld
Proofreader: Elizabeth Hui

ISBN-13: 978-1-61238-292-0
ISSN: 1531-8109

Printing History
1st Edition – 1987
18th Edition – April 2013
5 4 3 2 1

Front cover photo: Fallen trees in Upper Lundy Canyon west of Lundy Lake © David Toussaint/ gettyimages.com

Title page photo: Tioga pass, Yosemite National Park © Natalia Bratslavsky/123rf.com

page 3 © Jeffrey Banke/123rf.com; page 4 © Aaron Kohr/123rf.com; page 5 © Mark Rasmussen/123rf. com

Back cover photo: © John Beath

Printed in Canada by Friesens

Keeping Current

We are committed to making this book the most accurate and enjoyable camping guide to California. You can rest assured that every campground in this book has been carefully reviewed in an effort to keep this book as up-to-date as possible. However, by the time you read this book, some of the fees listed herein may have changed and campgrounds may have closed unexpectedly.

If you have a favorite gem you'd like to see included in the next edition, or see anything that needs updating, clarification, or correction, please drop us a line. Send your comments via email to feedback@moon.com, or use the address above.

MOON OUTDOORS

YOUR ADVENTURE STARTS HERE

Table of Contents

Preface

Writing this book, I felt a thrill of discovery. From the outset I was convinced that there remained great, unspoiled areas where paddlers today could still experience America's waterways as the explorers and Native Americans did in centuries past. I feared, however, that such areas would be fewer and farther between.

To my delight, in my research I learned of great paddling spots in every state from tiny Rhode Island to Alaska. Almost every new description, brochure, and photograph impressed or inspired me. I only hope that in this book I have managed to capture the rich selection of fine paddling and magnificent natural beauty the country has to offer.

For help with this book I am deeply grateful to my father, David, and wife, Kathleen. My father researched and wrote the introductions to each state, and Kathleen did much of the editing, proofreading, and data entry. I hate to think how long writing this book would have taken without their help.

I also am very grateful to the hundreds of outfitters across the country who supplied information, photographs, and kind words of encouragement. My thanks, too, go to Jim Thaxton and Bruce Kerfoot of the National Association of Canoe Liveries and Outfitters for their helpful support and advice. Other organizations that were of great assistance include the American Canoe Association, America Outdoors, the North American Paddlesports Association, and the U.S. Canoe Association.

Happy paddling.

Introduction

At 17 I took my first canoe trip. Three friends and I spent two glorious, carefree weeks swimming, fishing, and camping in the wilderness of Maine's Syslodobsis Lakes. At dusk we'd pitch our tents on small, breezy islands. Mornings we'd break camp early and paddle to a new lake or campsite.

I emerged from the woods amazed that such great trips could be so poorly publicized. In fact, we would have missed our Maine adventure altogether had I not spotted one of the tiny, intermittent advertisements our outfitter ran in *Field & Stream*.

Fifteen years later, minimal advertising is still the rule among many small canoe liveries. Owners of these businesses often are forced to take other jobs in the off-season to supplement their incomes. Such shoe-string operations predictably have little money left over for promotion.

Yet at the same time, I know there are others like me who glance over country bridges, spot enticing rivers, but haven't a clue where to rent a canoe, raft, or tube. In bookstores I have searched in vain for local or national guides to outfitters.

This book is an attempt to fill that gap. It is intended as a guide to tote along while traveling. Then, as you find yourself with some free time and a nice stretch of water, the book will guide you to a local outfitter for a day- or half-day paddle trip. The book also is intended to help you plan longer, more ambitious outings. Particularly as you leaf through the chapters on Maine, Minnesota, and most Western states, you will find a wide selection of week-long expeditions.

Before deciding where to spend your precious vacation time, you will want to do some careful research to ensure that the destination, equipment, food, guides, and service are exactly what you are looking for. Ultimately, you may want to write to five or more companies to request brochures and information. This book, with its outfitter listings and descriptions can help you find those chosen few.

Choosing a Destination

Whether or not you have some idea of where you would like to take your next trip, I urge you to browse through this book from cover to cover. I have spent months poring over outfitters' catalogs, yet I continue to be surprised at how easily some new trip or location catches my fancy.

You may well have the same response. One moment you may be tempted by an adventurous fly-in trip to the Alaskan wilderness, and the next you want to be sea kayaking off the Florida coast. Or, one minute you're set on hair-raising whitewater and the next you want a relaxing, scenic trip.

Here are some of the questions you might ask yourself. Do you want a guided or unguided trip? If guided, how large a group would you be comfortable traveling in? Do you want a whitewater or scenic trip? Do you want to paddle or are you happy to let a guide pilot the boat? On multi-day trips, do you want to camp or stay in lodges? Do you want to pitch in with camp chores or be pampered? Do you want to bring your kids?

Your answers to these questions will help you narrow the list of choices. For instance, if it is important to you to have solitude or be alone with friends and family, you may want to forego some of the most popular trips, where you will likely have other boats in view for most of your run. On the other hand, if it's famous whitewater stretches you're after, you may forgive or even take comfort in seeing others on the river.

How the Book is Organized

To help you with your choices, the book has state-by-state listings for the entire country. Each chapter begins with a brief introduction to many of the favorite paddling spots in each state, along with an overview of these areas' terrain, scenery, and wildlife. Some of the places mentioned are not served by commercial outfitters. These places are covered, however, as a service to those wanting to shuttle their own canoes, kayaks, or rafts. Material for the introductions was drawn from hundreds of sources, the most helpful of which are listed in the bibliography.

The introductions to each state are followed by listings of outfitters operating trips there. These listings give additional information on the particular areas each outfitter serves.

Finally, for additional information to help in selecting a destination, you may want to refer to the guidebooks listed in the bibliography, and write or call state departments of natural resources, state tourist boards, conservation groups, and any of the helpful paddle-sports associations listed in the "Resources" section at the end of the book.

Choosing an Outfitter

The companies in this book range from small, family operations to large, multi-state enterprises. Regardless of size, any outfitter should impress you with his or her concern for your having a safe, fun trip. Even if you are just planning a day trip, it is good to call ahead to make reservations. When you have the outfitter on the phone, ask some basic questions.

Will the outfitter provide you with a canoe or raft that is clean, in good condition, and equipped with properly sized paddles and PFDs (personal flotation devices)? Will you receive instruction on paddling, water conditions, hazards, and safety? Will you need to shuttle the boat on you cartop? If the outfitter provides the shuttle, how much extra, if any, will that cost? What is the outfitter's policy on refunds due to rain or low or unsafe water conditions? Does the outfitter have a trip to match your level of ability? On guided trips, are the guides experienced and mature? Is the outfitter licensed by the state or certified by a trade association?

When asking such questions, it is also a good idea to confirm that the trips offered are exactly as listed here in the outfitter descriptions. The outfitter information in this book was supplied by the outfitters themselves via written questionnaires and should, therefore, be accurate. However, because schedules and offerings change, and because Starfish Press cannot independently confirm each listing's accuracy, it is a good idea to double check trips and services before making a booking.

After making these inquiries, you should be satisfied both with the answers themselves and with the manner of the person on the phone. I might add that, if your experiences are like mine, I expect you will be very pleased with the service of the outfitters you encounter. The outfitters I've patronized and the hundreds more that I have written and spoken to in preparing this book have been extremely helpful.

Safety

Many of the country's largest outfitters have had tens of thousands of paddlers run wild whitewater runs without a single drowning or serious injury. Nevertheless, there is always certain inherent risk in paddling, for which all participants must have a healthy respect.

The United States Coast Guard, the American Canoe Association (ACA), and the American Red Cross have developed excellent safety education books, films, and instructional programs. To learn more about safety, contact your local Coast Guard or Red Cross office, or write to the American Canoe Association to request a copy of the free flier *Welcome Paddler* (see the "Resources" section for the address and phone number).

The ACA offers another excellent primer on safety, a poster titled "River Canoeing," which cites these common causes of avoidable accidents: alcohol consumption, not wearing life jackets, insufficient skill, inability to "read" river conditions, paddling alone, poorly maintained equipment, inadequate flotation, no spare paddle, no first aid kit, improper dress, high water, cold water, dams, downed trees, undercut rocks, paddling a remote river, and changing river conditions.

To be a safe canoeist, it is essential that you learn to take the proper precautions to avoid unnecessary risk. In particular, you should never attempt more difficult rapids than you are comfortable with, unless accompanied by a skilled guide, instructor, or trip leader. If in doubt, take an easier trip.

As you may know, rapids are rated on an international scale of difficulty. These ratings, cited throughout this book, are as follows:

Class I: Moving water with a few riffles and small waves. Few or no obstacles.

Class II: Easy rapids with waves up to 3 feet and wide, clear channels that are obvious without scouting. Some maneuvering is required.

Class III: Rapids with high, irregular waves often capable of swamping an open canoe. Narrow passages that often require complex maneuvering. May require scouting from shore.

Class IV: Long, difficult rapids constricted passages that often require precise maneuvering in very turbulent waters. Scouting from shore is often necessary, and conditions make rescue difficult. Generally not possible for open canoes. Boaters in covered canoes and kayaks should have the ability to Eskimo roll.

Class V: Extremely difficult, long, very violent rapids with highly congested routes, which nearly always must be scouted from shore. Rescue conditions are difficult, and there is significant hazard to life in the event of a mishap. Ability to Eskimo roll is essential for boaters in kayaks and closed canoes.

Class VI: Difficulties of Class V carried to the extreme of navigability. Nearly impossible and very dangerous. For teams of experts only, after close study has been made and all precautions have been taken.

A final note on safety — heavy rain, storms, spring runoff, fallen trees, and other hazards can suddenly make waters treacherous. For that reason, you should always inquire about water and weather conditions before beginning any trip. This book, intended as a general guide, cannot possibly anticipate such hazards. Also, while every effort has been made to be make this book as accurate as possible, there may be typographical errors or errors in the information submitted to us by outfitters. As a result, the author and Starfish Press assume no liability for any loss or damage caused or alleged to have been caused by information in this book.

Conservation

Paddlers can take an enormous toll on rivers. Recognizing this risk, paddlers and outfitters increasingly adhere to the wilderness ethic of packing out trash, not cutting live trees for firewood, building fires in fire rings or not at all, avoiding glass beverage containers, and practicing catch-and-release fishing. Many outfitters also go a step further by sponsoring river clean-up days in which they supply canoes free to paddlers who agree to pick up trash along the river.

As you read this book and plan your trips, you can contribute to this effort by questioning outfitters whose trips you consider about what they do to protect the environment.

For our part, at Starfish Press, we have volunteered to donate 10 percent of our net profit from the sales of *Paddle America* to American Rivers, the country's foremost river conservation group.

American Rivers

Here is a brief statement from American Rivers describing the organization and its activities:

> American Rivers, a non-profit founded in 1973, is the nation's leading river conservation organization. Its mission is to "preserve and restore America's river systems and to foster a rivers stewardship ethic."
>
> America has more than 3.5 million miles of rivers, comprising more than 100,000 streams. Healthy river systems, however, are a finite and vanishing resource. The vast majority have been drained, dammed, channelized, over-developed, and/or choked with pollution. Many, if not most, of our rivers are in danger of losing their most basic natural features, capacities and ecological balance.
>
> The loss of natural rivers and the degradation of river systems in the U.S. has critical implications that go far beyond the

river courses that American Rivers seeks to protect. Rivers are at the heart of natural ecosystems; the free-flowing, wild character of a river is an indication that an entire ecosystem is healthy and is providing crucial habitat and "highways" for innumerable species — very probably including some which are threatened or endangered. Additionally, natural rivers are valuable for paddling and fishing opportunities, their floodplains, clean water, aesthetic beauty, and the personal replenishment which many seek in rivers.

Yet, many of the rivers that are being systematically destroyed through the nation's development policies constitute our most important water supplies, have enormously important recreation and aesthetic value, and provide irreplaceable habitat for plants, fish, and wildlife.

American Rivers protects rivers across the nation from numerous threats: ecologically destructive — and harmful — dams, water diversions, dredging, adverse development (including mining and clear-cutting along river banks), and pollution.

If you are interested in joining American Rivers or obtaining more information about a river in your area, contact American Rivers at (202) 547-6900, 801 Pennsylvania Ave., S.E., Suite 400, Washington, D.C. 20003.

The Outfitters Included in this Book

The outfitters in this book are ones who responded to a written questionnaire mailed to more than 2,200 outfitters across the country. We did not solicit or accept payment for these listings. If your outfitting company or a company you know of is not included, please send its name and address to us so we can include it in future editions. Please send these names plus any suggestions or corrections to Nick Shears, Starfish Press, P.O. Box 42467, Washington, DC 20015.

Paddle America

Alabama

Alabama is well-served by rivers offering varied paddling from lazy floating to Class V white water. They are spread out over the state, from the Appalachians to the plateaus, the Piedmont, and the Gulf Coast plain. You can take your choice of cold mountain streams and warm pastoral rivers, with scenery to match. But John H. Foshee, author of Alabama Canoe Rides and Float Trips (Univ. of Alabama Press), says there is unfortunately a dark side to the story. He writes that Alabama tends to "dam every piece of water that moves" and allows too much riverside development and pollution.

However, the fishing is good. State tourist brochures claim that Lake Eufaula on the Chattahoochee River is the Big Bass Capital of the world. Similarly, they boast that Weiss Lake on the Coosa River is the Crappie Capital of the world.

Alabama's most popular canoeing river is the Cahaba, which flows from Trussville, near Birmingham, to its confluence with the Alabama River near Selma. Ideal for one-day trips, it is broken up by bridges or fords into segments with easy access. The Cahaba's upper section, through rocky territory, gets very low in the summer except when heavy rains suddenly turn it into a torrent. But below Centerville, where it starts meandering across the plain, it is floatable all year round. The river is surprisingly undeveloped and is rich in water lilies and fish.

The Little Cahaba is described by Foshee as an "excellent training river." It offers outfitted trips of four, six, and ten miles, but paddlers should call ahead (205) 926-7382) to check water levels.

The Locust Fork of the Black Warrior River offers more of a challenge to whitewater buffs. Located in Blount County, north of Birmingham, this well-known stream has a seven-mile Class III run down to the covered bridge at Nectar. It takes the paddler through rolling, forested country and is runnable from late winter until June after heavy rain. But there is said to be a long-standing antagonism between river-runners and the local private landowners.

The Mulberry Fork of the Black Warrior, in the same Nectar-Garden City area, has an eight- to eleven-mile stretch with Class I-II rapids. It is an unspoiled river, with scenic bluffs and rock formations alternating with low hills and wooded banks. Again, this stream is only runnable in late winter and after spring rains. Some stretches can be quite hazardous at high water.

Also close to Birmingham is the Blackburn Fork, which flows down from Inland Lake on a ten-mile course to its confluence with Calvert Prong. It continues as the Blackburn Fork — alternatively dubbed Little Warrior River — to join the Locust Fork described above. The countryside is mostly forested and unspoiled, with bluffs and rock formations.

For the real adventurer, Little River Canyon in season is about as exciting as anyone could wish. This run, not far from Mobile, has a so-called Suicide Section on its upper reach just below Desoto Falls. Richard Penny, in his Whitewater Sourcebook (Menasha Ridge Press, Birmingham, AL), calls the name "slightly hysterical." But he rates it as Class V-VI and describes it as "totally aggro." Below the 2.5-mile Suicide Section comes a three-mile stretch rated Class IV-V followed by a six-mile Class III-IV run down to Canyon Mouth. The time to tackle the Little River Canyon is November to May.

Paddlers preferring safe and easy floats will enjoy the Escatawpa, which runs almost due south, wandering westward across the Mississippi state line as it heads for the Gulf. It displays a sharp contrast between its black water and its many sugar-white sandbars that are fine for picnics and camping. The Escatawpa offers slow flatland canoeing, with adequate water depth all year round. Much the same is true of the Mobile-Tensaw River Delta, one of the largest delta systems in the country. The scenery in this area is a mixture of hardwoods and bottom swamp, alive with white-tailed deer, otters, raccoons, and birds, including swallowtail kites. Bass, brim, and catfish are among the freshwater fish and many marine species that can be caught in the brackish waters upstream from Mobile Bay.

Sunshine Canoes
Bob Andrews
5460 Old Shell Road
Mobile, AL 36608
(205) 344-8664
Escatawpa River, Mobile Tensaw River Delta
Max. rapids: None
Sunshine Canoes offers guided trips by canoe and kayak on the Escatawpa and the Mobile-Tensaw River Delta. It also rents canoes and kayaks. River trips can cover up to fifty miles and last anywhere from three hours to five days. The Escatawpa is unspoiled, with no development of any kind along its banks. Its many sandbars offer innumerable opportunities for swimming, picnicking, and camping. During its season from May through September, Sunshine Canoes also provides lessons.

Alaska

Alaska is a wilderness canoeist's dream, with countless pristine canoe trails along ten thousand undammed rivers. Here paddlers can feel like explorers, traveling for days without seeing others. Outfitters offer rafts, canoes, and kayaks for trips on a score of waterways, many of which are accessible only by private airplane.

The Talkeetna is a favorite whitewater river. Tours on the river last up to six days and take stalwart rafters through the Sluice Box, a continuous Class IV rapid within a deep 14-mile canyon that is the the longest runnable rapid in North America. Adding to the thrills, floaters can view grizzly bears, wolves, moose, and caribou. They can also enjoy excellent fishing in this salmon spawning river. Although the Talkeetna lies not far north of Anchorage, floaters fly in aboard a small plane, viewing Mt. McKinley and other Alaska Range peaks on the way.

Most Alaskan rivers are remote, but the ultimate escape from civilization is to the arctic north. For there in the Arctic National Wildlife Refuge bordering the Beaufort Sea and Canada's Northern Territories is an 18-million acre wilderness that is home to some 180,000 caribou as well as Dall sheep, wolves, musk oxen, grizzlies, and numerous waterfowl and birds of prey. Some have compared the coastal plain to East Africa's Serengeti, and wildlife biologists call it the last intact arctic ecosystem in America. A 10-day raft trip on the Canning River takes adventurous paddlers past high mountains, foothills, ice fields, and down into the tundra where the river flows into the Arctic Ocean.

For white water in the same area, one outfitter offers 10-day trips on a river with the improbable name of Hulahula, which runs through the highest peaks of the Brooks Range. It offers Class I-III rapids as well as excellent wildlife viewing and fishing. At the right time of year paddlers may be rewarded by the spectacle of the caribou migration.

Comparatively short floatplane flights eastward from Anchorage take paddlers to Tazlina and Klutina Lakes, where two- or three-day trips begin on rivers of the same names. Both offer Class III rapids with good scenery, wildlife, and fishing. And the Eagle, Matanuska,

Lionshead, and Six-Mile Creek rivers provide one-day whitewater paddling within easy driving distance from Anchorage.

For a complete change, sea kayakers may explore Prince William Sound and the nearby Kenai Fjords National Park, with their glaciers, seals, sea otters, and whales.

The river-boating season is short — May through September. High-water usually reaches its peak in July and August when warm spells melt the glacial ice. August is usually Alaska's wettest month.

Rafting on the Kongakut River. Courtesy of ABEC, Fairbanks, Alaska.

ABEC's Alaska Adventures
Ramona Finoff
1304 Westwick Drive
Fairbanks, AK 99712
(907) 457-8907
Kongakut River, Hulahula River, Koyukuk River, Alatna River, Noatak River
Max. rapids: III-IV

ABEC's Alaska Adventures runs guided trips of seven to 13 days on the Kongakut, Hulahula, Koyukuk, Alatna, Moatak, and other rivers in the Brooks Range. These trips, through pristine wilderness in remote areas of Alaska, offer spectacular mountain scenery and a chance to observe caribou, bears, moose, wolves, foxes, and other tundra wildlife. Guests can fish for grayling, Dolly Varden, pike, and lake trout. Custom river trips and backpacking expeditions are also available.

For its trips, which run from June to September, ABEC requires that participants have camping experience and be in good health.

Adventures & Delights
Intec, Inc.
P.O. Box 21-0402PA
Anchorage, AK 99521
(907) 276-8282
*Prince William Sound, Kenai Fjords,
Resurrection Bay*
Max. rapids: None
TASK
Adventures & Delights offers
guided and unguided sea kayak tours
in Prince William Sound, Kenai Fjords
National Park, and Resurrection Bay.
On four-to-five-day trips, kayakers
can explore fjords where ice drops
from 300-foot-high tidal glaciers to
form icebergs where harbor seals
haul out and sea otters play. Other
wildlife to see include bears, eagles,
moose, wolves, and sea birds.

Trips also feature views of orange
and gray granite cliffs and seaside
waterfalls, camping on black-sand
beaches, and walks on glaciers and islands covered in wildflowers. These
tours are suitable for beginning and
experienced kayakers and are available between May and September.

Air Adventures
Mike McBride
P.O. Box 22
Kenai, AK 99611
(907) 776-5444, FAX (907) 776-5445
Cook Inlet, Bristol Bay
Max. rapids: III-IV
Air Adventures flies paddlers to
remote sites for outfitted and guided
river raft trips of one to seven days on
tributaries of Cook Inlet and the Bristol Bay region. Trips with Class I to V
rapids run through pristine wilderness with views of snow-capped
mountains, boreal forest, and abundant wildlife, including moose, bears,
caribou, sheep, goats, otters, beavers,
eagles, and other birds. These areas
also feature good fishing for trout,
char, grayling, and various species of
salmon.

The season for Air Adventures'
trips is May to October.

Alaska River Adventures
George Heim
1831 Kuskokwim Street
Suite 9
Anchorage, AK 99508
(907) 276-3418, (907) 595-1422
*Lake Greer, Talkeetna River, Copper
River*
Max. rapids: III-IV
Alaska Wilderness Guides Association
Alaska River Adventures offers
guided raft and kayak trips of one to
10 days on numerous rivers in the far
north, above the Arctic Circle; in Bristol Bay; and on the Talkeetna, Copper, and other rivers in southern
Alaska. Most trips are easy for participants in good health who enjoy
camping. A few trips are more
demanding.

The waters traveled are among the
most beautiful, fish-filled wild rivers
in the world. Fishing for salmon,
trout, char, grayling, lake trout, and
pike is particularly good. On these
trips, paddlers can also enjoy the
varied terrain, ranging from arctic
desert to spectacular mountains, and
the remarkably abundant wildlife,
which includes moose, bears,
caribou, eagles, and wolves.

Alaska Whitewater
Mary Matisinez
P.O. Box 142294
Anchorage, AK 99514
(907) 337-RAFT
*Eagle River, Tonsina River, Klutina
River, Tazlina River, Copper River,
Talkeetna River*
Max. rapids: III-IV
Alaska Whitewater runs one- to 14-
day guided raft trips on six pristine
glacier rivers amid snow-capped
mountains, glaciers, and tundra with
"no dams, no houses, and no
bridges." Guests can also view

5

moose, caribou, bears, eagles, wolves, and other wildlife.

Trips run between May and October and range in difficulty from easy flat-water scenic floats to Class III-IV whitewater. Most trips are by paddle rafts, but oar boats are available too.

Alaska Whitewater also offers generous provisions beyond the usual life jackets and paddles, including wet suits, dry bags, booties, rainjackets, extra wool gear, and tents.

Colorado River and Trail Expeditions
Vicki and David Mackay
5058 S. 300 West
Salt Lake City, UT 84107
(801) 261-1789
Colorado River, Green River, Glacier Bay
Max. rapids: III-IV

Colorado River & Trail Expeditions runs guided raft trips of five to 12 days on the Colorado River in Utah and Arizona, the Green River in Utah, and Glacier Bay and the Arctic National Wildlife Refuge in Alaska. These trips offer excellent whitewater and magnificent scenery in remote locations. Their difficulty varies with the river and season. Generally, all trips are fine for people in good health and good physical condition.

During its May-September season, Colorado River & Trails also offers educational trips, which study photography, history, natural history or ecology.

Denali Floats
Tom Waite
Box 330
Talkeetna, AK 99676
(907) 733-2384
Susitna River, Chulitna River, Talkeetna River
Max. rapids: III-IV

Denali Floats runs one- to 10-day guided raft trips on three Alaskan rivers between June and September. Trips are suitable for all skill levels and offer beautiful views of Mt. McKinley, excellent fishing, and a chance to spot moose, bears, beavers, and eagles. Fishing is for salmon and trout.

Rafting on the Nenana River. Courtesy of Nate Mullins, Denali Raft Adventures, Inc., Denali National Park, Alaska.

Denali Raft Adventures
James Raisis
Drawer 190
Denali National Park, AK 99755
(907) 683-2234
Nenana River
Max. rapids: III-IV
Denali Raft Adventures offers exciting guided raft trips on the glacier-fed Nenana River in Denali National Park. Trips range in length from two to six hours with a scenic trip good for adults and children ages 5 and older, and whitewater trips for those 12 and older.

The season is from mid-May to mid-September, with good wildlife viewing for moose, caribou, Dall sheep, and grizzly bears.

Denali West Lodge
Jack and Sherri Hayden
Box 12
Lake Minchumina, AK 99757
(909) 733-2630
Nowitna River, Kantishna River system
Max. rapids: None
Alaska Wilderness Guides Association
Denali West Lodge runs canoe trips on remote wilderness rivers in Alaska's vast interior. Set on the western edge of Denali National Park and Preserve, the lodge is more than 100 miles from the nearest highway and is accessible only by seaplane or boat.

Guests at the lodge stay in private log cabins and are free to hike or canoe around Lake Minchumina alone or with guides. Available, too, are "flightseeing" tours of Denali with an afternoon of fishing and canoeing on an alpine lake; a canoe trip on the Nowitna River in the Nowitna Wild-

A 35-lb. king salmon caught on the Deshka River. Courtesy of Ouzel Expeditions, Anchorage, Alaska.

7

life Refuge; and trekking through Mystic Pass in the Alaska Range.

Denali West Lodge accommodates only six guests at a time. Its two owners, residents of the Alaska bush for 18 years, have backgrounds in gold mining and dog-sled racing, and have logged thousands of hours of bush flying. With this experience and extensive knowledge of Alaskan wildlife and wilderness, Jack and Sherri Hayden can design an adventure trip to match any guest's interests.

Eagle River Raft Trips
Donna Robinson
P.O. Box 142294
Anchorage, AK 99514
(907) 337-7238
Eagle River
Max. rapids: III-IV
Eagle River runs one- to two-day guided raft trips between May and October. Offering both flat-water and whitewater trips on the Eagle River, the outfitter can treat paddlers "age 8 to 100" to panoramic mountain scenery and views of moose, eagles, and bears. Fishing is for trout and salmon.

Eagle River Raft Trips supplies wet suits, booties, rain jackets, and extra wool gear if necessary. Located just 15 minutes from Anchorage, the outfitter offers free pickup at the Anchorage airport.

Gary King's Alaskan Experience
Gary King
202 E. Northern Lights Blvd.
Anchorage, AK 99502
(907) 276-5425, (800) 777-7055
Rivers throughout Alaska
Max. rapids: III-V
Gary King's Alaskan Experience is a travel agency that books one- to 10-day kayak and raft trips throughout Alaska. Claiming the distinction of being the largest booking agency for outdoor travel in Alaska, Alaskan Ex-

perience offers trips with dozens of outfitters for paddler of all skill levels. Trips run on remote, pristine streams and rivers known for fine salmon fishing and chances to spot moose, caribou, and bears.

Trips booked by Alaskan Experience are available between June and September. The agency writes: "We take the risk out of selecting your Alaskan outfitter as we are in Alaska and know firsthand the outfitters whose trips we sell."

Glacier Bay Sea Kayaks
Bonnie Kaden
P.O. Box 26
Gustavius, AK 99826
(907) 697-2257
Glacier Bay
Max. rapids: None
Glacier Bay Sea Kayaks offers two- to 10-day unguided kayak trips for paddlers wanting to explore the tidewater glaciers and pristine wilderness of Glacier Bay in Glacier Bay National Park.

The outfitter recommends its trips for novice and experienced kayakers alike, reporting a perfect safety record in 12 years of operation. The company does recommend, however, that paddlers on its trips be experienced campers.

Trips run between May 15 and September 15 and offer chances to spot humpback whales, Orcas, brown and black bears, and several species of sea birds.

Hawk, I'm Your Sister
Beverly Antaeus
P.O. Box 9109
Santa Fe, NM 87504
(505) 984-2268
Tatshenshini River
Max. rapids: III-IV
Hawk, I'm Your Sister of Santa Fe
specializes in women's wilderness
canoe and raft trips. Its year-round
program is geared to "women of all
ages, shapes, sizes and skill levels"
with guided trips in five states and
four foreign locations. Its aim is to
"teach you the language of the
forests, canyons, deserts and waterways" in a safe and non-competitive
environment. It takes paddlers on the
Abiquiu Lake in New Mexico and on
the Rio Grande in Texas, with other
excursions as far afield as Alaska,
Peru, and China.

Jacques Adventure Company
Jerry Jacques
4316 Kingston Drive
Anchorage, AK 99504
(907) 337-9604
Talkeetna River
Max. rapids: III-IV
Jacques Adventure Company offers a variety of guided oar-boat and
paddle-boat trips. These include half-
day raft trips in Denali Park near Mt.
McKinley; one-day trips on the wild
Six-Mile Creek; three- and six-day
trips on the Talkeetna River; and 12-
day trips on the Copper River starting
at the ghost town of McCarthy.

The outfitter also offers custom
river trips in Alaska, fishing trips of
one to 10 days, and natural history
and river trips in the Magadan and
Siberia regions of the former Soviet
Union. Trips, which run between
June and August, range in difficulty
and are suitable for guests age 12 and
older.

Keystone Raft & Kayak Adventures
Mike Buck
P.O. Box 1486
Valdez, AK 99686
(907) 835-2606
Lowe River, Tonsina River, Talkeetna River, Kennecott RIver, Nizina River, Chitina River, Copper River, Tatshenshini River
Max. rapids: V+
Alaska Wilderness Guides
Keystone Raft & Kayak Adven-
tures offers guided and unguided
kayak and raft trips through pristine
Alaskan wilderness. One of the most
spectacular and exciting river runs is
on the Lowe River through Keystone
Canyon. A popular day adventure,
with Class III-IV rapids, is a Tonsina
River trip. For action-packed white
water and excellent fishing, Talkeetna River trips are exceptional. And
Chitina and Cooper River trips in the
Wrangell Mountains offer beautiful
mountain and glacier scenery, plus a
chance to explore ghost towns. Finally, Tatshenshini River offers breathtaking tundra and glacier scenery with
giant icebergs and abundant wildlife.
Trips range from very easy to very
demanding. Among the wildlife to
see are bears, eagles, goats, sheep,
and moose. Fishing for salmon, trout,
and grayling is excellent. Trips run
from May to September.

Nichols Expedition
Chuck and Judy Nichols
497 North Main
Moab, UT 84532
(801) 259-7882
Copper River, Koyukuk River, Green River, Main Salmon River
Max. rapids: III-IV
Utah Guides and Outfitters, Idaho Guides and Outfitters
Nichols Expeditions runs guided
kayak and raft trips on the Copper
and Koyukuk Rivers in Alaska, rafting

9

trips on Idaho's Main Salmon, and "wilderness quest" workshop tours on Utah's Green River. The Alaska trips run through remote, pristine wilderness and offer many chances to see caribou, Dall sheep, moose, bears, sea eagles, harbor seals, and other wildlife. Lasting 8-15 days, these paddle raft tours are fine for beginners in good shape. They range through a region of glaciers, waterfalls, and nameless peaks. Guests can also enjoy excellent food and exciting fishing for salmon, char, arctic grayling, and northern pike.

Operating year-round, Nichols Expeditions also offers sea kayaking on the Sea of Cortez and Magdalena Bay in Baja, Mexico, as well as trekking in Thailand and the former Soviet Union.

Nova Riverrunners Inc.
Chuck Spaulding and Jay Doyle
P.O. Box 1129
Chickaloon, AK 99674
(907) 745-5753
Rivers throughout Alaska
Max. rapids: V+
National Forest Recreation Association

NOVA Riverrunners offers kayak rentals and guided kayak and raft trips on wilderness rivers throughout Alaska. Its easiest trip is a one-day float in an oar boat just a one-and-a-half hour drive from Anchorage in the Chugach and Talkeetna Mountains. At the other extreme is the Class V+ Six-Mile Creek paddle-boat run for which paddlers must pass a tough whitewater test to confirm their ability to handle the rigors of the trip.

Other offerings between May and October include a 27-mile trip along the edge of Matanuska Glacier and a three-day trip to remote Salmon Spring River, which offers great fishing and an abundance of bears. Other wildlife to be seen include moose, caribou, bison, beavers, and eagles.

Watching caribou along the Noatak River. Courtesy of ABEC, Fairbanks, Alaska.

Ouzel Expeditions, Inc.
Paul and Sharon Allred
7540 E. 20th Avenue
Anchorage, AK 99504
(907) 338-0620
Upper Cook Inlet, Bristol Bay
Max. rapids: I-II
Ouzel Expeditions runs guided raft trips on 26 scenic rivers in Alaska. Trips of six to eight days are generally by oar boat on Class I and II rivers, offering excellent opportunities to enjoy the wild scenery, fishing, and views of grizzly bears, caribou, and moose.

Especially proud of its fishing expeditions, Ouzel flies its guests to Alaska's interior to enjoy wilderness fishing for rainbow trout, Dolly Varden, arctic grayling, northern pike, and king, sockeye, silver, calico, and pink salmon. Ouzel Expeditions uses only debarbed single hooks and maintains a catch-and-release policy on all rivers. Guests may, however, keep two king salmon or three other salmon during the course of a trip

Ouzel's season runs from June to September.

Quest Expeditions
Paul Jackson
4651 Reka #11
Anchorage, AK 99508
(907) 333-7703
Canning River, Hulahula River, Sheenjek River, Franklin Creek, Kobuk River, Nigu-Killick-Colville Rivers, Naotak River
Max. rapids: III-IV
Quest Expeditions runs adventurous, expedition-style trips of five to 14 days in Alaska's Arctic National Wildlife Refuge (ANWR). The ANWR is the calving grounds of a herd of 180,000 "Porcupine" caribou and home to Dall sheep, wolves, musk oxen, grizzly bears, nesting waterfowl, shore birds, and raptors. Trips in this 18-million-acre wilderness

pass through high mountains, foothills, and coastal plains, offering beginning or moderate white water, fine fishing, and stunning views of wildflowers, ice fields, and abundant wildlife. Trips are also run in the Gates of the Arctic and Kobuk Valley National Parks, and the Noatak Preserve.

Most trips are of moderate difficulty, in authentic expedition style, requiring guests to paddle and otherwise pitch in. Easy river trips and cabin rentals on remote lakes are also available.

The National Outdoor Leadership School
Nancy Siegel
River Manager
Box AA
Lander, WY 82520
(307) 332-6973
Prince William Sound, other Alaskan waters, Green River
Max. rapids: IV
America Outdoors, Colorado River Outfitters Association, Utah Guides and Outfitters Organization
The National Outdoor Leadership School specializes in teaching a wide array of backcountry skills including kayaking, rafting, mountaineering, rock climbing, glacier travel, backpacking, and cross-country skiing. Its rafting trips run through Desolation Canyon on the Green River in Utah and Lodore Canyon on the Green River at the Colorado-Utah border. NOLS also offers sea kayaking in Alaska and Baja, Mexico. These instructional trips range in length from 14-31 days, with some trips geared for teenagers 16 and older and some for paddlers 25 and older. All trips are physically challenging; paddlers must be in good shape and excellent health.

These trips, which run between June and late October, feature beautiful scenery and sufficient challenge to ensure that all participants can test and improve their paddling skills.

Spirit Walker Expeditions
Nathan Borson
Box 240PA
Gustavus, AK 99826
(907) 697-2266, (800) 478-9255 (AK)
Icy Strait, Gulf of Alaska
Max. rapids: None
 Spirit Walker Expeditions offers guided sea-kayak trips of one to seven days on Icy Strait, the Gulf of Alaska, and numerous smaller bays and inlets. Paddlers pass along wild, rocky coasts, through narrow inlets among the islands of the inside passage, and over colorful reefs inhabited by starfish, sea anemones, and crabs. Travel by kayak permits silent approaches to view seals, sea lions, river otters, whales, deer, and bears. Trips also feature fresh, gourmet meals; fishing for salmon, trout, and halibut; and comfortable camp sites on wilderness beaches or amid spruce or hemlock forests.
 Trips run from May to October and are of little to moderate difficulty, suitable for anyone fit enough to walk a few miles.

Wapiti River Guides
Gary Lane
Box 1125
Riggins, ID 83549
(208) 628-3523, (800) 488-9872
Rivers throughout Alaska, Grande Ronde River, Owyhee River, Salmon River
Max. rapids: V+
Oregon Guides and Packers Association, Idaho Outfitters and Guides Association
 Wapiti River Guides, with trips in Idaho, Oregon, and Alaska, specializes in small personalized trips of moderate difficulty "for ages 3 to 103, families, and nature lovers." The outfitter's trips are distinctive, too, for their guides' emphasis on natural history and Native American culture, and for the fine scenery.
 Trips, ranging in length from one to 12 days, also allow time for interesting side hikes and viewing elk, deer, bald eagles, bobcats, cougars, bears, bighorn sheep, minks and other wildlife. Fishing is for steelhead, trout, and bass.

Wilderness: Alaska/Mexico
Ron Yarnell
1231 Sundance Loop
Fairbanks, AK 99709
(907) 479-8203
Noatak River, Hulahula River, Kongakut River, Koyukuk River, Alatna River, Kobuk River, Killik River, Jago River, Sheenjek River
Max. rapids: III-IV
Alaska Wilderness Guides Association
 Wilderness Alaska/Mexico offers guided trips of eight to 12 days in Alaska, Mexico, and Belize. The Alaska trips run on the Noatak, Hulahula, Kongakut, Koyukuk, Alatna, Kobuk, Killik, Jago, and Sheenjek Rivers between June and September. Highlights of these trips include the arctic light, midnight sun, and the abundant tundra wildlife, including caribou,

grizzly bears, musk oxen, wolves, Dall sheep, moose, and foxes. Paddlers also can fish for arctic char, grayling, lake trout, sheefish, and salmon. Most river trips are open to beginners; some require previous rafting experience.

From December to April, the company offers trips in Mexico and Belize, exploring jungle, Mayan ruins, and coral reefs.

Arizona

To many people, boaters and landlubbers alike, mention of rafting American rivers immediately conjures up the image of the Grand Canyon. No wonder, for this awesome chasm rivals Mount Everest among the world's greatest natural wonders, and the ideal way to explore it is by raft or kayak. Words hardly do the Grand Canyon justice. But Major John Wesley Powell, who made the first documented runs of the canyon in 1869-72, came close when he called its billion-year-old cliffs "the library of the gods" whose colorful strata formed the leaves of "one great book." Paddlers and trail riders can read this open book of geology at close range as they explore the 217-mile-long canyon with its mile-high walls. It is a place to linger, to contemplate the gigantic cross-section of the earth's crust laid bare by the Colorado River, to touch rocks more than 1,500,000,000 years old. Sightseers crowding the canyon rim far above can admire the spectacle from afar. But they cannot handle these primeval rocks or search the valley for sights of fossils.

Commercial floating through the canyon began in 1938, aboard rudimentary wooden boats very different from today's rafts and kayaks. Now it has become big business, to the point where paddlers who do not join an outfitted trip have to wait years for a permit to navigate on their own. Its rapids can be scary — up to Class V+ — and even the best kayakers sometimes overturn in heavy waves. They find the water extremely cold, sometimes less than fifty degrees at the Lees Ferry put-in close to the Utah state line. It has been aptly said that the Grand Canyon is one of the few places on earth where one may suffer heat prostration and hypothermia within a single ten-minute period. (Summer air temperatures may exceed 100 degrees.)

All kinds of pontoons are available, from small oar-powered and paddle rafts to huge motorized craft that carry 20 passengers on cushioned seats. Regardless, guides typically cook lavish meals for clients to eat at campsite tables. Bedrolls or foam rubber sleeping pads are provided for added comfort. Some outfitters helicopter people in and out of the canyon. Purists resent these intrusions on the peace and quiet of what remains of the wilderness. Many outfitters refuse to join the motorized contingent. One makes a point of stressing in his brochure: "All our trips are oar-powered. Given a choice, we think you would prefer the sounds of the canyon and the river, not the sound of a motor." But the canyon is so huge that its majesty can still overwhelm the visitor, especially at sunset as the motors fall silent, the rocks change color, and the campfires crackle.

Since completion of the Glen Canyon Dam in 1964, the natural flow of warm and muddy water through the world's biggest gorge has changed to a cold, crystal-clear river with a steadier flow. The Colorado can be floated as well in April or October as in midsummer. People who want to walk into the many beautiful side canyons and look for wildlife such as bighorn sheep should try to pick the cooler months of spring and fall.

Obviously the Grand Canyon with its 200 rapids is Arizona's star attraction, but despite its lack of rainfall the state is not without a supporting cast of minor rivers. Close to Phoenix, raft trips are offered down the Gila, Salt, and Verde Rivers with modest Class I-II rapids. These year-round scenic tours introduce rafters to the Sonoran Desert. They also provide memorable views of tall cliffs, cactus, mesquite groves, and wildlife including bald eagles and wild horses.

Adventures West, Inc.
P.O. Box 9429
Phoenix, AZ 85024
(602) 493-1558, (800) 828-9378
Colorado River
Max. rapids: V+
Adventures West runs guided three- to eight-day oar-boat trips in the Grand Canyon between May and September. Trips feature the natural wonders of the Grand Canyon and some of the largest white water in North America. The wild ride is exciting but suitable for guests age 12 and older.

Adventures West prides itself on experience, the safety of its trips, and the quality of its meals and guides. Wildlife to see include bighorn sheep and hawks. Fishing is for trout, chubb, and carp.

American River Touring Association
Star Route 73
Groveland, CA 95321
(800) 323-2782, (209) 962-7873
Colorado River, Middle Fork and Main Salmon Rivers, Selway River, Merced River, Tuolumne River, Klamath River, Rogue River, Illinois River, Umpqua River, Green River, Yampa River
Max. rapids: IV
America Outdoors, Oregon Guides and Packers, Idaho Outfitters and Guides, Utah Guides and Outfitters
ARTA offers a total of 16 raft trips in five Western states. The trips, in California, Oregon, Utah, Idaho, and Arizona, are by oar rafts, paddle rafts, oar/paddle combination rafts, and inflatable canoes.

15

Grand Canyon. Courtesy of Expeditions, Inc., Flagstaff, Arizona.

Most trips are of Class III difficulty and appropriate for novices and families, as well as those with more experience. Other trips of up to V+ difficulty challenge even the most advanced paddler. Depending on the location, the trips feature such added attractions as wildflowers, side streams, swimming holes, Indian ruins, warm water, abundant wildlife, good hiking and fishing, and hot springs.

ARTA, a non-profit company, also offers whitewater schools, professional guide training, and family discounts.

Arizona Raft Adventures
Robert Elliott
4050 E. Huntington Drive
Department P
Flagstaff, AZ 86004
(800) 786-7238
San Jose River
Max. rapids: II-III

Arizona Raft Adventures runs guided raft trips of six to 14 days on the Colorado River through the Grand Canyon, offering tremendous scenery, fishing, hiking, and white water. These expeditions are not difficult unless guests opt for the six-day canyon trip, which includes a strenuous seven-and-a-half mile hike and requires good physical conditioning. Guests can also control the degree of difficulty by the type of boat they select. Oar boats, motor boats, paddle boats, and paddle/oar combination boats are available.

Grand Canyon. Courtesy of Western River Expeditions, Salt Lake City, Utah.

On all trips, guests can also enjoy side hikes, pristine campsites, and spotting ringtail cats, bighorn sheep, mule deer, birds, and other wildlife. Trips run from April to October.

Arizona Raft Adventures also offers trips operated by other outfitters in Idaho, Utah, and Costa Rica.

Arizona River Runners

Bruce Winter
P.O. Box 47788
Phoenix, AZ 85068
(602) 867-4866, (800) 477-7238
Colorado River
Max. rapids: V+
America Outdoors

Arizona River Runners runs guided six- to eight-day oar-boat trips in the Grand Canyon from May to September. As guides do the rowing, trips are not strenuous and are fine for children as young as eight. Guests are

free to enjoy the beauty of the Grand Canyon's "billions of years of rock formations," and view various birds and perhaps bighorn sheep.

Arizona River Runners has been in business for more than 20 years and its guides have all been with the company for more than five seasons.

Canyoneers, Inc.

Gaylord and Joy Stavely
Box 2997
Flagstaff, AZ 86003
(602) 526-0924, (800) 525-0924 (outside AZ)
Colorado River
Max. rapids: V+
America Outdoors, National Forest Recreation Association, Grand Canyon River Guides

Canyoneers runs two- to 14-day guided trips in the Grand Canyon in pontoon rowboats and pontoon motorboats. Rowing boats carry four to six passengers and offer an exciting, wet ride, while motorboats are more comfortable, with individual, cushioned seats. Trips by either craft are suitable for guests in general good health.

Trips, which run between April and September, are led by knowledgeable guides and allow ample time for fishing and hiking in side canyons.

Cimarron Adventures and River Company

Denny Carr, Jon Colby, Dave Insley
7714 East Catalina
Scottsdale, AZ 85251
(602) 994-1199
Verde River, Salt River, Gila River
Max. rapids: I-II
America Outdoors

Cimarron Adventure and River Company runs guided raft trips on scenic rivers in the Sororan desert. Trips range in length from one to three days, offering excellent birdwatching and wildlife observation and views of towering cliffs, seigneur cactus, and mesquite groves in a unique desert landscape. Among the wildlife to be seen are eagles, coyotes, wild horses, and desert bighorn sheep.

Cimarron also offers night rafting, combined jeep/raft trips, executive fishing trips, paddle/saddle trips, and hiking tours in the Camelback and Superstitious Mountains.

Colorado River and Trail Expeditions
Vicki and David Mackay
5058 S. 300 West
Salt Lake City, UT 84107
(801) 261-1789
Colorado River, Green River, Glacier Bay
Max. rapids: III-IV
Colorado River & Trail Expeditions runs guided raft trips of five to 12 days on the Colorado River in Utah and Arizona, the Green River in Utah, and Glacier Bay and the Arctic National Wildlife Refuge in Alaska. These trips offer excellent whitewater and magnificent scenery in remote locations. Their difficulty varies with the river and season. Generally, all trips are fine for people in good health and good physical condition.

During its May-September season, Colorado River & Trails also offers educational trips, which study photography, history, natural history or ecology.

Expeditions, Inc.
Dick and Susie McCallum
Rt. 4, Box 755
Flagstaff, AZ 86001
(602) 744-8176, (602) 779-3769
Colorado River
Max. rapids: V+
Expeditions Inc., a family-run business, offers five- to 16-day trips on the Colorado River through the Grand Canyon. Guided trips are by canoe, kayak, or raft and offer ample time each day to hike, explore side canyons, and swim. On guided tours, guests can choose between oar-powered boats and paddle boats.

Expeditions Inc. also offers kayak rentals and can supply a support boat for running kayaks through the Grand Canyon. Both "kayak-support" and rafting trips includes complete camping equipment and meals.

Scenery is spectacular, with Class V rapids. All trips start and finish in the Grand Canyon. Guests can also enjoy fishing for trout and viewing bighorn sheep, coyotes, and foxes.

Grand Canyon Expeditions Company
Michael R. Denoyer
P.O. Box O
Kanab, UT 84741
(801) 644-2691, (800) 544-2691
Colorado River
Max. rapids: V+
Grand Canyon Expeditions runs guided raft and dory trips through the Grand Canyon on the Colorado River. Trips last eight days by motorized raft or 14 by oar boat. These expeditions begin and end in Las Vegas, with bus service to and from the Grand Canyon. The company provides gourmet meals and makes all other arrangements, leaving guests free to enjoy the Canyon's scenic and geological wonders. Guests can spot mule deer, bighorn sheep, and other wildlife; fish for rainbow, brook, and cutthroat trout, and hike in side canyons. In addition, special history, archaeology, astronomy, geology, photography, and ecology trips are available.

Grand Canyon Expeditions' trips, suitable for anyone aged eight or older, run between April and September.

Grand Canyon. Courtesy of Ron Smith, Grand Canyon Expeditions.

James Henry River Journeys
James Katz
P.O. Box 807
Bolinas, CA 94924
(415) 868-1836, (800) 786-1830
Colorado River, Salmon River, Rogue River, Tatshenshini-Alsek Rivers, Noatak River, Stanislaus River, Carson River, Klamath River
Max. rapids: III-IV
Idaho Outfitters and Guides
James Henry River Journeys runs guided canoe, kayak, and raft trips in California, Arizona, Idaho, Oregon, and Alaska. In California, the outfitter offers trips with Class II-III rapids, of one to three days, on the Stanislaus, East Fork of the Carson, and the Lower Klamath. In Arizona, the company runs Grand Canyon trips, with Class IV+ rapids, of 6, 8, 9, 13, and 14 days. Trips in Idaho, of 4, 5 or 6 days, run on the Class III-IV Main Salmon.

In Oregon, trips of 3, 4, and 5 days run on the Class III Rogue. Finally, in Alaska the company offers a natural history expedition on the Tatshenshini-Alsels Rivers.

Many special-interest trips are also available. These include Salmon River Bluegrass, Country, Folk, and Cajun Music Trips; Whitewater Workshops; Organizational Development and Teambuilding; Wine Tasting and Gourmet Cuisine; Lodge Trips on the Rogue and Salmon; Rogue and Salmon Natural History Trips; Alaska Nature Photography; and Alaska Wilderness Literature.

All trips run through especially scenic wilderness areas and are carefully planned to move at a leisurely pace, allowing ample time for side hikes, fishing, photography, and general relaxation. As a result, participation is open to anyone active and in good health. The company's season runs from May to September.

Laughing Heart Adventures
Dezh Pagen
Trinity Outdoor Center
P.O. Box 669
Willow Creek, CA 95573
(916) 629-3516, (800) 541-1256
Colorado River, Green River, Trinity River, Klamath River, Eel River, Sacramento River, Smith River, Russian River
Max. rapids: III-IV
NACLO, ACA
Laughing Heart Adventures offers "consciousness raising" canoe outings on wild and scenic rivers throughout the West and Mexico. Before trips start, guides interpret the geology and natural and human history of an area. Guides also gear some special trips toward specific goals such as stress reduction, holistic health, music and art appreciation, college credit, and environmental politics.

Laughing Heart's guided trips are by canoe, kayak, or raft. Rentals of canoes, kayaks, rafts, and tubes also are available. Trips run from one to seven days year-round. Kayak and canoe lessons and trips are available for paddlers of all skill levels.

Moki Mac River Expeditions, Inc.
Richard, Clair and Robert Quist
P.O. Box 21242
Salt Lake City, UT 84121
(801) 268-6667, (800) 284-7280
Colorado River, Green River
Max. rapids: V+
Utah Guides and Outfitters, NACLO

Moki Mac River Expeditions runs guided canoe, raft and "funyak" trips of 1-14 days on the Colorado and Green Rivers. Runs on the Colorado go through the Westwater, Cataract, and Grand Canyons, and on the Green River through the Desolation, Labyrinth, and Stillwater Canyons. Oar boats are available on all runs; motorized boats are available in Cataract Canyon and the Grand Canyon; and oar-boat/funyak trips run through Desolation Canyon. The Grand Canyon has the largest, most frequent rapids, Desolation Canyon is milder, and Cataract Canyon offers great excitement during the high-water runoff season.

Moki Mac also rents canoes for trips through the Labyrinth and Stillwater Canyons. All trips, set on the Colorado Plateau, offer chances to spot eagles, cranes, Canada geese, bighorn sheep and the occasional bear. Guests can also fish for catfish and trout. Moki Mac's season is from April to October.

Outdoors Unlimited
John Vail
6900 Townsend Winona Road
Flagstaff, AZ 86004
(602) 526-4546, (800) 637-RAFT
Colorado River
Max. rapids: V+

Outdoors Unlimited runs guided kayak and raft trips of five to 12 days on the Colorado River through the Grand Canyon. Twelve-day trips traverse the entire length of the Grand Canyon, while five- and eight-day trips run on either upper or lower sections. These partial trips begin deep in the heart of the canyon, requiring a strenuous nine-mile hike with a 5,000-foot change in altitude. Trips are either in five-person oar boats or six- or seven-person paddle boats.

All trips offer Class V rapids, spectacular scenery, and a chance to view bighorn sheep and other wildlife. Outdoors Unlimited's season is from May to October.

Western River Expeditions
Larry Lake
7258 Racquet Club Drive
Salt Lake City, UT 84121
(801) 942-6669, (800) 453-7450 (outside UT)
Colorado River, Green River, Main Salmon River
Max. rapids: III-IV
America Outdoors

Western River Expeditions runs guided raft trips and rents rafts and inflatable kayaks on the Colorado River in Colorado, Utah, and Arizona; the Green River in Utah; and the Main Salmon in Idaho. Green River trips, by oar or paddle raft, provide thrilling whitewater and views of towering red rock cliffs and arches, deep gorges, frontier cabins, and Indian petroglyphs. Colorado River tours offer spectacular scenery in Cataract Canyon, Westwater Canyon, and the upper and lower Grand Canyon. Rapids are moderate to large, and paddlers can swim, take side hikes, and view historic Indian and Old West sites. Finally, trips on the Main Salmon involve scenic blue-green waters, pine-covered mountains, stops at hot springs and abandoned mining camps, and camping on whitesand beaches. All trips are suitable for anyone in good health above the minimum age set for each trip. During Western River's March-September season, some trips can be combined with a ranch stay.

Whitewater Voyages
William McGinnis
P.O. Box 20400
El Sobrante, CA 94820-0400
(510) 222-5994, (800) 488-RAFT
Colorado River, Kern River, Merced River, Tuolumne River, Cache Creek, American River, Yuba River, Klamath River, Stanislaus River, Trinity River, Middle Fork Salmon River, Rogue River
Max. rapids: III-IV
America Outdoors, American River Recreation Association

Whitewater Voyages offers an extensive array of trips, with guided oar- and paddle-boat runs in California, Arizona, Oregon, and Idaho. Trips by kayak and raft range in length from one to five days and in difficulty from Class II to Class V. With runs on nine Wild and Scenic Rivers and on more California rivers than any other outfitter, Whitewater Voyages has trips for paddlers of all level of experience.

The outfitter also has specialty trips, including whitewater schools, family trips, low-cost river-cleanup trips, "teambuilding" trips and excursions in the former Soviet Union to paddle with Russians as part of project R.A.F.T.

21

Arkansas

Many of Arkansas' 9,000 miles of streams are great for floating by canoe, raft, or johnboat. The state helps paddlers by putting out a "floater's kit" describing 17 favorite waterways with maps, access points, preferred seasons, fishing, and scenery on each river, along with an outfitters' directory. Copies of this handy guide are available from the Arkansas Department of Parks and Tourism, 1 Capitol Mall, Little Rock, AR 72201.

Big Piney Creek is a classic Ozark stream. Only 67 miles long, it rises in the Ozark National Forest and offers both wild and calm water as it heads for its confluence with the Arkansas River at Lake Dardanelle. Along one 10-mile stretch, from Treat to Long Pool, its rapids boast such names as Roller Coaster, Surfing Hole and, ominously, Cascades of Extinction. The canoe season begins in late fall and can run until mid-June if the month is rainy. Along the creek's steep wooded hillsides, paddlers may spot deer, turkeys, and even black bears. Fishing for smallmouth bass is best in late spring or early summer.

For good family floating, the Caddo River in west central Arkansas is hard to beat. Originating in the Ouachita Mountains, the Caddo provides good pastoral scenery, excellent fishing, and peaceful waters with occasional Class I-II rapids.

Famous for its trout fishing is the White River, a 720-mile stream that follows a circuitous course, like a giant questionmark, from northwestern Arkansas to the Mississippi on the state's southeastern border. Its best-known section is just below Bull Shoals Dam, where cold water from deep in the lake is discharged at the right temperature for rainbow, brown, and cutthroat trout. Arkansas stocks the stream generously, and the resulting great fishing draws thousands of anglers every year. Some brown trout reach world-record size of 33 lb. or more. Above Bull Shoals Dam the river can only be floated from October-May. But below the dam it is good for year-round paddling and can be very swift when all the turbines are running.

Crooked Creek and the Buffalo River, both tributaries of the White River, are well worth exploring. Crooked Creek has deep pools, fast chutes, and clear water. The Buffalo, with nearly 95,000 acres of public land along its 150 miles, has superb scenery and great fishing. For white water, the Mulberry River is exciting in early spring, when its Class II-III rapids are at their height. Then it becomes an easy float until mid-June. From then on, as the floater's kit puts it, the best floating is "on an air mattress at one of the local swimming holes." At that point, paddlers should head for the Spring River in northcentral Arkansas, floatable year-round because of its massive inflow of cool water from Mammoth Spring. The river offers great trout fishing below Dam No. 3 and its South Fork is known for bass, catfish, and walleye. Call the Corps of Engineers at 501-324-5150 for information on river levels.

Arrowhead Cabin and Canoe Rentals, Inc.
John Carter and Philip Ward
209 E. Portia Terrace
Hot Springs National Park, AR 71913
(501) 767-5326
Caddo River, Little Missouri River, Cossatot River
Max. rapids: I-II
Arrowhead Cabin & Canoe Rentals, set in the Ouachita National Forest, offers canoe trips with long Class I-II rapids and only short and infrequent pools. Unguided one- to two-day trips run on the crystal-clear Caddo River, which has a rocky bottom and excellent fishing for smallmouth bass, catfish, Kentucky bass, and sunfish. Sharp-eyed paddlers can glimpse a wide variety of wildlife along the Caddo, including bears, turkeys, beavers, whitetail deer, and may kinds of waterfowl.

The company also offers canoe rentals for trips on the Little Missouri and Cassatot Rivers and is applying for guide permits for the Caddo, Little Missouri, and Cassatot.

Arrowhead Cabin and Canoe Rental also features a campground, cabins, and what the *Arkansas Times* named the best swimming hole in

Arkansas. Arrowhead's season runs from February to October.

Cossatot Outfitters
Marty Cox, Vickie Loftice
Route 1, Box 121
Lockesburg, AR 71846
(501) 286-2948, (501) 398-4458
Cossatot River, Little Missouri River, Saline River
Max. rapids: III-IV
Cossatot Outfitters offers one-day guided raft trips and canoe rentals for intermediate paddlers. The season runs from January to April or year-round, depending on rainfall.

The three rivers served are clear, unspoiled, and offer good white water, especially the Cossatot, which the National Park Service rates as "probably the most challenging" whitewater float in Arkansas.

Also notable is the little Missouri for its exciting drops and rapids, and the Saline River, site of the Arkansas Canoe Association's annual slalom and downriver races since 1984.

Gunga-La Lodge River Outfitters

Kenten Hunnell
Rt. 1, Box 147
Lakeview, AR 72642
(501) 431-5606, (800) 844-5606
Crooked Creek
Max. rapids: III-IV
White/Norfork River Outfitters
Association

Gunga-La Lodge, set in the Ozarks, offers one- to seven-day canoe and rafting trips on Crooked Creek and the White River. These trips are suitable for both beginners and advanced paddlers, and feature fine fishing and scenery, with views of mountain bluffs, woodlands, and historic river towns where supplies can be replenished on extended trips.

Wildlife to be seen include minks, muskrats, beavers, deer, coyotes, herons, and eagles. Fishing is for rainbow, cutthroat, and brown trout, and smallmouth and black bass.

The Lodge also offers well-equipped log cabins, guided float trips, and rentals of canoes, rafts, johnboats, and camping gear.

Moore Outdoors

Kerry and Debbie Moore
Route 2, Box 303M
Dover, AR 72837
(501) 331-3606
Big Piney Creek
Max. rapids: III-IV

Moore Outdoors offers guided raft trips and canoe and raft rentals for trips of one to three days on Big Piney Creek and the Illinois Bayou. Big Piney Creek has challenging Class II-III rapids, requiring previous white water canoeing experience. The creek is clear and clean, offering excellent fishing for catfish and smallmouth and largemouth bass. The creek also boasts beautiful wilderness scenery of high bluffs, waterfalls on side streams, and banks lined with pines, hardwoods, ferns, and wildflowers. Paddlers also can spot deer, beavers, minks, squirrels, ducks, and, in winter and early spring, bald eagles.

Moore Outdoors' season runs from January to June.

Ouachita Canoe Rentals

Tim and Sandy Williamson
SR 2, Box 200
Mount Ida, AR 71957
(501) 326-4710, (501) 867-2382
Ouachita River, Caddo River
Max. rapids: I-II

Ouachita Canoe Rentals, open year-round, offers one- to four-day trips on Ouachita River in the Ouachita National Forest. Trips on the Caddo River are also available by special request. With Class I rapids, all trips are fine for families and paddlers of all ages.

The Ouachita trips feature picturesque slate bluffs, gravel bars, and bluff shelters and excellent fishing for smallmouth and largemouth bass, catfish, bream, and crappie. Wildlife includes deer, beavers, turkeys, minks, otters, blue herons, bald eagles, and bears.

Ouachita Canoe Rentals also offers custom trips, a campground with showers, and cabin rentals. Its proprietors, Tim and Sandy Williamson, also operate "Rocky Shoals Float Camp," located two miles east of Ouachita Canoe Rentals.

Rocky Shoals, which can be reached at (502) 807-2382, offers camping, cabins, canoe lessons and rentals on the Ouachita, and combined hiking/canoeing trips, where guests hike the Ouachita Trail one day and float the Ouachita River the next.

Southfork Canoe Resort
Jerry Lawson
Rt. 3, Box 124A
Mammoth Spring, AR 72554
(501) 895-2803
Spring River, South Fork, Spring River, North Fork
Max. rapids: I-II

Southfork Canoe Resort is nestled in the Ozarks on the South Fork of the Spring River, famous for its beautiful scenery and fine fishing for small and largemouth bass, catfish, and walleye.

Southfork offers one to three-day canoe and kayak trips from April to September on the South Fork and North Fork of the Spring River. These trips can be guided or unguided, have Class I-II rapids, and are suitable for paddlers of all levels of experience. They pass through the Ozark hill country, with abundant deer, turkeys, and small game.

The company also offers a campground, store, modern cabins, electric hookups, hot showers, and a canoe shop.

Turner Bend
Brad Wimberly
HC 63, Box 216
Hwy 23 North
Ozark, AR 72949
(501) 667-3641
Mulberry River
Max. rapids: I-II

Turner Bend offers unguided whitewater canoe trips on the Mulberry River, which has Class I-II rapids and is one of the most challenging rivers in the Ozarks at high-water levels. Trips range in length from two to 26 miles, are offered March 1 to June 15, and require some paddling experience. These stretches of the Mulberry feature high bluffs, tree-lined banks, occasional views of deer, turkeys, and beavers, and fishing for catfish and small and largemouth bass.

Turner Bend also offers a year-round campground (without hookups), store, canoe shuttle service, hot showers, and shuttle service for hikers along the Ozark Highlands Trail.

Woodsman's Sports Shop & Fishing Service
Morrell Woods
HCR 61, Box 461
Norfork, AR 72658
(501) 499-7454
White River, Buffalo River
Max. rapids: I-II

Woodsman's offers one- to five-day guided and unguided canoe trips on the White and Buffalo Rivers in the Ozarks, with Class I and II rapids and cold, clear waters. These rivers offer easy paddling and excellent fishing for rainbow trout, brown trout, cutthroat, trout and small- and largemouth bass.

The unspoiled setting in northern Arkansas offers high bluffs, wooded hillsides, and abundant wildlife, including deer, squirrels, rabbits, and wild turkeys.

Woodsman's also has a campground with cabins and R.V. hookup, and is open year-round.

Wright Way Canoe Rental

Stephen R. Wright
P.O. Box 180
Highway 8 West and 27 North
Glenwood, AR 71943
(501) 356-2055
Caddo River
Max. rapids: I-II

Wright Way Canoe Rentals runs one- to seven-day canoe trips on the Caddo, specializing in outfitting small groups for customized overnight trips for beginners and experts alike. Most stretches of the Caddo offer Class I white water. After a good rain, however, experienced canoeists can find Class II and III white water above Caddo Gap.

Guided and unguided trips run year-round and offer excellent fishing for bream, catfish, and smallmouth, brown, white, Kentucky, largemouth, and rock bass. The Caddo also offers find swimming holes and abundant sand and gravel bars for camping.

California

With its streams churning and charging out of the Sierra Nevada range, California is practically made for river runners. Superb white water, crystal-clear rivers, lush forests, dramatic canyons, unspoiled wilderness — what more could a paddler ask? On top of everything else, California boasts the Cherry Creek/Upper Tuolumne run, which has been called "the Mount Everest of rafting" because of its phenomenal 105-feet-per-mile average gradient. This ferocious nine-mile dash in the Stanislaus National Forest has nearly continuous Class IV+ and V rapids. Strictly for experts, it is said to be the most challenging stretch of runnable white water in America and the standard by which Class V runs are measured.

Starting in the north, Hell's Corner Canyon on the Upper Klamath River offers 20 miles of tough Class IV+ rafting astride the Oregon state line. Rafters able to take time out from running 40 major rapids can spot abandoned settlers' cabins on the banks and visit lava caves once used by Indians. Further downstream, the Lower Klamath winds through forested mountains on a 28-mile stretch below Happy Camp, offering Class III floating with possible glimpses of bears, beavers, otters, ospreys, bald eagles, and great blue herons. Both of these relatively remote California runs can be enjoyed from mid-May until late summer.

Several stretches of the Trinity River, once a focus of intense and highly destructive gold mining, offer fine canoeing and rafting. Halfway down its course the Trinity churns through Burnt Ranch Gorge, a seven-mile long, 2,000-foot-deep chasm. A Class V adventure, this run takes the rafter at breakneck speed through giant boulder gardens and narrow passageways where both strength and skill are needed to dodge obstacles. Another tough challenge in this area is the California Salmon River, which like the Trinity has been officially designated Wild and Scenic. The Cal-Salmon, with its North and South Forks, remains a very beautiful river that runs through true wilderness country in the Salmon Mountains. It has mostly Class III runs with some impassable gorges. At least one outfitter offers two-day and three-day trips on a Class V section of the Cal-Salmon through a twisting gorge in the Klamath National Forest.

East of San Francisco, the Stanislaus River cuts through Mother Lode country in central California. Due to releases from the recently-built New Melones Reservoir, the Main Stanislaus now has excellent water flow all summer long. Once California's most popular river, the Stanislaus is back in business with Class III (formerly Class IV-V) rapids bearing names like Cadillac Charlie, Death Rock, and Widow Maker. The North Fork of the Stanislaus offers another great run within easy distance of city life. It goes five miles to Calaveras Big Trees State Park and combines Class IV rafting with forests of pines and sequoias and opportunities to visit historic gold rush towns.

Also in mid-California is the Tuolumne (pronounced tu-WAL-o-me) River, yet another gold-mining stream that runs from Yosemite National Park to join the San Joaquin River. Fed by releases from Hetch Hetchy Reservoir, the Tuolumne is runnable from March to October. It provides superb Class IV white water in an unspoiled canyon not far from the Yosemite Park's western entrance. Designated a National Wild and Scenic River, the Tuolumne takes rafters past places steeped in gold rush and Indian history.

For the real whitewater enthusiast, the ultimate challenge is the Cherry Creek/Upper Tuolumne run, mentioned above. This lies immediately upstream from the trip just described (and is generally known as the Cherry Creek, even though it covers only one mile of that stream and eight miles of the Upper Tuolumne). Its roaring chutes, holes, ledges, and falls go by such names as Miracle Mile, Lewis' Leap, and Jawbone. Outfitters require clients to pass stiff physical and Class V skill tests before participating in this daunting voyage.

California's most popular river, the South Fork of the American River, flows past the scene of James Marshall's 1848 find that touched off the Gold Rush. This trip east of Sacramento takes paddlers on clear, sparkling waters through Class III-IV rapids. The South Fork moves from rolling hill country to canyons and culminates in the American River Gorge with its white water and wildflowers. The most notorious rapid in this stretch is called Satan's John or Satan's Cesspool.

The North Fork American contains the Giant Gap run, which ranks among the most pristine of wilderness trips. It is also the most closely regulated stretch of river in the country, with (in 1991) only four guided trips allowed per week. The Giant Gap is a Class V springtime run featuring a 2,000-foot-deep sheer canyon with waterfalls cascading into the river. On one tour, rafters must descend a switchback trail to the put-in, with packhorses carrying their gear. Paddlers on the

Middle Fork American, another exciting run, raft through a 30-yard tunnel blasted out by gold miners. The Middle and South Forks American are California's only rivers that can be run consistently all year-round. Another certified Wild and Scenic whitewater river is the Kern in the Sequoia National Forest. The Lower Kern is only a short drive from the Los Angeles metropolitan area. One of the river's toughest sections is an Upper Kern run covering 17 miles down to the town of Kernville. It is a rigorous Class V test of every paddler's mettle, but is runnable only from April through June. To reach the put-in at Forks of the Kern for another nearby trip, paddlers must hike three miles down a rocky trail into a canyon, carrying backpacks. Pack animals carry river equipment and food for the Class V run through a spectacular 1,000-foot-deep chasm. For somewhat less energetic floaters, the Kern offers Class IV rapids elsewhere on its turbulent course, notably on a 20-mile Lower Kern trip starting at Isabella Lake.

Just north of the Bay Area runs the comparatively small Russian River, an easy float for beginners. Handsome redwoods line the stream as it slices through coastal hills to the sea. Although crowded at weekends, it offers canoeists a view of varied bird and marine life.

Sea kayakers paddle in San Francisco Bay, Tomales Bay, Humboldt Lagoons and sheltered river estuaries, where one can view seals as well as marine birdlife.

Adventure Connection, Inc.
Nate Rangel
P.O. Box 475
Coloma, CA 95613
(800) 556-6060 CA, (916) 626-7385
American River, Klamath River, Stanislaus River, Kaweah River
Max. rapids: IV
America Outdoors, California Professional Outfitters Association

Adventure Connection runs an eight-day whitewater rafting school and a variety of one- and two-day guided rafting trips. Trips on the South Fork of the American are suitable for first-time paddlers but enjoyed by experienced rafters as well. Rafting on the river's Middle Fork offers beautiful wilderness. More advanced are the company's trips on the North Fork American, Upper Klamath, and Kaweah.

Trips run through the Sierra foothills, offering views of deer, beavers, otters, eagles, and herons, and fishing for kokone and brown and rainbow trout.

Adventure Connection, open year-round, also offers special family discounts and charter coach transportation from southern California.

Chamberlain Falls on the North Fork of the American River. Courtesy of Sierra Shutterbug Photography.

Adventure Sports Unlimited
Dennis Judson, Virginia Wedderburn
303 Potrero Street #15
Santa Cruz, CA 95060
(408) 458-3648
Mokelomne River, American River, Kings River, Big Sur, Carmel Bay, Point Lobos, Point Reyes, Elkhorn Slough
Max. rapids: III-IV
Adventure Sports Unlimited offers guided and unguided canoe and sea-kayak trips of two to three days. Sea-kayak trips begin with instruction in a heated pool, followed by a trip to Big Sur, Carmel Bay, Pt. Lobos, Elkhorn Slough, or Pt. Reyes. These trips offer pristine beaches and clear water, ideal for viewing whales, sea lions, sea otters, seals, birds, and other coastal and marine wildlife. Sea-kayak trips vary in difficulty to suit anyone from beginners to kayak surfers.

River trips run on the Mokelomne, American, and King Rivers. Adventure Sports, open year-round, emphasizes instruction, togetherness, and gourmet food on all its trips.

Adventure Whitewater
Gene Allred, M.D.
P.O. Box 321
Yreka, CA 96097
(800) 888-5632
Salmon River, Scott River, Klamath River, Trinity River
Max. rapids: V+
America Outdoors
Adventure Whitewater offers raft rentals and guided kayak and raft trips for gentle Class II to expert Class V runs. Trips feature great white water and spectacular mountain scenery of snow-capped peaks, deep granite gorges, and heavily forested slopes. Set in the Marble Mountains

Tuolumne River. Courtesy of Sierra Mac River Trips, Sonora, California.

and Trinity Alps, the trips offer fishing for trout, steelhead, and salmon and chances to view bears, deer, coyotes, otters, eagles, ospreys, and herons.

Ahwahnee Whitewater Expeditions
Jim Gado and Cris Barsanti
P.O. Box 1161
Columbia, CA 95310
(209) 533-1401, (800) 359-9790
Tuolumne River, Merced River, Stanislaus River
Max. rapids: III-IV
America Outdoors

Ahwahnee Whitewater Expeditions runs one- to two-day guided oar- and paddle-raft trips for beginning, intermediate, and advanced paddlers. The minimum age for paddlers is 7 on the Stanislaus and 12 on the Merced and Tuolumne Rivers.

The Stanislaus sports exciting Class III rapids; the Tuolumne boasts Class III to IV+. Both rivers have sparkling, clear water, with some gentle rapids that are safe to swim. Along the way, guests can enjoy excellent trout fishing, wildflowers, remote wilderness canyons, gold rush artifacts, hiking, swimming, and wilderness camping. Guests also have a chance to spot otters, deer, foxes, coyotes, eagles, hawks, ospreys and waterfowl.

During the season, which runs from April to October, Ahwahnee also offers a special Mexican gourmet trip and a wilderness ranch/raft package.

American River Recreation
Don Hill
P.O. Box 465
Lotus, CA 95651
(916) 635-4516, (803) 333-RAFT
American River, Merced River, Carson River, Klamath River, Cal-Salmon River
Max. rapids: III-IV
America Outdoors

American River Recreation offers guided raft trips from March to October for paddlers of all skill levels. Highlights include skilled guides, an excellent safety record, a wide range of rivers and trips, and reasonable prices. Trips run from March to October and pass through varied terrain, including high desert, canyons, and gorges. Guests can also enjoy lessons, fishing for brown and rainbow trout, and viewing deer, ospreys, herons, eagles, and otters.

Kids enjoying the ride on the South Fork of the American River. Courtesy of Sierra Shutterbug Photography.

American River Touring Association
Steve Welch
Star Route 73
Groveland, CA 95321
(800) 323-2782, (209) 962-7873
American River, Merced River, Tuolumne River, Cal-Salmon River, Klamath River, Rogue River, Illinois River, Umpqua River, Green River, Yampa River, Salmon River, Selway River
Max. rapids: V+
America Outdoors, Oregon Guides and Packers, Idaho Outfitters and Guides, Utah Guides and Outfitters

ARTA offers a total of 16 raft trips in five Western states. The trips, in California, Oregon, Utah, Idaho, and Arizona, are by oar rafts, paddle rafts, oar/paddle combination rafts, and inflatable canoes.

Most trips are of Class III difficulty and appropriate for novices and families, as well as those with more experience. Other trips of up to V+ difficulty challenge even the most advanced paddler. Depending on the location, the trips feature such added attractions as wildflowers, side hikes, swimming holes, Indian ruins, warm water, abundant wildlife, good hiking and fishing, and hot springs.

ARTA, a non-profit company, also offers whitewater schools, professional guide training, and family discounts.

Beyond Limits Adventures, Inc.
Mike Doyle/Dave Hammond
P.O. Box 215
Riverbank, CA 95367
(209) 529-7655, (800) 234-RAFT (CA)
*Stanislaus River, American River,
Yuba River, Trinity River, Klamath
River, Scott River, New River*
Max. rapids: V
America Outdoors

Beyond Limits Adventures offers
one- to four-day trips ranging from
"mild to wild," with guided raft trips
and rentals of canoes, kayaks, and
rafts. The company's specialty, however, is Class IV-V rafting in self-bailing boats with skilled, friendly guides
and excellent food.

Set on the pristine, challenging
rivers of the Sierras, Beyond Limits
trips features scenery of giant sequoias, sheer granite domes, and
deep canyons. Also, lucky paddlers
may sight otters, eagles, and bears,
and catch trout, salmon, and steelhead.

CAL Adventures
Rick Spittler
University of California - Berkeley
2301 Bancroft Avenue
Berkeley, CA 94720
(415) 642-4000
*American River, Klamath River,
Trinity River*
Max. rapids: III-IV
America Outdoors

Cal Adventures offers an excellent
array of raft, kayak, and sea-kayak
trips and classes at very reasonable
rates. A unique outfitter, Cal Adventures is part of the Department of
Recreational Sports at the University
of California, Berkeley.

Despite its link to the university,
Cal Adventures' programs are available to the public. Among the offerings are a three-part sea-kayak class;
12 sea kayak trips; one- and two-day
raft trips on the America, Klamath,

and Stanislaus Rivers; a three-part
whitewater kayaking course; kayak
roll clinics and pool sessions; and five
one-day kayak river trips.

Cal Adventures also offers year-
round rentals of kayaks, rafts, sea
kayaks, and camping gear.

California Canoe & Kayak
Keith Miller
8631 Folsom Blvd.
Sacramento, CA 95826
(916) 381-6636
*San Francisco Bay, Tomales Bay,
Drakes Estero (sea kayaking),
American River, Stanislaus River,
Klamath River, Trinity River,
Nokelumne River, Eel River*
Max. rapids: IV
America Outdoors

California Canoe and Kayak offers
one- to five-day trips year-round,
suited for paddlers 15 or older. Between the guided and unguided
canoe and sea-kayak trips, the company offers access to a wide range of
waters and terrain, including limestone canyons, lush rain forests, and
scenic coastal waters.

Among the wildlife to be seen are
eagles, herons, otters, beavers, and
seals. Fishing is for trout and salmon.
California Canoe & Kayak also has
outposts in Pt. Richmond (415) 234-
0929 and Redwood City (415) 364-
8918.

Chuck Richards Whitewater, Inc.
Box W.W. Whitewater
Lake Isabella, CA 93240
(619) 379-4685
Kern River
Max. rapids: V
*American Rivers, NFRA, America Out-
doors*

Whitewater, Inc. offers guided and
unguided canoe, kayak, and raft trips
on three sections of the Kern River.
With Class III, IV, and V rapids, trips
feature "slambang action for adults"

on crystal-clear waters. Paddlers pass through pine and sequoia forests and enjoy views of granite spires and cliffs, deer, beavers, and eagles. Fishing is for brown and rainbow trout. Trips range in length from one to three days and the season runs from May 1 to October 31.

Earthtrek Expeditions
Jerry Ashburn
23342 Madero, Suite B
Mission Viejo, CA 92691
(714) 472-8735, (800) 229-8735, FAX
(714) 472-6047
American River, Klamath River
Max. rapids: IV
America Outdoors
Earthtrek Expeditions has a wide assortment of one- to four-day trips for rafters and sea kayakers in Topock Gorge and the Grand Canyon in Colorado and the goldrush country of California.

Paddlers can choose among trips of varying difficulty and accommodations ranging from historic inns to primitive wilderness campgrounds. Trips run from April to October, offering excellent wilderness scenery and chances to fish and view abundant wildlife.

Earthtrek also offers group rates, charter-bus service, and bicycling and skiing trips.

Echo: The Wilderness Company
Richard Linford and Joseph Daly
6529 Telegraph Avenue
Oakland, CA 94609
(510) 652-1600, (800) 652-3246 (CA)
Tuolumne River, Rogue River, Salmon River, American River, Cal-Salmon River
Max. rapids: III-IV
Idaho Outfitters and Guides Association, Oregon Guides and Packers, America Outdoors
ECHO runs guided trips on the Main Salmon and Middle Fork in Idaho; the Rogue in Oregon; and the Tuolumne, American, and Cal-Salmon in California. The company has one- to 12-day trips available for paddlers at all skill levels and offers a variety of boats, including inflatable kayaks, oar rafts, paddle rafts, and oar/paddle rafts.

ECHO also offers a large number of special trips, including Fly-Fishing on the Middle Fork; White (and Red) Wine and White Water; Bluegrass on White Water; River Trips for Kids; White Water School; Aikido and Nature; the Rogue String Quartet; Field Sketching Workshop; Whale Watching, Baja; Rainforests and Rapids, Costa Rica; Baja Sea Kayaking; Colorado River through the Grand Canyon; and Lodge Trips on the Main Salmon and Cal-Salmon.

ECHO's seasons runs from April to September.

James Henry River Journeys
James Katz
P.O. Box 807
Bolinas, CA 94924
(415) 868-1836, (800) 786-1830
Tatshenshini-Alsek River, Noatak River, Stanislaus River, Carson River, Klamath River, Rogue River
Max. rapids: III-IV
Idaho Outfitters and Guides
James Henry River Journeys runs guided canoe, kayak, and raft trips in California, Arizona, Idaho, Oregon, and Alaska. In California, the outfitter offers trips with Class II-III rapids, of one to three days, on the Stanislaus, East Fork of the Carson, and the Lower Klamath. In Arizona, the company runs Grand Canyon trips, with Class IV+ rapids, of 6, 8, 9, 13, and 14 days. Trips in Idaho, of 4, 5 or 6 days, run on the Class III-IV Main Salmon. In Oregon, trips of 3, 4, and 5 days run on the Class III Rogue. Many special-interest trips are also available. These include Salmon River Bluegrass,

Pop-up on the the South Fork of the American River. Courtesy of Sierra Shutterbug Photography.

Country, Folk, and Cajun Music Trips; Whitewater Workshops; Organizational Development and Teambuilding; Wine Tasting and Gourmet Cuisine; Lodge Trips on the Rogue and Salmon; Rogue and Salmon Natural History Trips; Alaska Nature Photography; and Alaska Wilderness Literature.

All trips run through especially scenic wilderness areas and are carefully planned to move at a leisurely pace, allowing ample time for side hikes, fishing, photography, and general relaxation. As a result, participation is open to anyone active and in good health. The company's season runs from May to September.

Kings River Expeditions
Justin Butchert
211 N. Van Ness
Fresno, CA 93701
(209) 233-4881
Upper Kings River
Max. rapids: III-IV
America Outdoors, NFRA

Kings River Expeditions runs one- and two-day guided raft trips on the Upper Kings River between the Sequoia and Sierra National Forests. The season begins in April and is followed by a period of high water stretching from the middle of May through the middle of June. The outfitter recommends that only physically fit adults raft during this early part of the season. From mid-June until August, the water warms considerably, making trips suitable for children as young as nine.

Guests enjoy the Kings River's clear, clean water and wilderness setting in a moderately steep tree-filled canyon. Fishing is for trout and bass, and the wildlife seen include hawks, bears, and foxes.

Laughing Heart Adventures
Dezh Pagen
Trinity Outdoor Center
P.O. Box 669
Willow Creek, CA 95573
(916) 629-3516, (800) 541-1256
Trinity River, Klamath River, Eel River, Sacramento River, Smith River, Russian River, Green River, Colorado River
Max. rapids: III-IV
NACLO, America Outdoors

Laughing Heart Adventures offers "consciousness raising" canoe outings on wild and scenic rivers throughout the West and Mexico. Before trips start, guides interpret the geology and natural and human history of an area. Guides also gear some special trips toward specific goals such as stress reduction, holistic health, music and art appreciation, college credit, and environmental politics.

Laughing Heart's guided trips are by canoe, kayak, or raft. Rentals of canoes, kayaks, rafts, and tubes also are available. Trips run from one to seven days year-round. Kayak and canoe lessons and trips are available for paddlers of all skill levels.

Libra Expeditions
Jon Osgood
P.O. Box 4280
Sunland, CA 91041
(818) 228-4121, (800) 228-4121 in CA
Stanislaus River, American River
Max. rapids: V
America Outdoors, Friends of Rivers, American River Recreation Association

Libra Expeditions specializes in paddle-boat raft trips, rewarding paddlers with exceptionally well-appointed campsites that feature professional cooks, hot showers, and rental tents, tipis and sleeping bags. Trips are for one or two days and run through California's gold-rush region, offering views of steep canyons, spring wildflowers, falcons, deer, and otters. Fishing is for trout and bass.

Libra Expeditions' season is from April to October.

A Beyond Limits Adventures' trip on the North Fork of the Yuba River. Courtesy of Rapid Shooters/Dennis Stiff.

O.A.R.S.
George Wendt
P.O. Box 67
Angels Camp, CA 95222
(209) 736-4677, (800) 466-7238 (CA),
(800) 346-6277 (U.S.)
*American River, Cal-Salmon River,
Stanislaus River, Tuolumne River,
Merced River, Rogue River, Snake
River, San Juan River, Colorado River
Max. rapids: III-IV
America Outdoors*
O.A.R.S. runs guided dory, raft,
and kayak trips in five Western states.
It offers tours in California on the
American, Cal-Salmon, Merced, Stan-
islaus, and Tuolumne Rivers; in Ore-
gon on the Rogue; in Arizona on the
Colorado; in Wyoming on the Snake,
and in Utah on the San Juan River.
These outings last one to 13 days
and, depending on the class of river,
are fine for children, novices, families, and intermediate and expert rafters. O.A.R.S. trips provide fishing,
swimming, camping, side hikes, wildlife viewing, and other activities.
Tours run from April to October.

Outdoor Adventures
Bob Volpert
P.O. Box 1149
Point Reyes, CA 94956
(415) 663-8300
*Tuolumne River, Kern River, Salmon
River, Rogue River
Max. rapids: V+
America Outdoors, Idaho Outfitters
and Guides, Oregon Outfitters
Association*
Outdoor Adventures specializes in
guided raft trips and raft rentals on
federally designated wild and scenic
rivers in Idaho, Oregon, and California. In Idaho, six-day trips are available on the Middle Fork of the Salmon
and the Salmon River. Included are
all shuttles from Boise, tents and
sleeping bags, delicious on-river
meals, quality guides, and Avon rafts.

In Oregon, three- and four-day
trips are available on the Rogue
River, featuring lively rapids, wonderful hiking trails, and abundant
wildlife. On these trips, the last night
is spent at Half Moon Bar, a rustic
lodge by the river where paddlers
can enjoy hot showers, comfortable
beds, and home-cooked meals.
In California, Outdoor Adventures
offers two-day trips on the Tuolomne
River, three-day trips on the Forks of
the Kern, and one-day trips on the
Upper Kern. These California trips
offer some of the wildest white water
in the country during the spring runoff in April and May. During this time,
wetsuits and previous rafting experience are required. All other Outdoor Adventures trips are fine for
families and beginners. The company's season is from April to October.

Ouzel Outfitters
Kent Wickham
Box 827
Bend, OR 97709
(503) 385-5947, (800) 788-RAFT
*Rogue River, Owyhee River, North
Umpqua River, Deschutes River, Mc-
Kenzie River, Salmon
Max. rapids: III-IV
Oregon Guides and Packers*
Ouzel Oufitters specializes in trips
of one to five days on the "loveliest
and liveliest" rivers in the Northwest.
These rivers include the Rogue, North
Umpqua, McKenzie, Lower and Mid-
dle Owyhee, and Deschutes Rivers in
Oregon; the Lower Salmon in Idaho;
and the Lower Klamath River in
California. All trips but the Middle
Owyhee runs have class III-IV rapids
and are fine for families and guests of
all levels of experience to paddle in
paddle rafts, inflatable kayaks, or
guide-accompanied, "row-your-own"
oar-rafts. The Middle Owyhee run,
with class IV-V rapids, is a challenging, expedition-like trip for adven-

turous, experienced rafters only. Ouzel Outfitters' trips run between May and September. Depending on the river traveled, guests can view bears, deer, eagles, and otters, and fish for bass, trout, steelhead, and salmon.

River Travel Center
Raven Earlygrow
15 Riverside Drive
Point Arena, CA 95468
(800) 882-7238, (707) 882-2258
All commerically run rivers
Max. rapids: V+
America Outdoors

River Travel Center represents more than 100 outfitters offering canoe, raft, kayak, sea kayak, and dory trips in the West and overseas. With knowledge of thousands of trips, River Travel Center can assist you in selecting the destination, trip, and outfitter that is right for you. The company specializes in arranging trips by telephone, providing quick, reliable, and convenient service.

Trips range in length from to 18 days and are available year-round.

Sierra Mac River Trips
Marty McDonnell
P.O. Box 366
Sonora, CA 95370
(209) 532-1327, (800) 457-2580
Tuolumne River, American River, Stanislaus River
Max. rapids: V+
America Outdoors

Sierra Mac runs Class III-IV guided raft trips of one to three days. The difficulty of the trips offered varies enormously. For novices, there are oar-boat and moderate paddle-boat trips. At the other extreme are several Class V trips, including the famed Cripple Creek run, which has a phenomenally steep gradient of 110-feet per mile and is widely considered the most challenging in the entire United States. A training seminar and Class V paddler's test are required for this expert's thrill ride.

Sierra Mac, with more than 26 years' experience, runs trips from March to October. In addition to the paddling adventure, guests can enjoy spectacular wilderness scenery, trout fishing, and a chance to view eagles, great blue herons, deer, kit foxes, and coyotes.

Sunshine River Adventures
Jim Foust
P.O. Box 1445
Oakdale, CA 95361
(209) 881-3236, (800) 829-7238
Stanislaus River, Mokelumne River
Max. rapids: III-IV
America Outdoors

Sunshine River Adventures has guided and unguided canoe and raft trips offering the full range of difficulty, from Class I float trips to Class IV adventure. Among the highlights of these trips is the guided cave tour in the West's largest limestone gorge along the Stanislaus Canyon.

Sunshine's tours, of one to three days, are offered April to October 31 at guaranteed lowest rates. Trips permit viewing of deer, otters, beavers, muskrats, ospreys, eagles, falcons, and hawks.

Tributary Whitewater Tours
Daniel J. Buckley, L.A. Hall
20480 Woodbury Drive
Grass Valley, CA 95949
(916) 346-6812
Yuba River, American River, Carson River, Klamath River, Stanislaus River, Kaweah River, Trinity River, New River, Salmon River, Scott River, Sacramento River, Eel River
Max. rapids: V+
America Outdoors

Tributary Whitewater Tours runs one- to six-day guided raft and inflatable kayak tours on 17 Northern

Mushroom Falls on the upper Tuolumne River. This Class V trip is widely regarded as one of the most challenging in the country. Courtesy of Sierra Mac River Trips, Sonora, California.

California rivers. Trips range from gentle family floats suitable for the young, old, and disabled, to Class V trips for experts only. Depending on the river, guests can choose paddle, oar, or paddle-oar boats. Also, on Class III rivers, paddlers can opt to use exciting one-person inflatable kayaks, These boats are maneuverable, easy to master, and ideal for running some of California's beautiful rivers during the summer, when the water is too low for larger rafts.

Whatever their size, all of Tributary's boats are self-bailing, which makes them more agile and comfortable in big water than conventional rafts. Special charter trips and group discounts are also available during Tributary's season of March.

Turtle River Rafting Company
Richard Demarest and David Wikander
P.O. Box 313
1308 Old U.S. Highway 99
Mt. Shasta, CA 96067
(916) 926-3223, (800) 726-3223
Klamath River, Trinity River, Sacramento River, Scott River, Eel River, Smith River
Max. rapids: V+
America Outdoors
Turtle River Rafting Company runs guided kayak and raft trips and rents kayaks for trips of one to 10 days on the Klamath, Upper Klamath, Scott, Cal-Salmon, Trinity, Upper Sacramento, Owyhee, Smith, and Eel Rivers. Depending on the river and time of year, these trips range in difficulty from Class II to Class V. Families are encouraged to participate, in accord-

"Satan's Cesspool" rapid on the South Fork of the American River. Courtesy of Sierra Shutterbug Photography.

ance with the following minimum age requirements: four for "Kid's Klamath"; six for "Gentle Klamath"; eight for Main Klamath, Trinity, and Owyhee; 12 for upper Sacramento and Middle Eel; and 15 for Upper Klamath, Scott, and Cal-Salmon.

These trips range in length from one to 10 days and feature wild and scenic canyons, waterfalls, clean beaches, excellent food, and abundant wildlife, including bears, eagles, otters, turtles, herons, and deer. During its April-to-October season, Turtle River also offers custom trips for men, women, musicians, and aspiring whitewater guides. "Personal growth" workshops are also available.

White Magic Unlimited
Jack Morison
P.O. Box 5506
Mill Valley, CA 94942
(415) 381-8889, (800) 869-9874
Colorado River
Max. rapids: V+
White Magic Unlimited runs guided raft trips of six, eight, and 13 days on the Colorado River through the Grand Canyon. The trips offer world-class white water, waves of up to 20 feet, and spectacular scenery. White Magic, an adventure travel company, also offers rafting and trekking expeditions in the former Soviet Union, China, Nepal, Chile, Ecuador, the Galapagos Islands, and Costa Rica.

Whitewater Voyages
William McGinnis
P.O. Box 20400
El Sobrante, CA 94820-0400
(510) 222-5994, (800) 488-RAFT
Colorado River, Kern River, Merced River, Tuolumne River, Salmon River, Cache Creek, American River, Yuba River, Klamath River, Stanislaus River, Trinity River, Rogue River
Max. rapids: V+
America Outdoors, American River Recreation Association

Whitewater Voyages offers an extensive array of trips, with guided oar- and paddle-boat runs in California, Arizona, Oregon, and Idaho. Trips by kayak and raft range in length from one to five days and in difficulty from Class II to Class V. With runs on nine Wild and Scenic Rivers and on more California rivers than any other outfitter, Whitewater Voyages has trips for paddlers of all level of experience.

The outfitter also has specialty trips, including whitewater schools, family trips, low-cost river-cleanup trips, "teambuilding" trips, and excursions to the former Soviet Union to paddle with Russians as part of project R.A.F.T.

Wild Water Adventures
Al Law, Melinda Allan
P.O. Box 249
Creswell, OR 97426
(503) 895-4465, (800) 289-4534
Klamath River
Max. rapids: III-IV
Oregon Guides and Packers Association

Wild Water Adventures specializes in running guided and unguided inflatable kayak trips on wilderness rivers. Trips in rafts and inflatable kayaks range in length from one-half day to nine days and run on rivers ranging from mountain streams to desert waterways and from scenic floats to crashing white water. On these trips, in addition to paddling, guests can fish, view Indian pictographs and pioneer ruins, and spot deer, eagles, otters, hawks, minks, beavers, and other wildlife.

During the season, which runs from March to November, and year-round for "wetsuiters," guests can also take inflatable kayak lessons, learning brace strokes, ferrying, river rescue, and how to "read" rivers. Kayaking students can enjoy instruction by Melinda Allan, coauthor of *The Inflatable Kayak Handbook.*

Wilderness Adventures
Dean Munroe
P.O. Box 938
Redding, CA 96099
(800) 323-7238
Sacramento River, Scott River, Wooley Creek
Max. rapids: V

Wilderness Adventures runs a number of remarkable trips on rivers along the California-Oregon border. Among the unusual offerings is a raft trip begun on the Class V Woodley Creek after a horseback ride into the Marble Mountain Wilderness. Another exciting trip, called "Hell and High Water," combines all the Class V sections of the Salmon, Scott and Upper Klamath into a weekend trip.

Trips range in length from one to four days, are offered from April to October, and are suited for intermediate to advanced paddlers. Set in wilderness areas, trips offer fishing for trout and views of eagles, ospreys, minks, otters, and beavers.

41

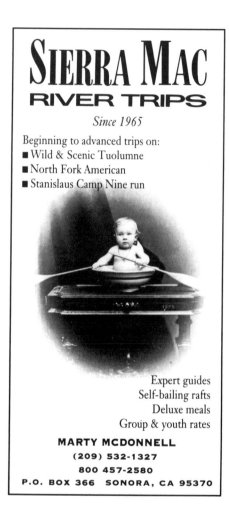

Colorado

As a classic Rocky Mountain state, Colorado offers whitewater enthusiasts innumerable rapids to run amid stunning scenery. Rivers that start as snow-fed mountain torrents plunge through deep canyons to irrigate distant deserts. They include some of the greatest American arteries: the Arkansas, the Colorado, the North Platte, and the Rio Grande. Rapids bear names that quicken the pulse: Pinball, Zoom-Flume, Widow-Maker, Needle Eye, Stovepipe, and the notorious Snaggletooth.

This is exciting country. Take, for instance, the furious Pine Creek Rapids that run just below Granite on the Arkansas River. Except in August, when the flow abates, this gorge is rated Class V. Among expert kayakers, running Pine Creek Rapids ranks as a test of manhood — or womanhood. More popular is the six-mile run a little further downstream on the Arkansas, which has been the scene of many national championships and the annual Colorado Cup. This Class IV river segment, which begins at a campground about ten miles upstream from Buena Vista, attracts kayakers from far and wide.

But the most popular of all Arkansas River runs is Brown's Canyon, a Class III rafting and kayaking trip that goes 10 miles from Nathrop to a highway bridge six miles above Salida. Many commercial rafts crowd this canyon on a busy summer day, with paddlers savoring the thrills of its excellent white water. But only seasoned kayakers attempt to run the 1,500-foot-deep Royal Gorge, a Class IV challenge that lies between Parkdale and Canon City. The black-walled chasm has some spectacular scenery including a suspension bridge said to be the world's highest.

A gentler float may be enjoyed on the Upper Colorado, starting near Kremmling and taking rafters through narrow Little Gore Canyon with its Class II rapids. On the second day of this 28-mile, two-day trip, one emerges into ranchland. A perfect outing for families, this tour offers natural hot springs, 100-year-old miners' cabins, and a stagecoach road. Below Grand Junction, with its waters swelled by the influx of the Gunnison, the celebrated Colorado moves sedately through Ruby and Horsethief Canyons before crossing the state line and entering turbulent Westwater Canyon (see *Utah*).

The North Gate Canyon stretch of the North Platte, where this undammed river flows northward across the Wyoming state line, is described by one outfitter as "the best-kept secret in Colorado." The canyon contains many Class III-IV rapids, and rafters running the entire 30-mile trip eventually come out of forested Medicine Bow mountain wilderness into the rolling hill country of southern Wyoming. The only time to paddle this stretch is late May through June.

The Dolores River in southwestern Colorado offers a great combination of canyon white water and colorful desert panoramas. But like the North Platte, its rafting season is short — from early May to mid-June. The Dolores, a tributary of the Colorado, invites trips through aptly-named Ponderosa Gorge and Slick Rock Canyon. Their toughest rapid is Snaggletooth, an infamous Class IV-V obstacle, which most rafters portage. Slick Rock is uniquely colorful with its red, white, and orange sandstone, prickly pear cactus, and pinon and juniper trees sprouting from the canyon walls.

Then there is the famous Gunnison River. Just downstream from the Black Canyon of the Gunnison National Monument with its many dams is Gunnison Gorge, where the river flows freely again and provides Class II-IV white water all summer long. This is rugged wilderness country: a spectacular narrow canyon with black cliffs and a river alternating between smooth pools and surging rapids. The put-in is at the foot of a mile-long narrow trail; rafts and equipment have to be carried down by packhorses.

Small rafts, canoes, and kayaks can float Colorado sections of the Rio Grande before it crosses into New Mexico and on to Texas. But a more rewarding river in the southern part of the state is the Animas. Its upstream rapids are hazardous for all but experts, but just north of Durango is an easy 10-mile run, and a pleasant 20-mile trip into the Animas Valley, close to the New Mexico state line.

American Adventure Expeditions

Ray and Penny Kitson
P.O. Box 1549
Buena Vista, CO 81211
(800) 288-0675
Arkansas River, Animas River,
Colorado River, Piedra River
Max. rapids: V+
America Outdoors, Arkansas River
Outfitters Association

American Adventure offers guided oar- and paddle-boat trips on four Colorado rivers set high in the Rockies amid the largest concentration of 14,000-foot peaks in the lower 48 states. Lessons and one- to seven-day trips are available for all skill levels from novice to expert. Along the way, guests can fish for trout and perhaps spot elk, deer, bears, and mountain lions.

Trips run from April to October. With experienced guides and fine equipment, American Adventures offers a satisfaction guarantee.

Arkansas River Tours

Box 1032-PA
Buena Vista, CO 81211
(719) 395-8949, (800) 321-4352
Arkansas River
Max. rapids: V+
America Outdoor, Arkansas River
Outfitters Association, Colorado River
Outfitters Association

Arkansas River Tours specializes in guided paddle rafting trips on the Arkansas in south central Colorado, with trips to suit paddlers of all skill levels. Trips last one to three days, run between May and August, and pass through high-desert terrain that offers scenic mountain views and chances to spot bighorn sheep, ouzels, and hawks.

Most trips are in self-bailing rafts; however, guests in groups of three or more may choose to run one-day trips in inflatable kayaks.

The owners of Arkansas River Tours also operate Four Corners Rafting. (See separate listing.)

Aspen Kayak School

Kirk Baker
P.O. Box 1520
Aspen, CO 81611
(303) 925-6248
Roaring Fork River, Colorado River,
Arkansas River, Crystal River, Green
River
Max. rapids: III-IV
American Canoe Association

Aspen Kayak School has more than 20 years' experience and an excellent safety record offering kayak instruction and rentals. Its trips run from one to 12 days and include offerings for paddlers of all skill levels. For novices there are trips with good beginner water, and for intermediate and advanced kayakers, there is an excellent variety of Class III and IV runs.

The scenery of the trips vary greatly as well, ranging from the alpine terrain of the Rockies to the high desert of the Colorado plateau. Wildlife to be seen include deer, foxes, and black bears, and fishing is for rainbow and brown trout.

Bighorn Expeditions

Pitchfork Enterprises, Inc.
P.O. Box 365
Bellvue, CO 80512
(303) 221-8110
Dolores River, Green River, Rio
Grande
Max. rapids: III-IV
America Outdoors, Utah Guides and
Outfitters

Bighorn Expeditions offers two- to eight-day guided oar-boat trips on the Rio Grande River in Texas, the Dolores River in Colorado, and the Green River in Utah. Unlike most outfitters offering oar-boat trips, Bighorn encourages guests to do the rowing.

45

Rafting on the Arkansas River. Courtesy of ECHO Canyon River Expeditions, Canon City, Colorado.

The company provides 11-foot, one-person rafts that are lively and river-worthy but small enough for easy handling. Trips include thorough lessons and begin on calm stretches, so they are fine for those with no rowing experience. Those wishing to row, however, should be in good physical condition. If you are unsure of your conditioning or prefer to concentrate on photography or bird-watching, you can elect to ride on one of the company's larger, guide-operated rafts.

Bighorn's trips run March to November through scenic canyon terrain and offer good instruction in whitewater boating and wilderness ethics.

Bill Dvorak's Kayak and Rafting Expeditions
Bill and Jaci Dvorak
17921 U.S. Highway 285
Nathrop, CO 81236
(719) 539-6851, (800) 824-3795
Arkansas River, Colorado River, Gunnison River, Green River, North Platte River, Dolores River, Middle Fork and Main Salmon River, Rio Grande, Salt River
Max. rapids: V+
America Outdoors, Colorado River Outfitters Association, Utah Guides and Outfitters, and New Mexico River Outfitters Association

Dvorak's Kayak and Rafting Expeditions runs a wide array of guided and unguided trips through 29 canyons on a total of 10 rivers in Colorado, Utah, and New Mexico. Scenery ranges from alpine to desert, and whitewater ranges from Class I to Class V. Guests also have a choice of touring by canoe, kayak, or raft. With this selection of locations and trips, Dvoraks has offerings to suit any individual or group.

Trips run for one to 13 days between March and October and permit time for trout fishing and viewing deer, elk, bears, eagles, beavers, and coyotes.

Brown's Royal Gorge Rafting
Mark Brown
45045 U.S. Highway 50
Canyon City, CO 81212
(719) 275-5161, (719) 275-7238
Arkansas River
Max. rapids: V+
America Outdoors

Brown's Royal Gorge Rafting runs guided oar-raft and paddle-raft trips on the Arkansas River. These trips last one to two days and range in difficulty from family trips to adventures for experienced paddlers only. On all outings, participants can enjoy the Arkansas' beautiful mountain and canyon scenery and views of mountain sheep, deer, and other wildlife. Anglers also can fish for trout.

Brown's Royal Gorge Rafting's season runs from April to October.

Colorado River Runs, Inc.
Joe Kelso
Star Route Box 32
Bond, CA 80423
(303) 653-4292, (800) 826-1081
Colorado River, Eagle River, Arkansas River
Max. rapids: III-IV
Colorado River Outfitters Association, America Outdoors

Colorado River Runs offers guided one-day raft trips on the Colorado, Eagle, and Arkansas Rivers. The trips,

suitable for guests of all ages, offer excitement, isolation, gorgeous Rocky Mountain scenery, and a chance to view deer, eagles, and coyotes.

The company, which has been in business for 18 years, runs trips from May through October.

Echo Canyon River Expeditions
Dave and Kim Burch
45000 US Highway 50 W.
Canon City, CO 81212
(800) 748-2953, (719) 275-3154, (719) 632-3684
Arkansas River, Piedra River, Gunnison River, Lake Fork River, Colorado River
Max. rapids: V+
Colorado River Outfitters Association, Arkansas River Outfitters Association

Echo Canyon's raft trips range from "mild to wild" and are suitable for people of all ages. Trips range in length from one to three days and run on five Colorado rivers, offering spectacular scenery, trout fishing, and a chance to view deer and bighorn sheep.

Echo's trips, by oar or paddle boats, are offered between April and September.

Far Flung Adventures, Inc.
Steve Harris/Mike Davidson
P.O. Box 377
Terlingua, TX 79852
(915) 371-2489, (800) 359-4138 (reservations)
Gunnison River, Dolores River, Arkansas River
Max. rapids: V+
America Outdoors, Rio Grande Guides Association

Far Flung Adventures specializes in taking rafters on camping trips through the ruggedly beautiful Big Bend region of Texas as well as in other states in the U.S. and Mexico. Its tours last from one to seven days in a season running from January to

December. It caters to everyone from novices to whitewater experts capable of meeting Class V+ challenges.

The remoteness of the Rio Grande's Big Bend National Park, its canyons and wildlife combine with good fishing to make these trips unforgettable. Far Flung Adventures offers paddling lessons as well as camping, fishing, and swimming.

Four Corners Paddling School
Nancy Wiley
Box 379
Durango, CO 81302
(303) 259-3893
Animas River, Dolores River
Max. rapids: III-IV
Four Corners Paddling School offers canoeing and kayaking classes for paddlers of all levels, novice to advanced. Classes are small, with five or fewer students per instructor, and the instructors are exceptionally well-qualified, each with many years of teaching experience.

The founder and director of the school, Nancy Wiley, was selected by Canoe Magazine in 1987 as one of the top 10 kayakers in the United States. She has devised a number of special clinics, too, including rolling clinics, women's clinics, A.C.A. kayak and canoe instructor certification, private lessons, squirt clinics, slalom-gate training clinics, and hole-playing clinics.

Classes are offered for two-day to four-day sessions during the June-to-September season. Trips run on the Animas and Delores Rivers, which flow from high alpine snowfields to deep desert canyons, offering a unique and diverse river experience.

A young rafter ready for action. Courtesy of Dvorak's Kayak & Rafting Expeditions, Inc., Nathrop, Colorado.

Four Corners Rafting
Karen Dils
Box 1032-PA
Buena Vista, CO 81211
(800) 332-7238, (719) 395-8949
Arkansas River, Dolores River
Max. rapids: V+
America Outdoors, Arkansas River Outfitters Association, Colorado River Outfitters Association
Four Corners Rafting runs guided oar- and paddle-raft trips on the Arkansas and Delores Rivers. Trips on the Arkansas vary widely in difficulty, offering family-class to adventure-class white water. The high-mountain setting features spectacular vistas of 14,000-foot mountains and a chance to fish for trout

Rafting on the Arkansas River. Courtesy of ECHO Canyon River Expeditions, Canon City, Colorado.

and view deer, bighorn sheep, ouzels, and hawks.

Three- to six-day trips are available on the Delores River, which boasts fun white water, Indian ruins, and changing, captivating scenery, including red sandstone, juniper trees, ponderosa, and desert terrain.

Four Corners' season runs from May to August. The company's owners also run Arkansas River Tours. (See separate listing.)

Holiday River Expeditions of Idaho
Frogg Stewart
P.O. Box 86
Grangeville, ID 83530
(208) 983-1518
Salmon River, Colorado River, Green River, Yampa River, San Juan River, Lochsa River, Snake River
Max. rapids: III-IV
Idaho Outfitters and Guides Association, Utah Outfitters and Guides Association, America Outdoors

Holiday River Expeditions runs one to six day trips on 12 sections of eight rivers in Utah, Colorado, and Idaho. Guided trips are by kayak or raft, with both oar and paddle boats available. Paddlers can also rent rafts

49

Rafting on the Arkansas River. Courtesy of ECHO Canyon River Expeditions, Canon City, Colorado.

during the April-to September season. Overall, trips range from "mild to wild" and are suited for all ages and abilities.

The company has been in business for 25 years, has an excellent safety record, and pays great attention to detail in training guides and maintaining equipment and vehicles.

Holiday River Expeditions also offers several distinctive specialty trips, including a whitewater guide school, kayak school, canoe trips on the Colorado River, and "ghost boats," a chance to run rapids in meticulously crafted replicas of boats from the past.

Joni Ellis River Tours, Inc.
Joni Ellis
Box 764
Dillon, CO 80435
(303) 468-1028, (800) 477-0144
Upper Colorado River, Blue River, Arkansas River
Max. rapids: III-IV
America Outdoors and Colorado River Outfitters Association
Joni Ellis River Tours runs one-day guided trips on the upper Colorado River, Blue River, and Arkansas River. The upper Colorado run is a scenic, introductory whitewater trip that passes through beautiful Little Gore Canyon and includes stops at natural hot springs and historic miners' cabins. The Arkansas River trip

through Browns Canyon is one of Colorado's most exciting family whitewater trips. The Blue River tour puts in at 9,000 feet, offering gorgeous alpine scenery and two miles of continuous white water, making it an excellent choice for both families and whitewater enthusiasts.

Joni Ellis runs tours from May to September and offers guests the choice of paddle rafts, oar rafts, and inflatable kayaks. Wildlife to see include eagles, hawks, migratory birds, deer, and beavers.

Mad Adventures, Inc.
Roger Hedlund/Jack Van Horn
Box 650
Winter Park, CO 80482
(303) 726-5290, (800) 451-4844
Upper Colorado River, Arkansas River
Max. rapids: III-IV
America Outdoors

Mad Adventures runs one-day guided paddle-raft trips on the Arkansas and upper Colorado Rivers. Trips on the Colorado have mild white water and terrific scenery and are well-suited for families. The Arkansas trips, for experienced paddlers only, have challenging white water and spectacular canyons with 800-foot-high walls.

Among the wildlife to be seen are deer, elk, beavers, golden eagles, and ospreys. Guests may also fish for rainbow, cutthroat, and brown trout.

Moondance River Expeditions, Ltd.
Nonny and Bear Dyer
310 West First Street
Salida, CO 81201
(719) 539-2113
Arkansas River
Max. rapids: V+
America Outdoors, Colorado River Outfitters Association, Arkansas River Outfitters Association

Moondance runs one- to five-day guided raft trips on a 100-mile stretch of the Arkansas River from north of Buena Vista to Canyon City, Colorado. The areas is home to hot springs, mountain lions, and spectacular mountain scenery.

Trips run from May to September and are by oar boat, paddle boat, or oar/paddle combination boats. With this selection, Moondance can accommodate guests with all levels of ability and experience, and is proud to offer trips accessible to the disabled, elderly, and young children.

Moondance, appropriately, also offers moonlight float trips. These trips run for five nights each lunar cycle and consist of six miles of Class I and II water.

Mountain Waters Rafting
Casey D. Lynch
P.O. Box 2681
108 West 6th Street
Durango, CO 81302
(800) 748-2507
Animas River, Piedra River
Max. rapids: V
America Outdoors, Colorado River Outfitters Association

Mountain Waters Rafting offers guided oar- and paddle-raft trips lasting one and two days. Runs on the lower Animas are excellent trips for families and novices. Trips on the upper Animas and Piedra are for experts only, with rapids of up to Class V. The upper Animas trips are notable, too, for including a shuttle aboard the Durango-Silverton Narrow Gauge Railroad.

On all trips, guests can enjoy the high-desert scenery, glimpses of remnants of Durango's wild-west history, and a chance to view deer, beavers, otters, muskrats, eagles, hawks, and other wildlife. The season runs from May to September.

Noah's Ark Whitewater Rafting
Chuck and Lindy Cichowitz
P.O. Box 850
Buena Vista, CO 81211
(719) 395-2158
Arkansas River
Max. rapids: III-IV

Noah's Ark runs one- to three-day guided and unguided raft trips on the Arkansas River. The difficulty of trips varies greatly, depending on the section of river chosen and whether one travels by oar or paddle boat. The easiest trips are fine for families and children age six and up. The toughest trips are challenging for advanced paddlers. On the river, guests have chances to fish for trout and view eagles and deer.

The company also offers a riverfront campground and rock-climbing and rappelling courses.

Pagosa Rafting Outfitters
Wayne Wells
Box 222
Pagosa Springs, CO 81147
(303) 731-4081
Upper San Juan River, Piedra River,
Upper Animas River, Conejos River
Max. rapids: III-IV
Colorado River Outfitters Association,
America Outdoors

Pagosa Rafting Outfitters runs one- to three-day oar- and paddle-raft trips of one to three days. Trips on the San Juan and Conejos rivers are fine for families, offering intermediate white water and great views of wilderness, ghost towns, and abandoned historic railroads. Trips on the Piedra and upper Animas are more demanding, restricted to teens and fit adults.

The Piedra run starts high in the mountains of the San Juan National Forest and offers spectacular vistas, craggy canyons, beautiful forests, and some of the most challenging white water in the Four Corners area. The upper Animas trip has even more

Fly-fishing. Courtesy of Dvorak's Kayak & Rafting Expeditions, Inc., Nathrop, Colorado.

challenging white water, including stretches of almost continuous Class IV rapids. This trip is exclusively for fit adults who have some river-running experience and are prepared for vigorous paddling.

Pagosa's season runs from April to September. The company also offers horseback and jeep trips and tours of Indian cliff dwellings.

Performance Tours Rafting
Kevin and Mary Foley
P.O. Box 7305
110 Ski Kill Road
Breckenridge, CO 80424
(303) 453-0661, (800) 328-7238
Arkansas River, Blue River, Colorado River
Max. rapids: V+

Performance Tours Rafting offers guided raft trips and raft rentals on the Arkansas, Blue, and Colorado Rivers. Trips last from one to three days and run amid the greatest concentration of 14,000-foot peaks in the country. In addition to the beautiful mountain scenery, guests can enjoy blue-ribbon trout fishing and the chance to spot deer, elk, eagles, hawks, bighorn sheep, and mountain lions.

With a choice of rivers and paddle and oar boats, Performance Tours has trips to suit guests of all ages. The company's season runs from May to September.

Raftmeister
Debbie K. Marquez
P.O. Box 1805
Vail, CO 81658
(303) 476-7238
Eagle River, Arkansas River, Colorado River
Max. rapids: III-IV
Colorado River Outfitters Association, America Outdoors

Raftmeister runs guided kayak and raft trips of one to three days on the Eagle, Arkansas, and Colorado Rivers. On the Arkansas, guests can run the Numbers or Brown's Canyon. The Numbers, for more experienced paddlers, features numerous Class IV rapids; Brown's Canyon, also a great whitewater trip, is slightly less overwhelming. The Eagle offers exhilarating rides for whitewater enthusiasts on its upper stretches, while Lower Eagle provides great adventure for families. Wildlife float trips on the Eagle are also available in the morning when wildlife is particularly abundant. On the Colorado, guests can ride the Upper Colorado, an historic, scenic family trip, or the Shoshone/Glenwood Canyon, a scenic and thrilling run.

With this wide choice of rivers, Raftmeister can accommodate guests of all ages and skill levels. The company's season is from May to October.

Raven Adventure Trips
Art and Virginia Krizman
P.O. Box 108
Granby, CO 80446
(303) 887-2141, (800) 332-3381
Arkansas River, Colorado River, North Platte River
Max. rapids: V+
America Outdoors, Colorado River Outfitters Association, Arkansas River Outfitters Association

Raven Adventure Trips runs one- to three-day guided raft and inflatable kayak trips on the Arkansas, Colorado, and North Platte Rivers. The Arkansas, renowned for its exhilarating Class III-IV white water, is nestled in central Colorado between the Collegiate Peaks and the Sangre de Cristo Mountains. On Arkansas River trips, guests eight and older may choose oar or paddle boats.

The Colorado River trips, with Class II-III rapids, are perfect for first-time rafters, families, and groups of all types. Guests age six and older can enjoy beautiful scenery, historic cabins, and hot springs. Trips on the Colorado are by raft or inflatable kayaks, as are trips on the North Platte River.

The North Platte trips, set in northern Colorado at over 8,000 feet, run through the remote Northgate Canyon, a designated wilderness area. The minimum age for the North Platte trips is 14. On Raven Adventure's trips, which run from May to September, guests can view elk, deer, bears, bighorn sheep, and bald and golden eagles. Fishing is for brown and rainbow trout.

River Runners, Ltd.
11150 US Highway 50
Salida, CO 81201
(719) 539-2144, (800) 525-2081, (U.S.)
(800) 332-9100 (CO)
Arkansas River
Max. rapids: V+
Colorado Rafting Association, Colorado River Outfitters Association, Arkansas River Outfitters Association
River Runners' one- to three-day guided trips are on the Arkansas River. With offices at the beginning, middle and end of the "raftable" Arkansas, the company offers access to many different stretches of river. Between this selection and guests' choice of oar-, paddle, and paddle-assisted boats, the company has trips for people of all ages.

All trips pass through areas of gorgeous scenery, whether high among the peaks of the continental divide or deep within towering canyons. Trips also offer fishing for brown trout and chances to view owls, eagles, hawks, deer, elk, and mountain sheep. The season runs from May to September.

River Runners runs a riverside campground and offers horseback rides, pack trips, and scenic jeep tours of ghost towns.

Slickrock Adventures
Cully Erdman
P.O. Box 1400
Moab, UT 84532
(80) 259-6996
Dolores River, Green River, Payette River
Max. rapids: III-IV
America Outdoors
Slickrock Adventures runs guided kayak and raft trips of 5-13 days on Utah's Green River, Colorado's Dolores River, and Idaho's Payette River. Its most popular beginners' runs are raft and kayak trips on 85 miles of the Green River, through Desolation and Gray Canyons. Paddlers have time to play in over 60 easy rapids, and enjoy views of tall cliffs, sandy beaches, and cottonwoods.

The Dolores emerges from lush meadows and forests to descend into a desert canyon. Continuous white water in the upper canyon gives way to widely-spaced, easier drops below. This allows Slickrock to choose stretches to match each group's ability. Green River kayak trips run through Labyrinth and Stillwater Canyons, offering peaceful, flat-water paddling through the heart of Canyonlands, with spectacular side canyons, petroglyphs and Indian ruins. Finally, on the Payette, Slickrock offers a whitewater kayak clinic featuring incredible white water and beautiful canyons. Open all year, Slickrock also offers paddling trips in Belize and Mexico.

Western River Expeditions
Larry Lake
7258 Racquet Club Drive
Salt Lake City, UT 84121
(801) 942-6669, (800) 453-7450 (outside UT)
Colorado River
Max. rapids: III-IV
America Outdoors
Western River Expeditions runs guided raft trips and rents rafts and inflatable kayaks on the Colorado River in Colorado, Utah and Arizona; the Green River in Utah and the Main Salmon in Idaho. Green River trips, by oar or paddle raft, provide thrilling whitewater and views of towering red rock cliffs and arches, deep gorges, frontier cabins, and Indian petroglyphs. Colorado River tours

offer spectacular scenery in Cataract Canyon, Westwater Canyon or the Upper and Lower Grand Canyon. Rapids are moderate to large, and paddlers can swim, take side hikes, and view historic Indian and Old West sites. Finally, trips on the Main Salmon involve scenic blue-green waters, pine-covered mountains, stops at hot springs and abandoned mining camps, and camping on white sand beaches.

All trips are suitable for anyone of good health above the minimum age set for each trip, depending on its difficulty. During Western River's March-September season, some trips can be combined with a ranch stay.

Courtesy of Dvorak's Kayak & Rafting Expeditions, Inc., Nathrop, Colorado.

Wilderness Aware Rafting
Joe and Sue Greiner
P.O. Box 1550 SP
Buena Vista, CO 81211
(719) 395-2112, (800) 462-7238
Dolores River, North Platte River, Gunnison River, Arkansas River, Colorado River
Max. rapids: III-IV
America Outdoors, Arkansas River Outfitters Association, Colorado River Outfitters Association

Wilderness Aware Rafting runs one- to 10-day guided raft trips on rivers in Colorado and Texas, offering "family white water to wild water" for adventurers age 6 to 86. Guests may choose either paddle or oar boats. Also, on some Class II and III sections during multi-day trips, guests may try one- and two-person self-bailing inflatable kayaks. These small, maneuverable kayaks make it easy to explore nooks and crannies not reachable in larger craft.

Among the wildlife to be seen on these rivers are deer, bighorn sheep, otters, and beavers. Fishing is for brown and rainbow trout.

Wildwater, Inc.
Robert Breckinridge
317 Stover Street
Fort Collins, CO 80524
(303) 224-3379, (800) 369-4165
Arkansas River, North Platte River, Colorado River, Poudre River
Max. rapids: V+
Colorado River Outfitters Association

Wildwater Inc. offers rentals and kayak trips on some of the best wildwater stretches in the state, including the Poudre, Colorado's only designated wild and scenic river. Trips range from "mild to wild" and last from one to six days. Canoes, kayaks, rafts, and tubes are available for rent.

Wildwater's season runs from May to September, with June and early July offering exceptional high-mountain "big water." Wildlife to see include deer, bears, and bighorn sheep. Guests also can fish for trout.

Connecticut

Float through the Connecticut hills on a sunlit autumn day when the fall foliage is ablaze and watch migrating birds head south for winter. Take the broad Connecticut River down the middle of the state or the Housatonic's fast water in the Berkshire Hills. On a calm summer day, take a sea kayak or canoe into the estuaries along the shore of Long Island Sound. Or just set out on a placid pond or lake for a day's cruising and fishing. Connecticut has all this to offer, plus interesting historic sites and museums.

The Connecticut River, formerly badly contaminated by industrial pollution, has been largely restored. Fish have returned to this waterway, which in earlier centuries had been famous for salmon and shad spawning. Bird life is abundant, trees line the riverbanks, and some handsome old houses may be seen — or even visited — from the water.

North of Hartford, the Connecticut has a series of easy rapids for 4 1/2 miles below Enfield Dam. But most canoeists prefer to skirt them by using the adjacent canal. At Middletown the river widens and deepens as it passes between forested hills. Then come several state parks and forests affording paddlers plenty of places to picnic and camp. And once it passes Hadlyme the mile-wide river becomes tidal for the rest of its journey past Essex to its sea outlet at Old Saybrook.

The Housatonic in the northwest corner of the state offers paddlers a different experience. It provides various degrees of white water — up to Class IV+ at Bull's Bridge Gorge, where seasonal guided raft trips are available — as well as gentle floating. An appealing stretch of the Housatonic is the scenic 10 miles from the Massachusetts state line southward to the Falls Village Dam. It provides smooth floating through pastures and a tree-lined Berkshires valley replete with otters and other wildlife.

Below Falls Village, paddlers find a mixture of flat water and white water on another 10-mile section of the river, down to Housatonic Meadows State Park. Several restaurants offer lunch at the well-known Covered Bridge in West Cornwall, and there are various picnic sites. But the water level on this segment of the Housatonic, and on the next section down to Kent School, varies widely depending on the season and rainfall. Outfitters caution that they may have to postpone or cancel trips, or move them to other sections of the river. The Mystic River in southeastern Connecticut is only a few miles long and largely tidal. It offers easy canoeing in calm weather and takes paddlers to the Mystic Seaport Museum with its ancient whaling vessels.

Clarke Outdoors
Mark Clarke
Box 163, Route 7
West Cornwall, CT 06796
(203) 672-6365
Housatonic River
Max. rapids: III-IV
NEPSA, NACLO, ACA

Clarke Outdoors runs one-day guided and unguided canoe, kayak, and raft trips on the Housatonic River in the Berkshire foothills from March to November. Canoe and unguided raft trips are 10 miles long, passing under the scenic covered bridge of West Cornwall. These trips have flat water and Class I and II rapids.

Kayak lessons and canoe clinics are also available, as are seasonal Class III and IV guided raft trips through the Housatonic's Bulls Bridge Gorge. Lessons are led by Mark Clarke, a six-time national open canoe champion, and other ACA-certified instructors.

North American Canoe Tours
David Harraden
65 Black Point Road
Niantic, CT 06537
(203) 739-0791
Farmington River, Connecticut River
Max. rapids: III-IV

North American Canoe Tours offers canoe and tube rentals for trips on the Farmington River between May and September. Canoe trips last one to three days and pass through scenic countryside, offering a chance to fish for trout and spot birds, deer, and beavers.

Elsewhere in Connecticut, NACT rents canoes on the Connecticut River in Hadden, Hopeville Pond State Park in Griswold, Squantz Pond State Park in New Fairfield, Burr Pond State Park in Thompson, and Lake Waramaug State Park in New Preston. NACT also offers trips in Everglades National Park and on the Suwanee River. (See description under Florida.)

The Mountain Workshop
Sue and Corky Clark
P.O. Box 625
Ridgefield, CT 06877
(203) 438-3640
New England rivers and lakes,
Everglades, Allagash River
Max. rapids: I-II

The Mountain Workshop offers guided one- to 12-day canoe and kayak trips on rivers and lakes in New England, the Allagash in Maine, and Florida's Everglades.

Trips are best-suited for adventuresome beginners seeking personalized instruction.

Delaware

Paddling in the First State is mostly on tidal waters within marshes and swamps. Canoeists should not be put off by the bloodthirsty names of some of the rivers, like Murderkill, Broadkill and Slaughter Creek. It is in fact a very peaceful and friendly place. More to the point is the need to time each trip in accordance with the tides coursing in and out of Delaware Bay from the Atlantic. Most Delaware streams ebb and flow as they glide eastward into the bay through flatlands and wildlife refuges. But there are rivers in southern Delaware, notably the Nanticoke, that flow southwest into Chesapeake Bay. Many of the state's 50 small lakes and ponds have good beaches and great freshwater fishing.

From Wilmington, the nearest rivers to paddle are the Appoquinimink and Blackbird Creek in New Castle County. Of these, Blackbird Creek is the prettiest. It passes through attractive unspoiled marshland, where the wall of reeds opens up from time to time to allow vistas of farmland on high ground.

Further south, the Smyrna and Leipsic rivers also take the paddler through vast wetlands, where the view is usually limited by tall reeds. But the Leipsic traverses the Bombay Hook National Wildlife Refuge with its wealth of waterfowl.

Slaughter Creek provides another rewarding bird sanctuary experience as it runs through Prime Hook National Wildlife Refuge. The upper stream starts out amid forests of pine and cedar, then the lower creek winds its way through salt marshes to Cedar Creek.

The Prime Hook refuge has two other canoe trails worth exploring, both on Prime Hook Creek. One is a 10-mile float from Del. Rte. 1 to the refuge headquarters, the other a circuit tour. But it is easy to go astray amid the confusing maze of major ditches and side channels. Prime Hook Creek is mostly sheltered from the wind by trees or reeds, and although it is tidal the ebb-and-flow range is weak and the current is gentle.

Beaston's Marina

Steven D. Beaston
Bayview Park
Bethany Beach, DE 19930
(302) 539-3452
Little Assawoman Bay, Assawoman Canal
Max. rapids: None

Beaston's Marina rents canoes from April to November for outings in the salt-marsh region of Little Assawoman Bay and Assawoman Creek. This is flat water that takes paddlers through a wildlife refuge abounding in waterfowl: ducks, geese, ospreys, herons and egrets. Crabbing and perch fishing are local pastimes.

Beaston's Marina is a small family business catering to individual tourists' needs. Canoes can be rented for up to a fortnight.

Waples Mill Pond Canoeing

H.H. Plummer
Routes 1 and 5
RD 1, Box 138
Milton, DE 19968-9723
(302) 684-8084
Prime Hook Wildlife Refuge, Prime Hook Creek
Max. rapids: None

Waples Mill Pond Canoeing has been in business for 15 years. Open year-round, it rents canoes for day trips in Prime Hook National Wildlife Refuge, Prime Hook Creek, and nearby areas. Longer trips can be arranged.

Prime Hook Creek is a unique ecosystem. Its upper five miles are strictly freshwater before it turns salty close to the sea. Scenery changes from woodland to coastal marshes with tall reeds. Wildlife ranges from whitetail deer and grey foxes to otters, opossum, raccoons, ospreys, and great blue herons. Anglers fish for largemouth bass, crappie, perch, pickerel, and bluegill.

Florida

Land of lazy waters, sparkling springs, abundant wildlife — Florida is a place to float idly into the wilderness and consort with nature. Alligators rather than unrunnable rapids are Florida's hazards to be avoided. Birds are ubiquitous: gleaming white egrets, slender blue herons, and keen-eyed kingfishers. Observant paddlers may also see rare species such as bobcats, wild hogs, or even a Florida panther stalking the riverbanks. Armadillos are found in some parts of the state, while otters, raccoons and opossums are common. All told, Florida has more than 1,700 rivers, streams, and creeks running to a total length of more than 10,000 miles. Some stem from great springs gushing millions of gallons a day of crystal-clear water.

The Everglades in the south and Okefenokee Swamp in the north are justly famed as back-country havens of natural beauty. Half land, half water, the 1.4-million-acre Everglades National Park provides a habitat for endangered plants and animals. Essentially a 50-mile-wide, slow-moving river, the Everglades consist largely of mangrove swamps and sawgrass marshland. Canoes may be rented in Flamingo, the southernmost point, and Everglades City in the northwestern corner of the park. Several canoe trails are marked, but paddlers are advised to pick up charts of the maze-like waterways and file trip plans before setting out. Okefenokee Swamp, smaller but just as fascinating, is accessible from Waycross, Georgia (see Georgia).

The Withlacoochee River in westcentral Florida — as distinct from its northern namesake, which flows into the state from Georgia — is an easy float for paddlers of all ages. Clean and largely undeveloped, the Withlacoochee provides fishing for catfish, largemouth bass, and brim, along with glimpses of interesting wildlife on its wooded banks.

Further south runs the Peace River, an artery that drains much of westcentral Florida into the Gulf at Punta Gorda. An unspoiled stream, the Peace has overhanging trees along its banks. Paddlers find plenty of sandbanks and swimming holes — places to pause and look out for alligators, wild boars, turkeys, and a wide variety of birds.

On the Alabama state line in the Florida panhandle, the Perdido is a safe and secluded river with white sandy beaches. But one writer advises sticking to its lower stretches to avoid the many abandoned bridges, log jams, and other obstacles upstream.

Just a few miles to the east of the Perdido is the Blackwater River State Forest, the largest state forest in Florida. It is the home not only of the Blackwater, with its dark, tannin water, but of Juniper and Coldwater Creeks as well. All three offer cool, unpolluted water amid attractive scenery, with riverbeds of white sand.

A favorite river near Orlando is the Wekiva, a tranquil stream that has been designated Wild and Scenic. Rich in fish and wildlife, it is said to have the cleanest water in the state. Equally appealing are the Wekiva's tributaries, the Little Wekiva and Rock Springs Run, which is great for tubing. The run to Blue Springs State Park on the St. John's River (into which the Wekiva flows) is to be avoided at weekends, when it is liable to be crowded.

Elsewhere in Florida, the Loxahatchee River is said to be the only remaining wild and natural river in the southeast part of the state. Situated within Jonathan Dickinson State Park near the coast, the Loxahatchee is well-preserved and home to abundant wildlife.

Adventures Unlimited
Jack, Esther, Mike, and Linda Sanborn
Route 6, Box 283
Milton, FL 32570
(904) 623-6197, (904) 626-1669
Coldwater Creek, Sweetwater Creek,
Blackwater River
Max. rapids: None
NACLO, Florida Association of Canoe
Liveries and Outfitters
   Adventures Unlimited offers canoe, kayak, raft, and inner tube rentals on four Florida wilderness streams: Coldwater Creek, Blackwater River, Perdido River, and Sweetwater Juniper. These spring-fed rivers flow at an average depth of two feet over soft, sandy bottoms through pine and cedar forests of Northwest Florida.
   White-sand beaches dot the banks and are perfect for swimming, sunning, and camping. Adventures Unlimited offers trips of one to three days, cabin and camping gear rentals, and a chance to spot deer, turkeys,

bobcats, foxes, squirrels, ducks, raccoons, and turtles. Fishing is for bass, bream, pickerel, and catfish.

Adventures Unlimited-Perdido River
David and Linda Venn
160 River Annex Road
Cantonment, FL 32533
(904) 968-5529
Coldwater River, Perdido River, Blackwater River, Sweetwater-Juniper
Max. rapids: None
   Adventures Unlimited-Perdido River offers one- and two-day trips along the Perdido River, renting canoes, kayaks, and inner tubes.
   The river is scenic and secluded, with white-sand beaches and clear-to tea-colored water. The calm waters are suitable for paddlers of all ages and encourage fishing and wildlife viewing. Fishing is for bass, bream, and catfish, and the wildlife to see includes deer, beavers, otters, and snakes.

61

Paddling on Coldwater Creek. Courtesy of Carter Photography/Adventures Unlimited, Milton Florida.

Adventures Unlimited also offers cabin rentals and tent and R.V. camping during its April-to-October season.

Back Country Tours, Inc.
Alan McGroary
39 Hollis Street
Pepperell, MA 01463
(508) 433-9381, (800) 649-9381 (in MA)
Blackwater River, Sweetwater River, Juniper River
Max. rapids: I-II
Back Country Tours, Inc., specializes in guided canoe trips and canoe rentals on "lesser known, uncrowded scenic waterways." Its trips run on the Souhegan and Merrimack rivers in New Hampshire; the Sauantacook and Nissitissit Rivers in Massachusetts; the Connecticut and Nashua Rivers in New Hampshire and Massachusetts; the Delaware River in New York, Pennsylvania, and New Jersey; the Blackwater, Sweetwater, and Juniper Rivers in Florida; and nine lakes near Long Pond Mountain in New York's Adirondacks. Several of these excursion are "vacation" trips of three to seven days that offer lodging at campgrounds, cabins, or bed-and-breakfast inns. All trips are suitable for beginners and experienced paddlers.

Back Country Tours' season runs from July to November.

Biscayne National Underwater Park Co.
Captain Ed Davidson
P.O. Box 1270
Homestead, FL 33030
(305) 247-2400
Shoreline of the southern tip of Florida, Biscayne Bay
Max. rapids: None
Biscayne National Underwater Park offers one-day canoe rentals for

exploring the longest stretch of
mangrove shoreline on Florida's east
coast. The water is clear, shallow,
and calm, making canoeing easy for
families and allowing paddlers to
view fish, stingrays, and manatees.
The park's clean, uncrowded waters
are also an excellent place to swim.

Bob's Canoe Rental and Sales
L.L. Plowman
4569 Plowman Lane
Milton, FL 32570
(904) 623-5457
*Blackwater River, Coldwater Creek,
Juniper Creek*
Max. rapids: I-II
*NACLO, Florida Association of Canoe
Liveries and Outfitters*
Bob's Canoe Rental offers canoe,
kayak, pedal boat, and inner-tube rentals year round on clear and blackwater rivers and creeks of Northwest
Florida. Good currents and calm
waters make paddling easy for
families, beginners, and advanced
paddlers alike. Trips last one to three
days and offer views of white-sand
beaches, wildflowers, flowering trees,
birds, raccoons, and turtles. Fishing is
for bass, bream, bluefish, and catfish.
Bob's prides itself on its many
years' experience and friendly personal service. The outfitter also offers
a picnic ground with grills, tables, a
game areas, and a white-sand beach.

Canoe Escape, Inc.
Joe and Jean Faulk
9335 East Fowler Avenue
Thonotosassa, FL 33592
(813) 986-2067
Hillsborough River
Max. rapids: None
*NACLO, Florida Association of Canoe
Liveries and Outfitters*
Canoe Escape, Inc., runs one-day,
self-guided trips through the cypress
swamps and hardwood hammocks of
the Hillsborough River. Set in a

wilderness park just minutes from
Tampa, the river varies from a narrow, twisting stream beneath a tree
canopy to a broad, sunlit river. In all,
25 miles of riverfront and 16,000
acres within the park are protected as
wilderness, offering habitat for many
wading birds, including limpkins,
wood storks, ibises, herons, egrets,
and birds of prey, as well as deer,
wild hogs, river otters, turtles, and alligators. Fishing is for bass, panfish,
catfish, and speckled perch.
Downstream paddling on this
placid river is easy for paddlers of all
ages. Trips run year-round.

Canoe Outfitters of Florida, Inc.
Eric and Sandy Bailey
16346 N. 106th Terrace
Jupiter, FL 33478
(407) 746-7053
Loxahatchee River
Max. rapids: None
*NACLO, Florida Association of Canoe
Liveries and Outfitters*
Canoe Outfitters of Florida has
one-day canoe trips on a section of
Loxahatchee River designated as part
of the Wild and Scenic river system.
Trips pass through pristine
countryside with 500-year-old
cypress trees and other native vegetation sheltering ospreys, eagles, owls,
snakes, and turtles.
Trips also offer a chance to camp,
see manatees, and fish for bass, brim,
snook, and tarpon.

Canoe Outpost - Peace River
Charlotte Bragg
Route 7, Box 301
Arcadia, FL 33821
(813) 494-1215
Peace River, Everglades National Park
Max. rapids: None
*NACLO, Florida Association of Canoe
Liveries and Outfitters*
Canoe Outpost — Peace River
runs guided and unguided canoe

trips on the Peace River, a placid blackwater river suitable for canoeists of all ages. Trips last from one to seven days and pass through unspoiled wilderness that offers fishing for bass, catfish, bream, and snook, and a chance to see alligators, birds, deer, wild boars, and turkeys.

Estero River Tackle & Canoe
Paula Stuller
20991 S. Tamiami Trail
Estero, FL 33928
(813) 992-4050
Estero River, Estero Bay and environs
Max. rapids: None
NACLO, ACA, Florida Association of Canoe Liveries and Outfitters

Open year-round, Estero River & Tackle has half-day and full-day canoe and kayak rentals on the Estero River. The river is tidal and spring-fed, suited for leisurely canoeing and excellent saltwater fishing for snook, mangrove snapper, and sea trout.

An acclaimed four-and-a-half mile Florida-designated canoe trail leads to Estero Bay through a picturesque semitropical landscape.

Camping is available at the nearby Koreshan State Historical Site.

Katie's Wekiva River Landing
Katie Moncrief
190 Katie's Cove
Sanford, FL 32771
(407) 322-4470, (407) 628-1482
Wekiva River, Little Wekiva River, Rock Springs Run, St. John's River
Max. rapids: None
NACLO

Katie's Landing has guided trips and canoe and kayak rentals on sandy bottomed, spring-fed rivers. The waters are clean, gentle, and suitable for paddlers of all ages.

Paddling on the Santa Fe River. Courtesy of Santa Fe Canoe Outpost, High Springs, Florida.

The rivers are zealously protected, designated as scenic and wild waters, outstanding Florida waters, an aquatic preserve, and a Florida State Canoe Trail. The water is so clear and clean that paddlers can easily see many varieties of aquatic vegetation and fish, including catfish, large-mouth bass, bream, and spec. Other wildlife to be seen include deer, raccoons, otters, black bears, alligators, turtles, herons, red-shouldered hawks, ospreys, and bald eagles.

Trips range in length from one to three days and are available year-round. Katie's Landing also offers cabin rentals, tent and R.V. sites, and a well-stocked country store.

Key West Kayak Co.

Jim and Ellen McCarthy
P.O. Box 4411
Key West, FL 33040
(305) 294-6494
Atlantic Ocean, Gulf of Mexico, mangrove creeks
Max. rapids: None

Key West Kayak Co. offers guided and unguided sea-kayak trips in the clear, shallow waters of the Atlantic Ocean and back country of the Gulf of Mexico. Trips last a half day or full day and concentrate on finding a wide variety of wildlife for paddlers to see. The clear waters allow easy viewing of sharks, rays, fish, sponges, coral, and other marine life. As they paddle on open water and down mangrove-lined creeks, guests can also see herons and egrets and fish for tarpon, bonefish, snapper, and barracuda.

Key West Kayak's trips, which run year-round, are leisurely, require no previous kayaking experience, and are fine for paddlers of all ages.

North American Canoe Tours

David Harraden
65 Black Point Road
Niantic, CT 06357
(813) 695-4666
Suwannee River, Everglades National Park
Max. rapids: None

NACT runs one- to seven-day guided and unguided canoe and kayak trips in the Everglades, offering guests a chance to see alligators, manatee, bottlenose dolphins, sea turtles, and a variety of birds. Guided canoe trips run for seven days and six nights through the backcountry of Everglades National Park, and include all camping gear and meals. These trips run between December and March. Those wanting to explore on their own can also rent all supplies and receive help in planning their trips.

NACT also runs trips on the Suwannee River in Georgia that start at the Okefenokee Swamp and wind down to White Springs, Florida. NACT has it headquarters in Niantic, Connecticut, and can be reached there during the off-season.

Santa Fe Canoe Outpost

Jim and Sally Wood
P.O. Box 592
High Springs, FL 32643
(904) 454-2050
Santa Fe River
Max. rapids: None
NACLO, Florida Association of Canoe Liveries and Outfitters

Santa Fe Canoe Outpost offers canoe and kayak rentals for trips of one to seven days on the Santa Fe, Suwanee, and Ichehicknee Rivers. These spring-fed waters are crystal-clear and offer easy paddling and excellent fishing for bass, mullet, gar, catfish, and perch. The banks, thickly wooded with cypress trees, provide secluded sites for wilderness camping and shelter abundant wildlife, including alligators, deer, beavers, turtles, snakes, otters, wild boars, and a wide variety of birds.

Santa Fe Outpost, open year-round, also offers custom trips, guided, full-moon night trips, and complete or partial outfitting for those needing camping gear.

Turner's Camp
Dennis and Alicia Lowe
3033 Hooty Point
Inverness, FL 32650
(904) 726-2685
Withlacoochee River, Gum Slough
Max. rapids: None

Turner's Camp offers one-day guided canoe tours and rentals on Withlacoochee River and Gum Slough. Trips are five or 10 miles long, on placid waters suitable for paddlers of all ages.

The Withlacoochee is a scenic river in a mostly undeveloped setting. Gum Slough is clear, spring-fed, and completely undeveloped. On both waters paddlers can see deer, wild hogs, alligators, otters, bald eagles, ospreys, and anhinga. There is also good fishing for largemouth bass, catfish, and eight varieties of panfish.

Turner's Camp, open year-round, also offers cabin rentals and tent and R.V. camping.

Wilderness Southeast
711 Sandtown Road
Savannah, GA 31410
(912) 897-5108
Everglades - 10,000 Islands
Max. rapids: None

Wilderness Southeast is a non-profit educational corporation that leads small groups on guided expeditions to teach participants about the natural history of unique wilderness ecosystems. Among the offerings is a four-day sea kayaking trip along Georgia's wild barrier islands, which

Paddling in the Everglades from a base aboard a houseboat. Courtesy of Wilderness Southeast.

permits ample time for exploring marshland, beaches, and tidal creeks, and for sighting dolphins, shorebirds, and other abundant wildlife. Also in Georgia is a five-day canoe trip through the wilderness of Okefenokee Swamp, which explores the peat prairies, towering cypress forests, and sandy pine islands. On these trips, paddlers can also see frogs, alligators, owls, river otters, and cranes.

In Florida's Everglades, Wilderness Southeast has seven-day canoe and sea-kayak trips spent exploring wild beaches, isolated coastal islands, and mangrove estuaries. Paddling these waters, guests can see herons, egrets, alligators, bald eagles, sea turtles, manatees, dolphins, and a great variety of other wildlife. On

A nature-study trip in the Everglades. Courtesy of Wilderness Southeast, Savannah, Georgia

Everglades trips, guests sleep aboard a moving base of two houseboats.

Wilderness Southeast, with trips year-round, also has expeditions to Costa Rica, the Amazon, the Virgin Islands, and the Great Smoky Mountains. Teen backpacking, sailing, and marine science trips are also available.

**Withlacoochee R.V. Park &
Canoe Rental, Inc.**
Louis Baggett, Jr.
P.O. Box 114
Lacoochee, FL 33537
(904) 583-4778
Withlacoochee River
Max. rapids: None
Withlacoochee R.V. Park and Canoe rental offers one- and two-day canoe rentals for trips through lush wilderness on the Withlacoochee in westcentral Florida. Trips pass along placid waters through unspoiled cypress swamps and pine forests, site of ancient campgrounds of the Seminole Indians.

The Withlacoochee is a "blackwater" river, its waters tea-colored from the tannins in the vegetation. Fishing is for bass, brim, and catfish, and the wildlife to be seen includes birds, alligators, turtles, wild hogs, and deer.

Campsites are available for tents and R.V.s at the outfitter's campground, which is open year-round.

Georgia

Northern Georgia's mountainous terrain is superb watersports country, offering a broad selection of rivers that enthrall novices and experts alike. There, for instance, is the Chattooga, whose fabled white water divides Georgia from South Carolina (for Chattooga River description see *South Carolina*). But while rafters brave the Chattooga rapids, less adventurous souls canoe quiet Georgia streams in search of wildlife lurking among mountain laurel and rhododendron. And down in the southeastern corner of the state lies Okefenokee Swamp, a naturalist's delight.

Start in the north with the Chestatee, where an easy day-trip run begins near Dahlonega and ends at Lake Sidney Lanier. It takes floaters through an area that was the scene of America's first gold rush, which began in 1828, 20 years before James Marshall's historic find at Sutter's Mill in California. Dahlonega itself, with its gold museum, is worth exploring. The lower Chestatee is runnable year-round, but the upper Chestatee, with its Class I-III rapids, is much affected by water levels.

Another great stream for beginners — except at high water — is the Etowah, which can be run from Dahlonega to Rome. It is a river of rare beauty, enriched by thickets of mountain laurel, hemlock, and rhododendron along its banks, interspersed with high rock bluffs and farmland. In the Chattahoochee National Forest the upper Etowah is little more than a stream, and it can only be run in early spring or after heavy rains. But the scenery is beautiful, there are ledges and rock gardens, and plenty of places to camp and fish. The middle stretch of the Etowah has a 10-foot waterfall to portage and numerous Class II rapids. Further downstream the river turns calmer but still contains some easy rapids.

The Amicalola Creek is in fact a full-fledged river, spiced with lively Class II-III rapids and splendid scenery. It takes its name from a Cherokee phrase for tumbling water, and its upper east fork tumbles over Amicalola Falls. The state park named for these falls marks the southernmost end of the Appalachian Trail. Rapids on the Amicalola such as Edge of the World and Off the Wall are quite demanding. The river is normally only runnable in the spring.

Also in this general area is the Toccoa River, which rises in Union County and flows northward through Blue Ridge Lake and onward into Tennessee. It has gentle Class I-II rapids, excellent scenery, clean water, and good fishing. Southwest of the Toccoa runs Talking Rock Creek, which probably gets its name from the echo off its cliffs. Talking Rock Creek actually runs through a handsome gorge with sheer walls up to 100 feet high. Access is difficult and water levels fluctuate greatly, so novices are advised to run it only when the water is low to moderate. But the rapids are seldom tougher than Class I-II.

Georgia has two other notable attractions for the canoeist: the Chattahoochee and Okefenokee. Like the Chestatee, the Chattahoochee River starts by running to Lake Sidney Lanier near the northern mountains. But then the Chattahoochee gathers strength and widens to a major artery, heading first for Atlanta and then bordering Alabama on its way southward to cross into Florida on its way to the Gulf of Mexico. Upstream of Atlanta the Chattahoochee provides some enjoyable woodland canoeing, followed by several miles of floating past many of Atlanta's finest suburban homes. But below Atlanta its charms diminish as dams and power boats proliferate.

Okefenokee Swamp, covering an area of more than 600 square miles, is an experience — like Florida's Everglades — not to be missed. The name is a corruption of the Indian word Owaquaphenoga, meaning "trembling earth." Anyone boating in the swamp can see why; one can step "ashore" and find oneself swaying on an island of densely matted floating vegetation. Some of these islands may already be occupied by basking alligators. Four-fifths of the swamp belongs to the Okefenokee National Wildlife Refuge, which allows canoe trips in rented or privately-owned boats. The slow-moving rainwater, stained to tea color by tannic acid, is decked with waterlilies, bladderwort, and other plants. The surface is so smooth that it reflects cypress, tupelo, oak, and other trees with mirror-sharp clarity. Besides alligators, snakes, deer, otters, and many varieties of birds turn this great unspoiled wilderness into a nature lover's paradise.

An alligator seen in the Okefenokee Swamp. Courtesy of Wilderness Southeast.

Appalachian Outfitters
Ben and Dana LaChance
Highway 60 South
P.O. Box 793
Dahlonega, GA 30533
(404) 864-7117, (800) 426-7117
*Chestatee River, Amicalola Creek,
Etowah River, Toccoa River, Talking
Rock Creek*
Max. rapids: III-IV
*Georgia Canoe Association, NACLO,
ACA*
Appalachian Outfitters runs
guided and unguided canoe trips on
five Georgia Rivers. These trips range
in length from one-half day to two-
and-a-half days, and are of varying
difficulty, with challenging ledges,
rapids, and rocks gardens to test the
skills of experienced paddlers.

Trips pass through quiet, beautiful
terrain in the Appalachians, with hemlock and pine forests and laurel- and
rhododendron-lined banks. Fishing is
for small and largemouth bass, trout,
perch, crappie, bream, red-eye bass,
and catfish. Among the wildlife to be
seen are deer, beavers, otters, great
blue herons, ospreys, turtles, and
wood ducks.

Appalachian Outfitters also offers
professional guides and experienced
instructors to teach basic and
whitewater canoeing skills, guide
trips on less-traveled rivers, and run
outdoor-adventure camps for
children.

Raft, GA.
Robert A. Reichert
P.O. Box 7363
Marietta, GA 30065
(404) 971-0707, (404) 971-6553 (off-
season)
Chatahoochee River
Max. rapids: I-II
Raft, Ga. offers rentals for day trips
on the Chattahoochee near Atlanta.
The trips are mostly on flat water
with some Class I and II rapids,
suitable for paddlers of all ages and
levels of experience. Wildlife to see
include beavers, snakes, and raccoons. Fishing is for trout and bream.

Raft, Ga.'s seasons runs from May
through September.

S.C. Foster State Park
Georgia Department of Natural
Resources
Route 2, Box 131
Fargo, GA 31631
(912) 637-5274, (912) 637-5325
Okefenokee Swamp
Max. rapids: None
S.C. Foster State Park offers canoe
rentals for day trips on Billy's Lake in
Okefenokee Swamp and for overnight camping trips in the Okefenokee National Wildlife Refuge.
Paddling is easy on the swamp's calm
waters, which cast mirror-like reflections and are tea-colored from tannic
acid. The swamp iis a slow-flowing
river, supporting varied plant life including water lilies, bladderwort,
neverwet, bald cypress, pond
cypress, tupelo, oaks, and pines.
There is fishing for bass, bream, catfish, jack, and perch, and a chance to
see includes snakes, alligators, deer,
foxes, squirrels, otters, and many
species of birds.

Wilderness Southeast
711 Sandtown Road
Savannah, GA 31410
(912) 897-5108
Everglades - 10,000 Islands
Max. rapids: None
Wilderness Southeast is a non-
profit educational corporation that
leads small groups on guided expeditions to teach participants about the
natural history of unique wilderness
ecosystems. Among the offerings is a
four-day sea kayaking trip along
Georgia's wild barrier islands, which
permits ample time for exploring
marshland, beaches, and tidal creeks,
and for sighting dolphins, shorebirds,
and other abundant wildlife. Also in
Georgia is a five-day canoe trip
through the wilderness of Okefenokee Swamp, which explores the
peat prairies, towering cypress
forests, and sandy pine islands. On

these trips, paddlers can also see
frogs, alligators, owls, river otters,
and cranes.

In Florida's Everglades, Wilderness Southeast has seven-day canoe
and sea-kayak trips spent exploring
wild beaches, isolated coastal islands,
and mangrove estuaries. Paddling
these waters, guests can see herons,
egrets, alligators, bald eagles, sea
turtles, manatees, dolphins, and a
great variety of other wildlife. On
Everglades trips, guests sleep aboard
a moving base of two houseboats.

Hawaii

Jungle rivers and sea kayaking are the twin delights of Hawaii for paddlers. Streams splash out of the verdant mountains on Kauai Island, cascading over waterfalls into deep valleys. Then they slow down and merge into 10 rivers that provide Class I waters ideal for family floating. These mini-rivers are insignificant by world standards but they can be floated year-round and are worth exploring for their scenery alone. Paddlers may find themselves in a pool at the foot of a spectacular waterfall, surrounded by tropical jungle. Looking up, they can admire fluted ridges in the forested hills above.

None of the other islands have canoeable rivers. But sea kayaking can be enjoyed at Kauai, off Oahu Island, and possibly elsewhere in the Aloha State. Paddlers avoid the northern shores of the island chain when these are battered by heavy winter waves. Nevertheless, experienced sea kayakers contend with Pacific surf equivalent to Class IV whitewater. Some use "surf-skis" — lightweight ultra-thin kayaks up to eight yards long (for the two-person craft) and less than twenty inches wide — for surfing and racing. From the ocean, day-trippers can explore caves and remote beaches so shut off by rugged cliffs (Na Pali) that they are virtually inaccessible to shore hikers. They can look for whales, seals, and turtles, fish for barracuda, or snorkel among reefs sparkling with small multicolored tropical fish.

Kayak Kauai
Micco and Chino Godinez
P.O. Box 508
Hanalei, HI 96714
(808) 826-9844, (808) 822-9179
10 rivers on Kauai
Max. rapids: III-IV
American Canoe Association
    Kayak Kauai offers guided and un-guided canoe and kayak trips of one to five days on Kaui's jungle rivers and on the coastal waters of Hawaii's Big Island. With Class I rapids, the river trips are perfect for beginners, families, and anyone seeking a relaxing, scenic trip. These rivers offer stunning views of fluted ridges, hanging valleys, and towering waterfalls. Also, thanks to the rivers' remote setting, water quality is excellent.
    Equally scenic but more strenuous are the sea kayaking trips. These trips offer a chance to see sheer cliffs, sea caves, waterfalls, remote beaches, dolphins, tropical birds, flying fish, turtles, and wild goats. Paddlers also can fish for barracuda, ahi, ulua, and olopu.
    Kayak Kauai, open year-round, also offers combination paddle/snorkeling trips to barrier reefs.

Idaho

The Snake, the Salmon, Hells Canyon — these are names to set the imagination soaring. In this land of mighty rivers and rugged mountains, Lewis and Clark floated their fragile rafts into the unknown. Anyone entering this Idaho wilderness today can only be awestruck at the daring and endurance of these first white explorers.

Today the adventure is less daunting, but still to be savored. The Middle Fork of the Salmon, the Main Salmon (the original "River of No Return"), the Lower Salmon, the Snake, the Payette, Lochsa, Owyhee, Moyie, and St. Joe rivers — all told they provide hundreds of miles of magnificent floating for rafters of all tastes and abilities.

The Salmon's Middle Fork offers some of the best white water in the West. Rafters may begin their 100-mile journey at nearly 6,000 feet altitude in the crisp cool air of a conifer forest. Then as sidestreams swell the current, the river churns through more than 100 rapids, rated Class I-IV. In June, when the spring runoff is at its peak, whitewater enthusiasts are in their element. July and August bring medium flows and warmer weather, allowing paddlers to relax in the biggest wilderness of the lower 48 states, the 2.3-million-acre River of No Return Wilderness. Forests and granite cliffs contrast with Alpine meadows ablaze with Indian paintbrush and other wildflowers. Bighorn sheep and mule deer eye passing rafts; eagles soar above. And at day's end, paddlers can wallow in soothing hot springs.

Congress has designated the Middle Fork as a Wild and Scenic River to ensure that it will remain forever free from dams, powerboats, roads, and pollution. Six-day river tours start from the tiny frontier town of Stanley, with its miners' log cabins and dirt streets. Near the lower end of Middle Fork lies Impassable Canyon, whose craggy cliffs rise higher than the walls of the Grand Canyon. It is indeed virtually impassable except by raft, and its Class IV rapids provide a whitewater climax to the trip.

Shoshone Indians called the Main Salmon Aggipah — big fish water — but never tried to run it in their frail canoes. Nor did Lewis and Clark dare attempt its formidable mile-deep canyon. But today it attracts many rafters, some as early as April or May to admire its big game and wildflowers. Whitewater enthusiasts come in June and July as the melting snow sets the river rampaging over classic rapids like Elkhorn and Big Mallard. Families enjoy the calmer waters of midsummer and fishermen bring their rods for the October-to-November steelhead season. People stop to study Indian pictographs, examine prospectors' cabins, and try their luck at panning for gold.

Lower Salmon (or Salmon River Canyons) trips generally begin from Whitebird and take the rafter through volcanic canyons down to the Salmon's confluence with the Snake. Often they take in a section of the Snake as well. Since the Lower Salmon is usually too high to float in June, outfitters tend to run trips from July through September. This is a favorite season for family rafting, with white sandy beaches providing ideal campsites beside 70-degree water for swimming. Yet the Lower Salmon is not without excitement, as its rapids still give rollercoaster rides.

The Snake provides the biggest rapids in the Pacific Northwest as it courses through Hells Canyon, flanked by snow-capped peaks 8,000 feet above sea level. Dividing Idaho from Oregon through the the deepest canyon in North America, the Snake ranks as another National Wild and Scenic River. Described as a fisherman's paradise, it is rife with trout and smallmouth bass. Outfitters offer five-to-six-day trips, sometimes combined with horseback trail riding.

Most challenging is the Lochsa River, a raging torrent with the wildest white water in Idaho. Its season is May through July and outfitters recommend previous paddling experience. From the Bitterroot Mountains to its confluence with the Selway and Clearwater rivers, the Lochsa charges through more than 40 major rapids. No Idaho stream offers more continuous white water, yet paddlers can relax under the stars on islands amid white pines and cedars.

Less traveled is the Owyhee amid the desert canyons of southwestern Idaho, raftable only during the spring snowmelt. It is a naturalist's delight with nesting ducks and geese, otters, beavers, and desert bighorn sheep, which scale the canyon walls. Indian rock carvings and miners' cabins, adorned with old cooking stoves and waterwheels, are also common. Another river raftable only in springtime is the Moyie, a whitewater stream for beginners as well as experts. The Moyie lies in the northeast corner of the Idaho panhandle and crosses the Canadian border. A little further south is an appealing stream for family rafting, the St. Joe. Near Boise, the state capital, runs the Payette, known for its white water and scenery. And the beautiful Clearwater, formed at Three Rivers from the Selway and the Lochsa, is famous for its steelhead fishing.

Tappan Falls on the Middle Fork of the Salmon. Courtesy of Bill Bernt, Aggipah River Trips, Salmon, Idaho.

Aggipah River Trips
Bill Bernt
P.O. Box 425
Salmon, ID 83467
(208) 756-4167
*Middle Fork, Lower, and Main
Salmon Rivers
Max. rapids: III-IV
Idaho Outfitters and Guides
Association*

Aggipah River Trips runs paddle-raft, oar-raft, dory, and inflatable kayak trips on the Salmon River. Trips last three to six days and allow time for stops to fish, look at old prospector's cabins and Indian pictographs, pan gold, pick berries, and soak in hot springs. During summer trips, guests invariably see bighorn sheep and eagles and often spot deer, minks, and otters. During spring trips, deer, elk, and bighorn sheep are common and it's not unusual to see mountain goats and bears.

Aggipah also offers one-day scenic float trips near Salmon, horse-back/float combination trips, and lodge trips in which guests stay in lodges each night. With the various boat and lodging offerings, Aggipah has trips suitable for guests of all tastes and ages.

American River Touring Association
Steve Welch
Star Route 73
Groveland, CA 95321
(800) 323-2782, (209) 962-7873
*Middle Fork and Main Salmon
Rivers, Selway River, Merced River,
Tuolumne River, Klamath River,
Rogue River, Illinois River, Umpqua
River, Green River, Yampa River,
Colorado River
Max. rapids: IV
America Outdoors, Oregon Guides
and Packers, Idaho Outfitters and
Guides, Utah Guides and Outfitters*

ARTA offers a total of 16 raft trips in five western states. The trips, in California, Oregon, Utah, Idaho, and Arizona, are by oar rafts, paddle rafts, oar/paddle combination rafts, and inflatable canoes.

Most trips are of Class III difficulty and appropriate for novices and families, as well as those with more experience. Other trips of up to Class V+ challenge even the most advanced paddler. Depending on the location, the trips feature such added attractions as wildflowers, side streams, swimming holes, Indian ruins, warm water, abundant wildlife, good hiking and fishing, and hot springs.

ARTA, a non-profit company, also offers whitewater schools, professional guide training, and family discounts.

Arizona Raft Adventures

Robert Elliott
4050 E. Huntington Drive
Department P
Flagstaff, AZ 86004
(800) 786-RAFT
Main and Middle Fork Salmon Rivers
Max. rapids: III-IV
America Outdoors

White Magic Unlimited runs guided raft trips of six, eight, and 13 days on the Colorado River through the Grand Canyon. The trips offer world-class white water, waves of up to 20 feet, and spectacular scenery. White Magic, an adventure travel company, also offers rafting and trekking expeditions in the former Soviet Union, China, Nepal, Chile, Ecuador, the Galapagos Islands, and Costa Rica.

Canoe Sport Idaho

Phil Lansing
3920 Twilight Court
Boise, ID 83703
(208) 345-3689
Owyhee River
Max. rapids: V+
Idaho Outfitters and Guides Association

Canoe Sport Idaho runs three- to five-day guided canoe trips on the Owyhee River in Nevada, Idaho, and Oregon. The Owyhee is federally designated "Wild and Scenic" in Oregon and is under study for wilderness status in Idaho. Canoe Sport's trips run through the Owyhee Canyon, which is magnificent, rarely visited, and just right for canoes. The landscape features thousand-foot canyon walls, vast trackless steppes, beautiful mountain ranges, and untrammeled native range land. Among the wildlife to be see are bighorn sheep, prairie falcons, otters, deer, and antelope. Fishing is for rainbow trout and smallmouth bass.

Canoe Sport's season runs from May to July and its trips are suitable for beginning and advanced canoeists. Trips feature small groups, solitude, and gourmet food.

Canyons Incorporated

Les and Susan Bechdel
P.O. Box 823
McCall, ID 83638
(208) 634-4303, (208) 634-4304
Middle Fork and Main Salmon Rivers
Max. rapids: III-IV
Idaho Outfitters and Guides Association, America Outdoors

Canyons Incorporated runs six- to 12-day guided trips on the Main Salmon River and the Middle Fork of the Salmon. Guests choose the degree of challenge they want: oar rigs, paddle rafts, duckies, hard kayaks, and canoes. With this range of offerings, there's a trip and boat to fit anyone

A five-year-old treasures her first steelhead, caught along the Salmon River. Courtesy of Bill Bernt, Aggipah River Trips, Salmon, Idaho.

from a complete beginner to an expert. Both the Main Salmon and Middle Fork of the Salmon offer spectacular scenery, clear water, and tremendous fishing. Guests also can view Indian pictographs and remnants of the gold-mining boom.

Lessons are also available, as Canyon's guides are certified canoe/kayak instructors with many years of experience. Owners Les Bechdel and his wife, Susan, have led river expeditions on four continents. Les is a leading authority on white water and co-author of the book River Rescue. He is also a four-time national champion who has represented the United States in five world championships.

Cascade Raft Company
Steve Jones
P.O. Box 6
Garden Valley, ID 83622
(800) 292-7238
Payette River, Main Salmon River
Max. rapids: III-IV
Idaho Outfitters and Guides Association, America Outdoors

The Cascade River Raft Company specializes in guided paddle raft and kayak trips on the Payette River in Boise National Forest. One-day trips on the Main Payette, South Fork, and North Fork each have their own distinct character, ranging from gentle, scenic trips to exciting runs through steep canyons and Class III-IV rapids. Also available are two- and three-day trips on the South Fork of the Payette, a six-day trip down the Main Salmon, custom tours lasting up to 18 days, and rafting/horsepacking trips.

Cascade Raft's trips run between May and October and feature good opportunities to fish for rainbow, cutthroat, and brown trout and view bears, moose, elk, deer, otters, beavers, and birds.

Castaway Fly Fishing Shop
Joe Roope
3620 N. Fruitland
Coeur d'Alene, ID 83814
(208) 765-3133
Coeur d'Alene River, St. Joe River
Max. rapids: I-II
Castaway Fly Fishing Shop offers customized trout-fishing trips on the Clark's Fork River in Montana and the St. Joe and Coeur d'Alene Rivers in Idaho. These dory trips last one to three days and pass through pristine wilderness with abundant wildlife and excellent fishing for rainbow and cutthroat trout. Among the wildlife to see are elk, deer, bears, beavers, and sheep. Castaway's season runs from May to October.

Echo: The Wilderness Company
Richard Linford and Joseph Daly
6529 Telegraph Avenue
Oakland, CA 94609
(510) 652-1600
Middle Fork and Main Salmon Rivers, Rogue River, Tuolumne River, American River, Cal-Salmon River
Max. rapids: III-IV
Idaho Outfitters and Guides Association, Oregon Guides and Packers, America Outdoors, California chapter
ECHO runs guided trips on the Main Salmon and Middle Fork in Idaho; the Rogue in Oregon; and the Tuolumne, American, and Cal-Salmon in California. The company has one- to 12-day trips available for paddlers at all skill levels and offers a variety of boats, including inflatable kayaks, oar rafts, paddle rafts, and oar/paddle rafts.

ECHO also offers a large number of special trips, including Fly-Fishing on the Middle Fork; White (and Red) Wine and White Water; Bluegrass on White Water; River Trips for Kids; Whitewater School; Aikido and Nature; the Rogue String Quartet; Field Sketching Workshop; Whale Watching, Baja; Rainforests and Rapids, Costa Rica; Baja Sea Kayaking; Colorado River through the Grand Canyon; and Lodge Trips on the Main Salmon and Cal-Salmon.

ECHO's seasons runs from April to September.

Eclipse Expeditions
Wayne and Gloria Ferguson, Dan Clemens
P.O. Box 1043
Salmon, ID 83467
(800) 366-6246
Main Salmon River
Max. rapids: III-IV
Idaho Outfitters and Guides Association, America Outdoors
Eclipse Expeditions has three- to six-day guided kayak, raft, and dory trips on the Main Salmon in the 2.3 million-acre Salmon River Wilderness Area.

Trips run between May and November, offering personal service for small groups and fine opportunities to fish and view wildlife. Eclipse also offer specialty trips, including photography seminars, continuing education trips, lodge trips, and steelhead fishing.

High Adventure River Tours
Randy McBride
P.O. Box 222
Twin Falls, ID 83301
(208) 733-0123
Snake River
Max. rapids: III-IV
Idaho Outfitters and Guides Association

High Adventure River Tours has one-day guided and unguided trips on two sections of the Snake River. The Hagerman stretch is ideal for beginning rafters, offering Class I, II, and III rapids and fine fishing for rainbow and German trout. For those seeking more adventure, the company offers trips on the Murtaugh stretch, which has Class III and IV rapids and passes through the scenic 400-foot deep Snake River Canyon.

Both stretches boast abundant wildlife, including deer, ducks, and occasional eagles or coyotes.

Holiday River Expeditions

Dee Holladay
544 East 3900 South
Salt Lake City, UT 84107
(801) 266-2087, (800) 624-6323
Snake River, Main and Lower Salmon Rivers, Lochsa River, Colorado River, Green River, San Juan River, Yampa River
Max. rapids: V+
Utah Guides and Outfitters

Holiday River Expeditions rents canoes and rafts and runs guided canoe, kayak, and raft trips on the Colorado, Green, San Juan, and Yampa Rivers in Utah and the Snake, Main Salmon, Lower Salmon, and Lochsa Rivers in Idaho. These trips last 1-12 days, offer oar and paddle options, and range in difficulty from beginners' runs to expert-level whitewater adventures. Floaters pass through pristine areas with spectacular scenery ranging from arid desert canyons to alpine forests. Along the way, guests can camp, swim, fish for trout, and catfish, and spot deer, bighorn sheep, raptors, otters, and beavers.

Holiday's season runs from April to October.

Holiday River Expeditions of Idaho

Frogg Stewart
P.O. Box 86
Grangeville, ID 83530
(208) 983-1518
Salmon River, Colorado River, Green River, Yampa River, San Juan River, Lochsa River, Snake River
Max. rapids: III-IV
Idaho Outfitters and Guides Association, Utah Outfitters and Guides Association, America Outdoors

Holiday River Expeditions runs one to six day trips on 12 sections of eight rivers in Utah, Colorado, and Idaho. Guided trips are by kayak or raft, with both oar and paddle boats available. Paddlers can also rent rafts during the April-to September season. Overall, trips range from "mild to wild" and are suited for all ages and abilities.

The company has been in business for 25 years, has an excellent safety record, and pays great attention to detail in training guides and maintaining equipment and vehicles.

Holiday River Expeditions also offers several distinctive specialty trips, including a whitewater guide school, kayak school, canoe trips on the Colorado River, and "ghost boats," a chance to run rapids in meticulously crafted replicas of boats from the past.

Hughes River Expeditions, Inc.

Jerry Hughes
P.O. Box 217
Cambridge, ID 83610
(208) 257-3477
Snake River, Main Salmon River, Owyhee River, Bruneau River
Max. rapids: V+
Idaho Outfitters and Guides Association

Hughes River Expeditions specializes in "first-class service on spectacular rivers." Trips last three to seven days and vary in difficulty with the river and type of boat selected. Oar rafts, paddle rafts, drift boats, and inflatable kayaks are available for trips on the Snake River, Middle Fork of the Salmon, Salmon River Canyon, Owyhee, and Bruneau. All trips offer excellent food, scenery, fishing, equipment, and supplies.

Of the rivers, Owyhee and Bruneau are exceptionally pristine, passing through desert canyonlands that are part of some of the country's most remote wilderness. The Bruneau, "an Idaho secret," is a guides' favorite.

Hughes River Expeditions also offers an array of three- to six-day fishing trips. Guests fish for smallmouth bass, cutthroat trout, rainbow trout, steelhead, white sturgeon, and channel catfish.

James Henry River Journeys
James Katz
P.O. Box 807
Bolinas, CA 94924
(415) 868-1836, (800) 786-1830
Main Salmon River
Max. rapids: III-IV
Idaho Outfitters and Guides

James Henry River Journeys runs guided canoe, kayak, and raft trips in California, Arizona, Idaho, Oregon, and Alaska. In California, the outfitter offers trips with Class II-III rapids, of one to three days, on the Stanislaus, East Fork of the Carson, and the Lower Klamath. In Arizona, the company runs Grand Canyon trips, with Class IV+ rapids, of 6, 8, 9, 13, and 14 days. Trips in Idaho, of 4, 5 or 6 days, run on the Class III-IV Main Salmon. In Oregon, trips of 3, 4, and 5 days run on the Class III Rogue. Finally, in Alaska the company offers a natural history expedition on the Tatshenshini-Alsek Rivers.

Bighorn sheep sighted along the Salmon River. Courtesy of Bill Bernt, Aggipah River Trips, Salmon, Idaho.

Paddle America

Many special-interest trips are also available. These include Salmon River Bluegrass, Country, Folk, and Cajun Music Trips; Whitewater Workshops; Organizational Development and Teambuilding; Wine Tasting and Gourmet Cuisine; Lodge Trips on the Rogue and Salmon; Rogue and Salmon Natural History Trips; Alaska Nature Photography; and Alaska Wilderness Literature.

All trips run through especially scenic wilderness areas and are carefully planned to move at a leisurely pace, allowing ample time for side hikes, fishing, photography, and general relaxation. As a result, participation is open to anyone active and in good health. The company's season runs from May to September.

Kingfisher Expeditions
Steve Settles
P.O. Box 1095
Salmon, ID 83467
(208) 756-4688
Middle Fork and Main Salmon Rivers
Max. rapids: III-IV
Idaho Outfitters and Guides Association

Kingfisher Expeditions runs one- to six-day guided raft and dory trips on the Main Salmon and Middle Fork of the Salmon. Trips feature exciting rapids, good food, and ample time to swim, hike, fish, and soak in hot springs. Guests can also view Indian pictographs, pioneer's cabins, and abundant wildlife.

Kingfishers trips are great for families and all those age eight and up. Also available are float/horseback packages through the Bighorns Crags and one- to five-day steelhead fishing trips.

McKay Bar Corporation
Brent Estep
3190 Airport Way
Boise, ID 83705
(208) 344-1881, (800) 635-5336
Middle Fork and Main Salmon Rivers
Max. rapids: V+
Idaho Guides and Outfitters Association

MacKay Bar Corporation offers kayak rentals and guided trips by kayak and dory on the Middle Fork of the Salmon and the Main Salmon. Trips range in length from three to 11 days and in difficulty from easy to extremely challenging.

As one of the largest and oldest outfitters in Idaho, MacKay features excellent service, experience staff, and trips and lessons suitable for all ages during its April-to-October season.

Middle Fork Wilderness Outfitters
Kurt and Gayle Selisch
P.O. Box 2222
Hailey, ID 83333
(208) 788-9168
Middle Fork Salmon River
Max. rapids: III-IV
Idaho Outfitters and Guides Association

Middle Fork Wilderness Outfitters runs guided kayak, raft, and dory trips on the Middle Fork of the Salmon for guests age eight to 70. These trips last four to six days, include both oar-boat and paddle-boat options, and feature gourmet food, clean and comfortable camping, and views of the famous, rugged canyons and wilderness of Idaho's backcountry.

On these trips, which run from June to September, guests can view bighorn sheep and other wildlife and fish for rainbow, cutthroat, and Dolly Varden trout.

Norman H. Guth, Inc.
Norman H. Guth
P.O. Box D
Salmon, ID 83467
(208) 756-3279
Main and Middle Fork Salmon Rivers
Max. rapids: III-IV
Idaho Outfitters and Guides
Association

Guth runs three- to six-day guided raft and kayak trips on the Middle Fork and Main Salmon River. Six-man oar/paddle combination rafts offer wet and wild trips, while rafts with custom spray shields and fixed seats offer more comfortable trips suitable for young children. Also available are spring and fall steelhead or trout fishing trips, spring bear hunting, and a spring camera safari, which is a boat and hiking trip for photographing deer, elk, mountain goats, sheep, mountain lions, and bears.

The Guth family, in its third generation as outfitters, led President Carter and his family on a trip down the Middle Fork in 1978. In addition to rafting, fishing, and hunting trips, the family also operates a lodge and cabins along the Main Salmon served by jet boats.

Northwest River Co.
Doug Tims
P.O. Box 403
Boise, ID 83701
(208) 344-7119
Selway River
Max. rapids: V+
Idaho Outfitters and Guides Association, America Outdoors

Northwest River Co. offers guided four- and five-day raft trips on the Selway River from June 2 to July 21. Early in the season, high water levels make for difficult rapids that challenge experienced paddlers and are too difficult for most beginners. Later trips are great for anyone.

All Northwest River Company's trips on the Selway offer excellent rapids, water quality, and trout fishing in an exceptionally scenic area of granite mountains and virgin stands of pine, cedar, and fir. Wildlife to see includes bears, mountain lions, moose, deer, elk, birds of prey, and waterfowl. Fishing is for cutthroat trout and Dolly Varden.

Orion Expeditions, Inc.
James L. Moore and Emily Johnston
1516 11th Avenue
Seattle, WA 98122
(206) 322-9130, (800) 553-7466
Middle Fork and Lower Salmon Rivers
Max. rapids: V+
Idaho Outfitters and Guides,
America Outdoors

Orion Expeditions offers whitewater and calm-water guided trips by raft and kayak on many of Washington's and Idaho's most exciting rivers, such as the Middle Fork Salmon, Lower Salmon, Skagit, Wenatchee, Sauk, Deschutes, and the legendary Skykomish. Some are of Class V+ difficulty and strictly for experts while others are suited to beginners. The landscape varies from Alpine to high desert canyon scenery. Orion's season runs from December to October and its trips, led by experienced and competent guides, last from one to six days.

Elk, bighorn sheep, black bears, eagles, and ospreys may be seen, and the rivers contain several species of trout.

Outdoor Adventures

Bob Volpert
P.O. Box 1149
Point Reyes, CA 94956
(415) 663-8300
Middle Fork and Main Salmon Rivers
Max. rapids: III-IV
America Outdoors, Idaho Outfitters
and Guides, Oregon Outfitters
Association

Outdoor Adventures specializes in guided raft trips and raft rentals on federally designated Wild and Scenic rivers in Idaho, Oregon, and California. In Idaho, six-day trips are available on the Middle Fork of the Salmon and the Salmon River. Included are all shuttles from Boise, tents and sleeping bags, delicious on-river meals, quality guides, and Avon rafts.

In Oregon, three- and four-day trips are available on the Rogue River, featuring lively rapids, wonderful hiking trails, and abundant wildlife. On these trips, the last night is spent at Half Moon Bar, a rustic lodge by the river where paddlers can enjoy hot showers, comfortable beds, and home-cooked meals.

In California, Outdoor Adventures offers two-day trips on the Tuolomne River, three-day trips on the Forks of the Kern, and one-day trips on the Upper Kern. These California trips offer some of the wildest white water in the country during the spring run-off in April and May. During this time, wetsuits and previous rafting experience are required. All other Outdoor Adventures trips are fine for families and beginners. The company's season is from April to October.

Ouzel Outfitters

Kent Wickham
Box 827
Bend, OR 97709
(503) 385-5947, (800) 788-RAFT
Lower Salmon River
Max. rapids: III-IV
Oregon Packers and Guides

Ouzel Oufitters specializes in trips of one to five days on the "loveliest and liveliest" rives in the Northwest. These rivers include the Rogue, North Umpqua, McKenzie, Lower and Middle Owyhee, and Deschutes Rivers in Oregon; the Lower Salmon in Idaho; and the Lower Klamath River in California. All trips but the Middle Owyhee runs have class III-IV rapids and are fine for families and guests of all levels of experience to paddle in paddle rafts, inflatable kayaks, or guide-accompanied, "row-your-own" oar-rafts. The Middle Owyhee run, with class IV-V rapids, is a challenging, expedition-like trip for adventurous, experienced rafters only.

Ouzel Outfitters' trips run between May and September. Depending on the river traveled, guests can view bears, deer, eagles, and otters, and fish for bass, trout, steelhead, and salmon.

R & R Outdoors, Inc.

Rob and Rex Black
HC2 Box 500
Pollock, Idaho 83547
(208) 628-3830, (800) 777-4676
Salmon River
Max. rapids: III-IV
Idaho Outfitters and Guides
Association

R & R Outdoors, Inc. runs one- to 13-day guided raft trips on the Salmon River from June to September, and fishing float trips from February to December. Offering both oar boats and paddle boats, R & R has trips suitable for river runners of all levels of ability.

R & R also offers several vacation packages that include a night in the outfitter's comfortable guest lodge, barbecue, and a "lumberjack breakfast" at the start or end of the trip. On the river, R & R supplies all meals and tents, and offers guests ample opportunity to fish, view wildlife, and explore wilderness canyons and valleys.

ROW (River Odysseys West), Inc.
Peter Grubb
P.O. Box 579-PA
Coeur d'Alene, ID 83814
(208) 765-0841, (800) 451-6034
Snake River, Middle Fork and Main Salmon Rivers, Lochsa River, Moyie River, Owyhee River, St. Joe River, Selway River
Max. rapids: III-IV
America Outdoors, Idaho Outfitters and Guides Association, Oregon Packers and Guides

ROW, one of the country's best-known outfitters, offers a wide array of trips on Idaho rivers to suit adventurers of all ages and levels of ability. Trips vary in length from one to 17 days and offer wilderness scenery ranging from desert to high alpine terrain.

In addition to its diverse offerings, ROW also takes particular pride in the quality of its guides and its annual "Family Focus" trips, which are designed with special activities for children. On ROW's trips, which run between May and October, paddlers may see bears, moose, bighorn sheep, mountain goats, river otters, deer, elk, and eagles. Fishing is for cutthroat and rainbow trout, smallmouth bass, and sturgeon.

Dave Warren on the Main Salmon. Courtesy of Warren River Outfitters, Salmon, Idaho.

Salmon River Experience
812 Truman
Moscow, ID 83843
(208) 882-2385 (year-round)
(208) 628-3589 (June-August)
Salmon River, Snake River
Max. rapids: III-IV
Idaho Outfitters and Guides
Association

Salmon River Experience runs one-to five-day guided trips on the Main Salmon and Snake Rivers. The one- and two-day Salmon trips take in some of the river's most spectacular rapids on scenic stretches lined with white, sandy beaches. The three- to five-day trips run on the lower gorge through steep rock canyons that are accessible only by water. Fishing is good and wildlife is abundant. Deer, elk, moose, bears, mountain goats, and eagles can be seen.

Excellent meals and guided oar boats ensure comfort and safety for beginners, but even the most advanced boaters find challenge in inflatable kayaks. SRE's season runs from June to September and includes special trips, such as a "mining history" trip and two-day and three-day mountain bike/rafting trips. The mountain bike portion of the latter runs through the Nez Perce National Forest high above the Salmon River, next to the Gospel Hump Wilderness Area, offering breathtaking views, visits to ghost towns, and chances to view wildlife.

Salmon River Outfitters
Steven Shephard
P.O. Box 307
Columbia, CA 95310
(209) 532-2766, (209) 795-4041
Salmon River
Max. rapids: III-IV
Idaho Outfitters and Guides
Association

Salmon River Outfitters offers six-day guided raft and canoe trips on the Salmon River between June and October. By specializing on the Salmon River and running only one trip at time, the company provides knowledgeable, personal service. Salmon River Outfitters also provides all equipment and excellent food.

Silver Cloud Expeditions
Jerry Myers
P.O. Box 1006
Salmon, ID 83467
(208) 756-6215
Salmon River
Max. rapids: III-IV
Idaho Outfitters and Guides
Association

Silver Cloud Expeditions provides guided kayak, raft, and dory trips of one to six days on the Salmon River. These trips offer beautiful wilderness camps, stunning scenery in the second-deepest canyon in North America, and a chance to view golden eagles, bighorn sheep, river otters, and other wildlife. The Salmon River also offers excellent trout fishing. In addition, guests on these trips can snorkel, pan for gold, hike, swim, soak in hot springs, explore historical sites, eat good food, and enjoy nightly programs on natural history, fly fishing, gold mining, and other topics.

The trips, offered between March and October, vary widely in difficulty. Novices and families with children age seven and up can choose to ride in oar boats rowed by guides; the more adventurous may prefer to paddle rafts or inflatable kayaks.

Slickrock Adventures
Cully Erdman
P.O. Box 1400
Moab, UT 84532
(801) 259-6996
Payette River, Green River, Dolores River
Max. rapids: III-IV
America Outdoors

Slickrock Adventures runs guided kayak and raft trips of 5-13 days on Utah's Green River, Colorado's Dolores River, and Idaho's Payette River. Its most popular beginners' runs are raft and kayak trips on 85 miles of the Green River, through Desolation and Gray Canyons. Paddlers have time to play in over 60 easy rapids, and enjoy views of tall cliffs, sandy beaches, and cottonwoods. The Dolores emerges from lush meadows and forests to descend into a desert canyon. Continuous white water in the upper canyon gives way to widely-spaced, easier drops below. This allows Slickrock to choose stretches to match each group's ability. Green River kayak trips run through Labyrinth and Stillwater Canyons, offering peaceful, flat-water paddling through the heart of Canyonlands, with spectacular side canyons, petroglyphs, and Indian ruins. Finally, on the Payette, Slickrock offers a whitewater kayak clinic featuring incredible white water and beautiful canyons. Open all year, Slickrock also offers paddling trips in Belize and Mexico.

Wapiti River Guides
Gary Lane
Box 1125
Riggins, ID 83549
(208) 628-3523, (800) 488-9872
Salmon River, Grande Ronde River, Owyhee River, rivers throughout Alaska
Max. rapids: V+
Oregon Guides and Packers Association, Idaho Outfitters and Guides Association

Wapiti River Guides, with trips in Idaho, Oregon, and Alaska, specializes in small personalized trips of moderate difficulty "for ages 3 to 103, families, and nature lovers." The outfitter's trips are distinctive, too, for their guides' emphasis on natural history and Native American culture, and for the fine scenery, which includes caves, spires, pictographs, petroglyphs, and historic sites.

Trips, ranging in length from one to 12 days, also allow time for interesting side hikes and viewing elk, deer, bald eagles, bobcats, cougars, bears, bighorn sheep, minks, and other wildlife. Fishing is for steelhead, trout, and bass.

Warren River Expeditions, Inc.
Dave Warren
Box 1375
Salmon, ID 83467
(208) 756-6387
Main Salmon River
Max. rapids: III-IV
Idaho Outfitters and Guides Association

Warren River Expeditions runs three- to eight-day guided and unguided trips on the Main Salmon, offering paddlers raging white water and the scenic beauty of Idaho's "Frank Church - River of No Return" Wilderness. Guided trips are by canoe, kayak, or raft, with trips available for guests of all ages. All kayak schools and kayak support trips are run in conjunction with regularly scheduled raft trips. This allows kayakers to spend time on the river with non-kayaking family and friends.

During the season of April to October, the outfitter also offers kayak rentals, lessons, and lodge accommodations.

Western River Expeditions
Larry Lake
7258 Racquet Club Drive
Salt Lake City, UT 84121
(801) 942-6669, (800) 453-7450 (outside UT)
Main Salmon River, Colorado River, Green River
Max. rapids: III-IV
America Outdoors

Western River Expeditions runs guided raft trips and rents rafts and inflatable kayaks on the Colorado River in Colorado, Utah, and Arizona; the Green River in Utah; and the Main Salmon in Idaho. Green River trips, by oar or paddle raft, provide thrilling whitewater and views of towering red rock cliffs and arches, deep gorges, frontier cabins, and Indian petroglyphs. Colorado River tours offer spectacular scenery in Cataract Canyon, Westwater Canyon or the Upper and Lower Grand Canyon. Rapids are moderate to large, and paddlers can swim, take side hikes and view historic Indian and Old West sites. Finally, trips on the Main Salmon feature scenic blue-green waters, pine-covered mountains, stops at hot springs and abandoned mining camps, and camping on white sand beaches.

All trips are suitable for anyone of good health above the minimum age set for each trip, depending on its difficulty. During Western River's March-September season, some trips can be combined with a ranch stay.

White Otter Outdoor Adventures
Randy Hess
P.O. Box 2733
Ketchum, ID 83340
(208) 726-4331, (208) 838-2406
Main Salmon River
Max. rapids: V+
Idaho Outfitters and Guides Association

White Otter Outdoor Adventures has personable, experienced guides and more than 20 years' experience running trips on wild rivers. The company offers one-day guided kayak and raft trips and rentals of canoes, kayaks, and rafts. Its trips on the Snake River have Class IV and V rapids and are designed for experienced rafters looking for the best in whitewater excitement.

Trips on the headwaters of the Salmon are calmer, suited for beginners, families, and those seeking more time for fishing, photography, and viewing wildlife. The Salmon is also an excellent river for beginners to learn kayaking in open, inflatable kayaks.

During the season from May to October, White Otter also offers dinner trips, gourmet food, and side trips to the Yankee Fort Dredge, the ghost town of Custer, and a working gold mine.

Illinois

Smoothed by ancient glaciers, Illinois is bordered by the Mississippi, Ohio, and Wabash Rivers and Lake Michigan. The hills of the Illinois Ozarks in the southern tip of the state mark where the glaciers stopped their planing action. Across the rest of the state, most rivers are slow and meandering. Illinois is not known for white water or crystal-clear water; it is after all the home of Big Muddy River, Little Muddy River, and Muddy Creek. But one of Illinois' great assets for paddlers is its helpful tourist office, which publishes a highly informative map of the canoeing rivers, showing put-ins, dams, and nearby roads. Included is a brief description of each river and a detailed listing of the access sites giving their exact location and stating whether parking is available. Fishermen are also well served: the state puts out a 60-page illustrated fishing guide packed with data on what to catch where on Illinois fishing waters. Both publications may be obtained from the Illinois Department of Commerce and Community Affairs, 620 East Adams Street, Springfield, IL 62701.

The Big Muddy River in southern Illinois meanders slowly through the scenic Shawnee National Forest in its lower reaches, and its diverse wildlife makes it — in the words of the state guide — "a year-round delight for the naturalist who isn't in any hurry to get downriver." Lusk Creek in the same Shawnee Forest area is described as one of the state's most picturesque float trips, with its canyons, bluffs, tall trees, wildflowers, and wildlife. The 18-mile float down to its confluence with the Ohio at Golconda entails portages at low water but allows good fishing, birdwatching, and mushroom-hunting.

Although only an hour's drive from Chicago, the Kankakee in northern Illinois is said to be one of the few natural, unspoiled rivers of the Midwest. Canoeists of all ages enjoy this gentle stream, which was paddled by LaSalle when he explored the region in the late 1600s. It provides good shoreline scenery and great fishing for species ranging from catfish and crappie to bass and walleye.

Due south of the town of Kankakee is the Middle Fork of the Vermilion River, the only National Wild and Scenic River in Illinois. Its run through Kickapoo State Park gives paddlers a taste of Class I-II canoeing on clean water over a gravel riverbed. Deer, wild goats, wild turkeys, and blue herons may be seen; anglers go for smallmouth bass, crappie, walleye and bluegill.

The best white water in the state is on the Vermilion of the Illinois, often dubbed Big Vermilion, which runs into the Illinois River near Starved Rock. Its six-foot waves are for seasoned canoeists only, who love its wild course through forests of flowering trees and between high bluffs topped with white pine and juniper.

Close to the Wisconsin state line runs the Sugar River, which flows rapidly through a secluded landscape. Replete with riffles and deep pools, the Sugar's attractions include a stone bluff where Indians marked the half-way point between Lake Michigan and the Mississippi. Although much of the land has been cleared, enough cover survives for the area to remain a major flyway for migrating ducks and geese.

Immortalized by the poetry of Edgar Lee Masters, the Spoon River in western Illinois is an appealing stream in its own right. Its setting is primitive and it runs through unspoiled old towns. When water is high it can be turbulent and demanding.

Elsewhere, paddlers can enjoy waters ranging from the Chicago River, canoeable all the way down to Chicago's Loop, to the Cache River tucked away in the far south near the Kentucky state line. The mysterious Cache winds its way through a maze of bald cypress and tupelo trees in an area resembling Louisiana bayou country. Its hazards include logjams and poisonous snakes, but it is a naturalist's dream.

Country Canoe
Stanley Hayes
824 Jackson
Pecatonica, IL 61063
(815) 239-1246
Sugar River
Max. rapids: None
Country Canoes offers canoe rentals for one- to four-day trips on the Sugar and Pacetonica Rivers, which have clear, fast waters that run through wetlands and swamps, sand hills and bluffs, hardwood forests, prairies, and bogs.

With Class I rapids, the trips are easy enough for beginners. Also, as trips end at the outfitter's headquarters, paddlers can travel at whatever speed they choose without having to worry about being early or late for the shuttle. Country Canoes' season runs from May to November.

Recreation Ventures
(Kickapoo Canoe Rental)
Charles Pickett
Route 2, Gravat Road
Danville, IL 61832
(217) 443-4939
Middlefork River
Max. rapids: I-II
Kickapoo Canoe Rental rents canoes for one-day trips on the Middlefork River, Illinois' only designated National Scenic River. The Middlefork runs through unspoiled wilderness and has clean, Class I-II white water that offers moderate challenge and smallmouth, crappie, walleye, and bluegill fishing. Paddlers also can spot deer, wild goats, turkeys, and blue herons.

The season runs from April to September.

Reed's Canoe Trips
Orville and Dorothy Reed
907 N. Indiana Avenue
Kanakee, IL 60901
(815) WE CANOE
Kanakee River
Max. rapids: None
NACLO
Reed's Canoe Trips offers one- and two-day canoe and kayak trips on the Kankakee River, one of the most unspoiled canoeing rivers in the Midwest.

The Kankakee is wide, with flat water, making trips easy for beginners and experienced paddlers alike. Its clean waters and many small islands and sandbars make the river ideal for swimming, picnicking, and exploring, with overnight camping available at private campgrounds, the Kankakee River State Park, and the La Salle State Fish and Wildlife Area.

The river also boasts especially good fishing for bass, walleye, northern pike, catfish, and crappie. The Kankakee consistently produces state-record catches and is widely regarded as one of the best fishing streams in Illinois.

Indiana

Indiana's Blue River, well-named for its aqua-blue color, runs through some of the most appealing country in the Hoosier State. First explored by Squire Boone, brother of Daniel Boone, it rises in Washington County, due north of Louisville, and flows southwest to the Ohio. Traces of the Indian tribes that Squire Boone encountered can still be found today. The most spring-fed of all Indiana's streams, the Blue winds through many "half canyons" — cliffs rising on one side or the other. These limestone bluffs are dotted with caves and old quarries in what is known as Indiana's Cave Country. Hardwood forests and hills add to the scenery, so it is no surprise that the Blue was the first river chosen for Indiana's Natural and Scenic Rivers System.

Much of the riverbed is covered with rocks and sediment, and rapids contain gravel bars. But the level drops at a rate of merely four feet per mile, so the rapids are rated only Class I-II. A favorite run is from Milltown to Rothrock Mill, a 13-mile trip that takes about five hours to float. It contains the best rapids on the river but is only runnable from April through June or after heavy rainfall later in the season. Paddlers must be sure to take out at the access site before the Rothrock Mill Dam since the dam is extremely dangerous. There are other good floats above Milltown, especially in springtime. But above Fredericksburg the water level gets too low.

Long the most popular, and probably the most beautiful, stream in the state is Sugar Creek, named by the pioneers for the many sugar maples in the area. This clean river runs 90 miles southwest from Tipton County (north of Indianapolis) to join the Wabash. Its course takes it through or beside several state parks and other public lands well-equipped with campgrounds and other recreational facilities. The scenery is an attractive mix of cliffs and pleasant woodland, with covered bridges and plenty of good fishing. Canoeists paddling on their own should check water levels before setting out on Sugar Creek, which can be hazardous when the river is high. At other times it is a gentle Class I-II float. Crawfordsville is a popular put-in.

Another very clean and scenic Indiana river is the Tippecanoe in the northcentral portion of the state. It runs through wooded countryside with abundant deer, beavers, herons, ducks, and geese. Lacking rapids, the Tippecanoe is a good paddling river for anyone. It has strong appeal for fishermen, who can find many varieties of bass, blue catfish, flathead, perch, sunfish, and crappie.

Sticklers for accuracy say that the name Whitewater River is a bit of a misnomer. True, this river has many rapids and the steepest gradient in the state — six feet per mile on average — but it does not contain genuine white water. Running north-south in the eastern part of Indiana, it flows through farmland in two forks and then in one before heading east into Ohio.

Cave County Canoes
112 Main Street
P.O. Box 145
Milltown, IN 47145
(812) 633-4993, (812) 633-4806
Blue River
Max. rapids: I-II
NACLO

Cave Country Canoes, Inc., rents canoes, kayaks, and rafts for one- to three-day trips on the Blue River. Most sections of the river are suitable for family canoeing, with Class I-II rapids, but previous paddling experience is required for one section during springtime when water levels are higher.The many springs that feed into the Blue give it its aqua-blue color and its name. Two-hundred-foot limestone bluffs with cave entrances and a canopy of huge sycamore trees shade the river. Paddlers can see deer, muskrats, beavers, and blue herons, and fish for smallmouth and largemouth bass, goggle-eye, and bluegill.

Cave Country Canoes prides itself on quality service and promises no long waits for bus shuttles. During its April 1-to-October 31 season, the outfitter offers riverside camp sites for tents and R.V.s, two large bunkhouses for group outings, and a bathhouse with hot showers.

Germany Bridge Canoe Trips
Paul and Maxine Bardsley
RR #3, Box 329
Rochester, IN 46975
(219) 223-2212
Tippecanoe River
Max. rapids: None
NACLO

Germany Bridge Canoe Trips offers canoe and tube rentals on the Tippecanoe River for one- to five-day flat-water trips. The river is clean and scenic, passing through wooded country with abundant deer, beavers, ducks, geese, and herons. Fishing is very good, especially for smallmouth bass, channel catfish, and northern pike.

Trips run from April to November and are suitable for paddlers of all ages.

Canoeing on Sugar Creek. Courtesy of Lee Merriman, Turkey Run Canoe Trips, Rockville, Indiana.

Turkey Run Canoe Trips
Bev Chaplain
311 West Ohio Street
Rockville, IN 47872
(317) 597-2456, (317) 569-6705
Sugar Creek
Max. rapids: I-II

Turkey Run Canoe Trips rents canoes and tubes for one- and two-day trips on Sugar Creek, a scenic canoeing stream lined with sandstone cliffs, woods, and sandy beaches. Both the flat-water and mild whitewater trips are fine for families and children age six and older. Along these trips, which run between April and October, paddlers can swim, view deer and turkeys, and fish for smallmouth bass and catfish. Camping at campgrounds enroute is also available.

Dam Bait Shop
Bob Harms, Joyce Sweet
Box 112B
201 North Main Street
Linn Grove, IA 51033
(712) 296-3611
Little Sioux River
Max. rapids: None

The Dam Bait Shop rents canoes for leisurely half-day to seven-day trips on the Inkpaduta Trail of the Little Sioux, with its great scenery, fishing, and wildlife. Outings can be organized to allow paddlers to camp either in developed campgrounds or in primitive sites, with access to their vehicles in either case.

Walleye, crappie, carp and catfish can be caught in this typical prairie stream. The company's season runs from April 1 through October.

Iowa

Less than 1,200 feet separate the highest from the lowest elevation in the Hawkeye State, so Iowa's rivers mostly meander idly across the plain. But despite its lack of white water, Iowa offers paddlers a wide variety of canoe trails with first-rate fishing in its rivers and lakes. The state puts out an excellent brochure (see below). All Iowa's streams flow into the Missouri or the Mississippi, which respectively form the western and eastern borders of the state. Some, like the Turkey River in the northeast "Little Switzerland" corner of Iowa, have a strong current with gentle rapids. Others, like the Boone River, have high rock walls, caves, and Indian burial sites. The scenery is generally unspoiled and attractive.

Reaching nearly 500 miles, the Des Moines River is the longest in the state. Six miles south of Fort Dodge, the Des Moines provides a scenic float over the eleven-mile stretch from Kalo to Lehigh. Described as an ideal one-day excursion, this trip runs past sandstone bluffs, caves, and ravines with plenty of good fishing spots and places to explore. One interesting site is Boneyard Hollow, a deep ravine where prairie Indians slew buffalo, deer, and elk by driving them over the cliff and retrieving their carcasses for meat, hide, and bones.

In Little Switzerland the Upper Iowa River is a popular stream for both canoeists and fishermen, who can wade easily on its gravel bed. The entire 55-mile stretch from Lime Springs, close to the Minnesota state line, to Decorah can be floated in a couple of weekends. The Upper Iowa, which flows directly into the Mississippi and is unconnected with the Iowa River, features old mill sites, limestone bluffs, wooded banks, and the 200-foot-high stone pillars known as Chimney Rocks.

A unique experience — portaging three blocks down the main street of town — is a quirk of paddling the Turkey River at the Clayton County seat of Elkader. There is one dam above and one below town. It must be the only portage in recreational canoeing that offers a grocery store and several eating places along the way. State officials advise those portaging on a Saturday to arrange wheeled transport so as to avoid "totally disrupting business in the town."

The Iowa River, running diagonally southeast across the state to the Mississippi, is a meandering prairie stream flowing through some historic territory. Near the put-in below the Alden Dam is Mormon Bridge, named after a pioneer group that lost many members in the severe winter of 1844-45. Further downstream at Steamboat Rock are the sites of early gold rushes amid forested recreational areas and limestone bluffs. In Hardin County, the river runs through a greenbelt, offering one of the loveliest floats in Iowa.

The Little Sioux is another typical prairie stream, with a sand, mud, and gravel bottom and high mud banks. It flows at barely one mile per hour, dropping an average of only two feet per mile. It is rich in wildlife, notably white-tailed deer, raccoons, beavers and otters, which are now being reintroduced after having been hunted nearly to extinction. When floating the westward-flowing Little Sioux in the northwest corner of the state, paddlers should visit the Sanford Museum at the Cherokee take-out.

Another Iowa river of considerable historic interest is the Wapsipinicon (Wapsi) in the northeast. On it lies the village of Waubeek, settled by New England whaling families in the 1850s who moved to the heartland to remove any temptation for their menfolk to continue their hazardous seafaring tradition. Their old homes still display harpoons, ships' bells, and other emblems of their maritime life. The most scenic stretches are between Waubeek and Anamosa, and at Pinicon Ridge Park north of Central City.

The Raccoon River offers a good weekend trip through unspoiled timberland in central Iowa. Although the float runs right down to Des Moines, it feels pleasantly remote from civilization. And catfish, smallmouth bass, and walleye are plentiful.

For detailed descriptions of Iowa canoe trails and fishing, write the state's Department of Natural Resources, Wallace State Office Building, Des Moines, Iowa 50319-0034, and ask for their 40-page leaflet, *Iowa Float Trips.*

Turkey River Canoe Trips
Eleanor Gossman
102 South Main
Elkader, IA 52240
(319) 245-1010, (319) 245-1434
Turkey River, Volga River
Max. rapids: I-II

Turkey River Canoe Trips rents canoes for trips of up to three days on both the Turkey and Volga rivers with their attractive uncrowded scenery. Paddlers may view the historic Motor Mill and Keystone Bridge as they float these streams, whose rapids rate only Class I-II. Bass, catfish, trout, and walleye may be found, and the wildlife includes deer, wild turkeys, and eagles.

Turkey River Canoe Trips' season runs from May 1-October 21.

University of Iowa Rec Services
Wayne Fett
Touch the Earth
E216 Field House
Iowa City, IA 52242
(315) 335-9293, (315) 335-5256
Upper Iowa River, Wolf River, Red River, Wisconsin River, Upper Iowa River, BWCA, Ocoee River, Chattooga River, Nantahala River, St. Francis River, Poudre River
Max. rapids: I-II

University of Iowa Recreation Services offers guided canoe, kayak, and raft trips and rents canoes for trips in Iowa on the upper Iowa River; in Minnesota in the Boundary Waters Canoe Area; in Wisconsin on the Wolf, Red, and Wisconsin Rivers; and in the southeast on the Ocoee, Chattooga, Nantahala, St. Francis, and Poudre Rivers. These trips, open to students and the general public, feature a low student-to-instructor ratio and are geared for beginning to intermediate paddlers. All trips run through scenic, remote, and wild areas. Trips last one to four days.

The department of recreation services, open year-round, also offers rock climbing, cross-country skiing, backpacking, and bicycle touring.

Kansas

Rivers meandering through the vast wheatfields of the Great Plains, banks lined with willow and cottonwood — this is canoeing in the Sunflower State. But it is not the whole story; in parts of Kansas paddlers find forests, bluffs, sandhills, and wetlands. Official tourist brochures boast that 10,000 miles of Kansas streams are "fishable" and that the state has 10 canoe trails on waters suitable for river-runners of all skill levels.

Kansas rivers flow east or southeast across the rolling Great Plains. Many become unfloatable after long periods of drought, such as occurred in 1991. This is especially true of the Kansas River, otherwise known as the Kaw. Paddlers who intend to float — not drag — their canoes on the 59-mile stretch of the Kaw above Topeka should first check with the U.S. Army Corps of Engineers at Tuttle Creek (913-539-8511) and Milford Lake (913-238-5714) on outflows from these upstream reservoirs. When waterlevels suffice, paddlers find ideal picnic sites on the river's large, clean sandbars. But overnight campers will want to seek sheltered spots out of the wind to pitch their tents. Bald eagles may be seen in winter and a wide variety of songbirds, shore birds, and waterfowl are common during other seasons. Deer, coyote, beavers, and muskrats can also be observed. For a change of pace, some paddlers combine the 17-mile float from Edwardsville to Kansas City with a leisurely riverboat cruise and dinner on the broad Missouri.

Further south in eastern Kansas is the Marais des Cygnes river, which passes through farmland, towns, and picturesque wooded areas. As its name (Marsh of Swans) implies, it is a favorite stopover for aquatic birds on their annual migrations. Its muddy banks, lined with oaks, sycamores, and willows, provide a habitat for numerous amphibians and reptiles. The canoeing trail includes the 14 miles of the river down to the town of LaCygne, plus the ensuing 18 miles to the end of the waterfowl area beside the Missouri state line.

Some of the best scenery and wildlife observation in Kansas is found on the Fall River in the southeast corner of the state. It also offers Class I-II white water on its upper reaches to challenge novices and provide fun for experienced canoeists. But the Fall is floatable only in the spring and after heavy rainfall. It is a great fishing river, well-stocked with spotted bass, channel cat, and crappie and white bass in season. Almost all of this 12-mile trail is through land owned by the Corps of Engineers and is open to public access, fishing, and hunting. The put-in is at Highway K-99 bridge close to Eureka.

Southwest of Wichita runs Grouse Creek, another good stream for wildlife, fishing, and scenery. All of the four-mile trail starting just south of Silverdale, next to the Oklahoma state line, is within the Kaw Wildlife Area. It is a clean and lively river running through woods, with catfish a favorite catch.

Voyageur canoe on the Missouri River. Courtesy of Ottertail Outings, Manhattan, Kansas.

Ottertail Outings
Jefferson M. Brown
5630 Bayers Hill Road
Manhattan, KS 66502
(913) 537-9403
Kansas River, Missouri River
Max. rapids: None
   Ottertail Outings runs unique guided canoe trips aboard a replica of the birch-bark trading canoes used on trading routes in Canada and the United States by voyageurs, French-Canadian fur traders of the 1600s to 1800s. Voyageur canoes, 26-feet long, would typically carry eight to 10 people and more than 2,000 pounds of cargo. Ottertail's replica is of the same dimensions and is equipped with traditional wooden seats, thwarts, and ribs. Only its hull, made of fiberglass and kevlar, is different.

   Ottertail offers custom trips within a 200-mile radius of Manhattan, Kansas, for groups of four to six. Reservations are available daily during summer school vacations and on weekends during the school year. The canoe is also available for historic festivals, and guides are available on request to appear is historic costume to tell the story of voyageur traders.

Kentucky

Stretching from the Appalachians to the Mississippi, the Bluegrass State has plenty of rain and no shortage of navigable rivers for the paddler to explore. All of the main Kentucky streams — the Cumberland, Green, Kentucky, Licking, Salt, and Tennessee — flow northwestward into the great Ohio River. And the Ohio, which forms the state's entire northern border, pours all this Kentucky water into the Mississippi.

Elkhorn Creek is perhaps Kentucky's most popular canoeing stream because of its easy accessibility from big cities, its gentle white water, and natural beauty. Flowing northwest to its confluence with the Kentucky River north of Frankfort, it is also close to Louisville, Lexington, and Cincinnati. Elkhorn Creek has attractive scenery with a mixture of sheer cliffs, tall trees, wildflowers, and fertile farmland. Fish include bass and bluegill, while the wildlife ranges from deer to raccoons and muskrats. Rapids are mostly mere riffles or Class I, with the only Class II stretch below Forks of the Elkhorn, where the north and south branches converge. The Kentucky River is a broad, slow stream with nothing more difficult than Class I, an invitation to leisurely cruising.

By contrast, the lower Rockcastle River in south central Kentucky offers intense Class III-IV white water that demands technical skill. This is an exhausting 17-mile run, and its last six miles, known as the Lower Narrows, is full of twisting blind drops that should be scouted one by one. As Bob Sehlinger puts it in his *Canoeing and Kayaking Guide to the Streams of Kentucky*, it is white water that "lambastes the paddler with every challenge in the book." The time to do it, by canoe or raft, is April through June. The upper sections of the Rockcastle provide 25 miles of easy paddling for families and beginners through forested hills and farmland in the heart of the Daniel Boone National Forest.

The Big South Fork of the Cumberland River comes northward from Tennessee through a remote region, the Big South Fork National Recreation Area (see Tennessee). Access is difficult but it offers several good canoe and rafting trips varying from Class I to Class IV or even Class V at times. Parts of the Big South Fork are best in the fall, when the hills are filled with changing colors. Just above Cumberland Falls the Cumberland offers a 17-mile run that is good for beginners. Below the falls is a five- to seven-mile run of Class II-III white water that includes rapids dubbed Screaming Right-Hand Turn, Stair Steps, and the Last Drop. Guided raft trips suitable for families and novices are available through this scenic wilderness.

One of the toughest whitewater rivers in the East is the Russell Fork of the Levisa through Breaks Interstate Park on the Virginia-Kentucky state line. Long considered unrunnable, the Russell Fork drops an incredible 500 feet in two and one-half miles. One of its Class IV-V rapids, appropriately named El Horrendo, is more of a waterfall than a drop. October, when water is released from the reservoir dam, is the time to raft this formidable 10-mile run.

The Licking River is runnable all year below Falmouth, where its South Fork joins the mainstream. Access points are scarce, but the scenery is attractive, with hardwood trees lining the banks as the broad, clean river winds gently through hilly valleys to its confluence with the Ohio. Deer, otters, and many birds may be observed, while anglers reel in bass, muskie, sauger, crappie, and catfish.

The upper North Fork of the Kentucky River provides an interesting insight into traditional local mountain lifestyle, with views of old frame houses, wooden footbridges, and porch rockers in riverside communities. The paddling is easy Class I. The Middle Fork is also populated, but the natural scenery is beautiful as the narrow stream winds through the hill country with Class I-II rapids.

Other popular Kentucky streams are the Red River, which flows through a beautiful gorge on its way to join the Kentucky River, the Green River, one of Kentucky's longest, and the Nolin, a tributary of the Green. The Red River mostly runs through extremely attractive countryside and its upper section is normally navigable from December to May. The middle section is just as scenic, but the lower river is less appealing after it emerges from Red River Gorge. The Green River, which empties into the Ohio opposite Evansville, Ohio, has two good canoeing stretches downstream from Green River Lake Dam. Much of the lower reach runs through Mammoth Cave National Park and is rich in natural history, with its riverside caves, forests, and wildlife. The Nolin flows through the same park to join the Green and offers similar scenery, although canoeists must portage several dangerous dams. All three rivers have easy rapids except where the old mill dams create Class II+ hazards.

"Devil's Jump" on the Cumberland's Big South Fork. Courtesy of Sheltowee Trace Outfitters, Whitley City, Kentucky.

Canoe Kentucky
Bess and Ed Councill
7265 Peaks Mill Road
Frankfort, KY 40601
(502) 227-4492, (800) K-CANOE-1
Kentucky River, Elkhorn Creek, Red River, Green River, Nolin River, Nolin Lake
Max. rapids: I-II
NACLO

Canoe Kentucky offers guided trips and canoe rentals on 12 streams from 10 "mini-liveries" around the state. With maximum rapids of Class I and II, these streams are well-suited for beginners, families, campers, fishermen, and intermediate paddlers. Among the attractions of the rivers served are the gorges, natural bridges, and breathtaking scenery of the Red River; the riffles, ledges, and 200-foot rock walls of Elkhorn Creek; and the abundant wildlife, fine scenery, riverside camping, and caves of the Green and Nolin Rivers.

Trips run from one to 10 days between April and November and offer good opportunities to fish for bass and muskie and view great blue herons, turkeys, hawks, deer, and waterfowl. The company also offers classes in basic and intermediate canoeing and rafting.

Rockcastle Adventures Canoe Livery
Jim Honchell
P.O. Box 662
London, KY 40741
(606) 864-5987, (606) 864-5407
Rockcastle River, Cumberland River, Buck Creek, Wood Creek, Laurel Lake, Cumberland Lake
Max. rapids: III-IV

Rockcastle Adventures offers canoe and kayak rentals on the Rockcastle River, Back Creek, Wood Creek, Laurel Lake, and Lake Cumberland. Most popular is an 11-mile trip on the upper Rockcastle, which features gentle current and light rapids, and passes through the heart of the scenic Daniel Boone National Forest. This trip, and the two- and three-day trips on the Upper Rockcastle, are fine for novices and families.

Also popular is a challenging 17-mile day trip on the Lower Rockcastle, which passes through spectacular gorges and boasts tough Class I-IV white water. This trip is for experienced canoeists only.

On these and other trips, paddlers can camp, spot deer and waterfowl, and fish for bass, drum, redeye, catfish, and walleye. During the March-to-October season, the company also offers hiking and caving trips.

Sheltowee Trace Outfitters
Richard Egedi, Sr.
P.O. Box 1060
Whitley City, KY 42653
(606) 679-5026, (800) 541-7238
Cumberland River, Rockcastle River
Max. rapids: III-IV
NACLO
Sheltowee Trace Outfitters offers canoe, raft, and tube rentals and guided raft trips on the South Fork of the Cumberland, Rockcastle, and Cumberland Rivers. Family and beginner raft trips on the Cumberland feature exciting Class II and III rapids,

scenic canyons, swimming, and views of wilderness waterfalls. Family and beginner trips of one and two days run on the Cumberland and Rockcastle Rivers on scenic sections with gentle currents and light rapids.

Wild water raft and canoe trips run on the Rockcastle and South Fork of the Cumberland — some of the most demanding water in Kentucky and Tennessee. These trips feature tight turns, large rocks, narrow chutes, and other challenges to thrill even the most skilled paddlers.

All trips run through wilderness areas with abundant deer, foxes, rabbits and other small wildlife, and good fishing for bass, walleye, and catfish. During its March-to-October season, the company also offers shuttle service for hikers and backpackers.

Cumberland River below Cumberland Falls. Courtesy of Sheltowee Trace Outfitters, Whitley City, Kentucky.

The gorge section of the Big South Fork of the Cumberland River. Courtesy of Sheltowee Trace Outfitters, Whitley City, Kentucky.

Still Waters Canoe Trails
Beth and Dave Strohmeier
249 Strohmeier Road
Frankfort, KY 40601
(502) 223-8896
Kentucky River, Elkhorn Creek
Max. rapids: I-II

Still Waters Canoe Trails offers one- and two-day canoe rentals for trips on Elkhorn Creek and the Kentucky River. Elkhorn Creek is a scenic stream with mostly Class I rapids and quiet pools. Noted for its smallmouth bass fishing, the Kentucky River has Class I rapids and is bounded by tall hills and cliffs. All trips but one five-mile, Class II section of Elkhorn Creek are fine for beginners.

The shores of both streams have colorful wildflowers, stately trees, and abundant wildlife, including deer, raccoons, muskrats, and blue herons. The two streams also have good fishing for largemouth and smallmouth bass, bluegill, and catfish.

Thaxton's Canoe Rental
Ann Thaxton and Sue Beagle
RR2, Box 391
Falmouth, KY 41040
(606) 472-2000, (606) 654-5111
South Fork, Middle Fork, Main Fork of the Licking River
Max. rapids: I
NACLO, ACA, USCA, AWA

Thaxton's Canoe Rental rents canoes, kayaks, and tubes for one- to 10-day trips on the Licking River and its tributaries. The Licking River Valley, first explored by legendary frontiersmen Simon Kenton and Daniel Boone, is a region rich in history and teeming with sportfish, birds, and animals. The Licking River's exceptionally clear waters are ideal for novices and advanced paddlers. Thaxton's, the oldest family-owned canoe rental in the state, was the first to offer guided moonlight floats, tube trips, kayak and sea kayak rentals and interpretive floats. Trips run between March and November.

Louisiana

Paddling in Louisiana is chiefly on lazy bayou streams, creeks, and lakes. Many local floaters are fishermen or naturalists drawn by the state's rich resources of fish and wildlife. With its great alluvial Mississippi delta, marshlands, and prairie to the south and its rolling country to the north, Louisiana is no place for white water. The state's highest point is just 535 feet above sea level. But in the so-called "uplands" there are numerous clear and lively streams with sand or gravel bottoms where fishermen may test their skill against wary spotted bass. State tourist brochures list no fewer than 66 rivers as suitable for canoeing and tubing. But in Louisiana's hot, humid, sub-tropical climate, few paddlers feel particularly energetic. Many just loll in their boats with a cane pole and a box of worms, hoping the catfish and bream will bite.

Among the streams served by canoeing and tubing outfitters are the Amite and Bogue Chitto Rivers and Pushepatapa Creek in the southeast, with the Quiska (Whisky) in the Shreveport region of the northwest. The scenery varies from vast marshlands to forests, which cover half the state.

White-tailed deer and wildcats frequent wooded swamps beside the rivers, while muskrats, minks, opossums, raccoons, wild hogs, and skunks roam the lowland woods. In the coastal bayous the paddler may see occasional alligators and coypus (beaverlike animals).

Nearly half the wild ducks and geese in North America are said to winter in the state's coastal marshes. All told, more than 100 bird species, notably the brown pelican, Louisiana's state bird, live there. Close to the coast speckled trout, redfish, crabs, shrimp, and oysters abound in the brackish waters of the largest estuary marsh in the nation. Further inland, Louisiana lakes and rivers have been well-stocked with striped and hybrid bass. Fish of up to thirty pounds are often caught in Toledo Bend and other lakes.

Atchafalaya Basin Backwater Tours

John Faslun
P.O. Box 128
Gibson, LA 70356
(504) 575-2371
Big Bayou Black, Tiger Bayou
Max. rapids: None

Atchafalaya Basin Backwater Tours offers guided powerboat trips and rentals of pirogues (canoe-like dugouts) for exploring the deep swamp country of the Atchafalaya Basin. The waters travelled — the Big Bayou, Black Bayou, and Tiger Bayou — are clean, beautiful, and unspoiled. The bayous are home to 17 kinds of fish, 16 types of animals, and 18 species of birds.

Paddling tours cover five miles roundtrip and are best suited for teens and fit adults. Trips run year-round.

Maine

With its great wilderness of forests, mountains, and five thousand streams and rivers, Maine rivals the West in remote canoeing territory. Here is a paradise for those wanting to escape the congestion of the city. One can lose oneself in the vast hinterland of Maine and not see another soul for days on end. Whitewater rivers, scenic streams, and lakes abound. The bays and rocky coves of the Atlantic coast also beckon.

The best-known of Maine's attractions for river-runners is the Allagash Wilderness Waterway, nearly 100 miles of lakes and river coursing northward. This is a land of gentle, quiet rapids and boundless forests alive with beavers, moose, deer, and the occasional bear. The fishing is great and the birdlife prolific. The entire trip from Telos Lake in the south to its confluence with the St. John River at Allagash can be canoed comfortably in a week. But paddlers with time to spare can easily spend a second week savoring side trips and studying wildlife along this original federal Wild and Scenic River. A favorite detour is to Allagash Lake, a pristine spot that can only be reached by poling a canoe up six miles of riffles from Chamberlain Lake.

Allagash Wilderness Waterway may be paddled anytime between May and October, although the water may be too high in May and June and rather low in late summer. Outfitters recommend some prior canoeing experience for the Allagash since the Chase Rapids (below Churchill Lake) present nine miles of Class II white water. There are four portages enroute.

For real whitewater enthusiasts the West Branch of the Penobscot River, claimed to be the most exciting river in the East, offers a 12-mile run that starts with rugged Class V rapids. The trip begins in spectacular Ripogenus Gorge, where the river drops 70 feet per mile for the first two miles. Then it alternates between calm stretches and Class III-IV white water as it passes Baxter State Park and Mount Katahdin, Maine's highest peak. The dam-controlled river can be run all summer long, with the greatest flow in May and June.

Novices and others not seeking white water enjoy paddling the Upper West Branch of the Penobscot, a four-day, 50-mile trip between the dam at the foot of Seboomook Lake and the start of the rugged West Branch run at Ripogenus. There are no difficult rapids, no portages, and half the floating is on lakes.

Definitely not for the faint-hearted is the Dead River, a Class III-V stream that shows it is very much alive by providing the longest stretch of continuous white water in the East. This 15-mile run through a remote wilderness canyon begins at Grand Falls and ends near the village of West Forks. It can only be floated when dam water is released; the big releases come in May.

The Kennebec, into which the Dead River flows at The Forks, boasts the largest river gorge in New England and some mighty rapids on its upstream portion. Starting at Harris Dam, adjoining Indian Pond, the Class IV-V rapids along the upper four-mile section are particularly daunting in the spring. But the remaining eight miles of this run are gentle and appealing for families with children, who may skip the upper gorge and start their float at Carry Brook.

Rapid River is one of the fastest streams east of the Mississippi, plunging 100 feet per mile as it flows from Lake Richardson to Lake Umbagog in a wonderfully rustic region of Maine woods. With its Class IV rapids, Rapid River is challenging at all times, but especially when water releases occur. Lake Umbagog is rich in wildlife and — by one recent report — habitat for a nesting pair of bald eagles.

Up north, the large St. John River runs parallel to the Canadian border through magnificent forest wilderness offering long stretches of solitude along the 83-mile course down to Allagash Village. Some of the trip involves heavy white water and is strictly for experienced paddlers. It can only be run from mid-May through mid-June when the run-off is right.

Canoeists and fishermen can also sample Maine's 2,500 lakes which, seen from the air, gleam like jewels in the forest. The largest, of course, is Moosehead Lake, which despite its many tourist facilities is still largely undeveloped and a favorite choice for anglers after trout and salmon. There are also organized "canoe safaris" for nature photographers in search of moose in the surrounding woods.

Sea kayakers revel in a totally different experience: paddling among dozens of islands off Penobscot Bay amid seals, porpoises, and — if they are lucky — various species of whales. Among the many sea birds they see are puffins, gannets, cormorants, fulmars, kittiwakes, and ospreys. All told, this stretch of the Maine coast is one of the best sea-kayaking regions in the country.

Allagash Wilderness Outfitters
Rick and Judy Givens
Box 620 HCR 76
Greenville, ME 04441
(207) 695-2821, (207) 723-6622
(winter)
Allagash River, Penobscot River
Max. rapids: I-II
NACLO
   Allagash Wilderness Outfitters offers full or partial outfitting for three- to eight-day trips on the Allagash, Penobscot and St. John Rivers and many other waterways and lakes in northern Maine. Both flat-water and moderate whitewater trips are available to suit paddlers of all skill levels. Trips pass through unspoiled spruce and fir forests and offer excellent fishing for trout, perch, and landlocked salmon. Moose, deer, bears, beavers, loons, and waterfowl are also abundant.
   The outfitter's season runs from May to September.

Back Country Tours, Inc.
Allan McGroary
39 Hollis Street
Pepperell, MA 01463
(508) 433-9381, (800) 649-9381 (in MA)
Connecticut River, Nashua River
Max. rapids: I-II
   Back Country Tours, Inc., specializes in guided canoe trips and canoe rentals on "lesser known, uncrowded scenic waterways." Its trips run on the Souhegan and Merrimack Rivers in New Hampshire; the Sauantacook and Nissitisit Rivers in Massachusetts; the Connecticut and Nashua Rivers in New Hampshire and Massachusetts; the Delaware River in New York, Pennsylvania, and New Jersey; the Blackwater, Sweetwater, and Juniper Rivers in Florida; the St. John in Maine, and nine lakes near Long Pond Mountain in New York's Adirondacks. Several of these

excursion are "vacation" trips of three to seven days that offer lodging at campgrounds, cabins, or bed-and-breakfast inns. All trips are suitable for beginners and experienced paddlers.
   Back Country Tours' season runs from July to November.

Downeast Rafting Inc.
Ned McSherry/Rick Haddicott
P.O. Box 119
Center Conway, NH 03813
(603) 447-3002, (800) 677-RAFT
Kennebec River, Dead River, Penobscot River, Rapid River, Swift River
Max. rapids: V+
   Downeast Rafting provides guided raft trips on the Kennebec, Dead, Penobscot, Rapid and Swift Rivers, which run through the Maine woods with their wealth of wildlife. These one-day trips are offered from mid-April to October. Rafters experience Class III-IV whitewater on some streams and Class V on the technical Penobscot.
   Downeast's guides are some of the most experienced and personable around. All the company's Kennebec and Dead River packages include lodging at its inn or campground, meals, grilled lunch on the raft trip and a video/slide show of the trip at the end. Various other package tours, including guided fishing trips and even combined skiing-rafting trips, are available.

A paddler negotiates Ledge Falls on the Kennebec River. Courtesy of Northern Outdoors, The Forks, Maine.

Eastern River Expeditions
John Connelly
Box 1173
Greenville, ME 04441
(207) 695-2411, (800) 634-7238
Dead River, Kennebec River,
Penobscot River, Moose River, Gauley
River
Max. rapids: V+
Maine Professional River Outfitters
Association, America Outdoors
    Eastern River Expeditions offers
canoe rentals and guided raft and in-
flatable-kayak trips on five rivers in
Maine, New York, and West Virginia.
In Maine, paddlers can choose
among whitewater trips on the Ken-
nebec, Penobscot, and Dead Rivers.
Most Maine trips are fine for novice
paddlers, combining excellent wilder-
ness scenery with Class II-IV white
water. Trips on the Dead and

Penobscot Rip Gorge, however, require excellent conditioning.
Penobscot Rip Gorge also requires intermediate or advanced paddling
skills. Advanced rafting experience is
a prerequisite for trips on New York's
Moose River and West Virginia's
Gauley River, which have Class IV-V
rapids.
    All trips, of one to two days, pass
through wilderness offering camping
spots, clear water, fishing, and chances to spot deer, coyotes, loons,
ducks, beavers, foxes, great blue
herons, and other wildlife.

Explorers at Sea, Inc.
D. Gay Atkinson, II
P.O. Box 469, Main Street
Stonington, ME 04681
(207) 367-2356
Penobscot Bay
Max. rapids:
TASK

Explorers at Sea offers half-day to five-day sea kayaking trips along the mid-coast of Maine off Stonington, a fishing village with nearly 100 islands just south of town. One- and two-day trips are designed for beginning sea kayakers, while the trips of three to five days are geared to paddlers with basic canoe or kayaking skills and camping experience.

The bays traveled are dotted with spruce-clad, granite islands, many of which are public and open for exploring and camping. These trips offer excellent chances to view eagles, ospreys, seals, and porpoises. Also, on special "whale and seabird" cruises, paddlers often see large groups of Atlantic white-sided dolphins and several kinds of whales. Among the many birds seen are loons, greater and sooty shearwaters, puffins, gannets, Wilson's storm petrels, red and rednecked phalarapes, great cormorants, fulmars, kittiwakes, and razorbills.

Explorers at Sea also offers family adventures and Baja Mexican expeditions. Its season runs from May to September.

Gilpatrick's Guide Service
Gil Gilpatrick
P.O. Box 461
Skowhegan, ME 04976
(207) 453-6959
Allagash River, St. John River,
Penobscot River
Max. rapids: III-IV
Maine Professional Guides
Association

Gilpatrick's Guide Service offers one-week, guided and unguided canoe trips on the Allagash, St. John, and Penobscot Rivers. All trips run through pristine wooded wilderness of spruces, firs, and occasional hardwoods. Wildlife is abundant, especially moose, deer, bald eagles, ospreys, geese, and ducks. Also, anglers enjoy fishing for brook trout, lake trout, and whitefish.

As these trips have Class III and IV rapids, those renting canoes should have whitewater experience. However, beginners are welcome on guided trips where the outfitter's master Maine guides give lessons enroute. Gilpatrick's season is from May to October.

Libby Sporting Camps
Matt Libby
Drawer V
Ashland, ME 04732
(207) 435-8274, (207) 435-6233
Penobscot River, Upper Allagash
River, Aroostook River
Max. rapids: III-IV
Maine Guides Association, Maine
Sporting Camps Association

Libby Sporting Camps runs guided canoe and kayak trips and rents canoes for wilderness trips of one to 10 days for paddlers of all skill levels. Trips run on the Upper Penobscot, Allagash, and Aroostock in Maine and the Atikonak in Labrador. All expeditions runs through pristine pine forests and offer striking views of mountains, waterfalls, and abundant

111

"The Cribworks" rapid on the Penobscot River, Maine. Photo by Jan Lorimer, North Country Rivers, Inc., Vassalboro, Maine.

wildlife, including moose, deer, bears, otters, eagles, ospreys, and beavers. There is also excellent fishing for landlocked salmon and brook trout.

Maine Outdoors
Don Kleiner
RR 1, Box 3770
Union, ME 04862
(207) 785-4496
Saint George River, Flagstaff Lake, Rangeley Lakes, Chesuncook Lake
Max. rapids: None
Maine Professional Guides Association

Maine Outdoors offers leisurely canoe trips led by a registered Maine guide and naturalist from May through September. Novices or experienced canoeists can enjoy a half-day outing or three-day canoe and camping trip down the scenic St. George's River or on unspoiled lakes surrounded by mountains.

A three-day canoe trip on Flagstaff Lake in western Maine offers warm water, sandy beaches, island camping, and a chance to visit Maine's only ghost town. Paddlers can retrace Benedict Arnold's trail to Quebec. The deeper, colder Rangeley Lakes have excellent trout and salmon fishing. After a trip up Chesuncook Lake, guests can spend two nights in a 19th-century hotel in Chesuncook, a village accessible only by water or air, and explore the back-country areas once traveled by Thoreau. While paddling on these waters, guests may see bald eagles, moose, deer, and ospreys.

Maine Sport
Stuart and Marianne Smith
Route 1
Rockport, ME 04856
(207) 236-7120, (207) 236-8797
Penobscot Bay, St. Georges River, St.
Croix River, Penobscot River, Ken-
nebec River
Max. rapids: III-IV
NACLO, ACA
 Maine Sport offers guided canoe, kayak, and raft trips and canoe and kayak rentals for trips on Penobscot Bay, Georges River, West Branch Penobscot, Kennebec River, and many lakes. Raft trips last one day and canoe trips from one to three days. All excursions are of little to moderate difficulty, suitable for beginners as well as experienced paddlers.

 What is distinctive about many of these trips is that waterways are interconnected, allowing paddlers to travel rivers, lakes, and tidewaters on a single trip. Also, the wilderness areas traveled feature abundant birds, deer, moose, seals, and other wildlife, depending on location. Fishing is good, too, for both freshwater and saltwater species.

 Maine Sport, which offers trips from April to October, also operates a well-stocked paddle store with a wide array of canoes, kayaks, and paddle gear.

Maine Whitewater, Inc.
James A. Ernst
P.O. Box 633
Gaddabout Gaddis Airport
Bingham, ME 04920
(207) 672-4814, (800) 245-MAIN
Dead River, Penobscot River, Ken-
nebec River
Max. rapids: V+
 Maine Whitewater, Inc., runs one-day guided rafting trips on the Penobscot, Kennebec, and Dead Rivers. These dam-controlled rivers offer consistently good Class III-V white water

from May to September. State-licensed guides are chosen for their "love of adventure and outgoing personalities."

 Both the Penobscot and Kennebec trips begin in gorges. The Penobscot River winds along the base of Mount Katahdin and the Kennebec trip features a stop at 90-foot Mukie Falls. Moose, deer, ospreys, and bald eagles may be seen along these rivers.

North Country Guide Service
Steve Roderick
RFD #1, Box 2840
McFalls, ME 04256
(207) 539-8483
Allagash River
Max. rapids: I-II
Maine Professional Guides Association
 North Country Guide Service runs guided trips of six or seven days on the Allagash Wilderness Waterway and Allagash River. These trips, with Class I-II rapids, are easy, relaxing, and fine for people of all ages. All canoes are equipped with motors, which gives paddlers a rest when they want one. As a result, guests can be assured of travelling greater distances. Six-day trips, for instance, cover 98 miles.

 On these trips, paddlers can enjoy clean waters, protected wilderness, and certain success at spotting moose and deer at close range. Ducks, geese, eagles, and osprey are also abundant. Fishing for brook trout, lake trout, salmon, and whitefish is excellent. North Country's season runs from May to September.

113

Canoeing on the 135-mile St. John River Trail. Courtesy of Back Country Tours, Inc., Pepperell, Massachusetts.

North Country Rivers
Jim Murton
P.O. Box 47
E. Vassalboro, ME 04935
(207) 923-3492, (800) 348-8871
Penobscot River, Kennebec River, Dead River, St. John River, Allagash River, Moose River
Max. rapids: V+
America Outdoors

North Country Rivers offers guided canoe, kayak, raft, and dory trips and canoe and kayak rentals on the Penobscot, Kennebec, Dead, St. John, Allagash, and Moose Rivers. With the many Class I-II rivers to choose from, all paddlers, from beginners to experts, can find a trip to suit their skills. On all trips, guests can enjoy Maine's vast, pristine wilderness, with good fishing for trout and landlocked salmon, and a chance to spot moose, bears, deer, eagles, and ospreys. North Country Rivers' season is from April to October.

Northern Outdoors
Wayne and Suzie Hockmeyer
P.O. Box 100, Route 201
The Forks, ME 04985
(207) 663-4466, (800) 765-RAFT (7238)
Kennebec River, Moosehead Lake
Max. rapids: III-IV
America Outdoors, Maine Professional River Outfitters

Northern Outdoors offers guided raft trips on the Kennebec and Penobscot Rivers from two outfitting locations, the Forks Resort Center and Penobscot Outdoor Center. The West branch of the Penobscot is a steep, turbulent, ledge-drop river, which is extremely challenging and best-suited for paddlers with some rafting experiences. Trips on the Penobscot also offer spectacular scenery, with excellent views of Mount Katahdin, Ripoganus Gorge, waterfalls,and abundant wildlife, including moose, deer, and bald eagles.

Trips on the Kennebec River pass through the biggest river gorge in New England — the Kennebec Gorge. Guests may elect to run either a 12-mile trip with white water that is among the biggest in the East, or a lower eight-mile trip, which is gentler and very safe. The river also boasts pristine wilderness scenery and views of moose, deer, and bald eagles. Trips on both the Penobscot and Kennebec last one or two days and offer good trout and salmon fishing.

During its April-to-October season, Northern Outdoors also offers cycling, horseback riding, bass fishing, inflatable kayak trips, camping, cabins, and deluxe lodge rooms.

Penobscot River Outfitters
Richard LeVasseir
P.O. Box H
Medway, ME 04460
(207) 746-9349, (800) 794-KAMP
(Maine only)
Penobscot River, Allagash River
Max. rapids: III-IV
Penobscot River Outfitters offers guided and unguided canoe and kayak trips of one to seven days on the East or West Branches of the Penobscot River and the Allagash Wilderness Waterway. Trips vary in difficulty, with runs to suit beginners and experienced paddlers. The scenic East Branch of the Penobscot has great fishing, is little-traveled, and has some challenging stretches of white water. The West Branch, also very scenic, is clean and has good fishing for salmon, trout, bass, and pike. Paddlers on all trips have a good chance of spotting moose, deer, eagles, beavers, otters, and bears. Penobscot River Outfitters' trips run from May to October.

NORTH COUNTRY GUIDES SERVICE

Allagash River Canoe Trips

Steve Roderick
Registered Maine Guide
R-1 Box 2840
McFalls, Maine 04256
Tel. (207) 539-8483

Saco Bound Inc.
Ned McSherry
P.O. Box 119
Center Conway, NH 03813
(603) 447-2177, (603) 447-3801
Max. rapids: None
NACLO, Saco River Recreational Council
The Saco River is a perfect stream for family floating, and Saco Bound is ideally placed for enabling paddlers to relish it. Saco Bound rents canoes and kayaks from May 1-October 15 for periods of half a day to three days, with ample campsites available on beaches and sandbars along a 43-mile route. The company runs guided day trips with barbecue lunches on Tuesdays and Thursdays in July and August.

During the summer months the crystal-clear stream is warm and levels average three to four feet, with

115

Moose feeding. Courtesy of Northern Outdoors, The Forks, Maine.

deeper holes for swimming. Early October is the time to experience brilliant fall foliage, when the White Mountains are ablaze with color.

Sunrise County Canoe Expeditions, Inc.

Martin Brown
Box 152
Cathance Lake
Grove Post Office, ME 04638
(207) 454-7708
St. Croix River, St. John River, Machias River
Max. rapids: III-IV
NACLO, Maine Professional Guides Association, America Outdoors

For almost 30 years, Sunrise Country Canoe Expeditions has specialized in open-canoe expeditions, offering lessons, rentals, and guided trips. In Maine, the outfitter runs trips on the St. Croix, Machias, and St. John Rivers. These trips have rapids of Class I-III, range in length from four to eight days, and are set in remote, unspoiled wilderness. The St. Croix and St. John trips have easy to moderate rapids and are suitable for novices as well as more experienced paddlers. Trips on the Machias are more difficult, offering fine technical white water over the course of an extended wilderness journey.

Sunrise Country Expeditions also offers trips in Quebec, Labrador, arctic Quebec, and Baffin Island in Canada; down the desert canyons of the Rio Grande in Texas; and the jungle gorges of Costa Rica.

Unicorn Expeditions

Jay Schurman
P.O. Box T
Brunswick, ME 04011
(207) 725-2255, (800) UNICORN
Kennebec River, Penobscot River, Dead River
Max. rapids: V+
America Outdoors

Unicorn Expeditions offers guided canoe, kayak, and raft trips and canoe rentals for trips of one to six days on the Kennebec, Penobscot, and Dead Rivers in Maine; the Hudson and Moose Rivers in New York; and the Deerfield River in Massachusetts. These trips range widely in difficulty to suit all skill levels from beginner to expert. Moose River trips have some of the wildest white water in the Northeast; the dam-controlled Penobscot and Kennebec Rivers ensure Class V white water all summer long; and the Hudson's spring high water offers 16 miles of exhilarating Class III and IV rapids.

Among the wildlife to see on these trips are moose, bald eagles, bears, deer, and ospreys. There is also fishing for bass, salmon, and trout. During its April-to-October season, Unicorn also offers "getaway" packages, which include rafting and lodge or inn accommodations.

Voyagers Whitewater
John P. Kokajko
Route 201
The Forks, ME 04985
(207) 663-4423
Kennebec River, Dead River,
Penobscot River
Max. rapids: III-IV
America Outdoors
Voyagers Whitewater runs raft trips of one and two days on the Kennebec River, Dead River, and West Branch of the Penobscot. These trips offer exciting white water on clean wilderness rivers. No prior rafting experience is required, but participants should be in good health and capable of vigorous physical activity. On these trips, which run between May and October, paddlers can also fish for trout and look for moose, deer, bears, foxes, and other wildlife.

Wilderness Expeditions
John Willard
Box 41
Rockwood, ME 04478
(207) 534-2242, (800) 825-9453
Kennebec River, Penobscot River,
Dead River, Moose River, Allegash
River, St. John River, Moosehead River
Max. rapids: V+
Wilderness Expeditions runs guided canoe, kayak, and raft trips and rents canoes and kayaks for trips of one to seven days on Moosehead Lake, the Allagash Wilderness Waterway, and the Kennebec, Penobscot, Dead, Moose, and St. John Rivers. With this range of offerings, the outfitters has organized trips for paddlers at all levels, from novice to expert, which feature wilderness scenery and moose, deer, bears, eagles, ospreys, beavers, and other wildlife. And for those who prefer to set their own dates and trip schedules, the company provides full or partial outfitting and helpful route suggestions. Boating runs from April to October.

As part of the Birches Resort, Wilderness Expeditions also offers horseback riding, ice fishing, and "cabin tent" and cottage rentals.

Woodland Acres, Camp N'Canoe
Chris and Sue Gantick
RR 1, Box 445
Brownfield, ME 04010
(207) 935-2529
Saco River
Max. rapids: I-II
Saco River Livery Association
Woodland Acres Camp N'Canoe offers shuttles and canoe rentals for one- to three-day trips on the Saco River in the foothills of the White Mountains. The river, which runs under several covered bridges, has clean water and lots of sandbars for camping, swimming, and picnics. Moose, loons, beavers, raccoons, and deer can be seen along its banks. Fishing is for brown trout, smallmouth bass, and pickerel.

Canoe trips on the Saco are suitable for "novices, families and lazy people," but more accomplished paddlers can take longer trips with some Class II rapids. Rentals are available from May 15 to October 15.

Maryland

Where Maryland's northwestern panhandle reaches up into the Appalachians, it takes in a famous stretch of the Youghiogheny River known as the "Upper Yough." Whitewater experts call it one of the world's most difficult commercially rafted rivers. It begins to get scary at Bastard Falls, dropping an average of 116 feet per mile. Along one 3.5 mile section of the river alone, the Upper Yough has more than 20 Class IV and V rapids sporting such odd names as Snaggle Tooth, Meat Cleaver, Powerful Popper, Lost-n-Found, Cheeseburger, and Double Pencil Sharpener.

By contrast, the Pocomoke River at the other end of the state meanders placidly through the coastal flats of the Delmarva (Delaware-Maryland-Virginia) peninsula between Chesapeake Bay and the Atlantic. With its wealth of blue herons, ospreys, eagles, ducks, and fish, its greatest appeal is to birdwatchers and anglers.

Like its neighbors to the north and south, Maryland encompasses three great geological divides: the Appalachian mountains, the Piedmont's rolling plateau, and the coastal plain reaching to the Chesapeake Bay and the Atlantic. The Potomac traverses all three as its winding course divides Maryland from Virginia.

The Potomac has a great advantage for paddlers who like to step ashore and see the sights — much of its eastern bank is part of the C & O National Historical Park. Canoeists can stroll the towpath to the nearest disused lock and admire the skilled stonework of Irish immigrants who built the Chesapeake and Ohio canal in the 19th century. They can tour Antietam battlefield, close to the river at Shepherdstown. Or they can take in a short stretch of the Shenandoah (see West Virginia) before exploring historic Harpers Ferry, where the two rivers converge.

The Potomac can be paddled year-round and is remarkably clean. Even in the heart of Washington, D.C., the Potomac is again a robust fishery with terrific bass fishing. The best white water and perhaps the finest scenery are to be found on the 10-mile stretch upstream from the capital to Great Falls. These falls themselves should be portaged. So should Little Falls and Brookmont Dam, an innocent- looking two-foot weir that has, in the words of one authority, "a reversal that will stop you and never let you go."

The Savage River, flowing through Savage River State Forest in northwestern Maryland, is as famous a whitewater river as the Upper Yough. Its five miles of Class III-IV rapids (Class IV-V at high water) fed by dependable reservoir releases have made it a favorite venue of national slalom and whitewater racing. It was the scene of the 1972 Olympic trials and it was selected again for the 1992 U.S. Olympic Whitewater Slalom Team trials.

Other canoeing rivers in the Maryland hills include Antietam Creek, runnable in winter and spring, and the North Branch of the Potomac, which is also floatable in late summer and early fall, after dam releases from Bloomington Lake. Close to Baltimore but only runnable in winter and spring after heavy rain is a three-mile trip down Gunpowder River through Gunpowder Falls State Park.

Harpers Ferry River Riders, Inc.
Mark Grimes
P.O. Box 267
Knoxville, MD 21758
(301) 834-8051
Shenandoah River, Potomac River, Tygart River
Max. rapids: III-IV

Harpers Ferry River Riders offers one-day guided raft and tube trips and canoe rentals on the Shenandoah, Potomac, and Tygart Rivers. Trips on the Potomac and Shenandoah, with Class I-III rapids, are fine for beginners and offer scenic views of historic Harpers Ferry, wooded mountains, and abundant wildlife, including great blue herons, egrets, nesting bald eagles, turtles, geese, deer, and ducks. The two rivers also feature good fishing for smallmouth and largemouth bass, catfish, panfish, and carp.

The Tygart River, also scenic, has more challenging white water with up to Class V rapids. The outfitter's season is from April to October.

Laurel Highlands River Tours
Mark and Linda McCarty
P.O. Box 107
Ohiopyle, PA 15470
(412) 329-8531, (800) 4 RAFTIN
Upper Youghiogheny River
Max. rapids: V+
America Outdoors

Laurel Highlands River Tours, one of the oldest whitewater companies in the East, claims to have the largest fleet of equipment anywhere. It operates on the Cheat River as well as the Lower, Middle and Upper Youghiogheny from bases in Albright, W.Va., Ohiopyle, Pa. and Friendsville, Md. In a season running from March to October, it offers guided raft trips and rents both rafts and canoes for floats on both rivers. All are one-day trips.

The "Yough" has the most popular whitewater in the East and the Cheat is famed for its spring thrills. Canoeing and kayaking instruction is available and acommodations range from camping to luxury motels.

Rafters brave the fierce rapids of the Upper Youghiogheny. Courtesy of Laurel Highlands River Tours, Ohiopyle, Pennsylvania.

Mountain Streams and Trails Outfitters

Michael McCarty and Ralph McCarty
P.O. Box 106, Route 381
Ohiopyle, PA 15470
(800) 245-4090
Upper Youghiogheny River
Max. rapids: V+
America Outdoors

Mountain Streams and Trails operates on all three sections of the Youghiogheny as well as the Class III-IV Cheat, the challenging Tygart, isolated Big Sandy Creek, and the Class III-VI Upper and Lower Gauley rivers. It runs guided raft and kayak trips in addition to renting canoes, kayaks, and rafts, tailoring its trips to suit the needs of every paddler.

The company has skilled guides, trained in first aid and equipped with radios. They take guests through the spectacular panorama of maples, pines, and rhododendrons that blanket the walls of the Middle and Lower Yough River canyon, habitat for deer, beavers, bears, ospreys, herons and an occasional wildcat. One-day and two-day tours are offered during a March-October season.

Passages to Adventure
Benjy Simpson
P.O. Box 71
Fayetteville, WV 25840
(304) 574-1037, (800) 634-33785
Upper Youghiogheny
Max. rapids: V+
America Outdoors, Association for Experiential Education
   Passages to Adventure provides guided canoe, inflatable kayak and raft trips as well as renting canoes and inflatable kayaks on the Cheat, New, and Gauley Rivers in West Virginia and the Upper Youghiogheny in Maryland.
   With this variety, the company caters to all paddlers, from beginners to experts. The wild Cheat River has challenging, technical rapids that come in quick succession down a majestic canyon. The Lower New River offers huge rolling waves, giving a "rollercoaster" ride that is the company's most popular trip. The Upper New is wide, scenic, and has Class II rapids — ideal for families and first-time rafters. The Upper Gauley has superb whitewater that requires previous paddling experience. The Lower Gauley has huge waves but doesn't require prior experience. Finally, the Upper Yough is famous for its extremely technical Class IV-V+ rapids.

Pocomoke River Canoe Co.
Barry R. Laws
312 N. Washington Street
Snow Hill, MD 21863
(301) 632-3971
Pocomoke River, Nassawango Creek
Max. rapids: None
   Pocomoke River Canoe Co. offers guided canoe trips and canoe rentals of one to three days on the Pocomoke River and Nassawango Creek. These trips are especially good for novices, nature lovers, and bird watchers, offering views of un-

spoiled regions on the Eastern Shore and particularly abundant wildlife, including great blue herons, eagles, otters, ospreys, and ducks. Fishing is for bass, gar, and other freshwater fish.

Rainy Day, Inc.
Donald and Mabel Rogers
11238 Adkins Road
Berlin, MD 21811
(301) 641-5029
Pocomoke River, Chesapeake Bay
Max. rapids: None
   Rainy Day, Inc., rents canoes for flat-water, scenic trips on Pocomoke River and in the bay behind Assateague Island at the Assateague Island National Seashore. These trips, which require no paddling experience, offer a peaceful way to explore wetlands and coastal waters; fish for flounder, spot, sea bass, and crabs, gather clams, and spot Assateague wild ponies, sika deer, and abundant waterfowl. Camping and swimming are also available.
   Rainy Day's season is from April to October.

River & Trail Outfitters
Lee Baihly
604 Valley Road
Knoxville, MD 21758
(301) 695-5177
Shenandoah River, Potomac River, Antietam Creek
Max. rapids: None
   River & Trail Outfitter runs guided and unguided canoe and raft trips on the Shenandoah and Potomac Rivers. The company also rents tubes on Antietam Creek. An excellent beginners' raft trip and intermediate canoe trip is the "Staircase," a six-mile run down the Shenandoah to its confluence with the Potomac at Harpers Ferry. Highlights of this Class I-III trip include a mile-long series of rapids and ledges that demands attentive pad-

Rafters on the Lower "Yough." Courtesy of Wilderness Voyageurs, Ohiopyle, Pennsylvania.

dling. A more challenging raft trip is a seven-mile run on the North Branch of the Potomac. This guided trip has Class I-III rapids in close succession, with waves and rollers up to six feet high. Canoe lessons and several other canoe trips are available. These include "Taylor's Landing," an 11-mile flat-water trip on the upper Potomac; the "Needles," a half-day run on the Potomac that includes a challenging mile-long rock garden with Class I-II rapids.

One- to three-day trips on the calm waters of the lower Shenandoah are also available. Many of these trips boast excellent bass fishing and a chance to spot herons, ospreys, bald eagles, and deer. River & Trail's season runs from April to November.

Upper Yough Expeditions
Gary Davis and Dave Martin
P.O. Box 158
Friendsville, MD 21531
(301) 746-5808, (800) 248-1UYE
Upper Youghiogheny River
Max. rapids: V+
NAPSA

Upper Yough Expeditions runs thrilling half-day whitewater trips on the Upper Youghiogheny. Trips, in guided rafts, are 11 miles long and include dozens of spectacular rapids. The 3.5-mile "heart" of the Upper Yough is virtually one huge rapid in itself. This stretch alone has more than 20 Class IV and V rapids. Experienced rafters are preferred on these trips and the Class V trips the outfitter offers on the Top Yough, Russell Fork, Big Sandy, North Branch of the Potomac, and Savage Rivers.

Also available are free camping and a free sauna. Upper Yough Expeditions' season runs from March to November.

USA RAFT
Mary Kay Heffernan
P.O. Box 277
Rowlesburg, WV 26425
(304) 454-2475, (800) USA RAFT
*North Fork Potomac River, Gauley
River, Cheat River, Tygart River, New
River, Upper Youghiogheny River,
Nolichucky River, Ocoee River, Nan-
tahala River, French Broad River*
Max. rapids: II-III
America Outdoors
USA Raft is the reservation and
marketing company for Appalachian
Wildwaters, Rough Run Expeditions,
and Expeditions, Inc. Its staff can
help you choose the ideal raft or
"funyak" trip from among 30 different
outings on ten of the best whitewater
rivers in the East — the New, Gauley,
Cheat, and Tygart in West Virginia;
the Upper Youghiogheny and North
Fork of the Potomac in Maryland; the
Nolichucky and Ocoee in Tennessee;
and the Nantahala, French Broad,
and Nolichucky in North Carolina.

With this selection of trips, rivers,
and outfitters, USA Raft can offer outings to suit paddlers of all skill levels
at locations convenient to residents
throughout the Middle Atlantic and
Southeast. Open year-round, USA
Raft also provides package trips that
include meals and lodging. And, for
winter paddling, it has one- to nine-
day trips on the Rio Grande in Texas.

White Water Adventures, Inc.
Robert and Shirley Marietta
P.O. Box 31
Ohiopyle, PA 15470
(412) 329-8850, (800) WWA-RAFT
(992-7238)
Upper Youghiogheny River
Max. rapids: V+
America Outdoors
White Water Adventurers runs
guided raft and kayak trips on the
Lower, Middle, and Upper
Youghiogheny as well as renting
canoes, kayaks, and rafts from March
to November. Paddlers can take their
pick; the dam-controlled Yough is
rated Class V on its upper section and
Classes III and II on its lower and
middle stretches respectively. Trips
are suitable for "folks from 12-100
who are willing to paddle a bit and
have a good time."

A highly professional staff and the
best modern equipment are
mainstays of the company, which offers lessons and provides a guide for
every raft on the steep and technical
Upper Yough. Trout, walleye and
bass can be caught on the Yough as it
winds through the Laurel Highland
Mountains.

In West Virginia, White Water Adventures of Cheat River Canyon runs
"very thrilling" guided raft trips from
March to July through Class IV-V
rapids on the free-flowing Cheat
River. The stream cuts through a very
steep canyon in an historic part of
West Virginia. It has beautiful wildflowers and mountain laurel, along
with deer, wild turkeys, and grouse.

One of the oldest outfitters on the
Cheat river, the company has very
professional guides with the latest
equipment. Rafts generally hold eight
people and the day trips cover a 12-
mile distance.

123

Massachusetts

P addling may be enjoyed in the Mayflower State anywhere from the coastal lowlands and islands around Cape Cod to the wooded Berkshire Hills in the west. The four thousand miles of rivers in Massachusetts include the great Connecticut River, which flows north-south across the state, and the wide Merrimack, which swings across the northeast corner past Lowell. Historic sites and fall colors greatly enhance the state's sightseeing appeal.

Some of the best canoe trails in Massachusetts are on the Deerfield River, which runs through the rolling Berkshires to join the Connecticut River at Greenfield. But it is essential to time it right: the Deerfield varies from a rampaging stream at high water to a placid float. There is Class IV wild water and equally wild scenery on the upper river near Vermont. From Shelburne Falls downstream the river is less hazardous but its levels can still change very swiftly, depending on dam releases and rainfall or sudden thaws. The Deerfield is described as the last wilderness river in southern New England. Its fish include trout and bass and its wildlife ranges from beavers and bear to hawks and eagles.

The Nashua, which flows north across the New Hampshire state line to its confluence with the Merrimack in Nashua, has become cleaner in recent years. Fish and wildlife are returning, with flocks of 40 to 50 great blue herons seen at Pepperell Pond, a beautiful spot rich in animal and plant life. A gentle paddle on the Nashua can reveal tracks of raccoons, deer, beavers, muskrats, and turtles. Another great Massachusetts river for naturalists is the Ipswich in the northeast corner of the state, which passes through an Audubon bird sanctuary.

Paramount among all the rivers in southern New England is the Connecticut. By the time it reaches Massachusetts it is already a broad waterway, runnable at all water levels and well-supplied with campsites. One attractive section of the river is the 21 miles of flat water upstream from Northampton. Here the scenery is rural and unsullied by civilization except for occasional powerboats. Between Northampton and Holyoke the stream cuts through the Holyoke Range, with Mt. Nonotuck and Mt. Tom on the right and Mt. Holyoke on the left. It then turns urban through Holyoke and Springfield.

The Merrimack, also swollen to a wide river before it enters Massachusetts from New Hampshire, is navigable at all times. It runs through a mixture of woodland and towns as it parallels the state line to the sea and becomes tidal after it passes through Lawrence.

The Blackstone River flows southwards from Worcester, with scenic stretches between milltowns. Parts of the canal built to connect Worcester and Providence are still intact, and the area around Rice City Pond is a state recreation area. The river has some white water but many dams that must be portaged.

For a different kind of experience altogether, paddlers visit Cape Cod, where canoeists and kayakers can explore both freshwater and saltwater habitats of many kinds of wildlife. These include lakes, streams, estuaries, salt marshes, and bays, where paddlers can find harbor seals, gray seals, ospreys, many kinds of fish, and even an occasional whale.

Back Country Tours, Inc.
Allan McGroary
39 Hollis Street
Pepperell, MA 01463
(508) 433-9381, (800) 649-9381 (MA)
Connecticut River, Nashua River
Max. rapids: I-II
Back Country Tours, Inc., specializes in guided canoe trips and canoe rentals on "lesser known, uncrowded scenic waterways." Its trips run on the Souhegan and Merrimack Rivers in New Hampshire; the Sauantacook and Nissitissit Rivers in Massachusetts; the Connecticut and Nashua Rivers in New Hampshire and Massachusetts; the Delaware River in New York, Pennsylvania, and New Jersey; the St. John in Maine; the Blackwater, Sweetwater, and Juniper Rivers in Florida; and nine lakes near Long Pond Mountain in New York's Adirondacks. Several of these excursion are "vacation" trips of three to seven days that offer lodging at campgrounds, cabins, or bed-and-breakfast inns. All trips are suitable for beginners and experienced paddlers.

Back Country Tours' season runs from July to November.

Cape Cod Paddle Ventures
Lorimer Richards
Box 455
Orleans, MA 02653
(508) 240-2770, (800) 438-2610
Cape Cod Bay, Nantucket Sound, freshwater ponds and lakes
Max. rapids: None
Cape Cod Paddle Ventures offers one- to three-day guided and unguided canoe and kayak trips on Cape Cod Bay, Nantucket Sound, many salt marshes, tidal inlets, and freshwater ponds and lakes. Most trips are easy enough for beginners, while some require good stamina and the ability to handle variable winds on open water.

Guided trips, led by a former schoolteacher and Sierra Club guide, acquaint paddlers with the region's natural history and abundant wildlife.

125

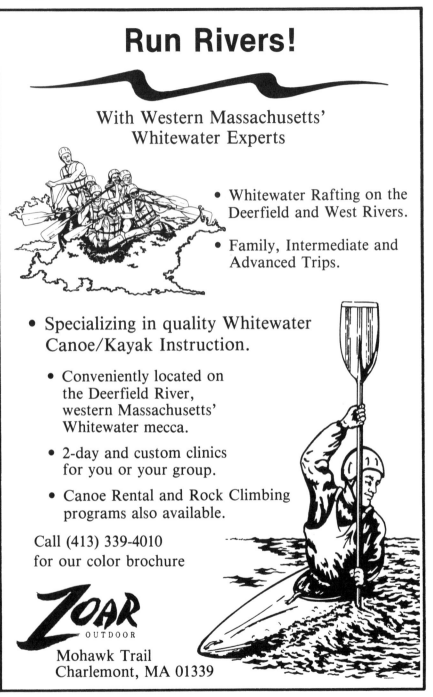

Among the many animals to see are whales, seals, turtles, waterfowl, herons, egrets, and terns. The waters contain plentiful striped bass, cod, bluefish, flounder, and freshwater species. Paddling instruction is also available. Cape Cod Paddle Venture's season runs from April to November.

Charles River Canoe and Kayak
Larry Smith, David Jacques
2401 Commonwealth Avenue
Newton, MA 02166
(617) 965-5110
Parker River, Ipswich River, Charles River, North River, Sudbury River, Lake Cochituate, Massachusetts coastline
Max. rapids: None
NACLO
Charles River Canoe and Kayak specializes in guided and unguided canoe and sea kayak trips in eastern Massachusetts. These trips, which last one day, are on the Parker, Ipswich, Charles, and Connecticut Rivers and along the coast. The outings feature clean water in scenic natural areas close to water. Paddlers on Charles River's trips, which run from April to October, can also enjoy canoe, kayak, and rowing lessons, picnic trips, moonlight on the Charles, and an overnight trip on the Connecticut River in Vermont.

The Outdoor Centre of New England
Tom Foster
10 Pleasant Street
Millers Falls, MA 01349
(413) 659-3926
Millers River, Deerfield River, Ashuelot River, West River
Max. rapids: III-IV
The Outdoor Center of New England claims to be the best technical paddling school in the Northeast. The company has a broad array of paddling classes for all levels, beginner to expert, in canoeing, kayaking, and sea kayaking. Canoeing instruction is in solo open canoes, solo decked canoes, tandem canoes, canoe poling, and marathon canoeing. Kayaking instruction includes rolling clinics, squirt clinics, over-40 classes, and recreational racing classes. In sea kayaking courses, students learn paddling and rescue technique on scenic rivers, lakes, and coastal areas.

The Outdoor Centre, open March to October, runs its river paddling classes on the Millers, Deerfield, Ashuelot, and West Rivers. During its season, the company also offers a "North Woods Week" paddling vacation, women's workshops, and instructor certification workshops.

Zoar Outdoor, Inc.
Bruce Lessels
Mohawk Trail, Box 245
Charlemont, MA 01339
(413) 339-4010
Deerfield River, West River
Max. rapids: III-IV
America Outdoors
Zoar Outdoor, Inc., rents canoes and kayaks and leads guided trips by canoe, kayak, and raft on the Deerfield and West Rivers. Its one-day trips vary in difficulty to suit paddlers of all levels, from beginner to expert.

All trips pass through the rolling wooded hills of the Berkshires, offering excellent scenery, and a chance to spot beavers, deer, bears, coyotes, foxes, hawks, and eagles. The rivers also offer good fishing for trout and bass.

Zoar Outdoor's season runs from April to October.

Michigan

Michigan is a favorite state for recreation, with fishing rivaling winter sports as the most popular outdoors pastime. Fishermen find brook, brown, and rainbow trout on rivers throughout the state. But those who prefer just to paddle and float find plenty of opportunities for good canoeing, kayaking, and tubing.

The Sturgeon River just south of Mackinac Strait no longer lives up to its name as a source of caviar. But it is an excellent trout stream, and with its average drop of almost 14 feet per mile it is the fastest river in the Lower Peninsula. To call it "challenging" is an exaggeration, but with its brisk current, hairpin turns, and other obstacles it is not recommended for novices, non-swimmers, or small children. The nearby Pigeon River, designated as one of Michigan's Wild and Scenic streams, flows through Pigeon River State Forest. A clear river, it is home to the only elk herd east of the Mississippi and other wildlife including beavers, muskrats, turkeys, porcupines, turkeys, foxes, and herons.

A little further south, near the town of Grayling, the well-known Au Sable begins its journey eastward to Lake Huron flanked by its North and South Branches. The name Grayling harks back to happier days for fishermen some 150 years ago, when the abundance of grayling in the Au Sable attracted anglers from far and wide. Since then, the grayling has become extinct in the river's waters, but brook, brown, and rainbow trout are still plentiful. Although several dams interrupt the river's flow, the Au Sable is an ideal stream for family canoeing. Portages are clearly marked, the water is clean, and much of the river runs through unspoiled territory where primitive camping is free. Average water depth on the 32-mile stretch below Mio Dam — the National Scenic River section — is between one and three feet and guaranteed by the dam. Beavers, deer, ducks, otters, wild minks, and bald eagles may be seen during a leisurely float.

The Muskegon is the longest of Michigan's rivers and navigable almost from its source near Houghton Lake in the middle of the Upper Peninsula to its outlet into Lake Michigan at Muskegon. The Muskegon has only one difficult stretch, at Big Rapids, and one strenuous portage, at Hardy Dam. Otherwise it rates as another good family paddling stream. Much of the land it traverses is state property and many campgrounds line its 170-mile course. The fishing is varied from place to place: the best trout are upstream near Evart and there are good runs of salmon and steelhead from Muskegon up to Croton Dam.

Another long river is the Manistee, which flows more than 150 miles southwest from the Otsego Lake area to its mouth at Manistee on Lake Michigan. With its remoteness, its campgrounds, and its clean water it is described as one of the Lower Peninsula's finest rivers for expedition canoeing and camping. Here, again, the fishing is varied and excellent, ranging from salmon downstream to walleyes, smallmouth bass, and northern pike above Tippy Dam and brown or brook trout upstream.

Very popular among canoeists is the Pine River, which flows into the Manistee at Tippy Dam Pond. It gets so crowded on Saturdays that some outfitters urge customers to come on Sundays or weekdays. The Pine is claimed to be Michigan's best fast-water canoeing river. It runs through the Manistee National Forest, and in order to keep the river banks unspoiled, camping is forbidden within a one-quarter mile corridor on each side of the stream except at developed campgrounds.

Further south within Manistee National Forest, the Pine River runs parallel to the Muskegon into Lake Michigan. Its lower section, covering the last 60 miles before the river delta begins, is an appealing run. It offers good fishing, many interesting wildlife species — notably turtles — and a glimpse of the high rollways that were used during the lumber boom of the 19th century to pile and store logs.

Finally the Upper Peninsula, where the most celebrated stream is the Big Two Hearted River, made famous by Ernest Hemingway when he used it for the title of his short story about the Fox River. It is the only Wilderness River in Michigan and claimed to be one of the top ten trout streams in America. But it is plagued by black flies in early summer and logjams year-round. Although there is an easy 4-6 hour float down the lowest stretch of the river, several portages are needed to skirt logjams further upstream.

Alcona Canoe Rental, Inc.
Kevin Ornatowski
6351 Bamfield Road
Glennie, MI 48737
(517) 735-2973, (800) 526-7080
AuSable River
Max. rapids: None
RCA, NACLO
Alcona Canoe Rental runs guided canoe and raft trips on the Au Sable River and rents canoes, rafts, and tubes. All trips on this national scenic river are easy enough for beginners and families and offer great trout, walleye, and bass fishing. Paddlers can also spot wildlife, including deer, bald eagles, minks, beavers, otters, ducks, and geese.

Trips through this wooded wilderness last from one to seven days and pass through federal land where camping is free and motorized boats are prohibited. During its April-to-October season, Alcona also offers cabin rental, primitive camp sites, and a camp store.

Carl's Canoe Service
Mark and Val Miltner
7603 West 50 Mile
Cadillac, MI 49601
(616) 862-3471
Pine River
Max. rapids: I-II
RCA
Carl's Canoe Service rents canoes and kayaks for one- to three-day trips on the Pine River. These trips have Class I-II white water and are for intermediate and advanced paddlers only.

The Pine River runs clean and cold through undeveloped woodland that is 95 percent state and national forest. Passing through the Pine's deep river valley, paddlers can glimpse deer, raccoons, minks, beavers, muskrats, ducks, and otters. Trout fishing is especially good, as the river is a natural trout stream. During the April-

to-November season, camping is also available at state and federal parks along the river.

Note: The owners of Carl's Canoe Service also operate Marrik's Pine River Canoe Service. Both liveries can be reached at the same phone number.

Double R Ranch
Richard Reeves
4424 Whites Bridge Road
Smyrna, MI 48887
(616) 794-0520
Flat River
Max. rapids: None
Double R Ranch rents canoes for one-day trips on the Flat River. This flat-water river is good for novices and those seeking a peaceful, scenic trip. The river also offers good fishing for smallmouth bass and pike, and a chance to spot blue herons, turtles, and other wildlife.

The livery's season runs from May to October.

**Grand Rogue Campgrounds —
Canoe and Tube Livery**
Wendell Briggs
6400 West River Drive
Belmont, MI 49306
(616) 361-1053
Grand River, Rogue River
Max. rapids: None
RCA
Grand Rogue Campground offers canoe trips on the Grand River and tubing on the Grand and Rogue Rivers. Trips last from one to four hours and are easy enough for beginners and families with small children. The Grand is a wide, slow-moving scenic river. The Rogue River, also scenic, is faster. Along both rivers floaters can spot ducks, deer, cranes, raccoons, and turtles and fish for bass, trout, pike, and walleye.

Guests can also enjoy Grand Rogue's modern campground with

Paddle America

tent and R.V. camping, washroom, laundry, and campstore. The season runs from May to October.

Happy Mohawk Canoe Livery
735 Fruitvale Road
Montague, MI 49437
(616) 894-4209
White River
Max. rapids: None
RCA

Happy Mohawk Canoe Livery rents canoes, rafts, and tubes for one- and two-day trips on the White River, through the Manistee National Forest. Trips wind through scenic, wooded wilderness inhabited by abundant wildlife, including deer, raccoons, minks, muskrats, waterfowl, and many types of turtles.

The flat-water river can be canoed safely by anyone, and has especially clean water, with good fishing for salmon, steelhead, pike, bass, bluegill, and perch. During the May-to-October season, camping is also available at the the modern, fully equipped White River campground.

Hiawatha Canoe Livery
Michael and Carol Quinlan
1113 Lake Street
Roscommon, MI 48653
(517) 275-5213, (800) 736-5213
Au Sable River
Max. rapids: I-II

Hiawatha Canoe Livery offers guided and unguided canoe and tube trips on the Au Sable River, through the scenic, unspoiled Mason Wilderness. Trips on the Au Sable last from one to seven days, are easy enough for beginners, and feature excellent fishing for trout and bass.

Hiawatha's season runs from April to November.

Hinchman Acres, Inc.
Sam Giardina
702 N-M-33
Mio, MI 48647
(517) 826-3267
Au Sable River
Max. rapids: None
Michigan Recreational Canoeing Association

Hinchman Acres rents canoes and tubes for one- to 14-day trips on the Au Sable River. Paddling is easy and the wilderness setting offers fine trout fishing and a chance to view deer, beavers, ducks, otters, minks, and bald eagles. Campgrounds are available at many spots along the river, and on the stretch between Mio and Oscoda, paddlers can set up camp wherever they want.

Horina Canoe Rental
James Horina
Highway M-37, Route 1
Wellston, MI 49689
(616) 862-3470
Pine River
Max. rapids: I-II
RCA, NACLO

Horina rents canoes for one- to three-day trips on the fastest sections of the Pine River. These runs have Class I and II rapids and are for intermediate and advanced paddlers only. Trips run through the protected Manistee National Forest, which treats paddlers to scenic views of woodlands, high sandbanks, and beautiful clay formations, and plentiful wildlife, including deer, geese, ducks, beavers, minks, and otters.

The cool, shady Pine River also boasts excellent fishing for brown, rainbow, and brook trout. Horina's season runs from April to October.

Tubers prepare for a trip on the Muskegon River. Courtesy of Sawmill Canoe Livery, Big Rapids, Michigan.

Indian Valley
Bill Mulder
8200 108th Street SE
Middleville, MI 49333
(616) 891-8579
Thornapple River, Cold Water River
Max. rapids: I-II
Michigan Association of Professional Canoe Outfitters, RCA

Indian Valley rents canoes, kayaks, tubes, and rafts on the Thornapple and Cold Water Rivers for trips of one or two days. These trips pass through secluded, wooded wilderness where paddlers can swim, camp, fish for pike and bass, and view loons, ducks, turtles, and the occasional bear. The rivers, with Class I-II rapids, offer easy paddling for guests of all ages.

Indian Valley, open from April to December, also offers tent and R.V. camping and a bathhouse with hot showers.

Marrik's Canoe Service
Mark and Val Miltner
7603 West 50 Mile
Cadillac, MI 49601
(616) 862-3471
Pine River
Max. rapids: I-II
RCA

The owners of Marrik's operate Carl's Canoe Service, also on the Pine River. See the description above under Carl's Canoe Service.

Mead's Canoe Livery
Tony Quinlan
11724 Steckert Bridge Road
Roscommon, MI 48653
Au Sable River— South Branch
Max. rapids: None
RCA

Mead's Canoe Livery rents canoes for one-day trips on the South Branch of the Au Sable, a flat-water wilderness river. Trips are easy, well-suited for beginners and families, and offer camping, fishing for trout and pike, and views of deer, wild turkeys,

Paddle America

beavers, and eagles. Mead's season
runs from May to November.

Northland Outfitters
Tom and Carma Gronback
Highway M-77
P.O. Box 65
Germfask, MI 49836
(906) 586-9801
*Manistique River, Manistique Lake,
Fox River, Big Island Lake Complex*
Max. rapids: None
Northland Outfitters rents canoes
and kayaks for one- to eight-day trips
on Manistique River, Fox River, Manistique Lake, and the Big Island Lake
Complex. All trips run through the
scenic wilderness of the Hiawatha National Forest, the Seney National
Wildlife Refuge, or both. Paddlers on
these trips can enjoy wilderness
camping, fishing for trout, bass, muskie, pike, and perch; and viewing the
abundant wildlife, including deer,
bears, moose, bald eagles, and more
than 200 species of birds. A particularly good fishing-canoeing trip can be
had at Big Island Lake Complex,
whose 12 islands are ideal settings for
fishing base camps. Northland's
season is from May to October.

Old Log Resort
Mark and Jeanette Knoph
1070 M-115
Marion, MI 49665
(616) 743-2775
Muskegon River
Max. rapids: None
RCA
Old Log Resort rents canoes and
kayaks on the Muskegon, a flat-water
river easy enough for first-time paddlers. Trips last one to four days and
pass through scenic wilderness, offering a chance to camp, view eagles,
bears, deer, otters, bobcats, beavers,
and muskrats, and fish for pike, smallmouth bass, and walleye. The season
runs from April to November.

Penrod's Canoe Trips
Gale Humes
100 Maple, P.O. Box 432
Grayling, MI 49738
(517) 348-2910
Au Sable River
Max. rapids: None
RCA, NACLO
Penrod's Canoe Trips rents canoes
and kayaks on the Au Sable River for
one- to seven-day trips. Paddling is
easy and safe for all ages, as the river
has a swift current, few obstructions,
and an average depth of only 18 inches for the first 25 miles. Trout fishing is good and wildlife is plentiful,
expecially deer, otters, minks,
muskrats, beavers, and ducks.
Camping is available at state
forest, state park, and private
campgrounds along the river.
Penrod's also rents comfortable riverside cabins on wooded sites. The
season is from April to October.

River Raisin Canoe Livery
Charles and Cherry Haddix
P.O. Box 136
Carleton, MI 48117
(313) 269-2004
Raisin River
Max. rapids: None
River Raisin Canoe Livery rents
canoes and kayaks for one- and two-
day trips on the River Raisin, a gentle
wilderness river. The river offers
good fishing for walleye, pike, bass,
and bluegill and a chance to spot
deer, foxes, raccoons, minks, and
muskrats. Also distinctive about the
scenery are the grapevines that hang
from trees along the banks.
The season runs from May to October.

River's Edge Campground

Bill Mudget
P.O. Box 189
Holton, MI 49425
(616) 821-2735
White River
Max. rapids: None
RCA

River's Edge Campground rents canoes, kayaks, and tubes for easy family trips on the flat-water White River. The river is clear, has a sandy bottom, and offers good fishing for pike, salmon, trout, and bass. Trips last one to three days and pass through wooded wilderness with plentiful deer, beavers, raccoons, and other wildlife. The season runs from May to October.

River's Edge also offers primitive "pumps and privies" camping on private wooded sites.

Riverside Canoe Trips

Tom and Kathy Stocklen
5042 Scenic Highway
Honor, MI 49640
(616) 325-5622, (616) 882-4072
Platte River
Max. rapids: None
Michigan Recreational Canoe Association, NACLO

Riverside Canoe Trips rents canoes, kayaks, rafts, and tubes for trips of two hours to two days on the Platte River. Trips on the Lower Platte are gentle, scenic, and ideal for families. Runs on the Upper Platte feature, fast, clean, spring-fed waters. This stretch has no rapids but does have narrow sections with quick turns and overhanging branches, requiring prior paddling experience. On all trips, paddlers leave early or late in the day and have a good chance to see deer, beavers, muskrats, wild turkeys and other wildlife. In addition, the Platte River, Platte Lake, Loon Lake, and Lake

Michigan offer good fishing for salmon, trout, bass, and other species.

During its March-October season, Riverside also offers sunset canoe trips, a general store, and camping at nearby sites.

Russell Canoes and Campgrounds

Robert Russell
146 Carrington Street
Omer, MI 48749
(517) 653-2690, (800) 552-4928 (MI)
Rifle River
Max. rapids: None
RCA, NACLO

Russell Canoes and Campgrounds rents canoes and tubes on the scenic, flat-water Rifle River. Trips last one to five days and are safe and fun for novices and families, as well as more advanced canoeists. The stretches paddled are through clean, wooded, wilderness terrain, with lots of wild deer, turkeys, eagles, and turtles. Fishing, too, is good, especially for trout, bass, suckers, salmon, and walleye.

During the May-to-October season, tent and R.V. camping is also available. The 140-site campground has modern washrooms, laundry facilities, and a camp stores.

Sawmill Tube and Canoe Livery

Donn and Lori Trites
230 Baldwin Street
Big Rapids, MI 49307
(616) 796-6408
Big Muskegon River
Max. rapids: I-II
RCA

Sawmill Tube and Canoe Livery offers guided and unguided canoeing and tubing trips on the Muskegon River. The river is wide and gentle, well-suited for novice and intermediate paddlers. The Muskegon also offers exceptionally good fishing for trout, bass, northern pike, crappie, walleye, and perch.

Trips last from one to seven days and pass through unspoiled areas with abundant wildlife, including eagles, deer, blue herons, beavers, otters, geese, and ducks. Sawmill's season runs from April to October.

Sawyer Canoe Company
Robert D. Gramprie
234 S. State Street
Oscoda, MI 48750
(517) 739-9181
Au Sable River
Max. rapids: None

Sawyer Canoe Company rents canoes on the scenic, flat-water Au Sable River. Trips run for one to seven days and are fine for beginners. Paddling is easy, as the Au Sable has a steady four-to-six mph current and is free of rapids and obstructions. A wilderness river, the Au Sable runs through unspoiled forests and sandhills, and offers views of deer, otters, beavers, muskrats, squirrels, and rabbits. Paddlers also enjoy good fishing for bass, brook trout, walleye, lake trout, steelhead, and salmon. Sawyer's season runs from May to October.

Skip's Huron River Canoe Livery
Skip and Jane McDonald
3780 Delhi Court
Ann Arbor, MI 48103
(313) 769-8686
Huron River
Max. rapids: I-II
RCA, NACLO

Skip's Huron River Canoe Livery rents canoes and open kayaks for beginner and intermediate trips on the Huron River. With gentle rapids and small rock dams, the Huron offers some challenge in addition to its acclaimed scenery and smallmouth-bass fishing. Trips last one-half day and run between April and October. Camping is also available.

Sportsmans Port Canoes and Camp
Mary Barber
RR #1
Wellston, MI 49689
(616) 862-3571
Pine River
Max. rapids: I-II
NACLO, RCA

Sportsman's Port runs guided and unguided canoe trips on the Pine River, one of the most challenging rivers of Michigan's lower peninsula. Trips, best suited for paddlers with some canoeing experience, run through wooded wilderness featuring clay hills, clean water, and abundant wildlife, including deer, otters, beavers, wild turkeys, and eagles.

During the May-to-October season, the company also offers shuttle service and camping at its campground, which is equipped with hot showers and a store.

Sturgeon and Pigeon River Outfitters
Scott Anderson
4271 S. Straits Highway
Indian River, MI 49749
(616) 238-8181
Sturgeon River, Pigeon River
Max. rapids: I-II
Michigan Recreational Canoeing Association, NACLO

Sturgeon and Pigeon River Outfitters rents canoes, kayaks, and tubes on the Sturgeon and Pigeon Rivers. Both rivers are crystal-clear and premier trout streams. The Sturgeon is the fastest, most challenging river in the lower peninsula. Canoeists on the Sturgeon must have basic paddling and maneuvering skills, The Pigeon is gentler, requires no prior experience, and is designated a Michigan Wild and Scenic River. The Pigeon runs through the Pigeon River State Forest, home of the only elk herd east of the Mississippi. Both rivers have abundant wildlife, including deer, elk, beavers, muskrats, blue herons, turkeys, and foxes.

The season runs from May to October.

Sylvania Outfitters, Inc.
E23423 Highway 2 West
Watersmeet, MI 49969
(906) 358-4766
Ontonagon River System
Max. rapids: III-IV
Michigan Recreational Canoeing Association, NACLO

Sylvania Outfitters rents canoes and kayaks for one- to six-day trips on the Ontonagon River. Some of the trips are fine for novices; other have Class III-IV rapids and are for advanced paddlers only. All trips are through unspoiled wilderness with plentiful deer, otters, raccoons, eagles, loons, and ducks. Fishermen also enjoy good fishing for trout, smallmouth and largemouth bass, northern pike, and walleye. Sylvania's season runs from April to October.

Tomahawk Trails Canoe Livery
A. Anderson
P.O. Box 814
Indian River, MI 49749
(616) 238-8703
Sturgeon River, Pigeon River
Max. rapids: I-II
Recreational Caoeing Association

Tomahawk Trails rents canoes, kayaks, and tubes for one- and two-day trips on the Sturgeon and Pigeon Rivers. Trips on the Sturgeon are challenging, requiring previous paddling experience. The Pigeon is a scenic "family river," good for beginners and children. Both rivers have good trout fishing and offer chances to glimpse elk, deer, beavers, turtles, and eagles. Tomahawk's season runs from May to November.

Troll Landing
Ervin and Marion Schilke
2660 Rifle River Trail
West Branch, MI 48661
(517) 345-7260
Rifle River
Max. rapids: None
RCA

Troll Landing rents canoes, kayaks, and tubes for trips of one to three days on the Rifle River. Paddling on the flat-water Rifle River is not difficult, as the river is clear and shallow, with a steady seven-mile-per-hour current. Paddlers of all ages can enjoy these scenic trips as they wind through pine and hardwood forests on the lookout for deer, ducks, and beavers. During the April-to-September season, guests can also fish for brown trout and steelhead.

Two Hearted Canoe Trips, Inc.
Richard and Kathy Robinson
Rainbow Lodge
P.O. Box 386, Co. Rd. 423
Newberry, MI 49868
(906) 658-3357
Two Hearted River
Max. rapids: I-II
RCA

Two Hearted Canoe Trips rents canoes for one- to three-day trips on the Two Hearted River in the scenic wilderness of northern Luce County. One-day trips are easy but the longer runs are somewhat strenuous, requiring two or three portages of a couple hundred feet.

The scenery in this remote, unspoiled area is beautiful, with large white pines, hardwoods, and abundant wildlife, including bears, deer, moose, raccoons, otters, beavers, and eagles. Trout fishing is also very good.

During its April-to-November season, the livery also offers primitive campsites, motel rooms, and a well-stocked camp store.

U-Rent-Em-Canoe Livery
Michael J. Hawthorne
685 W. State Street
Hastings, MI 49058
(616) 945-3191
Thornapple River, Kalamazoo River, Gun River
Max. rapids: I-II
NACLO, Michigan Recreational Canoeing Association

U-Rent-Em-Canoe Livery runs guided canoe trips and rents canoes, kayaks, rafts, and tubes on the Thornapple River and all nearby fishing lakes. Trips on the Kalamazoo River and Gun River are also available by request. River trips wind through wooded wilderness with abundant deer, waterfowl, and birds. Paddling is easy enough for novices, yet small rapids and other minor obstacles keep things interesting. One- and two-day trips are available.

All trips are on clean waters offering good fishing for bass, pike, panfish, trout, and muskie. The livery's season is from April to October.

U-Rent-Em Canoe Livery

Hastings, Michigan 49058
(616) 945-3191

Livery address:
685 W. State Street
Mailing address:
522 W. Grand Street

Mike Hawthorne
Beverly Kurr

Uncommon Adventures
Michael Gray
P.O. Box 6066
East Lansing, MI 48823
(517) 339-3479
Lake Michigan, Lake Huron, Lake Superior, Michigan rivers
Max. rapids: None
RCA, NACLO

Uncommon Adventures offers guided and unguided canoe and kayak trips on many of Michigan's beautiful lakes and winding streams. In addition to lovely scenery, these trips provide good opportunities to spot black bears, moose, loons, and raptors. Guided trips also feature excellent food.

The company offers a wide assortment of other trips, including canoeing in Florida's keys, Ontario's wilderness, and New York's Adirondack Mountain lakes; sea kayaking tours of Georgian Bay, Isle Royale National park, Florida's keys, St. John (U.S. Virgin Islands), and the Pacific coast of Costa Rica; and windsurfing in Michigan. Land-based cross-country skiing and backpacking trips are also available.

Uncommon Adventures runs one- to 10-day trips year-round.

Vic's Canoes, Tubes and Rafts
Ray and Mary Ellen Spyker
Salmon Run Campground, RR 2
Grant, MI 49327
(616) 834-5494
Muskegon River
Max. rapids: None
RCA, NACLO

Vic's rents canoes, tubes, and rafts for one- and two-day trips on the Muskegon, a wide river with gentle rapids, suited for beginners and experienced paddlers alike. Trips pass through pine and birch woods, offering views of deer, eagles, small game, ducks, herons, and other wildlife. The river's clean water also makes for good fishing for rainbow trout, smallmouth bass, steelhead, salmon, and walleye.

All trips begin or end at Salmon Run Campground, which offers comfortable tent and R.V. camping with hot showers, laundry rooms, a camp store, and swimming pool. The season is from April to October.

White Birch Canoe Livery & Campground
Bob and Pat Holt
5569 Paradise Road
Falmouth, MI 49632
(616) 328-4547
Muskegon River, Dead Stream Swamp
Max. rapids: None

White Birch Canoe Livery & Campground rents canoes for one-hour to 14-day trips on the Muskegon River, West Branch of the Muskegon, and Dead Stream Swamp. The outfitters, priding themselves on their trip planning, have planned routes for everyone from senior citizens to marathon paddlers.

The Muskegon River passes through protected state land, making it ideal for camping and viewing deer, raccoons, otters, beavers, herons, ducks, ospreys, sandhill cranes, eagles, and wild turkeys. Also, the river's clear, clean water offers excellent fishing for pike, bass, panfish, and walleye.

Minnesota

Mention canoeing in Minnesota and most paddlers immediately think of the Boundary Waters Canoe Area. This million-acre wilderness of forested lakes has a unique appeal. Here along a 150-mile stretch of the Canadian border, the roads peter out and travelers must move by water. Along 1,200 miles of canoe routes linking a thousand lakes by way of streams and portages, the silence is broken only by the dip of a paddle, the splash of fish, the rustling of aspen leaves, and the haunting call of the loon. Since motorboats are generally banned from BWCA waters, no engines sully the air and shatter the calm of most of the lakes in this federally-protected region. Amid the pines and birches along the shoreline lie 2,000 designated campsites. And deep in the forest lurk moose, bear, wolves, deer, beavers, and otters.

To the canoeist, lured perhaps by the writings of local naturalist Sigurd Olson, this is paradise. We see the pristine waterland today very much as the Ojibwe Indians and the French voyageurs found it centuries ago. Minnesotans call it the world's greatest canoe country.

Those BWCA lakes where motorboats are allowed are mostly at the access points on the edge of the area: the Gunflint Trail at the eastern end and the Ely area in the west. Gunflint Trail, site of many canoe liveries, leads northward from Grand Marais on Lake Superior. Ely is about a two-hour drive north of Duluth.

Adjoining the BWCA to the west is Voyageurs National Park, a smaller area open to motorized boats as well as canoes. Here canoeists must share the 34 lakes with everything from houseboats to bass boats and cabin cruisers. And the bigger lakes, like Rainy Lake astride the Canadian border, can be treacherous for canoeists in rough weather. But the only way to explore Voyageurs, too, is by boat. Visitor centers, a renovated 1913 hotel, campsites, and skilled naturalist and fishing guides are all available.

Both inside and outside the boundary waters Minnesota has 23 rivers offering everything from white water to lazy floats. Nineteen of them, including those mentioned below, are state-designated canoe streams.

Great for wildlife viewing, for example, is the Big Fork, which runs northward toward the Canadian border to empty into the Rainy River at Smokey Bear State Forest. Its middle stretch from Big Fork to Big Falls is punctuated with Class I and II rapids. It is known as a pleasant wilderness trip for novices who are cautious, prepared to portage, and have backcountry skills. The Big Fork also has good walleye and muskie fishing.

The upper reaches of the Cloquet, which runs into the St. Louis near Brookston, is said to be one of the state's most pristine rivers. It has Class I, II, and III rapids as it passes through deep forests of pine, birch and aspen.

The crystal-clear Crow Wing, flowing from a lake near Akeley in the middle of the state, is a popular float for novices. It glides through Crow Wing State Park, with many campsites and reminders of Indians and fur traders as it heads for its confluence with the Mississippi.

Where the St. Croix marks the state line close to the Twin Cities, this National Scenic Riverway requires only novice to intermediate skills. The most popular section is below Dalles, where the river widens and flows through a wooded valley with steep stone bluffs. But Class II-IV expertise is needed near St. Croix Falls Dam, which itself requires a mile-long portage.

Whitewater skills are also needed on the Class II-IV section of the scenic Kettle River from Banning State Park to Sandstone, roughly halfway between the Twin Cities and Duluth.

Fuller details of these and other Minnesota rivers are given in the leaflet Explore Minnesota Canoe Rivers, available from the state's Office of Tourism, 375 Jackson St., 250 Skyway Level, St. Paul, MN 55101, tel. (800) 657-3700 or (in Twin Cities) 296-5029. Paddlers can obtain free river maps showing access points, campsites, rest areas, portages, dams, waterfalls, and white water, from the Department of Natural Resources, 500 Lafayette Road, Box 40, St. Paul, Minn. 55155, tel. (612) 296-6157 or (800) 652-9747 (toll-free in Minnesota). Call these numbers also for weekly water level reports.

Arrowhead Canoe Outfitters
Kim Holzman
HC 1, Box 3299
Ely, MN 55731
(218) 365-5614, (800) 245-5614
BWCA
Max. rapids: None

Arrowhead Canoe Outfitters offers guided and unguided canoe trips of one to 30 days in the Boundary Waters Canoe Area and Quetico Provincial Park. This vast wilderness features beautiful forests, thousands of crystal-clear lakes, excellent fishing, and abundant wildlife, including loons, osprey, bald eagles, moose, wolves, coyotes, red foxes, raccoons, black bears, minks, weasels, and beavers. Anglers can fish for walleye, pike, trout, bass, crappie, and perch.

Arrowhead's routing service gives paddlers the choice of a leisurely course or a fast trip through many lakes. Guests also can choose between basic and deluxe outfitting packages, which feature top-quality boats and food. Guided trips are available for those interested in archaeology, history, photography, or just a smoother, more enjoyable trip. Arrowhead's season is from May to November.

Bear Track Outfitting Co.
David and Cathi Williams
Box 937
Grand Marais, MN 55604
(218) 387-1162
BWCA, Isle Royale National Park
Max. rapids: I-II

Bear Track Outfitters runs guided and unguided canoe and sea kayak trips of three to 30 days in the Boundary Waters Canoe Area. Guests can choose among a wide array of equipment, including eight types of tandem canoes and six types of solo canoes. Also available are towing service across Saganaga and Seagull Lakes, camping gear rentals, provisions, lodging in rustic cabins, fly-in canoe tours, and guided fishing trips.

Bear Track, open year-round, also offers backpacking, snowshoeing, and cross-country skiing trips. On these various trips, guests can see moose, bears, wolves, deer, beavers, otters, and minks; and fish for walleye, northern pike, bass, and lake trout.

Canadian Border Outfitters
Patrick and Chickie Harristhal
Box 117
Ely, MN 55731
(218) 365-5847, (800) 247-7530
BWCA
Max. rapids: None
Ely Outfitters Association

Canadian Border Outfitters offers guided and outfitted canoe trips in the Boundary Waters Canoe Area and Quetico Provincial Park. Trips last from three to 10 days, are suited for paddlers of all ages, and leave from all entry points in the Ely area. Canadian Border's base is at Moose Lake, 18 miles northeast of Ely. The base offers tow boats, fishing licenses, tackle, maps, meals, motel rooms, and a bunkhouse.

All trips give paddlers a chance to spot moose, bear, eagles, deer, minks, otters, osprey, and loons. Anglers can enjoy excellent fishing for northern pike, walleye, smallmouth bass, lake trout, and panfish. The outfitter's season is from May to October.

Canadian Waters, Inc.
Jon and Dan Waters
111 East Sheridan Street
Ely, MN 55731
(218) 365-3202, (800) 255-2922 (reservations)
BWCA
Max. rapids: None
NACLO

Canadian Waters offers guided and outfitted canoe trips in the Boundary Waters Canoe Area and Quetico Provincial Park. Trips last from three- to 20 days, with seven-day trips being the most popular. Canadian Waters takes particular pride in its canoes, claiming to have the world's largest outfitting fleet of light, Old Town Oltonar canoes. The outfitter also offers several special services, including towing, guide service, motorboat fishing, and airport shuttle service.

A canoe on Gillis Lake. Courtesy of Gunflint Northwoods Outfitters, Grand Marais, Minnesota.

On all trips, guests can enjoy wilderness scenery; a chance to view moose, deer, bears, eagles, osprey, minks, otters, and beavers, and fishing for smallmouth bass, walleye. northern pike, and lake trout. Canadian Waters' season runs form May to September.

143

Canoe Country Escapes
Eric Durland
194 South Franklin Street
Denver, CO 80209
(303) 722-7706
BWCA
Max. rapids: I-II
NACLO
Canoe Country Escapes offers guided and unguided canoe trips in the Boundary Waters Canoe Area and Quetico Park. Trips, which last five to 10 days, are tailored to suit a wide range of paddlers. Most popular are the pampered lodge-to-lodge trips in which guests spend four nights in comfortable lodges and two at well-tended campsites set up before guests' arrival. Also available are traditional guided and outfitted trips, family trips, and trips for seniors. Outfitting and lodge accommodations at the start and end of Canoe Country's tours are provided through Gunflint Northwoods (see separate listing).

Canoe Country Outfitters
Robert R. Olson
629 East Sheridan St.
P.O. Box 30
Ely, MN 55731
(218) 365-4046
BWCA
Max. rapids: None
Canoe Country Outfitters offers guided and outfitted canoe trips in the Boundary Waters Canoe Area and Quetico Provincial Park. Trips last from three to 30 days, are fine for paddlers of all ages, and boast excellent fishing for walleye, northern pike, smallmouth bass, and lake trout. Guests also can view moose, bears, deer, loons, and wolves.

Canoe Country has two bases, one in downtown Ely and one at Moose Lake. Between the two, the outfitter claims to serve all major entry points, providing customers with "the best route selection, scenery, fishing, and

Canoeists pause for a rest in the BWCA Courtesy of Top of the Trail Outfitters, Grand Marais, Minnesota.

seclusion." Also available are fly-in canoe trips, camping, and cabins at the Ely and Moose Lake bases, airport pickup, and a choice of "light" or "ultralight" outfitting. The outfitter's season runs from May to October.

Clearwater Canoe Outfitters & Lodge
Margy Nelson and Jim Holzman
355 Gunflint Trail
Grand Marais, MN 55604
(218) 388-2254, (800) 527-0554
Lake Superior, Isle Royale, BWCA
Max. rapids: I-II
Clearwater Canoe Outfitters and Lodge offers guided and outfitted

A floatplane, with canoes lashed aboard, shuttles paddlers to a remote region of the BWCA. Courtesy of Top of the Trail Outfitters, Grand Marais, Minnesota.

trips to Lake Superior's Isle Royale and in the Boundary Waters Canoe Area and Quetico Provincial Park. Guided trips to Isle Royale use Hydra Sea Runner kayaks, last five days, and require no previous kayaking experience. Custom guided trips in the BWCA and Quetico Park are also available.

Outfitted trips of any length desired are by canoe or 14-foot sailboat. Many of these are fine for novice paddlers and campers; other "marathon trips" require excellent conditioning and prior experience. Clearwater take particular pride in its canoes and other equipment, claiming that its standard equipment is equivalent to what other outfitters call their "ultra-lightweight" outfitting.

All trips offers abundant wildlife, including moose, bears, beavers, otters, eagles, osprey, wolves, and deer. Also, anglers can enjoy excellent fishing for bass, walleye, lake trout, northern pike, and rainbow and brook trout. Clearwater's season is from May to October.

Gunflint Northwoods Outfitters
Bruce and Sue Kerfoot
750 Gunflint Trail
Grand Marais, MN 55604
(800) 328-3325
BWCA
Max. rapids: III-IV
NACLO

Gunflint Northwoods Outfitters runs guided and unguided canoe and kayak trips of two to eight days in the Boundary Waters Canoe Area and

A cozy campsite in the BWCA Courtesy of Gunflint Northwoods Outfitters, Grand Marais, Minnesota.

Quetico Park. With primarily flat-water, canoeing trips are suited for all ages and anyone interested in multi-day trips in the world's largest canoeing wilderness. The outfitting company particularly prides itself on its extensive canoe and equipment offerings, breads and homemade snacks, and thorough trip planning.

During Gunflint Northwoods' May-to-October season, the outfitter also offers lodging in its bunkhouse and modern cabins. On its trips, paddlers can view moose, beavers, bald eagles, otters, and loons, and fish for walleye, smallmouth bass, lake trout, and northern pike.

Headwaters Canoe Outfitters
Andy Kuik
12404 Land End Lane, SE
Bemidji, MN 56601
(218) 751-2783
Mississipi River, Turtle River
Max. rapids: III-IV

Headwaters Canoe Outfitters offers guided trips and canoe rentals on the Mississippi, Turtle, Big Fork and Little Fork Rivers. Trips last one to seven days and range in difficulty from beginners' runs to trips for experts only. The areas traveled are clean, scenic, require few portages, and offer a good change to spot eagles, deer, beavers, otters, and muskrats. Also, anglers can enjoy fishing for walleye, nothern pike, perch, and bass.

Headwaters' season runs from May to October.

147

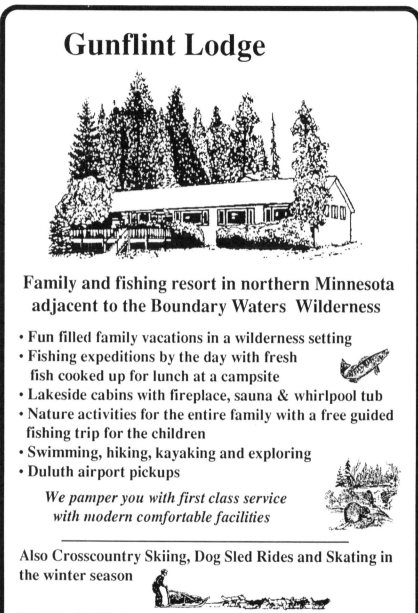

Huntersville Outfitters

F.A. and Dorothy Kennelly
RR 4, Box 317
Menahga, MN 56464
(218) 564-4279
Crow Wing River
Max. rapids: I-II

Huntersville Outfitters outfits canoe trips of one to 12 days on the Crow Wing River. The river is remarkably clear, with sandy beaches and excellent swimming areas. All trips are fine for beginning and advanced paddlers alike, as the intermittent rapids are exciting but not dangerous. The river also boasts historical sights, such as boat landings used by the Hudson Bay Company, and excellent fishing for walleye, northern pike, and bass. This wilderness area has abundant wildlife, too, including deer, foxes, coyotes, eagles, ducks, beavers, and otters.

Huntersville's season runs from May to October.

Ketter Canoeing

Betty L. Ketter
101 79th Avenue N
Minneapolis, MN 55444
(612) 560-3840, (612) 561-2208
Mississippi River, Rum River, Crow Wing River, Elk River
Max. rapids: I-II

Ketter Canoeing rents canoes and kayaks for trips on the Mississippi, Run, Crow Wing, and Elk Rivers. The outfitter also offers shuttle service for those who bring their own boats.

Midwest Mountaineering

Rod Johnson
309 Cedar Ave. South
Minneapolis, MN 55454
(612) 339-3433

Midwest Mountaineering is a retail store in Minneapolis that rents canoe and kayaks.

Moose Lake Wilderness Canoe Trips

Tom and Woods
P.O. Box 358
Ely, MN 55731
(800) 322-5837
BWCA
Max. rapids: None
NACLO

Moose Lake Wilderness Canoe Trips offers guided and outfitted canoe trips in the B.W.C.A. and Quetico Provincial Park. The outfitter says its specialty is "the finest equipment and facilities at reasonable rates." Trips run between May and October, boast excellent fishing for walleye, bass, northern pike, and lake trout, and offer a chance to spot moose, bear, wolves, eagles, and beavers.

Nor'wester Lodge

Carl and Luanna Brandt
Gunflint Trail
Grand Marais, MN 55604
(218) 388-2252, (800) 9912-4FUN
BWCA
Max. rapids: None

Nor'wester Lodge outfits canoe trips of three to 14 days in the Boundary Waters Canoe Area. Trips, leaving from 15 entry points, all offer excellent wilderness scenery; a chance to spot moose, beavers, minks, and bald eagles, and to fish for trout, walleye, bass, and northern pike. Nor'wester's season is from May to September.

Seagull Lake Canoe Outfitters

Debbie, Mark and Roger Hahn
920 Gunflint Trail
Grand Marais, MN 55604
(218) 388-2216, (800) 346-2205 (reservations)
BWCA
Max. rapids: I-II
NACLO, Minnesota Canoe Assocation

Seagull Outfitters offers guided and outfitted canoe trips in the Boundary Waters Canoe Area and

Quetico Provincial Park. Trips last from three to 10 days and are of minimal to moderate difficulty, with most routes suitable for anyone in good health. All trips offer pristine wilderness scenery; a chance to spot moose, bald eagles, otters, and loons; and excellent fishing for walleye, smallmouth bass, northern pike, and lake trout.

Seagull specializes in deluxe, ultralight outfitting and also offers special-interest packages, fly-in trips to remote areas, towing, partial ourfitting, and a complete store. The outfitters, whose season runs from May to October, has discounts for children under 16, repeat customers, and those who begin their trips in May or September.

Top of the Trail Outfitters
Jeff Drew
HC 64, Box 1001
Saganaga Lake
Grand Marais, MN 55604
(800) 869-0883
BWCA
Max. rapids: None
Minnesota Tourism Association

Top of the Trail Outfitters offers guided canoe trips and canoe and kayak rentals in the Boundary Waters Canoe Area and Canada's Quetico Provincial Park. Trips, of three to 20 days, are all on flat water but vary in difficulty of portages. Paddlers on all trips can enjoy viewing the abundant wildlife, which includes moose, beavers, otters, minks, bears, eagles, osprey, foxes, and wolves. Fishing is excellent, too, especially for walleye, northern pike, smallmouth bass, and lake trout. Top of the Trail's season runs from May to October.

Voyageur North Outfitters
John and Lynn O'Kane
1829 East Sheridan
Ely, MN 55731
(218) 365-3251, (800) 848-5530
BWCA
Max. rapids: None

Voyageur North Outfitters offers guided canoe trips and canoe and kayak rentals in the Boundary Waters Canoe Area and Quetico Provincial Park. Trips last from two to 14 days, offering chances to spot moose, otters, loons, and eagles. Fishing is also excellent, given the area's plentiful trout, northern pike, walleye, bass, crappie, and sunfish.

Voyageur North specializes in careful trip planning and in providing quality, ultra-light equipment. During its April-to-October season, the outfitter also offers bunkhouse accommodations, a Finnish sauna, guided fishing trips, and fly-in trips for fishing or canoeing.

Wilderness Adventures
Loy Householder
943 East Sheridan Street
Ely, MN 55731
(218) 365-3416, (800) 843-2922
BWCA
Max. rapids: V+
Ely Area Outfitters Associaiton

Wilderness Adventures is a small, "low-volume" outfitter, "specializing in personal service and the latest lightweight equipment." The outfitter offers guided and outfitted trips of two to 30 days in the Boundary Waters Canoe Area and Quetico Provincial Park. Trips range from very easy to difficult, depending on the distances covered and the number and difficulty of portages. All trips offer a chance to spot moose, bears, eagles, beavers, otters, and wolves, and to fish for walleye, northern pike, bass, and panfish. Wilderness Adventures' season run from May to September.

Mississippi

Since Mississippi's highest point is just 806 feet above sea level, nobody comes to the Magnolia State in search of white water. But canoeists enjoy a broad range of rivers, lakes, and ponds with abundant fish and other wildlife. Scenery varies from the Piney Woods country to the bayous and beaches of the Gulf of Mexico. Museums and archaeological sites remind visitors that more Indian tribes lived in Mississippi than in any other southeastern state. And many reminders exist of the state's more recent past: antebellum homes, the Natchez Trace, and impressive Civil War battlefields.

For fishing and sheer boating convenience, with boat ramps, camping, picnicking, and rest stops along the way, it is hard to beat the Pearl River and its main tributaries. The Pearl drains much of southern Mississippi and is rich in bass, catfish, perch, bream, and crappie. As it meanders past the state capital of Jackson and down to the Gulf, the Pearl widens and develops sandbars at its bends. Deer, beavers, opossum, raccoons, foxes, and wild turkeys lurk along its banks under stands of mixed hardwood, loblolly, sycamore, and willow. Hundreds of different wildflowers color the woods from spring until fall. The Pearl River Basin Development District has created 17 parks to date, strategically spaced along a "pleasure boatway" from Neshoba County to the coast. The facilities make it easy for floaters to relax and enjoy the river's beauty.

But perhaps the most popular float in Mississippi is Black Creek. And despite its summer crowds, this river-for-all-seasons also has a strong appeal to those who want to escape civilization. From its headwaters in Lamar County, it enjoys a Wild and Scenic designation as it passes through the one-half million acre DeSoto National Forest. Many sections of Black Creek are remote, picturesque, and full of wildlife. Paddlers find plenty of places to camp overnight, surrounded by trees and flowering shrubs. But elsewhere much of the land is privately owned, and boaters should get written permission from landowners before pitching tents and lighting fires.

Between Black Creek and Pearl River flows another delightful stream, Wolf River, noted for its clean water and its white sandy beaches overhung by magnolias, cypresses, and live oaks. It empties into the Bay of St. Louis, where stately mansions in the towns of Long Beach and Pass Christian overlook the Gulf.

Many other Mississippi streams can be canoed with enjoyment. Ten of Mississippi's twenty-seven state parks offer rental canoes and most have fishing boats for hire. But state authorities warn paddlers to take care. "Navigable streams in Mississippi are deceptively slow and gentle," Pearl River Basin officials caution in a bright red handout to floaters. "Water levels are unpredictable...dangerously low levels exist during summer and fall months."

Black Creek Canoe Rental
Pat and Terry Gibbs
P.O. Box 414
Brooklyn, MS 39425
(601) 582-8817
Black Creek, Red Creek, Pascagoula River, Beaverdam Creek
Max. rapids: None
NACLO

Black Creek Canoe Rental rents canoes for trips of three hours to three days on Black Creek, Beaverdam Creek, and Red Creek in southeastern Mississippi. These trips offer relaxing floats through remote, scenic areas, clean water, good fishing for bass, catfish and bream, and chances to see deer, wild turkeys, wood ducks, owls, great blue herons, and beavers. Most trips are suitable for families with children.

A wide stream with broad white sandbars that are perfect for camping, Black Creek is one of the most popular float trips in the state. One stretch of the stream, which flows through the half-million-acre DeSoto National Forest, is designated as wild and scenic, and another lies within the 35,000-acre Pascagoula River Wildlife Management Area. Beaverdam Creek, which flows into Black Creek, is a narrow stream sheltered by a canopy of giant trees. Red Creek flows for 85 miles through some of

the most beautiful pine and hardwood forests in the area.

Black Creek Canoe Rental prides itself on personal attention to clients' needs and the variety of floats available. The outfitter's season runs from March 1 to October 31.

Bogue Chitto Water Park
Pearl River Basin Development District
Route 2, Bos 223P
McComb, MS 39648
(601) 684-9568
Bogue Chitto River
Max. rapids: None

The Bogue Chitto Water Park is a state park where paddlers can take scenic tube and canoe trips year-round. These outings run on the Bogue Chitto River through protected woodlands where floaters can spot deer and wild turkeys, fish for catfish and bass, and stop at large sandbars to swim or picnic. Canoe and tube rentals are available from three private liveries that serve the park's waters: Ryal's Rentals (684-4948), Riverview Grocery (249-3670) and Choo Choo (no phone).

Bogue Chitto Water Park also offers trailer sites with water and electricity, primitive camping, boat launching, picnic grounds, a nature trail, and a bathhouse.

Wolf River Canoes, Inc.
Joseph Feil
21652 Tucker Road
Long Beach, MS 39560
(601) 452-7666
Wolf River
Max. rapids: I-II

Wolf River Canoes, Inc. offers guided and unguided canoe trips of one to three days on the Wolf River. Day trips are safe and fun for anyone age 7 to 70. On longer trips, paddlers encounter small rapids, but these stretches, too, are easy to negotiate, even for beginners.

The Wolf River is very clean and undeveloped. The river banks boast magnolia, cypress, and live-oak trees and many beautiful, white-sand beaches. Paddlers also can spot deer and alligators and fish for bass, catfish, gar, and sunfish. Wolf River Canoes, open year-round, also offers shuttle service and a bath house.

Missouri

Amid the forested hills of the Ozarks flow spring-fed rivers famed for their natural beauty and crystal-clear water. It was here, in the heart of southeastern Missouri, that the National Park Service established the nation's first scenic riverway. It spans 134 miles of the Jacks Fork and Current Rivers, and rangers boast that these Class II streams remain "nearly as wild as the day Indians lightly trod the Ozark trails." This park, the Ozark National Scenic Riverways, lies 175 miles south of St. Louis and 250 miles southeast of Kansas City.

One of the best floats in the park is on the Jacks Fork from Buck Hollow, where Mo. 17 crosses the river, to Alley Spring. This is where the park is at its wild and scenic best. You can paddle it year-round if you can read the currents and don't mind some bumps. But the best time is in the spring when the water is high. It's a fast, long, one-day trip or a lazy two-day run.

Johnboats, canoes, rafts, kayaks, and tubes can be rented. Limestone cliffs, some with caves to explore, enliven the wooded riverbanks. Big Spring, near Van Buren, is the nation's largest single-outlet spring, gushing an average 277 million gallons of water a day. Many paddlers prefer to float the upper reaches of the Jacks Fork and Current Rivers in winter or spring to avoid portaging around gravel bars exposed in the summertime. Yet these bars provide cool and relatively mosquito-free campsites. Floaters should watch out for trunks and roots of fallen trees, especially in the spring flood season. Rampant poison ivy as well as the occasional copperhead are riverbank hazards. But fishermen will find trout and bass lazing in shady pools.

Further west, in southcentral Missouri, Eleven Point River meanders gently through a different section of the Ozark hills. Another spring-fed stream in the Class II category, it winds through steep bluffs, forested valleys and low-lying pastures. About half the lands within the Eleven Point River National Scenic River area belong to the National Forest System; the rest are private but dotted with scenic easements.

Near Steelville, some 90 minutes southwest of St. Louis, are popular vacation resorts offering a wide range of activities, including floating on the Upper Meramec and Huzzah Rivers. Two hours south of St.

Louis is the Black River, claimed by locals to be the clearest stream in the Ozarks. Its East Fork offers Class III-IV whitewater in the spring but summer floaters may be confined to the main stream. Around Lebanon near Springfield is the unspoiled Niangua River with its gentle waters and profusion of fish and wildlife. Access to the Big Piney, rated one of the best fishing rivers in Missouri, is found 10 miles west of Licking on Rte. 32. It offers a slow and easy float.

Of the mighty Missouri and Mississippi, a state tourist official says: "Some adventurous people do float the Mississippi and Missouri rivers but, to my knowledge, have to provide their own craft, do their own shuttling, etc." He also says that some floating is no doubt done on the slow-moving, often muddy streams of north Missouri. But he knows of no canoe outfitters to serve them. Nor is he aware of any outfitters specializing in lakeside rentals, although doubtless canoes and other boats are available at resorts and marinas.

For more information, the Missouri Division of Tourism warmly recommends *Missouri Ozark Waterways*, a $2.00 book by Oscar Hawksley, published by the state's Department of Conservation, Public Affairs Section, P.O. Box 180, Jefferson City, Mo. 65102-0180.

Akers Ferry Canoe Rental
Gene and Eleanor L. Maggard
HCR 81, Box 90
Salem, MO 65560
(314) 858-3224, (800) 333-5628
Upper Current River
Max. rapids: I-II
NACLO, Missouri Canoe Association,
Akers Ferry Canoe Rental rents canoes and tubes for trips of one to nine days on the upper Current River, which has crystal-clear waters, numerous springs and caves, along with good trout and bass fishing. Paddlers on these trips can also enjoy camping, swimming, and a chance to spot deer, beavers, minks, and turkeys. The livery's trips, available year-round, are fine for all paddlers.

The owners of Akers Ferry Canoe Rental also operate two other liveries near Salem: Wild River Canoe Rental (858-3230) and Round Spring Canoe Rental (858-3224).

Black River Floats
Carmen Shaffer, Larry Morgan
P.O. Box 1
Lesterville, MO 63654
(314) 637-2247, (314) 223-7473
Black River
Max. rapids: None
Black River Floats rents canoes, rafts, and tubes for one- and two-day trips on the Black River, a scenic Class I and II river safe for beginning canoeists. Trips pass through the beautiful scenery of Johnson Shut-Ins State Park, Elephant Rocks State Park, Sutton's Bluff, and Mark Twain National Forest. Abundant wildlife includes deer, turkeys, and beavers. Also, anglers can enjoy fishing in the Black River's clear water for smallmouth bass, goggle-eye, and perch. Black River Floats' season runs from April to October. However, off-season floats are available if reserved in advance.

Blue Springs Campground and Canoe Rental

Doyle Isom, Jr.
P.O. Box 540
Thickety Ford Road
Bourbon, MO 65441
(314) 732-5200, (800) 333-8004
Upper Meramec River
Max. rapids: I-II
Mid Missouri Canoe Liveries Association

Blue Springs Campground & Canoe Rental offers guided canoe and raft trips and canoe, raft, and tube rentals on the Upper Meramec River. Trips last one to five days and offer "easy, recreational floating" for families, groups, and fishermen. The stretches floated are scenic, with crystal-clear water, bluffs, wooded hillsides, caves, and plentiful blue herons, deer, wild turkeys, and other wildlife. Paddlers also can enjoy good fishing for trout and bass.

The campground offers tent and R.V. camping, cabin rentals, cookouts, hayrides, trail rides, and a store. The season runs March to November.

Boiling Springs Resort & Campground

Alicia Kuhn
Route 7, Box 124
Licking, MO 65542
(314) 674-3488
Big Piney River
Max. rapids: I-II
Missouri Canoe and Floaters Association

Boiling Springs Resort and Canoe Rental rents canoes and tubes on the gentle, scenic Big Piney River for trips of one to five days. The Big Piney offers relaxing trips for families, beginners, and anyone wanting a "slow and easy float." Deer, turkeys, and beavers abound, and the river boasts excellent fishing for bass, goggle-eye, catfish and perch.

Boiling Springs, open from April to November, also offers johnboat rentals, cabins with showers and electric kitchens, and a campground with modern restrooms and hot showers.

Carr's Canoe Rental

Gary and Carol Smith
HCR-1, Box 137
Eminence, MO 65466
(314) 858-3240, (314) 226-5459 (home)
Current River
Max. rapids: I-II

Carr's Canoe Rental rents canoes for one- to 10-day trips on the Current River. Camping is available along the river and at nearby Round Spring Campground. Carr's is owned by the proprietors of Current River Canoe Rental, located six miles north. See the separate listing in this chapter for further details.

Cherokee Landing

Gary and Cheryl Stephens
Route 4, Box 303
Bonne Terre, MO 63628
(314) 358-2805
Big River
Max. rapids: None

Cherokee Landing rents canoes and tubes for one-day trips on less-traveled stretches of the Big River, a placid, scenic river fun for beginners and experienced paddlers alike. The trips feature views of cliffs, caves, and abundant wildlife, including deer, beavers, and raccoons. The clear waters also boast good fishing for bass, catfish, bluegill, and crappie.

Cherokee Landing's trips run from April to October.

Family floating on the Current River. Courtesy of Eminence Canoe Rental.

Clearwater Stores, Inc.
Jim Wohlschlaeger
Route 3, Box 3592
Piedmont, MO 63957
(314) 223-4813
Black River
Max. rapids: I-II

Clearwater Stores, Inc., rents canoes for one- and two-day trips on the scenic Black River in the East Ozarks. An excellent stream for beginners as well as experienced floaters, the Black River offers fine hill-country scenery; views of turkeys, deer, beavers, ducks, and blue herons; and fishing for bass, walleye, catfish, and perch. Tent and R.V. camping is available at Clearwater Lake, adjacent to the outfitter's base. Paddlers also can camp free along the river. Clearwater Store's season runs form March to October.

Courtois Canoe Rental & Campground
Marvin Hanks
P.O. Box 122
Steelville, MO 65565
(314) 786-7452
Courtois Creek, Huzzah Creek,
Meramec River
Max. rapids: I-II

Courtois Canoe Rental rents canoes, kayaks, rafts, and tubes for trips of one to four days on the Courtois Creek, Huzzah Creek, and the Meramec River. All trips are gentle, scenic floats of minimal difficulty that are safe and fun for paddlers young and old. Of particular appeal are the crystal-clear, spring-fed waters and the unspoiled Ozark wilderness offering scenic views of bluffs, oak forests, and wildlife. Fishing is good, too, for smallmouth and largemouth bass.

Courtois Canoe Rental, open year-round, operates a secluded, riverfront campground with a modern bathhouse, general store, and restaurant.

Fast-water canoeing on the Black River. Photo by Jack Kiser, courtesy of Black River Floats, Lesterville, Missouri.

Current River Canoe Rental
Gary and Windy Smith
HCR 62, Box 375
Salem, MO 65560
(314) 858-3250 (summers),
(314) 226-5517 (winters)
Current River
Max. rapids: I-II

Current River Canoe Rental rents canoes and tubes for one- to seven-day trips on the Current River in the heart of the Ozark National Scenic Riverways. Classified as a Class I, or occasionally as a Class II river, the Current is fun for beginners as well as experienced canoeists. The river is crystal clear and especially scenic, offering views of cliffs and bluffs and several large caves, one of which takes two hours to explore on tours led by the National Park Service. Wildlife to see includes turkeys, deer, otters, squirrels, rabbits, birds, turtles, and fish — smallmouth bass, trout, and goggle-eye.

During Current River's May-to-October season, R.V. and tent lodging is available at Pulltite Campground at the outfitter's base.

Eminence Canoes, Cottages, and Campground
Wes and Patti Tastad
P.O. Box 276, Hwy. 19 N.
Eminence, MO 65466
(314) 226-3642, (314) 226-3810
Current River, Jack's Fork River
Max. rapids: I-II
NACLO, Missouri Canoe Association

Eminence Canoe Rental, Cottages & Campground offers guided and unguided canoe, kayak, raft, and tube trips on the Jacks Fork and Current Rivers in the Ozark National Scenic Riverways Park. Trips last from one to seven days and are suited for all paddlers, novice to expert, depending on the time of year and section of river selected. The season runs year-round and the scenery includes forests, bluffs, and the largest concentration of caves and springs in the United States. Among the wildlife to see are bobcats, mountain lions, deer, beavers, minks, eagles, and buzzards. The fish to catch include smallmouth and largemouth bass, trout, and goggle eye.

Eminence Canoe also offers cottages and a private R.V. and tent campground with modern washroom.

Fagan's Canoe & Raft Rental
Linda and Joe Fagan
P.O. Box 796
Steelville, MO 65565
(314) 775-5744, (314) 885-2947 (winter)
Meramec River
Max. rapids: I-II
Mid-Missouri Liveries Association, State of Missouri Floaters Association

Fagan's Canoe & Raft Rental offers guided and unguided canoe and raft trips on the Meramec River. Trips last from one to five days, are fairly easy, and are best suited for fishermen, families, single canoeists and large groups. The area is distinctive for its scenic bluffs, caves, springs, and abundant wildlife, including deer, turkeys, birds, muskrats, minks, and squirrels. Fishing in the Meramec's cool, clear water also is exceptional, especially for brown trout but also for bass, perch, drum, goggle-eye, and suckers.

Fagan's is open year-round, but winter trips require advance reservation.

Franklin Floats
Bob and JoAnn Franklin
Route 1, Box 9
Lesterville, MO 63654
(314) 637-2205
Black River, Taum Sauk Lake
Max. rapids: III-IV

Franklin Floats rents canoes and tubes for one- to three-day trips on all forks of the Black River and on Taum Sauk Lake. At high water the East Fork of the Black River has exciting rapids to challenge advanced paddlers. Otherwise, all trips are fine for anyone, including novices. All paddlers can enjoy the Ozark countryside with its springs, caves, bluffs, and abundant deer, turkeys and herons. The waters also offer good fishing for smallmouth and largemouth bass, crappie, catfish, bluegill and goggle-eye.

Lodging is available in riverfront cabins and at camp sites along the river. Franklin Float's season is from April to October, but off-season trips are available by request.

Griffin's Canoe & Campground
James Griffin
Route 16, Box 1010
Lebanon, MO 65536
(417) 588-3353
Niangua River
Max. rapids: I-II

Griffin's Canoe & Campground, open year-round, rents canoes for one- and two-day trips on the scenic Niangua River in the Ozarks. These gentle float trips, fine for young and old, range in length from two-and-a-half to 40 miles. The Niangua offers wilderness scenery; views of deer, turkeys, and other wildlife; and excellent fishing for trout and bass.

Griffin's Campground features tent and R.V. camping, hot showers, and a spring-fed fishing pond stocked with bass, bluegill, and catfish.

Fall canoeing on the Elven Point River. Photo by Carole Nance, courtesy of Hufstedtler's Canoe Rentals, Alton, Missouri.

Hi-Lo Campground & Canoe Rental
Linda A. Skains
Route 1, Box 176G
Tecumseh, MO 65760
(417) 261-2590, (417) 261-2368
Bryant Creek, White River— North Fork
Max. rapids: I-II

Hi-Lo Campground & Canoe Rental rents canoes, kayaks, and tubes for one- to three-day trips on Bryant Creek and the North Fork of the White River. Trips range in difficulty, with stretches to suit paddlers of all levels of experience. On both the Bryant and North Fork, paddlers can enjoy views of wooded banks, springs, 19th century water mills, and wildlife, including deer, blue herons, otters, and wild turkeys. Also, the North Fork offers trout fishing and the Bryant has fishing for bass, rock bass, channel catfish, walleye, trout, and bluegill.

Camping also is available during Hi-Lo's April-to-November season.

Hufstedler's Canoe Rental & Campground
Mike Brooks
Riverton Rural Branch
Alton, MO 65606
(417) 778-6116
Eleven Point River
Max. rapids: III-IV
Missouri Canoe Outfitters and Liveries Association

Hufstedler's Canoe Rental and Campground offers canoe and tube rentals and guided canoe and dory trips on the Eleven Point River, a designated National Wild and Scenic River. Trips of eight to 44 miles run through pristine wilderness with towering 300-foot bluffs, clear water, and abundant wildlife, including deer, coyotes, mountain lions, beavers, turkeys, owls, bats, and bald eagles. Fishing for rainbow trout, bass, and pike is excellent.

Hufstedler's, open year-round, also offers a large, wooded campground with a modern bathhouse and free firewood.

Indian Springs Lodge
Greg Schmucker
P.O. Box T
Highway 8 West
Steelville, MO 65565
(314) 775-2266, (800) 392-1110
Meramec River
Max. rapids: I-II
Indian Springs Lodge rents canoes, kayaks, and tubes for one-day trips on the Meramec River. This slow, easy river is fine for paddlers of all ages and offers wilderness scenery; good fishing for trout, bass, catfish, and sucker; and a chance to view deer, bald eagles, great blue herons, turtles, and trout.

Paddling on the spring-fed Meramec is available year-round. In addition, Indian Springs Lodge offers a campground, bar, live bands, hiking trails, a pool, cabins, motel rooms, a restaurant, tennis, horseshoes, and other recreation.

Jack's Fork Canoe Rental
Gene and Eleanor L. Maggard
P.O. Box 188
Eminence, MO 65466
(314) 226-3434, (800) Jacks Fork
Current River, Jack's Fork River
Max. rapids: I-II
Jacks Fork Canoe Rental offers guided canoe and johnboat trips and rents canoes, rafts and tubes on the Current and Jacks Fork Rivers. These trips last one to 14 days, pass through a scenic wilderness of woods and high bluffs, and offer excellent bass and trout fishing. Paddlers can also

enjoy camping, swimming, and views of deer, turkeys, minks, and beavers. Jacks Fork Canoe Rental's season is from April to November.

Jeff's Canoe Rental
Jeff Vroman
Box 204A
Annapolis, MO 63620
(314) 598-4555
Black River
Max. rapids: I-II
Jeff's Canoe Rentals rents canoes, rafts, and tubes for one- to three-day trips on the scenic, crystal-clear Black River. Trips are easy enough for beginners and boast fine views of rocky bluffs, springs, and wildlife, including deer and wild turkeys. Anglers also can enjoy fishing for smallmouth bass, catfish, bluegill, and goggle-eye.

All trips start upriver and end at the outfitter's base at the Highway K Bridge. Jeff's Canoe Rental's season runs from Memorial Day to Labor Day.

K-Mark Canoe Rental
Dee and Sue Rayfield
Box 186
Annapolis, MO 63620
(314) 598-3399
Black River
Max. rapids: I-II
K-Mark Canoe Rental offers guided and unguided canoe trips of one and two days on the gentle, scenic Black River in the Ozark foothills. On K-Mark's trips, paddlers can enjoy wilderness scenery, abundant wildlife, and excellent fishing for bass, crappie, catfish, and perch.

During the April-to-October season, the outfitter also offers shuttle service for paddlers who bring their own canoes.

Meramec Canoe Rental
Doyle and Vicki Isom
P.O. Box 57
Sullivan, MO 63080
(314) 468-6519, (800) 334-6946
Meramec River
Max. rapids: I-II
Missouri Canoe Association

Meramec Canoe Rental rents canoes, rafts, and tubes at Meramec State Park for trips of one to five days on the Meramec River. These scenic trips offer views of caves, bluffs, and wildlife, including deer and wild turkeys. Group discounts are available.

The state park, open from March to November, also offers cabin rentals, barbecues, and a restaurant.

Muddy River Outfitters
Robert Hoenike
4307 Main Street
Kansas City, MO 64111
(816) 753-7093
Big Piney River
Max. rapids: I-II

Muddy River Outfitters offers one- and two-day guided and unguided canoe and kayak trips on the clear, calm waters of the Big Piney River. These trips, suited for beginners and advanced canoeists, are organized from the tour company's headquarters in Kansas City. The guided trips feature camping on a ridge above the river, a break to explore a mammoth cave, and a stop on the drive back to Kansas City at either an Ozark winery, an outdoor flea market, or at Arrow Rock, a restored historic town.

Muddy River also offers several out-of-state tours, including trips to the Grand Canyon, Yellowstone, and the Badlands.

Neil Canoe Rental and Campground
Martha Gossett
Highway M, P.O. Box 396
Van Buren, MO 63965
(314) 323-4447
Current River
Max. rapids: I-II

Neil Canoe Rental & Campground rents canoes, johnboats, and tubes on the Current River. Canoe trips last one to five days, offering easy paddling, crystal-clear water, good fishing for bass and goggle-eye, and beautiful views of large bluffs, dense forest, and abundant wildlife. Among the wildlife to watch for are deer, wild turkeys, raccoons, rabbits, and birds. The river also has many gravel bars that make good places to stop to picnic or swim.

Neil Canoe Rental's season is from April to October.

Onondaga Cave State Park & Canoe Rental
Doyle and Vicki Isom
Highway H, Box 114
Leasburg, MO 65535
(314) 245-6600, (800) 334-6946
Meramec River
Max. rapids: I-II
Missouri Canoe Association

Onondaga Cave State Park & Canoe Rental rents canoes and tubes on the Meramec River, a clear, clean river with scenic bluffs, good bass fishing, and nearby caves, including Onondaga, the largest cave in Missouri. Canoe and tube rental are available for trips of one to five days from March to November. During this time, paddlers also can camp at the state park's campground.

Ozark Sunrise Expeditions, Inc.

Guy M. Thomas
Route 4, Box 10 C
Joplin, MO 64804
(417) 782-5272
Shoal Creek, Buffalo River, Mullberry River, Frog Bayou
Max. rapids: I-II

Ozark Sunrise Expeditions, Inc., offers guided and unguided canoe trips on Shoal Creek, Buffalo River, Mulberry River, and Frog Bayou. All trips are relatively easy and offer excellent Ozark scenery, including bluffs, caves, and views of deer, turkeys, beavers, and eagles. Trips also feature many good spots to camp and fish for bass, panfish, and catfish.

Open year-round, OSE offers tents and R.V. camping, moonlight canoe trips, dark night tube parties, sunrise breakfast floats, and "adventure programs" such as orienteering and rappelling, and guided hunting and fishing trips.

R&W Canoe Rental & Campground

Rick and Wanda Beasley
Route 16, Box 884
Lebanon, MO 65536
(417) 588-3358
Niangua River
Max. rapids: I-II

R&W Canoe Rental and Campground rents canoes for one- and two-day trips on the scenic, gentle Niangua River. Paddlers can spot birds, deer, muskrats, turtles, beavers, and otters among the lush greenery on the Niangua, and fishermen can enjoy angling for shasta, brown and rainbow trout, goggle eye, bass, bluegill, and perch. Gravel bars along the river provide good stopping points for swimming in the Niangua's clear, spring-fed waters.

R&W also offers a riverfront campground. The season runs from March through October.

Ray's Canoe Rental

Route 8, Box 754
Steelville, MO 65565
(314) 775-5697
Upper Meramec River, Humpy Creek, Moose River
Max. rapids: I-II
Missouri Canoe Association

Ray's Canoe Rental rents canoes and tubes for trips of one to five days on the upper Meramec River, described as "sporty but safe." The chal-

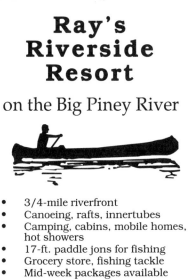

lenge on this generally placid Ozark stream comes in negotiating narrow stretches. The Meramec also offers fine wilderness scenery along its wooded banks, views of Meramec Spring and abundant wildlife, and excellent trout and bass fishing in its clear, spring-fed waters. Ray's, open from March to November, offers lodging in a bed and breakfast, its camping area, or a rustic cabin.

Ray's Riverside Resort

John and Joe Ann Wilder
Route 7, Box 418
Licking, MO 65542
(314) 674-2430
Big Piney River
Max. rapids: I-II

Ray's Riverside Resort runs guided and unguided trips of one to six days on the clean, clear, spring-fed Big Piney River. Trips are of little or moderate difficulty and offer pretty wooded scenery and views of limestone bluff, rabbits, deer, and wild turkeys. Guided trips are by canoe or raft and unguided trips are by canoe, raft, or tube. Riverfront camping and fishing for smallmouth bass and rock bass are also available.

Richard's Canoe Rental

Karen Richard
Route 2
Alton, MO 65606
(417) 778-6186
Eleven Point River
Max. rapids: I-II

Richard's Canoe Rental offers guided and unguided canoe and raft trips of one to seven days on the Eleven Point River, a scenic river easy enough for beginners. Trips pass through protected national forest land with wilderness scenery and plentiful beavers, bears, turtles, minks, and other wildlife. The river's clear water also has excellent fishing, with abundant trout, bass, goggle-eye

and perch. Rentals and guided trips are available year-round.

Riversedge Campgrounds

Johnny Beil
Box 90, Peola Road
Lesterville, MO 63654
(314) 637-2422
Black River
Max. rapids: None

Riversedge Campgrounds rents canoes and tubes for one-day trips on the Black River, a crystal-clear "family" river offering good swimming, scenery, and fishing for bass, goggle-eye, and catfish. Canoe trips of eight and 15 miles are available. The shorter and more popular trip ends at the campground, which has 110 campsites, one-half mile of beachfront, and modern bath houses. The campground also offers hayrides, trail rides, and weekend specials that include camping, a float trip, and a barbecue or hog roast. Riversedge's season runs from April to October.

Sunburst Ranch Inc.

Albert S. Eckilson
HCR 68, Box 140
Caulfield, MO 65626
(417) 284-3443
White River — North Fork
Max. rapids: III-IV

Sunburst Ranch rents canoes for one- and two-day trips on the North Fork of the White River. Trips run between April and November, with Class III rapids in the spring and Class II rapids in the summer and fall. Paddlers can enjoy fine Ozark scenery of bluffs, springs, caves, and abundant wildlife. The White River is also a trophy trout stream with outstanding fishing for rainbow and brown trout, smallmouth bass, and goggle-eye.

Paddlers can also "rough it in style" at a campground halfway along a two-day trip.

Montana

Montana's Rockies give rise to some of the finest canoeing, rafting and fishing rivers in the world. The Big Sky State is a place to rejoice in the wilderness, to commune with nature, to recall the wild and woolly West and retrace the routes taken by early explorers. Here are the sources of the mighty Missouri and its great tributary, the Yellowstone. These two rivers drain six-sevenths of the state and flow majestically across the great arid plain that comprises more than half of Montana. Their headwater streams, the Big Hole, the Beaverhead, the Jefferson, the Madison, the Gallatin, the Smith and the Bighorn, provide some of the best floating in the state. And there is more good paddling on the western side of the continental divide, where the Bitterroot, the Blackfoot and the three-pronged Flathead converge on the Clark Fork. The Clark Fork, navigable throughout its course through Montana, then joins the Columbia bound for the Pacific.

Start in the west with the Bitterroot, which Lewis and Clark originally named "Clark's River." They called it a handsome stream with clear water and a gravel bed. Unfortunately it is no longer pristine today: much of its downstream section towards Missoula has been spoiled by riprapping with rocks and old car bodies to protect mobile homes in the floodplain. But further upstream the Bitterroot is rich in wildlife and the entire river is flanked by the scenic Bitterroot Range to the west and the Sapphire Range in the east.

Also very popular with Missoulans is the Blackfoot River, especially in its lower stretches. One favorite outing is a six-mile trip at Johnsrud State Park. It has Class III rapids in May and June but can be run all summer long. The most difficult white water on the Blackfoot is further upstream, above the confluence with the Clearwater.

The Clark Fork itself has been much cleaned up since the grim fish kills caused by pollution in earlier years. Its trout and other aquatic life have returned in strength, and the river has become another popular float in western Montana. The 22-mile run starting at Alberton Gorge in Mineral County — again not far from Missoula — is a good Class II-III trip runnable all year round except when the river is frozen. It is tricky at peak water levels, when the rapids come close to Class V, but quite safe in July and August.

Further north, on the fringe of Glacier National Park, the Flathead offers varied paddling on its Main Stem, Middle Fork and North Fork. The Main Stem has a Class III six-mile run just below Flathead Lake for which a permit is needed from the Flathead Indian Reservation. This is a scenic journey between high cliffs that provide nesting sites for birds of prey. Following this Buffalo Rapids stretch, the entire lower portion of the river is gentle floating on clear water past rocky bluffs, badlands and wildflowers, with many species of birds.

The Middle Fork of the Flathead is reputedly Montana's wildest river. Its remote upper section is too rugged for most floaters in May, when its flow may surge from a low level of 900 cubic feet per second to more than 11,000 cfs. But in June and July it poses a tempting Class III-IV challenge for experienced rafters. Access to this wilderness grizzly-bear region is by plane to the Schaefer Meadows airstrip. Further downstream, the non-wilderness section of the Middle Fork is more frequented because of its easy access. This, too, has rapids that demand expertise, notably in the John Stevens Canyon run where the narrow stream drops thirty-five feet per mile along a five-mile stretch.

Among the headwaters of the Missouri, the Big Hole is a much-loved and famous river. It sets out as a narrow stream near the Continental Divide and flows into the Jefferson near Twin Bridges. Clear and cold, it curves through 150 miles of wide valleys and narrow canyons. For the fisherman, perhaps its chief attraction is that it contains grayling as well as more common species of trout.

The Madison takes the floater through Bear Trap Canyon, a whitewater wilderness run which includes Kitchen Sink, a Class IV rapid. This is great fishing territory, and at the end of the day the paddler can wallow in the water of the Bear Trap Hot Springs. Also heading northward from Yellowstone National Park to join the Missouri is the Gallatin, with its deep canyon and continuous Class III whitewater.

The Yellowstone, the longest undammed river in the lower 48 states, is famous both for its history in pioneer days and its fishing. The upstream stretch from Gardiner, where the river leaves the Yellowstone Park, down to Livingston is known as Paradise Valley. It runs between the jagged Absaroka Mountains and the Gallatin Range and is alive with trout, Canada geese, eagles and deer. One of its highlights is Yankee Jim Canyon, a four-mile whitewater stretch that attracts many summer rafters. Less crowded is the next section between Livingston and Big Timber, where the river begins to braid. Then the Yellowstone changes gradually to a warm prairie river, earn-ing its name from the yellowish bluffs on its flanks and attracting a wide range of wildlife.

The only section of the Missouri to have been included in the National Wild and Scenic Rivers system is the 150-mile stretch between Fort Benton and the James Kipp Recreational Area. This is untouched by the many dams that check Mighty Mo's progress through Montana. It attracts paddlers and fishermen from far afield and its rapids rate no more than Class I.

Finally, three more great Montana fishing rivers. The Jefferson, a Missouri tributary, abounds in trout and is said to provide some of the West's finest fly fishing. The Beaverhead, which flows into the Jefferson, is claimed to be Montana's best trophy trout stream. And the Smith, which runs into the Missouri above Great Falls, provides not only great trout fishing but also a 60-mile float through a beautiful limestone canyon with walls up to a thousand feet high. Fly fishermen on the Smith can view golden eagles, mule deer, elk, black bear, minks, and otters feeding on the riverbanks.

Al Gadoury's 6X Outfitters
Allen Gadoury
P.O. Box 6045
Bozeman, MT 59715
(406) 586-3806
Nelson's Creek, Armstrong Creek, DePuy Spring Creek, Yellowstone River, Missouri River
Max. rapids: III-IV
Al Gadoury's 6X Outfitters offers guided dory trips for fly fishermen on Nelson's, Armstrong's, and DePuy's Spring Creek and on the Yellowstone and Missouri Rivers. Gadoury floats these blue-ribbon trout streams in a 15-foot McKenzie-style drift boat equipped with swivel bucket seats and casting yokes fore and aft. Day trips on these catch-and-release waters run from March to November, and offer Class III-IV rapids and views of waterfowl, deer, blue herons, sandhill cranes, and minks.

Al Wind's Trout Futures
Al Wind
P.O. Box 485
Twin Bridges, MT 59754
(406) 684-5512
Smith River, Big Hole River, Beaverhead River, Blackfoot River, Jefferson River, Madison River
Max. rapids: III-IV
Fishing Outfitters Association of Montana
Al Wind specializes in guided oar-boat trips for people who enjoy beautiful river scenery and the challenge of fly-fishing for trout. Trips last one to five days and include expert fly-fishing instruction and descriptions of the area's entomology, trout biology, geology, wildlife, and pioneer days. Trips run on six rivers, all in distinctive wilderness ranging from 7,000 to 2,000 feet in elevation. On some rivers, it's not uncommon for the terrain to go from meadow to forest to canyon in a single day.

A 4-lb. brown trout caught on the Missouri River. Courtesty of Jerry Nichols, Western Waters, Missoula, Montana.

During Wind's May-to-October season, guests can fish for brook trout, rainbow trout, brown trout, grayling, sockeye salmon, and bass. The wildlife to see include eagles, osprey, herons, ducks, bighorn sheep, deer, and elk.

Bar RL Outfitters
R. J. Luchall
2230 Emory Road
Ronan, MT 59864
(406) 675-4256
Clark Fork River, Bitterroot River
Max. rapids: I-II
Montana Outfitters and Guides Association

Bar RL Outfitters runs one- to five-day guided raft and dory trips on the Clark Fork and Bitterroot Rivers. With Class I and II rapids, these trips are not difficult and are well-suited for families with children age 12 and older. The company also offers trips into the Selway Bitterroot Wilderness Area for paddling and fishing on four high Alpine lakes "teeming with fish of all sizes." Rainbow, brown and cutthroat trout can be caught.

Of the scenery Bar RL says," Montana rivers and lakes are all beautiful and pristine — ours are no exception." Wildlife viewing is excellent, too, with chances to see mountain sheep, elk, deer, bears, and mountain goats. The season runs from May to September.

BAR SIX OUTFITTERS

Dillon, MT 59725
Terry Throckmorton
406-683-4005

60 miles of scenic rafting and some of the finest trout fishing Montana has to offer--on the famous Smith River.

Also, one-day rafting and excellent fishing trips on the Big Hole and Beaverhead Rivers of Southwest Montana.
(family owned and operated)

Bar Six Outfitters
1975 Sullivan Lane
Dillon, MT 59725
(406) 683-4005
Big Hole River, Smith River, Beaver-head River
Max. rapids: I-II
Montana Outfitters and Guides Association

Bar Six Outfitters runs guided and unguided raft trips on the Bighole, Smith, and Beaverhead Rivers, which offer great scenery, fishing, and fun, gentle rapids. Trips pass through beautiful and varied terrain consisting of towering limestone cliffs, caves, timbered mountains, and green meadows. Abundant wildlife can be seen, too, including beavers, minks, deer, elk, bears, otters, hawks, and eagles.

Trips, which last one to five days, also feature exceptional fishing for grayling and brown, rainbow, and cutthroat trout. The season runs from May to July.

Big Timber Fly Fishing
Channing W. Welin
HC 89 Box 4316
Big Timber, MT 59011
(406) 932-4368
Yellowstone River, Boulder River
Max. rapids: III-IV
Fishing Outfitters Association of Montana

Big Timber Fly Fishing runs guided fly-fishing trips in dories on the Yellowstone and Boulder Rivers, which are large and relatively under-fished. Trips last one to three days and pass through scenic terrain where the mountains meet the plains. Trout and Rocky Mountain white fish are the main types of fish caught during the July-to-October season.

The company also offers tubing trips and fishing on select private lakes. Among the wildlife to see are waterfowl, raptors, deer, and many non-game species.

Bighorn-Yellowstone Guide Service
D.L. Tennant
1809 Darlene Lane
Billings, MT 59102
(406) 252-5859
Bighorn River, Missouri River, Yellowstone River
Max. rapids: I-II
Fishing Outfitters Association of Montana

Bighorn-Yellowstone Guide Service offers guided drift-boat trips and canoe rentals on the Bighorn, Missouri, and Yellowstone Rivers. Don Tennant, who has more than 40 years' experience floating, fishing, and working on rivers as a professional biologist, leads all guided trips himself. Fishing for brown and rainbow trout is superb. On guided trips, Tennant offers the guarantee "no fish — no pay."

Canoe rentals offered on rivers with mild white water are fine for

Fly-fishing on the Smith River, one of Montana's many terrific trout streams. Courtesy of Brian D. Nelson/Diamond N Outfitters, Missoula, Montana.

anyone age nine to 90. All trips boast terrific scenery, fine fishing, and excellent wildlife viewing of deer, beavers, minks, muskrats, eagles, osprey, geese, ducks, and numerous songbirds. The season runs from April to November.

Castaway Fly Fishing Shop
Joe Roope
3620 North Fruitland
Coeur d'Alene, ID 83814
(208) 765-3133
Clark's Fork River
Max. rapids:

Castaway Fly Fishing Shop offers customized trout-fishing trips on the Clark's Fork River in Montana and the St. Joe and Coeur d'Alene Rivers in Idaho. These dory trips last one to three days and pass through pristine wilderness with abundant wildlife and excellent fishing for rainbow and

cutthroat trout. Among the wildlife to see are elk, deer, bears, beavers, and sheep. Castaway's season runs from May to October.

Castle Mountain Fly Fishers
Shane Dempsey
Box 370
White Sulphur Springs, MT 59645
(406) 547-3366
Smith River, Yellowstone River,
Whitetail Lake
Max. rapids: I-II

Castle Mountain Fly Fishers offers guided canoe and raft trips and rents canoes and rafts for fly fishermen, families, and anyone seeking a wilderness experience. Trips run on the Smith River, Yellowstone River, and Whitetail Lake, through scenic areas with limestone cliffs and unspoiled wilderness. On these trips, of one to six days, guests can camp, swim, view wildlife, and fish for brown trout, rainbow trout, native trout, brook trout, and whitefish. Among the wildlife to see are muskrats, ducks, whitetail deer, mule deer, elk, antelope, and black bears. During Castle Mountain Fly Fishers' April-to-October season, the company also offers fly fishing lessons, fishing on private streams, and lodging before and after trips.

Diamond N Outfitters
Brian D. Nelson
P.O. Box 20193
Missoula, MT 59801
(406) 543-3887 (summers),
(406) 674-5540 (winters)
Clark Fork River, Bitterroot River, Blackfoot River, Rock Creek River, Missouri River, Smith River, Big Hole River, Beaverhead River
Max. rapids: III-IV
Fishing Outfitters Association of Montana, Trout Unlimited, West Montana Fish and Game Association

Diamond N Outfitters runs guided oar-boat fishing expeditions on eight rivers. The guides are excellent teachers of beginning and advanced fly-fishing techniques, and run trips of one to seven days.

Set in the heart of the northern Rockies, expeditions run through scenic terrain of canyons, mountains, meadows, and forests. The rivers boast excellent fishing for rainbow, brown, and cutthroat trout on trips between March and November. Wildlife viewing is good, too, with chances to see deer, elk, bears, eagles, minks, beavers, and otters. Custom trips can also be arranged.

Diamond R Expeditions
Pete and Tanya Rothing
3108 Linney Road
Bozeman, MT 59715
(406) 388-1760
Madison River, Gallatin River, Jefferson River, Yellowstone River, Missouri River
Max. rapids: None

Diamond R Expeditions offers one-to seven-day guided canoe trips on five scenic rivers. Trips are on flat water and are well-suited for novices and families. All trips feature blue-ribbon trout fishing, beautiful scenery, clear water, and abundant wildlife, including waterfowl, beavers, osprey, deer, herons, and cranes.

During its June-to-October season, Diamond R also offers horseback riding and pack trips, drift fishing, and a special combination, package consisting of a four-day pack trip in the Gallatin National Forest, two days floating on area rivers, and a one-day mini-tour of Yellowstone National Park.

E.W. Watson & Sons
Edwin W. Watson
152 Springville Lane
Townsend, MT 59644
(406) 266-2845, (800) 654-2845
Missouri River, Canyon Ferry Lake, Madison River
Max. rapids: None
Montana Outfitters and Guides Association

E.W. Watson & Sons Outfitting runs guided canoe and raft trips on the Missouri River, Madison River, and Canyon Ferry Lake. These flat-water trips are easy enough for beginners and feature clear, clean water, beautiful mountain scenery, and excellent fishing for brown and rainbow trout. Trips last one to six days and can include a combination of paddling and horseback riding when packing up to secluded camps at high mountain lakes. Among the abundant wildlife to see on these trips are deer, elk, blue herons, osprey, and eagles.

E.W. Watson's season is from July to September. The outfitter also offers trail riding, camping, and hunting trips.

Fishing Headquarters, Inc.
Dick Sharon and B. Thibeault
426 North Montana Street
Dillon, MT 59725
(406) 683-4634, (406) 683-6660
Beaverhead River, Big Hole River, Jefferson River, Madison River, Yellowstone River, Red Rock River
Max. rapids: I-II

Fishing Headquarters, Inc. runs guided raft and dory trips and rents tubes on the Beaverhead, Big Hole, Jefferson, Madison, Yellowstone, and Red Rock Rivers. Trips last one to two days and are geared for anyone who can fish or wishes to learn. These rivers offer scenic views of high mountains, riverside cliffs, and abundant wildlife, including deer, moose, elk, and bighorn sheep. The fishing, especially on the Beaverhead and Big Hole Rivers, is exceptional, with excellent chances to land grayling, and brown, rainbow, brook, and cutthroat trout. Fishing Headquarters' season runs from May to October.

Glacier Wilderness Guides
Randy Gayner
Box 535PA
West Glacier, MT 59936
(406) 888-5466, (800) 521-RAFT
Flathead River - Middle Fork, Flathead River - North Fork, Glacier National Park waters
Max. rapids: III-IV
Montana Outfitters and Guides

Glacier Wilderness Guides leads guided oar-boat and paddle- raft trips on the Middle Fork and North Fork of the Flathead River. These trips, of one

to eight days, pass through beautiful mountain wilderness along the boundary of Glacier National Park. On these excursions, guests can fish in the Flathead's pristine waters for cutthroat, rainbow, and Dolly Varden trout. Guests can also view abundant wildlife, including deer, elk, black bears, grizzly bears, mountain goats, and other animals and birds. These trips range in difficulty to suit both beginning and intermediate river runners.

During its May-to-October season, Glacier Wilderness also offers combined hiking/rafting trips, strictly fishing outings, day hikes and backpacking trips of four to six days. Equipment rentals are available.

Hawk, I'm Your Sister
Beverly Antaeus
P.O. Box 9109
Santa Fe, NM 87504
(505) 984-2268
Missouri River, Smith River, Abiquiu Lake, Rio Grande
Max. rapids: III-IV

Hawk, I'm Your Sister of Santa Fe specializes in women's wilderness canoe and raft trips. Its year-round program is geared to "women of all ages, shapes, sizes and skill levels" with guided trips in five states and four foreign locations. Its aim is to "teach you the language of the forests, canyons, deserts and waterways" in a safe and non-competitive environment. It takes paddlers on the Abiquiu Lake in New Mexico and on the Rio Grande in Texas, with other excursions as far afield as Alaska, Peru and China.

Rafting on the Missouri River. Courtesy of Jerry Nichols, Western Waters River Trips, Missoula, Montana.

Jerry Malson Outfitting
Jerry and June Malson
22 Swamp Creek Road
Trout Creek, MT 59874
(406) 847-5582
Northwestern Montana rivers
Max. rapids: I-III
Montana Outfitters and Guides Association

Jerry Malson Outfitting offers dory fishing trips and scenic float trips on the rivers of northwestern Montana. These trips, which run from late spring to early fall, are set in a beautiful mountainous area that resembles Glacier National Park. In addition to the scenery, guests on these trips can enjoy fishing for bass, trout, and pike and viewing deer, elk, ears, moose, and other wildlife. Dory trips last seven to 14 days. Jerry Malson also offers hunting trips and an outfitting and guide school.

Magellan Guide Service
Barry Morstad
P.O. Box 6132
Bozeman, MT 59714
(406) 388-1675
Yellowstone River, Madison River, Jefferson River, Gallatin River
Max. rapids: I-III
Fishing Outfitters Association of Montana

Magellan Guide Service runs guided oar-boat fishing trips on several rivers in southwestern Montana, including the Madison, Yellowstone, Jefferson, and Gallatin. These rivers, known for their fine trout fishing, boast sparkling, spring-fed waters passing through broad valleys amid high mountain peaks. Wildlife viewing is excellent, with good opportunities to spot deer, elk, bald and golden eagles, waterfowl, muskrats, otters, and shorebirds.

Magellan also offers a one-week "Ultimate Angling Tour," which includes fishing on a number of fine rivers and lakes and lodging in the famous Gallatin Gateway Inn, one of Montana's oldest railroad hotels, now completely refurbished.

Montana High Country Tours

Russ Kipp
1036 East Reeder
Dillon, MT 59725
(406) 683-4920
Smith River, Beaverhead River, Big Hole River, Pioneer Mountain lakes
Max. rapids: III-IV
Montana Outfitters and Guides Association

Montana High Country Tours offers guided float trips on three of Montana's best trout streams, the Beaverhead, Big Hole, and Smith Rivers. An extended 61-mile, six-day trip through the remote Smith River Canyon is a specialty and an excellent family vacation. The trip features great fishing, towering limestone canyon walls, and abundant wildlife, including deer, elk, bears, moose, sheep, mountain goats, and antelopes. The company also offers jeep, horseback, and llama trips to Alpine lakes in the Pioneer Mountains. The season is from May to September.

Montana Trout Guide Service

Monte Meredith
P.O. Box 565
Billings, MT 59103
(406) 947-2471, (406) 656-5407
Big Horn River, Big Spring Creek
Max. rapids: None

Montana Trout Guide Service offers guided, one-day fly-fishing trips on the Big Horn River and Big Spring Creek. These dory trips run year-round and feature terrific fishing for rainbow and brown trout on blue-ribbon trout streams where the average fish size is between 16 and 18 inches.

The dories pass through an historic and scenic area with abundant wildlife, including pheasants, deer, ducks, geese, herons, and eagles.

Pioneer Outfitters

Cliff and Chuck Page
Alder Creek Ranch
Wise River, MT 59762
(406) 832-3128
Big Hole River, Beaverhead River, Pioneer Mountain lakes
Max. rapids: I-II

Pioneer Outfitter specializes in float fishing on the Big Hole and Beaverhead Rivers on day trips or by the week. The emphasis is on trout fishing, as both rivers are blue-ribbon streams with excellent fly hatches between May and September. Trips are by oar boat through gentle Class I and II rapids and are perfect for older children and adults.

The company also offers high-country pack trips into remote, roadless areas of the Pioneer Mountains. These trips also boast excellent fishing, scenery, and wildlife viewing.

Point of Rocks Guest Ranch

Max Chase
Rte. 1, Box 680
Emigrant, MT 59027
(406) 333-4361
Yellowstone River, Missouri River, Spring Creek
Max. rapids: None

Point of Rocks runs guided fishing trips and rents tubes on Spring Creek and the Yellowstone and Missouri Rivers. This region, just north of Yellowstone National Park, is exceptionally beautiful and offers excellent fishing for brown, cutthroat, and rainbow trout. Guests on these trips, which run year-round, can also enjoy viewing deer, antelopes, elk, bears, and other wildlife.

Randy D. Rathie
Box 471
Ennis, MT 59729
(406) 682-4162
Madison River, Big Hole River
Max. rapids: None
Montana Outfitters and Guides
Association, Trout Unlimited, Ducks
Unlimited
Randy Rathie, an outfitter for more
than 25 years, runs guided oar-boat
fishing trips on scenic flat-water rivers
in southwestern Montana. Trips last
one day, are not demanding, and are
well-suited for both beginning and experienced trout fishermen. Wildlife to
see include deer, elk, bears, eagles,
hawks, and waterfowl. Rathie also offers horseback trips, tubing, lake
trips, wildlife photography trips, and
camping at high mountain lakes.

Rimrock Outfitting
Robert Stroebel
1520 Foothill Drive
Billings, MT 59105
(406) 248-4861
Bighorn River, Yellowstone River,
Missouri River, Madison River,
Gallatin River, Smith River
Max. rapids: V+
Montana Outfitters and Guides
Association
Rimrock Outfitting is a small company that specializes in customized
guided trips and rentals to suit guests'
needs. Guided whitewater and fishing trips, by canoe, raft, or dory, are
available on six rivers, as are rentals
of canoes, rafts, and tubes.
Trips last one to four days and
pass through prairie and mountain
country. All trips offer superb fishing
for walleye, northern pike, and especially trout. Also, deer, elk, moose,
bighorn sheep, turkeys, and antelope
can often be seen during Rimrock's
May-to-November season.

Roy Senter
726 North D Street
Livingston, MT 59047
(406) 222-3775
Yellowstone River
Max. rapids: None
Roy Senter offers float fishing and
scenic trips on the Yellowstone River.
These dory trips, offered between
April and October, pass through a
beautiful mountainous region with excellent trout fishing and plentiful
birds and other wildlife.

Royal L - Bighorn Lodge
Joe Caton
Bighorn River, MT 59075
(406) 666-2340, (406) 666-2389
Bighorn River
Max. rapids: I-II
Bighorn River Foundation
Royal L - Bighorn Lodge runs one-
to five-day guided and unguided raft
and dory trips on the Bighorn River.
With only gentle Class I and II rapids,
the runs are enough for guests of all
ages and boast "sensational" fishing
for rainbow and brown trout.
The areas also offers unspoiled
wilderness and a chance to view
deer, bears, and numerous types of
birds. The company's season runs
from April to October.

Spring Creek Outfitters
Bob Bouee
P.O. Box 328
Big Timber, MT 59011
(406) 932-4387
Yellowstone River, Boulder River
Max. rapids: III-IV
Montana Outfitters and Guides
Association
Spring Creek Outfitters runs one-
to seven-day oar-boat trips for blue-
ribbon trout fishing on Spring Creek
and the Yellowstone and Boulder
Rivers. Trips include personalized fly-
fishing instruction and a chance to
view abundant wildlife, including

deer, elk, bears, and antelope. Scenery is excellent, too, with all floats passing through the middle of Gallatin National Forest and the Absoraka Beartooth Wilderness.

Spring Creek also offers customized horsepack trips for Alpine fishing, camping, and photography.

Sundown Outfitters
Lyle Reynolds
Box 95
Melrose, MT 59743
(406) 835-2751
Bighole River, Beaverhead River, Jefferson River
Max. rapids: None
Sundown Outfitters runs oar-boat fly-fishing trips for beginners and pros alike. A wide array of fish can be caught, especially on the Big Hole River, where it is possible to catch brown, rainbow and brook trout and grayling all in one eight-hour float. Float trips last one day, with two fishermen and a guide per boat.

Surrounded by the Lost Pioneer and Highland Mountains, trips offer terrific scenery and a chance to view moose, bighorn sheep, and deer. Sundown's season runs from May to September.

Taylor Outfitters
Paul E. Taylor
Box 991
Dillon, MT 59725
(406) 681-3166
Big Hole River, Beaverhead River, Madison River, Ruby River
Max. rapids: I-II
Taylor Outfitters offers guided and unguided canoe and raft trips on the Jefferson, Madison, Beaverhead, and Big Hole Rivers. With Class I and II rapids, these trips are relatively easy, allowing beginners and experts time to fish for trout, whitefish and grayling, enjoy the mountain scenery, and view elk, deer, moose, geese, and

ducks. Trips last from one to seven days and run between June and October.

Taylor Outfitters has an unusual and scenic headquarters. It is based at a ranch on the Jefferson River, where the owners raise elk and play host to abundant deer and waterfowl.

The Canoeing House
Al Anderson
RR 1, Box 192
Three Forks, MT 59752
(406) 285-3488
Jefferson River, Madison River, Gallatin River, Missouri River, Yellowstone River, Big Hole River
Max. rapids: I-II
The Canoeing House offers canoe rentals and guided canoe and driftboat trips on six rivers. The rivers all boast excellent trout fishing and Rocky Mountain scenery. Trips run from one to five days and, with gentle Class I and II white water, are fine for novices. One particularly scenic trip the company offers, from Divide to the "Headquarters of the Missouri," was the same 125-mile stretch selected as a Sierra Club National Float Trip.

In addition to fine fishing, all trips offer good opportunities to spot eagles, beavers, minks, deer, antelopes, herons, and cranes.

The Montana Fisherman
Carl A. Mann
234 Ridgeway
Lolo, MT 59847
(406) 837-5632, (406) 273-6966
Clark Fork River, Bitterroot River, Flathead Lake
Max. rapids: None
Montana Outfitters and Guides Association
The Montana Fisherman offers oarboat raft trips on placid waters of the Clark Fork River, Bitterroot River, and Flathead Lake. Trips last one or two

days and run between April and October.

The company takes pride in organizing relaxing, scenic trips with excellent fishing for rainbow trout, cutthroat trout, lake trout and white fish. Guests also enjoy mountain landscape and seeing deer, eagles, ducks, geese, osprey, and blue herons.

Tom's Sport Shop and Guide Service

Tom Bugni
1210 Harrison Avenue
Butte, MT 59701
(406) 782-6251, (406) 723-4753
Big Hole River, Lower Madison River, Lower Gallatin River, Jefferson River, Yellowstone River, Missouri River, Beaverhead River
Max. rapids: None
Floaters of Montana

Tom's Sport Shop and Guide runs drift-boat fishing trips on one to three days on the Big Hole, Lower Madison, Lower Gallatin, Jefferson, Yellowstone, Missouri, and Beaverhead Rivers. These guided trips run through the heart of the Rockies, offering beautiful scenery; abundant elk, geese, ducks, and other wildlife; and excellent fishing for rainbow, brown, brook, and cutthroat trout. Tom's season runs from May to September.

Western Rivers

Fred Tedesco
P.O. Box 772
East Helena, MT 59635
(406) 227-5153
Smith River, Missouri River system, Clark Fork River system, Flathead Lake
Max. rapids: None

Western Rivers runs guided and unguided raft trips on the Smith River, Missouri River, Clark Fork River, and Flathead Lake. These trips offer excellent trout fishing, pure

waters, good campsites, and spectacular views of limestone canyons, mountains, and deer, elk, beavers, and eagles. Western Rivers' season is from April to October.

Western Waters

Gerald R. Nichols, Jr.
333 Knowles Street
Missoula, MT 59801
(406) 728-6161
Clark Fork River, Madison River, Missouri River, Big Hole River
Max. rapids: III-IV
Fishing and Floating Association of Montana

Western Waters is a family-run whitewater and fishing guide service. Whitewater trips by oar boat run on the Clark Fork River, which offers big water and wild rides between May and June. During this time, trips are limited to guests age 12 and older. From July to October, the age limit is six and older. Trips last from one to three days and can accommodate anyone from novices to experts. The Clark Fork River is particularly scenic, with gorgeous canyons and abundant wildlife, including deer, bears, moose, elk, osprey, eagles, and ducks.

Fishing trips run on the Madison, Missouri, and Big Hole Rivers. All three are clean and famous for their trophy trout fishing.

During its May-to-November season, Western Waters also offers horseback riding, sightseeing trips, and hikes to mountain lakes.

177

Wild River Adventures
Bob Jordan
P.O. Box 272
West Glacier, MT 59936
(406) 888-5539, (800) 826-2724
Middle Fork and North Fork Flathead River
Max. rapids: III-IV

Wild River Adventures specializes in oar- and paddle-raft trips on exceptionally scenic rivers bordering Glacier National Park. Trips on the Middle Fork of the Flathead range from mild to wild, with the greatest challenge coming in the high-water months of May to July. From July until the end of the season in September, rapids are more mild, making trips suitable for families with small children.

Trips on the North Fork of the Flathead are relaxing and scenic, offering fine trout fishing and good views of wildlife and Glacier's peaks. Wild Adventures also offers guided fishing trips and horseback trips though the Great Bear Wilderness.

Yellowstone Raft Company
Julia Page, Peter White
Box 46
Gardiner, MT 59030
(406) 848-7777
Yellowstone River, Gallatin River, Madison River
Max. rapids: III-IV
America Outdoors, American Rivers

Yellowstone Raft Company runs one-day guided trips on the Yellowstone, Gallatin, and Madison Rivers. Guests can opt for oar rafts, paddle rafts, or inflatable kayaks to suit the level of excitement they seek. The scenery is beautiful on all trips, especially those that run along the boundary of Yellowstone National Park, offering striking mountain views to the north and south. Among the wildlife to be seen are deer, antelope, bears, merganser, mallards, osprey, and great blue herons.

During the May-to-September season, the company also offers tubing, trout fishing excursions, and riverside barbecues.

Nebraska

Nobody heads for the prairies in search of white water. But the canoeist finds much to enjoy on Nebraska's many rivers. These include the North Platte and Platte which cross the state like a broad blue belt from Scottsbluff near the Wyoming border to where their waters merge with the Missouri just south of Omaha. There is a put-in on the North Platte right beside the Wyoming state line for a 61-mile trail to the Bridgeport State Recreation Area. It traverses some spectacular scenery and affords a great view of Scottsbluff National Monument and other rocky outcroppings along the way.

On the Platte itself, the Nebraska Game and Parks Commission recommends a 55-mile stretch at the eastern end of the state, from Fremont to a point just short of the confluence with the Missouri. But the commission warns that river flows vary considerably, especially along this lower segment, and suggests early spring and late fall as the best paddling seasons. Energetic canoeists can start their Platte River trip by paddling 75 miles down the Elkhorn River, its tributary. This, too, is an appealing float as the Elkhorn winds between willows and cottonwoods, then through steep, high bluffs covered in cedars and hardwoods. The ideal time for the Elkhorn is March through early July, although there is often enough water in September-October.

More challenging is a 70-mile section of the Dismal River near the center of the state. This trip, officially described as "definitely not for the novice," passes the Nebraska National Forest to Dunning. Wildlife enthusiasts will enjoy the Calamus River in north central Nebraska, with its abundance of ducks, herons, prairie chickens, pheasants, beavers, muskrats, turtles and other species. The 50-mile Calamus trail starts as a narrow and largely treeless stream, with more vegetation further down. Timber is so scarce that campers are advised to bring their own charcoal if they plan to cook. Ranchers have put up many fences across the river, some of which must be portaged.

Last but not least is the Niobrara River with its clean water and tall canyons forested with pine, birch and oak. Here in the Valentine region of northern Nebraska the canoeist can find fast water — Class I — during a season which runs from April through September. Bobcats, buffalo, minks, elk, otters, beavers, and wild turkeys can be seen, while catfish and trout may be landed early and late in the year.

For river level information on the North Platte call the Game and Parks Commission at Alliance, (308) 762-5605; for the Lower Platte, call the Two Rivers State Recreation Area at Valley, (402) 359-5165, and for the Elkhorn call the Fremont SRA, (402) 721-8482.

Brewers Canoers
Randy and Rich Mercure
P.O. Box 14
Valentine, NE 69201
(402) 376-2046, (402) 376-3548
Niobrara River
Max. rapids: None
Brewers Canoe runs guided and unguided canoe trips of one to two days on the gentle, scenic Niobrara River. The Niobrara, easy enough for novices, flows through canyons, lush river valleys, and birch woods. It offers fishing for catfish and trout and chances to spot deer, turkeys, eagles, buffalo, and elk.

Brewers Canoe's season runs from May to October.

Graham Canoe Outfitters
Douglas and Twyla Graham
HC-13, Box 16-A
Valentine, NE 69201
(402) 376-3708
Niobrara River
Max. rapids: I-II
Graham Canoe Outfitters runs guided and unguided canoe trips of one to two days on the Niobrara River. This prairie river is swift but gentle, offering easy paddling for novice and experienced canoeists alike. Trips run through the heart of the sand hills in a scenic river valley featuring views of cliffs, pine and deciduous woods, and abundant wildlife, including deer, turkeys, eagles, hawks, beavers, raccoons,

Class I rapids on the Niobrara River. Courtesy of Alan Stoker/Rocky Fork Outfitters, Valentine, Nebraska.

Swimming and paddling downriver on the Niobrara. Courtesy of Alan Stoker/Rocky Fork Outfitters, Valentine, Nebraska.

and ducks. The Niobrara's clean waters also offer fishing for catfish and trout.

Graham Canoe Outfitter's season is from April to November.

Oregon Trail Wagon Train
Kevin Howard
Route 2, Box 502
Bayard, NE 69334
(308) 586-1850
North Platte River
Max. rapids: None
Oregon Trail Wagon Train rents canoes for half-day trips on the North Platte River, a clean, gentle river suited for paddlers of all ages. These relaxing float trips offer a chance to paddle old fur-traders' routes, fish for catfish, trout, pike, and carp; and watch for deer, wild turkeys, coyotes, ducks, and geese.

During its May-to-October season, Oregon Trail also offers chuck-wagon cookouts and wagon train treks in authentic-style covered wagons.

Canoeists explore the shoreline along the North Platte River. Courtesy of Oregon Trail Wagon Train, Bayard, Nebraska.

Rocky Ford Outfitters

Alan and Mary Stokes
Box 3
Valentine, NE 69201
(402) 497-3479 (summers),
(712) 642-4422 (winters)
Niobrara River
Max. rapids: I-II

Rocky Ford Outfitters offers guided canoe trips and canoe and tube rentals on the Niobrara River. Trips last one to five days and are easy enough for beginners. The river has clean, fast-flowing water and offers scenic views of high canyon walls forested with pine, birch and oaks. Paddlers can body surf through chutes, fish for catfish and trout, and glimpse deer, wild turkeys, bobcats, minks, otters, and beavers.

Rocky Ford also offers camping, a bath house with showers, family cabins, a bunkhouse, and a camp store. The season is from April to September.

Nevada

The driest state in the Union with an average annual rainfall of less than eight inches, Nevada is known more for its deserts than its rivers. And indeed there is very little rafting or canoeing in the state. Most of Nevada's rivers run literally into the sand. Only a few have outlets to the sea: the Virgin and Muddy rivers join the Colorado in the southeastern corner of the state, while the Owyhee, Bruneau, and Salmon flow northward to Idaho's Snake River. All the others run into depressions (known as sinks) or closed lakes. The snow-fed Humboldt River, for instance, flows 300 miles southwestward from the mountains in the northeast, only to vanish in the Humboldt Sink.

Such canoeing as exists is chiefly on the lakes - notably Lake Tahoe on the California state line, Pyramid Lake to the north, and Lake Mead behind Hoover Dam on the Colorado River. But the vast majority of lake fishermen use power boats. Rafts can be rented on the Truckee River near Fanny Bridge, close to the point at which it leaves Lake Tahoe, for a leisurely float on this quiet stream.

In good years there is some white water on the East Fork of the Carson River. But one National Forest Service ranger said that if there was any raft rental business left on this river, "it has dwindled away almost to nothing with the drought we've been having."

Nevada claims to be the most mountainous state in the Union, in number of mountains and ranges within any given area. But after six years of drought, mountain streams are so shallow that rafting is preferable to canoeing even on their lower reaches. Their headwaters are mostly too narrow for either rafting or canoeing. The rafting outfitters based in Nevada tend to operate chiefly on California rivers just across the border.

183

Davis Whitewater Expeditions
Lyle Davis
P.O. Box 86
Winnemucca, NV 89445
Snake River, Owyhee River
Max. rapids: V+

Davis Whitewater Expeditions offers guided kayak and raft trips on the Owyhee River and on the Snake River through Hell's Canyon. These tours pass through deep, narrow, high-desert canyons, offering pristine wilderness; excellent fishing for trout, bass, catfish, and sturgeon; swimming, and a chance to spot bears, otters, elk, goats, sheep, and raptors.

Trips are small and personal, provide good food and last three to six days. Davis' expeditions, which run between April and October, vary greatly in difficulty from gentle, scenic excursions to very demanding Class V adventures. Both oar-powered and paddle trips are available.

New Hampshire

With over 100 inches of snowfall a year, New Hampshire's mountains spawn some excellent whitewater streams. The snag is that many of them are only runnable when the snow thaws in the spring or after heavy rains. The gung-ho whitewater enthusiast must seize the moment, which is sometimes hard to catch. But less adventurous canoeists can paddle almost anytime on slower rivers fed by periodic dam releases. What could be more blissful than floating a clear stream amid brilliant fall foliage with the White Mountains soaring in the background?

One of the most popular paddling rivers in New Hampshire is the Androscoggin along a 30-mile stretch from Errol to Berlin. It is the only run in the state that combines summer-long canoeing over a good distance with enjoyable Class I-II white water. Between its three sets of rapids this section of the Androscoggin has long spells of flat water and several campsites accessible by both car and canoe. Due to lakes and dams, the river's clean water maintains a fairly steady flow all summer long.

Another dependable stream for summer canoeing is the Pemigewasset, which has a short 2.5-mile whitewater run starting at Bristol Gorge, near Bristol. It is rated Class II-III and Class IV at high water. Upstream, the East Branch of the Pemigawasset has a six-mile Class IV run down to North Woodstock that provides a hairy adventure in April. But it is also runnable in May and after heavy rains. The name Pemigawasset is an Indian term that has been evocatively translated as "valley of the winding water among the mountain pines."

The long Connecticut River divides New Hampshire from both Quebec to the north and Vermont to the west before heading down through Massachusetts to the sea. The actual state line follows the low water mark along the Vermont side, so the full river's breadth belongs to New Hampshire. Paddlers on the broad and stately Connecticut can still see traces of the river's earlier use as a waterway to float logs downstream to lumber mills. These include log cribs — massive artificial islands built of logs and boulders — and iron rings in the rocks to which log-boom chains were attached. Floaters of today can marvel at the toughness of the river men and their teams of horses who kept the logs moving past the icy rapids.

The Mad River, which runs into the Pemigawasset north of Plymouth, is one of those whitewater streams that experts have to catch during the few weeks a year when it is runnable. True to its name, the Mad River comes tumbling like crazy out of the White Mountains when the snows melt in April. It provides 8-12 miles of nearly continuous Class III-IV white water as it roars down the attractive Waterville Valley toward Campton Upper Village.

For a change of pace, the Saco River is a great cruising stream, with its clean water, scenic beauty, and abundance of free and open campsites on its sandy beaches and sandbars. Canoeists can make the 40-mile eastbound trip from Weston's Bridge across the Maine state line to Hiram in three days and there are several access points for shorter floats.

Near Conway in eastern New Hampshire the Swift River provides good whitewater rafting during its short season from April until mid-May. Crashing out of the heart of the White Mountains, the Swift offers eleven miles of Class III-IV rapids as it parallels the Kancamagus Highway, both above and below the Lower Falls scenic area. When it is up, the stream demands considerable technical skill from paddlers negotiating its ledge drops and steep descents.

Back Country Tours, Inc.
Allan McGroary
39 Hollis Street
Pepperell, MA 01463
(508) 433-9381, (800) 649-9381 (MA)
Merrimack River, Connecticut River, Nashua River, Souhegan River
Max. rapids: I-II

Back Country Tours, Inc., specializes in guided canoe trips and canoe rentals on "lesser known, uncrowded scenic waterways." Its trips run on the Souhegan and Merrimack rivers in New Hampshire; the Sauantacook and Nissitissit Rivers in Massachusetts; the Connecticut and Nashua Rivers in New Hampshire and Massachusetts; the Delaware River in New York, Pennsylvania, and New Jersey; the Blackwater, Sweetwater, and Juniper Rivers in Florida; and nine lakes near Long Pond Mountain in New York's Adirondacks. Several of these excursion are "vacation" trips of three to seven days that offer lodging at campgrounds, cabins, or bed-and-breakfast inns. All trips are suitable for beginners and experienced paddlers.

Back Country Tours' season runs from July to November.

Canoeing the gentle Saco River. Courtesy of Downeast Rafting, Center Conway, New Hampshire.

Balloon Inn Vermont Vacations
Scott Wright
RR 1, Box 8
Fairlee, VT 05045
(802) 333-4326, (800) 666-1946
Connecticut River
Max. rapids: I-II

Balloon Inn Vermont rents canoes from May-October for self-guided trips on the Connecticut River between Woodsville, N.H. and Orford, N.H. These trips, of one to three days, include lodging at historic inns along the river. With only Class I-II rapids to contend with, paddling is only moderately difficult, even for beginners. Along the way, floaters can enjoy the natural beauty of the river valley, and fishing for trout, pike, bass, and walleye. The company also offers bicycling, hiking, and balloon trips.

Downeast Rafting Inc.
Ned McSherry/Rick Haddicott
P.O. Box 119
Center Conway, NH 03813
(603) 447-3002, (800) 677-RAFT
Kennebec River, Dead River,
Penobscot River, Rapid River, Swift
River
Max. rapids: V+

Downeast Rafting provides guided raft trips on the Kennebec, Dead, Penobscot, Rapid and Swift Rivers, which run through the Maine woods with their wealth of wildlife. These one-day trips are offered from April to October. Rafters experience Class III-IV rapids on some streams and Class V on the technical Penobscot.

Downeast's guides are some of the most experienced and personable around. All the company's Kennebec and Dead River packages include lodging at its inn or campground, meals, grilled lunch on the raft trip and a video/slide show of the trip at the end. Various other package tours, including guided fishing trips and even combined skiing-rafting trips, are available.

Northern Waters Inc.
Ned McSherry
P.O. Box 119
Center Conway, NH 03813
(603) 447-2177, (603) 447-3801
Androscoggin River, Lake Umbagog
Max. rapids: III-IV
NACLO

Northern Waters rents canoes and runs paddling clinics on the Androscoggin and Magalloway rivers, which have everything from flat water to Class III rapids. This remote region of northern New England is noted for its excellent scenery, fishing and camping. But camping is limited to designated sites.

Northern Waters does not rent kayaks for whitewater and will only rent canoes for whitewater to experienced paddlers. But it runs a whitewater school for varying periods and skill levels. The season lasts from mid-June to Labor Day.

Saco Bound Inc.
Ned McSherry
P.O. Box 119
Center Conway, NH 03813
(603) 447-2177, (603) 447-3801
Max. rapids: None
NACLO, Saco River Recreational
Council

The Saco River is a perfect stream for family floating, and Saco Bound is ideally placed for enabling paddlers to relish it. Saco Bound rents canoes and kayaks from May 1-October 15 for periods of half a day to three days, with ample campsites available on beaches and sandbars along a 43-mile route. The company runs guided day trips with barbecue lunches on Tuesdays and Thursdays in July and August. During the summer months the crystal-clear stream is warm and levels average three to four feet, with deeper holes for swimming. Early October is the time to experience brilliant fall foliage.

Canoeing the class II and III rapids of the Androscoggin River. Courtesy of Downeast Rafting, Center Conway, New Hampshire.

New Jersey

To many paddlers, canoeing in New Jersey means the Pine Barrens. This 2,000 square-mile area in South Jersey is actually more a land of bush and brush than pines. But it is sparsely populated and its flat, sandy soil is laced with streams, swamps, and marshes. Some rivers are 40 feet wide, but the typical stream is only half that and some are so narrow that there is barely room for two canoes abreast. Since the water is tinted by tannic acid from cedars, paddling in the pinelands is often called "brown water" canoeing. Local wildlife includes beavers, otters, Pine Barrens tree frogs, eagles, and ospreys, along with some unusual plants.

The Wading River is the most popular in the Pine Barrens, with its various campgrounds and outfitters, easy canoeing, and convenient access. On summer weekends there may be hundreds of canoes on its winding waters. Another popular stream is the Batsto, which stems from marshland and then, like the Wading, flows through the Wharton State Forest. The nearby Mullica River has extensive savanna marshes and its sandy banks are great for picnicking and swimming.

Toms River, probably named after a Thomas Luker who settled among the Indians around 1700, is the most frequented river in the area outside Wharton State Forest. The river courses through stands of holly, pine, and deciduous trees.

Cedar Creek, designated Wild and Scenic by the state of New Jersey, is relatively pristine. It passes an old iron forge, former cranberry bogs, and marshes before turning into a fast-flowing stream. It, too, offers glimpses of interesting wildlife.

Much farther north, only ten miles from busy Newark Airport, lies what sounds like a most unlikely canoeing site. Yet the locals at Cranford in Union County say that the Rahway River offers tranquil canoeing past old mansions and mills. Stocked with trout and home to carp and catfish, the Rahway also sports good fishing.

Also of note, of course, is the mighty Delaware River, which divides the state from Pennsylvania and attracts thousands of boaters on summer weekends. Floating in canoes, kayaks, tubes, and rafts, they enjoy spectacular views, notably at the Delaware Water Gap. In this recreation area not far from the New York state line, the wooded Tammany and Minsi Mountains rise steeply to about 1,200 feet above the river. Paddlers wishing to escape the crowds on this stretch may explore a hidden section of the Delaware named Walpack Bend, just downstream from Bushkill, Pennsylvania, and accessible only by canoe. It provides both flat and white water as the river follows its rocky streambed. (See *Pennsylvania*.)

Further south, novices should watch out for dangerous rapids at Foul Rift, one mile below Belvedere Bridge, and the hazards in the Lumberville-Lambertville area.

Canoeing the Egg Harbor River. Courtesy of Winding River Campground, May's Landing, New Jersey.

Saco Bound Inc.
Ned McSherry
P.O. Box 119
Center Conway, NH 03813
(603) 447-2177, (603) 447-3801
Max. rapids: None
NACLO, Saco River Recreational Council

The Saco River is a perfect stream for family floating, and Saco Bound is ideally placed for enabling paddlers to relish it. Saco Bound rents canoes and kayaks from May 1-October 15 for periods of half a day to three days, with ample campsites available on beaches and sandbars along a 43-mile route. The company runs guided day trips with barbecue lunches on Tuesdays and Thursdays in July and August.

During the summer months the crystal-clear stream is warm and levels average three to four feet, with deeper holes for swimming. Early October is the time to experience brillant fall foliage, when the White Mountains are ablaze with color.

Adams Creek Rentals, Inc.

Robert Wayne Adams
694 Atsion Road
Vincentown, NJ 08088
(609) 268-0189
Mullica River, Batsto River
Max. rapids: None
   Adams Canoe Rentals rents canoes
and kayaks for one- and two- day
trips on the Mullica and Batsto Rivers.
These gentle, clean, flat-water
streams offer easy paddling, beaches
for swimming and scenic, wooded
banks. Wildlife is abundant and
there's fishing for pike, catfish, and
some smallmouth bass. The livery's
season runs from April to November.

Cedar Creek Campground

Debra Fleming
1052 Route 9
Bayville, NJ 08721
(908) 269-1413
Cedar Creek
Max. rapids: None
   Cedar Creek Campground offers
relaxing one-day trips on Cedar
Creek, designated "wild and scenic"
by the state of New Jersey. These
easy floats are fine for beginning
canoeists and anyone wanting a tranquil, scenic trip. Paddlers pass
through the heart of the New Jersey
Pine Barrens and offer views of cedar
groves, cranberry bogs, deer,
beavers, shorebirds, and waterfowl.
Along the way, they can also fish for
catfish, and pickerel.
   The campground, just ten miles
from the Atlantic Ocean and Bernegat
Bay, offers wooded tent and R.V.
sites, modern restrooms, a swimming
pool and hot tub, and a fully-
equipped convenience store and deli.
The season runs from April-November.

Cranford Boat and Canoe Co.

Frank Betz
250 Springfield Avenue
Cranford, NJ 07016
(908) 272-6991
Rahway River
Max. rapids: None
   Cranford Boat & Canoe Company
rents canoes and kayaks for one- day
trips on the Rahway River, a tranquil,
scenic stream which meanders
through the township of Cranford
and the Union County Park system.
These trips offer views of old mansions, mills, deer, and many bird
species.
   The Rahway's clean waters also
offer carp, catfish, and trout fishing.
The season runs from March to
December.

Mick's Canoe Rental, Inc.

Wayne A. Wilson and Carl R. Zirkel
Route 563, Box 45 (Jenkins)
Chatsworth, NJ 07040
(609) 726-1380
*Wading River, Oswego River, Oswego
Lake, Harrisville Lake*
Max. rapids: None
NACLO
   Mick's Canoe Rental rents canoes
and kayaks on the Wading River, Oswego River, Oswego Lake and Harrisville Lake. Trips on these rivers last
one or two days. They run almost entirely within Wharton State Forest and
follow a meandering course through
pine oak and cedar forest. Gravel
bars and swimming holes are plentiful, giving paddlers many chances to
swim in the rivers' clean, spring- fed
waters or fish for pickerel, catfish,
and perch. Guests can also enjoy
watching deer, turtles, frogs, snakes,
beavers, hawks, and occasional
ospreys during the livery's April-
November season.

Children tubing on the Egg Harbor River. Courtesy of Winding River Campground, May's Landing, New Jersey.

Paradise Lake Campground

Walter D. Lohman
Route 206, P.O. Box 46
Paradise Lake Road
Hammenton, NJ 08037
(609) 561-7095
Robinson's Creek, Mullica River
Max. rapids: None

Paradise Lake Campground offers canoe rentals on Robinson's Creek and the Mullica River. These flat-water trips pass through the protected scenic pine and oak woods of Wharton State Forest. On these trips, paddlers can swim, camp and fish for bass, pickerel, catfish, sunfish, and perch. They can also spot occasional deer, otters, beavers, and raccoons.

During its April-to-October season, Paradise Lake Campground also offers tent and R.V. camping with hot showers.

Winding River Campground

James A. Horsey
R.D. 2, Box 246
Mays Landing, NJ 08330
(609) 625-3191
Great Egg Harbor River
Max. rapids: None

Winding River Campground rents canoes and tubes for day trips on the Egg Harbor River, a scenic, wooded flat-water river. Trips are easy and allow plenty of time for leisurely fishing for pickerel, eel, and catfish, and watching for turtles, deer, ducks, geese, and other wildlife. During the May-to-September season, the campground also offers tent and R.V. camping, cabin rentals, a heated pool, and a general store.

New Mexico

N ew Mexico is the land of the Rio Grande, a monarch among rivers. The second longest river in the nation, the "Great River" rises on the Continental Divide in the southern Colorado Rockies and flows southward through the middle of the New Mexico desert. Then it forms the boundary between Texas and Mexico before discharging into the Gulf of Mexico at Brownsville. Only the Missouri-Mississippi system surpasses its nineteen-hundred-mile length.

Most people think of New Mexico as dry and parched. But during the May-June spring runoff the Upper Rio Grande in the north rages with a fury to tax the skills of the most daring river runner. Some of its rapids are unrunnable and paddlers must struggle over portage trails several hundred feet high. The Rio Grande Gorge starts just north of the Colorado-New Mexico state line and continues for fifty miles to Taos Junction. A charter member of the National Wild and Scenic Rivers system, the Gorge offers sheer rock walls up to two hundred feet high, rising to eight hundred feet at the Red River confluence. One 12-mile stretch of the Gorge contains thunderous whitewater that ranks as Class VI and extremely hazardous. Guided raft trips traverse the so-called Taos Box well south of this dangerous area but still within the Gorge. It is an exciting 16-mile trip with Class III-IV rapids, 600-foot vertical cliffs and impressive canyon scenery. One outfitter promises a "frisky" run certain to get everyone wet.

The Lower Rio Grande Gorge offers the Pilar Canyon run, a popular family frolic through five miles of Class III rapids. The season for these Rio floats runs from April to early July.

Westward of the Rio Grande in northern New Mexico lies the Rio Chama, another Wild and Scenic river. The upper section from Plaza Blanca to El Vado Lake is an interesting day trip past meadows in a deep canyon. Its rapids are chiefly Class III and may involve some portaging; rafting on El Vado Lake is inadvisable because of strong winds. More popular is the 33-mile run from El Vado Dam to Abiquiu Lake, a two-day trip that runs through vivid red sandstone canyons with plenty of forests and wildlife. Here the rapids are rated Class I-III and the time to go is usually from late April to early July.

A beautiful trip in southwestern New Mexico is the Wilderness Run on the Gila River, some 32 miles of paddling through wide green canyons with springs, lots of wildlife and Class II-III rapids. But the water flow is usually either too much or too little so that the paddling season may be only a week or two in some years. Check with the National Weather Service or the U.S. Geological Survey for flow levels if you want to run this one on your own.

East of Santa Fe the Pecos River changes from a turbulent mountain stream to a pastoral float as it runs from Cowles to Villanueva State Park. The last 25 miles of this stretch passes several picturesque Spanish Colonial villages as the Pecos flows through rocky canyons. It is runnable in May-June during rainy years. Although it rates only Class I-II, its hazards include many dangerous fences, low bridges and several dams that must be portaged.

Bill Dvorak's Kayak and Rafting Expeditions
Bill and Jaci Dvorak
17921 U.S. Highway 285
Nathrop, CO 81236
(719) 539-6851, (800) 824-3795
Arkansas River, Colorado River, Green River, Gunnison River, North Platte River, Dolores River, Middle Fork and Main Salmon River, Rio Grande, Salt River
Max. rapids: V+
America Outdoors, Colorado River Outfitters Association, Utah Guides and Outfitters, New Mexico River Outfitters Association

Dvorak's runs a wide array of guided and unguided trips through 29 canyons on a total of 10 rivers in Colorado, Utah, and New Mexico. Scenery ranges from Alpine to desert, and whitewater ranges from Class I to Class V. Guests also have a choice of touring by canoe, kayak, or raft. With this selection of locations and trips, Dvorak's has offerings to suit any individual or group.

Trips run for one to 13 days between March and October and permit time for trout fishing and viewing deer, elk, bears, eagles, beavers, and coyotes.

Far Flung Adventures, Inc.
Steve Harrison/Mike Davidson
P.O. Box 377
Terlingua, TX 79852
(915) 371-2489, (800) 359-4138 (reservations)
Rio Chama
Max. rapids: Rio Grande
America Outdoors, Rio Grande Guides Association

Far Flung Adventures specializes in taking rafters on camping trips through the ruggedly beautiful Big Bend region of Texas as well as in other states in the U.S. and Mexico. Its tours last from one to seven days in a season running from January to December. It caters to everyone from novices to whitewater experts who can meet Class V+ challenges.

The remoteness of the Rio Grande's Big Bend National Park, its canyons and wildlife combine with good fishing to make these trips unforgettable. Far Flung Adventures offers paddling lessons as well as camping, fishing and swimming.

Hawk, I'm Your Sister
Beverly Antaeus
P.O. Box 9109
Santa Fe, NM 87504
(505) 984-2268
Abiquiu Lake
Max. rapids: III-IV
Hawk, I'm Your Sister of Santa Fe specializes in women's wilderness canoe and raft trips. Its year-round program is geared to "women of all ages, shapes, sizes and skill levels" with guided trips in five states and four foreign locations. Its aim is to "teach you the language of the forests, canyons, deserts and waterways" in a safe and non-competitive environment. It takes paddlers on the Abiquiu Lake in New Mexico and on the Rio Grande in Texas, with other excursions as far afield as Alaska, Peru and China.

Kokopelli Rafting Adventures
Jon Asher, Dennis Holmes
1702 Medio
Santa Fe, NM 87501
(505) 988-5799, (505) 986-1152
Rio Grande, Rio Chama
Max. rapids: III-IV
America Outdoors
Kokopelli Rafting Adventures runs guided paddle-raft trips on the Rio Grande and Rio Chama. Two half-day trips on the Rio Grande are the "Race Course," five miles of challenging, continuous rapids, and Otowi Bridge to Buckman Crossing, a short float trip through beautiful canyon scenery. A full-day trip on the Rio Grande, Whiterock Canyon to Frijoles Canyon, is nine miles of moderate rapids and still water, combined with a scenic canyon hike. Overnight trips through Whiterock Canyon are also available. Finally, the company offers a full-day Rio Chama trip, a winding, eight-mile course thorough magnificent, multi-colored canyon walls. Kokopelli also has seminars in art,

music, map and compass, archaeology, and tracking.
New Mexico trips run between April and October. In November, February, and March, the company has trips in Texas' Big Bend National Park.

New Wave Rafting Co.
Steve and Kathy Miller
Route 5, Box 302A
Santa Fe, NM 87501
(505) 984-1444
Rio Grande, Rio Chama
Max. rapids: III-IV
New Mexico River Outfitter Association
New Wave Rafting of Santa Fe offers half-day to three-day guided raft trips on the Rio Grande and Rio Chama for "anybody with a sense of adventure." They run through great scenery: high desert country and the Rio Grande volcanic gorge. Beavers and muskrat can be seen, and anglers may hook brown and rainbow trout.
The full-day Taos Box trip on the Rio Grande traverses sixteen miles of wilderness gorge with "rapids guaranteed to get you wet." This exciting trip, with its Class IV+ white water, is not for the timid. Less demanding are the Class II-III rapids on the Rio Chama, where floaters spend two nights and three days paddling 30 miles through canyons of vividly colored sandstone.

Wolf Whitewater
Jack O'Neil
P.O. Box 666
Sandia Park, NM 87047
(505) 281-5042
*Rio Grande - Upper Taos Box, Rio
Grande - Lower Pilar Canyon*
Max. rapids: III-IV
America Outdoors

Wolf Whitewater of Sandia Park
has a "very frisky" full-day
whitewater rafting trip on the Rio
Grande Gorge (Taos Box) for people
aged 12-60. It also offers half-day
runs in the five-mile Pilar Canyon
stretch of the same gorge for family
floaters aged 8-80, in both paddle
and oar rafts. In addition, the company provides skilled canoe and
kayak instruction.

The scenery on this Wild and
Scenic River is superb, with 600-foot
canyon walls along a seventeen-mile
chasm. Muskrat, beavers and birds of
many species may be found, along
with trout fishing.

New York

Endowed with an abundance of mountain streams, rivers and lakes, New York has it all. Up in the southern Adirondacks the headwaters of the mighty Hudson provide great scenery and rugged whitewater. In the southwestern Adirondacks the Moose River system combines grand wilderness with rapids that even experts treat with respect. Less than two hours drive from New York City flows the Delaware, with its scenic 76-mile run from Hancock to Port Jervis (see *Pennsylvania*). In the Catskills, not far from the Delaware's headwaters, slalom races are held the first weekend in June on Esopus Creek's exciting whitewater. Out at the western end of the state the Genesee cuts across from Pennsylvania and empties into Lake Ontario at Rochester, offering attractive paddling through Genesee Valley.

The Hudson is the first river that comes to mind when one thinks of New York waterways. The Hudson River Gorge provides 16 miles of almost continuous whitewater as the river rushes through a vertical-cliff canyon. Outfitters offer one-day rafting trips from the end of March until the beginning of June, resuming from Labor Day to Columbus Day. The Gorge rapids are roughest in April-May after the snowmelt and spring rains, some reaching into the Class IV+ category. With such thrills at hand, it is no surprise that the Gorge trip attracts more than twenty thousand rafters a year. Some are also drawn to the area by the excellent trout, pike and bass fishing, and by the abundant wildlife ranging from loons and hawks to bears and beavers.

For the rugged outdoorsman prepared to face the rigors of April in the Adirondacks, the Moose River offers some of the toughest rapids in the East. At least two of them, Tannery and Mixmaster, are Class V and definitely not for the novice. Wet suits and extra woolens are needed for protection against the cold since April is the only month the river is runnable. Rafts frequently overturn amid these complex rapids with their wide ledges and massive boulders.

Esopus Creek in the Catskills is another exciting stream set in mountain grandeur. The 25-mile canoe trail above Ashoken Reservoir depends after the April-May runoff upon water releases from upstream dams. So paddlers should check with the New York City

Board of Water Supply in Prattsville before planning summer trips. At high water, the Esopus is a trip for seasoned rapid-runners.

The Genesee meanders through a pastoral landscape in the foothills of western New York State and offers the birdwatcher much to view through his binoculars. The stretch to paddle is from Genesee, just across the Pennsylvania line, to Portageville — a well-named spot since the waterfalls just downstream in Letchworth State Park are strictly for riverbank sightseeing. But the park's 600-foot-deep gorge of shale and sandstone also contains a six-mile stretch with gentle rapids that makes a great raft trip for families. These tours begin in early April and run through October.

Long Islanders with a penchant for fishing, wildlife and easy canoeing can take a five-mile float on the Nissequogue River, in the middle of the island's North Shore near the town of Kings Park. It offers saltwater fish such as flounder in its estuary as well as trout and striped bass upstream.

Not to be omitted in any listing of New York's aquatic delights are the innumerable lakes, especially in the Adirondacks. One of our favorites for canoeing is Cranberry Lake in a particularly unspoiled area west of Tupper Lake. But the choice is so wide that everyone can take his pick.

Adirondack River Outfitters
Box 563
Watertown, NY 13601
(800) 525-RAFT
Hudson River, Moose River, Black River, Scandaga River
Max. rapids: V+
Adirondack River Outfitters Adventures runs guided white-water raft trips on the Hudson, Moose, Black, and Scandaga Rivers. From one of its four outposts, ARO also rents inflatable kayaks and from another it rents canoes.

Trips on the Hudson feature rapids over a mile in length, with waves cresting 10 feet high. This 17-mile course is the most popular spring run in the Adirondacks. Although rated class IV, the Hudson

thrills paddlers but is not as demanding as the Moose or Black Rivers.

Trips on the Moose have intimidating rapids resembling small waterfalls. Rated as Class IV-V, Moose trips are best suited for rafters with prior white-water experience.

The most challenging of all Adirondack white-water runs is the "Big Water Black," a spring high-water trips that has a continuous and potentially dangerous three-mile rapid. Paddlers on this Class IV-V trip must have prior white-water experience. Later in the season, the "Summer Black" trip offers a challenging white-water run of towering waves and foaming hydraulics. With 14 sets of rapids packed into seven miles of river, this Class IV trip boasts more ac-

"Rocket Ride" on the Black River. Courtesy of Adirondack River Outfitters, Watertown, New York.

tion per mile than any other New York white-water run.

Finally, ARO offers trips on the Class III Scandaga, which has gentle, forgiving waves that are ideal for novice rafters and families with children.

ARO's paddle trips last one day and are available between May and October. From September to November, the company also offers oar-boat, salmon-fishing trips on the Black.

Adventure Calls
Terry Shearn
20 Ellicott Avenue
Batavia, NY 14020
(716) 343-4710
Genesee River
Max. rapids: III-IV

Adventure Calls has guided raft trips over Class III-IV rapids on the remote Cattaragus Creek and the Genesee River. Although these floats are of medium difficulty, they can be enjoyed by anyone in good health. The season starts as early as March and runs until October.

Floaters ride through a 600-foot-deep gorge and heavily wooded countryside, with a great variety of undisturbed flora. The wildlife includes deer, beavers, hawks and vultures, while the fishing covers bass, trout and salmon. Camping is available.

Adventure Sports Rafting. Co., Inc.
John Starling
P.O. Box 775
Indian Lake, NY 12842
(518) 648-5812, (800) 441-RAFT
Hudson River, Moose River
Max. rapids: V+

Adventure Sports Rafting runs guided raft trips on both the Hudson and the Moose rivers, through wilderness countryside accessible only by raft. It has a double season, from March to June and again from Labor Day to Columbus Day.

The Hudson River Gorge trip provides 16 miles of almost continuous whitewater between vertical cliffs rising from the river's edge. No experience is necessary, although the rapids range from Class III-IV to Class V+. Customers must, however, be aged at least 16.

Deer, frogs, eagles, ospreys and ravens may be spotted in this remote region. Bass and several species of trout tease the angler.

Battenkill Sportsquarters
Walter Piekarz Jr.
RD 1, Route 313
Cambridge, NY 12816
(518) 677-8868, (800) 676-8768
Battenkill River
Max. rapids: I-II
NACLO

Battenkill Sportsquarters runs guided canoe and kayak trips and rents canoes, kayaks and tubes on the Battenkill River. The Battenkill is exceptionally clean, with excellent fishing for brown trout, speckled trout, and sunfish. Its waters, with Class I rapids, are well-suited for paddlers of all levels of ability. Sportsquarters trips last one to two days and pass through a scenic region of farm land and woods inhabited by deer, owls, rabbits, ducks, beavers, and other wildlife. Sportsquarters' season runs from April to October.

Bob's Canoe Rental, Inc.
Bob Koliner
P.O. Box 529
Kings Park, NY 11754
(516) 269-9761
Nissequogue River, all Long Island waters
Max. rapids: None

Bob's Canoe Rental, which describes itself as the oldest and finest canoe livery on Long Island, offers both guided canoe trips and rental canoes. The company is located on the Nissequogue River, an unspoiled river corridor in the midst of Long Island's North Shore. Group tours go to all Long Island waters.

During the season, which runs from St. Patrick's Day to Thanksgiving, canoeists can fish for saltwater fish such as bluefish, fluke and flounder in the estuaries as well as trout and bass in the headwaters. Shorebirds, foxes, raccoons, opossums and turtles are among the local wildlife.

Canoe Center
Brian Hart
7875 Fotch Road
Batavia, NY 14020
(716) 344-4734
Black Creek, Tonawanda Creek, Genesee River
Max. rapids: I-II

Canoe Center provides guided canoe trips suitable for all comers and rents canoes and kayaks from the beginning of May through September. Paddlers can explore Black Creek, Tonawanda Creek and the Genesee River, all offering good bass, pike and trout fishing. Floating on the quiet, winding rivers, one can look for deer and a variety of other animals and birds among the trees and fields. No rapids are rated harder than Class I-II.

Campsites are available and Canoe Center also provides quality instruction in canoeing and kayaking.

Kayaker runs "Hole Bros" rapid on the Black River. Courtesy of Adirondack River Outfitters.

Eastern River Expeditions

John Connelly
Box 1173
Greenville, ME 04441
(207) 634-7238, (800) 695-2411
Moose River, Gauley River, Kennebec River, Penobscot River, Dead River
Max. rapids: V+
Maine Professional River Outfitters Association, America Outdoors

Eastern River Expeditions offers canoe rentals and guided raft and inflatable-kayak trips on five rivers in Maine, New York, and West Virginia. In Maine, paddlers can choose among whitewater trips on the Kennebec, Penobscot, and Dead Rivers. Most Maine trips are fine for novice paddlers, combining excellent wilderness scenery with Class II-IV white water. Trips on the Dead and Penobscot Rip Gorge, however, re-quire excellent conditioning. Penobscot Rip Gorge also requires intermediate or advanced paddling skills. Advanced rafting experience is a prerequisite for trips on New York's Moose River and West Virginia's Gauley River, which have Class IV-V rapids.

All trips, of one to two days, pass through wilderness, offering camping spots, clear water, fishing, and chances to spot deer, coyotes, loons, ducks, beavers, foxes, great blue herons, and other wildlife.

Lander's River Trips

Richard Lander
Box 376
Narrowsburg, NY 12764
(914) 252-3925, (800) 252-3925
Upper Delaware River
Max. rapids: I-II
NACLO, NAPSA

Lander's River Trips rents canoes, kayaks, rafts and tubes for trips of one to four days on the upper Delaware River. This scenic river, of which 72 miles lies within a National Park, offers wilderness scenery and views of deer, bears, eagles, ospreys, herons, and beavers. The Delaware's clean waters also offer excellent fishing for bass, trout, shad, walleye, perch, sunfish, suckers, and eels.

The outfitter offers trips along calm stretches for beginners, and through white water for experienced river runners. Also, as the company operates three, conveniently spaced campgrounds, paddlers on overnight trips can avoid having to carry camping equipment on the river. Rentals are available between April and October.

Middle Earth Expeditions

Wayne Failing
HCR 01 Box 37
Lake Placid, NY 12946
(518) 523-9572
*Hudson River Gorge, any lakes or
rivers in the Adirondacks*
Max. rapids: V+
*New York State Outdoor Guides Association, Hudson River Professional
Outfitters Association*

Middle Earth Expeditions provides guided trips through white water of up to Class V+ difficulty by canoe on any Adirondack lakes or rivers and by raft through the Hudson River Gorge. A small, low-volume company, it sets out to meet the needs of each individual customer, from the beginner to the expert. With this personal attention, trips can range from one to seven days during the season, which runs from April 1 to October 15.

Middle Earth Expeditions offers lessons and camping is available. The scenery in this great wilderness area is superb. So are the wildlife and the fishing.

Port Jerry Marina

Rich and Mary Kolver
HCR Box 27
Bolton Landing, NY 12814
(518) 644-3311
Lake George
Max. rapids: None

Port Jerry Marina on beautiful, crystal-clear Lake George rents canoes which customers can paddle in May-September to state-owned camping islands in the lake. Experienced canoeists, for whom the lake is best suited, can view deer, beavers, otters, turtles and many different kinds of birds. Fishing is for small and largemouth bass, northern pike and lake trout. Camping is available, and the lake is good for swimming.

Racquette River Outfitters, Inc.

Carol Kennedy/Rob Frenette
P.O. Box 653
Tupper Lake, NY 12986
(518) 359-3228
all Adirondack canoe routes
Max. rapids: None

Racquette River Outfitters services all the Adirondack canoe routes with guided canoe trips and rentals of both canoes and kayaks. It plans custom trips to fit paddlers' vacation needs and schedules, varying in difficulty from leisurely to challenging.

Customers enjoy clean waters with good fishing amid grand mountain scenery. On the hillsides the canoeist may see whitetail deer and black bear while eagles and ospreys circle overhead. Otters and loons swim on the surface and anglers hook smallmouth bass, lake trout, brook trout, walleye, pike and salmon. Camping is available and the season runs from May to October 15.

Town Tinker Tube Rental

Harry G. Jameson, III
P.O. Box 404, Bridge Street
Phoenicia, NY 12464
(914) 688-5553
Esopus Creek
Max. rapids: I-II
American Rivers, NYSHTA

Town Tinker Tube Rental has rented its tubes to over 350,000 customers during its 12 years in business beside Esopus Creek. Tubers wallow in a clean stream that takes them through five miles of beautiful wooded scenery in the Catskill Mountains. The upper half of the stretch is for experienced tubers who revel in Class I-II whitewater.

Wildlife and fish are abundant, with the Esopus famous for its trout. The season runs from May 1 through September and camping is available.

Small waterfalls feed into the Black River. Courtesy of Adirondack River Outfitters, New York.

Unicorn Expeditions
Jay Schurman
P.O. Box T
Brunswick, ME 04011
(207) 725-2255, (800) UNICORN
Hudson River, Moose River
Max. rapids: V+
America Outdoors

Unicorn Expeditions offers guided canoe, kayak, and raft trips and canoe rentals for trips of one to six days on the Kennebec, Penobscot, and Dead Rivers in Maine; the Hudson and Moose Rivers in New York; and the Deerfield River in Massachusetts. These trips range widely in difficulty to suit all skill levels from beginner to expert. Moose River trips have some of the wildest white water in the Northeast; the dam-controlled Penobscot and Kennebec Rivers ensure Class V white water all summer long; and the Hudson's spring high water offers 16 miles of exhilarating Class III and IV rapids.

Among the wildlife to see on these trips are moose, bald eagles, bears, deer, and osprey. There is also fishing for bass, salmon, and trout. During its April-to-October season, Unicorn also offers "getaway" packages, which include rafting and lodge or inn accommodations.

Whitewater Willie's Sales & Rental Inc.
William O. Elston
17 West Main Street
Port Jervis, NY 12771
(800) 233-RAFT
Delaware River
Max. rapids: I-II
NACLO

Whitewater Willie's Sales and Rentals has canoes, rafts and tubes for rent by paddlers interested in fishing and exploring Hawks Nest Gorge on the Delaware River. The fishing is excellent, including shad, trout, bass, pike and eel. Floaters may view a very wide variety of wildlife as they negotiate Class I-II rapids.

The company offers paddling lessons, and campsites are available. Whitewater Willie's season runs from May 1-October 12.

North Carolina

North and South Carolina belong together like Siamese twins, bound by a shared river system flowing from the Blue Ridge Mountains in the west toward the Atlantic in the east. Tumbling in youthful exuberance through steep gorges with waterfalls and rapids, these rivers slacken their pace as they develop middle-age spread, cross the rolling Piedmont hills and descend to the coastal plain. Headwaters of the 341-mile Savannah River arise in the western mountains of North Carolina to form the waterway that divides South Carolina from Georgia. The Broad, Catawba and Yadkin Rivers also originate in the Blue Ridge, with the Yadkin flowing into the mighty Pee Dee. As they run southeast these rivers connect the Carolinas like arteries linking vital bodily organs. And further east the Cape Fear and Black Rivers follow a similar course before disgorging their waters at Wilmington.

In its western mountains North Carolina has many thrills to offer the river-runner, especially among the surging waves and high waters of spring and early summer. Among favorite rivers is the dam-controlled Nantahala just south of the Great Smoky Mountain National Park. Raftable from March to October, the Nantahala Gorge is a beautiful float which provides easy paddling for families and novices. The chasm is deep and forested with rhododendron and mountain laurel. Outfitters offer guided and unguided half-day trips on the eight-mile run, which is mostly rated Class II. At the end, the exciting plunge through Nantahala Falls provides a Class III climax to test beginners' newly-learned skills. Small wonder, then, that over 100,000 rafters run the Nantahala every season.

The French Broad River provides good family rafting as it, too, churns through spectacular gorges in the Pisgah National Forest. In places, the mountains rise more than 1,000 feet above the river. Its water flow, however, is not as dependable as the Nantahala's in the summer. On the eight-mile stretch between Barnard and Hot Springs the French Broad has Class II-IV rapids alternating with placid pools.

The free-flowing Nolichucky has a great one-day Class III-IV springtime float across the Tennessee state line through what is claimed to be the deepest gorge in the Southeast. Mountains of the Pisgah and Cherokee National Forests rise fully 2,000 feet above the water. Guided "ducky" (inflatable kayak) trips are popular when the water level drops in the summer.

Big Laurel Creek has exciting spring rafting for whitewater connoisseurs close to its confluence with the French Broad near Hot Springs. When in full spate, this is a very fast river with Class IV rapids and big ledge drops. At one point it drops eighty feet in a half-mile stretch of furious rapids.

Lovers of nature who enjoy more placid waters like to bask in the upper reaches of the New River in the northwestern corner of North Carolina. The North and South Forks which converge just south of the Virginia state line provide 100 miles of gentle paddling through forested mountains and pastoral valleys, enlivened by deer, wild turkeys, wild ducks, and herons.

The Haw River, a favorite Piedmont float for city dwellers in central North Carolina, provides great scenery, canoeing and wildlife. It offers easy rapids on its rocky course through a narrow valley before it runs into Lake Jordan close to Durham.

In the coastal plain of eastern North Carolina are the great rivers that flow into Albemarle and Pamlico Sounds: the Neuse, the Pamlico, with its highly scenic Tar River tributary, the Roanoke and the Chowan. Paddlers on the Roanoke should watch for great fluctuations in flow when dam waters are released. There is much fishing on the Roanoke just below Lake Gaston when the rockfish (striped bass) are spawning.

For those who yearn for a complete escape from urban civilization, Ocracoke Island on North Carolina's Outer Banks offers naturalist-guided trips in open kayaks. These take the paddler along the island's Pamlico Sound shore and inlets with their wealth of sea birds, turtles, otters, fish, shellfish and saltmarsh wildlife. Since almost the entire island belongs to the Cape Hatteras National Seashore, this is sea kayaking in a wonderfully unspoiled setting. But take industrial-strength bug repellent in July and August.

Blue Ridge Outing Company

Bob and Cindy Mattingly
Highway 74/441
Whittier, NC 28789
(704) 586-3510
Tuckasegee River
Max. rapids: I-II
NACLO

Blue Ridge Outing Co. offers guided canoe and raft trips and canoe, raft, and tube rentals on the Tuckasegee River. Trips last one day and are of easy to moderate difficulty, with some runs suitable for all ages, including young children. The Tuckasegee, a clean mountain river, runs through a scenic gorge and offers paddlers a chance to spot fish, birds, beavers, and turtles. The river also has excellent fishing for trout, smallmouth bass, and catfish.

The season runs from April to October.

Carolina Wilderness

Glenn Goodrich
P.O. Box 488
Hot Springs, NC 28743
(800) 872-7437
French Broad River, Nolichucky
River, Big South Fork Gorge
Max. rapids: III-IV

Carolina Wilderness offers guided raft trips and canoe and raft rentals for one- and two-day trips on the French Broad River, Nolichucky River, and Big South Fork Gorge. The French Broad River trips, easy enough for beginners, pass through a scenic forest gorge. The Nolichucky trips, which are more challenging, travel through the deepest gorge in the Southeast.

Carolina Wilderness, with three riverside outposts, also offers hot showers, inflatable "funyak" trips, and hot barbecue lunches on full-day guided trips. The outfitter's season runs from March to November.

Rapids on the French Broad River draw grins all round on trip by Carolina Wilderness, Hot Springs, North Carolina. Courtesy of Whitewater Photography.

An inflatable kayak gives a paddler an exciting ride through "On the Rocks Rapid" on the Nolichucky River during a trip run by High Mountain Expeditions. Photo by Johnny Meeks, courtesy of Blue Ridge Mountain Images.

Fast River Rafts and Rentals
Nolan Whitesell
Box 51, U.S. 19 West
Nantahala Gorge
Bryson City, NC 28702
(704) 488-2386, (800) GET-RAFT
(reservations)
Nantahala River
Max. rapids: III-IV
North American Paddle Sports Association

Fast River Rafts & Rentals offers guided and unguided canoe, inflatable kayak, and raft trips on the Nantahala River. The stretches paddled have exceptionally clear, clean water with continuous Class II and III white water, suitable for beginning and intermediate rafters and intermediate and advanced canoeists. All paddlers can enjoy the spectacular mountain scenery as the Nantahala winds its way through a deep, heavily forested gorge with views of hardwoods and abundant birds and small game. The river also offers good fishing for brown and rainbow trout.

Raft trips are available between May and September. Canoe trips run year-round.

French Broad Rafting Company
Ron and Sandy West
1 Thomas Branch Road
Marshall, NC 28753
(704) 649-3574, (800) 842-3189
French Broad River
Max. rapids: III-IV

French Broad River Rafting Company offers guided one-day raft trips on the French Broad River. These trips, with Class III-IV rapids, are exciting but not strenuous and are fine for paddlers age eight and older, as the company always includes a guide in each of its rafts. All trips offer challenging water, the striking mountain scenery of Pisgah National Forest, and a chance to spot herons, deer, ospreys, and muskrats. The river also has excellent fishing for bass, catfish, muskie, and gar.

The outfitter's season runs from April to November.

Great Smokies Rafting Co.
Ray McLeod, Manager
3 Highway 19 West
Bryson City, NC 28713
(800) 277-6302
Nantahala River
Max. rapids: III-IV

Great Smokies Rafting Co. offers guided and unguided raft trips on the Nantahala River, an especially clear river with excellent scenery, trout fishing, and Class II-III white water. Trips last a half day and are fine for families with children age seven and older.

The company's trips run through the beautiful Nantahala Gorge, which features brook, rainbow, and brown trout, and birds, deer, occasional turkeys, and other wildlife. The company's season is from April to October.

High Mountain Expeditions
Dave and Jacquelyn Jonston
P.O. Box 1299
Blowing Rock, NC 28605
(704) 295-4200
Nolichucky River, Watauga River, Wilson Creek
Max. rapids: V+
America Outdoors

High Mountain Expeditions runs guided raft and inflatable kayak trips of one to two days on the Nolichucky River, Watauga River, and Wilson Creek. Trips range from easy to wild, with runs to suit all ages and experience levels. The "section 5" Watauga trip is ideal for families with very small children, offering fast-moving water, Class I-II rapids, pastoral scenery, and abundant Canada geese and ducks. The "section 3" Watauga trip is a small-raft or "funyak" trip on a narrow, Class III stretch of the river

in a beautiful forested setting. Watauga Gorge is a heart-pounding Class V trip for experienced, energetic paddlers only. Wilson Creek is a creek-rafters treat, running through a narrow gorge with steep granite walls and Class III-IV white water in one of the country's deepest gorges east of the Grand Canyon.

High Mountain Expeditions, open year-round, also offers caving, backpacking, and hiking trips.

Nantahala Outdoor Center
41 U.S. Highway West
Bryson City, NC 28713
(704) 488-2175, (800) 232-RAFT
Nantahala River, French Broad River, Ocoee River, Nolichucky River, Chatooga River
Max. rapids: III-IV
America Outdoors

Nantahala Outdoor Center (NOC) runs guided and unguided trips of one to 21 days on five rivers in North Carolina, South Carolina, and Tennessee. Trips are by canoe, raft, or inflatable kayak.

Nantahala River trips, run near Great Smoky Mountain National Park, offer an excellent whitewater experience for beginners and families. Runs on the French Broad River, another ideal river for family rafting, wind through a spectacular gorge in the Pisgah National Forest. The Ocoee is a favorite of whitewater enthusiasts, with big waves and constant action on its course through Cherokee National Forest. The Nolichucky offers high-water excitement in spring, gentler rafting and kayak trips in late spring and early summer, and stunning scenery at any time. The Chattooga boasts some of the finest white water in the Southeast as it tumbles through the Chattahoochee and Sumter National Forests. NOC has Chattooga trips to match any paddler's skill, beginner to

Kids ride up front for the best view of the excitement on this Carolina Wilderness trip on the Nolichucky River. Photo courtesy of Whitewater Photography, Marshall, North Carolina.

advanced. NOC also offers lessons during its March-to-November season.

New River Outfitters
Randy Revis
P.O. Box 433
Highway 221 S
Jefferson, NC 28640
(919) 982-9192
New River
Max. rapids: I-II

New River Outfitters offers guided canoe trips and canoe and tube rentals for trips of one to six days on the New River, a designated Wild and Scenic River. Most trips have Class I rapids, making them ideal for beginners, families, groups, and canoe campers. Set in the mountains, the stretches paddled offer views of cliffs, pasture land, and deer, wild turkeys, ducks, herons, and other wildlife. The New River also offers excellent fishing for smallmouth bass, trout, and rock bass. New River Outfitters rents camping gear and operates an historic general store offering food, supplies, mountain crafts, and regional specialties. The season runs from April to October.

Ride the Wind
Tony Sylvester
Box 352
Ocracoke, NC 27960
(919) 928-6311
Pamlico Sound and estuary waters
Max. rapids: None

Ride the Wind offers guided and unguided sea-kayak trips on Pamlico Sound and estuary waters along Cape Hatteras National Seashore. Trips last from one-half day to two days, are suitable for beginners and veteran sea kayakers, and offer a chance to explore scenic, unspoiled marshland and spot many species of fish, birds, crustacea, mollusks, and plants. In these shallow waters paddlers also can stop to fish and gather clams, oysters, scallops, or crabs. And on guided trips, paddlers can receive kayaking instruction and learn about the area's natural history.

During its April-to-November season, Ride the Wind also offers guidebooks, apparel, and supplies at its Ocracoke headquarters.

River Runners' Emporium
H.M. DuBose
201 Albemarle Street
Durham, NC 27701
(919) 688-2001
Haw River and other North Carolina rivers
Max. rapids: III-IV

River Runners' Emporium rents canoes and kayaks year-round for trips on local rivers, principally the Haw River.

Rock Rest Adventures
Joe Jacob
Route 2, Box 424
Pittsboro, NC 27312
(919) 542-5502
Haw River, Cape Fear River, Black River
Max. rapids: III-IV
NACLO

Rock Rest Adventures rents canoes on the Haw River and leads guided trips in North Carolina, Alaska, and Florida. On the Haw, the 30-mile segment from Swepsonville to Lake Jor-

Paddlers enjoy a group outing on the French Broad River. The trip is by Carolina Wilderness; the photo is by Whitewater Photography, Marshall, N.C.

dan offers the best in canoeing, beautiful scenery, and wildlife observation. Below Swepsonville, the Haw flows through a narrow valley with slopes lined with hardwoods and pines and topped by 200-foot bluffs. Here the river has numerous islands, footholds for alder, willow, river birch, and sycamore. Deer, turkeys, great blue herons, ospreys, kingfishers, beavers, and raccoons are abundant. Also, bass, sunfish, and crappie fishing is good. The Haw River livery service runs from March to November.

Rock Rest Adventures' guided trips are to the Cape Fear River and Black River in North Carolina, the Nenana River and Swan Lake system in Alaska, and the Everglades in Florida.

Rolling Thunder River Company
Ken and Dina Miller
P.O. Box 88
Almond, NC 28702
(704) 488-2030, (800) 344-5838
Nantahala River, French Broad River, Nolichucky River, Ocoee River, Chattooga River
Max. rapids: III-IV
America Outdoors

Rolling Thunder River Co. runs guided canoe, kayak, and raft trips and rents canoes, kayaks, rafts, and "funyaks" on five rivers in North Carolina, Tennessee, and South Carolina. Trips on the Nantahala have Class II-III rapids, are easy enough for beginners and families, and pass through the beautiful Nantahala Gorge. Full-day, wild-water raft trips are available on the Ocoee. These trips, with Class III and IV rapids, are suitable for anyone age 12 and older. Private canoe and kayak instruction on the Ocoee is also available.

On the Chattooga, Rolling Thunder offers an exciting overnight whitewater canoe trip with Class II-IV rapids, spectacular scenery, and abundant wildlife. No experience is necessary on this guided trip. Finally, a combination French Broad River-Nolichucky River raft trip is available. This two-day expedition includes a night of camping at one of the company's base camps.

Rolling Thunder's season runs from April to October.

USA RAFT
Mary Kay Heffernan
P.O. Box 277
Rowlesburg, TN 26425
(304) 454-2475, (800) USA RAFT
French Broad River, Nantahala River, New River, Gauley River, Cheat River, Tygart River, Upper Youghiogheny River, North Fork Potomac River, Nolichucky River, Ocoee River, Rio Grande
Max. rapids: II-III
America Outdoors

USA Raft is the reservation and marketing company for Appalachian Wildwaters, Rough Run Expeditions and Expeditions, Inc. Its staff can help you choose the ideal raft or "funyak" trip from among 30 different outings on ten of the best whitewater rivers in the East: the New, Gauley, Cheat, and Tygart in West Virginia; the Upper Youghiogheny and North Fork of the Potomac in Maryland; the Nolichucky and Ocoee in Tennessee, and the Nantahala, French Broad, and Nolichucky in North Carolina.

With this selection of trips, rivers, and outfitters, USA Raft can offer outings to suit paddlers of all skill levels at locations convenient to residents throughout the Middle Atlantic and Southeast. Open year-round, USA Raft also provides package trips that include meals and lodging. And, for winter paddling, it has one- to nine-day trips on the Rio Grande in Texas.

North Dakota

$L$and of Sitting Bull, Lewis and Clark, Custer and Teddy Roosevelt, the state of North Dakota epitomizes the West. Through it glides the mighty Missouri in the west and the Red River in the east, dividing it from Minnesota. These two river systems drain most of North Dakota. Out of the western Badlands run the Little Missouri, the Knife, the Heart, the Cannonball and Cedar Creek, all emptying into the Missouri on its southward journey. Tributaries of the Red River, which runs north to Canada's Hudson Bay, include the Pembina, the Goose, the Park and the Sheyenne. The Souris also flows north, from the center of the state, and the James runs from eastern North Dakota into South Dakota.

Such a great prairie state is no place for white water, even in the Badlands where the highest butte tops 3,500 feet. But the scenery varies widely, from agricultural plains and river bluffs to wooded slopes and rugged hills. Many of North Dakota's canoeing waters are seasonal, so paddlers should check water levels with the state's Canoe Hotline in Bismarck (in-state 1-800-472-2100, or out-of-state 1-800-437-2077) before setting out.

North Dakota's only State Scenic River is the Little Missouri, which offers a panoramic view of the wild Badlands. This fine stream can, however, only be paddled in May. It provides many recreational opportunities as it runs through Theodore Roosevelt National Park and Little Missouri State Park, including camping and horseback riding. Bison roam the Roosevelt park along with mule deer, coyotes, red foxes, and bobcats, while the occasional golden eagle or prairie falcon soars above the river valley.

For those who prefer to canoe later in the season, the Sheyenne is a good bet. Runnable from May through July, this river cuts through rolling hills, wide bottomland forests, open prairie, and agricultural land. Lake Ashtabula is well-known for its fishing and the scenic river below its dam is especially popular with canoeists, as is the neighboring James.

In the northeast corner of the state, the Pembina meanders through a valley of woodland tranquillity. Pembina Gorge, extending from Walhalla to the Canadian border, is known to biologists as a meeting place of North America's central grasslands and forests, home to many unusual plant and animal species. The Pembina's mild white water attracts paddlers for canoeing, rafting, and tubing in the spring and early summer. Ashore, moose and elk thrive in the woods, the last surviving native forest of significant size in the state.

The Red River along the Minnesota border cuts through farmland and small tracts of prairie rich in native grasses and wildflowers. Fishing is popular among anglers from cities along its route, but canoeing, in May and June, is hampered by many dams that must be portaged.

The Souris River, which loops down from Canada and returns northward after traversing 80 miles of North Dakota, is a wildlife haven. Thousands of birds stop to feed and rest every year in its three national wildlife refuges, two of which contain guided canoe trails varying from three to 13 miles in length. But here, again, paddlers should watch out for lowhead dams.

Finally, the great Missouri itself is a favorite local playground for canoeists as well as power boaters, water-skiers, and fishermen. It provides excellent canoeing from May to September. But state authorities say that because of its swift current, the Missouri is best suited for experienced paddlers. Its many sandbars and gentle river bluffs make it an attractive float, good for picnicking and sunbathing.

For more detailed broadsheets describing each river's main characteristics, with maps and tables, contact the state's Parks and Recreation Department, 1424 W. Century Ave., Suite 202, Bismarck, N.D. 58501, tel. (701) 224-4887.

North Dakota State University
Outing Center, Memorial Union
Fargo, ND 58105
(701) 237-8241
BWCA, Crow Wing River
Max. rapids: None

The Outing Center, a non-profit organization at NDSU, offers guided canoe trips and canoe rentals on the Crow Wing River and in Minnesota's Boundary Waters Canoe Area. Guided trips are chiefly for NDSU students, faculty, and staff, who receive preference in making reservations. However, the general public is encouraged to participate on a "space available" basis. Canoe rentals and rentals of full camping equipment are available at very reasonable rates.

Guided trips run from 1-7 days and canoe rentals are by the day or week. Canoeing on both the Crow Wing River and BWCA is easy, flatwater paddling in clear waters with good scenery and fishing for trout, walleye, northern pike, bass, and panfish. The Outing Center's canoe trips and rentals are available from May to October. In the winter, the Center rents cross-country skis and snowshoes.

213

Ohio

P̲addlers find plenty of interesting canoe trails in Ohio. Some rivers, even in the flat northwest corner of the state, have rapids rated up to Class IV in springtime or after dam releases. Others offer a totally different kind of appeal, such as wetland canoeing through swampland alive with muskrats, raccoons, waterfowl, hawks, and owls.

Popular for family paddling is the Mohican River system near the center of the state. The Main Branch and the Black Fork can be paddled year-round, unlike the Clear Fork, which is runnable only from December to June. Lake Fork is open 10 months of the year, from December to September. Of these four, Clear Fork offers the most unspoiled scenery. This Class I stream runs through Clearfork Gorge, a National Natural Landmark, in pine-forested hill country. Lake Fork is less remote but allows two miles of secluded paddling before running into the popular Main Branch.

The Black Fork, with its riverside campgrounds, restaurants and carryouts, is crowded in the summer season with family paddlers. As a result, this slow-moving Class I stream — often called the Muddy Fork — may not be everyone's choice. The Main Branch, too, tends to be crowded with Black Fork paddlers in its ten-mile section closest to Loudonville. But elsewhere it offers more secluded floating through a wide, forested valley.

South of Springfield is the Little Miami River, Ohio's first stream to be federally designated Wild and Scenic. Regarded by some as the state's prettiest river, the Little Miami is popular between April and October each year. During its 105-mile course to the Ohio River it flows mostly between cornfields and wooded hills.

Just north of Springfield is a stretch of the Mad River that ranks as another of Ohio's best canoeing streams. Sycamore and cottonwood trees form a canopy above a narrow channel some two to three feet deep. Despite its name, the Mad River is sane and friendly, a gentle stream of crystal-clear water with few riffles to disturb its surface. It is a fine trout stream, flowing through a wide plain of wheat and cornfields in its northern reaches before entering built-up areas south of Springfield.

Elsewhere in Ohio the Sandusky and Maumee Rivers in the northwest offer Class III-IV rapids at high-water season. The Sandusky rates as a state scenic river from Upper Sandusky to Fremont. Paddlers enjoy its tree-lined seclusion and plentiful wildfowl. Where the broad Maumee flows down to Lake Erie at Toledo it offers great fishing, especially at spawning time in April-May. Canoeists more interested in scenery may prefer to stay further upstream, amid the sycamores and cottonwoods of the agricultural plain west of Napoleon. The Maumee is good for family floating and often offers views of deer and birds on its banks and islands.

Barefoot Canoes, Inc.
Bill Barefoot
3565 W. Frederick-Gingham Road
Tipp City, OH 45371
(513) 698-4351
Stillwater River, Great Miami River
Max. rapids: None
 Barefoot Canoes, Inc., offers guided and unguided canoe trips of one to three days on the Stillwater River and Great Miami River. These scenic, flat-water trips are perfect for families and paddlers of all ages. The rivers wind along unspoiled, tree-lined banks and offer excellent fishing for bass, bluegill, northern pike and catfish. The quiet setting is also good for spotting turtles, ducks, cranes, raccoons, deer, squirrels, and other wildlife.
 Barefoot Canoes, which also has liveries in Troy and West Milton, is open from April to October. During this time, the company also offers camping, bonfires, moonlight floats, and field games.

Mohican Canoe Livery
Doug Shannon
State Route 3
P.O. Box 263
Loudonville, OH 44842
(419) 994-4097, (419) 994-4020
Mohican River, Black Fork River,
Clear Fork River
Max. rapids: None
NACLO, Ohio Canoe Association
 Mohican Canoe Livery rents canoes, kayaks, rafts, and tubes for trips of one to six days on the Mohican, Black Fork, and Clear Fork Rivers. All trips are easy enough for beginners and offer attractive woodland scenery with views of large cliffs, turtles, birds, and beavers.
 During its April-to-November season, Mohican Canoe Livery also offers horseback riding, a waterslide, and other family amusements.

215

The Great Miami River is acclaimed as one of Ohio's prettiest rivers. Courtesy of Barefoot Canoes, Tipp City, Ohio.

Mohican Reservation Campgrounds and Canoeing

Christopher J. Snively
23270 Wally Road
Loudonville, OH 44842
(800) 766-CAMP
Mohican River, Clear Fork River, Black Fork River, Tuscarawas River, Muskingum River
Max. rapids: I-II

Mohican Reservation Campground & Canoeing rents canoes, kayaks, rafts, and tubes for trips of one to six days on the Mohican, Clear Fork, and Black Fork Rivers. Paddling is easy on these rivers, allowing families, beginners, and advanced canoeists time to enjoy the area's wooded, hilly scenery and views of deer, raccoons, pheasants, squirrels, buzzards, turkeys, and rabbits. Paddlers can also fish for muskie, walleye, catfish, carp, bass, and sucker.

Tent and R.V. camping is available at riverfront and shaded sites. The campground's facilities include modern restrooms, hot showers, a camp store, and playing fields.

Mohican Reservation Campground & Canoeing is open from April to November.

Mohican State Park Canoe Livery

Michael Dresch
3129 T.R. 629
Loudonville, OH 44842
(419) 994-4135, (800) 442-2663
Mohican River, Clear Fork River, Black Fork River
Max. rapids: None
NACLO

Michigan State Park Canoe Livery rents canoes and kayaks for one-day trips on the Clear Fork, Black Fork, and Mohican Rivers. The rivers are forgiving, suitable for beginning and experienced paddlers, and offer scenic views of rolling high hills and wildlife, including deer, raccoons, and birds. Paddlers also can enjoy fishing for bass, sucker, and saugeye, and hiking and camping in the surrounding woodlands.

The livery's season runs from April to November.

New World Expeditions

William P. Cacciolfi
209 Xenia Avenue
Yellow Springs, OH 45387
(513) 767-7221
Rivers worldwide
Max. rapids: V+

New World Expeditions offers guided canoe, kayak, raft, and dory trips and rents kayaks. An adventure travel company, New World Expeditions runs trips world-wide for paddlers of all levels of ability. Paddle trips last one to 30 days and offer a range of activities, including fishing, camping, and lessons.

NTR Canoe Livery

Ann Swain
State Route 212
P.O. Box 203
Bolivar, OH 44612
(216) 874-2002
Tuscarawas River
Max. rapids: None

NTR Canoe Livery rents canoes, kayaks, and tubes on the Tuscarawas River for trips of one to two days. The trips are easy and scenic, passing through wooded wilderness that offers camping spots and views of deer, beavers, blue herons, and other native wildlife. Paddlers can also enjoy fishing the clear waters for northern pike, bass, bluegill, and crappie.

Raccoon Run Canoe Rental

Thomas Fellenstein
1129 State Road
Geneva, OH 44041
(216) 466-7414, (216) 466-8360
Grand River
Max. rapids: I-II

Raccoon Run Canoe Rental offers guided and unguided one- and two-day canoe trips on the scenic and exceptionally clear Grand River. The trips, which are fine for paddlers of all ages and abilities, have stretches that pass through deep, picturesque gorges. Paddlers also can spot deer, beavers, foxes, minks, and raccoons, and anglers can fish for northern pike, muskie, smallmouth bass, trout and crappie. Camping, swimming, and lessons are also available.

Raccoon Run's season is from April to November.

Rivers Edge Outfitters

Rhett and Andrea Rohrer
3928 State Route 42 S
Waynesville, OH 45068
(513) 862-4540, (800) 628-2319
Little Miami River
Max. rapids: I-II
NACLO, Ohio Canoe Livery Association, North American Paddlesport

Rivers Edge Outfitters rents canoes and kayaks for one- to five-day trips on the Little Miami River, a state and nationally designated scenic river. The Little Miami, a classic meandering midwestern river, is suitable for all skill levels and is set in a peaceful landscape of rolling wooded hills, cliffs, gorges, meadows, and fields. In addition to the scenery, paddlers can enjoy fishing for smallmouth bass, rock bass, sunfish, and bluegill, and spotting wildlife, including deer, beavers, muskrats, minks, raccoons, herons, ducks, geese, hawks, and owls.

The livery, which adjoins the 800-acre Spring Valley Wilderness Area, has a spacious riverfront campground with a modern bath house, paddle sports shop, and picnic area. Also available during the April-to-October season are hayrides and a "float and feast" trip that concludes with a barbecue or pig roast.

217

The Stillwater River, a scenic, unspoiled flatwater river with good fishing. Courtesy of Barefoot Canoes, Tipp City, Ohio.

Riverside Landing
Hancock Park District
819 Park Street
Findlay, OH 45840
(419) 423-6952
Blanchard River
Max. rapids: None

Hancock Park District Riverside Landing rents canoes for one-day trips on the Blanchard River. The river has no rapids but is not suitable for novices, as paddling skills are required to skirt occasional logjams. Trips pass through scenic, unspoiled parkland and surrounding woods, offering views of deer, raccoons, and squirrels, and fishing for white bass, carp, bluegill, and catfish. The park also offers hiking and biking trails and primitive camping.

The park, open year-round, rents canoes between May and September.

Oklahoma

Oklahoma features two great river systems, the Red and the Arkansas. The Red River, which forms the state's boundary with Texas, draws water from southern Oklahoma. Most of the north and east of the state is drained by the Arkansas River and its long tributaries that reach into the panhandle.

For canoeists, the best paddling is in eastern Oklahoma, notably on the Illinois River above and below the town of Tahlequah. The Illinois runs through the heart of the Oklahoma Ozarks, a land of clear, swift streams and steep-sided river valleys. Especially on the upper 70 miles designated scenic, floaters enjoy interesting and sometimes challenging waters amid oak-hickory forest with abundant wildlife.

The Illinois has easy Class II rapids, waves up to three feet, and wide, clear channels. Although water levels vary, the Illinois is a river for all seasons. The river also has many campsites along the way, which are shown on maps of the river published by the Oklahoma Scenic Rivers Commission, P.O. Box 292, Tahlequah, OK 74465. The commission's "floater's guide" leaflet says 80,000 canoe trips are taken on the Illinois every year. Many of these paddlers are fishermen, for the river is said to be one of the few in Oklahoma that have the clean, clear conditions needed by smallmouth bass. All told, nearly 70 kinds of fish populate the Illinois.

Spring River Canoe Trail in the extreme northeast corner of the state runs through three separate state parks. These contain boat ramps, campgrounds, and other facilities in attractive Ozark foothills, close to a popular resort, the Grand Lake O' the Cherokees.

Grand Lake itself covers nearly 60,000 acres and boasts 10 state parks, many marinas, campgrounds, accommodations, and restaurants. Power boats, waterskiers, and sailboats abound, but canoeists can find sheltered coves to paddle in peace. Fish are plentiful: crappie, three species of bass, channel catfish, bluegill, and hybrid striper. Grand Lake's chief attraction for naturalists is that it is a favorite stopping-place for migrating white pelicans. The occasion is marked with a Pelican Festival in September.

Fort Gibson Lake, further south between Tulsa and Tahlequah, also attracts paddlers. Like Grand Lake, it has many tourist facilities: 26

parks and recreational areas, lakeside cabins, boat docks, and restaurants. Fort Gibson Lake has plentiful black bass, white bass, and catfish for what is claimed to be some of the best fishing in the country. The Oklahoma Department of Wildlife Conservation manages a 4,500-acre waterfowl refuge and a 17,300-acre public hunting area with deer, quail, doves, ducks, geese and rabbits.

Arrowhead Camp
Bill and Mary Blackard
HD 61, Box 201
Tahlequah, OK 74464
(918) 456-1140, (800) 749-1140
Illinois River
Max. rapids: I-II
Arrowhead Camp offers canoe rentals for trips of one to three days on the Illinois River. These tours pass through a scenic region of bluffs, hills, and woods. The Illinois is clean and clear, with good fishing for catfish, bass, and crappie. Along its banks are deer, raccoons, rabbits, birds, and other wildlife. Paddling is easy on these trips, which have gentle Class I-II rapids.

During its May-September season, Arrowhead offers cabin rentals, bunkhouse lodging, and both tent and R.V. camping. A camp store with ice, groceries, tackle, and other supplies is also available.

Blue Hole Canoe Floats, Inc.
Chet and Susan Brewington
Route 1, Box 144
Quapaw, OK 74363
(918) 542-6344
Spring River
Max. rapids: None
Blue Heron Canoe Floats rents canoes for trips of two hours to two days along a 29-mile stretch of the Spring River. These trips are scenic, passing through a region of bluffs and pine forest inhabited by deer, cranes, and eagles. Also, the river

boasts good fishing for crappie, bass, and catfish.

These Spring River trips, available from May to September, are on flat water and are fine for beginners, families and groups, as well as experienced paddlers.

Cedar Valley Camp (Ltd.)
Richard King
Star Route 1, Box 101
Proctor, OK 74457
(918) 456-4094
Illinois River
Max. rapids: I-II
Cedar Valley Camp offers guided canoe trips and canoe rentals on the Illinois River. This small family-owned business with but 20 canoes specializes in low prices and personal service. Its trips, with mainly Class I rapids, are fine for families and beginners as well as more experienced paddlers. Trips last from 1-4 days and pass through a scenic, heavily wooded region around Sparrowhawk Mountain. Along the way, paddlers can view abundant wildlife, including deer, foxes, eagles, and great blue herons. Anglers can enjoy excellent fishing in the Illinois' clear spring-fed waters for a wide variety of fish, ranging from smallmouth bass to 50-lb. flathead catfish.

Cedar Valley Camp's season lasts from Memorial Day to Labor Day. However, trips in the early spring and late fall are available by reservation.

Paddling on the Illinois River. Courtesy of Eagle Bluffs Resorts, Tahlequah, Oklahoma.

Diamond Head Resort
Tom Eastham
HC 61, Box 264
Tahlequah, OK 74464
(800) 722-2411
Illinois River
Max. rapids: I-II
Diamond Head Resort rents canoes and rafts for trips of one to three days on the Illinois River. These trips are easy outings suitable for families and novices, as well as experienced paddlers. Along the Illinois, paddlers can enjoy fishing, camping, swimming, and views of rocky bluffs and wildlife, including deer, raccoons, and birds. Diamond Head's season runs from April to October.

Eagle Bluff Resorts
Jeff and Vicki Bennett
H.C. 61, Box 230
Tahlequah, OK 74464
(800) 366-3031
Illinois River
Max. rapids: I-II
Eagle Bluff Resorts offers guided and unguided canoe and raft trips of one to four days on the Illinois River. These pass through a scenic region of rolling hills, bluffs, and hardwood forests. With only minor rapids, the Illinois is easy paddling for novices and families as well as experienced canoeists. While underway, paddlers can also enjoy fishing for brown bass and catfish, and glimpsing occasional deer, beavers, and other wildlife.

Eagle Bluff Resorts, open from April-November, provides riverside tent and R.V. camping, cabin rentals, a modern shower house, a guest lodge with dining room, a snack shop, and catered riverside meals.

Kamp Paddle Trails
Katherine and David Pickle
Route 1, Box 1320
Watts, OK 74964
(918) 723-3546
Illinois River, Lake Tenkiller
Max. rapids: I-II
Kamp Paddle Trails is a summer camp for boys and girls which also rents canoes to the general public. The camp, set on the Illinois River in the foothills of the Ozarks, specializes in teaching young people to canoe, camp, enjoy nature study and protect the environment. Camp sessions run from the start of school summer vacation through the first week in August. From then until November 1, Kamp Paddle rents its canoes to others, for trips of 1- 4 days. Canoe rentals are also available to the public in the spring and early summer, provided spring rains do not make the river dangerously high.

Paddlers can run 146 gentle Class I-II rapids over a 75-mile stretch of the Illinois, enjoying free camping, and varied fishing amid profuse wildlife. Trips are not difficult but require previous river paddling experience.

Peyton's Place Canoes
Route HC-61, Box 231
Tahlequah, OK 74464
(918) 456-3847, (800) 359-0866
Illinois River
Max. rapids: I-II
Peyton's Place has both canoes and rafts for use on the scenic Illinois River with its rich wildlife and fishing. The oldest canoe camp on the river, Peyton's has a campground, airconditioned cottages, a convenience store and shuttle equipment.

Fine for family floats year-round, the clean river is good for swimming as well as bass, bream and channel cat fishing. Trips are through beautiful woodland with deer, beavers, raccoons, herons, egrets, and eagles.

Tenkiller Valley Ranch
Larry and Paula Tharp
P.O. Box 231
Gore, OK 74435
(918) 489-5895, (800) 299-5895
Illinois River
Max. rapids: I-II
Tenkiller Valley Ranch rents canoes and rafts for one- day trips on a 12-mile stretch of the Lower Illinois River below the Lake Tenkiller Dam. This stretch features sparkling clear waters, scenic bluffs and woods, gravel bars, and several swimming holes complete with rope swings. Fishing is especially good on this stretch, which is stocked with trout, and also contains abundant striped bass, walleye, pike, black bass, crappie, channel catfish, and sand bass. Sharp-eyed paddlers may also see deer, squirrels, red foxes, raccoons, beavers, muskrats, ferrets, cranes, herons, and kingfishers.

The outfitter's trips, offered from May-September, have only minor rapids and are easy enough for beginners and families.

Oregon

Rugged Oregon is surrounded on three sides by water — the Pacific to the west, the mighty Columbia River to the north and the Snake River along much of the Idaho state line to the east. Within these borders, this land of forests and mountains contains other rivers that invite exploration. Among them are the whitewater Rogue River in the southwest, the John Day, Oregon's longest river, the Deschutes in the northwest, and the Owyhee in the southeast. Paddlers can find daunting rapids with names like Bodacious Bounce and Widowmaker, as well as white sandy beaches, deep gorges, sparkling clear water, desert canyons, and endless pine forests. Oregon's abundant wildlife includes bighorn sheep, bears, deer, minks, otters, bald and golden eagles, ospreys and herons.

The Rogue River is a charter member of the National Wild and Scenic Rivers club founded by Congress in 1968. Paddlers who put in near Grants Pass can spend several days traveling through a wilderness of forested canyons, rock slides, cascading side streams, and fern-shrouded grottoes. Its numerous rapids are mostly moderate, Class III-IV, and billed as suitable for both beginning and seasoned rafters. The 33-mile wild section of the Rogue is so popular that permits for individual boaters are issued by lottery for trips between June 1 and September 15. The chance of winning is said to average one in 10. For a sure thing, book with an outfitter. Fishing for steelhead begins in early September and lasts until mid-November, while salmon are caught in spring and summer.

The Deschutes cuts through the arid desert of central Oregon on its way north to join the Columbia. In this semi-wilderness the paddler floats past desert hills and rocky canyons. With rapids no tougher than Class III+, the Deschutes is good for families and experienced floaters alike.

Only expert paddlers should run the Middle Owyhee with its Class IV-V rapids. Of these adventurers, only the most daring attempt the notorious Widowmaker rapids in the steep-sided canyon. Below this obstacle the walls of the chasm widen and, for the last seven miles of the trip down to Rome on US 95, boaters must paddle on flat water, often against strong afternoon headwinds.

Rafters tackle Class IV "Blossom Bar Rapid" on the Rogue River. Courtesy of Wildwater Adventures, Eugene, Oregon.

While the Middle Owyhee can only be run between March and May, the Lower Owyhee — from Rome to Owyhee Lake — is runnable from April through June. This downstream section is also less fearsome, with somewhat easier Class III-IV rapids. It is therefore accessible to thrill-seeking novices as well as experts. Its pristine desert canyon wilderness, with its multi-colored rock turrets, offers interesting geology and birdlife.

Another exciting whitewater trip is the North Umpqua — the name derived from an Indian word meaning satisfaction. Recently designated a state and federal scenic waterway, the Umpqua has become one of Oregon's favorite whitewater rivers. This trip through Class III-IV rapids is an ideal weekend outing. Runnable from April through July, the North Umpqua winds its way through a narrow, forested gorge. Its waters near Steamboat Creek have long been beloved by anglers, including Zane Grey, who wrote books on game fishing as well as his popular novels of the American West.

Gentler floating through grand scenery is to be found on the 275-mile John Day River. The Upper John Day between Service Creek and Clarno in northcentral Oregon is normally floatable only in April and May. But it offers Class II-III rapids and superb views of ranch country amid the Blue Mountains. The Lower John Day from Clarno down to Cottonwood Canyon Bridge is runnable until late July and has easy Class I-II rapids for novices. It runs through semi-arid canyonland where paddlers feel the solitude of Oregon's great wide spaces.

Adventure Whitewater
Gene Allred, M.D.
P.O. Box 321
Yreka, CA 96097
(800) 888-5632
Salmon River, Scott River, Klamath River, Trinity River
Max. rapids: V+
America Outdoors

Adventure Whitewater offers raft rentals and guided kayak and raft trips for gentle Class II to expert Class V runs. Trips feature great white water and spectacular mountain scenery of snow-capped peaks, deep granite gorges, and heavily forested slopes. Set in the Marble Mountains and Trinity Alps, the trips offer fishing for trout, steelhead, and salmon and chances to view bears, deer, coyotes, otters, eagles, osprey, and herons.

American River Touring Association
Steve Welch
Star Route 73
Groveland, CA 95321
(800) 323-2782, (209) 962-7873
Rogue River, Illinois River, Umpqua River, Green River, Yampa River, Colorado River, Middle Fork and Main Salmon Rivers, Selway River, Merced River, Tuolumne River, Klamath River
Max. rapids: V+
America Outdoors, Oregon Guides and Packers, Idaho Outfitters and Guides, Utah Guides and Outfitters

ARTA offers a total of 16 raft trips in five Western states. The trips, in California, Oregon, Utah, Idaho, and Arizona, are by oar rafts, paddle rafts, oar/paddle combination rafts, and inflatable canoes.

Most trips are of Class III difficulty and appropriate for novices and families, as well as those with more experience. Other trips of up to V+ difficulty challenge even the most advanced paddler. Depending on the location, the trips feature such added attractions as wildflowers, side streams, swimming holes, Indian ruins, warm water, abundant wildlife, good hiking and fishing, and hot springs.

ARTA, a non-profit company, also offers whitewater schools, professional guide training, and family discounts.

Echo: The Wilderness Company
Richard Linford and Joseph Daly
6529 Telegraph Avenue
Oakland, CA 95609
(510) 652-1600
Rogue River, Main Salmon River, Middle Fork Salmon River, Tuolumne River, American River, Cal-Salmon River
Max. rapids: III-IV
Oregon Guides and Packers, Idaho Outfitters and Guides Association, America Outdoors, California chapter

ECHO, one of the country's best-known outfitters, runs guided trips on the Main Salmon and Middle Fork in Idaho; the Rogue in Oregon; and the Tuolumne, American, and Cal-Salmon in California. The company has one- to 12-day trips available for paddlers at all skill levels and offers a variety of boats, including inflatable kayaks, oar rafts, paddle rafts, and oar/paddle rafts.

ECHO also offers a large number of special trips, including Fly-Fishing on the Middle Fork; White (and Red) Wine and White Water; Bluegrass on White Water; River Trips for Kids; White Water School; Aikido and Nature; the Rogue String Quartet; Field Sketching Workshop; Whale Watching, Baja; Rainforests and Rapids, Costa Rica; Baja Sea Kayaking; Colorado River through the Grand Canyon; and Lodge Trips on the Main Salmon and Cal Salmon.

ECHO's seasons runs from April to September.

Paddle rafters at "Martin's Rapid" on the McKenzie River. Courtesy of Wildwater Adventures, Eugene, Oregon.

James Henry River Journeys
James Katz
P.O. Box 807
Bolinas, CA 94924
(415) 868-1836, (800) 786-1830
Rogue River, Stanislaus River, Carson River, Upper Klamath River, Colorado River, Tatshenini-Alsek River
Max. rapids: III-IV
Idaho Outfitters and Guides

James Henry River Journeys runs guided canoe, kayak, and raft trips in California, Arizona, Idaho, Oregon, and Alaska. In California, the outfitter offers trips with Class II-III rapids, of one to three days, on the Stanislaus, East Fork of the Carson, and the Lower Klamath. In Arizona, the company runs Grand Canyon trips, with Class IV+ rapids, of 6, 8, 9, 13, and 14 days. Trips in Idaho, of 4, 5 or 6 days,

run on the Class III-IV Main Salmon. In Oregon, trips of 3, 4, and 5 days run on the Class III Rogue. Finally, in Alaska the company offers a natural history expedition on the Tatshenshini-Alsek Rivers.

Many special-interest trips are also available. These include Salmon River Bluegrass, Country, Folk and Cajun Music Trips; Whitewater Workshops; Organizational Development and Teambuilding; Wine Tasting and Gourmet Cuisine; Lodge Trips on the Rogue and Salmon; Rogue and Salmon Natural History Trips; Alaska Nature Photography; and Alaska Wilderness Literature.

All trips run through especially scenic wilderness areas and are carefully planned to move at a leisurely pace, allowing ample time for side hikes, fishing, photography, and general relaxation. As a result, participation is open to anyone active and in good health. The company's season runs from May to September.

Northwest Outdoor Center
Bill Stewart, John Meyer, Herb Meyer
2100 Westlake Avenue N.
Seattle, WA 98109
(206) 281-9694
Rogue River
Max. rapids: III-IV
TASK
Northwest Outdoor Center was founded in 1980 to provide safe, high quality boating instruction in the Pacific Northwest. It has since expanded into providing guided sea and river kayaking trips and renting both kayaks and canoes. Most of its floats are in sheltered flat water, suitable for beginners. Sea kayaking tours run through Puget Sound and the scenic San Juan Islands, while river paddling is on five rivers in the beautiful Cascades and the Rogue in Oregon. NWOC operates trips varying from three hours to five days and its season runs year-round.

Many wildlife species may be admired, from whales and seals to bald eagles, migratory waterbirds and shorebirds.

Northwest Passage
Rick Swetzer
130 Greenleaf Avenue
Wilmette, IL 60091
(708) 256-4409, (800) RECREAT
Wolf River, Pike River, Peshtigo River, Red River, Wisconsin River, Current River, Rio Grande, Everglades, BWCA, Lake Michigan, Lake Superior
Max. rapids: III-IV
Northwest Passage offers guided raft trips on the New, Gauley and Cheat Rivers in West Virginia; canoe trips on the Wolf, Pike and Peshtigo Rivers in Wisconsin, the Current River

in Missouri, the Rio Grande in Texas, the Everglades in Florida, and the Boundary Waters Canoe Area in Minnesota; and sea kayak trips on Lake Michigan in Illinois and Lake Superior in Michigan. Most of these trips, which last two to seven days, are designed for beginners; some require prior experience. Depending on the location, these trips offer excitement, challenge, remoteness and beauty.

An adventure travel company, Northwest Passage also offers skiing, hiking, cycling, backpacking, scuba diving, dogsledding, and rock climbing. Outings run year-round in the U.S., the Arctic, New Zealand, Tasmania, Costa Rica, Argentina, Canada, Belize, Turks and Caicos, Crete, Lapland, and southern Africa.

O.A.R.S.
George Wendt
P.O. Box 67
Angels Camp, CA 95222
(209) 736-4677, (800) 466-7238 (CA), (800) 346-6277 (U.S)
Rogue River, San Juan River, American River, Cal-Salmon River, Merced River, Stanislaus River, Tuolumne River, Colorado River, Snake River
Max. rapids: V+
America Outdoors
O.A.R.S. runs guided dory, raft and kayak trips in five Western states. It offers tours in California on the American, Cal-Salmon, Merced, Stanislaus and Tuolumne Rivers; in Oregon on the Rogue; in Arizona on the Colorado; in Wyoming on the Snake, and in Utah on the San Juan River. These outings last one to 13 days and, depending on the class of river, are fine for children, novices, families, intermediate, and expert rafters. O.A.R.S. trips run between April and October and provide fishing, swimming, camping, side hikes, wildlife viewing and other activities.

227

Kayaker David Gilmore jumps a 15-ft. waterfall on Brice Creek in an inflatable kayak. Photo by Melinda Allan, courtesy of Wildwater Adventures, Eugene, Oregon.

Ouzel Outfitters
Kent Wickham
Box 827
Bend, OR 97709
(503) 385-5497, (800) 788-RAFT
*Rogue River, Owyhee River, North
Umpqua River, Deschutes River,
McKenzie River, Salmon*
Max. rapids: III-IV
Oregon Guides and Packers
　Ouzel Oufitters specializes in trips
of one to five days on the "loveliest
and liveliest" rives in the Northwest.
These rivers include the Rogue, North
Umpqua, McKenzie, Lower and Mid-
dle Owyhee, and Deschutes Rivers in
Oregon; the Lower Salmon in Idaho;
and the Lower Klamath River in
California. All trips but the Middle
Owyhee runs have class III-IV rapids
and are fine for families and guests of
all levels of experience to paddle in
rafts, inflatable kayaks, or guide-accompanied, "row-your-own" oar-
rafts. The Middle Owyhee run, with
class IV-V rapids, is a challenging, expedition-like trip for adventurous, experienced rafters only.
　Ouzel Outfitters' trips run between
May and September. Depending on
the river traveled, guests can view
bears, deer, eagles, and otters, and
fish for bass, trout, steelhead, and salmon.

River Adventure Float Trips
Mel and Diane Norrick
P.O. Box 841
Grants Pass, OR 97526
(503) 476-6493
Rogue River
Max. rapids: III-IV
Oregon Guides and Packers
　River Adventure Float Trips runs
guided raft and dory trips on the
Rogue River in southern Oregon.
These oar-boat trips, of one to four
days, are exciting but not strenuous.
However, for those who want to pad-
dle, the company brings inflatable

kayaks for guests to use along select
stretches. While underway, guests
can enjoy wilderness scenery with
views of woods, canyons, eagles,
osprey, herons, egrets, deer, and, occasionally, bears, minks, and otters.
Anglers also relish the Rogue's excellent fishing for steelhead, salmon,
and sturgeon.
　On multi-day trips, guests stay in
rustic, comfortable river lodges. But
for those wanting to rough it, camping trips are available in June and
August. Fall steelhead fishing trips are
also available. River Adventure's
season runs from May to November.

River Adventure Float Trips
Mel and Diane Norrick
P.O. Box 841
Grants Pass, OR 97526
(503) 476-6493
Rogue River
Max. rapids: III-IV
Oregon Packers and Guides
　River Adventure Float Trips runs
guided raft and dory trips on the
Rogue River in southern Oregon.
These oar-boat trips, of one to four
days, are exciting but not strenuous.
However, for those who want to paddle, the company brings inflatable
kayaks for guests to use along select
stretches. While underway, guests
can enjoy wilderness scenery with
views of woods, canyons, eagles,
osprey, herons, egrets, deer, and, occasionally, bears, minks, and otters.
Anglers also relish the Rogue's excellent fishing for steelhead, salmon,
and sturgeon.
　On multi-day trips, guests stay in
rustic, comfortable river lodges. But
for those wanting to rough it, camping trips are available in June and
August. Fall steelhead fishing trips are
also available. River Adventure's
season runs from May to November.

Paddle rafting. Courtesy of Ouzel Outfitters, Bend, Oregon.

ROW (River Odysseys West), Inc.
Peter Grubb
P.O. Box 579-PA
Coeur d'Alene, ID 83814
(208) 765-0841, (800) 451-6034
Snake River
Max. rapids: III-IV
*America Outdoors, Idaho Outfitters
and Guides Association, Oregon
Guides and Packers Association*

ROW, one of the country's best-known outfitters, offers a wide array of trips on Idaho and Oregon rivers to suit adventurers of all ages and levels of ability. Trips vary in length from one to 17 days and offer wilderness scenery ranging from desert to high alpine terrain.

In addition to its diverse offerings, ROW also takes particular pride in the quality of its guides and its annual "Family Focus" trips, which are designed with special activities for children. On ROW's trips, which run between May and October, paddlers may see bears, moose, bighorn sheep, mountain goats, river otters, deer, elk, and eagles. Fishing is for cutthroat and rainbow trout, smallmouth bass, and sturgeon.

Solitude River Trips, Inc.
Al and Jeana Bukowsky
P.O. Box 907
Merlin, OR 97532
(503) 476-1876
Owyhee River
Max. rapids: III-IV
Idaho Outfitters and Guides Association, America Outdoors

Solitude River Trips offers guided kayak, raft, and dory trips of five and six days on the Middle Fork of the Salmon River. These trips offer challenging whitewater, terrific fly-fishing for rainbow and cutthroat trout, and stunning, varied scenery, which includes alpine meadows, rock-strewn gorges, and desert. These trips, available with either paddle-boat or oar-boat option, are easy enough for people of all ages. Along the way, participants can enjoy swimming, camping, lessons, and a chance to spot deer, elk, sheep, goats, bears, cougars, and eagles. Solitude's season is from June to September.

Wapiti River Guides
Gary Lane
Box 1125
Riggins, ID 83549
(208) 628-3523, (800) 488-9872
Grande Ronde River, Owyhee River, Salmon River, rivers throughout Alaska
Max. rapids: V+
Oregon Guides and Packers Association, Idaho Outfitters and Guides Association
Wapiti River Guides, with trips in Idaho, Oregon, and Alaska, special-

izes in small personalized trips of moderate difficulty "for ages 3 to 103, families, and nature lovers." The outfitter's trips are distinctive, too, for their guides' emphasis on natural history and Native American culture, and for the fine scenery, which includes caves, spires, pictographs, petroglyphs, and historic sites.

Trips, ranging in length from one to 12 days, also allow time for interesting side hikes and viewing elk, deer, bald eagles, bobcats, cougars, bears, bighorn sheep, minks and other wildlife. Fishing is for steelhead, trout, and bass.

Rafting on the Owyhee River in Oregon, a great wilderness trip in April or May. Courtesy of Turtle River Rafting Company, Mt. Shasta, California.

Wenatchee Whitewater Scenic River Trips
Bruce Carlson
P.O. Box 12
Cashmere, WA 98815
(509) 782-2254, (800) 74 FLOAT
Deschutes River, Wenatchee River, Tieton River, White Salmon River, Deschutes River
Max. rapids: III-IV

Wenatchee Whitewater Scenic River Trips offers guided raft trips on the Wenatchee, Tieton, White Salmon, and Deschutes Rivers. These trips pass through the beautiful North Cascades, featuring scenic forest, canyons, wildflowers, and abundant wildlife, including deer, eagles, ospreys, minks, otters, ducks, herons, and geese. Anglers also can fish for salmon, steelhead, and rainbow trout.

Trips last one to three days, run between April and September, and range widely in difficulty, from scenic, flat-water trips to Class IV whitewater. Wenatchee Whitewater also offers parties, barbecue grills, campfires, day care, volleyball, moonlight floats, inflatable kayak trips, and scenic floats led by naturalist guides.

Whitewater Voyages
William McGinnis
P.O. Box 20400
El Sobrante, CA 94820-0400
(509) 222-5994, (800) 488-RAFT
Rogue River, Colorado River, Kern River, Merced River, Tuolumne River, Cache Creek, American River, Yuba River, Klamath River, Stanislaus River, Trinity River, Middle Fork Salmon River
Max. rapids: III-IV
America Outdoors, American River Recreation Association

Whitewater Voyages offers an extensive array of trips, with guided oar- and paddle-boat runs in California, Arizona, Oregon, and Idaho. Trips by kayak and raft range in length from one to five days and in difficulty from Class II to Class V. With runs on nine Wild and Scenic Rivers and on more California rivers than any other outfitter, Whitewater Voyages has trips for paddlers of all levels of experience.

The outfitter also has specialty trips, including whitewater schools, family trips, low-cost river-cleanup trips, "teambuilding" trips and excursions in the former Soviet Union to paddle with Russians as part of project R.A.F.T.

Wild Water Adventures
Al Law, Melinda Allan
P.O. Box 249
Creswell, OR 97426
(503) 895-4465, (800) 289-4534
Rogue River, Owyhee River, Deschutes River, McKenzie River, John Day River, North Umqua River, Grande Ronde River, Upper Klamath River, North Santiam River
Max. rapids: V+
Oregon Guides and Packers Associaiton

Wild Water Adventures specializes in running guided and unguided inflatable kayak trips on wilderness rivers. Trips in rafts and inflatable kayaks range in length from one-half day to nine days and run on rivers ranging from mountain streams to desert waterways and from scenic floats to crashing white water. On these trips, in addition to paddling, guests can fish, view Indian pictographs and pioneer ruins, and spot deer, eagles, otters, hawks, minks, beavers, and other wildlife.

During the season, which runs from March to November, and year-round for "wetsuiters," guests can also take inflatable kayak lessons, learning brace strokes, ferrying, river rescue, and how to "read" rivers. Kayaking students can enjoy instruction by Melinda Allen, coauthor of the *Inflatable Kayak Handbook*.

Kayaker demonstrates a brace while "hole riding" on the McKenzie River. Photo by Melinda Allan, courtesy of Wildwater Adventures, Eugene, Oregon.

Wilderness Adventures
Dean Munroe
P.O. Box 938
Redding, CA 96099
(800) 323-7238
Upper Klamath River, Cal-Salmon River, Scott River, Wooley Creek
Max. rapids: V+

Wilderness Adventures runs a number of remarkable trips on rivers along the California-Oregon border. Among the unusual offerings is a raft trip begun on the Class V Woodley Creek after a horseback ride into the Marble Mountain Wilderness. Another exciting trip, called "Hell and High Water," combines all the Class V sections of the Salmon, Scott and Upper Klamath into a weekend trip.

Trips range in length from one to four days, are offered from April to October, and are suited for intermediate to advanced paddlers. Set in wilderness areas, trips offer fishing for trout and views of eagles, ospreys, minks, otters, and beavers.

233

Pennsylvania

The Keystone State is a wide land of mountains, plateaus and plains, watered by big rivers as well as some of the most exciting whitewater streams in the East. Along its eastern border flows the majestic Delaware, rivaled by the mid-state Susquehanna and the Allegheny and Monongahela rivers in the west. Pennsylvania's backbone is the massive range of Appalachian ridges that divides the Allegheny Plateau in the northwest from the Atlantic coastal plain in the southeast. This topography defines a river system which offers the rafter and canoeist everything from wilderness thrills to placid floating on streams lined with campgrounds and restaurants.

For sheer popularity the Delaware River has few rivals. Surprisingly free of dams for a river flowing through such a thirsty conurbation, the Delaware brings clean water down from the Catskills of New York. Its 76-mile stretch from Hancock to Port Jervis has long been a favorite canoe trip. It takes three days and can be run in April-May and again in September-October. In the summer months paddlers depend upon adequate releases from Cannonsville and Pepacton reservoirs. The scenery is superb. But Edward Gertler, in his excellent book *Keystone Canoeing* (Seneca Press, 1988), writes that the upper Delaware on a crowded summer weekend has "hundreds of boaters, in all stages of ineptness, with no concept of river currents, canoemanship, or even that a life vest is not just a funny-shaped seat cushion. Many do not really care, their minds pickled by drugs or alcohol. They drown and injure themselves on this simple river with amazing frequency." Gertler adds that some "river pirates" even direct neophytes into rough sections of rapids in the hope that they will capsize, spilling valuables into the water which can be looted before the victims slog their way ashore. Despite all this, he says that most Delaware canoeists have a first-class time.

The West Branch of the Susquehanna drives through relatively empty, unspoiled countryside in the heart of Pennsylvania. It is flanked by mile upon mile of forest and the paddler can camp freely almost wherever he chooses.

Whitewater buffs head for the hills, and in Pennsylvania the best rapids lurk in the state's southwest corner adjoining Maryland and

West Virginia. The Youghiogheny — pronounced Yokagaynee or simply "Yok" for short — is a Mecca for paddlers from Pennsylvania, Ohio, Maryland, Virginia and West Virginia. The river's most exciting whitewater is on the Upper Yough across the border (see Maryland). Within Pennsylvania the Middle Yough still offers plenty of scope for novice and family floating on gentle Class I-II waters. The Yough flows through the Laurel Mountains, with rhododendron and mountain laurel adorning steep canyon walls. While other streams dry up in the summer, the dam-controlled Yough just keeps rolling along.

The Lower Yough ranks as an intermediate stream with Class III- IV rapids, good for novices and veterans alike. And the scenery, largely protected by the Ohiopyle State Park, is great. According to one recent count, 100,000 rafters enjoy the 7.5 miles of whitewater from Ohiopyle Falls through the park to Bruner Run every season.

Much beloved among Pennsylvania and New York paddlers is the Lehigh River in the Pocono Mountains. This popular stream is less than three hours drive from New York City and barely two hours from Philadelphia. Many floaters start at White Haven, right next to Interstate 80, and head 26 miles downstream to the town of Jim Thorpe. But the whole river provides interesting canoeing. In the summer its rapids are tame, but until May and on subseqent weekends when water is released from the Francis E. Walters Dam (check with outfitters for dates) they are exciting. The trip through the Lehigh Gorge State Park combines grand scenery with plenty of thrills for novices.

Pine Creek is another popular river, described by some as the crown jewel of Pennsylvania's scenic wilderness regions. Its chief attraction is the wooded gorge claimed to be Pennsylvania's "Grand Canyon" but bearing little resemblance to the original. Runnable usually from the "ice-out" in mid-March to mid-June and again from mid-September to mid-November, it has mostly gentle rapids and good scenery.

Rafting on the Lower Youghiogheny. Courtesy of Laurel Highlands River Tours, Ohiopyle, Pennsylvania.

Adventure Tours Canoe & Raft Trips
John Jacobi
P.O. Box 175
Marshalls Creek, PA 18335
(717) 223-0505
Delaware River
Max. rapids: I-II
NACLO

A family business, Adventure Tours rents canoes and rafts as well as running guided canoe and raft tours on the Delaware. Trips last from two hours to two weeks during a season running from April to October. They are geared to experts as well as beginners, although no rapids are rated above Class I-II.

On the river segments covered, the Delaware is above national purity standards, and it offers good swimming, camping and fall foliage. Pike, muskie, shad, bass and walleye are plentiful.

Blue Mountain Outfitters
Douglas Gibson
103 State Road
Marysville, PA 17053
(717) 957-2413
Susquehanna River, Juniata River
Max. rapids: I-II

Blue Mountain rents canoes and kayaks for trips of up to three days on the Susquehanna and Juniata Rivers, plus smaller tributaries when water levels permit. The company custom-tailors its trips to meet individual and group needs.

Waters in the area offer a unique blend of quiet floating with Class I-II rapids for those who seek more of a challenge. Numerous islands provide good sites for picnicking and camping. Among the scenic farmlands and mountains the paddler can see blue herons, egrets, Canada geese and kingfishers while the fisherman angles for bass, muskie and catfish.

Chamberlain Canoes
Bob Sweeney
P.O. Box 155, River Road
Minisink Hills, PA 18341
(800) 422-6631
Delaware River
Max. rapids: I-II
NACLO, ACA, U.S. Canoe Association
Chamberlain Canoes rents canoes, rafts and tubes for trips on the scenic Delaware River lasting from an hour or two to five days. Paddlers can explore the Delaware Water Gap recreation area, with its 38 miles of river. Open April-October, the company is geared to meet each customer's personal needs, with delivery and pickup according to his/her schedule. Overnight camping is free.

The Delaware, with Class I-II rapids, is suitable for novices and families. They may fish for bass, shad, walleye, muskie, trout and striper while looking out for bear, deer, fox, small game and birds including eagle and osprey.

Cook Forest Canoe Livery
Carl Lipford
Box 14, Route 36
Cooksburg, PA 16217
(814) 744-8094
Clarion River
Max. rapids: I-II
NACLO
Cook Forest Canoe Livery, located on the Clarion River in the heart of Cook Forest State Park, specializes in family canoeing. The Clarion's clean, clear waters appeal to many as they course through a scenic wilderness. Rapids are nowhere more difficult than Class I-II. The 22-year-old livery rents canoes, kayaks and tubes for one to three days during an April-November season.

Paddlers can glimpse deer, bear and raccoons as they float through the woods, and fish for trout and

bass. Campgrounds, picnic areas and hiking trails abound.

Delaware River Canoe Adventures, Inc.
Thomas W. McBrien IV
R.D. #1, Box 154-B
Route 611
Easton, PA 18042
(215) 252-0877, (215) 982-5697
Delaware River
Max. rapids: I-II
NACLO
A small, friendly family business, Delaware River Canoe Adventures provides canoe, kayak, raft and tube rentals for use on over 175 miles of the Delaware River. Open from mid-April to mid- November, this enthusiastic young company has no long lines. Its trips encounter only Class I-II rapids and are suitable for beginners and advanced paddlers.

Trips last from one to ten days, ranging through a varied landscape. Two national parks and 50 islands are to be found on this long stretch of the Delaware, with its excellent campsites, abundant wildlife and numerous fish.

Evergreen Outdoor Center
William Nesbit
RD #5, Union Deposit Road
Harrisburg, PA 1711-4708
(717) 657-9476
Susquehanna River, Lehigh River, Delaware River, most central PA streams
Max. rapids: III-IV
NACLO
Evergreen Outdoor Center rents canoes and runs guided canoe trips on the Susquehanna, Lehigh and Delaware rivers, along with most central Pennsylvania streams. It helps paddlers plan their trips, choosing easy flat water or Class II whitewater. Lessons are given by certified instruc-

Canoeing the Delaware River. Courtesy of Kittatinny Canoes, Dingman's Ferry, Pennsylvania.

tors well versed in all the streams traveled. Camping is available.

Trips run 1-10 days during a season lasting from mid-April to mid-October. They cover some excellent native trout and bass streams unaffected by drought. Paddlers see limestone springs along with deer, hawks, eagles and other wildlife.

Jim Thorpe River Adventures, Inc.
David and Robert Kuhn
1 Adventure Lane
Jim Thorpe, PA 18229
(717) 325-2570, (717) 325-4960,
(800) 424-RAFT
Lehigh River
Max. rapids: III-IV

Jim Thorpe River Adventures rents rafts and has one-day and two-day guided kayak and raft trips on the Lehigh River, with its beautiful mountain scenery and profusion of wildlife. Open from March to October, the company caters to beginners and intermediate paddlers, with its toughest rapids rated Class III-IV.

Anglers fish for bass, trout and pickerel in the Lehigh's waters. The company offers lessons, camping is available and the river is good for swimming.

Kittatinny Canoes
Ruth Jones
Star Route Box 360
Dingmans Ferry, PA 18328
(800) FLOAT KC
Delaware River
Max. rapids: I-II
NACLO, America Outdoors

Family-owned for three generations, Kittatinny Canoes offers trips on over 100 miles of the Delaware River. Canoes, kayaks, rafts and tubes are all available, for periods of up to seven days. Beginners can start on flat water and experienced paddlers can enjoy Class I-II whitewater. The Delaware is crystal clear, with tall cliffs, forested mountains and wooded islands. Eagles, osprey and many other birds and animals may be seen, with bass, shad, muskies and pike awaiting the fisherman.

Kittatinny's season runs from April to October. It also offers lessons and camping.

Laurel Highlands River Tours
Mark and Linda McCarty
P.O. Box 107
Ohiopyle, PA 15470
(412) 329-8531, (800) 4 RAFTIN
Middle Youghiogheny River, Lower Youghiogheny River, Cheat River
Max. rapids: III-IV
America Outdoors

Laurel Highlands River Tours, one of the oldest whitewater companies in the East, claims to have the largest fleet of equipment anywhere. It operates on the Cheat River as well as the Lower, Middle and Upper Youghiogheny from bases in Albright, W.Va. Ohiopyle, Pa. and Friendsville, Md. In a season running from March to October, it offers guided raft trips and rents both rafts and canoes for floats on both rivers. All are one-day trips.

The "Yok" has the most popular whitewater in the East and the Cheat is famed for its spring thrills. Canoeing and kayaking instruction is available and acommodations range from camping to luxury motels.

Mountain Streams and Trails
Michael S. McCarty
P.O. Box 106, Route 381
Ohiopyle, PA 15470-0106
(800) 245-4090
Lower, Middle, and Upper Youghiogheny River, Cheat River, Gauley River, Tygart River, Big Sandy Creek
Max. rapids: V+
America Outdoors

Mountain Streams and Trails operates on all three sections of the Youghiogheny as well as the Class III-IV Cheat, the challenging Tygart, iso-lated Big Sandy Creek and the Class III-VI Upper and Lower Gauley rivers. It runs guided raft and kayak trips in addition to renting canoes, kayaks and rafts, tailoring its trips to suit the needs of every paddler.

The company has skilled guides, trained in first aid and equipped with radios. They take guests through the spectacular panorama of maples, pines and rhododendrons that blanket the walls of the Middle and Lower Yough River canyon, habitat for deer, beaver, bear, osprey, heron and an occasional wildcat. One-day and two-day tours are offered during a March-October season.

Northbrook Canoe Company
Ezekiel Hubbard
1810 Beagle Road,
Northbrook
West Chester, PA 19382
(215) 793-2279, (215) 793-1553
Brandywine Creek
Max. rapids: I-II
NACLO

Based directly on the Brandywine River, Northbrook Canoe has canoes and tubes for rent to people who enjoy paddling gentle waters amid diverse scenery and wildlife. These leisurely trips last anywhere from one to six hours and are available from April to October. Ideal for beginners and families, they take paddlers through no riffles more difficult than Class I-II.

Observant floaters can admire herons, raccoons, foxes, otters, and turtles while fishing for bass, trout, and other fish.

Rafting on the Lower Youghiogheny. Courtesy of Laurel Highlands River Tours, Ohiopyle, Pennsylvania.

Pack Shack Adventures, Inc.
John C. Greene and Family
88 Broad Street
P.O. Box 127
Delaware Water Gap, PA 18327
(717) 424-8533
Pine Creek, Delaware River, Broadheads Creek
Max. rapids: III-IV
NACLO

Pack Shack Adventures specializes in five-day canoeing/camping trips for scouts, other youth groups and families. These and other guided tours are by raft and canoe on Pine Creek, the Delaware River and Broadheads Creek with its spring wildwater. In addition, Pack Shack rents canoes, rafts, kayaks and tubes.

The most difficult rapids on these waters are Class III-IV. The Pine River is noted for its trout while bass fishing is great on the Delaware, with its plush green valley and distant mountains. Paddling lessons are available. Campers help out with light chores.

Pine Creek Outfitters, Inc.
Chuck Dillon
RD #4, Box 130B
Wellsboro, PA 16901
(717) 724-3003
Pine Creek
Max. rapids: I-II
NACLO

Pine Creek Outfitters offers guided trips and rents rafts and canoes for trips of one to three days through Pine Creek Gorge, Pennsylvania's "Grand Canyon." Experienced and knowledgeable guides take rafters nearly 20 miles through the gorge from the March ice thaw until the water gets too low to float — usually mid-June — and again from mid-September to mid-November.

Various overnight camping and inn-to-inn tours are also provided. The wilderness scenery, fishing and wildlife are excellent.

Pocono Whitewater Adventure Center
Douglas Fogal
Route 903
Jim Thorpe, PA 18229
(717) 325-3656
Lehigh River
Max. rapids: III-IV
America Outdoors

Pocono Whitewater Adventure Center runs guided raft trips and rents rafts on the scenic Lehigh River with its 1,000-foot deep gorge. Rapids are rated Class III-IV and trips last one to two days. The company's season lasts from March to November and its customers enjoy swimming as well as paddling this popular stream.

The river is clean and undeveloped despite its proximity to major population centers. Rafters may catch a glimpse of bear, deer and hawks, while anglers go for trout and bass.

Riversport
Robert Ruppel
213 Yough Street
Confluence, PA 15424
(814) 395-5744
Youghiogheny River, Big Sandy River, Cheat River, Casselman River
Max. rapids: III-IV
NACLO

An excellent paddling school in the Pennsylvania area, Riversport runs one-day canoe and kayak trips as well as renting rafts, canoes and kayaks. It operates on the challenging and beautiful Youghiogheny, Big Sandy, Cheat and Casselman rivers from March to November.

Riversport's trips are suitable for youngsters, adults and senior citizens in good health. Its lessons teach the skills beginners and intermediate paddlers need to run the Class III-IV rapids of nearby rivers, with their hemlocks, rhododendrons, mountain laurel and rich wildlife.

Shawnee Canoe Trips
Shawnee Group
Box 93
Shawnee on Delaware, PA 18356
(717) 424-1139
Delaware River
Max. rapids: I-II
NACLO

Shawnee Canoe Trips rents canoes, kayaks and tubes for periods of one day to two weeks and serves the Delaware Water Gap area. These are mostly flat-water floats with a few rapids along the way, suitable for novices and experienced paddlers alike. Most of the trips go through the national park with its beautiful mountainsides and wealth of wildlife. Bass, pickerel and muskie lurk in the waters, plus shad in the spring. Lessons are also available during Shawnee's May-to-September season.

USA RAFT
Mary Kay Heffernan
P.O. Box 277
Rowlesburg, WV 26425
(304) 454-2475, (800) USA RAFT
Upper Youghiogheny River, New River, Tygart River, Gauley River, Cheat River, North Fork Potomac River, Nolichucky River, Ocoee River, Nantahala River, French Broad River, Nolichucky River, Rio Grande
Max. rapids: V+
America Outdoors

USA Raft is the reservation and marketing company for Appalachian Wildwaters, Rough Run Expeditions, and Expeditions, Inc. Its staff can help you choose the ideal raft or "funyak" trip from among 30 different outings on ten of the best whitewater rivers in the East: the New, Gauley, Cheat, and Tygart in West Virginia; the Upper Youghiogheny and North Fork of the Potomac in Maryland; the Nolichucky and Ocoee in Tennessee; and the Nantahala, French Broad, and Nolichucky in North Carolina.

With this selection of trips, rivers, and outfitters, USA Raft can offer outings to suit paddlers of all skill levels at locations convenient to residents throughout the Middle Atlantic and Southeast. Open year-round, USA Raft also provides package trips that include meals and lodging. And, for winter paddling, it has one- to nine-day trips on the Rio Grande in Texas.

White Water Adventurers, Inc.

Robert and Shirley Marietta
P.O. Box 31
Ohiopyle, PA 15470
(412) 329-8850, (800) WWA-RAFT
(992-7238)
Upper, Middle, and Lower Youghiogheny River, Cheat River
Max. rapids: III-IV
America Outdoors, West Virginia Eastern Professional Outfitters

White Water Adventurers runs guided raft and kayak trips on the Lower, Middle and Upper Youghiogheny as well as renting canoes, kayaks and rafts from March to November. Paddlers can take their pick; the dam-controlled Yough is rated Class V on its upper section and Classes III and II on its lower and middle stretches respectively. Trips are suitable for "folks from 12-100 who are willing to paddle a bit and have a good time."

A highly professional staff and the best modern equipment are mainstays of the company, which offers lessons and provides a guide for every raft on the steep and technical Upper Yough. Trout, walleye and bass can be caught on the "Yok" as it winds through the Laurel Highland Mountains.

In West Virginia, White Water Adventurers of Cheat River Canyon runs "very thrilling" guided raft trips from March to July through Class IV-V rapids on the free-flowing Cheat River. The stream cuts through a very steep canyon in an historic part of West Virginia. It has beautiful wildflowers and mountain laurel, along with deer, wild turkeys, and grouse.

White Water Rentals

Robert Marietta
P.O. Box 31
Ohiopyle, PA 15470
(412-329-8850, (800) WWA-RAFT
Middle and Lower Youghiogheny River
Max. rapids: III-IV
America Outdoors

Whitewater Rentals has rafts, canoes and kayaks for one-day use on the Middle and Lower Youghiogheny. Its professional staff is skilled at outfitting individual paddlers according to their particular needs. Trips range from mild water suitable for family floating to wild Class III-IV rapids.

The "Yok" is very clean and provides outstanding cold-water fishing for rainbow and brown trout, walleye and bass. Whitewater Rentals operates from March to November. Its clients enjoy the rugged mountain landscape with its hardwoods and mountain laurel.

Whitewater Challengers, Inc.

Kenneth Powley
P.O. Box 8
White Haven, PA 18661
(717) 443-9532
Hudson River, Moose River, Lehigh River
Max. rapids: V+
NACLO

Whitewater Challengers runs guided raft and kayak trips and rents rafts for the Lehigh, Hudson and Moose rivers, with their varying demands on paddlers' skills. The Lehigh is Class II and suitable for novices, the Hudson is an adventurous Class IV and the Moose is for Class V experts only.

Conveniently located near major interstate highways, the company has a superb 17-year safety record and is dedicated to guest satisfaction. Its paddling waters are clean, scenic, and full of fish and wildlife ranging from eel and carp to bear, hawk and blue heron. During its March-October season, Whitewater Challengers also offers paddling lessons.

Whitewater World
Douglas Fogal
Route 903
Jim Thorpe, PA 18229
(717) 325-3656
Hudson River, Moose River, Cheat River
Max. rapids: V+
America Outdoors
Operating in the Adirondacks during spring and fall, Whitewater World runs one- and two-day guided raft trips on the Hudson, Moose, and Cheat Rivers. These are clean, scenic streams with Class V+ rapids, coursing through a remote mountain wilderness area.

Whitewater World uses the latest self-bailing rafts and has a new assembly area. It describes its Adirondack runs as "extremely pretty and wild for the East." Bear, moose and deer can be seen, while the fish include trout and bass.

Wilderness Voyageurs, Inc.
Lance Martin
P.O. Box 97
Ohiopyle, PA 15470
(412) 329-5517, (412) 329-4752,
(800) 272-4141
Middle and Lower Youghiogheny River
Max. rapids: III-IV
America Outdoors
Wilderness Voyageurs, operating on the Middle and Lower Yough,

rents canoes, kayaks, rafts and duckies and provides guided trips in all these craft. With professional river guides dedicated to giving a quality wilderness experience, the company has an outstanding safety record.

Half-day to one-day trips start downstream of an impressive 20- foot waterfall and run seven miles through a wilderness gorge. The season runs from April 1 to October 15 and Wilderness Voyageurs can accommodate people of all ages on gentle floats or through Class III-IV whitewater.

Rhode Island

Tiny Rhode Island has a surprising amount to offer paddlers content to relax, fish, and birdwatch. Great Swamp, near Kingston in the south, is a state wildlife management area and home to sun turtles, water moccasins, herons, mallards, wild turkeys, deer, opossums, and redwing blackbirds. Seabirds such as herons, egrets, and sandpipers can be admired near the coast. Wood River in Exeter has good trout, bass, and pike fishing.

Great Swamp, famous for the colonists' defeat of Narragansett Indians led by King Philip (Metacomet) in 1676, can be reached along the tiny Chipuxet River from a put-in at West Kingston. The trip starts under a forest canopy, and canoeists may have to duck under low branches. Next one passes through marshy wetlands, finally emerging on Worden Pond. Here the paddling can be heavy going when headwinds whip up whitecaps.

Narrow River, also known as the Pettaquamscutt, runs southward parallel to the Narragansett Bay shore until it flows into the sea at Narrow River Inlet. It is a tidal waterway, allowing paddlers who time it right to ride the ebb tide when they set out and the flood tide when they return. Small ocean fish known as "buckies" spawn in the upper reaches of the river every spring. A pastoral stretch upstream turns built-up and popular with summer powerboats further down, and only daring paddlers attempt the surf at Narrow River Inlet.

Wood River, in western Rhode Island, is a particularly appealing stream — not just for its fish and wildlife but also its wooded scenery in the Arcadia Management Area. Its most popular section runs for 13 miles to the village of Alton.

In the northwest corner of the state the Pascoag even offers the paddler a taste of fast water. Soon after the put-in at Harrisville, the river runs over two dams. One is easily runnable but the second can be a tricky three-foot drop when the river is high. Further downstream the scenic Pascoag provides a good marshy area for fishing and picnicking before it turns lively again and becomes the Branch River. At this point there is a dam by an old factory that must always be portaged, and finally a 100-yard dash of shallow rocky rapids.

Quaker Lane Bait and Tackle
Michael S. Betwick
4019 Quaker Lane
North Kingstown, RI 02852
(401) 294-9642
Wood River
Max. rapids: I-II
NACLO

   Quaker Lane Bait and Tackle rents canoes, kayaks and johnboats for trips of one to three days on the scenic Wood River. This river, with only gentle rapids, is fine for beginners as well as seasoned canoeists. Its clean waters offer great fishing for trout, bass, and pike, and its tranquil, wooded setting shelters deer, otters, birds, and other wildlife for paddlers to observe. Quaker Lane, open year-round, has helpful staff on hand seven days a week, from 4.30 a.m. to 8 p.m., to help paddlers plan trips and get underway.

South Carolina

Compared to its neighbors, South Carolina has only a tiny slice of the Appalachian Mountain system which stretches from Pennsylvania to northern Georgia. Only some 500 square miles of South Carolina terrain, in the extreme west, can be termed mountainous. As a result, most river paddling in the state is relatively serene.

But there is one great exception — the celebrated Chattooga River which marks the state line between South Carolina and Georgia. Familiar to moviegoers as the setting for the whitewater film *Deliverance*, the Chattooga has some of the most exciting rapids in the East. One of the nation's first Wild and Scenic Rivers, it attracts tens of thousands of rafters annually as it churns through the scenic Sumter and Chattahoochee national forests. Yet the river is less crowded than many other famous streams, since rafts are spread out over a 20-mile distance.

The Chattooga's hairiest section is the eight-mile stretch from the US 76 bridge to Lake Tugaloo. There the river roars through a remote and inaccessible canyon, dropping nearly 50 feet per mile. Rafters must negotiate Class IV-V rapids with names like Corkscrew and Sock-Em-Dog in quick succession. Their only chance to admire the scenery — lofty cliffs, handsome rock formations and waterfalls — is when the river slackens its headlong rush in the late summer and fall.

For a more relaxing experience, the Edisto River gives floaters a fine opportunity to view wildlife: alligators, otters, snakes, foxes, white-tailed deer, bobcats, wild turkeys and bird species from kingfishers to hummingbirds. The Edisto canoe and kayak trail offers 56 miles of pastoral paddling within easy reach of Charleston. The river is claimed to be the nation's longest free-flowing black water stream — the term black water denoting its dark tannin-rich color.

Canoes, kayaks and johnboats find their place under the moss-draped live oaks and black maples of the Edisto all summer long. The river can be run safely by novices and access is easy at many points. Fishing is first-rate for largemouth bass, bream, catfish, jackfish and crappie. Floaters can interrupt their gentle progress down this scenic river to picnic and camp on the sandbars and banks of its upper reaches, or at developed campgrounds further downstream.

Carolina Heritage Outfitters
S. Scott Kennedy
General Delivery
Canadys, SC 29433
(803) 563-5051
*Edisto River, Santee River, Savannah
River, Black River*
Max. rapids: None
NACLO
Carolina Heritage Outfitters runs
guided and unguided canoe and
kayak trips of one to 10 days on the
Edisto, Santee, Savannah, and Black
Rivers. These flat-water rivers are fine
for beginners and any paddler look-
ing for a serene trip through scenic
southern low country, featuring cy-
press trees, tupelo swamp, and good
fishing for bream, bass, and catfish.
On these trips, which run year-round,
paddlers can also spot many types of
birds, reptiles and small game.

Edisto River Canoe & Kayak Trail Commission.
P.O. Box 1763
Walterboro, SC 29488
(803) 549-9595, (803) 549-5591
Edisto River, Combahee River
Max. rapids: None
The Edisto River Canoe & Kayak
Trail Commission offers guided
canoe and kayak trips on the Edisto
River, the world's longest black-water
river. Trips last a half day or full day,
run year-round, and are easy enough
for beginners. Along the way, paddlers can view river otters, deer, turkeys, ducks, alligators, snakes, and
other wildlife. Anglers can also fish
for red breast, catfish, and bass. Wildflowers bloom along the banks in
spring and fall, amid giant live oaks,
red swamp maple, black willows,
cypress, tupelo, gum, and tall pines.
Along the Edisto River Canoe and
Kayak Trail are two state parks, Col-
leton (803) 538-8206 and Givhan's
Ferry (803) 873-0692. Both offer
canoeing and picnicking.

Nantahala Outdoor Center
41 U.S. Highway 19 West
Bryson City, NC 28713
(704) 488-2175, (800) 232-RAFT
*Chattooga River, Nantahala River,
French Broad River, Ocoee River,
Nolichucky River*
Max. rapids: V+
America Outdoors
Nantahala Outdoor Center (NOC)
runs guided and unguided trips of
one to 21 days on five rivers in North
Carolina, South Carolina, and Ten-
nessee. Trips are by canoe, raft, or inflatable kayak.
Nantahala River trips, run near
Great Smoky Mountain National Park,
offer an excellent whitewater experience for beginners and families.
Runs on the French Broad River,
another ideal river for family rafting,
wind through a spectacular gorge in
the Pisgah National Forest. The
Ocoee is a favorite of whitewater enthusiasts, with big waves and constant action on its course through
Cherokee National Forest. The
Nolichucky offers high-water excitement in spring, gentler rafting and
kayak trips in late spring and early
summer, and stunning scenery at any
time. The Chattooga boasts some of
the finest white water in the
Southeast as it tumbles through the
Chattahoochee and Sumter National
Forests. NOC has Chattooga trips to
match any paddler's skill, beginner to
advanced.
NOC also offers lessons during its
March-to-November season.

Rolling Thunder River Company
Ken and Dina Miller
P.O. Box 88
Almond, NC 28702
(704) 488-2030, (800) 344-5838
Chattooga River, Nantahala River,
Ocoee River, French Broad,
Nolichucky River
Max. rapids: III-IV
America Outdoors
   Rolling Thunder River Co. runs
guided canoe, kayak, and raft trips
and rents canoes, kayaks, rafts, and
"funyaks" on five rivers in North Car-
olina, Tennessee, and South Carolina.
Trips on the Nantahala have Class II-
III rapids, are easy enough for beginners and families, and pass through
the beautiful Nantahala Gorge. Full-
day, wild-water raft trips are available
on the Ocoee. These trips, with Class
III and IV rapids, are suitable for
anyone age 12 and older. Private
canoe and kayak instruction on the
Ocoee is also available.
   On the Chattooga, Rolling
Thunder offers an exciting overnight
whitewater canoe trip with Class II-IV
rapids, spectacular scenery, and abundant wildlife. No experience is necessary on this guided trip. Finally, a
combination French Broad River-
Nolichucky River raft trip is available.
This two-day expedition includes a
night of camping at one of the
company's base camps.
   Rolling Thunder's season runs
from April to October.

South Dakota

South Dakota is good canoeing country, with rivers flowing through interesting scenery into the mighty Missouri. The state government has made it easy for paddlers to plan trips with its excellent leaflet, *Canoe South Dakota,* and separate brochures on the James River and Big Sioux River canoe trails. (Write the Game, Fish and Parks Department, 445 East Capitol, Pierre, SD 57501, for copies.)

Streams in the eastern part of the state drive through rolling hardwood forests while western creeks cascade from the Black Hills and converge into prairie rivers. The landscape runs the gamut from glacial plain croplands through short-grass prairie hills to steep chalk bluffs and ponderosa pine-covered foothills.

Some South Dakota rivers can be paddled year-round, others only in the spring and early summer, after snowmelt or rain. Some offer lazy floating while others have lively currents or require portages around dams and livestock fences. Campsites and parks flank a few rivers, while other streams wander through empty grasslands.

One of the state's favorite canoeing rivers is the Big Sioux, much of which can be floated all summer. Its slow current takes it on a winding course through a thin belt of timber with a variety of wildlife, from white-tail deer to painted turtles. The 52-mile stretch from Sioux Falls to Newton Hills — along the Iowa border — can be paddled comfortably in four days. Markers placed 300 feet upstream of lowhead dams warn of danger ahead, and portage signs indicate take-out points. For up-to-date water levels, call the Newton Hills State Park weekdays at (605) 987-2263. Canoeists wanting to explore the upper segments of the Big Sioux can start at Brookings, but there is only enough water during spring and early summer. In season, the entire 270-mile distance from Brookings to the river's confluence with the Missouri can be canoed.

The James River, a prairie stream that flows north-south through the state, has been called the longest unnavigable river in the world. But this does not apply to canoeists, who can float a 76-mile trail (from a put-in near Mitchell to Olivet) until early July, and sometimes through the summer. Normally this is a five-day trip but it can vary with current and winds. The slow-moving, curving river contains many species of wildlife including wood ducks. Six lowhead dams, three of them close to Mitchell, must be portaged but eight access points are available. For information on water levels, call the Mitchell Parks and Recreation Department at (605) 996-7180 weekdays.

Whitewater enthusiasts enjoy Split Rock Creek, which rises near the Pipestone National Monument in Minnesota and follows a picturesque course through Minnehaha County to join the Big Sioux near East Sioux Falls. The stream runs through Palisades State Park and parts of it run between sheer cliffs of red quartzite.

State officials recommend two segments of the Missouri for canoeing: the 40-mile stretch from Fort Randall Dam to Running Water, opposite the Nebraska town of Niobrara, and the 60-mile run from Gavins Point Dam to Ponca State Park, Nebraska. On both stretches the river is wide and clear, with sandbars and small islands. The lower section, which has several developed campsites and picnicking areas, has been designated a National Recreation River within the National Wild and Scenic River system.

In western South Dakota, the Belle Fourche River offers scenic floating through rolling plains dotted with buttes, peaks, and pinnacles. A popular run, water level permitting, is on Spearfish Creek and the Red Water River to the Belle Fourche and on to its confluence with the Cheyenne. The Cheyenne itself, flowing through remote grassland and rolling hills, has a good 55-mile run ending at the SD 63 bridge. Other recommended canoe trails in western South Dakota are on the White, Little White, Little Missouri, Moreau, and Grand rivers.

Cottonwood Corral
Jerry and Deanna Mueller
Route 1, Box 241
Yankton, SD 57078
(605) 665-9589
Lewis and Clark Lake, Missouri River, James River, Yankton Lake
Max. rapids: None
Cottonwood Corral rents canoes from mid-April to mid-October for relaxed paddling, fishing, camping and swimming in Lewis and Clark Lake, Yankton Lake and adjoining rivers. The river paddling — on the Missouri above and below the lakes and on the James — is relatively easy. Anglers go for walleye and bass, among other fish. Wildlife in the area consists chiefly of birds.

Missouri River Outfitters
124 Court Street
Vermillion, SD 57069
(605) 624-4823
Missouri River
Max rapids: None
Missouri River Outfitters offers guided and unguided canoe trips of one to four days on the Missouri River and area lakes and ponds. The stretches paddled boast exceptionally clean water and attractive scenery of bluffs, trees, islands, and sandbars. These gentle, flat-water trips also offer fishing for catfish, walleye, carp, sturgeon, and sauger. Bird watchers can enjoy views of eagles, turkey buzzards, and blue herons. MROs season runs from April to October.

Tennessee

T ennessee's star year-round attraction for thrill-seeking paddlers is the dam-controlled Ocoee River, proposed site of the 1996 Olympic whitewater events. Less than an hour's drive east of Chattanooga, the Ocoee winds through a deep and beautiful gorge in the Cherokee National Forest. Over a five-mile stretch its level drops at an average rate of 50 feet a mile, making it a continuous Class III-IV whitewater experience. Its rapids have such colorful names as Hell's Hole, Broken Nose, and Double Trouble. But local rafting outfitters say that with their experienced guides, the adventure is safe for everyone. Nearby is the Hiwassee River, also offering Class III-IV rapids as well as a glimpse of deer, raccoons, and numerous bird species.

Elsewhere in the Appalachians, too, Tennessee boasts some of the most challenging whitewater and spectacular scenery in the East. But the hazardous rapids on many mountain streams are runnable only in the winter and early spring. For example, there are two awesome gorges in the state's northeast corner along the border with Virginia and North Carolina. Paddlers on the Doe River thrill to the excitement of a narrow torrent confined between the 1000-foot bluffs of Cedar Mountain and Fork Mountain. The Doe's Class IV gorge on the seven-mile stretch above the town of Hampton is strictly for advanced canoeists prepared to scout the hazards.

In the same area, the celebrated Watauga River gorge cuts its way across the North Carolina state line. With rapids of up to Class V difficulty, gradients reaching 200 feet per mile, huge boulders, and hazardous drops, it should be attempted only by experts. Even they should be accompanied by a person familiar with the river in all its moods. But both the Doe and the Watauga can only be run from December to April, or after heavy rains.

Another of Tennessee's spectacular whitewater runs is the Big South Fork Gorge — a trip to be taken in the spring runoff weeks between late March and early May. This Class III-IV run on the Big South Fork of the Cumberland River is within the Big South Fork National River and Recreation Area. The nearby Obed River is the state's only National Wild and Scenic River, a pristine wilderness stream. Another springtime run through a handsome gorge, the trip from Obed Junction to Emory River, provides many Class III-IV rapids with such names as "Rockgarden" and "Oh My God."

For family canoe trips, the Elk River in south central Tennessee is a good bet, with its gentle current and profusion of trout, bass, blue herons, and basking turtles. Also in the middle of the state is the Harpeth State Scenic River, with many historic sites, mills, and Indian mounds. Here, too, floaters find easy paddling and good catches of smallmouth bass, brim, crappie, and catfish. The Sequatchie River canoe area near Dunlap northwest of Chattanooga offers clean water, fishing, and wildlife including foxes, minks, muskrats, blue herons, wood ducks, and Canada geese.

Around Gatlinburg, in the Smokies, families can enjoy rafting on the Nantahala, Big Pigeon, and French Broad Rivers in waters providing varying degrees of excitement. And the Buffalo River, which parallels the Tennessee River for part of its length, has great fishing.

The Buffalo River Canoe Rental Co.

Alf M. and Patricia Ashton
Route 4, Box 510
Flatwoods, TN 37096
(615) 589-2755, (615) 589-5403 (home)
Buffalo River
Max. rapids: I-II
NACLO, Tennessee Association of Canoe Liveries and Outfitters

Buffalo River Canoe Rental Co. offers guided canoe, kayak, raft, and flat-bottom boat trips and canoe, kayak, and raft rentals on the Buffalo River. The river, with Class I-II rapids, is challenging but fine for beginners. Its clear, cool, spring-fed waters also offer excellent fishing for smallmouth bass, largemouth bass, rock bass, crappie, pike, trout, catfish, and perch. The river is scenic, with views of rock bluffs, deer, turkeys, ducks, geese, and beaver. Trips run from one to seven. days.

During the March-to-October season, Buffalo River Canoe Rental also operates an attractive, primitive campground at the river's edge.

Canoe the Sequatchie

Scott and Ernestine Pilkington
U.S. Highway 127 South & River
Box 211
Dunlap, TN 37327
(615) 949-4400
Sequatchie River
Max. rapids: I-II
Tennessee Association of Canoe Liveries and Outfitters

Canoe the Sequatchie rents canoes for trips of one to seven days on the Sequatchie River. The river, fine for beginners and experienced paddlers, has exceptionally clean water and good fishing for smallmouth bass, rock bass, and sunfish. On its course through a unique rift valley, the Sequatchie offers many scenic spots to picnic, swim, and watch for deer, beaver, foxes, raccoons, minks, muskrats, great blue herons, wood ducks, and Canada geese.

Canoe the Sequatchie's season runs from April to October.

Cherokee Adventures, Inc.
Dennis Hedelman
Route 1, Box 605
Erwin, TN 37650
(615) 743-7733, (800) 445-7238
Nolichucky River, Gauley River, Russell Fork River
Max. rapids: V+
America Outdoors

Cherokee Adventures, Inc., runs guided raft and funyak trips of one to six days on the Nolichucky, Gauley, and Russell Fork Rivers. Trips on the Nolichucky, in national forest wilderness, run through the 2,000-foot Nolichucky Canyon. The Upper Nolichucky run, with Class III-IV rapids, is for paddlers 12 and older; the minimum age for trips on the Lower Nolichucky (Class II-III), is five. The Gauley and Russell Fork trips, with Class V-VI white water, run in the fall and are for experienced paddlers only. On these rivers, in quiet moments, paddlers can hope to spot deer, bears, and rabbits. There also is fishing for trout, muskie, bass, and catfish.

Cherokee Adventures, which runs trips from March to October, offers free riverfront camping for rafters on the Nolichucky.

Elk River Canoe Rental
Don and Lou Ann Townsend
Route 1, Box 20
Kelso, TN 37348
(615) 937-6886
Elk River
Max. rapids: None
NACLO

Elk River Canoe Rental rents canoes for trips of one to seven days on the Elk River. This scenic, flat-water river has clean, clear water, a gravel bottom, and steady flow throughout the season. Paddling is easy, allowing time to enjoy the Tennessee hill country of rocky bluffs, woodlands, and wildflowers. Along the way, paddlers can also enjoy fishing for trout, smallmouth and largemouth bass, and many types of panfish. On the banks, herons, wild turkeys, minks, beaver, muskrats, and deer are often seen. Elk River Canoe Rental's season runs from April to November.

Flatwoods Canoe Base
Richard and Julia Rotgers
Route 4, Box 612 B
Highway 13
Flatwoods, TN 37096
(615) 589-5661
Buffalo River
Max. rapids: I-II

Flatwoods Canoe Base rents canoes for trips of one to seven days on the Buffalo River from Natchez Trace to Blue Hole Bridge. With Class I-II rapids, the river is safe for beginners yet challenging for experienced canoeists. The clear, spring-fed waters offer good fishing for black perch, bream, smallmouth bass, and catfish. Paddlers also can enjoy beautiful views of limestone bluffs, waterfalls, wild flowers, fall foliage, and wildlife, including turtles, beaver, raccoons, and deer.

Flatwoods' season runs from May to October.

Hiwassee Outfitters Ocoee
Carlo J. Smith
P.O. Box 62
Reliance, TN 37369
(615) 338-8115
Ocoee River, Hiwassee River
Max. rapids: III-IV
NACLO

Hiwassee Outfitters runs half-day guided raft trips on the Hiwassee and Ocoee Rivers from two separate outposts. Trips on the Hiwassee, where the outfitter also offers raft and tube rentals, are perfect for families and inexperienced paddlers. The Hiwassee is a state scenic river and one of the

253

finest trout streams in the East. Trips on the Ocoee River, with Class III-IV rapids, are challenging, fun, and feature the spectacular wilderness scenery of Cherokee National Forest and the Smoky Mountains.

Trips on both rivers run between March and November and also offer good opportunities to view deer, bears, raccoons, beaver, and many species of birds.

Nantahala Outdoor Center
41 U.S. Highway 19 West
Bryson City, NC 28713
(704) 488-2175, (800) 232-RAFT
Ocoee River, Nolichucky River,
Chatooga River, Nantahala River,
French Broad River
Max. rapids: V+
America Outdoors

Nantahala Outdoor Center (NOC) runs guided and unguided trips of one to 21 days on five rivers in North Carolina, South Carolina, and Tennessee. Trips are by canoe, raft, or inflatable kayak.

Nantahala River trips, run near Great Smoky Mountain National Park, offer an excellent whitewater experience for beginners and families. Runs on the French Broad River, another ideal river for family rafting, wind through a spectacular gorge in the Pisgah National Forest. The Ocoee is a favorite of whitewater enthusiasts, with big waves and constant action on its course through Cherokee National Forest. The Nolichucky offers high-water excitement in spring, gentler rafting and kayak trips in late spring and early summer, and stunning scenery at any time. The Chattooga boasts some of the finest white water in the Southeast as it tumbles through the Chattahoochee and Sumter National Forests. NOC has Chattooga trips to match any paddler's skill, beginner to advanced.

NOC also offers lessons during its March-to-November season.

Ocoee Inn Rafting
Jerry Hamby
Route 1, Box 347
Benton, TN 37307
(615) 338-2064, (800) 221-7238 (TN),
(800) 272-7238
Ocoee River
Max. rapids: III-IV
America Outdoors

Ocoee Inn Rafting runs guided raft trips on the Ocoee, through five miles of exciting Class III-IV whitewater. These trips, fine for anyone over 12, are all in light, self-bailing rafts, a point of pride for the company. Paddlers pass through the beautiful Ocoee River Gorge, known for its mountain wilderness scenery. Trips run from April to November.

In addition to rafting, the Ocoee Inn offers rustic motel rooms, cabin rentals, family-style meals, and a boat dock on Lake Ocoee, where guests can rent canoes, pontoon boats, and fishing boats.

Ocoee Rafting, Inc.
John and Diana Holloran
P.O. Box 461
Ducktown, TN 37326
(615) 496-3388, (800) 251-4800
Ocoee River
Max. rapids: III-IV
America Outdoors

Ocoee Rafting Inc. runs guided one-day trips on the Ocoee River, site of the 1996 Olympic whitewater events. The trips feature continuous Class III-IV rapids but are fine for beginners and anyone over 12. The Ocoee, running through the Cherokee National Forest, also offers beautiful wilderness scenery, trout and bass fishing, and plentiful wildlife, including deer, beaver, and, occasionally, bears.

Ocoee Rafting's season runs from March to November. During this time, guests on river trips can camp for free at the company's campground, equipped with hot showers and attractive sites.

Outdoor Adventures of Tennessee
Doug and Connie Simmons
P.O. Box 109
Welcome Valley Road
Ocoee, TN 37361
(615) 338-8634, (800) OARSMEN
Ocoee River
Max. rapids: III-IV
America Outdoors

Outdoor Adventures of Tennessee offers guided raft trips and tube rentals for half-day trips on the Ocoee. With Class III-IV rapids, the Ocoee is suitable for beginners and exciting for experienced paddlers as well. Set in the Cherokee National Forest, the Ocoee trips feature wilderness scenery and views of soaring birds and other wildlife.

During its March-to-November season, the outfitter also offers a picnic area and camping on wooded sites.

Outland Expeditions
Lamar Davis
6501 Waterlevel Highway S.E.
Highway 64
Cleveland, TN 37323
(615) 478-1442, (615) 478-3553,
(800) 827-1442
Hiwasseee River, Lower Ocoee River
Max. rapids: III-IV

Outland Expeditions offers guided raft trips and canoe, kayak, raft, and tube rentals on the Ocoee and Hiwassee Rivers. The Ocoee trips cover five-and-a-half miles of continuous Class III-IV white water, a challenging and exciting run for beginners and experts alike. Hiwassee trips are leisurely, scenic, and particularly good for beginners, families, and trout fisher-

men. On both rivers, paddlers may be able to spot black bears, woodchucks, deer, and other wildlife.

Outland's season runs from March to November. During this time, the company offers free camping on wooded sites at its headquarters.

Quest Expeditions
Keith Jenkins
P.O. Box 499
Benton, TN 37307
(615) 277-4537, (800) 277-4537
Ocoee River
Max. rapids: III-IV
America Outdoors

Quest Expeditions specializes in guided raft trips for small groups on the Ocoee River. These trips last a half day and are challenging, fun whitewater runs with Class III-IV rapids, and are suitable for almost anyone. Ocoee trips, which run between April and October, also offer beautiful mountain scenery. In addition, to its Ocoee runs, Quest offers fall and winter river trips on Class IV rapids through North America's last remaining tropical rain forest.

RAFT USA
Mary Kay Heffernan
P.O. Box 277
Rowlesburg, WV 26425
(304) 454-2475, (800) USA RAFT
Ocoee River, Nolichucky River, New River, Gauley River, Tygart River, Cheat River, Upper Youghiogheny River, Potomac River, Nantahala River French Broad River
Max. rapids: III-IV
America Outdoors

USA Raft is the reservation and marketing company for Appalachian Wildwaters, Rough Run Expeditions and Expeditions, Inc. Its staff can help you choose the ideal raft or "funyak" trip from among 30 different outings on ten of the best whitewater rivers in the East: the New, Gauley,

Cheat, and Tygart in West Virginia; the Upper Youghiogheny and North Fork of the Potomac in Maryland; the Nolichucky and Ocoee in Tennessee, and the Nantahala, French Broad, and Nolichucky in North Carolina.

With this selection of trips, rivers, and outfitters, USA Raft can offer outings to suit paddlers of all skill levels at locations convenient to residents throughout the Middle Atlantic and Southeast. Open year-round, USA Raft also provides package trips that include meals and lodging. And, for winter paddling, it has one- to nine-day trips on the Rio Grande in Texas.

Rafting In The Smokies/Pigeon River Outdoors, Inc.

Andrew R. MacKinnon
P.O. Box 592, Highway 321 N.
Gatlinburg, TN 37738
(615) 436-5008, (800) 776-7228
French Broad River, Nantahala River, Big Pigeon River
Max. rapids: III-IV
America Outdoors

Rafting in the Smokies runs guided oar-raft and paddle-raft trip on the French Broad, Nantahala, and Big Pigeon Rivers. The Nantahala trips, for beginners and intermediate paddlers, feature the dramatic wilderness scenery of Nantahala Gorge, good trout fishing, and crystal-clear water. The Big Pigeon River offers a challenging, roaring five-mile run through the Great Smoky Mountains National Park and Pisgah National Forest. This trip is for intermediate to advanced paddlers. Finally, the French Broad River offers a quiet, scenic trip on the placid waters for guests young and old. The French Broad River has bass fishing; the Nantahala has trout fishing.

Rafting in the Smokies/Pigeon River Outdoors runs trips between March and October.

River Sports Outfitters

Ed McAlister
2918 Sutherland Avenue
Knoxville, TN 37919
(615) 523-0066
French Broad River, Nolichucky River, Little River
Max. rapids: V+
ACA

River Sports Outfitters offers guided canoe, kayak, and raft trips and rents canoes and kayaks for trips on the French Broad, Nolichucky, and Little Rivers. These trips, of one to 18 days, run year-round through unspoiled wilderness, offering fine scenery, trout fishing, swimming, and camping. River Sport Outfitters has trips for paddlers of all abilities, and also offers river adventures in Costa Rica and the Grand Canyon.

Rolling Thunder River Company

Ken and Dina Miller
P.O. Box 88
Almond, NC 28702
(704) 488-2030, (800) 344-5838
Ocoee River, Chattooga River, Nantahala River, French Broad, Nolichucky River
Max. rapids: III-IV
America Outdoors

Rolling Thunder River Co. runs guided canoe, kayak, and raft trips and rents canoes, kayaks, rafts, and funyaks on five rivers in North Carolina, Tennessee, and South Carolina. Trips on the Nantahala have Class II-III rapids, are easy enough for beginners and families, and pass through the beautiful Nantahala Gorge. Full-day, wild-water raft trips are available on the Ocoee. These trips, with Class III and IV rapids, are suitable for anyone age 12 and older. Private canoe and kayak instruction on the Ocoee is also available.

On the Chattooga, Rolling Thunder offers an exciting overnight whitewater canoe trip with Class II-IV rapids, spectacular scenery, and abundant wildlife. No experience is necessary on this guided trip. Finally, a combination French Broad River-Nolichucky River raft trip is available. This two-day expedition includes a night of camping at one of the company's base camps.

Rolling Thunder's season runs from April to October.

Tip-A-Canoe Stores, Inc.
D.J. Spear
1279 Highway 70
Kingston Springs, TN 37082
(615) 254-0836, (615) 646-7124
Harpeth River
Max. rapids: I-II
Tennessee Association of Canoe Liveries and Outfitters

Tip-A-Canoe Stores, Inc., rents canoes on the Harpeth River for trips of one to four days. With Class I-II rapids, the river is easy enough for beginners, and offers fishing for smallmouth bass, brim, crappie, and catfish. Paddlers can enjoy the river's natural beauty, with its bluffs, tree-lined banks, and beaver, otters, deer, ducks, birds, and other wildlife. Designated a state scenic river, the Harpeth also has historic significance, named for two bandit brothers, "Big" and "Little" Harp, who terrorized the region during the late 18th century. Various Indian artifacts remain to be seen. These include mounds, mills, tunnels, carvings, and paintings.

During its March-to-November season, Tip-A-Canoe offers primitive camp sites, picnic supplies, canoe accessories, and custom trips.

Texas

Clear and cold, the spring-fed streams of the Hill Country attract more canoeists than any other rivers of Texas. This area stretches from the central section of the Texas-Mexico border to the Colorado River in the east. Many of its streams are seasonal and susceptible to flash flooding due to high runoff after heavy rains. But the San Marcos, for instance, runs year-round and its clean water appeals to novice and expert paddlers alike. Located between Austin and San Antonio, it is mostly flat water and only one of its rapids is classified. Naturalists can find several species of plants and wildlife that are said to be unique in the world. While paddlers fish for bass, perch, catfish and bluegill, they can observe hawks, owls, kingfishers and herons overhead.

Hill Country streams typically contain whitewater rapids, small waterfalls and boulder gardens. River banks are lined with tall bald cypress, sycamore, pecan and live oak trees, and cliffs are crowned with mesquite, cedar and yucca. The Guadalupe River, flanked by rolling hills and rocky bluffs, has rapids for both novice and expert as well as good fishing.

Further west lies the Mountain Region, with the Rio Grande offering some of the most exciting scenery and canoe water in the state. At the heart of this country is the Big Bend National Park, a truly spectacular wilderness of desert canyons. With sheer walls rising 1800 feet or more, the Big Bend ravines rank behind only the Grand Canyon and Hell's Canyon on Idaho's Snake River.

Big Bend's deserts abound with cacti, while river cane, mesquite, salt cedar and cottonwood line the Rio's banks. Canoeing and rafting can be enjoyed all year, but many paddlers say the best period is from Thanksgiving to Easter. In summer the river is at its lowest and the air temperature often rises above 110 degrees. The river is highly susceptible to flash flooding, especially during spring and fall. One of the most popular trips in the Big Bend is Santa Elena Canyon, a 17-mile float between 1500-foot canyon walls. It is enlivened by the "Rock-slide" rapid, side canyons, fern-covered waterfalls and cool swimming holes. Wildlife along this stretch includes eagles, rare peregrine falcons, bank beavers, wild burros and javelina.

Elsewhere in Texas the scenery may be less awesome but the rivers are still appealing to many paddlers. The forested region of East Texas has a wealth of slow-moving, coffee-colored streams which owe their hue to tannic acid. And in the coastal area many vacationers enjoy paddling the bayous, rivers and streams.

Big Bend River Tours
Beth Garcia
P.O. Box 337
Terlingua, TX 79852
(915) 424-3219, (800) 545-4240
Rio Grande
Max. rapids: III-IV
America Outdoors
Big Bend River Tours runs year-round guided raft tours through the dramatic wilderness of canyons and whitewater that comprises the Big Bend National Park. Trips last anywhere from half a day to three weeks. Most are suitable for rafters of all ages and skill levels. Within this mysterious and alluring desert-mountain country may be found deer, javelina, fox, beaver, and more bird species, including eagles, peregrine falcons and hawks, than in any other National Park.

BBRT's friendly guides enjoy describing the flora and fauna, geology, folklore, and history as they steer the rafts through the canyons with rapids of up to Class III-IV difficulty. Floaters can enjoy fishing, camping, swimming and paddling lessons.

Bighorn Expeditions
Pitchfork Enterprises, Inc.
P.O. Box 365
Bellvue, CO 80512
(303) 221-8110
Rio Grande, Dolores River, Green River
Max. rapids: III-IV
America Outdoors, Utah Guides and Outfitters
Bighorn Expeditions offers two- to eight-day guided oar-boat trips on the Rio Grande River in Texas, the Dolores River in Colorado, and the Green River in Utah. Unlike most outfitters offering oar-boat trips, Bighorn encourages guests to do the rowing. The company provides 11-foot, one-person rafts that are lively and river-worthy but small enough for easy handling. Trips include thorough lessons and begin on calm stretches, so they are fine for those with no rowing experience. Those wishing to row, however, should be in good physical condition. If you are unsure of your conditioning or prefer to concentrate on photography or bird-watching, you can elect to ride on one of the company's larger, guide-operated rafts.

Bighorn's trips run from March to November through scenic canyon terrain and offer good instruction in whitewater boating and wilderness ethics.

Paddle America

Far Flung Adventures, Inc.
Steve Harrison/Mike Davidson
P.O. Box 377
Terlingua, TX 79852
(915) 371-2489, (800) 359-4138
(reservations)
Rio Grande, Abiquiu Lake
Max. rapids: V+
America Outdoors, Rio Grande
Guides Association
Far Flung Adventures specializes
in taking rafters on camping trips
through the ruggedly beautiful Big
Bend region of Texas as well as in
other states in the U.S. and Mexico.
Its tours last from one to seven days
in a season running from January to
December. It caters to everyone from
novices to whitewater experts seeking Class V+ challenges.
   The remoteness of the Rio
Grande's Big Bend National Park, its
canyons and wildlife combine with
good fishing to make these trips unforgettable. Far Flung Adventures offers paddling lessons as well as
camping, fishing and swimming.

Hawk, I'm Your Sister
Beverly Antaeus
P.O. Box 9109
Santa Fe, NM 87504
(505) 984-2268
Rio Grande, Abiquiu Lake, Missouri
River, Smith River
Max. rapids: III-IV
   Hawk, I'm Your Sister of Santa Fe
specializes in women's wilderness
canoe and raft trips. Its year-round
program is geared to "women of all
ages, shapes, sizes and skill levels"
with guided trips in five states and
four foreign locations. Its aim is to
"teach you the language of the forests, canyons, deserts and waterways" in a safe and non-competitive
environment. It takes paddlers on the
Abiquiu Lake in New Mexico and on
the Rio Grande in Texas, with other
excursions to Alaska, Peru and China.

An oar-raft trip on the Rio Grande.
Photo by Jim Hudson, Rio Grande
River Tours, Lajitas, Texas.

High Trails Co.
Bob Narramore
3610 Marquis Drive
Garland, TX 75042
(214) 272-3353
Rivers and lakes in Texas
Max. rapids: III-IV
   High Trails, located at Garland,
close to Dallas, rents canoes, kayaks
and rafts for paddling on the rivers
and lakes of Texas, Oklahoma and
Arkansas. Although not itself on a
river, the company is within driving
distance of many good paddling
waters in all directions. Open year-
round, it loads rivercraft on
customers' cars or aboard its own
trailers for large groups.

Some of the rivers its clients paddle, like the Guadalupe, are challenging. Mostly they are clear streams offering great fishing and camping, along with glimpses of wildlife ranging from deer and nutria to many kinds of birds.

Kimbo's
Rocky Shepler
HCR 4, Box 73
Canyon Lake, TX 78133
(512) 964-3113
Guadalupe River, Canyon Lake
Max. rapids: None

Kimbo's rents rafts and tubes from March-October for day-trip paddlers on the attractive Guadalupe River and Canyon Lake. The waters involved are clean and cold, with what is claimed to be the best rainbow trout fishing in Texas. Anglers can also catch catfish, perch, striper and walleye. Floats are easy, safe and suitable for families and large groups.

Set in the Texas hill country, the Guadalupe gives paddlers a view of cliffs and large trees. Deer, turkeys, armadillo, buffalo, Texas longhorn cattle and birds also enliven the scenery.

Lajitas Trading Post
Bill C. Ivey
Star Route 70, Box 436
Terlingua, TX 79852
(915) 424-3234
Rio Grande
Max. rapids: III-IV

Lajitas Trading Post rents rafts for floats of up to Class III-IV difficulty through the spectacular canyons of the Rio Grande. The scenery is rugged, with chasms 1,500 feet deep amid the desert landscape. During the year-round season, Lajitas arranges half-day to ten-day trips suitable for people of all ages and levels of experience.

Camping is available, swimming is good and fishermen angle for catfish.

Paddlers enjoy a fresh-cooked meal on the Rio Grande. Photo by Jim Hudson, Rio Grande River Tours, Lajitas, Texas.

Rio Raft Co.
John F. Guenzel
P.O. Box 2036
Canyon Lake, TX 78130
(512) 964-3613
Guadalupe River
Max. rapids: I-II
NACLO

Rio Raft Company rents canoes, rafts, and tubes for one-day trips on the Guadalupe River above and below Canyon Dam. The Guadalupe passes through a region of sheer bluffs, limestone cliffs, rolling green hills, and tall cypress and pecan trees. In this area, attentive floaters can also spot turkeys, deer, hawks, squirrels,

261

Rafting on the Rio Grande. Photo by Jim Hudson, Rio Grande River Tours, Lajitas, Texas.

cranes, and turtles. The river has deep pools and small rapids, making for easy trips for novices and intermediate paddlers. Also, the river's cold, clear waters offer fishing for bass, perch, and rainbow and brown trout. Rio Raft's rentals are available year-round.

Roy's Rentals
Roy L. Vordenbaum
HCR 3, Box 869
New Braunfels, TX 78132
(512) 964-3721
Guadelupe River
Max. rapids: I-II
NACLO
　Roy's Rentals, located between Austin and San Antonio, rents canoes, tubes and rafts for paddling down the Guadalupe River from Canyon Lake to New Braunfels. From March to September, its courteous staff helps novices and experienced paddlers arrange one- to two-day trips of varying difficulty. At high water the river with its Class I-II rapids gains added excitement.

　Unlike large parts of Texas, the countryside along this stretch of the Guadalupe has rolling hills and riverside cliffs. Deer and ducks are plentiful, and the fish include catfish, rainbow trout, perch and bass.

Spencer Canoes/Shady Grove Campground
Pat Spencer
Route 1, Box 55R
Martindale, TX 78655
(512) 357-6113
San Marcos River
Max. rapids: I-II
NACLO

Spencer Canoes/Shady Grove Campground, conveniently based at Martindale between Austin and San Antonio, rents canoes and takes canoeists for guided trips on the San Marcos River. This is a clean, spring-fed river that is both beautiful and isolated. It has several unique plant and wildlife species. The company prides itself on the personal service it gives clients, ranging from novices to experts, during its year-round season.

The San Marcos is mostly flat water, with only one rapid that even rates Class I, so it is ideal for beginners. Its banks are relatively undeveloped and the river is well-stocked with fish.

TG Canoe Livery
Duane and Evelyn TeGrotenhuis
P.O. Box 177
Martindale, TX 78655
(512) 353-3946
San Marcos River, Blanco River
Max. rapids: I-II
NACLO

TG Canoe Livery calls itself a personable Mom and Pop business which sets out to ensure that individuals and groups alike have safe and enjoyable canoeing. Operating year-round, it rents canoes and provides guided day-trip paddling on the San Marcos and Blanco Rivers.

The San Marcos is said to be the cleanest river in Texas and it combines lush vegetation with small, interesting rapids. In addition to its rich birdlife, the river contains bass, perch, catfish, bluegill and gar.

Utah

Utah boasts 400 miles of raftable rivers ranging from the Green and Colorado to their lesser-known tributaries such as the Yampa, the San Rafael and the San Juan. Spectacular red-rock canyons, exotic wildlife, some of the most exciting white water in the West, easy rapids, calm floating — Utah has it all. You can sign up with Utah outfitters for Grand Canyon rafting expeditions (see *Arizona*), which typically start at Lee's Ferry, just south of the Utah-Arizona state line. If you want still more, you can go on package tours that combine horseback or mountain-bike riding with river running. Or you can take special educational trips on which expert guides discuss history, folklore, geology, or natural history.

If Utah cannot match the majesty of Arizona's unique Grand Canyon, it comes close. Utah's Green River gorge is as deep as the Grand Canyon and the rapids in the Colorado's Cataract Canyon rival any in the Grand Canyon for power and difficulty.

From Sand Wash on the Green River, floaters can take a four- or five-day trip over some 60 rapids — exciting but not technically difficult — alternating with swift, calm water. They pass through Desolation Canyon, a craggy chasm with sculpted cliffs and towering peaks on either side. It was Major John Wesley Powell who gave Desolation Canyon its name during his epic 1869 descent of the Green and Colorado Rivers. But although its colorful rock strata remain unchanged, it is not so desolate or deserted today. This rafters' favorite offers views of pine-covered desert mesas and cool, refreshing pools and side streams.

Elsewhere on the Green River floaters may enjoy Labyrinth and Stillwater Canyons, great places for canoeing, and the one-day run through Gray Canyon near Interstate 70. Fishermen take special delight in the stretch of the Green River just below Flaming Gorge Dam in the far northeast corner of the state. It is said to boast some of the best fishing water in the world, with the largest trout population of any river in the lower 48 states.

Upstream on the Colorado is Westwater Canyon, with its narrow Black Granite Gorge and its feisty rapids: Funnel Falls, The Steps, Last Chance, and Skull Rapid. On the upper canyon's calmer stretches, rafters may float in silent contemplation of a wilderness in which beavers, muskrats, raccoons, and great blue herons make their home, along with occasional golden eagles.

In Cataract Canyon, within Canyonlands National Park, rafters on the Colorado encounter 26 rapids bearing such names as Brown Betty, Mile Long, and the Button, followed by the Big Drops. This white water is described as "truly awesome" in the spring runoff season from late May through most of June. The scenery is fantastic, with the gorge deepening to 2,000 feet and its colorful walls crowned with buttes. Rafters also can hike to Indian ruins and view the confluence of the Green and Colorado rivers.

Adrift Adventures
Mike Hughes
P.O. Box 577
378 N. Main Street
Moab, UT 84532
(801) 259-8594, (800) 874-4483
Colorado River, Green River
Max. rapids: V+
Utah Guides and Outfitters, America Outdoors

Adrift Adventures runs guided raft trips of one to seven days on the Colorado and Green Rivers, passing through the stunning red-rock canyons of Canyonlands National Park. The trips vary greatly in difficulty, depending on the river, time of year, and whether guests elect to ride in an oar boat or paddle themselves. On all trips, beginners and experts alike can enjoy the spectacular rock formations and abundant Indian ruins, pictographs, and petroglyphs. Guests also can view wildlife, including bighorn sheep, deer, otters, beavers, and cougars.

Adrift Adventures' season is from March to November. During that time the company also offers jeep trips, jetboat tours, and mountain bike trips.

American River Touring Association
Steve Welch
Star Route 73
Groveland, CA 95321
(800) 323-2782, (209) 962-7873
Green River, Yampa River, Colorado River, Middle Fork and Main Salmon Rivers, Selway River, Merced River, Tuolumne River, Klamath River, Rogue River, Illinois River, Umpqua River
Max. rapids: III
America Outdoors, Oregon Guides and Packers, Idaho Outfitters and Guides, Utah Guides and Outfitters

ARTA offers a total of 16 raft trips in five Western states. The trips, in California, Oregon, Utah, Idaho, and Arizona, are by oar rafts, paddle rafts, oar/paddle combination rafts, and inflatable canoes.

Most trips are of Class III difficulty and appropriate for novices and families, as well as those with more experience. Other trips of up to Class V+ difficulty challenge even the most advanced paddler. Depending on the location, the trips also feature wildflowers, side streams, swimming holes, Indian ruins, warm water, abundant wildlife, good hiking and fishing, and hot springs.

ARTA, a non-profit company, also offers whitewater schools, professional guide training, and family discounts.

Bighorn Expeditions
Pitchfork Enterprises
P.O. Box 365
Bellvue, CO 80512
(303) 221-8110
Green River, Dolores River, Rio Grande
Max. rapids: III-IV
America Outdoors, Utah Guides and Outfitters

Bighorn Expeditions offers two- to eight-day guided oar-boat trips on the Rio Grande River in Texas, the Dolores River in Colorado, and the Green River in Utah. Unlike most outfitters offering oar-boat trips, Bighorn encourages guests to do the rowing. The company provides 11-foot, one-person rafts that are lively and river-worthy but small enough for easy handling. Trips include thorough lessons and begin on calm stretches, so they are fine for those with no rowing experience. Those wishing to row, however, should be in good physical condition. If you are unsure of your conditioning or prefer to concentrate on photography or bird-watching, you can elect to ride on one of the company's larger, guide-operated rafts.

Bighorn's trips run from March to November through scenic canyon terrain and offer good instruction in whitewater boating and wilderness ethics.

Bill Dvorak's Kayak and Rafting Expeditions
Bill and Jaci Dvorak
17921 US Highway 285
Nathrop, CO 81236
(719) 539-6851, (800) 824-3795
Arkansas River, Colorado River, Green River, Gunnison River, North Platte River, Dolores River, Middle Fork Salmon and Main Salmon River, Rio Grande, Salt River
Max. rapids: V+
America Outdoors, Colorado River Outfitters Association, Utah Guides and Outfitters, and New Mexico River Outfitters Association

Dvorak's runs a wide array of guided and unguided trips through 29 canyons on a total of 10 rivers in Colorado, Utah, and New Mexico. Scenery ranges from Alpine to desert, and whitewater ranges from Class I to Class V. Guests also have a choice of touring by canoe, kayak, or raft. With this selection of locations and trips, Dvoraks has offerings to suit any individual or group.

Trips run for one to 13 days between March and October and permit time for trout fishing and viewing deer, elk, bears, eagles, beavers, and coyotes.

Colorado River and Trail Expeditions
Vicki and David Mackay
5058 S. 300 West
Salt Lake City, UT 84107
(801) 261-1789
Green River, Colorado River
Max. rapids: III-IV

Colorado River & Trail Expeditions runs guided raft trips of five to 12 days on the Colorado River in Utah and Arizona, the Green River in Utah, and Glacier Bay and the Arctic National Wildlife Refuge in Alaska. These trips offer excellent whitewater and magnificent scenery in remote locations. Their difficulty varies with the river and season. Generally, all trips are fine for people in good health and good physical condition.

During its May-September season, Colorado River & Trails also offers educational trips, which study photography, history, natural history or ecology.

Eagle Outdoor Sports

Rex Mumford
P.O. Box 375
North Salt Lake, UT 84054
(801) 451-7238, (800) 369-6635
Green River, Yampa River
Max. rapids: III-IV
*Utah Guides and Outfitters, Green
River Guides Association*

Eagle Outdoor Sports runs guided
kayak and raft trips on the Green
River from Flaming Gorge Dam to the
Colorado state line, and on the Green
and Yampa Rivers in Dinosaur National Monument. These trips last four to
five days and feature clean water,
beautiful canyon scenery, private
campsites, trout fishing, and plentiful
deer, elk, bighorn sheep and smaller
wildlife. Trips are by oar- or paddle
raft and are fine for families. The minimum age is six for scenic trips and 11
for whitewater runs. Eagle Outdoor
Sports' season lasts from May to September.

Flaming Gorge Lodge

Craig W. Colletti
Greendale U.S. 191
Dutch John, UT 84023
(801) 889-3773
Green River
Max. rapids: I-II

Flaming Gorge Lodge offers
guided raft and dory trips and raft rentals of one to three days on the Green
River. Guided trips are by oar boat
and geared for those who want to
sample the Green River's excellent
fishing for cutthroat, rainbow, brook,
and brown trout. Raft rentals for self-
guided float trips run on the river just
below Flaming Gorge Dam. These
trips feature gentle rapids and scenic
canyons, and are fun and safe for
families and paddlers of all ages.

Open year-round, Flaming Gorge
Lodge also offers motel rooms, con-
dominium units, a general store, and
shuttle service. Nearby campgrounds
are also available.

Four Corners School

Janet Ross
East Route
Monticello, UT 84535
(801) 587-2859, (800) 525-4456
San Juan River
Max. rapids: III-IV

Four Corners School offers guided
raft trips on the San Juan River. These
trips last five to eight days and pass
through a region of spectacular
geological formations, Anasazi ruins
and abundant wildlife, including raptors, deer, coyotes, and lizards. With
Class III-IV rapids and the choice of
either paddle or oar boats, floating
the river is not strenuous. However,
guests should be fit enough to participate in 3-6 mile day hikes to archaeological sites and rock
formations. Four Corners' trips run
from April to September.

Holiday River Expeditions

Dee Holladay
544 East 3900 Street
Salt Lake City, UT 84107
(801) 266-2087, (800) 624-6323
*Colorado River, Green River, San
Juan River, Yampa River, Snake
River, Main and Lower Salmon River,
Lochsa River*
Max. rapids: V+
Utah Guides and Outfitters

Holiday River Expeditions rents
canoes and rafts as well as running
guided canoe, kayak, and raft trips on
the Colorado, Green, San Juan, and
Yampa Rivers in Utah and the Snake,
Main Salmon, Lower Salmon, and
Lochsa Rivers in Idaho. These trips
last 1-12 days, offer oar and paddle
options, and range in difficulty from
beginners' runs to expert-level
whitewater adventures. Floaters pass
through pristine areas with spectacular scenery ranging from arid

desert canyons to alpine forests. Along the way, guests can camp, swim, fish for trout, and catfish, and spot deer, bighorn sheep, raptors, otters, and beavers.

Holiday's season runs from April to October.

Holiday River Expeditions of Idaho

Frogg Stewart
P.O. Box 86
Grangeville, ID 83530
(208) 983-1518
Salmon River, Colorado River, Green River, Yampa River, San Juan River, Lochsa River, Snake River
Max. rapids: III-IV
Idaho Outfitters and Guides Association, Utah Outfitters and Guides Association, America Outdoors

Holiday River Expeditions runs one to six day trips on 12 sections of eight rivers in Utah, Colorado, and Idaho. Guided trips are by kayak or raft, with both oar and paddle boats available. Paddlers can also rent rafts during the April-to September season. Overall, trips range from "mild to wild" and are suited for all age.

The company has been in business for 25 years, has an excellent safety record, and pays great attention to detail in training guides and maintaining equipment and vehicles.

Holiday River Expeditions also offers several specialty trips, including a whitewater guide school, kayak school, canoe trips on the Colorado River, and "ghost boats," a chance to run rapids in meticulously crafted replicas of boats from the past.

Hondoo Rivers and Trails

Pat Kearney
Box 98
Torrey, UT 84775
(801) 425-3519, (800) 33 CANYONS
Green River
Max. rapids: I-II
Utah Guides and Outfitters, Worldwide Guides and Outfitters

Hondoo Rivers and Trails runs guided kayak and raft trips on the Green River. Trips last up to six days and are designed for beginning and intermediate paddlers who want to learn whitewater skills and become comfortable with progressively larger rapids. Oar-boat trips are also available for families with young children and anyone preferring a less challenging ride. On Hondoo's trips, which run between May and October, guests can enjoy canyon scenery, swimming, sandy beaches, warm water, and fishing for catfish. In this remote, wilderness area, one can often spot deer, geese, eagles, and an occasional bear or bighorn sheep.

Lake Powell Tours, Inc.

Mark P. Slight
P.O. Box 40
St. George, UT 84771-0040
(801) 673-1733
San Juan River, Lake Powell
Max. rapids: I-II

Lake Powell Tours offers small guided kayak and raft trips and rents kayaks for trips of two to five days on the San Juan River and Lake Powell. River trips are good for beginners but also offer enough eddies and rapids to interest intermediate and advanced kayakers. On all tours, paddlers can enjoy the soothing desert landscape, unusual geology, and views of beavers, birds, deer, snakes, and bighorn sheep. One can also fish in Lake Powell for bass and trout and on the San Juan for catfish. Lake Powell Tours' season is from April-October.

Laughing Heart Adventures
Dezh Pagen
Trinity Outdoor Center
P.O. Box 669
Willow Lake, CA 95573
(916) 629-3516, (800) 541-1256
*Green River, Trinity River, Klamath
River, Eel River, Sacramento River,
Smith River, Russian River, Colorado
River*
Max. rapids: III-IV
NACLO, American Canoe Association
Laughing Heart Adventures offers
"consciousness raising" canoe outings on wild and scenic rivers
throughout the West and Mexico.
Before trips start, guides interpret the
geology and natural and human history of an area. Guides also gear
some special trips toward specific
goals such as stress reduction, holistic
health, music and art appreciation,
college credit, and environmental
politics.
Laughing Heart's guided trips are
by canoe, kayak, or raft. Rentals of
canoes, kayaks, rafts, and tubes also
are available. Trips run from one to
seven days year round. Kayak and
canoe lessons and trips are available
for paddlers of all skill levels.

Moki Mac River Expeditions, Inc.
Richard, Clair and Robert Quist
P.O. Box 21242
Salt Lake City, UT 84121
(801) 268-6667, (800) 284-7280
Colorado River, Green River
Max. rapids: V+
Utah Guides and Outfitters, NACLO
Moki Mac River Expeditions runs
guided canoe, raft and "funyak" trips
of 1-14 days on the Colorado and
Green Rivers. Runs on the Colorado
go through the Westwater, Cataract,
and Grand Canyons, and on the
Green River through the Desolation,
Labyrinth, and Stillwater Canyons.
Oar boats are available on all runs,
motorized boats are available in

Cataract Canyon and the Grand
Canyon, and oar-boat/funyak trips
run through Desolation Canyon. The
Grand Canyon has the largest, most
frequent rapids, Desolation Canyon is
milder and Cataract Canyon offers
great excitement during the high-
water runoff season.
Moki Mac also rents canoes for
trips through the Labyrinth and
Stillwater Canyons. All trips, set on
the Colorado Plateau, offer chances
to spot eagles, cranes, Canada geese,
bighorn sheep, and the occasional
bear. Guests can also fish for catfish
and trout. Moki Mac's season is from
April to October.

NAVTEC Expeditions
John and Chris Williams
321 North Main
Box 1267
Moab, UT 84532
(801) 259-7983
Colorado River
Max. rapids: III-IV
NAVTEC Expeditions offers
guided kayak and raft trips of half a
day to four days on the Colorado
through Westwater, Fisher Towers,
and Cataract Canyons. These trips feature spectacular canyon scenery, red-
rock cliffs and white-sand beaches,
with abundant great blue herons,
mule deer, beaver, bighorn sheep,
and other wildlife. Guests can elect
either paddle boat or motor raft trips
to suit their adventurousness.
NAVTEC's trips on the Colorado run
between April and October. From
December to March the company offers whale-watching trips on the Sea
of Cortez in Baja, Mexico.

Nichols Expeditions
Chuck and Judy Nichols
497 North Main
Moab, UT 84532
(801) 259-7882, (800) 635-1792
Green River, Copper River, Koyukuk River, Main Salmon River
Max. rapids: III-IV
Utah Guides and Outfitters, Idaho Guides and Outfitters

Nichols Expeditions runs guided kayak and raft trips on the Copper and Koyukuk Rivers in Alaska, rafting trips on Idaho's Main Salmon and "wilderness quest" workshop tours on Utah's Green River. The Alaska trips run through remote, pristine wilderness and offer many chances to see caribou, dall sheep, moose, bears, sea eagles, harbor seals, and other wildlife. Lasting 8-15 days, these paddle raft tours are fine for beginners in good shape. They range through a region of glaciers, waterfalls, and nameless peaks. Guests can also enjoy excellent food and exciting fishing for salmon, char, arctic grayling, and northern pike.

Operating year-round, Nichols Expeditions also offers sea kayaking on the Sea of Cortez and Magdalena Bay in Baja, Mexico, as well as trekking in Thailand and the former Soviet Union.

O.A.R.S.
George Wendt
P.O. Box 67
Angels Camp, CA 95222
(209) 736-4677, (800) 466-7238 (CA) , (800) 346-6277 (U.S.)
San Juan River, American River, Cal-Salmon River, Merced River, Stanislaus River, Tuolumne River, Rogue River, Colorado River, Snake River
Max. rapids: III-IV
America Outdoors

O.A.R.S. runs guided dory, raft and kayak trips in five Western states. It offers tours in California on the American, Cal-Salmon, Merced, Stanislaus, and Tuolumne Rivers; in Oregon on the Rogue; in Arizona on the Colorado; in Wyoming on the Snake, and in Utah on the San Juan River. These outings last one to 13 days and, depending on the class of river, are fine for children, novices, families, intermediate, and expert rafters. O.A.R.S. trips provide fishing, swimming, camping, side hikes, wildlife viewing and other activities.

O.A.R.S. tours run from April to October.

An oar-boat trip on the Green River. Photo by Norm Shrewsbury, courtesy of Sheri Griffith Expeditions.

The National Outdoor Leadership School
Nancy Siegel, River Manager
Box AA
Lander, WY 82520
(307) 332-6973
Green River, Prince William Sound, other Alaskan waters
Max. rapids: III-IV
America Outdoors, Colorado River Outfitters Association, Utah Guides and Outfitters Organization
The National Outdoor Leadership School specializes in teaching a wide array of backcountry skills including kayaking, rafting, mountaineering, rock climbing, glacier travel, backpacking and cross-country skiing. Its rafting trips run through Desolation Canyon on the Green River in Utah and Lodore Canyon on the Green River at the Colorado-Utah border. NOLS also offers sea kayaking in Alaska and Baja, Mexico. These instructional trips range in length from 14-31 days, with some trips geared for teenagers 16 and older and some for paddlers 25 and older. All trips are physically challenging; paddlers must be in good shape and excellent health.

These trips, which run between June and late October, feature beautiful scenery and sufficient challenge to ensure that all participants can test and improve their paddling skills.

Sheri Griffith River Expeditions
Sheri Griffith
P.O. Box 1324
2231 S. Highway 191
Moab, UT 84532
(801) 259-8229, (800) 332-2439
Colorado River, Green River, Dolores River
Max. rapids: III-IV
America Outdoors, Utah Guides and Outfitters, National Canoe Association
Sheri Griffith River Expeditions runs guided canoe, kayak, and raft

trips of 1-6 days through Westwater and Cataract Canyons on the Colorado River, Desperation Canyon on the Green River, and along the Dolores River. All trips are through protected lands — national parks and landmarks, wild and scenic rivers — where permit curbs limit the number of boats and ensure a true wilderness experience. On all trips, guests can enjoy exciting rapids, spectacular redrock canyons, excellent food and a chance to view bighorn sheep, golden eagles, and other wildlife.

Guests can choose between oar boats, paddle boats, inflatable kayaks and motorized J-rig rafts. Trips are of minimal to moderate difficulty, depending on river and choice of boat. During its May-Sept. season, Sheri Griffith also offers special family trips, luxury trips, holistic river trips, and combination mountain bike/raft trips.

Slickrock Adventures
Cully Erdman
P.O. Box 1400
Moab, UT 84532
(801) 259-6996
Green River, Dolores River, Payette River
Max. rapids: III-IV
America Outdoors
Slickrock Adventures runs guided kayak and raft trips of 5-13 days on Utah's Green River, Colorado's Dolores River, and Idaho's Payette River. Its most popular beginners' runs are raft and kayak trips on 85 miles of the Green River, through Desolation and Gray Canyons. Paddlers have time to play in over 60 easy rapids, and enjoy views of tall cliffs, sandy beaches, and cottonwoods.

The Dolores emerges from lush meadows and forests to descend into a desert canyon. Continuous white water in the upper canyon gives way

Paddle rafting on the Green River. Photo by Norm Shrewsbury, courtesy of Sheri Griffith Expeditions.

to widely-spaced, easier drops below. This allows Slickrock to choose stretches to match each group's ability. Green River kayak trips run through Labyrinth and Stillwater Canyons, offering peaceful, flat-water paddling through the heart of Canyonlands, with spectacular side canyons, petroglyphs, and Indian ruins. Finally, on the Payette, Slickrock offers a whitewater kayak clinic featuring incredible whitewater and beautiful canyons. Open all year, Slickrock also offers paddling trips in Belize and Mexico.

Western River Expeditions
Larry Lake
7258 Racquet Club Drive
Salt Lake City, UT 84121
(801) 942-6669, (800) 453-7450 (outside UT)
Colorado River, Green River, Main Salmon River
Max. rapids: III-IV
America Outdoors, Professional River Outfitters
   Western River Expeditions runs guided raft trips and rents rafts and in-

flatable kayaks on the Colorado River in Colorado, Utah and Arizona; the Green River in Utah and the Main Salmon in Idaho. Green River trips, by oar or paddle raft, provide thrilling whitewater and views of towering red rock cliffs and arches, deep gorges, frontier cabins, and Indian petroglyphs. Colorado River tours offer spectacular scenery in Cataract Canyon, Westwater Canyon or the Upper and Lower Grand Canyon. Rapids are moderate to large, and paddlers can swim, take side hikes and view historic Indian and Old West sites. Finally, trips on the Main Salmon involve scenic blue-green waters, pine-covered mountains, stops at hot springs and abandoned mining camps, and camping on white sand beaches.

   All trips are suitable for anyone of good health above the minimum age set for each trip, depending on its difficulty. During Western River's March-September season, some trips can be combined with a ranch stay.

Vermont

The Green Mountain State is graced with many rivers to take paddlers through its pastures, gorges, and mountain forests. Most Vermont streams are made for tranquil floating, not for crashing down thunderous rapids. Such white water as exists is modest by New York or Maine standards. Vermont's charms are different: relaxed paddling under covered bridges, past red barns and through wooded valleys dotted with inviting country inns. Of course the ideal time to go is in the fall when the foliage can be admired in all its glory.

Of the three big rivers that cut through the Green Mountain Range, the Winooski is the most scenic. It flows westward from its source in the cheesemaking area of Cabot to empty into Lake Champlain at Burlington. The Winooski is dammed at intervals and must be portaged, but is runnable all summer. It has deep gorges and views of Mount Mansfield to the north and Camel's Hump to the south.

Spaced further north, flowing parallel to the Winooski, are the Lamoille and Missisquoi Rivers, both of which also help feed Lake Champlain. One Lamoille run combines gentle floating past woods and meadows with occasional easy rapids. The Missisquoi takes a loop across the Canadian border before returning to Vermont. Both are appealing rivers.

The White River is one of the most beloved canoe trails in New England. It provides easy Class I-II rapids and water so pure that it was chosen as a spawning-ground by the Atlantic Salmon Restoration Project. On its way down to join the Connecticut River, the White flows through a scenic valley that was once a main Indian route between lower New England and Montreal.

The Black River in northcentral Vermont offers a slow, meandering float downstream from Albany, providing paddlers with pretty scenery and deep forests as it follows a curving valley. The Clyde River, which flows northwest from Island Pond, provides a Class-II run when the water level is right. Its lower stretch is secluded and has been called one of Vermont's best canoeing trails. Like the Black, the Clyde flows into Lake Memphremagog astride the Canadian border.

Near the pleasant little town of Waitsfield at the foot of the Green Mountains, the Mad River flows northward to its confluence with the

Winooski below Middlesex. It offers easy Class I-II rapids amid scenic forest. New Englanders seeking Vermont's best white water head for the West River on the first weekends of May and October. This stream in southern Vermont has lively Class II-IV rapids, scene of whitewater kayaking championships, in a gorgeous Green Mountain setting. It can only be run when the Ball Mountain Dam releases water — currently just those two weekends. Pick the October date if you want to combine paddling with fall foliage.

The Connecticut is a river on a totally different scale. More than 400 miles long, it divides Vermont from New Hampshire as it rolls majestically down toward Long Island Sound. Since the state line is drawn at the low-water mark on the Vermont side, the upper Connecticut actually belongs to New Hampshire.

Paddling on the Winooski River. Courtesy of Karen Krough/Battenkill Canoe, Arlington, Vermont.

Balloon Inn Vermont Vacations
Scott Wright
RR 1, Box 8
Fairlee, VT 05045
(802) 333-4326, (800) 666-1946
Connecticut River
Max. rapids: I-II
   Balloon Inn Vermont rents canoes from May-October for self-guided trips on the Connecticut River between Woodsville, N.H. and Orford, N.H. These trips, of one to three days, include lodging at historic inns along the river. With only Class I-II rapids to contend with, paddling is only moderately difficult, even for beginners. Along the way, floaters can enjoy the natural beauty of the river valley, and fishing for trout, pike, bass, and walleye. The company also offers bicycling, hiking and balloon trips.

BattenKill Canoe
Jim Walker
Vermont Canoe Trippers
Box 65, Historic Route 7A
Arlington, VT 05250
(802) 362-2800, (800) 421-5268
*Winooski River, Lamoille River, Missisquoi River, Clyde River, White River,
Black River, Connecticut River
Max. rapids: III-IV*
BattenKill Canoe offers guided
and unguided canoe trips of two to
ten days on the Winooski, Lamoille,
Missisquoi, Clyde, Black, Connecticut, and White Rivers. These outings
are exceptionally well organized and
widely varied to suit all skill levels
and tastes. Participants can choose
either whitewater or scenic trips, with
lodgings either at country inns or at
secluded riverside camp sites. Also
available throughout the March-November season are instructional trips
for all skill levels; river sampler trips
that offer paddling on a different river
each day; historic tours retracing explorers' routes, and fall foliage trips.
With this array of offerings, Batten-Kill gives paddlers a chance to view
scenic regions throughout the state,
from mountain to lush flatlands.

Clearwater Sports
Barry Bender
Route 100
Waitsfield, VT 05673
(802) 496-2708
*Mad River, Winooski River, White
River, Waterbury Reservoir
Max. rapids: III-IV*
Clearwater Sports offers guided
canoe, kayak, and raft trips and rents
canoes, kayaks, rafts, and tubes for
trips on the Mad, Winooski and
White Rivers as well as Waterbury
Reservoir. Guided one-day canoe
trips are available, along with escorted full-moon outings which include dinner as well as adventurous
paddling. For kayakers, Clearwater of-

fers two-day courses for beginners
through advanced paddlers. Sea
kayaking lessons are also available.
Canoeists and kayakers can run
rapids that challenge novices, intermediate paddlers, and — at high
water — advanced paddlers, too. The
scenery, fishing, and wildlife are
great. Clearwater also offers windsurfing, hiking, and mountain biking
during its April-October season.

Smugglers Notch Canoe Touring
Bette and Kelley Mann
Route 108S
RR 2, Box 4319
Jeffersonville, VT 05464
(802) 644-8321, (800) 937-MANN
*Lamoille River, Clyde River, Missisquoi
River, Winooski River, Black River,
Barton River, Greer River Reservoir
Max. rapids: I-II*
Smugglers Notch Canoe Touring
offers guided and self-guided canoe
trips of one or two days on the Lamoille, Clyde, Missisquoi, Winooski,
Black, and Barton Rivers as well as
the Greer River Reservoir. The scenery on these trips is picturesque, with
views of the Green Mountains, pristine countryside, and pine and maple
forests. There is also abundant wildlife, including hawks, loons, deer,
beavers, and sometimes bears and
moose. Paddlers can also enjoy fishing for sea trout, perch, and bass.
These trips, on placid waters, are fine
for all canoeists.

Stowe Action Outfitters
Dan Susslin
Box 2160
Stowe, VT 05672
(802) 253-7975
*Winooski River, Lamoille River,
Waterbury Reservoir
Max. rapids: I-II*
Stowe Action Outfitters provides
guided canoe trips and canoe and
tube rentals on the Winooski and

Lamoille Rivers and Waterbury Reservoir. These trips run on scenic, flatwater waterways that are well-suited for family trips and beginners. Guided canoe trips last half a day, with longer outings available by special arrangement. Rentals are for one- and two-day trips. On all outings, paddlers can enjoy fishing for rainbow, brown and brook trout, and watching for deer, moose, otters, eagles, falcons, and other wildlife. Stowe's season runs from March to November.

The Village Sport Shop
John G. Hibsman
P.O. Box 173, 74 Broad Street
Route 5
Lyndonville, VT 05851
(802) 626-8448
Connecticut River, Passumpsic River, Black River, Willoughby Lake
Max. rapids: I-II
The Village Sport Shop rents canoes for trips of one to five days on the Connecticut, Passumpsic and Black Rivers and on Lake Willoughby. The rivers, with Class I-II rapids, require whitewater paddling experience in the spring. However, by June 1 water levels have dropped enough to make all trips suitable for beginners as well. The trips pass through some of the loveliest country in Vermont, complete with covered bridges, red barns, sugar houses and lush forests. The region also contains moose, deer, foxes and bears, along with good trout, perch, bass, and pickerel fishing. The Village Sports Shop's season is April-October.

A covered bridge along the Battenkill River. Courtesy of Karen Krough/ BattenKill Canoe, Arlington, Vermont.

Virginia

Canoeing in Virginia naturally centers on the mountain streams in the west. The Old Dominion, like its neighbors to the north and south, stretches from mountains to the sea. Down in the Tidewater area adjoining Chesapeake Bay the land is divided into peninsulas by the broad Potomac, Rappahannock, York, and James Rivers. But most whitewater and recreational canoeing is done in the Shenandoah Valley between the Blue Ridge and the Allegheny Mountains.

Shenandoah, an Indian name, is said to mean "daughter of the stars." As a canoeing waterway, the South Fork of the Shenandoah is a favorite for paddlers from the Washington-Baltimore area. It can be run year-round and it has enough Class I-III rapids to lend spice to the trip and challenge novices. Outfitters run trips of various lengths along the meandering stretch of river between Luray and Front Royal. Here the hill scenery is mostly unspoiled as the South Fork winds its way along the George Washington National Forest. Local game species include bears, raccoons, deer, wild turkeys, quail, grouse, bald eagles, and hawks. Anglers enjoy excellent fishing for small and largemouth bass, perch, catfish, carp, and bluegill. A canoeing trip can also be combined with visiting one of the many caves in the area or hiking a woodland trail.

Further southwest along the valley lies another good canoeing area, the James River Basin around Lexington. Here flow the headwaters of the James and many smaller streams, including the Maury. It is a region of beautiful scenery, mostly gentle rapids, clean water, good fishing, relaxation, and solitude.

But not all the rapids in the James River Basin are easy. Whitewater buffs flock to the Maury in its upstream Goshen Pass area. Outfitters say this is probably the most popular whitewater run in Virginia. Depending on water levels, the rapids rate Class II-III and possibly Class IV for the first three miles. Next are nine miles of Class II-III white water before the river turns tame in its lower reaches. The Maury joins the James at Glasgow, ten miles south of Buena Vista.

The James is mostly easy Class I-II paddling in this headwater region. The only exception is its Balcony Falls stretch, which rates Class II+. Canoeists exploring the lower reaches of this river find that the most interesting stretch along the 185-mile section from Lynchburg to Richmond is a 13-mile trip just downstream from Scottsville. The area is fairly wild, with a nearby railroad as the only sign of civilization. There are over 300 islands along this stretch, as the river splits up into a skein of narrow channels. At low water there are various rapids, none tougher than Class II.

Far down at the James River estuary is Tidewater country, an area steeped in history. Paddlers roam rivers and creeks that the Jamestown settlers explored when they set foot in the New World in 1607. A leisurely tour of the new indoor museum at Jamestown, with its expert guides, is highly recommended. The waters of the James estuary, the Pagan and Blackwater Rivers, and neighboring creeks yield bass, catfish, and sea trout. The wildlife includes beavers, otters, muskrats, and birds of prey.

Downriver Canoe Co.
John Gibson
Route 1, Box 256-A
Bentonville, VA 22610
(703) 635-5526
South Fork Shenandoah River
Max. rapids: I-II
NACLO

Downriver Canoe Company rents canoes on a remote section of the South Fork of the Shenandoah River, which flows north between Shenandoah National Park and George Washington National Forest. The river is especially scenic, flanked by the Appalachian Mountains and offering views of beavers, otters, bald eagles, turtles, and other wildlife. Anglers also will enjoy the South Fork's profusion of smallmouth bass, as well as good fishing for bluegill, perch, catfish, and largemouth bass.

Trips last one to five days and are ideal for novices as well as experienced canoeists. The river's Class I-II rapids are fun and exciting but not dangerous. Downriver's season is from April- October.

Front Royal Canoe Co.
Don Roberts
P.O. Box 473
Front Royal, VA 22630
(703) 635-5440
South Fork Shenandoah River
Max. rapids: I-II
NACLO, PERO

Front Royal Canoe Co. rents canoes, tubes, and flat-bottom boats on the South Fork of the Shenandoah. These trips offer views of the Blue Ridge Mountains and abundant wildlife, including deer, squirrels, beavers, and occasional bears and bobcats. Anglers also can enjoy fine fishing on this clean mountain river for smallmouth bass, catfish, panfish, muskie, and largemouth bass.

Canoe trips last from one to seven days, are fine for paddlers aged six and older, and are available from March-November. On overnight trips free camping is available on government land. Tube trips cover three miles and last 3-4 hours. FRCC also has a store offering bait, tackle, and other paddling supplies.

Harpers Ferry River Riders, Inc.
Mark Grimes
P.O. Box 267
Knoxville, MD 21758
(301) 834-8051
Shenandoah River, Potomac River,
Tygart River
Max. rapids: I-II

Harpers Ferry River Riders offers one-day guided raft and tube trips and canoe rentals on the Shenandoah, Potomac, and Tygart Rivers. Trips on the Potomac and Shenandoah, with Class I-III rapids, are fine for beginners and offer scenic views of historic Harpers Ferry, wooded mountains, and abundant wildlife, including great blue herons, egrets, nesting bald eagles, turtles, geese, deer, and ducks. The two rivers also feature good fishing for smallmouth and largemouth bass, catfish, panfish, and carp.

The Tygart River, also scenic, has more challenging white water with up to Class V rapids, requiring previous paddling experience. The outfitter's season is from April to October.

James River Basin Canoe Livery, Ltd.
RFD #4, Box 125
Lexington, VA 24450
(703) 261-7334
James River, Jackson River, Cowpasture River, Calfpasture River, Tye River, Maury River, South River, Piney River
Max. rapids: III-IV
ACA, AWA

James River Basin Canoe Livery rents canoes and tubes on the James, Maury, Jackson, Cowpasture, Calfpasture, Tye, and Piney Rivers and Catawba, Craig, Buffalo, Kerrs, and Irish Creeks. With this array of trips, the livery has canoeing with fast water, flat water, game fish, camping, beautiful scenery, and other attractions.

Some trips feature high cliffs, others are pastoral, and all have views of the Blue Ridge Mountains. Along the way, paddlers can spot deer, herons, otters, beavers, turtles, turkeys, and ospreys, and fish for rock bass, smallmouth bass, perch, and bluegill. Floaters can select Class I, II or III runs, which last from 1-7 days. The livery's season runs from April-November.

Massanutten Canoe Co.
Jack Lockhart and Preston Matthews
Route 1, Box 34A
Bentonville, VA 22610
(703) 636-4724
South Fork Shenandoah River
Max. rapids: I-II

Massanutten Canoe Co. offers guided and unguided canoe trips of one to three days on the South Fork of the Shenandoah. These trips offer great wilderness scenery of protected national forest, the Massanutten Mountains, Indian fish dams, and abundant wildlife, including deer, beavers, turtles, eagles, owls, foxes, and hawks. For fishermen, the South Fork also offers good catches of bass, bluegill catfish, and carp.

Massanutten's trips run year-round, weather permitting, have Class I-II rapids, and are fine for beginners and experts alike.

Shenandoah River Outfitters
Route 3, Box 144
Luray, VA 22835
(703) 743-4159
South Fork Shenandoah River
Max. rapids: I-II

Shenandoah River Outfitters rents canoes and tubes on the South Fork of the Shenandoah for trips of 1-7 days. These trips are scenic, passing between two mountain ranges, and offering views of cliffs, caves, farmland, and abundant wildlife, including deer, ducks, and turkeys. Also, fishing in the Shenandoah is especially good, particularly for smallmouth bass, sunfish, perch, largemouth bass, catfish, crappie, and muskie. These trips are not difficult, offering only Class I-II whitewater, which is ideal for beginning whitewater paddlers.

Shenandoah River Outfitters, open all year, also offers a free steak dinner and lunch for groups of 20 or more.

Smithfield Paddler, Inc.
Gary Parsons
15017 Mill Swamp Road
Smithfield, VA 23430
(804) 357-4165
Pagan River, Cypress Creek, Jones Creek, Blackwater River, James River
Max. rapids: None
NACLO

Smithfield Paddler offers guided and unguided canoe and kayak rentals on the Pagan, Blackwater, and James Rivers, and on Cypress and Jones Creeks. These trips provide easy paddling for families, groups, and nature lovers on flat-water rivers. On these one-day outings, paddlers can view historic ruins and other remains dating back to the 1600s. The area also displays wilderness scenery and opportunities to view beavers, otters, hawks, eagles, egrets, and muskrats. Anglers also can enjoy excellent fishing for largemouth and smallmouth bass, catfish, and sea trout. Smithfield's season runs from April to November.

Washington

Breathtaking is the word for Washington's scenery: majestic mountains, evergreen forests, semidesert flatlands and snow-fed rivers slicing through to the Pacific. This is the land of the Cascades, of Mount Rainier, Mount Baker and the Olympic National Park. Many paddlers are content to take in the spectacle by floating on lakes amid snow-capped peaks.

For those with zest for more excitement, the Evergreen State has an abundance of fast-flowing wilderness rivers. They vary greatly in difficulty with the flow of water. In the spring — April through June — they are typically in spate from melting snow. From July until the end of the season in September they are fed by dam releases or melting glaciers. In any event the water is always cold, whether one is paddling in the mountains or the desert. Wet suits are recommended for whitewater runs, and floaters should check water levels before setting out.

The most popular river in the state is the Wenatchee, which runs off the east flank of the Cascades — the warmer and sunnier side. Its rapids rate as Class III+ and some previous paddling experience is recommended during peak run-off. With a highway beside the river for much of the run, civilization is never far away.

By contrast, superb scenery is to be found along the Sauk River, which flows through dense forest between snowy mountains on the west side of the Cascades. The Upper Sauk run, starting some 16 miles from Darrington, is eight miles long and has tough rapids at the beginning and the end which demand expert paddling. The Middle Sauk trip down to Darrington from the White Chuck River confluence is still more challenging, with its Class III-IV rapids rising to Class V at peak river levels. The Sauk is known for its rapid fluctuations in water flow, which may double from one day to the next. Parts of it are very difficult to scout because of the terrain and the whole river is subject to logjams.

One of the tougher rivers in the state is the Skykomish, with an eight-mile run rated Class III-V. The put-in is near Index, just off US 2 and only an hour's drive northeast of Seattle. Its most famous rapid is the Class V Boulder Drop which many paddlers prefer to portage. The

Skykomish is a very clean river with magnificent views of 5,000-foot mountains, and its banks are forested with evergreens and hardwoods.

Only 30 miles from Seattle is the Green River Gorge, a boulder-choked chasm with Class III-IV rapids dropping into deep green pools. Although it is one of the state's most beautiful river canyons, its waters are dam-controlled, with releases at unpredictable intervals. So outfitters cannot schedule trips through this lush rain forest gorge except at short notice, and then only in the spring.

A great float for families all summer long is the Skagit within North Cascades National Park. Although several dams control its flow, the Skagit is still relatively unspoiled and scenic, with salmon spawning in the fall and bald eagles circling overhead during the winter. The put-in for the nine-mile Class II-III run is near Newhalem and paddlers enjoy views of high Cascades peaks.

Washington State is not only blessed with magnificent mountains and rivers; it also has the superb San Juan Islands. They are said to be the only place in the world where sea kayakers can watch whales. But there is much more besides: largely unspoiled forested islands, historic sites, and plenty of wildlife, including dolphins, seals, sea turtles, water birds, and bald eagles. Fishermen pursue salmon, cod, and rockfish.

Downstream River Runners, Inc.
Casey Garland
12112 NE 195th
Bothell, WA 98011
(206) 483-0335
Suiattle River, Nooksack River, Wenatchee River, Methow River, Tieton River, Skykomish River, Sauk River, Green River, Grande Ronde
Max. rapids: V+
America Outdoors, Professional River Outfitters of Washington
Downstream River Runners conducts "mild to wild" guided trips on the Eagle, Upper Skagit, Suiattle, Nooksack, Wenatchee, Methow, Tieton, Skykomish, Sauk, Green, Cascade and Klickitat rivers, as well as streams in Oregon. Some of these are recommended for beginners, others have rapids of Class V+ difficulty.

Downstream prides itself on quality and safety, with all its river guides certified as Swiftwater Rescue Technicians. Open from March to September, it provides instruction and runs trips of one to five days' duration. It offers 25 different wetsuit sizes to protect against hypothermia on the cold mountain streams.

MacKaye Harbor Inn
Mike Bergstrom
Route 1, Box 1940
Lopez Island, WA 98261
(206) 468-2253
Puget Sound
Max. rapids: None
  Mackaye Harbor Inn, a beachfront
bed and breakfast on Lopez Island,
rents kayaks and conducts guided
kayak trips among the San Juans between April and October. The tours,
for beginners as well as intermediate
paddlers, take guests along a beautiful shoreline in one of the world's
loveliest island regions. They can
view many marine birds as well as
seals, otters and deer, while eagles
soar above. Salmon and cod are
among the local fish.

North Cascades River Expeditions
Gerald and Lori Michalec
P.O. Box 116
Arlington, WA 98223
(206) 435-9548, (800) 634-8433
Methow River, Skagit River,
Wenatchee River, Green River, Klick-
itat River, Noosuck River, Skyokmish
River, Tieton River, Deschutes River
Max. rapids: III-IV
Professional River Outfitters of
Washington
  North Cascades River Expeditions
provides guided raft trips on many
rivers: the Methow, Skagit, Suiattle,
Wenatchee, Green, Klickitat, Nook-
sack, Skykomish, Tieton, White Sal-
mon and Deschutes. It offers begin-
ners' and advanced trips, mostly
through rugged mountains, with the
advanced paddlers running Class III-
IV rapids. The season extends from
March 1 through September.
  Padlers can fish for salmon and
steelhead trout, and view bears, otters, ospreys, eagles, and other
wildlife.

Northwest Outdoor Center
Bill Stewart, John Meyer, Herb Meyer
2100 Westlake Avenue North
Seattle, WA 98109
(206) 281-9694
Skykomish River, Wenatchee River
Max. rapids: III-IV
TASK
  Northwest Outdoor Center was
founded in 1980 to provide safe, high
quality boating instruction in the
Pacific Northwest. It has since expanded into providing guided sea
and river kayaking trips and renting
both kayaks and canoes. Most of its
floats are in sheltered flat water,
suitable for beginners. Sea kayaking
tours run through Puget Sound and
the scenic San Juan Islands, while
river paddling is on five rivers in the
beautiful Cascades and the Rogue in
Oregon. NWOC operates trips varying from three hours to five days and
its season runs year-round.
  Many wildlife species may be admired, from whales and seals to bald
eagles, migratory waterbirds and
shorebirds.

Orion Expeditions, Inc.
James L. Moore and Emily Johnston
1516 11th Avenue
Seattle, WA 98122
(206) 322-9130, (800) 553-7466
Skagit River, Sauk River, Snoqualmie
River, Wenatchee River, Klickitat
River, Deschutes River, Skykomish
River, Methow River, Cispus River,
Tieton River, White Salmon River
Max. rapids: V+
Washington Outfitters and Guides,
America Outdoors
  Orion Expeditions offers
whitewater and calm water guided
trips by raft and kayak on many of
Washington's most exciting rivers,
such as the Middle Fork Salmon,
Lower Salmon, Skagit, Wenatchee,
Sauk, Deschutes, and the legendary
Skykomish. Some are of Class V+ dif-

ficulty and strictly for experts while
others are suited to beginners. The
landscape varies from Alpine to high
desert canyon scenery. Orion's season runs from December to October
and its trips, led by experienced and
competent guides, last from one to
six days. Guests can see elk, bighorn
sheep, black bear, eagles and osprey
may be seen, and fish for several
species of trout.

Pacific Water Sports, Inc.
Lee Moyer
16055 Pacific Highway South
Seattle, WA 98188
Puget Sound
Max. rapids: None
NACLO, NAPSA, TASK

Pacific Water Sports has been serv-
ing paddlers for 20 years, renting
canoes and kayaks, giving paddling
instruction and running guided trips.
It teaches sea kayaking on Puget
Sound and whitewater kayaking on
inland rivers, using classrooms, pools
and lakes for instruction.

Guided trips run from one to two
days and PWS is open year-round.
Tours include such destinations as
Squaxin and Jetty Islands, as well as
catering to birdwatchers and fishermen. The scenery is impressive in the
Sound, the San Juans, inland lakes
and mountain streams.

Sea Quest Expeditions
Zoetic Research
P.O. Box 2424
Friday Harbor, WA 98250
(206) 378-5767
Puget Sound
Max. rapids: None
TASK

Sea Quest Expeditions is different
from most outfitters in that it sets out
to give sea kayakers a learning experience as well as an outdoor adventure. Owned by a non-profit research
and education organization, it has
skilled biologists as guides to
describe the natural history of the San
Juan Islands. They lead sea kayak expeditions to, among other places, the
best whale-watching areas in North
America. No previous kayaking experience is needed, trips last from
one to three days, and paddlers camp
on uninhabited islands accessible
only by boat.

In addition to minke and orca
whales, the marine life includes dolphins, seals, sea turtles and sea birds.
Salmon and bottomfish may be
caught.

Wenatchee Water Sports, Inc.
Morey S. Zimmerman
15735 River Road
Leavenworth, WA 98826
(509) 763-3307
Wenatchee River
Max. rapids: III-IV
NACLO

Wenatchee Water Sports is a rafting, kayaking and canoe livery with
experienced river guides, located on
scenic land with unspoiled views of
the Wenatchee River and Big Jim
Mountain. Open May-September, the
company caters to people of all ages
with both rentals and guided trips
varying from one to seven days.
Tubes are also rented.

Wildlife to be seen in this alpine
setting includes mountain lion, bear,

deer, coyote, beaver and many bird species such as osprey and bald eagle. Salmon and trout tempt fisherman.

Wenatchee Whitewater Scenic River Trips
Bruce Carlson
P.O. Box 12
Cashmere, WA 98815
(509) 782-2254, (800) 74 FLOAT
Wenatchee River, Methow River, Tieton River, White Salmon River
Max. rapids: III-IV

Wenatchee Whitewater Scenic River Trips offers guided raft trips on the Wenatchee, Tieton, White Salmon, and Deschutes Rivers. These trips pass through the beautiful North Cascades, featuring scenic forest, canyons, wildflowers, and abundant wildlife, including deer, eagles, osprey, minks, otters, ducks, herons, and geese. Anglers also can fish for salmon, steelhead, and rainbow trout.

Trips last one to three days, run between April and September, and range widely in difficulty, from scenic, flat-water trips to Class IV whitewater. Wenatchee Whitewater also offers parties, barbecue grills, campfires, day care, volleyball, moonlight floats, inflatable kayak trips, and scenic floats led by naturalist guides.

West Virginia

Mountainous West Virginia calls itself the undisputed Whitewater Capital of the East, with nearly 2,000 miles of streams coursing through the Appalachians. More than 60 rivers in the state may be rafted, kayaked, or canoed, and some, notably the Cheat, the Gauley, and the Tygart, are very challenging. These rivers have rapids rated up to Class V+, demanding great skill, especially during the spring runoff. Less adventurous paddlers enjoy the Shenandoah with its pastoral scenery as it meanders through the eastern panhandle of West Virginia to join the Potomac at historic Harpers Ferry. (See *Virginia*.) But even the Shenandoah has Class III rapids on its Staircase segment to enliven the journey.

The Cheat River in the north of the state is a wild stream that winds through an impressive canyon with massive boulders, overhanging rock walls, and waterfalls. It has 38 rapids in eleven miles, including Big Nasty and Even Nastier. They are rated Class II-IV except in high water when some reach Class V. When the flow slackens in midsummer the Cheat allows paddlers to pause to relish the scenery.

The Gauley River, variously listed as number seven or eight in the world in difficulty, features more than 100 rapids on a 26-mile stretch that drops 670 feet. The toughest part is the upper Gauley, with its steep chutes and rocks that test the skills of even the most experienced paddlers. The Lower Gauley has huge waves and still ranks as Class III-V, but demands less technical expertise and can be rafted safely by less experienced paddlers. But since the river is controlled by Summersville Dam, the whitewater season is short — only 22 days in the fall when the sluicegates are opened. With space so limited, many of the kayakers and rafters who flock to the Gauley from throughout the United States and Canada make reservations a year ahead. So early booking is essential. But in the summer, when water levels are lower, the river still offers enjoyable family rafting.

The uncrowded Tygart in northcentral West Virginia contains Wells Falls, which rates as the most powerful runnable drop in the whole Monongahela River basin. Another Tygart thrill is Valley Falls, described as a short but incredibly intense 25-foot water slide. The most demanding of the Tygart's raftable stretches is the Gorge. It consists of Class II-III whitewater with intervening technical Class IV-V rapids. Placid Tygart Lake, which curves for 13 miles through wooded valleys, is a popular boating center with its campsite, cabins, lodge, and restaurant.

Despite its name, the New River is said to be the world's second oldest river after the Nile. Its celebrated gorge, dubbed the Grand Canyon of the East, has walls 700 to 1,300 feet high. Named in this section the New River Gorge National River, the stream drops 240 feet in 14 miles, creating the biggest white water in the east. The Upper New is comparatively gentle, suitable for leisurely floating and fishing. The middle section offers moderate Class II-III rapids. Only in its lower, and most popular, section does the New unleash its full fury. The New River season runs from mid-March through November, with the greatest rafting challenge in April and May.

The Greenbrier, a major tributary of the New River, and the South Branch of the Potomac, in the eastern mountains, rank among the best canoeing waters in West Virginia. The 150-mile Greenbrier flows through superb Allegheny scenery containing old logging communities, farmlands, and state forests. The South Branch altered course in 1985 when floods permanently changed its streambed. Paddlers able to travel at short notice can float the more remote Bluestone and Meadow with their Class III-V rapids and great mountain scenery. But these rivers, in the south and central sections of the state, are only raftable when swollen by spring rains.

ACE Whitewater Ltd.
Jerry Cook
Box 1168
Oak Hill, WV 25901
(800) 223-2641
New River, Gauley River, Russell Fork River
Max. rapids: V+
America Outdoors

ACE Whitewater offers guided canoe, kayak, and raft trips on the New and Gauley Rivers in West Virginia and the Russell Fork River in Virginia and Kentucky. On the New River, paddlers can enjoy all 52 miles of the 1,000 foot-deep New River Gorge, with rapids of up to Class V.

The Gauley offers 26 miles of clean water in the wilderness of the Gauley River Recreational Area. Depending on the river and season, these trips range from mild to wild, from family fun to world-class whitewater. Trips last one to five days.

During its March-November season, ACE also offers horseback riding, camping, hot showers, use of its recreation lodge, and base camp hiking trails and fishing lakes.

Wild whitewater on the Lower New River. Courtesy of Whitewater Information, Glen Jean, West Virginia.

Eastern River Expeditions
John Connelly
Box 1173
Greenville, ME 04441
(207) 695-2411, (800) 634-7238
Gauley River, Kennebec River, Penobscot River, Dead River, Moose River
Max. rapids: V+
Maine Professional River Outfitters Association, America Outdoors
Eastern River Expeditions offers canoe rentals and guided raft and inflatable-kayak trips on five rivers in Maine, New York, and West Virginia. In Maine, paddlers can choose among whitewater trips on the Kennebec, Penobscot, and Dead Rivers. Most Maine trips are fine for novice paddlers, combining excellent wilderness scenery with Class II-IV white water. Trips on the Dead and Penobscot Rip Gorge, however, require excellent conditioning. Penobscot Rip Gorge also requires intermediate or advanced paddling skills. Advanced rafting experience is a prerequisite

for trips on New York's Moose River and West Virginia's Gauley River, which have Class IV-V rapids.

All trips, of one to two days, pass through wilderness, offering camping spots, clear water, fishing, and chances to spot deer, coyotes, loons, ducks, beavers, foxes, great blue herons, and other wildlife.

Harpers Ferry River Riders, Inc.
Mark Grimes
P.O. Box 267
Knoxville, MD 21758
(301) 834-8051
Tygart River, Shenandoah River, Potomac River
Max. rapids: V+
Harpers Ferry River Riders offers one-day guided raft and tube trips and canoe rentals on the Shenandoah, Potomac, and Tygart Rivers. Trips on the Potomac and Shenandoah, with Class I-III rapids, are fine for beginners and offer scenic views of historic Harpers Ferry, wooded mountains, and abundant wildlife, in-

Riding a rapid on the Cheat River. Courtesy of Laurel Highlands River Tours, Ohiopyle, Pennsylvania.

cluding great blue herons, egrets, nesting bald eagles, turtles, geese, deer, and ducks. The two rivers also feature good fishing for smallmouth and largemouth bass, catfish, panfish, and carp.

The Tygart River, also scenic, has more challenging white water with up to Class V rapids, requiring previous paddling experience. The outfitter's season is from April to October.

Laurel Highlands River Tours
Mark and Linda McCarty
P.O. Box 107
Ohiopyle, PA 15470
(412) 329-8531, (800) 4 RAFTIN
Middle Youghiogheny River, Lower Youghiogheny River, Cheat River
Max. rapids: III-IV
America Outdoors
   Laurel Highlands River Tours, one of the oldest whitewater companies

in the East, claims to have the largest fleet of equipment anywhere. It operates on the Cheat River as well as the Lower, Middle and Upper Youghiogheny from bases in Albright, W.Va. Ohiopyle, Pa. and Friendsville, Md. In a season running from March to October, it offers guided raft trips and rents both rafts and canoes for floats on both rivers. All are one-day trips.

The Yough has the most popular whitewater in the East and the Cheat is famed for its spring thrills. Canoeing and kayaking instruction is available and acommodations range from camping to luxury motels.

289

Lower New River. Courtesy of Whitewater Information, Glen Jean, West Virginia.

Mountain River Tours, Inc.
Box 88 Sunday Road
Hico, WV 25854
(800) 822-1386
New River, Gauley River, Meadow River, Greenbrier River, Russell Fork River
Max. rapids: V+
America Outdoors

Mountain River Tours runs guided kayak and raft trips on the New, Gauley, Meadow, Greenbrier and Russell Fork Rivers. Trips pass through lush green forests with 1,000-foot rocky cliffs, and range widely in difficulty, from gentle runs through scenic wilderness to awesome Class V adventures. With this array of offerings, the company arranges trips to suit paddlers of all ages.

Taking pride in being flexible, Mountain River Tours will adapt trip times, meals, and river trips as desired. The company offers tours of two hours to five days and a choice of duckies or rafts. The season runs from March to November.

Mountain Streams and Trails
Michael S. McCarty
P.O. Box 106, Route 381
Ohiopyle, PA 15470-0106
(800) 245-4090
Cheat River, Gauley River, Tygart River, Big Sandy Creek, Youghiogheny River
Max. rapids: V+
America Outdoors

Mountain Streams and Trails operates on all three sections of the Youghiogheny as well as the Class III-IV Cheat, the challenging Tygart, isolated Big Sandy Creek and the Class III-VI Upper and Lower Gauley rivers. It runs guided raft and kayak trips in addition to renting canoes, kayaks and rafts, tailoring its trips to suit the needs of every paddler.

The company has skilled guides, trained in first aid and equipped with radios. They take guests through the spectacular panorama of maples, pines and rhododendrons that blanket the walls of the Middle and Lower Yough River canyon, habitat for deer, beaver, bear, osprey, heron and an occasional wildcat. One-day and two-day tours are offered during a March-October season.

New River Scenic Whitewater Tours, Inc.
P.O. Box 637
Hinton Bypass
Hinton, WV 25951
(304) 466-2288, (800) 292-0880
New River, Gauley River, Bluestone River, Greenbrier River
Max. rapids: V+
America Outdoors

New River Scenic Whitewater Tours offers guided canoe and raft trips as well as canoe and "funyak" rentals on the New, Gauley, Bluestone, and Greenbrier Rivers. All trips offer beautiful mountain scenery, exciting rapids, good fishing for smallmouth bass, catfish, and redeye, and abundant wildlife such as beavers, deer, muskrats, rare turtle species, falcons, herons, and migratory birds.

Rapids on these trips range from mild to wild, to suit everyone from young children and seniors to the most adventurous, skilled paddlers. Trips last from one-half to three days; special fishing trips are also available.

New River Scenic Whitewater Tours also offers oar-powered raft trips during its March-October season.

Northwest Passage
Rick Swetzer
1130 Greenleaf Avenue
Wilmette, IL 60091
(708) 256-4409, (800) RECREAT
New River, Gauley River, Cheat River, Wolf River, Peshtigo River, Pike River, Current River, Rio Grande, Everglades, BWCA, Lake Michigan, Lake Superior
Max. rapids: III-IV

Northwest Passage offers guided raft trips on the New, Gauley and Cheat Rivers in West Virginia; canoe trips on the Wolf, Pike and Peshtigo Rivers in Wisconsin, the Current River

Pillow Rock Rapids on the Upper Gauley River. Courtesy of USA Raft, Rowlesburg, West Virginia.

A family oar-boat trip on the Upper New River. Courtesy of Whitewater Information, Glen Jean, West Virginia.

in Missouri, the Rio Grande in Texas, the Everglades in Florida, and the Boundary Water Canoe Area in Minnesota; and sea kayak trips on Lake Michigan in Illinois and Lake Superior in Michigan. Most of these trips, which last two to seven days, are designed for beginners; some require prior experience..

An adventure travel company, Northwest Passage also offers skiing, hiking, cycling, backpacking, scuba diving, dogsledding, and rock climbing. Outings run year-round in the U.S., the Arctic, New Zealand, Tasmania, Costa Rica, Argentina, Canada, Belize, Turks and Caicos, Crete, Lapland, and southern Africa.

Passages to Adventure
Benjy Simpson
P.O. Box 71
Fayetteville, WV 25840
(304) 574-1037, (800) 634-3785
Cheat River, New River, Gauley River, Upper Youghiogheny River
Max. rapids: V+
America Outdoors, Association for Experiential Education

Passages to Adventure provides guided canoe, inflatable kayak, and raft trips as well as renting canoes and inflatable kayaks on the Cheat, New, and Gauley Rivers in West Virginia and the Upper Youghiogheny in Maryland.

With this variety, the company caters to all paddlers, from beginners to experts. The wild Cheat River has challenging, technical rapids that come in quick succession down a majestic canyon. The Lower New River offers huge rolling waves, giving a "rollercoaster" ride that is the company's most popular trip. The Upper New is wide, scenic and has Class II rapids — ideal for families and first-time rafters. The Upper Gauley has superb whitewater that requires previous paddling experience. The Lower Gauley has huge waves but doesn't require prior experience. Finally, the Upper Yough is famous for its extremely technical Class IV-V+ rapids.

River Riders, Inc.
Mark Grimes
Route 3, Box 1260
Harpers Ferry, WV 24525
(304) 535-2663
Shenandoah River, Potomac River, Tygart River
Max. rapids: V+
River Riders offers guided raft and tube trips as well as canoe rentals on the Shenandoah, Potomac, and Tygart Rivers. All three rivers feature mountain scenery, clean water, and good fishing for smallmouth and largemouth bass, catfish, carp, and panfish. The Shenandoah and Potomac, with Class I-III rapids, are fine for beginners. They also offer good views of historic Harper's Ferry.

Tygart trips, with Class V rapids, are for experienced paddlers only, and offer exceptional challenge. River Riders' trips last either a half or a full day and run from April to October.

RIVERS
Karen Calvert
P.O. Drawer 39
Lansing, WV 25862
(304) 574-3834, (800) 879-7483
Upper and Lower New River Upper and Lower Gauley River, Cheat River
Max. rapids: V+
America Outdoors
Rivers runs "mild to wild" guided raft and kayak trips on the New, Gauley, and Cheat Rivers. The New River offers breathtaking scenery and fun, moderate rapids. The Cheat features thrills for early-season rafters, and the Gauley offers the ultimate whitewater experience for paddlers who crave non-stop action. All trips run through wild, unspoiled gorges in a historic region of coal-mining and lumber towns. Varying with the river and season, difficulty ranges from Class I-III for families with young children, Class IV- V for adults and children over 12 and Class V for experienced rafters.

Open March-October, Rivers also offers camping, cabins, multi-day trips, ducky outings, kayak clinics, float-fishing trips, motel packages, an outfitter shop, hiking, and horseback riding.

Riversport
Robert Ruppel
213 Yough Street
Confluence, PA 15424
(814) 395-5744
Big Sandy River, Cheat River, Casselman River, Youghiogheny River
Max. rapids: III-IV
NACLO
An excellent paddling school in the Pennsylvania area, Riversport runs one-day canoe and kayak trips as well as renting rafts, canoes and kayaks. It operates on the challenging and beautiful Youghiogheny, Big Sandy, Cheat and Casselman rivers from March to November.

Riversport's trips are suitable for youngsters, adults and senior citizens in good health. Its lessons teach the skills beginners and intermediate paddlers need to run the Class III-IV rapids of nearby rivers, with their hemlocks, rhododendrons, mountain laurel, and rich wildlife.

Songer Whitewater, Inc.
Len and Susie Hanger
P.O. Box 300
Fayetteville, WV 25840
(304) 658-9926, (800) 356-RAFT
*New River, Gauley River, Greenbrier
River, Bluestone River, Meadow River*
Max. rapids: V+
America Outdoors

Songer Whitewater runs guided
raft trips of one to four days on the
New, Gauley, Greenbrier, Bluestone,
and Meadow Rivers. All trips are
through scenic mountains and gorges, with the most popular excursions running through large,
nationally protected areas with big
rapids and especially clean air and
water. These areas also boast good
fishing for bass, catfish, and muskie,
and opportunities to spot deer,
turkeys, and other wildlife.

Songer, whose season runs from
March to November, has trips to suit
all skill levels — novice to expert.

USA RAFT
Mary Kay Heffernan
P.O. Box 277
Rowlesburg, WV 26424
(304) 454-2475, (800) USA RAFT
*Gauley River, Cheat River, Tygart
River, New River, Upper
Youghiogheny River, North Fork
Potomac River, Nolichucky River,
Ocoee River, Nantahala River,
French Broad River*
Max. rapids: V+
America Outdoors

USA Raft is the reservation and
marketing company for Appalachian
Wildwaters, Rough Run Expeditions
and Expeditions, Inc. Its staff can
help you choose the ideal raft or
"funyak" trip from among 30 different
outings on ten of the best whitewater
rivers in the East — the New, Gauley,
Cheat, and Tygart in West Virginia;
the Upper Youghiogheny and North
Fork of the Potomac in Maryland; the

Nolichucky and Ocoee in Tennessee,
and the Nantahala, French Broad and
Nolichucky in North Carolina.

With this selection of trips, rivers,
and outfitters, USA Raft can offer outings to suit paddlers of all skill levels
at locations convenient to residents
throughout the Middle Atlantic and
Southeast. Open year-round, USA
Raft also provides package trips that
include meals and lodging. And, for
winter paddling, it has one- to nine-
day trips on the Rio Grande in Texas.

White Water Adventures of Cheat River Canyon
Robert and Shirley Marietta
P.O. Box 31
Ohiopyle, PA 15470
(412) 329-8850, (800) WWA-RAFT
(992-7238)
*Cheat River, Upper, Middle and
Lower Youghiogheny River*
Max. rapids: III-IV
*America Outdoors, West Virginia
Eastern Professional Outfitters*

White Water Adventures runs
guided raft and kayak trips on the
Lower, Middle and Upper
Youghiogheny as well as renting
canoes, kayaks and rafts from March
to November. Paddlers can take their
pick; the dam-controlled Yough is
rated Class V on its upper section and
Classes III and II on its lower and
middle stretches respectively. Trips
are suitable for "folks from 12-100
who are willing to paddle a bit and
have a good time."

A highly professional staff and the
best modern equipment are mainstays of the company, which offers
lessons and provides a guide for
every raft on the steep and technical
Upper Yough. Trout, walleye and
bass can be caught on the Yough.

In West Virginia, White Water Adventurers of Cheat River Canyon runs
"very thrilling" guided raft trips from
March to July through Class IV-V rap-

ids on the free-flowing Cheat River. The stream cuts through a very steep canyon in an historic part of West Virginia. It has beautiful wildflowers and mountain laurel, along with deer, wild turkeys, and grouse.

Whitewater Information
P.O. Box 243
Glen Jean, WV 25846
(304) 465-0855, (800) 782-RAFT
New River, Gauley River, Bluestone River, Greenbrier River
Max. rapids: V+

Whitewater Information offers guided canoe, raft, and dory trips as well as canoe, raft and tube rentals on the New, Gauley, Bluestone, and Greenbrier Rivers. Trips on the Lower New River cover some of the best whitewater rafting in the East, and can be run all season from April through October. The Upper New is great for scenic family floats and overnight excursions. And the Gauley offers wild excitement on one of the country's most challenging whitewater rivers. All rivers provide terrific mountain scenery, good fishing, and abundant wildlife.

Trips last one or two days and can be tailored to almost anyone's wishes. During its April-November season, the company also offers guided fishing trips on the New and Gauley Rivers. Acclaimed in outdoors magazines, these tours offer great fishing for many species from bass and walleye to yellow perch.

A paddle/oar boat trip on the Gauley River. Courtesy of New River Scenic Whitewater Tours, Hinton, West Virginia.

Paddling an inflatable kayak through Surprise Rapids on the Lower New River. Courtesy of USA Raft, Rowlesburg, West Virginia.

Whitewater World
Douglas Fogal
Route 903
Jim Thorpe, PA 18229
(717) 325-3656
Cheat River
Max. rapids: V+
America Outdoors

Whitewater World has guided raft trips on the Cheat River with its thrilling Class V+ rapids. Only for the experienced, these spring floats from May to June last one and two days. The company keeps the size of its groups small, uses up-to-date equipment and serves steak dinners.

Part of the appeal of Whitewater World trips is the amount of time actually spent rafting the rapids. Deer may be spotted on the riverbanks and bass caught in the fast-moving water.

Wisconsin

From the whitewater rivers in the north to the rolling Mississippi in the west and vast Lake Michigan in the east, Wisconsin has a wide variety of floats for every taste. All told, the state has 144 canoe trails covering nearly 3,500 miles of rivers. One of the best is the Flambeau, with its tranquil upstream waters and turbulent Class III-IV white water in its southern reaches. Still more challenging is the Peshtigo, whose upper waters flow through the beautiful Nicolet National Forest and contain some of the most difficult whitewater in the Midwest. And state officials warn that parts of the Menominee River separating Wisconsin from Michigan are so dangerous that they should be run only by experts in decked boats.

Canoeists in search of gentler trips are drawn to the Wisconsin River. On its lower reaches, where the 430-mile-long river bends westward to join the Mississippi, the Wisconsin provides lovely scenery and many islands. Canoes may be rented at many locations from Wisconsin Dells to Muscoda. Far upstream, on the quiet stretch between McNaughton and Rhinelander, ospreys, eagles, and blue herons delight floating birdwatchers.

All told, the Wisconsin Department of Natural Resources (whose Parks and Recreation Dept. can be reached at P.O. Box 7921, Madison, WI 53707, phone 608-266-2181) lists 32 canoeing rivers. These include the delightfully-named Kickapoo River in the southwest, known as "the crookedest river in the world."

The Yellow River in the northwest may be choked by aquatic growth in the summer, but the nearby Apple River, which runs into the Mississippi near Minneapolis, is recommended for family floating in tubes. World-famous for trout fishing is the Bois Brule River in the state's far northwest close to Lake Superior. But state officials warn that a section below the Hwy 2 bridge is hazardous and should only be attempted with a knowledgeable guide. Another well-known fishing stream is the Lower Wolf River in the east, where anglers chase walleye and white bass.

Canoeing is possible on the sloughs and backwaters of the Mississippi, but not on the river itself because of its heavy commercial traffic and currents. Some outfitters offer sea kayaking on Lake Michigan.

9 Mile Resort

Herb and Carm Echeler
Route 1, Box 205
Park Falls, WI 54552
(715) 762-3174
North Fork Flambeau River
Max. rapids: III-IV

9 Mile Resort rents canoes for trips of one to four days on the Flambeau River. These trips vary in difficulty, to suit novices and advanced paddlers. The first 30 miles below 9 Mile Resort is tranquil and good for beginners. The next 15 miles has Class III-IV rapids to challenge experienced canoeists.

Along the way, paddlers can enjoy the scenic northwoods country of the Flambeau State Forest, which offers free camping; good fishing for bass, walleye, muskie and sturgeon; and abundant wildlife, including osprey, deer, bears, otters, ducks, and bald eagles. 9 Mile Resort's season runs from May to October.

Bender's Bluffview Canoe Rentals

Ruth Huerth Bender
614 Spruce Street
Sauk City, WI 53583
(608) 643-8247
Wisconsin River
Max. rapids: None

Benders Bluffview Canoe Rentals rents canoes on the Wisconsin River, the "river of a thousand islands." This wide, gentle river offers good fishing, camping on beautiful sand islands and scenic surroundings of high bluffs and woodlands. Trips on the river last one to five days and are fine for paddlers of all ages. Along the way, canoeists can fish for walleye, bass, and catfish. They can also admire bald eagles, osprey, wild turkeys, turkey vultures, and deer.

Benders Bluffview Canoe Rentals' season runs from May to October.

Blue Heron Tours, Inc.

Roland Zuelsdorf
101 Main Street
Horicon, WI 53032
(414) 485-2942, (414) 485-4663
Horicon Marsh, Rock River
Max. rapids: None

Blue Heron Tours rents canoes on the Rock River and Horicon Marsh. During these one-day flat-water trips paddlers can observe a spectacular array of wetlands wildlife in the Horicon Marsh Wildlife Area and the adjacent Horicon National Wildlife Area. Lush grasslands and miles of waterways shelter waterfowl, songbirds, muskrats, deer, and a variety of upland game. The area, a wildlife refuge since 1943, is also well known as a stopover point for more than 200,000 Canada geese during their spring and fall migration. The area also has good fishing for bullhead.

Brookside Campground

John and Martha Schillberg
Route 3, Box 128
409 10th Avenue East
Osceola, WI 54020
(715) 294-3197
St. Croix River
Max. rapids: None

Brookside Campground rents canoes for half-day trips on the St. Croix River, a scenic flat-water river that offers easy canoeing for paddlers of all ages. The river is clean, has good fishing for bass, northern pike, and panfish, and is flanked by beautiful limestone walls and sandy beaches. Paddlers also can sometimes spot deer, muskrats, and eagles. Brookside's season runs from May to October.

Flambeau River Lodge

Robert B. Felske
N7870 Flambeau Road
Ladysmith, WI 54848
(715) 532-5392
North and South Fork Flambeau River
Max. rapids: I-II

Flambeau River Lodge rents canoes on Class I-II sections of the North and South Forks of the Flambeau River for trips of one to five days. These trips, fine for paddlers of all ages, run through unspoiled old-growth forest, offering views of bald eagles, osprey, blue herons, deer, and other wildlife. Along the North Fork, paddlers can also camp at free sites maintained by the Department of Natural Resources. There's no camping on the South Fork.

Flambeau River Lodge, open year-round, also has its own private tent and R.V. campground, a dining room and bar.

Fox River Marina, Inc.

Russell F. Williams
P.O. Box 1006
501 South Main Street
Oshkosh, WI 54902
(414) 236-4220
Fox River, Wolf River
Max. rapids: None

Fox River Marina rents canoes for trips of one to 14 days on the calm, scenic Fox and Wolf Rivers, and three large lakes. The river trips, fine for beginners and advanced paddlers, pass through protected, unspoiled pine forests that offer camping and a chance to spot deer, badgers, turtles, ducks, and geese. The rivers also offer fishing for trout, bass, and perch.

Fox River Marina, open from May to October, also rents sailboats, fishing boats, pedal boats, and pontoon boats on Lake Winnebago.

Kosir's Rapid Rafts

Dan Kosir
H.C.R. Box 172 PA
Athelstane, WI 54104
(715) 757-3431
Peshtigo River, Menominee River
Max. rapids: III-IV

Kosir's Rapid Rafts runs guided raft trips and rents kayaks and rafts on the Peshtigo and Menominee Rivers. These rivers offer continuous stretches of Class III-IV whitewater but are fine for beginners as well as experienced paddlers. Both rivers are also extremely clean, offering good fishing for bass, northern pike, walleye, and trout. The Menominee features 200-foot high cliffs, and both the Menominee and Peshtigo offer opportunities to spot deer, bald eagles, and occasional otters.

During Kosir's season, which runs from April to October, the outfitter also offers camping, cabin rentals, and a restaurant and bar.

Northern Waters

Wayne Overberg
P.O. Box 2087
6009 Highway 70 W.
Eagle River, WI 54521
(715) 479-3884, (715) 479-2966
Rivers of northern Wisconsin, Lake
Superior
Max. rapids: I-II
NACLO

Northern Waters offers guided canoe and sea-kayak trips and rents canoes, sea kayaks, and tubes for trips of one to three days. The canoe trips, on several Northern Wisconsin rivers, have Class I- II rapids and are fine for both novices and experienced canoeists. Sea kayaking trips, also easy enough for beginners, are on Lake Superior. On guided trips, guests wanting lessons can learn paddling skills from the outfitter's ACA-certified instructors. On all trips, paddlers can also enjoy pristine wilderness, clean waters, good camping, fishing for bass, walleye, muskie, and northern pike as well as views of eagles, ospreys, bears, deer, beavers, otters, and other wildlife.

Northern Waters' season runs from May to October.

Northwest Passage
Rick Swetzer
130 Greenleaf Avenue
Wilmette, IL 60091
(708) 256-4409, (800) RECREAT
Wolf River, Pike River, Peshtigo River, Red River, Wisconsin River, Current River, Rio Grande, Everglades, Boundary Waters Canoe Area, Lake Michigan, Lake Superior
Max. rapids: III-IV

Northwest Passage offers guided raft trips on the New, Gauley and Cheat Rivers in West Virginia; canoe trips on the Wolf, Pike and Peshtigo Rivers in Wisconsin, the Current River in Missouri, the Rio Grande in Texas, the Everglades in Florida, and the Boundary Water Canoe Area in Minnesota; and sea kayak trips on Lake Michigan in Illinois and Lake Superior in Michigan. Most of these trips, which last two to seven days, are designed for beginners; some require prior experience. Depending on the location, these trips offer excitement, challenge, remoteness and beauty.

An adventure travel company, Northwest Passage also offers skiing, hiking, cycling, backpacking, scuba diving, dogsledding, and rock climbing. Outings run year-round in the U.S., the Arctic, New Zealand, Tasmania, Costa Rica, Argentina, Canada. Belize, Turks and Caicos, Crete, Lapland, and southern Africa.

Old Homestead
Don and Arlene Kuba
Route 1, Box 446
Gordon, WI 54838
(715) 376-4491
Eau Claire River, St. Croix River
Max. rapids: III-IV

Old Homestead rents canoes on the Eau Claire and St. Croix Rivers, two clean, secluded streams with trips fit for all paddlers from beginners to experts. Trips last from two hours to five days and offer camping, good fishing for walleye, northern pike, bass, and panfish, and a chance to spot deer, bears, eagles, hawks, and other wildlife. Old Homestead's season runs from April to October.

Quest Recreation
John Wright
Highway 8 and 35
St. Croix Falls, WI 54024
(800) 992-2692
St. Croix River
Max. rapids: None

Quest Recreation rents canoes for trips of one to six days on the St. Croix, one of the eight original wild and scenic rivers. A gentle river, the St. Croix is fine for paddlers of all ages. It offers unspoiled wilderness, good fishing, and abundant deer, raccoons, eagles, and other wildlife. Quest's season is from May to September.

Riverview Hills
Albert J. Bremmen
Route 1, Box 307
Muscoda, WI 53573
(608) 739-3472
Wisconsin River, Pine River
Max. rapids: None

Riverview Hills rents canoes for trips of one to seven days on the Wisconsin and Pine Rivers. On the Wisconsin River alone the outfitter offers access to 100 miles of river along which to paddle, swim, fish, and camp. The rivers feature scenic bluffs, canyons, woods, clean water and good fishing for walleye, crappie, bass, catfish, sturgeon, bluegill, and sunfish. Paddlers on these gentle flat-water trips can also enjoy viewing deer, beavers, squirrels, turkeys, ducks, seagulls, foxes, and other wildlife. Riverview Hills' season runs from May to September.

Rutabaga, Inc.
Gordy Sussman
820 South Park
Madison, WI 53715
(608) 256-4303, (800) 236-6646
Lake Superior, BWCA
Max. rapids: None
NAPSA
Rutabaga rents canoes and kayaks from its location in Madison. Customers generally rent touring kayaks for trips on Lake Michigan and canoes for touring the Boundary Waters. The outfitter's staff also offers solo canoes and advice on where to paddle.

Shotgun Eddy, Inc.
1715 Westfield Avenue
Green Bay, WI 54303
(414) 494-3782
Wolf River
Max. rapids: III-IV
Shotgun Eddy, Inc., rents rafts for half-day and full-day trips on the Wolf River. The river has Class III-IV rapids, but is easy enough for beginners age 16 or older. In fact, 90 percent of the outfitter's customers are first-time rafters. In addition to the rapids, paddlers also can enjoy the river's exceptionally clear, spring-fed waters and its wilderness scenery of canyons, waterfalls, and abundant birds, fish, raccoons, and other wildlife. The banks are also free of litter, as no bottles or cans are allowed on the river.

During the May-to-October season, Shotgun Eddy also operates a rustic campground.

Sea Isles Boat Livery
Ronald C. Schams
107 First Avenue South
Onalaska, WI 54650
(608) 783-5623
Black River, Mississippi River, Lake Onalaska
Max. rapids: None
Sea Isles Boat Livery rents canoes for flat-water trips on the Black River, Mississippi, and Lake Onalaska. These waters offer excellent fishing for bluegill, crappie, bass, catfish, walleye, and northern pike. The livery also operates a camp store and a 30-site campground with electric hook-ups, shaded riverside sites, and a modern bath house.

St. John Mine Canoe Rental
Harry D. Henderson
129 Main Street
Potosi, WI 53820
(608) 763-2121
Grant River, Platte River, Mississippi River
Max. rapids: I-II
St. John Mine Canoe Rental offers guided and unguided canoe rentals for trips on the Grant, Platte, and Mississippi Rivers. These rivers, with Class I-II rapids, are especially well suited for beginners and families. The trips pass through the scenic, unglaciated "Hidden Valley" area of southwest Wisconsin, offering views of rocky ledges, steep bluffs, and woodlands. The wildlife includes deer, muskrats, otters, blue herons, several species of duck, and many smaller birds.

Paddlers on these one- to three-day trips can also enjoy primitive camping, excursions to the nearby historic lead mines and miners' homes, and fishing for smallmouth bass, northern pike, catfish, suckers, and bluegill. St. John Mine's season is from May to October.

Trek & Trail
Greg Swevak, Ken Pobloske
Granary-Wagon Trail Resort
Highway ZZ
Ellison Bay, WI 54210
(414) 854-9616
Lake Michigan, Lake Superior, Lake Huron, Green Bay
Max. rapids: None

Trek & Trail Inc. offers guided sea-kayak trips and sea-kayak rentals for one- to 14-day trips on Lake Superior and Lake Michigan. From the company's base on the Apostle Islands National Lake Shore, paddlers can quickly reach colorful sea caves, shipwrecks, lighthouses, and an abandoned fishing village. En route one can also fish for lake trout and salmon and view wildlife, including eagles, osprey, deer, otters, loons, cormorants, and possibly bears. On guided trips, paddlers can also receive basic or advanced instruction, learn about the region's geology and natural history, and enjoy combination sailing/kayaking trips, which enable kayakers to reach some of Lake Superior's most remote and spectacular areas.

Some extended trips and ones including long crossings of open water require previous sea-kayaking experience. However, no experience is necessary for most trips. In fact, 95 percent of Trek & Trail's guests have never kayaked before. The company, whose season runs from May to October, also runs a paddle sport retail and mail-order shop.

University of Iowa Rec. Services
Wayne Fett
Touch the Earth
E216 Field House
Iowa City, IA 52242
(319) 335-9293, (310) 335-5256
Wolf River, Red River, Wisconsin River, Upper Iowa River, BWCA, Upper Iowa River, Ocoee River, Chattooga River, Nantahala River, St. Francis River, Poudre River
Max. rapids: III-IV

University of Iowa Recreation Services offers guided canoe, kayak, and raft trips and rents canoes for trips in Iowa on the upper Iowa River; in Minnesota in the Boundary Waters Canoe

Area; in Wisconsin on the Wolf, Red, and Wisconsin Rivers; and in the southeast on the Ocoee, Chattooga, Nantahala, St. Francis, and Poudre Rivers. These trips, open to students and the general public, feature a low student-to-instructor ratio and are geared for beginning to intermediate paddlers. All trips run through scenic, remote, and wild areas. Trips last one to four days.

The department of recreation services, open year-round, also offers rock climbing, cross-country skiing, backpacking, and bicycle touring.

Whitewater Specialty
Bill Kallner
N3894 Hwy. 55
White Lake, WI 54491
(715) 882-5400
Wolf, Red, Peshtigo, and Menominee Rivers
Max. rapids: III-IV
Whitewater Specialty offers guided, instructional canoe and kayak trips on the Wolf, Red, Peshtigo, and Menominee Rivers in northern Wisconsin. On these one-day trips, professional instructors teach participants how to paddle skillfully, safely, and confidently and how to break complex rapids down into manageable parts. These trips, geared for paddlers of all experience levels, feature challenging, clean whitewater, outstanding scenery, and many opportunities to view bald eagles, ospreys, herons, ducks, otters, deer, mink, and other wildlife. Paddlers also can fish for trout. Whitewater Specialty is open from May to September.

Wild River Outfitters
Marilyn Chesnik and Jerry Dorff
15177 Highway 70
Grantsburg, WI 54840
(715) 463-2254
Upper St. Croix River, Namekagon River
Max. rapids: I-II
Wild River Outfitters rents canoes on the Upper St. Croix and Namekagon Rivers, both part of the National Wild and Scenic River system. Trips last one to six days, have Class I-II rapids and are suitable for beginners and anyone interested in a scenic, enjoyable trip. The rivers are clean and clear and have good fishing for largemouth and smallmouth bass, walleye, northern pike, muskie, catfish, and sturgeon. They also offer many scenic, secluded campsites and opportunities to see native wildlife, including deer, bears, raccoons, otters, foxes, bald eagles, blue herons, ducks, and geese.

During its April-to-November season, Wild River Outfitters also offers a campground with hot showers and a camp store that sells bait, tackle, and camping supplies.

Wolf River Trips, Inc.
Clair Flease
Route 3, Box 122
New London, WI 54961
(414) 982-2458
Little Wolf River
Max. rapids: I-II
Wolf River Trips rents canoes and tubes for one-day trips on the Wolf River. The river, with gentle Class I-II rapids, is fine for beginners and offers clean water good for swimming and fishing for black bass. For all trips, a shuttle bus takes paddlers to upstream put-ins for floats back to the campground. The campground, open from May to October, offers tent and R.V. sites, swimming, tennis, hiking and volleyball.

Wyoming

Where the Great Plains meet the Rocky Mountains, the classic western state of Wyoming bestrides the Continental Divide. Wyoming's cold, clear waters therefore flow both ways: eastward toward the Gulf and the Atlantic, westward to the Pacific. Mountains, desert, grasslands, and wild rivers make for some of the best recreational country in the world, with fine rafting, kayaking, and canoeing. The Snake, the North Platte, and the Big Horn are particular favorites, and parts of three great river systems — the Missouri, the Colorado and the Columbia — have their headwaters in Wyoming's mountains.

Outfitters run several popular trips on the Snake River, which rises in Yellowstone National Park and flows southward through the Grand Teton National Park before crossing into Idaho through a magnificent canyon. This Grand Canyon of the Snake offers whitewater rafting amid great scenery. Some of the rapids are rated Class III-IV, but guided oar-boat trips are billed as very safe floats for families with children. The canyon walls display intriguing geological formations, and wooded meadows offer comfortable camping with a chance of seeing eagles and ospreys overhead.

Further upstream, people can float on the Snake's headwaters or take a very gentle 10-mile paddle from Dead Man's Bar to Moose Village. Since the latter trip is entirely within the Grand Teton National Park, it runs beneath the beautiful alpine backdrop of the Grand Tetons and is rich in wildlife. Paddlers may spot moose, elk, beavers, deer, herons, and ospreys, especially in the early morning and at dusk. In addition to running rivers, visitors to the national parks can paddle on trout-rich Yellowstone and Jackson Lakes.

In the southeast corner of Wyoming near the Colorado state line, the North Platte comes roaring northward through North Gate Canyon. This is wild country where rafters battle rugged white water — mostly Class III-IV but up to Class V+ at high water — as the river thunders through canyons and past meadows, wildflowers, and forests. Bighorn sheep, black bears, elk deer, beavers, golden eagles, bald eagles, herons, and Canada geese may be glimpsed from the river. Trips through the North Gate Canyon also begin across the Colorado state line (see Colorado). The 64-mile stretch of the North

Platte between the Colorado border and the Wyoming town of Saratoga has been nationally designated a blue ribbon trout fishery. It is said to be Wyoming's best trout stream, with 3,200 catchable trout (rainbow, brown and cutthroat) per mile. As a rule, Wyoming's rivers are best run in June and July. The choice is wide: every paddler to his (or her) taste. The upper reaches of the Green River, the source and fount of the Colorado, provide a 16-mile Class II day trip near the town of Pinedale. Greys River is a real high-country stream in the 3,440,000-acre Bridger-Teton National Forest bordering Grand Teton and Yellowstone National Parks. The 43-mile section starting at the Corral Creek Campground is only Class II, but other stretches are virtually unrunnable.

In the Shoshone National Forest, the first National Forest in the United States (created by President Benjamin Harrison in 1891), the North Fork of the Shoshone River offers a nine-mile day trip from Wapiti to Buffalo Bill Reservoir. Its rapids rate Class II and it has the advantage that it can be run until early August. The broad Big Horn River, running vertically through the north-central area of the state, provides good scenery and great fishing all summer long. There are no rapids in the Thermopolis area and the waters are uncrowded.

Barker-Ewing Scenic Float Trips
Dick and Barbara Barker
Box 100
Moose, WY 83012
(307) 733-1800, (800) 365-1800
Snake River
Max. rapids: None
America Outdoors
    Barker-Ewing Scenic Float Trips offers half-day scenic trips on the Snake River in Grand Teton National Park. These cover 10 miles and offer spectacular views of the Teton Mountains and plentiful wildlife, including moose, elk, deer, bald eagles, ospreys, beavers, otters, and occasional bison and bears. These flatwater outings, suitable for all ages, are led by experienced guides who interpret the park's wildlife and natural history. During Barker-Ewing's

season, which runs from May to September, the company also offers cookout tours that provide either breakfast or dinner.

Flagg Ranch Village
P.O. Box 187
Moran, WY 83013
(307) 733-8761
Snake River
Max. rapids: III-IV
    Flagg Ranch Village offers guided oar-boat trips and canoe rentals for trips of one to four hours on the Snake River. These family-oriented trips offer spectacular views of the Teton Mountains and wilderness in Grand Teton National Park. Guests also can view abundant wildlife and fish for trout. Flagg Ranch's season runs from June 1 to July 30.

Great Rocky Mountain Outfitters, Inc.
Thomas H. Wiersema,
Robert G. Smith
Box 1636, 216 E. Walnut Ave.
Saratoga, WY 82331
(307) 326-8750
North Platte River
Max. rapids: III-IV
Great Rocky Mountain Outfitters, Inc. offers guided canoe, raft, and dory trips and rents canoes and rafts on the North Platte River. These trips offer spectacular wilderness and rural scenery that can vary enormously over the course of a multi-day trip, to include mountain terrain, cottonwoods, hay fields, limestone bluffs, and desert. In these areas, guests can see an equally wide array of wildlife, including bighorn sheep, elk, deer, antelope, beavers, foxes, coyotes, bald eagles, golden eagles, and herons. A nationally known blue-ribbon trout stream, the river yields record catches of walleye and brown, brook, rainbow, and cutthroat trout.

Trips last from half a day to five days and run between April and November. The company also offers guided hunting trips, fishing trips, and combine hunting and fishing trips.

Heart 6 Ranch
The Garnick Family
P.O. Box 70
Moran, WY 83013
(307) 543-2477
Snake River, Buffalo River, Yellowstone lakes, Jackson lakes
Max. rapids: None
Heart 6 Ranch provides guided raft and dory trips and canoe rentals on the Snake and Buffalo Rivers and Jackson and Yellowstone Lakes. These trips run at the base of the Tetons, offering spectacular mountain scenery and abundant wildlife, including elk, moose, deer, bears, eagles,

coyotes, and marmots. Paddling is on flat water, which makes it easy for people of all ages. Anglers also enjoy excellent trout fishing.

Heart 6 Ranch's season runs from June 1 to September 15.

O.A.R.S.
George Wendt
P.O. Box 67
Angels Camp, CA 95222
(209) 736-4677, (800) 466-7238 (CA).
(800) 346-6277
Snake River, San Juan River, American River, Cal-Salmon River, Merced River, Stanislaus River, Tuolumne River, Rogue River, Colorado River
Max. rapids: III-IV
America Outdoors
O.A.R.S. runs guided dory, raft, and kayak trips in five Western states. It offers tours in California on the American, Cal-Salmon, Merced, Stanislaus and Tuolumne Rivers; in Oregon on the Rogue; in Arizona on the Colorado; in Wyoming on the Snake, and in Utah on the San Juan River. These outings last one to 13 days and, depending on the class of river, are fine for children, novices, families, intermediate, and expert rafters. O.A.R.S. trips provide fishing, swimming, camping, side hikes, wildlife viewing and other activities.

O.A.R.S. tours run from April to October.

Richard Brothers, Inc.
James Richard
2215 Rangeview Lane
Laramie, WY 82070
(307) 742-7529
North Platte River
Max. rapids: V+
America Outdoors
Richard Brothers offer guided raft trips and raft rentals on the North Platte River through North Gate Canyon. These trips run through mag-

nificent canyon country of pine, spruce, fir, and aspen forests. These harbor abundant wildlife ranging from elk, deer, black bears, and bighorn sheep to eagles, herons, and Canada geese. The wild and free-flowing North Platte has technical Class III-IV rapids, which the company runs in oar boats for guests of all ages. Paddle raft trips are more demanding, requiring experience. Whitewater trips of one and two days are scheduled each weekend from mid-May through July 4. Custom trips of 1-7 days are also available, along with 3-5 day trips contracted through the National Audubon Society and American Wilderness Alliance. During Richard Brothers May-to-July season, the company also offers drift boat trout fishing trips for serious fly fishermen.

Sands Wild Water River Trips
Charles Sands
P.O. Box 696
Wilson, WY 83014
(307) 733-4410, (800) 223-4059
Snake River
Max. rapids: III-IV
Sands Wild Water River Trips offers guided oar- and paddle-raft trips on the Snake River. These outings, which last from half a day to two days, pass through a spectacular river canyon in the Tetons that offers exciting Class III-IV rapids, interesting geology, and spectacular views of surrounding mountains. Participants can also enjoy viewing abundant bald eagles, osprey, ducks, geese, beavers, otters, and other wildlife.

Oar-boat trips are fine for guests of all ages. Paddle-boat trips are best suited for active adults and teens. During Sands' season, which runs from May to September, guests can also camp at the company's "Pine Bar" campsite, set in a forest with beautiful mountain meadows.

Snake River Kayak and Canoe School
Donald S. Perkins
P.O. Box 3482
145 West Gill
Jackson, WY 83001
(307) 733-3127, (800) 824-5375
Hoback River, Snake River, Gros Ventre River
Max. rapids: III-IV
America Outdoors, ACA
Snake River Kayak & Canoe School offers guided and unguided canoe, kayak, and raft trips for paddlers of all levels of ability. These trips, which last from three hours to two days, run on the Hoback, Snake, and Gros Ventre Rivers through the spectacular mountain country in and around Grand Teton National Park and the Jackson Hole Valley. Both oar-boat and paddle-boat trips are available, making Class III-IV whitewater runs accessible to guests of all ages. Day trips run in morning, afternoon, and evening, include a hearty

Lewis & Clark
River Expeditions

Whitewater & Scenic
River Expeditions
Exceptional Meals

Corner of Gill & Glenwood
P.O. Box 720, 145 W. Gill,
Jackson Hole, Wyoming 83001
307-733-4022   1-800-824-5375

Classes, Tours
and Rentals

Fun, Instructional
Tours for the
Timid Souls

Snake River Kayak & Canoe School

homemade meal, and last for either three or six hours. Special scenic trips and combination "pedal & paddle" trips are also available. Finally, the company also offers a complete array of kayak, raft, and canoe lessons.

On all of Snake River Kayak & Canoe School's trips, guests have an excellent chance of spotting wildlife, including ospreys, eagles, deer, moose, and bears. The company's season runs from May to September.

Wind River Canyon Outfitters
Daniel E. Miller
P.O. Box 269
Thermopolis, WY 82443
(307) 864-3617
Big Horn River, Wind River, North Platte River, Shoshone River
Max. rapids: None

Wind River Canyon Outfitters runs guided drift-boat fly- and spin-fishing trips on the Bighorn, Wind, North Platte, and Shoshone Rivers. These half-day and full-day trips offer exceptional fishing for rainbow, brown, and cutthroat trout and beautiful scenery in this region bounded by the Big Horn and Absaroka Mountains. On these trips, which run from April to October, guests can also see abundant deer, waterfowl, birds of prey and other wildlife.

In addition to fishing, the outfitter also offers or can arrange hunting, horse-packing, sightseeing, and photography.

Resources

America Outdoors, David Brown, exec. dir., P.O. Box 1348, Knoxville, TN 37901, tel. (615) 524-4814.

American Canoe Association (ACA), Jeffrey Yeager, exec. dir., 7432 Alban Station Blvd., Suite B226, Springfield, VA 22150, tel. (703) 451-0141.

American Rivers. 801 Pennsylvania Ave. SE, Suite 303, Washington, D.C. 20003, tel. (202) 547-6900.

American Whitewater Affiliation, Phyllis Horowitz, exec. dir., P.O. Box 85, Phoenicia, NY 12464, tel. (914) 688-5569.

National Association of Canoe Liveries & Outfitters (NACLO), Jim Thaxton, exec. dir., R.R. 2, Box 249, Butler, KY 41006-9674, tel. (606) 472-2205, FAX (606) 472-2030

National Organization for River Sports (NORS), Eric Leaper, exec. dir., 314 N. 20th St., P.O. Box 6847, Colorado Springs, CO 80934, tel. (719) 473-2466.

North American Paddlesports Association (NAPSA), Neil Wiesner-Hanks, exec. dir., 12455 N. Wauwatosa Road, Mequon, WI 53092, tel. (414) 242-5228.

Trade Association of Sea Kayaking (TASK), Kitty Graham, P.O. Box 84144, Seattle, WA 98124, tel. (206) 621-1018.

U.S. Canoe Association (USCA), Jim Mack, exec. dir., 606 Ross Street, Middletown, OH 45044, tel. (513) 422-3739.

U.S. National Park Service, (202) 208-4747.

Note: if your local canoe club is not listed in the phone book, contact ACA or the USCA. Chances are these associations can direct you to a nearby member club.

Bibliography

Following is a selection of some of the best guidebooks on canoeing and rafting in the United States.

A Canoeing and Kayaking Guide to the Streams of Florida, by Elizabeth F. Carter and John L. Pearce, 1985-87, Menasha Ridge Press, Hillsborough, N.C.

A Canoeing and Kayaking Guide to the Streams of Kentucky, By Bob Sehlinger, 1978, Thomas Press, Ann Arbor, Mich.

A Canoeing and Kayaking Guide to the Streams of Ohio, by Richard Combs, 1983, Menasha Ridge Press, Hillsborough, N.C.

Adirondack Canoe Waters, North Flow, by Paul Jamieson, 1986, Adirondack Mountain Club, Glen Falls, N.Y.

Adirondack Canoe Waters, South and West Flow, by Alec C. Proskine, 1985, Adirondack Mountain Club, Glen Falls, N.Y.

AMC River Guide, Massachusetts, Connecticut, and Rhode Island, ed. by Steve Tuckerman, 1990, Appalachian Mountain Club Books, Boston, Mass.

AMC River Guide. Maine, Ed. Katharine Yates and Carey Phillips, 1991. Appalachian Mountain Club, New York, N.Y.

An Illustrated Canoe Log of the Shenandoah River and its South Fork, by Louis J. Matacia and Owen S. Cecil III, 1974, Matacia, Oakton, Va.

Back to Nature in Canoes: A guide to American Waters, by Rainer Esslen, 1976, Columbia Publishing Co., Frenchtown, N.J.

The Big Drops: Ten Legendary Rapids, by Robert O. Collins and Roderick Nash, 1978, Sierra Club Books, San Francisco, Calif.

Brown's Guide to the Georgia Outdoors, ed. by John W. English, 1986, Cherokee Publishing Co., Atlanta, Ga.

California Whitewater: A Guide to the Rivers, by Jim Cassady and Fryar Calhoun, 1990, North Fork Press, Berkeley, Calif.

Canoe Camping, Vermont and New Hampshire Rivers, by Roioli Schweiker, 1985, Backcountry Publications, Woodstock, Vt.

Canoe Guide, by Indiana Dept. of Natural Resources, 1975, Dept. of Nat. Resources, Indianapolis, Ind.

Canoe Trails of the Deep South, by Chuck Estes et al., 1991, Menasha Ridge Press, Birmingham, Ala.

Canoeing and Rafting: The Complete Where-to-go Guide to America's Best Tame and Wild Waters, by Sara Pyle, 1979, Morrow, New York, N.Y.

Canoeing Guide: Western Pennsylvania and Northern West Virginia, by American Youth Hostels, Inc., 1975, AYA Pittsburgh Council, Penn.

Canoeing Maine #1, by Eben Thomas, 1979, Thorndike Press, Thorndike, Maine.

Canoeing Maine #2, by Eben Thomas, 1979, Thorndike Press, Thorndike, Maine.

Canoeing Mass., Rhode Island and Conn., by Ken Weber, 1980, New Hampshire Pub. Co., Somersworth, N.H.

Canoeing Michigan Rivers, by Jerry Dennis, 1986, Friede Publcations, Davison, Mich.

Canoeing the Jersey Pine Barrens, by Robert Parnes, 1990, Globe Pequot Press, Chester, Conn.
Canoeing Waters of California, by Ann Dwyer, 1973, GBH Press, Kentfield, Calif.
Canoeing Western Waterways, the Mountain States, by Ann Schafer, 1978, Harper & Row, New York, N.Y.
Canoeing White Water: River Guide, Virginia, Eastern West Virginia, North Carolina, Great Smoky Mountain Area, by Randy Carter, 1974, Appalachian Books, Oakton, Va.
Canoeing Wild Rivers, by Cliff Jacobson, 1989, ICS Books, Merrillville, Ind.
Canoeing: Trips in Connecticut, by Pamela Detels and Janet Harris, 1977, Birch Run Press, Madison, Conn.
The Complete Guide to Whitewater Rafting Tours, by Rena K. Margulis, 1986, Aquatic Adventure Publcns., Palo Alto, Calif.
The Concord, Sudbury and Assabet Rivers, by Ron McAdow, 1990, Bliss Publishing Co., Marlborough, Mass.
Carolina Whitewater, by Bob Benner, 1981, Menasha Ridge Press, Hillsborough, N.C.
Cataract Canyon via the Green or Colorado Rivers, by Donald L. Baars, 1987, Canon Publishers, Evergreen, Colo.
Down the Wild Rivers: A Guide to the Streams of California, by Thomas Harris, 1972, Chronicle Books, San Francisco, Calif.
Downstream, A Rafting and Tubing Guide to Florida's Rivers and Streams, by Robert Tabor, 1978, SSAM Publishing Company, Ft. Pierce, Fla.
Exciting River Running in the U.S., by Elizabeth Medes, 1979, Contemporary Books, Chicago, Ill.
The Floater's Guide to Colorado, by Doug Wheat, 1983, Falcon Press Publishing Company, Helena, Mont.
The Floater's Guide to Montana, by Hank Fischer, 1986, Falcon Press Publishing Company, Helena, Mont.
Guide to Floating Whitewater Rivers, by R.W. Miskimins, 1987, F. Amato Publcations., Portland, Ore.
Idaho Whitewater: The Complete River Guide, by Greg Moore and Don Mc-Claran, 1989, Class VI Whitewater, McCall, Id.
Illinois Country Canoe Trails, by Philip E. Vierling, 1979, Illinois Country Canoe Guides, Chicago, Ill.
Introduction to Water Trails in America, by Robert Colwell, 1973, Stackpole Books, Harrisburg, Penn.
Keystone Canoeing, by Edward Gertler, 1988, Seneca Press, Silver Spring, Md.
The Lower Canyons of the Rio Grande, by Louis F. Aulbach and Joe Butler, 1988, Wilderness Area Map Service, Houston, Texas.
Maryland and Delaware Canoe Trails, by Edward Gertler, 1983, Seneca Press, Silver Spring, Md.
Midwest Canoe Trails, by John W. Malo, 1978, Contemporary Books, Chicago, Ill.
Mississippi Solo, by Eddy L. Harris, 1988, N. Lyons Books, New York, N.Y.
New Mexico Whitewater, by New Mexico State Park Division, Natural Resources Dept., 1983, Santa Fe, N.M.
Niobrara River Canoeing Guide, by Duane Gudgel, 1990, Plains Trading Co. Archives, Valentine, Neb.
No Two Rivers Alike: 50 Canoeable Rivers in New York and Pennsylvania, by Alec C. Proskine, 1980, Crossing Press, Trumansburg, N.Y.

Paddle America

Northern Georgia Canoeing, by Bob Sehlinger and Don Otey, 1980, Menasha Ridge Press, Hillsborough, N.C.

One and Two Day River Cruises: Maryland, Virginia, West Virginia, by H. Roger Corbett, Jr., and Louis J. Matacia, 1973, Blue Ridge Voyageurs, Oakton, Va.

Oregon River Tours, by John Garren, 1991, Garren Publishing, Portland, Ore.

Paddle Routes of Western Washington, by Verne Huser, 1990, Mountaineers, Seattle, Wash.

Paddle Washington, by Dave LeRoux and Martha Rudersdorf, 1984, Neah Bay Books, Seattle, Wash.

River Runners Guide to Utah and Adjacent Areas, by Gary Nichols, 1986, Univ. of Utah Press, Salt Lake City, Utah.

Rivers of the Southwest, by Fletcher Anderson and Ann Hopkinson, 1987, Pruett Publishing Co., Boulder, Colo.

Running the Rivers of North America, by Peter Wood, 1978, Barre Publishing, Barre, Mass.

Sierra Whitewater, by Charles Martin, 1974, Fiddleneck Press, Sunnyvale, Calif.

The Soggy Sneakers Guide to Oregon Rivers, by Willamette Kayak and Canoe Club, 1980, Corvallis, Ore.

Southern Georgia Canoeing, by Bob Sehlinger and Don Otey, 1980, Menasha Ridge Press, Hillsborough, N.C.

Still Waters, White Waters: Exploring America's Rivers and Lakes, by Ron M. Fisher, 1977, Nat. Geographic Soc., Washington D.C.

Verde River Recreation Guide, by Jim Slingluff, 1990, Golden West Publishers, Phoenix, Ariz.

Washington Whitewater I: A Guide to 17 of Washington's Most Popular Whitewater Tours, by Douglass A. North, 1988, Mountaineers, Seattle, Wash.

Washington Whitewater II: A guide to 17 of Washington's Lesser Known Whitewater Trips, by Douglass A. North, 1987, Mountaineers, Seattle, Wash.

Washington Whitewater, by Douglass A. North and Lynn Conant, 1984, North Publishing, Seattle, Wash.

West Branch of the Penobscot and the Kennebec Gorge, by Ron Rathnow, 1989, Menasha Ridge Press, Birmingham, Ala.

Whitewater Adventure, Running the Great Wild Rivers of America, by Richard Bangs, 1989, Thunder Bay Press, San Diego, Calif.

Whitewater Rafting in Eastern North America, by Lloyd D. Armstead, 1989, Globe Pequot Press, Chester, Conn.

Whitewater Rafting in Western North America, by Lloyd D. Armstead, 1990, Globe Pequot Press, Chester, Conn.

The Whitewater Source Book, by Richard Penny, 1989, Menasha Ridge Press, Birmingham, Ala.

Whitewater, Quietwater: A Guide to the Wild Rivers of Wisconsin, Upper Michigan and Northeast Minnesota, by Bob and Jody Palzer, 1983, Evergreen Paddleways, Two Rivers, Wis.

Wild Rivers of North America, by Michael Jenkinson, 1981, E.P. Dutton, New York, N.Y.

Wildwater: Exploring Wilderness Waterways, by Buddy Mays, 1977, Chronicle Books, San Francisco, Calif.

Wildwater: the Sierra Club Guide to Kayaking and Whitewater Boating, by Lito Tejada-Flores, 1978, Sierra Club Books, San Francisco, Calif.